"The Binding of Isaac": from the mosaic floor of the Beth Alpha synagogue (6th cent.).

The Encyclopedia of the Jewish Religion

EDITED BY

Dr. R. J. ZWI WERBLOWSKY

DEAN OF THE FACULTY OF THE HUMANITIES
PROFESSOR OF COMPARATIVE RELIGION
HEBREW UNIVERSITY, JERUSALEM

AND

Dr. GEOFFREY WIGODER

INSTITUTE OF CONTEMPORARY JEWRY,
HEBREW UNIVERSITY, JERUSALEM

ADAMA BOOKS, NEW YORK

Updating: Dr. Shmuel Himelstein

Library of Congress Cataloging in Publication Data

Werblowsky, R.J. Zwi (Raphael Jehudah Zwi), 1924-
The encyclopedia of the Jewish religion.

1. Judaism-Dictionaries. I. Wigoder, Geoffrey, 1922- II. Title.
BM50.W45 1986 296'.03'21 86-10932
ISBN 0-915361-53-1

Adama Books, 306 West 38 Street, New York, N.Y. 10018
Printed in Israel

PREFACE

There is no dearth of encyclopedias of Jewish knowledge in English — from the somewhat antiquated but still unsurpassed scholarly 12 volumes of the *Jewish Encyclopedia* (1901–1906) to the recent one-volume *Standard Jewish Encyclopedia* (1962). However, while every Jewish encyclopedia of necessity devotes much attention to aspects of the Jewish religion, practically all the extant encyclopedic works are designed to embrace all facets of Jewish life, culture, and history. A list of the tractates of the Mishnah would be followed by a list of Jewish Nobel Prize winners, and a modern Jewish actor may receive as many lines as a medieval kabbalist. There is room, therefore, for an encyclopedia of Jewish religion, providing the interested layman with concise, accurate, and non-technical information on Jewish belief and practices, religious movements and doctrines, as well as the names and concepts that have played a rôle in Jewish religious history.

The adjective "religious" is notoriously difficult to define. The editors have let themselves be guided by the facts and norms of Jewish tradition but are aware that some of their inclusions or exclusions may not escape the charge of arbitrariness. Thus the halakhic tradition of Judaism inevitably leads to the inclusion of terms and concepts which elsewhere would be regarded as belonging to the sphere of jurisprudence rather than religion. It might be argued with some measure of justification that the formulas of congratulation form part of the folkloristic and not of the religious tradition of the Jews. There are no hard and fast rules for choosing or omitting names of tannaitic teachers or medieval codifiers. The tradition of historical Judaism being what it is, certain subjects, which may elsewhere be treated in secular terms, also possess a religious dimension or background (e.g. Zionism). The editors felt that in addition to the central subjects of Jewish theology, philosophy, liturgy, ritual, and religious institutions, certain marginal themes ought not to be neglected (e.g. the influence of Judaism on other religions as well as the reciprocal influence upon it).

In a concise work of this nature, the treatment of each entry is necessarily limited. However, extensive cross-references — indicated by small capitals — give an immediate key to complementary entries, providing additional information relevant to the subject (but it should be noted that cross-references are only used where the subject-matter of the article referred to supplements the article being read). Moreover, references in major sources (particularly the Bible and Talmud) are indicated, thus furnishing the reader who wishes to pursue the subject further with an immediate guide. A Hebrew-English index has been appended for the benefit of those who are versed in the relevant Hebrew terminology.

Hebrew words have been transliterated according to the *Sephardi* pronunciation and italicized — except for those words which have passed into common English usage. Biblical citations are based on the Jewish Publication Society of America's translation of the Bible (1917). Personal or place names that appear in the Bible have been retained in the form familiar to the English reader.

While it is not the task of an encyclopedia of religion to serve as a textbook of theology or ritual practice, the editors hope that they have struck a fair mean between concrete (though non-technical) detail and valid (though not unduly simplifying) generalization, and have been accurate and unbiased in their presentation of the facts.

CONTRIBUTORS TO THE ENCYCLOPEDIA OF THE JEWISH RELIGION

ABRAHAMS, Prof. Rabbi ISRAEL, Capetown

COHEN, Dr. JACK J., Jerusalem

FENSTER, Rabbi MYRON, New York

FISCH, Rabbi Dr. SOLOMON, Jerusalem

GOLDBERG, Rabbi Dr. ABRAHAM, Jerusalem

GOLDMAN, Rabbi JACOB, Jerusalem

HEINEMANN, Dr. JOSEPH, Jerusalem

JAKOBOVITZ, Rabbi Dr. IMMANUEL, New York

JACOBS, Dr. NOAH J., Jerusalem

KATSCH, Prof. ABRAHAM I., New York

LEVI, Dr. LEO, Jerusalem

LEVINE, Dr. I.H., Jerusalem

MANTEL, Dr. HUGO, Ramat Gan

O'DELL, Dr. JERRY, Jerusalem

RABIN, Prof. CHAIM, Jerusalem

RABINOWITZ, Rabbi A.H., Ramat Gan

RABINOWITZ, Prof. Rabbi LOUIS I., Jerusalem

ROTH, Prof. CECIL, Jerusalem

SAGER, SHMUEL, Jerusalem

SCHIMMEL, Rabbi SHMUEL, Jerusalem

TOMASCHOFF, AVNER, Jerusalem

WEINER, Rabbi HERBERT, South Orange, N. Jersey

ABBREVIATIONS

abbr.	abbreviation
Ant.	Antiquities of the Jews (Josephus)
Arab.	Arabic
Aram.	Aramaic
A. Z.	Avodah Zarah*
b.	born
B.C.E.	Before the Common Era (=B.C.)
Bekh.	Bekhorot*
Ber.	Berakhot*
Bik.	Bikkurim*
c.	circa
C.E.	Common Era (= A.D.)
cent.	century
Chron.	Chronicles
d.	died
Dan.	Daniel
Dem.	Demai*
Deut.	Deuteronomy
Deut. Rab.	Deuteronomy Rabbah
E.	East
Ecc.	Ecclesiastes
Eccl.	Ecclesiasticus
Eduy.	Eduyyot*
Eruv.	Eruvin*
Est.	Esther
Exod.	Exodus
Exod. Rab.	Exodus Rabbah
Ezek.	Ezekiel
ff.	following
fl.	flourished
Fr.	French
Gen.	Genesis
Gen. Rab.	Genesis Rabbah
Ger.	German
Git.	Gittin*
Gk.	Greek
Hab.	Habakkuk
Hag.	Haggai
Ḥag.	Hagigah*
Ḥal.	Ḥallah
Heb.	Hebrew
Hor.	Horayot*
Hos.	Hosea
Ḥul.	Ḥullin
Is.	Isaiah
Jer.	Jeremiah
Josh.	Joshua
Judg.	Judges
Ker.	Keritot*
Ket.	Ketubbot*
Kidd.	Kiddushin*
Kil.	Kilayim*
Kin.	Kinnim*
Lam.	Lamentations
Lam. Rab.	Lamentations Rabbati
Lat.	Latin
Lev.	Leviticus
Lev. Rab.	Leviticus Rabbah
lit.	literally
Maas.	Maaserot*
Macc.	Maccabees
Mak.	Makkot
Makh.	Makhshirim*
Mal.	Malachi
Matt.	Matthew
Meg.	Megillah*
Men.	Menuḥot*
Mic.	Micah
Mid.	Middot*
Mik.	Mikvaot*
M.K.	Moed Katan*
Mt.	Mount
N.	North
Nah.	Nahum
Naz.	Nazir*
Ned.	Nedarim*

* Talmudic tractate

Neg.	Negaim*
Neh.	Nehemiah
Nid.	Niddah*
Num.	Numbers
Num. Rab.	Numbers Rabbah
Obad.	Obadiah
Ohal	Ohalot*
Pes.	Pesaḥim*
pl.	plural
Prov.	Proverbs
Ps.	Psalms
R.	Rabbi
Rev.	Revelations
R.H.	Rosh ha-Shanah
S.	South
Sam.	Samuel
Sanh.	Sanhedrin*
Shab.	Shabbat*
Shek.	Shekalim*
Shev.	Shevuot
Span.	Spanish
Suk.	Sukkot*
Taan.	Taanit*
Tem.	Temurah*
Ter.	Terumot*
Toh.	Tohorot*
Uktz.	Uktzin
W.	West
Y.	Yerushalmi (the Palestinian Talmud)
Yad.	Yadayim*
Yev.	Yevamot
Yidd.	Yiddish
Zav.	Zavim*
Zech.	Zechariah
Zeph.	Zephaniah
Zev.	Zevaḥim

TRANSLITERATION

א is not transliterated
בּ = b
ב = v
גּ, ג = g
דּ, ד = d
ה = h
ו = v (where not a vowel)
ז = z
ח = ḥ
ט = t
י = y
כּ = k
כ = kh
ל = l
מ = m
נ = n
ס = s
ע is not transliterated
פּ = p
פ = ph
צ = tz
ק = k
ר = r
שׁ = sh
שׂ = s
תּ, ת = t

◌ָ = a
◌ַ = a
◌ֹ, וֹ = o
◌ֻ, וּ = u
short ◌ָ = o
◌ֵי, ◌ֵ = ei
◌ֶ = e
◌ִ = i
◌ֵ = e
◌ֱ = e
◌ֳ = o
◌ֲ = a

vocal *sheva* = e
silent *sheva* is not transliterated

A

A FORTIORI AND A MINORI, see **HERMENEUTICS**

AARON: First HIGH PRIEST; great-grandson of Levi; elder brother of MOSES and his spokesman before Pharaoh. A. and his descendants were selected to serve as PRIESTS; together with his sons he was duly anointed by Moses upon the completion of the Tabernacle. A. officiated in the Holy of Holies for almost forty years until his death in the wilderness. Other descendants of the tribe of Levi were appointed to perform varied services in the Tabernacle (and later in the Temple), but to A. and his descendants — the *kohanim* (priests) — was reserved the direct and immediate contact with the sanctuary and altar. As God, in whose service they officiated, was regarded as their lot, they received no inheritance in Canaan (Num. 18:20). A. is frequently mentioned as a symbol of the priesthood in general, and in rabbinic literature his name was a byword for piety and the pursuit of peace (cf. *Avot* 1:12). The rabbis also depicted and extolled the bond of brotherly love between Moses and A.

AARON BEN ELIJAH (c. 1330-1369): KARAITE theologian, born in Nicomedia in Asia Minor but spent most of his life in Constantinople. He was the only Karaite scholar to seek a philosophical basis for Karaite beliefs. His *Etz Ḥayyim* ("Tree of Life") is modeled on Maimonides' *Guide to the Perplexed,* though it is closer to the Arab *Kalam* school and more negative toward Aristotelianism and Greek philosophy. According to A., the Pentateuch was meant for all mankind and could never be altered or supplemented by an Oral Law. A.'s other works include *Gan Eden* ("Garden of Eden"), a Karaite code dealing with the commandments, and *Keter Torah* ("Crown of Law"), a commentary on the Pentateuch based on literal interpretations of the text. Some of his religious poems were incorporated into the Karaite liturgy.

AARON BEN JACOB HA-COHEN (late 13th-early 14th cents.): Codifier. Born in S. France, he lived in Majorca after the expulsion of the Jews from France in 1306. His main work is *Oreḥot Ḥayyim* ("Paths of Life"), a compilation of ritual laws and customs. This influential code became especially popular in its abbreviated form called *Kol Bo* ("Everything in it"), which eventually superseded the original version.

AARON OF KARLIN, see **KARLIN**

AARON BEN JOSEPH HA-LEVI (d. c. 1305): Spanish talmudist and codifier; disciple of Naḥmanides. He is best known for his *Bedek ha-Bayit* ("Breach of the House"), a critique of *Torat ha-Bayit,* a halakhic work by the leading contemporary Spanish rabbinical authority Solomon ben ADRET. Adret sharply countered in turn with *Mishmeret ha-Bayit.*

AARON BEN JOSEPH THE PHYSICIAN (c. 1250-c. 1320): Karaite scholar. Little is known of his life, though he probably resided in Constantinople. He determined the authoritative version of the Karaite liturgy, introducing poems by Spanish Hebrew authors as well as some of his own compositions. His works include *Sepher ha-Mivḥar* ("The Choice Book"), a philosophical commentary on the Pentateuch based on the literal meaning of the text; commentaries on the prophetic books and Hagiographa; and a Hebrew grammar *Kelil Yophi* ("Perfect Beauty"). His writings, especially *Ha-Mivḥar,* were extremely influential in Karaite circles during the 14th and 15th cents. and were the subjects of a number of supercommentaries.

AARON BEN MOSES BEN ASHER, see **BEN ASHER**

AARON BEN MOSES HA-LEVI OF STAROSELYE (c. 1766-1828): Ḥasidic rabbi of the ḤABAD school, pupil of R. Shneour Zalman of Lyady, and author of commentaries on the TANYA. He endeavored to introduce elements of emotion and fervor into the predominantly intellectual attitudes of the *Ḥabad.*

AARON (ABU AHARON) BEN SAMUEL (9th cent.): Mystic and religious poet. Born in Baghdad, he migrated to Europe and traveled throughout Italy, bringing to western Jewry a knowledge of the mystical traditions that had developed in Babylonia. He also acquired a reputation as a wonder-worker and was dubbed the "father of mysteries". His pupil, Moses ben Kalonymos of Lucca, carried his teachings from Italy to Germany where they influenced the early German Ḥasidim (the ḤASIDEI ASHKENAZ).

AARON BERECHIAH BEN MOSES OF MODENA (17th cent.): Italian kabbalist; author of ethical works, chiefly on the subject of prayer. His best-known book is *Maavar Yabbok* ("The Ford of the Jabbok") dealing with deathbed conduct and confessions and the laws governing burial and mourning.

AARON HA-LEVI OF BARCELONA (late 13th-early 14th cent.): Spanish talmudist; author of *Sepher ha-Ḥinnukh* ("The Book of Education") in which the 613 precepts are enumerated in their pentateuchal order and expounded according to rabbinic tradition. The book was translated into Latin and French.

AARON SAMUEL KAIDANOVER, see **KAIDANOVER**

AB, see **AV**

ABARBANEL, see **ABRAVANEL**

ABAYE, see **ABBAYE**

ABBA (Aram. "father"): Honorary title conferred upon some of the *tannaim* and *amoraim*; according to Maimonides, it was synonymous with "rabbi". The title passed into Christian usage to denote high ecclesiastical office; cf. medieval Latin *abbas*; Italian *abbate*; German *Abt*; French *abbé*; English *abbot*.

ABBA ARIKHA, see **RAV**

ABBA GULISH (or **ABBA GULYASH**): Pagan priest in Damascus who, according to legend, became converted to Judaism in Tiberias and returned to Damascus to lead a mass conversion movement among the idol worshipers. The legend appears to be based on the historical fact of extensive conversions to Judaism which took place in 4th cent. Damascus.

ABBA MARI BEN MOSES HA-YARḤI (Don Astruc of Lunel; late 13th-early 14th cent.): Talmudist. A. headed the group of rabbinical scholars in S. France who opposed the philosophical and secular studies pursued by the followers of Maimonides and influenced Solomon ben Adret to issue a decree in 1305 forbidding anyone under the age of 30 to read philosophy, science (excepting medicine), and allegorical interpretations of the Bible. His *Minhat ha-Kenaot* ("The Zeal Offering") incorporated the correspondence between Jewish scholars in France and Spain relating to the Maimonist controversy.

ABBAHU (c. 279-320): Palestinian *amora*; headed the rabbinical academy at Caesarea. A distinguished preacher, he was noted for his modesty and humanity; his better-known sayings include "Where a repentant sinner stands, even a completely righteous man may not stand" (*Ber.* 34a) and "The world exists through the man who effaces himself" (*Ḥul.* 89a). He was highly respected by the Roman representatives and so gained added stature among his colleagues. A. sharply opposed sectarians and Christians, and his scriptural expositions were often directed to polemical ends. He decreed that the Samaritans should be regarded as gentiles. A. probably headed the group of "Rabbis of Caesarea" credited with redacting the juridical section of the Palestinian Talmud.

ABBAYE (real name Naḥmani; 278-338): Babylonian *amora*. A poor man, he emphasized the importance of physical labor, and in order to be free to study and teach by day he used to cultivate his small landholding at night. In his early childhood and youth he studied together with his colleague Rava and in later life — when A. was head of the academy at Pumbedita and Rava at Maḥoza — they argued together over many points of the law (with six exceptions, Rava's decision was accepted as the norm). Their discussions, which ranged over all aspects of the law, became a byword for acumen and keen argument and are regarded as among the finest examples of talmudic dialectics. A. was among the first rabbis to distinguish between the literal (*peshat*) and exegetical (*derash*) interpretation of biblical text. On A.'s death the Pumbedita academy was closed and Rava was recognized as head of all the Babylonian talmudic academies.

ABBREVIATIONS (Heb. *rashei tevot* "beginnings - or initials - of words"): Contractions of single words or groups of words are found in the writings and inscriptions of many peoples from early times In Hebrew this practice is at least as old as the 2nd cent. B.C.E., as evidenced by its appearance on Maccabean coins. The Talmud, as well as all rabbinic writings down to the present, makes very extensive use of the system of word a., which are usually indicated by dots, strokes, or double strokes over the first, second, or third letter of a word, while the remaining letters of the word are eliminated. Very common is the practice of substituting a stroke for the last one or two letters of a word (especially for plurals). Where the initials of several words are contracted to form a single element, the a. is indicated by one or two strokes over the line between the last two letters. The habit of abbreviating groups of words to one word (cf. UNESCO and similar formations in modern English usage) is very old in Hebrew. Books (*Tanakh*, *Shass*), names (*Rashi*, *Rambam*), concepts (*Taryag*), titles (*Admor*), etc. are known by a. that have become words in their own right. A. also played a role in rabbinic and mystical exegesis (see Notarikon) — e.g. for the purposes of gematria — as well as in magic.

ABEL, see **CAIN**

ABIATHAR: Priest of the family of Eli and son of Ahimelech. Chief priest at the sanctuary of Nob, A. was the sole survivor of Saul's massacre of the priests of that city for the assistance they had afforded David on his flight from Saul. A.

thereupon joined David's party, accompanying him on his wanderings and serving him as keeper of the priestly oracle (EPHOD). He was appointed chief priest when David ascended the throne and was one of the king's closest advisers. Because of A.'s support for the succession of Adonijah he was banished by Solomon to Anathoth where it has been conjectured he founded the priestly family from which later originated the prophet Jeremiah.

ABIATHAR BEN ELIJAH HA-COHEN (c. 1040-c. 1110): Last Palestinian *gaon.* He succeeded his father R. Elijah to the gaonate (1083) but was deposed by the Egyptian exilarch David ben Daniel who aspired to dominate Palestinian Jewry. A. fled to Syria (1093) but returned to his position the following year after the fall of David ben Daniel. An account of these events is contained in A.'s *Megillat Evyatar* ("Scroll of A.") which was discovered in the Cairo *genizah.*

ABIB, see **AVIV**

ABIHU, see **NADAB AND ABIHU**

ABITUR, see **IBN ABITUR**

ABLUTION: Washing or cleansing the body generally for a religious purpose. Jewish law deals with both total and partial a. Total a. takes the form of IMMERSION in a ritual bath (MIKVEH). Before immersion the body must already be scrupulously clean so that nothing may interpose between flesh and water; even the nails are pared to ensure that no dirt remains beneath them. The body must be totally immersed at one time. Immersion (*tevilah*) is a religious act specifically undertaken to achieve the ritual PURITY required for participation in certain religious ceremonials. Thus not only did the High Priest immerse himself before conducting the service on the Day of Atonement but each priest who participated in the Temple service was also required to undergo immersion, beside washing his hands and feet from the laver. The Mishnah attributes to Ezra a decree that each male should immerse himself before reciting the morning prayer or studying. Matutinal immersion was practiced by the HEMEROBAPTISTS and by pious ascetics, mystics, and Ḥasidim of later times. (For the occasions which require *tevilah* by law — as distinct from pious custom — see IMMERSION). Partial a. is of two kinds: (1) the washing of the hands and feet as prescribed by the Bible for priests ministering in the Temple; (2) the washing of hands prescribed by the rabbis for various occasions (e.g. before partaking of bread, after leaving a privy, on waking from sleep). In these cases the hands are regarded as having contracted a limited form of impurity which does not apply to the entire body; hence it is sufficient to pour water over them alone. Vessels which have contracted certain types of ritual uncleanness, or which were manufactured outside the Land of Israel, should also be immersed before use.

ABNER OF BURGOS (c. 1270-1340): Spanish apostate. A physician by profession, he was baptized at the age of 50 taking the name Alfonso of Valladolid. A. wrote several bitter attacks on Judaism and particularly on the Talmud. He was responsible for having the ALEINU prayer banned by Alfonso XI of Castile (1336). His works served as the basis for Christian anti-Jewish polemics and evoked a counter-polemical literature among Jews (e.g. Ḥasdai Crescas' *Or Adonai* and Ibn Pulgar's *Ezer ha-Dat*).

ABOAB: Family of Spanish origin. (1) *IMMANUEL A.* (c. 1555-1628): Author. Born in Portugal to Marrano parents, he escaped in his youth to Italy where he reverted to Judaism. His Spanish *Nomologia,* directed to Marranos, endeavors to prove the veracity of the Oral Law. (2) *ISAAC A.* (14th-15th cents.): Talmudic scholar; author of the homiletic classic *Menorat ha-Maor* ("The Candlestick of Light"), in which he collected ethical rabbinic teachings and arranged them according to subject-matter. The work achieved widespread popularity, was translated into Yiddish, Spanish, and German, and contributed largely to the dissemination of rabbinic ethics among the medieval Jewish masses. (3) *ISAAC DE FONSECA* A. (1605-1693): Rabbi. At the age of 21, he was appointed *Ḥakham* in Amsterdam. In 1642 he journeyed to Brazil with the Amsterdam Jews of Portuguese origin and officiated at Recife as the first rabbi and first Jewish author in the Western Hemisphere. After the Portuguese reconquest (1654) A. returned to Amsterdam where he headed a rabbinical academy. His works include a Spanish translation of and commentary on the Pentateuch. A. was a member of the rabbinical tribunal which pronounced the sentence of excommunication on Spinoza.

ABOMINATION: The usual English translation of the Hebrew word *toevah,* applied to something utterly detested and offensive on religious grounds. Thus sheep and shepherds were considered an "abomination" to the Egyptians (Gen. 46:34). It is usually applied however to that which is offensive to God and as such the term has both ritual and spiritual connotations. Examples of ritual a. include the eating of unclean animals (Deut. 14:3), the worship of idols (Deut. 7:25-26), the offering of maimed animals as sacrifices (Deut. 17:1), recourse to magic and divination (Deut. 18:12), and the "bringing of the harlot's hire and the price of a dog" into the Temple (Deut. 23:19). Among the spiritual and moral transgressions which also constitute a *toevah* is the use of false weights and measures; indeed "all that doeth unrighteously" are called an "a. to the Lord" and the author of

Proverbs lists seven such examples of abominations: "a proud look, a lying tongue, hands that shed innocent blood, a heart that deviseth wicked imaginations, feet that run to mischiefs, false witness, and sowing discord among neighbors" (6:16-19). A. is also the English translation of the Hebrew terms *sheketz* or *shikkutz,* a detestable object (e.g. Lev. 7:21; Dan. 11:31) and *piggul,* unclean sacrificial flesh (e.g. Lev. 7:18).

ABORTION: In contrast to most non-Jewish legislation in ancient and medieval times, Jewish law — as mentioned in the Bible, Talmud, and codes — makes very little reference to a. (and none at all to criminal a.), probably because it was generally unknown among Jews. The only direct biblical mention of the subject stipulates liability for monetary compensation in the case of an attack on a pregnant woman resulting in the a. of her unborn child, provided "no harm follow"; otherwise the attacker shall pay with "life for life" (Exod. 21:22-23). The rabbis interpreted this proviso to mean that no such compensation is due if fatal harm befalls the mother, since the offender would then incur capital liability. Jewish law extends full human rights only to a born and viable being, and accordingly the Mishnah rules in favor of embryotomy when a mother is in "hard travail" and her life cannot otherwise be saved, so long as the head or greater part of the child has not yet emerged from the birth canal (*Ohal.* 7:6). Several rabbinic responsa have sanctioned therapeutic a. where a hazard exists (whether for physical or psychological reasons) to the mother's life, but not in the case of a forbidden union or from fear of giving birth to abnormal children.

ABRAHAM: The founder of the Hebrew people and the first PATRIARCH. The scriptural narrative of his life begins with the call of God received by A. at the age of 75 and instructing him to leave his homeland and proceed to an unknown destination which later proved to be the Land of Canaan (Gen. 12:1-5). Midrashic legend however provides accounts of his early years and tells how A. smashed his father Terah's idols after having arrived at a belief in one God through meditation on the orderliness of the universe. He and his wife Sarah converted others to the knowledge of the true God (according to the rabbinic interpretation of Gen. 12:5 "the souls which they had gotten in Haran"), and A. is therefore regarded as the Father of MONOTHEISM and the spiritual father of all those who "come under the wings of the Divine Presence" by accepting Judaism. Converts to Judaism are consequently known as "sons of A.". God made a COVENANT with A., promising to make him the father of a mighty people to be bound in a special relationship to God; the sign of this covenant was to be CIRCUMCISION (Gen. 14). The supreme test of A.'s faith in God was the command to sacrifice his son ISAAC (see AKEDAH) — according to the Midrash the last of the ten trials through which A. passed. His name serves as the symbol of HOSPITALITY and kindness (cf. Gen. 18), and the rabbis credited him with instituting the MORNING PRAYER (on the basis of Gen. 22:3). The personality of A. played an important role not only in Jewish, but also in Moslem lore, since the Arabs were considered the descendants of A.'s son ISHMAEL.

ABRAHAM, APOCALYPSE OF: Pseudepigraphal work extant only in a Slavonic version. Written originally in Hebrew or Aramaic, it is the work of a Jewish author though it was later interpolated by Christian hands. As it contains an allusion to the destruction of the Temple, it must have been written after 70 C.E., most likely in the 2nd cent. The contents fall into two distinct sections, the first of which recounts Abraham's conversion from the idolatry of his father Terah to the worship of the one true God. The second section, a commentary on Gen. 15, is of a more apocalyptic nature: Abraham is spirited to heaven, and a version of human history — beginning with Adam and Eve and ending in the destruction of the Temple — is unfolded before his eyes. Finally, however, the coming of the Messiah is revealed to him together with the ingathering of the exiles and the last judgment.

ABRAHAM, TESTAMENT OF: Pseudepigraphal book recounting the last days of Abraham, his death, and ascension to heaven. The original language of this work was either Hebrew or Aramaic and it is extant in two different Greek versions, from which language it was subsequently translated into Arabic, Ethiopic, Slavonic, and Rumanian. Written c. 2nd cent. C.E., the book is basically Jewish, but a number of Christian interpolations have been added. The angel Michael is sent to bring Abraham's soul to heaven, but Abraham is reluctant to follow him. God then shows Abraham the entire world and has him transported to heaven where he witnesses the judgment of other souls. Abraham returns to earth, but when the angel of death visits him in all its awesomeness, Abraham yields and his soul is borne heavenward by the angels. This book closely follows the pattern of the ancient *aggadah* which, in similar fashion, describes the death of Moses.

ABRAHAM ABELE OF GOMBIN (c. 1635-1681): Polish rabbi, best-known for his *Magen Avraham* ("Shield of Abraham"), a commentary on the *Orah Ḥayyim* section of the *Shulḥan Arukh* meant to reconcile the views of Joseph KARO and Moses ISSERLES when they diverged. His work, which was widely studied by the Jews of Germany and Poland, greatly influenced *Ashkenazi* ritual.

ABRAHAM BAR ḤIYYA (11th-12th cents.): Spanish philosopher and scientist. His writings, on a wide variety of subjects, include a homiletic-ethical work *Hegyon ha-Nephesh ha-Atzuvah* ("Meditation of the Sad Soul") and the philosophic-eschatological *Megillat ha-Megalleh* ("Scroll of the Revealer") which fixed the date for the coming of the Messiah at 1358 C.E. His philosophical thought was strongly influenced by Neo-Platonism, although in certain respects he was also a pioneer of the Aristotelian trend in Jewish thought. A.'s works were among the first scientific and philosophical books written in Hebrew and much of the terminology he coined later passed into general usage.

ABRAHAM BEN ABRAHAM: Name given to male proselytes. These have included: (1) A 7th cent. monk in the Mt. Sinai monastery, who became a Jew, married a Palestinian woman and was a noted exponent of Judaism. (2) A Hungarian proselyte who was converted c. 1170. According to *Tosaphot* (*Kidd.* 71a) he interpreted the saying of R. Ḥelbo "converts are noxious as the scab" as meaning that converts are so expert and zealous in the performance of the commandments that they accentuate the shortcomings of Jews who are remiss in this respect. (3) A proselyte in Augsburg who was burnt at the stake in 1264 for defacing sacred Christian images. (4) A French convert, originally head of the order of Franciscan monks in France. He was burnt at the stake in Germany in 1270. (5) A convert at Cordova in Spain; author of a polemic work extolling Judaism.

ABRAHAM BEN ALEXANDER KATZ OF KALISK (d. 1810): Ḥasidic rabbi. Originally a student of Elijah of Vilna, he was attracted to Ḥasidism and became a pupil of Dov Ber of Mezhirich. A. returned to his native Kalisk (White Russia) and rapidly gathered a large following whom he instructed in his doctrines of faith, fervor, and DEVEKUT. His ḥasidic teaching and his contempt for traditional rabbinic scholars were important factors contributing to the ban on the ḥasidic movement imposed in Vilna in 1772 and the anti-ḥasidic persecutions by the MITNAGGEDIM. In 1777, together with Menahem Mendel of Vitebsk, A. led 300 Ḥasidim to Palestine where he settled first in Safed, and later in Tiberias. He sharply attacked R. SHNEOUR ZALMAN OF LYADY, regarding his more intellectual approach as a deviation from true ḥasidic doctrine, which, he maintained, should be based on simple faith.

ABRAHAM BEN AZRIEL (13th cent.): Bohemian talmudist. His *Arugat ha-Bosem* ("The Bed of Spices") includes extensive comments on Sabbath and festival *piyyutim* and on penitential prayers.

ABRAHAM BEN DAVID OF POSQUIÈRES (known as *Ravad*; 1120-1198): Talmudist. The outstanding French authority of his time, he was constantly requested to adjudicate disputed legal problems, and his decisions, which were noted for their independence and profound talmudic expertise, were recognized as authoritative; his responsa were collected in *Temim Deim* ("Perfect Knowledge"). He wrote erudite and often aggressive strictures (*hassagot*) on the halakhic works of Alfasi, Zerahiah ha-Levi, and Maimonides, which apart from their intrinsic importance served to maintain in W. Europe a critical approach toward halakhic codification. These have not survived in their entirety though many of his criticisms were incorporated into later editions of these codes. A. objected to Maimonides' setting himself up as a final arbiter on halakhic matters without indicating the sources of his decisions; he opposed the formulation of religious dogmas as being contrary to the nature of Judaism; in general he was fearful lest codifications replace study of the talmudic sources themselves. A. also wrote a comprehensive and lucid commentary on the *Siphra* which served to popularize that Midrash; scholarly commentaries on the mishnaic treatises of *Eduyyot* and *Kinnim*; and a work on family purity *Baalei ha-Nephesh* ("The Book of the Scrupulous"). A. was reputed to have been attracted by mystical thought and an early kabbalistic work has been attributed to his authorship.

ABRAHAM BEN DOV BER OF MEZHIRICH, see **ABRAHAM MALAKH**

ABRAHAM BEN ELIJAH OF VILNA (c. 1750-1808): Talmudist; son of ELIJAH BEN SOLOMON the Vilna Gaon. A. studied secular science as well as rabbinic literature; he was the first scholar to investigate the historical development of midrashic literature. His works include a critical edition of *Aggadat Bereshit* and a critical appraisal of 130 minor Midrashim.

ABRAHAM BEN ḤASDAI HA-LEVI, see **IBN ḤASDAI**

ABRAHAM BEN ISAAC OF NARBONNE (known as *Ravad* II; c. 1110-1179): S. French talmudist; head of the Narbonne academy and rabbinic court (hence also known as A. *Av Bet Din*). His *Ha-Eshkol* ("The Cluster"), an abbreviated version of Judah ben Barzillai's *Sepher ha-Ittim*, was the first major work of codification to appear in S. France and had a great influence on subsequent halakhic literature, remaining authoritative in France and Italy until the appearance of JACOB BEN ASHER's code. A. was also the author of many responsa.

ABRAHAM BEN MOSES MAIMONIDES (1186-1237): Temporal and spiritual head (NAGID) of the Jewish community in Egypt, succeeding his father MOSES BEN MAIMON. Like his father, A. was also physician to the caliph. He was responsible for many enactments, one of which — prohibiting the issuance of a ban of excommunication by an individual rabbi — became generally accepted. He was the author of rabbinic responsa, a commentary on the Pentateuch, philosophical writings defending his father's thought, and *Kitab al-Abidin* an encyclopedic work on Jewish religion, ethics, and philosophy. The last work is informed by deep mystical piety, and in it, as well as in some of his practices, A. appears to have been influenced by the ascetic mystics of Islam (the *sufis*).

ABRAHAM BEN NATHAN HA-YARḤI (c. 1155-c. 1215): Talmudist; born in S. France, eventually settling in Spain. His major composition is *Manhig Olam* (*"Universal Guide"*; generally known as *Ha-Manhig*) in which he recorded the synagogal and liturgical usages prevalent in the communities of France, Germany, England, and Spain, and explained their origin and development according to rabbinic sources (many of these sources not otherwise surviving).

ABRAHAM BEN SAMUEL ḤASDAI, see **IBN ḤASDAI**

ABRAHAM BEN SAMUEL ZACUT (ZACUTO), see **ZACUTO**

ABRAHAM GERSHON OF KUTOV (d. c. 1760): E. Galician talmudist and kabbalist; brother-in-law of the BAAL SHEM TOV whose teachings he originally opposed though he eventually became one of his most faithful followers. A. was the first of the Ḥasidim to settle in Palestine (1744) where he received a warm welcome and began to disseminate the doctrines of ḤASIDISM.

ABRAHAM IBN DAUD, see **IBN DAUD**

ABRAHAM IBN EZRA, see **IBN EZRA**

ABRAHAM IBN ḤASDAI, see **IBN ḤASDAI**

ABRAHAM IBN TIBBON, see **IBN TIBBON**

ABRAHAM JOSHUA HESHEL ("The Rabbi of Opatov [Apt]"; c. 1745-1825): Polish ḥasidic rabbi. He conveyed his teachings in strange and exaggerated utterances which formed the subject of careful study by his pupils. A. himself believed in transmigration and stated that his own soul had had ten previous existences — as high priest, king, exilarch, and so forth. In his sermons, he stressed the importance of "loving and fearing God" in contrast to the stress by the ḤABAD Ḥasidim on intellectual contemplation. A. differentiated between Divine love, which man can and must attempt to imitate, and Divine justice, which cannot be compared or analogized to human concepts. His sermons were collected by his pupils in the volumes *Torat Emet* ("Law of Truth") and *Ohev Yisrael* ("Lover of Israel").

ABRAHAM MALAKH (c. 1741-1776): Ḥasidic rabbi; son of DOV BER OF MEZHIRICH. Noted for his extreme asceticism, he isolated himself from society and subjected himself to rigid mortifications. The Ḥasidim venerated A. believing him an angel (*malakh*) who had adopted human form. His commentary on the Pentateuch *Ḥesed le-Avraham* ("Kindness to Abraham") criticized contemporary Ḥasidism for its degeneration and called for its purification through DEVEKUT. SHNEOUR ZALMAN OF LYADY was greatly influenced by A., whose teachings had a deep effect on ḤABAD doctrines.

ABRAVANEL, ISAAC BEN JUDAH (1437-1508): Biblical commentator, philosopher, statesman, and communal leader. Though an influential minister at the court of Ferdinand and Isabella of Spain, he failed to dissuade them from executing the expulsion of Spanish Jewry. He himself fled to Italy where his talents soon brought him into the forefront of public activity. His literary productions cover many subjects in the realm of biblical exegesis, philosophy, and theology. A.'s political experience is much in evidence in his biblical commentary dealing with the entire Bible except the Hagiographa. While drawing heavily on his forerunners, he did so with a keen critical sense and occasionally accepted the opinions of Christian scholars when they did not conflict with the Jewish faith. Compared to the classical medieval exegesis, his treatment of the Bible is copious and discursive, yet lucid and popular. Instead of commenting on individual verses he divided the Pentateuch into thematic sections, prefacing each by a number of varied queries, the answers to which constituted the bulk of his commentary. The commentary itself is largely philosophical and eschews philological or kabbalistic explanations of the text. Nevertheless, though rejecting philosophical allegory, A. held that the Bible contained an esoteric as well as literal meaning. A rationalist by training as well as by inclination, his position remained strictly traditional, and though much absorbed in philosophy, he maintained that it must take second place to religion. He also opposed the tendency to sum up the totality of Judaism in a given set of dogmatic principles and held that all elements of the *Torah* equally shared Divine authority and significance. His original view of Messianism is expressed in his commentary to the Book of Daniel wherein he also attacks Christian scholars for manipulating the biblical text in order to suit their own particular standpoint. In his commentary, he affirms belief in the coming Messiah, who he thought would appear in the year 1503 and whose advent would be preceded by the resurrection of the dead; the tribulations associated with the expulsion from Spain were thus regarded as the period of trial before the coming of the Messiah. A.'s philosophy is neither original nor free from internal contradictions. His main purpose was to liberate Jewish philosophy — especially that of Maimonides — from those elements which detract from complete faith. He differed from Maimonides in his conception of the source of prophecy, which he held lay not in the Active Intellect but in God Himself. A. believed that Israel is the recipient of special Divine Providence whereas other nations receive providence only indirectly, through the working of natural law. A.'s works, which include commentaries on *Avot*, the Passover *Haggadah*, and Maimonides' *Guide to the Perplexed*, were eagerly read by the Spanish exiles, and their forecast of an imminent messianic era helped pave the way for the initial success of David Reuveni and Solomon Molkho. But on the other hand his philosophical speculations — the last link in the chain of medieval Jewish philosophy — exercised little future influence, partly because of the growing counter-attraction of kabbalistic thought. His biblical commentaries were not studied long by Jews but in Latin translations they influenced Christian scholars in the 16th-18th cents.

ABRAVANEL, JUDAH BEN ISAAC (known as Leone Ebreo or Leo Hebraeus; c. 1460-1521): Italian philosopher, poet, and physician; son of Isaac Abravanel. His Latin work *De coeli harmonia* ("On the Celestial Harmonies") has not survived and his reputation rests on his posthumously published *Dialoghi d'Amore* ("Dialogues on Love"), one of the first philosophical works written in Italian. Modeled structurally after the Platonic dialogue, this book seeks to define the nature of spiritual and intellectual love, regarded by A. as the principle dominating all existence and reaching its apotheosis in the love of God (*amore intellectivo di Dio*), which permeates the entire universe and through which all creatures attain their perfection. God is identified with Love; hence the soul reaches God by loving Him. The mutual love which exists between God and the universe creates a powerful "circle of love" turning upon every section of the cosmos from the highest celestial sphere to the lowest earthly stone. From this central theory derives a wealth of reflections on religion, metaphysics, mysticism, ethics, esthetics, logic, psychology, cosmology, mythology, astrology, and astronomy. A.'s humanist thought is influenced both by the neo-Platonist philosophy cultivated in the 15th cent. "Platonic Academy" of Florence and by the works of Maimonides and Ibn Gabirol. His typically Renaissance work had a considerable influence on 16th cent. European thought and lyric poetry (e.g. Michelangelo, Tasso, Camoëns, Montaigne, Bruno, Spinoza) and was followed by a large number of imitative treatises, though by the end of the 16th cent. it was virtually forgotten. It was not widely known in Jewish circles.

ABROGATION OF LAWS, see ANTINOMIANISM

ABSTINENCE, see ASCETICISM

ABTALION, see SHEMAIAH

ABU ISSA AL-ISFAHANI (8th cent.): Founder of Jewish sect in Persia. He proclaimed himself the Messiah Son of Joseph, the last of the five forerunners of the Messiah Son of David — the others having included Jesus and Mohammed — and declared his mission to be the establishment of Jewish political independence. The first Jewish sectary after the destruction of the Second Temple, his unorthodox interpretations of the commandments led to far-reaching innovations among his followers (e.g. seven daily prayers instead of three, prohibition of divorce, ban on the consumption of meat and wine). Many Persian Jews accepted his messianic claim and some 10,000 joined him in rebellion against the Abbasid rulers in Persia. A. was killed in the fighting, though his followers believed he survived; the sect ("Isanites" or "Isfahanites") persisted for some time and still numbered a few adherents in 10th cent. Damascus. A. and his disciple Yudghan influenced Anan, the founder of Karaism.

ABUDARHAM (or ABUDRAHIM), DAVID BEN JOSEPH (14th cent.): Spanish commentator on the liturgy. The composition of his popular and encyclopedic prayer-book *Sepher Abudarham* ("Book of A.") was motivated by the lack of understanding among Jews of the synagogal service and liturgical customs and practice. His authorities included both Talmuds, the *geonim*, and later commentators; many of his references are unknown from any other source. A. fully expounded the prayer book, *piyyutim*, and the *Haggadah*, described divergences in local customs, explained the calendar, and elucidated rabbinical regulations governing prayer and benedictions.

ABULAFIA, ABRAHAM BEN SAMUEL (13th cent.): Spanish mystic. Moved by what he called "the spirit of prophecy", A. went to Rome to convert Pope Nicholas III to Judaism and was saved from being burnt at the stake only by the Pope's sudden death. His predictions of the imminent end of the world led to the charge of messianic pretensions, for which he was persecuted by the rabbis, notably Solomon ben Adret. A. founded a new school in mysticism which instructed in the attainment of the spirit of prophecy (called "Prophetic Kabbalah") through contemplation of the letters of the Hebrew alphabet. In accordance with his theory of the configuration of these letters as the constituent elements of God's name, A. held that the true path to ecstasy — the highest stage of contemplation —

lay in meditation upon the Divine name, and that his "science of letter-combination" (*ḥokhmat ha-tzeruph*) provided the means to the attainment of the harmonious movement of pure thought. A. is one of the major representatives of the ecstatic trend — a mixture of emotionalism and rationalism — which greatly influenced later kabbalists, especially the 16th cent. school at Safed, although his work was not widely known and little of it appeared in print. He called his method "The Path of the Names" in contrast to the kabbalistic doctrine — or path — of the *sephirot*. A. himself regarded his theories as the logical continuation of Maimonides' *Guide* which he deeply admired and to which he wrote a commentary.

ABULAFIA, MEIR BEN TODROS HA-LEVI (c. 1170-1244): Castilian talmudist. He was the first European scholar to attack Maimonides for his theory of resurrection (which A. believed would be corporeal) and other doctrines, thus precipitating the bitter 30-year Maimonist controversy. He was regarded as the leading contemporary Castilian rabbinic authority and many scholars, including Naḥmanides, submitted their halakhic queries for his decision. His main work is the Aramaic *Peratei Peratim* ("Minute Details"), which consisted of novellae on the entire Talmud; only the sections on *Bava Batra* and *Sanhedrin* have survived. Writing at great length, A. carefully analyzed all possible applications of the law; he explained difficult words by reference to Arabic.

ABULAFIA, TODROS BEN JOSEPH (1225-c. 1285): Spanish kabbalist and chief rabbi of Castile; nephew of Meir ben Todros Abulafia. Though he was close to the court, the asceticism which he practiced as well as preached was in sharp contrast to the general licentiousness of contemporary Jewish courtiers. He denounced the laxity of the Jews of Castile and demanded high standards of morality and religious observance. A.'s mystical teachings stressed the gnostic elements in Kabbalah. His *Otzar ha-Kavod* ("The Treasury of Glory"), a mystical commentary on talmudic legends, is a difficult work replete with esoteric references.

ACADEMIES: Institutions for the study of both the Written and ORAL LAW were held by the ancient rabbis to be so essential a feature of Jewish history that they could not conceive of a time when no a. existed. The *aggadah* is replete with stories of the patriarchs — especially Jacob — studying at the famous a. of Shem and Eber (cf. *Gen. Rab.* 68:11). The idealization of the a. is such that R. Ḥama ben Ḥanina states "A. never ceased to exist in the history of our forefathers" (*Yoma* 28b). According to rabbinic tradition, the chief exponents of the Law were carried away into Babylonian exile together with King Jehoiachin (*Gitt.* 88a). Babylonia certainly became a great center of Jewish learning, so much so that HILLEL, who went from Babylonia to Palestine is generally thought to have taken with him the rich heritage of Babylonian scholarship. In Jerusalem, during the Second Temple Period, there are already definite historical references to an a. on the Temple Mount (*Suk.* 53a; *Tos. Sanh.* 7:1). Even while it stood, the Temple, generally a Sadducean stronghold, had begun to lose something of its hold upon the people as the prime expression of Jewish religious life. Spiritual leadership of the people was passing to the PHARISEES, and the schools of Hillel and Shammai (see BET HILLEL AND BET SHAMMAI), both belonging to the Pharisaic tradition, made the study of the *halakhah* the basis of all Jewish spiritual and intellectual endeavor. After the destruction of the Temple, the a. no less than the local synagogue replaced the Temple as the center of Jewish religion and Jewish nationhood. The lasting character of rabbinic Judaism was completely forged in the a. set up at YAVNEH, but there soon grew up other centers of Jewish learning. Several outstanding pupils of R. JOHANAN BEN ZAKKAI established a. at Lydda, Pekiin, Sikhnin, Benei Berak, and elsewhere in Palestine. But it was at Yavneh that the great work of establishing the definite form of prayer, of determining the biblical canon, and of codifying the Oral Law was begun. The period of the BAR KOKHBA revolt (131-135 C.E.) was one of great crisis for the Palestinian a. and many scholars left for Babylonia, Rome, and elsewhere. After the rebellion Jewish learning in Palestine was able to recover only in Galilee where the official academies of the Patriarchs were set up, first at Usha, then Sepphoris, Bet Shearim, and Tiberias. Here the official MISHNAH as determined by R. SIMEON BEN GAMALIEL and R. JUDAH HA-NASI was developed to its final stages of formulation. The Mishnah and TOSEPHTA brought to an end the period of the TANNAIM. Henceforth the work of the a. was to interpret the Mishnah and its parallel literature. This began the period of the AMORAIM which lasted in Palestine until the completion of the Palestinian TALMUD at the end of the 4th cent., in the a. of Tiberias. Apart from Tiberias, the academy of R. Abbahu in Caesarea contributed much to the Palestinian Talmud, and there were other centers at Sepphoris and Lydda. As a result of Byzantine oppression the a. of Palestine began to decline in the early 5th cent., and many scholars left for Babylonia. Not until the Arab conquest in the mid-7th cent. were they ever to recover in any measure, but it was already too late to overtake the firmly-established hegemony of the Babylonian schools.

The history of a. in Babylonia before the period of the Bar Kokhba rebellion can only be guessed. Definite historical information becomes available, however, with the Bar Kokhba period. The students of R. Akiva fled abroad — R. Yose (Yosi) ben Ḥalaphta to Cappadocia, R. Meir to Asia Minor, R. Eleazar ben Shammua and R. Johanan Ha-Sandlar to Nisibis, and R. Nehemiah to Babylonia. The students of R. Ishmael, R. Jonathan and R. Josiah, went to Hutzal. They either established their own temporary schools or joined the few already existing ones. Of the latter, the most famous were those of Judah ben Bathyra, already in existence before the destruction of the Temple, and of Hananiah nephew of R. Joshua at Nehar Pekod established around the end of the 1st cent. Hananiah had attempted to take over the hegemony from the Palestinian a. after the Bar Kokhba rebellion by assuming their prerogatives of establishing the dates for the festivals, of intercalating the years, and so forth. Only after a hard struggle did the students of R. Akiva, who reassembled in Usha in Palestine after the end of the persecutions, succeed in forcing Hananiah to relinquish these usurped rights. The students of R. Ishmael, however, did not return to Palestine. Remaining in Hutzal-Nehardea in Babylonia and at Nisibis, they provided a strong stimulus to Babylonian study. During the patriarchate of R. Judah Ha-Nasi in Palestine, Abba bar Abba was spiritual head of the Babylonian community in Nehardea. There were frequent exchanges in questions of *halakhah* between him and the scholars of Palestine. His son Samuel inherited this leadership and was recognized head of the first generation of *amoraim* in Babylonia. Samuel's distinguished colleague R. Abba bar Abba, known as Rav, returned from Palestine and established the great academy at Sura in south Babylonia. At this time the number of students at the a. was at its maximum. In addition to the 1,200 regular students at the academy of Rav (*Ket.* 106a), who probably received most of their material support from the resources of the academy, there assembled twice a year in the months of *Adar* and *Elul* (KALLAH MONTHS) students from all parts of Babylonia, to hear lectures on the particular tractate assigned each half year for home study. Taken over also by the academy at Pumbedita (which had replaced that of Nehardea, destroyed in 259), the institution of the *Kallah* months thrived with the passing of the generations. The Pumbedita academy was removed by Rava to his native Maḥoza where it was augmented by many pupils fleeing Roman persecution in Palestine. His successor Naḥman bar Isaac returned to Pumbedita, while his contemporary Pappa located his academy at Naresh, near Sura. During this period the editing of the Babylonian Talmud according to the varying traditions of Pumbedita and Naresh may be seriously considered to have begun. The close of the Talmud marks the end of the Amoraic Period. The SAVORAIM continued the work of the a. but limited themselves to adding explanatory notes to the Talmud and to polishing its literary form. With the Arab conquest, the Gaonic Period marked by a revival of the a. of Pumbedita and Sura was inaugurated. At the same time new Jewish centers developed in N. Africa, Spain, Italy, and the Rhine country. Yet Saadyah, *gaon* of Sura in the early 10th cent., and Sherira and Hai at Pumbedita in the latter 10th and early 11th cents. successfully maintained the prestige of the Babylonian a. The a. eventually removed to Baghdad, and the 12th cent. traveler Benjamin of Tudela found ten a. in Baghdad. The great days of the Babylonian a. were by now definitely past. Three important new a. had been set up during the 10th cent.: that of Shemariah in Cairo, Hushiel in Kairouan, and Moses ben Enoch in Cordova. The academy at Kairouan achieved its prime stature under Hananel, son of Hushiel, at the end of the 10th cent. Hananel wrote what may perhaps be considered as the first comprehensive commentary to the Talmud, and is considered the inaugurator of the "rabbinic" period. Contemporary with Hananel was the second great luminary of N. Africa, Isaac Alfasi, whose academy was at Fez. Meanwhile the French-German center had begun to develop. Its great name in the 10th cent. was R. Gershom who headed the Mayence school and whose pupils were the teachers of Rashi. A. sprang up in many places during the period of the tosaphists; Jacob of Orleans even established an academy in London during the 12th cent. Jehiel of Paris took his academy of about 300 students to Palestine in 1306. Provence and Spain also had many a., two especially important ones being those of R. Asher in Toledo and Solomon ben Adret in Barcelona. Padua in Italy was famed for its academy in the early 16th cent., Holland for its *Etz Ḥayyim* academy in the 18th cent. During the 18th cent. there were important a. in Altona-Hamburg, Frankfort-on-Main, Metz, Nikolsburg. The first great academy in E. Europe was set up in Cracow during the early 15th cent. by Jacob Pollak, who inaugurated the new system of pilpulistic study. So great was the attraction that hundreds of students flocked to him, and Cracow became the chief center of Jewish study. His pupils established their own a. all over Poland. Apparently all a. simultaneously studied the same tractate of the Talmud according to a set order. During the vacation periods both students and teachers would find their way to the great cities of Poland where the students could listen to any master they chose. The centers in the Turkish empire (Salonica, Constantinople) and particularly Palestine experienced a revival in Jewish learning following the Spanish expulsion, and during the 16th cent. important a. were set up in Safed by Jacob Berab and Joseph Karo, and in Jerusalem by Levi Ibn Ḥabib. It was during the 19th and early 20th cents. that the great center of Jewish learning moved east in Europe to Russia and Lithuania. The academy of Volozhin was founded in 1803 by R. Ḥayyim, pupil of the Gaon, Elijah of Vilna. The pilpulistic method of earlier Polish study was in great measure abandoned, and emphasis was placed on the analysis of the text as taught by the Gaon of Vilna. At first R. Ḥayyim supported his students out of his own funds, but later, as expenses increased, sent out emissaries. It was Volozhin that set the pattern for many other Lithuanian, Russian, and Polish academies. Among those of international fame may be mentioned: Slobodka, Mir, Telz, Ponivezh, Radom, Lomzeh, Minsk, Vilna, Kovno, Radin, Kamanetz. Prime emphasis was on the study of the halakhic parts of the Talmud (the *aggadah* being frequently omitted). The pupils would listen to a daily lecture of about two hours, spending the rest of the time in preparation and review. A different system of study developed in the a. of Hungary and Galicia, especially in that of Moses Sopher in Pressburg with the emphasis more on the study of the codes which had little place in the curriculum of the Lithuanian-type academy. The destruction of European Jewry during World War II forced the closing of these a. Some found temporary haven in places like Shanghai and Japan. Many transferred to the U.S. (e.g. Telz, in Cleveland) and Palestine (e.g. Mir, in Jerusalem). The talmudic academy struck its first roots in America in 1886 with the opening of the *Etz Ḥayyim yeshivah* in New York. The Isaac Elchanan academy was founded in 1897. Beginning with the 1930's, higher schools of Jewish talmudic learning began to multiply rapidly. A characteristic of both the earlier and later schools was the introduction of secular studies alongside the regular intensive Talmud program. The two great centers of talmudic study today are Israel and the U.S. where scores of talmudic a. exist and where Talmud is also studied in universities and Jewish theological schools. See also METIVTA: YESHIVAH.

ACADEMY ON HIGH: The Midrash quotes R. Ḥanina as saying "The Holy One, blessed be He, is destined to set up an academy of His own elders; that is the meaning of the verse (Is. 24:23) 'And the Lord of Hosts shall reign in glory on Mount Zion and in Jerusalem, and before His (own) elders will be glory.'" Over that academy the Almighty Himself presides, sitting at the head of the half-circle which was the traditional form of seating for the earthly SANHEDRIN (*Lev. Rab.* 11:8). Upon their own death, the scholars and those who supported them are merely transferred from the earthly to the heavenly academy where they continue their studies under this Divine presidency. The phrase "Academy on High" is also used for the *familia* — the Council of Angels with whom the Almighty is said to consult. The traditional formula permitting worship with transgressors, which precedes the *Kol Nidrei* prayer, beginning "By authority of the Academy on High and the Academy on Earth" was introduced by R. Meir of Rothenburg in the 13th cent.

ACCENTS: Signs employed in the biblical text to mark sentence structure and the manner of cantillation; in Hebrew, *taamei ha-mikra*. These signs, like the vowel-signs (see ALPHABET), were introduced in the 8th-9th cents. C.E., and like the latter, exist in three different systems: Babylonian, Palestinian, and Tiberian. Similar though less developed systems exist among the Samaritans, in Syriac and in Arabic. The Tiberian system is the only one now in use. It has two distinct sets of signs: one for Psalms, Job, and Proverbs, the other for the remaining books. Each set consists of Dividing or Disjunctive a. (12 in the Psalms, etc., 18 in the other books) and Connecting or Conjunctive in the non-Tiberian systems. They alternate to some extent with the hyphen (*makkaph*) connecting 2-4 words, of which only one then receives an accent. The dividing a. are in four grades of disjunctive force, which may be compared in their syntactic effects to full stops, semicolons, and commas, but in fact occur much more frequently than the corresponding English signs. As a general rule, a divider occurs after every two or three words, often in the middle of a clause. The choice of individual signs is governed by complicated rules. If properly understood, the a. can be of great value in determining the structure and meaning of biblical sentences, and have been extensively used in this way by the Jewish medieval commentators (Abraham Ibn Ezra wrote "Take no notice of any commentary that does not rely on the a."). On the other hand, the ancient translations sometimes divide the sentences differently from the accepted version. One rabbinic tradition holds that the a. were given to Moses on Sinai, forgotten, and revived by Ezra. The kabbalists found mystic significance in the a. The musical interpretation of the a. in cantillation varies greatly from one Jewish group to another. The public reading of the Law and the *haphtarah* must be done according to the a. and their traditional cantillation. Since the Scroll of the Law has neither vowel points nor a. (and hence is also without verse dividers), the reader must prepare himself and there are versions printed for this purpose without vowels and a. (*tikkun ha-kore*). On the other hand, since the 9th cent., experts have prepared model codices with all vowels and a. for the guidance of readers and scribes; these are called in the orient "crown" (*keter torah*, Arabic *taj*), among Karaites "sanctuary" (*mikdashyah*). The most famous is the Aleppo Codex written by Aaron BEN ASHER from which the Tiberian tradition is derived.

ACCIDENT: The laws of liability for damage caused by a. is one of the most fully developed branches of Jewish civil law. In their analysis of the brief passages in Exod. 21:28-36; 22:4-5 that deal with various kinds of damage inflicted on persons or property, the rabbis regard the individual cases cited not as haphazard choices but as the four standard types of accidents, each of which causes injury in a different way but all imposing the onus of liability on the person responsible. The four — "the ox, the pit, the crop-devouring animal, and fire"— are the primary causes of a. and injury; every other instance is derivative. Thus the first represents injury caused in the course of normal activity, the second, by a stationary thing, the third, accidents caused not in public places but the private property of the person injured, and the fourth, consequential damage (*Bava Kamma* 1:1). Accidental manslaughter was punishable by exile to one of the CITIES OF REFUGE where the culprit had to remain until the death of the reigning High Priest (Exod. 21:13; Deut. 19:1-7, 11-13).

ACCIDENTS: In philosophy: ATTRIBUTES or qualities that are not essential to a thing. One of the persistent problems in Jewish as in general theology is the question of the Divine attributes, i.e., the determination of the unique qualities of GOD. Attributing qualities (such as goodness, greatness, etc.) to God may seem to imply that there is something "accidental" about Him viz., something added to His essence or being. But on the other hand, God must be defined as that Being in whom there are no accidents. Hence the medieval Jewish philosophers attempted to interpret and explain away the qualities of the Bible attributed to God and which seemed to imply that God possessed attributes accidental to His essence. Thus the human emotions and reactions attributed to God, such as love, wrath, etc., could not be considered as essential to the Divine Being; these biblical expressions were therefore interpreted as figures of speech or as concessions to the limitations of human understanding.

ACHAN: Member of the tribe of Judah in the period of Joshua's conquest of Canaan. A. committed sacrilege by helping himself to the consecrated spoil of Jericho. This act reflected on the entire nation and in punishment the Israelites suffered a severe reverse in their attack on Ai. When A.'s guilt was traced, he and his family were stoned to death (Josh. 7:1-26). The Talmud finds a mitigation of judgment in A.'s ultimate confession (*ibid.* 20) and maintains that this saved him from eternal punishment (*Sanh.* 43b-44).

ACOSTA (DA COSTA), URIEL (orig. Gabriel; 1585-1640): Religious skeptic; born in Portugal of MARRANO parents. His study of the Bible led him to doubt Christianity and he escaped with his family to Amsterdam (1615) where he discovered, however, that the Judaism to which he had converted was different from the idea he had formed of it during his studies. Recognizing only his literal understanding of the Bible as Jewish, he attacked, orally and in print, both the general rabbinic tradition and the particular doctrines of immortality and resurrection. As a result he was excommunicated from Judaism. Poverty and isolation forced him to recant (1633), but he soon repeated his attacks on rabbinic Judaism and was again put under ban. In 1640 he recanted once more but was required to subject himself to flogging and public penance. Having undergone the ordeal he wrote a short autobiography and then committed suicide. His tragic fate and abortive spiritual odyssey have inspired several novels and dramas by modern authors.

ACROSTICS: Literary device, employed especially in verse. A. are generally composed in alphabetic order or from personal names or words. Alphabetic a. are found in the Bible (e.g. Ps. 34; Ps. 119; Prov. 31:10-31; Lam. 1-4; Nah. 1-2:10). A. became frequent in Hebrew literature from the Gaonic Period on, especially in the liturgy (e.g. *Ein K-Elohenu, An'im Zemirot,* the *Seliḥot* prayers), where this usage facilitated the memorization of prayers (particularly important in the pre-printing era). They are often based on the author's name or on a biblical quotation.

AD MEAH (VE-ESRIM) SHANAH (Heb. "Until a hundred [and twenty] years"): Expression of good wishes, used especially in referring to the elderly (e.g. on the occasion of their birthday). The term is derived from the 120 years lived by Moses, which is hence regarded as the ideal life-span.

ADAFINA (or **ANI**): Among *Sephardi* Jews, a Sabbath dish consisting of beans, peas, meat, and eggs; also known as *ḥamin,* it is analagous to the *Ashkenazi cholent*. The Inquisition regarded the preparation and consumption of this dish as an indication of the observance of Jewish practices.

ADAM (Heb. "man"): Biblical designation of the first man, progenitor of the human species; also "man" in the general sense. A.'s origin is related in two distinct biblical accounts: (1) Gen. 1:26-30 is a brief account. Man was created by God on the sixth day of creation, both male and female, in the Divine image; he was to multiply and rule over all life. (2) Gen. 2-3 is more comprehensive. God fashioned man out of earth, breathed into his nostrils the breath of life, and charged him with tending and keeping the GARDEN OF EDEN. EVE, A.'s helpmeet, was created from his rib. Succumbing to temptation, they ate of Eden's forbidden "Tree of Knowledge" for which they were expelled and punished. Critical scholarship recognizes here the narrative of two different authors, possibly two ancient Israelite epic tales. The narratives are projected from two different points of view. The first portrays man against the background of universal Creation while the second evaluates the Universe from the viewpoint of man. Both however are alike in presenting man as God-like, and both are purely monotheistic in conception. There are certain affinities with parallel Mesopotamian and Egyptian tales but the biblical story is unique in the grandeur of its ethical concept. Elaborations of the A. story are found in the post-biblical pseudepigrapha and Apocrypha. Christian Patristic writings stress A.'s fall and ORIGINAL SIN. Talmudic treatment, some of it also reflected in the Koran, discusses God's purpose in creating man and also man's relations to the Heavenly Hosts as well as to lower forms of creation. Kabbalists maintained that A. received a revelation from God, the secrets of which were preserved by the mystics, and thus they speak of a "mystical Adam," the ADAM KADMON.

ADAM AND EVE, BOOK OF: Pseudepigraphic work which has been preserved in four versions — Greek, Latin, Armenian, and Slavonic. Its original language was apparently Hebrew, while the non-Greek versions appear to have been made from the Greek translation. The book contains legends associated with the history of Adam and Eve after their expulsion from Eden, their repentance, and burial. The conjectured date of composition is the late Second Temple Period. The authorship has been ascribed to Jewish mystic circles, possibly the Essenes. A number of apocryphal *Books of Adam* of Christian origin have also survived.

ADAM KADMON (Heb. "Primordial Man"): Kabbalistic symbol of the world of the SEPHIROT wherein the Divine macrocosm is pictured in the image of the human microcosm, as the material form of man, the creature, is held to reflect the spiritual form of existence of God, the Creator. The notion of a mystical "Primordial Man" seems to go back to earlier, gnostic types of speculation. The term *A.K.* is found in the *tikkunim* of the ZOHAR, whereas the Zohar itself uses the term *adam de-le-ela* ("celestial man"). According to Isaac LURIA who developed this symbol in an original way, *A.K.* is the first configuration of the Divine light flowing from God, the EIN-SOPH, into the primordial "space" made possible by *tzimtzum* (i.e., the withdrawing of the Creator within Himself). *A.K.* is thus the highest form of the manifestation of the Divinity after the process of *tzimtzum*. The *sephirot* come into existence when they break out as lights from the eyes, ears, nose, and mouth of *A.K.* The Lurianic doctrine of TIKKUN is based upon the analogy between biblical Adam, on the anthropological plane, and *A.K.*, on the ontological plane. Thus Man before his fall is a kind of cosmic being reflecting the entire world of existence as symbolized in *A.K.*

ADAR: 12th month of the Jewish religious year, 6th of the civil; falls approximately in March. The name is of Assyrian origin (*adaru*) and its zodiacal sign is *Pisces*. The feast of PURIM, which falls on *Adar* 14 (and *Shushan Purim* on the 15th) imparts a festive character to the entire month; hence the rabbinic dictum "When *A.* comes in, joy increases" (*Taan.* 29a). According to rabbinical tradition, *Adar* 7 is the anniversary of both the birth and the death of Moses and was a date for rejoicing — or alternatively fasting — among various Jewish communities (the fast-day was observed in 17th cent. Europe in Turkey, Italy, and N. Europe and the custom spread to ḥasidic circles). *Adar* 9 was traditionally held to be the date for the split between the school of Hillel and the school of Shammai, and was decreed as a fast-day. *Adar* 13 was Nicanor day — the anniversary of Judah the Maccabee's defeat of the Syrian general, Nicanor, in 161 B.C.E. — observed originally as a festival but later becoming the Fast of ESTHER. *Adar* 16 was a feast-day as according to tradition Nehemiah recommenced the rebuilding of the walls of Jerusalem on that day. *Adar* 20 being the date of ḤONI HA-MEAGGEL's miraculous invocation of rain was observed at one time as a feast-day. In leap years, all anniversaries are observed in the second month of A. — ADAR SHENI. A. lasts 29 days in an ordinary year; 30 days in a leap year.

ADAR SHENI (Heb. "Second month of *Adar*"): Intercalated month inserted in leap years after the month of ADAR (see CALENDAR). In such years all observances and regulations relating to the month of *Adar* are transferred to A.S. In the case of deaths occurring in *Adar*, the KADDISH prayer is recited in the First *Adar* when the first anniversary falls in a leap year but in A.S. in all subsequent leap years. A.S. has 29 days.

ADAT YISRAEL (or *Adas Yisroel*; Heb. "Congregation of Israel"): Name assumed by the separatist Orthodox movement founded in Berlin in opposition to the extant Jewish community of that city, which also included REFORM groups. By

1885, the movement received legal recognition as a separate community with its own synagogues, school system, ritual slaughtering system, ecclesiastical court, hospital, and burial grounds. Its aims were strictly traditional, i.e., the upholding of the biblical and talmudic laws and institutions as codified in the *Shulḥan Arukh.* The final decision to secede was taken in 1864 upon the death of the Orthodox rabbi Michael Sachs, after the extreme liberal wing of the Berlin community had summoned Abraham Geiger to become communal rabbi. The Berlin *A.Y.* was a significant center of Orthodox separatism next only in importance to the community in Frankfort-on-Main. It influenced the foundation of similar communities in E. Europe, Britain, and the U.S.

ADDIR BI-MELUKHAH (Heb. "Mighty in Kingship"): Alphabetical acrostic hymn listing Divine epithets and based on a legend in *Gen. Rab.* 6:2. It was introduced by *Ashkenazim* into the Passover *Haggadah* in the Middle Ages. Its date is obscure but it was probably written in France or Germany. See Addir Hu.

ADDIR HU (Heb. "Mighty is He"): Alphabetic acrostic hymn containing a prayer for the speedy rebuilding of the Temple. It was added to the Passover *Haggadah* in 15th cent. Germany (in the Avignon rite it was recited on all festivals). Originally *A.H.* was sung only on the second *Seder* night and addir bi-melukhah on the first, but since the 18th cent. both have been sung on both nights.

ADDITIONAL SERVICE, see **MUSAPH**

ADDITIONAL SOUL, see **NESHAMAH YETERAH**

ADLER: British family of rabbis. *NATHAN MARCUS A.* (1803-1890), Chief Rabbi of the British Empire from 1845, was largely responsible for the foundation of Jews' College and the United Synagogue and author of *Netinah la-Ger* ("A gift to the stranger") a standard commentary on Targum Onkelos. His son *HERMANN A.* (1839-1911) succeeded him as Chief Rabbi.

ADLOYADA (Aram.): *Purim* carnival. The name derives from the rabbinic remark that on *Purim* a man should revel until he does not know (*ad delayeda*) to distinguish between "blessed be Mordecai" and "cursed be Haman".

ADMOR (abb. of Heb. *Adonenu Morenu ve-Rabbenu* — "Our master, teacher, and rabbi"): Hebrew title given by the Ḥasidim to their Tzaddikim and rabbinical authorities.

ADON OLAM (Heb. "Eternal Lord"): Dogmatic hymn of unknown authorship probably dating from the Gaonic Period (although it has also been ascribed to Solomon Ibn Gabirol). It extols in poetic form the Unity, timelessness, and providence of God in whom it also expresses faith and trust. *A.O.* is generally recited at the beginning of the Morning Service in the *Ashkenazi* rite and in many rites at the conclusion of the Additional Service as well. In some rites it is sung after the Evening Service on Sabbaths and festivals. Many Jews recite this prayer before falling asleep (which may have been the original intention of its author) and it is also customary to say it on a deathbed. In Morocco, it was recited while leading the bride under the bridal canopy.

ADONAI (Heb. "My Lord"): Metonym traditionally substituted for the Divine name YHWH (the Tetragrammaton). Already by the time of the Septuagint translation (2nd cent. B.C.E.), A. was used at all times in Bible reading; a talmudic tradition reports that the original pronunciation was revealed by the rabbis to their disciples once or twice every seven years (*Kidd.* 71a) but even that practice eventually lapsed. Subsequently, sanctity was also attached to the word *A.* itself and religious Jews refused to pronounce it, substituting instead *Ha-Shem* ("The [Divine] name") or the artificial combination *Adoshem.* It became customary also to avoid writing the word *A.* and to substitute the abbreviation יי׳, ה׳, or ד׳. See also God, Names of

ADOPTION: A legal fiction whereby the relationship of parent and child is regarded as existing between persons not so naturally related. There are in the Bible cases of a., such as Sarah's wish that the child of her handmaid by Abraham be regarded as her son (Gen. 15:2), the a. by Jacob, with symbolic ceremony, of his two grandsons as his sons (Gen. 48:5), or Mordecai's a. of Esther (Est. 2:7). There are also aggadic statements to the effect that "whosoever rears an orphan in his home is regarded as having given birth to him", "whosoever teaches the son of his friend *Torah* is deemed to be his father" (*Sanh.* 19b). Nevertheless, a. is not recognized as legal in Jewish law and the a. of a child does not relieve the adopting parents of the consequences of childlessness (e.g. exempting the mother from levirate marriage or *ḥalitzah* in the case of the death of the husband) nor can such a child legally claim inheritance should his foster-father die intestate. In modern Israel a form of a. has been evolved whereby, without overcoming the religious difficulties, the rights of the child to care, maintenance, and inheritance are legally assured.

ADOSHEM: Artificial combination of Adonai ("My Lord") and *Ha-Shem* ("The Name" [of God]) frequently substituted as the Divine name in place of *Adonai* (itself a substitution for the Tetragrammaton) which is regarded by many Jews as too holy to pronounce.

ADRET, SOLOMON BEN (known from his initials as *Rashba;* 1235-1310): Spanish rabbinical authority. For over 40 years rabbi in Barcelona he was regarded as the outstanding spiritual leader of Spanish Jewry of his time. His halakhic responsa (over 2,000, out of some 16,000 have been published) are outstanding for their clear exposition, beside containing valuable historical and cultural information. He deals with all facets of religious, family, and civil law, and his decisions greatly influenced the development of Jewish law, laying the foundation for the subsequent authoritative code (*Turim*) of JACOB BEN ASHER and the SHULḤAN ARUKH. A. also wrote novellae on the Talmud, only a section of which (on 15 tractates) has been published, combining the erudite traditions of both French and Spanish rabbinical scholarship. The novellae concentrate on discussions of selected portions which A. keenly analyzes, reconciling apparent contradictions. His other works include a commentary on rabbinical legends, works on the laws practiced in the home and on the laws of the Sabbath and festivals. A. also had a knowledge of philosophy and defended Maimonides in the revived Maimonist controversy; he opposed both rationalistic allegory and excessive mysticism. He did not object to secular scientific or philosophical pursuits as such but opposed overconcentration in these fields to the detriment of the study of the *Torah*; so while refusing to ban such studies outright, he forbade them to students under the age of 30 (1305). A. also engaged in polemics and replied to the Dominican Raymond Martini's *Pugio Fidei* with a work setting out to prove the eternity of the *Torah* and the importance of the practical commandments.

ADULT: Nowhere in the Bible is there any clear indication of the age at which a minor attains his majority. The only relevant statements are that an able-bodied male was liable to military service from the age of 20 (Num. 1:3) and that the levite entered into the service of the sanctuary at the age of 25 (Num. 8:24) or 30 (Num. 8:23). Rabbinic law, however, established the appearance of the first signs of puberty as the onset of majority and laid this down generally as happening at the age of 12 years and 1 day in the case of females, and 13 years and 1 day in the case of males (*Nid.* 52a). On attaining the age of 12 years and a day a female ceased to be a minor and entered the category of *naarah* ("girl") in which she remained for six months until she became fully adult. The attainment of such majority does not however come automatically with age. The ages were selected as the normal period during which the first signs of puberty (two pubic hairs) appear. Where no such signs are evident, minority could extend to the age of 20, and in some cases even 35. Naturally, child-bearing would establish the majority of a female even in the absence of other signs. A person who attains his majority is regarded as responsible in all religious and ritual matters. In the Mishnah, 13 is described as the age "for the fulfillment of commandments" (*Avot.* 5:24). The desirability for a *Ḥazzan* to have a beard established the minimum age of a regular officiant at 18 or 20. Recent Israeli law has raised the age of consent for marriage of a female to 17 years and a day.

ADULTERY: Jewish law defines a., which is proscribed in the Ten Commandments (Exod. 20:13), as any sexual relations between a married woman and a man other than her husband. The crime (if properly witnessed) carries the death penalty for both offending parties (Lev. 20:10). Relations with a "betrothed woman" (i.e., who has *kiddushin* but not *nissuin;* see MARRIAGE) involve an even greater guilt (Deut. 22:23-24), as does the action of an adulterous woman of priestly descent (Lev. 21:9). The trial of a woman suspected of faithlessness (SOTAH) by the ordeal of "the bitter water that causeth the curse" (Num. 5:11 ff.) was suspended at the time of the Mishnah (*Sot.* 9:9). Any intrusion into a marriage by a. irrevocably destroys its sanctity, and it must be dissolved by divorce, even if the husband forgives his guilty wife (*Sot.* 25a). As added deterrents to a. the subsequent marriage between the two offending parties is also forbidden (*loc. cit.*) and any offspring produced by a. is bastard (*mamzer*) and debarred from marriage with anyone except his or her like or a proselyte. Jewish law, by branding a. as a penal crime, differs from modern systems of law in regarding the act not as a private or purely moral delict but as an offense against the social order; hence the warning attached to the proscription of a.: "and thou shalt put away the evil from Israel" (Deut. 22:22). Indeed, a. — together with incest — is one of the three cardinal crimes (the other two being idolatry and bloodshed) which must not be committed even if the alternative is death. While capital guilt ensues only from a. as defined above, biblical and rabbinic writings strongly condemn any sexual relations and intimacies outside marriage, including those between a married man and any woman other than his wife (which are not proscribed as a. proper since biblical and talmudic law tolerated polygamy in principle). To avoid temptation to such promiscuous relations, the rabbis prohibited all private meetings between individuals of opposite sexes except between spouses or between parents and children.

AFAM: Abbreviation formed from the names of the 3 NW Italian communities — Asti, Fossano, and Moncalvo — that followed the old French liturgical rite.

AFIKOMAN, see **APHIKOMAN**

AFTERNOON SERVICE, see **MINḤAH**

AGE, see **ADULT**

AGENT (Heb. *shaliah*): The main point of the Jewish law of agency is expressed in the dictum "A person's a. is regarded as the person himself" (*Ned.* 72b; *Kidd.* 41b). Therefore any act committed by a duly appointed a. is regarded as having been committed by the principal, who therefore bears full responsibility for it with consequent complete absence of liability on the part of the a. A number of results stem from this basic premise. The a. must be of the same legal status and standing as his principal. The appointment of a minor, imbecile, or deaf mute as an a. is invalid, as is any appointment by them (*Bava Kamma* 6:4). Similarly, the death of the principal automatically voids the agency. Betrothal or divorce by proxy is effected by appointing the proxy as an a. The a. is regarded as acting in his principal's interest and not to his detriment, and in any dispute as to whether the a. exceeded the terms of his agency this consideration is taken into account. The only exception to the plenipotentiary powers of the a. within the terms of his agency is the rule that "One cannot be an agent for a transgression" (*Kidd.* 42b); the law of agency applies only to legal acts, and a person committing a crime as the a. of a principal is held responsible for his act.

AGGADAH (or *Haggadah*): The non-legal contents of the Talmud and Midrash, including — often by way of biblical exegesis — ethical and moral teaching, theological speculation, legends, folklore, gnomic sayings, prayers, historical information, praise of Israel and the Holy Land, interpretation of dreams, and expressions of messianic faith and longing. Many theories have been advanced as to the source of the name *aggadah*. Some derive it from the Hebrew *huggad* (things which are "said", "spoken" — in contrast to biblical stories, which are written). Others take it from the rabbinic expression used in expounding Scripture, *maggid ha-katuv* ("Scripture states"). Still others connect it with the scriptural verse *ve-higgadeta le-vinekha* ("and thou shalt tell unto thy son," Exod. 13:8), which implies the relating of something other than Law and ordinances. The Mishnah contains relatively little *a.*, and that usually appears at the end of treatises, or after individual sections within the treatise, as a kind of epilogue to the completed study of a unified segment of legal subject matter. On the other hand, about a third of the Palestinian Talmud and approximately a fourth of the Babylonian Talmud is comprised of *a.* Here, too, it is frequently introduced to mark off one section of legal study from another. The *a.* serves not only as a kind of relief from strenuous, concentrated halakhic discourse, but also to keep the ethical ideals of the Law ever fresh and meaningful, complementing the HALAKHAH though lacking its binding character. It elaborates and develops the stories of Scripture so as to draw from them the maximum of moral instruction. Unlike *halakhah, a.* need not derive from an ancient recognized source, but may be the free individual creation of every generation. The *a.* is rich in literary forms, including parable, metaphor, personification, satire, poetry. It plays with homonymous roots, it computes the numerical value of letters to gain new information, it substitutes letters to reveal new nuances of meaning in Scripture, it even interprets individual letters of a particular word as the abbreviation of a series of words. The Bible is the source and fountainhead of the *a.* even more than the *halakhah*, for *a.* concerns itself as much with the Prophets and the Hagiographa as it does with the Pentateuch. Like *halakhah*, too, *a.* developed rules (MIDDOT) for the exposition of Scripture, and here again the number of its rules is greater (e.g. the thirty-two rules ascribed to Eliezer ben Yose ha-Galili) and their application much freer. Some of these hermeneutic rules have been found to resemble the ancient methods for the interpretation of dreams and oracles, and similarities have been pointed out between the dream interpretation of the rabbis and the *Onirocriticus* of Artemidorus. Whereas only few rules could be admitted for the elaboration and elucidation of *halakhah*, almost every currently established literary device could be used in *a.* There were ancient traditions of *a.* just as there were of *halakhah*, and they are usually introduced by a phrase such as *masoret aggadah* ("it is an aggadic tradition"). Thus the Midrash *Shoher Tov* to Ps. 18:32 relates the aggadic tradition that Judah killed Esau after the death of Isaac. *Tanhuma* (58:17) mentions a "tradition" that Jerusalem will only be rebuilt after the ingathering of the Diaspora. Collections or "books" of *a.* seem to be very old. The Jerusalem Talmud (*Kil.* 32b) notes an aggadic book on the Psalms which was known at the time of R. Judah. A talmudic passage (*Sanh.* 57b) suggests the existence of a collection of *a.* on Genesis. R. Johanan (Y. *Horayot* 48b) stated that he knew all the *a.* except for that to Proverbs and Ecclesiastes. That these collections were actually committed to writing is implied by a report to the effect that R. Johanan and Resh Lakish read from such a book on the Sabbath (*Tem.* 14b); or by such statements as "one who reads *a.* from a book will not quickly forget it" (Y. *Ber.* 9). As a natural extension of the Aramaic exposition of the *Torah* reading in the synagogue, *a.* was also the source of the sermon which it finally dominated to the exclusion of *halakhah*. Even in the academies students would ask their teachers for "instruction in *a.*" when the latter were too tired to teach *halakhah*. Although *a.* has no systematic philosophy, it deals in its own way with basic theological and moral problems. Many non-Jewish concepts found their way into *a.* and almost all the schools of Greek thought left traces there. The first book of edited *a.* does not antedate the 4th cent. The aggadic sections of the Talmud were collected in the *Ein Yaakov* of Jacob IBN ḤAVIV. A special appendix to the YALKUT SHIMONI contains a collection of all the *a.* in the Palestinian Talmud. Modern study of *a.* began with Zunz. There have been several modern collections, notably that of Louis Ginzberg, who, in his *Legends of the Jews* (1909-28), arranged the *a.* according to the chronological order of the Scriptures. The *Sepher ha-Aggadah* of Bialik and Ravnitzki has brought widespread popularity to *a.* in modern Israel. See also HOMILETICS.

AGGADAT BERESHIT (Heb. "Legend of Genesis"): Midrash on Genesis composed of 28 homilies each of which is subdivided into 3 parts, connected respectively with verses in Genesis, the prophetical books, and the Hagiographa. *A.B.* is based on other Midrashim, especially the early Midrash *Tanḥuma.* It dates from the 12th cent. approximately.

AGGADAT ESTER (Heb. "Legend of Esther"): Midrash on the Book of Esther. Its sources are talmudic and midrashic, though the compiler was not aware of ESTHER RABBAH. Its origin is apparently Yemenite and the quotations from Alfasi and Maimonides indicate a date not earlier than the 13th cent.

AGGADAT MASHIAḤ (Heb. "Legend of the Messiah"): Collection of homilies describing the messianic era, preserved in the Midrash *Pesikta Zutarta* which was written in the late 11th or early 12th cent. It is composed of early legends and was edited by R. TOBIAH BEN ELIEZER.

AGLA: A Divine name composed according to kabbalists from the initials of the phrase *Attah gibbor le-olam adonai* ("Thou art mighty forever, O Lord"). During the Middle Ages Christians in Germany used the phrase as a talisman against fire and inscribed it — together with a cross — on wooden bowls; they interpreted the letters as initials of the German phrase *Allmächtiger Gott, Lösche Aus* ("Almighty God, extinguish the conflagration").

AGNOSTICISM: As originally formulated in the 19th cent. by T. H. Huxley, a. designated an attitude of suspended judgment, particularly in religious matters. In this sense, it was hardly compatible with traditional Jewish religion, which considered God's reality as well as certain other beliefs as absolutely certain on the authority of revelation. Even Job, however much he questioned God's justice, never doubted His existence and power. Agnostic tendencies, denying the possibility of metaphysical knowledge, existed in ancient Greek as well as medieval philosophy. SAADYAH GAON criticized the view that it was proper for man to refrain from believing anything or from affirming any objective reality. Whereas this radical type of a. was never approved in Jewish philosophy, another kind of a., based on the transcendence of God, was much favored by theologians. According to MAIMONIDES, man can "comprehend only the fact that He exists, but not His essence" (*Guide* 1:58). The a. of Maimonides extends to all that is beyond man's earthly experience, as when he writes "we can obtain no knowledge of the essence of the heavens" (*loc. cit.*). A. can become dogmatic as a result of a proneness to attribute unknowability to that which is merely unknown, e.g. when Maimonides wrote of the impossibility of an "iron ship flying through space" (in his *Eight Chapters*). On the other hand, agnostic insistence that the human mind cannot grasp the whole of reality ("If I knew Him, I would be He," wrote Saadyah) often functioned as a wise methodological reservation, inducing men to concentrate on intellectually manageable problems.

AGRARIAN LAWS: All laws and ordinances, whether of pentateuchal or rabbinic origin, which concern AGRICULTURE—especially the tilling of the soil — apply as a rule only in the Land of Israel (unlike most other commandments which must be observed everywhere). However, even in the Land of Israel the status enjoyed by any one part of the country depends on whether it was within the historic boundaries established and thus "sanctified" by the first and second "conquests" (that of Joshua and the post-exilic one respectively). A.L. are treated systematically in the first order of the Mishnah (called ZERAIM — "seeds"); they are discussed in detail in the Palestinian Talmud, but are dealt with only incidentally in the Babylonian. The underlying assumption is that the Land of Israel belongs to God (Lev. 25:23) and hence is holy ground. By observing certain restrictions and separating parts of the harvest as an offering, or as gifts to the priests, levites, and poor, the owner of the soil will become conscious of his status as a mere "steward" who only acts in behalf of the true "owner". The a.l. include:

PEAH (the corner of the field, gleanings, and the "forgotten sheaf"; Lev. 19:9-10; 23:22; Deut. 24:19-22): All of these are to be left in the field for the benefit of the poor. This is not usually observed today in Israel.

KILAYIM (the mixing of two or more kinds of seed in one field or the grafting of different kinds of fruit-trees; Lev. 19:19; Deut. 22:9). It is forbidden to grow *k.* or even to preserve them when they grow accidentally; in some cases the resultant produce must not be eaten or even be put to any other use. *K.* is observed in the State of Israel today.

SHEMITTAH (the Year of Release — the seventh year; Exod. 23:10-11; Lev. 25:1 ff.): During the *Shemittah* all main types of agricultural work are prohibited; produce growing on its own is considered ownerless property (HEPHKER) and may be taken from the field by anyone in need. In Israel today, the prohibition of agricultural work in the *Shemittah* is mostly circumvented through a formal sale of all land to gentiles. In Temple times, the fiftieth year was the JUBILEE, when the land was restored to its original owners.

TERUMAH and MAASEROT (heave-offering and tithes; Num. 18:8 ff.; Deut. 14:22-27; 26:12-15): As long as these have not been set aside, the produce may not be eaten. Nowadays, in a formula worked out Rabbi ABRAHAM ISAIAH KARLITZ, known as *Hazon Ish*, an amount somewhat in excess of 1% of the produce is "redeemed" on a coin, and the balance may then be used. The amount set aside must be disposed of in a dignified manner. Originally, the *terumah* was given to a priest, the first tithe to a levite who in turn separated a "tithe of a tithe" for the priest; and a "second tithe" had to be consumed by the owner and his family in Jerusalem; however, it might also be "redeemed." Every third year a "poor man's tithe" was set aside in place of the "second tithe."

ḤALLAH (a portion of dough to be given to the priest; Num. 15:17-21): Today *ḥ.* is burned. Applies also outside Israel.

ORLAH: The prohibition against eating or making use of the fruit of a newly planted tree during the first three years of its growth; and *Revai*, the obligation to "redeem" the fruit of the fourth year of the vineyard (Lev. 19:23-25). Observed in Israel.

BIKKURIM: The FIRST FRUITS of the seven kinds of produce for which the Land of Israel is famed according to Deut. 8.8 (cf. Exod. 23.19; Deut. 26:1 ff.). The *bikkurim* were taken to the Temple in solemn procession and offered there to the priest.

AGRAT (or IGIRIT) BAT MAḤALAT: In popular mythology a demon queen controlling 180,000 angels of destruction; traveling about in her chariot, she seeks to harm living creatures. According to the Talmud, R. Ḥanina ben Dosa limited her activities to the Sabbath eve and Wednesdays, while the *amora* Abbaye endeavored to banish her altogether but was not completely successful. According to the Zohar, A. will exist until the messianic era when God will destroy the spirit of uncleanness.

AGRICULTURE: The economy envisaged for the children of Israel by the laws of the Pentateuch was purely agricultural. The Holy Land was to be divided according to tribal areas and each family within the tribe was to receive its portion. Alienation of this ancestral land could only be temporary; in addition to the cancellation of debts every SABBATICAL YEAR, all land had to be returned to its original owners in the JUBILEE year. As a result the price of land was reckoned according to the number of crops it would produce until the Jubilee year. To such an extent was a. regarded as the essential occupation of the Jews in biblical times that the term "Canaanite" was regarded as synonymous with "trader" (Zech. 14:21; Hos. 12:8). Many of the Israelite feasts — particularly the three pilgrim festivals — have an agricultural basis and application. Thus Passover was a herdsman's and farmer's festival; Pentecost was the festival of the new grains; while Tabernacles was the gathering-in of the autumn harvest. The common element of these festive occasions was thanksgiving to God for His blessings. Many religious laws apply to agricultural produce and animal husbandry. According to the rabbis most of them are of biblical authority only in the Land of Israel, but many were given lesser rabbinical sanction outside Israel. Some apply only to the period of the Temple, others to all time (see AGRARIAN LAWS). The details of these various laws are dealt with exhaustively in the Talmud, though only the Palestinian Talmud has tractates developing the relevant Mishnah tractates, as these laws had a greater application in the Land of Israel. With the modern resettlement of the Jews in Palestine and their re-involvement with agricultural pursuits, especially after the establishment of the State of Israel, many of these laws, hitherto academic, have taken on practical application (though some of them, like FIRST FRUITS and the second TITHE, applied only in Temple times). On the other hand such laws as tithes, HEAVE-OFFERINGS, ORLAH, Sabbatical Year and Jubilee, and the law of the firstborn of animals are regarded as applicable at the present day. Apart from *orlah*, however, it is tacitly conceded that modern economic conditions do not permit the literal application of these laws. Advantage is taken of every legal loophole and even legal fiction to fulfill the spirit of these laws without necessarily applying the letter, so that their incidence might not weigh too heavily upon the farming community. This applies particularly to the laws of the Sabbatical Year, concerning which most agricultural settlements act in accordance with the far-reaching concessions worked out by the late Chief Rabbi Kook. Agricultural products sold to the public in Israel are certified to the effect that "Tithes and heave-offerings have been duly taken".

AGUDAT ISRAEL, see **RELIGIOUS PARTIES**

AGUNAH: A married woman in danger of remaining in permanent "widowhood" owing to the disappearance of her husband and the lack of decisive evidence establishing his death. In such cases the rabbis have in many respects relaxed the usual rigidity of the laws of EVIDENCE (e.g. by permitting the testimony of a single witness). While absence *per se* cannot dissolve a marriage, the prolonged absence of a husband — where willful desertion or enforced detention such as captivity can be ruled out — creates a presumption of death. Where this presumption of the missing husband's death is fortified by circumstances it may be accepted as corroboration of evidence which in itself would be insufficient to prove death. In modern wars the number of missing men whose presumed death cannot be proven has increased greatly. To protect wives from becoming *agunot* (pl.), many rabbis have instituted the custom that soldiers upon enlistment sign a declaration authorizing the grant of a DIVORCE to their wives in the event of their being officially declared as "missing, presumed dead". Proposals advocating the introduction of a conditional form of marriage that would spare a woman from becoming an *a.* because of malevolent desertion by her husband have been rejected by leading rabbinical authorities who feel that such extreme measures — if at all feasible — could rob marriage of its sanctity and also lead to many errors. Among Conservative Jews in the U.S., a similar controversy has developed. In the 1930's Rabbi Louis Epstein led an effort in the Rabbinical Assembly to solve the *a.* problem by halakhic means, principally by inserting a codicil to the KETUBBAH according to which the groom would authorize the Rabbinical Assembly *Bet Din* to declare his marriage null and void retroactively should *a.* conditions prevail as a result of his (unproved) death. This solution has not met the official approval of the Rabbinical Assembly, but many Conservative rabbis have, in any case, chosen to ignore the traditional law. Reform Jews are not guided at all by halakhic rules regarding the *a.*

AḤA (AḤAI) OF SHABḤA (c. 680-c. 752): Babylonian rabbi who taught for many years at Pumbedita. His *Sepher Sheiltot* ("Book of Problems") was one of the first rabbinic works to appear after the redaction of the Babylonian Talmud. It contains a discussion of many problems raised in the immediate post-talmudic era and incorporates valuable source-material from the late Talmudic, Saboraic, and early Gaonic Periods. Directed both to scholars and educated laymen, it contains Aramaic homilies arranged according to the weekly pentateuchal readings and the order in which the 613 precepts are mentioned in the Pentateuch; it constitutes the first endeavor at codification of talmudic material. The book has survived only in a truncated form but was an important source for subsequent rabbinical authorities, codifiers in particular.

AḤAD HA-AM (pen-name of Asher Ginzberg; 1856-1927): Writer and Zionist philosopher. Born of a ḥasidic family in the Ukraine, he achieved the reputation of a brilliant young talmudist before he began to study Western philosophy. His two visits to Palestine (1891 and 1893) resulted in two famous essays in which he severely criticized the current ideas and practices of colonization. He remained an uncompromising critic of Herzl's political Zionism and to it opposed his own "cultural Zionism". A.H.'s thinking was based on 19th century evolutionary and social philosophies, but with an undercurrent of deep religious feeling. Zionism must tackle the spiritual "problem of Judaism" before it could hope to solve the social and political problems of the Jews. He viewed the Jewish people as a collective unit, a "national ego" endowed with a will to survive, a creative urge and a cultural-spiritual personality. This organism had realized its form of life, "Hebraism", through the struggles between priesthood and prophecy and through the practical ethos of Pharisaism. But in exile the organism lost its health; deprived of territory and state, the spirit also degenerated, Hebraism became Judaism, collective awareness gave way to individualism. A spiritual fastening upon Palestine by the Jews would turn it into a spiritual center for Jews everywhere and lead to a revival and rejuvenation of the Jewish soul and body politic.

AḤARONIM (Heb. "Latter Ones"): Later rabbinical authorities, as distinguished from RISHONIM (the first authorities). The term is common in later rabbinic terminology though the demarcation is fluid; sometimes the 12th cent. tosaphists are called *a.*, elsewhere the designation is applied only to authors writing after the completion of the *Shulḥan Arukh* in the 16th cent.

AHASUER, see **WANDERING JEW**

AHAVAH (Heb. "love"): Opening word of prayer recited every morning and evening immediately before the *Shema.* The morning version begins with the words *Ahavah Rabbah* ("Great love") and the evening one with *Ahavat Olam* ("Everlasting love"; the *Sephardi* rite uses this formula also in the morning). Both versions are mentioned in the Talmud (*Ber.* 11b), possibly reflecting the difference in Palestinian and Babylonian usage. The prayer which was probably part of the Temple service, incorporates an expression of thanksgiving for the gift of the Law, a prayer for redemption, and an entreaty for spiritual illumination and the ability to perform the Divine commandments.

AḤER, see **ELISHA BEN AVUYAH**

AHIJAH THE SHILONITE: Israelite prophet who — in order to preserve the pristine nature of Israelite religion — encouraged the revolt of Jeroboam against Solomon (his forecast of Jeroboam's success by rending his garment into twelve pieces is the first recorded example of prophetic symbolism). His subsequent disappointment with Jeroboam's attitude to traditional religion led A. to foretell the destruction of the dynasty (I Kings 11:29-40; 14:1-18). Rabbinical tradition designated A. as one of the seven righteous mėn whose combined lifespans cover the history of the world (the others being Adam, Methusaleh, Shem, Jacob, Amram, and Elijah). In ḥasidic legend A. figures as the mystical teacher of the BAAL SHEM TOV.

AḤIKAR, BOOK OF: Book popular in ancient Aramaic-speaking countries. Its first section contains an account of the life of the legendary Aḥikar, adviser to the Assyrian king Esarhaddon; sentenced to death as a result of a plot, A. was saved through the mercy of the executioner. The second part consists of proverbs and ethical sayings in the familiar style of WISDOM LITERATURE. The book originated in an Assyrian Aramaic environment but was given a Jewish ascription in Second Temple Palestine (cf. *Tob.* 1:21) where it was widely read though it left no trace in sacred literature — probably because its character was markedly alien to its Jewish readers. In the 5th cent. B.C.E., the book was well-known to the Jews of S. Egypt and considerable excerpts have been discovered among the Elephantine papyri. Translations of the book have been preserved in Syriac, Arabic, Ethiopian, Armenian, Rumanian, Turkish, and Slavonic.

AHITHOPHEL: Adviser to David, noted for his wisdom ("The counsel of A. was as if a man inquired of the word of God" — II Sam. 16:23). A. later went over to the rebellious Absalom, but his advice, which might have meant success for the rebellion, was rejected in favor of the counter-proposal made by Hushai the Archite (acting on the command of David). Seeing that his counsel went unheeded, A. committed suicide. In later Jewish tradition A. became the archetype of an evil, provocative, over-proud adviser (the rabbis say he is denied a share in the world to come) while in medieval literature he is depicted as a Mephistophelian figure to whom is ascribed a "Book of Lots" dealing with the divination of future events. According to a midrashic legend, A. was the grandfather of Bathsheba and teacher of Socrates.

AKAVIA BEN MAHALALEL: Sage of the late Second Temple Period. Several of his halakhic sayings are quoted in tannaitic literature. A. differed from the majority of contemporary scholars on a number of issues connected with the laws of purity and was excommunicated for resolutely refusing to change his views; however he instructed his son to accept the views of the majority. His best-known saying is "Consider three things, and thou wilt not come within the power of sin... know whence thou comest — from a putrefying drop; whither thou goest — to a place of dust, worms, and maggots; and before whom thou wilt have to give an account — before the Holy One Blessed be He" (*Avot* 3:1).

AKDAMUT MILLIN (Aram. "introduction"): *Piyyut* recited in *Ashkenazi* synagogues on the morning of the Feast of WEEKS (where two days are observed it is said on the first) immediately prior to the Reading of the Law; in some rites, it is read after the first verse of the portion of the Law. Originally intended as an introduction to the Aramaic translation of the Decalogue which was recited in the synagogue on this festival, it was composed by R. Meir ben Isaac Nahorai of Worms (11th cent.). The poem contains a doxology and the reply of Israel to its persecutors, describing the ultimate bliss assured for Israel and the punishment foreseen for hostile nations. A. is a 90-line acrostic based on a double alphabet and the author's name. Its traditional melody has become a central characteristic of the *Ashkenazi* service on the Feast of Weeks.

AKEDAH (Heb. "binding," cf. Gen. 22:9): The binding of ISAAC — the dramatic incident related in Gen. 22 when ABRAHAM, with supreme self-denial, was prepared to carry out the Divine command to offer up his only son by SARAH as a sacrifice to God. The *a.* has given to the Jewish people the ideals of unquestioning acceptance of the Divine command and of MARTYRDOM as the supreme expression of the Sanctification of God's name (KIDDUSH HA-SHEM). The account of the *a.* forms the scriptural reading for the second day of the New Year and is included as a voluntary reading in the daily prayers. R. Abbahu explained the sounding of the SHOPHAR on the New Year: "The Holy One, blessed be He, said 'Sound the ram's horn before me that I may remember in your favor the binding of Isaac the son of Abraham, and I will account it to you as though you had bound yourselves before me'" (*R.H.* 16a). The MERITS of the *a.* are often invoked in liturgical and penitential compositions, and the Additional Service of the New Year, formulated by Rav in the 3rd cent., includes the passage, "Remember the binding whereby Abraham our father bound his son Isaac on the altar, and suppressed his compassion in order to perform Thy will with a perfect heart... O remember the binding of Isaac this day in mercy unto his descendants." This passage — like Gen. 22:1 — emphasizes that the test was upon Abraham rather than Isaac. A famous *seliḥah* in the *Ashkenazi* rite relates all martyrdoms suffered by the Jews in the Middle Ages to the *a.* of Isaac. In the *Sephardi* rite a poetic version of the *a.* is sung before the sounding of the *shophar.*

AKIVA (ben Joseph; c. 40-c. 135): *Tanna.* Pupil of R. Joshua and R. Eliezer, A. laid the foundations for the exposition of the ORAL LAW as later codified in the Mishnah, and is credited with having arranged the Oral Law into its divisions of Mishnah, Tosephta, *Siphra,* and *Siphrei.* He is especially noted for his hermeneutic exposition of Scripture, finding a basis for the Oral Law in almost every peculiarity or superfluity in the language of the Bible. His method was opposed by his great contemporary R. Ishmael who taught that "Scripture speaks in the language of men" i.e., it must be interpreted straightforwardly and literally. The additions and explanations which A. gave to the early Mishnah teachings of his masters were later incorporated in the collections of his pupils: R. Meir, R. Judah, R. Yose, and R. Simeon. R. Judah Ha-Nasi in completing his Mishnah used the collections of A.'s pupils so A. is truly called the "father of the Mishnah". A. participated in political missions, traveling to Rome to help secure the reversal of Domitian's legislation against the Jews. He was a prime supporter of the Bar Kokhba revolt. Arrested as a rebel and imprisoned for a long period, he was finally executed at Caesarea. A.'s life and death made a profound and lasting impression on Jewish history and legend; his martyrdom became in tradition the exemplary type of love of God and faithfulness to Judaism.

AKIVA, ALPHABET OF: Midrash dealing with the letters of the Hebrew alphabet and interpreting their names and forms, often in a fanciful manner; dating from possibly the 8th-9th cents. Before the throne of the Almighty the various letters vie for the honor of beginning the story of creation. Another version of this work enumerates the allegorical connotations inherent within each individual letter. This work has been falsely ascribed to R. AKIVA on the basis of *Men.* 29b according to which Akiva was to give a halakhic interpretation to each letter of the alphabet.

AKKUM (abb. for Heb. "worshiper of stars and constellations"): Idol-worshiper. The term was frequently used in rabbinic literature where it was substituted for *nokhri* or *goy* (gentile) to indicate that the reference was to an idolater or heathen and not to a Christian.

AKNIN, JOSEPH BEN JUDAH IBN, see **IBN AKNIN**

AL HA-NISSIM (Heb.: We thank Thee "for the miracles"): Eulogy inserted into the AMIDAH and GRACE AFTER MEALS on the festivals of PURIM and ḤANUKKAH. After the initial formula, a brief account of the events commemorated on the festival is recited. The version that has become accepted is first known from the prayer-book of R. AMRAM.

AL ḤET (Heb. "For the Sin"): Formula of confession recited in the Afternoon Service preceding the Day of Atonement and in every service on the Day of Atonement except the Concluding Service. The congregation first says the prayer silently and then repeats it aloud together with the cantor. The list of sins is in alphabetical order (the *Sephardi* version giving one sin for each letter, the *Ashkenazi,* two) and is uttered in the first person plural, the confession being offered as a corporate and not an individual act. An early version is known from the Gaonic Period and is mentioned by R. Aḥai of Shabḥa; there is evidence that the formula derives from Temple times.

AL TIKREI (Heb. "Read not"): Midrashic device by which biblical phrases are reinterpreted by slight changes such as revocalization. For example, the end of the talmudic tractate *Berakhot* (64a) quotes the verse (Is. 54:13) "And all thy children shall be taught of the Lord and great shall be the peace of thy children" and states "Read not (*al tikrei*) 'thy children' (*banayikh*) but 'thy builders' (*bonayikh*) i.e., the sages".

ALBALAG, ISAAC (late 13th cent.): Philosopher who lived in N. Spain or S. France. A. was responsible for disseminating the ideas of Averroes among Jewish thinkers and was one of the chief Jewish exponents of the "double truth" theory — originating at that time in Christian Averroist circles — according to which there is no compromise between conflicting truths of theology and of philosophy. Each establishes its rules in its own manner, and a thesis may be true and false at the same time — philosophically true and theologically false, or vice versa. He translated Alghazzali's *Tendencies of the Philosophers* into Hebrew and added his own comments where he disagreed with the author's views.

ALBO, JOSEPH (14th-15th cents.): Spanish religious philosopher and pupil of Ḥasdai Crescas; participated in the Christian-Jewish DISPUTATION of Tortosa in 1413-14. His *Sepher Ikkarim* ("Book of Principles") provides a final major statement of medieval Jewish philosophy which, though undoubtedly affected by the atmosphere of Christian attacks on Judaism, represents a positive attempt to determine the roots of Jewish religion. As in all medieval Jewish philosophy, A. considers first the question of salvation, and finds his answer in the proper conception of law. A.'s preoccupation with law and his relegation of belief in the coming of the Messiah to the level of a secondary, rather than a primary, principle of the Jewish faith may well be his response to the Christian emphasis on faith and Messianism. The major point in his system is the delineation of the various kinds of law which guide mankind. He enumerates conventional, natural, and Divine law, and attributes ultimacy only to the last. Conventional and natural law suffice to care for man's earthly needs for peace, economic security, etc. Only Divine or revealed law can assure man of salvation. By setting forth basic principles A. intended to enable men to distinguish between true and pseudo-Divine laws. He set forth three such principles — belief in the existence of God, revelation, and retribution — under which he subsumed what he called the *shorashim* (secondary or derivative roots or principles). In typical medieval fashion, A. tried to advance arguments for Divine law based on human reason and experience, but in the last analysis he had to rest his case on revelation and belief in the reality of miracles.

ALCHEMY: The English form of the Arabic word for "the chemistry," now generally used to denote the theoretical and experimental study of chemistry as developed in late antiquity and throughout the Middle Ages up to the 18th cent. A. was as much a natural (and at times even mystical) philosophy as an experimental science and was closely connected with astrological beliefs and various forms of MAGIC (e.g. in its concern with the transmutation of metals, the elixir of life, the philosopher's stone, etc.). Though certainly not of Jewish origin, a. was studied by Jews such as Maria Hebrea who also made important contributions to it. References to a. in the Talmud are dubious, and there is little a. in KABBALAH, though many mystics and kabbalists studied or even practiced it (e.g. Ḥayyim VITAL who subsequently rejected it and Samuel Falk, the *Baal Shem* of London). Judah Ha-Levi, Maimonides, and many other thinkers were antagonistic to a.

ALEINU (Heb. "It is incumbent upon us"): Prayer proclaiming Divine sovereignty over Israel and the world; though probably composed earlier, it was placed by RAV in the 3rd cent. as the introduction to MALKHUYYOT, the ten scriptural verses declaring the sovereignty of God which are selected from the three sections of the Bible and are read in the New Year Additional Service. Thus A. was originally part of the New Year service, but from the 12th cent. on it began to be used as the concluding prayer for all services — morning, afternoon, and evening throughout the year — and spread to all rites. The prayer was the object of slanderous accusations. The phrase "for they prostrate themselves to vanity and emptiness and pray to a god who cannot save them" was misconstrued as a specific attack upon Christianity and was therefore deleted from the *Ashkenazi* ritual in order to prevent libels and persecutions; the *Sephardim* (who recite only the first paragraph of the prayer in their daily service) still retain it. The prayer, a confident and triumphant proclamation of God's kingship, was invested during medieval times with special solemnity and awe and is particularly associated with martyrdom. The martyrs of Blois (1171) are said to have been heard singing the *a.* from the burning pyre.

ALEXANDER SUSLIN HA-COHEN (d. 1349): German rabbi, martyred in Erfurt. His *Aggudah* ("Collection") collates and codifies earlier rabbinic decisions as well as his own novellae and had a significant influence on subsequent *Ashkenazi* codifiers, especially Mölln and Isserles.

ALEXANDER SUSSKIND OF GRODNO (d. 1794): Kabbalist and author of ethical works; lived in White Russia. His emphasis on the importance of KAVVANAH in the observance of the commandments and on joy in Divine worship led R. Naḥman of Bratzlav to call A. "a Ḥasid before Ḥasidism". A.'s main work *Yesod ve-Shoresh ha-Avodah* ("The Foundation and Root of Worship") is an ethical work touching upon many aspects of everyday life.

ALEXANDER YANNAI, see PHARISEES

ALFASI, ISAAC (1013-1103): Talmudic authority and codifier. Born in Algeria, he studied with R. Hananel in Kairouan and settled in Fez where he lived until the age of 75. He was then forced to flee to Spain where he headed the community at Lucena. A. was an important link in the process of transferring the center of talmudic studies from east to west. The last of the Babylonian *geonim*, R. Hai, died when A. was 20 and by way of the intermediary role of the N. African academies, Spain began to emerge as the new focus of talmudic learning; A. was the first major rabbinical authority to teach in Spain. Hundreds of his responsa have been preserved written originally in Arabic and addressed to communities in Spain and N. Africa. His *Sepher ha-Halakhot* ("The Book of Laws") is one of the basic works of Jewish legal codification. Its twofold objectives were: 1) to extract the legal subject-matter from the Talmud and to determine halakhic rulings; 2) to present a digest of the Talmud which would facilitate and popularize its study. His brief explanations, inserted into the original Talmud text, brilliantly clarify difficult and obscure points. Writing at the conclusion of the Gaonic Period, A. was able to present an authoritative summation of gaonic thought and legislation while concentrating as well on the actual Talmud text, which by that time was often neglected. *Sepher ha-Halakhot* influenced all subsequent scholars and codifiers notably constituting a primary source for Maimonides; it was also in turn the subject of numerous other works, both critical and supporting, and during the following centuries in W. Europe — particularly Spain — rabbinical study was based not on the Talmud but on A.'s work.

ALGAZI, ISRAEL JACOB BEN YOMTOV (c. 1680-1757): Rabbi and kabbalist. About 1740, he left his native Smyrna and settled in Jerusalem where he served as RISHON LE-ZION. He was greatly revered by *Sephardi* Jewry and was the author of rabbinic and kabbalistic works. His son YOMTOV BEN ISRAEL JACOB A. (1727-1802), chief rabbi of Jerusalem, was an outstanding halakhic authority.

ALIBI, see **WITNESS**

ALIENS, see **STRANGERS**

ALIMONY: The allowance made to a woman from her husband's estate for her maintenance, granted by law when she is divorced or legally separated from her husband. In Jewish law there is no provision for separation, but on the other hand the provision for divorce applies equally to widowhood. A. was legally unknown in biblical times and no provision existed for the maintenance of a divorced wife or a widow from her husband's estate. Various attempts were made in the early Talmudic Period to ensure some relief for the woman in these circumstances, and the final form of the remedy, which is in force to this day, was evolved in the first cent. B.C.E. The KETUBBAH, the marriage settlement in writing, had been introduced some time previously, securing the wife a fixed sum from her husband's estate in the case of divorce or widowhood. In order to obviate various fraudulent and undesirable practices, Simeon ben Shetaḥ, the head of the Sanhedrin, decreed that although the amount stipulated in the *ketubbah* remained in the provision of the husband, during the period of widowhood it was made a lien upon the estate. The woman's right to her *ketubbah* was thus absolutely guaranteed (*Ket.* 82b) and she was not even entitled to release her husband from his obligations under it.

ALIYYAH (Heb. "ascent", "going up"): A word applied to three different kinds of ascent.

1) Ascent to heaven.
2) Ascent to the land of Israel and particularly Jerusalem, whether for *aliyyat regel*, the pilgrimage on the occasion of the three annual PILGRIM FESTIVALS, or for permanent settlement in the land.
3) The privilege of being called up to the Reading of the Law at public readings in the synagogues.

1) The only explicit reference in the Bible to a miraculous ascent to heaven is that of the prophet Elijah (II Kings 2:1-13). The Midrash (*Gen. Rab.* 25:1) strenuously denies such an ascension to Enoch, against the views of the "sectarians" (*minim*) who so interpreted Gen. 5:24, but apocalyptic literature regarded both him and Moses (the latter on the basis of his ascent of Mt. Sinai) as having made the ascent to heaven and returned to earth; they are both the subjects of apocalypses bearing their respective names and centering on their ascension. Other figures who ascended to heaven according to apocalyptic and rabbinical literature include Isaiah, Baruch, Ezra, and even post-biblical rabbis such as Ishmael ben Elisha. In some instances the ascent is described as a journey to a permanent paradise, in others it is temporary and followed by a return to earth.

2) The comparative geographical elevation of the Land of Israel as compared with low-lying Egypt is the basis of the Hebrew usage whereby one "goes down" from Israel to Egypt (cf. Gen. 12:10) and one "goes up" from Egypt to Israel (cf. Gen. 13:1). From here the word was extended to apply to journeys from any country to Israel, whether in pilgrimage or for permanent settlement, and it is not improbable that there was added the conception of a spiritual ascent as well. Biblical law requires every male Israelite to make the *aliyyat regel* (foot pilgrimage), and visit the Temple three times a year on the occasions of Passover, Pentecost, and Tabernacles, which were therefore called the "Foot" or Pilgrim Festivals (Exod. 23:14). According to II Kings 12:26-33, Jeroboam I, the first king of the seceding northern kingdom, set up golden calves in Dan and Bethel and changed the dates of the festivals in order to create a barrier between his newly established kingdom and Judea, and to wean his people from their ancient loyalties. The popularity of these pilgrimages during the period of the Second Temple is seen from the figure given by Josephus of 256,500 paschal lambs slaughtered for the Festival of Passover in 66 C.E., thus implying a pilgrimage of some 3,000,000 (*Wars*, 6:9). After the destruction of the Second Temple such pilgrimages were made as voluntary acts of piety. With the EXILE, the rabbis of the Talmud and subsequent ages went to great lengths to emphasize the importance of permanent settlement in Israel, apart from the duty of pilgrimage. "One should rather dwell in Israel even among a non-Jewish majority than outside Israel even in the midst of a Jewish majority", "He who dwells in the land of Israel is regarded as having God ever with him, but he who dwells outside Israel is as one who hath no God" are two of the many statements stressing the religious duty of dwelling in the land of Israel; they both stem from the aggadic discussion of the mishnaic law which states that a man can force his family to follow him to settle in Israel, and if the wife refuses to do so she loses

her marriage settlement in case of divorce (*Ket.* 110b ff.). But even in amoraic times, faced with the problem of a considerable emigration from Babylon to Israel, the 3rd cent. Babylonian R. Judah expressed himself strongly against *a.* from Babylon to the land of Israel, going so far as to declare it a biblical transgression (*ibid.*). Similarly during the 12th and 13th cents., when *a.* from England, France, and Germany was assuming considerable proportions as a result of the increasing insecurity of the Jews in those countries, the tosaphist R. Ḥayyim Cohen declared that the religious duty to settle in Israel no longer applied, since it was too difficult to observe all the many additional commandments applicable in the Holy Land and the penalty for transgressing them was severe. Another reason given was the danger of travel (*Tosaphot in loc.*) R. Meir of Rothenburg (13th cent.) takes up a middle position and in a responsum enjoins *a.* to Israel only if one's economic livelihood is assured there. The precepts of the Talmud and the later expositions of Jewish religious law were a major factor during the ages of the Diaspora in keeping alive the burning passion for permanent *a.* This was exemplified throughout the centuries by the settling in Palestine of distinguished rabbinical leaders (e.g. Naḥmanides in 1266, Obadiah of Bertinoro in 1488, Joseph Karo and other leaders of Jewish mysticism in the 16th cent., Isaiah Horowitz in 1621, Judah Ḥasid and 1,500 followers in 1700, Menahem Mendel of Vitebsk and 300 ḥasidim in 1777). The kabbalists found profound mystical significance in the Land of Israel and the Zohar says "Happy is he whose lot it is during his lifetime to live in the Holy Land for such a one draws down the dew from heaven upon the earth and whoever is attached to the Holy Land during his lifetime becomes attached ever afterwards to the heavenly Holy Land" (*Aḥarei Mot*, 72). This tradition continued among the ḥasidim among whom there was a continual *a.* to the Land of Israel. With the growth of modern Zionism, religious factors and motivations have continued to play an important part in the mass *a.* of Jews from all parts of the world.

3) The universal custom today is for the whole Pentateuch to be read in the course of a year by a series of continuous readings each Sabbath morning. In addition, excerpts from the Pentateuch are read in the synagogue every Sabbath afternoon, Monday and Thursday mornings, and on festivals. On Sabbath morning, the portion is divided into a minimum of seven sub-sections, and eight individuals (a section of the last portion being read a second time for the eighth person who reads the prophetic lesson) are honored by being asked up to the reading; this "calling up" is called an *aliyyah* ("going up" to the READING OF THE LAW"). The choice of the word is due to the fact that whereas in ancient times one "went down" to conduct the prayers (the reading desk being recessed in the floor), the *Torah* was read from an elevated platform (cf. Neh. 8:4). Only males above the age of 13 are called up. A *cohen* (a Jew of priestly descent) is called first, followed by a levite, and then ordinary "Israelites". In the absence of a *cohen*, a levite or Israelite is called first; in the absence of a levite and the presence of a *cohen*, the *cohen* is also called to the second portion. Custom regards the third *a.* (the first one available to an Israelite) and the sixth as the most important. On the Day of Atonement, the reading is divided into six portions; on the three pilgrim festivals and the New Year, five; on New Moons and intermediate days of festivals, four; on Sabbath afternoons, weekdays, fast-days, *Ḥanukkah* and *Purim*, three. Until the 13th cent. the person called up read the portion himself; for those unable to read, a reader was appointed. By the 14th cent., however, the custom was universally adopted that the appointed reader recite the portion for all, so as not to put the ignorant to shame, and the person called up only recites the relevant blessings. The only exception is in the case of a boy's attaining his religious majority (BAR MITZVAH) which he himself signalizes by reading the portion to which he is called. In most rites a person is called up by his first name and patronym.

ALKABETZ, SOLOMON BEN MOSES HA-LEVI (c. 1505 - before 1584): Hebrew poet and homilist. He studied mystical literature in his native Turkey with Joseph KARO and then moved to Palestine where he settled in Safed and headed a kabbalistic group engaged in mystical studies and devotional practices. His many pupils included Moses CORDOVERO. A.'s religious poetry written under a marked kabbalistic influence, is noteworthy for its elevated devotional content. Most famous is his poem LEKHAH DODI, which is recited in synagogues of all rites every week at the commencement of the Sabbath. His other works include mystical commentaries on the Bible.

ALKALAI, JUDAH SOLOMON ḤAI (1798-1878): Rabbi and proto-Zionist. While serving as rabbi in Serbia, he became acquainted with Balkan national aspirations and in 1834 his booklet *Shema Yisrael* ("Hear, O Israel") proposed a man-inspired return of the Jewish people to the Holy Land. This was in contrast to the familiar pious viewpoint that such a return would come about only through a miraculous Divine intervention. A. believed that natural redemption must come prior to supernatural intervention. He expounded his program of self-redemption in a series of booklets and disseminated his views in the course of extensive European journeys. His practical suggestions reached fruition in Herzl's program while many of his views paved the way for the religious Zionist movement.

ALLEGORY: The presentation of one subject matter under the guise of another, as by figurative speech and extended metaphor. Allegorical interpretation seeks to discover a meaning other than that suggested by the plain and literal sense of the text. It has been a favorite method of Bible interpretation since the earliest stages of exegesis. It is motivated by four distinct factors:

1) The desire to derive moral and ethical lessons from biblical texts. 2) the belief that since the Bible was the revealed word of God, such passages as on the surface appear to be banal and unimportant must possess a hidden meaning: "Woe unto the man who asserts that the *Torah* intends only to relate commonplace things and secular narratives... When angels wish to descend to earth they have to don earthly garments; how much more so is this true of the *Torah*... The narratives of the *Torah* are merely its outer garment" (Zohar 3:52). 3) Portions of the Bible may lose their practical application (e.g. the sacrificial system after the destruction of the Temple), or their literal meaning may no longer be in consonance with modern views. The veneration which surrounds the text demands that an allegorical interpretation be given to such passages in order to preserve allegiance to the text. 4) When Jews came into contact with systems of thought which were apparently in conflict with that of the Bible, they often resorted to allegorical interpretation in order to place the Bible on equal footing with the prevailing philosophy whose validity they accepted.

These factors led to various types of allegorical interpretation. The Talmudic Period in Palestine and Babylon produced the symbolic a. characteristic of the MIDRASH. Thus, *Ḥul.* 92a proposes no less than six different allegorical interpretations of the butler's dream in Gen. 40:10, e.g. "The vine is Jerusalem, the three branches are the Temple, the King, and the High Priest, the buds are the young priests, the ripe grapes are the drink offerings." The Song of Songs was the subject of extensive allegorical interpretations in Jewish (as in Christian) literature. Contact between Judaism and Hellenism produced philosophical allegorization of the Bible, particularly in the Alexandrian school and its outstanding exponent PHILO (1st cent.). The encounter with Greco-Arabic philosophy in the late Middle Ages led to a new wave of allegorical exegesis, exemplified also by MAIMONIDES' *Guide to the Perplexed.* Some philosophers, like SAADYAH and ALBO, advised moderate use of the allegorical method while it was totally rejected by literalist Orthodoxy. The kabbalists understood Scripture as mystical a.

ALLITERATION: Literary device based on repetition of sound. A. was a common figure of speech in Hebrew literature already in biblical times. It became particularly frequent in medieval religious poetry and liturgy where it was even used to excess. The *paytan* Kallir, for example, employs a. in much of his verse.

ALMEMAR (from Arab. *al-minbar* "platform"): Raised platform in the center of the SYNAGOGUE on which is situated the desk for reading the Scroll of the Law. In medieval times, it became a dominating feature of the synagogue and designers were constantly faced with the problem of creating a balance between the two foci of the ark and the *a.* In Central and E. Europe, the *a.* was often integrated with the central vault-carrying pile of masonry. In Spain the platform was placed at the western end of the synagogue. In *Sephardi* synagogues — where the *a.* is called *tebah* (Heb. "box") — the precentor also recites the prayers from the *a.* though in other rites he generally stands before the ark. Some rabbinical authorities (e.g. Maimonides, Isserles) hold that the *a.* must be in the center of the building but Karo and most modern rabbis do not regard this as essential and in recent times — especially under Reform influence — it has often been combined with the ark platform. Among *Ashkenazim* the *a.* is also known as *bimah.*

ALMS, see CHARITY

ALMUKAMMAS, DAVID BEN MERWAN (9th-10th cents.): Philosopher; living in Babylonia. A. was the first to introduce the philosophy of the Arab *Kalam* school into Jewish thought. His *Esrim Perakim* ("Twenty Tractates") deals primarily with proofs for the existence of God and His attributes, clearly following the *Kalam* doctrine of Divine attributes which stresses their difference from human attributes. God's attributes are identical with His being and cannot affect His unity. Two of A.'s tractates are polemic attacks on Christianity for maintaining that God has form, a view inconsistent with pure monotheism; another section (now lost) polemicized against Islam. A., who wrote in Arabic, cites Greek and Arab authorities, but never quotes the Bible.

ALNAKAWA, ISRAEL BEN JOSEPH (d. 1391): Spanish scholar; martyred in his native Toledo. He wrote the ethical work *Menorat ha-Maor* ("The Candlestick of Light"), which was probably the original for the better-known work of the same name by Isaac ABOAB. The book deals with practical aspects of religious life and incorporates a wealth of maxims, gathered from talmudic *aggadah*, later rabbinic sources, and the Zohar.

ALPHABET, HEBREW: The Hebrew a. is an offshoot of the Canaanite a., the first purely alphabetic script. In the course of its history, **Hebrew**

employed two distinct forms of this a. The first was the ancient Hebrew a., used until the First Exile, identical in its monumental form with the Phoenician a. This script continued in use to some extent after the Exile: it appears on practically all Jewish coins, throughout some Dead Sea mss., and in other Dead Sea mss. for writing Divine names only. In general use it seems to have been replaced by an Eastern Aramaic script, itself derived from the Canaanite a. Only the Samaritans retained the Ancient Hebrew a. In the first two cents. C.E. the Aramaic a. (*ketav ashuri*) developed into the specifically Jewish Square Script (*ketav merubba*). The rabbis taught that the *Torah* was given to Moses in the Hebrew language and in the ancient script and that in the time of Ezra, it was given in the Aramaic language and script (*Sanh.* 21b). At various times cursive forms developed locally. The so-called RASHI SCRIPT, sometimes used in printing parts of religious works, is based on a medieval Spanish cursive. Jews used the Hebrew a. extensively in writing such vernacular languages as they happened to speak, such as Aramaic, Arabic, Persian, Turkish, Berber, Spanish, Provençal, Italian, medieval and modern German, Judeo-Spanish (Ladino, Spaniolic), and Yiddish. Until fairly recent times religious Jews avoided using "gentile" scripts which were supposed to trouble the spiritual purity of the eyes. At first the vowels were left without any indication. In the course of time certain letters (*y*, *v*, ', *h*) also came to serve as vowel indicators. This use was gradually extended to cases where there was already a vowel, so that *y* came to mark *i* and *e*, and *v* marked *u* and *o*. This system of *matres lectionis* is only partly, and rather inconsistently, used in the standard Hebrew Bibles. The occurrence of "defective" and "full" (*plene*) spellings is regulated by tradition, and failure to observe it can invalidate a *Torah* scroll or a divorce document. In the 7th-9th cents. various systems arose — one of which subsequently came into general use — for writing all vowels by new signs added above, below, and (rarely) inside the letters. This complement to the Hebrew a. did not, however, become an integral part of it. Vowel signs must not appear in a ritual *Torah* scroll; they are not used in documents, nor do they appear in most books for practical use.

Soon after fixing the vowel point system, there began a controversy which has continued until modern times between those who acknowledged the late introduction of this innovation and those who held that the vowel signs had been revealed to Moses by God, along with the consonant text of the Pentateuch and were thus of equal inviolability. Today the way in which the text is vocalized is held to be of absolute authority in Orthodox circles, while other Jewish Bible students of conservative leanings, who would not nevertheless agree that the consonant text could be faulty and need emendation, are yet willing to accept for exegetical purposes alternative vocalizations of the same consonant skeleton, such as are possible with many Hebrew words. The order of the Hebrew a. was apparently fixed from its very invention. The fixed order is employed as a literary device in alphabetic (acrostic) psalms whose verses open with successive letters of the a. It was apparently the Greeks who first took this fixed order as a device for using the letters of the a. as numerical signs (the Israelites used special number symbols). The method was adopted in the first centuries C.E. by Jews, and is still extensively employed. It gave rise to GEMATRIA, in which the numerical values of the letters of a word are added together and compared with those of other words for exegetical, homiletic, and mystical uses. The method of inserting the letters in *Torah* scrolls is minutely regulated by *halakhah* and custom; of special interest are the "crowns" (TAGIN) placed over seven of the letters. The religious significance of the Hebrew a. is mainly bound up with the writing of Divine names. While the Tetragrammaton must not be written at all under ordinary circumstances, and when written by a *Torah* scribe, only after proper ritual purification, all other names, substitutes, and abbreviations for the Divine name also partake of holiness and must not be destroyed or exposed to defilement. Mystic powers were ascribed to the letters of the a. by the kabbalists, and permutations and combinations of letters played a great role both in magical practice (AMULETS) and mystical meditation. An outstanding exponent of this letter-mysticism was Abraham ABULAFIA whose *Ḥokhmat ha-Tzeruph* ("The Science of Letter Combinations") assumed that the Hebrew letters were keys to the realm of prophetic illumination.

ALROY, DAVID (12th cent.): Pseudo-messiah. He succeeded his father Samuel as head of a messianic movement in N.E. Caucasia and after the movement there was suppressed transferred his activities to Kurdistan. He changed his name from Menahem to David in order to stress his similarity to King David. A. gained a large following when he agreed to wage war upon the Sultan, but his sudden death (possibly by assassination) brought the revolt to an end. A group of his followers ("Menahemites") in Azerbaijan continued to believe in his messiahship after his death.

ALSHEIKH, MOSES BEN ḤAYYIM (c. 1507-c. 1600): Rabbinical scholar and prolific Bible exegete. He left his native Turkey and settled in Safed where he served as *dayyan* in the court of his teacher Joseph KARO. Apart from his responsa, he is best known for his voluminous homiletic commentaries on the Bible which were greatly influenced by Isaac ABRAVANEL. His interpretations tend to the allegorical as a compromise between the rationalist and esoteric approaches to textual commentary.

ALTAR: Structure on which SACRIFICES are offered. Found among most ancient peoples, it is first mentioned in the Bible when Noah built an a. after being saved from the Flood (Gen. 8:20). Abraham, Isaac, Jacob, and Moses built altars as an expression of thanksgiving or in order to mark a significant occasion, e.g., upon entering into a covenant with God (Exod. 24:4). According to the Bible (Exod. 20:21-23) the a. was to be made of a mound of earth. If made of stones, they had to be untouched by iron since this metal represented bloodshed and weapons of war. It was furthermore forbidden to ascend the a. by steps (Exod. 20:26) or to follow the idolatrous custom of planting trees around it (Deut. 16:21). Specifications were laid down for the portable a. of the desert sanctuary, made of wood and overlaid with bronze, measuring $5 \times 5 \times 3$ cubits; it had four corners or "horns". Another a. overlaid with gold, measuring $1 \times 1 \times 2$ cubits, served for incense. When Joshua crossed the Jordan he built an a. of stones upon which he inscribed "the second Law of Moses" (Josh. 8:30-32). During the period of the Judges and Kings numerous local altars ("HIGH PLACES") existed. The command for one central a. is formulated in Deut. 12:5-14, and the historical books of the Bible as well as rabbinic tradition assume that all altars except the one in God's chosen sanctuary (i.e., in Jerusalem after the building of Solomon's temple) were illegal. According to the biblical account, Solomon's a. measured $20 \times 20 \times 10$ cubits (II Chron. 4:1). The golden incense a. was also installed (I Kings 7:48). Upon the division of the Monarchy the Israelite kings waged a schismatic struggle against the central a. at Jerusalem. According to the Talmud, the only legitimate a. outside the Temple precincts was that of 12 stones (symbolizing the unity of the tribes) built by Elijah in order to vindicate the lordship of God against the priests of Baal. Upon their return from Babylonian Exile, the Jews erected an a. before rebuilding the Temple. The sanctity of the a. made it a haven for the unintentional manslayer who traditionally seized the "horns" at the corners of the a. (see ASYLUM). In the Second Temple Period the a. was the focus of popular piety, and during the Feast of Tabernacles in particular, it was the center of great rejoicing during the ritual of circumambulation. When the Second Temple was laid waste Johanan ben Zakkai comforted his colleagues saying: "You have another means of atonement as powerful as the a., and that is the work of charity, for it is said: 'I desired mercy and not sacrifice' (Hos. 6:6)." The detailed description of the a. found in the Bible served as the basis for allegorical and mystical elaboration in later aggadic and kabbalistic literature.

ALTER OF GUR, see **GER**

AM HA-ARETZ (Heb. "People of the Land"): 1) In biblical usage — the mass of indigenous population as distinct from the noble class. 2) After the first Exile — part of the rural population who had remained in their homeland and assimilated with the surrounding peoples. 3) In the Talmud — a vulgar part of the people, lax in religious observance, particularly with regard to tithes and ritual purity. 4) In later parlance — an ignoramus. The copious though varied references to the *A.H.* in the Talmud stem from the beginning of the Second Temple Period when Ezra and Nehemiah decreed the separation of the homecoming exiles from the lawless *"Ammei Ha-Aratzot"* (pl.). In the subsequent period of the Great Synagogue this separation led to the formation of the Ḥasidim — the pious — or *Perushim* (PHARISEES) — those setting themselves apart. These in turn formed associations of the strictly observant called ḤAVERIM for the protection and furtherance of the Pharisaic interpretation of the *Torah.* The ensuing antagonism between the opposing factions is attested by R. Akiva's confession that while still an *A.H.* he was eager to break the bones of the learned "like those of an ass". The growing estrangement between learned Pharisee and ignorant *A.H.* is considered to have provided a fertile ground for early Christendom. Talmudic definitions of an *A.H.* vary: He is one who does not give the tithes as prescribed or one unobservant of the laws of purity, or one who does not read the *Shema* twice a day. Others see in him one who spurns the laws of *tzitzit, mezuzah,* or *tephillin,* or a father who fails to instruct his sons in *Torah.* Extenuating or even sympathetic consideration of the *A.H.* is also to be found in the Talmud despite the prevailing intergroup friction; one such utterance even bids "Heed the sons of the *A.H.* for they will be the living source of the *Torah.*"

AMALEK: Ancient nomadic people who lived in the Sinai desert between Egypt and the land of Canaan. According to the Bible (Gen. 36:12) they were of Edomite stock. At Rephidim, the Children of Israel — then on their way from Egypt to Mt. Sinai — were treacherously attacked by Amalekites whom they repelled after a battle of varying fortunes. Thereafter A. was regarded as Israel's inveterate foe whose annihilation became a sacred obligation (Exod. 17:16; Deut. 25:19), and once performed was to be remembered as a religious duty at least once a year (on the Sabbath preceding PURIM; see SABBATHS, SPECIAL). Saul's failure to fulfill the commandment of total annihilation (I Sam. 15) led to the annulment of the rights of his descendants to succeed to the throne of Israel. The Amalekites suffered defeat at the hands of David (II Sam. 8:11) and were finally wiped out during the reign of Hezekiah (8th cent. B.C.E., cf. I Chron. 4:43). Rabbinic literature dwells on A.'s role as Israel's permanent arch-enemy. HAMAN's origin is also described as Amalekite (his cognomen "Agagi" is taken to indicate his descent from Agag, king of A.). Whenever the Jews failed to abide by the Covenant, A. is said to have prevailed over them. Moreover, it is said that the struggle between the two peoples will continue until the coming of the Messiah, when God will destroy the last remnants of A.

AMEN (Heb. "So be it"): Expression occurring 14 times in the Bible and signifying assent to an oath (e.g. Deut. 27:15), agreement or corroboration (e.g. I Kings 1:36), or blessing and praise of God (Ps. 41:14). The term was also used as a public response after the prayers and blessings of the priests and levites (cf. Neh. 8:6; I Chron. 16:36; Ps. 106:48) although in the Temple it was part of a larger formula (Ps. 72:18-19). In synagogue practice, *a.* is the response to every BENEDICTION. According to the rabbis, it is obligatory to say *a.* on hearing a blessing and the person who says it is regarded as if he had recited the blessing himself, just as a person who says *a.* after an oath is regarded as if he himself had sworn (*Shev.* 29a). A. is rarely said by the person who himself makes the benediction. The rabbis suggested homiletically that the word is derived from the initials of the phrase *El Melekh Ne'eman* ("God, Faithful King") (*Sanh.* 111a) The term passed into Christian and, to some extent Islamic, usage.

AMIDAH (Heb. "standing", i.e., a prayer to be recited in a standing position): Main section of all obligatory prayers; it is also known as *tephillah* — the prayer *par excellence,* and by *Ashkenazim* popularly as *shemoneh esreh* ("eighteen" benedictions). All the prescribed prayers (SHAHARIT, MINHAH, MAARIV on weekdays, together with MUSAPH on Sabbaths and festivals and NEILAH on the Day of Atonement) incorporate the *a.* in one of its forms as their central feature. On weekdays the *a.* consists of 19 BENEDICTIONS (formerly, eighteen), while on Sabbaths and festivals it has only seven (with the exception of the additional service on ROSH HA-SHANAH which has nine). The authorship of the *a.* is ascribed to the Men of the Great Synagogue (see LITURGY); it undoubtedly was already current during the last centuries of the Second Temple Period. It underwent its final editing at Yavneh under R. Gamaliel II who laid down the exact order and contents of its benedictions, and also introduced the nineteenth benediction — a prayer "against the heretics", probably aimed originally at the Judeo-Christians (see MINIM). On weekdays, the structure of the *a.* is as follows: The first three benedictions, which also constitute the oldest section of the *a.*, are in praise of God: (1) the first (AVOT) refers to Him as the "God of the Fathers" and extols His greatness; (2) the second (*gevurot*) is in praise of His power (with the addition during the winter months of a petition for rain); (3) while the third (KEDUSHAH) extols His holiness. The order of the intermediate, petitionary benedictions is as follows: (4) prayer for knowledge (into which a HAVDALAH prayer is inserted on Saturday evening); (5) for repentance; (6) for forgiveness; (7) for redemption (see GEULLAH); (8) for healing of the sick (which may include a private prayer specifying a particular individual); (9) for the blessing of agricultural produce (with the interpolation during the winter months of a prayer for rain); (10) for the ingathering of the dispersed; (11) for righteous judgment; (12) for the punishment of the wicked and the heretics; (13) for the reward of the pious; (14) for the building of Jerusalem; (15) for the restoration of the Davidic dynasty; (16) for the acceptance of prayers. The last three (possibly dating from the Maccabean Period) render thanks (especially the middle one; the first of these three is a request for the restoration of the Temple service and the last — which follows upon the priestly blessing — is a prayer for peace). The *a.* concludes with meditation *Elohai Netzor* which is regarded as an individual prayer and is therefore not repeated by the reader. In this form, which has a total of 19 benedictions, the *a.* is common to all rites today; but in the old Palestinian rite nos. 14-15 were combined into one single benediction, giving a total of only 18. The petitionary prayers fall into two categories: general human needs (both spiritual and material) and national aspirations of Israel: all are formulated in the first person plural, since the *a.* is essentially a congregational prayer (though it must be recited by the individual, even when he is unable to join a MINYAN). In congregational worship the *a.* is first said silently and then repeated aloud by the reader (except the *a.* of the Evening Service which is not repeated). The recitation of the full *kedushah* in the third benediction and of the priestly blessing before the last one require a *minyan.* The times at which each *a.* must be recited correspond to the natural divisions of the day (morning, noon, evening), but were associated, especially after the destruction of the Temple, with the times of the daily sacrifice (morning and late afternoon). Similarly, the *Musaph a.* came to take the place of the additional sacrifices on Sabbaths and festivals (Num. 28-29). It was permissible to recite more than the required number of *amidot* on weekdays as "voluntary prayers," corresponding to voluntary sacrifices in Temple days, but this custom no longer prevails.

AMITTAI: Name of two 9th cent. synagogal poets in Oria, in S. Italy. The first A. composed poems in the style of the early Palestinian *piyyutim* some of which were adopted into the Italian and German rites and which also influenced the 30 known *piyyutim* of his grandson A. ben Shephatiah. The latter's penitential prayer *Adonai, Adonai, El Raḥum* has been incorporated into the Concluding Service for the Day of Atonement. He also wrote dirges on the anti-Jewish outbreaks in his time (especially the compulsory conversions enforced under the Byzantine emperor, Basil I) while several of his poems poignantly express the Jewish longing for Zion.

AMMI BAR NATHAN (3rd-4th cents.): *Amora;* headed the Tiberias academy and together with his colleague R. ASSI regularly toured Palestine to encourage religious study. A. was responsible for the Jewish judiciary and strove to ensure that *dayyanim* be chosen on their merit and not — as had been the tendency — for their wealth.

AMMON AND MOAB: Inveterate enemies of Israel in the Biblical Period, specifically excluded from "the congregation of the Lord" (Deut. 23:4-5). This commandment meant that an Israelite woman was forbidden to marry anyone of Ammonite or Moabite origin; however Israelite men were permitted to marry Ammonite or Moabite women (cf. Ruth). In the course of time, the attitude toward males relaxed and R. Joshua permitted the conversion of such males on the grounds that the original peoples could no longer be distinguished; a priest was even permitted to marry the daughter of such a convert (*Yev.* 77a).

AMNON OF MAINZ: Legendary martyr of the Crusader Period. According to the traditional story which is set at the time of the High Holy Days, A. refused the demand of the Archbishop of Mainz that he accept Christianity. In punishment his limbs were cut off; taken to synagogue for the New Year the dying rabbi recited the prayer *U-Netanneh Tokeph* which thereafter was incorporated into the High Holiday liturgy. The prayer, in fact, is of earlier origin and a copy was discovered in the Cairo GENIZAH.

AMORA (from Heb./Aram. *amar*, to speak, interpret): Name given to the rabbinic teachers in both Palestine and Babylonia during the period of the Talmud. They are thus distinguished from the teachers of the Mishnah who are called TANNA. There is no real difference between the *tannaim* and the *amoraim* (pl.) either in method or in area of exposition; the distinction is only chronological and is marked by the external fact that the period of the *tannaim* ends with the compilation of the Mishnah. In the same way as the later teachers of the Mishnah commented on the traditions received from the early teachers, and the compiler of the Mishnah and his contemporaries preserved their comments on the completed Mishnah in the TOSEPHTA, the comments of the *amoraim* on both the Mishnah and Tosephta were collected in the compilation known as the TALMUD. Neither is there any real difference between the Palestinian and Babylonian *amoraim*, except that the period of the latter's activity was longer. Hence the full literary development of the Talmud which came only with the later *amoraim* is entirely missing in the Palestinian Talmud, which was edited a century before the Babylonian. Palestinian *amoraim* are distinguished in title from those of Babylonia in that the former are called RABBI, indicating complete judiciary competence in all matters of law, whereas those in Babylonia are called *rav*. The two groups kept in close contact through the frequent visits of scholars specially appointed to bring the teachings of Palestine to Babylonia and vice versa. The great academies of amoraic instruction were in Tiberias, Sepphoris, and Caesarea in Palestine, and in Nehardea, Sura, and Pumbedita in Babylonia. The total number of *amoraim* mentioned in the sources exceeds 3,000.

AMORITES: Early Semitic inhabitants of Palestine; the Bible applies the name both generically to the early population of the country and more particularly to one of the tribes annihilated or assimilated by the Israelites. In talmudic times, the A. were regarded as the prototype of the early Canaanite population and were taken as the chief bearers of a false faith. Evil customs and superstitions were known as "the ways of the A." (*Shab.* 67a) as the rabbis applied the name A. to all idolaters.

AMOS: The earliest of the literary prophets although his book is placed third among the Minor Prophets. Born in the 8th cent. B.C.E. in the Judean town of Tekoa south of Bethlehem, A. prophesied during the reign of Uzziah king of Judah and Jeroboam II king of Israel. A. was living a simple pastoral existence when a Divine summons led him to the shrine of Bethel where he uttered his fiery remonstrances against the moral corruption of his generation. There he defended his prophetic calling, dissociating himself from the professional prophets and soothsayers until he was evicted by the head priest Amaziah. The prophet shocked his self-satisfied audience by proclaiming the impending doom of the then flourishing nation. His admonitions were clothed in language and imagery full of great force as well as great beauty. The burden of his message insists upon universal ethical monotheism and uncompromising moral demands. With the zeal of an iconoclast A. inveighed against prevailing misconceptions such as the popularly longed for "Day of the Lord". This, he averred, meant a day of judgment, not of bliss. Of all nations Israel was the most vulnerable to Divine retribution because of its status as a "chosen people," a status which had been falsely interpreted as conferring unconditional benefits. Though no opponent of the sacrificial cult as such, A. proclaimed it ineffectual unless matched by sincere devotion to the will of God. Of unequaled pathos is the prophet's denunciation of a corrupt aristocracy and its merciless oppression of the poor under the guise of a hypocritical claim to a unique relationship with God. Though foretelling destruction, his prophecy ends with a description of Israel's latter-day restoration. According to the Talmud (*Mak.* 24a) all 613 commandments of the Bible were summed up in A.'s single dictum "Seek Me and live!"

AMRAM BAR SHESHNA (9th cent.): *Gaon*: head of the Sura academy. The first complete prayer-book — the *Seder Rav Amram* ("Order of Prayers of Rabbi Amram") — is traditionally ascribed to his authorship. This practical code greatly influenced *Sephardi* ritual and contained both the text and order of the prayers and halakhic legislation governing synagogue practice and the observance of the holidays. His responsa throw vivid light on the conditions of Jewish life in his time.

AMULET (Heb. *kamea*): Object worn as a charm against evil (sickness, ill-fortune, the "evil-eye", etc.). In Jewish custom, an a. usually contains verses from the Bible which refer to protection against harm, such as "I will put none of the diseases upon thee, which I have put upon the Egyptians, for I am the Lord thy healer" (Exod. 15:16), or sacred letters and symbols, names of angels, etc. The Tosephta (*Shab.* 5:9) speaks of an "effective amulet" (*kamea mumḥeh*) as being one which has healed three times, "whether it be an a. of writing or an a. of herb roots" (Rashi on *Shab.* 61a explains the word *kamea* as having reference to anything which can be made into a knot). The Mishnah, too, gives indirect recognition to the propriety of the wearing of amulets, reflecting the prevalent attitude of the time when it teaches that only "an a. which has not yet proven its effectiveness" may not be worn in the street on the Sabbath (*Shab.* 6:2). Amulets were very common throughout the ancient Middle East and have been frequently uncovered in archeological excavations. In mishnaic, talmudic, and gaonic times they were also widely worn. The later KABBALAH gave a further impetus to the wearing of amulets, increasing belief in the efficacy of the Divine name represented by various letter-combinations. Whereas previously the rabbis had never given specific approval, the preparation of amulets now often became a rabbinic function. Kabbalistic formulas, moreover, were as common as scriptural verses in amulets. The use of amulets is still prevalent among oriental Jews. Not all amulets are worn; some are hung on the walls of a birth-chamber as protection against LILITH, or are placed wherever real or imaginary danger lurks. See also MAGIC; SUPERSTITION.

ANAGRAM: Literary device by which the letters of a word or sentence are transposed to form a new word or sentence. The system occurs in the Bible and was often used in talmudic and midrashic literature as a basis for aggadic interpretations of biblical texts. Under the influence of the Midrash and also of Arabic literature, the a. became a favorite device of medieval Hebrew poetry and was also frequently used in Kabbalah (and in AMULETS). European alchemists derived the method from the Kabbalah.

ANAN BEN DAVID (8th cent.): Founder of the KARAITE sect (originally known as the Ananites). According to legend, A. envied his younger brother's election to succeed their father as exilarch in Babylon. A., who had probably already been attracted earlier to unorthodox religious groups, thereupon began to advocate opposition to the Oral Law, taking as his motto "search the Scriptures thoroughly"; he united existing dissident groups around his anti-Rabbinism. In 767, after proclaiming himself exilarch, he was condemned to death as a rebel by the caliph but was saved on declaring that his faith differed from that of his brother. His *Sepher Ha-Mitzvot* ("The Book of Precepts") claimed to contain strictly biblical commandments and often relied on Sadducean tradition, but in fact many matters were explained in it according to rabbinic tradition and methodology (especially the use of analogy). The result was a rigorous and often gloomy interpretation of Judaism. A. introduced changes in methods of intercalation and the determination of months; stressed hyperstringent Sabbath observance and introduced a number of fast days; and permitted in theory the consumption of meat with milk though in practice he entirely forbade the consumption of meat (except deer), fowl (except pigeon), and wine. He recognized Jesus and Mohammed as prophets sent respectively to the Christians and Moslems. Subsequent Karaism modified many of A.'s doctrines though continuing to venerate him as the "principal teacher".

ANATHEMA, see **EXCOMMUNICATION**

ANCIENT OF DAYS (Aram. *attik yomin*): Designation for God found in the Book of Daniel (7:9 ff.) and used frequently in mystical literature.

ANENU (Heb. "answer us"): Prayer inserted on fast-days in the *Shema Kolenu* blessing in the repetition of the AMIDAH at the Morning and Afternoon Services. It beseeches God to "answer in time of trouble". The earliest formulation is in the Palestinian Talmud (*Ber.* 4:3) but the existing versions contain a number of divergences, that of the *Ashkenazi* rite being closest to the original.

ANGELS: Conceived of as supernatural, celestial beings, a. play a role in Jewish thought and literature from earliest biblical times, yet angelology has never become a major systematized branch of Jewish theology. Some scholars maintain that belief in a. is of foreign origin, and aroused the opposition of certain religious authorities. The study of angelology is nevertheless important for the understanding of the evolution of Jewish religious ideas. Various names are applied to angelic beings in Scripture. Like the Greek word from which "angel" is derived, the Hebrew word *malakh* signifies primarily a "messenger" or "agent"; it is as God's messenger that the *malakh* becomes an "angel". Other designations for spiritual entities are: *benei Elohim* or *benei elim* ("sons of God", Gen. 6:4; Ps. 29:1); *kedoshim* ("holy ones", Ps. 89:6, 8); *ir* ("watcher" or "envoy", Dan. 4:10, 14); and sometimes simply *ish* ("man", Gen. 18:2; 32:25). More distinctive appellations are reserved for the supernatural creatures connected with the Divine Throne or Chariot: SERAPHIM (Is. 6:2); CHERUBIM (Ezek. 10:3; cf. Gen. 3:24); *ḥayyot* ("living creatures", Ezek. 1:5); OPHANNIM ("wheels", Ezek. 1:15 ff.). Notwithstanding the variety of generic names by which a. are called and the use of descriptive expressions indicative of their mission, such as "the angel which hath redeemed" (Gen. 48:16), "the angel that destroyed" (II Sam. 24:16), "an interpreter" (Job 32:23), etc., it is significant that with the exception of certain post-exilic references, these heavenly spirits are depicted in the Bible as lacking individuality, personal names, and/or hierarchical rank. In the course of their duties they assume many forms, the shape varying with their task. Most often, especially in the earlier narratives, they appear as human beings. But irrespective of their commission they remain completely obedient to the Divine will. Even Satan, the "adversary", is none other than the Lord's official prosecutor and is subservient to His authority. The concept of rebellious a. belongs to post-biblical Jewish literature. Angelic functions are numerous and, as a rule, beneficent. Thus, they come to the aid of Hagar, apprise Abraham that a son will be born to him, guard the Israelites against the pursuing Egyptians, protect them during their wanderings in the wilderness, interpret the visions of Zechariah and Daniel. At other times a. (to be distinguished from the DEMONS of a later epoch) are given punitive missions — to destroy Sodom and Gomorrah (Gen. 19), punish the citizens of Jerusalem (Ezek. 9), smite the camp of Assyria (II Kings 19:35). In heaven they surround God's throne, and form His Council and Court (I Kings 22:19 ff.). They also constitute the celestial choir which has sung unceasing praise to the Creator since the beginning of time (Job 38:7). Inconsistencies discernible in the portrayal of angelic activities (e.g. the "sons of God" marrying the daughters of men, Gen. 6:2 ff.) appear to be due to the fact that varied strands of thought and belief combine to form the fabric of biblical angelology. In some instances forces deified by heathen people were reduced to the status of a. and thus brought under the control of the One God. At other periods it was felt that the very transcendental character of God postulated the presence of intermediary beings to mediate between Him and the world. In many passages the angel merely personifies a Divine attribute, or embodies His will in history, or is an objectivization of the prophet's vision. It is noteworthy, however, that in large parts of the Bible a. are conspicuously absent. It is conjectured that the prophetic and priestly circles, as well as the so-called Deuteronomic school, were opposed to the doctrine of a. inasmuch as it derogated from the absolute divinity of the One God. The Babylonian Exile had a marked effect on Jewish angelology. Rabbinic tradition attested to this Babylonian-Persian influence in the statement: "The names of the a. were brought by the Jews from Babylonia" (Y. *R.H.* 1:2). The a. became individualized, were given specific names, and were graded, like Babylonian spirits, into different ranks. Ezekiel speaks of seven a., six of whom wrought destruction, while the seventh acted as a scribe. Zechariah saw "a man riding upon a red horse", who was chief of those who "walk to and fro through the earth" (1:8-19). The new conception of the Deity was so transcendental that it was no longer God but "the angel that talked with me" who instructed the prophet (1:9, 14, etc.). In the Bible this process reaches its climax in the Book of Daniel. Here the a. are classified; two high-ranking a. have individual names (MICHAEL and GABRIEL); and national Guardian Angels (*sarim*) are introduced for the first time (Dan. 8:16; 10:20, 21). The evolution of angelology advanced still further in the post-biblical apocalyptic literature, especially in *Enoch, Jubilees, The Testament of the Twelve Patriarchs,* and the *Sibylline Oracles.* The world of a. now becomes so bizarre and chaotic as to leave an impression of unbridled imagination. Essentially, the a. serve as the media of revelation and the instruments by which God governs the world. Their numbers are astronomical; their varieties almost endless. All the elements and phenomena of nature are given tutelary spirits. Certain angelic categories are of special interest. Thus frequent reference is made to the Angel of Peace and it is said "the very angel of peace shall strengthen Israel" (*Test. of Dan.* 6:5). The seven (or four) archangels are usually deemed to be the highest angelic echelon (*Enoch* 20:1-8). They may be identifiable with the "watchers" of Daniel, the "a. of the presence" (see Is. 63:9), and the "ministering a." of rabbinic ideology. Mystic lore devoted special attention to the Divine Chariot (Ezek. 1-3). At the other end of the scale, the Fallen a., who for their sins were cast from heaven to the netherworld (see Gen. 6:4; Is. 14:12-15) are given prominence in the apocalyptic works, but find no place in rabbinic literature. It is they who begot the demons and seducers of women. They were subjugated by the archangels but not annihilated. This polarization of the angel world into good and evil spirits is a major feature of angelology to which it appears the Essenes made a considerable contribution. The Sadducees, on the other hand, seem to have been strenuously opposed to it. A highly developed angelology is also found in the Talmud, Midrash, and the Palestinian Targum. Under Magian and Zoroastrian influence the angelic hosts proliferated, but in rabbinic Judaism, unlike Persian Mazdaism, the evil spirits — even the *malakhei ḥabbalah* ("a. of destruction") — remained under the supreme control of the one God. There are many aggadic sayings on the subject of a: they are made of fire, or of fire and water divinely harmonized; some are transitory and live only to sing a single hymn of praise to the Creator, others are eternal. A few have cosmic proportions. It was a moot point as to whether the permanent a. were formed on the second, fourth, or fifth day of Creation. They certainly were not created on the first day lest it be thought that they were God's partners in the creative process. They are called *elyonim* ("higher beings") to distinguish them from the *taḥtonim* ("lower beings"), the denizens of the earth. They have no will of their own, but loyally carry out the Divine commands. Mostly they seek the good of pious men and the well-being of Israel in particular. Wherever no personal agent is mentioned in the Bible, the *aggadah* tends to fill the vacuum with a. Thus they are given an important role in the creation of man, the sacrifice of Isaac, and the story of Esther. There are 70 (Deut. 32:8; cf. Septuagint) or 72 (corresponding to the divisions of the Zodiac?) guardian a. of the nations. They constitute the Divine Council and the Court. Individual Israelites also have guardian a. One angel is given each Jew with the fulfillment of a commandment, and two accompany him constantly. On Sabbath eve a good and evil angel accompany each worshiper as he returns from the synagogue. In the sanctuary on high the *malakhei ha-sharet* ("ministering a.") perform the priestly functions, with Michael acting as a kind of high priest. There are seven heavens, each in the charge of an archangel. Of special eminence is the *Malakh ha-Panim* ("Angel of the Presence") also called Amshapands and identified with Enoch. There are numerous allusions to A. of Destruction. The most terrible of the destroying angels is the *Malakh ha-Mavet* ("The Angel of Death"), who waits at the bedside of the sick. At the tip of his sword hangs the lethal drop of venom. Originally, the A. of Death, like other a., personified a function of the Divine will, but gradually he acquired a definitely demonic individuality. He is linked, and at times identified, with Satan (who tempts and accuses), the evil inclination, and SAMAEL, the prince of demons. All the great Jewish philosophers, except Philo, adopted a rationalistic view of a. Ibn Daud, Maimonides, and Gersonides identified them with the Pure Intellects who governed the planetary bodies. Saadyah Gaon and Judah Ha-Levi regarded them as manifestations of prophetic visions created for a specific mission; Ha-Levi, however, considered the a. of the "higher world" as eternal. In the Kabbalah, both speculative and practical, angelology assumes its most extravagant forms. Whereas the Talmud (Y. *Ber.* 9:13) depicts the a. as servants of God, and prohibits supplicating them for help, ancient mystical texts (*Heikhalot*, Zohar and later kabbalistic literature) attributed to them the most extraordinary powers; in consequence, despite the disapproval of many rabbinic authorities, appeals were made to them in the form of AMULETS, incantations, and even through interpolations in the liturgy. Kabbalistic angelology remained nevertheless essentially monotheistic. Most rabbinic texts agree that man, in spite of his bodily materiality, ranks above the a. References to a. are still preserved in the traditional liturgy. They occur, *inter alia,* in the *musaph kedushah*, the *seliḥot*, and in the *shopharot* passages. The "ministering a." and the "a. of peace" are addressed in the hymn *Shalom Aleikhem* ("Peace be to you"), which is recited after the Evening Service on Friday night. Generally speaking contemporary Judaism regards allusions to a. in Scripture and in the liturgy as of poetic and symbolic significance rather than of doctrinal import or factual significance.

ANI MAAMIN, see **CREED**

AN'IM ZEMIROT, see **SHIR HA-KAVOD**

ANIMAL SACRIFICES, see **SACRIFICES**

ANIMAL WORSHIP: Worship or religious reverence paid to either living animals or animal representations as symbols of the divine. Animal images were common in ancient religions, and appear even in Israelite history in a religious context (e.g. the NEHUSHTAN — the "brazen serpent" — made by Moses and destroyed by Hezekiah). A.W. comes under the general prohibition of IDOLATRY. As calves and bulls were common symbols of fertility and strength, evidence of calf-worship also appears in the Bible (II Kings 12:28-30; see CALF, GOLDEN).

ANIMALS, TREATMENT OF: Extraordinary solicitude for a. is one of the most distinctive features of Jewish ethics. God's "remembrance" extends to the beasts and cattle in Noah's ark (Gen. 8:1) and later the animals of Nineveh (Jon. 4:11), and His "salvation" is granted to man and beast alike (Ps. 36:7). This attitude explains the numerous laws on the treatment of a. designed to protect them against pain, disease, hunger, and overwork. Among relevant biblical laws are the precepts to assist a. in loading and unloading their burdens (Exod. 23:5; Deut. 22:4), not to "muzzle the ox when he treadeth out the corn" (Deut. 25:4), not to remove a bird's eggs or young in the presence of the mother (Deut. 22:6, 7), and to include domestic a. among the beneficiaries of the Sabbath ordinance of rest (Exod. 20:10; 23:12; Deut. 5:14). The rabbis developed these laws further; e.g. they insisted that it was unlawful to eat until one had first fed one's a. or birds (*Git.* 62a). The infliction of unnecessary cruelty on a. is accounted a biblical offense; the definitions of "necessary" (medically or otherwise) and "unnecessary" pain are discussed in rabbinic law. Thus, according to some recent responsa, no objections are to be raised against animal vivisection for medical research, provided every measure is taken to guard against unnecessary torture.

ANINUT (Heb.): Interval between death and burial; during this period the mourner is called *onen*. The *onen* is absolved from observing all *Torah* precepts e.g. praying or laying *tephillin*. He is forbidden to eat meat or drink wine. Should a Sabbath intervene during this period, the *onen* must observe the precepts as usual.

ANOINTING: In religious usage a. signifies consecration by the application of OIL, as distinct from secular a. for hygienic and cosmetic reasons (the latter being forbidden during mourning and on fasts, Mishnah *Yoma* 8:1). A. was an integral part of the solemn act of the consecration of High Priests and kings to their respective offices. In the consecration of Aaron as High Priest, the altar and the sanctuary vessels, as well as Aaron himself, were anointed with oil (Lev. 7:10-12) and by this act were "sanctified". So central was the act of a. to the ceremony that the consecration as a whole is called "the day of his a." (Lev. 6:12) and Aaron's successor is referred to as "the anointed priest that shall be in his stead from among his sons" (Lev. 6:15). Similarly, the priest appointed for purposes of war (Deut. 20:2) is invariably referred to in the Talmud as "the priest anointed for war" (e.g. Mishnah *Sot.* 8:1). According to the Talmud kings were consecrated by a. only on the inauguration of a new dynasty, but not when a son succeeded his father without opposition. Thus in the southern kingdom of Judah, in which all the kings were of the dynasty of David, only kings whose succession was disputed were anointed, e.g. Solomon because of the rival claim of Adonijah (I Kings 1:39); Joash, because of the opposition of Athaliah (II Kings 11:12); and Jehoahaz because of the claims of his older brother Jehoiachim (II Kings 23:30). The phrase *meshiaḥ adonai* ("A. of the Lord"), however, is used for a king (e.g. I Sam. 24:6) and from this phrase is derived the word MESSIAH (Heb. *mashiaḥ* — "anointed one") the scion of the House of David who will bring salvation. In Is. 45:1 Cyrus, who is destined to bring about the restoration of the Jews to their land, is called the anointed of God. A. plays no part in Jewish ritual today.

ANTHROPOMORPHISM: The attribution to God of such human qualities as human form (a. proper, e.g. God's figure, hands, eyes, etc.) and human emotions (anthropopathism, e.g. God loves, is angry, etc). A., which is taken for granted in many primitive and pagan religions, becomes a problem when the concept of a spiritual and transcendent God conflicts with apparent a. in authoritative texts (e.g. the Bible, rabbinic AGGADAH, etc.). 19th cent. scholars claimed to have discovered evidence of a gradual evolution from an anthropomorphic to a more spiritual conception of God in the biblical texts, but this is now held to be an oversimplification. On the one hand biblical writers do not hesitate to resort to a. (God walks in the Garden of Eden, passes over the houses of the children of Israel, dwells in Zion, is moved by love or feelings of revenge, etc.) but on the other hand they frequently use qualifying language. Many of the definite anthropomorphisms are obviously not meant to be taken literally but are the language of imagery. The TARGUMIM (Onkelos in particular) as well as the hellenistic philosophers (PHILO) rendered this anthropomorphistic imagery by qualifying circumlocutions or interpreted it allegorically, so as to avoid all danger of misunderstanding. Rabbinic usage too did not shy away from a. and it was attacked by the KARAITES and others for its alleged primitive crudity. The great medieval Jewish philosophers, Maimonides in particular, undertook to "interpret" all objectionable anthropomorphisms, viz. to "translate" them into abstract, conceptual language (see ATTRIBUTES). For their part the mystics and kabbalists evolved new — to some minds shocking — anthropomorphisms as well as theories and concepts to deal with them. Ultimately the problem is one of enabling human beings to speak validly both of a God (in theology) and to a God (in prayer) who is utterly transcendent. The choice seems to be between saying nothing at all (the "mystic silence") and daring to speak of Him in human terms — i.e., in the only language men possess to indicate that God is actively meaningful in human life (e.g. as Creator, Father, King, Lover, Redeemer, etc.). The conviction of God's spirituality and transcendence as it finally developed in Judaism was so radical and deep, that the most daring a. could be used without risk or danger.

ANTICHRIST, see **ARMILUS**

ANTINOMIANISM: Opposition to and negation of traditional Law. Tendencies and movements denying the validity of the practical commandments or, at least, encouraging their neglect, appeared in different periods and for varying reasons. In hellenistic Egypt, and again in the later Middle Ages, the substitution of symbolic and allegorical meanings for the literary meaning of the *Torah* tended to undermine strict observance of the Law by reinterpreting it philosophically. Paul's doctrine of the "fulfillment" and hence the abolishment of the Law by Jesus presents a different type of a. The Church Fathers considered the Hebrew Scriptures and their Law merely as an allegory foretelling and preparing for the coming of the founder of Christianity. Christian gnostics of the 2nd-4th cents. contrasted the God of the Old Testament, whom they considered the lower "demiurge" and an often evil creator, to the Most-High and absolutely good God. With the rise of the Reformation early Protestantism for a while struggled with the idea of giving binding sanction to part of Old Testament Law but this tendency was soon defeated as a "Judaizing" heresy. The Kabbalah furnished latent seeds for a. Although the mystics recognized four concurrently valid methods of interpreting Scripture (the literal, the aggadic, the allegorical, and the mystical), only the last was the main concern of the Zohar. A sharper note of mystical a. is struck by the author of the *Raaya Mehemena* in his contemptuous criticism of literal exegesis and methods of study used by the halakhic scholars. In the books of *Pelia* and *Kanah* even talmudic discussions of the law are considered meaningless except as they are given kabbalistic interpretation. All this latent a. exploded in the Sabbataian movement where it gave birth to the notion of the "holy sinner". SHABBETAI TZEVI's provocative breaches of the Law took on special sanctity, if not in his own eyes, then at least in those of his followers who considered them mystical acts of TIKKUN. A. then became ritualized, and its underlying heretical mysticism issued forth in the radical nihilism of some of the Sabbataian sects. It has been argued that the Sabbataian debacle contributed to the formation of the intellectual atmosphere that produced the Reform movement in the 19th cent., though of course the a. of modern liberal, let alone Reform Judaism, has very different ideological and theological foundations.

ANTIOCHUS IV EPIPHANES (reigned 175-163 B.C.E.): Syrian king and ardent hellenizer. After conquering Egypt, he was ordered by the Romans to withdraw; his consequent bitterness influenced his attitude to his Jewish subjects especially as they rejected his claims to divinity. A. visited Jerusalem and despoiled the Temple. Subsequently a rumor that he had died led to riots in Jerusalem which were suppressed with great cruelty. A violent anti-Jewish policy was introduced whereby observance of the commandments (especially the Sabbath and circumcision) was forbidden, books of the Law were burnt, the Temple altar was desecrated by idol-worship, and orders were issued to erect altars to Greek gods throughout the country. Jews who resisted were mercilessly slaughtered and many sold into slavery. The persecution of A. led to the HASMONEAN revolt.

ANTIOCHUS, SCROLL OF: Pseudepigraphic work describing the HASMONEAN revolt. Dating probably from the 7th cent. C.E. the book consists of legends and is without value as a historical source; it nevertheless passed into the old Italian and Yemenite *Ḥanukkah* rites, being read from a scroll in the synagogue.

ANTI-SEMITISM: Hatred of, and hostility to, the Jews. The term is used in both a general and a particular sense. In general it is applied to all manifestations of hatred of the Jewish people throughout the ages, and as such it has a long history. It even precedes the enmity of the Christian Church toward the Jews for their alleged crime of deicide and their refusal to accept Jesus. In fact, the classical expression of animosity toward the Jews is found as early as the Bible in the statement of Haman, "there is a certain people scattered abroad and dispersed among the people in all the provinces of the kingdom, and their laws are diverse from all people, neither keep they the king's laws, therefore it is not for the king's profit to suffer them" (Est. 3:8). That verse contains many traditional aspects of anti-Semitism; the dispersion and homelessness of the Jews, the suspicions aroused by their strange customs which gives rise to "the dislike of the like for the unlike", the accusation that as an alien element they are potentially harmful to the State (cf. Exod. 1:10), and that in any case they are disloyal to it. Lastly comes the belief in their dispensability as a useless element. Much of the early hatred of the Jews was based upon the Jewish rejection of paganism; the Jewish refusal to worship images led to a series of clashes with the Hellenistic and Roman authorities and to the antagonism to Jews expressed, for example, in certain classical authors. Other peoples accepted the existence of the gods of other nations; only the Jews refused absolutely to acknowledge such existence or to send tribute. Moreover Jewish religious practices (e.g. marriage customs, dietary laws) cut them off from social intercourse with their neighbors. The necessity for Jews to live in close proximity to one another (for the proper observance of the Sabbath etc., and in order to be close to a synagogue), as well as their inability to perform certain communal or national obligations (e.g. military service) for religious reasons, also stressed their apartness. Pagan (hellenistic) anti-Semitism was rife in the 1st cent. B.C.E. and the 1st cent. C.E., particularly in Alexandria, and was probably accentuated by Jewish proselytizing activities and the concomitant Jewish denigration of the practices of other religions. However it was only in the Christian world that anti-Semitism assumed tragic proportions. Though Christianity denied all other religions, it found itself in a particularly hostile position with regard to the "mother religion" from which it claimed its descent but which had rejected it. The spread and ultimate political success of Christianity led to the emergence of the doctrine that the Jews were hated by God, who had rejected them for their sinfulness and obstinacy. Jews were gradually forced out of every sphere of political influence and deprived of civil and political rights. In due course the Church's attempts to erect barriers between Jew and non-Jew were translated into legislation affecting all aspects of Jewish life. Conversion to Judaism became an offense punishable by death and a movement for the destruction of synagogues and forced CONVERSION of the Jews was strong from the 5th cent. on. Exclusion of Jews from economic life was the next objective, and in the later Middle Ages expulsions were frequent. Hatred of the Jews was fed by liturgical and other (e.g. dramatic) commemorations of the crucifixion of Jesus, and was liable to erupt with particular violence at the Easter season, the occasion for organized attacks on the Jews. Religious a. reached its first climax in the period of the Crusades, and the Fourth Lateran Council (1215) passed a series of anti-Jewish measures. In this atmosphere many anti-Jewish libels — notably the BLOOD LIBEL — received universal credence throughout the Christian world. The ultimately religious nature of Christian a. was demonstrated by the fact that baptism automatically removed all disabilities from a Jew. In fact, discrimination and persecution had the avowed purpose of producing conversion and there is no record of church discrimination against converted Jews earlier than 16th cent. Spain. The doctrine of the medieval church that by their crime of deicide and their refusal to accept the divinity of Jesus the Jews had become the "spawn of the devil" and the enemies of God was largely responsible for the concept that Jews as a group were inherently wicked and depraved, and had to be treated accordingly. In the Moslem world, anti-Semitic developments were far less extreme. There was little specific a. and Jews were treated (or ill-treated) like other infidels. The end of the Middle Ages did not bring any major changes. The Counter-Reformation in the Catholic world renewed and increased anti-Jewish legislation and enforced the introduction of the ghetto system. Protestants in general followed the medieval pattern and Luther advocated an extreme anti-Jewish policy. In the 19th cent., the religious foundations of Christian Europe were weakened and with them religious prejudices, except in Czarist Russia and wherever the church continued to press an anti-Semitic policy. In the 19th cent. "scientific" a. gradually took the place of "religious" a. The Jews were said to represent a distinct and inferior ethnic Semitic group different from the Nordic or Aryan people among whom they lived. Hence their integration and assimilation into their environment, even if possible, would corrupt society and bring about the decline of prevailing standards. Modern a. is thus built on racial, not religious, foundations and the adoption of the prevailing faith no longer provides an escape route for persecuted Jews. Modern racial a. reached its tragic apogee with the rise of Hitler and his infamous "Final Solution" of the Jewish problem. Responsible contemporary church leaders, realizing the dangers of a. as well as the common ground of men of all faiths, have condemned a. and are making efforts to spread attitudes of tolerance and understanding to those circles in which the traditional Christian forms of a. still persist.

ANUSIM, see **MARRANOS**

APAM, see **AFAM**

APHIKOMAN (Greek word of uncertain origin): Name given to the piece taken from the middle of the three unleavened breads on the *Seder* table on Passover eve and eaten at the conclusion of the meal by all present. The paschal meal in the Temple ended with the tasting of the paschal lamb, and the *a.* symbolizes this custom. The tradition is for the celebrant to hide half of the middle piece of *matzah* before reciting the HAGGADAH; this is meant to arouse the curiosity of the younger participants and the custom has developed for children to remove the *a.*, hide it elsewhere, and refuse to reveal its whereabouts until it has been ransomed by the promise of a gift.

APIKOROS: Rabbinical form of the name of the Greek philosopher Epicurus. According to Jewish tradition, he believed that the soul perished with the body and that the pleasures of this-world are the highest happiness. The Talmud therefore applied the name to all heretics and the term was eventually used to refer to all unbelievers and skeptics. Maimonides classed as *apikorsim* those who disbelieve in prophecy in general, those who deny the prophecy of Moses, and those who do not believe that God knows man's thoughts. They were regarded as completely wicked and without any lot in the future world. The *Shulḥan Arukh*, which defines an *a.* as one who rejects the Divine origin of the *Torah* as well as prophecy, deems him worthy of death. Since medieval times, the term has also been applied in popular parlance to Jews who are lax in traditional observance. See HERESY.

APOCALYPSE (Gk. "uncovering", "disclosure"): Divine revelation made known in a dream, vision, or trance; the appellation subsequently came to denote the literature devoted to such revelations — in particular the Jewish and Christian writings which purported to discern the mysteries of creation, the cosmos, and the END OF DAYS. Though apocalyptic is closely related to and, to some extent, stems from PROPHECY, the two are not to be equated. The biblical prophets spoke out with the conviction of Divine inspiration when they interpreted the significant events of the day, or exhorted, admonished, and consoled their listeners. Furthermore, the prophetic message — even in those instances when it utilized "visions", "symbols", and other literary forms closely associated with apocalyptic — was directed primarily at the contemporary scene and aimed at a definite, active, and immediate response. The Apocalyptics, on the other hand, beheld the events of the past or of the ultimate future, and lacking prophetic status, they sought to invest their words with authority by writing under the pseudonym of a venerated biblical personality. Thence the designation Pseudepigrapha ("false writings") which was applied to the majority of apocalyptical books. Unlike the prophets of old, the Apocalyptics actively challenged contemporary reality, but preferred to dwell on the theme of a sudden, miraculous Divine intervention which was to redeem and restore Israel. The exact origins of A. are obscure, though its roots were firmly planted in the soil of biblical prophecy. Apocalyptic thought was doubtless greatly influenced by the ancient popular concept of a DAY OF THE LORD — the day on which God would bring the sinners, both Jew and Gentile, to judgment. Traces of A. are to be found in the Bible (cf. Zech. 9-14) culminating in the Book of DANIEL which is sometimes erroneously referred to as the source of A. Though Daniel is among the earliest of the extant apocalyptical works (one or more sections of the Book of ENOCH may be even earlier) and the only one which found its way into the canon of the Bible, its apocalypticism is by no means primitive and would seem to presuppose an older, well-developed apocalyptic tradition. The Apocalyptics used prophetic themes, but elaborated them and practically changed their original meaning. Furthermore, apocalyptic literature tended to be deliberately vague and ambiguous. It employed an elaborate system of imagery (cf. particularly Dan. 7-8) in which animals, birds, reptiles, and half-human, half-beast monsters played a leading rôle. ANGELOLOGY played an important part in a. and GEMATRIA and other symbolic devices were employed to enhance the mystery of their message. The apocalyptic writer's favorite literary scheme was to assume the name of a biblical personage long since deceased and recount the subsequent historical events leading up to the writer's own time as though these events were still in the future — a prophecy *ex post facto*. Thinly disguised contemporary happenings and personalities were then portrayed with, however, apocalyptical trappings. The fact that the "prophecy" in the first part of the apocalypse had been fulfilled gave added authority to the vision of the future. In point of fact, the narration of past and present history served merely as a point of departure from which the Apocalyptist could launch into his description of the as-yet-unknown future. Fantasy was given free reign: the exact date of the "end of days" was calculated, the advent and reign of the MESSIAH were described at length, a detailed account of the DAY OF JUDGMENT was given, and the blessings of the "world-to-come" were enumerated. These elaborate and fanciful prophecies were not mere "daydreams", for they contained the very essence of the apocalyptic message — namely, that the advent of the messianic age was at hand, when the righteous of Israel would be redeemed, the sinners damned. Apocalyptical literature flourished for roughly three and a half centuries, from the 2nd cent. B.C.E. to the middle of the 2nd cent. C.E. and A. must be regarded within the setting of this historical background: Israel had returned from the Babylonian Exile, Jerusalem had been restored, the Temple rebuilt, but contrary to all expectations, the Messiah had not come. The situation, far from improving, had gradually deteriorated. The former glories of the united kingdom under David and Solomon seemed more unattainable than ever. The present was insecure, the future dubious. Particularly in the last two centuries B.C.E. the horizon had begun to blacken with the dark clouds of the impending storm which was to destroy the Temple and leave Jerusalem desolate. It became increasingly evident that the very existence of the Jewish nation was at stake. A. attempted to provide the answer: the coming days would bring even greater hardships, yet it was wrong to despair. The powerful, evil forces at work in the world bore witness to the imminent dawn of a new era. The greater the trials, the nearer the day of deliverance, for these tribulations were in reality the "birth-pangs of the Messiah" (*ḥevlei ha-mashiaḥ*). The growing political tensions acted as a catalytic agent on apocalyptical thought, causing it to turn further and further away from the reality of life and to focus on the coming messianic era. In many cases a type of optimistic fatalism developed. Man was engulfed in powers well beyond his control, but however dark the present might seem, God in His might would prevail. A. was not, as has long been held, a specific trend within Pharisaism, but a general widespread and heterogeneous acute-eschatological movement in the Jewish community in the latter days of the Second Temple. As the DEAD SEA SCROLLS have shown, a. was cultivated in sectarian circles. Although apocalyptical literature expresses various and conflicting views, one central belief was shared by all the various sects and groups comprising this movement, and served as the cornerstone of A.: Divine intervention in human affairs was imminent, and the day of judgment and salvation was at hand. Illustrations of this acutely eschatological orientation can be found in the writings of the *Qumran* Community as well as in the New Testament. A more reserved attitude developed among the Pharisees who, while accepting messianic beliefs and preserving many apocalyptic traditions, rejected the more extreme forms of imminent eschatology. Their concern was not with the final apocalyptic events, but with daily practice and with the study and observance of the Law. With the exception of Daniel, all writings of an apocalyptic character were ranged among the "external books" (see APOCRYPHA), e.g. the Books of ENOCH, JUBILEES, FOURTH ESDRAS, etc. Jewish elements are still recognizable in the Christian apocalypse, the Revelation of John, which forms the last book of the New Testament. Apocalyptic writings were also produced during the Middle Ages, reflecting the historic experiences and the messianic hopes of their authors.

APOCRYPHA AND PSEUDEPIGRAPHA: The body of Jewish religious literature, written between the 2nd cent. B.C.E. and the 2nd cent. C.E., which was not included in the canon of the Hebrew Bible. Most of these works originated in Palestine and the majority were written either in Hebrew or Aramaic. Generally speaking, the Apocryphal writings antedate the Pseudepigrapha. Whereas the Apocrypha — containing didactic, prophetical, historical, legendary, and Apocalyptical Literature — are similar in character to the Hagiographa, the Pseudepigrapha, with few exceptions, are primarily apocalyptic in content. Though this body of literature enjoyed considerable popularity for some three centuries, it was subsequently thrust aside by the rapidly growing body of talmudic literature and was all but lost to the Jewish tradition. The preservation of these writings is due in great measure to the Christian Church; in many cases, the original Hebrew or Aramaic of the texts has been lost, but the literature itself has been preserved in a secondary (Greek, Latin, Armenian, Coptic, Ethiopian, etc.) translation. The word Apocrypha (Gk. "hidden" or "secret") refers specifically to fourteen (or sixteen) books which were included in the SEPTUAGINT and VULGATE but not in the Hebrew Bible. Eleven of these books were subsequently declared canonical by the Catholic Church while the remainder, though "extra-canonical", were accorded a special status of esteem. The Apocrypha consist of the following books: I and II *Maccabees* (in some instances III and IV *Maccabees* are also included), I and II *Esdras, Ecclesiasticus, Wisdom of Solomon, Tobit, Judith, Prayer of Manasseh, Additions to Esther, Bel and the Dragon, Song of the Three Holy Children, The History of Susannah,* and *Baruch* (of which chap. 6 is referred to as the *Epistle of Jeremiah*). The Apocrypha are of later origin than the canonical books of the Bible (though *Ecclesiasticus* may be somewhat older than the canonical book of Daniel) and, as a body, never quite measured up to the standard of literary excellence or to the degree of spiritual insight attained by the books of the Bible. The designation Pseudepigrapha (Gk. "with false title") has been affixed to the remaining books of this period which were not incorporated in the Septuagint, the Vulgate, or the Hebrew Bible. This appellation was due to the contemporary practice of ascribing a work to a famous historical personage in order to enhance the book's authority and spiritual stature. Though the division between the Apocrypha and Pseudepigrapha is far from consistent (several books of the Apocrypha are properly speaking "pseudepigrapha", cf. *Wisdom of Solomon, Baruch,* and the *Epistle of Jeremiah,* while some of the Pseudepigrapha are not written under a pseudonym at all, cf. *Book of Jubilees*), it is nonetheless justified by the diversity between the two groupings in content and subject matter. The Apocrypha are a type of inferior Hagiographa, but the Pseudepigrapha — concentrating as they do on the Advent of the Messiah, the Coming of Judgment, and the End of Days — mark a departure from Scripture. While similar themes are touched upon in the Bible, they are neither elaborated nor carried to such disproportionate lengths as in the apocalyptical "visions" and "revelations" described by the Pseudepigraphal writers. The Pseudepigrapha generally were not accepted into the Christian canon, but they were nonetheless preserved as semi-sacred literature by various Christian communities for the reason that, with minor interpolations, they could readily be adapted to the Christian interpretation of the life, mission, and second coming of Jesus. Indeed, the Jewish origin of some of the Pseudepigrapha was for some time suspect. Until the recent discovery of the DEAD SEA SCROLLS, most of the Pseudepigrapha were known only in the form of a secondary translation but a number of them have now been found in the original. Among the better-known works of the Pseudepigrapha are: *Psalms of Solomon, Testament of the Twelve Patriarchs, Book of Jubilees, Apocalypse of Baruch, Book of Enoch, Assumption of Moses, Ascension of Isaiah,* and the *Sibylline Oracles.* For some time, scholars were prone to ascribe the Pseudepigrapha to the Pharisees, but it is now becoming increasingly apparent that this body of apocalyptic writings stems rather from the widespread eschatological movement, embracing *inter alia* the Essenes and related sects, which was prevalent in Palestine from the last two centuries B.C.E. down to the end of the first century C.E. The phenomenon of the neglect of most of this body of Jewish literature — the Apocrypha and Pseudepigrapha — by its own people, and its subsequent "adoption" by the Christians, is due to two major factors. First, with the emergence of rabbinical Judaism as "normative Judaism" *per se*, after the destruction of the Second Temple, the Scriptures and their oral traditions became the foundations of Jewish spiritual life. The apocryphal books not only lacked canonical authority but, for the most part, were neither biblical interpretations nor commentaries, and hence did not draw their inspiration directly from the Bible. In the process of studying and interpreting the Bible, that is, in the development of talmudic literature, those non-canonical books which had no direct bearing on the Bible were carried out of the mainstream of Jewish tradition and became historical flotsam. Secondly, the Pseudepigraphal writings were not merely passively neglected but actively rejected by the Pharisees and their successors. The acute-eschatological orientation of these books, which expected and emphasized an immediate Divine intervention in history, hindered their authors from coming to grips with the very real problem of continued religious existence in the midst of political upheaval. The Pharisees, in their factual and realistic approach to the spiritual welfare of Israel, could not accept the far-fetched conclusions of the apocalyptical adherents, though they did in fact later incorporate several of these concepts in the Talmud. The early Christians were undoubtedly associated with the same general eschatological movement out of which the Pseudepigrapha arose. The Church accepted these writings and, with minor changes, introduced them into Christian tradition. See also entries on the individual books.

APOLOGETICS: The defense of a position in the face of critical challenge. The apologetic defense of Judaism and the Jewish people is generally considered to have originated in hellenistic Alexandria. Beginning in the mid-2nd cent. B.C.E., and continuing for several centuries, works like the SIBYLLINE BOOKS and the WISDOM OF SOLOMON attempted to portray the superiority of Jewish ethics and practice over the allegedly immoral views and behavior of the pagan world. Philo's work was also meant to demonstrate that Judaism contained in the most perfect form all the intellectual and moral achievements and ideals of hellenistic philosophy and piety. As against its usual pejorative connotation, a. must be considered a natural form of reaction to criticism, whether from hostile or objective sources or from self-questioning. On occasion Jewish a. has exaggerated its case, but for the most part it has been a record of dignified restatement of Jewish concepts in the light of anti-Jewish attack or genuine cultural difference. Frequently its purpose was not so much to convince others as to heighten Jewish morale. A complete statement of the content of Jewish a. would necessitate an analysis of each environment to which Jews have felt the need of responding. Thus, Josephus, in his *Contra Apion*, was reacting to the anti-Semitic calumnies then current in Alexandria. In presenting his account of Jewish history he also essayed a summary statement of the religious and moral values of normative Judaism: "...The laws given us are disposed after the best manner for the advancement of piety, for mutual communion with one another, for a general love of mankind, also for justice, for sustaining labors with fortitude, and for a contempt for death." Later Jewish a. reasserted Judaism against Greek philosophy, Christianity, Islam, (JUDAH HA-LEVI's *Kuzari* dealt with all three) and — in the modern period — also against scientific positivism, and defended Jews against various forms of prejudice and anti-Semitism. Apologists have not only defended Judaism, but also made valuable and permanent contributions to Jewish thought and tradition. Thus the intellectual achievement of Maimonides literally transformed Judaism. His demonstration of the compatibility of Judaism with Aristotelian philosophy gave new content and meaning to many traditional concepts such as prophecy, the hereafter, etc. By applying philosophical methods of reasoning, he further spiritualized the Jewish conception of God. Jewish a. is less "apologetic" than the term indicates. Occasionally, and with great courage, Jews have gone on the attack. Thus, the Moslems were charged at various times with moral laxity and Islam with distorting the Bible. Joseph Kimḥi (12th cent.) began the practice of countering Christian attacks by circulating Jewish replies which often contained vigorous criticism of Christian morality and theology. Moses Mendelssohn's *Jerusalem* (1783) was a milestone in Jewish a., marking the opening of the Jewish struggle for emancipation. 19th and 20 cent. a. had to defend Judaism against the Ritual Murder libel and recrudescent anti-Semitism generally. In the work of H. COHEN, ROSENZWEIG, BAECK, BUBER, and others, religious and philosophical a. reached new peaks. As a reflection of the spiritual level both of the general society and of the Jewish people Jewish a. will undoubtedly continue to be developed as Jews wish to defend, interpret, or reconstruct their cultural theory and their way of life in interaction with their environment. See also POLEMICS AND POLEMICAL LITERATURE.

APOSTASY: Abandonment of the faith and practice of Judaism for another religion. The first large-scale a. from Judaism seems to have occurred during the events preceding the Maccabean Revolt of 168-165 B.C.E.; it occurred mainly among the upper strata of Jewish society in Jerusalem who had abandoned traditional practice for the hellenistic way of life. That the abandonment of Jewish practice by early Judeo-Christians was regarded as a. can be gauged from the fact that Irenaeus (*Adversus Haereses* 1.262) interpreted *Acts* 21:21 to mean that James, the leader of those Judeo-Christians and his followers the EBIONITES "repudiated the apostle Paul, maintaining that he was an apostate from the Law". The most famous apostate mentioned by name in the Talmud is Elisha ben Avuyah, a contemporary of R. Akiva and teacher of R. Meir, and one of the most distinguished rabbis of his era. After his apostasy the rabbis referred to him merely as *Aḥer* ("another one"). As a bitterly persecuted minority, Judaism inevitably regarded a. (which later came to mean mainly conversion to Christianity) as a despicable act of desertion, treason, and weakness. Hatred of a. grew as many apostates, either to still their consciences or to demonstrate their zeal in their newly-adopted faith, took a prominent part in anti-Jewish polemics and denunciations. Among the most notorious were the leaders on the Christian side of the three famous medieval DISPUTATIONS: Nicholas Donin in Paris in 1240, Pablo Christiani in Barcelona in 1263, and Geronimo da Santa Fé (Joshua Lorki) in the Disputation at Tortosa in 1413-1414. Another outstanding medieval apostate, who did untold harm to his former coreligionists, was Solomon Levi, rabbi of Burgos, who apostasized after the pogroms of 1391 and as Paul de Santa Maria, archbishop of Burgos, became a member of the triumvirate forming the Regency Council during the minority of the king, Juan II. His harsh decrees against the Jews, aimed at humbling their pride and breaking their spirit, succeeded in causing a wave of conversion. Another famous apostate, Johann Pfefferkorn (16th cent.) advocated the confiscation of the Talmud in Germany. A. to Islam was not infrequent, but the apostates evinced little of the active anti-Jewish activity that was so frequently the case in the Christian world. The status of apostates in religious law was frequently discussed in rabbinic literature, e.g. with regard to the question whether a penitent apostate required a ceremony of readmission to Judaism; or whether the wife of an apostate required a valid divorce or his sister-in-law *ḥalitzah*.

APPARITIONS: The preternatural or unexpected appearance of phantoms or spirits is virtually unknown in the Bible, the sole exception being the raising up of Samuel's spirit (I Sam. 28). Angels, on the other hand, frequently appear to convey the will of God. Necromancy is forbidden in the biblical code but other forms of contact between the living and the dead are not specifically banned. It is doubtful whether the legendary appearance of Elijah to various talmudic and medieval rabbis (e.g. R. Joshua ben Levi) comes within the category of genuine visual a. The frequent mention in the early responsa of a decision being "shown me from Heaven" is too vague to be identified. Kabbalistic literature abounds in formulas for and accounts of contact with celestial spirits, departed saints, and even demons, but it is doubtful whether these refer to actual a. or to inner experiences.

APPROBATION, see **HASKAMAH**

APT, RABBI OF, see **ABRAHAM JOSHUA HESHEL**

AQUILA (end 1st-early 2nd cent. C.E.): Proselyte who translated the Bible into Greek. His version, which was literal to the extent of violating Greek syntax, was influenced by R. AKIVA's principles of interpretation. It was inspired by the rabbinical school of Yavneh and meant to meet the demand for a translation more in accord with the Jewish spirit than the SEPTUAGINT which was serving as the basis for Christian polemics. A. incorporated rabbinical interpretations and strove to avoid translations which could be interpreted other than according to Jewish tradition. The version was widely used by Jews in Greek-speaking countries; it is quoted in the Talmud but only fragments have been preserved. A. was identified in rabbinical sources with ONKELOS.

ARAKHIN (Heb. "Estimations"): Fifth tractate in the Mishnah order of *Kodashim,* with commentary in both Talmuds. It discusses the amount paid for the redemption of persons, houses, or fields vowed to the Sanctuary (Lev. 25-27).

ARAM, ARAMEANS: Group of ARAMAIC-speaking Semitic tribes who settled in the Fertile Crescent, particularly in the Syrian region, in the 2nd millennium B.C.E. Apart from spreading their language to the extent that it became the international tongue of Western Asia even before the Persian Period, the Syrian Arameans exercised comparatively little cultural influence on the surrounding peoples; this applied equally to their religion though exceptions are to be seen, for example, in the introduction of the Damascus cult in Jerusalem by Ahaz (II Kings 16 ff.; II Chron. 28:3) and in the Elephantine papyri. The Arameans worshiped both their own traditional gods and those of the areas in which they settled (e.g. Phoenician, Hittite, and Assyrian deities); the chief god of the Syrian Arameans was HADAD. Although the Israelites and A. were bitter enemies from the time of David, they were regarded as a single family in patriarchal times; Aram was the homeland of Abraham, to which his family looked for their wives (cf. Deut. 26:5). At one period, it appears that the Israelite religion exercised a certain influence in A. (cf. the story of Naaman in II Kings 5 and the names of certain Aramean rulers e.g. Jehobad).

ARAMA, ISAAC BEN MOSES (c. 1420-1494): Spanish rabbi. Influenced by Christian example he adopted the practice of delivering philosophical sermons, and his discourses on the weekly pentateuchal readings and the Five Scrolls form the basis for his best-known work *Akedat Yitzḥak* ("Binding of Isaac"). Although A. was of a philosophical bent, he put religious truth before philosophical truth. He believed in various methods of Bible interpretation but stressed that the plain meaning was primary. He postulates three basic Jewish tenets, namely belief in creation, in the *Torah,* and in reward and punishment in a future world. His book was extremely popular and was imitated by subsequent philosophic preachers.

ARAMAIC: Semitic language closely related to Hebrew. Its written use is documented in Syria from the 9th cent. B.C.E.; it appears slightly later in Babylonia, where it seems gradually to have ousted the Babylonian-Assyrian language from everyday speech. Under the Achaemenids, A. became the administrative language of the western half of the Persian Empire (Imperial A.), and as such appears in the documents of the Jewish military colony at Elephantine in Egypt (6th cent. B.C.E.). In all probability the use of A. in portions of the biblical books of Ezra and Daniel also represents this Imperial A., though biblical A. is somewhat modernized in spelling and grammar. The use of A. as a trade language (*lingua franca*) and as the everyday language of mixed populations spread widely. In some places local A. dialects turned into literary languages, the most important being Syriac. Among Jews, a number of such literary dialects formed at various places and times: (1) early Judean A., preserved in inscriptions and in some texts of the DEAD SEA SCROLLS: (2) the A. of the TARGUMS, which differs from one to the next; (3) the Galilean dialect of the Palestinian Talmud; (4) Samaritan A.; (5) the A. of the Babylonian Talmud; (6) the later Babylonian A. of the *geonim*; (7) the A. of the *Zohar*; (8) the modern spoken A. of the "Kurdish" Jews of N. Iraq, of which the Zakho dialect has been especially used in religious works. As a language of religious importance, A. has been considered only slightly inferior to Hebrew. Although, according to the rabbis, "the ministering angels do not understand A." (*Shab.* 12b), A. penetrated into the liturgy, e.g. the KADDISH, the KOL NIDREI, and the opening of the Passover *Haggadah* (HA-LAḤMA ANYA). The A. *Targum* Onkelos of the Pentateuch acquired a sanctity almost equal to that of the original, expressed in the halakhic obligation to read the weekly portion in private "twice in Hebrew, once in the *Targum*". When in the 10th cent. the community of Fez abolished the recitation of the *Targum,* the scholar Judah Ibn Kuraish wrote a treatise pointing out the importance of this reading. Under the influence of the Zohar, A. became the principal language of Jewish mysticism. The Lurianic movement and Ḥasidism introduced further A. prayers into the liturgy. But above all the position of A. was assured by the fact that both the Babylonian and the Palestinian Talmud are in that language, at least as far as the amoraic parts of the discussions are concerned.

ARBA KANPHOT, see **TZITZIT**

ARBA KOSOT (Heb. "four cups"): The four glasses of wine obligatorily consumed during the course of the Passover SEDER service. Rabbinical explanations of the custom vary: there are midrashic traditions that the four cups correspond to four references to "redemption" in Exod. 6:6-7, to four references to Pharaoh's cup in Gen. 40, to the four times the word "cup" is applied to punishments traditionally to be meted out to the nations of the world, and the four times the word is used in connection with the consolations that Israel will eventually receive (Y. *Pes.* 10). The four cups are drunk after the sanctification (*kiddush*), after the conclusion of the first part of the *seder*, after Grace, and following the conclusion of the second part of the service.

ARBAAH MINIM, see **FOUR SPECIES**

ARBA PARASHOT, see **SABBATHS, SPECIAL**

ARBAAH TURIM, see **SHULḤAN ARUKH**

ARBITRATION (Heb. *borerut*): The determining of a dispute between parties by a mediator chosen or agreed to by them. The Talmud discusses whether in civil disputes the application of the strict letter of the law is preferable to an attempt to reach a compromise between the disputing parties. Moses is regarded as the protagonist of the former method and Aaron as the prototype of the latter. Both views are argued with considerable vigor; the *halakhah* rejects the view of R. Yose that "it is forbidden to effect a compromise, and whosoever does so is a sinner" and accepts the opposing view that "to effect a compromise is praiseworthy" (*Sanh.* 6b). The Jewish law of a. is a consequence of this ruling, and is specifically stated to be an instrument of the rule that compromise is to be preferred over the letter of the law (*Ḥoshen Mishpat* 12:2). A. takes place either before a duly constituted *Bet Din*, with the litigants given the right to demand the disqualification of any of the rabbis, or by what is called *Zabla ve-Zabla* (a phrase made up of the initial letters of the sentence "One chooses [an arbitrator] to represent him, and the other does likewise") whereby each litigant chooses an arbitrator and these two arbitrators agree on a third, independent of the wishes of the litigants. The decision of the arbitrators is final. In most western *Batei Din* the rabbis hear disputes in accordance with the Arbitration Laws of their specific countries, so that their decisions are enforceable in the civil court.

ARCHANGELS, see **ANGELS**

ARCHISYNAGOGUS (Gk. "head of the synagogue"): Title of the honorary official who supervised the religious aspects of synagogue affairs; occurring frequently in hellenistic and Roman Jewish communities during the last centuries B.C.E. and the first centuries C.E. He was the spiritual head of the community and was responsible for regulating services, designating preachers or readers from the Pentateuch, and inviting strangers to address the congregation. The *a.* was probably also responsible for the construction of the building. He represented the community in its dealings with the secular authorities. Although not necessarily a person of great learning, he required an extensive acquaintance with ritual and liturgical practice. It is possible that once elected he served until retirement or death.

AREVIT, see **MAARIV**

ARI, see **LURIA, ISAAC BEN SOLOMON**

ARISTEAS, LETTER OF: Pseudepigraphic Greek composition of Alexandrian Jewish origin, giving a legendary account of the preparation of the SEPTUAGINT translation of the Bible. According to this work, which probably dates from the latter half of the 2nd cent. B.C.E., 72 Jewish scholars went from Palestine to Egypt at the invitation of the Egyptian king Ptolemy II Philadelphus (285-246 B.C.E.), and though working separately they all translated the Bible into identical Greek in 72 days. The story is based on a tradition already current in 3rd cent. Alexandria; the writer injected into it views he wished to propagate — such as the importance of Greek friendship for Jews, the value of a Helleno-Jewish rapprochement, and the compatibility of Judaism and hellenic religion. On the other hand, he stressed Jewish distinctiveness and praised the practical commandments, even though explaining them symbolically.

ARISTOTELIANISM: Aristotelian philosophy did not enter Jewish circles until the 10th cent., and then largely through Arabic translations, with later medieval Jewish philosophers also benefiting from Hebrew translations made from the Arabic. Though the available versions were actually abbreviations of the original, they managed to preserve the basic text, and Jewish reaction to Aristotle was therefore based on accurate understanding. Aristotle's influence on Jewish theology and philosophy reached its fruition and classic statement in the work of MAIMONIDES (12th cent.) and its effects were profound and lasting. It gave new scope and discipline to the reasoning capacities of the mind and the medieval Jewish philosophers were not slow in bringing these to bear on the basic notions of religion (revelation, faith *versus* knowledge, immortality, etc.). On the one hand A. offered the possibility of a purer, less primitively anthropomorphic, conception of God; on the other hand it was admitted, even by Maimonides, to harbor dangers. Jewish rationalism wholeheartedly adopted Aristotle's views on the incorporeality, pure actuality, and eternity of God, but had to reject his theory of the eternity of the universe and of God as the unmoved Mover. God the Creator could not be considered coeval with the universe, and God as an active force was not the philosopher's passive and unmoved Mover. Since Aristotle could not disprove the biblical view of God's creativity, it was held that Judaism was intellectually justified in retaining its ancient position of *creatio ex nihilo*. On the other hand, Aristotle's influence proved effective in changing both the general mood of Jewish philosophy and some of its particulars. Jewish philosophers now went to great pains to prove what in its own terms required no proof, namely revelation. In so important an issue as individual providence, Maimonides sides with Aristotle against Jewish tradition, in holding that Divine providence operates in behalf of the human species rather than the individual. Maimonides explains miracles by building them into the original Divine order of things. Through Maimonides, A. exerted a continuing influence on Jewish thought.

ARK OF THE COVENANT: A wooden chest measuring 2½×1½×1½ cubits (c. 45"×27"×27") which Moses was commanded by God to construct to contain the two Tablets of the Law (Exod. 25:10-22). It was lined with gold within and without, and surrounded with a golden mold. Each side had two golden rings at the corners, through which two staves were inserted, making the a. portable. Superimposed upon the top was the *kapporet* — a golden slab of the same proportion, flanked by two CHERUBIM whose outstretched wings covered the seat of Divine revelation. This a. was carried by the levites throughout Israel's wanderings in the wilderness; when not mobile, it was placed in the Holy of Holies inside the Tabernacle, where it was beheld only by the High Priest on the Day of Atonement (Lev. 16:1-16). After the conquest of Canaan the a. was placed in the sanctuary at Shiloh but was occasionally removed from there to accompany the Israelites onto the battlefield. On one such occasion it fell into the hands of the Philistines (I Sam. 4:1-5) but a series of misfortunes subsequently compelled them to return it to Israel. David then brought it to Jerusalem where it was later installed in the temple of Solomon (I Kings 8:1-11). There is no biblical reference to the ultimate fate of the a. It was still in existence during the latter days of the First Temple (cf. Jer. 3:16 and II Chron. 35:3), though there was no a. in the Second Temple. According to a later tradition, it was hidden under the floor of the Temple. The Bible has several designations for the ark: "A. of Covenant", "A. of Testimony", "A. of God, Lord of the Universe", "A. of the God of Israel", "Holy A.", etc. Comparison with pre-Islamic parallels renders a Mosaic date for the ark eminently feasible, pointing to a nomadic rather than a sedentary way of life. Comparative research claims a similarity between the ancient custom of depositing important documents at the feet of a god and the placing of the Tablets below the *kapporet*. Closer identification of ancient non-Israelite sacred vessels with the a. is, however, purely conjectural, the Israelite cult alone stressing the aniconic character of worship. The rabbis discussed at length the nature and significance of the a. According to the Talmud (*Men.* 29a) a fiery image of the a. descended from Heaven and served Moses as a prototype for the one he was to build.

ARK OF THE LAW (Heb. *aron ha-kodesh;* among *Sephardim* called *heikhal*): While originally referring to the ARK OF THE COVENANT in the Tabernacle and Temple, which contained the two "Tablets of the Law" (Exod. 25:10 ff.), the term a. came to be used invariably for the shrine or closet in which the Scrolls of the Law are kept in the SYNAGOGUE. In talmudic times, it was called *tevah* ("chest"), it was portable and brought into the synagogue only when needed for the service; but for over a thousand years it has become customary to build the a. into the focal "eastern wall" (i.e., the one facing in the direction of Jerusalem) of the synagogue. Hence it forms the synagogue's most important architectural feature and is usually beautifully designed and ornamented. In *Ashkenazi* and some other synagogues a curtain (called *parokhet;* Exod. 27:21) is hung before the a.; in front of it is a raised platform, reached by a number of steps (used by the priests when pronouncing the priestly blessing); the eternal lamp (*ner tamid*) is arranged before or near it. Prominent in modern times among the decorations of the a. and of the curtain is a representation of the Tablets of the Law. The opening of the a. for the purpose of taking out or returning the Scrolls of the Law on the occasion of public reading is conducted in solemn ceremony, with the congregation rising to its feet.

ARK OF NOAH: God commanded NOAH (Gen. 6:14-16) to build an enormous three-storeyed ark of gopher wood coated with bitumen. In it Noah and specimens of all animal life were saved from the FLOOD. A parallel Babylonian legend refers to an a. of considerably larger proportions built by Utnapishtim in order to escape the evil design of the gods. Rabbinic literature (e.g. *Sanh.* 108b) adds more details to the biblical description of the a. and elaborates the moral concern of the story. The a. is said to have been built from cedars planted 120 years before the Deluge in order to grant humanity an ample opportunity for repentance.

ARMILUS: Eschatological figure found in the literature of the Gaonic Period. The origin of the name, of which there are many variants, is obscure. It is possibly a corruption of "Romulus", the mythical founder of Rome; another derivation connects it with Ahriman, the Persian god of evil who wages incessant war with Ahura-Mazda, the good deity. Saadyah (*Emunot ve-Deot* 8:6), the first authority to summarize eschatological traditions, describes A. as the king of Edom (Christian Rome) who at the end of days will slay the Messiah son of Joseph, conquer Jerusalem, and cruelly persecute the Jewish people till his final defeat by the Messiah son of David. A similar account is given by Hai Gaon who regards the war with A. as preceding that with Gog. Other sources (*Midrash Va-Yosha, Nistarot de-Rabbi Shimon ben Yoḥai*) call A. the successor of Gog and depict him as a monstrosity. His head is bald, his forehead leprous, one of his eyes is large and the other small, he is deaf in the right ear and maimed in the right arm, and his left hand is two and a half ells long. In some late pseudepigraphs A. is stated to be the horrendous offspring of evil men, or Satan, coupled with a beautiful marble statue of a girl in Rome. He claims to be the Messiah or even God, and is accepted as such by the sons of Esau, but is rejected by the Jews. In the ensuing struggle the Ephraimite Messiah and a million Jews are slain, but A. is vanquished by God or the Davidic Messiah. The composite A. legend appears to have been influenced by older concepts such as Ezekiel's Gog and Magog, the Persian Ahura-Mazda and Ahriman, the Christian Christ and Antichrist, and certain pagan myths; it forms part of the eschatological *aggadah* that visualizes the messianic era as the ultimate victory of the forces of good, represented by the Messiah, over the power of evil.

ARON HA-KODESH, see **ARK OF THE LAW**

ART: The Jewish attitude toward a. has been marked by historical ambivalence. The positive attitude toward religious a. appeals to the statements in Exodus (31:1-6; 35:30-35; 36:1-4) that the a. manifested by Bezalel and his co-workers in the erection of the Sanctuary in the wilderness was a form of wisdom deriving from Divine inspiration. This, however, in context, applies only to the architecture and religious appurtenances of worship in the Sanctuary. The development of the plastic arts among Jews has come up against the alleged prohibition forbidding such activity contained in the Second Commandment and in the much more detailed passage in Deut. 4:16-18 which enumerates among things forbidden to reproduce, "the likeness of male or female... of any beast on earth... any winged fowl, creeping thing... fish". The interpretation of the extent of this prohibition varied widely throughout the ages. There were periods when the most extreme interpretation was adopted, even including prohibition against portrait painting ("likeness"), while at other times the most liberal view prevailed. Even the authoritative statement of Jewish law in the classical codes only prohibits sculpturing the full human figure in the round, or the combination of the four figures of the Divine Chariot in the first chapter of Ezekiel. Anything less than that, such as sculpture of the head, animals, or painting of any kind, depended upon the particular spirit prevailing at the time, or the views of individual rabbis. Thus with regard to portrait painting there is the clear and explicit ruling given by Maimonides (*Mishneh Torah,* Laws of Idolatry, 3:10) "The prohibition on reproduction for decorative purposes refers to the human figure alone. For this reason one must not fashion a human figure in wood, in plaster, or in stone. This applies however only to a round figure. If it is sunken (*intaglio*) or done in paint upon a board or *tabula,* or if figures are woven in tapestry, it is permitted." This view is subscribed to by such eminent *Ashkenazi* authorities of the Middle Ages as R. Meir of Rothenburg (Responsa, No. 97), his disciple Mordecai ben Hillel (*A.Z.* 840) and Jacob ben Asher (*Yoreh Deah* 141). An instructive example of the change of religious climate with regard to the plastic arts is afforded by two responsa published by David Kaufmann who wrote "The fable of the hatred entertained by the synagogue against all manner of art even in the Middle Ages and modern times should at last succumb to the evidence of facts and of literary documents. The horror of plastic art gradually disappeared among Jews along with the fear of idolatry which was the most important motive of the Lawgiver... As a matter of fact both painting and sculpture were admitted in the synagogue." The first of the responsa deals with the sculptured lions in the *Sephardi* synagogue of Pesaro, which had been transferred to that town from Ascoli. For centuries they stood without any voice of criticism being raised against their propriety, when suddenly some famous rabbis prohibited them in the middle of the 17th cent. This prohibition brought forth a defense of the established custom by R. Abraham Joseph Solomon Graziano. In the second responsum, Samuel Archivolti, rabbi of Padua, in 1611 declared himself to be against paintings on the walls of the synagogue there (*Jewish Quarterly Review,* O.S. IX 254-269). Since the publication of these responsa overwhelming evidence that a. was permitted in ancient times has been produced by archeological excavations in the Middle East. To cite a few examples — the remarkable paintings on the walls of the 3rd cent. synagogue at Dura-Europos in Syria which include biblical scenes, the full-sized figures of biblical heroes, and even the depiction of the "hand of God"; and the discovery of the mosaics of the early synagogues at Bet Alpha, Nirim, and Ḥamat near Tiberias, which include human and animal figures. At Ḥamat, the figured mosaic was overlaid at a later period with one on which no human figures appeared — evidence of a stricter interpretation. With regard to the adornment of the synagogue with works of art, an additional consideration obtruded unconnected with the prohibition of art as such — on the contrary conceding its esthetic aspect. It stated that artistic representations tended to distract the worshiper from a proper concentration upon his devotions. Such a ruling, when strictly enforced, included in the prohibition any kind of embellishment whatsoever, even of birds, flowers, etc. Thus, in the 12th cent., Eliakim ben Joseph of Mainz ordered the removal of stained-glass windows from the synagogue of Cologne containing reproductions of serpents and lions, though a little earlier Ephraim ben Joseph had permitted the painting of synagogue walls with figures of animals, birds, and horses. Even this prohibition, however, allowed room for a liberal interpretation; as long as the paintings were not directly opposite the eyes of the worshiper, they could be permitted. In a responsum the liturgical author Abudraham states that it was his custom to close his eyes when he had to say his prayers in front of an adorned tapestry or painted wall. Jewish artists devoted special attention to ritual objects and lovingly designed spice boxes, wine cups, Sabbath lamps, *Ḥanukkah* candelabra, *Torah* scroll coverings, and similar objects associated with religious practice. The Scroll of Esther, the Passover *Haggadah*, and marriage contracts provided outlets for painters and were frequently illustrated and illuminated as on occasion were the Bible and the prayer-book. The prevailing tendency today, even among Orthodox circles, is in the direction of the most elastic and liberal interpretation of the prohibitions. In progressive Jewish thought, the attitude toward art has been positive; Mordecai Kaplan and his Reconstructionist School have advocated emphasis on all aspects of art as an integral element in Jewish religious experience.

ARTICLES OF FAITH, see **THIRTEEN ARTICLES OF FAITH**

ARTIFICIAL INSEMINATION: A.I. on humans is a fairly recent operation. The rabbinic principles involved are however already set out in the Talmud, which discusses whether a High Priest is permitted to marry a virgin who is pregnant; the answer given is affirmative and the circumstances of her pregnancy explained as being due to an accidental impregnation through water in which she had bathed and which had previously been fertilized by a male (*Ḥag.* 15a). Most modern responsa hold that a. i. by donor does not constitute adultery and the child so conceived is not a bastard (*mamzer*), but the legitimate child of the donor and the inseminated woman. Nevertheless, virtually all Jewish religious authorities agree in prohibiting and condemning the practice unconditionally. This opposition stems not so much from the intrinsic illegality of the act as from the fear of abuses to which its legalization would lead, however great the benefits in individual cases. Through the generation of many children whose fathers' identity would be known only to the attending physicians, the paternity of all children would become open to some doubt, and the safeguards against incestuous marriages could eventually collapse. Some responsa have suggested that children so conceived might have to be subjected to the marriage restrictions applicable to semi-foundlings. None of these considerations applies to a.i. from the husband (where necessary because of some physical impediment to normal intercourse). This practice is therefore generally permitted under certain conditions.

ARUKH, see **NATHAN BEN JEHIEL**

ARYEH LEIB BEN ASHER GINZBURG (c. 1695-1785): Talmudist, living from 1720 in Minsk where he founded and headed a *yeshivah* attracting pupils from many parts of E. Europe and noted for its development of PILPUL. Later he was rabbi in Volozhin and in his later years in Metz. His best-known work is *Shaagat Aryeh* ("Lion's Roar"), responsa on halakhic topics arranged according to the order adopted in the *Oraḥ Ḥayyim* code of the *Shulḥan Arukh.*

ARYEH LEIB OF SPOLA (1725-1812): Ḥasidic rabbi; pupil of Phinehas of Koretz. He traveled extensively, visiting small towns and villages and acquiring a reputation as a *tzaddik* and wonder-worker. In his later years he clashed frequently with R. Naḥman of Bratzlav, then living near Spola, and when mediation proved futile, R. Naḥman had to leave the region. The controversy was continued by their disciples even after the death of the two original figures.

ASARAH BE-TEVET, see **FAST DAYS**

ASCAMA, ASCAMOT, see **HASKAMAH**

ASCENT OF SOULS, see **ALIYAH**

ASCENT TO THE TORAH, see **ALIYAH**

ASCETICISM: The practice of religious austerities to expiate past sins or to achieve spiritual perfection. The dominant tendency in Judaism does not encourage a., since the body is not considered as inherently evil. The pleasures of this world should not be suppressed, but enjoyed in moderation and with gratitude to God. The only ascetic practice formally prescribed is FASTING. The FLOGGING which pious persons undergo on the eve of the Day of Atonement is not so much ascetic flagellation, as a symbolic expiation of transgressions for which the Law prescribes the punishment of stripes; moreover the ceremony is not general but is left to personal piety. According to one rabbinic dictum, man will be accountable at his judgment for permissible pleasures deliberately rejected (Y. *Kidd.* 4:12). A similar view is expressed by R. Eleazar Ha-Kappar who explains the sin-offering of the Nazirite (Num. 6:11) as an expiation of his guilt in "denying himself the use of wine which the *Torah* permits", adding that "if a man who only denies himself wine is termed a sinner, how much more so is this true of one who is an ascetic in all things" (*Naz.* 19a). One of the main forms of a., CELIBACY, is ruled out by the first precept "Be fruitful and multiply", and celibates are traditionally debarred from certain religious functions. When under the crushing blow of the Destruction of the Temple "large numbers in Israel adopted ascetic practices, binding themselves neither to eat meat nor to drink wine" R. Joshua ben Hananiah opposed them vigorously (*Bava Batra* 60b). Ascetic tendencies nevertheless existed at all periods and often dominated Jewish piety, though they were especially marked in sectarian circles. The ascetic practices adopted by the ESSENES and related sects in the Second Temple Period went far beyond the discipline of holiness enjoined by the Pharisees. KARAITE a. was exemplified by the MOURNERS OF ZION. Medieval moralist and mystical literature bears witness to the increasing importance of the ascetic ideal. The subject is discussed at some length in BAḤYA Ibn Pakuda's book *The Duties of the Hearts.* A., he holds, is necessary for the purpose of controlling man's passions and purifying his soul from earthly dross. Only an ascetic can achieve that solitude and abandon to God which lead to the ultimate purpose of the religious life, the perfect love of God. Baḥya agrees that these ascetics — Nazirites and saints — are a minority, a kind of spiritual counterpoise to the majority at the other extreme who tend to lose themselves to the world, and he concludes that the form of a. most in keeping with the precepts of the *Torah* consists in leading a life of moderation while participating in the world with all its struggles and temptations. Maimonides' teaching of the Golden Mean (*Ḥilkhot Deot* 2) is strongly influenced by Aristotelian Ethics, and his doctrine of moderation is far less severely ascetic than the widely read penitential tracts of Jonah of Gerona, for example. Mystic circles always practiced ascetic disciplines, and the preparations of the MERKAVAH mystics involved strict fasts and other practices. But it was mainly the KABBALAH, particularly in the 16th and 17th cents., that developed traditional a. into a system of mortification in which penitential and mystical motives combined. Much of the ascetic tradition survived also in ḤASIDISM, in spite of the original ḥasidic teaching that communion with God was to be attained not through mortification but through joy. Modern Jewish writers, in keeping with the tendency of the age, generally emphasize the affirmation of life in Judaism and treat a. as an alien or at least marginal phenomenon.

ASERET HA-DIBROT, see **TEN COMMANDMENTS**

ASERET YEMEI TESHUVAH, see **TEN DAYS OF REPENTANCE**

ASHAMNU (Heb. "We have trespassed"): Ancient formula of confession, listing 24 sins in alphabetic order. It was probably uttered in a somewhat different form by the High Priest in the Temple; the alphabetic arrangement dates from gaonic times. It is now said in all synagogue services on the Day of Atonement. Like the AL HET prayer *a.* is recited in the plural by the entire congregation, implying corporate responsibility for misdeeds and for failing to prevent them being committed by others. The worshiper beats his breast on reciting each sin as an expression of contrition.

ASHER BEN JEHIEL (known as *Rosh*; c. 1250-1327): Codifier. The leading pupil of R. Meir of Rothenburg, he was regarded as the spiritual leader of German Jewry after the death of R. Meir; but when conditions in Germany grew too difficult, he left the country and eventually headed the rabbinical academy at Toledo in Spain. His authority was recognized by Jews of all communities, and his responsa (of which over a thousand have been published) constitute a rich source both for halakhic development and Jewish history of the 13th-14th cents. His simple and logical glosses on the Talmud were collected and printed in all subsequent Talmud editions. His legal decisions were noted for their intellectual independence and rigor; he laid down that a *dayyan* must give decisions on the basis of the Talmud alone, while later authorities could be quoted only as additional support. Contemptuous of non-talmudic subjects, he bitterly opposed any attempt to give secular subjects precedence over religious ones, and prohibited secular studies to students under the age of 25. In his teachings A. combined the acumen of the tosaphists with the logic and orderliness of the Spanish scholars. His chief halakhic work, the compendium *Piskei ha-Rosh* covers all halakhic practices of the time and was the basis for all subsequent codifications including the *Tur* of his son JACOB BEN ASHER.

ASHERAH: Name of goddess, mate of El in the Canaanite pantheon. In the popular fertility cult she appears as the female counterpart of BAAL, and many clay figurines assumed to represent her have been found in Palestine. The name A. was also applied to a wooden pole representing the goddess and placed near her altars. A variant form of her name is Ashtoreth. The injunction to destroy the cult-objects of A. is repeatedly mentioned in the Pentateuch. Her cult is reported to have spread to Judah (through Maachah, mother of King Asa) and Israel (through Jezebel).

ASHI (4th-5th cents.): Babylonian *amora,* for 52 years head of the Sura academy which he brilliantly re-established at Mata Meḥasya. A. was regarded as the spiritual head of the Babylonian community. His great achievement was the redaction of the Babylonian Talmud on the basis of the amoraic discussions of the Mishnah. The amoraic traditions he received were fixed and edited but lacked any order or arrangement; A. clarified and sifted the various versions to determine the final form. (Further additions — including A.'s views — and changes were introduced before the compilation was definitively concluded but the form underwent no material modification). He was assisted in his work by the circle of scholars he established in Mata Meḥasya; according to tradition, the work took 30 years to complete.

ASHKENAZ (pl. **-IM**): The name Ashkenaz is first mentioned in the genealogical table of the descendants of Noah (Gen. 10:3) as the name of the eldest son of Gomer the son of Japheth. Though the Targum and the Midrash, probably on grounds of assonance, identify the third son, Togarmah, with Germany, from the Gaonic Period (c. mid-9th cent. on) the name Ashkenaz became identified with Germany (as *Sepharad* in Obad. 1:20 was identified with Spain). Jewish communal and social life as well as Jewish scholarship developed in Christian Europe from the three Rhineland communities of Speyer, Worms, and Mayence in the 10th cent. Thence they spread westward to France through Rashi and his descendants and eastward to Germany and Bohemia establishing a unity of custom, ritual, and law differing from the parallel tradition developing in what was then Moslem Europe — Spain. As a result the word Ashkenaz, from having a purely geographical connotation became applied to a religious and cultural tradition of those who followed the custom which had its origin among German Jews. With the drift of German Jews over the eastern borders of their country into the Slavonic lands in the 16th cent., and the adoption by the Jews in those countries of the traditions (and language, namely YIDDISH) of the German Jews the word *Ashkenazi* received an even wider connotation. Although in the purely liturgical sphere there is a difference between the *Ashkenazi* and the Polish ritual, the word is generally applied to all Jews of European origin and customs, i.e., to all Jews of the Western tradition (apart from comparatively small groups of Jews of Spanish and Portuguese origin and tradition) in the same way as the name SEPHARDI is generally applied to all Jews of Oriental countries who follow the parallel Spanish tradition. Thus the Jewish communities of the U.S., England, and the countries of the British Commonwealth are largely *Ashkenazi*. These two main divisions of world Jewry have persisted to the present. Despite the generally successful attempt to weld the State of Israel into one cohesive national entity, the present population is still divided into these two well-defined groups, the *Ashkenazim* from Europe and the countries of Western civilization and the *Sephardim* from the countries of the Orient and N. Africa, and the difference is marked in such spheres as religious customs, Hebrew pronunciation, and synagogal cantillation. Israel legislation provides for both an *Ashkenazi* and a *Sephardi* Chief Rabbi.

ASHKENAZI, BEZALEL (16th cent.): As chief rabbi of Cairo, he became embroiled in a controversy with the *Nagid* (the head of the Egyptian Jewish community) as a result of which the office of *nagid* was abolished. In 1588 A. went to Jerusalem where he was appointed chief rabbi and became the teacher of Isaac LURIA. He traveled widely as an emissary and under his influence *Purim* was fixed as a day for sending contributions to the Jews in Palestine. His chief work is *Shittah Mekubbetzet* ("Collected Interpretation"), a compilation of comments on the Talmud by *Ashkenazi* and *Sephardi* scholars from the end of the Gaonic Period onward. This work preserved many valuable interpretations unknown from other sources.

ASHKENAZI, TZEVI HIRSCH, see **ḤAKHAM TZEVI**

ASHMODAI, see **ASMODEUS**

ASHREI (Heb. "Happy are they"): The alphabetic 145th Psalm read daily in the Morning (twice) and Afternoon Services; it is prefixed by two extra verses — Ps. 84:5 (which begins with the word *ashrei*) and Ps. 144:15. The Talmud quotes the saying of R. Eliezer "Whoever recites the 145th Psalm [thrice] daily is assured of entering the world to come" (*Ber.* 4b). It also quotes the verse "Happy are they who dwell in Thy house" to explain the ancient pious custom of spending an hour in the synagogue prior to the service.

ASMAKHTA (Aram. "support"): Talmudic term used in two unrelated connections. The first is merely a designation that the scriptural verse cited in support of a case of the Oral Law is not meant to imply that this particular Oral Law actually derives from a scriptural verse. The *a.*, therefore, is a device to give rabbinic legislation some tie, however slight, with Scripture, and thus demonstrate that even the purely rabbinic part of the Oral Law was "foreseen" and alluded to in the Bible. The second use of the word *a.* is as a legal term referring to the undertaking of an obligation in case of the fulfillment, or non-fulfillment, of certain conditions. Any such undertaking is considered illegal by the *halakhah*, regardless of the fulfillment of the condition, although the authorities differ as to the exact nature of the condition which makes any document containing such an obligation invalid. Most authorities would consider an advance promise to deliver property in case of non-payment of a debt, or to pay more than the amount originally borrowed when this is not returned within a certain period, as being in the nature of a fine and therefore not binding. Ways and means, however, were developed by later halakhic authorities to overcome the illegality of an advance promise.

ASMODEUS (Heb. *Ashmedai*): Evil spirit. First mentioned in the Book of TOBIT as the king of the demons who fell in love with Sarah the daughter of Raguel and slew all those who wished to marry her until Tobit, instructed by the angel Raphael (A.'s chief antagonist), rendered him harmless and married her. A. is to be identified with Ashmedai the king of the DEMONS (*Pes.* 110a) of whom a long account appears in the Talmud (*Git.* 68a-b) relating how Solomon managed to capture him and force him into service for the building of the Temple. Later aggadic legend depicts A. as a merry trickster rather than an evil demon, while according to some sources his influence is actually beneficent and is directed to guarding the moral order of the universe. The name A. seems to be derived from *Aeshura Daeva,* the Persian god of anger.

ASSEMBLY, GREAT, see **KENESET GEDOLAH**

ASSI (3rd cent.): Babylonian *amora.* His authority was widely recognized throughout Babylonia, and a number of his ordinances are quoted in the Talmud. He was a contemporary of RAV and often differed from him, many of their controversies having been recorded. Another R. Assi (3rd-4th cent.) was a Palestinian *amora* who, together with his colleague R. AMMI BAR NATHAN, were known to the Babylonian rabbis of his time as "the Palestinian judges".

ASSIMILATION: The process by which individuals or groups lose their national, religious, or cultural identity through absorption into their environment. The process may vary in degree and intensity, from the adoption of foreign language and behavior (e.g. in matters of food and clothing) to complete a. Minorities being particularly exposed to a., it is not surprising that already in ancient times Jews bore foreign (e.g. Greek) names and read the Scriptures in the language of the dominant culture. Similarly, modern synagogue services in many Western countries, especially in the Reform movement, are often adaptations of the patterns of the dominant type of Christian (Protestant or Catholic) type of service. Jewish absorption of outside influences has taken place at all times to a greater or lesser degree, but a. as a large-scale social phenomenon has appeared in the modern age for the first time since the Hellenistic Period. Until now, the segregation of Jewish life limited the scope of a., and total conversion to the dominant religion was the only alternative to a full Jewish life. Conversion was again restricted by the modern, racial form of anti-Semitism, but on the other hand the modern age with its "open society" provided new possibilities of a. Traditional Jewish law has always implicitly and explicitly (cf. ḤUKKAT HA-GOYYIM) combated a., but with the emergence of the national movement (see ZIONISM) anti-Zionist Orthodoxy has shown that, like anti-Zionist liberalism, it could also renounce Jewish nationalism while claiming to maintain Jewish group-consciousness and loyalty on a purely religious basis. The social and cultural spectrum of Jewish life in Israel and the diaspora indicates that there are different types and levels of a. and that these are not necessarily incompatible with Jewish identification and commitment.

ASSUMPTION, see **ALIYAH**

ASSYRIA: Ancient W. Asian empire. From the time of Shalmaneser III (859-824 B.C.E.), the Hebrew people fought frequently against the Assyrians and it was the armies of A. under Shalmaneser V and Sargon II who brought to an end the kingdom of Israel and deported many of its inhabitants (see TRIBES, TEN). The prophets characterized the succeeding Assyrian invasions as Divine scourges. Isaiah saw A. as the rod of Divine ire destined to rule the earth but be broken by Israel (10:5 ff.). His intuition was fulfilled in the sudden arrest of Assyrian progress before the gates of Jerusalem (700), and the subsequent Assyrian withdrawal probably assisted the prophet in impressing on the people his monotheistic message. Isaiah, Micah, and Zephaniah all looked on A. as the final enemy prior to the establishment of Divine rule on earth.

ASTROLOGY: Study which assumes and professes to interpret the influence of heavenly bodies on human affairs. According to the Talmud: R. Ḥanina said "The planet of a person decides whether he shall be wise or wealthy, and Israel has its planet.' R. Johanan said 'Israel has no planet; as it is written (Jer. 10:2): 'Thus saith the Lord, Learn not the way of the heathens, and be not dismayed at the signs of the heaven, for the heathens are dismayed by them'" (*Shab.* 156a). This talmudic quotation on planetary influence thus represents two points of view, but it should be noted that the opponents of astrological belief (R. Johanan, R. Judah, Rav) confine themselves to denying such influences upon Israel "which has no planet" but do not deny its efficacy for others. The Midrash (*Gen. Rab.* 44:14) interprets Gen. 15:5 as meaning "And he took him outside the scope of astrology" and has God say to Abraham "Thou art a prophet and not an astrologer". There is ample evidence however that the more rational view was not accepted, despite the definite element of DETERMINISM and absence of free will inherent in this belief. Belief in a. has been widespread throughout the ages, not only among the common people. References to it as both valid and reliable abound in rabbinical literature and it was accepted without question by medieval authorities. In fact it was held that, unlike animals, every human being is born under the influence of a particular planet (*Shab.* 53b, 146a). Rava stated explicitly that "Length of life, children, and sustenance depend not on merit but on one's planet" (*M.K.* 28a), and "lucky" days and periods are often taken into account. The only medieval authority roundly condemning belief in a. is Maimonides who includes it in his code among the prohibited superstitions such as witchcraft, sorcery, and soothsaying, and concludes the chapter with one of his few statements in the *Mishneh Torah* in which he allows his own views to prevail over the statements of the Talmud: — "These and similar things are all lies and deceit... it is not fitting for Israel to be attracted by these follies or to believe that they have any efficacy. Whosoever believes that they are possible — though the *Torah* has forbidden their practice — is but a fool" (Laws of Idolatry 11:16). The universal Jewish phrase of congratulation *Mazzal Tov* ("Good Luck" literally, a good constellation) is a relic of the belief in a.

ASTRONOMY: Like all sciences in ancient and medieval times a. was studied for its religious implications — but for the Jews there was never any question of star-worship; the stars as part of the heavenly host are themselves conceived as worshiping God. They also influenced terrestrial events (see ASTROLOGY). The Bible contains no reference to the science of a. The apocryphal Book of Enoch devotes several chapters to movements of heavenly bodies, to determining the relative length of nights and days, etc. The necessity for the accurate fixation of the CALENDAR for religious purposes made the authorities of the Mishnaic Period adept in a. Their main expertise was in determining which months were to be regarded as *plene* (full months of 30 days) and which as having only 29. A full month was called "a month big with foetus" (*ubbar*) and since the prerogative of fixing the New Moon was jealously guarded by the Sanhedrin, the general name for astronomical calculations was *Sod ha-Ibbur,* ("The secret of intercalation"). Notable astronomers in talmudic times included R. Joshua ben Hananiah, whose statement that a certain star "rises once in seventy years" has been taken to refer to Halley's Comet, 1,500 years before its "official" discovery (*Hor.* 10a), and Samuel who although he claimed that "the paths of heaven are as clear to me as the paths of [my native] Nehardea" nevertheless pleaded ignorance of the incidence of comets (*Ber.* 58b). In the Middle Ages the Jews, especially in Spain, were among the outstanding astronomers of their time.

ASYLUM: The Bible grants the right of a. to one who has committed unpremeditated murder or manslaughter, so as to avoid summary vengeance at the hands of the next-of-kin. The murderer had to proceed immediately to the nearest city of refuge to await trial (Num. 35:9-25; Deut. 19:1-7). He was to remain in the city of refuge until the death of the High Priest (Num. *loc. cit.*) and was under no circumstances to leave it "lest his life be forfeit to the blood avenger". Originally six cities were to be set aside for refuge (Num. 35:13-15), but the additional stricture, "and beside them thou shalt give forty and two cities" (*ibid.* 6) is understood by the Babylonian Talmud (but not the Palestinian Talmud) to mean that all the forty-eight cities of the levites (listed in I Chron. 6:39-66) were to be considered cities of refuge. Care had to be taken to ensure that the cities of refuge were sufficiently scattered throughout the country (Deut. 19:3); the roads leading to them had to be signposted, and precautionary measures taken to ensure the safe arrival of the murderer at the place of refuge (*Mak.* 2:5). By implication (cf. Exod. 21:14) the ALTAR was also considered a place of refuge, but this applied only a) to the altar of the permanently established temple in Jerusalem; b) to the top of the altar but not to its horns; and c) to a priest performing the temple service. A. is also granted to a bondman who, having fled his master, enters the territory of Israel (Deut. 23:16). The rabbis stress that a. is afforded not to protect the unintentional murderer so much as to give him the opportunity to expiate his deed.

ATONEMENT: The doctrine of a. rests upon the belief that there exists a relationship between man and God according to which God looks favorably upon man and desires his well-being. That relationship is disturbed when man fails to act in accordance with the will of God. God does not however desire the perdition of man for upsetting that relationship: "As I live, saith the Lord, I have no pleasure in the death of the wicked but that the wicked turn from his way and live. Turn ye, turn ye from your evil ways" (Ezek. 33:11). Thus God desires the restoration of the desirable norm through the forgiveness of sin. Forgiveness depends upon man's expiation of his sin, and it is that expiation which constitutes a. A. can be effected in a number of ways. It may be achieved through the payment of compensation for wrong committed, through suffering, through the performance of certain rituals, and through REPENTANCE and the rectification of one's way of life. The Hebrew word for a. (*kapparah*) is derived from a legal term signifying "ransom" or compensation (paid e.g. by the owner of an ox that has gored a man; Exod. 21:3), and thence passed into ritual and theological use. The Talmud insists that sacrifices were accepted as a. only for those sins committed in ignorance or unwittingly, but that for those committed deliberately no sacrifice could avail. Thus an element of repentance was introduced into the sacrificial rite, which was an act of contrition. Among the common people however a tendency developed to regard the sacrifice in itself as a propitiatory offering which would avert Divine wrath for a sin committed deliberately, and sacrificing could serve as an a. for all sins. The prophets inveighed sharply against this belief, stressing instead the moral aspects in such passages as "Shall I come before Him with burnt offerings, with calves a year old? He hath showed thee, O man, what is good, and what doth the Lord require of thee, but to do justly, and love mercy and walk humbly with thy God" (Micah 6:6-8) or the statement of Hosea "Take with you words and return unto the Lord... so will we render the calves of our lips" (14:2). With the destruction of the Temple and the automatic abolition of the sacrificial system these and similar verses formed the basis of the doctrine of the existence of alternatives to the sacrificial system. These alternative means of a. can be effected through suffering, repentance, prayer, and good works. In the first category come the statements that "sufferings wipe out transgressions" (Y. *Sanh.* 10) and "death wipes out transgressions" (*Shev.* 8b) though "death expiates together with repentance" (*Yoma* 8:8). Repentance is the broad highway to a. and rabbinical literature is replete with references to the efficacy of repentance; the effectiveness of the Day of Atonement depends on sincere repentance (see ATONEMENT, DAY OF). Virtually every aspect of "good works" is mentioned as a means of a. e.g. "now that there are no sacrifices, a man's table acts as an a." (*Ber.* 58a); "acts of kindness bring a." (*R.H.* 18a); "Charity brings a." (*Bava Batra* 9a); and "good works avert the evil decree" (*Taan.* 16a). Repentance must at all times be accompanied by change of conduct, and sincerity is a basic component of a. Generally speaking, the doctrine of vicarious a. plays very little rôle in Judaism, although suggestions of it are not entirely absent, e.g. in the statement (*Lev. Rab.* 20:7) "the death of the righteous atones [for the world]".

ATONEMENT, DAY OF (Heb. *Yom Kippur*): The most solemn occasion of the Jewish calendar, falling on *Tishri* 10. Although strictly observed as a 25-hour FAST (in accordance with the biblical injunction "and ye shall afflict yourselves"), it formally belongs to the category of FESTIVALS (Lev. 23:26-32). The biblical commandment regulating its observance (Lev. *loc. cit.*) indicates no link with the holiday observed a few days earlier on *Tishri* 1 (see PENITENCE, TEN DAYS OF), but modern scholars hold all *Tishri* festivals to be parts of the ancient NEW YEAR celebration. The rabbis insist that the Day itself will not effect forgiveness of sin unless accompanied by sincere REPENTANCE (*Yoma* 8:8-9). During Temple times, the D. of A. was the occasion of an elaborate sacrificial ceremony based on Lev. 16. This consisted of two parts. The first was the sacrificial service in the Temple, at which the HIGH PRIEST pronounced the threefold confession of sins in behalf of himself, the priests, and all Israel. The climax came when, clothed in white linen, he entered the HOLY OF HOLIES (the one occasion during the year when this was permitted) to sprinkle the blood of the sacrifice and to offer incense. The second part consisted of hurling the scapegoat which "shall bear upon him all their iniquities" — i.e., to which the sins of the community had been symbolically transferred — to his death in the wilderness (see AZAZEL). There is no historical source material concerning the observance of the D. of A. in First Temple times but there is much material depicting celebration of the day in the Second Temple (e.g. Ecclesiasticus 50 which describes the celebration during the High Priesthood of Simeon Ha-Tzaddik, c. 200 B.C.E., and the Mishnah tractate *Yoma*). A mishnaic statement that the D. of A. was one of the happiest days in Israel when the maidens danced in the vineyards has been found puzzling in view of the solemn nature of the Day; one suggestion is that the celebration of the young people should be connected with the feast which the High Priest made for his friends when he emerged safely from the Holy of Holies (*Yoma* 7:4). With the destruction of the Temple, the LITURGY was transferred as far as possible to the synagogue. The ancient sacrifice is commemorated by the *Avodah*, an elaborate poetical description of the Temple ceremony included in the Additional Service. The taking of KAPPAROT before the D. of A. was once widespread and still remains in extremely Orthodox and certain Oriental communities. The FESTIVAL PRAYER is divided into five services of which the first is the Evening Service preceded in most rites by the recitation of KOL NIDREI; hence the eve of the Day has come to be known as *Kol Nidrei.* (Many Reform congregations omit this prayer and recite one of the psalms to its melody). The main features of the day are the "five mortifications": abstention from 1) food, 2) drink, 3) marital intercourse, 4) anointing with oil, 5) wearing (leather) shoes. Moreover all Sabbath work prohibitions also apply on the D. of A. The prayers of the day stress confession of sins and supplications for forgiveness. Like all congre-

ABLUTION: Ewer and laver, 1900. Designed by Ernest Brandon — after the Larnaka laver of the 12th cent. B.C.E. ("Jewish Chronicle" photograph).

AMULET: From Hayyim Vital's *Shaar ha-Yihudim ve-Tikkun*.

APHIKOMAN: The *Seder* celebrant breaks and passes the *aphikoman*; from Bernard Picart's *Cérémonies et coutumes religieuses* (Amsterdam, 1723).

ARK: The ark of the synagogue at Curaçao, 1732. (Foto Fischer).

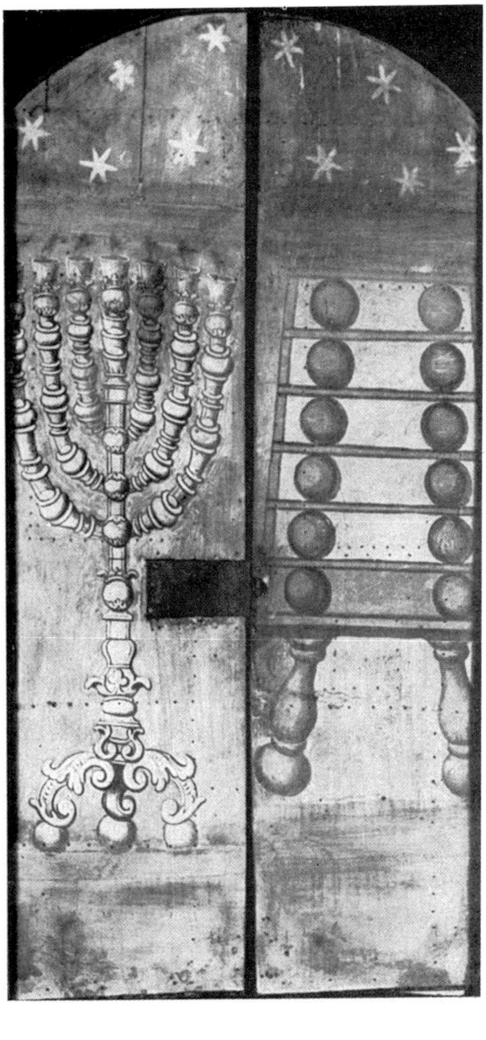

ARK: Outside and reverse of outer doors of ark for the Scrolls of the Law; originating from Tobitschau, Moravia, first half of 18th cent.

ARK, CURTAIN (*parokhet*): Silk, embroidered;
Italy, 1681. Harry G. Friedman Collection (Photo: Ambur Hiken).

ART: Fresco from Jewish catacombs in Rome.

ATONEMENT, DAY OF: Belt worn by *kohanim*.
Germany, 18th-19th cent.; Feinberg Collection, Detroit.

ATONEMENT, DAY OF: Painting by Maurycy Gottlieb (1856-1879).
Tel-Aviv Museum.

ATONEMENT, DAY OF: from Bernard Picart's *Cérémonies et coutumes religieuses* (Amsterdam, 1723).

BENEDICTION: Blessing over the Sabbath candles; copper engraving by Boris Schatz (1866-1932).

BIBLE: King David, from the Kennicott Bible, Bodleian Library, Oxford.

בְּרָא אֱלֹהִים אֵת הַשָּׁמַיִם וְאֵת הָאָרֶץ : וְהָאָרֶץ הָיְתָה תֹהוּ וָבֹהוּ וְחֹשֶׁךְ
עַל־פְּנֵי תְהוֹם וְרוּחַ אֱלֹהִים מְרַחֶפֶת עַל־פְּנֵי הַמָּיִם : וַיֹּאמֶר אֱלֹהִים יְהִי
אוֹר וַיְהִי־אוֹר : וַיַּרְא אֱלֹהִים אֶת־הָאוֹר כִּי־טוֹב וַיַּבְדֵּל אֱלֹהִים בֵּין הָאוֹר
וּבֵין הַחֹשֶׁךְ : וַיִּקְרָא אֱלֹהִים לָאוֹר יוֹם וְלַחֹשֶׁךְ קָרָא לָיְלָה וַיְהִי־עֶרֶב
וַיְהִי־בֹקֶר יוֹם אֶחָד : וַיֹּאמֶר אֱלֹהִים יְהִי רָקִיעַ בְּתוֹךְ הַמָּיִם
וִיהִי מַבְדִּיל בֵּין מַיִם לָמָיִם : וַיַּעַשׂ אֱלֹהִים אֶת־הָרָקִיעַ וַיַּבְדֵּל בֵּין הַמַּיִם
אֲשֶׁר מִתַּחַת לָרָקִיעַ וּבֵין הַמַּיִם אֲשֶׁר מֵעַל לָרָקִיעַ וַיְהִי־כֵן : וַיִּקְרָא
אֱלֹהִים לָרָקִיעַ שָׁמָיִם וַיְהִי־עֶרֶב וַיְהִי־בֹקֶר יוֹם שֵׁנִי :

וַיֹּאמֶר אֱלֹהִים יִקָּווּ הַמַּיִם מִתַּחַת הַשָּׁמַיִם אֶל־מָקוֹם אֶחָד וְתֵרָאֶה
הַיַּבָּשָׁה וַיְהִי־כֵן : וַיִּקְרָא אֱלֹהִים לַיַּבָּשָׁה אֶרֶץ וּלְמִקְוֵה הַמַּיִם קָרָא יַמִּים
וַיַּרְא אֱלֹהִים כִּי־טוֹב : וַיֹּאמֶר אֱלֹהִים תַּדְשֵׁא הָאָרֶץ דֶּשֶׁא עֵשֶׂב מַזְרִיעַ
זֶרַע עֵץ פְּרִי עֹשֶׂה פְּרִי לְמִינוֹ אֲשֶׁר זַרְעוֹ־בוֹ עַל־הָאָרֶץ וַיְהִי־כֵן :
וַתּוֹצֵא הָאָרֶץ דֶּשֶׁא עֵשֶׂב מַזְרִיעַ זֶרַע לְמִינֵהוּ וְעֵץ עֹשֶׂה־פְּרִי אֲשֶׁר
זַרְעוֹ־בוֹ לְמִינֵהוּ וַיַּרְא אֱלֹהִים כִּי־טוֹב : וַיְהִי־עֶרֶב וַיְהִי־בֹקֶר יוֹם שְׁלִישִׁי :
וַיֹּאמֶר אֱלֹהִים יְהִי מְאֹרֹת בִּרְקִיעַ הַשָּׁמַיִם לְהַבְדִּיל בֵּין הַיּוֹם וּבֵין

ב   א

BIBLE: First page of the Book of Genesis; from the Bomberg Bible, 16th cent.

gational prayers they are couched in the plural, confession and forgiveness being sought in behalf of "the whole congregation of Israel" (Num. 25:26). The formulae of confession include one that is composed of alphabetically arranged synonyms for transgression (ASHAMNU) and a longer alphabetical list enumerating a comprehensive catalogue of sins (AL HET). It is noteworthy that with one possible exception all the sins mentioned appertain to the moral and ethical aspects of Judaism and not to its ceremonial side.

Formerly it was the custom for Jews to remain in the synagogue for the entire day and the four services, with their many additional hymns, litanies, and confessions, are deliberately designed so that prayer should continue throughout the day. The reading of the Law during the Morning Service relates to the ritual of the D. of A. (Lev. 16; Num. 19:7-11) while the prophetical reading (Is. 57:14 — 58:14) emphasizes the spirit of devotion and penitence without which the ritual is worthless. The Law is read again at the Afternoon Service with the pentateuchal selection devoted to forbidden marriages (Lev. 28); the prophetical reading is the Book of Jonah with its message of Divine forgiveness for genuine repentance. The fifth service, NEILAH or Concluding Service, is dominated by the thought that the Day of Judgment is coming to an end and the Divine verdict is about to be sealed. It concludes with the declaration of God's unity, the sounding of the SHOPHAR, and the prayer "Next year in Jerusalem" (in Israel: "Jerusalem Rebuilt"). The TALLIT is worn at all five Services. The custom of many *Ashkenazi* congregations of wearing a white KITTEL at the services is no longer extensively practiced.

ATTAR, ḤAYYIM BEN MOSES (1696-1743): Moroccan kabbalist who settled in Jerusalem in 1741. His works include novellae on the Talmud and a pentateuchal commentary *Or ha-Ḥayyim* ("Light of Life") which became particularly popular in ḥasidic circles. The *Keneset Yisrael yeshivah* founded by A. in Jerusalem became after his death the *Or ha-Ḥayyim yeshivah* and was taken under *Ashkenazi* supervision.

ATTRIBUTES: Permanent qualities of a substance which determine its nature. They generally stand in contrast to ACCIDENTS the absence of which would in no way detract from the nature of a thing. In the history of philosophy, discussions of a. almost always concern the nature of God. In traditional Jewish texts like the Bible and the prayer-book God's a. are set forth in unquestioned terms, i.e., the conception of God as Creator, Judge, One, Omnipotent, Omniscient, Eternal, etc. is never analyzed. The a. merely attest to the sense of human dependence on a Power which compels reverence and obedience. When they began to be analyzed, however, God's a. became philosophical and theological problems with implications for the understanding of the nature of God, His unity, and His transcendence. Jewish philosophers from Saadyah on have dealt with the difficult problem of how to assert anything positive about God. If it is assumed, with most Jewish philosophers, that man cannot know what God is like and that God's nature cannot in any way be said to resemble man's, then it becomes impossible to talk meaningfully about God's a. Indeed Gersonides (14th cent.), attacked the prevailing Maimonidean view that there is nothing in God's a. susceptible to human grasp. Maimonides had declared that assertions about God's thinking can have no real cognitive significance, since God thinks in a way unknown to man. This led Gersonides to the conclusion that if such be the case, man cannot legitimately assert anything about God's a. To escape this conclusion he challenged the premise and insisted that Divine and human a. were distinct merely in the measure of their perfection, but not in their essence. This solution of Gersonides, however, was not generally accepted by medieval Jewish philosophers. The whole trend of Jewish philosophy was to seek a definition of God's a. which would set them apart from any human associations. But there was always the problem of finding something in God about which man could talk intelligibly. Hence the various divisions made by philosophers into those qualities which could be asserted about God and those which had to be treated obliquely. Saadyah, for example, denied that God possesses positive a. except in regard to His existence, unity, power, and wisdom, which are one in fact, although not in man's thought about God. This objection against articulating any distinctive a. which do not actually imply each other is respected throughout the Jewish philosophical tradition. Baḥya, in making a distinction between the essential a. and those which describe God's actions, lists the former as His existence, unity, and eternity. He hastens to add that they are really one. Moreover, even when affirmed positively, their real meaning is to negate the possibility of God's possessing the opposite attribute. Thus God cannot be multiple or have parts; nor can He be in time. Judah Ha-Levi lists three groups of a. — the active ones (those indicating God's power to affect human fate), the relative ones (in which, for example, God's blessedness is set forth), and the negative (which include the essential a. that can be expressed only negatively). Maimonides listed various kinds of positive a. and concluded that none of them could legitimately be asserted of God who can be described only negatively, i.e., in terms not of what He is but of what He is not. Jewish thought down to the present day has shied away from definitive statements regarding the nature of God. See THIRTEEN ATTRIBUTES.

ATZERET, see **WEEKS, FEAST OF**

AUGURY, see **DIVINATION**

AUTO-DA-FÉ, see **INQUISITION**

AV: Fifth month of the Jewish religious year, 11th of the civil year; also called *Menaḥem* ("Comforter") *Av* either as a reference to the Divine Father (*av*) comforting Himself after the destruction of the Temple which took place in that month, or to the name of the Messiah who will traditionally be born on *Av* 9. *Av* always has 30 days and its zodiacal sign is the lion; the name of the month is not mentioned in the Bible.

Av 1 is the date observed as the anniversary of the death of Aaron; *Av* 9 is a fast-day (see AV, NINTH OF); *Av* 15 is a day of rejoicing (see AV, FIFTEENTH OF); *Av* 24 was observed as a feast by the Pharisees to mark the annulment of the Sadducee decree that a daughter should have equal inheritance rights.

The first 9 days are observed as a sorrowful period and the Sabbath before *Av* 9 was at one time known as the Sabbath of Punishment, later as the Sabbath of Vision (*Shabbat Ḥazon*, from the opening word of the prophetic portion from the Book of Isaiah). It became customary during these nine days not to eat meat or drink wine or perform marriages. However festivities falling on a particular day — such as a circumcision feast — are observed as usual during this period.

AV, FIFTEENTH OF: Popular festival in Second Temple times. According to the Talmud, on this day eligible maidens went out in borrowed white garments (so that the poorer ones among them would not be shamed) and danced in the vineyards, and the young men present would select their wives from among them (*Taan.* 4:8). The day was probably originally a nature festival; and as it was regarded as the climax of the period of solar heat it was also the festival of the wood-offering — the last day for bringing wood to the Temple altar; after this date the trees were no longer dry enough and wood-hewing ceased until the spring sap began to rise six months later on *Shevat* 15th (NEW YEAR FOR TREES).

AV, NINTH OF: Day of Mourning upon which, in the words of the Talmud, "disasters recurred again and again to the Jewish people". In point of fact only the fall of Betar, the last stronghold of Bar Kokhba captured by the Romans in 135 C.E., possibly occurred on that day. According to II Kings 25:8-9 the First Temple was burned on the 7th of the month, and according to Jer. 52:12 it was on the 10th, but the Talmud (*Taan.* 29a possibly influenced by the fall of Betar) explained that it took place on the 9th, and all subsequent major catastrophes which happened about that time were ascribed to that sad day. The Second Temple was destroyed on *Av* 10 but later tradition also set back this date to the 9th. The Karaites, however, observe the fast on the 10th. The Mishnah (*Taan.* 4:6) adds to the list of tragic events on *Av* 9 the decree against the entrance of the children of Israel into the Holy Land after the incident of the Twelve Spies, and the plowing up of Jerusalem in 136 C.E. Isaac Abravanel, himself one of the exiles, repeatedly maintains that the Expulsion of the Jews from Spain in 1492 took place "on that selfsame day, on the day of the 9th of *Av*, when disasters repeatedly occurred" whereas the actual date, the last day of July, was a few days earlier. *Av* 9 is observed as a fast, the only one aside from the biblical fast of the Day of Atonement to start at nightfall and last for 24 hours. The essential features of the special liturgy for the day are the reading of the Book of Lamentations and the recital of *kinot* (dirges) composed not only in commemoration of the events of that day but for all the tragic occasions of Jewish history. In many synagogues these are read by dim candlelight and while sitting on the floor or on low benches, as a sign of mourning. A unique feature of the commemoration is that prayer-shawls and phylacteries are donned not in the Morning but at the Afternoon Service, which also includes a moving prayer for the occasion. If the date falls on a Sabbath, the observance is postponed until the next day. The Midrash (*Lam. Rab.* 1) states "The Messiah, the Savior, was born on the day that the Temple was destroyed" and Jews have traditionally believed that the Messiah would be born on *Av* 9; consequently in certain Oriental communities, the women anoint themselves with oil after midday of the fast. It is a custom to visit the cemetery where one's loved ones are buried on that day. Since the Old City of Jerusalem was captured by Israel during the Six Day War large numbers of people, often in excess of 100,000, have made it a custom to visit the Wailing Wall, a relic of the Western Wall of Temple, on the eve of *Av* 9 or during the following day. Reform Jews do not observe *Av* 9 as a fast-day.

AV BET DIN, see **BET DIN**

AV HA-RAḤAMIM (Heb. "Merciful Father"): Martyrs' memorial dirge; probably composed after the Crusader massacres of 1096. It is found only in the *Ashkenazi* rite. The prayer was originally said twice a year (on the Sabbath before Pentecost and before *Av* 9) but it later became customary to recite it every Sabbath (except on New Moons, festivals, and Sabbaths preceding the New Moon).

AVADIM (Heb. "Slaves"): Minor tractate appended to the Talmud dealing with the manumission of SLAVES and related topics.

AVELEI-ZION (Heb. "Mourners for Zion" cf. Is. 61:2): Groups of Jews who after the destruction of the Second Temple observed daily mourning customs and ascetic practices and devoted much of their time to prayer for the hastening of redemption. The Talmud refers to the custom of these "abstainers" (*perushim*) not to eat meat or drink wine (cf. *Bava Batra* 60b). The KARAITES who settled in 9th cent. Jerusalem adopted the customs of the A.Z., and their leaders stated that the object of the Karaite settlement in Jerusalem was to mourn the destroyed Temple. All traces of the A.Z. are lost after the conquest of Jerusalem by the Seljuks in 1071 but some of their customs reached other communities, and the 12th cent. traveler Benjamin of Tudela reports that he encountered A.Z. in Germany and Yemen.

AVELUT, see **MOURNING**

AVENGER OF BLOOD, see **BLOOD REVENGE**

AVERAH (Heb. lit. "crossing over" the line of right conduct; pl. *averot*): Trespass, transgression; the opposite of MITZVAH. *Averot*, like *mitzvot*, are divided into two main classes: those committed by man against his fellow-man, and those committed by man against God. Only for the latter is the Day of Atonement effective; the former are not atoned for "until his fellow be appeased" (*Yoma* 85b). The three cardinal *averot* are the shedding of innocent blood, adultery, and idolatry — rather than transgress these, a man must sacrifice his life; all other *averot* may be transgressed if human life is at stake (*Sanh.* 74a). Jewish moralists generally assume that *averot* are committed not because of inherent wickedness but on account of spiritual lethargy and lack of awareness.

AVINU MALKENU (Heb. "Our Father, Our King"): Prayer of supplication recited during the Ten Days of Penitence (except on Sabbath and the Afternoon Service prior to the Day of Atonement) and on fast-days (except *Av* 9); each line begins with the words *A.M.* The Talmud (*Taan.* 25b) relates that the basic formula was recited by R. Akiva on the occasion of a drought; many additions were made later, probably on account of continued tribulations and persecutions. By later talmudic times, the prayer contained 19 verses, on the analogy of the blessings of the *amidah*; by gaonic times the prayer had 29 verses, and later (in the *Ashkenazi* rite), 44. In Reform usage, the prayer is recited only on the New Year and the Day of Atonement.

AVIV: First month of the year according to the biblical nomenclature, corresponding to NISAN. The word probably originally referred to the ripening of the corn and was later applied to the spring season in general.

AVODAH, see **ATONEMENT, DAY OF**

AVODAH ZARAH (Heb. "Idolatry"): Tractate in the Mishnah order of *Nezikin* with commentary in both Talmuds. It deals with laws concerning the prohibition of IDOLATRY and the attitude to be adopted toward idols and their worshipers. The purpose of the legislation, which is based essentially on the pentateuchal prohibitions directed against idol-worship and close contact with idolaters, is to guard against idolatry in particular and to avoid heathen customs in general.

AVOT (Heb. "PATRIARCHS"): First blessing in the AMIDAH, so called because of its reference to "the God of Abraham, the God of Isaac, and the God of Jacob", the eulogy of "God of our fathers", and its concluding reference to God as the "shield of Abraham". According to legend, the blessing was instituted by Abraham when escaping from Ur.

AVOT (Heb. "Fathers", also *Pirkei Avot* "Chapters of the Fathers"; popularly known in English as "Ethics of the Fathers"): Mishnah tractate in the order of *Nezikin*; it has no *gemara* in either Talmud. The name A. probably refers to the early rabbis (300 B.C.E. — 200 C.E.) who composed the various aphorisms and wise, moral sayings collected in the tractate. The original object of the work may have been to illustrate the character of the *ḥasid* as developed under Pharisee training. A. is the sole mishnaic tractate devoid of halakhic content, nor does it contain aggadic narrative. Its chief emphasis is on the value of *Torah* study and the observance of the commandments. Regarded as a basic exposition of Jewish ethical ideals, it was read in the Sura academy after the Sabbath afternoon service, and by the 11th cent. had been incorporated into that service; local custom differed, but in general, the *Ashkenazim* read A. in the synagogue between Passover and the New Year, and *Sephardim* in their home between Passover and Pentecost and, in some instances, in the Sabbath Morning Service. The tractate contains five chapters to which has been added a sixth, dating from amoraic times, in praise of the *Torah.* The first chapter — the only one arranged chronologically — traces the chain of tradition from Moses down to the school of R. Johanan ben Zakkai. A. became extremely popular and was the subject of many commentaries (e.g. AVOT DE-RABBI NATAN) and translations.

AVOT DE-RABBI NATAN (Heb. "*Avot* of Rabbi Nathan"): Tractate appended in Talmud editions after the tractate *Avot*. In form it is a *tosephta* or homiletic commentary to *Avot* ascribed to R. Nathan the Babylonian (2nd cent.), although internal evidence indicates a later date of composition. It incorporates a number of ethical sayings attributed to famous rabbis which are not quoted in *Avot*; thus a complete chapter is devoted to sayings by Elisha ben Avuyah the main point of which is the worthlessness of *Torah* study when not accompanied by good deeds. A. contains the only explicit reference in talmudic literature to the heresy of the Sadducees in denying resurrection and the doctrine of reward and punishment in the future world.

AVTALYON, see **SHEMAIAH**

AZ YASHIR MOSHEH, see **MOSES, SONG OF**

AZAZEL: A. is mentioned in Lev. 16 in connection with the ritual of the Day of Atonement; the High Priest would cast lots over two he-goats, designating one "for the Lord" and the other "for A." and confess over the latter all the iniquities of the children of Israel. Thereafter the goat was sent away "by the hand of a man that is in readiness into the wilderness". In talmudic times the goat was thrown from the top of a precipice near Jerusalem and if the tuft of scarlet wool fastened to it turned white (cf. Is. 1:18), this was taken as a sign of God's forgiveness. The meaning of the word A. is variously explained: "the place of sending away [the goat]" (Septuagint); "scapegoat" (Vulgate); "rugged mountain" (Talmud). The ritual is generally taken to symbolize the complete removal of the people's transgressions. The concept of A. may have a pre-Israelite origin connected with the worship of *seirim* — goatlike demons (cf. Lev. 17:7), but in Judaism it became the symbol of the casting out of sinfulness from Israel's borders (cf. Lev. 14:1-7; Zech. 5:5-11). In apocalyptic and late aggadic as well as kabbalistic literature A. is conceived of as a fallen angel and even as a prototype of SATAN.

AZHAROT (Heb. "exhortations" so-called after the initial word of an early composition of this nature dating from the Gaonic Period): Liturgical poems dealing with the enumeration and explanation of the 613 precepts (the numerical value of the word *azharot* in Hebrew is 613). They are recited in the *Shavuot* liturgy, especially among the *Sephardim*, before the Afternoon Service. A. were written by early *paytanim* and by many famous medieval rabbis and poets including Saadyah and Ibn Gabirol; however these compositions also aroused opposition such as that expressed by Abraham Ibn Ezra who compared one who recites A. to one who enumerates a list of herbs without any appreciation of their remedial properties.

AZRIEL AND EZRA OF GERONA (13th cent.): Spanish kabbalists who played an important rôle in the transmission of kabbalistic lore from France to Spain. They influenced their younger contemporary NAḤMANIDES and pioneered in composing an organic system of speculative Kabbalah out of scattered teachings. Azriel's commentary on the liturgy and Ezra's on the Song of Songs were used by the author of the Zohar. The teaching of the two men became identified and only recent scholarship has distinguished between them.

AZULAI, ḤAYYIM JOSEPH DAVID (known as *Ḥida*; 1724-1806): Rabbi, kabbalist, and bibliographer; born in Jerusalem, eventually settled in Leghorn. He wrote some hundred works on *halakhah*, homiletics, ethics, kabbalah, etc. The first Jewish scholar to study systematically the Hebrew manuscripts of Italy and France, he is best-known for his vast bibliographic guide to Hebrew literature *Shem ha-Gedolim* ("Name of the Great Ones").

B

BAAL (Phoenician—Canaanite: "Lord"): CANAANITE deity. Although the Canaanite pantheon was presided over by El, it was his son B. who played the most prominent part. B. was the fertility god and was also known under the name of HADAD — god of thunder. The Phoenicians referred to him as *Baal Shamim* lord of heaven. His sister was the ferocious Anath. UGARITIC texts describe B.'s slaying of the seven-headed dragon Lotan (sometimes identified with LEVIATHAN) and also depict B.'s contest with Yam-Nahar (the encroaching waters) and the struggle against the god of the underworld Mot (identical with the Hebrew word meaning death, but in this context representing the barren wilderness). B. worship entailing lascivious fertility rites and human sacrifice troubled much of Israel's ancient history. Some abandoned God outright for B., others purported to worship God through the ritual of B., while still others conceived of God as the national guardian, with B. the dispenser of fecundity. During the reign of Ahab and Jezebel, Baalism threatened to supplant the worship of the God of Israel, and Elijah's dramatic vindication of the Lord at Mt. Carmel (I Kings 18:19-40) halted the scourge only temporarily. In Judah Baalism was encouraged by Jezebel's daughter Athaliah, but after her death and under the influence of Jehoiada the priest (II Kings 11:15-20) the practice ceased for some time. Prophetic opposition to Baalism had the unqualified support of the reformer kings Hezekiah and Josiah but some Baalist practices continued until the Babylonian Exile.

BAAL KERIAH or **BAAL KORE** (Heb.): The person who reads from the Scroll in the synagogue at the READING OF THE LAW.

BAAL NES (Heb. "miracle master"): Term popularly applied to saintly individuals reputed to have worked miracles. Originally the term meant someone to whom a miracle had happened, and was applied to specific rabbis who had been miraculously saved from danger, e.g. R. MEIR BAAL HA-NES. In later (ḥasidic) usage a miracle worker was called *Baal Mophet*.

BAAL SHEM (Heb. "master of the [Divine] name"): Title found in the literature of the Middle Ages and especially in mystical and later ḥasidic works, denoting a person who used the magic power of the Divine names (the Tetragrammaton, viz. *shem ha-mephorash,* as well as other combinations of letters) to perform miracles. The title came to be used also for healers and exorcisers who wrote amulets (*kemiot*) in which were inscribed the names of God. *Baalei Shem* (pl). were frequent from the 16th cent. on especially among the Jewries of Germany and Poland, and after that time the title was widely applied to those who healed the sick, particularly the mentally sick, by means of charms and herbs. The literature of the period is replete with stories concerning such *Baalei Shem.* The founder of ḤASIDISM, Israel ben Eliezer first became known as a *Baal Shem* of this type (see BAAL SHEM TOV).

BAAL SHEM TOV, ISRAEL BEN ELIEZER (c. 1700-1760): Founder of ḤASIDISM. Little is known of his life and there exist no reliable biographical documents. According to legend, he was orphaned while a child and spent a great deal of his time in solitude and meditation in the woods and fields around his home town in Podolia. For many years he was assistant to a teacher and acted as sexton of the *bet midrash.* Until his "disclosure" (Heb. *hitgalut,* an important concept in Ḥasidism, signifying the disclosure of one's true worth and message), he studied assiduously, acquiring wide knowledge of both the revealed and secret law, but concealed his knowledge and affected the personality of a simple, unlettered Jew. He then traveled in Podolia, Volhynia, and Galicia where by virtue of his prayers and amulets (*kemiot*), he achieved a reputation as a healer of the sick and a comforter to those in need, so that he soon became known as a BAAL SHEM (or BAAL SHEM Tov i.e., "master of the good Name" abbreviated to *BeSHT*). However the charms which he distributed contained none of the holy names of God, but only his own and his mother's name "Israel son of Sarah". Folklore has woven a halo around his personality and his life, which it describes from birth to death as a miraculous chain of events: Elijah the prophet foretold his birth; his soul was a spark from that of the Messiah; and he was taught both exoteric and secret *Torah* by Elijah himself. About 1740, the period of solitude and concealment ended and the time for his "disclosure" arrived. He thereupon settled in Medzibozh where he established a *bet midrash* which attracted admirers and scholars from far and near. They came for guidance in the service of God, to receive B.'s blessing, and beseech his prayer and intercession for their spiritual and physical welfare. He declared that his mission was "to stir the hearts of those seeking communion with God. This contains nothing new. It adds nothing. It is merely a reminder, a strengthening of that faith which has somehow been forgotten." While drawing heavily upon the kabbalistic doctrines of Isaac LURIA, he invested them with new meaning and thus created an original and distinctive type of MYSTICISM. B. did not himself commit his teachings to writing; they were handed down orally and preserved in numerous sayings recorded by his pupils. His sayings inculcated joy and warmth in his followers and warned against sadness and mortification which "stultify the heart". Even the most simple may serve the omnipresent God by means of inner joy. Many stories are found in ḥasidic folklore describing B. and the great leaders of Ḥasidism at prayer. True prayer was pictured as a state which freed the personality from the trammels of the body and allowed fusion of the soul with God. When B. prayed, it was said that his entire body used to tremble, that those present were seized with shivering, and that the building would shake. The emphasis on "intention" (KAVVANAH), which formed one of the major points of controversy concerning the movement, was a further basic tenet of B. *Kavvanah*, he said, is the "soul of the deed". The central pillar of his teaching was love — love for God, for the *Torah*, for Israel — and all other facets of Ḥasidism may be considered as being directed toward its realization. His *bet midrash* and the shrine erected over his grave became centers of pilgrimage. His movement was continued by two of his pupils, R. JACOB JOSEPH OF POLONNOYE, whose writings include many of B.'s authentic sayings, and R. DOV BER OF MEZHIRICH who succeeded B. as the leader of Ḥasidism.

BAAL TEKIAH (Heb.): The person who sounds the SHOPHAR.

BAAL TEPHILLAH (Heb. "master of prayer"): The person who leads the prayer in synagogue or at the *minyan;* the SHELIAḤ TZIBBUR.

BAAL TESHUVAH (Heb.): A penitent. See REPENTANCE.

BABEL, TOWER OF: A structure erected after the Flood by the inhabitants of Shinar (Babylonia) for the purpose of reaching Heaven (Gen. 11:1-9). Looking down upon the builders and finding their purpose ill-conceived, God confounded their speech and scattered them over the earth. The object of the story is to show that the cradle of humanity was also the provenance of man's first rebellion against God, which resulted in man's estrangement from man. God's omnipotent rule was, however, beyond the challenge of mankind. Although etymologically "Babel" probably means *Bab-ili* "gate of God", the Bible derives it from the Hebrew root *balal* "to confuse". The polemical point of the story was probably inspired by the high temple-towers (*ziggurat*) in Babylonia. Talmudic comment ascribes a variety of motives to the builders of the Tower, dwelling upon the arrogance and heartlessness of the people branded as *dor ha-pelagah,* the generation of secession.

BABYLONIAN EXILE, see **EXILE**

BABYLONIAN TALMUD, see **TALMUD**

BACHARACH, JAIR ḤAYYIM (1638-1701): German rabbi. His best-known work is the responsa collection *Ḥavvot Yair* ("Villages of Jair"). A systematic student of rabbinical literature, he strongly opposed casuistry. He was also the author of poetic and mystical works.

BACHELOR, see **CELIBACY**

BAECK, LEO (1874-1956): German rabbi, theologian, and scholar. Born in Lissa (Posen), he worked in various German communities; after 1912 in Berlin, where he also taught at the *Hochschule für die Wissenschaft des Judentums.* The recognized head of German Reform Judaism, he became the spiritual leader of German Jewry as a whole after the Nazi seizure of power in 1933. Refusing invitations from abroad, he remained at his post until deported (1943) to the Theresienstadt concentration camp, which he survived. After the war he settled in London. B. wrote on midrashic and historical (including New Testament) subjects, but his main concern was philosophical and theological. His interpretation of Judaism was determined partly by the German philosophical tradition, partly by the challenge of pre-World War I liberal Protestantism which presented Christianity as the highest form of universal, human spirituality. This preoccupation shows clearly in B.'s major works (*The Pharisees, Judaism and Christianity, The Essence of Judaism*). B. contrasted "classical" with "romantic" religion. Judaism is the classical religion of action, and hence the supreme expression of morality, whereas Christianity is the romantic religion of emotion. This accounted for the authoritative character of *halakhah* and the absence of dogmatic theology in Judaism. Judaism has a "theology of teachers" and not that of an authoritative ecclesiastical body. The experience which that theology strives to elucidate is historic and national — i.e., particularistic — in substance, although its reference is universal. B. was the last great figure in the German Reform rabbinate, and one of the outstanding personalities of modern liberal Judaism. He was the initiator and first president of the World Union for Progressive Judaism.

BAHIR, BOOK OF: One of the oldest kabbalistic texts. Mystic tradition ascribes *B.* (Heb. "Shining") to R. Neḥuniah ben Ha-Kaneh (1st cent. C.E.). Modern scholarship believes it to have been edited in 12th cent. Provence but to incorporate ancient texts which had been transmitted to Europe from the East. This view regards the book as the main channel through which early oriental gnostic ideas found their way into the mainstream of Jewish mystical thought. The Spanish school of kabbalists was familiar with *B.* or with the texts upon which it is based. The book is written in pure Hebrew and in a terse though at times strange and obscure style. Like many later kabbalistic texts, it is concerned with letter mysticism, stressing both the shapes and sounds of the letters and vowels. The doctrine of the SEPHIROT, later so important in the Kabbalah, is hinted at by a reference to the ten *maamarot* ("sayings") instrumental in the process of creation. Much of the technical terminology used in *B.* later became a part of the basic vocabulary of the Kabbalah. Some examples are the image of the spiritual "tree" symbolizing the chain of creative power which forms and maintains all existence, and terms like the worlds of *beriah* - "creation" and *yetzirah* - "formation". The book also contains the first reference, in kabbalistic literature, to the doctrine of the TRANSMIGRATION of souls.

BAḤUR (Heb. "chosen one"): In the Bible, a person in the prime of his youth and vigor (cf. Ecc. 11:9; 12:1). As the word was often juxtaposed with *betulah*, a "virgin" (Deut. 32:5; Is. 62:5; Lam. 1:16), it was regarded in later Hebrew as the equivalent of an unmarried man and its use is now largely confined to this meaning, as the general title given both to a bachelor and particularly, to an (unmarried) *yeshivah* student.

BAḤUR, ELIJAH (also known as Elijah Levita; c. 1468-1549): Scholar. Born in Germany, he lived in Italy where he taught Hebrew to Christian ecclesiastics and humanists. In addition to important works — many of which were translated into Latin — on Hebrew grammar, biblical language, and *masorah* (his work *Masoret ha-Masoret* lucidly explains masoretic tradition and terminology and influenced scientific Bible study among Jewish and non-Jewish Renaissance circles), he also wrote a talmudical lexicon (*Tishbi*) and an Aramaic dictionary (*Meturgeman*), and translated from Hebrew into Yiddish (notably the Book of Psalms).

BAḤYA BEN ASHER IBN HALAWA (d. 1340): Spanish kabbalist and homilist. His moralistic works (e.g. the ethical *Kad ha-Kemaḥ*) and commentaries on the Bible, in which he also expounded kabbalistic ideas, were extremely popular. His commentary on the Pentateuch according to the fourfold method of interpretation (PARDES, i.e., literal, philosophical, homiletical, and mystical) — saw more than twenty editions.

BAḤYA BEN JOSEPH IBN PAKUDA (late 11th cent.): Philosopher and moralist; author of *Ḥovot ha-Levavot* ("Duties of the Hearts"), one of the most popular works of spiritual and ethical guidance in Judaism. Little is known of his life except that he lived in Moslem Spain and was a judge (*dayyan*) at a rabbinic court. It was perhaps in his latter capacity that he became sensitive to the dangers of a one-sided emphasis on outward punctiliousness in the observance of the Law (the "duties of the limbs") leading to neglect of the inward, spiritual "duties of the heart". B.'s work takes as its model the books of Moslem mystics which conduct the reader through the various stages of the inner life toward spiritual perfection and loving communion with God. Despite his indebtedness to the literature of Moslem mysticism and Arabic Neo-Platonism, B.'s work is a classic of Jewish piety. In his understanding of man's nature and the path to perfection, B. follows the Platonic tradition. The soul, being of celestial origin, is placed by Divine decree within the body, in whose service it runs the danger of forgetting its supernatural calling. The growth of the soul is aided by the inspiration of reason (both a faculty residing in man and a supernatural entity) and by the revealed Law. The obligations imposed by the latter correspond to the benefactions God has showered on man, especially on the Jew as a member of the chosen people; they also specify the general duties suggested by simple reason, and in particular the duty of gratitude toward the Benefactor. The marvelous microcosmic structure of man serves a double purpose — that of leading man to God through the contemplation of creation, since God can be known in no other way, and that of inculcating man's duty of gratitude toward his Benefactor. To fulfill his duties to God without faltering and to accomplish his authentic mission, man must practice a number of virtues with unremitting diligence. Trust in God, first of all, rests on two principles: God knows what is good for man better than man himself; and man is free with respect to his intentions and decisions, the realization of his acts being solely determined by the Divine will. Further, a sound spiritual life requires the most perfect agreement of the conscience with one's outward performance (i.e., sincerity of purpose), humility, and the mending of the inevitable flaws in one's present carnal state. At no time must self-examination be allowed to relax. Ascetic discipline leads to the highest rung of spiritual life which is the love of God. B. eschews the more extreme forms of asceticism (e.g. permanent solitude and seclusion from society) and advocates a middle way, as also specified by the religious Law; the genuine ascetic is one who is always with God while at the same time performing his duties within society. B.'s work has been translated into many languages and was one of the most frequently printed guides to Jewish spiritual life.

BAILMENT: A bailment arises when one person (the bailee) is lawfully entrusted with the goods of another (the bailor) with the understanding that he will return them. The law of b. deals with the duty to return the articles held, in good condition. In assessing the responsibility and liability of the bailee, Jewish law recognizes four categories of bailee (*shomer*); these are (1) the gratuitous keeper (*shomer ḥinnam*); (2) the borrower (*shoel*); (3) the receiver of hire (*nosei sakhar*); and (4) the hirer (*sokher*) (Exod. 22:6-14; Mishnah *Bava Metzia* 7:8). The talmudic discussion of the subject is contained in the treatise Bava Metzia. See also Breach of Trust.

BAKKASHAH (Heb. "entreaty", "supplication"): Name given to *piyyutim* resembling *seliḥot*. There are two types of *b.*: the first consists of long works written in prose or rhymed verse and of philosophical or theological content; the second is a shorter composition (all known instances originate from Spain) of a strict rhyming pattern (a number of such hymns are recited in the *Sephardi* rite on the High Holidays). *"Bakkashot"* (pl.) is also the name given to a service of *piyyutim* printed at the commencement of *Sephardi* prayer-books from the 17th cent. on and recited by congregants while waiting for the commencement of the Morning Service. This custom probably originated in Lurianic circles in Safed, and spread to other countries. Originally said every morning, in the course of time it was restricted to Sabbaths.

BAL TASHḤIT (Heb. "do not destroy"): The biblical prohibition on destroying fruit-bearing trees even when laying siege to a city (Deut. 20: 19-20) was extended by the Talmud to cover all senseless destruction or waste. The rabbis permitted destruction with an ultimately constructive objective (e.g. cutting trees for building or in order to let other trees grow) as against negative and prohibited destruction.

BALAAM: Heathen prophet. According to the biblical account (Num. 22-24) Balak, king of Moab, requested B. to curse the Israelites when they approached his country on their way from the wilderness to Canaan but instead, under Divine inspiration, B. uttered blessings. B. is described as a typical heathen soothsayer but also as a genuine prophet of God. Talmudic tradition regards him as one of the prophets God raised among the nations, equal to Moses in prophetic power, but at the same time utterly wicked — on his advice the Midianites enticed Israel to immorality and idolatry. The fact that God spoke through the heathen B. is early evidence of the universalistic outlook of Judaism. The story of B.'s ass was much debated between literalist and allegoristic commentators; Maimonides held that B. dreamed that his ass spoke. The words of B., "How goodly are thy tents O Jacob, thy dwelling-places O Israel", are the first words uttered by the Jew each morning on entering the synagogue.

BAMAH, see HIGH PLACE

BAMBERGER, SELIGMAN BAER (Isaac Dov; 1807-1878): Rabbi and Orthodox leader in Germany. He was largely responsible for the victory of the Orthodox rather than the liberal viewpoint at a conference of Jewish leaders called by the Bavarian government in 1836 to report on Jewish religious problems. In 1840 he became rabbi of Würzburg where he founded a *yeshivah*, a Jewish school, and a teachers' training college. He opposed the secession of autonomous Orthodox communities (as advocated by Samson Raphael Hirsch) and held that the Orthodox cause should be fought for within the framework of the general community.

BA-MEH MADLIKIN (Heb. "Wherewith may one light [the Sabbath lamp]?"): The opening words of the second chapter of the Mishnah tractate *Shabbat*, recited during the Sabbath Eve service — in some rites before the main part of the service, in others after the *amidah*. The reading was originally introduced (in post-talmudic times) to allow late-comers to catch up with the service. *B.M.* is not recited when the Sabbath coincides with, or immediately follows, a holiday.

BAN, see ḤEREM

BANISHMENT: Expulsion from one's normal residence. Biblical law legislates b. only in the case of accidental slayers who find Asylum from blood-vengeance in the Cities of Refuge; the rabbis, however, insisted that this b. was no mere protective asylum, but had also an atoning function. B. is the major punishment which God visits on his people (see Exile), as it was in the cases of Adam and Cain. In the Second Temple Period, b. was occasionally decreed as a punishment in criminal cases. B. is not recognized in Jewish law as a normal form of punishment, though medieval courts resorted to it in order to rid the community of heretical individuals (see Ḥerem). In some periods mystics would take upon themselves voluntary exile (*galut*) or wanderings (*gerushim*) to promote mystical atonement.

BAPTISM: Ritual purification by total immersion in water (*tevilah*). In the Second Temple Period b. was practiced by many pietist groups and sects (cf. the Essenes, John the Baptist). It was required of converts to Judaism and became the distinctive conversion rite of the Christian Church (see *Mark* 1:9; *Acts* 2:38-41; 8:38; 19:3-5). In the course of time the practice of total immersion largely gave way in Christianity to a ceremonial sprinkling of water. See ABLUTION; HEMEROBAPTISTS; IMMERSION; MIKVEH.

BAPTISM, FORCED, see **CONVERSION, FORCED**

BAR KAPPARA (Eleazar; 3rd cent.): Palestinian scholar. A disciple of R. JUDAH HA-NASI, he made an independent collection of legal traditions (*Mishnat B.K.*). The Talmud quotes some of his sayings, epigrams, fables, and riddles.

BAR-MITZVAH (Aram. and Heb.): An adult male Jew obligated to perform the commandments; hence, the ceremony at which a 13-year-old boy becomes an adult member of the community for ceremonial purposes (including that of making up a MINYAN). Although one of the most widely observed of all Jewish rites, it is devoid of ancient authority or sanction. The term itself in its present-day connotation is unknown in the Talmud though it is found as a general term applying to an adult male (*Bava Metzia* 96a). The Talmud merely states that a male child reaches his religious majority upon attaining puberty, which as a general but not an exclusive rule is set at the age of 13 years and a day. From this age on, he is regarded as a responsible person, liable for the results of his own actions, and it is for this reason that R. Eleazar enjoins that when a child reaches this age the father should recite the blessing BARUKH SHE-PETARANI ("Blessed is He who has freed me from the responsibility for this child" — *Gen. Rab.* 63:14). The performance of all the duties of a Jew are now incumbent upon the youth (*Avot* 5:24). Since approximately the 14th cent. the term *B.M.* has been limited to refer to a boy on the attainment of his religious majority only. An elaborate ceremony has developed, generally divided into two parts: the religious ceremony in the synagogue and the subsequent social celebration. The synagogue ceremony normally takes place among *Ashkenazim* on the first Sabbath after the (Hebrew) actual thirteenth birthdate, though it can be held on any weekday when scripture reading takes place. One of the most characteristic visible expressions of the *B.M.* in observant circles is that the boy begins to put on PHYLACTERIES daily. In some communities of Baghdadi provenance, the first putting on of phylacteries on the day following the ceremony is made the occasion of a separate ceremony. In synagogue the *B.M.* boy is called to the reading of a portion of the law — usually the last portion (*Maphtir*) which gives him the opportunity of reading the prophetic lesson (*Haphtarah*). In the State of Israel the two are sometimes separated with the boy reading from the weekly portion at a weekday service on the actual date of his anniversary, and postponing the prophetical reading to the following Sabbath. The custom for the *B.M.* to be specially addressed in synagogue has become widespread though of comparatively recent origin. The celebration which follows the synagogue ceremony is usually a purely social gathering but in Orthodox circles, it is the custom for the boy to deliver a learned discourse (*derashah*). Rabbinic justification for the social celebration has been found in a midrashic interpretation of Gen. 21:8, "And Abraham made a great feast on the day that Isaac was weaned", to the effect that it refers not to his weaning from his mother, but from the "evil inclination" (*Gen. Rab.* 53:14) i.e., on his attaining his religious majority. The banquet thereby qualifies as a SEUDAT MITZVAH, i.e., a feast celebrating the fulfillment of a religious commandment. (See also BAT MITZVAH).

BAR YOḤAI, see **SIMEON BAR YOḤAI**

BARAITA (Aram. "outside teaching"; pl. *baraitot*): General term for all tannaitic teaching not included in R. Judah Ha-Nasi's compilation of the MISHNAH. Collections of such "outside teachings" are the TOSEPHTA (a work parallel to the Mishnah) and the halakhic Midrashim (which record tannaitic teachings in the form of a running commentary to the legal sections of the Pentateuch). Many *baraitot* do not belong to any collection but are found scattered in the Babylonian and Palestinian Talmuds, where those from the Tosephta and halakhic Midrashim are also to be found. The Talmud makes reference to standard collections of *baraitot* which no longer exist in the same form, such as those of R. Oshaya and R. Ḥiyya or the "mishnah" collection of Bar Kappara. Such collections were considered equal in importance to the Mishnah itself. *Baraitot* are usually introduced in talmudic discussion by set phrases, such as *tanya* ("it was taught"), *tanu rabbanan* ("the rabbis taught"), etc. For the most part they are quoted to explain and amplify the teachings of the Mishnah.

BAREHEADEDNESS, see **COVERING OF THE HEAD**

BAREKHI NAPHSHI (Heb. "Bless [the Lord], O my soul"): Psalm 104, thus named after its opening words. The psalm glorifies God as creator and sustainer of nature, and is traditionally recited on *Rosh Ḥodesh*. In some rites it is also recited, on Sabbath afternoons between Tabernacles and Passover.

BAREKHU: *"Barekhu et adonai ha-mevorakh"* ("Bless ye the Lord who is [to be] blessed") has become the customary synagogue formula of invitation to prayer. It is based on the phrase "Bless ye the Lord" which occurs frequently in the Bible (e.g. Ps. 135:19; Neh. 9:5). This formula serves as the opening of both the morning and evening prayers in the synagogue (those sections of the morning prayer now preceding *B.* did not originally form part of the obligatory synagogue prayers) and also serves as the introduction to the public reading from the *Torah.* It was also used for the *zimmun,* i.e., the invitation to GRACE, but was later replaced by the formula *nevarekh* ("let us bless") which is used today. While the reader chants *B.*, the congregation reads silently a prayer beginning *yitbarakh* (of which different versions exist in the various rites); when the reader concludes the invitation, the congregation responds aloud: "Blessed is the Lord who is [to be] blessed for ever and ever."

BARRENNESS: With the commandment to "be fruitful and multiply" (Gen. 1:28; 9:1) heading the list of Judaism's 613 precepts, b. has always been considered a great misfortune. "Give me children, else I die" (Gen. 30:1) was the anguished cry of Rachel, and the Hebrew Bible mentions other notable instances of the craving for children (e.g. Sarah, Rebecca, Hannah) where marriages were long barren. Conversely, the promise "there shall not be male or female barren among your cattle" (Deut. 7:14) was among the most cherished blessings, and the barren woman who ultimately gave birth became a symbol of supreme happiness extolled in song and prophecy (I Sam. 2:5; Is. 54:1; Ps. 113:9). The rabbis regarded the procreation of children as the principal purpose of marriage, codifying the duty to marry under the heading of "the precept of procreation". According to talmudic law, a man was compelled to divorce his wife if the marriage had remained barren for ten years (*Yev.* 64a). Although since medieval times no compulsion has been actually exercised in such cases, b. remains a valid cause for divorce or (where Jews are polygamous) a valid reason for taking a second wife.

BARUCH, BOOK OF: A number of pseudepigraphal works purporting to have been written by Baruch, the disciple and amanuensis of the prophet Jeremiah. 1) The Apocryphal *Book of B.* has been preserved in a Greek version which is probably a translation from the Hebrew. Though it may contain earlier material, it did not assume its present form until after the destruction of the Temple. This work comprises two sections, the first being a letter of B. which he reads to Jehoiachin and the exiles in Babylonia; this moves them to confess their sins and send money offerings to the Temple. The second section contains two poems: the first admonishes Israel to seek wisdom, and the second recounts the plight of the nation and promises future deliverance. 2) *The Syriac Apocalypse of B.* Its style as well as the experiences and visions recorded in it suggest that it was originally written in Hebrew after the destruction of the Second Temple. At God's bidding, B. leaves Jerusalem as the Chaldeans approach, and sees how the angels set fire to the city. There follows a series of visions describing the advent and reign of the Messiah. This APOCALYPSE is closely akin to IV ESDRAS and a number of its eschatological views have close parallels in talmudic literature. 3) The *Greek Apocalypse of B.*, written in the 2nd cent. C.E., (also extant in a shorter Slavonic version) shows a marked gnostic influence. It describes B.'s journey through the five (or seven) heavens, where the wonders of creation are disclosed to him. 4) The *Rest of the Words of B.*, first discovered in Ethiopic, has also been preserved in Greek, Armenian, and Slavonic versions. Though containing Christian interpolations, it is basically Jewish and relates how B. remained in Israel while Jeremiah accompanied the exiles to Babylonia, but returned at their head 66 years later. As this work postulates the existence of IV Esdras and the Syriac B., it cannot antedate the 2nd cent. C.E., and was written possibly after the Bar Kokhba revolt.

BARUCH OF MEDZIBOZH (d. 1810): Ḥasidic leader. A son of the BAAL SHEM Tov's daughter Odel, he was proud of his descent and often contemptuous of other ḥasidic *rebbes* of his day. B. was particularly bitter in his antagonism toward SHNEOUR ZALMAN OF LYADY, while many ḥasidic leaders found it difficult to maintain friendship with him. Intent on appearing "different" from his colleagues, he assumed a highly individual style of prayer and a rather extravagant style of life. At his court in Tulchin (Ukraine) he even kept a jester, and he also inaugurated the custom of the *ḥasidim* paying money to their TZADDIK. For all these practices he advanced mystical reasons.

BARUKH (Heb. "blessed" or "praised" — with regard to God the two words are identical in meaning): The opening word of the standard formula of BENEDICTION which is one of the basic forms of Jewish prayer. According to the Talmud many of the benedictions beginning with the formula "Blessed art thou, O Lord our God, King of the Universe" date back to the Men of the GREAT SYNAGOGUE.

BARUKH DAYYAN (ha-) EMET (Heb. "Blessed be the true Judge"): Benediction pronounced on hearing evil tidings (Mishnah *Ber.* 9:2) since a Jew praises God both in joy and in sorrow. The formula is generally recited on hearing the report of a death; close relatives say the full liturgical formula ("Blessed art thou, O Lord our God, King of the universe, the true Judge").

BARUKH HA-SHEM (Heb. "Blessed be the

Name" [i.e., of God]): Expletive, usually uttered on hearing good tidings.

BARUKH HU U-VARUKH SHEMO (Heb. "Blessed be He, and blessed be His name"): Response by the congregation to the mention of the Divine Name in the first half of a BENEDICTION ("Blessed art thou, O Lord"), the response to the second half being *amen.* If the listener intends to be included in the recitation of the benediction (e.g. in the *kiddush* or *havdalah*), the response is omitted.

BARUKH SHE-AMAR (Heb. "Blessed be He who spoke"): Opening words of the PESUKEI DE-ZIMRA.

BARUKH SHEM KEVOD MALKHUTO LE-OLAM VA-ED (Heb. "Blessed be His name whose glorious kingdom is eternal"): Phrase recited after the first verse of the SHEMA; it is said in an undertone to distinguish it from the rest of the *Shema* which is a biblical quotation. Only on the Day of Atonement is this phrase recited aloud; this is to recall its public exclamation by worshipers in the Temple when the High Priest uttered the Tetragrammaton on the Day of Atonement (*Yoma* 6:2). A talmudic legend (*Pes.* 56b) relates that when Jacob was dying he asked his sons if they indeed believed in the One God; their response was to state the *Shema* whereupon Jacob responded *barukh shem,* etc.

BARUKH SHE-PETARANI: Opening words of the blessing (quoted in *Gen. Rab.* 83) spoken by the father of a BAR MITZVAH boy ("Blessed be He who has freed me from the responsibility for this child") since the child is now considered to assume responsibility for his actions as a member of the religious community.

BASHYAZI, ELIJAH (c. 1420-1490): KARAITE scholar and theologian in Turkey. His work *Aderet Eliyahu* ("The Mantle of Elijah", also called *Sepher ha-Mitzvot*) was accepted as the last and outstanding compendium of Karaite religious law. It contains a statement of ten basic Karaite dogmas demonstrated philosophically.

BASTARD, see **ILLEGITIMACY**

BATHING, see **ABLUTION; MIKVEH**

BAT KOL (literally "daughter of a voice", i.e., "echo"): In rabbinic literature the term denotes a heavenly voice announcing God's decisions in matters of urgent importance. Traditionally the voice was that of the angel Gabriel. Legend reports instances of manifestations of the *B.K.* that were heard by individuals or even by groups of people; this differs from PROPHECY in which the Divine communication is received by a person already predisposed to be in spiritual communication with God. The *B.K.*, like other forms of heavenly pronouncement, was not necessarily accepted as authoritative in halakhic matters, since the rabbis held that the *Torah* "is not in heaven" (Deut. 30:12) and that religious decisions had to be arrived at by established human methods.

BAT-MITZVAH (Heb.): An adult female Jew obligated to perform the commandments; hence the ceremony on the occasion of a girl's reaching her religious majority (according to Jewish law at the age of twelve years and one day — a year earlier than the comparable ceremony, the BAR MITZVAH, in the case of a boy, but generally postponed to the age of 13 or even later). Conservative and Reform synagogues have introduced a confirmation-ceremony in the synagogue. This form of observance is generally condemned by Orthodox Jewry which looks askance at any participation of females in the synagogue service (although during the past century a number of Orthodox synagogues in the Western world have introduced a modified service in synagogue for girls attaining their religious majority, and the late British Chief Rabbi Dr. J.H. Hertz was a pronounced advocate of it). The Israel Chief Rabbi Nissim has advocated a religious ceremony to take place in the home of the occasion of *B.M.*

BAVA (Aram. "gate"): Section of book (=Heb. *shaar*). The first tractate of the Mishnah order of *Nezikin* was divided into three sections, each divided into ten chapters, with *gemara* in both the Palestinian and the Babylonian Talmud.

B. Kamma	("the first gate"), deals with the four principal types of damage to property and personal injury according to Exod. 21:33; 22:5 ff.
B. Metzia	("the middle gate") deals with found property, law of chattels, bailments, sales, interest, fraud, hiring, partnership.
B. Batra	("the last gate") deals with real estate, usurpations, hereditary succession, legal documents.

BEADLE, see **SHAMMASH**

BEARD: Among the ancient Hebrews and other oriental nations, the b. was considered a symbol of manhood and was carefully tended, trimmed (in later periods especially in honor of the Sabbath and festivals), and anointed. Its removal — except as a sign of mourning — was a disgrace (cf. II Sam. 10:4-5), though SHAVING was obligatory in certain purification ceremonies (cf. Lev. 14:9). The biblical injunction not to "mar the edges of your beard" in the fashion of pagan worshipers was interpreted by the rabbis as a prohibition against shaving in general, although ways have been devised to remove the b. without technically infringing this prohibition. The kabbalists, especially the followers of Isaac Luria, ascribed mystic significance to the b., and would not even trim it.

BEDIKAH (Heb. "examination"): As a halakhic term *b.* denotes various kinds of inspection or examination in connection with ritual and legal questions, more particularly with regard to the slaughtering of animals, when *b.* is made of: 1) the knife before slaughtering to make sure it is absolutely sharp; 2) the windpipe and esophagus to ascertain whether they have been properly cut; 3) the inner organs, particularly the lungs, to ascertain whether the slaughtered animal suffered from any serious disease. Examination of witnesses in court is called *bedikat ha-edim.* For the search for LEAVEN on the day before Passover, see BEDIKAT ḤAMETZ.

BEDIKAT ḤAMETZ (Heb. "search for leaven"): The biblical injunction "even the first day shall ye put away LEAVEN out of your houses" (Exod. 12:15) was interpreted by the rabbis as referring to the day preceding Passover, i.e., *Nisan* 14. To make sure that "there be no leaven found in your houses" (Exod. 12:19), the rabbis instituted a ceremonial search for leavened substances. *B.Ḥ.* takes place after dark on the eve of *Nisan* 14, when all holes and crannies are examined by candle light. As a formal religious ceremony, *b.ḥ.* is preceded by a benediction ("Blessed art thou... who hast commanded us concerning the search for leaven"). If leaven is found, it is burned on the next morning (*biur ḥametz*). Since *b.ḥ.* has become a highly formalized ritual, it is customary with some to hide small pieces of bread (according to the Lurianic kabbalists, ten in number) to make sure that the search will not be in vain. After the search an Aramaic formula is recited, renouncing ownership of any leaven that may have escaped detection. A similar formula is pronounced the next morning after the burning of the leaven.

BE-EZRAT HA-SHEM (Heb. "With the help of the Name [of God]"): Expression of pious hope; often written in initials at the head of letters, or used in speech in a way similar to the English "God willing".

BEHEADING (in Heb. *hereg,* "slaying"): One of the four types of CAPITAL PUNISHMENT known in talmudic law. The transgressions punishable by b. — in particular murder and idolatry — as well as the mode of execution are discussed in the talmudic tractate *Sanhedrin.*

BEHEMOTH: Animal described in Job 40:15-24; in pseudepigraphal and rabbinic lore, b., like the LEVIATHAN (cf. Job 40:25-32), was a legendary animal. In the messianic age there will be a fight between b. and leviathan. The righteous will be spectators at the fight and afterward feast on the flesh of the animals at the messianic banquet.

BEIT DIN, BEIT HILLEL, BEIT MIDRASH, etc., see **BET DIN, BET HILLEL, BET MIDRASH,** etc.

BEITZAH (Heb. "Egg"): Tractate of the Mishnah order *Moed,* containing five chapters in the Talmud (Palestinian and Babylonian). It deals with prohibited and permitted labor on festivals, hence its original title was *Yom Tov.* The popular title *B.* derives from its first word (the only tractate whose title is so derived), which introduces the laws concerning an egg laid on a festival day. The tractate also contains an important list of differences of opinion between BET HILLEL AND BET SHAMMAI.

BEKHOR, see FIRST-BORN

BEKHOROT (Heb. "Rights of first-born"): Fourth tractate of the Mishnah order *Kodashim* (with *gemara* in the Babylonian Talmud) dealing with laws concerning the FIRST-BORN of men and animals (Exod. 13:2, 12 ff.; Num. 18:15 ff.).

BELIAL: Biblical term (possibly a compound of *beli* and *yaal,* i.e., "worthless", "good-for-nothing") applied to subversive or wicked individuals. In apocryphal literature the name also occurs as Beliar, and is equated with Satan.

BELIEF, see **CREED; DOGMA; THIRTEEN ARTICLES OF FAITH**

BELLS: The *Torah*-Scroll decorations, often made of silver and mounted on the finials, are either in the form of two towers or of a crown, generally with little bells attached. The custom was probably inspired by the biblical description of the High Priest's robe (Exod. 28:33-35) whence also the association of b. with pomegranates (RIMMONIM).

BELZ: Town in Galicia; original seat of the ḥasidic dynasty of the Rokeaḥ family, established by Shalom of B. (1799-1856). The B. rabbis laid great stress on rabbinic learning. They were extreme in their insistence on a specific Jewish garb and appearance, any diminution of which diminished the "Divine Image" in which man was created. They exercised a great influence on the development of Galician Ḥasidism.

BE-MIDBAR, see **NUMBERS, BOOK OF**

BE-MIDBAR RABBAH, see **MIDRASH RABBAH**

BEN ASHER, AARON BEN MOSES (10th cent.): Palestinian Hebrew grammarian and masoretic scholar, one of the last representatives of the Tiberian school of masoretes, in which his family had figured prominently. He produced a carefully edited biblical text with vowel-points and accents which became the basis for subsequent Bible editions (see MASORAH). Maimonides corrected his own Scroll of the Law in accordance with the B.A. text which he declared authoritative. Some scholars maintained that B.A. was a Karaite but the theory has not been accepted.

BEN AZZAI, SIMEON (2nd cent.): *Tanna.* One of the great scholars of his generation, he died in his prime before being formally ordained; hence his name is not preceded by the title "rabbi". He remained unmarried — contrary to the requirements of rabbinic law — in order to **devote his**

time exclusively to study. Tradition connects him with a circle of mystics and attributes his premature death to a mystical experience (against the danger of which the rabbis frequently warned; cf. *Ḥag.* 14a).

BEN NAPHTALI, MOSES BEN DAVID (10th cent.): Palestinian masoretic scholar. He edited a text of the Hebrew Bible according to the traditions of his school which differed in many small details, mainly of vocalization and accent, from those of the BEN ASHER school. The generally adopted biblical text is the Palestinian (Tiberian) MASORAH (to be distinguished from the Eastern, i.e., Babylonian, version) as established by Ben Asher with occasional details from B.N.

BEN SIRA (or Sirach; 2nd cent. B.C.E.): Palestinian sage and teacher. His first name was Simeon (according to the Hebrew texts) or Jesus (i.e., Joshua) according to the Greek texts. A member of the class of scribes and learned men, he composed a book of proverbs, practical and moral maxims and counsels, and exhortations to love wisdom, similar in style and outlook to the biblical Book of Proverbs. It also contains liturgical texts, prayers, psalm-like poems and hymns. The book, known as the *Wisdom of Ben Sira* (*Ecclesiasticus* in Greek), was among the best-known of the apocryphal books and exerted considerable influence on talmudic and medieval moralists, and on many liturgical compositions. It identifies WISDOM with the observance of *Torah;* the highest wisdom is Divine and the wisdom of man comes from accepting and obeying the Divine will. The Hebrew text was lost and rediscovered only at the end of the 19th century in the Cairo *genizah*. For many centuries the book was known only through the Greek translation, made by the author's grandson, which was incorporated in the Septuagint.

BENÇAO: A *Sephardi* term corresponding to the *Ashkenazi* BENSHEN and denoting blessing in general, the particular form of prayer known as "benediction", and the Grace after Meals. The word has been corrupted into *besam.*

BENEI BETERA (or BATHYRA): A prominent family of scholars, 1st cent. B.C.E. — 1st cent. C.E. According to tradition they renounced their leading position, which they had held after the deaths of SHEMAIAH and Avtalyon, in favor of HILLEL whose appointment as president of the Sanhedrin they promoted. Several members of the family are mentioned in the Talmud.

BENE ISRAEL (Heb. "sons of Israel"): Native Jews of India, dwelling for the most part in Bombay and the surrounding area. Their origin is uncertain; according to B.I. tradition their ancestors — descendants of the Ten Tribes — arrived in India about the 3rd or 4th cent. C.E. The only Hebrew they had preserved was the *Shema,* while their holy days consisted of the New Year (observed for one day), a version of Tabernacles on *Tishri* 4, the Day of Atonement (when they fasted), *Purim,* Passover, the 9th of *Av, Ramzan* (a month-long fast during *Elul*), the fast of *Tammuz* 17, the fast of Gedaliah, and the feast of *Shevat* 15 commemorating Elijah's ascension to heaven. Their other Jewish observances were limited to the Sabbath, circumcision, and certain aspects of the ritual preparation of food. When first discovered by David Rahabi of Cochin about 300 years ago, they had retained only the slightest vestiges of Jewish custom but he succeeded in reconverting them to a full Judaism. A subsequent revival brought about at the end of the 18th cent. by Samuel Divekar led to their acceptance of the *Sephardi* ritual and tradition with very slight differences. Numbering an estimated total of 28,000, some 7,000 have immigrated to Israel. The fact that for many centuries they had been out of contact with rabbinic Judaism and hence ignorant of halakhic procedures for marriage and divorce has caused doubt about their personal status in Jewish law. Many rabbis therefore refused to sanction marriages between B.I. and other Jews. This led to friction between the B.I. and the Israel Chief Rabbinate.

BENEDICTION (Heb. *berakhah*): Any kind of blessing or praise; in LITURGY, prayer or praise of God that is formulated in a special style. In the technical latter sense, the term b. is applied only to a prayer which contains in its opening or concluding sentence, or in both, the words *barukh attah adonai* ("Blessed art Thou, O Lord"); if appearing at the beginning of the prayer, the formula continues with the words: *eloheinu melekh ha-olam* ("our God, King of the Universe"). After this unvarying formula comes the specific praise, appropriate to each particular prayer. Of all the various formulas of praise, e.g. in the Book of Psalms, the b. was eventually chosen to serve exclusively in any obligatory prayer. It is modeled on a biblical pattern (Ps. 119:12; II Chron. 29:10), though it underwent some modification. B. formulas are found frequently in the Dead Sea Scrolls, though there they are still interchanged with others (not all contain the word "Thou", and they refer to God by various names and epithets). By the 3rd cent. C.E., all the statutory forms of the b. had been fixed: a b. had to contain the word "Thou"; the Tetragrammaton (pronounced *adonai*) had to be used (and no other epithets of God); it had (when used as an opening formula) to contain mention of God's Kingship. While invariably commencing with a direct address to God, the b. continues, with very few exceptions, by referring to Him in the third person; on the other hand, any section of the obligatory part of the liturgy, which does not open with the b. formula, (such as all the intermediary benedictions of the AMIDAH), invariably uses the second person in addressing God. The exclusive use of the b. style for obligatory prayers was apparently intended to provide a special formula as a distinguishing mark by which normative standard prayers are differentiated from individual and private ones. Hence the Talmud lays down that "unnecessary" use of the b. (*berakhah le-vatalah*), including its use in non-obligatory prayer, is prohibited and regarded as a transgression of Exod. 20:7: "Thou shalt not take the name of the Lord thy God in vain." Since, however, no objection is raised to the use of the Divine name in private prayer as such, but only to its use in the b. formula, it is clear that the intention was to reserve the latter exclusively for statutory prayers. Hence the presence or absence of this formula at the beginning or end of any part of the liturgy can serve to determine if the prayer in question forms part of the obligatory service. Though at times individuals would use the b. to conclude their private prayers, this practice was definitely forbidden by later authorities. The b. is used both in synagogue and in private or domestic prayers as long as they are obligatory, e.g. KIDDUSH, GRACE. Three forms of b. are distinguished: the short form, which only opens with the b. formula; the long form, which both opens and concludes with it; and "a b. following upon a preceding one" in which the b. formula only serves as conclusion. The first type is very frequent for a short b., such as that spoken before partaking of any food; the third is used extensively in the longer portions of the obligatory daily prayers, such as the AMIDAH, the benedictions of the SHEMA and Grace after Meals, all of which consist of "series of benedictions", of which only the first belongs to the "long form", while all the subsequent ones no longer open but only conclude with *barukh*, etc.

Benedictions may be divided according to their contents and liturgical function into several main groups. Apart from the series of b.'s which constitute the main portions of all obligatory daily prayers, there are many, mostly of the short form, recited for certain occasions: 1) B. "of enjoyment", e.g. the b. before partaking of any food or drink. For each of the more important categories, especially bread, cake, wine, fruit, or vegetables, a special b. is used, e.g. "Blessed art Thou etc. who brings forth bread from the earth", "...who creates the fruit of the wine"; while for any other type of food or drink (meat, eggs, fish, sweets, etc.) there is one uniform b. "...by whose word all things came into being". Several additional special formulas were known in the old Palestinian rite but have fallen into disuse. To this category belong also various b. to be recited before enjoying the smell of flowers, spices, etc. Apart from GRACE, two b. are to be recited after the enjoyment of food or drink: the longer one (a condensation of Grace into one b. of the "long form") to be used after wine, cake, and those kinds of fruit mentioned in Deut. 8:8; and the shorter one, to be used after all other types of food or drink.

2) Before performing a MITZVAH, e.g. putting on TEPHILLIN, kindling the Sabbath lights, sounding the SHOPHAR. All b.'s recited over a *mitzvah* open "Blessed art Thou ...who has sanctified us by His commandments and commanded us..."; after this follow 2 or 3 words indicating which commandment is about to be performed. These b.'s are to be recited before the *mitzvah* is observed with only a few exceptions (e.g. the b. on the occasion of the ritual washing of one's hands, which is spoken after the ablution). If a commandment is performed for the first time, or for the first time in any particular year, the additional b. "Blessed... who has kept us alive... and made us reach this time" is recited.

3) Various b.'s of praise or thanksgiving, such as those to be recited upon seeing lightning, the ocean, a king, a great scholar, etc. or upon hearing either good or bad news, etc. With this group might also be counted the "blessings of the morning" (nowadays usually recited in synagogue before SHAḤARIT proper) e.g. "Blessed... who restores souls to dead bodies"; "who opens the eyes of the blind"; "who clothes the naked"; "who supplies my every want" etc.

4) Individual b.'s or arrangements of several b.'s to be recited on special liturgical occasions, e.g. *Kiddush*, HAVDALAH, SHEVA BERAKHOT, the blessing recited on seeing the New Moon, etc.

Occasionally the term *berakhah* is used in the liturgy in a non-technical sense concerning a blessing or prayer which does not contain the "*barukh*" formula, e.g. *birkat kohanim* (=the original PRIESTLY BLESSING); *birkat ha-ḥodesh* (NEW MOON, BLESSING OF). According to R. Meir a man should utter at least one hundred b.'s every day. The fact that at various times throughout the day the Jew is obliged to recite a blessing and thus turn his thoughts to God, is one of the most characteristic features of the discipline of sanctification. Everyday actions, such as getting up and dressing in the morning, eating or drinking, the observance of natural phenomena, or the receiving of glad or sad news, all provide occasion for praising God and thus take on religious significance. Through the b., a physical action becomes an act of worship. In the case of *mitzvot*, the preceding b. serve the purpose of preparing the mind of the worshiper to perform the *mitzvah* not as mere routine, but joyfully and as a conscious act of observance. Since the occasions for b. arise throughout the day — at home as well as at work — they help to overcome the cleavage between the "holy" and the "profane" in man's life and are designed to make man's entire life a continuous service of God. Traditionally the b.'s were attributed to the Men of the Great Synagogue. See also BLESSING AND CURSE.

BENEFIT: The enjoyment of certain rights is classified by rabbinic law as b. (*tovat hanaah*). Thus the tithe (given to the levites) and the heave-offering (given to the priests) are not considered the giver's property, but since he can choose the person to whom he gives these dues, he has some b. in the matter. The rabbis discuss the question whether b. is a property title and hence falls under the law of property, or whether it is merely the incidental enjoyment of a right.

BENJAMIN BEN MOSES NAHAVENDI (9th cent.): KARAITE scholar; considered one of the founders of the sect, the name of which he coined (until his time they had been known as Ananites). He lived in Nahavend (Persia), and was the first Karaite author to write in Hebrew. B. laid down the Karaite principles and methods of independent biblical study and interpretation, rejecting traditional rabbinical authority. He composed commentaries on the Bible (which were admired by Abraham Ibn Ezra) as well as codifications of ceremonial law.

BENSHEN or **BENSH:** *Ashkenazi* term, derived from Latin *via* the Old French *benedicere,* and meaning to "bless". Applied more particularly to 1) the blessing of children by their parents; 2) GRACE AFTER MEALS; 3) the recitation of the GOMEL blessing. It corresponds to the *Sephardi* term BENÇAO.

BEQUEST, see **INHERITANCE; WILLS**

BER OF LIUBAVICH, see **LIUBAVICH**

BER OF MEZHIRICH, see **DOV BER OF MEZHIRICH**

BERAB, JACOB, see **BERAV, JACOB**

BERAḤ DODI (Heb. "Make haste my beloved"): The opening words (derived from the Song of Songs 8:14) of a number of liturgical compositions recited in the *Ashkenazi* rite on Passover.

BERAKHAH, see **BENEDICTION**

BERAKHAH AḤARONAH (Heb. "last blessing" in contradistinction to the "first blessing" said before partaking of any food): The shorter form of GRACE AFTER MEALS said after partaking of (1) food other than bread prepared from the five primary grains; (2) wine; (3) food specified in Deut. 8:8 as characteristic of Israel. The *b.a.* briefly summarizes the ordinary grace after meals. After partaking of food which requires neither the full grace nor the *b.a.*, an even shorter blessing is recited (*bore nephashot*).

BERAKHOT (Heb. "Blessings"): First tractate of the Mishnah order of *Zeraim* with *gemara* in both Talmuds. It deals with the rules for the recitation of the *Shema*, prayers, and blessings and benedictions for various occasions. The *gemara* on *B.* abounds in aggadic statements which have provided, the foundations of Jewish teaching on prayer, piety, and devotion.

BERAV (or **BERAB**), **JACOB** (1474-1546): Talmudist. Born in Spain, B. became rabbi of Fez in Morocco at the age of 18. From there he moved to Egypt and finally settled in Safed. He was considered one of the foremost rabbinic authorities of his age, and in 1538 initiated the abortive attempt to renew rabbinic ORDINATION (*semikhah*, which had lapsed in the Amoraic Period) as a first step toward re-establishing the SANHEDRIN, reuniting the Jewish people under one spiritual authority, and hastening the advent of redemption. The scheme was opposed by R. Levi Ibn Ḥaviv of Jerusalem and by others, and after an acrimonious controversy ultimately failed.

BERERAH (Heb. "choosing", "selection"): A technical term of rabbinic law designating a situation the facts or the legal implication of which become definitely known only at some future time. The question is whether there can be retroactive recognition of such. The Talmud distinguishes between two kinds of *b.*; one where the present condition of doubt is due to the person, although the situation itself has certainty, and the other where the situation itself is doubtful. The first category of personal doubt is again divided into two aspects: one where the definite outcome depends upon the individual himself, and one where it depends upon the will or action of others.

BERESHIT, see **GENESIS**

BERESHIT RABBAH, see **MIDRASH RABBAH**

BERESHIT RABBATI: A Midrash on Genesis composed by MOSES HA-DARSHAN of Narbonne (11th cent.). It was mentioned and quoted by the 13th cent. Spanish Dominican Raymund Martini as *Midrash Bereshit Rabbah Major*; the Hebrew original has only recently been published.

BERLIN, ISAIAH BEN JUDAH LOEB (also known as Isaiah Pick; 1725-1799): German talmudist. He settled in Breslau and from 1793, was president of the *bet din* of Silesia. In addition to wide-ranging erudition, he possessed a developed critical sense and his textual emendations and notes to the Talmud have been printed in all editions since 1800, laying the foundation for the critical study of the Talmud. B. developed this approach in his notes on other major rabbinical classics.

BERLIN, NAPHTALI TZEVI JUDAH (known by his initials as the *Natziv;* 1817-1893): Russian talmudist. From 1854 he was head of the famous *yeshivah* of VOLOZHIN where he continued the tradition of the Vilna Gaon, opposing *pilpul* and advocating profounder study and logical understanding of texts based on a minute knowledge of sources. He wrote on the *Sheiltot* of AḤA OF SHABḤA as well as commentaries on the Bible and Jerusalem Talmud. One of the first rabbis to sympathize with Zionist aspirations, he actively supported the work of the *Ḥovevei Zion.* His son Meir Berlin (Bar-Ilan, 1880-1949) was the leader of the religious Zionist party *Mizraḥi.*

BERLIN RABBINICAL SEMINARY (*Rabbiner Seminar für das orthodoxe Judentum*): Seminary for the training of Orthodox rabbis, founded in Berlin in 1873 by Azriel Hildesheimer, one year after the establishment of the Berlin *Lehranstalt* for Reform rabbis. Students had to promise not to officiate in a synagogue that used ORGAN music. The B.R.S. was closed by the Nazis in 1938.

BERNAYS, ISAAC (1792-1849): German rabbi and orator, also known as Ḥakham Bernays; from 1821 chief rabbi of Hamburg. He opposed reform of the prayer-book and of religious observances, but modernized Jewish education, introducing German as the language of instruction in the Hamburg *Talmud Torah.* The first Orthodox rabbi to preach in German, B.'s sermons made a considerable impression on his contemporaries, including his pupil SAMSON RAPHAEL HIRSCH.

BERTINORO, OBADIAH OF (c. 1450-1510): Italian scholar. He went to Palestine in 1485 and settled in Jerusalem where he founded a *yeshivah* and was recognized as the chief halakhic authority in Palestine and Egypt. He wrote a graphic account of his journey to Jerusalem, which had taken two and a half years and led him through many oriental Jewish communities. B. is best known for his lucid commentary on the entire Mishnah, in which he incorporated the explanations of the Talmud and the medieval commentators. The commentary, directed to those who study the Mishnah without the *gemara,* rapidly became standard, and was printed in almost all subsequent editions of the Mishnah. A Latin translation was made for the benefit of Christian scholars.

BERURYAH (2nd cent. C.E.): Wife of the *tanna* R. MEIR and daughter of the martyr R. ḤANINA BEN TERADYON, she was renowned for both her scholarship and her piety. The Talmud tells many stories of her exemplary wisdom, kindness, and fortitude in adversity, and quotes many of her halakhic and aggadic sayings. On one occasion her legal opinion was accepted as authoritative.

BESAMIM, see **SPICES**

BESHT, see **BAAL SHEM TOV**

BE-SIMAN TOV, see **CONGRATULATIONS**

BET ALMIN: Another form of *Bet Olam* ("Eternal Home"); euphemism for CEMETERY.

BET DIN (Heb. "house of judgment", "court", pl. *battei din*): Jewish court of law guided by the principles of recognized HALAKHAH in dealing with matters of civil, criminal, or religious law. The command to appoint judges and establish courts of law is mentioned in Deut. 16:18. During the Temple and Mishnaic Periods there were three types of *battei din.* The lowest, which was found in almost all towns, consisted of three judges who had authority to adjudicate civil cases. The judges received their authorization from the heads of the academies or from the Patriarch. A higher court consisted of 23 judges, and was empowered to judge criminal cases. This court was sometimes called the "small Sanhedrin". Any town of 120 inhabitants had the right to appoint such a court. The highest type of court was known as the Great *Bet Din* or the SANHEDRIN. It consisted of 70 or 71 members, and during the Temple Period sat in the Chamber of Hewn Stone in the precincts of the Temple and was the source of final authority for the interpretation of law and the establishment of new legislation. It also appointed the judges of the lower courts. Following the destruction of the Temple, the Sanhedrin made its seat at Yavneh and was recognized as the central authority for all Jews, its two leaders being the *nasi* ("president") and *av bet din* ("head of the court"). Because of the gradual decline in the status and condition of Palestine Jewry, it steadily lost authority and eventually disappeared. Since membership depended upon an unbroken chain of ordination, it became impossible to reconstitute such a court. Yet Jewish centers continued almost everywhere to have courts, usually presided over by the leading rabbinic scholar of the vicinity. In many places these had almost complete autonomy. In Spain, Jewish courts were even granted criminal jurisdiction, delegated by the king. Among the courts of later Jewish history, the most famous was perhaps that of the Council of Four Lands which up to 1764 served as a court of final appeal for Polish Jewry. When Jewish autonomy broke down after the Emancipation Period, the authority of Jewish courts became for the greater part limited to ritual questions. In the State of Israel today the rabbinical courts enjoy official recognition in all matters of personal status. This is a continuation of the situation under the British mandate when Jewish courts were recognized as having the same authority as Moslem religious courts in the areas of marriage and divorce.

BET HA-MIKDASH, see **TEMPLE**

BET ḤAYYIM (Heb. "house of the living"): Euphemism for CEMETERY.

BET HILLEL AND BET SHAMMAI (Heb. "the house — i.e., the disciples — of HILLEL and the house of SHAMMAI): Two schools of *tannaim* flourishing in the 1st cent. C.E. The Talmud records more than 300 controversies on points of law between the two schools, whose attitudes seem to reflect the personalities of their founders: Shammai, strict and uncompromising, Hillel, kind and gentle. Some scholars maintain that differences between the schools also concerned political attitudes and not only the interpretation of the Law. Even after the formal cessation of the two schools, their controversies were continued among scholars until the assembly at Yavneh (c. 90 C.E.) ruled that *B.H.'s* views be accepted as final. According to the Talmud (*Eruv.* 13b) this decision was supported by a *bat kol* ("heavenly voice").

BET KENESET, see **SYNAGOGUE**

BET KEVAROT (Heb. "house of graves"): CEMETERY.

BET MIDRASH (Heb. "house of study"): Place for study of the Law, and, more specifically, of the rabbinic texts such as the Mishnah, Talmud, Codes, and Responsa. In the Talmudic Period, the term *b.m.* was almost synonymous with that of ACADEMY (*yeshivah*). The sanctity of the *b.m.* was considered greater than that of the synagogue (*bet keneset*), and rabbis of the Talmud preferred to pray in the *b.m.* rather than adjourning to the synagogue (*Ber.* 8a). During medieval times the *b.m.* came to be closely connected with the *bet keneset,* usually situated in the same building or close by. In Germany it was termed *klaus* (from the Latin, *claustrum,* cloister), and in E. Europe *kloiz.* It was here that senior students would spend most of their day, either in individual study or under the discipline of a *rosh yeshivah* ("academy head"). The *b.m.* was also a place for general popular study and almost all those who went to the synagogue for prayer would usually spend some time before or after prayer in the *b.m.* It also served as a communal library sometimes containing many hundreds of books of rabbinic literature. The antiquity of the institution goes back in Jewish legend to the *b.m.* established after the Flood by Shem and Eber, where the patriarchs are said to have studied. From the stories told in connection with Jacob and Esau it appears that the proper time for entering the *b.m.* was upon the completion of primary education at the age of 13. The term *b.m.* occurs for the first time in Ecclesiasticus (51:50) but seems to be referred to in Prov. 8:34. It was customary from talmudic times to recite a special prayer upon entering the *b.m.* The Talmud preserves several such prayers, such as that of R. Neḥunyah ben Ha-Kanah who, upon entering, prayed to be saved from errors of understanding or interpreting the *halakhah,* and, upon leaving, would give thanks to Heaven for having cast his lot "among those who dwell in the House of Study" (*Ber.* 28b). Study was pursued both day and night, as well as on Sabbaths and holidays. Students who spent their time in the *b.m.* were permitted to eat and sleep there (unlike in the synagogue). The *halakhah* permits the selling of a synagogue in order to build a *b.m.*

BET OLAM (Heb. "everlasting house"): Euphemism for CEMETERY.

BET SHEARIM: Jewish city at the end of the Second Temple Period and the first centuries following the destruction of the Temple; located about 1½ miles S. of the present Kiryat Tivon near Haifa. It attained special importance in 170, when R. JUDAH HA-NASI transferred his academy there, thus making it the seat of the SANHEDRIN. B.S. became a famous burial place for Jews both inside and outside Palestine; Judah Ha-Nasi and other members of his family were buried there. Since 1936, many catacombs and tombs as well as the remains of a synagogue have been unearthed at B.S. Most of the burials were secondary ones, the bones being placed in arcosolia or *kukhim,* a practice common among the Jews of Palestine in the Hellenistic and Roman Periods. The inscriptions on the doors, lintels, and walls above the tombs are in Hebrew, Aramaic, Greek, and Palmyrene.

BETROTHAL: MARRIAGE without preliminary b. (*shiddukhin*) is frowned upon in Jewish practice. Such b. does not create any matrimonial relationship and both parties are free to retract their promise of marriage. The aggrieved party, however, can claim reimbursement of loss actually suffered and demand compensation for humiliation. Suit for breach of promise is justified if the other side retracted any part of the agreed terms or if meantime some grave disqualification developed or came to light. The bridegroom, however, is urged on ethical grounds not to break off an engagement because of monetary disappointment. It is customary to draw up the terms of *shiddukhin* in a document called *tenaim* (i.e., conditions) which also specifies the penalties payable by the defaulting party. The non-fulfillment of the *shiddukhin* stipulations does not release the aggrieved party after marrage from his (or her) duties toward the spouse; the remedy to be sought is that for ordinary breach of contract.

BIBLE: The word "Bible" is derived from the Greek *biblia,* which is itself a translation of the Hebrew *sepharim* ("books") — the oldest term for biblical literature. In Hebrew the Bible is most commonly called *TaNaKH,* a designation formed from the initials of *Torah* ("Instruction", "Law"), *Neviim* ("Prophets"), *Ketuvim* ("Writings", "Hagiographa"). Other names are: *kitvei ha-kodesh* ("Holy Scriptures") and *mikra* ("Reading" — pointing to the fact that the Scriptures were read in public). Christians refer to the Hebrew Bible as the Old Testament (i.e., Covenant) in contradistinction to the "New Testament".

Canon: The Bible, which represents only a remnant of the far larger national literature of the ancient Israelites, was created over the course of more than a thousand years by a host of writers, many anonymous, and in various countries — the Land of Israel, Babylonia, and the adjoining areas. According to Jewish tradition, the Bible contains 24 books (though Josephus and others give the number as 22). These are enumerated as follows: *Torah* (also called *Ḥummash*, i.e., "five fifths" or Pentateuch) comprising Genesis, Exodus, Leviticus, Numbers, Deuteronomy (these names stem from the Septuagint; the Hebrew designations are based on the first significant word of each book) — 5 books. *Neviim* is divided into (a) *Neviim Rishonim* ("Former Prophets"): Joshua, Judges, Samuel (I & II), Kings (I & II); and (b) *Neviim Aḥaronim* ("Later Prophets"): Isaiah, Jeremiah, Ezekiel, the Twelve (Minor) Prophets — 8 books. *Ketuvim* contains Psalms, Proverbs, Job, the five *megillot* ("Scrolls"), Daniel, Ezra (including Nehemiah), Chronicles (I & II) — 11 books. If each volume is counted separately, the total number is 39. The body of sacred literature constituting the Bible is called the Canon (Greek for "measuring rod"; hence, "model", "standard"). In the Talmud canonical books are said "to defile the hands" (as a consequence of their holiness) and the verb *ganaz* "to hide" (i.e., remove from circulation) is applied to works excluded from the canon. Some of the latter are called APOCRYPHA (Greek for "hidden"), but many books excluded from the Hebrew canon are included in the SEPTUAGINT and thence in the Catholic Bible. Other uncanonical writings bear the name PSEUDEPIGRAPHA (Greek for "falsely inscribed") i.e., books spuriously attributed to biblical heroes (e.g. Enoch, Baruch). Though the ascriptions are imaginary, the spiritual quality of these works is often very high. The biblical canon evolved gradually. The process may have taken 500 years, and the tripartite division of the Bible possibly indicates the stages of canonization. It is conjectured that the *Torah* in its present form received scriptural status in the 5th cent. B.C.E.; the collection of the Prophets was completed about the beginning of the 2nd cent. B.C.E.; the composition of the Hagiographa was probably decided at the Synod of Yavneh (c. 90 C.E.), but at the beginning of the following century controversy still continued over Ezekiel, Proverbs, Song of Songs, Ecclesiastes, and Esther. Another theory holds that all three divisions developed concurrently and were finally canonized at the same time. All parts of the Bible are regarded as sacred and Divinely inspired; nevertheless, the Pentateuch enjoys a position of pre-eminence in Judaism. Among the factors determining the canonization of books was the presumed time of composition (the sacred book had to date from before the cessation of prophecy, which occurred according to Josephus in the reign of Artaxerxes Longimanus, i.e., Ahasuerus), the conformity of the work with the teachings of the *Torah*, and the language, which as a rule had to be Hebrew.

Text. Originally biblical mss. were not uniform (as the Dead Sea Scrolls, among other evidence, illustrate), and the text was consonantal, with only a few vowel-letters (like *Vav*, *Yod*, and *He*) used for partial vocalization. The desirability of having a standard text and the need to assist the reader, especially when the knowledge of Hebrew as a living language began to decline, in understanding and pronouncing the words correctly, gave rise to an intensive study of the scriptural text that extended over centuries and resulted in the division, and vocalization of Holy Scriptures, as well as the addition of signs for accentuation and intonation. The vast collection of notes aimed at preserving the purity and uniformity of the text is known as MASORAH ("tradition"), and the scholars (6th to 10th cents.) whose labors produced it are called Masoretes. They counted the letters; they indicated the *kerei* (how a word was to be read) when the *ketiv* (the written consonantal text) represented an unapproved reading; they pointed out *plene* and defective spelling, and numerous other peculiarities. Three vowel-systems were developed: Palestinian, Babylonian, and Tiberian. The first two are supralinear and the last which is used today, mainly infralinear. Aaron BEN ASHER (whose text has been generally adopted) and Moses BEN NAPHTALI (both of the 10th cent.) were the most famous Masoretes. Still later (13th cent.), numbered chapters and verses were introduced; but to this day the *Torah* and the Book of Esther (and in some communities other books as well) are always read in the synagogues from unvocalized, handwritten, parchment scrolls.

Language and Style. The Bible is written almost entirely in Hebrew. The only exceptions are Aramaic passages, which occur in Gen. 31:47; Jer. 10:11; Dan. 2:4-7:28; Ezra 4:8-6:18, and 7:12-26. The tapestry of Scripture is woven of both prose and poetry. The earlier narrative portions are written in pure, classical Hebrew, distinguished as a rule by a cadenced and elevated style; the later historical books are composed in less polished Hebrew, displaying Aramaic influence and looser syntactical construction. Biblical POETRY is not strictly metrical and has no rhyme but is marked by parallelism — "the rhyme of thought"; alphabetic acrostics are occasionally found. The prophetical utterances often combine exalted prose with poetry in a style that is at once noble, vibrant, and charged with deep emotion.

Content. The Bible is a great spiritual storehouse in which every facet of human life and experience and a variety of literary forms are represented: history and legend, poetry and prose, legal codes and fervent prayer, matter-of-fact statistics and chronologies, and prophetic exhortations. Though mainly concerned with the history of the Jewish people, its sweep is universal, and at the heart of everything is God, the Creator and Ruler of the universe. Genesis opens with an account of Creation, describes the origins of mankind, and ends with the close of the patriarchal age. The account of Israel's history begins in the Book of Exodus: the liberation from Egyptian bondage molds the Hebrews into a people, the Revelation at Mt. Sinai lays the foundation of their religion, and the erection of the Tabernacle gives them their first national shrine. For forty years the Israelites continue to wander in the wilderness and finally conquer parts of Transjordan. The Pentateuch concludes with the death of Moses. Apart from its narrative sections, the *Torah* contains considerable legislative material — hence also the customary translation of *Torah* as "LAW". The Former Prophets are historical works. They describe Joshua's conquest of Canaan, the troubled times under the Judges, the work of Samuel, the inauguration of the monarchy under Saul, its consolidation under David and Solomon, the partition of the country into two kingdoms, and the history of the divided monarchy till the destruction of the northern kingdom by Assyria (722 B.C.E.) and of Judah by Nebuchadnezzar (586 B.C.E.). The Later Prophets inclure the books of Isaiah, Jeremiah, Ezekiel, and the Twelve (Minor) Prophets (Hosea, Joel, Amos, Obadiah, Jonah, Micah, Nahum, Habakkuk, Haggai, Zephaniah, Zechariah, Malachi); the latter all combined are less in size than any one of the three major prophets. The Hagiographa is a literary miscellany. It comprises Psalms (a collection of devotional poetry); Proverbs (aphorisms on a variety of topics); Job (a philosophico-religious drama, mainly in poetic form, dealing with the problem of suffering); the *Megillot* ("Scrolls"), which include Song of Songs (a collection of love poems, read in the synagogue on Passover), Ruth (a tender idyll of the period of the Judges, read on Pentecost), Lamentations (elegies on the fall of Zion, read on *Av* 9), Ecclesiastes (reflections on the vanity of life, read on Tabernacles), Esther (a story of the persecution and deliverance of the Jews under Ahasuerus, read on *Purim*); Daniel (describing the history and visions of Daniel in Babylon); Ezra and Nehemiah (an account of the restoration of the Jewish people in the Persian Period); and Chronicles (a history, from a Judean and ecclesiastical viewpoint, of Israel from earliest times up to the Return under Cyrus in 538 B.C.E.).

Authorship. The talmudic view of the authorship of the various sections of the Bible is stated in *Bava Batra* 14b-15a; "Moses wrote his book (i.e., the *Torah*), the section of Balaam and Job; Joshua wrote his book and [the concluding] eight verses of the *Torah*; Samuel wrote his book, Judges, and Ruth; David wrote the Psalms incorporating therein the writings of ten elders, Adam, Melchizedek, Abraham, Moses, Heman, Jeduthun, Asaph, and the three sons of Korah. Jeremiah wrote his book, the Book of Kings, and Lamentations. Hezekiah and his council wrote [i.e., edited] Isaiah, Proverbs, Song of Songs, and Ecclesiastes; the men of the Great Assembly wrote [i.e., edited] Ezekiel, the Twelve Prophets, Daniel, and the Scroll of Esther. Ezra wrote his book and the genealogy of Chronicles down to himself". Modern scholarship does not accept this statement as factual. The critical tendency is to regard many of the biblical books as of composite structure, having been compiled from various sources and edited by one or more redactors. See BIBLE CRITICISM.

Theology. The vast expanse of time covered by the Bible and the great variety of minds that contributed to its making necessarily produced many levels of ethical and religious teaching in Scripture. Yet an underlying spiritual unity is apparent. Biblical religion may be defined as historico-ethical monotheism. God — Omnipotent, Omniscient, and All-Holy — is spirit and cannot be represented. He is known only by His acts. He created the world and by His providence continues to guide the course of history. Man is the peak of creation and is made in the Divine image. (The paradox of the imageless, infinite Deity reflected in corporeal, finite man has been a major theme in later theological discussion). God communes with man, and reveals Himself to mankind in various ways. The Prophets are the chosen instruments of His REVELATION, and are under compulsion to convey the Divine will to humanity. But man has free will; consequently he is accountable for his actions and receives punishment and reward. God is the Supreme Judge, and judges the whole world in righteousness (Gen. 18:25); but His grace far exceeds the severity of His punishment (Exod. 20:5-6). He seeks to save the sinner and readily forgives the penitent (Ezek. 18:23, 32). By creation, revelation, call to repentance and forgiveness God seeks man even before man seeks God.

It is generally taken for granted that ritual observance, being an act of worship, is an important link between man and God. But such worship must be wholeheartedly sincere, otherwise it becomes blasphemous, and the prophets denounced sacrificial rites, the holy days, and even prayer if divorced from righteous conduct (Is. 1:11 ff.). Idolatry and immorality are the two great dangers, and the prophets, pouring out their bitterest scorn on these man-made divinities, never tire of demanding social justice as the true service of God. The national aspect of biblical religion springs from its historical character. Israel is the "people of the covenant" of the Lord and His *segullah* ("special possession"). ELECTION, however, means not Divine favoritism but greater responsibility (Amos 3:2) and obedience under the COVENANT. In the final analysis Israel enjoys no higher status before God than other nations (Is. 19:25; Amos 9:7). Biblical prophecy envisages a Messianic era and "a new heaven and a new earth" when a new spirit will inform mankind. It is a vision of world peace and brotherhood, rooted in knowledge of the Lord emanating from Zion (Is. 2:2-4).

The Place of the Bible in Jewish Life. If the Jews are the human authors of the Bible, the Bible has in turn made the Jews the "People of the Book". It has served not so much as a compendium of early Hebrew history and literature, but as the perennial spiritual source of Jewish life. The *Torah* taken as God's word to Moses, and the prophetic and historical books as human utterance Divinely inspired, are the ultimate authority of Judaism in faith and practice. Both the *halakhah* and *aggadah* of Talmud and Midrash are but vast commentaries on the Holy Scriptures. The synagogal liturgy and worship are steeped in the biblical tradition. In every generation Scripture has been the foundation of Jewish education, and the study and interpretation of it formed a major part of Jewish scholarly and literary activity. Whereas in the many centuries of exile the B. was (in Heine's words) the Jews' "portable fatherland", in modern times it played an important part in shaping the self-awareness of Zionism and in stimulating both the rebuilding of Israel and the revival of the Hebrew tongue. The traditional faith in the unlimited meaningfulness of the B. is expressed in the rabbinic exhortation (*Avot* 5:25) "Turn it over again and again, for everything is in it". See entries on the individual books.

BIBLE COMMENTATORS, see **BIBLE EXEGESIS**

BIBLE CRITICISM: The critical study of biblical text. B.c. is generally classified as "lower" and "higher", although in practice the two categories tend to overlap. The former deals with textual problems; the latter with literary and historical questions such as authorship, date, composition, and purpose. Critical views concerning the Bible were already voiced by such scholars as Ḥivi Al-Balkhi (9th cent.), Moses Ibn Gikatilla (11th cent.), and Abraham Ibn Ezra (12th cent.). Spinoza (1632-77), who attributed the first 11 books of the Bible to Ezra, is regarded as the founder of modern b. c., and the French physician Astruc first formulated the documentary theory (1753). Higher criticism was given its classical form by Graf (1866) and Wellhausen (1876 and 1878) whose literary and historical theories constitute the basis of contemporary biblical studies. The documentary hypothesis, according to which the Pentateuch is a composite text made up of several sources or distinct "documents", is based on (a) the use of different names for God; (b) linguistic and stylistic variations; (c) discrepancies in both narrative and legal sections; (d) repetitions; (e) internal signs of composite structure. Variant readings in the ancient versions (augmented now by divergences in the Dead Sea Scrolls) and archeological discoveries likewise form part of the Bible student's critical apparatus. The principal conclusions of higher criticism are as follows: The Hexateuch (Pentateuch plus Joshua) is composed of extracts, fused together by redactors from four main documents, which can be further broken down into subdivisions. The documents are designated J (Jahwist, using the Divine name *YHVH*, 9th cent.), E (Elohist, using *Elohim*, 8th cent.), D (Deuteronomist, 7th cent.), and P (Priestly Code, 5th cent.). These or similar sources are also the component elements of the Former Prophets. Corresponding methods of analysis were applied to the Latter Prophets and Hagiographa with comparable results. In the last generation a reaction has set in against the most extreme conclusions of b.c. The documentary hypothesis remains dominant, but not unchallenged, and the new trend in biblical studies is toward greater conservatism.

BIBLE EXEGESIS: Exposition and interpretation of Scripture became necessary even before the canon of the BIBLE was finally determined, and oral comment probably accompanied the reading of the sacred text. In due course b.e. became a scientific discipline, supported by auxiliary sciences such as Hebrew and general Semitic philology, lexicography, and more recently archeology. Since all Jewish religious culture was related to the Bible and proceeded by way of interpreting Scripture, b.e. in its widest sense can be said to have been the major intellectual pursuit of the Jewish people for many centuries. Though traces of early exegesis and interpretation are preserved in the Bible itself, EZRA can be considered the father of the systematic exposition and teaching of Scripture

(Ezra 7:10; Neh. 8:1-8). Since he made the *Torah* the constitution of the new Jewish settlement in Israel, b.e. in the sense of expounding the Law assumed more than an academic interest and became a vital element of Jewish life and development. Two trends manifested themselves from the beginning: a naturalistic form of interpretation, later called PESHAT (the plain sense), and a homiletical method, termed DERASH (investigation) which sought to draw from the text halakhic and also religious and ethical teaching, or to find scriptural support for existing traditions. The latter type of exegesis (MIDRASH) is generally divided according to its content, into halakhic (legal, ritual) and aggadic (homiletic, non-legal) exposition. In time, HERMENEUTICAL rules were formulated: Hillel set out 7; Ishmael ben Elisha (whose principle, "The *Torah* uses the language of men", later became the watchword of rationalist commentators) 13, and Eliezer ben Yose 32 exegetical rules. Both the *peshat* and the *derash* types of interpretation were developed orally for generations before the body of exegesis cultivated in the schools was committed to writing. The effort to convey a relatively plain sense is discernible in the early Bible translations (e.g. TARGUM Onkelos, SEPTUAGINT) and in the work of the MASORETES. The *derash* was embodied chiefly in the two TALMUDS, the various MIDRASHIM (halakhic and aggadic), as well as the APOCRYPHA and Pseudepigrapha. However the Aramaic and Greek versions also contain considerable midrashic material. MYSTICISM, being related, like all else, to Scripture, also developed by uncovering hidden meanings in the sacred text. In particular the biblical account of Creation and the first chapter of Ezekiel provided fertile soil for esoteric teaching and mystical exegesis which reached its climax in the KABBALAH. Particularly important in the history of b.e. was PHILO, whose allegorical method of exposition (see ALLEGORY) was designed in order to interpret the Bible in terms of hellenistic thought. It paved the way for later Jewish philosophical interpretations of the Scriptures and served as a model for Christian allegorists. In the Talmudic and Gaonic Periods the exegetic pendulum swung far in the direction of *derash*, and although Jewish tradition subsequently came to recognize four methods of interpretation — *peshat*, *derash*, *remez* (allusion), and *sod* (mysticism), referred to by the mnemonic PaRDeS — the plain meaning of Scripture was frequently neglected in ordinary study (cf. the saying of R. Kahana in *Shab.* 63a). The reasons for this phenomenon were many, but undoubtedly the belief that God's word was an inexhaustible source of wisdom, and that its manifold meanings could be uncovered by recognized — albeit artificial — methods of exegesis, prevented concentration on the plain and literal meaning of the text. The exigencies of halakhic development as well as of edification through *aggadah* encouraged a tradition of often fanciful interpretation. A powerful impetus for exegetical studies was provided by the rise of Karaism (8th cent.). The KARAITES justified their rejection of the ORAL LAW (i.e., rabbinic tradition) by an appeal to Scripture and its evident meaning. The work of the Karaite exegetes, though not marked by great originality, nevertheless forced the rabbanite party to meet the challenge by exegetical efforts that could withstand criticism. The great defender of rabbinic orthodoxy against Karaism, SAADYAH Gaon, ushered in a new epoch of scriptural study. A pioneer in the field of philology and lexicography, his Arabic translation of the Bible was lucid without being slavishly literal, and his commentaries were distinguished by a more natural concept of scriptural exposition. The last two *geonim* (SAMUEL BEN HOPHNI and HAI) followed in his footsteps, but it was the Jewish scholars of Spain who were the true intellectual heirs of Saadyah, and many of their contributions to biblical scholarship remain significant to this day. The philological, lexicographical, and grammatical foundations of b.e. of the "golden age" were laid chiefly by Menahem ben Saruk and Dunash ben Labrat and developed by Judah Ḥayyuj and Ibn Janaḥ. Abraham IBN EZRA's brilliant commentaries sum up the mature erudition of the Spanish epoch. His uncompromising plain-sense approach is respectful of, yet unhampered by, traditional expositions, and even allowed for several obscurely worded critical suggestions (non-Mosaic Pentateuchal interpolations, and the composite authorship of the Book of Isaiah). Another eminent representative of the Spanish school is David KIMḤI whose commentaries are essentially based on plain exegesis, but pay more attention to midrashic tradition. In scriptural scholarship, as in his halakhic and philosophical writing, MAIMONIDES represents the zenith of Judeo-Spanish learning. His *Guide for the Perplexed* contains many exegetical discussions and detailed interpretations of passages, but his philosophical orientation and concomitant tendency to allegorical interpretation often produce that "philosophic Midrash" which assumed extreme proportions in later generations. At the opposite end of the scale stood the French and German Jewish exegetes, of whom Rashi was the most famous representative. He combined *peshat* with *derash*, while eschewing the more bizarre interpretations of the *aggadah*. The clarity of his annotations and his fine expository insight won unrivaled popularity for his Bible commentary. His grandson, R. SAMUEL

BEN MEIR, went still further along the road of *peshat*. NAHMANIDES' commentary on the Pentateuch is a classic of a different kind. Although a strict traditionalist, Naḥmanides remained true to his Spanish heritage in the rationalism of his exegesis, but he has room for Midrash and also sounds a new note in introducing allusions to "the hidden wisdom" of the Kabbalah. The latter becomes more explicit in the commentary of BAHYA BEN ASHER. Also among German ḤASIDIM mystical exegesis was cultivated, e.g., in the writings of ELEAZAR BEN JUDAH of Worms. The ZOHAR, the great classic of Spanish Kabbalah, which appeared at the end of the 13th cent., is essentially a kabbalistic Midrash. Biblical scholarship now suffered a decline; *derash* and *sod* gained increasing favor. A noteworthy exception is found in the discursive commentaries of Isaac ABRAVANEL, which were distinguished by general erudition and historic perspective; his work reflected the sunset of the Spanish epoch. Persecution continued to darken the mental horizons of Jewry. Study of the Talmud tended to replace that of the Bible, until attention to biblical studies almost became a sign of freethinking heresy. Moses MENDELSSOHN's German translation of the Scriptures and his *Biur* ("Commentary") were already a symptom of the new epoch that was dawning on Western Jewry. The *Biur* did not aim at originality but sought to reproduce the best interpretations of earlier expositors, yet it could not escape Orthodox condemnation. Among the most eminent Jewish commentators of the 19th cent. were the MALBIM and S.D. LUZZATTO. As the century advanced non-Orthodox Jewish scholars came increasingly under the influence of modern biblical criticism (Graetz, Geiger). In the mid-20th cent. many of the more extreme theses of classical criticism are no longer as popular as they used to be, and a more conservative tendency is developing. Leading Jewish Bible scholars of the 20th cent. (B. Jacob, U. Cassuto, Y. Kaufman, M. Z. Segal) — each to a different degree — seem to seek a middle way between higher criticism and Jewish exegetical tradition. (See BIBLE CRITICISM).

BIBLE, LOST BOOKS OF THE: The canonical books of the Bible represent only a remnant of early Hebrew literature, and Scripture itself mentions a number of source-books that have not survived. The oldest are two poetical works — *Book of the Wars of the Lord* (Num. 21:14) and *Book of Jashar* (Josh. 10:13; II Sam. 1:18). Among the historical books referred to are: *Words of Samuel the Seer*, *Words of Nathan the Prophet*, *Words of Gad the Seer* (I Chron. 29:29), *Chronicles of King David* (ibid. 27:24), *Acts of King Solomon* (I Kings 11:41), *Prophecy of Ahijah the Shilonite*, *Visions of Jedo the Seer* (II Chron. 9:29), *History of Iddo the Seer* (ibid. 12:15), *Chronicles of the Kings of Israel* (I Kings 14:19, etc.) and *Chronicles of the Kings of Judah* (I Kings 14:29, etc.) — the principal sources for the biblical Books of Kings and *Midrash* ("Commentary") *of the Book of Kings* (II Chron. 24:27).

BIBLE READINGS IN THE SYNAGOGUE, see **READING OF THE LAW**

BIBLE TRANSLATION: The primary purpose of translating the BIBLE was to meet the religious needs of Jews and Christians in worship and in study. Through translation the Bible, which has been rendered into more than a thousand tongues, exerted a formative influence on many languages, and enriched them with its idioms and phrases. The earliest translations were oral and in Aramaic; eventually they developed into the TARGUMS. They became a necessity when Palestinian Jews spoke ARAMAIC and needed a translation to follow the synagogue reading; the weekly portion was therefore read in both languages — twice in Hebrew and once in Aramaic according to the pious custom. Common to these versions are their fidelity to rabbinic exegesis and their avoidance of anthropomorphic and anthropopathic expressions. Of the pentateuchal Targums, that of ONKELOS (Aquila) is the oldest and adheres most closely to the original; the Palestinian Targum (Yerushalmi, Pseudo-Jonathan) contains much aggadic material; the third has been hitherto known as the fragmentary (Yerushalmi) Targum, but in 1956 a complete manuscript was discovered. There is also a SAMARITAN rendering of the *Torah*. The Targum to the Former and Latter Prophets, traditionally ascribed to Jonathan ben Uzziel, is in fact a continuation of Onkelos. The extant remains of a Palestinian Targum to the Prophets are fragmentary. The Targums to the Hagiographa, except for Psalms, are diffuse and of a midrashic nature. The Targum to Proverbs resembles the PESHITTA and is apparently of Christian origin. Though the Targums originated at an early period when Hebrew was first superseded by Aramaic, they received their final form in the 4th or 5th cent. C.E. The oldest written translation is the ancient Greek (*Koine*) version called the SEPTUAGINT ("*Seventy*", LXX). According to the Letter of Aristeas, the name derives from the fact that seventy-two Palestinian scholars translated the *Torah* (c. 250 B.C.E.) at the request of Ptolemy Philadelphus of Egypt. More probably the translation was undertaken for the benefit of the Alexandrian Jews. The rest of the Greek Bible was gradually completed by 100 B.C.E. The LXX is invaluable for the textual study of the Bible since the Hebrew original underlying it differed considerably from the Masoretic recension. The rendering of the earlier biblical books is fairly literal; that of the later books is more paraphrastic. In the 2nd cent. C.E. three further Greek translations were made. Aquila's is excessively literal and accords with R. Akiva's method of exegesis; the rendering of Symmachus is free and polished; Theodotion's, combining elegance with fidelity, is mainly a revision of the LXX on the basis of the Hebrew. These minor Greek versions are preserved in commentaries of the Church Fathers, who extracted them from Origen's *Hexapla*. The Syriac version, called *Peshitta* ("Simple"), was redacted in the 2nd cent. The Old Latin version or Itala (3rd cent.) is a translation of the LXX; but the Vulgate ("Common Edition"), composed by Jerome (4th cent.), is a graceful Latin rendering of the Hebrew and became the standard Bible of the Catholic Church. Later versions deserving mention include: Saadyah's in Arabic (*Tafsir*), 10th cent.; Moses Arragel's in Spanish, 1432; Martin Luther's in German, 1523-32; the English Authorized Version, 1611, and the Revised Version, 1885; the German translation of F. Rosenzweig and M. Buber, 1925-38; the English translation of the Jewish Publication Society of America, 1917, and its new rendering of the Pentateuch, 1962.

BIGAMY, see **POLYGAMY**

BIKKUR ḤOLIM, see **SICK, VISITING THE**

BIKKURIM, see **FIRST FRUITS**

BIKKURIM (Heb. "First fruits"): Last tractate of the Mishnah order *Zeraim,* containing three chapters with *gemara* in the Palestinian Talmud. It deals with the laws concerning the offering of FIRST FRUIT (cf. Exod. 23:19; Deut. 26:1-11), and contains a description of the *b.* ceremony in Second Temple times.

BILL OF DIVORCEMENT, see **DIVORCE**

BIMAH, see **ALMEMAR**

BINDING OF ISAAC, see **AKEDAH**

BIRDS; BIRDS' NESTS, see **ANIMALS, KINDNESS TO**

BIRKAT HA-KOHANIM, see **PRIESTLY BLESSING**

BIRKAT HA-MAZON, see **GRACE AFTER MEALS**

BIRKAT HA-MINIM (Heb.): The benediction (actually a curse) concerning MINIM. It constitutes the twelfth of the benedictions of the AMIDAH and was composed or copied from earlier sources by Samuel Ha-Katan at the request of R. Gamaliel who instituted it as a statutory part of the prayers. The liturgical cursing of heretical sectarians was meant to prevent them from participating in synagogue worship, and thus to force them out of the community. The text has undergone many changes and revisions, and the original wording cannot be reconstructed with certainty. The present opening *ve-la-malshinim* ("and for the informers") is a late substitution, but was particularly applicable in the medieval Jewish community.

BIRKHOT HA-TORAH: The blessings recited before studying the law and also before and after being called to the public reading of the *Torah.* The study of the law being considered a foremost religious duty, it has to be preceded, like any other religious performance, by the recitation of an appropriate BENEDICTION. Various formulae are quoted in the Talmud in the name of different teachers; some of them appear at the opening of the Morning Service which includes, in addition to prayers, also "study of *Torah*" in the form of quotations from the *Mishnah. B.H.* are also recited by individuals called to the reading of the Law (the original version being traditionally ascribed to Ezra on the basis of Neh. 8:4-6), the opening benediction being "Blessed art thou... Who hast chosen us from the nations and given us Thy law", and the concluding one "Blessed... Who hast given us the Law of truth, and hast planted everlasting life in our midst." Special blessings are also recited before and after the reading of the HAPHTARAH, and the reading of the Scroll of Esther on *Purim.*

BIRTH, see **CHILDBIRTH**

BIRTH CONTROL: According to the Midrash, the practice of b. c. goes back as far as the depraved generations before the Flood (*Gen. Rab.* 23:2, 4; Rashi on Gen. 4:19, 23). Explicitly the Bible mentions some form of b.c. only in connection with Onan whose conduct in "spilling his seed on the ground" while cohabiting with his wife was execrated as "wicked in the sight of the Lord" and punished by death (Gen. 38:9-10). There are references in the Talmud to the prevention of pregnancy and the subject is treated extensively in responsa works of the past two centuries, particularly in more recent times. While several Reform authorities sanction b.c. for social reasons in common with the more liberal Protestant views, the consensus of Orthodox rabbinical opinion strongly condemns the practice except for serious health reasons. Among the methods considered — always to be applied by the wife only — the highest preference is given to oral contraceptives, in principle already frequently mentioned in the Talmud and the codes as a "cup of sterility".

BIRTHDAY: No observances or celebrations are traditionally connected in Jewish custom with the anniversary of a person's birth, the sole such occasion mentioned in the Bible being Pharaoh's b. (Gen. 40:20). The only birthdays taken note of — because of their religious implications — are the 13th in the case of a boy (BAR MITZVAH) and the 12th for a girl (BAT MITZVAH).

BIRTHRIGHT: Rights inherent in the status of FIRST-BORN. B. is first mentioned in the Bible in connection with its sale by Esau to Jacob for "a mess of pottage" (Gen. 25:31-34). Jewish tradition ascribes particular significance to this sale, seeing in it the discarding of the spiritual heritage of Abraham by Esau who by virtue of his birth was entitled to be its inheritor. Before the institution of the hereditary priesthood, the first-born of each family was automatically designated as the spiritual leader of the home (Rashi on Gen. 25:31). In the Bible the hereditary "spiritual" b. is in several instances transferred from the first-born (Ham loses it to Shem; Ishmael to Isaac; Esau to Jacob; Reuben to Judah; Menasseh to Ephraim) thus illustrating the fact that entrance into the spiritual heritage (as opposed to the material inheritance which cannot legally be bypassed) is ultimately dependent upon merit. Maimonides codifies this principle when he states that although all hereditary offices pass to the first-born, this is only so when the first-born is fit to assume the responsibilities of office (*Hilkhot Melakhim* 1:7). See INHERITANCE.

BISHOP OF THE JEWS (in Latin *episcopus Judaeorum*): Term applied in medieval England to a *kohen*. In Germany it was sometimes used for a rabbi.

BITTER HERBS, see **MAROR**

BIUR, see **MENDELSSOHN, MOSES**

BIUR ḤAMETZ (Heb. "destruction of leaven"): The act of destroying, preferably by fire, any LEAVEN in one's possession on the morning of *Nisan* 14, in accordance with the rabbinic interpretation of Exod. 12:15 "even the first day shall you put away leaven out of your houses". To make sure that "no leaven shall be seen with you" (Deut. 16:4) during the PASSOVER festival, leaven should on the eve of the festival be either burned (*biur*) or disowned (*bittul*). Traditionally, both methods are followed, and after the burning, an Aramaic formula is recited by which ownership of any leaven that may have escaped detection is formally renounced. See also BEDIKAT ḤAMETZ.

BLASER, ISAAC BEN MOSES SOLOMON (also known as Reb Itzele Peterburger; 1837-1907): Russian rabbi and leader of the MUSAR movement. Rabbi of St. Petersburg 1862-1878, and from 1880-1891 head of the *yeshivah* in SLOBODKA, which was run on the lines of *musar* pietism. B. settled in Jerusalem in 1904. A disciple of R. Israel SALANTER, B. expounded his master's *musar* teaching in his work *Or Yisrael* ("Light of Israel").

BLASPHEMY (Heb. *gidduph*): The reviling of God, i.e., of His Holy Name, is punishable according to the Bible by stoning (Lev. 24:15-16). The Talmud restricts capital punishment to b. of the TETRAGRAMMATON: when using any other of the DIVINE NAMES or attributes, the blasphemer is subject only to corporal punishment (*Sanh.* 56a). B. — which is prohibited by one of the seven NOACHIAN LAWS — does not extend, as in other religions, to reviling of sacred institutions or customs. In order to avoid repetition of the b. during the trial, a special procedure, involving a substitution for the actual blasphemous phrase, is adopted in relating the evidence. However, since because of the substitution the court will not once have heard the exact words allegedly spoken by the accused and therefore cannot pronounce him guilty, the court is cleared upon the conclusion of the evidence and one of the witnesses repeats the exact words used. On hearing the blasphemous words the members of the court rend their garments as a sign of grief and pass sentence. Josephus, following a tannaitic tradition, records (*Ant.* 4:202) that the body of a person executed for b. was exposed unburied until sunset, the ignominy proclaiming the reprehensible and heinous nature of the crime. Despite the gravity of the offense, the blasphemer who does penance may nonetheless become reconciled with God. After Jewish courts no longer had authority to inflict the death sentence, b. was usually punished by EXCOMMUNICATION.

BLEMISH (Heb. *mum*): A physical defect which disqualified (1) a priest from performing his office in the Temple (Lev. 21:17-21; *Bekh.* chap. 7); and (2) an animal for use as a sacrifice (Lev. 22:20-25; *Bekh.* chap. 6). In addition to physical blemishes, the priest is further disqualified if he is born in unlawful wedlock, is in mourning, is in a state of drunkenness, or disheveled. Moral blemishes such as idolatry, homicide, or other major offenses, likewise disqualify him from the priestly office. Further blemishes which disqualify the levite from service include loss of voice (*Ḥul.* 24a) and being too young (Num. 4:43). Non-physical blemishes may also occur in the case of animals, e.g. if the animal had served as an object of worship. The reason for disqualification by b. is stated by the prophet Malachi (1:8) to be that a gift unacceptable to an exalted personality is surely so when the presentation is to God. Maimonides listed 50 types of b. disqualifying animals and 90 for priests. Blemishes on the person of parties contracting to a MARRIAGE — which could not have been known by the parties prior to the marriage, or which render intercourse between the parties unbearable — form valid reasons to vitiate the marriage bond. Moral blemishes are treated at length in numerous rabbinic passages, typical of which is the statement (*Kidd.* 70b) that "he who finds fault in others is influenced by the b. in himself."

BLESSING, see **BENEDICTIONS**

BLESSING AFTER DELIVERANCE FROM DANGER, see **GOMEL, BLESSING OF**

BLESSING AND CURSE: In Hebrew, the word *barakh,* commonly translated "bless", is used in the standard invocation to prayer (*barekhu et adonai* — "Bless ye the Lord") and in BENEDICTIONS for giving thanks and praise to God not only for His benefits but even for such misfortunes as one is called upon to suffer. "In exactly the same way as a blessing is uttered for boons, so is one uttered for misfortunes" (*Ber.* 54a). The common belief is that not only can God bring good fortune (blessing) or misfortune (curse) upon a person but that this power is also invested — albeit indirectly — in man, who can invoke God's b. or c. on others. The strength of this belief is illustrated by the competition of Jacob and Esau for the blessing of their father Isaac (Gen. 27). Prior to his death Jacob blessed his children (Gen. 49) and Moses the Children of Israel (Deut. 33). Balaam the heathen prophet was forced by a power greater than himself to turn his intended curses into blessings (Num. 23-24). The power of blessing and cursing is held to be very great; thus David on his deathbed urges his son Solomon to execute Shimei ben Gera because "he cursed me with a grievous curse" (I Kings 2:8) while the Talmud states "The curse of a sage — even when undeserved — comes to pass" (*Ber.* 56a) and "Regard not lightly the blessing of an ordinary person" (*Ber.* 7a). Specifically forbidden by the Bible is the cursing of God, parents, or the deaf; the penalty in the first two instances is death. See also PRIESTLY BLESSING.

BLESSING OF CHILDREN: Although the importance attached to parental blessing appears in many passages of the Bible (e.g. Gen. 27 and 49), the custom of blessing the children on the eve of the Sabbath (and in some rites also on Holy Days) is a much later innovation. The customary formula consists of the phrases "God make thee as Ephraim and Manasseh" (cf. Gen. 48:20) for boys, and "God make thee as Sarah, Rebecca, Rachel, and Leah" (cf. Ruth 4:11) for girls, followed by the Priestly Blessing (Num. 6:24-26). The parent places both hands on the head of the child while pronouncing the blessing. The b. is given to adult children as well. In the *Sephardi* rite the b. is also given after father or child have performed a religious function in the synagogue (e.g. *aliyah*). Special formulae of the b. exist for particular occasions, e.g. the eve of the Day of Atonement.

BLESSING OF THE NEW MOON, see **NEW MOON, ANNOUNCEMENT OF**

BLESSINGS OVER TORAH, see **BIRKHOT HATORAH**

BLESSING OVER LIGHTS, see **KINDLING OF LIGHTS**

BLOOD: Blood was regarded in the Bible as the vital element of all living things, as is clear from such verses as "the b. is the life" (Deut. 12:23). This is also the reason why Noah and his descendants were forbidden to consume the b. of animal flesh (Gen. 9:4): the consumption of b. was regarded as equivalent to eating the living animal. The prohibition against consuming b. is repeated several times in the Bible and is the basis of the detailed laws elaborated in the Talmud concerning the ritual preparation of meat. Even after an animal or bird belonging to a permitted species (Lev. 11:2-8; Deut. 14:4-6, 11) has been slaughtered in accordance with ritual regulations, the b. is still forbidden. The Talmud however limits the prohibition to b. in the arteries, which is removed by ritual slaughter or by cutting the veins, and to b. which has emerged on the surface of the meat. B. within the meat itself is permitted, but the surface b. must be removed by "kashering" (soaking the meat in water, salting, and rinsing) or by grilling the meat. Liver is regarded as containing so much b. that only grilling on an open fire is permitted. The b. of fish does not come under this prohibition, but so great was the abhorrence of b. by the rabbis that they extended the original prohibitions (e.g. by forbidding the eating of bread bloodstained from one's own gums); see DIETARY LAWS. Menstrual b. is considered especially unclean and the biblical regulations are further extended by the Talmud (see MENSTRUATION).

BLOOD AVENGER: The next of kin of a murdered man, duty-bound — in many societies — to avenge the murder on any member of the murderer's kin. Biblical law restricts blood vengeance to cases of accidental manslaughter, and provides ASYLUM in the six Cities of Refuge within the boundaries of which the slayer enjoys immunity from the b.a. (Deut. 19:1-10). Intentional murder must not be avenged by the b.a. but punished by regular processes of law (Exod. 21:12-14; Deut. 19:11-13). Royal authority seems to have intervened at times to halt blood vengeance (cf. II Sam. 14:11). The Talmud formulates detailed rules on the subject, but it is uncertain whether these reflect any particular historical reality. The rabbis discuss whether blood vengeance is a right or a sacred duty, who is permitted (viz. required) to act as b.a., etc. The Hebrew term for b.a. (*goel dam,* "blood redeemer") is indicative of ancient Israelite conceptions. God as *goel* ("redeemer") acts as Israel's next of kin in a relationship in which the functions of redeemer and avenger are identical.

BLOOD LIBEL: The accusation — frequently leveled in the Middle Ages, during the 19th cent., and propagated again during the Nazi Period —

that Jews use the blood of a Christian for their religious rites, particularly in the preparation of unleavened bread for Passover. The libel dates from pre-Christian times; Apion charged the Jews with annually fattening a Greek for sacrifice in the Temple (Josephus, *Against Apion* 2.8.95) and the Romans made the same charge against the early Christians. The first recorded accusation in the Middle Ages occurred in England, the alleged victim being William of Norwich in 1144. Hugh of Lincoln, who was found dead in 1255, is the subject of one of Chaucer's Tales. The accusation frequently served as an occasion or pretext for anti-Jewish outrages. Among the most notorious blood libels in the 19th-20th cents. were the Damascus Affair of 1840, the Tisza-Eslar accusation of 1882, and the accusation against Mendel Beilis in Russia, in 1912. During the Hitler persecution the allegation was constantly repeated by Streicher in his obscene anti-Semitic publication *Der Stürmer.* The allegation, which has been repeatedly proved as completely baseless, was formally and repeatedly denounced by the Popes.

BOAZ, see **JACHIN**

BODEK (Heb. "examiner"): Term applied to the official who inspects a slaughtered animal for its ritual fitness for consumption (see BEDIKAH). The inspection is usually carried out by the slaughterer himself, and a licenced ritual slaughterer is generally called *shoḥet u-vodek.*

BODY: The juxtaposition of b. and SOUL as representing the physical and spiritual, or evil and good, in man, is unknown to the Hebrew Scriptures. Indeed, there are no specific terms for b. and soul in biblical Hebrew. Man's creation is described as "the breath of life" breathed into the nostrils of man who was "formed of the dust of the ground" (Gen. 2:7). Even though "the dust returneth to the earth as it was, and the spirit returneth unto God who gave it" (Ecc. 12:7), no distinction between b. and soul is made during life. In rabbinic writings, the b. was sometimes regarded as the seat of passion and the cause of sin; yet both b. and soul were held jointly accountable for deeds committed. The human b. is deemed as the possession of God; man, as its custodian, is responsible for protecting it from mutilation, and Maimonides includes in his religious code a detailed regimen of diet, exercise, and other rules to ensure the health of the b. (*Hilkhot Deot* 4). In death, too, the b. is inviolable; hence the insistence on its speedy interment (cf Deut. 21:23) and the Orthodox opposition to CREMATION, DISSECTION, embalming, or any other violation of its integrity. The belief in the physical RESURRECTION, as well as in the incorporeality of God, belongs to the Thirteen Articles of Faith listed by Maimonides.

BOETHUSIANS: Religious-political party in the century preceding the destruction of the Second Temple, and for some time afterward. They were associated with the high priesthood and were close to, though not identical with, the SADDUCEES. Rabbinic tradition considers them primarily a religious sect, founded by Boethus, a heretical disciple of the mishnaic authority Antigonus of Sokho. Other scholars connect the B. with Simon ben Boethus, High Priest in King Herod's time; the family is thought to have belonged to the Benei Ḥezir, known from inscriptions up to the 2nd cent. C.E. The Talmud describes the B. contemptuously and characterizes them as arrogant and selfish.

BOOK: The high regard in which the Book of the Law (*Sepher Torah*) and other biblical and post-biblical books were held as instruments conveying or expounding God's will, and guiding man on the right path, has resulted in a Jewish tradition of love and reverence for books. Special laws govern the writing of and behavior toward biblical books in particular and religious books in general (e.g. a sacred b. that has fallen on the floor is immediately lifted up and kissed). Rabbinic and moralist literature devote much attention to inculcating respect for and care of books. Acquiring books and lending them to scholars and students who needed them was considered a meritorious religious act, particularly before the invention of printing when manuscripts were expensive and rare. Religious books that could no longer be used were not thrown away, but deposited in a storeroom or hiding-place; see GENIZAH.

BOOK OF CREATION, see **YETZIRAH, BOOK OF**

BOOK OF LIFE: The metaphorical concept of a B. of L. dates from the Bible (cf. Exod. 32:32; Mal. 3:16; Ps. 69:29); to be omitted or "blotted out" from the book means death. This idea was subsequently connected with the notion of an annual balancing of the heavenly books on the Days of Judgment, i.e., ROSH HA-SHANAH and the DAY OF ATONEMENT. In his examination of conscience during the penitential days, the Jew is bidden to think of there being three books — for the righteous, the average persons, and the sinners. If the individual's balance is positive, he will be inscribed in the B. of L. on the New Year, and the entry will be sealed on the Day of Atonement. Various additions containing references to the B. of L. are inserted in the *amidah* during the ten penitential days. The traditional New Year's wish "may you be inscribed [and sealed] for a happy year", refers to the same idea.

BOOK OF THE WARS OF THE LORD, see **BIBLE, LOST BOOKS OF**

BOOKS, BURNING OF: Jewish law forbids the burning of books that contain the Divine Name, even if they have become disused or are secular or heretical. Such books are put away to molder naturally (*Shab.* 116a; see GENIZAH). Despite this, R. Tarphon, in his vigorous denunciation of the "Books of the Sectarians" (probably in this context Judeo-Christians) declared that should such books come to his notice, he would unhesitatingly burn them "even should they contain the mention (of the Divine name)" (*ibid*). Thus the ceremonial burning of books became a symbol of arch heresy. Such a fate was actually meted out to the philosophical works of Maimonides during the fierce controversy which erupted over their doctrines, and they were publicly burnt in S. France in 1233. In recent years, the ceremonial burning by extreme Orthodox elements in New York of Mordecai Kaplan's Reconstructionist Prayer Book was a unique modern example. On the other hand Jewish books have often been consigned to the flames by non-Jewish authorities, notably the 24 cartloads of the Talmud burnt at Paris in 1242, the burning of Jewish books in Rome in 1332 and 1553, and the Nazi holocaust of all books by Jewish authors in 1933.

BOOKS, PROHIBITED: To the list of those who "have no share in the world to come" in the Mishnah (*Sanh.* 10:1), R. Akiva contributes "he who reads in external books", suggesting a prohibition against the reading of certain books. Among the books to which this ban applies (listed in the talmudic discussion in *Sanh.* 100b) the only one which can be positively identified is the Book of Ecclesiasticus from which the Talmud itself quotes extensively on various occasions. There is therefore reason to believe that the prohibition is only against public reading of such books and not private reading. Similarly the book of "Hamiram" (sometimes identified with Homer) mentioned as a forbidden book (*Y. Sanh.* 10:28), is regarded by R. Akiva as permitted, "as though one were reading an epistle". This assumption is strengthened by the fact that the term "external books" is applied to the Apocrypha which are "external" to the extent that they are not included in the canon (Mishnah *Yad.* 4:6). There is no equivalent in Judaism to the *Index Expurgatorius* of the Roman Catholic Church, though certain heretical books are by popular usage referred to in the Yiddish vernacular as *treif pasul* ("unfit and invalid"). In the Middle Ages, fierce controversy raged around rabbinical attempts to ban philosophical works, especially those of Maimonides, at least to readers under the age of 25. See CENSORSHIP.

BOOTHS, see **TABERNACLES, FEAST OF**

BORROWING, see **LOANS**

BRAZEN SEA (also **SOLOMON'S SEA**): A large basin for ritual ablutions in the Temple built by Solomon, said to hold "two thousand *baths*" — according to the Talmud, equal to a hundred and fifty times the size of a normal MIKVEH. According to the description in I Kings 7:23-26 it rested "upon twelve [brazen] oxen", an instance of animal representations in the Temple of Jerusalem.

BRAZEN SERPENT, see **NEHUSHTAN**

BREACH OF PROMISE, see **BETROTHAL**

BREACH OF TRUST: The only biblical laws relating to b. of t. refer to bailees. By analogy with the case of the guardian who must, if suspect, take an oath to the effect that "he has not put his hand to his neighbors' goods" (Exod. 22:10), others, such as a partner at the dissolution of joint interests who is suspected of wrongdoing by another partner, or a middleman suspected by a principal party, are obligated to take the same oath. An exception is the testamentary guardian who cannot be compelled to swear on mere suspicion but must however render full account. If a bailee falsely denies possession of the BAILMENT and his deceit is proved, he is rendered untrustworthy and consequently debarred from taking an oath or acting as a witness.

BREAD (Heb. *leḥem*): The Semitic word from which *leḥem* is derived originally designated a principal food, the main element of any meal. In Hebrew civilization this came to mean b., i.e., a baked dough prepared from one of the "five species of grain" (wheat, barley, rye, oats, and spelt). The blessing over the b. ("Blessed art thou... who bringest forth b. from the earth") is considered adequate for the whole meal and no separate BENEDICTIONS have to be recited over the individual elements. Hands should be ritually washed before partaking of b., and the full GRACE AFTER MEALS is recited only when b. has been eaten. A portion of the dough was formerly given to the priests (ḤALLAH), and twelve loaves of b. were kept on a golden table in the inner sanctuary of the Temple (see SHEWBREAD).

BREAKING OF THE VESSELS, see **KABBALAH; LURIA, ISAAC**

BREASTPLATE, see **EPHOD**

BREATH, see **SOUL**

BRIBERY (Heb. *shoḥad*): The conveyance of a gift in order to influence judgment; prohibited in Deut. 16:19. Whereas culpability extends both to the offer as well as to the receipt of b., the Bible directs its remarks in this connection primarily to the judge. The rabbis considered all forms of gift-taking by a judge as impairing his impartiality, no matter if the bribe was offered with a view to condemning the guilty or vindicating the innocent. The slightest courtesy or favor received often provided grounds for the self-disqualification of the judge. B. is mentioned as one of the twelve crimes which evoke the curse of Heaven (Deut. 27:25). The strictness of the laws concerning b. led in very early times, when the judge received no fixed stipend, to the practice of his receiving an equal fee from both parties. In order however to ensure the freedom and integrity of the judicial authority it gradually became the custom for communities to pay the judge's stipend from communal funds.

BRIDE, see **MARRIAGE**

BRIDEGROOM, see **MARRIAGE**

BRIDEGROOM OF GENESIS, BRIDEGROOM OF THE LAW, see **ḤATAN BERESHIT AND ḤATAN TORAH**

BROKERAGE: The function of an intermediary in any legal transaction. In Jewish law the broker is considered as an agent, but since he is paid for his services he is liable for loss, theft, or any personal negligence as is the paid bailee. In cases of dispute concerning the broker's activities, he may clear himself by oath if there are no witnesses and the broker insists that he was authorized to accept the terms realized. The marriage broker (*shadhan*), who acts as a go-between in arranging marriages, is also classed as a broker and is legally entitled to remuneration.

BUBER, MARTIN (1878-1965): Philosopher. He was active in the Zionist movement and achieved prominence in the intellectual life of Germany where he lived until settling in Palestine in 1938. His religious thought developed from mysticism to Jewish existentialism; he achieved distinction as a philosopher (*Life of the Dialogue, I and Thou*), as a biblical theologian and exegete (he translated the Bible into German together with Franz Rosenzweig), and as an interpreter of Ḥasidism. In his philosophy, B. was concerned with explaining the nature of the relation between man and his fellowman as an essentially personal, as distinct from objective, relationship. By extending his insights to the relationship between man and God, B. interpreted the Bible in a personal and "existential" fashion which made his thought a great influence on contemporary Christian theology. His views on man and the quality of genuinely human relationship have exerted considerable influence on philosophers, educationists, and even psychiatrists. As a humanitarian, socialist, and Zionist he believed, in terms of his philosophico-religious conception, that it was Israel's calling to respond as a nation to the challenge of a dialogic life with God. The elements of *halakhah* and practice which loom so large in the actual reality of historical Judaism play little or no rôle in B.'s religious philosophy. This may have been one of the reasons why his influence has been felt more strongly outside than inside traditional Judaism.

BURGLARY (Heb. *maḥteret*): A thief found breaking into a home may be killed by the owner (Exod. 22:1). It is assumed (*Sanh.* 62a) that the burglar, knowing that every man will do his utmost to defend his property, is prepared to kill if necessary. The owner may therefore anticipate the burglar and act first in self-defense. The Bible adds (*ibid.* v.2) "If the sun be risen upon him, there shall be blood-guilt for him", which is understood to mean that should it be clear that the thief has not come with the intention to kill but is nevertheless killed, the killer is guilty of a capital crime.

BURIAL AND BURIAL RITES: The only method of disposing of the dead according to traditional Jewish Law is by placing the body of the deceased in the earth or in sepulchers (see CATACOMBS). This practice is based on Deut. 21:23 which enjoins the decent disposal of the body of the publicly hanged criminal by burial on the selfsame day. Thus as even the convicted felon must receive an honorable b., it follows that to be denied b. is the greatest humiliation which can be inflicted on the deceased. The reverence attached to b. is an outstanding feature of Jewish practice. The task of ensuring a proper b. is regarded as one of the greatest acts of benevolence and the prohibition against deriving any benefit from the dead has resulted in the well-nigh universal custom of the responsibility for b. being assumed by communal organizations, known as "the Holy Brotherhood" (ḤEVRAH KADDISHA) rather than by private undertakers. According to Jewish law, b. must take place as soon as possible after death. The body is ritually washed (TAHARAH) and wrapped in a simple shroud. The use of a coffin is general in Western countries, as in biblical times (Gen. 50:26), but in Eastern countries and the State of Israel it is dispensed with. B. customs vary from country to country, but in general they are characterized by utmost simplicity. The body is borne to the grave on a bier and interred with a brief ceremony, all those present assisting in filling the grave, after which the mourners say KADDISH. Exhumation is forbidden except in two circumstances — for re-interment in a family grave or in the Land of Israel. Jews of priestly descent (*kohanim*) are forbidden ritually to contaminate themselves by contact with the dead or by too close a proximity (4 cubits) to a grave. *Kohanim* are therefore usually buried at the end of a row or in the front row to enable their relatives who are *kohanim* to visit the grave. Attendance at a funeral is regarded as an act of particular piety. After the interment those present form themselves into two rows through which the mourners pass, to be greeted with words of consolation. It is from this moment that official MOURNING commences. CREMATION — although forbidden by rabbinic tradition — is occasionally practiced by Reform Jews.

BURIAL SOCIETY, see **ḤEVRAH KADDISHA**

BURNING BUSH: The thorn-bush, possibly a wild acacia shrub, from which God spoke to Moses in the wilderness and called him to his prophetic mission (Exod. 3:1-10). The Divine appearance was in the form of a flame of fire, but though "the bush burned with fire... the bush was not consumed." The b.b. has often been taken, in homiletics and in art, as a symbol of Israel.

BURNT-OFFERING (Heb. *olah*, "that which is brought up"): A SACRIFICE which is burnt completely and therefore considered of particular holiness and slaughtered on the north side of the altar. It is *kalil* i.e., a WHOLE-OFFERING (Greek *holocaust*) completely offered upon the altar (after dissection), no part (other than the hide) being left for the consumption or use of either priest or donor. The *temidim* — daily morning and afternoon sacrifices in the Temple — were b.'s, as were the special Sabbath offering (Num. 28:10) and the New Moon offering (*ibid.* v. 11). The b., which according to rabbinic teaching atones for pride, could be brought as a voluntary sacrifice. It was obligatory in the service of the consecration of priests (Exod. 29:15); the purification of the leper (Lev. 15:15, 30); of women after childbirth (Lev. 12:6-8); and in connection with the vow of the Nazirite (Num. 6:11, 16). The b. was the only offering accepted from non-Jews.

BYZANTINE RITE: The prayer rite (MINHAG) of the Jews of the E. Roman Empire, akin in some respects to the Italian rite. The B.R. was contained in the *Maḥzor Romania* which was printed a number of times in the 16th and 17th cents., but was eventually superseded in Turkey and the Balkans by the *Sephardi* rite. Since the 18th cent. it has survived only in Corfu and Kaffa.

C

CABALA, see **KABBALAH**

CAIN AND ABEL: Oldest sons of Adam and Eve. The Bible (Gen. 4) relates the murder of the shepherd Abel by the farmer Cain as well as the latter's punishment. Legend tells that Cain was accidentally killed by his descendant Lamech. The rabbis cited Cain as an outstanding example of a sinner but also praised the sincerity of his repentance. In the 2nd cent. C.E. a gnostic sect, called the Cainites, practiced a thoroughgoing ANTINOMIANISM.

CALENDAR: The Jewish c., though extremely complicated, is so accurate that unlike the Julian and Gregorian calendars it has never had to be adjusted. Its special complications derive mainly from two factors: (a) the year is lunisolar ("bound lunar"); and (b) in fixing the c., religious convenience necessitated that certain festivals could not fall on certain days of the week (e.g. *Hoshana Rabbah* was not permitted to fall on a Saturday nor the Day of Atonement on Friday). Until Hillel II instituted a permanent c. based on calculations (c. 360), the fixing of the NEW MOON was determined by observation and the evidence of witnesses. During the earlier period, the practice of adding a second day to festivals (except for the Day of Atonement) was introduced for communities lying at a distance from Palestine, because it was doubtful on precisely which of two days the New Moon occurred. The length of the lunar month was established by the rabbis as 29 days, 12 hours, and 793 parts (thousandths). Ignoring the fraction, 12 lunar months in this system comprise 354 days. Since the solar year consists of 365 days (again ignoring the fractions), it was therefore necessary to make provision for a discrepancy of 11 days per year. This was achieved by intercalating seven leap months (Second ADAR) over the course of a 19-year-cycle. The 3rd, 6th, 8th, 11th, 17th, and 19th years are designated leap years and contain thirteen months (the year 5711, for instance, began such a cycle). Adjustments are made to provide for the fractions, and a completely recurrent cycle occurs every 371 years. With regard to the lunar months, the 12 extra hours accumulated over each month are provided for by making some months "defective" i.e., 29 days long, and others "full", consisting of 30 days. Ideally *Nisan, Sivan, Av, Tishri, Kislev,* and *Shevat* have 30 days and *Iyyar, Tammuz, Elul, Ḥeshvan, Tevet,* and *Adar* 29 (i.e., a strict alternation of full and defective months). However, because of the necessary adjustments, this regular alternation is not strictly followed, though no year may have less than five or more than seven "full" months. In a leap year *Adar* I has 30 days and *Adar* II 29. In the case of a "full" month both the 30th day of that month and the first of the next are celebrated as *Rosh Ḥodesh* (New Moon) since the second half of the 30th day actually belongs to the New Moon. In the case of *Rosh ha-Shanah,* the only festival of the Jewish c. to occur on the first of the month, it proved impracticable to rely on the observation of the New Moon of *Tishri,* as the information would have arrived too late to notify all the various communities of the advent of the NEW YEAR. It was therefore instituted that both the first day of *Tishri* and the second day of that month are to be observed equally as the New Year; thus of all the biblical festivals, *Rosh ha-Shanah* alone is observed for two days, even in the Land of Israel. (There was, however, a period during the Middle Ages when *Rosh ha-Shanah* was observed for one day only in Palestine). *Elul* is always defective, with the result that the 1st and 2nd of *Tishri,* are the two days of *Rosh ha-Shanah,* and are traditionally regarded as "one long day". As for the differentiation between NIGHT and DAY, the main concern of the rabbis was to establish the precise moment during the gradual onset of night between twilight and complete darkness when one day ends and the next begins, in order to determine the incidence, and more particularly the conclusion, of Sabbaths and festivals. Nightfall was established as that moment when three stars of the second magnitude become visible, estimated as the moment when the sun is seven degrees below the horizon. The Jewish c. is now reckoned from the date of creation which, on the basis of other biblical dates, is placed at 3760 B.C.E. To calculate Jewish dates one first deducts 1240 from Common Era date and then adds 5000 (for dates falling between *Rosh ha-Shanah* and Dec. 31 one adds another year); thus 1966 corresponds to the Jewish year 5726-7. A certain amount of agitation has occurred in recent years among non-Jewish circles for the reform of the c. in the interests of simplicity and business efficiency. Jewish opposition has been expressed to any proposal which would interfere with the invariable sequence of the seven-day week, since according to the Bible only the seventh day can be observed as the Holy Sabbath.

CALF, GOLDEN: Image for worship constructed by the Israelites at the base of Mt. Sinai while Moses was at the top of the mountain. After persistent importuning by the people, Aaron gathered together earrings and other gold ornaments, from which the calf was then fashioned. Upon discovering the calf Moses ground the gold to dust, but he managed to ward off Divine wrath from the Israelites (Exod. 32). Golden calves were not unusual in ancient Canaanite worship and were also established by Jeroboam at Dan and Bethel (I Kings 12:28-30). According to some scholars golden calves were not meant as actual representations of a deity but rather the pedestal upon which the invisible deity was enthroned. The sin of the g.c. is often stressed by the rabbis, who regarded it as the source of Israel's misfortunes (*Sanh.* 102a); they also endeavored to excuse and minimize Aaron's rôle in the incident.

CALF WORSHIP, see **ANIMAL WORSHIP**

CALUMNY, see **SLANDER**

CANAANITES: Ancient inhabitants of Palestine and Phoenicia. Canaanite mythology was in many ways more primitive than that of Egypt and Babylonia. At the head of the pantheon stood El and his consort Asherah. More important than these, however, was the storm and rain god Baal or Hadad, and the story of his death and resurrection is held by many scholars to symbolize the cycle of vegetation, as did also the ritual enactment of the death of Tammuz during the Canaanite New Year celebrations. This mythology, as well as the spirit of Canaanite fertility cults, were utterly alien to the Israelite ethos, some formal resemblances between Canaanite and Israelite temple ritual notwithstanding. The Bible repeatedly and insistently warns against Canaanite worship and customs (e.g. Exod. 23:23-4), and prohibits treaty or marriage relations with the C. (Deut. 7:1ff.) lest they seduce Israel away from the covenant with God and the Sinaitic code of morality (Lev. 18:3 ff.). Opposition to intermarriage is already reflected in the history of the patriarchs (Gen. 24:4; 28:6), though the Israelites did in fact later intermarry and contract alliances with the C. and often adopted Canaanite idolatry (e.g. Judg. 2:2; 6:8). But though Canaanite cultural influences are to be noted, and some even affected the literary forms of the Bible, Israelite religious culture succeeded in maintaining its original and revolutionary character largely uncontaminated.

CANDELABRUM, see **KINDLING OF LIGHTS; MENORAH**

CANDLES: In Jewish tradition the lighting of c. is characteristic of occasions both of joy and sorrow. As a symbol of joy it is an essential feature of the festive board on Sabbaths and festivals, the custom having been instituted by the Pharisees during the time of the Second Temple, and it has been suggested that the main reason for its introduction was in order to refute the Sadducees who interpreted Exod. 25:3 as a prohibition (later adopted by the Karaites) against the presence of light and fire on the Sabbath. The lighting of these c., together with the appropriate blessing, is the prerogative of the mistress of the household. A talmudic legend relates that the angels who accompany a man from the synagogue on Sabbath eve bless his home as soon as they see the lighted c. The verse, "For the soul of man is the light of God" (Prov. 20:27) has been taken as the origin of the use of c. in mourning rites. C. are kindled and placed at the head of the deceased, and are also lit during the week of mourning, on the anniversary of the death, and on the eve of the Day of Atonement. (See also Light; Menorah).

CANDLESTICK, see **MENORAH**

CANON, see **BIBLE**

CANOPY, see **ḤUPPAH**

CANTICLES, see **SONGS OF SONGS**

CANTILLATION, see **ACCENTS; CANTORIAL MUSIC**

CANTOR (Heb. *ḥazzan*): The term ḥazzan originally denoted a community official carrying out a variety of functions. The earliest references to the *ḥazzan* as leader of the congregation in synagogue prayer (*sheliaḥ tzibbur*) is found in the Palestinian Talmud, though they are regarded as later interpolations. At first there was no need for a professional rendering of the prayers as the congregation could be led by lay members. The necessity for a professional c. arose in the Gaonic Period because of the decline in knowledge of Hebrew and the incorporation into the service of piyyutim, many of which were the cantor's own compositions. The c.'s status in the community varied with the times. The qualifications for office were many, ranging from moral to artistic (e.g. *Taan.* 16a); the c. had to be of mature age, preferably married, with a pleasant voice and appearance, and well versed in scripture and liturgy. In the course of time, emphasis was laid almost exclusively on voice quality, and complaints were frequently leveled by the rabbis against the shortcomings of those cantors whose fervor was of a histrionic rather than religious nature. Various influences — including the operatic — shaped the singing style of cantors in the 19th cent. Several cantors of modern times have endeavored to raise the artistic standard of CANTORIAL MUSIC. With the emergence of modified services, characterized by less active participation of the congregation, the importance of the c. and choir has greatly increased. On the other hand Reform Judaism has tended to restrict the liturgical significance of the c., and in many congregations his function is performed by the rabbi assisted by a choir.

CANTORIAL MUSIC (Heb. ***ḥazzanut***): The term at first denoted only the melodic rendering of medieval *piyyutim* but later came to span the entire range of synagogal music. As such, its roots can be traced to the levitical songs of the Temple in which antiphonal or responsive singing must have played a significant part. Unlike the reading of the Bible, which is guided by a system of ACCENTS, c.m. possessed neither notes nor even predetermined melodies. The CANTOR was always free to exercise his own bent and talent, so long as he adhered to a certain traditional pattern. The Talmud (Y. *Bik.* 1) describes cantorial rendition as being of the recitative genre, stressing the text rather than the melody. Palestinian c.m., at its early stage, was uniform. Only with the rise of the Arab caliphate did c.m. assume diverse forms, the main division being between the *Ashkenazi* and *Sephardi* schools. There is also an independent Yemenite tradition as well as further subdivisions among the *Ashkenazim*, notably between Western and Eastern Europe. During the late Middle Ages the influence of church melodies occasionally made itself felt in *Ashkenazi* synagogue music, and rabbinic protests were voiced against these musical incursions. The *Sephardi* school developed under the influence of Arab music, while the *Ashkenazi* variant continued to be colored by European trends. In the late 16th cent. Solomon de' Rossi of Mantua attempted to introduce mensural and polyphonic music into the synagogue according to the style of the Italian Renaissance but his success was short-lived. The German Reformers of the early 19th cent. sought to modernize the synagogue service by imitating the style of contemporary church music. The 18th-19th cents. saw the beginning of systematic musical study by cantors: the Viennese cantor Solomon Sulzer set traditional material in modern forms, Lewandowsky composed c.m. in contemporary style, and Idelsohn initiated scientific research into c.m. Since 1948, the leading U.S. rabbinical seminaries have established schools of c.m.

CAPITAL PUNISHMENT: Although biblical law specifies the death sentence for various types of crime, this form of punishment was rarely carried out in practice. Rabbinic interpretation of biblical law made it almost impossible to sentence a person to death, by requiring first of all two witnesses to the crime and secondly that the perpetrator be given specific warning, prior to his actual committing of the crime, as to the gravity of the act and its punishment. Thus the death penalty in the Bible came to be in time no more than an indication of the seriousness of a sin. Indeed, a court which over a period of 70 years condemned even one person to death was considered by some rabbis of the Talmud to be a "bloodthirsty" court. The offenses for which biblical law orders the death penalty are: murder; adultery, incest and certain other sexual sins; blasphemy; idolatry; desecration of the Sabbath; witchcraft; kidnaping; striking or dishonoring parents. Capital cases may be tried only by a BET DIN of at least 23 judges. Methods of execution are by stoning, burning, slaying with a sword, and strangulation, depending upon the crime. Strangulation is the method of execution in all cases where the manner of capital punishment is not specifically described in the Bible. Hanging is not permitted as a method of execution, and the reference to hanging in Deut. 21:22 is interpreted as meaning exposure after death, to be imposed in the case of idolaters and blasphemers. According to later rabbinic interpretation, stoning should take the form of throwing the guilty person from an elevation. The rabbinic definition of burning (pouring molten metal down the throat of the condemned individual) also differs from what is ordinarily meant by the term, though the Sadducees disputed with the Pharisees on this question. Long before the destruction of the Temple, c.p. was not considered to be within the competence of the Sanhedrin and was placed in the hands of the Roman authorities. Rare cases of c.p. decreed by Jewish courts are mentioned, however, in the literature of the Middle Ages. In the State of Israel c.p. is abolished except in cases of genocide and wartime treason.

CAPTIVES: The Bible makes no provision for the treatment of c. taken by Israelites, with the exception of the laws concerning the marriage of an Israelite and a captive woman (Deut. 21:10-14). The Talmud and other Jewish sources did however concern themselves with the very real problems facing Jews in captivity. Taking the catastrophes enumerated in Jer. 15:3 as representing an ascending scale of punishment, the rabbis regarded captivity in foreign lands as worse than death or famine (*Bava Batra* 8a). Consequently, the ransoming of c. was regarded as the most sacred duty a Jew could fulfill, taking precedence over all other form of benevolence or charity. One was even permitted to use money originally collected for another cause in order to provide the necessary funds. A woman taken into captivity by foreign soldiers was on her release barred from marrying into the priesthood, and if the wife of a priest she had to be divorced. The extreme lengths to which Jewish communities were willing to go in order to redeem their brethren forced up the ransom price of Jewish c. and as a measure of self-protection an enactment was promulgated forbidding the ransoming of a captive at a price higher than the normal value, unless in exceptional circumstances (*Git.* 45a). Among the notable captives in Jewish history may be mentioned Moses ben Enoch (10th cent.), who was taken by a Moorish pirate in the Mediterranean. Ransomed by the Cordova community, he later laid the foundations for the study of Talmud in Spain. When R. Meir of Rothenburg (13th cent.) was imprisoned by Emperor Rudolf and held to ransom in Alsace he refused to allow his community to provide the necessary funds for his release, lest it encourage the authorities to blackmail other communities by imprisoning and holding their rabbis for ransom.

CARCASS (Heb. *nevelah*): The body of an animal or creature which died other than by valid ritual slaughter (SHEḤITAH) or as prey of a wild beast (see TEREPHAH) is called *nevelah.* A c. may not be eaten but is to be given to a resident alien or sold to a non-Jew (Deut. 15:21). One who touches or carries a piece of c. contracts ritual impurity. The law of c. applies both to animals which are normally permitted as food and to those which are forbidden. A limb torn from a living animal (EVER MIN HA-ḤAI) is also considered c.

CARO, JOSEPH, see **KARO, JOSEPH**

CASPI, JOSEPH BEN ABBA MARI (1297-1340): S. French commentator and philosopher; author of a commentary on Maimonides' *Guide to the Perplexed* and of Bible commentaries (stressing literal interpretations of the text). Some of his philosophical conclusions (e.g. regarding the eternity of the universe) and his naturalistic explanations of biblical miracles were condemned as heretical by many rabbinical authorities.

CASTRATION: The Hebrews were the only nation of antiquity to enact a religious prohibition against the emasculation of men and even animals. Originally the biblical interdict only stipulated the exclusion of castrated animals from serving as sacrifices on the altar (Lev. 22:24) and of him "that is crushed or maimed in his privy parts" from entering "into the assembly of the Lord," i.e., from marrying within the Jewish congregation (Deut. 23:2). In the Talmud and codes the prohibition is extended to include any impairment of the male reproductive organs in domestic animals, beasts, or birds as well as in man, as well as the c. of a person who is already impotent (*Shab.* 110b). The problems which this raised for animal husbandry are discussed in halakhic literature. See also STERILIZATION.

CASUISTRY, see **PILPUL**

CATACOMBS: Subterranean galleries with the sides hewn out to accommodate the dead; a burial vault. This method of BURIAL was typically Jewish and detailed descriptions of it are given in the Talmud. Many specifically Jewish c. have been discovered in Rome (where the system was also adopted by Christians) and they contain such characteristic Jewish symbols as the seven-branched candelabrum, the *lulav,* and the *etrog;* the inscriptions are in Greek and Latin, with some in Hebrew. Examples of this method of burial can be seen in the Herodian family sepulcher and the graves of the Sanhedrin in Jerusalem, as well as in the extensive array of 2nd-4th cent. sepulchers at BET SHEARIM used by Jews from all parts of the Middle East. This method of burial in Rome ceased with the sack of the city by Alaric in 410.

CATECHISM: A compendium of instruction, mostly in the form of questions and answers, designed for children and uneducated persons. It was especially favored as a means of instruction for prospective proselytes. The earliest known example of a c. is contained in the Didache, a Christian manual of instruction for converts dating probably from the 2nd cent.; research has shown that the c. part was originally a Jewish manual of instruction and was later adopted for Christian use. But as a rule Jewish religious instruction never resorted to the c.-type of literature, insisting rather on the study of the basic texts — Bible, Mishnah, and Talmud. Probably the earliest attempt to introduce the c. into Jewish literature was the *Lekaḥ Tov* of Abraham Jagel of Venice (1587). Although it went through a number of editions, the author's hope for its use as a textbook in schools was never fulfilled. Since the Emancipation Period, scores of such manuals have been published, being particularly favored by Reform Judaism in the 19th cent. Question and answer handbooks setting forth rules of circumcision and ritual slaughter (*sheḥitah*) have been very common.

CELIBACY: As the propagation of the race through MARRIAGE is a cardinal religious precept c. is strongly frowned upon by Jewish law, and celibates are scarcely ever mentioned in the Hebrew Bible or the Talmud. Neither the ascetic habits of the Nazirite (Num. 6:1-21) nor the sacred duties of the priesthood (Lev. 21:1-15) included c. among their restrictions and acts of self-denial, though, according to Josephus, c. was practiced among Essene groups. Rabbinic law particularly requires religious leaders to be married, and if not they are debarred from public office. C.

is condoned only in exceptional cases, like that of the talmudist Ben Azzai who said: "My soul is fond of the Law; the world will be perpetuated by others" (*Yev.* 63b); but far from being positively recommended, c. is only tolerated in such cases of men who are absorbed in religious studies and who do not feel the power of sexual temptation. While advocating self-control and a measure of abstinence, moralists and kabbalists insisted that religious perfection could be achieved only in the married state.

CEMETERY: A plot of ground set aside for the burial of the dead. Various names for c. are used in the Bible and Jewish tradition, such as "the house of graves" (Neh. 11:3), "the house of eternity", and the euphemistic "house of the living" (based on Job 30:23). Since dead bodies, and hence also graves, are a source of ritual impurity, the c. is usually situated beyond town limits. The c. is also invested with a certain sanctity, and any activity therein which might tend to show disregard for the dead, such as eating and drinking or pursuing mundane occupations, is forbidden. Frequently a c. also contains buildings for the performance of BURIAL RITES (see TAHARAH). Graves are usually allotted in strict rotation, conforming to the notion of death as the great leveler. Exceptions are priests, who are usually interred in plots accessible to relatives, and family graves. In some cemeteries special sections are set aside for men to be honored. Suicides as well as apostates and men of evil repute, are buried outside the line of graves, near the c. wall. According to Jewish law, however, this discriminatory practice does not apply in the case of a suicide of unsound mind, and as this is the usual verdict today the regulation is largely disregarded. Various customs exist with regard to visiting graves; this is generally done on anniversaries of deaths, on fast days, during the month of *Elul,* and on the eve of the Day of Atonement, but the rabbis warned against visiting cemeteries too often and suggested that visits should not be made more than once every thirty days. (See also CATACOMBS).

CENSORSHIP: Rabbinic law prohibits the reading of heretical or immoral books (cf. *Sanh.* 100b). To ensure that a book contained no objectionable matter, the custom arose of prefacing approbations (see HASKAMAH) by eminent rabbis to printed works. Regular c. of books existed mainly in relation to the non-Jewish world. The c. of Hebrew books for the purpose of removing words or passages considered offensive to Christianity was undertaken from time to time during the Middle Ages on the instructions of government or church authorities, and the practice was continued in Russia until the end of the Czarist regime. At its most extreme, c. took the form of seizing and burning all available copies of the Talmud and other works. More generally it consisted either of orders to replace such words as *goy* ("gentile") with "Samaritan" or "idolater" (to show that the reference was not to Christians) or of expunging whole passages. An example of this last type of c. was the extensive expurgation of the last chapter of Maimonides' *Mishneh Torah,* where whole passages were deleted which referred to Christianity (as well as Islam) as a relative advance — though one based on error — toward the acknowledgment by the entire world of the sovereignty of God. The Papal Bull of 1554 allowing Jews to possess only those books that were not considered blasphemous gave the signal for a systematic c. of Jewish books in Italy; as a result of this c., which was often undertaken by apostates, all passages regarded as hostile or contradictory to Christian doctrines were blacked out. To prevent Christian c. from tampering with Jewish books rabbinic authorities sometimes instituted their own pre-c. Another case of self-censorship is to be seen in the deletion by *Ashkenazi* Jews of a sentence from the *Alenu* prayer in the face of constant unjustified allegations that the passage in question was meant as a disparagement of Jesus. The *Sephardi* liturgy however retains the formula, and it has been restored in the *Ashkenazi* prayer book in the State of Israel. See BOOKS, PROHIBITED.

CENSUS: The Bible contains many accounts of a c. being taken of Israel, but at the same time there was also a prohibition against numbering people directly. This prohibition, which is very widespread, is based on the superstition that numbering implies limiting. In the case of the Bible there is also the idea that to take a c. is to take stock of one's own strength (particularly of one's military power) and hence to lack the necessary trust in God. This idea is reflected in the regulation in Exod. 21:2 "When thou takest the sum of the children of Israel after their number, they shall give every man a ransom of his soul unto the Lord when thou numberest them, that there be no plague amongst them when thou numberest them." When David persisted in taking a c. of the children of Israel despite the objections of his military commander Joab, a pestilence struck the people (II Sam. 24), i.e., the numbers he wanted to count decreased as a result of his action. Various stratagems are popularly employed to avoid counting persons. Thus it is common to tell whether a religious quorum of ten males is on hand by numbering those present through the recitation of a biblical quotation containing ten words (e.g. Ps. 28:9).

CENTRAL CONFERENCE OF AMERICAN RABBIS: An organization of REFORM Rabbis in the U.S. and Canada, with a few members in other parts of the world. Founded in 1889 by Isaac Mayer WISE, by 1964 it had a membership of over 800. The C.C.A.R. created a uniform prayer book for Reform Congregations (twice revised) and has produced other written aids to worship, including musical hymnals, a Passover *Haggadah,* and a rabbi's manual suggesting procedures for weddings, funerals, and other ceremonial occasions. In the early part of this century, the Conference tended to adopt a neutral or critical attitude toward Jewish nationalism despite the fervent pro-Zionist position of some prominent members like Stephen S. Wise and Abba Hillel Silver. A sharp reversal of this attitude commenced in the 1930's when the Conference began to adopt pro-Zionist attitudes. This was accompanied by a general tendency to return to Hebrew in the service, and a more positive attitude toward ritual in the synagogue and in family life. Another traditional position has been a strong belief in the need for separation of church and state in America, and also in the State of Israel. In addition to its stands on public issues the Conference, in conjunction with the UNION OF AMERICAN HEBREW CONGREGATIONS, handles internal rabbinic placement, and other practical matters.

CEREMONIAL LAWS (in Heb. *mitzvot maasiyyot* "practical observances"): The emphasis upon the importance and validity of c.l. as outward symbols and rituals which in their totality combine to create a specific way of life expressing itself in action is a chief characteristic of traditional Judaism, imposing a discipline whereby fealty to God is expressed by a series of actions apart from any specific theological beliefs or moral code. Outstanding examples of such ceremonies are the DIETARY LAWS and the injunctions mentioned in or derived from the first and third paragraphs of the SHEMA (Deut. 6:4-1 and Num. 15:37-41), concerning the putting on of phylacteries (TEPHILLIN), the fastening of a MEZUZAH to the doorpost of a house and on city gates, and the wearing of fringes (TZITZIT) on one's garment. Nearly every festival has its own specific ceremonial object or practice: unleavened bread on Passover, the SHOPHAR on the New Year, fasting on the Day of Atonement, the SUKKAH, FOUR SPICES, and HOSHANOT on the Festival of Tabernacles, the HAKKAPHOT on *Simḥat Torah*, KINDLING OF LIGHTS on Sabbath, KIDDUSH and HAVDALAH at the conclusion of Sabbaths and festivals. Although attempts have continually been made to interpret and justify these ceremonies as expressions of inner spiritual and moral thoughts and values, the absence in many instances cf an understandable reason was never accepted by Orthodox Jews as an excuse for abandoning any of these traditional practices. The rabbis describe c.l. such as the prohibition against eating swine's flesh or wearing garments of mixed wool and linen as "laws which are ridiculed by the Evil Inclination and the heathens", and they taught that "a Jew should not say 'I do not eat pork because I do not like it' rather 'I would like to eat it, but what can I do seeing that the *Torah* has forbidden it?'" (*Siphrei, Ked.* 20). Authority for such incomprehensible and paradoxical laws as that of the Red Heifer (Num. 19:1-22) is sought in God's sovereign will. Indeed one even learns that understanding the reason for a c.l. may be an inducement to neglect: "in two instances when dealing with the laws pertaining to kings (Deut. 17:16-17) the *Torah* states the reasons for its dicta and as a result the wisest of men (Solomon) went astray with regard to these laws" (*Exod. Rab.* 6:1). Theologically the purpose of c.l. is expressed by the benediction which precedes every performance of a ritual act: "Blessed art Thou O Lord... who has sanctified us by His commandments, and commanded us to..." Often there are indications that the purpose of the outward act is to inculcate an inner frame of mind. Thus when enjoining the wearing of ritual fringes the Bible adds "that you may look upon it, and remember all the commandments of the Lord and do them, that you do not go about after your own heart and after your own eyes, after which you used to go astray, that you remember and do all My commandments" (Num. 15:39-40) — the implication being that the outward action recalls man to his spiritual responsibilities. Similarly Exod. 12:26 ff. indicates that the Passover ritual is designed to elicit an understanding of the Exodus and its significance. The same thought finds vivid expression in a talmudic passage (*Men.* 43b), "Beloved are Israel, for the Holy One, blessed by He, has surrounded them with precepts — R. Eliezer ben Jacob said 'Whosoever has phylacteries on his head, phylacteries on his arm, fringes on his garment, and a *mezuzah* on his doorpost, is certain not to sin.'" An early example of the widespread tendency to invest an outer action with inner spirituality is to be found in a Mishnah (*R.H.* 3:8) dealing with two ceremonial acts of Moses, the holding of his hands aloft during the war against the Amalekites (Exod. 17:11) and the making of the Brazen Serpent (Num. 21:8): "'And it came to pass, when Moses held up his hand that Israel prevailed, and when he let down his hand Amalek prevailed.' Could then the hands of Moses promote victory or cause defeat? The passage teaches that when the people of Israel direct their thoughts on high and make their hearts subservient to their Father in Heaven, they prevail; otherwise they are defeated. Similarly the verse 'make thee a brazen serpent and set it on a standard, etc.'; could the serpent then decree death or life? No! It is to teach that when the people of Israel direct their thoughts on high and make their hearts subservient to their Father in Heaven, they are healed, otherwise they wither." Gradually under the influence of medieval mystics and philosophers, this tendency to find spiritual meaning in outward ceremonial acts became more and more common, and *kavvanot* ("spiritual meditations" or "thought concentrations") were composed on the inner meanings of these outward acts and introduced into the prayers. Their purpose was partly to prevent a purely mechanical performance of the ceremony. Nevertheless rabbinic thought continues to stress the elements of unquestioning obedience and insists that a rational interpretation of the c.l., however plausible and acceptable, does not necessarily explain the true reason for their injunction. The rabbis discuss whether "commandments require intention" or whether mere mechanical performance is sufficient (cf. *Eruv.* 95b) and though the former view prevails, the latter is also propounded with authority. R. Judah Ha-Nasi counseled, "Be as heedful of a light commandment as of a grave one, for thou knowest not the reward granted for the performance of each commandment"(*Avot* 2:1). In a similar vein the rabbis point out that the only two commandments which promise long life upon earth are the "gravest of the grave" — the duty of honoring parents (Deut. 5:2) — and the "lightest of the light" — the injunction to send a mother bird away before raiding her nest (Deut. 12:6, cf. *Kidd.* 39b). Among Conservative Jews, attitudes concerning c.l. range from those cited above to ones identified more with the Reform movement. In general Conservatism has interpreted revelation as an historical process whereby the Jewish people has sanctified its customs, thus investing them with a meaning and permanence lacking in mere folkways. However, given this consensual base, there is wide divergence of opinion among Conservative authorities as to the precise implications of a history-oriented interpretation of revelation. Some draw conclusions no different from those of Orthodoxy, while others call for varying degrees of change, from slight adjustments to the abrogation of whole ceremonies and rituals and the creation of new ones. Classic Reform rejected ceremonies altogether as it considered them to have only a time-bound significance. Modern Reform, however, is witnessing a return to many of the traditional forms, in an acknowledgment of their value as spiritual and educational instruments and as a means of fostering Jewish loyalty.

CHAIR OF ELIJAH, see **CIRCUMCISION; ELIJAH**

CHAJES, TZEVI HIRSCH (1805-1855): Galician rabbi and scholar. Together with Nachman Krochmal and S.J. Rapoport, C. was a pioneer of Wissenschaft in Galicia, but as an Orthodox Jew his conclusions were less extreme than theirs. He was the author of many studies, including introductions to Targums and Midrashim; *Torat Neviim* ("Law of the Prophets") which demonstrated the relationship between the Written and Oral Law; and an introduction to the Talmud which classified the legal content and analyzed aggadic methods and characteristics.

CHANGE OF NAME: The Bible relates several instances in which God changed a person's name (Abram to Abraham, Sarai to Sarah, Jacob to Israel); the c. of n. symbolically implies investing a person's life with new significance. The custom of changing the name of a person who is dangerously ill is mentioned in the Talmud (*R.H.* 16b) and explained as a method of avoiding the Divine decree and misleading the angel of death. This custom is still extant in Orthodox circles; the change is conferred at a short ceremony in which charity is donated in behalf of the invalid, a blessing is recited, a formula read announcing the new (additional) name, and a prayer recited asking "new life" for the bearer of the new name.

CHANTING, see **ACCENTS; CANTORIAL MUSIC**

CHAPLAINS: The appointment of specific chaplains as part of the military establishment is a comparatively recent innovation in military history, although the "priest anointed for war" — a talmudic term for the priest referred to in Deut. 20:2 — could possibly be regarded as a prototype. In modern times, the first Jewish c. were appointed during the U.S. Civil War, while the first Jewish chaplain to the British Army was officially appointed in 1892. The chaplaincy service was considerably developed during World War I. During World War II there were 311 Jewish c. in the U.S. forces, organized by a chaplaincy committee of the National Jewish Welfare Board representing Orthodox, Conservative, and Reform bodies. Jewish c. were also appointed in other countries, including France, pre-Fascist Italy, and pre-Nazi Germany. With the establishment of the State of Israel, a chief rabbi was appointed to the Israel army with the rank of *aluph-mishneh* (Lt. Col.) and serving under him a chaplaincy system to supervise *kashrut*, burials, etc. A chaplain is attached to each brigade and a chaplain-sergeant to each battalion.

CHARIOT MYSTICISM, see **MAASEH MERKAVAH**

CHARITY (Heb. *tzedakah*): The Hebrew word *tzedakah*, which in the Bible refers to any kind of righteous conduct, is limited in the Talmud to mean one aspect of righteousness, namely, the giving of alms or assistance to the poor through material gifts. For all other acts of benevolence or kindness the phrase GEMILUT HESED (or *ḥasadim*) is employed, and the distinction between the two types is defined by the following passage: "In three respects *gemilut ḥasadim* is superior to *tzedakah. Tzedakah* can be performed only with one's material possessions, *gemilut ḥasadim* both in kind and in personal service. *Tzedakah* can be given only to the poor, *gemilut ḥasadim* to both rich and poor. *Tzedakah* can be performed only for the living, *gemilut ḥasadim* for the living and the dead" (*Suk.* 49b). Although *tzedakah* is regarded as a lower expression of social virtue and ethics as compared to *gemilut ḥasadim* (the latter has "no fixed measure" and is of "the things the fruit of which man enjoys in this world, while the stock remains for him in the world to come" — cf. Mishnah, *Peah* 1:1 — and is one of the three pillars upon which the world stands — *Avot* 1:2), the rabbis nevertheless also extol the virtue of c. in the simple sense of almsgiving as one of the greatest of good deeds. Thus R. Eleazar finds in Prov. 21:3 proof that the giving of c. is greater than "the sacrifice of all the sacrifices". Provision for those in want has at all times been regarded among Jews as a sacred duty. The very use of the word *tzedakah* shows that the relief of poverty is a matter of duty and not voluntary philanthropy. This duty will never end as long as "the poor shall not cease out of the land" (Deut. 15:11), and the prophet enjoins man to "deal thy bread to the hungry, and that thou bringeth the cast-out poor to thy house. When thou seest the naked that thou cover him, and that thou hide not thyself from thine own flesh" (Is. 58:7). Failure to give c. constitutes "hiding thyself from thine own flesh". The rabbis lay greatest stress upon the spirit in which c. is given, and the extent of the consideration for the feelings of the recipient, rather than upon the act of giving or the amount. Referring to Deut. 15:11, they demand that not only "shalt thou surely give him" but "thy heart shall not be grieved when thou givest him"; the reward for c. is entirely according to the measure of kindness in it. Hillel in giving c. took into consideration the standard of living to which the recipient had been accustomed before falling upon evil days, and even provided one unfortunate with a horse and servant (*Kidd.* 67b). The rabbis estimated that people with means should expend 10-20% of their income on c. Under no circumstances was the recipient to be put to shame (*Ḥag.* 5a) and it is the highest form of almsgiving when the donor and recipient are ignorant of each other's identity. Maimonides (*Hilkhot Mattenot Aniyyim* 10:7-18) tabulated eight degrees of c., ranging from rehabilitative c. to c. given with feelings of resentment. Customary forms of c. have included HAKHNASAT KALLAH, MAOT HITTIM, the ransom of CAPTIVES, and provision for education, hospital services, old-age homes, and free burials.

CHASTITY: The Pentateuch, Prophets, Talmud, and later moralists inveighed persistently and vehemently against the evil of unchastity. Only the sin of immorality is serious enough to be described as "defiling the land" and causing it "to vomit out her inhabitants" (Lev. 18:25, 28). The sternest warnings in Jewish ethical writings are reserved for the denunciation of prostitution, promiscuity, surrender to passion, and particularly the entertainment of lewd thoughts. Jewish law erected numerous legal barriers as a protective guard against unchastity in deed, word, or thought. Accordingly a man should never be alone with a woman, ogle or jest with her, amorously look at her clothes or listen to her singing, or embrace and kiss her. The laws of c. extend also to relations between spouses, and the codes devote whole chapters to the proper norms of decency and c. of conduct and conversation to be observed in conjugal intimacies (*Even ha-Ezer* 24). But on the other hand this stringent attitude never developed to the point of prudery and Jewish religious writings — from the Bible to the Talmud and the latest responsa — are replete with detailed and frank references to SEX, and the study of these writings formed an integral part of Jewish education.

CHAZARS, see **KHAZARS**

CHERUB (Heb. *keruv*): Winged creatures with both human and animal characteristics first mentioned in the Bible as guarding the approach to the Tree of Life (Gen. 3:24). God is also described as riding upon a c. (II Sam. 22:11). Gold likenesses of celestial cherubim with outspread wings were depicted above the curtain of the Ark of the Covenant in the Tabernacle (Exod. 25:18-22, 37:7-9); in Solomon's Temple, the cherubim were placed on the ground in front of the ark. In each case the wings of the cherubim were meant to guard the ark and also served as a cover for the Divine glory emanating therefrom. In the vision of Ezekiel, the four-faced cherubim (one human face, the others of an ox, a lion, and an eagle) are pictured as the bearers of the Divine throne. The origin of the c. is probably to be found in Egyptian mythology and the motif is common in countries neighboring Israel (cf. Hittite griffins, Mesopotamian winged lions and bulls). According to the Midrash the cherubim were created prior to the Garden of Eden and are among the highest class of angels. They also figure prominently in mystical literature and are identified with God's invisible glory, an emanation of the great fire of the Divine Presence (possibly corresponding to the *logos*), and as the model used by God in the creation of man.

CHIEF RABBINATE: Since the cessation of the Sanhedrin there has been no basis in Jewish law for the institution of a C.R. since in theory every rabbi who has the necessary qualification of rabbinical ORDINATION (*semikhah*) possesses spiritual authority equal to that of every other rabbi. Nevertheless, throughout the ages it has become the practice in various countries to appoint one rabbi as the spiritual or representative head of the community, to whose authority all other rabbis within the area of his jurisdiction are subject. Three factors contribute to the institution of such an office: (a) the appointment of one man by the civil authorities in order to establish a channel of communication between the government and the Jewish community (see CROWN RABBI); (b) the voluntary acceptance by the Jewish community and its rabbis of one outstanding figure as Chief Rabbi; and (c) an appointment made by the Jewish community on its own initiative as a necessary consequence of its internal communal organization. In the first category belong the medieval appointments by the kings of Aragon and Castile of certain rabbis as District Chief Rabbis, the appointment of Arch-Presbyters by the kings of England and by the German emperors of Chief Rabbis who were responsible for the collection of the taxation imposed upon the community. The Chief Rabbis of France (in the years from 1807-1906), whose appointment was made by state-controlled Consistories first established by Napoleon, belong in a similar category. In the second category are such medieval figures as R. Solomon ben Adret of Barcelona, called El Rab d'Espana, and R. Meir of Rothenburg (who also belongs to the first category). The C.R. of the British Commonwealth is the most extensive and best organized example of the third category and has its parallels on a lesser scale in various European countries and in South Africa. In the U.S. and Canada the institution is unknown. The office of the Chief Rabbi (called the ḤAKHAM BASHI) in Turkey was established in the 15th cent. The C.R. occupies a unique position in Israel where — in continuation of the system introduced under the British mandate in 1920 — there are two Chief Rabbis (one *Ashkenazi* and one *Sephardi*) both for the country as a whole and for each large city. The governmental nature of their appointment, and the legislative situation whereby all questions of personal status are governed solely by rabbinical laws, invests the Israel C.R. with great practical authority aside from its natural prestige in the Orthodox Jewish world.

CHILDBIRTH: The Bible associates c. with pain from the very beginning of human history (see Gen. 3:16), but Jewish authorities never regarded the suffering of this curse as a mandatory obligation and they sanctioned its mitigation by the use of analgesics just as they favored man's efforts to overcome the parallel curse of hardship in tilling the soil (*ibid.* 17-19) through the use of agricultural machinery. According to biblical law, a mother was considered ritually impure for 7 days and pure after IMMERSION) for 33 after having a male (14 and 66 days for a female), following which she offered a sacrifice of purification (Lev. 12:1-8). In what is probably the first reference in literature to a caesarian section on a living mother, the Mishnah denies the rights of the first-born both to a first child "extracted through the wall (of the abdomen)" and to further children (*Bekh.* 8:2). A woman in confinement enjoys religious concessions in Jewish law. For the first three days she is deemed in mortal danger, and Sabbath or other laws may be disregarded for her needs as for any other gravely ill patient; from then until the seventh day religious laws may be violated for her if she so requests, while from then until the thirtieth day she is regarded as a patient who is not in danger, except insofar as fires may be made for her on the Sabbath to protect her from the cold. From the 15th cent. on it became a custom among European Jews for the mother to pay a special visit to the synagogue upon recovering from c. and an appropriate prayer was composed for the occasion. There are many folkloristic beliefs and customs associated with c., some of them censured in rabbinic writings for their superstitious nature.

CHILDREN: BARRENNESS and childlessness are regarded among Jews as the greatest of misfortunes. The cry of Abraham "O Lord God, what wilt Thou give me, seeing I go childless" (Gen. 15:2) and Rachel's lament "Give me children, else I die" (*ibid.* 30:1) are echoed by the talmudic statement which includes "him who is childless" (*Ned.* 64b) among the four types of living men who are considered as dead. A male is regarded as a child until attaining the age of 13 and a day; females a year earlier. A child is free of all legal and religious obligations and is not punishable for his misdeeds, though he is expected to begin accustoming himself to the practice of the precepts of Judaism as he approaches his majority. The Jewish religious attitude to c. is one of unbounded love, combined with a solid sense of sober responsibility. This love is expressed in such passages as the rhetorical question, "Is it possible for a father to hate his son?" (*Sanh.* 105a) and the statement "a man can be envious of anyone except his own son and his disciple" (*ibid.*). The passage in the New Year prayers, "If Thou dost regard us as Thy children, have mercy on us as a father to his child", conveys the accepted metaphoric transference of the father-child relationship to that between God and Israel. A parent discharges his responsibility toward his child by teaching him the precepts of Judaism, and the traditional belief is that a child who goes in the way of the Law not only ensures the continuity of Judaism but confers salvation upon the soul of his parent after death (the KADDISH, insofar as it became a prayer for mourners, derives from this idea). According to the Talmud, one of the three categories who will inherit the world to come includes those "who bring up their children in the way of the *Torah*" (*Pes.* 113a), and "he who has a son who toils in the *Torah* is regarded as not having died" (*Gen. Rab.* 49). The father is enjoined never to favor one child over another (*Shab.* 10b), and the bondage of the Israelites in Egypt is traced back to the favoritism shown by Jacob to Joseph. Similarly a father should never fail to fulfill the promises he has made to his children, lest he thus lead them to tell untruths (*Suk.* 46b). The ideal child is one who attends a school of religious study and to whom the rabbis (*Shab.* 119b) apply the verse, "touch not mine anointed" (I Chron. 16:20), in contrast to the "child brought up in captivity among the heathens". A striking exception to the otherwise universally accepted doctrine of a child's lack of responsibility and consequent freedom from punishment is to be noted in the law of the stubborn and rebellious child who may be put to death by the court (Deut. 21:18-21). The justification for this law put forth in the Talmud — that it is better for such a child 'to die innocent rather than guilty" since he is sure to grow up a criminal and eventually incur the death penalty (*Sanh.* 72a) — was obviously unsatisfactory, and the Talmud itself came to the conclusion that "the stubborn and rebellious son never existed and never will" (*ibid.* 71a), but that the law was promulgated merely as a dire warning. The talmudic discussion demonstrates that the rabbis viewed the responsibility for a child's rebelliousness as resting ultimately on the shoulders of the parents. (See also FATHER; MOTHER).

CHOICE (FREE CHOICE), see **FREE WILL**

CHOIR: The presence of a levitical c. at the Temple in Jerusalem is the earliest recorded evidence of regular and organized choral singing in Israel. The antiphonal character of the MUSIC is described in Neh. 12:31, but little else is known about the nature of this music though attempts have been made to link it with early Arab or Church music. Congregational singing during the first centuries after the destruction of the Temple was probably limited to short recitative responses to the officiant. The earliest report of a synagogal c. in the Diaspora comes from R. Nathan the Babylonian in 10th cent. Baghdad. A significant impetus to choral singing resulted from the gaonic introduction of *piyyutim* into the synagogue service. Evidence of the use of harmony is not to be found earlier than the 16th cent. By the early 17th cent. the Italian Jewish composer Solomon de' Rossi could take into account high professional standards in the performance of sacred music. However, in most Jewish congregations choral singing remained primitive until the early 19th cent. Jacobsohn introduced hymnal composition on a Protestant model as a part of the German REFORM program for the synagogue. Sulzer and Lewandowski developed the modern synagogue c. by adapting traditional melodies to the musical style of the period. Reform synagogues introduced mixed choirs (often composed of non-Jewish singers) and organ music, whereas in Orthodox services only unaccompanied singing by men and boys is permitted. Congregational singing — as distinct from c. performances — is a traditional custom in oriental synagogues and was a conspicuous feature of ḥasidic worship.

CHOLENT: Dish with a bean basis traditionally eaten by *Ashkenazim* for Sabbath midday dinner. As cooking on the Sabbath is forbidden, the *c.* is prepared on Friday afternoon and placed on a hot plate or oven to bake overnight. It is eaten after the Saturday morning service. The *Sephardim* prepare a similar hot dish for the Sabbath called *ḥamin.*

CHORIN, AARON, see **HORIN, AARON**

CHOSEN PEOPLE: The belief that the Jewish people has been chosen by God above all other peoples is frequently mentioned in the Bible, and occupies a prominent place in Jewish liturgy. Thus Deut. 14:2 states "For thou art a holy people unto the Lord thy God, and the Lord hath chosen thee to be a peculiar people unto Himself, above all the nations that are upon the face of the earth". The blessing recited by the person called up to the Reading of the Law is "Blessed art Thou... who hast chosen us out of all peoples and given us the *Torah*"; and the specific festival portion of the *amidah* begins "Thou hast chosen us from all peoples; Thou hast loved us and taken pleasure in us, and hast exalted us over all tongues". The doctrine of a c.p. is therefore central in Jewish theology, but there is difference of opinion as to its precise meaning. Interpretations vary from a narrow concept of superiority to attempts at ethical and even universalist formulations. The frequent biblical emphasis on the election of Israel led to the idea, also found in later rabbinic literature, that there was a moral or even racial excellence inherent in the Jewish people as such, and references are not wanting to the superiority of those who are "of the seed of Abraham our Father" (e.g.

Betz. 32b). Inevitably the doctrine of election also led to an ethnocentric view of world history. On the other hand the notion of a c.p. is also related to that of a "holy nation" (e.g. Exod. 19:5-6): "Now therefore if ye will obey My commandments and keep My covenant, then ye shall be a peculiar people unto Me above all people", and election is accounted for as an act of Divine love and faithfulness to the Divine promise (Deut. 7:6-9). In spite of their severe castigation of Israel's failings, the prophets generally assumed the permanence of Israel's election under the COVENANT. If election meant heavier responsibility and stricter standards rather than greater privileges (Amos 3:2), then Israel was proved to be God's c.p. also in exile and punishment (Jeremiah, Ezekiel). Although DEUTERO-ISAIAH had proclaimed that God's dealings with Israel would make the latter a source of light to all the nations, the idea was not systematically developed and Jewish commentators did not, as a rule, interpret the "Suffering Servant" of Is. 53 as a figure of Israel suffering for the sake of mankind. The emphasis on Israel's continued election became stronger when rival religions (e.g. the claim of the Church to be the "true Israel") or historical circumstances (e.g. oppression and persecution) contradicted Israel's claim to be the c.p. The treatment which medieval Jewry received at the hands of its neighbors was not such as to encourage universalist tendencies. Medieval philosophers paid relatively little attention to the doctrine of the c.p., the major exception being JUDAH HA-LEVI for whom Israel was a kind of spiritual superrace. The unique historic and cosmic status of Israel was a fundamental tenet of the KABBALAH, but rationalism, modernism, and EMANCIPATION made the notion of a c.p. increasingly problematical. Geiger still held that the Jewish people possessed a unique "gift for religion" and he and other REFORM thinkers tended to regard the dispersion as part of Israel's mission to serve as God's instrument in disseminating their specific insight of the relationship between the human and the Divine. This attitude has been modified subsequently and some groups (Reform, Reconstructionist) have repudiated the traditional doctrine of a c.p. and have deleted all references to it from the prayer-book. The socio-historical and spiritual rather than racial character of the traditional concept of the c.p. is clearly brought out by rabbinic law which accords to the convert all the rights and privileges of the born Jew. This attitude, the earliest expression of which is found in the biblical book of Ruth, was succinctly formulated by Maimonides: "Whosoever adopts Judaism and confesses the Unity of the Divine Name as is prescribed in the *Torah* is counted among the disciples of Abraham our father. These men are Abraham's household". This principle strictly applied in *halakhic* procedure: a convert discards his patronymic and becomes "the son (or daughter) of Abraham our Father".

CHRISTIANITY: The Christian religion grew out of Judaism and at first existed as a Jewish sect. The founder and early adherents were all Jews and much light has been thrown on their teachings by comparing them with both rabbinic doctrines and those contained in the DEAD SEA SCROLLS. C. has adopted not only the Hebrew Bible but much of its traditional interpretation as well, in addition to many elements from Jewish liturgy. JESUS preached the imminent advent of the Kingdom of Heaven but in spite of his anti-Pharisaic criticisms he was in many ways closer to the Pharisees than to their opponents, the Sadducees. He did not intend to abolish the traditional law (cf. *Matt.* 5:17); and his supplication prayer, known as the Lord's Prayer, bears a striking resemblance to the traditional "short prayer" (*tephillah ketzarah*). After the crucifixion, his followers regarded themselves as Jews who were committed to a belief in the messiahship of Jesus and his imminent return. It was PAUL who developed C. in a way that prepared for a complete break with the parent religion. Drawing on doctrines current in sectarian circles, he developed a theology that laid the foundation for gentile C.: Jesus' death had redeemed sinful man from his state of sin; the Law had been fulfilled and superseded (i.e., abolished), and salvation was now attainable through baptism and faith in the Messiah. With the growth of gentile C. the original Jewish Christians (EBIONITES, also called *minim*, i.e., "sectarians" or "heretics") became a minority of "heretics" even inside the Church. With the introduction of a solemn curse upon *minim* into the *amidah* prayer, the Jewish community finalized its breach with C. However C. could never regard Judaism as just another religion. The Church insisted that its roots were sunk deep in the history of Israel, that the events recounted in the NEW TESTAMENT were the fulfillment of the promises made in the Hebrew Bible (now called the Old Testament), that its founder was the Messiah expected by Jewish tradition, that it was the heir of God's covenant with Israel — in short, that it was the "true Israel". This position inevitably led to a complicated and ambivalent attitude toward Israel in which affirmation and utter rejection, acceptance and hatred were intertwined. In order to come into her own, the Church had to picture Israel as dispossessed, rejected, or even cursed. This "competitive" situation, aggravated by Israel's stubborn refusal throughout the centuries to be in any way impressed by the religious claims of C., has provided the basis for the tragic history of Christian ANTI-SEMITISM. The development and growth of this hatred can be traced through the books of the New Testament and beyond it to the writings of the CHURCH FATHERS and later authors. The destruction of the Temple and the disastrous failure of the first and second (Bar Kokhba) rebellions were taken as proof that Israel's historic role had come to an end, whereas C. continued to spread until it finally became the official religion of the Roman empire. (From the Jewish point of view Rome, with all its evil associations (EDOM), was henceforth identified with C.). Although Judaism was tolerated and given a status of its own in medieval Europe, Jews were subjected to humiliation, persecution, and frequent violence. The official theory claimed that Jews should be allowed to live, albeit in abject degradation, as a terrible warning to all those who would reject the Christian savior. Toward the later Middle Ages Christian anti-semitism became more violent. The CRUSADES, with their wholesale massacres of Jewish communities, the repeated accusations of ritual murder (see BLOOD LIBEL) and desecration of the Host, expulsions, forced CONVERSIONS and the activities of the INQUISITION brought Jewish suffering at the hands of C. to an unprecedented pitch. Theological DISPUTATIONS which at one time had been conducted in a spirit of relative fairness were increasingly forced upon the Jews in order to embarrass them. All the more extensive was the development of polemical literature (see APOLOGETICS) — both on a high philosophical plane and on a crudely derogatory (e.g. TOLEDOT YESHU) level. No doubt there were mutual influences between the two religions, in the sense both of adopting and rejecting certain ideas and practices, e.g. Maimonides exercised considerable influence on Albertus Magnus, Thomas Aquinas, and Meister Eckhart whereas Jewish theological doctrines were often formulated with polemical intent against Christian teachings. Christian influence is noticeable in such Jewish customs as *yahrzeit* and prayers for the dead. The Church dissociated its Easter date from that of Passover to avoid celebrating on the Jewish festival; conversely, Jewish customs were discontinued because they were also practiced by Christians e.g. kneeling at prayer (see also ḤUKKAT HA-GOYYIM). But these mutual influences affected the general moral climate as little as an interest in the Hebrew Bible changed the attitudes of later Protestant reformers. Luther's attitude to Judaism was the same as that prevalent in the earlier Middle Ages, while the Counter-Reformation in the Catholic Church served to revive and enforce even more severe anti-Jewish legislation (the yellow badge, the GHETTO system). Some English Puritans seemed ready to adopt a different attitude toward the Jews, but generally speaking it is only in recent times that Christian Churches and theologians, largely under the shock of Hitler's persecution, have begun to press for a radical revision of the Christian approach to Judaism. On the Jewish side theological evaluation of C. varied with the times and individual thinkers. It was generally admitted that C., like Islam, was different from paganism, and as a monotheistic faith could be considered as one of the ways by which Providence gradually led the gentiles toward true religion. It was never doubted, however, that C. was essentially a false religion and according to some authorities (e.g. Maimonides) it could not even be regarded as a genuinely monotheistic faith. Some modern thinkers (particularly Franz ROSENZWEIG) have assigned an especially important role to C. and describe its relationship to Judaism as a complementary one.

CHRONICLES, BOOK(S) OF (Heb. *Divrei ha-Yamim*): The last book in the Hagiographa section of the Hebrew Bible, describing the history of Israel and Judah up to the Babylonian Exile; in the Septuagint it is included among the historical books and placed between Kings and Ezra. Originally one work, it is now generally printed as two books (I Chronicles and II Chronicles) following the precedent of the Greek translation. C. contains (1) the genealogy of the Israelite tribes from Adam to the Davidic period, (I Chron. 1-9); (2) a description of the Davidic reign with the omission of the more reprehensible acts that are incorporated in the parallel book of Samuel and with added details concerning David's activities and the organization of his kingdom (10-29); (3) the Solomonic reign with emphasis on the Temple (II Chron. 1-9); (4) the subsequent history of Judah with a sympathetic and apologetic emphasis on the kingdom of Judah and the actions of its kings (10-36). The House of David as a centralizing force in the development of the nation and the significance of the Temple and Temple cult are the overall foci of the work. Also stressed is the role of the Zadokite priesthood and the levites. Much of the contents resembles other sections of the Bible (especially the Books of Samuel and Kings) but the style is later and is like that of the Books of Ezra and Nehemiah.

CHRONOLOGY, see **CALENDAR**

CHUETAS: A name given to the CRYPTO-JEWS or MARRANOS of the Balearic Islands; both "Marrano" and "Chueta" mean "pig" and are indicative of the contempt in which these people were held by "Old Christians". Like the Marranos, C. came into being as a result of the anti-Jewish violence and agitation of 1391 which spread from the mainland to the islands. The advent of the fiery Spanish Dominican friar Vicente Ferrer, who in 1415 stayed in Majorca for 6 months in pursuit of his missionary activity, caused the numbers of C. to swell. After the introduction of the Inquisition in 1488 a general amnesty was granted to all repentants but many cases of secret practice of Judaism were reported. Despite their forced conversion, the C. were confined to special ghettos and severe persecutions by the Inquisition occurred in 1678 and 1691; in 1782 they were allowed to reside in any part of the island. They are now completely assimilated to the general population, though their Jewish origin is known, and recent attempts to bring them back to the Jewish fold have failed.

CHURCH FATHERS: The writers and teachers of the Christian Church, from the post-apostolic age to about the 7th cent. Their interest in the Hebrew Bible and biblical exegesis led many C.F. to study Jewish interpretations and commentaries while others both in Palestine (e.g. Justin Martyr) and elsewhere (e.g. Chrysostom of Antioch) engaged in polemics against Judaism, some of them laying the foundations for medieval Christian ANTI-SEMITISM. The writings of the C.F. ("patristic literature") contain many references to Jews and Jewish teaching, and preserve valuable information not contained in Jewish sources: Jerome and others quote Jewish interpretations of Scripture; Eusebius cites from lost works of hellenistic Jewish writers; Origen provides information regarding the biblical text and its early translations, as well as the pronunciation of Hebrew, and also records some otherwise unknown rabbinic traditions. Since much in patristic literature reflects the background of Jewish-Christian polemics, study of these writings has been found to throw much new light on rabbinic texts, particularly aggadic statements and midrashic homilies.

CIRCUMCISION: Removal of the foreskin in an operation performed on all male Jewish children on the eighth day after birth, and also upon male converts to Judaism. C. was enjoined by God upon Abraham and his descendants (Gen. 17:10-12) and has always been regarded as the supreme obligatory sign of loyalty and adherence to Judaism. As the sign of the COVENANT (*berit*) "sealed in the flesh", c. came to be known as *berit milah* or the "covenant of our father Abraham". The presence of the foreskin was regarded as a blemish, and "perfection" was to be attained by its removal (cf. *Ned.* 31b). The generation born in the wilderness, however, was not circumcised, an omission repaired by Joshua (Josh. 5:2-9). In the Hellenistic Period many hellenized Jews, desirous of concealing the fact of their c., especially at athletics in the gymnasium, had another operation performed for this purpose (I *Macc.* 1:15). Similar action was taken during the Hadrianic persecution, which also included a prohibition against c. It was probably in order to prevent the possibility of obliterating the traces of c. that the rabbis added to the requirement of cutting the foreskin that of *periah* — laying bare the glans. To this is added a third requirement, *metzitzah* ("sucking of the blood"). This was originally done by the *mohel* (circumciser) applying his lips to the penis and drawing off the blood by sucking. For hygienic reasons a glass tube with a wad of cotton wool inserted in the middle is now generally employed or the blood is simply drawn off by the use of some absorbent material. Unless medical reasons interpose, the c. must take place on the eighth day after birth even if that day falls on a Sabbath. If it has been postponed for medical reasons, the ceremony may not take place on a Sabbath. The only exception permitted to the otherwise universal requirement of c. is if two previous children of the family have died as a result of the operation, i.e., in cases of hereditary hemophilia. The duty of circumcising the child is the responsibility of the father, but in his absence or in case of his failure to do so, the religious authorities are bound to see that it is performed. The occasion of a c. is regarded as a festive event for the whole community. The presence of one of the participants (the father, godfather, or *mohel*) in synagogue on that day justifies the omission of all penitential and supplicatory prayers. A sentence in the prayer of Elijah (I Kings 19:10), "for the children of Israel have forsaken Thy covenant" is taken by the rabbis to mean that they had abandoned the rite of c., which is always referred to (on the basis of Gen. 17:9) as the *berit* ("covenant"). It was therefore decreed that Elijah's zealousness should be commemorated by regarding him as the patron of c., and his spirit is therefore considered to be present at all circumcisions. This is the origin of the "Chair of Elijah", now an integral part of the ceremony. In oriental communities, where the ceremony takes place in the synagogue, such a chair is a permanent feature of the synagogue appurtenances. Among *Ashkenazim,* it is customary to appoint a couple as *kvatter.* The woman carries the child from his mother's room to the room where the ceremony takes place and gives him to her husband, who in turn hands him to the *mohel.* The *mohel* places the child upon the chair of Elijah and proclaims, "this is the chair of Elijah, may he be remembered for good", etc. He then lifts up the child, places him upon a cushion in the lap of the godfather (SANDAK, from Gk. *synteknos*), and in this position the operation is performed after the *mohel* recites the appropriate blessings. The father also recites a blessing to God "who has sanctified us by His commandments and commanded us to enter our sons into the covenant of Abraham" and according to some rites also says SHE-HEHEYANU. The *mohel* then recites a prayer dating from gaonic times, in the course of which a name is bestowed on the child. The c. ceremony is normally followed by a banquet which ranks as a *seudat mitzvah*, a meal of religious character. Special hymns are sung, and blessings for the parents, the *sandak*, the child, and the *mohel*, as well as for the advent of the Messiah and the "righteous priest", are inserted in the Grace after Meals. C. is enjoined upon male proselytes (and slaves) as an essential condition of their acceptance into the Jewish faith.

CIRCUMSTANTIAL EVIDENCE, see **EVIDENCE**

CITIES OF REFUGE, see **ASYLUM**

CITRON, see **ETROG**

CITY OF DAVID, see **JERUSALEM**

CIVIL COURTS: Jewish law contains a prohibition against having recourse to non-Jewish courts of justice. The prohibition originally derived from a fear of being inveigled into a recognition of idolatry (A.Z. 13a). Certain exceptions were made, e.g for the witnessing of documents, except in the case of writs of divorce or manumission (*Git.* 9b-10a). In the 2nd cent., however, R. Tarphon issued a blanket prohibition against Jews having any recourse to non-Jewish (heathen) courts, even if their dispensation of justice was identical with that of the Jewish courts. He quoted Exod. 21:1 in support of his decision (*Git.* 88b). In their desire and anxiety to maintain as far as possible the internal AUTONOMY of the Jewish communities in the Diaspora, medieval Jewish authorities insisted that Jews bring their disputes only before their own courts and harshly condemned those having recourse to c.c. even by mutual agreement. The only exception permitted was if the defendant failed to appear before the Jewish court (BET DIN) after three successive summonses, in which case the *bet din* issued permission to the plaintiff to apply to the civil authorities. The prohibition has fallen almost completely out of use in modern times. The sole occasion when systematic attempts are made to avoid recourse to c.c. is the case of disputes affecting the internal regulations of the community.

CIVIL LAW: Jewish c.l. may be defined as that area of Divinely authorized law which deals with matters other than criminal and ritualistic. C.l. occupies a modest place in the Bible, but as it developed in the Talmudic Period and later it came to constitute the main part of Jewish law. As found in the Bible c.l. reflects the life of a predominantly agricultural community, and there is little material dealing with commerce. With the development of commerce from the Second Temple Period onward, and the necessity of paying taxes to foreign rulers, the area of commercial law expanded greatly, as is reflected in the Mishnah and TALMUD. The laws of contract, expressed or implied, were studied in detail. The development of c.l. continued during the Gaonic Period and later in the literature of the RESPONSA and CODES. The basic Orders of the Mishnah concerned with c.l. are NASHIM and NEZIKIN (though these sections also deal with other matters). The former treats the laws of MARRIAGE and DIVORCE, PROPERTY rights of husband and wife, and the rights and obligations of SLAVES. The nature of CIVIL COURTS, legal procedure, the administration of OATHS, as well as most laws dealing with money matters, land, INHERITANCE, pledges, LOANS and interest, TORTS, and BAILMENTS are found in *Nezikin* — particularly in the first three tractates of this Order: *Bava Kamma*, *Bava Metzia*, and *Bava Batra*. Rabbinic sources distinguish between rules applicable in ritual law (*isura*) and c.l. (*mamona*) respectively. The principle of equity (e.g. in application of the biblical commandment "and thou shalt do that which is right and good") often enforced in order to mitigate any special severity which might arise from the strict application of the law in certain cases. Whereas no non-Jewish authority could change or influence ceremonial law, in matters of c.l. the "law of the land" (*dina de-malkhuta*) would be considered valid by rabbinic legislators for certain purposes. Nevertheless Jews were always urged to bring litigation to rabbinic courts and not to the "gentile courts". In many parts of the Diaspora rabbinic courts were given full jurisdiction by the government; elsewhere their status was that of a court of arbitration. In the State of Israel, litigants can choose to go to rabbinic instead of secular courts in civil suits.

CIVIL MARRIAGE, see **MARRIAGE**

CIVIL RIGHTS: The duties and privileges appertaining to full membership in a state. In most ancient societies membership in a group was determined by blood ties or tribal affiliation, and c.r. were inextricably bound up with and often indistinguishable from ritual and other privileges and obligations. Bible law clearly distinguishes between Jews and non-Jews (e.g. regarding the right to own land, hold slaves, etc.) and rabbinic law developed and refined these distinctions (see GENTILE; GER; PROSELYTE). While ensuring fair treatment of the gentile, rabbinic law, as codified by such authorities as Maimonides, left him with certain disabilities as compared to the Jew, who was a full member in what is conceived of as an essentially religious and not merely a "civil" community. The convert to Judaism acquired almost all c.r. Similarly, Jews could not fully share the life of the ancient pagan cities and states, though many of them obtained Roman citizenship, particularly after 212 (Edict of Caracalla). As a rule the Jewish communities preferred internal autonomy which enabled them to organize their lives in accordance with their own religious and legal traditions. This internal autonomy was of even greater importance when with the triumph of Christianity Jews were frequently deprived of citizenship and c.r. As outsiders in a "Christian society", excluded from the feudal system of relationships, they were often without any rights at all unless protected by a lord or sovereign (thus becoming his dependents or property), or by charters granted specially to them. Since the end of the 18th cent., enlightenment and progressive conceptions of equality and citizenship have gradually allowed Jews fuller c.r. But EMANCIPATION also seemed to entail an abandonment of traditional internal autonomy and a relegation of Jewish law to purely ritual or liturgical matters (e.g. military service could involve breaking the Sabbath or dietary laws; extension of state law to include Jews also had the effect of weakening the authority of rabbinic courts in matters of marriage and divorce); hence it was mistrusted and even opposed by many Orthodox Jews.

CLEAN AND UNCLEAN ANIMALS: Animals whose flesh is permitted by Jewish DIETARY LAWS are considered clean; those whose flesh may not be eaten are considered unclean. Clean and unclean animals are first mentioned in the Bible in the story of Noah who took into the ark seven pairs of clean but only two pairs of unclean animals. Lev. 11:1-47 and Deut. 14:3-25 list clean and unclean animals together with the principles by which they are classified. Clean quadrupeds are those which both chew the cud and have cloven hooves. This excludes, for example, the hare, which chews its cud but does not have cloven hooves, and the pig, which has cloven hooves but does not chew the cud. Marine animals considered clean are those having both fins and scales. All true fish come under the category of clean, while shellfish are excluded. No general principles are given to determine the cleanness of fowl, but about 20 unclean fowl are listed with the implication that all others may be eaten. The rabbis, however, endeavored to establish principles for determining clean fowl such as the fact that clean fowl have three digits of the foot in front and one in back, whereas unclean fowl perch with two digits in front and two in back. Such external signs, however, were not considered sufficient in themselves for determining whether an unknown fowl is fit to be eaten and the principle was laid down that only a definite tradition permitting the eating of a particular species of fowl could remove any doubt of its possibly belonging to an unclean "family". In general it may be said that the specific list of unclean fowl in the Bible includes birds of prey only, thus implying the permissible character of those not birds of prey. All reptiles and insects are prohibited, with the exception of four types of locusts, mentioned specifically by name, whose cleanness is determined in the Bible according to the principle that they have "knees above their legs to jump with upon the ground".

CLEANLINESS: Personal c. and hygiene are stressed in the Bible (Deut. 23:10-15), in rabbinic literature, and in all codes c. is not to be confused with the concepts and practices of *taharah* — ritual PURITY, but immersion in the ritual bath (MIKVEH), which is the major means of obtaining ritual cleanness, can be effective only if the body is scrupulously clean prior to immersion. In one or two instances, such as ABLUTION of the hands before partaking of bread or engaging in prayer, ritual and hygienic motives are intertwined. Halakhic insistence on ritual immersion at regular intervals, e.g. in the case of the menstruant woman and the frequent voluntary immersion of males naturally gave rise to a high level of personal hygiene among Jews. In fact, so important does Judaism consider personal c. that the obligatory abstention from washing on the Day of Atonement is taken to be an "affliction" (*Yoma* chap. 8). Personal hygiene is considered by the rabbis to extend also to modesty, decency, and c. of dress, an attitude voiced in an extreme fashion by the statement (*Shab.* 114a), "a scholar upon whose garment a speck of dirt is found is worthy of death". During the Middle Ages, Jews prided themselves on their clean habits and neatness of dress. Maimonides considered the achievement of c. in dress and body to be among the general objectives of the Bible, adding that an outer appearance of c. and propriety should reflect inner purity of heart.

CODES OF LAW: The basis of all Jewish law in its present form of observance is the Talmud. Yet only the expert can use the Talmud directly as a code of Jewish law. For the Talmud is not so much a book for deciding the law as it is for expounding the various possibilities of law. It is meant more for the scholar than for the judge. Very seldom does it give a direct answer to a problem when there is a variety of opinions on the subject. Nor could one easily find an answer in the Talmud to a specific legal problem because of the peculiar and unwieldy form of arrangement. For this reason systematic compilations of talmudic law and later decisions were composed at various periods. The transition from the amorphous form of talmudic discussion to the systematically arranged and infinitely detailed works of the later codifiers was, however a very gradual one. Early codifications are little more than abridged editions of sections from the Talmud. R. YEHUDAI Gaon's *Halakhot Pesukot*, the first post-talmudic codification, arranges its material according to topic (in contrast to the slightly earlier *Sheiltot* of R. AHA, where isolated points of law are discussed in connection with the scriptural readings of the week), but it is limited in scope to subject matter relevant only to the post-Temple period. The work served as a basis for many later abbreviations and expanded reworkings such as *Halakhot Ketzuvot*, *Halakhot Ketuvot*, and *Halakhot Ketannot*. The most important of these was the *Halakhot Gedolot* of R. Simeon Kayyara in the 9th cent. The next important landmark in the codification of talmudic law was the *Sepher ha-Halakhot* of R. Isaac ALFASI written in the 11th cent. This work, still widely studied, is arranged according to almost strict talmudic order and gives a synopsis of the legal discussion in the original talmudic language. By omitting all subject matter not directly relevant to the point of *halakhah* under discussion, Alfasi provided essentially an abridged version of the Talmud, though he occasionally digressed to give an original exposition justifying his determination of a point of law. He also makes use of the Jerusalem Talmud on many matters where the Babylonian Talmud is silent. Like the gaonic compilers before him, Alfasi deals only with those aspects of talmudic law relevant to Jewish life in the Diaspora in the post-Temple period. The first original compilation of Jewish law in plan, arrangement, and language is the code of MAIMONIDES, known as *Mishneh Torah* or *Yad Ḥazakah*, composed during the second half of the 12th cent. Unlike previous codifiers, Maimonides included all talmudic law, even that only having application in Palestine during the period of the Temple. His arrangement is not based on the order of the talmudic treatises, but on a systematic division of the legal subject matter. His language and style are reminiscent of the easy Hebrew of the Mishnah. Also important is Maimonides' *Sepher ha-Mitzvot* in which he lists the 613 precepts. At the same time that Maimonides was preparing his original compilation in Egypt, French scholars of the TOSAPHIST school compiled books of law in imitation of the method of Alfasi. Thus Abraham ben Isaac of Narbonne wrote his influential *Ha-Eshkol* toward the end of the 12th cent. The *Sepher Ha-Ittur* of his pupil, ISAAC BEN ABBA MARI, covers almost the entire body of rabbinic jurisprudence (i.e., civil and religious law, excluding only criminal law). Other books of law from both the French and German

schools in the 13th cent. include the *Even ha-Ezer*, the *Sepher ha-Terumah*, the *Rokeah*, the *Sepher Mitzvot Gadol* (*Semag*) and the *Or Zarua*. But the truly important works after Maimonides which mark a definite advance in codification start with the *Arbaah Turim* of JACOB BEN ASHER in Spain in the 14th cent. Jacob was the son of ASHER BEN JEHIEL who had made an abstract of halakhic material patterned after Alfasi, adding the views of later authorities. Jacob arranged the laws logically in four different divisions: 1. Laws of daily conduct, including prayer, Sabbath and festival observance. 2. Dietary laws. 3. Family law. 4. Civil law. This work combined French, German, and Spanish rabbinic tradition and interpretation. Jacob presents the views of the Talmud and the codifiers who preceded him in logical order, then gives his own views, which are usually based upon his father's decisions. This important work formed the basis for the shorter *Shulḥan Arukh* of Joseph KARO in the 16th cent. Karo as a rule follows Alfasi, Maimonides, and Asher ben Jehiel, usually siding with the majority view (two against one) where there is any difference of opinion. Moses Isserles added notes to the *Shulḥan Arukh* called the *Mappah*, wherein he incorporates strictly *Ashkenazi* views and customs, thus making it possible for the work to become accepted by Jews everywhere as the authoritative code. The *Shulḥan Arukh* has formed the subject of many commentaries and is the source of all subsequent attempts at codification, but it has never been superseded in Orthodox practice. Non-Orthodox (Conservative and Reform) developments of *halakhah* have so far not been codified in recognized compilations.

COFFIN: The practice in the ancient Middle East was to bury bodies in wood, stone, or clay coffins decorated with designs and inscriptions, but the only biblical reference to a c. is in the case of Joseph (Gen. 50:26). It appears that although the non-Israelite inhabitants of Palestine used coffins the Israelites had different BURIAL customs. In the Hasmonean Period Jews collected the bones of the dead (after the flesh had decayed) in small sarcophagi, and their use of coffins dates only from late Second Temple times. It was strictly forbidden to plunder or derive benefit from a c. In some places it became customary to remove the bottom of the c. to ensure the fulfillment of the verse "Thou art dust and unto dust shalt thou return" (Gen. 3:19). In the State of Israel today, burials are generally made without coffins.

COHEN, see **PRIESTS**

COHEN, HERMANN (1842-1918): German philosopher, regarded as the founder of the "Marburg" school of Neo-Kantian philosophy. He evinced little interest in Judaism until 1879 when he replied to the anti-Jewish attacks of the historian Treitschke. Initially he supported a theory of deliberate assimilation and stressed the similarities between Judaism and Christianity. Later it was the contrast between the two religions that he emphasized, particularly the absence in Jewish thought of the concepts of a mediator or of original sin. After his retirement from teaching in 1912, he increasingly devoted himself to religion in general (it had not played a part in his early thought) and to Judaism in particular (expressed most notably in his posthumously published *Religion of Reason from the Sources of Judaism*). He now held that the origin of man, and the faculty of reason, are to be found in God (as indicated in Zech. 12:1; Job 31:2) and are correlated with the Holy Spirit (*ruaḥ ha-kodesh*), a concept expressing a relationship and not an individual entity. Man is thus linked to God through this correlation; the source of the Law is in God but the source of the sense of duty is in man himself. Next to this idea of God, the other great concept in C.'s thought during this period was his idea of the Messiah, i.e., a belief in the triumph of good and the achievement of man's urge to perfection. Judaism, according to C., is a religion of ethical reason; ethics supplies its universal morality and religion its emphasis on the individual. Regarding the dispersion of the Jews as a positive aspect of their destiny, C. thought of Zionism as a historical retrogression.

COHEN, ISRAEL MEIR (*Ḥaphetz Ḥayyim;* 1838-1933): Rabbinical scholar and Orthodox leader in Lithuania. His *Ḥaphetz Ḥayyim* ("Desirous of Life"), dealing with laws of tale-bearing and slander, achieved such popularity that its author became generally known by the name of his book. C.'s most important composition was *Mishnah Berurah* ("Clear Teaching"), summarizing the views of diverse commentators on Karo's SHULḤAN ARUKH. He stressed the importance of studying the ritual connected with the Temple in order to be ready to apply it at the advent of the Messiah. By virtue of his saintliness of character he wielded great spiritual authority over Orthodox Jewry in his lifetime.

COHEN, SHABBETAI BEN MEIR (known as *Shakh* from the initials of his best-known work; 1621-1662): E. European talmudist. His exposition of sections of KARO's SHULḤAN ARUKH called *Siphtei Kohen* ("Lips of a Priest") was outstanding for its sharp analysis and its attempt to decide rulings in those instances where Karo and ISSERLES had differed. Like the *Turei Zahav of* DAVID BEN SAMUEL HA-LEVI (with whom C. conducted a sharp controversy), this book became a standard work and the subject of a considerable literature.

COLLEGES, see **ACADEMY; RABBINICAL SEMINARIES; YESHIVAH**

COLLEGIO RABBINICO ITALIANO: Rabbinical school founded in 1829 at Padua where its outstanding teacher was Samuel David Luzzatto. The school was subsequently transferred to Rome (1887) where its activities were on a small scale; Florence (1899) where under the influence of R. Samuel Hirsch Margulies many rabbinical leaders were trained; and back to Rome where it reopened in 1955 after having been closed during the later Fascist period.

COMMANDMENT, see **MITZVAH; PRECEPTS**

COMMANDMENTS, TEN, see **DECALOGUE**

COMMENTARIES, see **BIBLE COMMENTARIES; TALMUD**

COMMUNITY: The term c. is used to render a variety of Hebrew expressions (*kehillah, edah, kahal, tzibbur, kelal*), each with specific legal, social, and ethical connotations. The widest and at the same time most fundamental concept of the Jewish c. is that of a "people" or "nation". Within this general framework, the large c. of the "children of Israel" has organized itself into many types of individual communities in its unceasing endeavor to survive under changing conditions. Loose tribal associations gave way, in the period of the First Temple, to a growing centralization of wealth and power, which did not, however, affect the largely autonomous life of the small towns. With agriculture dominating trade and industry, Palestine's towns — seldom above 1,000 in population — were economically, and in a great measure politically, self-sufficient. The tradition of local autonomy (e.g. the "elders at the gate of the city" and the assemblies for purposes of worship) was to a great extent responsible for the later ability of the Jews to survive in exile. The disintegrating effects of the destruction of the Temple and deportation were countered by a new form of religious and national association, centered around the SYNAGOGUE. It appears that the Babylonian exiles gathered on Sabbaths for a service of prayer and for encouragement from their spiritual leader. But the synagogue was not merely a new type of center for worship; the congregation also marked a new form of local association, which, with variations, has served as the nucleus of Jewish c. organization in the Diaspora down to the present day. These local congregations, which fulfilled secular as well as religious functions, depended for whatever unity they were able to achieve upon the authority of the spiritual and lay leadership which guided them — elders, priests, prophets, teachers, rabbis. Spiritual leadership often transcended national territories, as evidenced by the authority wielded by the Palestinian patriarchs over the Jewish communities in the widespread Roman Empire, and of the Babylonian academies over the Jewries of North Africa and Spain. Religious authority and communal solidarity were so strong that when the Roman government deprived the Jewish courts of justice of their authority by converting them into courts of arbitration (398 C.E.) or when it suppressed the Palestinian patriarchate (425 C.E.), there was still no weakening of internal Jewish c. organization. Throughout the centuries, congregations, and the network of welfare and mutual aid activities which they fostered, served as effective cohesive agents in Jewish communities throughout the world. Such an organizational form was particularly effective in the small towns which made up the Jewish world of the medieval and early modern periods. The leaders of different communities sometimes met in COUNCILS AND SYNODS, thereby evolving patterns of organization transcending the local c. The modern trend toward a concentration of Jewish population in large cities, and the heterogeneity of thought and behavior characteristic of modern democratic societies, have largely destroyed the unified and homogeneous character of the traditional local c. New c. organizations on a national level are of different kinds. Sometimes European governments have sought to organize the Jewish c. for their own purposes (e.g. Napoleon's Sanhedrin). On the other hand many new types of organization have arisen representing the Jewish c. or sections of it but not necessarily composed of local synagogue congregations. Freedom of association in a democratic society, the phenomenon of ANTI-SEMITISM, and the establishment of the State of Israel have helped to pose the problem of the nature of the Jewish c. in a new and acute fashion. In both the sociology and theology of Judaism the precise nature of the Jewish c. continues to be a major issue, about which opinions range from the traditional conception originating in rabbinic and mystical theology of the c. of Israel (*Keneset Yisrael*) as a mystical body whose transcendent character is merely reflected in the earthly, historical people, to scientific sociological definitions of the c. in terms of its identifying traits, whether racial, cultural, or social.

COMPASSION (Heb. *raḥamim*): Compassion is regarded as one of the outstanding virtues and characteristics of the Jewish people. The Talmud states that "Whosoever shows c. to God's creatures is surely of the seed of Abraham, and he who fails to show c. is certainly not of such descent" (*Beitz.* 32a; cf. *Yev.* 79a) and Jews are referred to by the rabbis as "compassionate children of compassionate sires". The outstanding manifestation of c. is the feeling of a parent for his child which should be paralleled in the relationship between man and his neighbor. C. is a Divine attribute and God is often referred to as "the compassionate One (*ha-Raḥman*)"; thus, man's practice of c. is one of the main examples of *Imitatio Dei*: "As God is compassionate, be thou compassionate" (*Siphrei, Ekev* 89). Also, since "God's c. is extended to all His creatures" (Ps. 145:9) the c. of the Jew should likewise extend beyond the human race to the lowliest of God's creatures (*Gen. Rab.* 33:3). On the other hand misplaced c. often leads to cruelty and crime; the rabbis cite Saul as a case in point (cf. I Sam. 15:9; 22:17-19). A sharp emphasis is laid on the non-interference of c. with the proper exercise of legal rights, but the law states that "C. should figure in the making of legal judgments" (Mishnah *Ket.* 9:2).

COMPULSION, see **DURESS**

CONCUBINAGE, see **POLYGAMY**

CONFESSION (Heb. *vidduy*): The admission and acknowledgment of guilt or wrongdoing which might otherwise remain undisclosed. C. is a means of expiation and ATONEMENT for such wrongdoing and is one of the three essential elements of true REPENTANCE (the other two being regret for the action committed and resolve not to repeat it). Thus the sin-offering in the Temple was accompanied by c., and according to rabbinic doctrine there can be no remission of sin without c. The rabbis said that in a human tribunal, a man may possibly escape punishment by denying his guilt while when he pleads guilty he is sure to receive punishment; before God, however, the opposite holds true: denial of guilt excludes the possibility of remission of sin, whereas a contrite c. appeals to God's forgiving mercy. C. is made directly to God (and not through an intermediary), and may be said individually, in one's private prayers, or collectively in public congregational c., as on the Day of Atonement. The wording of the liturgical c. is based upon that given by the High Priest in the Temple, following the ordinance (Lev. 16:21), "and he shall confess... all the iniquities of the children of Israel, and all their transgressions in all their sins". Alphabetical enumeration of sins in congregational c. (e.g. AL ḤET; ASHAMNU) are couched in the plural rather than the singular, thus emphasizing the collective responsibility of the community for the sins of its individual members. Although there was originally no fixed wording for the c., traditional formulas emerged and were incorporated into the liturgy. Various formulas for private c.'s are also suggested in rabbinic literature, for example: "How shall a man make (private) c. on the eve of the Day of Atonement? He should say 'I confess before Thee for all the wrongs which I have committed. I have taken the path of evil. I hereby renounce all the wrongdoing which I have hitherto committed. May it be Thy will, O Lord my God, to pardon me for all my iniquities, forgive me for all my transgressions, and grant me atonement for all my sins'" (*Lev. Rab.* 3). Public confessions appear in the liturgies for penitential and fast days, as well as on every Monday and Thursday. Private c. is said by some at night before retiring, and also by a bridegroom and bride before their wedding. Since c. in general is recognized as having the power to effect atonement for sins, c. on one's deathbed became a matter of great importance, and is recommended in the Talmud (*Shab.* 32a), which cites the precedent of ACHAN (Josh. 7:19). A traditional formula was evolved, and is recorded by Naḥmanides (13th cent.), which incorporates the mishnaic petition "May my death be an atonement for all the sins... of which I have been guilty toward Thee" (*Sanh.* 6:2). The custom of confessing regularly to a trusted friend or master was practiced in some mystic circles, particularly in some of the 16th cent. kabbalistic brotherhoods, but failed to gain wider currency.

CONFIRMATION, see **BAR MITZVAH; BAT MITZVAH**

CONGRATULATIONS: Belief in planetary influence was widespread among the Jews (see ASTROLOGY) and though they have entirely lost their original astrological significance, the most common Jewish expressions of congratulation (*mazzal tov* = "good luck", lit. "[under] a good constellation"), *mazzal u-verakhah* ("luck and blessing"), and *be-siman tov* ("under a good sign") were originally connected with this belief. Other forms of c. include the phrases *yeyasher koḥekha* ("May God increase your strength") and (among *Sephardim*) *ḥazak u-varukh* ("Be strong and blessed"), both of which convey encouragement. Among *Sephardim* various c. are introduced by the word *tizkeh* ("may you be vouchsafed" — length of years, the performance of commandments, etc.). Toasts consist of the one word *le-ḥayyim* ("To life"); birthday c., of the phrase "may you live to 120 years". See also GREETINGS.

CONGREGATION, see **COMMUNITY**

CONSECRATION, see **DEDICATION; HOLINESS**

CONSENT, see **HASKAMAH**

CONSERVATIVE JUDAISM: Religious movement which developed in the U.S. in the 20th cent., inspired by the 19th cent. Historical School of Judaism in Europe. The challenge of the Emancipation to traditional Judaism, beginning in W. Europe with the 18th cent. Enlightenment and intensified during the first half of the 19th cent., met a positive reaction in the Historical School. One of the chief exponents of that School, Zacharias FRANKEL (1801-1875), is considered by Conservative Jews as the first seminal influence in the evolution of the philosophy of Conservatism. In his reconstruction of the history of rabbinic thought, Frankel prepared the way for C.J.'s commitment to scientific scholarship. Against the rising Reform movement of his time he reaffirmed the importance to Jewish life of the concepts of Jewish nationhood, the Land of Israel, and the Hebrew language. Frankel insisted that the observance of the *mitzvot* was vital to Judaism as a "religion of action". While he agreed with Reform thinkers concerning the need for development, he believed that the *halakhah* should be adapted in terms of its own spirit and modes of interpretation. His ideas were later taken up by the molders of the Historical School and by Conservative theoreticians. In the U.S., the forerunners of Conservatism in the Historical School — Isaac Leeser, Benjamin Szold, Marcus Jastrow, Alexander Kohut, and others — as well as later major figures of Conservatism such as Solomon Schechter and Louis Ginzberg, offered different and often conflicting theories which nonetheless found their way into Conservative thought. Another stream which ran into the Conservative confluence was Zionism, particularly that aspect of the Zionist movement identified with Aḥad Ha-Am and his concept of cultural nationalism. From the outset, Conservatism had espoused the Zionist cause, both in its spiritual aim of revitalizing the Jewish tradition and its political objective of securing a national homeland for the Jewish people. Aḥad Ha-Am had interpreted Jewish culture in moral and intellectual terms; Conservatism emphasized the religious strain of the Jewish tradition. Yet it was Aḥad Ha-Am's influence which dominated the Zionism of Conservatism, which did not exclude Herzlian Zionism, but viewed the political program as a means to a primarily spiritual end. In evolving its theory of Zionism, C.J. gradually reinterpreted the traditional concept of *kibbutz galuyyot* (the "ingathering of the exiles") and extended Aḥad Ha-Am's philosophy to include a positive approach to the Diaspora as a source of enrichment to Jewish life. Various attempts have been made to articulate a platform for Conservatism which would clarify the diversity of thought and practice that has always characterized the movement. Even such generally recognized concepts in Conservative ideology as catholic (the community of) Israel, Zionism, Jewish civilization, *halakhah*, and the principle of unity in diversity are subject to varied and contradictory interpretation. The movement has from the outset been a coalition. Historic ties and common loyalty to the JEWISH THEOLOGICAL SEMINARY (the spiritual and educational center of the movement) have served to hold the various strands together. As a movement, Conservatism is also united by its adherents' ties to tradition and their desire to have it strengthened by change from within rather than demands of convenience and conformity from without. Thus the ultimate distinctiveness of Conservatism is the ability of a diverse array of thinkers and followers to continue to function together and maintain their sense of unity and relatedness. Still, the coalition is in constant tension, particularly in matters of theology and ritual practice. Many Conservative leaders interpret theological concepts like revelation and the idea of a personal God in ways radically different from their predecessors and from each other — so different, in fact, as to be virtually mutually exclusive. It is thus difficult to define Conservative theology with any degree of preciseness. Solomon Schechter eschewed a theology of his own, though he wrote movingly about rabbinic theology and articulated the idea of God as revealed in Jewish history. To Louis Ginzberg, theology, which he identified with *aggadah,* was far less significant and vital for Jewish life than was *halakhah.* Abraham Joshua Heschel breathed an air of mysticism, Mordecai Kaplan one of naturalism. Conservative views on ritual range from Orthodoxy to Reform. Both majority and minority opinions in the RABBINICAL ASSEMBLY are recognized as legitimate expressions of Conservatism. C.J. is now endeavoring to make an impact on communities outside North America.

CONSISTORIES: Governing bodies of a Jewish communal district. The institution was established by the Napoleonic decree of 1808, which provided for the creation of c. of both clerical and lay participants throughout France with a central consistory in Paris under 3 "grand rabbis" and 2 laymen, responsible among other things for the maintenance of the Chief Rabbinate and the rabbinical seminary. The system still prevails in France and Belgium.

CONSOLATION, see **MOURNING**

CONTRACT, see **DEED**

CONTRACTION, see **TZIMTZUM**

CONTROVERSIES (internal): The existence or emergence of deviating views or movements (schismatic, heretical, or sectarian) inevitably produced c. in which one group attacked the other's positions and defended its own. C. often crystallized in literary works and were thus responsible for an important part of theological literature. The Bible, for instance, contains many polemics against paganism, while religious c. in post-biblical Judaism begin with the SAMARITANS and continue with the SADDUCEES, the KARAITES, the SABBATAIANS, and the ḤASIDIM, entering the modern period with the REFORM movement. The legal c. between the schools of Hillel and Shammai, as well as the bitter religious controversy over the philosophical works of Maimonides, were over matters of interpretation rather than fundamental faith. The breach with the Samaritans, on the other hand, resulted in a long drawn-out social and political struggle whose religious core was the question of whether Judaism was based on the Pentateuch alone or on the entire Bible — quite apart from the Samaritan claims in behalf of Mount GERIZIM. In hellenistic times, the Hellenizers, profoundly influenced by Greek philosophy, engaged in controversy with the representatives of traditional Jewish thought. Similarly, the Pharisees with their broader interpretations of the law disputed with the narrower Sadducee tradition. Sectarian c. (with ESSENES and others) are reflected in the DEAD SEA SCROLLS, while c. with Jewish-Christians are preserved in rabbinic literature. The religious controversy between the Rabbinites and the Karaites reverted once again to the Sadducee controversy and inspired forceful attacks by the representatives of Rabbinic Judaism, particularly SAADYAH Gaon. The messianic movement launched by SHABBETAI TZEVI led to many bitter c., of which the FRANKIST and the EMDEN-EIBESCHUTZ c. were two offshoots. The rise of the ḥasidic movement in the second half of the 18th cent. for a time led to violent polemics in E. Europe between Ḥasidim and their opponents, the MITNAGGEDIM. The controversy between Orthodoxy and the Reform movement, which was initially directed against such individuals as Abraham Geiger, acquired an ideological tone after the first Reform Council at Brunswick in 1844; it has continued with varying degrees of intensity to the present day. For controversies with non-Jews, see DISPUTATIONS.

CONVERSION, FORCED: The forced conversion of the Idumeans (Edomites) to Judaism by John Hyrcanus (135-105 B.C.E.) is the only such recorded case in history. On the other hand Jews have been the victims of forced conversions throughout their history, and the rabbis issued special enactments to provide for Jews who were unable to observe their religion openly, as happened during the times which immediately preceded and led up to the Maccabean revolt in 168 B.C.E. Forced conversions to Christianity as a result of mob violence occurred in the Roman Empire during the 4th-6th cents., and it later became state policy in Visigothic Spain and elsewhere. During the CRUSADES many Jewish communities, especially in the Rhineland, were given the alternative of baptism or death; in most cases they chose the latter alternative, as for instance at York (England) in 1190 where the entire community immolated itself before the Christian attackers. When after the persecutions those who had adopted the dominant faith to save their lives applied to return to the Jewish fold, all rabbinical authorities, notably Rabbenu GERSHOM and RASHI, insisted that they be treated with the utmost tact and consideration, and any mention of their previous lapse was forbidden. If after their f.c. they had made efforts to practice Judaism secretly, they were not regarded as apostates. Even Maimonides, who ruled in his *Mishneh Torah* that a Jew should accept death rather than abandon a single commandment under compulsion, admitted that apostasy under threat of death was not to be punished. The Almohadic persecution in Spain and N. Africa in 1148 produced a wave of forced conversions and was the occasion of the publication by Maimon (Maimonides' father) of the *Iggeret ha-Shemad,* in which he encouraged the forced converts to "hang on by their fingertips"; Maimonides for his part permitted the outward assumption of Islam to save one's life, since the Moslems — unlike the Christians — required only a formal declaration of adherence to their faith and did not insist on the abandonment of Jewish practices. Forced conversions under Moslem pressure also produced the Daggatun — a Moroccan Berber tribe, traditionally of Jewish origin, and the JEDID AL-ISLAM in 19th cent. Persia. The most extensive f.c. in Jewish history occurred in Spain following the widespread anti-Jewish excesses which began in Seville in 1391; these converts were called MARRANOS (Heb. *anusim* i.e., "forced converts"). A considerable number of Jews remained loyal to the faith despite every pressure and peril, and it was they who were expelled from Spain in 1492. Many of them proceeded to Portugal where, in 1496, they were forcibly dragged to the baptismal font or regarded as having automatically adopted Christianity; in later centuries these Portuguese Marranos seized every opportunity to return to Judaism. Problems in Jewish law arose as to the Jewishness of the descendants of forced converts and Marranos who were unable to return to Judaism; it was agreed that such a person, upon returning to Judaism was not required to undergo the obligatory ceremony for proselytes. See also CRYPTO-JEWS.

CONVERSION FROM JUDAISM, see **APOSTASY**

CONVERSION TO JUDAISM, see **PROSELYTE**

CORDOVERO, MOSES BEN JACOB (known as *Remakh;* 1522-1570): Kabbalist of the Safed school; brother-in-law of Solomon ALKABETZ and disciple of Joseph KARO. The most profoundly systematic thinker among kabbalists, his literary works, of which the most famous are the highly technical *Pardes Rimmonim* ("Pomegranate Orchard") and the more popular *Tomer Devorah* ("Deborah's Palm Tree"), offer a full discussion of kabbalistic mystical theology and practical, devotional guidance respectively. A problem to which he made a particularly significant contribution was that of the relationship of EIN SOPH, the hidden Divine Ground, to the SEPHIROT in which the Divine becomes manifest. C.'s solution, which is a synthesis of the kabbalistic concepts of *atzmut* (essence or substance of the Divine) and *kelim* (instrument or "vessels" of its manifestation) raises the problem of the theistic viz. panentheistic character of his teaching; some scholars have even claimed that much of Spinoza's thought has its origin in C.'s ideas. Though soon ousted by the victorious new Kabbalah of Isaac LURIA, C.'s writings influenced many subsequent kabbalists.

CORNERS, see **PEAH**

CORPORAL PUNISHMENT, see **FLOGGING**

CORPSE: Dead human body. In biblical times, all who came into contact with a c. were rendered ritually unclean as was also the building where the c. was situated together with all inhabitants and any uncovered vessels inside. Purification was then effected by sprinkling on the third day after defilement all contaminated persons and objects with water containing ashes of the RED HEIFER and further sprinkling, on the seventh day, together with the immersion of the person defiled and his clothes (Num. 19:14-22). These regulations are expanded in the Mishnah tractate *Oholot.* BURIAL of a c. was a religious obligation (Lev. 21); only the High Priest and Nazirites were absolutely forbidden to come into contact with a c. In rabbinic law the prohibition against contact with a c. applied to all members of priestly families; hence *kohanim* cannot remain under the same roof with a c., attend burials, or visit the cemetery. In all cases where contact was permitted, subsequent washing of the hands was made obligatory. For animal bodies, see CARCASS.

COSMOGONY AND COSMOLOGY: Doctrines and speculations regarding the origin and nature of the universe. Whereas Jewish ideas about the structure of the cosmos were influenced by mythological, philosophical, and scientific notions current in the non-Jewish (near-eastern, hellenistic, medieval, etc.) environment, the basic cosmogonic-religious principle of Judaism was determined by the first chapter of the Bible. God, the Creator, created "heaven and earth and all the host of them". Speculation concerning the connotations of the words "heaven", "earth" and "created", was a constant subject of inquiry. Traditional Jewish teaching (the rabbis, PHILO, and most medieval philosophers) insisted that creation was made from nothing (*ex nihilo*), but some thinkers, apparently with the support of the biblical account itself, held that the universe was fashioned from pre-existent, formless matter. (For biblical c. cf. Gen. 1-2; Ps. 104; Job 38). With the early rabbis c. was a systematic discipline (MAASEH BERESHIT), the study of which was, however, restricted to the initiated (Mishnah *Ḥag.* 2:1) because of the dangers — in particular of dualist and gnostic heresies — which it harbored for the average mind. Nevertheless much cosmogonic and cosmological speculation is enshrined in talmudic and midrashic AGGADAH, and it is prominent in the PIRKEI DE-RABBI ELIEZER, the *Midrash Konen,* and the mystical HEIKHALOT writings. The last-named also influenced the c. of the KABBALAH in which man, i.e., the Jew, is held to occupy a key position in the cosmos. This anthropocentric tendency reached its acme in the teachings of Isaac LURIA regarding the "breaking of the vessels" and the cosmic TIKKUN. Whereas kabbalistic c. was greatly influenced by the Neo-Platonic tradition, most medieval philosophers followed the Aristotelian system. Maimonides summarized his cosmological views in his code (*Hilkhot Yesodei ha-Torah*) and thereby codified the Ptolemaic system, according to which the earth, surrounded by concentric, incorporeal, and "intelligent" spheres was held to be the center of the universe. Throughout ancient and medieval times c. was closely allied to theology in general and mysticism in particular, particularly since religious language always used cosmic terminology: things Divine are "heavenly" as contrasted with things material and earthly; the spirit soars to "higher spheres" (hence the influence of c. on mystical experience), etc. Modern science rendered a completely literal acceptance of the traditional imagery, and of biblical cosmography in particular, a virtual impossibility. There are still literalists and fundamentalists in Orthodox circles, but the general tendency is to agree that the biblical account of creation is to be read for its moral and religious message rather than for its "scientific" meaning.

COSTUME: The only biblical injunctions in the matter of dress are the prohibition against the wearing of SHAATNEZ (cloth woven of wool and linen; Lev. 19:19), the commandment to place fringes upon the four corners of one's garments (Num. 15:37-41), and that against the "abomination" of wearing the dress or accouterments of the opposite sex (Deut. 22:5), though the commentators largely limit this prohibition to men wearing such dress for lewd purposes. During the Talmudic Period, however, the duty of adopting distinctive Jewish garb was raised to the level of a biblical commandment, based upon an interpretation of Lev. 18:3, "Neither shall ye walk in their ordinances". The Midrash declares that one of the four factors contributing to the redemption of the Children of Israel from Egypt was that "they did not change their [distinctively Jewish] garments [for prevailing Egyptian fashions]" (*Lev. Rab.* 32:5). The law against Jews wearing the garments of gentiles makes it clear that the prohibition is confined, in the words of Joseph KARO, to "garments peculiarly distinctive of the gentiles" or, as ISSERLES puts it, "to such garments that suggest brazenness or have an idolatrous connection", but nonetheless the custom developed for Jews to adopt a unique c. as a demonstration of their Jewish identity. During the late Middle Ages Polish Jews adopted the then obsolete dress of the Polish noblemen, the fur-trimmed hat (*shtreimel*), and the long caftan, to which the Ḥasidim added, for religious reasons, a girdle round the waist (to distinguish the "pure" upper part of the body from the "impure" lower). This garb is still worn by Ḥasidim and in certain ultra-Orthodox Jewish circles. Despite the injunction that the four-fringed garment has to be "seen" (Num. 15:39), it is usually worn as an undergarment except during religious services. Among extremely religious Jews, however, there is a tradition allowing the fringes to hang out. Change of garments was obligatory, where possible, on Sabbaths and festivals (*Shab.* 113a) and scholars were also supposed to wear distinctive clothing (*Ber.* 43b; *Shab.* 114a; *Bava Batra* 57b). The Jewish badge ordained by the Fourth Lateran Council (1215) in order to prevent social mixing between Jews and Christians inspired later authorities to insist that Jews wear some distinguishing article of apparel (such as a badge or hat). However, the apparently distinctive c. of Jews portrayed in medieval manuscripts and prints is more often than not only the particular dress of that country and period, common to both Jews and non-Jews.

COUNCILS AND SYNODS: Gatherings of rabbis, sometimes in conjunction with laymen, for the purpose of safeguarding the Jewish religion, regulating the inner life of the Jewish COMMUNITY and its relationship with the outer world, or framing extra-legal communal enactments which would thereafter be binding upon all those represented. Antecedents may be discerned in the GREAT ASSEMBLY and rabbinical meetings after the destruction of the Second Temple, such as that at Yavneh (c. 90) where the biblical canon was determined, or at Usha (c. 138) where halakhic rules were laid down. C. and S. as distinctive aspects of voluntary Jewish self-government developed in the Jewish communities of the Rhineland and N. France at the beginning of the second millennium C.E. The first synod in medieval Jewish history was convened c. 1150 by the brothers Samuel ben Meir and Jacob Tam, grandsons of Rashi, and was followed by a second in 1160. Two of their enactments — the prohibition against having recourse to gentile courts of law, and an important amendment to R. Gershom's prohibition against polygamy — are indicative of the nature of the regulations adopted at these synods. Two important synods were held at Mainz in 1220 and 1223 under the leadership of the most distinguished rabbis of the day, Eliezer ben Judah and Eliezer ben Joel Halevi. The enactments passed there became generally accepted by *Ashkenazi* Jewry. Gradually these synods extended the scope of their activities to include every phase of the religious, economic, social, and family life of the Jews. In Spain, the available evidence shows that C. and S. were convened by the king for financial and civil matters. In 1552 Middle Eastern rabbis convened at a synod in Jerusalem to determine the sabbatical year. The most important and long-lived synod in Jewish history was the Polish Council of Four Lands, which consisted of thirty delegates — both rabbinical and lay — and met twice yearly at the fairs of Lublin and Jaroslav. This council embraced every possible aspect of Jewish activity. In the religious sphere, for instance, it safeguarded strict observance of the law and bitterly fought the followers of Shabbetai Tzevi and the Frankists. It lasted for some two centuries from 1550. Synods in St. Petersburg were convened on several occasions during the 19th cent. by the Russian government, the last in 1879 to satisfy governmental interest in Jewish marriage and divorce laws. One of the most famous of modern synods was the Grand Sanhedrin convoked by Napoleon in 1807 which recognized the authority of civil law and set up a central Jewish communal administration in France.

The rabbinical conferences at Brunswick in 1844, Frankfort in 1845, and Breslau in 1846 laid the groundwork for the modern Reform movement. It was at the Frankfort conference that Zacharias Frankel parted company with the Reformers and became one of the founders of the Historical School (later Conservatism). One of the most decisive meetings in the history of Reform took place in 1885 in Pittsburgh, Pennsylvania, and produced the platform which guided that movement for several decades. The Central Conference of Reform Rabbis met in 1937, at Columbus, Ohio, and reversed the opposition to Jewish nationalism expressed in the 1885 platform. In the course of time U.S. Reform rabbis began to abandon the anti-Zionism of the 19th cent. Each convention of the Central Conference of American Rabbis (Reform), the Rabbinical Assembly of America (Conservative), and the Rabbinical Council of America (Orthodox) takes stands on problems in contemporary Jewish life.

COUNTING OF OMER, see **OMER, COUNTING OF**

COURT OF GENTILES, see **TEMPLE**

COURT OF WOMEN, see **TEMPLE**

COURTS, see **BET DIN; SANHEDRIN**

COVENANT (Heb. *berit*): An agreement by which two contracting parties freely enter into a special kind of relationship (e.g. of solidarity, friendship, obedience, etc.). A c. could be made between man and his fellow or between man and God and was usually confirmed by some kind of ritual symbolizing the union of the partners. Such bonds between men are illustrated by the biblical accounts of the c. between Jacob and Laban (Gen. 31:44) and that between the king and the people during the reign of Zedekiah (Jer. 34). In the former, God is invoked as a witness of the sanctity of the c. (Gen. 31:53); the latter solemnly provided for the release of all Hebrew slaves, and its subsequent breach by the slave-owners was also regarded as a breach of the basic c. between God and the people of Israel (Jer. 34:14-16). The account in Jeremiah (34:18-19) also describes the ceremonial part of the c., which consisted of the two parties passing between the two halves of a calf. Similarly at the "c. between the pieces" (*berit bein ha-betarim*) between God and Abraham (Gen. 15:9-17), the "furnace of smoke and the flame of fire which passed between the pieces" represented the Presence of God as one of the contracting parties; cf. the Hebrew idiom *karat berit* (literally "cutting a c.") for "making a c.". The c. which God made with Abraham and subsequently confirmed to Isaac and Jacob is fundamental to the theological understanding of the development of Judaism. The original c. with the patriarchs was renewed, this time with the whole people, at Sinai (Exod. 24) where the people accepted the obligations of the law ("the two tablets of the c."; cf. Exod. 31:18; 32:15 ff.). The c. was renewed again by EZRA. God's eternal fidelity to his c., in spite of Israel's backsliding, is a major theme in AGGADAH and liturgy (cf. also Lev. 26:42-45). Outward signs serve to testify to the permanent validity of a c. e.g. CIRCUMCISION — *berit milah*, the "*berit*" *par excellence* — for the c. of Abraham; the Sabbath, Exod. 31:16-17). Other, more specific, covenants conferred the priesthood upon the House of Aaron (Num. 25:12-13) and kingship upon the House of David (Ps. 132). A c. involving mankind as a whole, and indeed the entire natural order, was made with Noah (Gen. 9:12-15); according to Jeremiah (33:19-21, 25-26) the specific covenants with Israel and David are everlasting. The traditional idea of a c. between God and His people is presupposed by the prophets and forms the background of their preaching.

COVENANT OF ABRAHAM (BERIT MILAH), see **CIRCUMCISION**

COVERING OF THE HEAD: There is little basis in Jewish law for the Orthodox custom of going about with covered head, or even for the covering of the head during prayer and other religious exercises. It is an outstanding example of CUSTOM assuming the force of Law. The most explicit reference to it in the Talmud is the statement of R. Joshua ben Levi that one should not walk four cubits "with upright stature" in view of the verse, "the whole world is full of His glory" (Is. 6:3), to which R. Huna ben Joshua added that he would never walk four cubits bareheaded, since "the Divine Presence is above my head" (*Kidd.* 31a). Thus, covering the head became a sign of reverence and awe, and an acknowledgment of the omnipresence of God. The Bible prescribes that the High Priest don a miter (Exod. 28), but otherwise bareheadedness was originally the prevailing custom. Gradually it became usual to cover the head during prayer as a mark of piety. The Jews of Babylonia stressed the importance of covering the head, and the growth of Islam subsequently spread the concept of keeping the head covered during prayer. Yet it took a long time for this custom to gain universal acceptance. As late as the 13th cent., R. Isaac of Vienna expressed his disapproval of boys going up to read the *Torah* bareheaded: "And the custom of our rabbis in France of reciting blessings with uncovered head does not meet with my approval" (*Or Zarua*, 11:43). Solomon Luria (16th cent.) writes in a responsum (No. 72): "I do not know of any prohibition against pronouncing blessings with uncovered head... were it not for the fact that I am not accustomed to differ from the ancient teachers, I would be inclined to be lenient and utter blessings, or even recite the *Shema,* with uncovered head... the prohibition against uncovering the head even when not at prayer astonishes me; I do not know its source". The Vilna Gaon agreed with him that the prohibition was based on custom only. However the 17th cent. rabbi David Ha-Levi of Ostrog found religious prescription in his interpretation of the talmudic view of Lev. 18:3, "we shall not walk in their ordinances" (*ḥukkat ha-goy*): i.e., Jews should cover their heads at prayer because Christians do not. The prevalent custom among strictly Orthodox Jews is to keep their heads covered at all times during their waking hours, and all traditionalist Jews cover their heads when praying. The question of the validity of this custom has occupied Reform Jews in Europe and the U.S., and many Reform communities have abolished the custom of covering their head even during synagogal prayer.

COVETOUSNESS: Wrongful desire to possess what belongs by right to another. The tenth commandment (Exod. 20:17), which forbids c., is the only commandment in the Decalogue transgressable by thought rather than action, and rabbinic teaching takes it for granted that man can conquer his sinful desires. The later books of the Bible outspokenly condemn c. as a major sin undermining society and moral relationships (cf. e.g., Micah 2:1-2). God abhors the covetous man (Ps. 10:3); the rabbis regard the violation of the tenth commandment as a violation of the entire Decalogue. On the other hand spiritual "covetousness", which takes the form of a desire to emulate others in spiritual matters, is regarded as praiseworthy, on the grounds that "the envy of scholars increaseth wisdom" (*Bava Batra* 21a).

CREATION, see **COSMOGONY AND COSMOLOGY**

CREATION, BOOK OF, see **YETZIRAH, BOOK OF**

CREDIT, see **DEBT; LOANS**

CREED: An authoritative and binding summary of those articles of faith and the fundamental doctrines of a religious community, usually set out in the form of dogmatic statements or questions and answers (CATECHISM). Whereas the process of the formulation and adoption of such creeds has been a major feature of the history of Christianity, it has played almost no role in the spiritual development of Judaism. The absence of a supreme ecclesiastical body authorized to formulate a c. is not the sole reason for the virtual absence of creeds in Judaism, and it was often felt that the very idea of such formulation ran counter to certain fundamental tendencies in Jewish theology, which is concerned not only with beliefs but very largely with "commandments", of which R. Judah Ha-Nasi said "Be as heedful of a light precept as of a grave one for thou knowest not the grant of reward for each precept" (*Avot* 2:1). In the view of the ancient rabbis, faithful and devout observance of the commandments was more important than "faith" in the sense of formal assent to theological statements; hence the Midrash could put into the mouth of God the wish: "Would that they abandoned Me, but observed My commandments — since the light thereof will turn them again to Me" (*Lam. Rab.* Introd.). Man is judged by his actions and not by the c. he professes. The nearest approach to a c. in Judaism is to be seen in certain rabbinic statements emphasizing religious fundamentals or defining the actions or beliefs by which a person forfeits his share in the OLAM HA-BA or qualifies as an APOSTATE, viz., MUMAR. R. Simlai (*Mak.* 23b-24a) declared the eleven injunctions of Ps. 15, the six of Is. 33:16, the three of Mic. 6:8, and Hab. 2:4 ("The righteous shall live by his faith") to be the quintessence of the 613 PRECEPTS, while R. Akiva stated that the commandment "Thou shalt love thy neighbor as thyself" (Lev. 19:18) was the "great principle of the *Torah*" (*Siphra, Kedoshim* 4.) All these statements, however, cannot be said to constitute a c. PHILO (1st cent.) was the first philosopher to formulate something like a c., but his five principles (the existence and rulership of God, the Unity of God, the creation of the world, the unity of creation, and Divine Providence) left little mark on the subsequent history of Jewish theology. Of the various attempts made by the medieval philosophers to formulate a c., the most successful and enduring is Maimonides' statement of the THIRTEEN PRINCIPLES OF FAITH, but despite its popularity (the well-known hymn *Yigdal* is a poetic version) it has never been formally regarded as binding, and several thinkers objected to it on various grounds. Joseph ALBO in his *Ikkarim* opposed Maimonides, and maintained that there were only three basic DOGMAS: the existence of God, Divine REVELATION, and RETRIBUTION. No doubt there always was a body of beliefs or even dogmas held by Jews — though not necessarily identical at all times and in all groups — but these beliefs were generally implicit in law and practice, expressed in liturgy and prayer (e.g. the confession of the unity of God in the SHEMA, or of the RESURRECTION of the dead in the AMIDAH), or expounded in moral and homiletical literature, rather than formally defined in creedal statements. Since the 19th cent. creeds came to play a greater rôle in Judaism. The REFORM Movement, partly in imitation of the Christian Churches, partly in order to clarify and justify its own deviation from traditional rabbinic Judaism, tried to state its beliefs in declarations or "platforms" (cf. e.g. the Pittsburgh Platform) which partook of a creedal, though not necessarily dogmatic, nature. Creeds were also embedded in CATECHISMS which also were particularly popular in the 19th cent.

CREMATION: Disposal of a dead body by burning. C. is forbidden by Orthodox Jewish religious law which, in line with biblical tradition, considers it as a desecration of the dead. Even criminals on whom the death sentence had been carried out had to be buried with reverence, following the verse in Deut. 21:23, which is regarded as the basis for the law enjoining BURIAL as the only acceptable method for disposal of the dead. The Talmud (*Yev.* 78b) regards the three years' famine in the time of David as a punishment for the burning of the body of Saul (I Sam. 31:12). During the past century, the possibility of permitting c. has been discussed, but Orthodox authorities have not gone beyond allowing the ashes of a cremated person to be interred with a burial ceremony. Reform Judaism, on the other hand, permits c.

CRESCAS, ḤASDAI BEN ABRAHAM (c. 1340-1410): Spanish philosopher and CROWN RABBI of Aragon. His main work *Or Adonai* ("The Light of the Lord") is a closely reasoned critique of Aristotle and the Aristotelian rationalist tradition in Jewish thought, as represented in particular by MAIMONIDES. Steering a middle course between philosophic rationalism on the one hand, and a growing Spanish tendency toward mysticism on the other, C. rejected the traditional proofs for the existence of God and insisted that certainty in this matter rested solely on the authority of the Bible. He criticized Maimonides' formulation of thirteen principles of faith and proposed a list of eight principles. According to C., love of God, rather than specific beliefs regarding the nature of creation or an intellectual understanding of the Divine, was the main concern of Judaism. C., who lost a son in the anti-Jewish riots of 1391, also wrote a critique of the Christian religion to win back Jewish apostates. His theological work was continued and popularized by his disciple Joseph ALBO.

CRIME: No term corresponding exactly to the normal usage of the term c. exists in Jewish law, since no distinction is made, as regards PUNISHMENT and procedure, between punishable offenses of a purely ritual and those of a secular nature; e.g. murder and the breaking of the Sabbath (both punishable by death) would be classified as the same type of c. Various degrees of gravity of offense are recognized (see SIN), and rabbinic law distinguished sharply between civil law (*dinei mamanot*), involving monetary matters only, and criminal law (*dinei nephashot*, "laws involving persons" i.e., offenses involving capital or other physical punishment). The latter is administered according to special and rigid rules of procedure.

CRIMINAL PROCEDURE: Jewish criminal law and criminal court procedure are dealt with in the Mishnah tractate *Sanhedrin* (particularly chaps. 3-4). The differences in the treatment of civil and criminal cases is especially emphasized. Whereas the former may be tried in a court of three judges, the latter requires a court of at least 23. In criminal cases, the judges must consider first the arguments for acquittal before turning to any charges made against the accused. A majority of one is sufficient for acquittal, but a majority of two is required for condemnation. There can be no retrial once a man has been acquitted of a criminal charge, whereas there can be any number of retrials if he is found guilty. Any witness may be heard for the defense of the accused, but there are serious limitations to accepting witnesses for the prosecution. A man cannot be declared guilty on the day of the completion of the trial, but no delay is necessary before he is declared innocent. Judges must reconsider over and again before pronouncing a verdict. WITNESSES in criminal cases are given a severe warning to tell nothing but the truth and are cross-examined in a most painstaking manner. A court which perseveres in its cross-examination is considered especially praiseworthy. At least two witnesses are required to secure condemnation and almost the least contradiction renders their testimony invalid. Hearsay or circumstantial evidence is not tolerated in the court. Even where guilt was certain, many courts hesitated to pronounce a death sentence and would search for an argument to free the accused; rabbinic law exhibits an aversion against CAPITAL PUNISHMENT. Some rabbis are quoted as saying that a court which pronounced a death sentence even once in 70 years was a "bloody court". In periods of national emergency and the like men were put to death for such crimes as informing, but this was not usually a court procedure.

CRITICISM, BIBLICAL, see **BIBLE CRITICISM**

CROWN OF THE LAW, see **KETER TORAH**

CROWN OF ROYALTY, see **KETER MALKHUT**

CROWN RABBI: Rabbi appointed by the secular authorities as the official representative of the Jewish community vis-à-vis the government. From 1394-1401, for instance, Joseph Orabuena, physician to the king of Navarre was appointed as "rabi mayor de los judeos del reyna" and in 1432, Abraham Benveniste convoked a synod in Valladolid in his capacity as "rab de la corte". Such appointments were not necessarily made on the basis of the piety or scholarship of the nominee, and for this and other reasons they were looked at askance by the Jewish community. This dissociation was most pronounced in Czarist Russia where the Crown or "Kazyonnay" Rabbis were regarded as mere government puppets whose authority was completely ignored in all but purely official matters, while the real spiritual authority was vested in the "Dukhovner" or "Orthodox" rabbis, who were the real heads of the community.

CRUELTY: Although the Bible occasionally reports atrocities, especially against defeated enemies (e.g. II Sam. 12:31), its laws condemn all forms of c. or indifference to suffering. Particular consideration is urged toward the defenseless. The oppression of widows and orphans provokes the wrath of God (Exod. 22:21-23), and the warning against c. to strangers is often repeated on the grounds that "ye know the heart of a stranger, seeing ye were strangers in the land of Egypt" (*ibid.* 23:9). Rabbinical exegesis insists that the alleged LEX TALIONIS was never meant to imply mutilation of the offender but only his liability for monetary compensation (*Bava Kamma* 83b). In rabbinic Judaism characteristics of c. include an unforgiving temper and general lack of consideration for others. Thus, Maimonides in his code brands as cruel a man who refuses to accept a plea for forgiveness by another who wronged him, who treats or addresses his servant intemperately, and who fails to show compassion for the needy; such c., he says, is not to be found among the seed of Abraham and would cast doubts on a Jew's pedigree. See also ANIMALS, TREATMENT OF; COMPASSION.

CRUSADES: The holy wars proclaimed by the Christians in Western Europe at the end of the 11th cent. with the avowed purpose of wresting the Holy Sepulcher from the hands of the infidel Moslems; the c. marked a turning point in the history of the Jews of Christian Europe. From the prime objective of defeating the infidels in the Holy Land, Christians turned in an outburst of hate against the Jewish "infidels" in their midst. As early as 1094, Godfrey of Bouillon declared that he would avenge the blood of Jesus on the Jews, leaving none alive. The First Crusade of 1096 brought with it the virtual extermination of the ancient Jewish communities of Speyer, Worms, Mainz, and others. The tragedy is commemorated to the present day in the *Ashkenazi* rite in a Sabbath prayer (*Av ha-Raḥamim*) for "the holy congregations who laid down their lives for the sanctification of the Divine Name" and in the dirge *Arzei Levanon* found in the liturgy for *Av* 9. When the Crusaders finally reached Palestine and stormed Jerusalem (1099) they drove all Jews there into a synagogue and burned them alive. The pattern of anti-Jewish massacres, following resolute refusal on the part of the Jews to accept conversion to Christianity, was repeated throughout Europe during subsequent c. (especially the Second and Third).

CRYPTO-JEWS: Jews who, as a result of coercion — usually the threat of death — outwardly adopt the dominant faith while clandestinely continuing to maintain Jewish practices. The MARRANOS (and CHUETAS in Majorca) are the best-known examples, but Jewish history knows many other such C.J. (see CONVERSION, FORCED). The Crypto-

Judaism of the DONMEH, (those who continued to follow Shabbetai Tzevi even after his adoption of Islam), belongs to a different category. Their outward acceptance of Islam was a voluntary act undertaken to follow the example of their master. In 1838, the Jews of Meshed (Persia) were the victims of an outburst of mob violence and were faced with the alternatives of death or the adoption of Islam. Those who could not escape outwardly took the Islamic faith, but maintained their Jewish practices and religious exercises with extreme devotion (see JEDID AL-ISLAM).

CUPS: WINE occupies an important position in Jewish ritual and despite stern disapproval of drunkenness, is regarded in rabbinic lore as representing the essence of joy and goodness. The Cup of Benediction is an essential element of all joyous occasions, whether a circumcision, wedding, or *kiddush.* The *kiddush,* though it belongs strictly to the festive board, is in most rites included in the synagogue service, the origin of this practice being the hospitality for wayfarers formerly provided on synagogue premises. At the greatest home festival of the year, the Passover SEDER, four cups of wine (ARBA KOSOT) are drunk. There was controversy among the rabbis whether the *Seder* ritual required four or five cups. Since in Jewish tradition all doubtful cases will be resolved "when Elijah comes", custom decreed that a fifth cup be filled but not partaken of. This is the origin of the "Cup of Elijah" at the *Seder,* which, with the passage of time, was given a mystic interpretation as the cup kept in readiness for the advent of this prophet, who would come on the Festival of the Redemption from Egypt to herald the messianic redemption of the future.

CURSES, see BLESSING AND CURSE

CURTAIN ON ARK, see PAROKHET

CUSTOM (Heb. *minhag*): As a specific halakhic term, *minhag* denotes a religious practice dating from post-biblical times; not one introduced by an authority or based on biblical writ, but one which has nevertheless become sacred by virtue of long usage. Accepted c. is one of the formative contributing factors in the development of Jewish law and religious observance. This applies both to local *minhag,* i.e., customs which obtain in one locality only, as well as to customs which have been adopted universally. *Minhagim* (pl.) are considered as less binding than formal legal enactments, though in the event of conflict c. can take precedence over law (see Y. *Yer.* 12:1). The institution of the SECOND DAY OF THE FESTIVALS in the Diaspora is a striking example of an obsolete law surviving merely because it qualified as c. Originally the second day was instituted on account of doubt over the exact day of the festival, since the emissaries of the Sanhedrin could not reach the Jews in the Diaspora in time to notify them of the date of the New Moon. When the calendar became fixed by astronomical calculations this consideration no longer applied, but the question of the Babylonian Talmud, "now that we are acquainted with the calendar, why do we observe two days?" was answered, "because they sent a directive from Palestine stating, 'Adhere to the *minhag* of your ancestors which has been transmitted to you'" (*Beitz.* 4b). The COVERING OF THE HEAD is another example of an early custom that became solidly entrenched in traditional practice. According to rabbinic law local c. is binding not only upon natives of the locality but upon all those who take up their residence there though they come from places where the custom does not obtain. Discussing the difference of *minhag* regarding the permissibility of work on the eve of Passover, the Mishnah lays down the general rule that "in order to obviate conflicts, no one should depart from local *minhag*" (Mishnah *Pes.* 4:1). The Talmud records many differences in c. between the provinces of Judea and Galilee. The varieties of ritual and liturgical usage which have developed in various communities, and not only in the main divisions of *Sephardim* and *Ashkenazim,* are generally referred to as the *minhag* of such and such a group or community. Occasionally authoritative and powerful voices were raised in protest against slavish adherence to senseless or even objectionable c. Thus Maimonides did not hesitate to say of a prevalent c. "This is not a *minhag,* but an error, and even smacks of heresy", and R. Jacob Tam declared a certain custom "stupid", adding that the letters of the word *minhag* read backward as *gehinnom* ("hell") and that sages need not necessarily uphold foolish customs. In modern times migrations and other historical circumstances (e.g. REFORM) have led to the emergence of many new liturgical, religious, and semi-religious customs as well as to the erosion of old ones. These recent developments do not, however, qualify as *minhag* in the technical sense.

D

DAMAGES, see **TORTS**
SCROLLS
DAMASCUS DOCUMENT, see **DEAD SEA**

DANCE: Dancing, as a way of expressing joy and religious ecstasy, has been traditional in Judaism throughout the ages, from biblical times up to the present. The common root for dancing, *rakad*, suggests leaping and jumping, in contrast to the rhythmic round d., or *maḥol* (Jer. 31:3). The d. of Miriam and the women of Israel after the crossing of the Red Sea, the d. of the Israelites after making the Golden Calf, and David's joyful leaping and dancing in front of the Ark on its arrival in Jerusalem (II Sam. 6:14-16) are early examples of such expressions. In talmudic times the rabbis used to dance at weddings in the presence of the bride (*Ket.* 17a) but in all such traditional dancing, men and women danced separately. The unusual sight of R. Aḥa dancing with the bride (*ibid.*) aroused the disapproving comments of other rabbis, but he explained that d. had no erotic significance for him. The merrymaking which marked the Festival of Water Drawing included dancing (*Suk.* 53a) while in Temple times, the maidens danced in the vineyards on the feast of *Av* 15, and this was a recognized occasion for the young men to select their brides. In modern times the Ḥasidim, with their stress on *hitlahavut* (religious enthusiasm), have been the greatest exponents of dancing on festive occasions, and the Bratzlav Ḥasidim even dance daily after prayers. In general, religious tradition recognizes certain appropriate occasions for dancing, which include weddings and the celebrations during the week following the wedding, the Festival of Water Drawing, and above all the celebration of Simhat Torah at the close of the Festival of Tabernacles, when dancing with the Scrolls of the *Torah* takes place in the synagogue. The rabbis disapproved of mixed dancing, but the constant reiteration of this prohibition from the Middle Ages onward demonstrates that it was not always observed.

DANGER: Two biblical verses — "Only take heed to thyself and keep thy soul diligently" and "take ye good heed to your souls" (Deut. 4:9, 15) — were interpreted by the rabbis as a positive biblical commandment enjoining the duty of personal safety and the consequent avoidance of danger to life. The Talmud gives a long list of prohibitions enacted solely for the purpose of preventing d. to life. They range from such dangers as entering a ruined building (*Ber.* 3a) to drinking contaminated water (*Pes.* 112a) and not taking dietary precautions (*Ḥul.* 9b). In addition, the rule is laid down that "a man should never court danger in the hope that he will be miraculously delivered" (*Shab.* 32a). This injunction to preserve one's own life finds a forceful corollary in the doctrine of *pikuaḥ nephesh*, the sacred duty to go to any lengths to save the life of a human being. This duty is a major principle of law, taking precedence over and annulling all other prescriptions of Judaism with the sole exception of the three cardinal sins of idolatry, immorality, and the shedding of innocent blood (*Ket.* 19a). In particular all the laws of the Sabbath or even the Day of Atonement can be overridden in the face of this sacred duty (*Ber.* 61b; Mishnah *Yoma* 8:7). Where the saving of life is involved there must be no hesitation or delay, nor may the duty be delegated to another person, but "even the greatest in Israel" must perform it (Tosephta *Shab.* 16). All illnesses are regarded as endangering life, so that the laws of *pikuaḥ nephesh* also operate in the case of sickness and the instructions of the doctor must be followed. A person who persists in fasting on the Day of Atonement in defiance of his doctor's orders is regarded as having transgressed that holy day by his refusal to eat.

DANIEL: Book in the Hagiographa section of the Bible, written partly in Hebrew and partly in Aramaic and named after its central personality. Chapters 1-6 relate (in the third person) the miraculous incidents that occurred to D. and his pious colleagues, Judean exiles at the court of kings Nebuchadnezzar, Darius the Mede, and Belshazzar; chapters 7-12 consist of D.'s four apocalyptic visions (related in the first person) concerning the future of the "four kingdoms" (viz. Babylonia, Persia, Media, Greece). Rabbinical tradition ascribes its composition to the men of the Great Synagogue but modern scholars believe that the first part was written c. 300 B.C.E. and the second section in the reign of Antiochus Epiphanes (c.

165 B.C.E.), when its message of hope was designed to strengthen those who were downcast at the persecution of the righteous and the seeming triumph of the pagans. The ultimate message of the book is that God rules the universe; D. is the first biblical book to speak specifically of a life after death, though the reference is limited to the wholly righteous and the wholly wicked (12:2). It also contains important innovations in ANGELOLOGY; for instance, each nation has its guardian angel (and thus, Michael is angel of Israel). The figure of D. may be modeled on the D. cited in Ezek. 14:13-14; 20; 28:3, who was noted for his wisdom and is featured extensively in Ugaritic texts. The Book of D. formed the basis for much subsequent apocalyptic and mystical speculation, particularly for attempts to compute the date of the advent of the Messiah.

DANIEL BEN MOSES ALKUMISI (9th-10th cents.): KARAITE scholar from Persia. His writings, fragments of which have survived, were greatly respected by subsequent Karaite scholars. They include a *Book of Precepts* (written in Hebrew), which displays an attitude of stringency toward the ceremonies (especially Sabbath and dietary laws), and a commentary on the Bible which stresses a literal interpretation.

DANZIG, ABRAHAM BEN JEHIEL MICHAEL (1748-1820): Talmudic scholar of Vilna, author of *Ḥayyei Adam* ("Life of Man") and *Ḥokhmat Adam* ("Wisdom of Man"), both popular codifications based on the first two parts of KARO's *Shulḥan Arukh*. These works achieved widespread popularity as they lucidly guided laymen in practical matters of religion and ethics, and groups throughout Lithuania and elsewhere in E. Europe met daily to study *Ḥayyei Adam*.

DARSHAN (Heb. "expounder"): Term applied to a public teacher or preacher in the synagogue or school of study. The field of exposition by the *d.* may be *halakhah* or *aggadah*, but is most frequently a combination of both. EZRA is described as the first such "expounder". In talmudic times it was the general custom to conduct public teaching at the synagogue on all Sabbaths and holidays. In the Medieval Period this preaching in certain areas included also philosophic exposition and was delivered at wedding feasts and the like as well as in the synagogue. In Poland the *d.* came to be known as the MAGGID whose teaching or preaching was primarily devoted to aggadic and ethical instruction, as the practical objective of fostering religious observance was regarded as primary.

DAVEN (Yidd.): Common word among *Ashkenazim* meaning "to pray". The etymology is obscure.

DAVID (reigned c. 1010-970 B.C.E.): Second king of Israel; youngest son of Jesse, of the tribe of Judah. Born in Bethlehem where he herded his father's sheep. He is described as "skillful in playing and a mighty man of valor and a man of war, and prudent in affairs and a comely person and the Lord is with him" (I Sam. 16:18). Having despaired of Saul's reign, SAMUEL was sent on a clandestine mission to anoint D. as king (*ibid.* 1-13). The biblical account of the early relationship between D. and Saul is confused and contradictory. According to I Samuel 16, Saul suffered from depression and melancholia, and D. was brought to court in order to raise the king's spirit through his music. According to I Samuel 17 it was D.'s spirited reaction to the challenge of Goliath that drew the king's attention to him. The relationship between the two began to deteriorate with the public acclaim accorded to David's military prowess (I Sam. 18:6-9 ff.). Following an unsuccessful attempt on his life by Saul, whose daughter he had married, D. flew to Judah where he gathered around himself an army of 400 followers. At the age of 30 he was crowned king after Saul's death in the battle of Gilboa, and he proceeded to conquer JERUSALEM, which he made the capital of his kingdom. During his reign the kingdom expanded considerably as the tribes coalesced into a homogeneous political unit. Of immense importance to the future course of history was D.'s placing of the ARK in Jerusalem, signifying a cultic unification emphasized later by the erection of Solomon's Temple. The biblical record of D.'s life story (I Sam. 16 ff; the entire book of II Sam.; I Kings 1-2; I Chron. 10 ff.) faithfully portrays his complex character as statesman, warrior, poet, friend, and lover, in high as in low tide of fortune, sinning and repentant. Tradition ascribes to him the composition of many PSALMS and also the organization of Temple MUSIC. In later generations his exemplary qualities became the ideal of Israelite kingship, and God's covenant with D. was considered as firm and eternal as His covenant with Israel (cf. Jer. 33:19-26 and the many references in the liturgy); hence the future king and restorer of Israel's fortunes will be a scion of the House of David (Is. 9:5-6; 11:10; see MESSIAH). Aggadic treatment of D. is copious and in the main highly laudatory; it has also found its way into the KORAN. Christianity regards D. as an ancestor of JESUS. The degree to which his personality fired the popular imagination is best expressed in the adage "D. king of Israel lives forever" (*R.H.* 25a). The traditional site of his tomb has become the object of pilgrimages (see DAVID, TOMB OF).

DAVID, CITY OF, see **JERUSALEM**

DAVID, SHIELD (STAR) OF, see **MAGEN DAVID**

DAVID, TOMB OF: The Bible relates that David was buried "in the city of David" (I Kings 2:10). There are a number of references to the tombs of the House of David but these were apparently destroyed or obliterated after the Bar Kokhba rebellion of 132-135. The site was probably SE of present Jerusalem (near the village of Silwan). Popular traditions refused to accept the disappearance of David's tomb and various sites (especially in Bethlehem) came to be venerated. The present ascription of the tomb to the south of old Jerusalem on what is (erroneously) called Mount Zion dates back about a thousand years. For centuries the Arab custodian forbade Jews access to the tomb but after the establishment of the State of Israel in 1948 it became a center of Jewish pilgrimage, especially as Jews could no longer visit the WAILING WALL, which remained in the Jordanian section of Jerusalem. Since the capture of the Old City of Jerusalem by Israel in 1967, the T. of D. has lost much of its allure as a venue for pilgrimages.

DAVID BEN SAMUEL HA-LEVI (called *Taz* from the initials of his main work; 1586-1667): Polish talmudic authority, known for his *Turei Zahav* ("Golden Rows"), recognized as a standard commentary on KARO's *Shulḥan Arukh*. D.'s objectives were to re-establish Karo's original decisions by refuting subsequent criticisms, and to bring order to the voluminous comments that had appeared concerning the *Shulḥan Arukh*.

DAVID BEN SOLOMON IBN AVI ZIMRA, see **ZIMRA**

DAVID IBN MERWAN ALMUKAMMAS, see **ALMUKAMMAS, DAVID**

DAY: The Hebrew word *yom* can refer both to the period of daylight (as opposed to NIGHT-time) and to the entire span of 24 hours. The 24 hour d. is reckoned from evening to evening. In Jewish law part of a d. is often taken as a full d., e.g. in counting the days of mourning or in calculating the eighth d. after birth for circumcision. Many commandments may be fulfilled only during the daytime. A talmudic hour constitutes one-twelfth of the period of daylight and is therefore variable with the seasons.

DAY OF ATONEMENT, see **ATONEMENT, DAY OF**

DAY OF JUDGMENT: The final judgment of mankind by God, or one of His appointed, to be made at the end of days (*aḥarit ha-yamim*). Parallel to the biblical idea of reward and punishment in this world was the concept of the DAY OF THE LORD, i.e., the day upon which Israel would be exalted and her foes delivered up to Divine justice. This predominantly nationalistic idea was transformed by the prophets (particularly AMOS), who proclaimed that the Day of the Lord was to be a day of judgment and doom for all evildoers, including those among the people of Israel. The prophets warned of the coming Exile as the just punishment of God meted out to Israel for her sins. Once this terrible judgment was passed on Israel and the nation refined of its sinful dross, the REMNANT of the upright and righteous was to return (the ingathering of the exiles) and enjoy a long and prosperous life. These hopes of return are poignantly expressed in the post-exilic prophets, particularly HAGGAI and ZECHARIAH, who believed that the re-establishment of the Jewish community in Jerusalem and the rebuilding of the Temple heralded the dawn of the messianic era. Disappointment at the non-fulfillment of this hope was partially responsible for the gradual transformation of eschatological thought from the realm of immediate hope to that of apocalyptic speculation. According to the new conception, the final D. of J. had not yet occurred, for it would happen only at the end of days. The notion of the D. of J. thus became a major element of apocalyptic literature. It would witness not simply a judgment of Israel, but the judgment of mankind and the cosmos as a whole, and even the wicked angels were to be called to account (see ENOCH). In later apocalyptic literature, it is held that the RESURRECTION of the dead will occur before the D. of J., so that the dead may also be judged. There is a wide divergence of views regarding the D. of J. in pseudepigraphal and tannaitic literature. On that great and terrible day either God Himself or His anointed Messiah will judge the entire world and declare its fate. In earlier apocalyptic literature the eschatological D. of J. is identified with "messianic woes", the period of trial and tribulation preceding the advent of the Messiah. In later apocalyptic works (Syriac BARUCH, IV ESDRAS) the view is expressed that the messianic age is merely a transitional period from this world to a new era, described as the "World to Come" (OLAM HA-BA). Tannaitic literature also seems to distinguish between the Messianic Age and the World to Come. According to this view, which was also held in early Christian circles, the Messianic Era is a transitional one, and the D. of J. will occur at the end of the Messianic kingdom but before the advent of the World to Come. The world will be cleansed once and for all of its sinful element, and the unrighteous will be consigned to "everlasting abhorrence". The faithful and elect, however, will witness the New Jerusalem descend from the heavens and will live thereafter in a new world of eternal bliss. See ESCHATOLOGY; ROSH HA-SHANAH.

DAY OF THE LORD: Originally, the day on

which the Lord would reveal Himself to the nations in all His power and might to smash the enemies of Israel in punishment for their sins against His people. The prophet Amos gave a new meaning to this concept when he warned that not only the heathen nations would be judged, but also Israel itself. Thus, the concept of a DAY OF JUDGMENT, which was to play a leading role in the shaping of Jewish ESCHATOLOGY, evolved out of the prophetical D. of the L.

DAYS OF AWE (Heb. YAMIM NORAIM): The TEN DAYS OF PENITENCE.

DAYYAN (Heb. "judge"): Judge of a rabbinic court. The institution of rabbinic judgeship is an ancient one as is the provision for different types of courts. According to the Talmud the SANHEDRIN (Great Court) of the Chamber of Hewn Stone (*Lishkat ha-Gazit*) consisted of 71 judges; lower courts of 21 judges were to be found on the Temple Mount and in every community containing a population of at least 120 adult males. In smaller communities the courts had only three judges. This was not parallel to the modern system of appellate courts, but each court was of different jurisdiction. Money cases could be heard by courts of three, but capital cases, among others, only by courts of 23. A few special areas of national consideration were the sole prerogative of the Sanhedrin of 71. Jewish courts outside Palestine were limited in their jurisdiction in that they could not impose money fines. This was because judges outside Palestine were not considered *semukhim* ("ordained"); *semikhah* ("ordination") could be received only by those in Palestine where there was a direct line of ORDINATION. Judges of rabbinic courts everywhere are under this same limitation of not being "ordained", and however valid their jurisdiction, it is based on the premise that they act as *sheliḥim* ("representatives") of the former properly ordained magistrates. A *d.* must be learned in Jewish law, and it is expressly forbidden to appoint an unlearned *d.* who would have to rely upon the help of one so learned. Yet in those communities where no man may be found versed in Jewish law it is permitted to appoint as judges members of the aristocratic or ruling group. In the modern world, the jurisdiction of Jewish judges has become extremely limited. Even in the State of Israel, most cases of law are heard by general courts, and only matters of personal status are required by law to be heard by rabbinic judges.

DAYYENU (Heb. "It would suffice us"): Thanksgiving litany in the Passover SEDER service, of unknown authorship but possibly dating to the 6th-7th cent. C.E. It lists the accumulation of Divine favors for which Israel is grateful to God.

DEAD BODY, see **CARCASS; CORPSE**

DEAD, PRAYERS FOR, see **EL MALE RAḤAMIM; KADDISH; MEMORIAL SERVICE; YIZKOR**

DEAD SEA SCROLLS: Ancient scrolls and fragments written in Hebrew, Aramaic, and Greek, and discovered at various times from 1947 on, along the N.W. shore of the Dead Sea. A number of these scrolls are now in the permanent possession of the Hebrew University; others are in Jordan. The consensus of scholarly opinion is that the manuscripts originate from around the 1st cent. B.C.E. Archeological explorations of a ruin called Khirbet Qumran — near the site of the caves where the D.S.S. were discovered — unearthed an ancient settlement. This settlement appears to have been founded toward the end of the 2nd cent. B.C.E. and was temporarily abandoned after being badly damaged by an earthquake in 31 B.C.E. It was reinhabited, however, and remained in existence until its final destruction during the revolt against Rome (67-70 C.E.). The scrolls were most probably the possessions of the men who lived in this settlement, which contained a scriptorium (with a writing table and inkstands) and fragments of jars, similar to those in which the scrolls were found. The scrolls include a Manual of Discipline for the Qumran community. This manuscript, which bears the marks of an editing hand (several variant versions have been brought to light), begins with a section dealing with the life and aims of the righteous (the "Sons of Light") as opposed to those of the wicked (the "Sons of Darkness"). The two forces at work in this world, the spirit of truth and light and the spirit of evil and darkness, are also to be found in the heart of every man. From this Manual of Discipline it is evident that the men of Qumran thought themselves to be members of a special community which was both of this world and a part of the coming heavenly world (cf. the New Testament concept of the "kingdom of God"). The central section of this manuscript lays down the laws and ordinances of the community, and the Manual closes with a long hymn of praise and thanksgiving. Another scroll which helps to throw light on this community is the War Scroll, a manuscript which describes in detail the coming eschatological war between the "Sons of Light" and the "Sons of Darkness". The Thanksgiving Scroll contains a collection of the community's hymns and psalms. Of particular interest are the so-called "PESHER" commentaries written by members of this community on various biblical books. For the most part, these commentaries tend to give an acute-eschatological interpretation to scripture. Of great importance to biblical scholars are the scrolls and fragments of the great majority of the biblical books; these manuscripts constitute the most ancient copies of the Hebrew scriptures now extant. Fragments of several pseudepigrapha (cf. APOCRYPHA AND PSEUDEPIGRAPHA) were discovered, thus disproving the theory of the Christian origin of these works. In the course of subsequent excavations fragments of the Damascus Document were unearthed. This Document had been discovered in the *genizah* of a Cairo synagogue at the end of the 19th cent., but there was considerable dispute concerning its date and origin. The discovery of fragments of this manuscript among the D.S.S. has settled the question. A number of theories have been propounded concerning the origin and identity of this Qumran community. That it was a Jewish religious group or sect is beyond dispute; the archeological evidence and the scrolls themselves give overwhelming evidence to support this. The generally accepted view and the one which presents the least difficulties, is that this sect was identical with, or closely related to, the ESSENES described in detail by Josephus. The site of the ruins of this ancient settlement coincides almost exactly with Pliny the Elder's description of an Essene settlement on the W. shore of the Dead Sea. Several theological concepts attributed to the CALENDAR of their contemporaries, the PHARISEES and SADDUCEES, were firmly rejected by the members of the Qumran community, which held to a solar reckoning. Thus for them, the feasts and fasts as celebrated at the Temple in Jerusalem, were considered to be profane, since they were not held on their proper appointed days. Evidence of the regular ablutions practiced by this community and described by Josephus is to be found in the archeological ruins of Qumran as well as in the scrolls themselves. An extremely rigid and unyielding attitude toward the Law is also to be noted in the scrolls. Mention is made of a "Teacher of Righteousness", who was held in high esteem by the members of the Qumran community. Though this Teacher of Righteousness played an influential role in the shaping of the community, it is impossible to determine whether or not he was the founder of the group. The greatest significance of the D.S.S. is that they have necessitated a revision and reinterpretation of the Jewish religious scene during the latter years of the Second Temple. The origins of Christianity are also shown in a new light. The members of the Qumran community, like the early Christians, belonged to a movement which almost daily awaited the advent of the Messiah. Both Christian and Jewish scholars had tended to view Second Temple Judaism as having consisted almost exclusively of PHARISEES and SADDUCEES, and early Christianity was regarded as a unique phenomenon. Now, however, the literary treasure of a similar Jewish eschatological group has been discovered. Both of these groups claimed to be the true remnant of Israel, both regarded themselves as living under a "new covenant", and both believed they were living on the threshold of the new messianic era. Though their respective approaches were different (compare their attitudes to the Law, to ritual cleanness, and to the question of the calendar), they had much in common. The dualistic ideas expressed in the Gospel of John and in the writings of Paul were thought to be the result of Greek philosophical thought. Now there is direct evidence that such dualism pervaded certain religious elements of Judaism. The D.S.S. also attest to the fact that the period of the Second Temple was one of the most productive and vigorous in Jewish history.

DEAF, IMBECILE, AND MINOR: Group of persons deprived of legal rights in Jewish law because they are regarded as lacking understanding and responsibility. "Deaf" here refers to the deaf-and-dumb mute and excludes such categories as the dumb person who can hear or a person who has once possessed the powers of speech and hearing. According to the Talmud, members of this group cannot claim property by virtue of undisturbed possession, their business transactions are invalid, and they are barred as witnesses. They are exempt if they cause injury to others but if they themselves are injured, the person responsible is liable. Talmudic law sanctioned the marriage of a deaf-mute, and it could be consecrated by signs.

DEATH: Surprisingly little attention is devoted in the Bible to the fate of the soul after death. There is an implicit belief that the spirit survives death, but this assumption leads to no religious or moral conclusions. The spirit of a dead person simply descends to *Sheol*, the dark land of no return. On the other hand, special care was taken to ensure that the body had a proper BURIAL. Belief in a connection between the living and the dead led to necromancy and other practices. After God has taken back the spirit, the fate of the body is one of "dust to dust" (cf. Gen. 3:19; Ps. 104:29 ff.). A more clearly defined doctrine on the nature of the soul and of its relationship with the Divine Sphere, after death, emerged much later. By rabbinic times, death was thought to mark the end of man's striving upon earth, whereupon he receives his reward and punishment (RETRIBUTION) for the manner of his life. The Pharisees developed the doctrine of RESURRECTION. Thus, when R. Johanan finished reading the Book of Job, he used to say "the end of man is death; the end of the animal is slaughter. All are doomed to die. Happy then is he who was brought up in the *Torah*, whose labor was in the *Torah,* who in his life gave pleasure to his Creator, who grew up with a good name and departed this world with a good name" (*Ber.* 17a). "Let a man always engage in *Torah* and good deeds during his lifetime, for as soon as he dies he is unable to practice them... and thus did R. Johanan say: What is meant by the verse 'among the dead, free?' (Ps. 88:6). It is this: once a man dies he is free from the possibility of practicing *Torah* and good deeds" (*Shab.* 30a). In the words of R. Eleazar Ha-Kappar: "Not of thy will wast thou formed and not of thy will wast thou born, and not of thy will dost thou live, and not of thy will dost thou die, and not of thy will art thou to give just account and thou wilt in future have to give account and reckoning before the Supreme King of Kings" (*Avot* 4:29). In rabbinic thought d. came to the world through sin — either the sin of Adam or one's own personal sin. Though the rabbis list a number of individuals who died without sin (*Shab.* 55b), a prevalent idea in Judaism is that death constitutes a punishment for sinfulness and this view is supported by the doctrine that "there is not a righteous man on earth who doeth good and sinneth not" (Ecc. 7:20). Thus "Even Moses and Aaron died through their sin, as it is said, 'Because ye believed not in me'... Hence had ye believed in me, your time would not have come to depart" (*Shab.* 55a). As a result of this doctrine the rabbis go to great lengths to explain the death of children. The barrier between life and death is regarded as complete and impenetrable, though the view is expressed that the corpse remains sensate until the grave is covered over, or until the body disintegrates (*Shab.* 152a). Death brings with it a purging of sin (*Shab.* 8b) and acts as a kind of atonement (*Siphrei, Shelaḥ* 112). The rabbis stressed the natural aspect of death and tried to minimize the dread with which it was anticipated. Since the time of death was determined by God it must not be precipitated (see SUICIDE). It is forbidden by Jewish law to do anything to hasten death. Not only is euthanasia strictly forbidden, but anyone who performs the slightest action that may inadvertently hasten death is regarded as having shed innocent blood. A person should not be allowed to die alone, and relatives and friends should remain with the dying person to the end. As soon as a person dies his eyes are reverently closed; those present say the TZIDDUK HA-DIN and formally rend their garments. Based on a statement in the Talmud (*R.H.* 16b) to the effect that one of the things which can avert the decree of death is CHANGE OF NAME, a custom has developed of formally changing the existing name of a dangerously ill person by giving him a symbolic name such as Ḥayyim (life) or Joshua (salvation). A common superstition requires the pouring of all water in the vicinity of a person who has just died onto the ground, in the belief that the angel of death cleanses his knife in water. Another custom is to cover all mirrors in the house so as to avoid the bad luck of seeing the angel of death. See also IMMORTALITY.

DEATH, ANGEL OF, see **ANGELOLOGY**

DEATHBED CONFESSION, see **CONFESSION**

DEATH PENALTY, see **CAPITAL PUNISHMENT**

DEBT AND DEBTOR: The Bible insists that a creditor refrain from embarrassing his debtor or acting toward him in an exacting manner (Exod. 22:24). Debts were dissolved every seventh year (but see PROSBUL). All Israelites who had been sold into slavery for debt were released or redeemed in the JUBILEE YEAR. The debtor's goods could not be seized in the event of failure to meet his obligations, though at a later period this ruling had to be modified. According to post-biblical legislation, a loan (or a sale on credit) is presumed to fall due in thirty days, in the absence of any special terms. Where a date for payment has been set, neither the creditor nor his executors may present demands prior to the date originally agreed upon. After repayment, acquittance for cancellation of a bond is to be made by formally attested receipt (*shover*). Since gaonic times, the creditor could insist, at or after the time of contract, that the debtor repay only in the presence of witnesses. Upon partial repayment the creditor may insist on receiving a new bond for the remainder or give a *shover* for the part paid. For an orally incurred debt (where no bond exists) the debtor is entitled to a *shover* on payment. Transference of a debt from the creditor to a third party, to whom the creditor is himself indebted, is considered valid if the transference takes place in the presence of all three parties. Where a loan is contracted without formal bond, the real estate of the borrower is not subject to seizure by the creditor in the event of failure to repay the loan. USURY is condemned in the Bible; Jewish law is equally condemnatory of charging interest, although historical circumstances necessitated certain modifications in this respect. See also LOANS.

DECALOGUE (Gk. "ten words"): The Ten Commandments, given by God to Moses on Mount SINAI (Exod. 20; Deut. 5). The REVELATION of the d. was the central event of the GIVING OF THE LAW, and according to Exod. 20:18 it was heard by the whole people assembled at the foot of Mt. Sinai. The rabbis, however, specify (*Mak.* 24a, *Hor.* 8a) that only the first two commandments (which are couched in the first person) were heard directly by the people, the others (which use the second person in speaking of God) being transmitted by Moses. The two versions of the D. (Exod. 20 and Deut. 5) exhibit variant readings, the most striking of which occur in the fourth commandment, where they differ both in their opening word and in the reason given for the observance of the Sabbath. The Talmud says that the differences in the two versions occurred by a miracle, as "both were uttered simultaneously". Some commentators suggested that the first version was that of the first set of TABLETS which were smashed by Moses (Exod. 32:19), and the other represents the text of the second tablets. Abraham Ibn Ezra holds that only the D. in Exodus was uttered on Sinai, the version in Deuteronomy being phrased by Moses. According to the rabbis the D. was written "with white fire on a background of dark fire" and was spread equally over the two tablets — the first five commandments dealing with "duties of man toward God" being inscribed on one tablet and the second five concerning the "duties of man toward his fellow man" on the other. Most of the ten commandments refer to actions — either commanded or prohibited; only the last concerns a state of mind. The opening sentence, "I am the Lord thy God", is an assertion rather than a precept, and for that reason some authorities regard it as an introductory statement and not as the first commandment; instead they divide what is now the second commandment into two. Nevertheless there is general rabbinic consensus that belief in (viz., knowledge of) God, as implied by the first sentence, constitutes a positive commandment. The rabbis regard the D. as the quintessence of the Law and hold that all 613 PRECEPTS were somehow contained or alluded to therein. Liturgically the D. is less prominent than might be expected. It was recited together with the *Shema* in the Temple but not in congregational worship outside the Temple, and the rabbis objected to any such liturgical custom on the grounds that it might be construed as support of the heresy that the D. alone was valid *Torah* (*Ber.* 12a). However, when the D. is read in the synagogue as part of the Pentateuchal lesson, whether in the weekly portions of *Yitro* or *Va-Ethanan* or on the Feast of WEEKS, the congregation rises. On these occasions the D. is sung to a more solemn tune than that used normally for the biblical cantillation.

DEDICATION (Heb. *ḥanukkah*): Ceremony whereby a building is dedicated to a sacred purpose, or a plot of land to be used for a cemetery. There is explicit reference in the Bible to the formal d. of the three biblical sanctuaries: the d. of the Sanctuary in the wilderness (Num. 7), the d. of the Temple of Solomon (I Kings 8, II Chron. 5-6 as well as Ps. 30 — the Psalm of Dedication); and the d. of the Second Temple (the d. of the altar in Ezra 3:9-12 and of the Temple in Ezra 6:16-18). In the Post-Biblical Period, the rededication of the Temple by Judah the Maccabee three years after its desecration by the Syrians, instituted the eight-day Festival of ḤANUKKAH (I *Macc.* 4). Ceremonies for the d. of other sacred buildings are of comparatively late origin. It is possible that homes were dedicated in biblical times (Deut. 20:5), but if so the custom lapsed. Until recently *Ashkenazim* merely affixed the MEZUZAH and uttered the appropriate blessing, though an order of service for the d. of a home was evolved among *Sephardim*. In the 19th cent., the British Chief Rabbinate drew up a prayer form for the occasion, which includes Ps. 30 and 15, those verses of Ps. 119 which acrostically compose the word *berakhah* (blessing) and a special prayer of d. There is no standard or statutory service for the consecration of a synagogue, but it usually includes Ps. 30 and circuits of the synagogue with Scrolls of the Law. There is also an Order of Service for the d. of a cemetery including the recitation of penitential prayers at the Morning Service on the day of d. A curious medieval custom, sanctioned by R. JUDAH BEN SAMUEL HE-ḤASID but no longer practiced, was to kill a cock (the word *gever* in Hebrew means both "cock" and "man") and bury it as the first funeral in the newly dedicated cemetery.

DEED: Legal document. In the Bible the word *sepher* indicates a legal document (Deut. 24:10-12) and in rabbinic literature, *shetar*. The word *get*, originally also used by the rabbis for all documents, came gradually to refer only to a bill of DIVORCE. In Jewish law, every legal document consists of two parts: (1) the *tophes*, a general formula standardized for different types of documents; and (2) the *toreph* — an open portion containing the specific terms and nature of the individual contract, the names of the parties, date, time, etc. While for all normal transactions ready-made documents may be used, in the case of a bill of divorce the document must be specially prepared. Additional clauses may be added to the standard formula of a document; the addition of such clauses was in fact often encouraged in order to clarify exactly what the document meant to state. A formally attested document enjoys a presumption of validity; however, if this presumption is called in question, the document may be granted authentication (*kiyyum or henpek*) by a court. A document may serve in a dual capacity: it may act as the validating instrument (see KINYAN) in the purchase of land, or as proof that ownership was transferred by means of some other *kinyan*. In the case of a bill of divorce the actual transfer of the document from husband to wife (in front of witnesses) effects the divorce. The act of betrothal may be performed in like manner. While documents may be entered as valid evidence, witnesses may not testify in writing.

DEGREES, SONG OF, see **SHIR HA-MAALOT**

DEISM: In contrast to THEISM, d. is the view that God exists as the cause of the universe, but does not actively influence its operation. The universe created by the God of deistic thought has been compared to a clock which, once constructed and wound, functions independently of its maker. D., which reached its classical form in the 18th cent., was popular among the thinkers of the Enlightenment as "Natural Religion", i.e., religion without revelation. Traditional theism both biblical and rabbinic, is opposed to d., since it assumes God's constant PROVIDENCE and solicitude for His creation (and individual creatures) as well as His power to intervene in the course of nature and history (MIRACLES, REVELATION), and His moral judgment of human actions. Mystical thinkers (e.g. the kabbalists), far from attributing independent existence to the universe, held that it would return to utter nothingness and non-being if God's sustaining presence were withdrawn even for a moment.

DEITY, see **GOD**

DELMEDIGO, ELIJAH (1460-1497): Philosopher; born in Crete, lived in Padua. He was greatly influenced by Averroes and translated some of his works via Hebrew into Latin. D.'s *Beḥinat ha-Dat* ("The Examination of Religion") seeks to reconcile philosophy and religion, holding that each has its own domain and that they do not therefore conflict. Should philosophy and revelation seem to contradict each other, philosophy must defer. In particular, the philosopher must not tamper with the basic doctrines of Divine existence, revelation, and retribution.

DEMAY (Heb. "Produce on which tithes may not have been paid"): Third tractate in the Mishnah order of *Zeraim* with *gemara* only in the Palestinian Talmud. It deals with the laws for collecting TITHES in the case of produce purchased from a person who might be suspected of having neglected the tithe. Where such doubt occurred, the purchaser had to put aside the priestly heave-offering and also, in relevant years, the levitical tithe.

DEMOCRACY: Form of government in which sovereignty resides in the people. Although many of the values and moral principles underlying d. are affirmed by (and often derived from) the Bible, (e.g. Exod. 12:49 "One law shall be to him that is home-born and unto the stranger that sojourneth among you"), the way of life envisaged for the Israelites in the Bible cannot properly be termed a d. The Bible, it is true, greatly influenced the development of democratic ideas in 17th cent. England and 18th cent. America, and the organization of the ancient Israelite tribes, may also have been a kind of primitive d. Nevertheless, a system which provides for both an hereditary monarchy and an hereditary priestly caste cannot be so termed, even though kings often ruled by popular consent (Saul, David, Simon the Hasmonean). Deut. 17:14-20 and other scriptural passages envisage a limited constitutional monarchy, but the basic conception is essentially theocratic. The rabbis of the Second Temple Period further developed the theocratic or "nomocratic" principle (rule of the divinely revealed law). They recognized no political or spiritual prerogatives of the priesthood (except in matters of religious precedence) and rejected prophetic authority, since prophecy in this view had come to an end with Malachi. Within the body of sages qualified to interpret the law decisions were arrived at by the process of "counting and deciding" (i.e., by majority vote); failure to submit to the majority decision rendered a scholar a "rebellious elder" (*zaken mamre*). It is not so much the political theory underlying biblical and rabbinic law which has turned Jews into champions of d. as the social and moral values implicit in traditional Jewish teaching.

DEMONOLOGY: Belief in demons or evil spirits has played a relatively unimportant role in official Judaism, though prominent in popular practice. Jewish theology, as reflected in biblical and rabbinic literature, did not deny the existence of supernatural beings capable of harming persons, but the absolute sovereignty and omnipotence attributed to God by Jewish monotheism (Deut. 4:35) reduced the importance and power of such demonic forces. It was mainly under the influence of later dualistic systems with their dichotomy of cosmic good and evil that d. flourished. The apocalyptic writings already exhibit dualistic influences, originating in Persian teaching (Ormuzd and Ahriman); the Essenes seem to have cultivated an esoteric lore regarding evil spirits and to have practiced exorcism; Christianity developed the doctrine of the Devil; in the systems of medieval kabbalists, d. also plays a major role. In rabbinic Judaism, d. belongs primarily to the realm of *aggadah* and folklore, and rarely impinges on the *halakhah*. In the Bible all cosmic agencies, both beneficent and malign, are controlled by God's will. Forces of destruction are His messengers of punishment (e.g. Exod. 12:23) and even SATAN is only His servant (Job 1:2). But the survival of earlier animistic beliefs is attested to by the refer-

RIAL: Burial in the *Sephardi* cemetery, Amsterdam; from Bernard Picart's *Cérémonies et coutumes ligieuses* (Amsterdam, 1723).

CIRCUMCISION: Chair of Elijah in the Carpentras synagogue (Photo Franck)

CHARITY: Collecting-box. Germany, 18th cent.; Feinberg Collection, Detroit.

CIRCUMCISION: "The Child entering the Covenant' by Moritz Oppenheim (1800-1882); Jewish Museum, New York.

DIETARY LAWS: "*Kashrut* Problem" by Meyer de Hahn (1852-1895); Aronson Collection, Amsterdam.

DEAD SEA SCROLLS: A sheet from the Isaiah "A" manuscript; Israel Museum, Jerusalem.

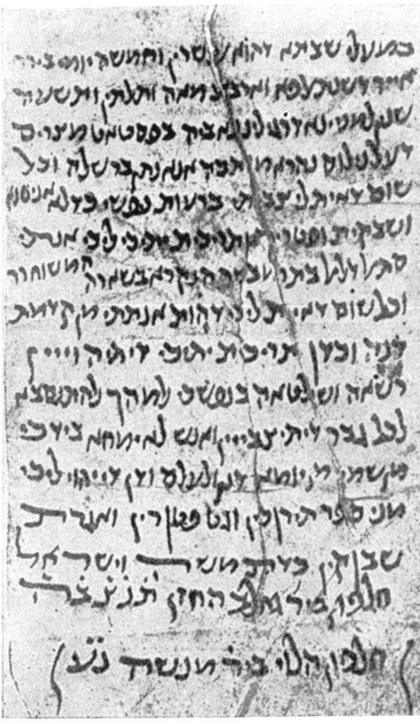

DIVORCE: Bill of divorcement (*get*); Fostat (Cairo), 1128 from "Paleographica Ebraica" by Carlo Bernheimer; Florence, 1925.

EDUCATION: "The Yeshivah" by Samuel Hirszenberg (1865-1908).

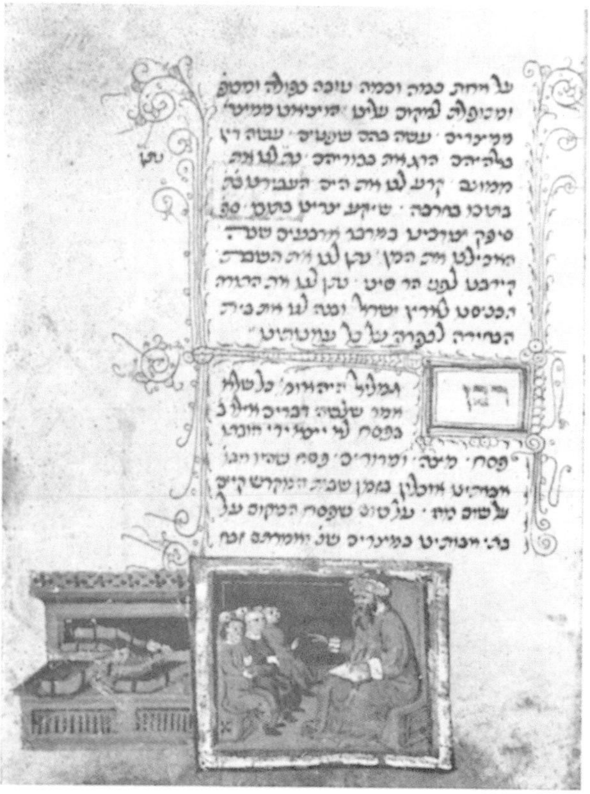

EDUCATION: Teacher and pupils; from the Forli prayer book, 1383. British Museum, London.

ESTHER, SCROLL OF (*megillah*): Silver chased with *Purim* revelers and Hebrew inscription "The Jews had light, gladness, joy, and honor"; Italian or French, c. 1700; Jewish Museum, London (Photo: Warburg Institute).

HAGGADAH: *Seder* service from 14th cent. *Haggadah*, possibly Spanish. British Museum, London.

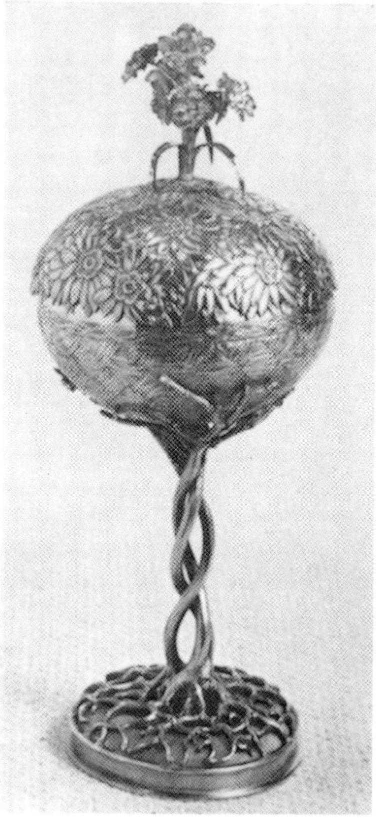

ETROG: *Etrog* case; Central Europe, 18th cent., Feinberg Collection, Detroit.

FIRSTBORN, REDEMPTION OF: from Bernard Picart's *Cérémonies et coutumes religieuses* (Amsterdam, 1723).

פירוש אברבנאל

מַעֲשֶׂה בְּרַבִּי אֱלִיעֶזֶר וְרַבִּי יְהוֹשֻׁעַ וְרַבִּי אֶלְעָזָר בֶּן עֲזַרְיָה וְרַבִּי עֲקִיבָא וְרַבִּי טַרְפוֹן שֶׁהָיוּ מְסוּבִּין בִּבְנֵי בְרַק וְהָיוּ מְסַפְּרִים בִּיצִיאַת מִצְרַיִם כָּל אֹתוֹ

בלילות עד שדרשה בן זומא שהוא שמעון
בן זומא והנה היה בן זומא זה קטן בשנים
ולכן לא נסמך ונקרא תמיד ע"ש אביו בן
זומא ולא זכה רבי אליעזר למה זכה בן ז
זומא שהוא נער ממנו ולא נעשה לו תורתו
גם וזה היה תמיהת ר"א בן עזריה · ולא
זכיתי לשון נצוח כמו מאן דזכי למלכא כ
כלומר לא נצחתי לחכמים בגמרא ותלמוד
שתאמר יציאת מצרים בכל לילות השנה
בפ' ציצית בק"ש של ערבית לפי שהייתי
יחיד והם רבים ואין דברין של אחד ב
במקום שנים · שדרשה בן זומא וכו' ומעתה ק"ו שאם בכל לילות השנה חייב להזכיר יציאת מצרים לזכרון אותו הנס כל שכן שיותר ויותר
ראוי לספרו בליל פסח שהוא הזמן המיוחד אליו ולכן כל המרבה לספר בו הרי זה משובח · ימי חייך העולם הזה לפי שהלילה נמשכת אחר
היום

HAGGADAH:
Page from *Haggadah* of 1740 depicting the rabbis who studied all night at Benei Berak; British Museum, London.

ḤEVRA KADDISHA: Engraved goblet of the Eisenstadt *Ḥevra Kaddisha*, 1712, showing funeral scenes.

HAVDALAH: by Hermann Struck (1876-1944).

HANUKKAH: *Hanukkah,* Silver lamp; Eastern Europe, late 18th cent.; Jewish Museum, New York.

HOSHANA RABBAH: *Hoshanot* from the Rothschild ms.; Italy, c. 1485; Israel Museum, Jerusalem.

ences to *seirim* (Lev. 17:7; "satyrs", Arabic *jinn*), *shedim* (Deut. 32:17; "demons"), AZAZEL (Lev. 16:8), LILITH (Is. 34:14), *ov* (Lev. 20:27; I Sam. 28; "ghost"), and the like. At times Scripture derisively applies demonic terminology to the pagan deities (Deut. 32:17). In rabbinic times, under Babylonian and Persian influence, d. — like ANGELOLOGY — assumed considerable importance in aggadic thought and general Jewish folklore. Many of the demons became individualized and were given specific names, often of foreign origin. The chief generic names are: *shedim, mazzikim* ("injurers"), *ruhot* ("spirits"), and *malakhei habbalah* ("angels of destruction"). These demons are invisible and their numbers legion. Partly like angels and partly like human beings, they possess wings, can fly from one end of the world to the other, and know the future (as do the ministering angels); like humans they eat and drink, procreate, and die (*Hag.* 16a). They live in ruins and desolate places, and are most active at night. As a rule they are malevolent, and the cause of various diseases; in Gehinnom they torture the wicked. But some are friendly and useful to man; these were employed, for example, in the construction of the Tabernacle and Temple. Their king is ASMODEUS (*Git.* 68a-b), or SAMAEL, or Azazel; AGRAT BAT MAHALAT is a queen of demons, as a Lilith who slays newborn infants. But Satan rules over them all. The only true defense against demoniac injury is the observance of commandments, though special prayers were also prescribed and AMULETS worn. The origin of demons is variously explained. Among other things it is said that they were created at twilight on the eve of the Sabbath (*Avot* 5:9); that they are the offspring of Lilith by Adam; that they are descended from "Fallen Angels" (cf. Gen. 6:1-4). In pseudepigraphic literature the guardian angels of gentile nations, as well as Satan himself, are also depicted as fallen angels. Medieval Jewish philosophers, with the exception of Abraham Ibn Ezra and Maimonides, accepted belief in demons. Kabbalists added the concept of the *kelippah* ("shell of evil") which wages an incessant war against the element of "holiness"; they also contributed to the increasing popularization of amulets. Later Jewish folklore referred to *letzim* ("mischievous imps"), and also absorbed many non-Jewish superstitions. In modern times scientific rationalism has tended to disperse the miasma of d., leaving the essence of Jewish creed and practice completely unaffected, as belief in evil spirits never did form an integral part of Jewish theology.

DENUNCIATION: The insecurity of the Jews in talmudic and medieval times, and their urgent need for solidarity in face of a hostile world, made d. the most heinous crime in the Jewish community and the informer (*malshin* or *moser, delator*) its most despicable character. Every step against him, even taking his life, was permitted in order to safeguard the interests of the community. When the imprecation against "sectarians" in the *amidah* prayer became obsolete (as sectarians no longer constituted a danger), the wording was changed so as to include all kinds of informers and slanderers (*malshinim*). R. Asher of Toledo refers to the death sentence carried out against informers (Responsa VIII 1.8), while Maimonides stated that in the Maghreb (W. Morocco) it was a "normal occurrence" for informers to be handed over to the non-Jewish authorities for punishment.

DERASH, DERASHAH, see **HOMILETICS; MIDRASH**

DEREKH ERETZ (Heb. "the way of the land"): Phrase used with varying connotations in rabbinic literature. In *Avot* 2:2 and 6:6 it means "a worldly occupation" while in *Num. Rab.* 31:23 it means "normal procedure". Its most common connotation, however, and the one to which the phrase became wholly limited, is "etiquette", or "correct conduct", implying dignified behavior and politeness. It is the subject of two post-talmudic treatises, DEREKH ERETZ RABBAH AND DEREKH ERETZ ZUTA. The rabbis ascribed such correct behavior to worthy biblical figures, and even to the Almighty Himself. The phrase "the *Torah* thus teaches us *d.e.*" is frequently found in rabbinic literature (e.g. in *Sot.* 49a, "the *Torah* thus teaches us *d.e.* that a man should first build his house, then plant his vineyard, and only then take a wife"; or *Bava Metzia* 87a — "the *Torah* teaches us *d.e.* that a man should always inquire after the welfare of his host"; or *Exod. Rab.* 35:2 — "The Holy One, blessed be He, thus teaches us *d.e.* that a man should refrain from using a fruit-bearing tree to build his house"). The laws of *d.e.* as found in rabbinical writings cover every conceivable aspect of man's life, his relationship with his wife, family, and friends. It regulates his ways of dressing and eating, his modes of address, procedure in visiting superiors, his use of language, and so forth; its importance was such that the rabbis state that "*D.E.* precedes *Torah*" and that "Without *d.e.*, there is no *Torah*".

DEREKH ERETZ RABBAH (Heb. "The major [Tractate on] Etiquette") and **DEREKH ERETZ ZUTA** ("The minor [Tractate on] Etiquette"): Two short independent treatises appended to the Babylonian Talmud at the conclusion of the tractate *Nezikin.* They contain ethical maxims covering such subjects as personal relationships, forbidden marriages, manners, the qualities required of a scholar, a list of those sins responsible for solar or lunar eclipses, and an extolment of the virtue of peace. Rules of conduct are illustrated with stories drawn from the lives of the early rabbis.

DERUSH (Heb.): A homiletic or aggadic interpretation. See AGGADAH; HOMILETICS; MIDRASH.

DESECRATION: Violation of the sacred or hallowed character of an object; diversion of purpose from the sacred to the PROFANE. Most such transgressions in Jewish law relate to the Temple ritual (e.g. the use of Temple objects for non-sacred purposes) and to the role of the priests (e.g. the ban which prohibits a High Priest from marrying an unsuitable wife or a deformed priest from participating in the Temple service). The punishment for d. is generally excommunication from the people of Israel (*karet*) or the death penalty (to be administered by Divine intervention).

DESECRATION OF THE NAME, see ḤILLUL HA-SHEM

DESECRATION OF THE SABBATH, see ḤILLUL SHABBAT

DESTRUCTION OF PROPERTY, see BAL TASHḤIT

DETERMINISM: The view that whatever happens is determined in advance, either by causal necessity or by God's knowledge or decree; the latter category is known as predestination. Though d. is accepted in one form or another by many religious philosophies, Judaism has tended to consider FREE WILL and the exercise of free choice as a pre-condition for the religious and moral life. Moral indeterminacy seems to be assumed both by the Bible, which bids man to choose between GOOD AND EVIL, and by the rabbis, who hold that the decision for following the good inclination rather than the evil (see YETZER) rests with every individual. D. is discussed by most philosophers in connection with the problem of free will. That the doctrine of free will is compatible with the theory of God's foreknowledge is asserted by Maimonides (*Hilkhot Teshuvah* V), who also emphatically rejects the doctrine of predestination. Modern philosophers discuss d. mainly in the light of scientific concepts of causality; the same problem was discussed under the heading of ASTROLOGY by medieval thinkers whose theories of stellar determination correspond to those of natural causality found in later periods.

DEUTERO-ISAIAH, see ISAIAH

DEUTERONOMY (Heb. *Devarim,* from its first distinctive word): The fifth and last book of the Pentateuch, containing Moses' farewell address to the Children of Israel, his final blessing and "song", and an account of his death. Moses reminds the people of their frequent disobedience and lack of faith in God, and he exhorts their fidelity. He stresses the blessing and happiness which result from obedience, and the curses which follow transgression; future sins of the people, he prophesies, will be severely punished, but eventually God will usher in an era of happiness and glory. D. recapitulates the main religious principles and legislation, including the DECALOGUE, contained in the previous three books but new laws are also added. An important feature of the book is its emphasis on a single central sanctuary where festivals are to be observed and sacrifices offered. It also insists on the uniqueness of God and His choice of Israel, from which derive the practical obligations due Him by the Israelites, such as the absolute rejection of idolatry. Modern scholars, who maintain that the Pentateuch is based on several documents, regard the Book of D. as an independent source. It is widely believed that D. is the "book of law" found by the prophet Hilkiah in the Temple in 621 B.C.E. during the reign of Josiah; the prophet's discovery provided the impetus for a religious reform in Judah (II Kings, 22-23).

DEUTERONOMY RABBAH, see MIDRASH RABBAH

DEVARIM, see DEUTERONOMY

DEVARIM RABBAH, see MIDRASH RABBAH

DEVEKUT (from *davak* Heb. "cleave"): Term used in the specific sense of cleaving, or loving adhesion, to God (cf. Deut. 11:22). Commenting on Deut. 13:5, the Talmud (*Sot.* 14a) asks "Is it possible to cleave unto God? Is it not said 'The Lord thy God is a devouring fire?'" and explains that *d.* means imitating His attributes of mercy and kindness (see IMITATION OF GOD). Halakhic codifiers (e.g. MOSES OF COUCY and MAIMONIDES), included *d.* among the positive commandments. Medieval philosophers and mystics used the term in the sense of "communion with God", and as such it meant the ultimate goal of religious life and spiritual endeavor. Under the influence particularly of kabbalists, and later of Ḥasidim, meditative as well as ecstatic *d.* became generally accepted ideals. *D.* involves the practice of DEVOTION (*kavvanah*), by which man removes the barriers between himself and God and establishes spiritual communion by "divesting himself of his material being" (*hitpashtut ha-gashmiyyut*).

DEVIL, see DEMONOLOGY; SATAN

DEVIR, see TEMPLE

DEVOTION: The Heb. term *kavvanah* means "intent" or "intention", in both a legal and moral sense, and d. in the sense of spiritual concentration, particularly accompanying religious exercises or the performance of a commandment, with a view to establishing DEVEKUT with God. The talmudic discussion of whether "the performance of a commandment requires *kavvanah*" (*Eruv.* 95b), and the rabbinic statement that *kavvanah* is essential to PRAYER (in particular the *Shema*), both refer to the general intent of one's action;

e.g. "When standing in prayer one should direct one's mind to God" (*Ber.* 31a). Medieval mystics developed the concept of d. to mean systematic meditation during prayer and this method reached its height in the mystical system of Isaac LURIA, and moralists and spiritual writers (like Nathan Hannover and Isaiah Horowitz) composed special prayers to be recited before the performance of such specific ritual obligations as donning *tephillin,* counting the *Omer,* and entering the tabernacle, with the purpose of giving expression to the spiritual meaning underlying the outward action. Such prayers are called *kavvanot.*

DEVOTIONAL LITERATURE: Religious literature found elsewhere than in sacred or otherwise official texts (Bible, Talmud, prayer book) and designed primarily to increase piety and devotion rather than theological learning. In a wider sense d. l. includes such compilations as the *Maamadot* (selections of scriptural and talmudic passages for daily reading), additional non-liturgical prayers to be said to satisfy private devotion, and moral and penitential writings. In addition to these compositions, many of which can be found in the larger and more comprehensive prayer books, there is d.l. proper, which was, in the main, the reading matter of ordinary pious folk, rather than of the scholars who followed the injunction to "meditate on (i.e., study) the *Torah* by day and night" (Josh. 1:8). D.L. was thus principally designed for ignorant persons and women, to whom the duty of *Torah* study did not fully apply. Hence most of this literature is written in the vernacular, Yiddish for *Ashkenazim* and Ladino for *Sephardim.* The best-known Yiddish collections are the *Teḥinnot,* or "supplications", and the renowned TZE'ENAH U-RE'ENAH (composed specifically for women).

DEW (Heb. *tal*): During the winter months a prayer for RAIN and d. ("Give d. and rain for a blessing upon the face of the earth") is inserted into the ninth of the EIGHTEEN BENEDICTIONS ("the blessing of the years"). The prayer is recited from the sixtieth day after the autumnal equinox; Dec. 3 or 4 (in Israel, from *Ḥeshvan* 7) until the first day of Passover (in *Sephardi* custom, an alternative benediction is inserted during the same period). Originally *Shemini Atzeret* should have been the starting date, but pilgrims were given time to return home before commencing recitation. Some rabbis suggested that the prayer should be offered during the appropriate season in one's individual country of residence, but, on the grounds of safeguarding Jewish unity, the suggestion was rejected. In summer months a prayer for d. is included by *Sephardim* and in the State of Israel in the second of the Eighteen Benedictions. A special *piyyut* for d. is recited in all rites in the Additional Service on the first day of Passover. According to the *aggadah,* God will send the "d. of resurrection" when the dead are about to be resurrected.

DIALECTICS, see **PILPUL**

DIASPORA, see **EXILE**

DIBBUK, see **DYBBUK**

DIETARY LAWS: Jewish d.l. apply only to animal foods, with the exception of 1) ORLAH (forbidden fruit): the prohibition against eating the fruit of a tree during the first three years after planting (Lev. 19:23); after the destruction of the Temple, the fruit of the fourth year was also forbidden (*ibid.* 19:24); 2) ḤADASH (new corn); the ban on eating bread made from a fresh crop of corn until the third day of the Festival of Passover (*ibid.* 23:14); 3) TEVEL (untithed produce): the ban on produce until the tithe has been set aside; this is applicable only in the Land of Israel; 4) KILAYIM (diverse kinds): prohibition against sowing diverse kinds of seed together; also applicable only in the Land of Israel (Deut. 22:9); 5) NESEKH (wine of libation): originally referring only to wine that had been used, or was suspected of having been prepared, for idolatrous libation, the prohibition was later extended to include any wine prepared or even touched by a non-Jew.

Permitted and Forbidden Animal Foods (see also CLEAN AND UNCLEAN ANIMALS): 1) Quadrupeds permitted for consumption are enumerated in Deut. 14:4-5, while Lev. 11:3 lays down the rule that "Whatsoever parteth the hoof and is wholly cloven-footed and cheweth the cud, that may ye eat." Both conditions are necessary (*ibid.* 4-7).

2) Only fish that have both fins and scales are permitted (*ibid.* 9-12). Fish which in their natural habitat have scales but shed them before or upon being taken from the water are permitted.

3) A number of birds are enumerated (*ibid.* 13-19) as forbidden, but no general characteristics are given in the Bible to distinguish permitted fowl from forbidden (distinguishing signs are mentioned by the Mishnah in *Ḥul.* 3 and by the Talmud in *Ḥul.* 65b). Since uncertainty exists as to the exact identification of the fowl listed as forbidden in the Bible, only those birds traditionally known as "clean" are used for food.

4) Winged animals that creep on the ground may not be eaten. Exceptions are listed in Lev. 11:20-22.

5) All kinds of worms, mites, snails, etc., are forbidden (*ibid.* 41).

Flesh may not be torn from a living animal (Gen. 9:4; *Sanh.* 59b), and all animals and birds, but not fish, require ritual slaughter (SHEHITAH). which alone renders the animal lawfully fit for consumption. A flaw in the performance of, or arising from, ritual slaughter renders the animal *nevelah* (carrion) and unfit for food. The term TEREPHAH originally designated the meat of animals mauled or torn by wild beasts but gradually became the term used to designate all food, especially meat, that is forbidden, for whatever reason, by law. In particular an animal found to be suffering from one or more of the defects or diseases listed in the Mishnah (*Ḥul.* 3) is called *terephah.* Maimonides lists seventy such cases under eight main headings:

Derusah — mauled by wild animals or birds;
Nekuvah — with a pierced or perforated membrane or organ;
Ḥaserah — defective (from birth);
Netulah — missing a limb, organ, or part;
Keruah — torn;
Nephulah — fallen, so that inner shock and consequent damage is suspected;
Pesukah — split;
Shevurah — broken.

Part of the abdominal fat (*ḥelev*) of the ox, sheep, and goat is forbidden (Lev. 7:23) as is the sinew of the hip, *nervus ischiadicus* (*gid ha-nasheh*, cf. Gen. 32:33). Permitted fat is called *shuman.*

The blood of fish is permitted; that of beasts and birds is forbidden (Lev. 17:12-14), hence all meat must be "kashered", or rendered fit for cooking, by a process called *meliḥah,* which consists of both soaking (for half an hour), covering with salt (for an hour), and thorough rinsing of the salt before the dish may be prepared for food.

Blood specks render eggs unfit for consumption. The products of unclean cattle, beast, birds, or fish (e.g. asses' milk, or caviar prepared from sturgeon roe) are also forbidden. Bee honey is an exception to this rule, as it is assumed that the bee merely sucks out and then discharges the nectar of a flower, and the honey does not contain any part of the bee itself.

Any mixture of meat and milk is strictly forbidden; separate sets of utensils must be provided for both the preparation and serving of meat and milk diets. Fish is not considered as meat in this respect. Milk foods may not be eaten for some time after the consumption of meat, and the same applies to meat after cheese. Custom varies as to the length of time (one hour, three hours, six hours) which should elapse (*Yoreh Deah* 89). Utensils which have been used in the preparation or serving of non-*kasher* foods, or for a mixture of meat and milk foods, may not be used subsequently for *kasher* foods. On the basis of the threefold repetition of the prohibition against seething a kid in its mother's milk (Exod. 23:19; 34:26; Deut. 16:21), it is forbidden to cook, eat, or benefit from a mixture of meat and milk foods. Food which is "neutral" (known in Yiddish as *parveh*) may be eaten with either milk or meat.

Attempts have been made to explain the d. l. on the basis of hygiene; according to such an explanation, *kasher* denotes any foodstuff which by virtue of its salutary nature is conducive to the proper nourishment of the human body without giving rise to disturbance after ingestion, while *terephah* signifies anything which, possessing more or less toxic qualities, is possibly instrumental in creating unhealthy symptoms in the human body. This theory holds that while much remains to be discovered to explain the d. l. in every detail, enough is known to warrant the conviction that their observance produces beneficial effects upon the human body (a view expressed by Maimonides cf. *Guide* 3:48). However, this apologetic attempt to understand the d. l. has been criticized as missing the basic intent of these precepts. On the verse "Thou shalt not eat any abominable thing" (Deut. 14:3), the *Siphrei* comments "that is, everything that the Word of God declares to be abominable", indicating that the only reason for refraining from these foods lies in the Divine prohibition concerning them. Thus also the *Siphrei* states "Let not a man say 'I do not like the flesh of swine'; on the contrary, he should say, 'I like it, but what can I do, seeing that the *Torah* has forbidden it to me?'" This suggests that the rabbis regarded the discipline of obedience and self-mastery as the real motivation for the d. l. In the Bible the observance of d. l. is held to be conducive to and a means of attaining the condition of holiness (Lev. 11:44-45) and prevents intimate association with "heathens". The nature of this holiness, according to both Philo and Maimonides, lies in the acquisition of self-control and the habit of mastering the appetites — "They accustom us to restrain the growth of desire, the indulgence in seeking that which is pleasant, and the disposition to consider the pleasure of eating and drinking the end of man's existence" (*Guide* 3:25).

The 19th cent. German Reform leader, Abraham GEIGER, held that the d. l. were anachronistic relics and that if not observed in their entirety should be totally abolished. In 1885 a conference of U.S. Reform rabbis at Pittsburgh affirmed that "all laws regulating diet are apt to obstruct modern spiritual elevation", and the American Reform leader Isaac Mayer Wise regretted the emphasis laid by Orthodoxy on these laws.

The Conservative Movement accepts the halakhic importance of d. l. but in practice tends to stress their educational significance rather than the actual letter of the law.

DIN (Heb.): A religious law; a lawsuit; a legal decision or judgment. R. Simeon ben Gamaliel postulated that *d.* was one of the three elements by which the world is preserved — the others being truth and peace (*Avot.* 1:18). In theological terminology *d.* signifies the Divine ATTRIBUTE of severe judgment and destructive punishment; it is held in check by Divine mercy (*ḥesed*) or compassion (*raḥamim*).

DIN TORAH (Heb.): Legal hearing conducted according to halakhic regulations.

DISABILITIES, see **CIVIL RIGHTS**

DISPENSATION (Heb. *heter*): Action by a competent halakhic authority to relax certain laws in order to alleviate a hardship which might arise should the strict application of the law be adhered to. As a principle of guidance it is to be understood that such power can only be exercised in the case of laws of rabbinic origin, or in connection with matters whose origin is in CUSTOM (*minhag*), but not in matters affecting biblical law. Thus the d. given by the Israeli Chief Rabbinate to allow land to be worked under certain conditions during the Sabbatical year is based on the premise that the prohibition regarding the Sabbatical Year is now based only on rabbinic ordinance. The *Ashkenazi* d. of one hundred rabbis, granted to one who may not ordinarily by law DIVORCE his insane wife in order to remarry, is premised on the fact that polygamy is permitted by the *Torah,* while monogamy is a rabbinic innovation.

DISPUTATIONS: Public CONTROVERSIES between representatives of opposing faiths. These verbal duels were a natural outgrowth of the desire to propagate one's faith by a public triumph in debate over one's opponents. An early example is the disputation between the Jews and the Samaritans mentioned by Josephus (*Ant.* 3:3-4); another is that recorded in the Mishnah (*A.Z.* 4:7) between philosophers in Rome and the Jewish elders. There are several references in the Talmud to discussions between rabbis and Romans (and other pagans) but the circumstances in which they were held are not specified. Early Christian literature reports many d. with Jews, all of them concluding with the Jewish protagonists' acceptance of Christianity. The name is however usually applied more specifically to the public d. forced upon Jews in the Middle Ages in a determined attempt to convert them to Christianity. The initiative in such d. was without exception taken by the Christians, and the Jews were ordered to appear at the behest of the authorities. The challenger was generally an apostate Jew who employed his knowledge of Judaism both to discomfit his opponents and to demonstrate publicly his loyalty to the new faith. The scales were naturally weighted heavily against the Jews. Of these medieval d., three were outstanding. The first was the d. of Paris in 1240, in which the challenger was the apostate Jew Nicholas Donin and his opponent R. Jehiel of Paris. As a result of this debate 24 cartloads of the Talmud were consigned to the flames in 1242. The most famous d. was at Barcelona in 1263. The Jewish champion Moses ben Naḥman (Naḥmanides) answered the charges of his opponent Pablo Christiani with such dignity and fearlessness that he completely vanquished him and was awarded a purse by the Spanish king. Nonetheless Naḥmanides found it politic shortly thereafter to leave Spain and move to Palestine. The longest d. was at Tortosa (1413/15), where the apostate Geronimo da Santa Fé (whose Hebrew name was Joshua Lorki) faced 22 of the most distinguished rabbis of the time. The disputation lasted for over 69 sessions, and was organized with all the outward trappings of a public entertainment. More unusual were the disputations in 1757 and 1759 — organized at the instigation of the Christian ecclesiastical authorities — between rabbinic spokesmen and FRANKISTS in Poland.

DISPUTE, see **MAḤLOKET**

DISSECTION: While the Talmud mentions several anatomical experiments involving d. — one, for instance, to investigate foetal development (*Nid.* 30b) and another to establish the number of bones in the human body (*Bekh.* 45a) — it strongly condemns any disfigurement of a corpse as an execrable violation of the rights of the dead (*Ḥul.* 11b). D. at European medical schools became common only in late medieval times, and the subject is not mentioned in rabbinic sources until 1737, when R. Jacob Emden in a responsum addressed to a Jewish medical student forbade his participation in the practice because of the prohibition against benefiting from the dead. Similar objections were subsequently raised by most leading rabbinical authorities, among them R. Ezekiel Landau of Prague, who granted his sanction only if that particular d. might be expected to save the life of another patient then at hand and suffering from a similar obscure disease. Religious opposition to d. contributed to the long delay in opening a medical school at the Hebrew University in Jerusalem, until with the establishment of the State of Israel the Chief Rabbinate agreed "to the use of bodies of persons who give their consent in writing, of their own free will during their lifetime, for anatomical dissections as required for medical studies, provided the dissected parts be carefully preserved so as to be later buried with all due respect according to Jewish law." See also POST-MORTEM.

DIVINATION: The art of foretelling the future by invoking the aid of external objects or movements. The collective name for such activity in the Bible was *kesem,* and the various kinds of d. are listed in Deut. 19:10-11 and translated as "observer of the times, enchanter, witch, charmer, consulter with familiar spirits, wizard, and necromancer". Recourse to such means of prescience is strictly forbidden as an "abomination". However certain forms of d. were practiced by the Israelite priesthood, probably through the EPHOD and the URIM AND THUMMIM. The distinction between forbidden and permitted d. largely depended on the methods employed: d. based on pagan practices was outlawed even though its efficacy was not doubted, whereas certain other practices were permitted. Thus in biblical times the Israelite could inquire of God through direct d. based on simple "lots" or priestly oracles. Later authorities also do not always entirely rule out the possibility of various forms of d., but Maimonides declares "Whosoever believes in them and their like, and thinks in his heart that they appertain to wisdom but that the *Torah* has forbidden recourse to them, is a fool and lacking in knowledge" (Laws of Idolatry 11:16).

DIVINE ATTRIBUTES, see **ATTRIBUTES OF GOD**

DIVINE NAMES, see **GOD, NAMES OF**

DIVINE SERVICE, see **PRAYER**

DIVORCE: A marriage is dissolved by a ceremony in which the husband gives his wife a bill of divorcement (*get*) in the presence of a competent rabbinical court. The court does not dissolve the marriage but merely supervises the complicated procedure, ensuring that it is in accord with religious law. An official of the court then makes a record of the d. and gives a certificate of the record to both parties. A court has jurisdiction, however, to make a declaration on the validity or nullity of a supposed marriage, in which case its decree is final. By the strict letter of the law, divorcement is an arbitrary right to be exercised by the husband whenever he might feel so inclined. From the earliest times, however, the MARRIAGE contract (KETUBBAH) contained stipulations protecting the wife from the husband's capricious misuse of this power. Since the time of R. Gershom (11th cent.), divorcing a wife against her will has been absolutely prohibited among *Ashkenazi* Jews (*Shulḥan Arukh, Even Ha-Ezer,* 119:6). For d. as it stands now, all that is required is the mutual consent of husband and wife. There are, however, specific grounds in Jewish law which entitle one of the parties to compel the other spouse to agree to a d. Among the main grounds are: 1) refusal of cohabitation; 2) apostasy; 3) loathsome chronic disease rendering marital relations impossible; 4) moral dissoluteness; 5) grossly insulting behavior; 6) ill-treatment; 7) well-founded suspicion of adultery committed by the wife; and 8) impotency of the husband. In such instances the party seeking the d. may apply to a rabbinical court, which sits as an investigating body to decide what degree of pressure may be exerted to prevail on the recalcitrant party to "agree" to a d. Although a husband's agreement obtained by coercion renders the *get* void, this is not the case where compulsion is so ordered by a rabbinical court. Even then a declaration of acquiescence on the part of the husband is essential. Since according to the letter of the law a Jewish marriage is in principle potentially polygamous, if a wife obstinately refuses to accept a d. which her husband is entitled to give, the husband can be granted permission to remarry without the dissolution of his former marriage. However, the remarriage of a Jewish woman without a *get* entails the most serious consequence for herself — her second union is considered an act of adultery and the issue of her second union are regarded as *mamzerim,* i.e., illegitimate in the worst sense and debarred from "entering into the congregation of the Lord" (Deut. 23:3). Rabbis therefore make every effort to secure a *get* for the woman. Where the d. was not dictated or justified by circumstances, it is considered to be a virtuous deed for a man to remarry his divorced wife. Remarriage with the first husband is however precluded if the wife has meantime married another man or if the husband is a priest. A divorcee (like a widow) may not remarry until ninety-one days have elapsed in order that the paternity of a child with which she may be pregnant might not be in doubt. The marriage of an adulterous wife and her consort after d. has been obtained is forbidden. A husband cannot divorce his wife if she is insane. If the wife is seen to be incurably insane, however, the signatures of one hundred rabbis are required to give the husband permission to marry a second time; this is by way of an exception to the 900-year-old enactment in *Ashkenazi* tradition against polygamous marriages. In any case the sick wife must first be provided for. At the time of d. the rabbinical court deals with monetary settlements and the custody of children. Maintenance to be paid after d. (alimony) is unknown in Jewish law, which sees d. as "complete severance". In deciding which one of the divorced parties is to vacate the joint dwelling, rabbis are guided by the maxim that the re-establishment of a homestead is more difficult for a man than for a woman. Other considerations, however, may reverse this rule. In countries where a *get* has no legal effect, rabbis will not arrange for a Jewish d. before a civil d. is granted. On the other hand civil d. is not recognized by rabbinical law unless it is supplemented by a d. according to religious procedure. Jewish law then provides for the easy technical dissolution of marriage. Under certain conditions separation is obligatory but where it is optional everything possible is done to discourage its hasty exercise. The Talmud quotes a saying : "The altar sheds tears for him who divorces his first wife." Indeed, the causeless d. of a first wife, even if valid, is deemed to be an act contrary to the will of the Almighty. Yet where continued life together is absolutely impossible, it is recognized that no impediment should hinder the release by d. See DOWRY.

DOGMA: Authoritative formulation of the tenets of a faith. Such formulation is alien to Judaism and was attempted only as a reaction to contact with other religions and philosophies. Generally speaking the tendency has been to stress the practice of Judaism rather than theological beliefs and articles of faith. Another restraining factor in this respect was the absence of a central ecclesiastical authority. Various Jewish thinkers, especially in the Middle Ages, felt the need to formulate the basic principles of Judaism. Influenced by Islam, the Karaites stated articles of faith, and under a similar impetus Jewish medieval thinkers endeavored to reduce Judaism to doctrines (see CREED). In his major work *Jerusalem*, Moses Mendelssohn reasserted that Judaism (as opposed to Christianity) has no d., the acceptance of which is a necessary prerequisite for salvation. Some thinkers have suggested that Judaism does have dogmas, in the form of certain common assumptions of faith, but no dogmatics in the sense of a systematic and detailed set of beliefs.

DOMAIN: Ownership of and control over the use of land. The rabbis distinguish between public and private d. in three instances. (1) For Sabbath observance, where they list four types of d.: a) private (*reshut ha-yaḥid*) where carrying is permitted on Sabbath; b) public d. (*reshut ha-rabbim*), such as streets and squares, where carrying is forbidden; c) semi-private d. (*karmelit*), e.g. fields, the sea, booths in a street, where carrying is forbidden; d) semi-public d. (*makom patur*) e.g. a trench. (2) In cases of ritual uncleanness, a private d. is one where there are less than three individuals; with three or more, it becomes public. (3) In cases of claim for damages, a public d. is any place or road to which there is public access; any person who causes injury there is himself liable to pay compensation.

DONMEH (Turkish: "apostates"): Crypto-Jewish sect in Turkey, derived from the followers of the pseudo-messiah SHABBETAI TZEVI. His adoption of Islam in 1666, which was received with consternation by most of those who had believed in him, still did not disillusion his most fanatical followers, who interpreted even this step as divinely ordained and directed toward the ultimate triumph of his messiahship. They followed his example, and ostensibly adopted the Islamic faith, but in secret maintained many Jewish practices and Sabbataian, Judeo-Spanish prayer-formulae, as well as certain antinomian doctrines and rituals of Sabbataian origin. Later the sect split into two or more groups, their main center being in Salonica. Many D. played a leading part in the Young Turk movement. Their main beliefs were in the Unity of God, in Shabbetai Tzevi as His anointed, and in the celebration of *Av* 9, normally the saddest day in Jewish history, as a holiday (the birthday of Shabbetai Tzevi). Recent research has added greatly to the previously scanty knowledge of the history and customs of this sect, and shows a greater affinity to Jewish tradition than had been surmised. Since the interchange of population between Greece and Turkey began in 1923 the D. as a group have been in a steady process of disintegration.

DOOMSDAY, see DAY OF JUDGMENT

DOUBT (Heb. *saphek*): In instances where (1) the law is undecided, or (2) the facts are uncertain, a state of doubt exists. The *halakhah* has evolved a detailed code of procedure and criteria by means of which each instance is to be resolved. The basic guide to be followed in resolving cases of d. is the general rule that doubts affecting biblical law are to be decided in conformity with the stricter view, while those involving laws of rabbinic origin are to be resolved according to the more lenient opinion (*Ḥul.* 9b). Exceptions to this rule are (1) doubts in monetary matters where, even in instances involving biblical law, the more lenient view is acted upon, since one cannot dispossess a property-holder without valid proof; and (2) instances which may involve danger to life, in which case that view is followed which will best obviate the suspected danger. The more lenient ruling adopted in connection with rabbinic law rests upon the assumption that the sages issued decrees only in cases of certainty. In all of these instances many qualifying factors exist. In cases involving double doubt (*sephek sepheka*) the lighter view is adopted, even in deciding matters of biblical law.

DOV BER OF MEZHIRICH (known as the *Maggid* i.e., preacher, of Mezhirich; d. 1772): Rabbi and teacher who succeeded to the leadership of the ḥasidic movement after the BAAL SHEM TOV's death. His main talent was as a teacher, and legend does not associate him, as it does the Baal Shem Tov, with miraculous stories. Though personally something of an ecstatic, his sermons and mystical teaching are clearly and logically composed, and show great learning. While using traditional kabbalistic terminology, he often gave the classical concepts a highly original interpretation of his own, as in his doctrine of *ayin* — the moment of "nothingness" to which each thing must return before it is re-created. Another tendency developed by him is the central rôle of the TZADDIK. Out of the group that gathered about him came the most famous schools of ḤASIDISM. His disciples included Shneour Zalman of Lyady, Aaron of Karlin, the brothers Zusya and Shmelke, and Levi Isaac of Berdichev. Though he wrote no books, he permitted his students to record his sermons and discussions, and these were published in several volumes (*Maggid deverav le-Yaakov, Or Torah,* etc.).

DOWRY (Heb. *nedunyah*): Property brought by a bride to her husband in the form of either movable or immovable goods. In biblical times, it was the bridegroom who paid a sum of money (*mohar*) to the bride's father (as is still the custom in the Arab world). The bridal d. is however also found in the Bible (e.g. Gen. 24:59-61; Judg. 1:15; I Kings 9:16) and by the Talmudic Period the tradition of a d. had become universal and the *mohar* unknown. According to Jewish custom, a bride should be dowered by her father (or his estate) in proportion to his means; a poor bride, out of charity funds. A man has no proprietary rights over his wife's property — acquired either before or after her marriage — but is granted as much of its income as he expends on the upkeep of the household. This grant is explained historically as being in consideration of his obligation to ransom his wife — a not uncommon need in ancient days. The donor of a gift to a wife may deny the husband the benefit of its income. Even a "rebellious" wife (one who does not fulfill her marital obligations) must be returned her d. in the event of DIVORCE. A wife may deliver to her husband by agreement the control and administration of all, or part, of her property, which must be fully restored to her — together with an additional amount (usually 50%) — upon dissolution of marriage. Such property and its assessed value are recorded in the marriage contract (*ketubbah*). By law, the husband is responsible for its deterioration and fall in market value, but may claim any rise in its value. A husband may not dispose of his wife's immovable property without her acquiescence.

DOXOLOGY, see **CREED; DOGMA; LITURGY**

DREAM: The Bible attached immense importance to dreams, as they were regarded as one of the main channels whereby God revealed His will to all the prophets (except Moses, cf. Num. 12:6-7), both Jewish (e.g. Joseph in Gen. 37 or Daniel in Dan. 2:19) and non-Jewish (e.g. Laban in Gen. 31:29, Pharaoh in Gen. 41 or Balaam in Num. 22:20). But with the exception of Joseph and Daniel (both of whom interpreted in foreign courts), dream-interpretation by Jews is absent from the Bible. One of the largest sustained passages devoted to a single subject in all the aggadic sections of the Talmud is that dealing with dreams and their interpretations, and it covers five folio pages (*Ber.* 55b-57a). The treatment ranges from profound psychological insight into the nature of dreams to pure folklore and superstition. Thus on the one hand it says "Just as there is no chaff without straw, so there cannot be a d. without nonsense," "Part of a d. may be fulfilled, but not the whole," and "A man sees in d. only what is suggested by his own thoughts." On the other hand the significance of various animals seen in a d. is interpreted in the manner of popular dream-books, e.g. an ass means salvation, a roan horse walking gently is a good sign, but if galloping, a bad one. A saddled elephant is a good omen of impending miracles, but an unsaddled elephant is a bad omen. There is also a number of paradoxical interpretations. Dreaming that one is naked depends upon the place of the dream; in Babylon, it is a sign of freedom from sin, in Palestine, of the absence of good deeds. The effect of these detailed interpretations, to which countless other examples are found scattered throughout the Talmud, was to give dreams a tremendous importance among the common people; it became customary to FAST after a bad d., and such a fast was deemed sufficiently important to be permitted even on the Sabbath (though later authorities tried to limit this permission to specific dreams; *Shulḥan Arukh, Oraḥ Ḥayyim* 288). A talmudic formula (*Ber.* 55b), to be uttered during the priestly blessing in the synagogue for the fulfillment of a good d. or the changing of a bad d. to a good one, is still found in some prayer books and recited in some places. It was to enable the recitation of this prayer that a pause was inserted between each of the three verses in the priestly blessing.

DRESS, see **COSTUME**

DRINK-OFFERING, see **LIBATION**

DRUNKENNESS: It is indicative of the almost complete absence of d. as a serious social and moral problem among Jews that the Talmud contains only one legal reference to the subject, namely that a person under the influence of alcohol is legally responsible for his actions unless he has attained the state of oblivion attributed to Lot (cf. Gen. 19:3, *Eruv.* 65a). A drunken person is forbidden to conduct a service (*Ber.* 31a), and the death of the two sons of Aaron (Lev. 10:1-4) is attributed by the rabbis to the fact that they entered the sanctuary in a state of intoxication (*ibid.* 9). The lighter side of d. is illustrated by the permission, if not the duty, to become so intoxicated on the holidays of *Purim* as to be unable to distinguish between "Blessed be Mordecai" and "Cursed be Haman" (*Meg.* 21a), but rabbinic authors are at pains to point out that this injunction should not be taken too seriously.

DRUSH, see **DERUSH**

DUALISM: The doctrine — metaphysical or moral — which holds that all being can be reduced to, or derives from, two ultimate and contrasting principles. (1) The ancient religion of Persia (Zoroastrianism) saw history as a cosmic struggle between the power of light and goodness on the one hand, and that of darkness and evil on the other. A slightly different form of d. was assumed by GNOSTICISM, which distinguished between a lower, evil deity, responsible for the creation of this world, and a higher, more transcendent, "good" deity. The source of these doctrines is man's experience of the radical opposition between GOOD AND EVIL. The prophets, however, insisted that God alone was the source of both light and darkness, good and evil (Is. 45:7) and the Mishnah condemned all forms of gnostic d. (*shetei reshuyyot* — "two powers") as heresy. Dualistic tendencies manifested themselves more than once in Jewish religious history (e.g. in apocryphal books such as JUBILEES and the TESTAMENTS OF THE TWELVE PATRIARCHS, in the writings of the DEAD SEA SECT, and in the medieval kabbalistic doctrine of evil, viz., the *sitra aḥra*), but they were kept in check by a basic and uncompromising MONOTHEISM. See also DEMONOLOGY; EVIL; SATAN. (2) A philosophical d., stemming from Greece (Plato) and opposing spirit to matter, exerted considerable influence on Jewish thinking and morals, both in the Hellenistic Period (cf. Philo) and later, particularly, in the Middle Ages. The logical consequence of this d. was contempt of the body, matter, and "this world", and a thoroughgoing ASCETICISM which, however, was partly inhibited by the rabbinic tradition that considered the physical universe and its enjoyment as essentially good, provided they are hallowed in the service of God. Modern writers tend to emphasize the biblical affirmation of the good and blessed life on this earth as a more adequate form of spirituality than one which negates matter. See also BODY; SEX; SIN.

(3) By positing a radical distinction between the absolute being of God the Creator, and the contingent, created being of all other things, the Bible and subsequent Jewish tradition affirmed another kind of d. Though created being derives from its Creator, the two still cannot be identified, as is done by the doctrines known as PANTHEISM or MONISM.

DUKHAN, see **PRIESTLY BLESSING**

DURAN: Family of Provençal origin. 1) *PROFIAT D.* (14th-15th cents.): Spanish philosopher. He suffered in the anti-Jewish persecutions of 1391 and wrote a bitter satire on Christianity *Al tehi ka-avotekha* ("Be not like your fathers"; known as *Alteca Boteca*) and the anti-Christian polemic *Kelimmat ha-Goyyim* ("Shame of the Gentiles"); this work quotes the Gospels to show that Jesus had no intention of leaving Judaism and endeavors to show that Christian dogma is untenable. D. cites many examples of the Bible being misquoted by Church Fathers, including Jerome. 2) *SIMEON BEN TZEMAḤ D.* (known as *Rashbatz,* 1361-1444): Philosopher and codifier, one of the outstanding rabbinical authorities in N. Africa. Over 800 of his responsa have been preserved. His encyclopedia *Magen Avot* ("Shield of the Patriarchs") incorporates a commentary on the tractate AVOT and discusses the philosophical fundamentals of Judaism. He accepted Maimonides' 13 principles of faith but reduced them to three basic dogmas — the existence of God, the Divine origin of the *Torah,* and the doctrine of reward and punishment. He sought to reconcile contradictory views of Jewish philosophers and also quoted kabbalistic and mystical sources.

DURESS (Heb. *ones*): According to talmudic law, a man is held responsible for his actions only if they are initiated and performed by his own free will (*Bava Kamma* 28b). This principle is derived from Deut. 22:25-28, according to which a betrothed virgin who has been raped is freed from all penalty, since she acted under compulsion. While various types of d. are recognized by *halakhah,* compulsion as grounds for extenuating circumstances refers only to physical violence or threat to the life of the person concerned (following the phrase in Lev. 18:5 "he shall live by them [commandments]" i.e., not die by them). Compulsion to commit one of the three cardinal sins — idolatry, murder, or an adulterous or incestuous act — is to be resisted even at the cost of life. However, one who from fear or under d. violates one of these three precepts, remains unpunished by human court. A divorce granted under d. is invalid and a woman who is forced to agree to wedlock is considered unmarried by law. Oaths or vows taken under d. are also invalid and carry neither obligation nor penalty. Similarly a gift bestowed under d. may be rescinded, but a sale or purchase concluded under similar circumstances remains valid. Saving one's life by means of another's property is permitted but compensation must be made to the owner of the property; likewise an injury caused under d. to one's fellow must still be compensated (*Bava Kamma* 27a).

DUTY: The Hebrew word for d. (*ḥovah;* the fem. form of *ḥov* "debt") conveys the notion of an obligation or due, payable by man to God or to his fellow man. By carrying out such a d. he becomes free of his indebtedness, hence the rabbinic idiom for fulfilling one's d. *"yotzei yedei ḥovato"*, means literally emerging from the hold of one's obligation. *Ḥovah* is distinct from *mitzvah* (see COMMANDMENT; PRECEPT) in that the latter term can also signify a commendable action (*reshut*); e.g. each of the three daily prayers is *mitzvah,* but whereas the morning and afternoon prayers are obligatory, the evening prayer is *reshut.* BAHYA IBN PAKUDA distinguishes between the "duties of the limbs [of the body]", i.e., ceremonial and practical obligations, and the "duties of the heart" (i.e., of the spiritual life). The rabbis considered those actions performed in obedience to a positively commanded d. as morally superior to voluntary good deeds (*Kidd.* 31a).

DYBBUK (Heb. literally "attachment"): The disembodied spirit of a dead person which finds no rest on account of the sins committed during life, and seeks a haven in the body of a living person, acting as an evil influence within him. Possession by a *d.* is often taken as a sign of hidden sin on the part of the person possessed. The *d.* can be exorcised by a religious rite. There is no mention of the *d.* in the Talmud or early kabbalistic literature. The emergence of the belief is connected with that of *gilgul* (the TRANSMIGRATION OF SOULS) developed by the disciples of Isaac LURIA. The belief became widespread from the 17th cent. onward and found expression in popular legends and in literature.

E

EAST, see **MIZRAḤ**

EBIONITES: Designation applied to members of a Judeo-Christian movement within the early Church. The derivation of the name has been a subject of debate, but it is generally held to derive from the Hebrew *evyon* ("poor"), a word which originally had an economic meaning but gradually assumed a theological connotation and was used as a self-appellation by the eschatological groups who, though they then appeared poor, oppressed, and lowly (*evyonim*), thought themselves destined to "inherit the kingdom of God" (cf. *Matt.* 5:3, "blessed are the poor in spirit", and the numerous references to *evyonim* in the DEAD SEA SCROLLS). There seem to have been several distinct groups within this movement, but each was firmly rooted in Jewish tradition. The E. were strict in their adherence to the Jewish Law and insisted that all devout Christians were bound by it. They observed the Sabbath and held their *agape* (love feast) on the Sunday. While some of them accepted the divinity of Jesus, they refused to ascribe to him any kind of transcendental nature. Other groups of E. completely rejected Jesus' divinity, but they held that he was the Messiah, chosen by God at the time of his baptism. Thus, the baptism of Jesus was a leading theme in the Ebionite gospel. The E. were firm in their rejection of Paul and his teachings which they regarded as heretical. As the Christian Church turned increasingly toward the gentiles, the gap between orthodox Christianity and the E. widened. Many E. returned to Judaism and as a unit the group drifted into obscurity in the 5th cent.

ECCLESIASTES, BOOK OF (Heb. *Sepher Kohelet*): Fourth of the five scrolls contained in the Hagiographa section of the Bible; read in the synagogue on the intermediate Sabbath of the Feast of Tabernacles (or in the absence of an intermediate Sabbath on *Shemini Atzeret*). Its 12 chapters present the meditations of an author who has failed to find spiritual comfort either in faith or in intellect but still endeavors to discover the purpose of human life with all its trials and tribulations culminating in senility, sickness, and death. His philosophy is summed up in the phrase "Vanity of vanities—all is vanity". This generally pessimistic outlook is accompanied by ethical advice postulating that no effort in life is worthwhile since, owing to predestination, nothing can be changed. Man must reconcile himself to the absence of justice in the world and seek consolation in a hedonistic approach to life. According to E., God — ruler of the universe — loves justice, but in this world all is fortuitous with only death certain. This defeatism runs contrary to the rest of biblical teaching which stresses the Divine rule of justice in the world and the eventual elimination of evil; the last few verses (according to critics, emanating from a later hand) provide a more conventional conclusion to the book. Some early rabbis did not want to admit the book to the canon, but the traditional ascription of its authorship to King Solomon ensured its inclusion. Modern scholars have surmised that it was written c. 3rd cent. B.C.E.

ECCLESIASTES RABBAH, see **MIDRASH RABBAH**

ECCLESIASTICUS, see **BEN SIRA**

ÉCOLE RABBINIQUE DE FRANCE, see **SÉMINAIRE ISRAÉLITE DE FRANCE**

EDELS, SAMUEL ELIEZER (known as the *Maharsha*; 1555-1631): Polish talmudic commentator. His *Ḥiddushei Halakhot* ("Legal Novellae"), appended to almost all editions of the Talmud, expands the talmudic text with acumen and profundity, and also explains the comments of Rashi and the *Tosaphot*. His *Ḥiddushei Aggadot* ("Aggadic Novellae") contains many rational interpretations of aggadic material.

EDEN, GARDEN OF, see **GARDEN OF EDEN; PARADISE**

EDUCATION: The duty to instruct the people in the commandments of God (cf. "and thou shalt teach them diligently unto thy children", Deut. 6:7) is often emphasized in the Bible. At first this religious e. — like practical e. in the arts of farming or shepherding — was a matter of parental precept and example, supported by traditions of folk tales and oral teachings. Literacy seems to have been widespread in ancient Israel (cf. Judg. 8:14), and toward the end of the First Temple Period there is evidence of formal religious instruction being given by the LEVITES (cf. II Chron. 7:7 ff.). The institution by EZRA of regular public readings of the TORAH, as well as the emergence of a non-priestly class of SCRIBES and scholars, gave a new impetus to e. The liturgical reading of the Pentateuch was accompanied by exposition and instruction. According to talmudic reports SIMEON BEN SHETAḤ established local schools for boys between 15 and 17, while the High Priest Joshua ben Gamala is said to have instituted elementary e. for boys from the age of 6. The Talmudic Period formulated the ideals and patterns of e. that remained characteristic of the Jewish community until the onset of the Modern Period. TALMUD TORAH ("study") in the sense of "laboring in the *Torah* for its own sake" was considered the most laudable kind of activity, and the ideal type of Jew was the scholar. Higher rabbinic e. was given in the BET HA-MIDRASH which was usually close by the SYNAGOGUE and tended to overlap some of the latter's functions. In Babylonia, non-professional scholars would leave their farms or trade for the semi-annual study-retreat (KALLAH). Elementary e. was given in *bet hasepher* (school) — known later as the HEDER — which was normally maintained by the community. The importance attached to school is evident in the rabbinic dictum that the world is "poised on the breath of schoolchildren". Rabbinic law obligates the father to teach his sons *Torah* as well as a trade. *Talmud Torah* was restricted to boys, and the rabbis were critical of formal e. for girls. Nevertheless there were women, both in the Talmudic and in the Medieval Periods, whose learning and competence in the Law were acknowledged by the rabbis. The tendency to restrict the curriculum to Jewish learning, and more particularly to talmudic studies, became even more marked in the medieval and post-Reformation GHETTO. While secular studies had never gone unopposed — even in the "golden" Spanish age — they were now completely neglected. Proposals by HASKALAH writers and others to reform the educational system aroused violent Orthodox opposition. With the entry of Jews into modern society and the spread of universal e. the place of the Jewish school was taken by the general school, and an often inadequate Jewish e. was given in the afternoons or on Sundays in "Hebrew School" or "religious classes" organized by the synagogues or communities. Post-emancipation Jewish schools were primarily meant to give a general e. with only a minimum of Jewish instruction. In more recent times a tendency toward a more markedly Jewish e. has asserted itself, partly through religious, partly under national (Zionist) inspiration. Many day schools self-consciously call themselves *talmud torah* or *yeshivah*, and alongside the old-style *yeshivot*, institutions have developed combining the traditional talmudic curriculum with a standard secondary e. Modern social and cultural trends have affected not only the methods, contents, and aims of these schools but also their underlying philosophies of e. But there is little doubt that the extraordinary emphasis and value placed by Jews on e. and study are a legacy of the Jewish religious tradition.

EDUYYOT (Heb. "Testimonies"): Tractate in the Mishnah order of *Nezikin* mostly comprising testimonies of scholars in the Yavneh court regarding doubtful cases. In each connection the statements of previous authorities are cited. The object of this tractate is to collect unimpeachable traditions. There is no internal connection between the various *halakhot* discussed.

EGER, AKIVA (1761-1837): Rabbi and codifier. He founded a distinguished *yeshivah* at Posen and bitterly fought secular education and the Reform movement, the latter particularly for reducing the use of Hebrew in prayer. E., recognized as one of the leading talmudists of his time, wrote important novellae on the Mishnah and Talmud. His responsa — 151 of which were published — are noted for their direct, concise, and often lenient consideration of the subject under discussion.

EGLAH ARUPHAH (Heb.): A heifer whose neck was broken in the event of an unsolved murder. According to Deut. 21:1-9, if a corpse was discovered in a field and the identity of the murderer could not be ascertained, the elders of the town closest to the body were commanded to take a heifer "which hath not been wrought with and which hath not drawn in the yoke" and break its neck "in a rough valley which neither be plowed nor sown". They then had to recite a formula proclaiming their innocence, the priests adding a prayer for the forgiveness of the people. According to the Mishnah (*Sot.* 9:9) the custom was discontinued after the occurrence of murders grew in frequency. The *E.A.* is a ritual meant to atone for land and persons involved in guilt on account of the shedding of unavenged innocent blood.

EḤAD MI YODEA (Heb. "Who knows one?"): Hymn of medieval origin and unknown authorship sung in *Ashkenazi* rites at the end of the SEDER service. It is composed of 13 riddles (possibly because the numerical value of the Hebrew word *eḥad* — "one" — is thirteen) and was inserted especially to maintain the interest of children participating in the service.

EIBESCHUTZ, JONATHAN (c. 1690-1764): Talmudist and kabbalist. When serving as rabbi in N. Germany, he was accused — especially by Jacob EMDEN — of being a secret believer in the messiahship of SHABBETAI TZEVI; the resultant controversy occupied rabbinical scholars throughout Europe, most German rabbis opposing E. and most Polish and Moravian rabbis rallying to his defense. Modern scholarship agrees with Jacob

Emden that E. was a Sabbataian. E. was an outstanding preacher and talmudist noted for his sharp acumen and PILPUL, impressive evidence of which he gave in his halakhic works *Urim ve-Tummim* and *Keret u-Pheleti.*

EIGHTEEN BENEDICTIONS, see **AMIDAH**

EIKHAH, see **LAMENTATIONS**

EIKHAH RABBATI, see **MIDRASH RABBAH**

EIN HA-RA, see **EVIL EYE**

EIN K-ELOHENU (Heb. "There is none like our God"): Hymn of praise to God recited in the *Sephardi* rite at the end of the Morning Service; among *Ashkenazim,* it is said only on Sabbaths and festivals at the conclusion of the Additional Service. An acrostic forming the word *Amen,* it is of early origin and is found in the prayer book of R. Amram and the *Maḥzor Vitry.*

EIN SOPH (Heb.): Kabbalistic term which over the centuries became associated with a number of meanings differing in nuance and, at times, in essential definition. The term means literally "without end", and its early pre-kabbalistic use was probably as a synonym for "limitless". In the Spanish and later Kabbalah, it was used for that aspect of the Godhead about which absolutely nothing could be thought or said — the *deus absconditus.* For most kabbalists it connoted the impersonal aspect of the Deity with which all relationship in human terms is impossible, though that aspect is the ultimate source of all creation. Only when the *E. S.* is limited or contracted by ATTRIBUTES which can somehow be grasped by the finite mind, can man have a conscious relationship with it. Some mystics try to illustrate the relationship between the hidden *E. S.* and the personal God of religion through the analogy of coal, the attributes of which are made manifest only by flame. However, with other kabbalists, the distinction between the *E. S.* and the manifest personal God of religion leads to a DUALISM verging on the heretical.

EIN YAAKOV, see **IBN ḤAVIV**

EINHORN, DAVID (1809-1879): Reform rabbi; born in Germany, officiated in Budapest until the authorities closed his synagogue, and from 1855 in the U.S. The spokesman of radical Reform in the U.S., he denied the continued authority of the Talmud, and introduced Sunday services, at which worship was conducted with uncovered head and to the accompaniment of ORGAN music. A brilliant orator and considerable rabbinical scholar, he preached that the ceremonial laws of Moses were only symbolical and that biblical miracles were allegories. E.'s prayer book *Olat Tamid* ("Perpetual Offering") was composed mostly in German with a small number of prayers in Hebrew; it omitted prayers for the revival of sacrifice, the return to Zion, and the resurrection of the dead. Its English version (prepared by his son-in-law, Rabbi Emil Gustav Hirsch of Chicago) formed the basis of the Union Prayer Book.

EL, see **GOD, NAMES OF**

EL ELYON, see **GOD, NAMES OF**

EL EREKH APPAYIM (Heb. "O God, slow to anger"): Short *seliḥah* prayer recited in the synagogue during the Morning Service on Mondays and Thursdays, prior to the Reading of the Law. It is omitted on the New Moon, the eve of Passover, *Av* 9, *Ḥanukkah,* and *Purim.* This prayer is found in the earliest prayer books (e.g. of R. Amram and *Maḥzor Vitry*).

EL MALE RAḤAMIM (Heb. "God, full of compassion"): Prayer for the repose of the souls of the dead. This prayer is recited in certain European rites after the Bible reading on Sabbaths and weekdays. Its current form is late, probably dating from the time of the Chmielnicki pogroms (1648-49), though the custom of praying for the repose of the dead dates back to earlier times. In many *Ashkenazi* communities it is also recited after a burial, on the 30th day after a death, and after the recitation of the YIZKOR prayer on the three Pilgrim Festivals and on the Day of Atonement. It corresponds to the *Sephardi* HASHKAVAH prayer.

EL MELEKH NE'EMAN (Heb. "God, faithful king"): A phrase interposed between the AHAVAH benediction and the recitation of the SHEMA; its initial letters form the word AMEN. The phrase was introduced either in order to preface the *Shema* with the basic idea of Divine kingship (which does not occur in the *Shema* itself) or else to bring the total number of words in the *Shema* to 248 corresponding to the 248 members, which according to the rabbis, were comprised in the human body. It is recited only when the *Shema* is said in private prayer.

ELDERS: In ancient times, the authoritative body ruling the people or state. The first such group to be appointed was during the time of Moses (Num. 11:16-17) but similar bodies are reported to have existed earlier both among the Jews in Egypt (Exod. 3:16) and at Sinai, where 70 e. were privileged to accompany Moses up the mountain (Exod. 24:1). On several subsequent occasions the e. are mentioned as a representative and advisory, though never a legislative, body. The Mishnah (*Avot.* 1:1) reports that the e. constituted a link in the chain of tradition between Joshua and the prophets. Reference to the e. is found in the Book of Ezra (10:8) and it is possible that they were the basis for the GREAT ASSEMBLY. Many scholars maintain that the e. participated in administering affairs of state until the Hasmonean Period and that their functions were eventually incorporated into those of the Sanhedrin. The e. doubtless included men noted for their sagacity and learning, and not necessarily for their great age. See also GEROUSIA.

ELEAZAR BEN AZARIAH (1st-2nd cents.): *Tanna.* While still in his teens, he succeeded R. GAMALIEL when the latter was temporarily deposed from the presidency of the Yavneh academy. After Gamaliel's reinstatement, E. continued to play a central role in the communal and religious life of his time. E. was an outstanding preacher and aggadist and is credited with some of the basic maxims of the Talmud, e.g. "Saving a life takes precedence over the Sabbath" (*Shab.* 132a), "The Day of Atonement does not atone for sins against one's fellow man until the person sinned against has been appeased" (Mishnah *Yoma* end), and "The Bible is written in human language" (*Kidd.* 17b, in defense of the literal interpretation of Scripture). He was also responsible for the HERMENEUTICAL principle according to which a biblical verse can be interpreted in the light of the preceding or following verse.

ELEAZAR BEN JUDAH OF WORMS (Eleazar Rokeaḥ, c. 1165-1238): Kabbalist, talmudist, and religious poet; pupil of JUDAH HE-ḤASID. He was responsible for popularizing the doctrines and practices of the German Ḥasidim, whose mystical system was based on letter and number mysticism. He was influenced by various oriental traditions connected with MERKAVAH mysticism and the Book of YETZIRAH. According to this system, from the absolute transcendent spirituality of God there emanated the "*kavod*" (glory) or "special cherub" which served as intermediary (or *logos*) between God and finite creation. But in spite of His transcendence, God is closer to the universe than the soul is to the body. All corporeal epithets attributed to God in the Bible should be attributed to the *kavod.* In E.'s many writings (the best-known, *Rokeaḥ,* is a code of ethical laws), *halakhah, aggadah,* and kabbalah are closely interwoven; they provide a comprehensive picture of early German Ḥasidim and were doubtless known to Moses de Leon, the putative author of the ZOHAR.

ELEAZAR KALLIR, see **KALLIR, ELEAZAR**

ELEAZAR ROKEAḤ, see **ELEAZAR BEN JUDAH OF WORMS**

ELECTION OF ISRAEL, see **CHOSEN PEOPLE**

ELEGY, see **KINAH**

ELEPHANTINE, see **YEB**

ELI TZIYYON (Heb. "Lament, O Zion"): Alphabetic hymn of medieval origin, recited in *Ashkenazi* rites on *Av* 9 after the reading of *kinot* (dirges). The traditional melody has influenced the chanting of other prayers recited during the THREE WEEKS.

ELIEZER BEN HYRCANUS (1st-2nd cents): *Tanna;* pupil of Johanan ben Zakkai and teacher of R. Akiva. After the destruction of the Temple, he headed the academy of Lydda and was a leading member of the Sanhedrin. His stringent halakhic opinions, based on the teachings of the School of Shammai, led to his excommunication after he refused to accept the majority ruling.

ELIEZER BEN NATHAN OF MAINZ (1090-1170): Codifier, religious poet, and one of the first German tosaphists. His main work was *Even ha-Ezer* ("The Stone of Help") which collected halakhic material from scattered sources; his work, a compendium of halakhic opinion with particular reference to the talmudic tractates of *Moed, Nashim,* and *Nezikin,* summarizes responsa and rabbinical rulings, explains customs, *aggadah,* and liturgy, and incorporates valuable material on 12th cent. Jewish life.

ELIEZER BEN YOSE HA-GALILI (2nd cent.): *Tanna;* pupil of R. AKIVA. A noted aggadist, he laid down 32 hermeneutical rules for the interpretation of the AGGADAH. These were preserved in a special *baraita* which is printed in Talmud editions after the tractate *Berakhot.*

ELIEZER OF TOUQUES (latter 13th cent.): French tosaphist. His arrangement of TOSAPHOT formed the basis of the standard version incorporated in subsequent editions of the Babylonian Talmud. It is based on abbreviations of the *tosaphot* of SAMSON OF SENS to which certain later views have been added.

ELIJAH: Prophet in the Kingdom of Israel, originally from Gilead in Transjordan. In the biblical narrative E. emerges as a stern, fearless, and uncompromising figure, zealously determined to uproot the idolatrous worship of Baal introduced by Jezebel, the Tyrian wife of Ahab. His zeal eventually earned the gentle rebuke of God in a vision (I Kings 19:11-12) which taught him that God is not always in the tempest, the earthquake, and the fire, but is in the "still small voice". E.'s dramatic encounter with the priests of Baal on Mt. Carmel (I Kings 18) and his fearless denunciation of Ahab (I Kings 21) after the king had engineered Naboth's execution in order to possess his vineyard are among the best-known incidents of his career. The figure of E. has been one of the most popular in Jewish tradition, though bearing a very different character from the biblical portrait. The fact that he did not die but was borne to heaven in a chariot of fire, and the prophecy in Malachi (3:23) in which he appears as the precursor of the Messiah who will "turn the hearts of the fathers unto the children and the hearts of the children unto their fathers" combined to produce the image of the ever-present prophet, wandering incognito over the earth, sometimes in the garb of a nomad, to aid in moments of distress and danger, appearing to mystics and scholars to teach them hidden truths, and acting as celestial messenger. The talmudic rabbi with whom legend most associates him was R. Joshua ben Levi. On one occasion R. Joshua in view of the Roman threat to destroy the town surrendered to the Romans a political fugitive who had taken refuge in his home town of Lydda. To show his displeasure at this act, E. terminated his visits to the sage. Ultimately he returned, and when R. Joshua pleaded that he had acted in accordance with the letter of the law, E. answered that such a law did not represent the highest ethical attitude of Judaism. To R. Anan he used to teach the "SEDER ELIYAHU" (*Ket.* 106a) which supposedly became the basis of the midrashic compilations known as *Tanna de-Vei Eliyahu Rabbah* and *Zuta*. Identified as he was with the "Angel of the Covenant" of Mal. 3:1, where the word *berit* suggested more specifically the BERIT MILAH, he came to be especially associated with the latter. He is thought to be present at every CIRCUMCISION ceremony as its guardian spirit and witness, and a special chair is reserved for him on such occasions, the person performing the ceremony announcing, "This is the Chair of Elijah, may he be remembered for good". E. is also associated with the SEDER celebration of Passover night, where the custom of the "fifth CUP" has given rise to the popular belief in his invisible presence. The prominence of E. in the HAVDALAH liturgy for the termination of the Sabbath (e.g. the popular hymn *Eliyahu ha-Navi*) is connected with his traditional rôle as precursor of the Messiah.

ELIJAH, APOCALYPSE OF: A Jewish apocalyptical work, written in Hebrew and generally dated in the Gaonic Period (6th-10th cents.), though it probably includes material of an earlier era. It purports to record the revelations made to Elijah on Mt. Carmel by the archangel Michael and contains all the main elements of classical ESCHATOLOGY e.g., the advent and reign of the MESSIAH, the war of GOG AND MAGOG, the RESURRECTION of the dead, the DAY OF JUDGMENT, and the coming of the heavenly Jerusalem.

ELIJAH, CHAIR OF, see **CIRCUMCISION; ELIJAH**

ELIJAH, CUP OF, see **CUP; ELIJAH**

ELIJAH BEN SOLOMON ZALMAN OF VILNA (known as the Vilna Gaon; 1720-1797): Rabbinical authority; one of the outstanding spiritual figures of E. European Jewry. His severely ascetic life was devoted to study and his encyclopedic knowledge spanned the whole gamut of Jewish lore. E.'s approach to the Talmud was characterized by keen logic and a critical sense aimed at establishing a correct text and understanding its plain meaning. Opposing contemporary trends of viewing the Talmud as the exclusive object of study, he stressed the importance of prior acquaintance with the Bible, and argued that a proper grasp of *Torah* required the knowledge of auxiliary sciences, several of which he himself mastered. Theologically an uncompromising fundamentalist, he asserted the eternal validity of every last detail of the *Torah* and averred that any challenge to the smallest item was a challenge to the whole; hence also his meticulous care for detail. His reputation rests particularly in the sphere of *halakhah*. He was profoundly versed in kabbalistic literature on which he wrote extensively but he had no sympathy with philosophy. E. stridently opposed the rising ḥasidic movement and in the ensuing controversy took rigorous measures to check the spread of Ḥasidism in Lithuania. His literary output included biblical exegesis, commentaries upon Mishnah, Midrash, Talmud, *Shulḥan Arukh*, and Kabbalah.

ELIMELECH OF LIZENSK (1717-1787): Ḥasidic rabbi. A disciple of Dov Ber of Mezhirich and brother of R. Sussya of Annapol, E. was accepted after the death of his master in 1755 as the leader of the ḥasidim of Galicia and Poland. Although he himself indulged in severe ascetic practices, he discouraged his followers from following his example. E. was among the first of the ḥasidic rabbis to develop the theory of the TZADDIK as the intermediary between man and God, especially in his *Noam Elimelekh* ("Delight of Elimelech").

ELISHA (9th cent. B.C.E.): Israelite prophet. Disciple and successor to ELIJAH, he continued his master's mission; through his encouragement of Jehu, he brought to a successful conclusion Elijah's struggle against the House of Omri and against Baal worship in Israel. Like Elijah, E. was forceful, courageous, and independent and strove to maintain the purity of the Israelite religion. Whereas Elijah was more the fighter-prophet, E. emerged during his 50-year ministry as the adviser-statesman and man of action. The folk tales that clustered around his personality attributed a series of miracles to his intervention and depicted him as the friend of the poor and oppressed. In general, the E. stories — like those of Elijah — stress the prophet's moral stature and rigor while illustrating his dominance in the religious life of the nation.

ELISHA BEN AVUYAH (2nd cent.): *Tanna*; teacher of R. Meir. His doctrines stress the virtue of ethical behavior without which mere legal observance is valueless. Deeply affected by the failure of the Bar Kokhba uprising (which he possibly opposed) and influenced by mysticism, he came to reject rabbinic Judaism (especially the theory of reward and punishment and the resurrection of the dead) and apparently accepted one of the then widespread branches of heretical gnostic thought. The Talmud (which in view of his defection never calls him by name but refers to him as *Aher* i.e., "another one") mentions his absorption in sectarian literature and hellenistic song; it also relates that he endeavored to influence students to abandon their talmudic studies.

ELOHIM, see **GOD, NAMES OF**

ELUL: Sixth month in the religious calendar and twelfth and last in the civil; *E.* has 29 days. The name is Babylonian and first occurs in Neh. 6:15. During Temple times, messengers would travel from Jerusalem to the Diaspora to announce the date of the New Moon of *E.* so that the following New Moon — the New Year (*Tishri*) — could be accurately determined. As it immediately precedes the Ten Days of Penitence, *E.* became a month of repentance and preparation for the Day of Judgment. In the *Ashkenazi* rite the SHOPHAR is sounded throughout the month after the Morning Service (except on Sabbaths and the eve of the New Year) in order to inspire a mood of penitence. *Sephardi* Jews call it the "month of mercy" and recite SELIHOT nightly throughout the month; *Ashkenazim* start their recitation on the Saturday evening preceding the New Year (unless the New Year falls on Monday or Tuesday, in which case the recitation of *selihot* is commenced a week earlier).

EMANATION: The process by which entities (personal or impersonal) proceed directly from a higher to a lower entity. Unlike the act of CREATION, which is an act of will of a personal Creator, e. is usually conceived as an impersonal and almost natural process, like the e. of rays from the sun. Doctrines of e. generally suppose a higher degree of affinity, or even a substantial identity, between the various forms of being — they may be higher or lower, spiritual or material etc., but ultimately all derive from a single source — whereas creation implies an essential discontinuity between the creator and all other beings. Doctrines of e. are prominent in GNOSTICISM, NEO-PLATONISM, and various mystical systems. The chief phase of Jewish MYSTICISM, i.e., the Kabbalah, combines gnostic and Neo-Platonic elements, and consequently the notion of e. (Heb. *atzilut*) is a major feature of the "Divine world". The origin of the doctrine of e. is concerned with the procession of the "Divine worlds" rather than with the origin of the cosmos as a whole; it describes the fullness of the manifest Godhead (SEPHIROT) as it emerges from the hidden depths of EIN SOPH. The symbolic and speculative elucidation of the nature and character of this process is one of the main themes of theoretical Kabbalah (e.g. in the ZOHAR and in the works of Moses CORDOVERO). Whether e. is restricted to the sphere of the Divine or whether it also extends to the lower worlds is a matter of controversy between kabbalistic schools.

EMANCIPATION: The e. of the Jews — the legal acceptance of their equality with fellow citizens of other faiths as regards both the privileges and responsibilities of citizenship, and the abolition of all discriminatory legislation which had had the effect of making the Jews at best a tolerated group — is closely connected in Western history with the struggle for religous freedom and the separation of Church and State. In the Western world, as long as Christianity was regarded as the state religion or the state as a Christian state, it followed that those who did not profess that faith were *ipso facto* denied the privileges of full citizenship and CIVIL RIGHTS. Apart from its civil aspects, therefore, Jewish e. involved either the abolition of the identification of Church with State or the recognition of Judaism as an official religion. Thus the struggle for the admission of a Jew to the British parliament centered on the abolition of the OATH which a member had to take "on the true faith of a Christian" whereas in pre-Hitler Germany, Judaism was recognized as an official faith, to the extent that the government levied taxes on all professing Jews for the upkeep of Jewish religious and communal institutions. E. also involved relinquishment by the Jews of the internal legal jurisdiction over their members which they had hitherto exercised. It also ran counter to the conception of the Jews as a member of a distinctive ethnic or national group. The attitude of the protagonists of e. is expressed in the slogan of one of its most fervent Christian protagonists Clermont-Tonnerre "Everything for the Jews as individuals; nothing for the Jews as a people... we cannot have a nation within a nation". The emergence of the Jew from the GHETTO and his full participation in every aspect of national life caused fundamental and far-reaching changes in Jewish social and religious life. With the disappearance of those external forces which had had the effect of unifying the inner community, secularization and ASSIMILATION set in. Many abandoned Judaism entirely but even to those remaining within the Jewish fold e. brought profound changes. Closely connected with the movement for social and political e. was the REFORM Movement in religion which tended to the view that full e., along with its corollary — full equality and brotherhood between men — heralded the messianic age foretold by the prophets, and therefore, that the fullest identification with the state was the highest expression of religious loyalty. The state laws concerning divorce and other matters of personal status were regarded as binding and superseding traditional Jewish legislation. The talmudic rule *Dina de-Malkhuta Dina* (i.e., "the law of the state is Jewish law"), the original scope of which was restricted to civil matters not impinging upon religious law, was now comprehensively reinterpreted and all those laws which tended to maintain Jewish exclusiveness, notably the dietary laws, were declared obsolete or mere folkways. Other religious movements too were influenced by e. Even the philosophy of the Neo-Orthodox movement established by Samson Raphael HIRSCH was based on the principle that the strictest Orthodoxy was compatible with complete social participation in the cultural and civic spheres of national life. Similarly the universal use of the vernacular in sermons, and its introduction to varying extents in the liturgy, resulted directly from the impact of e.

EMBEZZLEMENT: The fraudulent conversion of money or property entrusted to one's care. E. differs from THEFT in that the actual possession of the property by the embezzler is lawful. In addition to the instance of the bailee (Exod. 22) the Bible lists other cases of fraudulent conversion (e.g. Lev. 5:20-26), and demands full restitution of the property involved. If the perpetrator denies his fraud on oath and it is later proven, or he himself admits it, he is obligated to restore (1) the property, plus (2) one fifth of its value, which goes to the person defrauded, and (3) to offer the sacrifice of a guilt-offering.

EMDEN, JACOB ISRAEL (known as *Yavetz;* 1697-1776): German talmudic authority. His independent spirit and acute critical sense led him into conflict with leading rabbis of his time. He regarded Sabbataianism as a mortal danger to Judaism and his extreme zeal on this subject led him into a celebrated controversy with Jonathan EIBESCHUTZ whom he accused of being a secret believer in the messiahship of Shabbetai Tzevi; E. based his charge on the formulae contained in amulets prepared by Eibeschutz and wrote some 25 polemical compositions in this connection. E. was also the author of about 40 halakhic works including a commentary on the Mishnah, responsa, and works on the Kabbalah (violently attacking its practical aspects and suggesting a late authorship for the greater part of the ZOHAR).

EMET VE-EMUNAH (Heb. "True and trustworthy"): First blessing after the reading of the three paragraphs of the *Shema* in the Evening Service. The Talmud states that whoever does not recite EMET VE-YATZIV in the Morning Service and *E.V.* in the evening has not fulfilled his obligations (*Ber.* 12a). The evening formulation differs from the morning one in accord with the biblical phrase "to declare... Thy trustworthiness (*emunatekha*) every night" (Ps. 92:2). The contents of this prayer vary in different rites.

EMET VE-YATZIV (Heb. "True and firm"): First blessing after the reading of the three paragraphs of the *Shema* in the Morning Service. It is mentioned in the Mishnah and Talmud (cf. *Ber.* 21a; Y. *Ber.* 1:9) but the original version was probably much briefer than the present form. As it concludes with the blessing of God as Redeemer of Israel, it is known as the Redemption blessing. The almost complete uniformity in the basic wording of the blessing in all rites attests to its early origin. The prayer professes faith in the unity of God and the eternal truth of Divine revelation.

EMISSARY, see **SHALIAḤ**

END OF DAYS, see **ESCHATOLOGY**

ENGAGEMENT, see **BETROTHAL**

ENLIGHTENMENT, see **HASKALAH**

ENOCH, BOOKS OF: Series of literary works purported to have been written by or about Enoch (Heb. *Ḥanokh*) who — though of minor significance in the Bible — is reported to have "walked with God" and to have been "taken" by God (Gen. 5:24); the latter phrase is interpreted to mean that E. was literally taken into heaven during his lifetime. Although a Book of E. is mentioned by both Jewish and Christian (notably *Epistle of Jude* 14) sources, it was deemed lost until the late 18th cent. when an Ethiopic translation was discovered. This work — perhaps the most outstanding example of Jewish messianism from the Second Temple Period — was probably a translation from a Greek version which was in turn a translation from the original Hebrew or Aramaic. The book is a compilation of various E. legends and "visions" which have been put together with some semblance of order. The various sections date from the 2nd and 1st cents. B.C.E. The "Book of Parables" (chaps. 37-71) — concerned primarily with the End of Days, the last judgment, and the future life — center about the character of the "Son of Man", a messianic figure who will judge the earth. In the late 19th cent. another version of the Book of E. was discovered, this time in Slavonic. The "Secrets of Enoch" as this work is called, antedates the destruction of the Second Temple. Though this version is akin to the Ethiopic one, it is by no means a mere edition of it. It incorporates the messianic concepts of Alexandrian Jewry as well as many Christian additions, substantiating the theory that a large body of E. literature was in circulation during the Second Temple Period.

EPHOD (Heb.): Upper garment worn by the High Priest, to which was fastened the breastplate of judgment containing the oracular URIM AND THUMMIM; the word is also used for the High Priest's entire mantic vestment (for a description of the e., cf. Exod. 28:6ff.; 39:2-5). Although forbidding divination in general, the Bible allowed the priestly

e. as a means of determining the Divine Will. The e. apparently fell into disuse (possibly at the insistence of the prophets) and is not mentioned after the time of David.

EPHRAIM MOSES ḤAYYIM OF SADILKOV, see **MOSES OF SADILKOV**

EPICUREAN, EPIKOROS, see **APIKOROS**

EPITAPH, see **TOMB**

EPITROPOS, see **GUARDIAN**

ERETZ ISRAEL, see **ISRAEL, LAND OF**

EREV (Heb. "eve"): The day in the Jewish CALENDAR commences with sunset, so that the term *e.* is used to refer to the day preceding the commencement of a holy day. The period of holiness is inaugurated some time before sunset and in Temple times (as again in the State of Israel) the *shophar* was sounded as a signal to cease work. The rabbis also advised to eat abstemiously on the eve of Sabbaths and festivals so as to derive the maximum enjoyment from the evening meal. The TAḤANUN prayer is omitted from the Afternoon Service on the eves of Sabbaths and festivals. On the eve of the New Year, *seliḥot* are recited (including a special one for this occasion — ZEKHOR BERIT). The eve of the Day of Atonement is a time for eating and also for appeasing one's fellow man who has been offended during the past year. The eve of Passover is the fast of the FIRST-BORN; the eve of the New Moon was observed as a fast called YOM KIPPUR KATAN.

ERROR: Jewish law distinguishes between a ritual transgression committed in error (*shogeg*) and one committed intentionally (*mezid*). The former carries no penalty except in the case of the transgression of a prohibition which had it been intentionally transgressed would have been punishable by *karet* (excommunication); in such a case the accidental transgressor must bring a sin-offering. The three exceptions to this rule are 1) the blasphemer; 2) one who fails to have himself circumcised; and 3) one who fails to bring the paschal offering. False adjuration uttered in e. involves a special sacrifice. If the Sanhedrin ruled in e. concerning a matter involving excommunication and the public acted in accord with its erroneous ruling a special sacrifice must be brought by the Sanhedrin (Lev. 4:13-21). Similarly a special sacrifice is to be brought by the High Priest (*ibid.* 2-13) and the prince (*ibid.* 22-26) for their errors.

ERUSIN, see **BETROTHAL; MARRIAGE**

ERUV (Heb. "blending"): The general term for three types of rabbinic enactment intended to promote the sanctity of the Sabbath. 1. *ERUV TEḤUMIM* ("*e.* of boundaries"). According to the rabbinic interpretation of Exod. 16:29-30 which commands "each man to sit in his place" on the Sabbath, there is no biblical prohibition on walking outside the limits of one's place of residence on the Sabbath unless this distance exceeds 12 miles. Rabbinic law, however, places the limit at 2,000 cubits (about two-thirds of a mile) from the point where the built-up area of a locality ends. In order to ease the stringency in case of need, the rabbis made it possible for a person to go another 2,000 cubits provided he had, before the Sabbath, placed food for two meals at the end of the permitted 2,000 cubits. The location of the food would then in theory be considered his place of residence for the Sabbath, thus permitting him a further 2,000 cubits from that point. Hence it became possible to walk from one town to another whenever the distance between the two was less than 4,000 cubits. 2. *ERUV ḤATZEROT* ("*e.* of courtyards"). According to the biblical Sabbath law one may carry things from a house into a courtyard even if many other houses open onto it — as long as the courtyard is enclosed, it is considered a "private domain". To promote the sanctity of the Sabbath, however, the rabbis prohibit such carrying unless the inhabitants of the courtyard symbolically make all their houses a single dwelling by each contributing some food to be placed in one of the houses belonging to the courtyard. Since there is now a "common" eating place, it is permissible to carry objects in the whole courtyard. The same procedure may be followed to make it possible to carry objects from all the courtyards into a common alleyway enclosed on at least three sides (and symbolically on a fourth), except that the food is placed not in the alleyway but in one of the courtyards. The name of the *e.* of alleyways is called *shituphei movaot* ("partnership of alleyways"). 3. *ERUV TAVSHILIN* ("*e.* of dishes"). This is intended to safeguard the eminence of the Sabbath when preceded by a festival day. Ordinarily one may cook on a festival day only for that day. However, when such a day precedes the Sabbath, cooking is permitted on that day also for the Sabbath provided one has symbolically begun the Sabbath preparation on the day preceding the festival by setting aside something cooked and something baked for the Sabbath, and making an appropriate benediction.

ERUVIN (Heb. "Blendings"): Tractate in the Mishnah order of *Moed* with commentary in both Talmuds It deals with laws concerning the various types of ERUV.

ESAU: Elder son of Isaac and twin brother of JACOB. The personalities of Jacob and E. in the Book of Genesis symbolize the character and origin of the two nations of Israel and Edom, which derived from a similar background but developed an enmity toward each other (Jacob is identified with Israel in Gen. 32:25-29 and E. with Edom in Gen. 36:1). E. is depicted as a hunter who sells his birthright to Jacob. His anger at Jacob for having obtained their father Isaac's blessing through cunning results in Jacob's flight to Haran; but on Jacob's return, twenty years later, E. shows only friendliness. The rabbis depict E. as the epitome of wildness and lust for power; the name E. (or Edom) is used as an eponym for Rome and in medieval Hebrew literature for any anti-Jewish regime, Christianity in particular.

ESCHATOLOGY: The concept of and teachings about the happenings and events which are to come to pass at the "end of days" (*aḥarit ha-yamim*) when the present era is to undergo a definite, basic change. In Jewish thought, eschatological phenomena include the ingathering of the dispersed Jewish exiles, the last great conflict between the forces of righteousness and the powers of evil (the war against Gog and Magog), the Day of Judgment, the advent of the reign of the Messiah, the resurrection of the dead, and the re-establishment of the original paradise on earth. E. as a religious phenomenon is by no means peculiar to Judaism. Traces of it are to be found in many of the world's religions. It has been suggested that Israelite e. was greatly influenced by Babylonian, Egyptian, Canaanite, and Persian eschatological thought. If so, Israel was no mere passive recipient of these influences, for she reformed and reinterpreted them so that an entirely new and unique system of eschatological thought evolved. Judaism never had a single doctrine of e., but rather a multiplicity of views, the expressions of various groups and individuals. Israelite e. therefore cannot be presented as a rational and coherent scheme. E. looks to the future, awakening both hope and expectation in the heart of the believer. It is difficult to determine exactly at what stage Israel's hope for a more perfect future developed into true eschatological expectation. For example, the disappointment and disillusionment with the worldly and unrighteous monarchs of Israel and Judah gave rise to a natural desire for a just, heavenly ordained monarch. This longing, when colored by e., led to the concept of the godly king *par excellence,* i.e., the Messiah who was to rule Israel at the dawn of the new, eschatological era. One of the basic influences on Israel's eschatological thinking was the popular concept of the Day of the Lord — a day on which God would pour out His wrath on the enemies of Israel — a nationalistic idea which under the influence of the prophets (Amos, Hosea) was transformed into the great concept of a universal Day of Judgment, a day when all mankind, including Israel, would be called upon to account for its sins. Suffering and repentance were then to be followed by the advent of a new era, a period of peace which was to comprehend all nature ("The wolf shall dwell with the lamb..." Is. 11:6) and a time of material prosperity approximating paradise itself (Amos 9:13; Joel 4:18). The Lord would establish His throne on Zion and all nations would pay homage to the true and only God. Though the early beginnings of eschatological thought in Israel cannot be precisely dated, by the time of the return from the Babylonian Exile a well-defined e. played a substantial role in the shaping of Jewish religious life in Jerusalem and was of particular importance in the rebuilding of the Temple. According to prevailing opinion, the Exile represented the ultimate punishment for the sins of Israel. Now that the Exile was ended, however, the returned exiles stood on the very threshold of the messianic era. All that remained to be done was the rebuilding of the Temple (cf. Hag. 2:6-9, 21-23; Zech. 3:8; 4:6-11, 13-14, 6:9-15; 8:2-13). Once again, however, hopes were dashed, for even after the Temple was rebuilt the long-awaited era of peace and prosperity failed to materialize. Contrary to expectations, Zerubbabel governor of Judah and a scion of the house of David, did not prove to be the long-awaited Messiah. These continual disappointments and political upheavals served to increase the apocalyptic element in eschatological thought. The "new era" became further and further removed from reality. This tendency can be readily observed in Daniel, one of the earliest apocalyptic books and the only one of that genre to make its way into the biblical canon. The division between the here and now and the coming messianic era had become much greater and more distinct. The "World to Come" assumed a transcendental character. Israel would be redeemed and saved by the wonderful and miraculous intervention of the Divine. There was even a tendency, later rejected by the *tannaim,* to ascribe a transcendental nature to the messianic deliverer, the so-called "Son of Man" (cf. Daniel and the "Parables" of Enoch; compare also the Logos section [1:1-18] of John where the transcendental nature of Jesus is proclaimed). But even at this later date (2nd cent. B.C.E.) there was no single, unified system of e. among the Jewish people; perhaps at no other time were views on the subject so divergent. The Sadducees seem to have rejected e. completely, the Pharisees — while holding to the general concept of e. and its related phenomena — took a "middle-of-the-road" position between the religious problems of everyday life and concern with the coming era, while the third group —

which was in actuality a large, conglomerous movement — so devoted itself to apocalyptical e. that it lost touch with reality. Among the various groups and sects related to this last acute-eschatological movement may be numbered the ESSENES, JOHN THE BAPTIST and his followers, the early CHRISTIANS, and numerous other groups of whom only scant information has survived (NEW TESTAMENT, DEAD SEA SCROLLS). During the 1st cent. C.E. eschatological thought reached its zenith in Jewish life; widespread eschatological expectations and a belief in the imminent deliverance of Israel were among the factors helping to fan the flames of the great revolt against the Romans which ended in the fall of Jerusalem and the destruction of the Temple (70 C.E.). With the emergence of Pharisaic (Rabbinical) Judaism as the "normative Judaism" after the destruction of the Temple, many apocalyptical concepts of e. found their way into the Talmud. In many cases, the more extreme elements of apocalyptical e. were either modified or rejected by the rabbinical sages. The Bar Kokhba Revolt (132-135) carried with it some eschatological overtones and in the period of extreme persecution immediately following this revolt, the *tannaim* (especially the students of R. Akiva) took comfort in the conviction that they were experiencing the "birth pangs" of the Messiah. Eschatological hope has remained an essential element of the Jewish religion. Belief in the world to come and in the advent of the Messiah were included by Maimonides in his THIRTEEN PRINCIPLES OF FAITH. This hope for a righteous society has been a continual source of comfort and challenge to Jewish life and thought throughout the ages, both in its traditional forms and in the attitudes of Reform and progressive thinkers who regard the messianic era as the attainment, through human means, of complete justice on earth.

ESDRAS, BOOKS OF: The Apocryphal works ascribed to E. (the biblical EZRA). (a) The Apocryphal Book of E. often referred to as III E. (so designated in the Septuagint where I Esdras is the biblical Ezra and II E. the biblical Nehemiah). This is for the most part a compilation of material from the canonical books of Chronicles, Ezra, and Nehemiah, though it also includes elements foreign to the biblical accounts; it dates from the 1st cent. B.C.E. (approx.). III E. recounts the history of the late First Temple Period, the fall of Jerusalem, the ensuing exile in Babylon, the return of Zerubbabel, and the rebuilding and re-establishment of Jerusalem. (b) The Apocalypse of Ezra, or IV E., is a major work of Jewish apocalyptic thought and one of the most inspiring compositions of the pseudepigrapha. Written in Hebrew shortly after the destruction of the Second Temple, it seeks to find an answer to the problem of suffering and in particular to the tragedy which had struck at the very roots of Jewish existence. The reply revealed to Ezra is that although the world has been created for the sake of Israel, Israel must undergo this period of purification on account of its sins. The book is eschatological in character and offers despairing mourners the consolations of the coming messianic age when the wicked will disappear and Israel triumph. IV E. (which has survived only in translation) is closely akin to the Apocalypse of Baruch and probably used common source material. Apart from the basic original work, it contains Christian additions.

ESHET ḤAYIL (Heb. "a woman of worth"): Description of the ideal wife (an alphabetical acrostic in Prov. 31:10-31) recited by the husband in the home on Sabbath Eve in the *Ashkenazi* and kabbalistic rites. The custom originated with the 16th cent. kabbalists in Safed for whom the term *E.Ḥ.* was a mystical metaphor for the SHEKHINAH; it is now generally recited in honor of the housewife.

ESNOGA (from *sinagoga*): Word used among *Sephardim* for a synagogue. Its use is attested to as early as the 13th cent. and occurs for the first time in the Zohar.

ESSENCE OF GOD: The intrinsic nature of God, as distinct from His existence and His manifestations. Jewish medieval philosophy tended generally to deny the possibility of saying anything valid about the e. of God who is conceived as utterly transcendent to His creation and to human understanding. Only His existence could be asserted, along with certain qualities or attributes. See ATTRIBUTES; GOD; MIDDOT.

ESSENES: Jewish religious sect which flourished in Palestine during the last two centuries B.C.E. and up to the Roman conquest in 70 C.E. The derivation of the name is subject to debate, though most scholars hold that it is the Greek translation of the Aramaic or Syriac equivalent of the Hebrew word *ḥasidim* ("pious"). Until recently the primary sources of information about this group were the works of JOSEPHUS and PHILO together with a report of the elder Pliny. More recent finds suggest that the Qumran sect also belonged to the Essene movement and that the DEAD SEA SCROLLS contain the sacred literature of that sect. It is possible that both the E. and the PHARISEES were related to the ḤASIDIM RISHONIM mentioned in I and II Maccabees and in the Talmud. By the middle of the 2nd cent. B.C.E. at the latest, the E. and the Pharisees had gone their separate ways. Essene HALAKHAH was on many points more strict and uncompromising than that of the Pharisees, particularly with regard to dietary and purity laws, and the observance of the Sabbath. They seem to have followed a CALENDAR of their own (see JUBILEES, BOOK OF), which resulted in different dates for celebrating festivals, including the Day of Atonement, and to have lived in an atmosphere of acute-eschatological expectation (see ESCHATOLOGY). According to Pliny, the E. were a "solitary race" who lived in a community located on the northwestern shore of the Dead Sea — a description which fits exactly the location of the ruins at Qumran. Philo, on the other hand, reports that there were some 4,000 E. scattered throughout the villages of Judea. Josephus mentions at least two distinct groups among the E., one practicing celibacy and the other permitting marriage. Thus, it is difficult to ascertain whether the E. were a small sect or a relatively large movement within Judaism of their day; there may have been a widespread ascetic movement of which the E. (like the THERAPEUTAE mentioned by Philo) constituted a branch. In any event, the ancient authors agree in describing the E. as a tightly knit, exclusive group, living together in communities and practicing communal ownership of wealth and goods. They rejected slavery and earned their livelihood by tilling fields and herding flocks; those who engaged in a trade placed their earnings at the disposal of the community. It was forbidden for an Essene to pass on the teachings of his sect to an outsider and anyone wishing to join their number had to undergo a period of testing and examination. Josephus reports that they did not offer sacrifices at the Temple, probably because they contested the legitimacy of the Jerusalem priesthood. An important feature of their rule was the communal meal, presided over by a priest. The E. were also especially conscientious in the reading and study of the Scriptures. Discipline was strict. The most extreme punishment was expulsion from the group — an act which according to Josephus was equivalent to a sentence of death by starvation if the expelled member continued to observe the peculiar dietary laws of the sect. Assuming that the E. and the Dead Sea Sect were identical their theology was as dualistic as possible while still remaining within the framework of monotheistic Judaism: God had divided the world into two parts, the community of the elect and "children of darkness" who live according to the flesh. The elect were the "true remnant of Israel" and the only ones to be destined for salvation after the apocalyptic events of the last days. There are many similarities between early Christianity and the E. and it has been suggested that JOHN THE BAPTIST was an Essene or was close to the E. Many early Christian doctrines (e.g. predestination and the election of grace), until recently thought to have originated from non-Jewish sources, can now be traced within the framework of Jewish — albeit sectarian — thought as expressed in the Dead Sea Scrolls. Of importance to the understanding of this movement is its predominantly sacerdotal character, which resulted in a doctrine of a messianic pair: a priestly Messiah of the house of Aaron, and a royal Messiah of the house of David. After the destruction of the Temple, the Essene sect presumably disintegrated and is not heard of again by that name though it may have continued to exist outside Palestine and have influenced later sectarian movements, e.g. the KARAITES. Further publication of, and research into, the Dead Sea finds may throw more light on the Essene question — either by supplementing present knowledge, or by disproving the hypothetical identification of the E. with the Qumran sect.

ESTHER, BOOK OF: Last of the five SCROLLS incorporated in the Hagiographa section of the Bible; read in the synagogue in the Evening and Morning Services of the feast of PURIM, commemorating the events recorded in the Book of E. In some communities (e.g. Tunis), it is also read in the home after the synagogue service so that the women may hear the reading. Unlike the rest of the five scrolls which are read in the synagogue on other occasions the Book of E. must be read from a parchment scroll. Regulations covering the reading of the scroll are contained in the talmudic tractate MEGILLAH. The book relates the deliverance of the Jews in the kingdom of the Persian ruler Ahasuerus from the annihilation planned for them by the chief minister, Haman; they are rescued through the intervention of the Jewish girl Esther whom the king has married. There is no confirmation of the events from any other source and the historicity of the book has been questioned. It was included in the biblical canon only after a rabbinic controversy centering on the absence of any mention of God in the book; its proponents put forward exaggerated claims, e.g. that the book was known to Moses (Y. *Megillah* 1:5). The book achieved wide folk popularity in the Diaspora as it contains a message of the triumph of justice, the downfall of opponents of Jewry, and the extension of Divine providence to Jewish communities in the Diaspora. The book inspired many midrashic works and commentaries and became a favorite object of Jewish folk art.

ESTHER, FAST OF (Heb. *Taanit Ester*): Fast day observed on *Adar* 13, the day preceding PURIM; if this should fall on a Sabbath, the fast (from sunrise to sunset), is observed on the previous Thursday. The custom of fasting on this date is first known from the 8th cent. but may be of a much older origin. It may have been as ancient as the

Purim festival itself, but *Adar* 13 also became Nicanor Day — celebrating the anniversary of Judah Maccabee's victory over Nicanor — and only when this custom fell into disuse was the day once again observed as a fast. If on the other hand the fast is of late origin, it may have been instituted as a restraint on the merrymaking of the *Purim* period. It is unconnected with the fast ordered by the biblical Esther (Est. 4:16) which occurred in *Nisan*. The fast is observed with particular stringency by Persian Jews.

ESTHER, FEAST OF, see **PURIM**

ESTHER, SCROLL OF, see **MEGILLAT ESTHER**

ESTIMATES (Heb. *arakhin*): Technical term used in connection with a special type of vow concerning a money-offering to the Temple. A person could vow either his own or another's "value" or "worth"; a vow involving "value" is called *arakhin*. While "worth" must be ascertained in each individual instance, "value" is estimated (Lev. 27) on a scale depending upon the age of the persons valued. Thus in the case of males from the age of one month to five years it is fixed at five shekels; from five to twenty years at twenty shekels; from twenty to sixty years at fifty shekels; and thereafter at fifteen shekels. For a female the values are, from one month to five years, three shekels; from five to twenty years, ten shekels; from twenty to sixty years, thirty shekels; and thereafter ten shekels.

ETERNAL LIGHT, see **NER TAMID**

ETHICAL LITERATURE, see **MUSAR**

ETHICAL WILLS: It is natural for a father to give a parting deathbed message to his children, as in the biblical instance of Jacob (Gen. 49:33). This example, and the various instances of last messages in the Talmud, e.g. the deathbed message of Judah Ha-Nasi (*Ket.* 103a-b) were verbal communications. In the Middle Ages, however, the custom developed for scholars to write testamentary dispositions to their children. Since these consisted not of the disposal of worldly possessions but of ethical advice, they have been called e.w. Among the most famous are those of R. Eleazar ben Judah of Worms, R. Asher ben Jehiel, his sons Judah and Jacob, R. Abraham (the father of Isaiah Horowitz), and R. Sheftel (his son). They are replete with statements enjoining humility and ethical conduct of the highest degree. "Keep away from taking oaths and vows, from levity and anger; do not envy the successful person; do not depend upon gifts but work for your livelihood. Rely not upon the broken reed of human support, nor place your trust in wealth... hearken to reproof; if men insult you, answer them not" is a typical extract from the ethical will of R. Asher.

ETHICS: The philosophy of moral behavior and principles. Among the basic problems of e. are: What is the nature of the GOOD? What is the good that man should choose, and why? What is the purpose of human life and what constitutes true happiness? Whereas general, philosophical e. studies these problems without reference to religious dogmas, the norms and principles of religious e. are founded on theological presuppositions (e.g. the existence of GOD, His purpose with man and with creation, REVELATION, the destiny of the SOUL in this world and in the hereafter, etc.). The question of the autonomy of e. was much discussed by medieval philosophers: is an action right because God commanded it, or did God command it because it is intrinsically right? Some thinkers tend to identify the spheres of e. and religion, while others hold that despite the overlap, there is an essential difference. Abraham, they suggest, was ready on purely religious grounds to obey God's command to sacrifice his son Isaac (Gen. 32), although on purely moral grounds he ought to have disobeyed. However, the analytical distinction between the realms of religion and e. belongs to later philosophical development. The difference is not recognized in most ancient religions, where ceremonial, ethical, legal, and cultic precepts appear together (cf. the biblical Holiness Code in Lev. 19-20). Yet the ethical element is prominent throughout the Bible. There is an urgent appeal to man's FREE WILL to choose the good which is also his true blessing and happiness (Deut. 30:15-20), and the Divine Will, as revealed in the TORAH, is that man do "that which is good and right in the sight of the Lord thy God" (Deut. 12:28). That which God requires of Israel (see Deut. 10:12 ff.) includes the "circumcision of the foreskin of the heart" no less than SACRIFICES and ritual obligation. There is an impressive ethical grandeur about the declaration that God is the advocate "of the fatherless and widow, and loveth the stranger" (*ibid.* verse 18). Altogether the biblical rejection of magic, divination, and similar pagan practices tended to make religion unequivocally a matter of "fearing the Lord and walking in all His ways, loving him and serving the Lord thy God with all thy heart and all thy soul". The historical books of the Bible as well as the prophets interpret history in moral terms: prosperity and disaster are regarded as Divine reward or punishment. History is to end with the ultimate triumph of good and evil (see ESCHATOLOGY). The great literary PROPHETS gave the ethical element of religion an even stronger emphasis. Their apparent rejection of sacrifices and ritual (cf. Is. 1:10-17; Jer. 7:9) may be no more than a passionate denunciation of a ceremonial worship that is not matched by SOCIAL JUSTICE and purity of heart. On the other hand some statements (cf. Jer. 7:22) seem to imply a radical rejection of all cultic religion in favor of a purely moral worship of God: "take thou away from me the noise of thy hymns... But let judgment flow as waters, and righteousness as a mighty stream" (Amos 5:23-4). A different attitude finds expression in WISDOM LITERATURE, but even its somewhat pragmatic e. of prudence and common sense is ultimately based on the fear of God and the knowledge of His commandments. A similar tendency is discernible in Jewish HELLENISM, and particularly in its greatest representative, PHILO of Alexandria: the moral life and the practice of virtue are nothing but conformity to the laws of the cosmos which the Creator established from the very beginning and which He revealed in His Law. The TALMUD, though primarily a record of legal discussions, contains a detailed though unsystematic rabbinic e., both implicitly in its HALAKHAH and explicitly in a wealth of moral dicta and maxims, as well as in parables and homiletic interpretations of Scripture. HILLEL's saying "what is hateful to you, do not unto your fellow man", and R. AKIVA's statement "Love thy neighbor as thyself — this is a basic principle of the *Torah*" are among the best-known of the rabbinic maxims; see also the Mishnah tractate AVOT, known as the "E. of the Fathers". In fact, rabbinic AGGADAH is the treasury of Jewish ethical teaching, which in general eschews excesses and recommends a golden mean (e.g. "a man should spend no less than one tenth of his income on CHARITY, and no more than one fifth, lest he become himself dependent on charity"), although the extreme and uncompromising e. of the *ḥasid* (the "pious") is also presented by many examples. *Halakhah,* too, at times uses ethical concepts, e.g. when ruling of certain actions that the agent "must be acquitted by the human court, but is guilty according to heavenly law", or when distinguishing between "matters between man and God" on the one hand, and "matters between man and his fellow" on the other as two classes of religious obligation. The concept of *li-phenim mi-shurat ha-din* implies an ethical norm of which the actual law is but the last limit, and hence the rabbis could say that Jerusalem was destroyed because people insisted on the letter of the law. Some teachers asserted that the one definite purpose of all the precepts of the *Torah,* including the purely ceremonial and cultic ones, was the moral improvement and refinement of MAN. This notion was taken up and elaborated in great detail by medieval thinkers (e.g. SAADYAH, MAIMONIDES; IBN GABIROL was exceptional in keeping his ethical treatise *Tikkun Middot ha-Nephesh* free of religious elements), usually in terms of their general philosophical systems (see NEO-PLATONISM, ARISTOTELIANISM). Similarly, later philosophers used the framework of Kantian e. or other modern philosophies (German idealism, EXISTENTIALISM) when expounding their systems of Jewish e. (e.g. Moritz Lazarus, *Die Ethik des Judentums*). Of greater practical influence on Jewish life was the ethical literature written with a definitely edifying, devotional, ascetic, or mystical purpose in view, e.g. BAḤYA IBN PAKUDA's *Book of the Duties of the Heart,* the *Book of the Pious* composed in the circle of R. JUDAH BEN SAMUEL HE-ḤASID, ISAIAH HOROWITZ's "*Two Tablets of the Covenant*", and — perhaps the most popular ethical classic — Moses Ḥayyim LUZZATTO's *Path of the Upright.* The essentially non-philosophical and non-mystical but pietistic MUSAR movement founded in the 19th cent. by R. Israel SALANTER again strongly emphasized ethical concerns in the Lithuanian *yeshivot* where talmudic learning and intellectual achievement had held pride of place. See also ASCETICISM; ETHICAL WILLS; RIGHTEOUSNESS.

ETHICS OF THE FATHERS, see **AVOT**

ETHROG, see **ETROG**

ETIQUETTE, see **DEREKH ERETZ**

ETROG (Heb. "citron"): One of the FOUR SPECIES carried and shaken in the TABERNACLES synagogue service; the custom, which was well established in Second Temple times, is based on Lev. 23:40 where the "fruit of a goodly tree" was traditionally interpreted as referring to the citron; the rabbis proffer midrashic explanations for the choice. The *e.* was featured widely as a Jewish symbol in classical times.

EULOGY, FUNERAL (Heb. *hesped*): Eulogies are of ancient origin. David's eulogies over Saul and Jonathan (II Sam. 1:17-27) and Abner (II Sam. 3:33-34) are biblical instances, and several are recorded in the Talmud which also discusses the question whether eulogies are meant for the benefit of the dead or the living. If a righteous man before his death asks that he be not eulogized, his request is respected only in his home but he is eulogized in the synagogue and the cemetery. It was customary on *Adar* 7, the traditional anniversary of Moses' death, to eulogize distinguished individuals who had died during the preceding year. In certain festival periods, eulogies are not permitted. Among *Sephardi* communities, it became customary to deliver the e. in the form of a talmudic discourse after the *sheloshim* (thirty days' period of mourning).

EUNUCH, see **CASTRATION**

EUTHANASIA, see **LIFE**

EVE (Heb. *Ḥavvah*): Wife of ADAM and the "mother of all living" (Gen. 2-4). Bible scholars regard the Eve stories as primitive traditions meant to explain the origin of mankind, the relationship between the sexes, woman's labor pains, and the inferior social position of women in the ancient world. The rabbis did not propound a doctrine of ORIGINAL SIN, and the taint of E.'s sin was in any case removed by the Israelites' acceptance of the Law.

EVE, see **EREV**

EVEL RABBATI (Heb. "Great [tractate on] mourning"; euphemistically called *Semaḥot,* i.e., joys"): Minor tractate, appended to the talmudic order *Nezikin.* It deals with laws concerning the dying, DEATH, FUNERALS and BURIALS, EULOGIES, MOURNING, etc. The version that has been preserved is incomplete; although its final form is post-talmudic, *E.R.* is based on an original that dates from the Tannaitic Period.

EVEL ZUTRATI (Heb. "Small [tractate on] mourning"; also euphemistically known as *Semaḥot de-Rabbi Ḥiyya,* i.e., "Rabbi Ḥiyya's joys"): Minor tractate of talmudic origin, referred to in early literature but not incorporated in editions of the Talmud. The manuscript was discovered only in the 19th cent. It deals with dying, DEATH, and the reward of the righteous and punishment of the wicked in the future world. The style of *E.Z.* clearly resembles that of EVEL RABBATI and it has been surmised that they originally constituted a single work.

EVEN HA-EZER, see **SHULḤAN ARUKH**

EVENING SERVICE, see **MAARIV**

EVER MIN HA-ḤAI (Heb. "a limb from the living"): The prohibition derived from Deut. 12:23 against eating a limb taken from a living animal, beast, or bird. The prohibition is considered one of the seven NOACHIAN LAWS (*Sanh.* 56a), derived from the verse "only flesh with the life thereof... shall you not eat" (Gen. 9:4) enjoined upon Noah. The rabbis ruled that although one may derive benefit from such a limb in certain ways e.g. by feeding it to an animal, it is forbidden to sell it or even give it to a non-Jew, since the Noachian laws are binding also on gentiles.

EVIDENCE: Testimony received in legal proceedings in proof or disproof of the facts under inquiry. Whosoever is in possession of direct knowledge of such facts is obliged (Lev. 5:1) to state them in testimony and it became customary to issue a ḤEREM on witnesses who refused to testify. However no legal decision can be concluded in capital or civil cases in matters of atonement, sacrifices, or involving flagellation or promotion or demotion in the priesthood, etc., on the evidence of a single witness (cf. Deut. 19:15 and *Siphrei in loco*). But while a single WITNESS is insufficient in law he must nonetheless attend court to testify since in many instances his testimony may be joined to that of another of whom he is unaware, or his e. might be sufficiently compelling to force the one testified against to substantiate his plea on OATH. The inadequacy of a single witness extends only to the legal status of persons or property, but in deciding the ritual status of an object his testimony is decisive. His e. is also extremely important in the case of an AGUNAH. No weight is added to the e. by increasing the number of witnesses above two — a pair having the same weight as a hundred. Where two witnesses are contradicted (*hakhḥashah*) by two others, the case is decided as if no witnesses were available for either side. Procedurally, the court is first addressed on the gravity of FALSE WITNESS, and then it crossexamines the witnesses in order to ascertain their reliability and trustworthiness. Two types of crossexamination are added in criminal cases: (1) *ḥakirah,* to establish the exact time and place of the criminal act, and (2) *bedikah,* to ascertain the exact nature of the crime. Once the testimony is recorded in court, it cannot be retracted. The litigant may however enter new evidence, in which event the court must retry the action. Persons known to earn their livelihood by gambling, or to have no regard for the law, or who are related to one of the litigants, or who have some interest in the case, and women (in most instances), are invalidated from giving testimony. Self-incrimination, except for admission of monetary liabilities, does not form valid ground for conviction since in Jewish law a person is debarred from testifying against himself. Circumstantial e., even of the most convincing nature, hearsay, or anything not actually heard or seen by the witness is invalid and inadmissible as e.

EVIL, see **GOOD AND EVIL**

EVIL EYE: A widespread and still extant superstition that the malignant and envious eye of an ill-disposed person can cause harm. From the concept of the *ayin raah* the "grudging eye" (Deut. 16:9) — in contrast to the *ayin tovah,* the "benign eye" (Prov. 22:9; cf. *Avot* 2:13-14) — there developed the idea of *ein ha-ra* ("the eye of the evil person") which is sometimes thought to be possessed by special individuals and to exert its harmful influence as a result of envy at the prosperity or good fortune of others. Formulae were drawn up to be said in times of prosperity in order to ward off any e.e. (cf. the Yiddish phrase *kainehora,* literally "without the e.e."). The belief in its potency is widespread in the Talmud, and according to the Midrash, Jacob enjoined his sons not to enter Egypt all through one gate in order to avoid the e.e. (*Gen. Rab.* 96). The descendants of Joseph were supposed to be immune from its effects; a proof adduced by the Talmud (*Ber.* 20a based on Gen. 49:22) by interpreting "Joseph is a fruitful vine" as "a fruitful son superior to the e.e.". As a result this verse is widely used by Oriental Jews in AMULETS to guard against the e.e.

EVIL INCLINATION, see **YETZER HA-RA**

EVIL SPIRITS, see **DEMONOLOGY**

EVOLUTION: The theory, generally associated with the name of Darwin, that the various animal species evolve from other and lower forms, and that man — related to the primates — is but the last link in the chain of e. E. provoked considerable controversy when first propounded in the 19th cent. and continues to exercise fundamentalist circles. Modern biological theories at first made little impact on Jewish thought. When scientific theories became more generally accepted, Orthodoxy still continued to reject them as heretical and as incompatible with the biblical account of creation. Attempts to interpret the biblical six days of creation figuratively as geological ages hardly got beyond homiletical apologetics; the basic philosophical problems of e. — which are not the congruence or incongruence of the biblical and scientific chronologies, but the transcendence or immanence of the creative act, the nature of purposiveness in the evolutionary process, and the moral implication of the "survival" factor — have so far not been tackled at all in Jewish thought. Although the creation account of GENESIS has traditionally been taken to be a "mystery" (see MAASEH BERESHIT) and creation itself understood as a supratemporal act, Orthodoxy has nevertheless tended to remain rigidly fundamentalist at the same time. Non-Orthodox thought on e. has hardly moved beyond superficial commonplaces. A theological understanding of the doctrine of creation in the light of evolutionary biology is still an outstanding need.

EXCOMMUNICATION: The exclusion of a person from membership in the community and from its rights and privileges. E. is employed either as a punishment for transgressions or as a sanction to ensure obedience to communal enactments. The regulations governing e. are carefully detailed in the Talmud and various safeguards were instituted from time to time to prevent the abuse of this powerful weapon when wielded in the interest of conformity. E. took three forms, of increasing severity. The mildest was *neziphah* ("rebuke"), lasting for only one day in Babylonia and seven in the Land of Israel. The punishment consisted merely in the offender having to retire to his house and refrain from social intercourse. On expressing regret at his conduct he was allowed to resume his normal life. A stronger form of e. was *niddui* ("banishment") which was imposed for a fixed period, usually of 30 days. During that period the person excommunicated was regarded as a pariah. He was completely ostracized except by the immediate members of his own family and had to fulfill all the regulations appertaining to a mourner. His children could be denied circumcision, tuition, or attendance at worship. Should these measures fail to bring him to penitence or conformity the most extreme form of e. — the HEREM ("ban") — was imposed with solemn ceremonial. This lasted for an indefinite period and the person placed under the ban was denied every amenity of social and religious life apart from the barest necessities. During the Middle Ages, when Jews had no other legal means for enforcing conformity, the *ḥerem* became the sanction behind the promulgation of communal enactments. Thus the phrase "*ḥerem* of Rabbenu Gershom", as applied to the famous enactments of R. Gershom outlawing polygamy and the divorce of a wife without her consent, etc., means that when the enactment was promulgated it contained the provision that, in the absence of any legal basis, a person transgressing it would be placed in *ḥerem*. Such sanction proved sufficient to ensure adherence. Two notable examples of the invocation of the *ḥerem* by the *Sephardi* community of 17th cent. Amsterdam concerned Uriel ACOSTA and Baruch (Benedict) SPINOZA. Since the 18th cent. e. has gradually lost its significance as a result of rabbis resorting to it too frequently and of the disintegration of the self-enclosed medieval Jewish community.

EXECUTION, see **BEHEADING; CAPITAL PUNISHMENT**

EXEGESIS, see **BIBLE EXEGESIS**

EXILARCH (Aram. *resh galut* "head of the exile"): Title of the head of Babylonian Jewry. The e. was a hereditary office, traditionally originating with King Jehoiachin and hence looked upon as maintaining, albeit in an attenuated form, the continuity of Davidic rule. The importance of the e. increased after the failure of the Bar Kokhba revolt (135 C.E.) when it rivaled and eventually surpassed the authority of the parallel Palestinian institution of NASI. The functions of the e. were more political and secular but his administration of internal justice in the Jewish community necessitated close collaboration with the rabbis in both tannaitic and amoraic times. Under the *geonim* (see GAON) the influence of the religious authorities extended and new exilarchs had to receive the approval of the heads of academies before their appointment was submitted to the caliph for approval.

EXILE: The enforced dwelling of the Jews outside the Holy Land. The Jewish people has been in exile from its ancestral land for a longer period than it has dwelt in it. Rabbinic tradition distinguishes between two exiles — the Babylonian e. and the e. following the destruction of the Second Temple (in addition to the earlier Egyptian e.). From a historical viewpoint, however, there was continuity in the life and development of the Diaspora (Gk. "dispersion", i.e., the Jews living outside the Holy Land). These two exiles have exercised a profound influence upon the whole development of the Jewish religion and way of life; indeed the features which characterized the Second Exile were already to be detected in the brief First Exile in Babylonia. Ezekiel's prophecies were made in Babylonia (cf. Ezek. 1:1-2) and exhibit three important effects of life in exile. (1) Insistence on the need for personal, as distinct from national, righteousness (cf. Ezek. 14); (2) Intimations of the foundation of the SYNAGOGUE, which as a "minor sanctuary" (Ezek. 11:16) was to be a substitute for the "major sanctuary", the soon-to-be-destroyed Temple; and (3) Implanting in the hearts of the people and undying hope for their eventual return and the rebuilding of the Temple (Ezek. 37). The rabbis noted other effects of the cultural contacts and influences to which Israel was exposed during the Babylonian e., e.g. the adoption of the square or "ARAMAIC" script (*ketav ashuri*) in place of the earlier Phoenician script (*ketav ivri*), the adoption of Babylonian names for the Hebrew months, and the development of the "names of the angels" i.e., ANGELOLOGY. They interpreted the verse "So they read in the book of the law of God distinctly, and gave the sense, and caused them to understand the reading" (Neh. 8:8) as referring to the translation of the Hebrew text into Aramaic, thereby drawing attention to the adoption by the exiles of the vernacular of their country of e. Under the influence of the second exile, which lasted some eighteen centuries, there was a vast extension of these primary effects, but the difference was of degree rather than of kind. The synagogue, which had developed during the period of the Second Temple as an ancillary to Temple worship, now took the latter's place entirely, and R. Johanan ben Zakkai deliberately transferred to the synagogue many of the rites and ceremonies which originally had belonged to the Temple (cf. *R.H.* 4:1-3; *Suk.* 3:12). In particular, the Additional (*musaph*) Service took the place of the additional sacrifices on the days on which they used to be offered, and the scriptural verses pertaining to the sacrifices for that particular day were combined with a fervent prayer for the restoration of Israel to its land and the renewal of Temple worship. This was only one of many alternations and additions made in the synagogue service for the purpose of keeping alive the faith in the ultimate return. A great variety of external influences penetrated and enriched Jewish culture during the second exile. The adoption of the prevailing systems of Greek philosophy as preserved and developed by the Arabs, and the introduction of Arabic rhyme and meter by the Hebrew poets of the Middle Ages, are obvious examples. The adoption of the vernacular was particularly marked in Arabic which was used by leading Jewish writers and thinkers. In Christian countries that particular influence was less marked, as rabbinic Hebrew remained the medium of religious literature. The Diaspora profoundly affected Jewish Law. With the destruction of the Temple and subsequent e., vast areas of Jewish law, such as the laws pertaining to sacrifices, the laws concerning local and national government, the agricultural laws which obtained only in the Land of Israel, became merely subjects for academic study, though they were passionately pursued with the double object of maintaining alive the belief in the restoration and of acquiring merit through study for its own sake. The area of practical Jewish law became correspondingly circumscribed. Until the advent of the modern era (cf. EMANCIPATION, ASSIMILATION, ZIONISM) e. was considered an unmitigated evil, a curse or punishment for Israel's sins or a redemptive suffering, and a provisional form of existence which would be terminated by the INGATHERING OF THE EXILES and messianic redemption. The latter either had to be patiently awaited or actively prepared for by piety and penitence. In early rabbinic and later mystical theology the notion of Israel's e. was complemented by that of God's own e. (*galut ha-Shekhinah* — the "e. of the Divine Presence"). This doctrine implied, on the one hand, that God himself shared Israel's sufferings, and on the other hand that even in e. Israel's communion with God was unbroken. With the establishment of the State of Israel and the partial ingathering of the exiles, the problem of the definition of e. has come to the fore and there is lively discussion whether the Diaspora Jewries in the free world should consider themselves as living in e| or not.

EXILES, INGATHERING OF: When Ezekiel in the Babylonian EXILE prophesied the eventual return of the Exiles to their native land, he addressed himself first to the Judean exiles and then extended his prophecy to include the exiles of the Northern Kingdom (the TEN TRIBES) who had been dispersed over a century earlier (Ezek. 37:16-28). Although in the Mishnah (*Sanh.* 10:3) opposing views are expressed as to whether the Ten Tribes are destined to return or not, the view prevailed that the ultimate restoration would include the Ten Tribes. It is this belief which explains the phrase *kibbutz galuyyot* ("the Ingathering of the Exiles") i.e., the Exiles of both Judea and Israel. The word "exile" refers to the condition, not the person. Whenever the liturgy incorporates prayers for the Ingathering of the Exiles (in the *ahavah rabbah,* the tenth blessing of the *amidah,* the prayer for the New Moon) the words are added "from the four corners of the earth" (cf. Deut. 30:4-5) and the reference is to the messianic future. Today, the phrase is employed to describe the immigration of Jews from the numerous communities of the Diaspora to the State of Israel.

EXISTENTIALISM: A modern movement in philosophy, concerned with the understanding of human existence in its concreteness rather than as an object of understanding or theoretical abstraction. In spite of certain "existentialist" features of early philosophy (as in Socrates Pascal), e. proper begins with the 19th cent. Danish Protestant thinker Kierkegaard. A basic attitude toward philosophy rather than a well-defined doctrine, e. encompasses atheistic thinkers (Heidegger, Sartre) as well as religious ones (e.g. Marcel). Franz ROSENZWEIG, one of the greatest modern Jewish thinkers, was one of the founders of the existentialist philosophy. Many modern thinkers believe that e. provides better tools than classical philosophy for interpreting the significance of religion. Martin BUBER's "I and Thou" philosophy and his interpretations of the Bible have exerted wide influence as major expressions of a religious e. which sees in religion no objective system of doctrine or law, but a relationship and mode of being realized in actual existence.

EXODUS (Heb. *yetziat mitzrayim*): The miraculous departure of the Israelites, led by Moses, from Egypt — the "Land of Bondage" — and their dry-shod crossing of the Red Sea in which the pursuing Egyptians were subsequently drowned (Exod. 12:29–15:21). Traditionally marking the beginning of Israel's history as a people, the e. became a symbol of God-given freedom and a potent factor in shaping Israel's religious consciousness. Explicit mention of the e. is made in no less than 160 passages of the Bible, while 67 injunctions of a religious, social, or national nature are directly related to it. Its theological significance lies in the manifestation of a "historical" God, i.e., a God who reveals Himself as acting in history, rather than one who is apprehended through rational deduction or mystic intuition; its great importance for the religious understanding of history is such that the rabbis held that the e. would be commemorated even in the messianic era. Liturgically the e. is commemorated daily in the SHEMA prayer, and annually in the celebration of the PASSOVER SEDER. Scholarly opinion is divided as to the date of the e. as well as the historicity of the details of the traditional account.

EXODUS, BOOK OF (called in Heb. *Shemot,* "names", after its first distinctive word): Second book of the Pentateuch. It continues the story of GENESIS and describes the transformation of the Israelite tribes into a people of God through the EXODUS, the covenant with God at Mount Sinai, and the building of the Tabernacle, as well as the development of Hebrew law against the background of the wanderings in the wilderness. Chaps. 1-17 are primarily narrative; 18-40 legislative. The book contains many of the fundamentals of Judaism — including the account of the revelation at Mount Sinai, the Decalogue, the ordinance of Sabbath and the three historic festivals. Certain resemblances have been detected between Israelite institutions and parallel legislation of the ancient Near East (e.g. the Hammurabi code) but the biblical version, aside from its strict monotheistic motivation, is infused throughout with a loftier and more humane spirit.

EXODUS RABBAH, see MIDRASH RABBAH

EXORCISM: The expulsion of foreign spirits that have possessed an individual. Mention of e. is rare in early Jewish literature. In the Bible the only clear examples are the possession of Saul by an evil spirit and its e. by David's playing the harp (I Sam. 16:14-23) and in the Apocrypha in the Book of Tobit. References in the Talmud are equally sparse. With the spread of Kabbalah, particularly the doctrine of the TRANSMIGRATION of Souls, this belief became powerfully reinforced, notably in E. Europe; a particular form of e. was the expulsion of a DYBBUK.

EZEKIEL: Third of the three major PROPHETS. A member of the priestly house of Zadok, he was the great prophet of the Babylonian Exile and is said to have been deported to Babylonia with King Jehoiachin in 597 B.C.E. (Other scholars hold that after his "call" in 593, he was active in Jerusalem leaving shortly before the fall of the city and continuing his prophetic ministry among the exiles in Babylonia). He was a younger contemporary of JEREMIAH and the Book of E. follows Jeremiah in the masoretic order of the prophetical books. More than his predecessors, E. freely describes the overpowering effect of the Divine call upon his mind and body. There are two main parts to the Book of E.: Prophecies announcing (1) the imminent fall of Jerusalem)chaps. 1-24(, and (2) the reconciliation with God and restoration of Jerusalem through the return of the exiles (chaps. 25-48). Though mainly concerned with the collective defection of the Jewish people, E., in the face of prevalent misconceptions regarding collective guilt, taught a doctrine of individual responsibility (18:2-31). At the same time he also stressed the concept of holiness and the priestly tradition. While harsh and uncompromising in his denunciations of all forms of idolatry and iniquity, E. countered a growing mood of despondency and lack of hope with his vision of the dry bones, a symbolic expression of hope and faith in Israel's ultimate regeneration (chap. 37). A majestic description of the ideal Temple as the center of a reconstituted theocracy concludes his prophetic message (chaps. 40-48). His descriptions of his visions of the Divine throne and glory became the basis for an entire branch of Jewish mysticism (MAASEH MERKAVAH), and also greatly influenced ANGELOLOGY and APOCALYPSE. Contradictions between Mosaic law and certain passages in the Book of E. (accounted for by critical scholarship in terms of differences between the priestly traditions of E. and those embodied in Leviticus) caused strong rabbinic opposition to the canonization of the prophetical book; according to the Talmud (*Shab.* 13b) the apparent contradictions were resolved by R. Hananiah ben Hezekiah. The rabbis ascribed the editing of the Book of E. to the men of the Great Assembly (*Bava Batra* 15a). Critics have been divided on the precise dating of E.'s prophecies.

EZRA: Priest and SCRIBE (descendant of ZADOK) who was primarily responsible for a series of religious reforms laying the spiritual foundations of the new Judean commonwealth. According to the traditional account (Ezra 7:14) he returned to Jerusalem at the head of 1,800 exiles, with full powers from the Persian king Artaxerxes to impose the law of the *Torah* on the community there (458 B.C.E.). E. journeyed from Babylon to Jerusalem at the head of the returning exiles bearing the sacred vessels of the TEMPLE and set about effecting reforms in the religious as well as civic conditions then prevailing in Judah. Mixed marriages with heathen wives were annulled (probably completing the breach with the SAMARITANS) and a vigorous program was launched for observing the Sabbath and Sabbatical Year and expounding the *Torah* to the common people. E. also revived the thanksgiving Feast of Tabernacles (Neh. 8:13-18). As the traditional founder of the GREAT ASSEMBLY, E. laid the basis for the future form of Judaism. The Talmud also ascribes to him the final decision on the text of the Pentateuch and the introduction of the square Hebrew script. The Book of E. (partly in Aramaic) appears tenth in the Hagiographa and is regarded as a single unit with the Book of Nehemiah. The narrative centers around the vicissitudes of the rebuilders of the Second Temple and is written from a priestly viewpoint. The relation of E.'s activity to that of NEHEMIAH, as well as their respective dates are a matter of controversy among modern biblical scholars. Rabbinic evaluation of E.'s initiative during the critical period of transition from the prophetic to the pharisaic era can be gathered from the talmudic observation that, had not Moses preceded, God would have given the *Torah* through E. (*Sanh.* 21b).

EZRA OF GERONA, see **AZRIEL OF GERONA**

EZRAT NASHIM (Heb. "Women's Court"): The court in the TEMPLE beyond which women were not allowed to pass. The term was subsequently used for that section of the SYNAGOGUE (either a special balcony or a partitioned section) where the women sit during the service. Separate seating for women has been abolished in Reform and most Conservative synagogues.

F

FAITH, see **CREED**

FAITH, ARTICLES OF, see **THIRTEEN ARTICLES OF FAITH**

FALAQUERA (or **Ibn Falaquera**), **SHEMTOV BEN JOSEPH** (c. 1225-c.1295): Philosopher and poet in Spain or S. France; author of many books aiming at reconciling Judaism with philosophy. His best-known work *Moreh ha-Moreh* ("Guide to the *Guide*") is a commentary to MAIMONIDES' *Guide to the Perplexed* which quotes extensively from Arab and Jewish philosophers.

FALASHAS: Members of a negroid people originally in regions north of Lake Tana in Ethiopia. It has been maintained that they are of Jewish ethnic origin, but more probably they are descendants of native Abyssinians converted to Judaism. The Jewish basis of their religion cannot be doubted. Their outstanding belief is in "The God of Israel, the Invisible, Creator of Heaven and Earth" and they adhere strictly to biblical laws concerning animals permitted for food, as well as the laws of ritual uncleanliness, and concerning contact with the dead. Their religious life is based on a literal interpretation of biblical prescriptions and is unacquainted with post-biblical teaching and customs. It revolves about the synagogue where the service is performed by priests. Sacrifices are offered on *Nisan* 14. They have no knowledge of Hebrew and use an Ethiopic dialect (*Ge'ez*) in prayer. In 1984-85 many F. were airlifted to Israel, and they are gradually being brought into the mainstream of Jewish observance.

FALK, JOSHUA BEN ALEXANDER HA-COHEN (c. 1550-1614): Talmudist in Lvov; best-known for his commentaries on JACOB BEN ASHER'S *Tur* and on the *Ḥoshen Mishpat* of the SHULḤAN ARUKH. The latter commentary (called *Sepher Meirat Einayim* "The Book which Enlightens the Eyes") is regarded as authoritative and is printed in all standard editions of the *Shulḥan Arukh.*

FALL OF MAN: The sin of Adam and Eve in eating the forbidden fruit, as a result of which they were expelled from Paradise, and toil, pain, and death entered the world (Gen. 2-3). The biblical narrative was later given radical and far-reaching interpretations: through the sin of its first ancestors, the whole human race "fell" from bliss and grace. Christian theology holds this "original sin" to have involved mankind in an inherent and congenital sinfulness and depravity from which only a special Divine act can "save" them. The rabbis generally held that all men die because of Adam's sin (a divergent view is expressed by R. Ammi in *Shab.* 55a) but did not teach a doctrine of original sin. There is, however, a view that the serpent transmitted to Eve a blemish which she passed on to all her descendants. At Mt. Sinai the Israelites were restored to man's original state of perfection, but this was undone again by the sin of the GOLDEN CALF. In kabbalistic literature the f. of m. is interpreted in extreme fashion: as a result of original sin (*ḥet kadmon*) evil entered the world, with disastrous consequences not only for the whole of creation but also for the sphere of Divine being, and the entire process of history is seen as a struggle to restore the fallen world to its pristine perfection. Medieval as well as modern thinkers interpreted the story in diverse ways as an allegory or "myth" expressing some philosophical or existential truth about the human situation.

FALLEN ANGELS, see **ANGELS**

FALSE WITNESS: The prohibition "thou shalt not bear false witness against thy neighbor" (Exod. 20:13) embraces all forms of slander, defamation, and misrepresentation whether of an individual, a group, a people, a race, or a faith, but is primarily directed against the giving of false testimony in court. The biblical injunction to do to the f.w. as he had proposed to do to his brother (Deut. 19: 19) applies only if a second pair of witnesses state in court "How can you testify ? You were with us that day in another place". In this way the testimony of the second two witnesses incriminates the first pair themselves without touching upon the criminal act in question before the court. This is called *hazammah.* The punishment is however only applied if the falsity of the witnesses is proven prior to the execution of the sentence. See also EVIDENCE.

FAMILY: From earliest biblical times, it was taken for granted that the f. was an integral part of the social structure. The tribe was an extension of the f. The first of the 613 precepts "Be fruitful and multiply" was interpreted by the rabbis as implying the prime duty of rearing a f. The Bible inculcates respect for parents (Exod. 20:12) and protection of INHERITANCE rights (e.g. Deut. 18:8; 21:15-17). The latter was of great importance in keeping the patrimony within the possession of the f. and even land that was sold reverted to the f. in the Jubilee year. The execution of justice was also often entrusted to the f. in early society and in the event of a murder, for example, the next-of-kin was obligated to seek revenge on the murderer. Wisdom literature abounds with advice on familial happiness (see e.g. Prov. 13:1; 15:5; 19:13; 26). The warm and intimate nature of the f. became a recognizable characteristic of Jewish life, which also preserved its patriarchal aspect (among oriental Jews until modern times). The mother occupies a somewhat lower position but is the object of reverence and love. In biblical times, the f. unit would often include concubines (especially when the wife was barren) but Judaism's natural tendency was toward the MONOGAMY which became the rule among western, and later also oriental, Jewry. The talmudic concept of the f. set the tone for the rich Jewish f. experience of the Middle Ages when Jewish life to a large extent centered around the home, especially on Sabbaths and festivals. Marital relations were strictly regulated by *halakhah* and great stress was laid on *taharat mishpaḥah* ("family purity") which included shunning forbidden relationships and observing the relevant laws of ritual cleanness, etc. Factors which broke up many homes — such as infidelity or drunkenness — were rare among Jews because of the influence of Jewish tradition as well as the external conditions of ghetto life. Pride was taken in illustrious descent (*yiḥus*), originally from the House of David or from the priestly families, but later from distinguished scholars. With the impact of Emancipation, Jewish f. life has tended to fall into patterns more closely resembling those of the environment although the long line of Jewish tradition often still serves as an influence to higher standards of morality. Since the 19th cent., the demand to pray in f. pews has grown and is now accepted in Reform and most Conservative synagogues. See also CHILDREN; FATHER; MOTHER; PARENTS.

FAST: Abstention from food as a sign of mourning or in expiation of sins. A major f. includes abstention from eating, drinking, sexual intercourse, and the donning of leather footwear. The only f. in Mosaic Law is the Day of Atonement on *Tishri* 10 (see ATONEMENT, DAY OF). The phrase "ye shall afflict your souls" (Lev. 23:27) was taken as a synonym for fasting and is the basis of the talmudic word *taanit* (in preference to the biblical word *tzom*). Physical abstention is regarded not as an end in itself but as a means to spiritual affliction and self-abasement. This finds eloquent expression in the portrayal of the true f. in Is. 58, which was adopted not only as the prophetic reading for the Day of Atonement, but was probably read on the occasion of each public f. The regulation of the Day of Atonement specifically mentions that it shall be observed "from evening to evening" (Lev. 23:32) i.e., for 24 hours. The only other f. to which this applies is *Tisha be-Av* (see AV, NINTH OF) observed in commemoration of the destruction of the Temple. The period of abstention for all other fasts is from daybreak until nightfall. All statutory fasts, apart from the Day of Atonement, are days of mourning in commemoration of tragic events in Jewish history. Four of them date back to the period of the First Temple or immediately after its destruction as is evidenced by the reference to "the fast of the fourth month and the fast of the fifth and the fast of the seventh and the fast of the tenth" (Zech. 8:19). The query of the people whether fasting was still obligatory after the return (7:3) and the prophecy that the fasts would be turned to "joy and gladness and cheerful feasts" (8:19) prove that they were instituted to commemorate that tragic period. These fasts are *Tammuz* 17 (SHIVA ASAR BE-TAMMUZ), *Av* 9, *Tishri* 3 (see GEDALIAH, FAST OF), and *Tevet* 10. To these was later added *Adar* 13 (see ESTHER, FAST OF). (A convenient mnemonic for these six fasts is "The Black and the White" [*Tisha be-Av* and the Day of Atonement] "The Long and the Short" [*Tammuz* 17 and *Tevet* 10, reversed in the Southern Hemisphere] and "The Man and the Woman" [Gedaliah and Esther]). All fasts falling on the Sabbath, except the Day of Atonement, are observed on another day (generally the following Sunday). In addition to these statutory fasts, public and private (individual) fasts were also instituted. The former were to ward off threatened calamities, most frequently in the case of severe drought, and almost the whole of the tractate TAANIT is devoted to the regulation of these fasts — which are days of supplication and a call to penitence in the hope that "repentance will nullify the evil decree". The purpose is conveyed in the standard words of admonition uttered by the head of the elders on these occasions: "Brethren, it is not written of the men of Nineveh that God saw their sackcloth and their fasting, but that God saw their works that they turned from their evil ways (Jonah 3:10); and the prophet Joel says (2:13) 'Rend your hearts and not your garments'" (Mishnah *Taan.* 2:1). Other common fasts were the f. of the first-born on *Nisan* 14; the f. observed by the bride and groom on their wedding day; the f. observed in certain kabbalistic circles on the eve of the New Moon (YOM KIPPUR KATAN); and fasts on *Yahrzeit.* Individual fasts were undertaken mostly as a result of evil DREAMS. Some extremely pious Jews fast every Monday and Thursday.

FAT, see **ḤELEV**

FATALISM: The belief in the inexorable operation of fate, to which everything is subject. Fate can be conceived of as impersonal (e.g. a cosmic law to which even the gods are subject, the rule or influence of the stars [see ASTROLOGY], natural causality, etc.) or as personal. In the latter case it may be interpreted as the will of an omnipotent God. A certain tension between f. on the one hand and indeterminacy due to the freedom of action of men and/or God on the other exists in monotheistic religions; see DETERMINISM; FREE WILL. Generally speaking, theological tradition emphasizes the element of freedom: everything — or at least Israel — is directly subject to God's will, but He permits Himself to be influenced by prayer, repentance, and good works. Other tendencies are also in evidence, but full-fledged f. could not develop in the religious climate of Judaism.

FATE, see **PROVIDENCE**

FATHER: In Jewish law the rights of the f. over his CHILDREN, as long as they are minors, is unbounded, and the respect due to PARENTS, enjoined in the Fifth Commandment and elsewhere in the Bible, is developed to an extraordinary degree. The f., however, has definite legal obligations toward his children, which are codified in the saying that "the f. is obliged to circumcise his son, teach him *Torah,* teach him a trade, and marry him off" (*Kidd.* 29b). There was originally no legal obligation on the f. to provide for his children's material needs, this being regarded as only a moral duty; hence the rabbinical application of the verse "Happy are they that keep justice, that do righteousness at all times" (Ps. 106:3) to the man who maintains his sons and daughters in their childhood (*Ket.* 50a). The 2nd cent. synod at Usha made it obligatory upon a f. to maintain his children during their minority (*ibid.* 49b). The only exception to the otherwise unbounded respect which is due to parents is when the parents order the child to transgress the precepts of Judaism, in which case the child must defy them. Later authorities stated that another exception can be made if the father objects to his child's choice of a bride or groom (after the child has reached his majority). Paternity requires no proof and if a man says "this is my child" he is believed. The child's communal standing is modeled after the f.'s, i.e., the son of a priest is a priest regardless of whether the mother belongs to a priestly family or not. A f. can punish his children only while they are minors (*M.K.* 17a). His legal responsibility toward them generally ends on their attaining their majority, which is the basis of the blessing uttered by the father on the religious confirmation of his son — "Blessed be He who hath relieved me of the responsibility for him". There is no provision in Jewish law for ADOPTION and these regulations apply only to a natural parent. The use of f. as a title of honor is rare in Judaism. It is laid down that only the three patriarchs may be called f. (*Ber.* 15b) and in rabbinical literature only Hillel and Shammai (*Eduy.* 1:4) and R. Akiva and R. Ishmael (Y. *Rosh ha-Shanah* 56a) are referred to as "the fathers of the world". On the other hand during the Tannaitic Period a number of rabbis were given the honorific title (as distinct from a cognomen, common in amoraic times) of ABBA (the Aramaic form of *av,* father) — generally those who maintained a specially high standard of saintliness and purity in their lives. The second in rank in the SANHEDRIN, after the *Nasi,* was given the title of *Av Bet Din* ("father of the court" *Ḥag.* 16b). The word is also applied to a teacher (while the "sons" of prophets are their disciples) and the Talmud regarded the "father" and "son" of the Book of Proverbs as teacher and disciple (*Ḥul.* 6a). See also CHILD; INHERITANCE; MOTHER.

FEAR OF GOD: Fear (i.e., awe) of God is regarded as the basis of Jewish religious awareness, and is repeatedly exhorted in the Pentateuch, e.g. Deut. 10:12: "And now, Israel, what doth the Lord thy God require of thee, but to fear the Lord". Fear of God is the "beginning of knowledge" (Prov. 1:7) and the "beginning of wisdom" (Prov. 10:10), and according to the Talmud the person who "possesses knowledge without fear of heaven is like a treasurer who possesses the outer keys but not the inner" (*Shab.* 31a-b; talmudic literature uses the alternative phrase "fear of heaven"). The purity of motive which is demanded in the service of God is emphasized by R. Antigonus of Sokho who states that one should serve God without any thought of reward, but "let the fear of heaven be upon thee" (*Avot* 1:3). Fear of heaven is entirely in man's hands, and the statement "everything is in the hands of heaven except for the fear of heaven" (*Ber.* 33b) is a key to the rabbinic doctrine of FREE WILL. Fear of God is to be distinguished from fear of Divine punishment, for as "fear and trembling" arising out of an awareness of the awesome and numinous quality of the Divine majesty, it is closely allied to the complementary attitude of love of God.

FEAST, see **FESTIVALS; SEUDAH**

FENCE [AROUND THE LAW] (Heb. *seyag*): Preventive rabbinic injunctions enacted to safeguard the observance of biblical commandments. The injunction to erect such safeguards is found in *Avot* 1:1 where it is given as one of the three precepts of the Men of the GREAT SYNAGOGUE. The "fence" consisted of a stringent intensification of the law to safeguard the original commandments. An example of such a "fence around the law", given in tannaitic sources, is the prohibition against eating the paschal sacrifice and other sacrifices after midnight, although according to biblical law they may be eaten until morning.

FESTIVAL PRAYERS: In their basic structure, f.p. do not differ greatly from daily prayers, except that to the three prescribed daily services, a fourth additional service (MUSAPH) is added (as also on Sabbaths and New Moon) corresponding to the additional sacrifice offered on these days in the Temple; on the Day of Atonement there is also a fifth concluding service (NEILAH). The AMIDAH, which forms the climax of each service, has only seven benedictions (as on Sabbath). The fourth benediction is devoted to the special significance and holiness of the festive day; the text used is identical for all festivals, except for the name of the appropriate festival. For *musaph* this text is enlarged by a request for the rebuilding of the Temple and the mention of additional sacrifices which are prescribed for the day in question. In the Additional Service of *Rosh ha-Shanah* there are nine benedictions; the three intermediate ones — after each of which the SHOPHAR is sounded, are concerned 1) with the holiness of the day and the kingship of God; 2) with God's remembrance; 3) with the *shophar*, and each contains 10 Bible verses appropriate to its theme. The section on kingship opens with the hymnic prayer ALEINU *le-shabbeaḥ* (used nowadays also as conclusion for each of the daily services). On the Day of Atonement, the worshiper adds at the end of the *amidah* the confession of sins (*vidduy*), while in the repetition by the reader this confession is included in the fourth benediction. The repetition of the *amidah* on *Rosh ha-Shanah* and the Day of Atonement and in some rites also on other festivals, is considerably enlarged by the insertion of extensive *piyyutim* (see also AMIDAH LITURGY). In the Additional Service of the Day of Atonement these include the *avodah*, i.e., a detailed poetic description of the Temple service of the day (various versions are used in different rites). The service of the eve of the Day of Atonement opens with KOL NIDREI. On the first day of PASSOVER and on SHEMINI ATZERET respectively *piyyutim* containing prayers for DEW and RAIN are inserted in the Additional Service (for TABERNACLES see also HOSHANOT). In every *amidah* of *Rosh ha-Shanah* and the Day of Atonement the third benediction is enlarged by a prayer for the establishment of the kingdom of God; and during the first ten days, of the month of *Tishri* requests that God "May remember us unto life" are added to the *amidah*, while the prayer AVINU MALKENU, containing a large number of brief requests, is recited twice daily. On all festivals appropriate portions from the Pentateuch and Prophets are read in the morning (see READING OF THE LAW); on the Day of Atonement also during the Afternoon Service. On the three pilgrimage festivals, HALLEL is recited after the Morning Service. On the Sabbath of the Passover week, the Song of Songs is read in synagogue; on the Feast of Weeks, the Book of Ruth; and on Tabernacles, the Book of Ecclesiastes (see SCROLLS, FIVE). The rest of the liturgy for festivals does not differ essentially from the weekday version. PESUKEI DE-ZIMRA are enlarged and followed by NISHMAT as on Sabbath. The SHEMA and its benedictions are the same as on weekdays, although in some rites *piyyutim* are interwoven in the latter. On the Day of Atonement the first verse of the *shema* and the following doxology (*barukh shem kevod malkhuto,* etc.) are chanted aloud by the entire congregation. The book containing the f.p. is called the *maḥzor*. Minor festivals — ḤANUKKAH, PURIM, ROSH ḤODESH — are generally treated like weekdays, except that additional sections, referring to the significance of the day, are added in the *amidah*. On all three occasions, there is a reading from the Pentateuch. On *Ḥanukkah* and *Rosh Ḥodesh, Hallel* is recited; on *Purim* the Book of Esther is read; and on *Rosh Ḥodesh musaph* is read. No uniform practice has emerged concerning *Yom Atzmaut* (the State of Israel's "Independence Day") but the tendency liturgically is to treat it like *Ḥanukkah* and *Purim*.

FESTIVALS: The Pentateuch enumerates five f. to be observed throughout the year: — the three PILGRIM FESTIVALS (PASSOVER, WEEKS, and TABERNACLES), the "day of blowing the trumpets" (see ROSH HA-SHANAH), and the Day of ATONEMENT which, although observed as a fast, is included among the f. *Rosh ha-Shanah* and the Day of Atonement are celebrated as purely religious occasions of judgment, atonement, and reconciliation with God, whereas historical and agricultural motives combine in each of the Pilgrim Festivals. Thus Passover is celebrated as both the f. of Spring and the anniversary of the Exodus from Egypt; Weeks, as the f. of the FIRST-FRUITS and the anniversary of the Revelation upon Mt. Sinai; and Tabernacles as the harvest f. and also the commemoration of the forty years wandering in the wilderness. Each has a liturgical name which does not occur in the Bible: "The Season of our Freedom" (Passover), "the Season of the Giving of our *Torah*" (Weeks), and "the Season of our Rejoicing" (Tabernacles). Doubt is expressed in the

Talmud whether SHEMINI ATZERET, with which the Festival of Tabernacles concludes (Num. 29:35), is to be regarded as a separate festival or as the concluding day of Tabernacles; the decision, as also expressed in the ritual of the day, is in the nature of a compromise. During the period of the First Temple, the NEW MOON was celebrated at least as a semi-festival, but it has since completely lost its festive character. *Rosh ha-Shanah* is now observed both in Israel and in the Diaspora for two days, and the Day of Atonement for one. The celebration of the other biblical festivals (first and last day of Passover, Weeks, first day of Tabernacles, *Shemini Atzeret*) has been extended in the Diaspora to two days (see SECOND DAYS OF FESTIVALS). Although the original reason for the extension no longer existed even in talmudical times, the custom was retained (see *Beitz.* 4b). On all these f. (apart from the intermediate days — ḤOL HA-MOED) abstention from work is obligatory. The Day of Atonement, being a "Sabbath of Sabbaths" (Lev. 23:32), is subject to the same prohibitions as the Sabbath. On the other f., unlike the Sabbath, carrying and the use of fire, both for cooking and other needs, are permitted. The second day of *Shemini Atzeret* has developed as the special festival of *Simḥat Torah,* on which the completion of the annual reading of the Pentateuch is celebrated with joy and merriment. To these major f. a number of later ones have been added on which the prohibition to work does not apply. These can be divided into full f. with their special ritual and liturgy, and the semi-f. which are little more than days commemorating events regarded as sufficiently significant to justify the omission of supplicatory prayers. To the former category belong *Ḥanukkah* and *Purim* (the latter, although its institution is recounted in the biblical Book of ESTHER, has the character of a post-biblical festi-

CALENDAR OF FIRST DAYS OF JEWISH FESTIVALS

Year	*Passover*	*Weeks*	*Rosh Ha-Shanah*	*Day of Atonement*	*Tabernacles*	*Ḥanukkah*	*Purim*
1986	April 24	Jun. 13	Oct. 4	Oct. 13	Oct. 18	Dec. 27	Mar. 24
1987	Apr. 15	Jun. 3	Sep. 24	Oct. 3	Oct. 8	Dec. 16	Mar. 15
1988	Apr. 2	May 22	Sep. 12	Sep. 21	Sep. 26	Dec. 4	Mar. 3
1989	Apr. 20	Jun. 9	Sep. 30	Oct. 9	Oct. 14	Dec. 23	Mar. 21
1990	Apr. 10	May 30	Sep. 20	Sep. 29	Oct. 4	Dec. 12	Mar. 11
1991	Mar. 30	May 19	Sep. 9	Sep. 18	Sep. 23	Dec. 2	Feb. 28
1992	Apr. 18	June 7	Sep. 28	Oct. 7	Oct. 12	Dec. 20	Mar. 18
1993	Apr. 6	May 26	Sep. 16	Sep. 25	Sep. 30	Dec. 9	Mar. 7
1994	Mar. 27	May 16	Sep. 6	Sep. 15	Sep. 20	Nov. 28	Feb. 25
1995	Apr. 15	Jun. 4	Sep. 25	Oct. 4	Oct. 9	Dec. 18	Mar. 16
1996	Apr. 4	May 24	Sep. 14	Sep. 23	Sep. 28	Dec. 6	Mar. 5
1997	Apr. 22	Jun. 11	Oct. 2	Oct. 11	Oct. 16	Dec. 24	Mar. 23
1998	Apr. 11	May 31	Sep. 21	Sep. 30	Oct. 5	Dec. 14	Mar. 12
1999	Apr. 1	May 21	Sep. 11	Sep. 20	Sep. 25	Dec. 4	Mar. 2
2000	Apr. 20	Jun. 9	Sep. 30	Oct. 9	Oct. 14	Dec. 22	Mar. 21
2001	Apr. 8	May 28	Sep. 18	Sep. 27	Oct. 2	Dec. 10	Mar. 9
2002	Mar. 28	May 17	Sep. 7	Sep. 16	Sep. 21	Nov. 30	Feb. 26
2003	Apr. 17	Jun. 6	Sep. 27	Oct. 6	Oct. 11	Dec. 20	Mar. 18
2004	Apr. 6	May 26	Sep. 16	Sep. 25	Sep. 30	Dec. 8	Mar. 8
2005	Apr. 24	Jun. 13	Oct. 4	Oct. 13	Oct. 18	Dec. 26	Mar. 25
2006	Apr. 13	Jun. 2	Sep. 23	Oct. 2	Oct. 7	Dec. 16	Mar. 14
2007	Apr. 3	May 23	Sep. 13	Sep. 22	Sep. 27	Dec. 5	Mar. 4
2008	Apr. 20	Jun. 9	Sep. 30	Oct. 9	Oct. 14	Dec. 22	Mar. 21
2009	Apr. 9	May 29	Sep. 19	Sep. 28	Oct. 3	Dec. 12	Mar. 10
2010	Mar. 30	May 19	Sep. 9	Sep. 18	Sep. 23	Dec. 2	Feb. 28
2011	Apr. 19	Jun. 8	Sep. 29	Oct. 8	Oct. 13	Dec. 21	Mar. 20
2012	Apr. 7	May 27	Sep. 17	Sep. 26	Oct. 1	Dec. 9	Mar. 8
2013	Mar. 26	May 15	Sep. 5	Sep. 14	Sep. 19	Nov. 28	Feb. 24
2014	Apr. 15	Jun. 4	Sep. 25	Oct. 4	Oct. 9	Dec. 17	Mar. 16
2015	Apr. 4	May 24	Sep. 14	Sep. 23	Sep. 28	Dec. 7	Mar. 5
2016	Apr. 23	June 12	Oct. 3	Oct. 12	Oct. 17	Dec. 25	Mar. 24

val). The minor post-biblical f. (some of them now of little consequence) include the NEW YEAR OF TREES (*Shevat* 15), the traditional date of the death of Moses (*Adar* 7), *Lag ba-Omer*, the SECOND PASSOVER, *Av* 15, and HOSHANA RABBAH. See FESTIVAL PRAYERS.

FINDING OF PROPERTY, see **LOST PROPERTY**

FINES: While any court can render a decision in litigation involving monetary statutes, the authority to levy a monetary penalty (*kenas*) as a punishment for wrongdoing, such as is explicitly stated in the Bible (e.g. "He whom God shall condemn shall pay double unto his neighbor", Exod. 22:8), rests only with those judges who have received ORDINATION in the Holy Land from teachers themselves so ordained. In practice certain categories of f. are levied by rabbinical courts up to the present despite the fact that ordination has long ceased to exist. The legal right for such adjudication is found in the principle of the delegation of authority by the ordained when special conditions prevail. F. for which one can only become liable on conviction in court but not when one freely admits to wrongdoing are payable to the injured party and not to the court or the state. Later rabbinical courts, however, ruled that f. should be paid to the communal fund in the case of certain public misdemeanors. F. could also be imposed for failure to observe public obligations (e.g. refusal to accept communal office).

FIRE: The use of f. as an element of ritual worship is common to all faiths. In Judaism however its use was limited to the f. on the altar used for the burnt-offering (Lev. 6:5) and the eternal lamp (*ner tamid*) which burned in the Temple (Exod. 27:20; Lev. 34:2). Both had to remain permanently alight. The LAMP is regarded as the symbol of God's presence among his people (*Shab.* 22b) and most synagogues have a *ner tamid* for that symbolic reason. Aaron's two sons forfeited their lives for offering up on the altar "strange f. which He had not commanded them"; and as a result "f. went forth from before the Lord and consumed them" (Lev. 10:1-2). The use of Sabbath lamps and the HAVDALAH torch are not connected with the ritual use of f. (See also LAMP, SABBATH; OIL).

FIRMAMENT, see **COSMOGONY**

FIRST-BORN: The Bible allots the first-born son a double portion of the inheritance from his father's real and personal estate (Deut. 21:17). This right does not apply to that which accrues posthumously to the estate. First-born (Heb. *bekhor*) in this connection refers only to the first-born male child of the father regardless of whether the child is first-born to its mother. Since in Jewish law it is not the testator's will which determines who shall be the heir and to whom the INHERITANCE should go, a father cannot by testation deprive his first-born of his right. He may however divide his property during his lifetime, thus equalizing the shares of his children; the property is then a gift bestowed during the lifetime of the owner and does not infringe upon the laws of inheritance. According to some authorities, however, a father violates a religious precept if he does not make provision for his first-born son to enjoy his BIRTHRIGHT; the first-born may however voluntarily renounce his right (*Bava Batra* 124a). A posthumously born child, although an inheritor, does not enjoy the right of primogeniture, and a child delivered by caesarian section is likewise excluded (*Bekh.* 8:2). On receiving his double inheritance the first-born also takes on proportionately double obligations affecting the estate: thus, he is obligated to pay a double share in settling the outstanding debts of his father. Kingship and other hereditary offices pass to the first-born provided he is suitable for the tasks of office. See also BIRTHRIGHT.

FIRST-BORN, FAST OF (Heb. *taanit bekhorim*): Fast traditionally observed by first-born (whether on the father's or mother's side) during all or part of the day preceding the Passover festival, i.e., *Nisan* 14. Until the first-born reaches maturity, his father fasts in his behalf. The fast is mentioned in tractate *Sopherim* (21:3) and was instituted in the Gaonic Period. Later it became customary to conclude the study of a talmudic tractate on that day, thereby permitting the breaking of the fast with the festive SEUDAT MITZVAH.

FIRST-BORN, REDEMPTION OF (Heb. *pidyon ha-ben*): The commandment to "redeem" the first-born refers to the male first-born on the mother's side — "whatsoever openeth the womb" — and applies to both man and beast (Exod. 13:1-16). *Humans*: The father is obliged to redeem his first-born son from the priest by payment of a ransom of five shekels or its equivalent in goods. The redemption is effected at a short religious ceremony when the child is 30 days old (if the 31st day falls on a Sabbath or festival, the ceremony is postponed until the eve of the following day) and the occasion is a festive one. Originally the first-born male in each family was to be consecrated to the service of God, thus forming a priesthood of the first-born in return for the deliverance of the Hebrew first-born during the night of the Exodus, when the Egyptian first-born were slain. Tradition asserts (*Zev.* 112b) that the Israelite first-born indeed served in the priesthood until the completion of the Tabernacle, whereupon they were exchanged for the tribe of Levi (Num. 3:12-13).

Priests and levites are exempt from the obligation to redeem their first-born since they are in fact consecrated to the service of God (*ibid.* 3:6-10). The obligation of redemption does not apply in the case of a child who was preceded by a miscarriage or a stillbirth, or who was delivered by caesarian section, since in these instances the child does not in fact "open the womb" of its mother.

Animals: The firstling of "clean animals" (i.e., those from which sacrifices can be brought) are automatically consecrated at birth and in Temple times were to be sacrificed as peace offerings. The firstling of an ass is to be either redeemed or destroyed. Since the destruction of the Temple the firstlings of animals are left to pasture and may not be used nor benefit derived from them unless a blemish occurs which would have invalidated them for sacrifice, in which case they may be slaughtered for food.

FIRST FRUITS (Heb. *bikkurim*): The biblical precept to bring the first ripe fruits, cultivated or wild, to the Temple (Exod. 23:19; 34:26; Deut. 26) applies according to the Talmud only in Temple times (since the f.f., which have the sacred status of the HEAVE-OFFERING, are to be placed "before the altar of the Lord") and affects only the produce of the Land of Israel — in which the rabbis included Transjordania and Syria. F.f. may be brought only from the seven kinds of produce for which the Land of Israel is praised — wheat, barley, figs, vines, pomegranates, olives, and honey (Deut. 8:8). The f.f. on appearance are to be tied with a marker and left to grow and ripen. They are then cut and brought with great ceremony to the Temple court. Psalms were chanted throughout the journey, which was made by as large a group of people as possible. The streets of Jerusalem were adorned and the bringers of the f.f. profusely welcomed. The main occasion for bringing the fruits was the Feast of WEEKS but they could be brought until the following *Ḥanukkah.* Placed in a basket (*ibid.* 26:2), the copiously decorated fruit was presented to the priest, while the donor recited the "confession" prescribed in Deut. 26:5-10, thereby expressing his faith in God, the Owner of the land, and thanksgiving for allowing him to hold it in trust. The priest then touched the basket and the fruit became his property. The entire ceremony was accompanied by the singing of Psalm 30 by the levitical choir of the Temple and followed by the sacrifice of peace-offerings. After the destruction of the Temple, when f.f. could no longer be brought, the rabbis regarded acts of charity as a substitute (*Lev. Rab.* 24) especially when extended for the support of scholars (*Ket.* 106a). The relevant legislation is discussed in the talmudic tractate, *Bikkurim*.

FIVE BOOKS OF MOSES, see **BIBLE**

FIVE SCROLLS, see **SCROLLS, FIVE**

FLAGELLATION, see **FLOGGING**

FLESH: Flesh is mentioned in the Bible in various senses: (1) of the body as a whole; (2) as a collective noun for mankind; (3) figuratively, as the impressionable side of human nature (Ezek. 35:26) or weakness (Is. 31:3); (4) as an article of food (Dan. 7:5). Originally forbidden to man as food (Gen. 1:29-30), it was later permitted with the qualification that it be not torn from a living creature (*ibid.* 9:3-4). In Sinaitic law the general permission to use animal f. for food was limited to particular species (Lev. 11) and to a particular manner of slaughter and preparation, while many regulations deal with the f. of an animal consecrated to the altar. The dualistic opposition of flesh and spirit taught by some Jewish groups (see DEAD SEA SCROLLS) and adopted by the NEW TESTAMENT was not favored by Rabbinic Judaism which encouraged neither the mortification of the f. nor the ascription to it of inherent sinfulness. While recognizing that human frailties stem from the nature of the body and the temptations to which it is subject, the consensus of Jewish precept and teaching, far from negating the "flesh", is directed to uplifting and "sanctifying" it.

FLOGGING: Punishment by the infliction of stripes as provided for in Deut. 25:1-3. Although the Bible prescribes a maximum of 40 stripes, the rabbis interpreted this as a maximum of 39, one third being administered on the chest and two-thirds upon the back. F. is the normal punishment for the active infringement of negative commandments where no specific mention is made of a death penalty. It is also considered to be sufficient punishment for severe violations of commandments where the punishment is traditionally decreed as *karet* ("cutting off"). Although there is no physical punishment for the failure to carry out a positive commandment, the rabbinical authorities were considered empowered to administer such punishment for the general welfare of the community in all cases where they saw fit.

FLOOD: The destruction of all living creatures by God because of man's wickedness, as told in Gen. 6:5-9:17. Only the righteous NOAH, his family, and representatives of the animal kingdom were allowed to escape in a floating ARK. The F. is described as a release of the primeval waters of chaos that had been restrained by the act of creation. Subsequently God vowed never to repeat this punishment, and proclaimed the RAINBOW as a sign of His COVENANT (Gen. 9:12-17). F. legends are known from many parts of the world. The biblical account shows many similarities with the Babylonian-Sumerian story of the f. as told by Utnapishtim to Gilgamesh. The Bible apparently refashioned the ancient oriental material in the light of its monotheistic and universalist conception of history as a moral issue. The Midrash develops this view of the F. by describing in detail the sinfulness of antediluvian mankind and Noah's attempts to make them repent. Some biblical critics hold that an analysis of Gen. 6-9 indicates that two originally distinct versions were woven into a single story.

FOLKLORE: Traditional popular arts, beliefs, and practices, and their study. Since many folk customs relate to the supernatural and were meant to ensure fertility, health, protection against evil and demonic influences, etc., they frequently border on religion. Jewish life is permeated by folkloristic elements, some of them native tradition, others derived from the non-Jewish environment. Thus the Bible reflects much ancient Semitic f., the Talmud contains a wealth of Babylonian f., and many of the f. elements recorded in midrashic literature have also been preserved in the oral traditions of Arabs in Palestine. Jewish law distinguishes between various kinds of folk belief and custom. Some are so closely bound up with religious observance that they practically enjoy the status of MINHAG. With others the pagan or gentile background is so patent that they were discouraged as being the "ways of the AMORITES". Certain forms of MAGIC and SUPERSTITION were merely tolerated. Occasionally a folk custom could establish itself as a popular religious ritual, in spite of rabbinic opposition (see KAPPAROT). In the 18th and early 19th cents. ḤASIDISM was productive of a rich religious f.

FOOD, see DIETARY LAWS

FORBIDDEN FOODS, see CLEAN AND UNCLEAN ANIMALS; DIETARY LAWS

FORGERY: Any alteration in the writing of a document, such as an erasure or the insertion of words between lines, is considered f. and thus renders the document illegal. In order to detect possible changes in documents, rabbinic legislation established the type of paper, ink, etc. which could be used for certain documents, thus making f. difficult. Yet it might sometimes be claimed that an entire document of completely proper appearance had been forged. In order to remove the complications involved in such a claim, any document could be submitted for certification by a court. Such certification would prevent any possible future claim that the document had been forged. Although f. is considered a sin, there is no prescribed punishment for it. At the most the person involved is disbarred from serving as a witness in other cases.

FORGIVENESS: F. of sin is a Divine ATTRIBUTE (Exod. 34:6-7) and the sixth of the AMIDAH blessings is a prayer for such f. The conditions for f. are CONFESSION, REPENTANCE, and the resolution to abstain from repeating the transgression. Since man should imitate the attributes of God, f. for injuries or offenses should be freely given by the injured party, but human f. involves the added need for rectifying any wrong and appeasing the person injured (*Yoma* 85b). See also ATONEMENT.

FORMER PROPHETS, see BIBLE; PROPHETS

FORNICATION, see ADULTERY

FOUND PROPERTY, see LOST PROPERTY

FOUR CUPS, see ARBA KOSOT

FOUR PARASHOT, see SABBATHS, SPECIAL

FOUR QUESTIONS, see MAH NISHTANAH

FOUR SPECIES (Heb. *arbaah minim*): Four plants taken and "waved" during the service on the festival of TABERNACLES. The biblical injunction for the festival enjoins "And ye shall take you on the first day the fruit of goodly trees, branches of palm trees, boughs of thick trees and willows of the brook and rejoice before the Lord your God seven days" (Lev. 23:40). Rabbinic tradition identified the "fruit of the goodly tree" with the myrtle. The f. s. are traditionally made up of one palm branch (LULAV), one ETROG, three sprigs of myrtle, and two willow twigs. In the service, the *lulav* is held in the right hand and the *etrog* in the left. The Bible does not explain the injunction, although from Neh. 8:15-16, it appears that Nehemiah (and later the Sadducees and Karaites) interpreted the verse to refer to the species used in building the *Sukkah*. The Midrash offers a wealth of allegorical interpretations (e.g. the qualities of the f.s. correspond to four types of Jews who make up the community, or the shapes of these species correspond to the organs of the human body — the heart, eye, lip, and spine). Modern scholars regard the f.s. as an ancient ritual of prayer for RAIN; rabbinic tradition confirms that one of the main concerns of the Harvest Festival was rain for the coming season. On each day of the festival (except the Sabbath) after reciting the appropriate benediction ("to take the *lulav*") the f.s. are waved in the four directions as well as upward and downward, and a circuit is made with them round the synagogue (in Temple times around the altar). On *Hoshana Rabbah* seven circuits are made.

FRANK, JACOB, see FRANKISTS

FRANKEL, ZACHARIAS (1801-1875): Rabbinical scholar; from 1854, director of the Breslau Rabbinical Seminary. He endeavored to combine traditional Judaism with European scholarship. F. opposed religious reforms, especially the replacement of Hebrew by German as the language of prayer and the omission of references to sacrifices and the return to Zion, but at the same time advocated liturgical changes and the modernization of Jewish education. He participated in the

Reform Synod at Frankfurt in 1845 but withdrew when it was decided that Hebrew prayers were not obligatory. F. opposed GEIGER's reform proposals and was one of the leaders of the countermovement which he called "Historical Positive Judaism" (and which led eventually to CONSERVATIVE JUDAISM). He was the author of many basic WISSENSCHAFT works notably *Darkhei ha-Mishnah* ("The Paths of the Mishnah").

FRANKISTS: Followers of Jacob Frank (1726-1791), the last of the pseudo-messiahs who emerged in the wake of the messianic movement started in 1665 by SHABBETAI TZEVI. Various groups of believers in Shabbetai Tzevi had continued to exist, including the DONMEH in Turkey and numerous secret societies in Poland and Galicia. Many of these groups practiced sexual license as part of a perverse mystical faith in the Messiah. Frank was brought up in one of these sects, became their leader, and eventually claimed to be the successor to Shabbetai Tzevi. He preached an antinomian doctrine and advocated a rapprochement with the Catholic Church similar to the adoption of Islam by Shabbetai Tzevi and the Donmeh (with whom Frank had personal contacts). After various disputations with the rabbis, in which Frank repudiated the Talmud, confessed a Trinitarian Judaism and even repeated the blood libel, the F. took the decisive step of baptism in Lemberg in 1759. Frank himself insisted on being baptized in Warsaw Cathedral with great pomp and with Emperor Augustus III as his god-father. Accused of heresy a year later he was incarcerated and remained in prison for 13 years during which time he became the "suffering messiah" in the eyes of his followers. In 1786 he settled in Offenbach near Frankfurt, where he and his beautiful daughter Eve presided over the secret headquarters of the sect and indulged in orgiastic rituals. After Frank's death the sect ceased to exist and the baptized F. completely merged with Polish society.

FRAUD: Jewish law strongly condemns all forms of f. and legislates appropriate punishments. Primarily f. annuls a contract while the injured party is entitled to damages. The Bible lists severe laws against false weights and measures (Lev. 19:35-36). If an article is faulty, the purchaser must be informed of the blemish prior to the sale otherwise the transaction comes under the category of f. Any false description gives the buyer the right to have the contract annulled and his money refunded.

FREEDOM: Although slavery (see SLAVES AND SLAVERY) was an accepted part of the economic system in ancient Israel, as elsewhere in the ancient world, the f. of the nation as well as of the individual was considered a supreme value and gift of God. The DECALOGUE begins with the affirmation "I am the Lord thy God, who brought thee out of the Land of Egypt, out of the house of bondage". Biblical legislation provides for the automatic liberation of even the gentile slave in the JUBILEE year and protected fugitive slaves ("Thou shalt not deliver unto his master a slave that is escaped from his master unto thee: he shall dwell with thee", Deut. 23:16-17). The ritual for the Hebrew slave who elects to continue his servitude (Exod. 21:6) is interpreted by the rabbis as a symbolic punishment of the man who has heard but failed to respond to the Divine proclamation of f. The gift of national f. is the main theme of the PASSOVER celebration, concerning which the rabbis taught "every man is bound to regard himself as though he had himself gone out of Egypt", and thanksgiving for f. occurs at various points in the daily liturgy. The political and social concept of f. was spiritualized in later theological literature (cf. e.g. JUDAH HA-LEVI's famous line "only the servant of God is truly free").

FREETHINKING, see **AGNOSTICISM**

FREE WILL: The notion that man's actions are determined by his f.w. and that he is, therefore, morally responsible for them becomes a religious and philosophical problem in the light of the belief in Divine omniscience, predestination or PROVIDENCE (see also DETERMINISM; FATALISM). Although the contradiction is often transcended in actual religious experience (cf. Jeremiah 4:3 ff. and 1:5), it remained a serious problem for reflective thought. Attempts to solve it often tended to curtail either man's f.w. or God's omniscience and omnipotence. The former solution not only outrages man's moral sense, but also calls in question the justice of God in rewarding virtue and punishing sin. On the other hand the limitations of God's sovereignty entails serious theological difficulties. Philosophical discussions of f.w. oscillate between these two poles, one side maintaining that every being, including God, is determined by the necessity of its own being, and cannot voluntarily do anything or leave it undone, while the other side asserts that God is not bound by necessity external to Himself. Freedom of choice seems to be presupposed in the Bible (cf. Deut. 30:19) and in particular in prophetic preaching. According to Josephus, the Sadducees, following Epicurus, denied the existence of Divine Providence and attributed everything to change; the ESSENES, on the other hand, were absolute determinists and attributed everything to predestination and the will of God (see also DEAD SEA SCROLLS); the Pharisees asserted both the sovereignty of God and the freedom of man, holding that not all things are predestined and that in certain matters man has freedom. Indeterminism and freedom in men's religious choice are asserted in such rabbinic statements as "Everything is in the hands of God except the fear of God" (*Ber.* 33b) or "The eye, ear, and nostrils are not in man's power, but the mouth, hand, and feet are" (*Tanḥuma, Toledot*) i.e., external impressions are involuntary but actions, steps, and words arise from man's own volition. The Jewish philosophers generally follow the Pharisaic tradition, defending f.w. even at the price of limiting the scope of God's foreknowledge. Philo forsakes his Stoic masters and holds that f.w. is a Divine part of Divine knowledge in such a way that it does not impinge on man's freedom. SAADYAH and JUDAH HA-LEVI held that God's knowledge of human actions, past and future, did not prejudge or determine them in any way. BAḤYA IBN PAKUDA limited f.w. to the mental acts of decision and choice; external acts, however, he claimed, were determined. CRESCAS alone among the Jewish philosophers, although aware of the demoralizing effect of his doctrine, denied f.w. in the interests of proving the sovereignty of God and His infinite attributes.

FREE-WILL OFFERING (Heb. *nedavah*): Sacrifice offered voluntarily, either as a result of the initiative of the individual (e.g. through a vow) or to mark a significant occasion (e.g. the building of the Temples). The f.o. could be a burnt-offering and was frequently sacrificed on feast days, since most of its meat could be consumed by the sacrificer.

FRINGES, see **TZITZIT**

FRONTLETS, see **TEPHILLIN**

FUGITIVE, see **ASYLUM**

FUNERAL, see **BURIAL**

FUNERAL ORATION, see **EULOGY**

G

GABBAI (Heb.): Originally meaning a "collector", and "tax gatherer", the term had a derogatory connotation (cf. Mishnah *Ḥag.* 3:6 and *Toh.* 7:6 and Tosephta *Bava Metzia* 8 "It is difficult to accept the repentance of *gabbaim*"). *Gabbaim* are listed among those whose evidence in court was invalid, as they were reckoned untrustworthy and dissolute (*Sanh.* 25b). In contrast, however, the *gabbaei tzedakah* ("charity collectors", "overseers of the poor") collected and distributed charity funds and were regarded as so honorable and worthy that they were not required to account for the funds. They were chosen only from the highest ranks of society, and their children were permitted to marry into the priesthood without investigation of their genealogy (*Kidd.* 76a). The Talmud, however, takes the precaution of insisting that in order to avoid suspicion they must carry out their collections in pairs. From this primary meaning the use of the title was extended in later ages to the cognate office of the treasurer of the synagogue or other communal institutions and then popularly to its wardens, even though they had no financial functions. See Parnas.

GABIROL, see **IBN GABIROL**

GABRIEL, see **ANGELOLOGY**

GAD: (1) Name of one of Jacob's sons (by Zilpah, the handmaid of his wife Leah) and hence of one of the twelve tribes. The tribe of G. dwelt E. of the river Jordan. The original meaning of the word *gad* (good fortune, deity of luck) appears in the account of his naming (cf. Gen. 30:11) and the word occurs in composite names in the Bible as well as in later literature. (2) Name of a prophet at David's court (II Sam. 24:11-14, 18-19).

GALANTE: Family of rabbis and scholars. (1) *ABRAHAM BEN MORDECAI G.* (born in Rome, d. 1588 in Safed), disciple of Moses Cordovero and one of the leading kabbalists in Safed. Author of a commentary on the Zohar. (2) *MOSES BEN MORDECAI G.* (c. 1520-c. 1612), brother of (1); kabbalist and author. From 1580 chief rabbi of Safed. (3) *MOSES BEN JONATHAN G.* (1620-1689), known as *Ha-Magen;* grandson of (1). Chief rabbi of Jerusalem and author of kabbalistic and halakhic works.

GALUT, see **DIASPORA; EXILE**

GAM ZO LE-TOVAH (Heb. "this too is for good"): Phrase often used in unpleasant circumstances and expressive of the faith that God's providence, even if apparently working harm, is ultimately for the good. The expression is said to have been a favorite maxim with R. Nahum of Gimzo.

GAMALIEL: Name of six Palestinian patriarchs (1st-5th cents. C.E.) of the House of Hillel. The best-known are (1) *GAMALIEL I "THE ELDER"*, also known as Rabban ("our master") G., (d. c. 50 C.E.), grandson of Hillel, head of the Sanhedrin at the time of the emperor Caligula. He introduced important judicial reforms including improvements in the legal status of women. Among his pupils was Paul (*Acts* 22:3) who mentions sympathetically his tolerance of the small Christian sect. (2) *G. II "OF YAVNEH"*, titular and spiritual heir to R. Johanan ben Zakkai as head of the academy at Yavneh (80-118 C.E.). In his efforts to centralize legislative authority he clashed with R. Joshua, was temporarily deposed, but was reinstated upon coming to terms with his antagonists. Many of his important halakhic dicta dealt with the need for religious readjustment and the determination of a uniform *halakhah* after the destruction of the Temple. Under him the Amidah received its final redaction and the three daily prayers were made obligatory. He was well versed in the sciences which he used in fixing the Jewish calendar. His knowledge of Greek, moreover, made him a spokesman of Judaism in encounters with paganism and Christianity. He did much to raise the prestige of the Palestinian patriarchate which lasted till the death of R. Gamaliel VI in 426.

GAMBLING: There are no references to games in the Bible and it seems that only under Greek and Roman influence were games such as dice-playing (*kubya*) adopted and indulged in by Jews. The rabbis were strongly opposed to all forms of g. which, although not classed as actual robbery (since appropriation against the will of the owner is an essential legal requirement for proving robbery in Jewish law), was considered closely akin to it; g. debts could not be legally claimed. Although the general tendency of rabbinic law is to forbid all manner of g., careful distinction is made between those who indulge in it as a pastime and those for whom it is a profession (*Sanh.* 24b). Thus g. pastimes were allowed even on the Sabbath, but professional gamblers were considered untrustworthy and invalid as witnesses, for "they waste their time in idleness and are not interested in the welfare of humanity" (*loc. cit.*). The numerous communal enactments against g. which are found in the medieval records of European Jewry show that g. was fairly widely indulged in and several instances of addiction are recorded. The custom of playing cards on Christmas eve and *Ḥanukkah* was fairly widespread among Orthodox Jews in Eastern Europe.

GAN EDEN, see **GARDEN OF EDEN**

GANZFRIED, SOLOMON (1804-1866): Hungarian rabbinic scholar. His best-known work is the *Kitzur Shulḥan Arukh* ("Abbreviated *Shulḥan Arukh*"), a convenient abbreviation in handbook form, of Joseph Karo's Shulḥan Arukh, giving the essential rules, *halakhot*, and customs in simple and clear language. The *Kitzur* soon became the Orthodox layman's indispensable guide and was translated into several languages.

GAON (Heb. "excellency", "eminence", "pride": pl. *geonim*): Title of the heads of the two leading academies in Babylonia following the period of the savoraim between the end of the 6th and the end of the 12th cents. The title is an abbreviation for the designation of their position as *resh metivta geon Yaakov* ("head of the academy which is the excellency of Jacob"). Although temporal power was held by the exilarchs, the rôle played by the *geonim* in this respect was also considerable. The two academies, Sura and Pumbedita, each of which was headed by a g., dated from early amoraic times. The fortunes of each academy usually varied in accordance with the distinction and authority of the g. who headed it. The first *geonim*, according to the famous "epistle" of Sherira Gaon, were Mar Ḥanan in Pumbedita (589) and Rav Mar bar Rab Huna in Sura (591). It was the exilarch who appointed the heads of the academies and since his association with Sura was closer than with Pumbedita this helped invest Sura with a kind of formal ascendancy. The *geonim* did much to foster and develop talmudic law. Their influence and authority extended to Jewish settlement everywhere, even in Palestine, for most of the Gaonic Period. It was Yehudai Gaon of Sura (appointed in 760) who wrote a systematic talmudic code known as *Halakhot Pesukot* ("Decided Laws"; known also as *Hilkhot Reu*), while at the same time the *Sheiltot* ("Discussions"), a series of halakhic-homiletic sermons or discourses following the weekly readings of the *Torah*, was the work of Aḥa ben Shabḥa, a Pumbedita scholar who left for Palestine when a younger colleague was appointed to head the academy. Natronai Gaon of Sura (853-856) prepared a brief arrangement of the daily prayers at the request of the community in Lucena, Spain. His successor Amram Gaon (856-874) followed this up by arranging a complete order of prayer for the use of communities in Spain, collecting material from both Talmuds and the homiletical Midrashim as well as relying upon the customs of the "two schools". At almost the same time Paltoi Gaon of Pumbedita (842-858) sent a copy of the Talmud accompanied by explanations to the Spanish communities. The greatest figure connected with Sura is Saadyah Gaon (appointed 928), famous in *halakhah*, liturgy, Bible commentary, and philosophy. Under him Sura reached its zenith, and upon his death in 942, the academy closed for 45 years. Reopened with the appointment of Tzemaḥ of Pumbedita, it achieved some prominence again with his successor Samuel ben Hophni (1003-13). By this time both academies were centered in Baghdad, having moved there toward the end of the 9th cent., although still retaining their distinctive names (much in the same manner as famous former European *yeshivot* still retain their old place names in their new locations in America today). The heyday of the Pumbedita academy was the 70-year period when it was headed by Sherira Gaon (968-98) and his son Hai (998-1038). It was Sherira especially who restored for a time the prestige of the Babylonian center which was being superseded by new settlements in the West. He and his son maintained contact with the communities in N. Africa and Spain through many responsa, the most important of which is the historical epistle written by Sherira in 992 for the Jews of Kairouan who had asked for a recorded tradition of the chain of scholars up through the Gaonic Period, as well as for information on the origins of the Mishnah and Talmud. Under Hai, Pumbedita continued as the leading world center of Jewish learning. He wrote thousands of responsa as well as commentaries on the Bible and Talmud. After his death the two academies, both in Baghdad, were united and had a continued existence for another 150 years. Samuel ben Ali (died c. 1207) was the last of the Baghdad *geonim*, whose influence by this time had become purely local as the new centers of the Diaspora had developed their own leadership. Palestine too had developed a competing gaonate originating toward the end of the 9th cent. and lasting till 1109. The *geonim* were responsible for broadening the *halakhah* and interpreting it on a talmudic basis. During their time the definitive versions of the Talmud and the Midrash were redacted, and they were responsible for making the Talmud the cornerstone of national life. They also fostered the amoraic tradition of the two annual Kallah Months. In addition they occupied themselves with the standardization of the liturgy and under their supervision the masoretic text of the Bible was determined. The activities of the *geonim* were threefold: 1) to reply to queries from communities who did not possess a copy of the Talmud or who required interpretations; 2) to train talmudic experts; 3) to determine the law in places where the Talmud had not reached a clear decision. The term *gaon* has remained in popular Jewish usage to describe an outstanding scholar.

GARDEN OF EDEN: God planted a garden in Eden (Gen. 2:8-3:24) and charged ADAM with keeping it. It was watered by a river which parted into four streams: Pishon, Gihon, Tigris, and Euphrates. Here Eve induced Adam to eat with her of the fruit of the Tree of Knowledge of Good and Evil, though this was forbidden by God. Thus they gained a new insight into life but at the same time forfeited God's trust. Man was ejected from the Garden lest he also partake of the Tree of Life and thereby secure immortality. The way to the Garden was henceforth barred by the flaming sword of the angelic guardians. Another version of the story is found in Ezek. 28:13-20. Several theories have been advanced as to the supposed site of the Garden but none is conclusive. Eden means "delight" in Hebrew but has also been derived from the Assyrian *Edinu,* meaning "plain" or "steppe". The Sumerian parallel to the G. of E. is Dilmun, where sickness and death were unknown and which became the abode of the immortals, including Utnapishtim, the Babylonian Noah. In the Sumerian and Babylonian myths, however, the story is governed by the contest of rival forces, human and divine, whereas the biblical account is wholly subservient to a moral design. The Christian doctrines of the FALL and Original Sin are based on interpretations of the biblical Eden story which are unknown in ancient Jewish exegesis, and it was only in medieval kabbalistic literature that doctrines like those of original sin and a primal fall were developed. Rabbinic texts distinguish between two Gardens of Eden: an earthly garden and a heavenly one, the latter being the abode of bliss (PARADISE) reserved for the souls of the righteous (see also HEAVEN).

GARTEL (Yidd. for "girdle", "belt"): Girdle made of black silk or wool, and worn by Ḥasidim at prayer, in obedience to the rabbinic injunction that when praying a division shall be made between the upper and lower halves of the body. The custom is also meant as a symbolic "girding of the loins" in the service of God.

GEDALIAH, FAST OF: Fast day commemorating the assassination of Gedaliah on *Tishri* 3, the day after *Rosh ha-Shanah* (*R.H.* 18b). Gedaliah ben Ahikam, a member of the Shaphan family which had supported the prophet Jeremiah, was appointed governor of Judah by Nebuchadnezzar after the destruction of the First Temple. Following G.'s murder at the hands of Ishmael ben Nethaniah, of the royal family, the remaining Jews fled to Egypt and the last vestige of Jewish self-government in Judah came to an end (II Kings 25:25; Jer. 40-1). The Bible states that the murder took place in the month of *Tishri* and later tradition dated it on the 3rd; some authorities suggested that it took place on *Rosh ha-Shanah* but that the commemoration was postponed until after the holiday. The F. of G. is already mentioned by the prophet Zechariah (7:5; 8:19). When *Rosh ha-Shanah* falls on Thursday and Friday, the fast is postponed to the following Sunday, *Tishri* 4. In the synagogue, SELIHOT are read at the Morning Service (as well as before the service in some rites).

GEHENNA, see GEHINNOM

GEHINNOM (or Gehenna; Heb. *Gei ben Hinnom* or *Gei Hinnom*): Valley outside the western wall of Jerusalem; mentioned in the Bible (Josh. 15:8; 18:16; II Kings 23:10; Jer. 7:31; Neh. 11:30) as a valley through which ran the boundary between the tribes of Benjamin and Judah. It was the site of TOPHETH, where child sacrifice was offered to MOLOCH. The valley also served for the incineration of the city's refuse and for the carcasses of animals and criminals. Jeremiah prophesied (7:32) that the valley would become a "valley of slaughter" and a burial place. Thus it assumed in post-biblical literature the connotation of hell, where the wicked are punished — though no such allusion to it exists in the Bible itself which refers to the abode of the dead only as SHEOL. The rabbis were divided as to the place of this G. (or hell), some placing it in the heavens. The form of punishment inflicted on the wicked is not clearly defined in the Talmud but is principally associated with fire. Maimonides interpreted the tradition of punishment of the wicked in G. as a denial of eternal life for them. The Zohar describes an upper G. and a lower G., the dross of the soul that is not purged in the lower G. being finally removed in the upper G.

GEIGER, ABRAHAM (1810-1874): Spiritual leader of REFORM Judaism in Germany, preacher and controversialist. The outstanding intellectual figure among the early Reformers, he was animated by the desire to liberate Judaism from its ceremonialism, to link it with European traditions, to organize it on modern scientific lines, and to interpret it in the light of an ethical universalism based on the prophets. His Reform principles and theological convictions are embodied in the prayer book which he published in 1854. It omits all references to angels, to the resurrection of the dead, to the restoration of the Temple, or the return to Zion. G. was opposed to the doctrine of Israel's election and all evidence of religious or national particularism. Among the innovations he introduced in the service were choral singing, confirmation exercises, and sermons in German. He favored the elimination of circumcision and the dietary laws, but opposed the tendency in certain Reform circles to observe the Sabbath on Sundays. His scholarly activities were based on a historical-critical study of the evolution of Judaism. He believed that Judaism ought to become a world religion that should take the place of Christianity, which he maintained was marred by basic misconceptions. His main work is his *Urschrift und Übersetzungen der Bibel* which deals with the text and translations of the Bible in their relation to the inner development of Judaism.

GELILAH (Heb. "rolling"): In the *Ashkenazi* rite, the rolling-up, i.e., closing, of the *Torah* scroll after the reading in the synagogue. One person performs the raising of the scroll (known as *hagbahah*), while another performs the g. In talmudic times the person who read the last section of the *Torah* rolled it up. In many congregations g. is now performed by children.

GEMAR ḤATIMAH TOVAH (Heb. "a final good sealing"): The traditional wish and greeting in the period between Rosh Ha-Shanah (when the individual's fate in the New Year is inscribed in the Book of Life) and the Day of Atonement (when the decree is sealed). Sometimes the wish *G.Ḥ.T.* is used until Hoshana Rabbah.

GEMARA (Aram. "completion" i.e., of the Mishnah): The usual designation for the comment on and discussions around the Mishnah. The Mishnah together with the g. make up the Talmud. There is a Palestinian and a Babylonian g. to the Mishnah but to many tractates no g. has been preserved.

GEMATRIA: The calculation of the numerical value of Hebrew words and the search for other words or phrases of equal value. Since every Hebrew letter has a numerical value, words and phrases could be added to make sums. G. as a method of exegesis is mentioned in the *baraita* of R. Eliezer, the son of R. Yose Ha-Gelili, on the "thirty-two hermeneutical rules", and was much used for aggadic and homiletical purposes; e.g. Jacob's words to his sons (Gen. 42:2) "go down (*redu*) to Egypt" are said to have initiated the Israelites' stay of 210 years in that country (the numerical value of *redu* = 210). While many scholars were critical of g. or took it as a kind of homiletical game, others considered it an important avenue to the hidden or implied meanings of Scripture. Under the influence of letter-mysticism which played an important part in esoteric tradition, g. became a major feature of kabbalistic exposition as well as of magical practice (e.g. in amulets).

GEMILUT ḤESED (Heb. "bestowal of loving-kindness"): Any act of kindness, consideration, and benevolence. The rabbis said that "he who has occupied himself with *Torah* but not with the performance of g.ḥ. is as though he had no God". "In three respects is *g.ḥ.* superior to charity: charity can be given only to the poor while *g.ḥ.* to both rich and to poor; charity can be given only to the living, *g.ḥ.* to both the living and the dead; charity can be given only in kind, *g.ḥ.* can be given both in kind and in personal service" (Tos. *Peah* 4:19). *G.Ḥ.* is unlimited in its application and is listed among those actions of which "man enjoys the fruit in this world, while the stock remains to him in the world to come" (*Peah* 1:1). It is also considered an attribute of God, who is described in the daily *amidah* as *gomel ḥasadim tovim* ("bestower of loving-kindness"). Because lending money to enable a person to stand on his own feet is *g.ḥ.* and considered superior to almsgiving which could humiliate the recipient, the term came to be applied more specifically to the lending of money free of interest to those in need of temporary financial assistance and *g.ḥ.* societies exist for this purpose.

GENESIS, BOOK OF: The first book of the Pentateuch, called in Heb. by its first word *Bereshit* ("In the beginning") and in Greek G. ("coming into being"). The book recounts the creation of the world and the history of humanity from Adam to the birth of Abraham (chaps. 1-11), and the history of the patriarchs from Abraham to the death of Joseph (chaps. 12-50). The B. of G. is meant to lay the foundation for the historical accounts, teachings, and legislation of the subsequent books of the Bible: monotheism; the sovereignty and providence of the Creator-God who is at the same time the source of morality; the emergence of peoples; the special relation of the patriarchs to God and the election of their seed to be God's people; and the promise of the land of Canaan as their ultimate home.

GENESIS RABBAH, see MIDRASH RABBAH

GENESIS ZUTARTA (Aram. "Lesser Genesis"): Apocryphal work of the 2nd cent. B.C.E., generally known as the Book of Jubilees.

GENIZAH (Heb. "hiding"): A hiding place or store room, usually connected with a synagogue, for the deposition of worn-out sacred books. It is also the place for storing books considered heretical but which contain the Name of God and hence are too sacred to be burned. Present-day Orthodox custom is to give cemetery burial to all such documents, which are accumulated in a special place set aside in the synagogue. Reference is made in the Talmud to R. Gamaliel's placing an Aramaic translation of the Book of Job, considered improper at the time, under the pillars of the building upon the Temple Mount. During the Middle

Ages, almost every synagogue allotted a room as a g. for old or imperfect books or ritual objects. Such synagogue hiding places for sacred books have often provided later generations with precious pages of books considered lost. The most famous such g. is that discovered in the synagogue of Fostat, Cairo (built in 882) which included part of the lost Hebrew version of Ecclesiasticus and other lost Hebrew works, extracts from Aquila's Greek translation of the Bible, the Zadokite Fragments which portray a halakhic system with affinities both to the Pharisaic tradition and to that of the Judean Desert sect (see DEAD SEA SCROLLS), variant text readings of Mishnah and Talmud, ancient liturgies and synagogue poetry from almost all places of known Jewish settlement at the time, as well as miscellaneous secular documents and letters, many of which are extremely valuable as historical sources. This discovery has thrown much new light on the history of the gaonate, the Karaites, and the conditions of Jews in Palestine and Egypt between 640 and 1100. A new kind of g. has come to light more recently with the discovery of the Dead Sea Scrolls.

GENTILES: The common English translation for the Hebrew *nokhri* or *goy,* a non-Jew. A Jew is a person either born of a Jewish mother or who has accepted the Jewish faith by undergoing conversion; all others are g. In Jewish law, g. are divided into different categories depending upon their acceptance of various basic standards of conduct; of these divisions and subdivisions, the most important are on the one hand, *akkum* (a word made up of the initial letters of the Hebrew phrase for "a worshiper of stars and planets") i.e., an idolater or pagan, and on the other, those who have abandoned idolatry and accepted the belief in one God. According to rabbinic opinion (A.Z. 64b) the latter type alone — i.e., those who accept the seven laws of Noah — can qualify for the status of a *ger toshav* (a "resident stranger") with defined rights in the community (see NOACHIAN LAWS). The rabbis said "The pious of all the nations of the world have a share in the world to come" and these are identified by Maimonides with those who accept Noachian laws as Divine revelation. As a result of this distinction the extremely severe laws applying to heathens and idolaters in the Bible and Talmud are not held to apply to Christians or Mohammedans. Another consideration however came into play which deleteriously affected the relationship between Jews and g. In their determined efforts to prevent assimilation and loss of identity as a small minority in the midst of a hostile majority, the rabbis deliberately set up barriers for the explicit purpose of preventing social intercourse with g. which could lead to intermarriage, etc. The injunction in Deut. 7:2-4, originally limited specifically to the seven Canaanite nations who inhabited the Land of Israel, was extended to include all g., and decrees were enacted to erect barriers against this danger (see ḤUKKAT HA-GOY). The partaking of meals with g. was forbidden, even when it did not infringe the dietary laws. Food cooked by g. was banned (Mishnah A.Z. 2:6) and the prohibition sometimes extended even to bread and oil. The prohibition against "non-Jewish wine" (*yayin nesekh*), originally promulgated against wine prepared for idolatrous worship, came within the general prohibition of the appurtenances of heathen or idolatrous worship, and was extended not only to wine manufactured by g. but to wine manufactured by Jews which had come into physical contact with g. (on the grounds that the intention of the g. was to consecrate it for their rites). A decree extended the prohibition even to non-libation wine "as a safeguard against the use of libation wine" (see NESEKH). The modern period, starting with the era of Emancipation, has witnessed a revolution in relations between Jews and g. Having emerged from ghetto conditions Jews maintain a close everyday contact with g.; on one level this has brought about the tendency to ASSIMILATION, while on another it has encouraged a more liberal approach to g. from the religious aspect, including interfaith activities.

GER (Heb. "sojourner", i.e., in a strange land): Originally meaning a stranger dwelling in the Land of Israel (cf. Lev. 19:33-34), the term g. subsequently came to signify the convert to the Jewish religion. Rabbinic law distinguished between the *ger toshav* who has renounced paganism and observes the seven NOACHIAN LAWS and the *ger tzedek*, the full "proselyte of righteousness" who is considered a Jew in every respect. See CONVERSION; GENTILES; PROSELYTE.

GER (or Gur): Townlet near Warsaw and former seat of the dominant ḥasidic dynasty of Poland, that of the Alter family. The dynasty was established by Isaac Meir Alter (1799-1866), a disciple of Bunim of Pzysha and colleague and successor of Menahem Mendel of Kotzk. He was a profound talmudic scholar, and author of the novellae *Ḥiddushei Ha-Rim* and other works. In 1877 (after an interregnum) Isaac Meir was succeeded by his grandson Judah Aryeh Leib (1864-1948) one of the few ḥasidic rabbis to adopt a positive attitude to the rebuilding of Palestine. He died in Jerusalem and was succeeded by his son Israel.

GERIM (Heb. "Proselytes"): One of the "minor tractates", which do not form part of the Talmud but were appended to it. Its four chapters deal with the rules and procedures of conversion to Judaism.

GERIZIM: The highest of the hills of Ephraim; S. of Nablus, the ancient Shechem. According to Deut. 11:29ff., G. was the mountain from which six of Israel's tribes were to pronounce the blessings upon the observant; Joshua carried out this ceremony immediately upon conquering the region. G. is fertile and endowed with natural water sources in contrast to its arid neighbor Mt. Ebal, which was appointed for the curse. When the SAMARITANS were denied participation in the building of the Second Temple, they built their own sanctuary on G. which was eventually destroyed by John Hyrcanus in 129 B.C.E. G. remains the focal point of the Samaritan ritual.

GERONDI: Name of family of scholars originating in Gerona in Spain. (1) *ZERACHIAH BEN ISAAC HA-LEVI G.* (12th cent.). A talmudist of rare critical acumen, his glosses (*Sepher ha-Maor*) to ALFASI's work provoked violent criticism from other scholars (e.g. ABRAHAM BEN DAVID OF POSQUIERES, NAḤMANIDES). He also wrote liturgical poetry. (2) *JONAH BEN ABRAHAM G.* (1180-1263), also known as R. Jonah the Pious. At first a zealous partisan in the campaign against the works of MAIMONIDES, he later repented and planned a pilgrimage to his tomb, but got no further than Toledo where he headed a rabbinic academy until his death. Best known for his commentary on Alfasi's digest of the tractate *Berakhot* and for his ascetic and moralist tracts.

GEROUSIA (Gk.): Council of elders. In the Roman period, the affairs of many Jewish communities in the Empire — including Palestine — were conducted by a *g*. The *g*. of Jerusalem was headed by the High Priest.

GERSHOM BEN JUDAH (c. 965-c. 1028; surnamed *Meor ha-Golah* "the light of the Diaspora"): Leading talmudic authority in W. Europe. He headed a rabbinic academy in Mainz where he laid the foundations of the tradition of *Ashkenazi* (Franco-German) scholarship by establishing correct readings and providing commentaries to the talmudic texts. He also prepared a copy of the biblical MASORAH. Only fragments have survived of his writings, but many of his explanations are embedded in RASHI's commentary on the Talmud. Many of the ordinances regulating the life of European Jewry bear his name, e.g. prohibitions of polygamy, of divorcing a wife without her consent, of shaming apostates returning to Judaism, of reading letters addressed to others, insistence on the requirement of securing the consent of both parties to a divorce, etc. Violators of these regulations were subject to excommunication; hence they were known as "ḤEREM ('ban') of *Rabbenu G.*". He also wrote penitential prayers (*seliḥot*) lamenting the persecutions suffered by his generation (his son — possibly also his wife — was forcibly baptized).

GERSONIDES, see **LEVI BEN GERSHON**

GERUSHIN (Aram. "driving out", hence also "banishment", "expulsion"): Technical term denoting DIVORCE. Among the kabbalists in the 16th cent. *g*. also meant peregrinations undertaken for the purpose of sharing the "exile of the SHEKHINAH" and gaining mystical illumination.

GESHEM, see **RAIN**

GET, see **DIVORCE**

GEULLAH (Heb. "REDEMPTION"): The name of various benedictions in the liturgy: 1) One of the petitions in the weekday AMIDAH; 2) Benediction giving thanks for the redemption from Egypt with which the main part of the HAGGADAH on Passover eve is concluded; and 3) Benediction following the SHEMA in the SHAḤARIT and MAARIV prayers. The first-mentioned is a prayer for redemption not in the messianic sense but for deliverance from hardships and trouble; the other two are concerned mainly with thanksgiving for the redemption from Egyptian slavery in the past. Hence the Talmud (*Pes.* 117b) rules that the former is to be concluded in the present tense ("Blessed... who redeems [or: the Redeemer of] Israel"), but the latter in the past ("...who has redeemed Israel"). This distinction, however, was not made universally and in the old Palestinian rite the *g*. after the *Shema* was concluded: "Blessed... the Rock of Israel and its Redeemer". Moreover, in the *g*. of Passover eve, a petition for future Redemption was inserted by R. Akiva, and in the *g*. after the *Shema* messianic prayers have been added in a variety of forms, mostly in PIYYUT style (see EMET VE-YATZIV; EMET VE-EMUNAH). *Piyyutim* composed for insertion into this benediction on festivals, etc. are also known by the name of *g*. According to the Talmud there must be no interruption between the *g*. and the ensuing *amidah* and hence the response "*amen*" is omitted after this particular benediction. Thus, in effect, the *shema* with its benediction and the *amidah*, though originally separate entities, became welded into one continuous order of prayer.

GEZERAH (Heb.): A "decree" (from *gazar*="cut"; cf. "decision"); hence a technical term for a rabbinic prohibition, as distinct from a positive enactment (TAKKANAH). In non-legal usage *g*. came to mean an evil or anti-Jewish decree and, by extension, anti-Jewish persecutions and pogroms (pl. *gezerot*).

GHETTO: Section of a town enclosed by a separate wall and designated by law as an exclusive living quarter for the Jews (as distinct from a section chosen by Jews because of their preference for living together for religious reasons as well as considerations of safety). The term derives from the name of the Jewish quarter established in Venice in 1516 (*geto nuovo*). In spite of the degradation, the overpopulation, and other dangers involved, Jewish life in the g. had its positive aspect, and there were many Jewish authorities who looked with apprehension upon the demolition of its walls. The enforced seclusion from the outer world developed a life apart and a close communion among its inhabitants which fostered not only outward religious life but a highly developed morality. The g. in fact formed a town within a town in which the precepts of Judaism could be inculcated and observed with little or no interference from without. As a result the only education provided for was religious, and life was regulated by Jewish law, including Jewish civil law; the age-old prohibition against taking one's lawsuits to a non-Jewish court could be and was rigidly enforced in the g. As a result a large section of *ḥoshen mishpat* (civil law) which was otherwise largely inoperative in the Diaspora, was fostered and applied.

GIANTS: Mythological g. rarely if ever occur in the Bible, though the descendants of the "sons of God" (Gen. 6:1-4) may have been such. *Anakim,* usually translated as g., are mentioned among the inhabitants of Palestine and must have impressed the Israelites by their physical stature (cf. Num. 13:22, 28, 32-3). The two g. whose measurements are specified are Og of Bashan (Deut. 3:11) and Goliath (I Sam. 17:4).

GIFT: The transference of the rights enjoyed in a particular object or piece of property to another. Such transfer becomes legally valid only upon effecting a KINYAN. A verbal promise (except in the case of HEKDESH) is not legally binding. An exception is made in the case of a dying person whose gift is valid even without a *kinyan.* A g. may be given for a limited period of time, after which it reverts to the owner. It may also be subject to conditions. The sending of gifts to friends forms part of the celebration of *Purim.* See also CHARITY; PEAH; PRIESTLY GIFTS; TITHE.

GIKATILLA, JOSEPH BEN ABRAHAM (1248-1305): Spanish kabbalist. His works (*Shaarei Orah, Ginnat Egoz,* etc.) are among the first systematic expositions of classical Spanish kabbalism during the period which also produced the ZOHAR.

GILGAL: Name of several places of religious significance in ancient Palestine; possibly marked originally by a heap (Heb. *gal*) of stones; cf. Gen. 31:46-47. The Bible mentions (1) a G. where Joshua built an altar and circumcised the people (Josh. 4-5); there Samuel judged the people and proclaimed Saul king (I Sam. 11:14); (2) a G. near Mount GERIZIM and Mount Ebal (Deut. 11:29-30); (3) a G. is mentioned in connection with Elijah and Elisha; and (4) a G. as the residence of a Canaanite king (Josh. 12:23).

GILGUL, see **TRANSMIGRATION**

GILLUI ROSH, see **COVERING OF THE HEAD**

GINSBERG, ASHER, see **AḤAD HA-AM**

GITTIN: Mishnah tractate in the order NASHIM with *gemara* in both Talmuds. It deals with the laws of DIVORCE, the bill of divorce (Heb. *get,* pl. *g.*), and remarriage after divorce.

GIVING OF THE LAW (Heb. *Mattan Torah*): Traditional designation of the REVELATION of Mount SINAI, as described in Exod. 19-20. On that occasion not only was the DECALOGUE given to Israel but — according to rabbinic doctrine — the whole *Torah* with its 613 precepts as well as the ORAL LAW. The G. of the L. is also described as the solemn COVENANT ratifying the special relationship between God and His chosen people (see Exod. 34:27-28; Deut. 4:10-15). The biblical account is further elaborated in rabbinic literature, where the event is described in superlative terms: the whole cosmos participated, and all the generations of Israel, including the future ones as yet unborn, were present at Mount Sinai. The Bible mentions no festival in commemoration of the event, but the rabbis computed from the biblical dates (Exod. 19:1, 15-16) that it occurred on *Sivan* 6. Hence the biblical festival of *Shavuot* (WEEKS) became the "feast of the G. of the L."

GLEANINGS: The remains of a crop after harvesting, which according to biblical law are to be left for the poor. Grain g. are called *leket*; vine g., *peret* (Lev. 19:9-10). A description of the practice is found in Ruth 2 where the gleaners are pictured as following the reapers to gather up what is left. Gleaning is limited to cornfields, orchards, and vineyards and may not take place in vegetable gardens. The owner of the field may derive no benefit from the g. nor should he discriminate among or help the gleaners. G. are exempt from the obligation of tithing. Non-Jewish poor were allowed to glean alongside the Jewish poor (*Git.* 59b). The subject is discussed in the talmudic tractate PEAH. The obligation to leave g. applied only to the Land of Israel but was also observed in Babylonia; it was not regarded as binding on Jewish agriculturalists elsewhere.

GNOSTICISM (from Gk. *gnosis* "knowledge"): A term describing the ideas and mystical theories — usually confined to a limited circle of initiates — of a number of sects that arose both within and around Judaism, Christianity, and paganism in the Roman world during the first and second centuries. The beginnings of g., however, seem to be earlier, and some scholars suggest that it originated in Jewish or Samaritan circles influenced by certain oriental ideas. While these sects differed widely from each other in style of behavior and in theories, most shared a number of beliefs. G. distinguished between the Supreme Divine Being and the demiurge, a secondary power responsible for creation and involved in the material world. DUALISM — the belief that the world is ruled by two opposing principles — was characteristic of most gnostic systems as was the tendency to divide the heavenly powers into pairs — male and female, left and right, etc.; the Supreme First Principle was conceived as an all-good Power, whereas the creator-demiurge was considered a lower, fallen and imperfect being. Some Christian gnostics, e.g. Marcion, identified the first principle with the New Testament "God of Love" and the "Creator-God" with the Old Testament Law which they labeled as evil. As against the biblical tradition which regarded creation as essentially good (Gen. 1:31), g. considered the material universe the result of a primordial fall from a state of pure, i.e., spiritual being. The soul too is thought to be in exile in the lower and basically evil material world into which it has fallen and from which it can be redeemed and returned to its celestial home by means of *gnosis* i.e., secret knowledge. The sense of irreconcilable conflict between the sphere of *Pneuma* ("spirit") and the "material" world of creation made for some affinities between g. and Neo-Platonic philosophy. Some of the gnostic sects demonstrated their liberation from the material world (of which morals and the Law form part) and the spiritual "freedom" to which they had attained by theoretical and practical ANTINOMIANISM. The early Church combatted the Christian forms of g. as a dangerous heresy. The Jewish struggle against g. is reflected in liturgical and other regulations directed against the MINIM. However, in spite of its struggle against gnostic heresy, Judaism and Jewish mysticism in particular (see MERKAVAH Mysticism; HEIKHALOT), absorbed certain gnostic themes and ideas. Tendencies of a gnostic character also appeared in medieval KABBALAH e.g. in the ZOHAR and particularly in the esoteric doctrines of Isaac LURIA.

GOD: The Supreme Being; the Creator of the universe; the Judge and Ruler of history; the Supreme Lawgiver.

The existence of G. is presupposed in the Bible from the very first sentence, and no attempt is made to prove it. His power and love are immediately experienced. He is conceived not in philosophical or abstract terms, such as first cause, but in imaginative pictorial ideas such as Father, Shepherd, Judge, and King. Though ideas of G. were present in the civilization in which the Bible came into being, the Israelite conception is unique. All others were based on mythological ideas, so that the gods were conceived to be subject to the laws of natural necessity. In the biblical idea of G., the Supreme Being has no mythological quality whatsoever. He has no body, no relatives, no human needs. He is the sovereign Lord of nature which is completely dependent upon Him. There is no force which is independent of His sovereign will and does not do His bidding. He is completely independent and there are no other divine beings to compete with Him for lordship. This gives rise to the pure MONOTHEISM of the Bible and later literature. There is a constant battle against IDOLATRY which is the substitution of some non-absolute force or entity for the Supreme G. of the Bible. G. and the world are distinct. He is the Creator of the world, and it is completely under His will. He maintains the regularities and lawfulness of nature. Nature is orderly not because of any inherent law, but because the Creator maintains that order. Man experiences the presence and power of God in seemingly contradictory ways. He is majestic, yet kind and compassionate. He punishes those who do wrong, yet He is quick to forgive. He is transcendent, beyond anything in the world; yet His wisdom is the source of human understanding. There is a special relationship between G. and Israel. Israel is G.'s chosen, not because of any special merit which the people of Israel possess, but because of G.'s own act of grace. Through G.'s relation to His people, His relationship to the world is also exhibited. Israel is to be G.'s witness. When Israel falls away from its task of being G.'s people, He sends prophets to admonish and chastise it. Through Israel, the rest of mankind will be brought to recognize G.'s sovereignty. Thus, Israel is the instrument of REDEMPTION. Another aspect of G.'s love for Israel is His activity as a lawgiver to His people. Through REVELATION G. relates Himself to man. The purpose of the Law (TORAH) is to make Israel a holy nation. The G. of the Bible, however, is not a national G.; He is the Lord of all nations. The fate of one people mirrors the universal facts of His kingship and fatherhood. His power and presence are experienced through great historical events like the Exodus from Egypt. Man has been given the freedom to obey or to defy G. When man disobeys, G. metes out His JUSTICE. In the End of Days (see MESSIAH), man will possess a new heart and all the disharmonies of history will be banished. Thus three aspects of G.'s relationship to the world are manifest in the Bible. Through CREATION, G. calls the world into being; through revelation G. speaks to man; and through redemption, G. will sanctify all existence.

Post-biblical literature reflects the beginning of philosophic influence on the formulation of the G. idea in Judaism. This influence came *via* the Greek philosophers whose view of G. was abstract and impersonal. The earliest traces of philosophic formulations in speaking of G. are found in the APOCRYPHA. The books originating in Palestine deal with the concept of G. in substantially traditional terms. Differences stem from the terminology rather than the content of the ideas. In the Alexandrine Apocrypha some change of conception is evident, but even these include works whose theology is a restatement of biblical teachings. In the TARGUM and SEPTUAGINT translation of the biblical books there are evidences of an attempt to avoid ANTHROPOMORPHISM. The writings of PHILO reveal a consistent effort to reinterpret the biblical view of G. in philosophic terms. This is the first attempt to harmonize the biblical and Greek philosophical traditions. His synthesis exerted far-reaching effects on the subsequent history of PHILOSOPHY and theology in the West. Philo placed great stress on G.'s complete transcendence and posited the existence of intermediaries through which G. influences creation. Of special importance is the LOGOS. The personal, direct relationship between G. and man was stressed in the talmudic and midrashic literature. Though the rabbis use circumlocutions for G. in order to increase respect for His holy name (see GOD, NAMES OF) they brought the Divine near to even the humblest heart. They would speak of G. as suffering together with His children, weeping over the destruction of the Temple, and rejoicing over piety and good works, and they would even describe Him as taking part in learned discussions or putting on TEPHILLIN. The rabbis were essentially carrying on the prophetic concept of G., though they expressed themselves in a more popular and picturesque way. As a reaction to the teachings of heretical sects and CHRISTIANITY, the rabbis laid great stress on the unity of G. Thus, the SHEMA was considered the most important confession of faith, and it was incumbent upon all Jews to recite it twice daily. The rabbis were especially careful to repudiate any suggestion that there were two powers (dualism) and insisted that G. has neither father, son, nor brother (*Deut. Rab.* 2). Of special importance in rabbinic literature is G.'s role as the Lawgiver. The *Torah,* which is G.'s gift to Israel, is highly exalted and even described as the purpose and instrument of creation. It is through the study of *Torah* that men know the will of God. The best source for the study of rabbinic theology is the LITURGY, which contains all the basic teachings of the rabbis concerning the Divine Being.

Medieval Jewish thought developed under the influence of the rediscovery and development of Greek philosophy by the Arabs. Jewish theologians reinterpreted their faith in the light of the new philosophy, especially Neo-PLATONISM and ARISTOTELIANISM. The philosophers of the Middle Ages were particularly concerned with such problems as the ATTRIBUTES of G., the relation between Divine foreknowledge and human freedom, and the presence of evil in the world. It was their aim to demonstrate that the biblical and talmudic teachings about G. were in conformity with the results of rational thinking. Thus they held that the existence of G. could be logically proved. Since the Creator is the cause of all bodies, He himself must be beyond all matter. He is free of all human and natural properties. The absolute unity of G. implies the spiritual nature of His essence. For were He not one, He would be many, and multiplicity is characteristic of corporeality; His oneness thus implies His incorporeality. Though G. is abstract and transcendent, He is not inactive. He reveals Himself to His prophets and directs the affairs of creation. Direct biblical expression about G., however, should be understood in a metaphorical sense. The greatest medieval Jewish philosopher, MAIMONIDES, was also the most extreme in stressing G.'s transcendence. He denied that man had the capacity to say anything meaningful about G. The existence of G., it was true, could be proved. But the meaning and nature of this existence were beyond human comprehension. Everything said about G. is allegorical, and all positive ways of describing Him clothe essentially negative statements. Thus, when one says that G. exists, the only real meaning of the statement is that His non-existence is unthinkable. Maimonides is the exponent of the so-called "negative theology" which was then developed in other directions by the mystics. Other thinkers, like JUDAH HA-LEVI, felt the aridity of the abstract formulations of G.'s nature and stressed the experience of the Divine action in history, especially in the crucial events in the annals of Israel. A bold solution of the problem of G.'s power and foreknowledge, and man's free will, is offered by ABRAHAM IBN DAUD. He concludes that G. restricts His omniscience and omnipotence deliberately so as to allow man freedom of choice. Another attempt to overcome the tension between the transcendent, absolutely unique G. of philosophy and the vital, real, and dynamic G. of religious experience was made in the medieval KABBALAH which taught the doctrine of the two aspects of the Godhead: the infinite, inaccessible "Mystery of Hiddenness" and the ten SEPHIROT of Divine manifestation. This profound and audacious conception often came under criticism for harboring the seeds of heretical deviations and, particularly, for coming dangerously close to polytheism.

Contemporary Jewish philosophy reflects the fundamental change in outlook that characterizes modern thought in general. Whereas medieval speculation was concerned with harmonizing revelation and reason (both elements being taken as authoritative), the period of the ENLIGHTENMENT called the authority of revelation into question. The Jewish religion must be authenticated as a manifestation of the human spirit and be shown as significant within the larger framework of thought, be it conceived as universal reason (Hegel), the dialectic of the mind (Kant), or human existence as such (EXISTENTIALISM). The first significant attack on the Jewish conception of G. was made by SPINOZA who denied the medieval attempt to derive the material world from a G. who is wholly transcendent to it, and propounded a thoroughgoing PANTHEISM. MENDELSSOHN taught that the basic ideas of religion — the existence of a personal G. and the immortality of the individual soul — were universal possessions of mankind because of their reasonableness. They need not wait for revelation to be known, since they were manifest at all times and everywhere. Mendelssohn summed up his view in his famous phrase: "Judaism is not a revealed religion, but a revealed law". The rise of Kantianism accentuated the division between theoretical and practical reason. The proofs which Kant adduced to destroy rational theology led to the idea that religion was dependent on ethics and fundamentally an expression of practical reason. Hermann COHEN produced the most impressive synthesis between Kantianism and Judaism. To him the idea of G. is indispensable both to theoretical and to practical reason. It establishes the necessary link between the two spheres by assuring the final realization of man's moral destiny within the natural order of being. The philosophy of Franz ROSENZWEIG is an elaboration of Schelling's positive philosophy combined with modern Existentialism. G., man, and the world are irreducible entities. The task of philosophy is to interpret the interrelation between G., man, and the world. G. and man are united in and through speech. The term "speaking" as used by Rosenzweig means "speaking to a person in all earnestness and devotion". G. speaks to man through revelation. He also calls the world into being through creation. This philosophy plays an important part in the thought of Martin BUBER. G. cannot be known in His essence. He can only be addressed, when man turns to Him in full devotion, in the full power of an "I" addressing a "Thou". Mordecai KAPLAN has been influenced by Naturalism. G. is conceived as a "force" or a "power" within the physical universe which makes for man's SALVATION. ḤASIDIC mysticism, which was based largely on the KABBALAH, at times came close to pantheism but generally remained orthodox. Modern interpretations (Buber, HESCHEL) are influenced by existentialism.

GOD, NAMES OF: N. of G. may be either conceptual (e.g. God, Creator) or proper. The latter sort predominates in ancient literature, but the original significance of such names is not always easily determined. The choice of one name rather than another generally depends on its significance, the occasion, and the specific traditions of the user. BIBLE CRITICISM has taken the two most important biblical N. of G. *YHVH* and *Elohim,* as indicative of two distinct biblical traditions. Of the two names, the Tetragrammaton, consisting of the letters *Yod He Vav He* (יהוה; *YHVH)* is the most frequent in the Bible, and rabbinic tradition considers it the essential name of God. The name seems to be connected with the phrase *ehyeh asher ehyeh* (translated as "I am that I am", Exod. 3:14). Interpreted as denoting eternal existence, the phrase became the symbol of MONOTHEISM. Because of its great holiness, the name was never pronounced ("the Ineffable Name") except once a year by the High Priest in the Holy of Holies on the Day of Atonement. According to a rabbinic tradition, once (or twice) in seven years the sages entrusted to their disciples the pronunciation of the Tetragrammaton, but the original pronunciation is now unknown; it is read rather as ADONAI. *Yah* (cf. Hallelu-yah) is thought to be a shortened form of *YHVH.* In vocalized texts, the four letters are given the pronunciation of the word *adonai,* giving rise to the erroneous hybrid form JEHOVAH in the English translation. Other N. of G. mentioned in the Bible, but classified by the rabbis as "secondary", are *El, Eloha, Elohim* with various suffixes, *Shaddai* (chiefly in Job), and *Zebaoth* (though the Talmud opines that the last is not a name of God but refers to the Hosts of Israel of which God is the Lord). The word *elohim* is also found in a secular sense, referring not only to heathen gods (e.g. Exod. 20:3) but also to human judges (e.g. Exod. 22:7). The rabbis, considering the N. of G. as symbols of His relationship to His creatures, held that *YHVH* expressed His ATTRIBUTE of MERCY, while *Elohim* referred to His attribute of JUSTICE. Both the essential and secondary names of God must be written "in holiness", and once written they must not be erased. To avoid "taking the name of the Lord in vain", the custom developed of pronouncing and sometimes writing *Adonai* as *Ha-Shem* ("the Name") — and even, for sake of assonance, as *Adoshem* — and *Elohim* as *Elokim. Adonai* is usually printed in prayer books as two *Yods* (יי); the prohibition against erasure does not apply to this abbreviation.

Other N. of G., which are descriptive rather than personal names and express Divine attributes (such as *Raḥum,* "Merciful"; *Elyon,* "The Most-High"; *Shaddai,* "The Mighty One"), do not fall under the prohibition against erasure as they can be applied to mortals as well (*Shav.* 35a). According to some authorities, however, (cf. *Tosephta*

Sot. 10a) the word *Shalom* ("peace") can occur as a Divine name, in which case it belongs to the former category. The sanctity attached to the Divine names and the prohibition of the Third Commandment against taking the name of the Lord in vain resulted in a growing disinclination to use the biblical N. of G. and in the Talmudic Period a series of circumlocutions evolved. The most common one, used almost exclusively in midrashic literature, is *Ha-Kadosh Barukh Hu* ("The Holy One, blessed be He") and in Aramaic *Kudesha Berikh Hu,* sometimes expanded into "The Supreme King of kings, the Holy One, blessed be He". Next in popularity and occurring mainly in invocations, is *Ribono shel Olam* ("Master of the Universe"). Also frequent is the name *Ha-Makom* ("the Place"), explained as "He is the place of the world but the world is not His place" and translated as "the Omnipresent". *Ha-Rahman* ("The All-Merciful") is a mishnaic form of the biblical *Rahum* (cf. in the Grace After Meals). Another frequent talmudic designation is the *Shekhinah* — "Divine presence". Philosophical and kabbalistic literature added further designations which, however, were technical terms and mystical symbols (e.g. First Cause, EIN-SOPH) rather than names. The medieval poets too coined many terms and epithets designating God. Esoteric tradition contains references to Divine names composed of 12, 42, and 72 letters, and the kabbalists considered the whole Pentateuch as a series of mystical names of God. This doctrine lent itself to the use of various combinations of Hebrew letters as powerful N. of G. for magical purposes, e.g. in AMULETS.

GODFATHER, see **SANDAK**

GOEL, see **BLOOD AVENGER; REDEMPTION**

GOG AND MAGOG: The anti-Messiah who in the great eschatological battle against the righteous host is to head the forces of evil. The concept is derived from Ezek. 38:2 where "Gog, of the land of Magog, the chief prince of Meshech and Tubal" is to lead a savage horde of nations from the North against Israel. He and his army will be defeated by the hand of the Lord on the mountains of Israel. Though Josephus (*Ant.* I, 6, 1) identifies the Magog mentioned in the Table of Nations (Gen. 10:3) with the land of the Scythians, it is more likely that this figure reflects the historical Gyges, king of Lydia. G. and M. (and not G. of the land of M.) are frequently mentioned in apocalyptic works; they also appear in the Dead Sea Scrolls and are vividly portrayed in talmudic literature where the war against G. and M. is identified with the "messianic wars" preceding the advent of the Messiah. G. and M. will be defeated by God Himself or by the Messiah ben Ephraim. This idea of eschatological warfare against G. and M. is echoed in Christian (e.g. *Rev.* 20:7-9) and Islamic traditions.

GOLAH, see **DIASPORA; EXILE**

GOLDEN CALF, see **CALF, GOLDEN**

GOLDEN RULE: Term applied in all European languages to the statement in the New Testament (*Matt.* 7:12; *Luke* 6:31) "Whatsoever ye would that men should do to you, do ye even so unto them, for this is the law, the prophets". In its negative formulation it is identical with the answer which Hillel gave to the inquiring heathen as being "the whole law" (*Shab.* 31a). Both forms of this rule (which was also enunciated by Confucius in the 5th cent. B.C.E.) should be compared with the positive "Love thy neighbor as thyself" of Lev. 19:18, and with Hillel's own maxim "Love thy fellow creatures" (*Avot* 1:12).

GOLEM (Heb. "shapeless mass"): The word occurs once in the Bible (Ps. 139:16) and there refers to an embryo; in medieval Hebrew it was used in the sense of "formless matter", but later came to mean a robot or mechanical monster magically created when its master infused life into a clay model by inserting one of the mystic names of God under its tongue. The *g.* would then obey the behests of his creator. The *g.* legends were associated with the magical interpretation of the Book of YETZIRAH and its letter-mysticism. In a responsum (no. 93), *Hakham* Tzevi Ashkenazi of Amsterdam (1658-1718) seriously discussed whether a *g.* might be counted as one in the religious quorum of ten, adding that his grandfather, R. Elijah of Chelm, had fashioned such a creature. A great danger, mentioned also in similar non-Jewish legends, was that the *g.* might get out of hand, and this fear agitated the minds both of Elijah of Chelm, and the creator of the most famous *g.* in Jewish legend, R. JUDAH LÖW BEN BEZALEL of Prague. The *g.* was rendered innocuous by removing the source of its animation, the Divine Name. The *g.* of the Prague rabbi acted as his servant, and to ensure its resting on the Sabbath he immobilized it every Friday afternoon. Once he forgot to do so, pursued it to the synagogue where he apprehended it just before the onset of the Sabbath and destroyed it by removing the Divine Name. In Hebrew (cf. *Avot* 5:10) and in colloquial Yiddish the word *g.* designates a stupid person.

GOLUS (*Ashkenazi* pronunciation of *galut* — Heb. for "exile", "banishment"): Term which, especially in its Yiddish usage, refers to life in the DIASPORA, particularly as regards its more degrading aspects of discrimination, humiliation, and danger to life.

GOMEL, BLESSING OF: Benediction of thanksgiving uttered after deliverance from danger. Basing itself upon Ps. 107, the Talmud (*Ber.* 54b) rules that a special blessing of thanksgiving is to be said on being delivered from one of four perils: after crossing the desert or the sea, on being freed from incarceration, or on recovery from a serious illness. It is recited in the synagogue on being called to the Reading of the Law. The blessing thus prescribed is called the blessing of g. from its formula, "Blessed art thou O Lord... who bestows favors (*gomel*) on those unworthy of them". Since the Psalm explicitly mentions thanksgiving "in the assembly of the people" after each of those deliverances, the blessing must be recited publicly and the congregation responds "He who hath bestowed good upon thee, may He bestow further good upon thee". In many congregations the blessing of g. is also recited by women at their first attendance in the synagogue after giving birth.

GOOD AND EVIL: The problem of good and evil is inherent in the doctrine of MONOTHEISM. DUALISM or pluralism can attribute good to one divinity and evil to another. A monotheistic faith, however, is faced with the difficulty that God, in apparently permitting the existence of evil, is either imperfect or not omnipotent. The difference is clearly seen in the change introduced into the liturgy when it quotes Is. 45:7 — possibly as a protest against Zoroastrianism, the prophet refers to God who "maketh peace and createth evil"; the prayer book alters this to "maketh peace and createth all things". It is impossible to speak of a systematic view of the problem in the Bible or the Talmud. As far as the Bible is concerned the view expounded in Genesis seems to be that everything created by God is good (1:31) but man's being endowed with freedom of will and the fact that "the inclination of man's heart is evil from his youth" (8:21) cause evil in the world, thus thwarting the Divine plan. The Book of Job is the one systematic attempt to deal with the problem. It posits two opposing views: that of the friends of Job who say that since God is wholly good, evil must be punishment for wrongdoing, and that of the summation of the book to the effect that God's ways are inscrutable. The Talmud also gives only general indications. "Whatever God does, He does for good" declares R. Akiva (*Ber.* 60b) and what appears to be evil is not necessarily so, since "there is no evil in which there is not good" (*Gen. Rab.* 68). This view is emphasized by the statement that death and the evil inclination are in fact "very good". However the rabbis affirm the existence of evil through the operation of man's bad inclinations (see YETZER TOV AND YETZER RA). They are also exercised by the problem of the prosperity of the wicked and the suffering of the righteous (e.g. *Ber.* 7a) which runs counter to their belief that evil is the wages of sin (see RETRIBUTION). If, however, God created evil, He also created the *Torah* to counteract it (*Kidd.* 30b). Most of the medieval philosophers adopt the Platonic view adumbrated by Philo, that evil is not a positive thing in itself but merely the absence of good, just as darkness is the absence of light. Maimonides adds that evil is but a negation of the positive good, and many evils of man are self inflicted. The mystics postulate a very real existence for evil and propound several solutions to the problem. They suggest that evil was a residue of the Divine or of a primeval world, and also that God created evil in order to challenge man to overcome it. The negation of evil has also been carried on into more recent Jewish theology (cf. Hermann Cohen's "Evil is non-existent. A power of evil exists only in myth"). According to Judaism the motive determines the good or evil nature of an action.

GOSPELS, see **NEW TESTAMENT**

GOSSIP, see **LASHON HA-RA**

GOVERNMENT, PRAYER FOR: The duty to pray for the welfare of the authorities in whatever land Jews happened to live was first stated by the prophet Jeremiah (29:7 — "Seek the peace of the city whither I have caused you to be carried captive, and pray for it unto the Lord") and reinforced by the Mishnah (*Avot* 3:2 "pray for the welfare of the government"). P. for the G. as a regular feature of the synagogue service is first attested to in the 14th cent. The customary formula *ha-noten teshuah* ("He who giveth salvation unto kings") probably originated in Spain. Various changes have been introduced into the wording of the prayer as a result of political and other circumstances, e.g. the change from autocratic monarchies to republican forms of government. In many congregations the prayer, or part of it, is said in the vernacular. It is usually recited on Sabbaths after the Reading of the Law.

GOY (Heb. "people"): Although in the Bible the term is used for any nation including Israel, it subsequently came to mean the non-Jewish nations in general and finally a member of any such nation, i.e., the non-Jew. See GENTILE.

GRACE AFTER MEALS (Heb. *birkat ha-mazon*); The obligation to recite the g. is inferred from the verse "And thou shalt eat, and be satisfied, and bless the Lord thy God for the good land He hath given you" (Deut. 8:10). The halakhic requirement concerning the complete g. applies only to a meal which includes bread. The g. consists of three benedictions: 1) *birkat ha-zan,* thanksgiving to God for the food He has provided; 2) *birkat ha-aretz,* thanksgiving for the gift of the land of Israel; 3) *boneh yerushalayim,* a petition for the rebuilding of Jerusalem. These three blessings formed the core of the g., but the rabbis added a fourth (*ha-tov veha-meitiv*) after the destruction of the Second Temple. In later times, prayers were added for the welfare of the host, for an honorable livelihood, etc. The verses commencing *ha-raḥman* ("The All-Merciful") are a late addition and the number varies according to different rites; Maimonides lists 3, *Maḥzor* Vitry 12, the *Sephardim* 18, the Roman rite 22, and modern *Ashkenazi* custom 9. Special prayers were included for the Sabbath, festivals, *Purim, Ḥanukkah,* and the New Moon. Under certain conditions, an abbreviated form of the g. is recited that corresponds more closely to ancient custom. The g. must be said at the place where the meal has been eaten. If three or more adult males have eaten together, they say g. as a group. One takes the lead by inviting his companions to join in the blessing. The formula of this invitation (*zimmun*) is: "Let us bless Him of Whose food we have eaten". Where there are ten or more males (MINYAN) the words "our God" are introduced into both the invitation and the response. The custom and formula are ancient and according to the Talmud were as old as SIMEON BEN SHETAḤ (Y. *Ber* 7:2). On weekdays, the g. is preceded in some rites by Ps. 137, and on Sabbaths, by Ps. 126. At circumcisions and wedding feasts, poetic interpolations are customary. There is also a special form for recitation in the house of mourners. If certain kinds of fruits or cake only are consumed, a shortened version, consisting of one benediction which contains all the main motifs of g., is used; after all other kinds of food, a still shorter version is recited. Recitation of g. is obligatory where food at least the size of an olive has been consumed. See BENÇAO; BENSHEN.

GRACE BEFORE MEALS: G. before meals consists of one single benediction which varies according to the types of food about to be consumed. For bread it reads: "Blessed... who brings forth bread from the earth" (see BENEDICTIONS) and must be preceded by the washing of the hands, for which the blessing is "Blessed... who hast commanded us concerning the washing of the hands".

GRAVE, see **BURIAL; TOMB**

GREAT ASSEMBLY, see **KENESET GEDOLAH**

GREAT SYNAGOGUE, see **KENESET GEDOLAH**

GREETINGS: The Bible contains a number of examples of formal g., e.g. Laban greets the servant of Abraham with the words "Come, blessed of the Lord" (Gen. 24:11); the Book of Ruth contains both the greeting "The Lord be with you", and the response "The Lord bless thee" (2:4); the longest is the greeting of David to Nabal "All hail and peace to thee, and peace be to thy house, and peace to all thou hast" (I Sam. 25:6). The Talmud goes to great lengths in detailing the etiquette of g. and their reply — who has to greet whom first, when to reply, etc. It states that readiness to be first in greeting is an act of special piety (*Avot* 5:10). Formal g. are customary on Sabbath (*Shabbat shalom,* "a Sabbath of peace" or, among *Ashkenazim, gut Shabbes,* "a good Sabbath"), the conclusion of Sabbath (*shavua tov* or *gut vokh,* "a good week"), festivals (*ḥag sameaḥ,* "a joyous holiday", *Moadim le-simḥah,* "joyous festival days", or among *Ashkenazim, gut yontov,* "a good holiday"), and New Year (*le-shanah tovah tikatev ve-teḥatem,* "May you be inscribed and sealed for a good year"). On performing a religious duty it is also customary to say a greeting (*ḥazak barukh,* "Be strong, blessed" or, among *Ashkenazim, yishar* [*yasher*] *koaḥ,* "May your strength increase"). The most customary greeting is *shalom aleikhem,* "Peace be with you" and to the one who enters a house *barukh ha-ba,* "blessed be he who enters". No g. are made in the house of mourning or on *Av* 9. See also CONGRATULATIONS.

GREGGER (GROGGER): Rattle sounded in the synagogue on *Purim* at each mention of the name of HAMAN in the course of the reading of the Scroll of Esther. The g. dates back to 13th cent. France and Germany. The custom among oriental Jews was to stamp the feet or knock two stones together at the mention of Haman's name but this has generally been superseded by the g. (although not in Persia).

GROOM, see **MARRIAGE**

GUARDIAN AND WARD: A guardian (*apotropos* or *epitropos*) is appointed either by the father prior to his demise or, when necessary, by the court. The ward may be an orphaned minor, a deaf and dumb mute, or an imbecile. A father may appoint whomever he wishes as guardian but a court must choose a responsible adult. The function of the guardian is not to legalize non-binding acts of his ward, but to represent either the deceased parent or the court who appointed him. He acts in the interest of the estate entrusted to him and is fully entitled to do all that he thinks fit in matters pertaining to this charge; he himself is only liable in the event of loss due to negligence or fraud. A partial guardian may be appointed to deal with either the liquid or real assets, with the court making alternative arrangements for other considerations. Full account of the estate is made before it is entrusted to the guardian and both he and the court retain copies of this account. The guardian is responsible for the general welfare, education, and upbringing of his ward, all expenses for which are charged to the estate. Only limited personal expenses needed for direct management of the estate may be used by the guardian.

GUIDE TO THE PERPLEXED, see **MAIMONIDES**

GUILDS: As medieval g., were organized on a Christian basis, Jews were automatically excluded, though rare instances are recorded of Jews being admitted to membership. The institution in many communities during the Middle Ages of the *ḥerem ha-yishuv,* whereby a local community could forbid the entry of newcomers, was the Jewish counterpart of the merchant g., and obtained only in those places where such g. existed. However in its wider connotation of associations for members of a particular trade or calling organized for mutual benefits, the guild had a long Jewish history. Nehemiah refers to the goldsmiths, merchants, and, possibly, the apothecaries who as organized groups assisted in the rebuilding of the walls of Jerusalem (Neh. 3:8, 32). In the description of the synagogue in Alexandria, destroyed by Trajan in 116, the Talmud relates that goldsmiths, silversmiths, metal workers, and weavers sat in separate groups "so that a poor man upon entering could recognize the members of his craft and apply to them for assistance in earning a livelihood" (*Suk.* 5b). In Rome, the Jewish limeburners had their own congregation. In the 19th cent., Jewish craft g., often with their own synagogues, flourished in E. Europe.

GUILT-OFFERING (Heb. *asham*): A g. was brought to the Temple in five instances: (1) In cases of false dealing (Lev. 6:6) where the offering follows upon full restitution; (2) in case of sacrilege (*ibid.* 5:15); (3) in case of intercourse with a betrothed bondwoman (*ibid.* 19:20); (4) in the case of a Nazirite who has become ritually unclean (Num. 6:12); and (5) in the case of a leper on the day of his ritual purification (Lev. 14:12). In addition to these offerings (called *vadday,* "certain", because they are brought in cases of definite obligation), a further g. (called *taluy,* "suspensive") is brought by one in doubt as to whether he has transgressed a biblical law, which if actually trangressed by error would have rendered him liable to bring a sin-offering e.g. if he consumed fats and later had doubts as to whether the fats had been of a forbidden variety.

GUR, see **GER**

GUTMACHER, ELIJAH (1796-1874): Ḥasidic leader and rabbi. A kabbalist and reputed miracle-worker, he held that the Jewish soul could find complete redemption only in the Holy Land. In 1860 he attended the rabbinic assembly convened by R. Tzevi Hirsch Kalischer in order to further the colonization of Palestine, in the cause of which he remained active for the rest of his life.

H

HA LAḤMA ANYA (Aram. "This is the bread of affliction"): Opening words of the introductory paragraph to the SEDER service. The passage is very old, though its exact date and provenance are still under discussion. The text is composite, made up of short sentences uttered by various authors on different occasions, and there are slight variations in the versions of the different rites, some of which precede *H.L.A.* with the words "In haste did ye go out of Egypt". The invitation to all that are hungry to come and partake of the Passover meal presupposes that the Temple is no longer in existence, as does also the conclusion "next year in Jerusalem... next year free".

ḤABAD: A word made up of the initial letters of the Hebrew words for wisdom (*ḥokhmah*), understanding (*binah*), knowledge (*daat*). In the world of ḤASIDISM it designated the school founded by R. SHNEOUR ZALMAN OF LYADY (1747-1813), whose principal and most influential literary work, entitled *Likkutei Amarim* ("Collections of Sayings") but better known as the TANYA (Hebrew word meaning "there is a teaching" with which the work begins), expounds the doctrine of *Ḥ.* Its basic thought is along the ḥasidic themes of DEVEKUT (constant communion with and "clinging" to God), "*hitlahavut*" (intensity of feeling at times bordering on ecstasy) and *kavvanah* i.e., DEVOTION, meditation, and concentration on "inner intent". *Ḥ.*'s insistence on the principle that "there is no place empty of Him" has more than once provoked the charge of PANTHEISM. The element in *Ḥ.* which distinguishes it from other ḥasidic schools is its emphasis on the importance of intellectual effort in religious striving. The "upper" SEPHIROT — the powers of contemplation, analysis, and understanding—must rule and guide the "lower" emotional impulses. The result of such intellectual effort ought to be an intensification rather than weakening of the emotional aspects of prayer and religious effort. Partly through its emphasis on the "systematizing" and organizational aspects of religious work and partly due to a succession of gifted leaders, *Ḥ.* Ḥasidism (as expressed in the LIUBAVICHER Movement) continued to win adherents even when other ḥasidic schools began to weaken. Not content with being a peculiar form of ḥasidic thought and piety, *Ḥ.* became a dedicated missionary movement, active in many parts of the world and attempting to counter the slackening of Jewish life by founding schools and orphanages, distributing literature and promoting study groups and religious festivals.

HABAKKUK: Prophet of the 7th cent. B.C.E.; author of the eighth book of the Minor Prophets. Nothing is known of his life or person. In vivid language he foretold the rise of the Chaldeans to the position of a dominant world power, the ferocity of their military campaigns, and the unbridled cruelty of their violent deeds. His prophecy actually dates from 626 B.C.E., when the "Chaldeans" conquered Nineveh, and under Nebuchadnezzar defeated the Egyptians at Carchemish (605 B.C.E.) and invaded Judah two years later. The perennial problem of why an omnipotent and all-merciful God should allow the rule of evil (in the form of the new Babylonian empire) to persist is poignantly discussed in chap. 1:1-4. Yet the prophet is consoled by his apocalyptic conviction of the ultimate doom of the wicked. Moreover he was assured "the just shall live by his faith" (2:4), a maxim that was seized upon by the Talmud (*Mak.* 24a) as the quintessence of the entire Bible. A Hebrew PESHER on the book was discovered among the DEAD SEA SCROLLS.

ḤABER, see **ḤAVER**

ḤABIB, see IBN ḤAVIV

ḤAD GADYA (Aram. "one kid"): Aramaic poem recited at the close of the Passover *Seder* service. Resembling a German folk song and composed on the pattern known to English readers from "The house that Jack built", it was written in the 15th cent. and may have been included in the HAGGADAH in order to amuse the children who were kept up late. It is not found in the *Sephardi* or Yemenite traditions. Literally, its theme is the retribution meted out for evil deeds, and various allegorical interpretations have been advanced by commentators. According to some it symbolizes the fate of the Jewish people among the nations; others have suggested that it describes the experiences of the soul in the human body from birth to judgment day.

HADAD: The chief god in the pantheon of the

Arameans; god of storm, thunder, and rain; identical with BAAL. Occurs also in personal names (cf. Ben-H.).

ḤADASH (Heb. "new"): Technical halakhic term for the new grain ripening in spring, which could not be eaten until "a sheaf of the first fruits" from the new harvest (OMER) was offered by the priests in the Temple on the second day of Passover, *Nisan* 16. Since the destruction of the Temple and the suspension of the *omer*-offering, eating *ḥ.* has been forbidden through *Nisan* 16, but the prohibition lapses automatically on the eve of the 17th.

HADASSAH: Another name for ESTHER (Est. 2:7).

HADASSI, JUDAH BEN ELIJAH (12th cent.): Karaite scholar. Born in Edessa in Asia Minor (hence his name), he was a member of the ascetic group known as the AVELEI-ZION. His encyclopedic work *Eshkol ha-Kopher* ("The Cluster of Camphor") gives a rhymed account of Karaite literature and scholarship from the 8th to the 12th cents.

HADLAKAT NEROT, see **KINDLING OF LIGHTS**

ḤAG, see **FESTIVAL**

ḤAG SAMEAḤ (Heb. "joyful festival"): Customary modern Hebrew greeting on religious holidays; many, however, prefer the more classical MOADIM LE-SIMḤAH.

HAGBAHAH (Heb. "elevating"): Raising of the open *Torah*-scroll in the synagogue so that the congregation may see the writing and testify, "This is the Law which Moses placed before the children of Israel". In the *Ashkenazi* rite *h.* takes place after the Reading of the Law and is immediately followed by GELILAH. Among *Sephardim h.* is performed by an honorary official or members of an honorary brotherhood (*levantodores*) before the Reading of the Law.

HAGGADAH, see **AGGADAH**

HAGGADAH (Heb. "narration"), **PASSOVER:** The set form in which the story of the EXODUS must be told on the first two nights of PASSOVER (in Israel, first night only) as part of the ritual *Seder* ("order") for those nights. The term *H.* is now used for the entire *Seder* ritual as well as for the special books containing that ritual. The obligation to relate the story of the Exodus, as well as the name *H.*, is derived from Exod. 13:8, "and thou shalt tell thy son in that day, saying: it is because of that which the Lord did for me when I came forth out of Egypt". The obligation of *H.* is to be observed not by the mere reading of the relevant Bible passages (as the Karaites do), but through the midrashic exposition and interpretation of these passages. This should be done in the form of an answer to questions posed by a child (to which the Bible refers frequently in this connection, e.g. Exod. 13:14). The questions were already standardized in the Mishnah (*Pes.* 10) in the form of the MAH NISHTANAH ("why is this night different", etc.); today there are four questions put by the youngest present and referring to the eating of MATZAH (unleavened bread), MAROR (bitter herbs), vegetables dipped in salt water or vinegar, and to the custom of eating in a reclining posture. In Temple days, the first question used to refer to the eating of the Passover sacrifice. When no children participate, the questions are read by an adult. The reply, which is the *H.* proper, is also given nowadays in a set form, beginning with *avadim hayinu* ("We were slaves to Pharaoh in Egypt") and containing details of the precept enjoining the narration of the story of the Exodus, the *baraita* dealing with the four types of sons, a detailed commentary on Deut. 26:5-8 (probably chosen because it contains a particularly concise account of the Egyptian slavery and the Exodus), an account and midrashic exposition of the Ten Plagues, and the thanksgiving hymn *dayyenu*. This is followed by HALLEL, the first two chapters of which (Ps. 113 and 114) are recited before the meal, the rest after. Originally, the meal preceded both the questions and the answers, as is evident from the order in the Mishnah and from the content of the questions. The *Seder* contains elements in addition to the *H.* proper. As any meal on a Sabbath or festival night, it opens with the KIDDUSH, and concludes with GRACE. A number of specific prescriptions must be observed; the eating of the paschal lamb (in Temple days), *matzah*, and *maror*. The Bible specifically prescribes that the paschal sacrifice be consumed by a company previously invited (Exod. 12:4); hence the corporate character of the *Seder*. Other features of the *Seder* derive from the fact that this festive meal was patterned on the ancient Greco-Roman banquet (in the style customary at the time of the Mishnah) so as to emphasize that on this night all Jews were free men. At such banquets it was usual for the guests to begin by drinking wine and eating appetizers such as vegetables dipped in vinegar or a fruit sauce (from which the HAROSET may have derived); then the guests would enter the dining room proper where they would partake of the main meal of bread and meat while reclining on couches; this again was accompanied by the drinking of wine. Lastly, after the meal, wine would be served once again. These three separate occasions on which wine was imbibed during such a banquet, with the addition of the extra cup required for the *kiddush*, were the source for the ruling that four cups of wine are obligatory during the *Seder*: the first for *kiddush*, the second just before the meal and after the *H.* has been concluded; the third, after Grace; the fourth after the conclusion of the *hallel*. A dispute as to whether a fifth cup was obligatory led to the custom of filling but not drinking still another cup of wine, subsequently called the cup of Elijah (see CUPS). Other *Seder* customs, too, such as the reclining position taken during the meal or the eating of vegetables dipped in salt water before the meal (*karpas*) reflect the same historical background, but all customs and rituals were in the course of time invested with symbolic meanings, expressive of the spiritual significance of the *Seder*. A number of BENEDICTIONS are recited in the course of the *Seder*, such as the benediction over wine (four times), over the *matzah*, *maror*, and vegetables, the GEULLAH after the conclusion of the *H.* and, finally, the blessing after the *Hallel*. With the conclusion of the obligatory part of the *H.* various songs of folk origin, e.g. ḤAD GADYA, are customarily sung. Among certain oriental communities a further embellishment is provided by the dramatic enactment of parts of the Exodus story by the males present. The *H.* is one of the most frequently printed Hebrew books. Many *Haggadot* (printed or handwritten) are beautifully illustrated and ornamented. In recent times some groups have produced "modern" *Haggadot* which omit part of the traditional formula and add new material, such as references to Jewish national revival. *Haggadot* of this type have been produced in Israel, especially by *kibbutzim*; the Israel Army has also published its own *H.* which aims at combining the customs of different communities.

HAGGAI: Hebrew prophet of the post-Babylonian era and contemporary of ZECHARIAH: author of the tenth book of the Minor Prophets consisting of four addresses delivered in 520 B.C.E. during the reign of Darius I. This was a time of widespread political convulsions to which H. gave a messianic interpretation, teaching that the time was now ripe for the rebuilding of the Temple. To the deprecatory remarks of the older generation the prophet retorted that the glory of the Second Temple would outshine that of the First. His rhetoric was effective, and the work of rebuilding was resumed under the leadership of Zerubbabel.

ḤAGIGAH (Heb. "festival offering"): Obligatory animal sacrifice brought by every worshiper to the Temple on each of the three PILGRIM FESTIVALS. It had to be not less in value than two silver pieces. The lame, blind, sick, or aged, and those incapable of going up to Jerusalem on foot were exempt from the obligation to bring the *ḥ*. After the prescribed parts (Lev. 3:15) had been offered on the altar the remainder was consumed by the person who had brought the sacrifice. In order that the paschal lamb, consumed on the first night of Passover, be eaten to fulfill the religious commandment only, and not to assuage hunger, a special *ḥ*. was brought on the eve of Passover and served as the main course of the evening meal before the paschal lamb was served.

ḤAGIGAH (Heb. "Festival Offering"): Last tractate in the Mishnah order MOED. It deals with the festival duties, pilgrimage to Jerusalem, rejoicing, and the *ḥ*-offering. This last subject also leads into a discussion of the degrees of ritual sanctity and purity. The second chapter of the *gemara* on *Ḥ*. is a major source of information on ancient rabbinic MYSTICISM.

HAGIOGRAPHA (Gk. "holy writings"): Term referring to all the biblical writings (Heb. *ketuvim*) which are classed neither as *Torah* (Pentateuch) nor as *Neviim* (Prophets). There are 11 such books: PSALMS, PROVERBS, JOB, the Five SCROLLS (SONG OF SONGS, RUTH, LAMENTATIONS, ECCLESIASTES, ESTHER), DANIEL, EZRA, NEHEMIAH, CHRONICLES. See BIBLE.

ḤAGIZ: Family of Palestinian scholars. 1) *JACOB Ḥ*. (1620-74), author of several halakhic works, was head of the *Bet Yaakov yeshivah* in Jerusalem, where NATHAN OF GAZA was one of his pupils. He sharply opposed SHABBETAI TZEVI's messianic pretensions. 2) *MOSES Ḥ*. (1672-c.1760), son of (1), was a prolific author and an ardent opponent of the Sabbataian heresy. He lived in Europe for some time, and in Amsterdam took part in ḤAKHAM TZEVI Ashkenazi's campaign against Nehemiah ḤAYYUN. Later he returned to Palestine and settled in Safed.

HAHAM, see ḤAKHAM

HAI GAON (939-1038): Last GAON of the academy at Pumbedita, which under his direction reached the zenith of its fame. A son of SHERIRA Gaon, H. was appointed AV BET DIN in 986 and became *gaon* in 998 after his father's retirement. H. wrote in Hebrew and Arabic on philosophical, exegetical, and philological problems, and also composed halakhic works and liturgical compositions. The number of his responsa to queries from all parts of the Jewish world runs into the thousands, and he was generally regarded as "the last of the *geonim* in time, but the first in eminence".

HA-KADOSH BARUKH HU, see GOD, NAMES OF

ḤAKHAM (or **HAHAM**, Heb. "sage", "wise man"): Originally used in a general, descriptive sense (e.g. in the Book of PROVERBS) the term subsequently became a specific title. In the Tannaitic Period the office indicated by the title *ḥ*. was ranked third in the SANHEDRIN, after the *nasi* (president), and the *av bet din* (head of the law court) (*Hor.* 13b). In *Sephardi* communities the title is given to fully ordained rabbis.

ḤAKHAM BASHI (Heb. and Turkish "chief sage"): Under Turkish rule, the title accorded a chief rabbi who was recognized by the government as the representative of the Jewish community (also for leading provincial rabbis). This title was borne by the chief rabbis of Turkey and Egypt and by the *Sephardi* chief rabbi of Palestine until 1918.

ḤAKHAM TZEVI (real name, Tzevi Hirsch Ashkenazi; c. 1660-1718): Rabbi and talmudic scholar. Born in Moravia, he studied in Salonica where he adopted *Sephardi* ways and customs. In 1710 he was appointed rabbi of the *Ashkenazi* community in Amsterdam but had to leave in 1714 as a result of quarrels with his own as well as the Portuguese community. His clash with the latter community and its rabbi Solomon Ayllon arose in connection with the visit of the Sabbataian adventurer Nehemiah Ḥayyun. Ḥ.T. was a stern and uncompromising character, and his career — like that of his son Jacob Emden — was marked by conflicts and quarrels.

HAKHNASAT KALLAH (Heb. "bringing in a bride" i.e., under the wedding canopy): The custom of assisting a poor girl to be suitably provided for on the occasion of her marriage. From a passage in the Talmud (*Suk.* 49b; see Rashi *in loco*), it appears that the essential virtue of this good deed lay in the secret manner in which it was performed, so that the bride should not be put to shame. *H.K.* is ranked as one of the few good deeds which takes precedence even over the study of the *Torah* (*Meg.* 3b). During the Middle Ages and up to the present day special societies have existed for the purpose of *H.K.* The inclusion of this virtuous custom in the prayer book version of Mishnah *Peah* 1:2, as being one of those acts "the fruits of which a man enjoys in this world, while the stock remains for him in the world to come", has no basis in rabbinical literature but is an example of the great value popularly attached to this act of charity.

HAKHNASAT OREḤIM, see **HOSPITALITY**

HAKKAPHOT (Heb. "circumambulations"): Processional circuits made on various ceremonial occasions. The term *h.* is applied to: (1) Circuits around the almemar in the synagogue: (a) during Tabernacles, a single circuit is made daily (except on Sabbath) with the worshipers carrying the four species and accompanied by the singing of the day's *piyyut*, in commemoration of the daily festival circuit around the altar in the Temple (*Suk.* 4:5); (b) on Hoshana Rabbah, there are seven such *h.* recalling the Temple custom and the seven circuits around Jericho (Josh. 6:15); (c) on Simḥat Torah (Ḥasidim outside Israel commence on *Shemini Atzeret*), male members of the congregation, led by children carrying flags, participate in carrying all the Scrolls from the ark in seven (or more) *h.*; (d) at the dedication of a new synagogue, seven *h.* are made with the scrolls. (2) Circuits at the cemetery: (a) the *Sephardim* make seven *h.* around the grave prior to burial; (b) it was formerly a custom to pray for the sick while circumambulating the cemetery; (c) in consecrating a new cemetery, an extension to an existing one, or a cemetery wall, seven *h.* are made, to the recitation of appropriate biblical passages; (3) Circuits at a wedding; in many communities the bride is led around the bridegroom three (or seven) times.

HALAKHAH (Heb. "law"): That part of Jewish literature, stemming especially from the talmudic and later periods, which deals with religious, ethical, civil, and criminal law. In a wide sense it may be defined as everything in Jewish writing which is not aggadah. Where the term is used in a strict sense, it may mean the abstract formulation of Jewish law, as opposed to Midrash which is always presented together with the biblical verse from which it is derived. The origin of the word is probably Aramaic and it occurs frequently in the Targums as the translation for *mishpat* ("rule", "law") and other related words. Until recently it has generally been connected with the root which means "road", and thus, subsequently, "custom", "law", i.e., the proper "path" in which one must walk. Recently, however, it has been suggested that it may be related to the tax term *helekh* (Ezra 4:13). In ancient Babylonian and Aramaic documents a land tax is called *halakhah.* Thus the term *halakhah* (*regula*, fixed rule) may have its origin in the name of the fixed land tax, the implied meaning being something fixed and permanent, a principle of justice, or a statement of law (in contrast to case law). And, indeed, although Judaism recognizes a constant development in the *h.*, its traditional basic conception is that of laws deriving from Sinai and even having primordial existence. The plural, *halakhot,* is often used to refer to a collection of laws. The *h.* itself recognizes several categories of authority, the highest being those laws which find explicit mention in the Five Books of Moses. Next in importance are those laws which are derived from an interpretation of the written text of the *Torah* by means of certain principles of interpretation called *middot* ("rules"; see Hermeneutics). Concomitantly there are oral traditions considered also as stemming from the Sinaitic revelation, but which cannot be obtained by interpretation of the written text. Some of these, however, find mention in the Prophets and Hagiographa, and often occur in translations of the Pentateuch, such as Targum Onkelos and the Septuagint. Below these two categories are those laws which enjoy only "rabbinic" authority, being in the main later enactments decreed by the authorities of a given time to provide for new situations of life or to form a "fence" for the preservation of pentateuchal law. The lowest category comprises those laws which derive only from CUSTOM, itself considered a part of Jewish law. The differentiation between pentateuchal and rabbinic law is more a delineation of essence than of time. Many laws of only "rabbinic" authority are considered almost as old as Sinai, and many are already mentioned in the Prophets and Hagiographa. Laws which find explicit mention in the Pentateuch are considered part of the WRITTEN LAW. All others go by the name of ORAL LAW. Opinion is divided as to whether a "new" law derived from an interpretation of Scripture may truly be termed pentateuchal. According to Maimonides, those laws deriving from the halakhic principles of interpretation may be termed pentateuchal only where a tradition exists that they were part of the Oral Law given to Moses at Sinai. Otherwise they are called *divrei sopherim* ("words of the Scribes", or "rabbinic"). Naḥmanides, however, considers both as part of the Written Law. Many rabbinic laws are also connected to scriptural verses, but this connection is considered to be no more than an artificial ASMAKHTA. Rabbinic law, even though secondary to biblical law, can upon occasion cancel biblical law. The rabbis are considered empowered to abrogate even the explicit law of Scripture in all matters of money or property, if they deem it necessitated by the exigencies of the case. This rabbinic right comes under the category of *hephker bet din hephker* ("the decree of the court can render property ownerless"). Even biblical religious law can be overruled where rabbinic enactment is limited to the negative aspect of prohibiting its performance, such as the prohibition against blowing the *shophar* on the New Year if it falls on a Sabbath. More than one tradition of what constituted "extra-biblical" law existed during the Second Temple Period. The strongest was the Pharisaic, which consequently became the only form of post-Temple Judaism. A second tradition was the Sadducean, adhered to mostly by priestly and aristocratic groups. A third was the Essene tradition, probably identical with that of the Judean Desert sect. The Samaritan tradition may be considered a fourth. Collections of this "extra-biblical" law were probably begun during the Second Temple Period, definite reference being made to the Sadducean *Sepher Gezerata* ("Book of Decrees"). Pharisaic collections of such laws were all oral, it being considered forbidden to put these in writing. These collections were also probably commenced during the Second Temple Period, but they did not begin to receive the form in which they were later known until the conscious formulation of the Oral Law in the MISHNAH, a task begun at Yavneh following the destruction of the Temple. The Mishnah represents the halakhic endeavors of several generations of scholars, which received final and definite form at the hands of R. Judah Ha-Nasi toward the end of the 2nd cent. C.E. The teachers of the Mishnah go by the name of *tannaim* and the TANNA leaving the greatest imprint on the "literary" form of the Oral Law was R. Akiva. His teachings were handed down in various traditions by his four chief disciples — R. Meir, R. Judah, R. Yose, and R. Simeon. The primary work of R. Judah Ha-Nasi was in selecting and arranging the laws from previous collections to form the definitive Mishnah. The Mishnah, then, is the prime literary formulation of the Oral Law, and for many generations it continued to be taught orally, and was only committed to writing long after its compilation. It was not meant, however, to be a compilation of completely binding law, for it contains many conflicting *halakhot*. Its prime purpose was to give an orderly presentation of the *h.* as taught in the various academies, serving as a textbook of instruction rather than a code or manual of legal decision. A parallel work to the Mishnah was the TOSEPHTA which included explanatory tannaitic instruction supplementing that of the Mishnah. The Mishnah itself became the chief instrument for instruction in both Palestinian and Babylonian academies. The post-mishnaic teachers, known as AMORAIM, articulated various rules for deriving the binding law from the Mishnah, and also expanded its doctrines in many ways. The teachings of the *amoraim* became the basis for the compilation of the two TALMUDS, one in Palestine (edited c. 400) and the other in Babylonia (edited c. 500). The Amoraic Period was followed by that of the SAVORAIM followed by that of the *geonim* (see GAON). The *geonim* originated the responsa form of halakhic writing and did much to complete the expansion of *h.* However, at all times from then on, the Talmud was the one work to which reference had to be made for authority. Since the Talmud is not in the form of a CODE, it was not long before orderly arrangements of talmudic law began to be compiled. The earliest such were the *Halakhot Pesukot* and *Halakhot Gedolot* of the Gaonic Period, followed by the codification of Isaac Alfasi. The greatest code was that of Maimonides, which was completed a thousand years after the Mishnah. Later efforts culminated in the *Shulḥan Arukh* of Joseph Karo in the 17th cent., which — with the addition of the *Mappah* of Moses Isserles — is still the standard basic reference book in Jewish law.

HALAKHOT GEDOLOT (Heb. "Great Laws"): Codification of rabbinic law dating from the Gaonic Period. Its author, R. Simeon Kayyara (8th cent.), drew on the HALAKHOT PESUKOT and other early codifications. In many cases *H.G.* follows the tradition of the academy of SURA and was therefore highly regarded there. It was the best-known halakhic digest until the appearance of Alfasi's code, and the first to enumerate the 613 PRECEPTS.

HALAKHOT PESUKOT (Heb. "Decided Laws"): Earliest halakhic codification after the TALMUD. Its author, R. YEHUDAI Gaon, summarized the conclusions of the Talmud while omitting the discussions, and thus created the model for a new type of halakhic digest. The Aramaic original of this work has recently been discovered and published.

HALBERSTAMM, ḤAYYIM (1793-1876): Talmudic scholar and ḥasidic leader. Known as the "*rebbe* of Sanz" (where he was the communal rabbi from 1830), his enthusiastic habits of prayer and charity drew many admirers. His public condemnation (1869) of the ostentatious way of life led by the ḥasidic rabbis of the RUZHIN-Sadagora dynasty resulted in a prolonged conflict among Ḥasidim.

ḤALITZAH, see **LEVIRATE MARRIAGE**

ḤALLAH (Heb.): That part of the dough separated out as a gift for the priest (Num. 15:7-21). Any dough consisting of the flour of wheat, barley, spelt, oatmeal, or maize, and no less in volume than approximately three pounds twelve ounces becomes liable for *ḥ.* at the conclusion of kneading. The amount to be separated out is one twenty-fourth of the "dough of the householder", or one forty-eighth of the "dough of the baker". *Ḥ.* partakes of the same status and law as the HEAVE-OFFERING (*terumah*) and was originally binding only in Israel. In order that the precept not be forgotten, however, the rabbis ordained its observance throughout the Diaspora and for all time. In the course of time, the separated portion could no longer be given to the priest, since after the destruction of the Temple he was precluded from observing the laws of ritual purity which alone would allow him to eat the sacred portion, and it was therefore burnt. Since it is usually the woman who bakes in the home, the precept of *ḥ.* is enjoined particularly upon her (*Shab.* 2:7) and a special blessing is prescribed for the occasion. The loaves used for Sabbath and festival meals are called *ḥallot,* since their preparation provides the housewife with the opportunity to perform the duty of separating out the *ḥ.* portion.

ḤALLAH (Heb. "Dough-Offering"): Tractate in the Mishnah order ZERAIM. Its four chapters, with *gemara* in the Palestinian Talmud, deal with the laws concerning the separation of the HALLAH.

HALLEL (Heb. "praise"): Name given to a group of psalms (113-118) recited in the synagogue after the Morning Service on the three PILGRIM FESTIVALS and on ḤANUKKAH. The custom originated in Temple times when *H.* was recited during the offering of the pilgrims' sacrifices, on Passover Eve, while the paschal lambs were being slaughtered, and again that night when they were eaten during the *Seder* (see HAGGADAH). Talmudic sources indicate different manners of reciting the *H.*, either antiphonically, with the reader and congregation chanting alternate verses, or by the reader reciting aloud the entire *H.* with the congregation responding *hallelujah* after each verse. Among *Ashkenazim* it is usual for the congregation to recite each chapter silently, and the reader to repeat the conclusions aloud; but some passages are sung jointly. The latter verses of Ps. 118 are read twice to preserve the symmetry that marks the first part of the psalm. In some congregations, the *H.* is also recited on Passover Eve in synagogue (and it is read again as part of the *Seder*). From the second day of Passover on (outside the Land of Israel, from the third day) an abbreviated *H.* (omitting the first parts of Ps. 115 and 116) is used. This shorter version ("Half *H.*") is also recited on the New Moon (*H.* was not read in ancient Israel on this occasion and is hence not obligatory). A BENEDICTION is recited before the reading of *H.* (though not on Passover Eve) and after it; authorities differ as to whether the blessing should be recited or omitted on the New Moon. On *Purim* no *H.* is read because according to the Talmud the reading of the Scroll of Esther takes its place. In most synagogues in the State of Israel today, *H.* is read on the Day of Independence (though generally without the benediction). On the Feast of Tabernacles the worshipers hold the LULAV and ETROG in their hand during *H.* and shake them while reciting Ps. 118:1-4, 25, and 29. It is customary for the congregation to stand during the recitation of *H.* The rabbis referred to Ps. 113-118 as the "Egyptian *H.*" after the reference to the Exodus in Ps. 114, and they called Ps. 136 the "Great *H.*".

HALLELUJAH (Heb. "praise the Lord"): Liturgical exclamation occurring at the beginning and end of many psalms; in the Talmudic Period it also served as a congregational response during the recitation of the Great HALLEL. The word has also become an inseparable part of the Christian tradition of praise and worship.

ḤALUKKAH (Heb. "distribution"): Financial support given from the end of the 18th cent. on to pious *Ashkenazi* Jews in the four "holy cities" of Jerusalem, Hebron, Safed, and Tiberias. From the beginning of Second Temple times, Diaspora Jewry sent assistance to Jerusalem (Ezra 1:6; 25:33) and the custom continued at all periods of Jewish settlement in the Holy Land. Thus in the Mishnaic Period, leading rabbis traveled extensively to collect money for the Palestinian academies; *sheliḥei tziyyon* ("emissaries of Zion") were sent abroad with a similar object in amoraic and gaonic times; while in 1623 Isaiah HOROWITZ, *Ashkenazi* rabbi of Jerusalem, organized fixed help from communities in Central Europe (see also MEIR BAAL HA-NES). The modern concept of *ḥ.* dates from the ḥasidic immigration of 1777. The 19th cent. saw the proliferation in the four cities of small communities (*kolelim*) which distributed the money collected abroad. By 1913 — when 80% of the *Ashkenazi* communities in Jerusalem lived on *ḥ.* — these were 29 *kolelim* e.g. *kolel* Austria-Galicia, *kolel* Holland-Germany, *kolel* Pinsk. Support from Europe came to an end with World War II, but Orthodox Jews in the U.S. still contribute considerable funds to maintain pious Jews in the Land of Israel who devote themselves to rabbinical studies.

HA-MAKOM YENAḤEM (Heb. "May God comfort you"): Opening words of the traditional formula of consolation addressed to mourners before they leave the cemetery after a burial. Visitors to a house of MOURNING during the SHIVAH use the same formula upon taking leave of the mourners.

HAMAN: Chief minister of King Ahasuerus of Persia. As related in the Book of ESTHER, he secured a royal decree for the destruction of the Jews, but his scheme was frustrated by Esther. H. and his sons died on the gallows he had prepared for Mordecai, Esther's cousin. H. is the central object of scorn in the celebration of the holiday of PURIM and his name is traditionally greeted with derisive interruptions of the synagogal reading of the Book of Esther. H. is identified as a descendant of Agag the Amalekite and his name has become synonymous with the practice of Jew-baiting. Scholars are divided as to the historicity of the story.

HA-MAVDIL (Heb. "He who distinguishes"): Hymn recited on the conclusion of the Sabbath and marking the differentiation between the holy Sabbath day and the secular week. Its authorship has been ascribed to the Spanish rabbi Isaac ben Judah Ibn Ghayyat (c. 1030-1089). It may have originally been written for the Day of Atonement *Neilah* Service. See HAVDALAH.

ḤAMETZ, see **LEAVEN**

ḤAMIN, see **CHOLENT**

ḤAMISHAH ASAR BE-AV, see **AV, FIFTEENTH OF**

ḤAMISHAH ASAR BI-SHEVAT, see **NEW YEAR FOR TREES**

HAMMURABI: Babylonian king, conqueror of Sumer and Akkad (19th or 18th cent. B.C.E.). An identification of H. with the biblical Amraphel is now generally rejected. His collection of laws, engraved on a large stele, was discovered in 1902. Comparative study of the Code of H. and the laws of Exod. 21-23 has revealed certain resemblances in style and subject matter, but the differences, stemming from separate social backgrounds and religious outlooks, are even more striking. In general the Babylonian code tends to be more utilitarian, secular, and cruel than the biblical; for instance, sons were to receive the death penalty for the crimes of their fathers, and whereas biblical law forbids the return of runaway slaves to their masters, H.'s penalty for those aiding such fugitives was death.

HA-MOTZI, BLESSING OF, see **GRACE BEFORE MEALS**

HANANEL BEN ḤUSHIEL (c. 990-c. 1055): Rabbinic scholar; called "Gaon" by later generations. Born in Kairouan, he succeeded his father as head of the academy there. His concise and lucid commentary on the Talmud — one of the first to be written — was much used by later commentators; it often compares the Babylonian and Palestine Talmuds. Of his commentary on the Bible, only citations in other works have survived. H. is considered as marking the transition from the Gaonic Period to that of the medieval rabbis (RISHONIM).

HANANIAH: Name of various persons in biblical and rabbinic history. 1) *H. BEN AZUR*; contemporary and opponent of JEREMIAH, branded by the latter as a "false prophet" (Jer. 28). 2) *H. BEN HEZEKIAH*; *tanna* in the 1st cent. C.E. He prevailed upon his colleagues to admit the Book of Ezekiel into the biblical canon. 3) *H.* the nephew of R. JOSHUA; *tanna* in the 2nd cent. C.E. He lived in Babylonia and was censured by R. Judah Ha-Nasi for arrogating to himself the strictly Palestinian right of fixing the CALENDAR. 4) *H. BEN JUDAH*; head of the academy of Pumbedita (10th cent.), father of SHERIRA Gaon.

HANANIAH, MISHAEL, AND AZARIAH: Three companions of DANIEL at Nebuchadnezzar's court (also known as Shadrach, Meshach, and Abed-Nego). According to Dan. 3, they were thrown into a fiery furnace for refusing to worship the king's image, and were miraculously saved. The *Prayer of Azariah* and *The Song of the Three Children* in the furnace occur in an apocryphal addition to the Septuagint version of the Book of Daniel, and thence passed into the Catholic Bible.

HANGING: H. was never a method of CAPITAL PUNISHMENT among Jews. According to the rabbis (*Sanh.* 75b) it was used only as a posthumous ignominy in conformity with the verse "and if a man have committed a sin worthy of death and he is put to death" — then — "thou shalt hang him upon the tree". The victim was however to be buried the same day, and it was strictly prohibited to leave the body suspended overnight (Deut. 21:22-3). The rabbis held that this posthumous ignominy applied only to one executed for blasphemy or idolatry. The condemned was hanged by his hands and not by the neck (*Sanh.* 46b). The body of a woman was not to be hanged.

ḤANINA BEN DOSA (1st cent.): Palestinian *tanna*; known for the ascetic simplicity of his life and for his saintliness. Many miracles were ascribed to him, and his prayer and intercession (especially for the sick, cf. *Ber.* 34b) were considered of particular efficacy.

ḤANINA BEN TERADYON (2nd cent.): Palestinian *tanna*; head of the academy at Sikni in Galilee, arrested for teaching *Torah* after it had been forbidden by the Romans. One of the TEN MARTYRS, he was wrapped in a Scroll of the Law and burned alive. His daughter BERURIAH, was the wife of R. MEIR.

HA-NOTEN TESHUAH, see **GOVERNMENT, PRAYER FOR**

ḤANUKKAH (Heb. "dedication"): Festival commemorating the rededication of the Second Temple by JUDAH THE MACCABEE on *Kislev* 25, 165 B.C.E., the third anniversary of its desecration by Antiochus Epiphanes. The concluding sentence of the special prayer for *Ḥ.* (AL HA-NISSIM) inserted in the *amidah* and Grace after Meals, "And thereupon Thy children came into the oracle of Thy house... kindled lights in Thy holy courts, and appointed these eight days of *Ḥ.* to give thanks and praises unto Thy great Name", accords with the statement in I Macc. 4:59: "And Judah and his brethren and the whole congregation of Israel ordained that the days of the dedication of the altar should be kept in their seasons from year to year for eight days from the 25th day of *Kislev*". Talmudic legend (*Shab.* 21b), in a poetic embellishment of the historical reason, states that the festival was instituted for eight days because the pure oil found in the Temple, though sufficient for one day only, miraculously burnt for eight days until new supplies could be provided; in fact, the length of the festival was probably determined by analogy to the eight day festival of Tabernacles (II Macc. 10). The main feature of the celebration is the kindling of the eight-branched candelabrum (*menorah*) from a light placed in a ninth socket (*shammash*), followed almost everywhere by the singing of the MAOZ TZUR hymn (originally in the *Ashkenazi* rite only). *Sephardim* also recite Psalm 30. The lights are inserted on successive nights incrementally from right to left, but the actual lighting is from left to right i.e., beginning with the most recent addition. The view of the School of Hillel that one light is kindled the first night and one successively added every following night prevailed over the opinion of the Shammaites that eight candles are lit on the first night and are thereafter decreased by one each night. In the absence of any males, the obligation to kindle the *Ḥ* lights falls on females. The candelabrum should be kindled in a prominently visible place "to advertise the miracle". The *Ḥ.* candelabrum has been an important object of Jewish art; originally it took the form of an oil lamp but in recent centuries its form has been modeled on the 7-branched candelabrum which was used in the Temple. *Ḥ.* is the only non-biblical festival on which the full *Hallel* (Ps. 113-118) is recited, and the special scriptural reading consists of the passage which describes the gifts brought by the princes for the dedication of the sanctuary in the wilderness (Num. 7). Work is not prohibited during the festival. The prophetical portion for the first Sabbath of *Ḥ.* (two Sabbaths occur in the festival only when the first day falls on a Sabbath) is Zech. 2:14-4:7, which includes the penultimate verse, "Not by might nor by power, but by My spirit, saith the Lord of Hosts". The emphasis laid by the rabbis on this verse is one example of the pronounced tendency on their part (possibly against the background of the dispute between the Pharisees and the Hasmoneans) to diminish the military aspect of the festival and concentrate instead on the aspect of the survival of religious values in the face of pagan and idolatrous opposition. In modern times, especially in the State of Israel, the opposite tendency is to be noted. A number of children's games became popular (notably spinning the *Ḥ.* top — *dreidl* or *trendl* in Yiddish, *sevivon* in Hebrew) and the custom also developed of giving children monetary gifts (*ḥanukkah gelt*) and presents.

ḤANUKKAT HA-BAYIT, see **DEDICATION**

ḤAPHETZ ḤAYYIM, see **COHEN, ISRAEL MEIR**

HAPHTARAH (Heb. "conclusion" i.e., of the biblical lesson): The reading from the prophetical books which follows the READING OF THE LAW in the Morning Service on Sabbaths and festivals; on fast days a *h.* is read during the Afternoon Service. The person called to read the *h.* (the *maphtir*) reads first a portion from the Pentateuch (generally a repetition of the last three verses of the previous section). Unlike the Reading of the Law, which must be performed from a handwritten scroll, the *h.* may be read from a printed text; only a few congregations (mainly in Jerusalem) use scrolls of the prophetical books. As the printed, vocalized text is easy to read, the *maphtir* usually reads the *h.* himself according to special cantillation; only in some congregations (including those where the *h.* is read from a scroll) is it chanted by a reader. Before the readings, a benediction is recited in praise of God "who has sent us true prophets"; another four benedictions follow the reading, one affirming faith in the eventual realization of the words of the prophets, two petitions of messianic content (for the rebuilding of Jerusalem and the coming of the Messiah), and one referring to the holiness and significance of the day (Sabbath or festival, respectively; this last blessing is omitted on fast days). The custom of conducting regular public readings from the Prophets goes back to Temple times, possibly to the Hasmonean Period. Its purpose was to conclude the public Reading of the Law — the main instrument for educating the people and strengthening their faith — with words of consolation and promises of messianic redemption, so as to encourage them in times of adversity. In later times the *h.* portion was no longer necessarily a prophecy of consolation, but was instead suited to the occasion of its recitation. Thus on a festival the *h.* is somehow connected with the day, while on Sabbaths it is chosen on the basis of its association with the pentateuchal portion for that day. On the four special Sabbaths (see SABBATHS, SPECIAL) the *h.* again refers to the specific occasion. On a Sabbath which is also the New Moon Is. 66 is read, as it refers to both Sabbath and *Rosh Ḥodesh.* On the three Sabbaths preceding *Av* 9, Jer. 1 and 2 and Is. 1 are read because of their character as prophecies of wraṭh, while on the seven following Sabbaths, "prophecies of consolation" (taken from Is. 40ff.) are chosen in most rites. The Chief Rabbinate of the State of Israel has ordained the reading of Is. 10:32; 11:12 for the annual Independence Day service. On those Sabbaths when two pentateuchal portions are read, the *h.* recited is generally that for the second portion. The *h.* often varies according to different rites, while the ones current today do not correspond with those mentioned in the Mishnah (*Meg.* 4:10). In many congregations it is considered a special honor to be called to read the *h.*,and it is given for instance to a *bar mitzvah* or a bridegroom; in others, it is customary to call boys below the age of thirteen for *maphtir* (but not for other parts of the reading). In the Talmudic Period a reading from the Hagiographa was incorporated into the Sabbath Afternoon Service.

ḤAROSET: A mixture of ground apples, walnuts, almonds, cinnamon, and other spices, combined into a thick paste with wine. It forms part of the *Seder* plate on Passover eve, serving as a dip for the bitter herbs. In ancient times *ḥ.* was used as a vegetable dressing. The Talmud (*Pes.* 116a) states that its clay-like appearance recalls the mortar used by the Israelite slaves in Egypt.

HARVEST AND HARVEST FESTIVALS: In biblical times the occasion of the h. was one of merrymaking and dancing; cf. the merrymaking at the grape h. (Judg. 9:27; Is. 16:10; Jer. 48:33). All three PILGRIM FESTIVALS are specifically referred to in the Bible as harvest festivals, and it has been suggested that this was their original import among the ancient Canaanites, with the Israelite religion adding specific historical motivations. Passover is the occasion for bringing "a sheaf of the first fruits of your harvest" (Lev. 23:10); this was the festival of the OMER when the offering of barley was brought to the Temple. The holiday of PENTECOST marks the time when "ye reap the harvest of your land" (Lev. 23:22) and the solemn ceremony of Thanksgiving (Deut. 26) took place when the wheat ripened and the FIRST FRUITS were brought to Jerusalem. TABERNACLES is called "the harvest festival" and "the feast of ingathering, which is the end of the year, when thou hast gathered in thy labors from the field" (Exod. 23:16; See also Exod. 34:22). It later became the sole harvest festival and hence the festival of rejoicing, *par excellence.*

ḤASDAI CRESCAS, see **CRESCAS, ḤASDAI**

HA-SHEM, see **GOD, NAMES OF**

HASHGAḤAH, see **PROVIDENCE**

HASHKAMAH (Heb. "early rising"): Term used to denote an early Sabbath morning service, ending before the commencement of the official or main service. The expression *hashkamat Bet ha-Midrash* signifies "timely attendance" at services (*Shab.* 127a).

HASHKAVAH (Heb. "causing to lie down", hence "laying to rest"): *Sephardi* term for the prayer for the dead, corresponding to the *Ashkenazi* YIZKOR.

HASHKIVENU (Heb. "Cause us [O Lord our God] to lie down [in peace]"): Opening words of the second benediction following the evening SHEMA (the first being the GEULLAH); a prayer for protection and peace during the night. The wording differs slightly in various rites, and there are certain differences between the weekday and Sabbath versions of the prayer.

ḤASID, JUDAH, see **JUDAH BEN SAMUEL HE-ḤASID**

HASIDEANS (from the Gk. transliteration of the Heb. *Ḥasidim* = the pious): An obscure Jewish religious sect which flourished during the 2nd cent. B.C.E. There are a few scant references to the H. in I and II MACCABEES. They apparently joined the rebellion against the religious persecution of Antiochus Epiphanes but fell easy prey to his soldiers because of their refusal to defend themselves on the Sabbath. Thereafter, Mattathias and his followers, including a great number of the H., decided to defend themselves even if attacked on the Sabbath. Once the struggle for religious freedom had been won, a breach developed between the H. and the HASMONEANS over the latter's interest in political affairs. In the Talmud and Midrash the H. are referred to as the *ḥasidim rishonim* ("the early pietists"), and accounts of their strict obedience to the Law border on legend, e.g. they refused to kill even snakes or scorpions on the Sabbath. The H. used to meditate for one hour before and one hour after their prayers, which they would not interrupt "even if a serpent were to wind itself around their ankle". As a distinct group the H. disappeared during the Hasmonean Period, but some of their principles and practices seem to have survived among the PHARISEES as well as among the ESSENES.

ḤASIDEI ASHKENAZ (Heb. "pious men of Germany"): Name given to German school of pietists and mystics in the 13th cent. ff.; outstanding among them were JUDAH BEN SAMUEL HE-ḤASID OF REGENSBURG (d. 1217) and his disciple, ELEAZAR BEN JUDAH OF WORMS. Their most influential composition was the SEPHER ḤASIDIM. Their system was heavily influenced by the MYSTICISM of the Babylonian *geonim*, which reached them largely, as recent research has suggested, through the mediation of the mystical works of AARON BEN SAMUEL of Babylonia, whose writings were kept a closely guarded secret, handed down from father to son. The *Ḥ.A.* paid particular attention to the cultivation of inner piety (through asceticism, humility, and strict morality) and the meticulous establishment of correct prayer formulae. They held that an invisible and incorporeal God made Himself manifest through His *kavod* (glory), and that it was to this personification of the Divine majesty as revealed to man that all anthropomorphic references to the Godhead in Scripture applied. The movement was a decisive event in the religious development of German Jewry and inspired it with a vitality to which can be partly ascribed its inner strength and devotion in the face of subsequent persecution.

ḤASIDEI UMOT HA-OLAM (Heb. "pious ones of the nations of the world"): Righteous gentiles who according to the Talmud (*Sanh.* 13:2) "have a share in the world to come" i.e., rank equally in merit and grace with the Jews (of whom with some exceptions, it is stated that "All Israel have a share in the world to come", *Sanh.* 10:1). Maimonides (*Hilkhot Melakhim* 8:11) defines the pious gentiles as those who adhere to the seven NOACHIAN LAWS which are binding upon all humanity, provided they are motivated by religious faith in God and His revelation, and not by purely intellectual reasons.

ḤASIDISM: Name given to a religious and mystical revival movement, originating in Southern Poland and the Ukraine in the 18th cent., spreading to other parts of Eastern Europe (Poland, Rumania, Hungary) and now found mainly in the State of Israel and the U.S.

The biblical noun *ḥasidim* ("pious ones") had been used before to designate religious groups of great piety and fervor (e.g. the HASIDEANS in the days of the MACCABEES, and the ḤASIDEI ASHKENAZ in medieval Germany), but there is no historic connection between these earlier groups and 18th cent. Ḥ. The ḥasidic movement was initiated by Israel ben Eliezer, known as the BAAL SHEM Tov (often abbreviated to *Besht*), and developed by his foremost disciple Dov BER of Mezhirich. The spectacular success of this Ḥ. has been attributed by some scholars to the peculiar circumstances in which Polish Jewry found itself at the time. They had suffered disastrous physical destruction during the Cossack uprising led by Chmielnicki in 1648; they lived in great poverty; their sense of desolation was heightened by the spiritual bewilderment and moral chaos that came in the wake of the failure of the messianic hopes engendered by the appearance of the false messiah SHABBETAI TZEVI. The poverty-stricken masses also labored under a sense of religious inadequacy, since they were unlearned and ignorant by rabbinic standards. It was to these people that the *Besht*, famed for his ecstatic prayer and as a "healer", brought the message of "serving God with joy" assuring the ordinary and even ignorant Jew that mystical communion with God was within his reach. The *Besht* taught by word of mouth and by personal influence; he wrote no books. One of his disciples, R. JACOB OF POLONNOYE d. 1794), formulated the teaching of the *Besht* and of Dov Ber of Mezhirich (d. 1773) who organized the growing movement. From Mezhirich, the main schools of the movement branched out in three directions: 1. The Ukrainian branch, whose outstanding figures were LEVI ISAAC OF BERDICHEV (d. 1802) and NAḤMAN OF BRATZLAV (d. 1810). 2. The Lithuanian branch which included R. Aaron of KARLIN and SHNEOUR ZALMAN of Lyady, the latter originating the ḤABAD school. 3. The Polish-Galician branch which included ELIMELECH OF LIZENSK (d. 1786), JACOB ISAAC, the Seer of Lublin, Israel of Kozniece, and many others. Although the ḥasidic teachers saw themselves in the line of classical Jewish tradition, and in particular that of the KABBALAH, Ḥ was sufficiently original, both in its doctrinal formulations and in the forms of social organization of religious life which it evolved, to appear as different and hence suspect in the eyes of contemporaries. Thus, the traditional theological proposition, "There is no place empty of Him", was understood by the Baal Shem Tov and his followers in a manner that went far beyond the orthodox notion of God's omnipotence. They held that meditation on this doctrine would dispel all fear and sadness, for how could there be fear or sadness if God is actually and essentially with man in every circumstance? In fact, how can evil exist if there is no place empty of God? The apparent PANTHEISM in this teaching was one of the reasons which prompted ELIJAH BEN SOLOMON OF VILNA, the famous talmudic scholar (d. 1797) to lead the MITNAGGEDIM (as the opponents of Ḥ. were called) in a determined campaign against the new and, in his eyes, heretical sect. The aftermath of the Shabbetai Tzevi debacle (see FRANK, JACOB) had made rabbinic leadership very heresy conscious. The ḥasidic doctrines of "joy" (*simḥah*), enthusiasm (*hitlahavut*), and communion with God (DEVEKUT) were all derived from Jewish sources. But in Ḥ. these theories were not only interpreted more radically, but were also expressed in song, dance, feasting, and rejoicing — to a degree which other Jews considered inappropriate. The *Mitnaggedim* were scandalized by the shouting and ecstatic twisting of the body which often accompanied the prayers of Ḥasidim. At its core, Ḥ. was a mystical movement stressing the quality of "inwardness" both in life and in learning. While never questioning the authority of the HALAKHAH, it emphasized its esoteric meaning and intent. The ḥasidic masters and writers drew much on kabbalistic literature, particularly the Zohar and the Lurianic writings, but interpreted the texts in terms of their own system. Mystical doctrines, which had formerly been reserved to a spiritual "elite", were now offered to the masses. Underlying all ḥasidic thought was the kabbalistic concept of this world as an emanation and reflection of "higher worlds". But even as the "higher" influenced the "lower", so could the "lower" influence the "higher". This theory was used by the ḥasidic masters to invest even ordinary acts in this "lower" world with cosmic significance. "If a person but moves his finger here, whole worlds move there". Another kabbalistic doctrine which gave even the simple man a sense of Divine mission was that of the "lifting of the holy sparks". These Divine "sparks" were buried everywhere in the world and covered by shells (*kelipot*). They yearned to be united with their Source. Man's task was to liberate these "sparks", to achieve the "unities" which would eventually bring about the time of the great TIKKUN ("repair") and usher in the messianic age. Since these sparks were embedded not only in human beings but even in the inanimate world, there was scarcely a moment when man could not be engaged in the redeeming activity of "liberating the sparks". An outwardly insignificant or even contemptible action as well as any ordinary labour could cloak a mystic *tikkun* of far-reaching consequences. More important than the outer act of work, or prayer, was *kavvanah* — the inner DEVOTION with which it was carried out. God would accept even the prayers or efforts of an ignorant man so long as they were accompanied by inner sincerity. This ḥasidic interpretation of the talmudic saying "God wants the heart" endowed the Jewish masses with a sense of religious dignity; at the same time it provided fuel for the suspicion of opponents that Ḥasidim were neglecting outer forms and observances of Judaism because of their concern with inner intent. The antagonism between the two communities was climaxed by a series of excommunication bans issued by Elijah of Vilna. For several generations bitterness continued between *Mitnaggedim* and Ḥasidim until the threat of a common enemy, namely modern Enlightenment, made them close their ranks. In fact, Ḥasidim remained strictly observant, but they evolved or adopted a number of customs and prayer patterns which distinguished them from the traditional *Ashkenazi* community. Most important of these was the use of the *Sephardi* prayer book (called *Nusakh Ari*) adopted by the Palestinian kabbalists. Though the differences between this "*Sephardi*" order of prayers and the order used by the *Mitnaggedim* were minor, they were another factor in the split between the communities. Some of the Ḥasidim also took the liberty of changing or extending the hours of prayer. All ḥasidic communities emphasized the special holiness and mystical significance of the third Sabbath meal — the SEUDAH SHELISHIT — which was held toward the evening and sometimes stretched into the late hours of the night. The meal was often accompanied by dances and songs, in a mood of *devekut* (at times ecstatic). At this time the REBBE or TZADDIK "gave *Torah*" as the Ḥasidim listened with rapt attention. Indeed the institution of the *tzaddik*, the "holy man" who was the leader of the ḥasidic community, became the major object of attack by the *Mitnaggedim*. The Ḥasidim looked upon the *tzaddik* as an intermediary with God and sometimes as a miracle worker. "God decrees and the *tzaddik* can annul His decree", was a talmudic saying they liked to quote in support of their belief in the extraordinary powers of the *rebbe* or *tzaddik*. They would, when visiting him, leave a *pitka* (note) inscribed with the names of members of their families and their own name, along with a request for the *tzaddik's* intervention. Attached to the *pitka* would be a *pidyon* (ransom i.e., a sum of money). There were *rebbes* like Shneour Zalman — who energetically opposed the superstitious elements that crept into faith in the *tzaddik*. But other *rebbes* (or ADMORIM) — like Elimelech of Lizensk — stressed the power of the *tzaddik* in both the terrestrial and spiritual spheres, and the help which a man could receive by binding (*hitkashrut*) his own imperfect being to the perfection of the *tzaddik*. The *tzaddik* could not only lift the prayers of the *Ḥasidim* but could help them liberate the "sparks of holiness" in their souls and raise them to a higher level. A *tzaddik*, in order to lift sparks, would occasionally have to "descend" to the lower levels where they were embedded. The greater the *tzaddik*, the lower he could descend — with safety. If he was not great enough, he might himself be caught in the evil *kelipot* (husks) and be led astray, as was Shabbetai Tzevi — who according to a ḥasidic interpretation, had "descended" too far and become a heretic. The institution of the *tzaddik* played a vital part in the development of Ḥ. and was, in many cases, abused by men who were not worthy of their rôle. During its early period, Ḥ. produced "a number of religious personalities of a vitality, a spiritual strength, and manifold originality, such as have never appeared together, in so short a time span in the history of religion" (according to Martin BUBER). But as the early generations of *tzaddikim* passed away, their places were often taken by men whose sole claim to the position was their descent from earlier holy men. The acceptance of the dynastic principle hastened the degeneration of the movement.

The great centers of ḥasidic influence were wiped out by the Nazi holocaust, but a number of dynasties have re-established themselves in the State of Israel and the United States. "The "courts" of the *rebbes* of BELZ and of GER still have thousands of followers in Israel and ḥasidic groups going back to Aaron of Karlin, Naḥman of Bratzlav, Sadagora, etc., can also be found in Israel. In the United States, there are a number of dynasties — the Bobover, Czarnobover (Twersky family), and Kopyezne (Heschel), etc. Among the largest ḥasidic groups now in the United States are the Satmarer and the LIUBAVICHER. The latter, under the direction of a descendant of Shneour Zalman, is particularly active, conducting an extensive network of schools and *yeshivot* in N. America, N. Africa, and Israel.

HASKALAH (Heb. "Enlightenment"): Movement among the Jews of E. Europe in the late 18th-19th cents. to acquire modern European culture and secular knowledge. It opposed the dominance of rabbinic Orthodoxy in Jewish life and the restriction of education and culture to talmudic studies. Spreading eastward from Berlin (see Moses MENDELSSOHN), *H.* shared many of the values of European Enlightenment, and attempted to steer a middle course between unbending Orthodoxy and radical ASSIMILATION. It wished to promote the process of EMANCIPATION by spreading general education and western culture among the masses, while at the same time fostering specifically Jewish cultural consciousness, mainly through an emphasis on the importance of pure (biblical) Hebrew as a literary medium. The character of *H.* activity differed in various countries (Germany, Russia, Galicia, Lithuania). In eastern Europe, *H.* was tantamount to westernization, and its efforts to substitute modern schools for the traditional *ḥeder* were violently resisted by the Orthodox; *H.* writers in Galicia countered with bitter satires, attacking the obscurantism, fanaticism, and superstitions of the Ḥasidim and the talmudists (cf. Erter's satire *Moznei Mishkal*), but these writers also advanced historical research considerably in their scholarly periodicals (*Bikkurei ha-Ittim*, 1820-31, *He-Ḥalutz*, 1852-89, *Kerem Ḥemed*, 1853-57). To counteract the excessive devotion to the Talmud and rabbinic theology, secular schools were founded and new pedagogic manuals of instructions written (Hartwig Wessely in Berlin, Herz Homberg in Galicia). Their severe rationalism notwithstanding, the *maskilim* (proponents of *H.*) were animated by a romantic desire of a return to nature (Y.L. Gordon) and by a high regard for manual work (schools of arts and crafts were opened at Tarnopol, 1819 and Odessa, 1826). They advocated an esthetic reform of the synagogue service, and in literature exhibited both a particular interest in ancient heroes (Saul, Samson) and an inclination to romanticism and hedonism (translations of the pastoral poetry of Haller, Gessner, Kleist, etc. as well as verses in honor of wine, women, and love appeared in the *Measseph*, the first literary periodical [1784-1811] of the *maskilim*). The opponents of *H.* feared that the movement would lead to the liquidation of historical Judaism, that it had too little regard for Jewish sentiment, tradition, and piety, and that its critical scholarship would undermine Orthodoxy and serve the purposes of Reform. By the end of the 19th cent. the movement had run its course. Some of its ideas and achievements were firmly established; others, however, were soon turned into anachronisms. On the one hand full cultural emancipation rendered a Hebrew H. unrealistic; on the other hand it became obvious that social emancipation had failed and that cultural reform would not stem the rising tide of ANTI-SEMITISM. Writers began to denounce *H.* as a betrayal of Jewish identity, but the growing awareness of Jewish nationhood as expressed in Zionism was in many ways a result of the influence of the *H.*, which had created a secular middle-class faithful to historic tradition and Hebrew culture, yet alive to western ideas.

HASKAMAH (Heb. "agreement", "approbation"): Official authorization prefixed to a book. With the introduction of printing it became customary to preface Hebrew books with an approbatory note by one or more recognized rabbinic authorities. This was originally instituted as a voluntary measure by Jewish authorities to avoid unnecessary friction with the Church. The *h.*, which was in the interest of both author and publisher, fulfilled a double purpose: in the absence of an official rabbinic censorship, it served as an *imprimatur*, assuring the reader that there was nothing heretical or otherwise objectionable in a book. Then the *h.* also contained a prohibition (sometimes phrased in the form of a ḤEREM) forbidding others to reprint the book within a specified number of years; thus it also assured the book's "copyright". Among *Sephardim* the communal rules and regulations agreed upon and adopted by the congregation were called *ascamot*.

HASMONEANS: Family name of the Hasmonean (or Maccabean) priestly dynasty. Mattathias, father of the five Maccabean brothers, raised the standard of revolt against the Syrian ruler Antiochus Epiphanes who was attempting to unify his realm by enforcing HELLENISM on all his subjects. Upon the death of Mattathias, his son JUDAH THE MACCABEE succeeded him as leader of the revolt. He succeeded in recapturing Jerusalem and purifying the Temple which was reconsecrated on *Kislev* 25 in the year 165 B.C.E. (see ḤANUKKAH). The right of religious self-determination was recognized two years later when the Jews were permitted to live according to the customs of their forefathers (I *Macc.* 6:59). This military triumph over the hellenistic forces proved a major factor in the development of Judaism, encouraging as it did the rise of pietists and WISDOM teachers. The Hellenist party dwindled in importance and the SANHEDRIN administered the country in accordance with Jewish traditional doctrine. However the original motivation of the H. was replaced by a desire for self-aggrandizement. Judah's successors appropriated the office of HIGH PRIEST which they combined with civil power. The militant policies of John Hyrcanus (135-104) formed one of the causes of his great quarrel with the PHARISEES. Originally he had supported them and packed the Sanhedrin with their adherents; but after breaking with them he relied for his support on the SADDUCEES. The two parties now emerged as bitter rivals and the conflict between them dominated the political and religious scene during the rest of the Second Temple Period. Alexander Yannai (103-76) sided with the Sadducees and plunged the country into civil war. The wounds of this conflict were healed only during the reign of his widow Salome Alexandra (76-67), under whom the Pharisees returned to their former position of influence under the leadership of SIMEON BEN SHETAH. They regained control of the Sanhedrin and revised Temple ritual according to their own traditions. With the death of Salome Alexandra the dynasty of the H. rapidly declined. After 63 the country was a Roman province and all major officials — including the High Priest — were Roman appointees. The H. no longer were the effective rulers, and were distrusted by the people for their surrender to Rome and their general display of decadence. The last traces of the family were destroyed by Herod. See also MACCABEES, BOOKS OF.

ḤATAM SOPHER, see **SOPHER, MOSES**

ḤATAN, see **MARRIAGE**

ḤATAN TORAH AND ḤATAN BERESHIT (Heb. "bridegroom of the law" and "bridegroom of Genesis"): Titles of two honorary functionaries at the synagogue service on SIMḤAT TORAH (which in the Land of Israel coincides with SHEMINI ATZERET). In this particularly solemn reading of the Law, the annual cycle is concluded and the new one begun. The person called up to the reading of the last portion of Deuteronomy is the *ḥatan Torah*; the one who follows with the first chapter of Genesis is *ḥatan Bereshit*. The functions are a coveted honor in the congregation. *Ḥ.T.* and *ḥ.B.* usually entertain the congregation in celebration of the occasion and are formally congratulated on the privilege of leading the community in the JOY of the festival.

HATRAAH (Heb. "warning"): According to talmudic law, a man cannot be sentenced to capital or corporal punishment for a crime unless he receives a specific warning (*h.*) beforehand not to commit that crime. The object of this legislation was to ensure that the person sentenced to extreme penalties was being punished for a misdeed committed willfully and not accidentally or in ignorance. Should the judges in such cases consider that the deed had been done willfully but no specific caution had been issued, the sentence was generally reduced to one of imprisonment.

HATRED: The Bible commands "Thou shalt not hate thy brother in thy heart" (Lev. 19:17); any hostile feeling amounts to h. H. of evildoers or of the enemies of God, however, which finds expression in the Bible (cf. e.g. Ps. 139:21-22), is considerably toned down by the rabbis, who emphasize the duty of hating not the sinner but the sin; hence the ideal course is to prevail upon the evildoer to repent. Groundless h. is considered by the rabbis as the greatest of all social vices. "The First Temple was destroyed because of the commission of the three cardinal sins of Judaism — idolatry, immorality, and murder — and the Second Temple because of their equivalent — groundless h." (*Yoma* 9b).

HATTARAT HORAAH, see **ORDINATION**

ḤATUNNAH (Heb.): Wedding. See MARRIAGE.

HAVDALAH (Heb. "differentiation" i.e., between the holy and secular): Prayer recited at the conclusion of Sabbaths and festivals to indicate the distinction between the sacred day that has ended and the weekday which is beginning. *H.* corresponds to KIDDUSH, which proclaims the sanctity of the day at its beginning. No work should be done and no food consumed after nightfall until *H.* has been recited. One form of *H.* is incorporated as part of the fourth benediction of the AMIDAH of MAARIV; but *H.* is recited again over a cup of wine as a separate benediction at the end of the service and then at home (it is unclear whether *H.* originated in the home or the synagogue). Traditionally *H.* was instituted by the men of the Great Assembly (*Ber.* 33b). The prayer enumerates the differences between "holy and profane", between "light and darkness", and between "Israel and the gentiles". At the conclusion of the Sabbath, it is customary to recite also a benediction over spices and over the light of a plaited candle. If a festival follows directly upon the Sabbath, a special form of *H.* is combined with the *kiddush.* In several versions ELIJAH is mentioned prominently in the *H.* service in view of the belief that his advent as harbinger of the Messiah will occur on a Saturday evening after the conclusion of the Sabbath.

ḤAVER (Heb. "companion"): Term used to denote a scholar and pious man, in accordance with the verse "I am a companion of all them that fear Thee and of them that observe Thy precepts" (Ps. 119:63). It was also a scholar's title, and a disciple who reached a standard of scholarship almost equal to that of his master was called *Talmid Ḥaver* (*Ber.* 27b). During the Second Temple Period the term was bestowed upon members of an association that observed the levitical rules prescribed for the handling of sacred food and was punctilious in matters of tithes; the opposite of *ḥ.* was AM HA-ARETZ. In the 16th cent. the title *ḥ.* was conferred upon young scholars. R. Moses Sopher (1762-1839) described the use of this title as a custom originating in Germany and states that in Moravia a rabbi with less than ten students in his college must not confer the title *ḥ.* without the permission of his district rabbi. The conferment of the title *ḥ.* was still in vogue in Germany up to the 1930's.

ḤAYYUN, NEHEMIAH (c. 1650-1730): Kabbalist and Sabbataian adventurer. Born and educated in Palestine, he served for some time as rabbi in the Balkans but later led a wandering life. He joined the sect of believers in the pseudo-messiah SHABBETAI TZEVI, and wrote kabbalistic works which he provided with forged rabbinic approbations and in which he expounded Sabbataian heresies under the cloak of mystical symbolism. His appearance in Amsterdam, where he was unmasked by Moses ḤAGIZ, caused a major scandal: ḤAKHAM TZEVI Hirsch Ashkenazi sided with Ḥagiz and issued a ban against Ḥ., who was supported by the *Sephardi* Chief Rabbi Solomon Ayllon. Ḥ. died in poverty in N. Africa; his son apostatized in Rome and made vicious attacks against the Jews.

ḤAZAK (Heb. "be strong"): Exclamation (usually *ḥazak ḥazak ve-nitḥazzak*) made by the congregation to the reader at the completion of the synagogal reading of one of the Five Books of Moses; see Josh. 1:6-9. *Sephardim* congratulate one who has performed a MITZVAH with the phrase *ḥ. u-varukh*, corresponding to the *Ashkenazi* expression *yishar koaḥ* (see CONGRATULATIONS).

ḤAZAKAH (Heb. "taking hold"): The presumptive right of one in possession to retain ownership or possession until such right is disproved. *Ḥ.* is an important principle of Jewish law, and is at the basis of its legal theory of ownership and possession, as well as of personal and ritual status. The state of a thing or person as it is known to have last existed forms the presumption in law for all questions involving present status. Not all presumptions have equal force in law, while presumptions of a general character may have to be tempered in the light of local custom. Undisturbed possession of land for a period of three years creates the presumption of a legal title. Where it is possible to verify the facts, a presumption is not relied upon. The transfer of land is effected by means of a KINYAN also called *ḥazakah.*

ḤAZAL: Word formed by the initials of the phrase *ḥakhameinu zikhronam li-verakhah* ("our sages of blessed memory"). Like *Rezal* (*rabboteinu zikhronam li-verakhah*, "our masters of blessed memory"), it refers to the teachers of the Talmudic Period.

HAZKARAT NESHAMOT, see **EL MALE RAḤAMIM; YIZKOR**

ḤAZON ISH, see **KARLITZ, AVRAHAM YESHAYAHU**

ḤAZZAN (Heb.): Communal official; in later usage also CANTOR; probably derived from the Assyrian *hazannu* — overseer or governor. Talmudic descriptions of the rôle of the *ḥ.* vary. During the Second Temple Period, one of his functions was to attend to the priestly robes and accompany pilgrims to the Temple. Another task was that of announcing the beginning and conclusion of the Sabbath. Among his synagogal duties was the care of the building and the education of the children. At times the *ḥ.* would also be charged with tending the sick and needy. The *ḥ* was often a poet and supplemented the service with his compositions; consequently, he stood beside the reader and eventually supplanted him.

ḤAZZANUT, see **CANTORIAL MUSIC**

HEAD, COVERING OF, see **COVERING OF THE HEAD**

HEALTH: The biblical exhortation to "take heed to thyself and keep thy soul diligently" (Deut. 4:9, cf. also Deut. 4:15) was traditionally interpreted as enjoining care for one's h. and physical well-being. From the verse "and surely your blood of your souls will I require" (Gen. 9:5) is derived the prohibition against inflicting any self-injury (*Bava Kamma* 91b, see SUICIDE). Rabbinic law prohibits any action likely to endanger h., and some authorities consider a vow to abstain from food for seven days to be automatically invalid since it endangers life. A person who insists on fasting on the Day of Atonement despite being forbidden to do so on medical grounds is considered to have committed a crime; under such circumstances fasting carries no merit but is, on the contrary, "nonsensical piety". In general, any laws (excepting those forbidding murder, idolatry, and adultery) can be violated where life is endangered (see DANGER). Many precepts of the *Torah*, though not in the first instance laid down for reasons of h., nevertheless contribute to bodily well-being. Thus the separation imposed by the laws of NIDDAH ensures that a woman has fully recovered from her menstrual condition and regained her vitality before renewing intercourse. Circumcision, observance of the dietary laws, washing the hands before meals, various ablutions and instructions regarding personal habits as well as a general insistence upon moderation in all things, all contribute to the physical well-being of those who perform them. (See also CLEANLINESS). The rabbis paid great attention to hygiene and h., enacting relevant legislation and proferring extensive advice on the subject.

HEATHEN, see **GENTILE**

HEAVE-OFFERING (Heb. *terumah*): First and most important of the presents separated out from the produce and donated to the priests; for this reason called *terumah gedolah* ("great" heave-offering). Biblically it has no fixed measure and a single stalk suffices to fulfill the obligation. The rabbis however declare that "the liberal-minded separate one fortieth of the produce, the moderately liberal one-fiftieth, and the miserly one-sixtieth". The h. is given to the priest and becomes his property. He must consume or use it only in such a manner and state as will not result in its becoming ritually unclean. It may not be eaten by a non-priest. The h. is still practiced by observant Jews in the Holy Land, but as it cannot be eaten nowadays even by priests, for reasons of ritual impurity, only a token quantity is separated and subsequently burned, as in the case of the HALLAH. See TITHES.

HEAVEN: The upper region of the universe according to traditional Jewish COSMOLOGY. "In the beginning the Lord created the heavens and the earth" (Gen. 1:1), but "the heavens are the heavens of the Lord and the earth hath He given to the sons of man" (Ps. 115:16); that is, h. is the abode of God and the celestial beings, while man has been given the earth for his habitation. The only specific mention made in the Bible of an ascension to h. is in the case of Elijah (II Kings 2:11); otherwise the Bible is geocentric in its outlook. It was only during the Second Temple and Talmudic Periods that the idea developed of h. as the abode of the righteous after death. Not infrequently, descriptions of this h. of the souls are influenced by descriptions of the post-messianic, eschatological "World to Come" (OLAM HA-BA) and vice versa, but ultimately the celestial abode of the souls was identified with the heavenly GARDEN OF EDEN (PARADISE). Later midrashic and kabbalistic literature went into great detail in depicting the life of the righteous in h., which has always been the popular symbol of immortality. Modernist thinking (also in Reform Judaism) tends to the philosophical view that h. refers to a spiritual state rather than a specific place.

HEBREW: The word is first found in Gen. 14:13 as an epithet of Abram (ABRAHAM). It is used in the Bible to indicate the Jewish people, who are otherwise called "the children of Israel" (see ISRAELITE). There is a difference of opinion as to the origin of the name — whether it means "a descendant of Eber" (Gen. 10:21; 11:16) or "the one from the other side" (Heb. *ever*) i.e., of the Jordan (cf. Josh. 26:37). Some scholars identify the word with the "Habiru", the first-known mention of whom occurs in the Tel-el-Amarna tablets, but if this is correct it is not an ethnic designation but seems to mean "wanderers".

HEBREW LANGUAGE (Heb. *Ivrit*): A branch of the Canaanite group of Semitic languages, possibly adopted by the Israelites after their settlement in the Land of Israel. The designation H. for the language is late, and in biblical times the language was known as *yehudit* ("Jewish"), cf. II Kings 18:26. Different forms of H. existed (or developed) at various periods (Biblical H., Mishnaic H., etc.) and the language, even when used for liturgical and literary purposes only, continually absorbed outside influences, particularly from vernaculars currently in use among Jews (Aramaic, Greek, Arabic, etc.). As the language in which the Bible was written, H. became for the rabbis the Holy Tongue and is commonly known by this name in rabbinic literature, which is often extravagant in its praise of the language (e.g. H. is "the language spoken by the angels" *Ḥag.* 16a). Although many of the rabbinic statements on the importance of teaching H. as a language (e.g. "When the child begins to speak, his father should speak to him in the Holy Tongue... and if he does not speak to him in the Holy Tongue... it is as though he had buried him", *Siphrei*, *Ekev* 46; or, "He who dwells in the

Land of Israel permanently, eats his food in a state of ritual purity, speaks in the Holy Tongue and reads the *Shema* morning and evening is certain of the life of the World to Come" Y. *Shab.* 1) were clearly meant to counteract tendencies to neglect H. in favor of the current vernacular, there is no doubt that to the rabbis the language was invested with a special sanctity *per se.* As a result the tendency developed, especially during the Middle Ages, to confine its use to sacred purposes such as prayer, study, correspondence of a religious nature. This tendency manifested itself again in the bitter opposition of some religious extremists in Palestine to the activities of Eliezer Ben-Yehudah (1858-1922) aimed at making H. the vehicle of ordinary communication. The value of H. was further enhanced by certain midrashic and mystical traditions, as a result of which a mystical theology of the H. language grew up and proved of great importance in kabbalistic speculation and practice. Although H. continued to be used by medieval Jewry and, indeed, served as the Jewish *lingua franca*, significant differences in the attitude to the language developed among different groups. Thus the Spanish Jews preferred Arabic not only for oral communication but also for philosophical, theological, and at times even halakhic writing; further, H. served as a purely literary medium, mostly for poetry, and Spanish writers insisted on purity of diction and rigid adherence to the forms and syntax of classical biblical H. and grammar, opposing innovations and the introduction of post-biblical terms. The Franco-German scholars on the other hand, though disregarding the niceties of H. grammar, were never averse to allowing mishnaic Hebrew and even Aramaic into their diction, and regarded H. as the sole medium for written communication and literature. H. became established as the sole language acceptable for liturgical purposes, although talmudic law (see Mishnah *Sotah* 7.1) explicitly permits the use of the vernacular for prayer (including the *Shema* and the *amidah*). In modern times, the vernacular has reappeared in the synagogue both for the sermon and, to greater or lesser degrees, in Reform and Conservative services.

HEBREW SCHOOLS, see **EDUCATION**

HEBREW UNION COLLEGE — JEWISH INSTITUTE OF RELIGION: U.S. Reform rabbinical seminary. Aside from training rabbis, it awards degrees for specialized studies and offers training programs for educators and cantors. It is located on three campuses, in Cincinnati, New York, and Los Angeles. There is also a H.U.C. School for Biblical and Archaeological Studies in Jerusalem. The H.U.C. was founded in Cincinnati in 1875 by Isaac Mayer Wise. In 1922, Stephen S. Wise founded the J.I.R. in New York. At the time of its founding, the latter institution, though affiliated with the Reform movement, differed from H.U.C. in attempting to embrace, through its curriculum and faculty, a wider perspective of liberal religion and a more positive attitude toward Jewish nationalism. The two institutions were merged in 1950, and Nelson Glueck (1900-1971) became the president of the combined school.

ḤEDER (Heb. "room"): Popularly applied to an elementary religious school of the type prevalent in E. Europe, often situated in a single room in the teacher's house. A frequent talmudic appellation for schoolchildren, "children of the house of their teacher" (*tinokot shel bet rabban*) suggests that a similar system obtained in talmudic times. Study hours in the *ḥ* were long and the teacher rarely had any pedagogical training. A minor official connected with the system was the *belfer* (from *behelfer* "assistant") who conducted the children from their homes to the *ḥ*. Under the influence of the *Haskalah* movement in the 19th cent. an attempt was made to modernize the system by the institution of the *Ḥeder Metukkan* ("improved *ḥ*."). Attempts to transplant the *ḥ*. system to western countries, where the prevalence of compulsory secular elementary education forced it into the position of an afternoon adjunct to the day school, did not have happy results, and the tendency now is toward other forms of Jewish education for children (day schools, Sunday classes, etc.). See Education; Talmud Torah.

HEIKHAL, see **ARK OF THE LAW; TEMPLE**

HEIKHALOT (Heb. "palaces"): The tradition of Jewish mysticism in the early Rabbinic and Gaonic Periods, which centered on the mystical ascent through the heavenly spheres and palaces (*heikhalot*) to the vision of the Divine Chariot (see Maaseh Merkavah; Throne of God), produced a body of literature known as the *H.* books. The mystical Midrashim describe the ecstatic experiences of the visionaries and abound in powerful hymns of praise to the Divine Majesty. Many of these hymns have become part of the *Ashkenazi* prayer book for the High Holidays, and their style has influenced the liturgical compositions of the great Spanish poets (e.g. Judah Ha-Levi and Solomon Ibn Gabirol).

HEIR, see **INHERITANCE**

HEKDESH (Heb. "sacred property"): Property sanctified to God. (1) Property owned by the Temple; (2) animals, wine, oil, or flour, etc. set aside for sacrificial purposes (*kodeshei mizbeaḥ*); (3) property set aside as a gift to the temple treasury (*kodeshei bedek ha-bayit*). *H.* may not be handled by a person in a state of ritual impurity and no use or benefit whatsoever may be derived from it. One who inadvertently makes use of or benefits from *h.* is obliged to bring a special sacrifice (*korban meilah*) to the Temple. *H.* may be redeemed by payment of its value plus a fifth to the Temple treasury. Unlike all other transactions in Jewish law, *h.* requires no KINYAN; property becomes *h.* and falls to the possession of the Temple treasury solely by the owner's declaration. In later times, *h.* was devoted to charitable, communal, or educational purposes.

HEKHALOT, see **HEIKHALOT**

ḤELEV (Heb.): Fat; in biblical usage more specifically certain portions of the intestinal fat of oxen, sheep, and goats, offered upon the altar (Lev. 3:3-17). Like BLOOD it was forbidden food for the Israelites. Maimonides (*Hilkhot Maakhalot Assurot* 7:5) explains the distinction between intestinal fat (*ḥelev*) which is forbidden food, and animal fat (*shumen*) which is part of the sinews and hence allowed.

HELL, see **GEHINNOM**

HELLENISM: The form of Greek civilization that spread through the Near East and Mediterranean lands after the conquests of Alexander the Great (365-323 B.C.E.) and which persisted well into the period of the Roman Empire. Whereas the history of H. in general is that of the absorption of oriental elements by Greek culture and the diffusion of these new syncretistic forms, the history of Jewish H. is concerned with the impact of hellenistic civilization on Judaism. After Alexander's conquest Palestine was under Greek rule and Judea was surrounded by an increasing number of hellenized gentile cities, and in the countries of the Diaspora (Egypt, Syria, Asia Minor, etc.) hellenization made rapid progress. Outside Palestine Greek became the language of the Jews, and in the 3rd cent. B.C.E. the Jews of Egypt were already using a Greek translation of the Bible (SEPTUAGINT). In Palestine the radical tendencies of hellenizing groups such as the TOBIADS, powerfully supported by the Seleucid rulers, finally led to the anti-hellenistic rising led by the MACCABEES. After the Maccabean victory, Palestinian Jewry was strong enough to absorb Greek influences without danger of being engulfed by H. as such. Toward the end of the Second Temple and in the Mishnaic Period, material life was predominantly hellenistic (synagogue architecture and decoration; tomb inscriptions in Greek, e.g. in BET SHEARIM; art), and many Greek words entered the Hebrew and Aramaic vocabulary — even as designations of major Jewish institutions and liturgical practices (e.g. SANHEDRIN). At the same time the rabbis opposed too close an acquaintance with, and study of, Greek culture. The upper classes, however, adopted a thoroughgoing hellenistic style of life, which was often assimilationist. In the Diaspora the influence of H. was naturally much stronger, though its pagan character precluded full participation of the Jews in the civic life of the hellenistic cities. Gentile H., which regarded Jewish MONOTHEISM and the worship of an invisible God as tantamount to atheism, also produced the first historic expression of ANTI-SEMITISM, in the form of riots and anti-Jewish literature. As a result much Jewish hellenistic writing, whether philosophical (see PHILO) or historical (see JOSEPHUS), was apologetic and propagandist in character, attempting to demonstrate the excellence and superiority of the Jewish laws and teachings. This literature, however, does not seem to have made an impression on the Greeks. Hellenistic influences are also present in Jewish writings that were not composed with gentile readers in mind, e.g. many of the APOCRYPHA AND PSEUDEPIGRAPHA; some of these works have survived only in Greek translation. The historical significance of the Hellenistic Period resides not only in its great and permanent influence on Jewish culture and rabbinic tradition, but also in its being a paradigmatic instance of the capacity of Judaism to enrich, without losing, itself by contact with a "universal" civilization.

HELLER, YOM-TOV LIPMANN (1573-1654): Rabbinic scholar and commentator on the Mishnah. At the age of 18, H. was appointed *dayyan* in Prague and subsequently served as (chief) rabbi in Vienna, Prague, and other cities. After the Thirty Years War he was forced to supervise the assessments of the heavily taxed Jewish community, and his enemies informed against him that he attacked Christianity in his writings. His best-known work is the logical and concise commentary *Tosaphot Yom Tov* ("Additions of Yom-Tov") printed (in full or abridged form) in the margin of subsequent editions of the Mishnah.

HEMEROBAPTISTS (Gk. "daily bathers"): A Jewish sect, mentioned by the Church Fathers, observing ritual IMMERSION every morning. Daily ABLUTIONS were practiced by several Jewish groups (including the ESSENES) and the h. may be identical with one of them, possibly with the *tovelei shaḥarit* ("dawn bathers") mentioned in the Talmud.

HENOTHEISM: Devotion to, and worship of, one God, but without denying the existence of other gods. Many scholars hold that the religion of the Israelites was henotheistic in its earlier stages (cf. e.g. Jephthah's message to the Ammonites, "Will you not possess what Chemosh your god gives you to possess? And all that the Lord our God has dispossessed before us, we will possess" — Judg. 11:24) and only later developed into a fully articulated, absolute MONOTHEISM.

ḤEPHETZ BEN YATZLIAḤ (10th cent.): Babylonian scholar, possibly a disciple of SAADYAH. His *Sepher Mitzvot* ("Book of Commandments"), a code arranged according to the 613 PRECEPTS, was highly regarded by Spanish scholars.

HEPHKER (Heb): Ownerless PROPERTY. Property may become ownerless (a) by voluntary formal renunciation on the part of the owner in the presence of three persons; (b) by compulsory renunciation by the owner of his right to the property, as ordered by a court; (c) by the death of a proselyte who leaves property but no Jewish heirs; or (d) by being lost by its owner who despairs of recovering it. Property found in deserts or at sea is treated as ownerless. *H.* becomes the property of the first person to acquire it by the usual means. *H.* is not subject to the law of tithing nor to laws benefiting the poor.

ḤEREM (Heb.): In its primary sense, *ḥ.* refers to property separated out — or "devoted" — for sacred purposes (Lev. 27:28) or with which contact is disallowed because of its objectionable nature, e.g. idolatrous appurtenances from which no benefit may be derived (Deut. 7:26). Ezra uses the term in the sense of confiscation of property (Ezra 10:8). The most familiar talmudic usage of the word refers to the isolation of an individual from the community by being placed under *ḥ.*, i.e., EXCOMMUNICATION. The *ḥ.* completely ostracizes the individual involved from all contact with his fellow Jews, and was the most formidable and potent weapon at the disposal of the Jewish community to guarantee both religious conformity and general order. It formed a major standby of the Jewish court for generations, since after due warning, a court may react to contempt by means of a *ḥ.* Authorities of all ages have resorted to this weapon in order to enforce major enactments, the most famous instance being the prohibition on pain of *ḥ.* against polygamy in *Ashkenazi* Jewry (the *Ḥ.* of R. Gershom). Overfrequent and illegitimate use of *ḥ.* along with the disintegration of the traditional closely-knit forms of community life, have deprived the *ḥ.* of its power and significance in modern Jewish life.

HERESY: Whereas Jewish law examines in detail those departures from orthodox belief which constitute h., the punishment is generally left to God, and there is little if any provision for earthly sanctions in such cases. Various terms are used for heretics. The generic name is MINIM, "sectarians", those who depart in their conduct and beliefs from the norms of Judaism; the term covers a multitude of sinners, and in specific context can refer to Gnostics, Judeo-Christians, Sadducees, etc. Alternate names are APIKORSIM ("Epicureans", "deniers") and *mumarim* ("those who have changed"). The usual and practically only punishment foretold for heretics is that they "forfeit their share in the World to Come" i.e., their punishment is in the hands of God and comes after their death, not by human courts during their lifetime. Thus the Mishnah (*Sanh.* 10:1) enumerates among those who forfeit their share in the World to Come those who deny the doctrine of resurrection, or the Divine origin of the *Torah,* while R. Eleazar ha-Modai specifies him "who profanes sacred things, puts his fellow to shame in public, despises the festivals, nullifies the covenant of Abraham, and makes the *Torah* bear a meaning other than its true one" (*ibid.* 3:15). Rabbinic authorities have never set up courts comparable to the INQUISITION for trying heretics, though severe sanctions such as the HEREM were applied at certain periods to deviationists whose doctrines and behavior might bring internal or external harm to the Jewish community. Outstanding victims of such sanctions were SPINOZA and Uriel ACOSTA. Whereas norms of behavior were spelled out in detail by the HALAKHAH, matters of faith were not sufficiently systematized to permit the establishment of generally accepted categories of h. In this respect the attempt of Maimonides to lay down certain principles of faith, the denial of which would apparently place those who reject them outside the pale of Judaism, represents a departure from the Jewish norm and was not allowed to go unchallenged. Writings belonging to heretics, even if valid scriptural scrolls, were not to be rescued from a conflagration on the Sabbath, and R. Tarphon went so far as to declare that he would deliberately commit them to the flames (*Shab.* 116b).

HERMENEUTICS (Heb. *middot*): Rules for interpreting the biblical text both for halakhic and aggadic purposes. The rules of h. are traditionally held to be as old as the text itself. Their origin is unknown but they were first classified by HILLEL who formulated seven exegetical principles by which the Bible is to be expounded:

1. *Kal va-Ḥomer*: an *ad fortiorem* inference which permits deductions from a minor to a major case.
2. *Gezerah Shavah*: Inference by word analogy (if two biblical passages contain words with similar or identical meanings, both laws, although different in themselves, are subject to the same application).
3. *Binyan Av mi-Katuv Eḥad.* Principles derived from a single verse and applied to a group of biblical passages.
4. *Binyan Av mi-Shenei Ketuvim*: Same as (3) but based on two passages.
5. *Kelal u-Pherat u-Pherat u-Kelal*: Limitations of a general principle derived from a particular, and vice versa.
6. *Ka-Yotze Bo be-Makom Aḥer*: Principles derived by virtue of similar passages (according to some authorities, 5 represents two rules, and 6 should be deleted).

7. *Davar ha-Lamed me-Inyano*: Deduction from context.

R. ISHMAEL amplified these to 13 principles and R. Eliezer ben Yose Ha-Gelili (according to post-talmudic literature) to 32. Most of these last are intended for aggadic interpretation, but some are valid for *halakhah* and appear also in the rules of Hillel and Ishmael. Other methods of biblical h. applied at different times included GEMATRIA, NOTARIKON, and interpretations of apparently superfluous words, prefixes, and suffixes. This last method characterized the approach of R. Akiva as opposed to R. Ishmael who held that "The Bible speaks in the language of men" i.e., it uses human speech and cannot form the basis of legal deductions. R. Ishmael's viewpoint tended to prevail and the later rabbis taught that "nothing can override the plain meaning of the text" (*Shab.* 63a). Malbim (1809-1870) in the introduction to his commentary on the *Siphra* suggested that all the rules of interpretation are implied in the text, and can be deduced from the unique logical syntax of the Hebrew language.

HESCHEL, ABRAHAM JOSHUA (1907-1973): Philosopher and scholar. Born in Poland of a well-known ḥasidic family (see ABRAHAM JOSHUA HESCHEL OF OPATOV), he settled in the U.S. in 1940. From 1945 H. served as professor of Jewish ethics and mysticism at the Jewish Theological Seminary in New York. His religious philosophy (*Man is Not Alone; God in Search of Man; Man in Search of God*) draws on both modern EXISTENTIALISM and ḥasidic tradition, and has therefore been described as "Neo-Ḥasidism".

HESSAḤ DAAT: (Heb. lit. "removal of one's mind"): Phrase used in Jewish religious law to convey the idea of a lack of attentiveness in religious duties, which because of their importance demand special mental awareness in their performance. As a result of *h.d.* such actions become invalid i.e., if the person performing them allows his attention to wander. Typical examples include the need to keep one's mind alert in the separation of heave-offerings, in the laws appertaining to ritual uncleanness, and in the preparation of the ashes of the Red Heifer. Different aspects of *h.d.* are combined in a statement of R. Zeira (*Sanh.* 97a: "A lost article, the Messiah, and (the bite of) a scorpion appear with *h.d.*"; the first instance merely means "absent-mindedness", the other two mean that they come when least expected.

ḤESHVAN, see **MARḤESHVAN**

HESPED, see **EULOGY**

HETTER, see **DISPENSATION**

ḤEVRAH (or **ḤAVURAH**) **KADDISHA** (Heb. and Aram. "holy brotherhood"): The term refers to Jewish communities as a whole in the YEKUM PURKAN prayer. Subsequently, however, it was almost exclusively applied to the "brotherhood" which undertakes to perform the religious task of the burying of the dead in accordance with Jewish law. The respect due to the dead, together with the strict prohibition against deriving any material benefit from a dead body, combined to make this a sacred, voluntary duty. Although there are references to such groups in earlier times (e.g. *M.K.* 27b), the institution of the formal *ḥ.k.* is ascribed to R. JUDAH LOEW BEN BEZALEL of Prague and it became a recognized institution in the 17th cent. Members were often present to hear deathbed confessions, to provide the funeral repast, and to comfort the mourners. The members hold a special banquet on a specific day of the year, preceded by a service at which special *seliḥot* are recited. Among *Sephardim* the *ḥ.k.* is called the Society of Lavadores or *ḥ.k. ḥesed ve-emet*.

HEZEKIAH: King of Judah, 720-692 B.C.E. The biblical books describe him as one of the most righteous kings. He renewed the pure monotheistic religion and purged the Israelite cult of all pagan influences and elements (some of which H.'s father Ahaz had introduced even into the Temple at Jerusalem). In his zeal to eradicate all idols he also destroyed the BRAZEN SERPENT of Moses. H. was a contemporary of the prophet ISAIAH, who wielded great influence in affairs of state, particularly during the crisis of Sennacherib's siege of Jerusalem. The Talmud depicts H. as an ideal king, worthy to be the MESSIAH. According to one rabbinic opinion his was indeed the messianic reign.

ḤIBBUT HA-KEVER (Heb. "the torture in the grave"): Belief that a person is judged in the grave during the first days after burial by being tortured by the ANGEL OF DEATH or other demonic beings unless he remembers his name. Hence it was recommended to learn by heart a biblical verse beginning and ending with the initial and final letters of one's name. Those who practiced charity, hospitality, and devotion in prayer are exempt from the test. The idea occurs in early eschatological *aggadah* and was developed by the kabbalists.

ḤIDDUSHIM, see **NOVELLAE**

ḤIDKA, FEAST (or **MEAL**) **OF RABBI:** The 2nd cent. *tanna* R. Ḥ. held (*Shab.* 117b) that the Sabbath should be honored by four meals and not the customary three (see SEUDAH SHELISHIT). Hence certain Orthodox Jews observe a fourth Sabbath meal called the meal of R. Ḥ.

HIGH FESTIVALS (or **HIGH HOLIDAYS**): Term for ROSH HA-SHANAH and the DAY OF ATONEMENT, the most solemn festivals of the Jewish year. See YAMIM NORAIM.

HIGH PLACE (Heb. *bamah*): Structure, usually of stones, used in biblical times for cultic purposes, and built generally on a hill (I Kings 14:23), though also at times in a valley (Jer. 7:31). The Canaanite h.p. contained an altar, MATZEVAH, and ASHERAH, visible symbols of the deity. According to rabbinic law sacrifices on a h.p. were legitimate until the building of the Tabernacle, which thereupon became the exclusive cult center in the wilderness. After the conquest of Canaan the ban on h.p.'s was temporarily suspended but was reintroduced when Shiloh became the center of worship, then lifted again until the completion of Solomon's Temple. Jeroboam I erected high places at Bethel and Dan (I Kings 12:29ff.) to draw the people away from the pilgrimage to Jerusalem. Although high places often served as altars for worshiping the God of Israel, they tended to become associated with pagan practices, and biblical books (e.g. Deuteronomy, Kings) reflect an unremitting struggle against them. The h.p.'s in Judah were extirpated by Josiah (II Kings 23:8ff), and none existed during the Second Temple Period.

HIGH PRIEST (Heb. *kohen gadol*): Head of the priestly hierarchy in ancient Israel and chief official in the Temple. In the Pentateuch the designation appears in only one passage (Num. 35:25, 28), though another verse dealing with a PRIEST who is "highest among his brethren" (Lev. 21:10) is taken to refer to the same functionary. Other biblical titles for the office include "anointed priest" (Lev. 4:3ff.) and "head priest" (II Chron. 29:11). The office was conferred upon the descendants of AARON, who was ordained as the first Head Priest (Exod. 28:1); the ceremony of initiation, as described in Exod. 29 and Lev. 8, lasted for seven days and consisted of ritual ablutions, solemn investiture with the garb of office (the priestly breeches, tunic, girdle and miter and the high priestly robe, EPHOD, BREASTPLATE, and frontlet), ANOINTING with sacred oil, and other rites. As chief officiant at the Temple in Jerusalem the H.P. was in charge of the Temple administration and treasury and was entitled to officiate at will at all sacrificial services. He also administered the Divine ORACLE, the URIM AND THUMMIM. He was the sole ministrant at the solemn service on the DAY OF ATONEMENT, when he officiated in white linen garments; his entry on that day into the HOLY OF HOLIES to burn incense and sprinkle the sacrificial blood constituted the climax of the religious year (Lev. 16). He had to marry a virgin, and was forbidden to incur ritual impurity by proximity to a dead body, or to mourn the dead. In later times political machinations often marred the dignity and integrity of the office of the H.P., who was also head of the SANHEDRIN (the body which appointed him). In the early Second Temple Period the H.P. also acted as the political head of the nation, recognized as such by foreign rulers who charged him with maintaining order and collecting and delivering taxes. The office was in the hands of the Zadokite family until taken over by the HASMONEANS. From the time of Herod, appointments were made at the whim of the ruler. The office came to an end with the destruction of the Second Temple in 70 C.E.

HIGHER CRITICISM, see **BIBLE CRITICISM**

HILDESHEIMER, AZRIEL (Israel; 1820-1899): German Orthodox scholar. After officiating in Eisenstadt (Hungary) where he founded a rabbinical school combining secular with religious studies, he moved to Berlin in 1869 and headed the ADAT YISRAEL congregation. A foremost opponent of REFORM, he founded (1873) and directed until his death the BERLIN RABBINICAL SEMINARY for the training of modern Orthodox rabbis. H. was a leader of the Neo-Orthodox movement and also published scholarly works including an edition of the HALAKHOT GEDOLOT.

ḤILLAZON: Conchiferous marine animal, possibly *helix jointhina*, the blue blood of which was used for dying the blue cord of the TZITZIT as prescribed in Num. 15:39 (*Men.* 44a). It was very scarce and supposedly appeared only once in seventy years. For this reason the rabbis allowed its use to be dispensed with. According to *Sanh.* 91a the *ḥ.* snail was also found in the mountains, but the ritually prescribed species was caught near the coast in territory held by the tribe of Zebulun (*Meg.* 6a). R. Joseph described the *ḥ.* fishing area as extending from Tyre in Phoenicia down to Haifa Bay. According to the Zohar it could also be found in the Sea of Galilee.

HILLEL (1st cent. B.C.E.): Rabbinic authority and Pharisaic leader. H. went to Jerusalem to study with Shemaiah and Avtalyon. He returned to Babylonia, but later went back to Jerusalem where he became the recognized head and *nasi* of the highest academy. He and his colleague SHAMMAI (with whom he basically differed on matters of legal interpretation, with H. advocating an attitude of leniency) constituted the last of the ZUGOT. H. assumed his office at a time when the whole structure of the religious and national life of the nation was in danger as a result of Herod's policies. He dedicated himself to the task of raising an academy for the study of the Law, and warned his contemporaries to shun politics but to "love peace and draw their fellow men to the *Torah*" (*Avot* 1:12). Neither Herod nor the Roman rulers hindered his endeavors which exerted a major influence on the development of Judaism. Indeed it is said of H. that like Ezra, who also came from Babylonia to Jerusalem, he restored the *Torah*, which had been neglected (*Suk.* 20a); he and Shammai were responsible for establishing the study of the ORAL LAW independently of biblical texts. H.'s virtues and his teaching that love of man is the essence of the Divine Law (*Shab.* 30-31) are reflected in the institutions he introduced, the best known of which is the PROSBUL. He also determined seven basic rules of HERMENEUTICS which enabled greater flexibility in the approach to Bible interpretation than was permitted by Shammai. H. was noted for his modesty, patience, and leniency; asked to define Jewish law in one sentence he replied "Do not unto others that which you would not have them do unto you" (*Shab.* 31a). See also BET HILLEL AND BET SHAMMAI.

HILLEL II (2nd half of the 4th cent.): Patriarch of Palestinian Jewry. He abolished the proclamation of a new month by observation of the NEW MOON and substituted for it a permanent CALENDAR, based on complicated but very exact calculations. This calendar and its adoption meant that the Diaspora no longer had to depend on Palestine for the fixing of dates, and it remains the standard Jewish calendar. H. was in correspondence with the Roman emperor Julian (called the Apostate), who addressed him with particular affection.

HILLEL BEN SAMUEL OF VERONA (1220-c. 1295): Philosopher and physician in Italy. A representative though unoriginal thinker, he did much to spread the ideas of MAIMONIDES, whom he ardently admired. His best-known work is *Tagmulei ha-Nephesh* ("The Rewards of the Soul") on the nature, immortality, and ultimate fate of the soul.

HILLEL, SCHOOL OF, see **BET HILLEL AND BET SHAMMAI**

ḤILLUL HA-SHEM (Heb. "profanation of the [Divine] Name", cf. Lev. 22:32): The special emphasis given to *ḥ.h.* in Jewish thought and religion derives from the concept that the honor of God is so bound up with the Jewish people that any praiseworthy act on the part of a Jew adds to the glory of God, and conversely, any unworthy or dishonorable act detracts from that glory and causes a profanation, not only of the good name of the Jew, but of God Himself. Consequently, *ḥ.h.* is usually associated with a disreputable act on the part of a Jew, especially vis-à-vis non-Jews. Thus a theft committed by a Jew from a non-Jew is regarded as an offense more heinous than a similar one committed against a Jew, since it brings about the added sin of *ḥ.h.* In some instances, *ḥ.h.* was punished by excommunication. A person publicly regarded as a representative of Judaism should be particularly careful to ensure that his conduct is above reproach, for fear of causing *ḥ.h.* Thus Rav said that were he to purchase meat and not pay the butcher immediately (i.e., use his rabbinic reputation for buying on credit), he would be guilty of *ḥ.h.* (*Yoma* 86a).

ḤILLUL SHABBAT (Heb.): The desecration or profanation of the SABBATH. So fundamental and central is the duty of Sabbath observance in Jewish thought and law that the Sabbath desecrator is equated with one who transgresses the entire *Torah* and is regarded, for certain purposes, as a non-Jew. Thus wine touched by a desecrator of the Sabbath is regarded as if it were touched by a non-Jew, and is hence unfit for Jewish use. The deliberate performance of one of the 39 types of work prohibited on the Sabbath constituted *Ḥ.S.* and was punishable by death; if done unintentionally, the offender had to bring a sin-offering to the Temple. The sacred duty of saving human life, however, may override the prescription of Sabbath observance.

HINNENI HE-ANI (Heb. "Behold me, poor [in good works]"): Opening words of a prayer recited by the reader at the beginning of the Additional Service on *Rosh ha-Shanah* and the *Day of Atonement* according to the *Ashkenazi* rite. Originally intended as a silent meditation, it has often been developed into a demonstration of cantorial virtuosity.

HIRING AND LETTING (Heb. *sekhirut*): Transactions by which the interested parties contract for the use of property or the labor power and skill of an individual. The hiring of labor power or personal service is governed by 1) the general considerate relationship between master and servant, employer and employees, as outlined in the Talmud and based on biblical legislation (e.g. Lev. 25:43); and 2) the specific terms of contract which may, however, be repudiated by the employee. H. and l. of property is subject to the same laws as selling (*Bava Metzia* 56b), both as regards manner of acquisition and deceit or overcharge. The liability of the lessee extends only to neglect but not to damage incurred in the normal use of the property hired. If no definite date is stated for termination of the lease, due notice must be given to the lessee. The period of notice varies with the type of property hired, the season of the year, and local custom (*Bava Metzia* 101b).

HIRSCH, SAMSON RAPHAEL (1808-1888): German rabbi, author, and founder of neo-Orthodoxy. In 1851, he relinquished a rabbinical post at Nikolsburg (Moravia) to answer a call from the Orthodox *Israelitische Religionsgesellschaft* of Frankfort-on-Main. From there he propagated his doctrine of *Trennungsorthodoxie* (orthodoxy of separation): Orthodox Jews, according to H., ought to organize themselves in completely autonomous congregations and refuse alliance or integration with larger communities if these were not committed to Orthodox ideals and practice. From Frankfort he started a countrywide movement of secession opposed to the majority view favoring integration, whose chief spokesman was Rabbi S. B. BAMBERGER of Würzburg. The Reichstag bill of 1878 permitting Jews to secede from the state-recognized religious community was passed largely as a result of H.'s efforts. His basic maxim was *Torah im Derekh Eretz* ("*Torah* together with secular knowledge"). This idea was first expressed in the *Nineteen Letters* and more copiously in *Horeb* and his monthly *Jeschurun*. His concept of Jewish nationality was purely religious and based on a fundamentalist attitude to biblical narrative and particularly to Sinaitic revelation. The biblical message, together with its rabbinically defined practical obligations, constituted the sole reason for the existence of the Jewish people. Israelite humanism was the highest pinnacle of human culture, of which classical humanism was but a preparatory stage. The Jewish mission was to exemplify the Divinely inspired doctrines of Judaism and these in turn would also inspire the rest of mankind. Religious and secular knowledge were complementary. Judaism was an organic this-worldly growth, hence the inimical effect of all attempts at Reform based on expediency and the rationalization of laxity in Jewish practice. Beside writings of a polemical and apologetic nature, H. also prepared German translations of and commentaries upon the Pentateuch, Psalms, and prayer book.

ḤISDA (3rd cent.): Babylonian *amora*. He and his colleague HUNA — both disciples of RAV — were called "the pious men of Babylonia" and increased the prestige of the academy of SURA. Many of his aggadic and halakhic dicta are quoted in both the Palestinian and the Babylonian Talmud. He was responsible for the prayer recited on setting out for a JOURNEY (*Ber.* 29b).

HISTORY: A historical conception is implicit in the Jewish religion. The Bible begins with an account of the Divine creation of the world — that is, an initial event, with which the subsequent h. of humanity must necessarily be linked. Judaism begins to receive its specific form with the historic account of the call of Abraham and the record of the patriarchs, leading on to the redemption from Egypt and the revelation at Sinai. Many of the basic observances of Judaism are linked with historical episodes: thus Passover recalls the Egyptian bondage and the Feast of Tabernacles the wandering in the Sinai desert. The Scriptures, the study of which was incumbent on the Jew as a fundamental religious duty, comprise in the Pentateuch and the Former Prophets the historical record of the Jewish people, while much of the rest — e.g. the Prophets — is incomprehensible without its historical background. Moreover, the Bible inculcates its moral lessons to a large extent by historic instances of immoral conduct resulting in the loss of Divine favor, as in the story of David (and Bathsheba) or of Ahab, or in stories of national apostasy resulting in political disaster, as repeatedly told in the Book of Kings. Later developments in Judaism tended, at the beginning at least, to emphasize historical aspects. Thus the final paragraph of the SHEMA (Num. 15:37-41) was apparently added specifically in order to bring in a reminder of the Exodus. The later feasts of *Ḥanukkah* and *Purim*, which were added to those ordained in the Pentateuch, commemorated historical episodes; the post-biblical FAST days were associated with historical misfortunes. Even the Feast of Pentecost had its basic agricultural associations diverted to the commemoration of the Sinaitic revelation; while the Day of Atonement became centered in its most solemn moments on the historic recollections of the Temple service (see AVODAH). The basic prayer of the Jewish liturgy, the AMIDAH, begins with a reference to God as the historic God of the three patriarchs, Abraham, Isaac, and Jacob, while the Grace after Meals stresses the historic connection of the people with the Land of Israel. The *Seder* service of Passover Eve, which became the most popular and universally observed Jewish religious ritual, was essentially an evocation of the circumstances of the Exodus from Egypt. Thus Judaism became not merely an historic religion, but a religion in which historic reminiscence and a sense of h. was utterly implicit at every turn. It is remarkable, therefore, that after a certain point this historic sense was lost. During the Second Temple Period and after, the present increasingly lost its meaningfulness and the historical orientation became focused on the ultimate fulfillment and end of h. (APOCALYPSE; ESCHATOLOGY; MESSIAH). The general outline of biblical h. and the historical association of religious observances was universally familiar, even to the most ignorant, however much embroidered by legend and fantasy. A general impression of later h., down to the fall of the Jewish state, was preserved in the *Ḥanukkah* liturgy and observances (later given literary form in the Scroll of Antiochus, modeled on the Book of Esther, which in some communities even entered into the liturgy), and on *Av* 9 by talmudic legends relating to the destruction of the Second Temple. But from this point onward historic ideas remained very vague and imprecise, being summed up in the liturgical phrase that "because of our sins we were exiled from our land", this being the reason for the beginnings of the Diaspora. Even the real occasions for the semi-festal days listed in *Megillat Taanit*, dating back to the period of the close of the Second Temple, came to be forgotten, and they were associated with trivial religious controversies.

The writings of Josephus marked the end of Jewish historiography for many centuries. Historic interest for the post-biblical period came to center on a completely different and essentially literary aspect of Judaism: in order to establish the authentic tradition regarding various halakhic problems, it was desirable to know the chronological sequence of the authorities quoted. It was basically to make this known that Sherira Gaon completed his Historical Epistle in answer to an inquiry sent by the elders of Kairouan (c. 992). The earliest consistent Jewish chronicles, such as the *Sepher ha-Kabbalah* of Abraham Ibn Daud (12th cent.), were intended to establish the continuity and reliability of the chain of rabbinic tradition as a convincing argument against the anti-rabbinic claims of the Karaites. Except for this, the historical purview of Judaism became increasingly restricted in this period. From the time of the Crusader massacres, historical elegies commemorating these persecutions began to figure in the liturgy, local fasts and some local festivities (often with the name "*Purim*") began to be instituted to celebrate local disasters or deliverances. However for the general sweep of Jewish h. from the period of the destruction of the Jewish state onward, there was little conception and indeed little interest. Only some national disasters of particular magnitude, such as the expulsion from Spain in 1492 or the Cossack massacres in Poland in 1648-9, entered fully into communal cognizance. To some extent, the exaggerated absorption in talmudic study as an overwhelming religious duty impeded historical knowledge. There was a tendency to overlook the study of the historical books even of the Bible, while the incipient chronicles of Jewish persecution which began to emerge in the 16th cent. were regarded as proper reading only for such days as *Av* 9, when the luxury of study was suspended and a scholastic vacuum ensued in Jewish religious education. H. thus hardly played any part at all, except insofar as it was comprised in the study of the Bible and of religious observances, though to be sure, this was inevitable in view of the fact that no general Jewish h. was written between the days of Josephus and those of the Protestant theologian Basnage at the beginning of the 18th cent. Clearly, it was impossible to include in the educational syllabus a subject in which no literature was available even for advanced study by adults. Only in the first half of the 19th cent. did systematic Jewish histories written by Jews begin to make their appearance. At the same time, h. began to figure for the first time in the syllabus of Jewish religious education, though confined as yet to the Biblical Period, down to Second Temple times. At the end of the 19th cent., Jewish histories down to contemporary times written specifically for educational purposes or for juvenile reading were published. Since then, many other successful works have appeared particularly in America, and h. is now regarded as an integral part of Jewish religious education. Meanwhile, Jewish historiography in its widest sense has been subject to constant development. To a great extent however, it has been centered around the various Jewish theological institutions and rabbinical seminaries in various lands. This has entailed two somewhat equivocal consequences: First, that the teaching of h. retained a theological complexion, and second, that the interest centered in theological and literary rather than in political or economic h. To this Heinrich Graetz, (1817-1891), the great master of Jewish h., added an unfortunate personal rationalistic prejudice against every manifestation of mysticism in Jewish life. Simon Dubnow (1860-1941), in his World H. of the Jewish People, beside attempting to redress the balance of Jewish historiography in favor of Eastern European Jewry (with full realization of the importance of Ḥasidism in Jewish life) at the same time stressed economic and social factors, and endeavored to make his h. basically secular in its approach. With this precedent, a new school of Jewish historians began to emerge, both in the Diaspora and in the State of Israel (where historians tend to approach the subject from the nationalistic and territorial standpoint). The emancipation of Jewish studies from their former dependence on theological institutions has assisted in developing a secular outlook. Yet the most eminent and versatile of contemporary Jewish historians, Salo Baron (b. 1895), in his monumental *Social and Religious History of the Jews,* insists on the integral importance and interconnection of the religious element throughout Jewish h. It was religion that brought the Jewish people into being, gave it cohesion and endowed it with phenomenal powers of resistance, and furnished it with the ideal of national resurgence that has influenced its recent renewal and the foundation of the State of Israel. At the same time, while the Jewish religion has conditioned Jewish h., Jewish h. in its turn, has conditioned the Jewish religion.

HITTITES: One of the seven nations mentioned in the Bible as inhabiting pre-Israelite Palestine (Gen. 15:20). They probably constituted an offshoot or colony of the powerful Hittite kingdom which flourished in Asia Minor in the 17th-13th cents. B.C.E. They left very little trace in Palestinian culture. The Bible scarcely mentions the great Hittite empire (cf. Josh. 1:4) although it makes a number of references to the Hittite kingdoms in Syria (e.g. II Kings 7:6).

ḤIVI AL-BALKHI (2nd half of the 9th cent.):

Freethinker and critic of the Bible. Born in Balkh (Afghanistan), he lived in Persia and caused considerable stir by his "two hundred critical comments on the Bible", pointing out impossibilities and contradictions, and provoking polemical rejoinders from SAADYAH and others.

ḤIYYA: Name of Palestinian *tanna*; co-redactor, with R. Hoshaiah, of the TOSEPHTA. Name also of several Palestinian and Babylonian *amoraim* including Ḥ. ben Abba, an important participant in halakhic discussions.

HOCHSCHULE FÜR DIE WISSENSCHAFT DES JUDENTUMS (Ger. "High School for Jewish Studies"): Institute for Jewish studies and for the training of reform rabbis opened in Berlin in 1872; for some time also known as *Lehranstalt für die Wissenschaft des Judentums.* It remained in existence until closed by the Nazis in 1942.

HOFFMANN, DAVID TZEVI (1843-1921): Bible and Talmud scholar; lecturer and, from 1899, principal of the BERLIN RABBINICAL SEMINARY. H. was a vigorous champion of Orthodoxy both against Reform and against anti-Semitic attacks on the Talmud and the *Shulḥan Arukh.* He wrote studies in early rabbinic literature and halakhic responsa (*Melammed le-ho'il*) and published editions of midrashic texts. His major work was his commentary on Leviticus and Deuteronomy which critically examined Graf-Wellhausen's theories of BIBLICAL CRITICISM.

ḤOL HA-MOED (Heb. "the weekday of the festival"): The intermediate days of the Festivals of Passover (3rd-6th day in the Diaspora, 2nd-6th day in Israel) and Tabernacles (3rd-7th day in the Diaspora, 2nd-7th in the Land of Israel). The pertinent regulations treat these days as a combination of weekday and festival. Only urgent work should be performed, although normal work is permitted if done with a distinguishing difference. Mourning is restricted, while marriages are not performed for the reason that one does not "commingle one joy with another". A special prayer, YAALEH VE-YAVO, is inserted in the *amidah* and Grace after Meals, HALLEL is recited (half-*Hallel* on Passover) as is the Additional Service, and special scriptural passages are read. There is a difference of opinion as to whether TEPHILLIN should be donned; *Sephardim* and Ḥasidim do not, while *Mitnaggedim* do, but without reciting the customary blessing. In Israel, where the festive aspect of these days is more pronounced than elsewhere, the custom of not donning the *tephillin* is almost universal. The talmudic tractate MOED KATAN ("Minor Festival") is devoted to the regulations governing *ḥ.h.*

HOLDHEIM, SAMUEL (1806-1860): Exponent of extreme Reform Judaism in Germany. In his Berlin congregation he introduced radical innovations such as services on Sunday, prayers in German, and family pews where the men, bareheaded, sat together with the women. He rejected the permanent validity of ceremonial law, disregarded the traditional marriage and divorce laws, and insisted on the primary functions of the rabbi as a teacher and preacher and not as an expert on ritual questions. Judaism for him was to be seen as part of the larger life of humanity, and as he believed that loyalty to its essential forms was compatible with allegiance to German nationality, H. strove for the complete integration of Jews into the German people, an accomplishment he regarded as a religious duty.

HOLINESS (Heb. *kedushah*): In an ethical sense h. signifies the attainment of moral purity and perfection through right conduct and especially by imitating the Divine ATTRIBUTES (see IMITATION OF GOD). Essentially h. is an attribute of God, who alone is "holy with every form of h." (*Y. Ber.* 9a), and the most common epithet for God in rabbinical literature is "The Holy One, blessed be He". Man attains h. to the extent that he consciously models his life and conduct upon the known attributes of God. "As He is merciful, be thou merciful; as He is gracious, be thou gracious" (*Shab.* 133b). Originally, however, h. was not an ethical term: the basic concept is rather one of "separateness", the Divine attribute of being apart from that which is not Divine. As a result of the COVENANT with God, Israel too became "separate" and accepted a state of h. which was to inform henceforth all its activities and even have physical implications (see HOLY CITY; HOLY LAND; HOLY PLACES). Israel is separated as a holy people; the priests and levites are separated as a holy caste responsible for the Temple ritual; the Sabbath is separated as a holy day; the Temple itself is separated as the place where man could worship the Divine Presence in the Holy of Holies. The obligation of h. falls on the individual as part of a holy people, and any shortcomings on the part of the individual reflect on the entire people. Failures in the ceremonial sphere cause a state of ritual impurity which must be expurged by a prescribed ritual. Apart from ceremonial h., stress came increasingly to be laid on h. in the ethical sense as it affected personal character. The prophets clashed with the priesthood over the question of emphasis; they did not negate ceremonial h. but proclaimed it meaningless without concomitant ethical h. The rabbinic code was devoted to sanctifying all of human life and with this object in mind a daily routine was prescribed by which the Jew would always feel himself part of a holy people. More specifically the rabbis on occasion connected h. with the prohibition against sexual licence, interpreting the verse "Ye shall be holy" (Lev. 19:2) as "ye shall be separated from sexual immorality" and adding that the word was always employed in connection with this aspect of right living (*Siphra, in loc.*). Accordingly Maimonides gives the title *Kedushah* ("holiness") to the fifth book of his code, which deals with sexual relationships. Similarly the rabbis connect h. with the dietary laws because of the juxtaposition (both in Lev. 11:45 and Lev. 20:26) of the prohibition against unclean animals, birds, and insects with the commandment to be holy. Nevertheless the "separation" implicit in h. is by no means to be regarded as a withdrawal from the world and its temptations, and Judaism has always opposed reclusion and extreme ASCETICISM. It insists on the attainment of h. by remaining separate from contaminating things while still living in their presence. It is this idea which runs through Lev. 19 — the so-called "Chapter of Holiness". The words "Ye shall be holy" are the keynote to the whole chapter and the various precepts must be read in connection with it. H. is not so much an abstract or a mystic idea as a regulative principle in the everyday life of men and women. It is attained not by flight from the world, nor by renunciation of human relationship of family or station, but by the spirit in which the obligations of life in its simplest and commonest details are fulfilled. According to the rabbis, man has only to set his feet upon the road to h. to receive Divine aid in its attainment: "If a man sanctify himself a little, he becomes sanctified much; if he sanctify himself below, he becomes sanctified from on high" (*Yoma* 39a). The classical exposition of the ladder of virtues by which man rises to h. was set forth in M. Ḥ. Luzzatto's *Mesillat Yesharim*. See also SANCTIFICATION.

HOLOCAUST, see **BURNT-OFFERING; WHOLE-OFFERING**

HOLY CITY: Traditional term for JERUSALEM. All cities which were believed to have been surrounded with a wall since the conquest of the land by Joshua are also invested with a special holiness, though less so than Jerusalem (Mishnah *Kelim* 1:6-7; *Arakh.* 8:6). Later sentiment also regarded three other cities in the Land of Israel as holy — Hebron, because of its association with the patriarchs and matriarchs; Tiberias, because of its importance after the Bar Kokhba War when it became the religious focus of the country; and Safed, the center of the Kabbalists in the 16th cent.

HOLY DAYS, see **FESTIVALS**

HOLY, HOLY, HOLY, see **KEDUSHAH**

HOLY OF HOLIES, see **TEMPLE**

HOLY LAND: "The Land of Israel is holier than any other land" (Mishnah *Kelim* 1:6). Not only for Jews is the Land of Israel holy, but also for Christians and to a lesser extent Moslems. The phrase "Holy Land" or rather "holy soil" is applied only once in the Bible to the Land of Israel (Zech. 2:16) but it is nevertheless clearly regarded as the land "which the Lord thy God careth for" (Deut. 11:12). Legally its sanctity was expressed in the fact that certain commandments could be fulfilled only in Israel. Consequently the question was raised whether the sanctity with which it was endowed after the conquest by Joshua ceased with the Babylonian Exile and whether all the land or only those portions which were occupied by the returned exiles was endowed with a permanent sanctity (Mishnah *Eduy.* 8:6; *Ḥul.* 7a). Over and above these legal considerations however, the sentiment of the Jewish people invested the land with imperishable holiness. The Talmud (e.g. *Ket.* end) provides many examples of the manner in which the rabbis gave expression to their love for the H.L. This love was re-echoed throughout Jewish literature, both lyrical and doctrinal, and finds its most vivid expression in the liturgy. Rabbinic and kabbalistic texts did not recoil from the most extravagant statements in glorifying the H.L., the merit of dwelling in it, and the spiritual graces (prophecy in particular) attainable in it. The holiness of the land led to the custom of taking to Israel for burial the remains of those who died abroad, and the rabbis said "Whoever is buried in the Land of Israel is as if he were buried beneath the altar". The custom elicited a vigorous protest from R. Judah Na-Nasi (2nd cent. C.E.), despite the fact that its first instances are those of Jacob and Joseph (*Gen. Rab.* 96:8). Throughout the centuries it was customary for Jews in the Diaspora to be buried with earth brought from the H.L.

HOLY PLACE: Every spot where God manifests Himself becomes holy, but it is His actual presence and not the memory of an event that bestows holiness on a place. Moses was bidden at the bush "Draw not nigh hither; put off thy shoes from off thy feet, for the place whereon thou standest is holy ground" (Exod. 3:5). Mt. Sinai was a h.p. for the period of the revelation only, during which time the people were forbidden to set foot there (Exod. 19:23). The Temple likewise was holy, and gentiles and those ritually unclean were forbidden to enter it. The holiest of all places in Jewish tradition was the Holy of Holies, which was barred to all but the High Priest, and even he could enter only on the Day of Atonement. Subsequent Jewish tradition has maintained the holiness of the temple site, which should, therefore, not be visited, because of the irremovable ritual impurity attaching to individual Jews in the post-Temple period. Among Oriental Jews, even outside the Land of Israel, various locations have been invested with the sanctity of a h.p. as the real or reputed sites of the graves of outstanding biblical and post-biblical figures. In many instances regular pilgrimages take place to these shrines on specific days. Thus in Hamadan in Persia the reputed graves of Esther and Mordecai were visited at the end of every month and on *Purim;* the Babylonian Jews venerated the site of the traditional grave of Ezra at Shatt-el-Arab at the confluence of the Tigris and Euphrates, and at Alkush near Mosul the grave of the prophet Nahum is venerated. In Israel, Mt. Meron — the burial place of R. Simeon bar Yoḥai, the traditional author of the Zohar — has become the site of a remarkable celebration on *Lag ba-Omer,* though the custom was strongly denounced as near idolatry by R. Moses Sopher among others. Many sites were "identified" as the graves of distinguished talmudic rabbis by the 16th cent. kabbalists in Safed and became the objects of the accepted tour of Orthodox pilgrims. From 1948 to 1967 many of the most venerated places were under Jordanian control and Jews were denied access to them, in spite of agreements that had permitted such visits. Since 1967 the CAVE OF MACHPELAH near Hebron, the TOMB OF RACHEL on the road from Jerusalem to Bethlehem, and especially the WAILING WALL (now referred to universally as the Western Wall) attract large numbers of pilgrims.

HOLY SCRIPTURES, see **BIBLE**

HOLY SPIRIT (Heb. *Ruaḥ ha-Kodesh*): The Divine spirit; spirit emanating from God. The expression occurs only three times in the Bible, where it is more or less synonymous with God (Is. 63:10) or else signifies His sustaining and inspiring presence (Is. 63:11; Ps. 51:13). Elsewhere biblical usage prefers "Spirit of God" (*Ruaḥ Elohim,* or *Ruaḥ YHWH, Ruaḥ El*) to denote the creative action of God (Gen. 1:2; Ps. 139:7; Job 33:4) as well as the powers of superior wisdom, statesmanship, and valor, which He imparts to man (e.g. Judg. 13:25; Is. 11:2), more particularly the gift of inspired speech (II Sam. 23:2; Joel 2:28-29). It is the latter sense which became especially associated with the later usage of the expression. According to the Talmud (*Sot.* 48b) the H.S. departed from Israel with the death of the last prophets, though a minor form of celestial communication still existed in the BAT KOL. Hence in some apocryphal writings H.S. refers either to the age of biblical prophecy or to the prophetic revival in the messianic age (cf. Joel *loc. cit*); in others the term is made to approximate the concept of an ever-present Divine WISDOM. The Targum often renders the "spirit of God" as the "spirit of Prophecy" and in this sense the term H.S. is often akin to the concept of SHEKHINAH. Rabbinic and medieval philosophical writers distinguished higher and lower forms of INSPIRATION and degrees of action attributed to the H.S., e.g. the direct inspiration of the Pentateuch, the "prophetic spirit" in the prophetic books proper, and the H.S. informing the HAGIOGRAPHA. Following R. Phineas ben Jair's dictum (Mishnah *Sot.* 9) "piety leads to the H.S.", it has been generally held — with many variations of form and emphasis — that the H.S. as a degree of spiritual perfection (viz. communion with God, DEVEKUT, and even illumination) can be attained by earnest striving, religious observance, ascetic discipline, and moral and intellectual perfection.

HOLY TONGUE, see **HEBREW**

HOMICIDE: "Thou shalt not murder" (Exod. 20:13) is one of the Ten Commandments; willful murder is a capital crime for which no expiation is possible other than the forfeiture of the life of the murderer (Num. 35:31-33). Failure to expiate the crime of murder renders society guilty (Deut. 19:10) and the land polluted (Num. *loc. cit.*). Thus, even in a case where the murderer is unknown, the Bible ordains the ceremony of EGLAH ARUPHAH (Deut. 21:1-9) in order to free society from the taint of innocent blood shed in its midst. While the prohibition of h. was formally and explicitly enjoined upon Noah — "Whosoever sheddeth man's blood, by man shall his blood be shed, for in the image of God made He man" (Gen. 9:6) — it seems to have been presupposed from creation. Thus Cain was called to account for Abel's murder without having first received a direct prohibition against h. The capital punishment suffered by the murderer serves both as an expiation for the community at large and as atonement for the criminal himself provided he repents and makes full confession of his guilt. Euthanasia (mercy killing) is also strictly forbidden in Jewish law; see also ABORTION. The only instances of what might be called justifiable h. are:

(1) Self-defense. This applies not only when one's life is directly threatened, but also when there exists reasonable certainty that one's life might be in danger (see BURGLARY).

(2) If a man pursues another with the intention of taking his life (*rodeph*), it is justifiable for anyone to prevent the attempted crime, even by taking the pursuer's life.

(3) If one sees another pursuing a victim with the intention of committing rape, adultery, incest, or unnatural sexual act (e.g. with another male), he is in duty bound to prevent the crime by taking the assailant's life.

In these instances the assailant is intent upon a crime that is punishable by death, or excision (*karet*); the taking of his life is condoned only where other means, such as wounding him, prove ineffective in preventing the crime. If such means could have been attempted, but were not, the rescuer is himself considered a murderer (*Sanh.* 74a). Moreover once the crime has been committed, it is forbidden to take the law into one's own hands. Accidental manslaughter is punished by banishment to one of the forty-eight CITIES OF REFUGE. The court trying a case of murder must consist of no less than twenty-three fully qualified judges who must not be aged, childless, or eunuchs (*Sanh.* 26b). While the court may acquit by a simple majority vote, a majority of at least two votes is necessary for a conviction. In the event of a death-sentence and execution, the judges must fast until evening. Circumstantial EVIDENCE, even of the most compelling kind, is not acceptable in court. To become guilty in law, intention of both the act and its result must be proven and the death of the victim must have resulted from the direct and immediate blow of the accused. If, after summing up the evidence, one of the judges is unable to render a decision, two more judges are added to the bench, a new trial commenced, and the previous proceedings rendered void. In rabbinic law CAPITAL PUNISHMENT can be imposed only after the fulfillment of conditions so stringent (e.g. two witnesses must have forewarned the murderer of the gravity of the crime he was about to commit; the Sanhedrin must be sitting in the Temple) that a death sentence was an extremely rare event. Where carried out, execution for h. was by means of the sword. If the crime of h. was found proved but the requisite conditions for the death penalty had not been fulfilled, rabbinic law provides for lengthy imprisonment. (See also HATRAAH; IMPRISONMENT).

HOMILETICS: The art of preaching. Homiletical expositions of the Bible, both halakhic and aggadic, are as old as the Bible itself. The Book of Deuteronomy can be classified as a sermon which elaborates on the Law and admonishes the people. The words: "And Moses assembled all the congregation of the children of Israel" (Exod. 35) followed by the giving of the laws of the Sabbath is taken by the rabbis to have been a Divine instruction to Moses to assemble congregations on Sabbath and preach to them about the Sabbath laws, while another tradition ascribes to Moses the practice of preaching on each festival about its observance and significance (*Yalkut* Exod. 408). The prophets' addresses were sermons on ethics and morality and on the devout observance of the Divine laws. Ezra and the men of the Great Assembly explained and expounded the Law (Ezra 7:10; Neh. 8:8), and Shemaiah and Avtalyon (1st cent. B.C.E.) were referred to as great preachers (*Pes.* 70b), while many *tannaim* used to preach on *aggadah* in addition to expounding the intricacies of the *halakhah* In talmudic times there were two types of preachers, one who lectured on *halakhah* and the other on *aggadah*. The *halakhah* preacher used to deliver only the gist of his legal pronouncement in Hebrew and an interpreter elaborated on it in the vernacular. The New Testament, Josephus, and Philo attest to the practice of preaching in the synagogue on Sabbaths and festivals as an integral part of the service. Many MIDRASHIM are in fact literary compilations based on sermons. The Midrashim PESIKTA DE-RAV KAHANA and PESIKTA RABBATI consist of complete sermons for various occasions written (unlike other midrashim) in the very words with which the preacher addressed his audience. In the Gaonic Period there flourished many distinguished expounders (*darshanim*) who delivered their sermons in Arabic, but these were not committed to writing. Many of the medieval philosophical and moralist compositions originated in sermons, e.g. the *Twelve Sermons* by Nissim Gerondi (14th cent.); *Menorat ha-Maor* by R. Isaac Aboab (14th cent.); *Nishmat Ḥayyim* by Manasseh Ben Israel (17th cent.); *Akedat Yitzḥak* by Isaac Arama (16th cent.). The custom of preaching in the vernacular was in vogue in several European countries. Thus in Amsterdam in the 17th cent., Manasseh Ben Israel and Isaac Aboab shared the pulpit and preached in Spanish, and their addresses attracted even non-Jewish listeners to the synagogue. In Italy, especially in Venice, the sermon was an institution; the language was generally Italian with a certain mixture of Hebrew. The scope of the sermon delivered in the ghetto was broad, and aimed at educating as well as inspiring. Preaching in Germany and France in medieval times was not widespread, probably because many *piyyutim* replaced the sermon and because more attention was paid to *halakhah* than to *aggadah*. A rabbi delivered sermons on only two occasions of the year — the Sabbaths before Passover and the Day of Atonement — explaining the laws and significance of the forthcoming holy days. The situation in E. European communities was similar. In the 17th and 18th cents. a new type of Yiddish-speaking preacher called the MAGGID appeared in Germany and E. Europe, and attracted large audiences. The *maggidim* were "free-lancers" traveling from town to town, and their homiletical expositions of Bible, Talmud, and Midrash were intended both to educate and to infuse a love for the higher values of life into the hearts of their listeners. Larger communities, such as Vilna, employed a permanent *maggid*. Preaching in the vernacular as a feature of the synagogue service was introduced into Germany by the Reform Movement in the early 19th cent. and by communities in other lands. Adolf JELLINEK brought his profound scholarship to the modern sermon, using talmudic and midrashic homiletical expositions as the basis of his preaching. Samson Raphael Hirsch established the German sermon also in Orthodox Judaism in Germany. A more recent tendency, especially in western communities, is to link the Sabbath sermon to topics of current events.

ḤONI HA-ME'AGGEL (Heb. Ḥoni the circle-drawer; 1st cent. B.C.E.); Sage. Ḥ. was considered a miracle worker, and his prayers were held to be particularly efficacious. During the civil war between the brothers Hyrcanus and Aristobulus he was asked by the former's party to put a curse on its opponents. According to Josephus Ḥ. prayed instead for peace between the brothers and was stoned to death. During a severe drought he drew a circle and refused to step out of it until God had answered his prayer for rain; his name is said to derive from this incident. The Talmud also makes him the hero of a legend according to which after a sleep of seventy years he awoke to find the world so changed and beyond recognition that he desired to die.

HONOR: Respect manifested for worth, merit, or rank. H. is in the first place due to God, the source of all h. (Prov. 3:9; Mal. 1:6), and according to the Bible also to parents (Exod. 20:12), the Sabbath (Is. 18:13), the aged (Lev. 19:32), and the God-fearing (Ps. 15:4). The rabbis also emphasize the h. due to one's teacher since "the father only ensures him life in this world, while the teacher brings him to the life of the World to Come" (*Bava Metzia* 33a). The rabbinic saying "Let the h. of thy friend be as dear to thee as thine own" (*Avot* 2:15) enjoins both the duty of self-respect and the h. due to others. H. is to be paid to royalty (*Exod. Rab.* 4), the patriarch (*Ket.* 17a), and the *Torah.* The Talmud discusses whether a person can renounce the h. which is due to him, and concludes that a king (*Ket.* 17a) and a teacher (*Kidd.* 32b) may not. At the same time the rabbis repeatedly and severely condemned the seeking of h. "H. flees from him who pursues it, but it pursues him who flees from it" (*Eruv* 13b).

HORAYOT (Heb. "decisions"): Tractate in the Mishnah order of *Nezikin* with *gemara* in both Talmuds. Its three chapters deal with the procedure to be followed in the case of erroneous decisions by the Sanhedrin or the High Priest and the sin-offering which is due in expiation (see Lev. 4).

HORIN (CHORIN), AARON BEN KALMAN (1766-1854): Hungarian Reform rabbi. As rabbi in Arad, he advocated extreme liberal principles (mixed marriages, introduction of organ music and the vernacular into the synagogue service, modifications of the *halakhah,* relinquishment of national messianic hopes such as the return to Zion) which brought him into conflict with the Orthodox rabbinate; the government finally had to intervene in his behalf.

HOROWITZ, ISAIAH (known as *Shelah* after the initials of his main work; c. 1565-1630): Kabbalist and moralist. Born in Prague, he served as rabbi in Posen, Cracow, Frankfort, Prague, and then in Jerusalem until he moved to Safed and Tiberias because of persecution by the local ruler. His *Shenei Luḥot ha-Berit* ("Two Tablets of the Covenant") is an encyclopedic compendium of kabbalistic theology, traditional philosophy, moralist teaching, and devotional and ascetic guidance. The book became an influential vehicle of Lurianic piety.

HOROWITZ, JACOB ISAAC (1746-1825): Ḥasidic leader. A disciple of Dov Ber of Mezhirich and R. Elimelech of Lizensk, he was one of the founders of popular Ḥasidism in Poland. His saintliness and charismatic powers earned him the title "the Seer of Lublin". H. interpreted the Napoleonic wars in an eschatological perspective, and ḥasidic legend connects his illness and death with his attempt to force the advent of the Messiah.

HOSANNA, see **HOSHANOT**

HOSEA: First book of the Minor Prophets. A contemporary of Isaiah, Amos, and Micah, H. came from the Northern Kingdom and prophesied during the latter half of the 8th cent. B.C.E. His execrations were uttered under the shadow of impending doom: the Assyrians under Tiglath-pileser III were advancing into the kingdom of Israel in 733 B.C.E., and by 721 Samaria fell. At the core of H.'s impassioned pleading stood the symbolism of a broken matrimonial life; it is unclear whether the prophet's utterances on this subject are metaphorical or an account of his actual experience. In any event the wife's harlotry epitomized Israel's unfaithfulness to the Lord, its breach of the covenant, its licentious liaison with Baal, and immoral behavior. With the pathos of a deceived yet ever-loving husband, H. beseeched his compatriots to return to God and thus save themselves. Though threatening dire punishment for Israel's defection, the prophet still presents God's mercy as the supreme force. There will be a new betrothal, he proclaimed, everlasting in justice, kindliness, and faith. It has been suggested that the first 3 chapters of the Book of H. are by a different hand from the rest of the book and date from an earlier period (possibly the reign of Jehu).

HOSHAIAH RABBAH (Heb. "H. the Great"; first half of the 3rd cent.): Palestinian *amora.* A celebrated authority on the Mishnah ("father of the Mishnah"), he was equally prominent as an aggadic teacher. His homilies (of which the opening chapter of GENESIS RABBAH is one — hence the whole *Midrash* has been attributed to him) reflect the religious discussions between Jews and Christians in Caesarea where H. had his academy. Most leading Palestinian *amoraim* of the next generation were his disciples.

HOSHANA RABBAH: The seventh day of the Feast of TABERNACLES. During this festival in Temple times the people made daily circuits round the altar, waving the FOUR SPECIES and crying "*hoshana*" (see HOSHANOT) while on the seventh day they circuited seven times. This day was therefore called *Hoshana Rabbah* i.e., "The Great *Hoshana*". The ceremony of the WATER DRAWING in a ritual of great merry making (*Suk*. 53a) took place the previous day, while *H.R.* itself was the occasion for the beating of the willow branches (symbolizing the dependence on RAIN) which was the climax of the festival (though opposed by the Sadducees and Boethusians because of the absence of scriptural authorization). During the Middle Ages a sober note was introduced into the celebrations by identifying *H.R.* with the last day of judgment and the culmination of the period of self-examination and repentance which begins 3 weeks earlier on the New Year. This aspect is especially stressed in *Sephardi* practice. The synagogue service combines all the normal ritual of the Intermediate Days (see ḤOL HA-MOED), together with a sevenfold circuit of the *almemar* with the Four Species, while appropriate *hoshana* hymns are recited. In the *Ashkenazi* rite the penitential character of the day is emphasized by the reader's wearing the white canonicals of the Penitential Days and by the recitation of the preliminary psalms read on Sabbaths and festivals. The beating of the willow branches continues the Temple custom. Such importance was attached to this day even in early times that when Hillel II (c. 360) instituted the fixed CALENDAR, he included the provision that the calendar should be adjusted so that *H.R.* would never fall on a Sabbath. In the 13th cent. Abudraham mentions the custom, which still prevails among pious Jews, of staying up the night of *H.R.* A special order of service (*tikkun*) was evolved for the occasion, which included the reading of the Book of Deuteronomy, Psalms, and passages from the Zohar. A number of superstitions grew up around this occasion and it was widely believed that a person who was to die during the coming year would not see the shadow of his head on the night of *H.R.*

HOSHANOT (from "*hosha-na*" hosanna, i.e., "O deliver"; Ps. 118:25): Prayers recited on the Feast of TABERNACLES during the HAKKAPHOT circuits. Written in the form of litanies, they consist of a large number of brief lines (usually arranged alphabetically), each of which opens and concludes with the response *hoshana* spoken by the congregation. They are generally simple in form, addressing God by different epithets or beseeching His deliverance "because of Thy truth, because of Thy covenant", etc.; some of the *h.* in use today, however, were composed by well-known *paytanim* such as Eleazar Kallir and are more complex. Originally, the *h.* were prayers for RAIN, recited on the Festival of Tabernacles because it marks the approaching rainy season, but rain is not explicitly mentioned in all *h.* as the desired object. The word *hoshana* was also popularly applied to the willow branch carried on HOSHANA RABBAH.

HOSPITALITY (Heb. *hakhnasat oreḥim*): Few social virtues rank higher in the scale of merit than the practice of h., which is included among "those things of which a man enjoys the fruit in this world while the stock remains with him in the World to Come" (*Shab*. 127a; *Peah* 1:2). On the basis of Gen. 18:1-8, Abraham is regarded in Jewish lore as typifying the virtue of h. The invitation now incorporated into the Passover *Seder* service — "Let all who hunger enter and eat" — was originally the exhortation uttered before all meals by R. Huna (*Taan*. 20b). The rabbis teach that the virtue of h. is to be extended to everyone — the poor, the ignorant, the stranger, and those of lower social status than the host — and they condemn various rabbis for their tendency to confine h. to their own class. "Let thy house be open wide, and let the poor frequent it" (*Avot* 1:5). The laws of h. are elaborated in detail in rabbinic literature, and the rabbis are as insistent on the duties of the host as those of the guests. The host should always have a cheerful countenance in order to make his guests feel at home. He should serve the guests himself. All kinds of dishes should be placed on the table so as not to embarrass the fastidious guest. As the guest is required to express his thanks to the host, the privilege of reciting the Grace after Meals is given to him "in order that he may thereby invoke the blessing of God on his host" (*Ber*. 58a), and in addition to statutory thanks, "the good guest also says 'Blessed be the host, may he be remembered for good'" (Y. *Ber*. 9). When a learned company was assembled and speeches were delivered in a private home "they opened their discourse with praise of the host" (*Ber*. 68a). During the Middle Ages, the practice of h. toward itinerant mendicants and traveling scholars, etc. was widespread; a Jew visiting a synagogue in a town other than his own would naturally be invited to the homes of the congregants for meals. *Hakhnasat Oreḥim* societies were established to provide shelter for travelers.

HOST OF HEAVEN: God is frequently described as the "Lord of hosts", the reference being sometimes to human armies (e.g. Exod. 7:4; 12:41), to the stars (Deut. 4:19; Is. 40:26), to the angels (Josh. 5:14 ff.), or to cosmic powers generally (Gen. 2:1). The h. of h. may have originally been a metaphor derived from the stars regarded as arrayed in order of battle (cf. Judg. 5:20, "The stars in their courses fought against Sisera"). In ancient polytheism the heavenly host was the object of worship (cf. *avodat kokhavim* "worship of the stars" — one of the rabbinic terms for paganism). Instances of such worship even in Israel are mentioned in the Bible. King Ahaz built altars "for all the host of heaven in the two courts of the house of the Lord", which were later destroyed by Josiah (II Kings 21:3-5; 23:5). The worship of the h. of h. seems to have taken place also on the rooftops of houses (Zeph. 1:5; Jer. 19:2). In the language of Jewish monotheism the expression became a poetical metaphor for both the heavenly bodies, and the retinue of angels. Both are pictured as singing the praises of the Creator (cf. Ps. 148:1-5 and the YOTZER benediction in the daily Morning Service).

ḤOVAH, see **DUTY**

ḤUKKAT HA-GOY (Heb. "statute of the gentile"; cf. Lev. 20:23): Developing the law in Lev. 20:23, the rabbis stipulated that a Jew was forbidden to copy GENTILE mores, especially if these partook of lewdness or loose morality or the manner in which the gentiles conducted their religious rites. The first category prohibited the wearing of a specifically gentile COSTUME, including even the manner of dressing one's hair. In the second may be noted such customs as attendance at circuses and stadia (see Rashi on Lev. 18:3). The ban on idolatrous rites extends also to customs which "have become part of their folly" such as superstitious practices (see Tosaphot on *Sanh.* 52a). Much of Jewish law was fashioned as a reaction to gentile customs, and although this particular attitude does not for the most part obtain in modern times, Orthodox voices are often still raised against the dangers of adopting non-Jewish habits. On the other hand, Jewish religious practice has always been influenced by its environment, as can be detected in such details as liturgical music and customs and synagogue architecture.

ḤULLIN (Heb. "profane things"): As a technical term *ḥ.* denotes anything that is not — by vow, dedication, or otherwise — "holy", i.e., reserved for priestly or ritual use. More particularly it refers to "profane" food, i.e., such as may be eaten without observing the rules of levitical purity (unlike sacrificial meat, heave- and dough-offering, etc.).

ḤULLIN: Tractate in the Mishnah order *Kodashim,* with *gemara* in the Babylonian Talmud. It deals with the laws concerning slaughtering (SHEḤITAH) for profane use as well as other prescriptions relating to the preparation of animal food (cf. BEDIKAH, BLOOD, MEAT), CLEAN AND UNCLEAN ANIMALS, and forbidden meats (see TEREPHAH). It is one of the main sources for the DIETARY LAWS.

ḤUMASH (Heb. from *ḥamesh* — "five"): The five books of Moses, or PENTATEUCH; synonymous with TORAH in the sense of the first division of the Hebrew Bible; a volume containing the Pentateuch, used in the synagogue by the congregation in following the Reading of the Law.

HUMILITY: The verse "And what doth the Lord require of thee but to do justly, to love mercy, and to walk humbly with thy God" (Micah 6:8) is stated by the Talmud (*Mak.* 24a) to contain within it the entire *Torah,* and the rabbis described the third of its prescriptions, h., as the greatest of Jewish virtues. It was an attribute of Moses, who was "exceedingly humble, above all the men that were upon the face of the earth" (Num. 12:3). H. is regarded as the outstanding characteristic of the "disciples of Abraham" in contrast to the "disciples of Balaam" (*Avot* 5:22). However, it must not be confused with servility, which is considered a vice despite the statement "Be exceedingly lowly in spirit" (*Avot* 4:4). R. Johanan emphasized the importance of h.: "In every passage where mention is made of the greatness of God, it is combined with mention of His h. This is written in the Pentateuch, repeated in the Prophets, and stated for a third time in the Hagiographa" (*Meg.* 31a).

ḤUMRA (Aram): The stricter of two possible rulings in a condition of halakhic doubt. Although indiscriminate preference for the more lenient ruling is condemned by the rabbis, they deny any virtue to a *ḥ.* for its own sake. In doubts regarding biblical law the stricter ruling applies, in matters of rabbinic law the more lenient solution should be adopted. Rabbinic law provides further directives as to when and to what extent doubts, mitigating circumstances, the nature of the issue etc. should affect the ruling.

ḤUPPAH (Heb.): Originally the bridal chamber in which the marriage was consummated (see Ps. 19:6; Joel 2:16) and where the nuptials continued for seven days. The word is now used for the canopy, symbolizing the chamber, under which the wedding ceremony takes place. It ranges in form from richly embroidered baldaquins to a simple *tallit* attached to poles by its four corners. The word is popularly employed as a term synonymous with the wedding ceremony.

HURVITZ, see **HOROWITZ**

HUSBAND, see **MATRIMONY**

ḤUSHIEL BEN ELHANAN (2nd half of the 10th cent.): Rabbinic scholar. Born in Italy, Ḥ. settled in Kairouan where he founded a flourishing academy and laid the foundations for subsequent rabbinic culture in North Africa. He was succeeded by his son HANANEL.

HYGIENE, see **HEALTH**

HYMNS, see **LITURGY; PIYYUT; ZEMIROT**

HYPOCRISY: The Talmud defines the hypocrite as "He who says one thing in the heart and another with his lips". H. is frequently condemned by the rabbis, and Gamaliel II forbade any student "whose inside is not like his outside" to enter his academy (*Ber.* 28a). A classic warning against the hypocrite is the deathbed advice of the Sadducee king Alexander Yannai to his Pharisee wife Salome Alexandra, "Fear neither the Pharisees nor the Sadducees, but those who do the deeds of Zimri and expect the reward of Phinehas" (*Sot.* 22b., the reference being to Num. 25).

I

IABNEH, see **YAVNEH**

IBN ATTAR, ḤAYYIM, see **ATTAR, ḤAYYIM BEN MOSES**

IBN AVI ZIMRA, see **ZIMRA, DAVID BEN SOLOMON IBN AVI**

IBN BAKUDA, see **BAḤYA IBN PAKUDA**

IBN DAUD, ABRAHAM (known by his initials as *Ravad*; c. 1110–c. 1180): Spanish philosopher, historian, and martyr. The first thoroughgoing Jewish Aristotelian, he tried to show in his main philosophical work *Emunah Ramah* ("Exalted Faith") — of which only a Hebrew translation of the Arabic original has survived — that science and religion were not at variance and that the distinctive doctrines of traditional Judaism were in complete harmony with Aristotelian philosophy. He followed the Islamic Aristotelians in his proofs of the existence of God and in his interpretation of prophecy (which, however, he limited in accordance with rabbinic teaching to the Jewish people in the Land of Israel). Prophecy is the highest attainment of the human spirit, and derives solely from pure intellect without the intermixture of imaginative faculties, which, for Maimonides, were to become an essential ingredient in the prophetic act. The problem of FREE WILL is solved by I.D. in the traditional Jewish manner of asserting that God limits His own omniscience. In his discussion of the soul, I.D. follows the Arab Aristotelian philosopher, Avicenna, but departs from Aristotle in denying the eternity of matter and upholding the doctrine of creation *ex nihilo*. The Bible contains the highest ethical precepts and these are not contradicted by philosophical speculation. The highest goal of man is conceived by I.D. in Aristotelian fashion as intellectual perfection and knowledge, which is in turn identified with faith. I.D. also wrote *Sepher ha-Kabbalah* ("The Book of Tradition") relating the chain of rabbinic tradition from Moses to his own time. Though primarily undertaken to refute Karaite denials of such a tradition, the work is of major importance for knowledge of the history of Spanish Jewry. He also wrote histories of the Second Temple and of Rome.

IBN EZRA, ABRAHAM (1092-1167): Spanish poet and exegete who during the last thirty years of his life was forced by poverty as well as a sense of mission to become a roving scholar, spreading Jewish studies among the Jews of Christian Europe. In his commentary on the Bible (on which some fifty supercommentaries have appeared), he sought a grammatical, literal understanding of the text even if it conflicted with rabbinic tradition. His wide knowledge of mathematics, astronomy, and astrology find ample expression in his commentary, which is replete with terse critical observation. I.E. was the first to suggest the ascription of the Book of Isaiah to two authors. His religious philosophy is in the medieval Neo-Platonic tradition and is not particularly original. *Yesod Mora* ("Foundation of Reverence"), apart from the commentary his best-known work, expounds the reasons for biblical commandments. He was also the author of grammatical works and a poet whose sacred verse is marked by lofty religious feeling.

IBN EZRA, MOSES (1070-1138): Spanish philosopher and poet. His major philosophic work *Arugat ha-Bosem* ("The Bed of Spices), dealing with the familiar problems of medieval philosophy (e.g. Divine attributes, creation, nature, and the intellect), shows a knowledge of Greco-Arabic thought. However his fame rests more upon his religious and secular poetry. A great part of his two hundred and twenty sacred compositions are scattered throughout *Sephardi* prayer books for the New Year and Day of Atonement. In these poems he calls upon man to search himself, to consider the emptiness of life and the vanity and illusion of mundane pleasures. His poetic paraphrase of the Book of Jonah was adopted in the Avignon rite for the Day of Atonement.

IBN GABIROL, SOLOMON (c. 1021–c. 1058): Spanish philosopher and poet. Little is known of his life after he left Saragossa at the age of 16. He seems to have suffered from melancholia and loneliness, and to have died young. His chief philosophical work "Fountain of Life" (Heb. *Mekor Ḥayyim*), written in Arabic, has survived only in a Latin translation, *Fons Vitae* (from which a modern Hebrew translation has been made), and in a few Hebrew excerpts translated by Shemtov Falaquera in the 13th cent. The *Fons Vitae* was known to Christian scholastics, who never suspected it to be the work of a Jewish author, since it had no specifically Jewish content and was neglected by Jews. It was only in 1845 that Solomon Munk discovered that its author "Avicebron" was identical with I.G. The work represents the climax of the Neo-Platonic tradition in medieval Jewish philosophy. The initial question, how can a material world derive from an utterly spiritual Being, is answered in Neo-Platonic fashion: by way of emanation from the Creator. From the Divine Will, which is in a sense identical with the Godhead yet also separate from it in its outward action, there proceeded the two basic principles of "general matter" and "general form". The chain of emanations ends with our corporeal world, in which, however, the initial Divine will is still present. Since man is a MICROCOSM partaking of both the intelligible and the corporeal worlds, he is able to grasp the immaterial, spiritual forms in things by his own powers and is not dependent, as Arab thinkers asserted, on an external intelligence for his illumination. By means of this conception of matter I.G. attempted to reconcile the Arab view of matter as metaphysically self-subsistent with the Jewish view of a transcendental God who created the world by an act of His Divine will. I.G.'s doctrine of the will subsequently (though indirectly) influenced kabbalistic formulation of the doctrine of Divine emanation. I.G.'s ethical work. *Tikkun Middot ha-Nephesh* ("Improvement of the Moral Qualities") is the first work of its kind by a Jewish philosopher, inasmuch as it presents an ethical system irrespective of religious tradition. As a Hebrew poet, I.G. ranks among the greatest. His secular poetry concerns wine, friends, life and love, as well as loneliness and bitter sorrow, and expresses both a gaiety bordering on frivolity, and despair at the vanity of life and worldly striving. In his sublime religious poetry, personal sorrow and joy have been transmuted into Israel's sorrow in its exile and joy in its communion with God. Many of I.G.'s penitential prayers have found their way into the prayer-book, and his powerful hymns on the glory of the Divine majesty form part of the *Sephardi* literature for the High Holidays. His greatest poem, *Keter Malkhut* ("Royal Crown") — partly a philosophico-theological meditation, partly a moving prayer —, is frequently recited as a private devotion after the Evening Service on the Day of Atonement.

IBN GIKATILLA, see **GIKATILLA**

IBN ḤAVIV (ḤABIB), JACOB (c. 1460-1516): Talmudist. After the expulsion from Spain, I.Ḥ. settled in Salonica, where he compiled his *Ein Yaakov* ("Eye of Jacob"), a comprehensive collection of the aggadic sections of both Talmuds with relevant commentaries, including his own. He himself completed only the tractates of *Zeraim* and *Moed* and the work was finished by his son Levi (c. 1480-1545); after 1525 chief rabbi of Jerusalem, where he opposed and defeated Berav's attempt to revive ORDINATION. *Ein Yaakov* became an extremely popular work among all sections of Jewry and was studied by groups specially formed for the purpose.

IBN LATIF, ISAAC (c. 1228-c.1290): Spanish kabbalist and philosopher. Unlike other kabbalists he was an admirer of Maimonides. I.L. developed a new trend in kabbalistic thought based on the natural sciences and Aristotelianism. In explaining the process of creation he followed the kabbalistic theories of emanation through SEPHIROT, but described the process in mathematical terms. I.L. firmly rejected the kabbalistic belief in metempsychosis.

IBN PAKUDA, BAḤYA, see **BAḤYA IBN PAKUDA**

IBN PALQUERA, see **FALAQUERA**

IBN SHEMTOV: (1) *JOSEPH IBN SHEMTOV* (c. 1400 – c. 1460): Spanish philosopher; son of (2). Unlike his father, he approved of the study of philosophy and wrote a commentary on Aristotle's *Ethics*. His main work *Kevod Elohim* ("The Glory of God") endeavors to reconcile the thought of Maimonides with the anti-philosophical views of certain Jewish scholars in I.S.'s own time, including those of his father. Common to philosophy and Jewish religious thought is a belief that the purpose of life is realizable through proper action and thought; philosophy enables man to fulfill himself as a natural and social being but the *Torah* enables the Jew to attain even higher fulfillment and Divine happiness. (2) *SHEMTOV IBN SHEMTOV* (d. 1430): Spanish kabbalist. In his *Sepher ha-Emunot* ("The Book of Beliefs") he attacked philosophical thought — particularly that of Maimonides — and advocated Kabbalah, which he held to be the correct interpretation of Jewish tradition. (3) *SHEMTOV BEN JOSEPH IBN SHEMTOV* (late 15th cent.): Spanish philosopher; son of (1). An admirer of Maimonides, his commentary on the *Guide to the Perplexed* — which he defends against the criticism of Ḥasdai Crescas — was incorporated in most editions of that work.

IBN TIBBON: Family of translators in S. France. They were responsible for the standard Hebrew translation of Jewish medieval philosophical classics from Arabic and for coining Hebrew philosophical terminology. Judah ben Saul I.T. (12th cent.) translated the main philosophical compilations of Saadyah, Baḥya Ibn Pakuda, and Judah Ha-Levi. His son Samuel (c. 1150-c. 1230) produced the classic translation of Maimonides' *Guide to the Perplexed* under the guidance of Maimonides himself. Samuel's son Moses (13th cent.) translated Ibn Tzaddik's *Olam Katan*, some of the writings of Maimonides, and Averroes' versions of Aristotle.

IBN TZADDIK, JOSEPH (1075-1149): Spanish philosopher and poet. Only a fraction of his poetry has survived, and his reputation rests largely on his religious-philosophical work *Olam Katan* ("Microcosm"), which is extant only in a Hebrew translation of the Arabic original. The author conceives of the human soul as a MICROCOSM or epitome of the universe, uniting in itself both the terrestrial and celestial worlds. God's existence is deduced from the creation of the world, and His absolute unity — which cannot be grasped by the finite mind of man — from the manifold character of objects. The end of man is to attain the highest knowledge, which is the knowledge of God, and to walk in His ways. I.T.'s conception of man shows great similarity to that of Maimonides who, however, claimed never to have read I.T.

IBN ZERAḤ, MENAHEM (d. 1385): Spanish codifier; author of *Tzedah la-Derekh* ("Provision for the Journey"), an encyclopedic work incorporating a concise halakhic codification intended for wealthy Jews who lacked the time for extended study. It also contained philosophical and ethical interpretations of halakhic rules and practices.

IDOLS, IDOLATRY: Idols are physical representations of gods, generally symbolizing the forces of nature; idolatry is the worship of such images and of the powers which they represent, and is often treated as synonymous with paganism. Jewish tradition finds the first protest against i. in Abraham's iconoclastic revolt against his idolatrous father Terah. MONOTHEISM has ever since become synonymous with the negation of idol worship: "I am the Lord thy God, who brought thee out of the land of Egypt, out of the house of bondage. Thou shalt have no other gods before Me. Thou shalt not make unto thee a graven image" (Exod. 20:2-3). Biblical literature is replete with references to Israel's reversion to idolatrous foreign cults, and the struggle against such practices constitutes one of the major features of biblical history. Legal prohibitions, passionate denunciation, and scathing sarcasm (particularly in Deutero-Isaiah) were among the weapons which the Law and the Prophets directed against idolatry and its attendant moral and spiritual degradation (orgiastic promiscuity, human sacrifices, necromancy, magic, divination, etc.). The most frequently mentioned idols in the Bible are the Canaanite BAAL and ASTARTE; references are often couched in the form of derogatory epithets such as: "vanity", "iniquity", "abomination", "carcasses", etc. It was only during the Babylonian Exile (586-516) that Israel was effectively weaned from idol worship. The varied attempts at reintroducing pagan cults into Judea during the Greco-Roman period met with the physical opposition of the Jewish masses. The Talmud devotes an entire tractate — AVODAH ZARAH ("idol worship") — to the regulation of the social and commercial intercourse between Jews and heathens. The problem as to which of the non-Jewish religions were to be considered as idolatrous has been discussed by medieval and later halakhists and theologians. Islam was generally considered a genuinely monotheistic religion, but many authorities classified Christianity as idolatry (because of its doctrines of the incarnation and the eucharist, and its use of images). Others held that Christianity, while not a "pure monotheism", was not idolatrous either since strict monotheism was enjoined on Israel only, Christians need not be considered as idolaters. Some authorities also distinguished between Catholic and Protestant forms of Christianity, the latter being considered as less idolatrous.

IDRA (Aram. "assembly"): Name of three kabbalistic works (*I. Rabbah, I. Zuta*, and *I. de-Vei Mashkanah*) incorporated in the ZOHAR and containing its most fundamental and revered doctrines. The date of composition is unknown but in final form the *I.* dates from the first part of the 13th cent. The kabbalists introduced *I. Rabbah* and *I. Zuta* into certain liturgies (e.g. the *tikkun* for the Feast of Weeks and *Hoshana Rabbah*). Many commentaries were written on all three works.

ILLEGITIMACY: Jewish law sharply differentiates between the MAMZER i.e., the child born out of forbidden union, and other types of i. Other illegitimate children are the *shetuki* (the child of an unmarried mother, who does not know his father's identity) and the *asuphi* (the foundling who does not know either parent) (*Kidd.* 4:1). Such children are regarded as of doubtful i. and any circumstantial evidence which can remove this doubt renders them legitimate (*Kidd.* 73b). They were permitted to intermarry with one another. An illegitimate person who died childless is regarded as intestate. A special type of i. is the *ḥallal*, the child of a priest by a woman whom he is forbidden to marry (a convert or widow). This child is illegitimate only with regard to succession to the priesthood.

ILLNESS, see **SICK, PRAYERS FOR**

ILLUY (Heb.): An exceptionally brilliant student; in particular a young talmudic prodigy.

IMAGES, see **IDOLS**

IMBECILE, see **INSANITY**

IMITATION OF GOD: Although the desire to be "like unto God" (cf. Gen. 3:5) is considered a sinful disregard of human limitations, certain of the attributes of God should, according to the rabbis, be taken as models for human behavior. Though the literal fulfillment of the biblical commandment (e.g. Deut. 10:20; 13:5, etc.) to "cleave" to God is impossible, yet man should "cleave to His qualities". Elaborating on Lev. 19:2—"Ye shall be holy for I the Lord am holy"—the rabbis taught "As He is merciful and gracious, so be thou merciful and gracious" (*Mekh.* 37a); similarly R. Ḥama bar Ḥanina said "Follow the attributes of God; as He clothes the naked, so do thou clothe the naked; as He visits the sick, so do thou visit the sick; as He comforts the mourners, so do thou comfort the mourners; and as He buries the dead, so do thou" (*Sot.* 14a). These and other texts show that it is God's qualities of mercy, compassion, and loving-kindness which are held up for imitation. The concept of I. of G. is particularly important in the moral teaching of the kabbalist mystics.

IMMERSION: The biblical statement "he shall bathe his flesh in water" (Lev. 15:16) and its variants refer to total i. of the body in a ritual bath (MIKVEH) or flowing river water. Ritual i. alone is effective in ridding one of ritual impurity. In all cases of i. the body must be scrupulously clean prior to the i. In modern Jewish Orthodox practice, the only mandatory bodily i. is that of the menstruating woman (NIDDAH) and the PROSELYTE. Pious custom among the very Orthodox requires i. by males prior to the onset of festivals, especially prior to Yom Kippur, and among certain groups, especially Hasidim, i. is practiced daily before the morning prayer. New or used vessels which have been purchased from a non-Jew also require i. (See also ABLUTION; BAPTISM; IMPURITY; PURITY).

IMMORTALITY OF THE SOUL: A doctrine of the immortality of the soul is not stated in the Bible and is not clearly defined in early rabbinical literature. Various eschatological notions were in existence (see ESCHATOLOGY; MESSIAH; OLAM HA-BA) — e.g. the passage in the Sabbath prayers "There is none to be compared to Thee in this world, neither is there anyone beside Thee for the life of the World to Come. There is none but Thee... for the Days of the MESSIAH, neither is there any like unto Thee... for the (days of) the RESURRECTION of the Dead," but considerable confusion prevailed among rabbinic authorities as to the exact connotation of these terms and the relationship between them. In particular, opinions diverged over whether the idea of the World-to-Come necessarily includes that of the i. of the s. Maimonides was severely criticized for minimizing the significance of the doctrine of resurrection and for his almost exclusive emphasis on the i. of the s. which was a privilege he confined to thinkers; he was obliged to write a special treatise on resurrection to correct the impression that he had denied this belief and he incorporated it in his Thirteen Principles. The belief that some part of the human personality is eternal and is freed from the body at death to enjoy a separate existence in the celestial spheres is taken for granted by the rabbis and became almost universally accepted in later Judaism, whereas in the Bible eternal life seems to apply only to God and the angels (cf. Gen. 3:22; Ps. 115:17). Belief in REWARD AND PUNISHMENT is also based on belief in the i. of the s. The rabbis laid down that "there is no reward for the fulfillment of the commandments in this world," and interpreted the biblical promise that "thy days may be prolonged", which is posited as the reward for fulfilling the commandment to honor parents (Deut. 5:16), as referring to "the world which is wholly good, and the world which is eternally long" (*Ḥul.* end). Belief in the i. of the s. is virtually axiomatic among medieval and later Jewish philosophers. The kabbalists also based their thought on this concept though they combined it with their belief in METEMPSYCHOSIS. Although Reform Judaism almost wholly denies the doctrine of resurrection, it accepts the belief in the i. of the s.

IMPRISONMENT: I. is mentioned in the Pentateuch as a temporary measure pending a decision on appropriate punishment (cf. Lev. 24:10-23 and Num. 15:32-36). It is nowhere considered by the *Torah* as a form of punishment, and offenders were at most placed in custody until the court could attend to their case and decide their ultimate penalty. The experience of Jeremiah (Jer. 37:15, cf. also II Chron. 16:7-10; I Kings 22:26-28) possibly indicates the use of i. for political offenders at a later period. Nonetheless penal institutions did exist in ancient times and the rabbis legislated i. as punishment in the case of certain offenses for which no other penalty is prescribed in the Bible, or for which circumstances demanded particular measures. As provided for in the Talmud, i. is extremely severe and is for life. The prisoner is to be incarcerated in a narrow cell and receives a scant diet. I. was applied: (1) To the incorrigible offender (*Sanh.* 9:5), but only in cases where the culprit had already received corporal punishment for transgression of a prohibition involving "excision" (*karet*); (2) When the court is certain that the culprit is guilty of murder but because of legal technicalities cannot pronounce a death sentence (if there is insufficient evidence in law to convict and execute a culprit in crimes other than murder, but also involving capital punishment, he is nonetheless acquitted); and (3) To one found guilty of causing a murder by hiring an assassin.

IMPURITY (Heb. *tumah*): People become ritually impure by being in certain states or in contact with impure persons or objects. States of impurity are: (1) a flux issuing from a man, or (2) from a woman (Lev. 15:2, 25); (3) menstruation (*ibid.* 15:19); (4) a woman after childbirth (*ibid.* 12:2); (5) leprosy (*ibid.* 13:1 ff.); (6) male semen (*ibid.* 15:15). Contacts that render impure are: (7) a corpse (Num. 19:11); (8) carrion (Lev. 11:26, 39); (9) creeping things (*ibid.* 11:29-31); (10) the burning of the Red Heifer (Num. 19:7); (11) the burning of certain sacrifices (Lev. 4:12, 21, 26; 16:27-28); (12) the leading away of the scapegoat (*ibid.* 16:26). A state of i. lasts for varying periods and is removed by IMMERSION in the MIKVEH, and in some cases also by the sprinkling of the ashes of the RED HEIFER (Num. 19). A person in a state of i. is precluded from entry into the Temple precincts, from partaking of sacred foods, or in the case of (2), (3), and (4), from marital contact. Leprosy precludes normal intercourse with other people. (See also ABLUTION; NIDDAH; PURITY).

INCENSE: The burning of i. was an essential element of the sacrificial system in Tabernacle and Temple times (Exod. 30:7-9). In its discussion of i. the Bible (*ibid.* 34-38) lists four ingredients, to which the Talmud (*Ker.* 6a) adds seven more, including one called *maaleh ashan*, which had the property of causing the smoke of i. to rise in a straight column. It was forbidden to use any i. other than the mixture prescribed. Extraordinary care was taken in its preparation, even to the extent of recommending the repetition of the phrase "pound well, pound well" during the mixing of i., since "such instruction is beneficial to the outcome". A special i. altar stood in the Temple in front of the Holy of Holies, and on the Day of Atonement the High Priest took a censer of burning i. inside the sacred chamber. The Bible warns "Whosoever shall make like unto it, to smell thereto, shall even be cut off from his people". Thus the use of the i. was strictly limited to the Temple, and i. plays no part whatsoever in present-day worship, though in commemoration of the ancient ritual certain biblical and rabbinic texts referring to the offering of i. are recited in the prayer service; the details vary according to different rites. The smelling of SPICES as part of the HAVDALAH ceremony has an entirely different origin.

INCEST: Sexual intimacy within the prohibited degrees of consanguinity listed in Lev. 18:6-18. The Talmud explains that the ban on relations with one's granddaughter automatically includes a ban on intercourse with one's daughter (which is not specifically listed in the Bible). The rabbis added to these "primary" incestuous unions a number of "secondary" ones, such as any paternal grandmother or a son's daughter-in-law, the general principle being to raise the degree of prohibition one stage higher. A marriage which would result in a primary union is completely invalid and does not even require a divorce to be dissolved, whereas a marriage between secondary degree relatives does require a divorce for its dissolution. Only the issue of a primary degree of i. is a MAMZER.

INDEMNITY: Injury to another's person is considered equivalent to damage inflicted upon his property (*Sanh.* 2b) and in both instances financial compensation and restitution are obligatory. In cases of personal injury, i. consists of payment reckoned on the following counts — (1) for the injury itself; (2) for the pain suffered; (3) for the medical expenses arising from the injury; (4) for loss of earnings incurred; and (5) for the indignity suffered. Pain and personal injury are estimated on a common basis for all but in estimating the amount due for indignity the sensitivity of the individual and the occasion of his humiliation as well as the standing and intention of the humiliator are all taken into account. A halakhic principle states that two punishments cannot be meted out for a single offense, and therefore one who is obligated to pay i. receives no corporal or other punishment. Crimes punishable by monetary i. are not considered criminal offenses.

INDEPENDENCE DAY: The anniversary of the proclamation of the State of Israel in 1948 (*Iyyar* 5) which is celebrated as a national holiday in the State of Israel and to some extent in the Diaspora. Various attempts have been made by religious authorities to establish the date as a religious festival, but a noticeable hesitation in certain religious quarters, and actual hostility on the part of extreme Orthodox elements (who do not see in the event a partial fulfillment of the biblical prophecies concerning the Return to Zion), have prevented the standardization either of a form of service or of ritual regulations. The recitation of Half-HALLEL has been generally adopted, though opposition is still expressed to the recital of the accompanying blessings. Similarly a lifting of the ban against the celebration of weddings during the period of the OMER — during which *Iyyar* 5 falls — has not been approved, though other mourning regulations are waived on this day.

INFORMING, see **DENUNCIATION**

INGATHERING, FESTIVAL OF, see **HARVEST FESTIVALS**

INGATHERING OF THE EXILES, see **EXILES, INGATHERING OF**

INHERITANCE: The acquisition of property by one person as heir to another. In Jewish law — unlike Roman law — the individual does not appoint heirs; rather they are determined by law. The basic rules governing i. are: 1) I. always passes in the direct line of immediate descent, i.e., either from father to son or from son to father. It does not pass from a son to his brother or to his father's brother, even though the father is deceased. The brother or father's brother inherit only from their father but not from the inheritor himself.

2) A daughter inherits only in the event of the absence of a male in direct line of descent. Thus, daughters do not inherit if brothers or their children exist. (This is bound up with the biblical concept of the completeness of the family — and its property — which is preserved by sons and not by daughters). If a brother dies leaving only daughters to succeed him, his daughters take precedence over the claims of their father's sisters.

3) A person born of illegal wedlock or out of wedlock cannot be excluded from his i. This does not apply to one born of a slave or of a non-Jewish mother.

4) Since by law an i. passes automatically through fixed patterns of relationship, it may pass to one deceased — and through him to his inheritors, or to one yet unborn.

Thus the order of i. is: 1) sons and their descendants (with a double portion to the FIRST-BORN); 2) daughters and their descendants (Num. 27:8-11); 3) father; 4) brothers and their descendants; 5) sisters and their descendants; 6) father's father; 7) father's brothers and their descendants; 8) father's sisters and their descendants. The maintenance of an unmarried daughter is a charge on the estate of the deceased and takes moral precedence even over the legal rights of the sons who were the heirs; provision for a daughter's dowry must also be made from the estate. A husband inherits from a wife; the reverse however is not the case, though the widow's maintenance is a prime charge on the husband's estate (unless she remarries). All the heirs, apart from the FIRST-BORN, who receives a double share, receive equal portions of the i. Property that cannot reasonably be divided or is used as a public utility is inherited wholly and not apportioned among the inheritors. The inheritors (unless they are minors) assume responsibility for all debts incurred by the deceased to the value of the inherited property which remains mortgaged to such debtors as exist. But if the deceased left no property or goods whatsoever, his would-be inheritors bear no responsibility for the deceased's debts. Possession by the heirs can be taken immediately after the owner's death unless the heirs are minors, in which case a guardian is appointed until they come of age. Since the order of i. is fixed in Jewish law the need for a will is largely obviated. It is however important for the granting of bequests outside the family or to its female members. A will is fully respected in Jewish law provided it does not completely disinherit those legally entitled to inherit. The legator may, if intending to disinherit, legally dispose of his property during his lifetime, so that the problem of disinheriting will not arise, but "the spirit of the sages is displeased with such procedure". The wishes expressed by a dying person concerning the disposal of his property are fully binding in spite of the lack of a formal legal DEED or KINYAN.

INITIALS, see **ABBREVIATIONS**

INJURY, see **TORTS**

INNOCENCE: In Jewish law, a person is presumed innocent until he is proved otherwise. Neither hearsay nor circumstantial EVIDENCE (especially in capital cases) is allowed to undermine this presumption. In criminal cases the presumption of i. is so strong that the accused must virtually have surrendered himself to the consequences of his act, in front of witnesses, in order to be found guilty (see WARNING), while self-incrimination has no validity in law. Presumption of i. is grounded in the essential trustworthiness and moral dignity accorded to the individual.

INQUISITION: An ecclesiastical court ("Holy Office") set up by the Catholic Church for the trial of heretics, i.e., those who had abandoned the religious tenets and beliefs of the Catholic faith in which they had been brought up or which they had adopted. It first became prominent in Europe in the 13th cent. when established to deal with the heretical Albigenses in S. France. Its operation was mainly entrusted to the Dominicans. It had no jurisdiction over persons other than members of the Church including such Jews as had, voluntarily or otherwise, formally adopted Christianity. These were regarded as guilty of heresy when reverting to Jewish practice and belief. The I. is best known for its relentless hunting down of the descendants of converted Jews (MARRANOS) in Spain in the 14th cent. and afterward. It was introduced into the united kingdoms of Castile, Aragon, and Navarre by Ferdinand and Isabella, and lasted for nearly 350 years, from the first auto-da-fe held in Seville in 1481 until its final abolition in 1834. Both the Spaniards and the Portuguese carried it to their overseas possessions in America and India. In N. Portugal alone, between 1565 and 1595, over 900 communities were victimized by the I. and estimates are given that the Spanish I. from its establishment until 1808 sentenced over 30,000 Marranos to be burned at the stake, while another 16,000 were punished *in absentia* by being burnt in effigy.

INSANITY: An insane person is one whose mind is permanently deranged. One who suffers temporary, occasional, or periodic bouts of i., or epileptic fits, is considered sane and responsible during his lucid periods. Examples of the symptoms of i. given by the rabbis are (1) going out alone at night; (2) sleeping in a cemetery; or (3) destroying that which is given to one (Tos. *Ter.* 1:3). It is not necessary for all of the symptoms to be present, and a rational explanation must be lacking for the symptoms. A generally muddle-headed and irresponsible attitude and demeanor is also considered evidence for i. A person suffering from i. is free from all religious obligations or punishment, is not responsible in law for any tort committed by him, and his dealings have no legal validity. He is classed together with the deaf and dumb mute and the minor. He is however to be compensated for any tort committed against him or his property. If adjudged dangerously insane he may be placed in protective custody in order to safeguard others. He is however to be periodically examined as to his state of mind, and on recovery is fully reinstated in all civil rights. Insane persons cannot marry, since the consent of both parties is necessary. A man who becomes insane after marriage cannot give his wife a bill of divorce; a woman who becomes insane after marriage can legally be divorced but the rabbis forbade such an action on humanitarian grounds, though in special cases they permitted the husband to take a second wife on receiving permission from a hundred rabbis.

INSPIRATION: The condition of being directly under Divine influence so that the spirit of God enters into man. Since i. emanates from God it is free from human error. Biblical prophecy is a classical example of i., and as a result the one criterion in selecting and determining the biblical canon was whether the books under review were "composed under Divine i." (*Meg.* 7a; Tos. *Yad.* 2:14). However, i. was not confined to the prophets. Bezalel, the architect of the sanctuary in the wilderness, was "filled with the spirit of God" (Exod. 31:3; 35:1); it came to the heathen prophet Balaam to enable him to utter his prophecies (Num. 24:2); and it also descended upon seventy elders (*ibid.* 11:17) and enabled them to prophesy. Although i. is considered to have ceased with the last prophets, Haggai, Zechariah, and Malachi (Tos. *Sotah* 13:2; *Sanh.* 11a), the Talmud does not hesitate to ascribe inspiration to the authoritative Aramaic translation of the Bible by Jonathan ben Uzziel (*Meg.* 3a), as Philo does to the Septuagint (*Vita Moysis* 2:7; *Letter of Aristeas* 305-317). Although nowhere in the Talmud is there explicit mention of different degrees of i. between the Pentateuch, the Prophets, and the Hagiographa — all having been "composed under Divine i." — such a difference is implicit in a comparison of the manner in which Moses received the Divine message with that of the later prophets. "If there be a prophet among you, I the Lord will make myself known to him in a vision, and will speak with him in a dream. Not so my servant Moses... With him will I speak mouth to mouth, even manifestly and not in dark speeches" (Num. 12:6-8), i.e., i. came to the other prophets while their cognitive faculties were in a state of suspended animation, in trances, dreams, and ecstasy, whereas Moses alone was inspired while in full possession of his normal cognitive faculties. This difference is succinctly expressed by the rabbinic statement that whereas other prophets saw God "through nine glasses" or "through a glass darkly", Moses saw Him "through one glass" or "through a clear glass" (*Lev. Rab.* 1:14). Maimonides on the other hand specifically lays down three descending degrees of i. for the three sections of the Bible (*Guide* 2:45). Reform Judaism rejects the doctrine of direct literal i. but nevertheless maintains that the spirit of God was manifested in the prophets, to the extent that the i. of the Bible is greater than that of any other work.

INSULT: I. is regarded as an injury in Jewish law and as such must be compensated for. In cases of bodily injury the i., or "shame", involved is considered an additional count in determining the extent of damages. The shame endured by one maimed by another as well as the shame suffered by the family of a girl robbed of her virginity are cases in point. The compensation for indignity "is in accordance with the standing of him that inflicts the indignity and him that suffers the indignity" (cf. *Ket.* 3:7). Insulting a scholar or the display of insulting behavior in court was usually dealt with by rebuke and partial ostracization of the culprit. The rabbis decreed that "one who insults his fellow in public has no share in the World to Come".

INTENT: This corresponds to two Hebrew terms KAVVANAH and *zadon*. *Kavvanah* refers to a state of mental concentration investing an act with religious intention. According to most authorities the fulfillment of the positive precepts does not require particular intention beyond the general *kavvanah* of implementing the word of God, and failure to take cognizance of the particular motive behind the precept does not invalidate its performance. However in those instances where the Bible itself expressly states the intention of the precept (e.g. the Tabernacle, in which case the Bible says "that your generations may know..." — Lev. 23:43), particular *kavvanah* is necessary. It is also necessary in those precepts where *kavvanah* is of the essence of the precept, such as in prayer. In medieval usage *kavvanah* came to mean specific devotional intention and, in particular, mystical meditation. *Zadon* is a legal term; to be culpable in law, intention (*zadon*) must be proven (see WARNING). Where such intention is lacking the

Bible stipulates compensatory ritual obligation in a limited number of cases (mainly those concerned with the performance of ritual, with purity, and with prohibitions involving excision from the community).

INTERCALATION, see **CALENDAR**

INTEREST, see **USURY**

INTERMARRIAGE: Marriage between a Jew and a non-Jew. The original biblical prohibition against i. is directed against the seven Canaanite nations, concerning whom it is enjoined, "Neither shalt thou enter into marriages with them; thy daughter shalt thou not give unto his son, nor his daughter shalt thou take unto thy son" (Deut. 7:3). Since the reason given, however, is that they will turn away thy son from following me and serve other gods" (*ibid.* 7:4), the Talmud (*A.Z.* 36b) extends the prohibition to all heathen nations, as indeed is understood by Ezra (9:12; 10:10-11). Since his time, in contrast to the period of the First Temple, all i. between Jews and non-Jews is forbidden by Jewish law and invalid, unless the non-Jewish partner has been first converted to Judaism. The child of a mixed or an invalid marriage (see Incest) is considered to have the faith and status of the mother. Thus the child of a Jewish father and a non-Jewish mother is regarded as non-Jewish while that of a non-Jewish father and a Jewish mother as Jewish. Since i. is invalid, no divorce is necessary to dissolve it. In modern Israel the prohibition has been applied to marriage with Samaritans and Karaites, despite some decisions in the past to the contrary.

INTERMEDIATE DAYS, see **ḤOL HA-MOED**

INVOCATION: Among the ritual innovations of U.S. Jewry is the practice adapted from the Christian environment of opening public meetings and dinners with a short prayer said by a rabbi. This i. "invokes" God's blessing on the endeavor for which the group has gathered and on the guest of honor or the sponsoring organization; at dinners it culminates in the blessing over the bread.

ISAAC: Second of the three Patriarchs; son of Abraham and Sarah. Both Abraham and Sarah laughed (Heb. *tzaḥak*) when God's angel promised them a son in their old age (Gen. 17:17; 18:12); hence the biblical derivation of Isaac's name (in Heb., *Yitzḥak*). Unlike his half-brother Ishmael, I. was to be the heir of God's promise to Abraham. He was circumcised when eight days old. His supreme trial came in the Akedah. Although this was primarily the story of Abraham's willingness to sacrifice his beloved son at God's bidding (Gen. 22:1-19), I.'s consent to be bound to the altar and sacrificed became symbolic of Kiddush ha-Shem, the willingness to forfeit life for the glory of God. At the age of 40, I. married Rebecca, who bore him Esau and Jacob. In old age he lost his eyesight and his wish to bestow the patriarchal blessing upon Esau was directed to Jacob through a ruse of Rebecca. He died at the age of 180 and was buried by Jacob and Esau in the patriarchal tomb of Machpelah (Gen. 35:28-29). Isaac's filial loyalty is depicted in many Midrashim as well as in Islamic lore. Rabbinic tradition credits I. with the introduction of the custom of praying each afternoon.

ISAAC, BINDING OF, see **AKEDAH**

ISAAC ARAMA, see **ARAMA, ISAAC**

ISAAC BEN ABBA MARI OF MARSEILLES (12th cent.): French codifier. His learned and comprehensive code of civil and religious law, *Ittur Sopherim* ("Scribal Separation"), was at first extremely influential but became largely overshadowed when Jacob ben Asher published his *Tur.*

ISAAC BEN ABRAHAM OF TROKI, see **TROKI, ISAAC BEN ABRAHAM OF**

ISAAC BEN JOSEPH OF CORBEIL (13th cent.): French codifier, known as *Semak* after the initials of his *Sepher Mitzvot Katan* ("Small Book of Precepts"). This was based on the large code of Moses ben Jacob of Coucy but was directed at a wider public. The book cited a minimum of sources and contained a clear formulation of rabbinical decisions. To promote its popularity, the author also included aggadic and ethical material.

ISAAC BEN MOSES OF VIENNA (also known as Isaac *Or Zarua;* 13th cent.): Codifier. His outstanding work, the code *Or Zarua* ("Light is Sown"), deals with religious, but not criminal and civil, law. It includes comments and addenda to all sections of the Talmud as well as extensive quotations from a wide variety of sources including the Jerusalem Talmud and gaonic and later responsa. Apart from its legal value, which led to frequent citation of the book by later authorities, it contains important information on Jewish life in medieval Europe.

ISAAC BEN REUBEN (or **MEIR**) (14th cent.): Codifier living in the German town of Düren. His code *Shaarei Dura* ("Gates of Düren"), also known as *Issur ve-Hetter* ("Prohibition and Permission"), deals with the dietary laws and was regarded as authoritative until replaced by the *Shulḥan Arukh.*

ISAAC BEN SAMUEL OF ACRE (c. 1250-1340): Kabbalist who journeyed from Palestine to Spain to examine the authenticity of the Zohar. His diary — which queries the antiquity of the Zohar — contains important information concerning the putative author of this work Moses de Leon. I. himself became an outstanding exponent of mystical thought and contemplative practice.

ISAAC BEN SHESHET BARFAT (known as

Ribash; 1326-1408): Spanish talmudist who spent his last years in Algiers; an outstanding halakhic authority. Many queries were addressed to him and his responsa were noted for their clarity, erudition, and acumen. His decisions were incorporated into many subsequent codes. A strict legalist, he warned against the study of philosophy and, even more, of Kabbalah. He wrote a number of dirges after the massacre in 1391 of the Jews in Spain. I.'s tomb, near Algiers, became a center of pilgrimage for N. African Jews.

ISAAC ELHANAN, see **SPEKTOR, ISAAC ELHANAN**

ISAAC ISRAELI, see **ISRAELI, ISAAC**

ISAAC OF ACRE, see **ISAAC BEN SAMUEL OF ACRE**

ISAIAH (Heb. *Yeshayahu*): Prophet living in the 8th cent. B.C.E.; the biblical book named for him constitutes the first in the section of Latter Prophets. Of noble family, his private life was subordinated to his prophetic ministry: his wife is referred to as the "prophetess" (Is. 8:3) and their two sons bore names symbolic of his message (Is. 7:3; 8:3). The decisive event of his life — the call to prophecy (Is. 6) — occurred in the year of King Uzziah's death in the form of an overpowering vision of God which came to I. in the Temple. His visionary experience of the contrast between human frailty and impurity on the one hand and the holy majesty of the Lord of Hosts on the other, determined the character of his preaching. "Belief" in God's active participation in history and in human ability to witness it through an act of faith (Is. 5:12; 7:9; 28:16) was the attitude which he demanded of the king and the nation, as every other policy meant putting one's trust in "flesh" instead of in the "spirit" i.e., God (cf. Is. 31:3). Hence also I.'s interventions in public affairs, particularly during the reign of King Hezekiah. I. saw all nations as mere tools in the hands of God. Pending the realization of the ideal, eschatological state of things (Is. 2:1-4; 11:1-10), Israel was to expect severe chastisement. Its only path of action as a people was complete trust in God, expressed in justice, pity and morality, which mean more in the eyes of God than sacrifices and Temple worship. According to legend, I. was put to death by King Manasseh. The book named after I. is generally ascribed by scholars to 3 authors: a) Chaps. 1-39, by the original prophet I., consisting of prophecies to Israel and Judah (specifically 1-12), prophecies concerning other nations (13-23) and the future Day of Judgment (24-27), a short apocalypse (34-35), and prophecies in connection with Sennacherib's march on Jerusalem (28-33) described in 36-39. b) Chaps. 40-55 by another prophet designated as Deutero-I. (Gk. "Second I.") who prophesied during the Babylonian Exile, before and during the time of the conquests of CYRUS. Unlike I.'s dire prophecy of judgment, Deutero-I.'s rhapsodic utterances celebrate God's salvation as made manifest in Israel's return to Zion. 52-53 contain the prophecies concerning the "suffering SERVANT" which the Christian church later interpreted as referring to Jesus. In Deutero-I. the universalist monotheism of the prophets found its most eloquent spokesman. c) Chaps. 56-66 are attributed by some scholars to yet another prophet, designated as Trito-I (Gk. "Third I.") because their main concerns (the SABBATH, SACRIFICES, the TEMPLE, the desperate state of the community) suggest a background similar to that of the prophecies of MALACHI and ZECHARIAH.

ISAIAH, ASCENSION OF: An apocryphal work of composite origin, extant only in an Ethiopic version, though Greek, Latin, and Slavonic fragments have also been found. In its present form the book is the work of a Christian writer, but its literary foundation is based upon a Jewish (perhaps sectarian) apocryphal legend, "The Martyrdom of Isaiah", to which allusions are also made in the Talmud. The content of the book is divided into two parts: an account of the martyrdom of ISAIAH who was sawn in half at the instigation of King Manasseh (chaps. 1-5), and an apocalyptic vision (entirely Christian in character) in which the prophet is transported through the seven heavens (chaps. 6-13).

ISHMAEL: Elder son of ABRAHAM. His mother was Hagar, Sarah's Egyptian handmaid and Abraham's concubine (Gen. 16:15). I. was circumcised by Abraham at the age of 13, an age at which the ceremony is still practiced among many Arab tribes. Expelled from his home because of Sarah's jealousy, he fled to the desert and lived by the bow. I. married an Egyptian wife, and his daughter married Esau, from whom the heads of the Edomite families were traditionally descended. Arabs trace their ancestry to I., and in Islam he is regarded as a prophet. In medieval Hebrew usage I. represents the Moslem world (i.e., the Arabs, and later the Turks), just as ESAU or Edom represent the Christian Roman world.

ISHMAEL BEN ELISHA (1st-2nd cents.): *Tanna*. Prominent in both halakhic and aggadic Midrash, he is responsible for the MEKHILTA to Exodus and for the famous school of HALAKHAH which bore his name — *Beit Rabbi Ishmael*. He formulated the thirteen HERMENEUTICAL RULES "by means of which the *Torah* is to be expounded" but these are in fact an amplification of the seven rules previously promulgated by Hillel. His work was largely devoted to the formulation of categories, classifications, and rules in connection with both biblical exposition and the Oral Law. I. formulated the principle that "the Bible speaks in ordinary language". His approach was rational and avoided extremes in the interpretation of biblical passages.

ISLAM: Religion founded by MOHAMMED (c. 570-632), the spiritual development of which owed much to Jewish contacts and influences. Jewish elements are much in evidence in the KORAN, as well as in certain beliefs and institutions of I., particularly in its uncompromising MONOTHEISM which made many medieval Jewish thinkers think more highly of I. than of Christianity. Mohammed became hostile to the Jews after being disappointed in his hope of their conversion to his religion, but he still did not consider them on the same footing as pagans. Jews and Christians, in fact all "peoples of the book" (i.e., peoples with Holy Scriptures), were to be tolerated, though made to suffer various indignities and disabilities. I. in its turn profoundly affected Judaism at a later period, and both Jewish medieval philosophy and ascetic piety (see BAHYA IBN PAKUDA) are indebted to the influence of Moslem thinkers and mystics. The opening of the *Shahādah* ("confession of faith", the first of the "five pillars" of I.), "there is no God but *Allah*", is the Islamic counterpart of the Jewish *Shema* (cf. also II Sam. 22:32 "For who is God save the Lord" and Ps. 18:32 "There is no God but the Lord"). Moslem orthodoxy does not recognize saints serving as mediators between the individual and his Creator, and has no priesthood. Any competent man of good character may conduct the prayer service. Religious leadership rests with scholars and teachers of the Law; the central Moslem concept of *shari'a* shows resemblance to the HALAKHAH of Judaism. The second "pillar" of I. is the obligation to pray five times daily — at sunrise, mid-day, mid-afternoon, sunset, and at night before retiring — and some scholars have suggested that the Arabian Jews also used to pray five times daily. At first Moslems turned toward Jerusalem when praying, but Mohammed later changed the direction to Mecca. Even so Jerusalem remains, after Mecca and Medina, the third most holy city of I., and according to a tradition one prayer in Jerusalem outweighs a thousand prayers elsewhere. The hours of prayer are announced by a crier (*muadhdhin*, or *muezzin*) from the tower of the mosque, a practice reminiscent of the custom followed in the Temple of Jerusalem, where, according to the Talmud, an appointed crier used to announce: "Arise, ye priests to your service, ye levites to your platforms, and ye Israelites to your stands". Instead of the Jewish Sabbath or the Christian Sunday, Mohammed chose Friday as "a day of assembly" (possibly influenced by the practice of the Jews in Arabia to begin the observance of the Sabbath early on Friday), but did not declare it a day of rest; work is permitted and the day is merely marked by special congregational services and sermons. The third "pillar" *zaqāt* ("alms") to the poor, the widowed, and the orphaned, was originally left to individual charity, but subsequently became a fixed tax. Every Moslem must make a PILGRIMAGE to Mecca at least once in his lifetime, unless physically or financially unable to do so. For regular corporate worship, the Moslem prays in the mosque, which, like the SYNAGOGUE on which it is modeled, is a house of worship without any images or figures. At first Mohammed also instituted a fast on the tenth day of the Moslem calendar year (*Ashura*, "the fast of the tenth"), obviously in imitation of the Jewish DAY OF ATONEMENT observed on *Tishri* 10, but subsequently revoked the obligation. Instead he instituted the fast of the month of *Ramadan* (the ninth month of the Moslem lunar year) which is observed for thirty days from sunrise to sunset. Moslems practice circumcision, and refrain from the consumption of blood, pork, or the flesh of any animal that "dieth of itself". The fifth pillar of I. is the *Jihad* i.e., the Holy War. All followers of Mohammed share the hope of "Islamizing" the non-Moslem world. This concept requires of the Moslem that he subdue the infidel, and he who dies in the war for *Allah* is considered a martyr and assured of entry into PARADISE. Jewry under I. has known occasional periods of fanatical persecution, but also of great cultural flowering (e.g. the "golden age" of Spanish Jewry). On the whole, Jewish life in the Middle Ages was less precarious under Moslem than under Christian rule. The extent to which Jews shared the culture of their Moslem neighbors is illustrated by the number of Jewish classics (philosophical, ethical, and even halakhic) written in Arabic, as well as by the influence of Moslem thinkers which these works exhibit.

ISRAEL, see **ISRAELITE**

ISRAEL, LAND OF (Heb. *Eretz Yisrael*): Traditional name, since rabbinic times, for the land (known subsequently as Palestine) promised by God to Abraham and his seed (hence also "Promised Land"), and never actually occupied to the full extent of the frontiers indicated in the patriarchal covenant (Gen. 15:18-19). Other boundaries are described in Num. 34:2-12, in other biblical books, and in the talmudic sources. In due course the L. of I. became a halakhic, and indeed theological, entity without reference to the territory actually held or occupied by Jews. The land was regarded as an inalienable gift of God to His people, and part of the Divine COVENANT. God's ultimate ownership of the land and Israel's "tenant" relationship were emphasized by certain AGRARIAN LAWS, and by SHEMITTAH and the JUBILEE in particular (cf. Lev. 25:23). Love for the L. of I. became a halakhic, and indeed theological concept and a high estimation of its value is expressed throughout Jewish history — in the Bible (cf. Deut. 11:12), the Talmud, the liturgy, religious thought and even in law. Thus the Talmud rules that "in the case of him who buys a house in the L. of I., the deed may be written even on the Sabbath by a non-Jew" (*Bava Kamma* 80b) and a wife who refuses to accompany her husband to settle in the L. of I. loses her rights under her marriage settlement. A further concept of increasing importance was that of the sanctity of the land. This concept was interpreted both mystically and legally, the latter interpretation emphasizing, with a view to the agrarian laws, that is was possible to fulfill the *Torah* more fully in the L. of I. Thus the Mishnah (*Kel.* 1:2) states "The L. of I. is holier than all other lands. Wherein lies its sanctity? In that from the L. of I. alone one may bring the *Omer*, the first fruits, and the two loaves which cannot be brought from another land" (see also HOLY LAND). In one instance of exaggeration the rabbis went so far as to say "Whoever lives outside the L. of I. can be regarded as an idolater", referring to I Sam. 26:19 as a proof (*Ket.* 110b). In the 12th and 13th cents. persecution and growing insecurity encouraged a tendency among W. European Jewry to settle in I., and many prominent rabbis joined the pilgrimages. The opponents of this ALIYYAH declared that the duty to reside in the L. of I. no longer obtained in their time because of the dangers involved in travel, while the tosaphist R. Ḥayyim actually states that the existence of those commandments which can be fulfilled only in the Land of Israel constituted a valid reason for not going, since their proper observance was extremely difficult and the consequent danger of sin was too great to be risked (on *Ket.* 110b; cf. Rashbam on Deut. 11:10). These however were exceptional views, and the general trend of Jewish attitudes and religious instruction has been toward the resettlement of the L. of I. NAḤMANIDES regarded the duty to dwell in the L. of I. as a positive biblical commandment. As the nature of the emotional and religious ties to the L. of I. largely depends on the views held with regard to existence in the DIASPORA, the classical REFORM Movement deleted from its prayer book all references to a return to the L. of I. The traditional prayer book has remained Israel-centered throughout the centuries of exile, and even the prayers for rain and dew in the *amidah* are said in conjunction with the appropriate seasons in the L. of I. According to the Talmud, PROPHECY is possible only in the L. of I. The concept of the Land of Israel has been developed to what may fitly be described as a theology of the Holy Land, in the Medieval Period by JUDAH HA-LEVI as well as by kabbalists and mystics, and in recent times particularly by Rabbi A. Y. KOOK.

ISRAEL BEN SAMUEL ASHKENAZI OF SHKLOV (c. 1770-1839): Talmudist. A pupil of Elijah the Vilna Gaon, he was for 12 years preacher in Shklov (White Russia) and co-editor of the Gaon's glosses on the *Shulḥan Arukh*. In 1809, he went to Palestine and settled in Safed where he founded a *yeshivah* and headed the community of *perushim* ("separatists", so called because they did not belong to the ḥasidic community in Safed which had been founded in 1757). He led the community through many difficult crises (plagues, Arab attacks, earthquakes) and in 1837 went to Jerusalem and founded another congregation of *perushim*. His major work is *Peat ha-Shulḥan* ("Corner of the Table") a codification of the rabbinic laws dealing with residence in the Holy Land (which had been omitted by Joseph Karo in his code).

ISRAEL OF RUZHIN, see **RUZHIN**

ISRAELI, ISAAC BEN SOLOMON (c. 855-955): N. African philosopher and physician. His *Sepher ha-Yesodot* ("The Book of Elements") and his commentary on the Book of YETZIRAH have survived in Hebrew translations of the Arabic original. A pioneer of medieval Jewish philosophy, he combined Neo-Platonic metaphysics with Aristotelian logic, physics, and psychology, bringing philosophy to the attention of Jews but without injecting Jewish content into his thought. His significance was as a compiler rather than as an original thinker. He developed his cosmogonical theories in the framework of his commentary on the first two chapters of Genesis.

ISRAELITE: According to the biblical account (Gen. 33:29), "Israel" ("God fights", or "He for whom God fights", or "He who fights with God") was bestowed as a name of honor on the Patriarch Jacob after his nocturnal struggle near the brook of Jabbok. The name also signifies the people composed of his descendants (the "children of Israel"), being applied (a) to the whole people (including Judah); (b) with the division of the kingdom after the death of Solomon, to the Northern Kingdom only (in contrast to the Southern Kingdom, known as Judah); (c) after the fall of the Northern Kingdom, to the members and descendants of the kingdom of Judah. The designation "children of Israel" was later almost entirely superseded by JEWS, but during the Emancipation Period and after, the derogatory associations connected with the word Jew brought about an artificial tendency, especially among Western and assimilated Jewry, to revive the term I. as a less offensive substitute for Jew. In the purely liturgical context an I. is a Jew who is neither a priest nor a levite (see READING OF THE LAW). When the Jewish State was established in 1948 it was decided to name it Israel; a citizen of the State is called an Israeli, a term which designates nationality and citizenship, but not faith.

ISRAELITISCH-THEOLOGISCHE LEHRANSTALT: Rabbinical and teachers' seminary established in Vienna in 1893. Adolf Schwarz was its first rector and under his guidance it developed into one of the most important RABBINICAL SEMINARIES in Europe, combining traditional rabbinic studies with general education. Many noted scholars (e.g. Bacher, M. Friedman-Ish Shalom, Aptowitzer) taught at the seminary, which closed in 1938 after the Nazi occupation of Austria.

ISRU ḤAG (Heb.; lit. "the binding of the festival offering"; cf. Ps. 118:27): The day after the termination of the three PILGRIM FESTIVALS. The Talmud comments "To add a day to the festival and honor it with feasting, is as if to have offered a sacrifice at the altar" (*Suk.* 45b). The day is considered a minor festival for liturgical purposes: no supplicatory or penitential prayers are said, and fasting and funeral eulogies are prohibited. This custom, expressive of the reluctance with which the passing of the festival is viewed, possibly goes back to a more ancient custom — deduced from Deut. 16:7 — of remaining an extra night in Jerusalem at the conclusion of the festival (*Ḥag.* 16a). In the Palestinian Talmud (*A.Z.* 1:1) the day is called *berei de-moada* i.e., "the son (or offshoot) of the festival".

ISSERLEIN, ISRAEL BEN PETHAHIAH (1390-1460): Austrian rabbinical authority. His major work was the book of responsa *Terumat ha-Deshen* ("The Fat Offering"), based on the Talmud and the works of earlier rabbis in Germany and France as well as on Alfasi and Maimonides. In instances where the ideas of more recent rabbis conflicted with those of earlier authorities, I. decided in favor of the more ancient sources. His objective was to point the way to a revival of the study of the Talmud, which had been largely replaced in Germany by the study of codes. His decisions tended to the stringent, although he was noticeably lenient in cases involving a possible conflict with Christians. I.'s writings constitute an important source for 15th cent. Austro-German Jewish history.

ISSERLES, MOSES (c. 1525-1572): Polish codifier. In 1552 he founded a *yeshivah* in his native Cracow which he headed and maintained until his death. When his contemporary Joseph KARO published the code *Bet Yoseph* based on the decisions of Alfasi and Maimonides and ignoring those of *Ashkenazi* authorities, I. wrote his own commentary on JACOB BEN ASHER's *Tur*, entitled *Darkhei Mosheh* ("Ways of Moses") to summarize the halakhic views of the *Ashkenazi* scholars. Fearing that Karo's popular abbreviated code *Shulḥan Arukh* would spread rapidly throughout Europe and oust *Ashkenazi* tradition, he wrote the complementary glosses, the *Mappah* ("Tablecloth"), adding *Ashkenazi* custom; the *Shulḥan Arukh* together with I.'s additions became the standard authority for *Ashkenazi* halakhic practice. I. was interested in secular as well as sacred knowledge and his *Torat ha-Oleh* ("Law of the Burnt-Offering"), a discussion of the symbolism of the Temple and the sacrificial system, contains positive views on philosophy, astronomy, and Kabbalah. Although a firm believer in the antiquity and revealed character of the Kabbalah, I. strenuously opposed its popularization.

IYYAR: Second month of the civil calendar and eighth of religious; zodiac sign – Taurus. It has 29 days and is referred to in the Bible as *Ziv*. The chief dates are: INDEPENDENCE DAY of the State of Israel: 5th; second PASSOVER: 14th; LAG BA-OMER: 18th; and Jerusalem Day: 28th.

J

JABNEH, see **YAVNEH**

JACHIN: Copper pillar at the right-hand entrance to Solomon's TEMPLE porch, the one on the left being called Boaz (I Kings 7:21). Their exact significance is uncertain and attempts have been made to relate them to similar pillars discovered in other Near Eastern shrines. A homiletic interpretation suggests that they symbolized the pillar of fire and pillar of cloud which accompanied the Israelites in their desert wanderings.

JACOB (Heb. *Yaakov*): Israelite PATRIARCH: son of ISAAC and Rebekah; also named Israel (Gen. 32:29). The third and eponymous forefather of the Jewish people, he was the younger twin of ESAU whose heel (Heb. *ekev*) he gripped at birth — hence the traditional derivation of his name (Gen. 25:26). The highly dramatic life-story of J. (Gen. 25-50) was marked by conflict and struggle in which he showed great courage and perseverance. In contrast to Esau's purely martial qualities J. is described as "a plain man, dwelling in tents" (Gen. 25:29) and more than once he had to resort to strategem and craft. Although apparently predestined to the patriarchal succession (cf. also Gen. 25:23) he nevertheless acquired the requisite blessing by questionable means (no effort is made to conceal his weakness), and for this he had to suffer harshly. His flight from his brother's wrath was followed by prolonged servitude to his uncle Laban, his struggle with the angel at the ford of Jabbok, the dreaded encounter with Esau and his 400 men, the early death of his beloved wife Rachel, and the presumed loss of his favorite son JOSEPH. Only at the end of his days, after the reunion with Joseph in Egypt, did J. find peace and rest — though again in exile. Archeological discoveries such as the Nuzi code, showing the close affinity between the customs of the Patriarchs and those obtaining in Mesopotamia at that period, have thrown light on many details in the biblical account of J. J.'s many trials are treated in rabbinic literature as symbolic of the plight and struggles of the Jewish people. The rabbis ascribe to J. the introduction of the evening prayer.

JACOB, BLESSING OF: The blessing over the tribes (Gen. 49) pronounced by the Patriarch Jacob on his deathbed. The sequence of short sayings, expressing the characteristics and historical condition of each tribe, is held by critical scholars to have been composed in the Judean kingdom during the reign of David or Solomon.

JACOB BEN ASHER (known as *Baal ha-Turim* i.e., author of the *Turim*; c. 1270-c. 1343): Codifier. Born in Germany, he emigrated to Spain together with his father, ASHER BEN JEHIEL and his brothers in 1303. A pietist who refused to accept an appointment as rabbi, J. remained in dire poverty throughout his life. His great code *Arbaah Turim* ("Four Rows") was directed toward bridging the gulf between the Franco-German and Spanish rabbinical schools of Jewish law. His sources included the two Talmuds, gaonic literature, and later commentators and codifiers, especially his father. Unlike Maimonides' code (*Mishneh Torah*), J. quotes all his sources and cites the opinions upon which his decisions (generally following those of his father) are based. Omitting those branches of *halakhah* which had become obsolescent with the destruction of the Temple, the work follows an original arrangement which subsequently became classic. The four parts are: 1) *Oraḥ Ḥayyim* ("Way of Life") dealing with the daily duties of man, including blessings, prayers, Sabbaths, festivals, etc.; 2) *Yoreh Deah* ("Teacher of Knowledge") embracing ritual law including dietary regulations, vows, mourning, etc.; 3) *Even ha-Ezer* ("The Stone of Help") dealing with family laws, marriage, divorce, etc.; and 4) *Ḥoshen Mishpat* ("Breastplate of Judgment") on civil law. This work rapidly became the standard code of Jewish law and was the basis for Joseph KARO's SHULḤAN ARUKH. J. also wrote a lengthy commentary to the Pentateuch, only a small section of which was printed.

JACOB BEN JACOB MOSES OF LISSA (c. 1762-1832): E. European rabbinic authority who strenuously opposed both Ḥasidism and the Reform Movement. The best known of his many works is *Derekh ha-Ḥayyim* ("The Way of Life"), a convenient manual summarizing everyday religious practice, frequently printed in editions of the prayer book.

JACOB BEN MEIR TAM, see **TAM, JACOB BEN MEIR**

JACOB BEN MOSES HA-LEVI MÖLLN (known as *Maharil*; c. 1365-1427): Rabbinical authority. His *Minhagim* ("Customs") reported the customs of German communities, particularly in the sphere of ritual. It was regarded as authoritative in view of J.'s commanding position among German Jews. The customs he recorded were in many cases incorporated by Moses ISSERLES into his additions to the SHULḤAN ARUKH and hence became standard *Ashkenazi* practice. J. was also the author of responsa, which together with the *Minhagim*, preserved a vivid picture of 15th cent. Jewish life in W. Germany.

JACOB BEN WOLF KRANZ ("The MAGGID of Dubno"; c. 1740-1804): Preacher who traveled extensively through Poland. His sermons gained much popular fame particularly for their brilliant use of parable; Moses Mendelssohn called J. "the Jewish Aesop". Given in the form of homiletical expositions on the sections of the Bible read in the synagogue, they were published posthumously.

JACOB ISAAC OF PRZYSUCHA (1765-1817): Polish *tzaddik* known as *Yehudi ha-Kadosh* ("the Holy Jew"). Toward the end of his life he separated from his master, R. Jacob Isaac Horowitz, known as the "seer of Lublin", and founded a new trend in Ḥasidism combining talmudic scholarship and a more speculative treatment of ḥasidic teaching. He opposed the popular Ḥasidism of the masses and their belief in wonder workers, thereby provoking the antagonism of many ḥasidic circles. Among his disciples were R. Simḥah Bunam of Przysucha (his spiritual heir and successor) and R. Menahem Mendel of Kotsk.

JACOB JOSEPH OF POLONNOYE (d. 1782): Ḥasidic writer; disciple of the BAAL SHEM TOV. His master was succeeded as leader and organizer of the rapidly growing ḥasidic movement by Dov BER OF MEZHIRICH, whereas J. J. became the literary exponent of ḥasidic teaching. His writings not only formulated and spread early ḥasidic doctrine, but also helped the adherents of the movement in defining their position and in defending it against the aggressive opposition of the MITNAGGEDIM. His best-known work, the *Toledot Yaakov Yoseph* ("The generations of Jacob Joseph"), offers a spirited exposition of the semi-pantheistic mysticism which characterizes ḥasidic thought and which seems to have been one of the main features in the thought and teachings of the Baal Shem Tov (who himself left no writings). Its many first-hand quotations make the work a primary source of information about the Baal Shem Tov. It also emphasizes the spiritual function and importance of the TZADDIK.

JACOB JOSHUA BEN TZEVI HIRSCH FALK (1680-1756): Talmudist; lived in Poland, later in Germany. His halakhic decisions, which relied to a great extent on the early codifiers, particularly Maimonides, enjoyed great authority. His best-known work *Penei Yehoshua* ("Face of Joshua"), consisting of novellae and glosses on the Talmud, is characterized by lucid and penetrating halakhic analysis. He supported R. Jacob EMDEN in his polemic against R. Jonathan EIBESCHÜTZ.

JACOB OF DUBNO, see **JACOB BEN WOLF KRANZ**

JAHRZEIT, see **YAHRZEIT**

JAHWIST THEORY, see **BIBLE CRITICISM**

JAPHETH BEN ALI (10th cent.): Karaite biblical scholar, living in Jerusalem. His Bible commentaries vigorously attacked the rabbinical commentators, particularly Saadyah Gaon, and are equally emphatic in their polemics against Islam and Chrisianity. J. is often quoted by Abraham Ibn Ezra.

JASHAR, BOOK OF, see **BIBLE, LOST BOOKS OF**

JEDID AL-ISLAM (Arab. "New Moslems"): A group of Persian crypto-Jews. In 1839, the Jews of Meshed in Persia were subjected to religious persecution, and the entire community was forced to adopt Islam. However they devoutly maintained their Jewish practices in secret. Gradually they managed to escape from their Marrano existence with at least a half of them (over 1,000 individuals) settling in Palestine. The synagogue which they founded in Jerusalem still exists.

JEHIEL OF PARIS (known in French as Sir Vives; 13th cent.): Talmudist; succeeded his master, R. Judah Sir Leon, as head of the Paris *yeshivah*. In 1240, he played a leading role in the DISPUTATION with the apostate Nicholas Donin. Despite J.'s defense, the Talmud was formally condemned and 24 carloads of copies were destroyed. J. later settled in Palestine where he founded a rabbinical school. He was the author of TOSAPHOT noted for their legal acumen.

JEHOVAH: English transliteration of the Divine name, based on a misunderstanding of the Hebrew text. The Tetragrammaton JHVH was regarded by Jews as too holy to pronounce and was therefore read ADONAI. To indicate this reading, the Masoretes vocalized the original name with the vowels of *Adonai*. The translators, however, took this as the actual vocalization of the Tetragrammaton, and produced the hybrid form, Jehovah.

JELLINEK, ADOLF (1821-1893): Rabbi, preacher, scholar; officiated in Leipzig, and from 1856 in Vienna. The most celebrated Jewish preacher of the period, his brilliant sermons — noteworthy for their midrashic exposition — attracted large congregations, including many non-Jews. Over 200 of his sermons were published and greatly influenced Jewish HOMILETICS. He inclined toward moderate Reform and opposed Zionism. As a scholar he belonged to the modern school of the WISSENSCHAFT DES JUDENTUMS. His extensive researches covered many fields, in particular medieval Jewish philosophy and Kabbalah (he was the first to compare the ZOHAR with the Hebrew texts of Moses de LEON). In his *Bet ha-Midrash,* he edited from manuscript many of the smaller and apocryphal Midrashim.

JEREMIAH: Second of the three Major PROPHETS. A priest from Anathoth, he began to prophesy in the thirteenth year of King Josiah (626 B.C.E.). The 41 years of his ministry spanned a crucial period in Israelite and world history alike, as Egypt and Babylonia were contending for the control of W. Asia after the foundering of the Assyrian Empire in 609 B.C.E. Feverish political maneuvering under Jehoiakim could not prevent the conquest of Jerusalem by Nebuchadnezzar (597) who carried the "flower of Judah" into Babylonian captivity. The victor appointed Zedekiah as vassal-king, but the latter, encouraged by false prophets and trusting in an Egyptian alliance, flouted J.'s prophetic demand to submit to the Babylonian yoke and rose against Nebuchadnezzar. The resultant fall of Jerusalem and destruction of the Temple in 586 marked the end of the Judean kingdom. There followed further deportations to Babylonia, while after the murder of GEDALIAH others fled to Egypt against the warnings and protests of J., who was forced to go with them. From the numerous personal and biographical references in the Book of J. there emerges a picture of the most tragic of all the Israelite prophets. Of an essentially tender and lyrical disposition, his soul was torn between love for his people and the dire compulsion of his prophetic mission (which he vainly tried to refuse) to announce doom and destruction. The inescapable call to prophecy, like "burning fire" in his bones, turned into intense anguish and profound despair as a result of the apparent failure of his mission. His message was rejected by king and people in favor of the more agreeable utterances of the "false prophets", and he was persecuted, imprisoned, and almost put to death. His personal career adds an individual depth to his prophecy, which reaches its climax in the message of the new covenant which God will engrave upon men's hearts. Scholars distinguish in the Book of J. between the prophet's speeches (dictated to his amanuensis BARUCH, see 36:1 ff.), a biographical account by Baruch, and some later additions. The rabbis also credited J. with the authorship of LAMENTATIONS and the Book of KINGS.

JERUSALEM: Ancient capital of the Davidic kingdom. It has been identified with the Salem mentioned in the time of Abraham (Gen. 14:8). Situated in hill country, it was not captured by Joshua and remained a Jebusite stronghold until conquered by David (i.e., by the tribe of Judah), though it was in the territory allotted to Benjamin. When David was appointed king over the whole nation, he transferred his capital from Hebron to J., where he reigned for over 33 years (II Sam. 5:5). Its importance was immeasurably enhanced by the building of the TEMPLE by Solomon (I Kings 6 ff.). J. became the Jewish HOLY CITY, to which were later added Christian and Moslem religious connections. Despite the powerful sentiment for the Land of Israel as a whole maintained throughout the centuries of Exile and Diaspora, it is rarely the land which is mentioned as the subject of the yearnings of the people, but almost exclusively "ZION" and J.; cf. "If I forget thee, O J., let my right hand forget its cunning" (Ps. 137:5); "Pray for the peace of J." (Ps. 122:6); "See the good of J." (Ps. 128:5), and the constant references to J. in the liturgy, particularly the 14th benediction of the weekday AMIDAH and the 3rd benediction of the GRACE AFTER MEALS. In Temple times, J. was the object of the thrice-annual festival pilgrimages. Wherever a Jew prays, he turns toward J. In rabbinic literature the earthly J. was conceived as the copy or reflection of a celestial archetype, the heavenly J., and the terms J. and Zion were invested by homiletic and mystical writers with symbolic and spiritual significances over and above their concrete meaning.

JERUSALEM TALMUD, see **TALMUD**

JESHURUN: Symbolic name for Israel (Deut. 32:15; 33:5, 26).

JESUS (Greek form of the Heb. name Joshua): Founder of CHRISTIANITY (d. 29 C.E.). The only source for our knowledge of the life and teaching of J. is the NEW TESTAMENT which, however, reflects the beliefs and struggles of the nascent Church rather than those of J.'s own day. The New Testament account, being often tendentious and unreliable, has to be used with great caution. Jewish references to J. (e.g. the Talmud and TOLEDOT YESHU) are late and merely polemical; the reference of JOSEPHUS is probably a Christian interpolation. It appears that J. was a Galilean Jew, and was influenced in his youth by the ascetic JOHN THE BAPTIST, who preached BAPTISM and repentance in preparation for the imminent coming of the KINGDOM OF GOD. During this period J. may also have absorbed some ESSENE and sectarian influences. He became a wandering teacher, roaming the country with a small band of followers, preaching in the synagogues, and urging the people to repent because the Kingdom of God was at hand. New Testament accounts of J.'s clashes with the PHARISEES and his diatribes against the Jews are exaggerated and probably reflect growing Christian hostility against the Jews who rejected the claims of the young Church. Nevertheless there is no reason to doubt that J. did clash with the Pharisees, who evidently resented the authority which he claimed and the liberties which he took regarding the Law, far more than they minded the insistence (which he shared with other moralists and teachers) that intention and right spirit were more important than outward performance. In spite of these conflicts, J.'s sayings exhibit many resemblances to contemporary rabbinic teaching, and he essentially belonged to the Pharisaic rather than the Sadducean or sectarian tradition, both in his observance of the Law and in his acceptance of specifically Pharisaic doctrines (e.g. the resurrection of the dead). Ultimately it was not so much his teaching as his conception of his messianic mission and destiny that was ultimately decisive. J. lived in the intense apocalyptic expectation of contemporary Jewish (sectarian rather than Pharisaic) ESCHATOLOGY, and apparently believed himself called to the messianic rôle of the SON OF MAN. In the course of his short ministry he seems to have come to the conclusion that his task also involved suffering and dying. After a messianic entry into Jerusalem just before the Passover, he was arrested as a potential revolutionary, and executed (i.e., crucified) by order of the Roman procurator Pontius Pilate — probably at the instigation of Jewish circles who feared the Roman reactions to messianic agitation. For some time his disciples and their followers, who believed that J. had risen from the dead and ascended into heaven, existed as a sect within the main body of Jewry, but soon the ways parted and Christianity became a distinct, and for a long time hostile, religion. Although the life and teachings of J. have exercized a great influence on the course and development of western civilization, they had no direct effect on Jewish thought; nevertheless their reconstruction by New Testament scholarship helps to illuminate the religious movements and messianic ferment in Judaism at the end of the Second Temple Period.

JESUS BEN SIRA, see **BEN SIRA**

JEW: Anglicized form of the Hebrew *yehudi.* Originally a tribal definition, it meant a member of the tribe of Judah. With the division of the kingdom in the reign of Rehoboam, the southern kingdom, consisting of the two loyalist tribes of JUDAH and Benjamin, took the single name Judah. Thus the word *yehudit* ("Hebrew") in II Kings 18:28 means, in its context, "the language of the kingdom of Judah". With the disappearance of the Northern Kingdom and the exile of its population, Judah alone remained to perpetuate the Israelite faith and nationality. The Judean exiles retained their identity as a people also during the Babylonian Exile. After their return to Jerusalem following the declaration of Cyrus, they came to be called by the name *yehudi.* The word became synonymous with the "descendants of Abraham" and is found in Est. 2:5 referring to "Mordecai... a Benjaminite" i.e., a member of the tribe of Benjamin which was part of that people now called Jews. Hence "Jew" developed into a common appellation (from Latin *Judaeus* from which the word "JUDAISM" has been derived to designate the faith of the Jews). In rabbinical sources the term is used in a purely homiletical as well as in a legal-theological sense; a statement such as "anyone who repudiates idolatry is called a J." (*Meg.* 18a) has homiletical significance only, whereas rabbinic law defines a J. as either a person born of a Jewish mother or one who has been converted to Judaism (PROSELYTE). The origin of the rule that a child born of a Jewish father and a non-Jewish mother is not considered a J. is obscure, but scriptural authority is adduced from Neh. 10:29, where it is said that Ezra obliged those Jews who had married foreign wives to put them away together with their children. The child of a Jewish mother, on the other hand, even if the father is not Jewish, has all the rights and privileges of a J. Whether, or the extent to which, a J. can lose his Jewish character, and the rights and responsibilities entailed by it, has been a matter of controversy. The talmudic statement, "an Israelite, even though he sin, remains an Israelite" (*Sanh.* 44a), has been interpreted so widely as to include even the sin of apostasy, but different authorities have held varying views regarding the loss of certain rights. Later authorities even ruled that a repentant apostate who wishes to return to his original faith must go through a ceremony of readmission: nevertheless, failure to do so would not deprive him of his rights as a J. The non-Jew who wishes to become a Jew has, after undergoing a course of instruction, formally to take upon himself the obligation of Judaism, and in the case of a male to undergo ritual CIRCUMCISION. All converts, in addition, have to undergo IMMERSION in a ritual bath (MIKVEH) in the presence of a properly constituted court. Such a convert is in every respect a J. and is considered to be on a par with a natural born J. He suffers from practically no disabilities, except that the female convert cannot marry a priest. Reform Judaism does not observe the talmudic regulations concerning CONVERSION, nor does it admit that the child of a non-Jewish mother and a Jewish father is not Jewish. In general it accepts a gentile into the Jewish fold upon his making an appropriate declaration after undergoing a course of study.

JEWISH CHRISTIANS: The abrogation, viz. "fulfillment", of the Law proclaimed by Paul (see CHRISTIANITY) led to adoption of the new faith by many gentiles. Most of the Jewish followers of JESUS, however, who had scrupulously maintained the ritual and ceremonial regulations of Judaism, continued to do so and became J.C., i.e., Jews who observed the Law while believing in Jesus. The varying extent of their belief differentiates the two main sects of these J.C., the EBIONITES and the Nazarenes. The former believed in Jesus' messianic character but denied his divinity and miraculous birth, while the latter accepted both though they maintained that the Law was binding on Jews only. It was in order to drive the J.C. from the Jewish religious communion that the Patriarch Gamaliel II instructed R. Samuel Ha-Katan to compose the imprecation which became an additional paragraph to the existing AMIDAH (c. 100 C.E.). In modern times attempts have been made by Jewish converts to Christianity to re-establish the conception of J.C. With the emergence of the State of Israel, and the corollary idea that Jewishness is a national and not a religious concept, a small movement of J.C. is trying to establish itself in Israel.

JEWISH INSTITUTE OF RELIGION, see **HEBREW UNION COLLEGE**

JEWISH OATH: As early as the 6th cent. the Emperor Justinian declared that Jews were inadmissible as witnesses against Christians. During the Middle Ages this disability was modified to the extent that a special OATH (*more Judaico*) was exacted from Jews. It took various forms, very often of a degrading and humiliating nature. The model for later legislation was the oath adopted by German courts in 1555 in which the Jewish witness had to call down upon himself all the curses in Lev. 26, Deut. 28, the plagues of Egypt, etc. Moses MENDELSSOHN succeeded in persuading the Prussian government to modify the oath but it remained in force in some countries until the beginning of the 20th cent. The imposition of this oath was based upon the false allegation that by the KOL NIDREI formula the Jew absolves himself from all oaths. The medieval J. O. is not to be confused with the modifications allowed by many law courts to make the procedure of oath-taking acceptable to Jews (e.g. substituting a Hebrew Bible for the New Testament).

JEWISH RECONSTRUCTIONIST FOUNDATION, see **RECONSTRUCTIONISM**

JEWISH SCIENCE: Religious movement, founded in the U.S. in 1924 by Morris Lichtenstein, and led after the founder's death by his wife Tehilla Lichtenstein. The name J.S. was chosen as a sign of opposition to Christian Science which, at the time, attracted many Jews. The philosophy of the movement was essentially optimistic, stressing the goodness of God, the efficacy of prayer, and the spiritual rather than ritual aspects of Judaism.

JEWISH THEOLOGICAL SEMINARY: New York RABBINICAL SEMINARY; academic center of the CONSERVATIVE Movement. Founded in 1886 under the leadership of Sabato MORAIS, the J.T.S. was reorganized in 1902 after the arrival, from Cambridge, of its second president Solomon SCHECHTER, during whose incumbency it became one of the outstanding theological schools in the U.S. and the cradle of Conservative Judaism. It is composed of a Rabbinical School, library, Teachers' Institute (including youth and adult education departments), College of Jewish Studies, Cantors' Institute and School of Jewish Music, Department of Radio and Television, and Institute for Religious and Social Studies. The Jewish Museum, New York, is an independent institution under the auspices of the J.T.S. The library is one of the world's major collections of books and manuscripts in Jewish studies. The Seminary has branches in Jerusalem and Los Angeles (The University of Judaism), and has an agreement for mutual support with the Seminario Rabinico Latino Americano in Argentina. It also operates the Schocken Institute for Jewish Research.

JEWS' COLLEGE: Training institution for Orthodox ministers and rabbis for the British Commonwealth. It was established in London in 1856. In addition to B.A. (Hons.), B.Ed. (Hons.), M.A. and Ph.D. degrees in Jewish Studies, it has a training section for cantors. Principals have included Michael Friedlander, Adolf Buechler, Isidore Epstein, H.J. Zimmels, and Nachum Rabinovitch. It is a recognized college of the University of London.

JHWH, see **GOD, NAMES OF**

JOB: A man of exemplary righteousness, mentioned together with Noah and Daniel (Ezek. 14:14). He also appears as the hero of a biblical work (third book of the Hagiographa) which bears his name. The prologue (chaps. 1-2) — in prose — portrays the righteous ways of J. who lived and prospered in the land of Uz. In the celestial council Satan cynically attributes J.'s exemplary piety to his good fortune, and he is granted a free hand to test Job's faith in God. Visited by a series of increasingly heavy misfortunes and ills J. is reduced to the depths of agony and despair, but withstands the temptation to "curse God". There follows a series of poetically phrased discourses on the possible causes and significance of J.'s suffering, delivered in the form of a discussion between J. and his four friends (Eliphaz, Bildad, Zophar, and Elihu), most of whom maintain the traditional popular view that suffering must be a consequence of sin, while J.

insists that he is not conscious of having committed any wrong (chaps. 3-37). Finally God answers J. out of a whirlwind, in an overpowering manifestation of His inscrutable omnipotence (chaps. 38-41). The book concludes with an epilogue (chap. 42) in which J. regrets his presumption in doubting God's ways; his health and vigor are restored and his former fortune even doubled. The setting and characters of the book are all non-Israelite, thus stressing the anonymous author's universalist conception of his central theme — innocent suffering and God's justice. The precise interpretation of the argument of the book depends in part on the views taken regarding the nature and composition of the text. Many scholars consider Elihu's speeches (chaps. 32-7) an awkward later addition. But it is generally agreed that God does not offer any rational answer to J.'s problem of innocent suffering. While disavowing the theological explanation's of J.'s friends, God humbles J. and forces him to realize that man cannot presume to ask God any questions. The book exhibits a unique combination of audacity and profound faith, climaxed by J.'s affirmation: "But as for me, I know that my Redeemer liveth, and that He shall stand up over my dust at the last" (19:25). Scholars differ as to the date of the book but agree that it belongs to the school of WISDOM LITERATURE. It has also been claimed that the book contains Edomite elements. Talmudic views of J.'s time and personality varied. Some rabbis suggested Mosaic authorship of the book (*Bava Batra* 14b), and held J. to be a contemporary of Abraham; others thought that "J. never existed but was a parable" (*ibid.* 15a; *Gen. Rab.* 57). According to the Talmud the book was recited by the High Priest shortly before the Day of Atonement and is still read by SEPHARDIM on the fast of *Av* 9. It is also one of the few biblical texts whose study is permitted during the period of MOURNING.

JOB, TESTAMENT OF: Pseudepigraphal work preserved in Greek, written in the form of a last testament of Job in which he reviews the events of his life in order to instruct his children in the ways of righteousness. Of Jewish origin, this book most probably stems from the 1st cent. C.E. Job, a convert from idolatry, generously shares his great wealth with the poor, but is afflicted by Satan. After a period of trial and tribulation, Job emerges triumphant; his former wealth and station are restored and at his death his soul is carried to heaven in a great chariot. The book was probably written in answer to the problem of pagan domination.

JOEL: Prophet; author of the second book of the Minor Prophets. His date and life story are not indicated. J. exhorted Israel to fast and repent and to invoke God's mercy, for the Day of the Lord was at hand, bringing destruction in its wake. On that Day the nations would be judged and Israel regain its glory on the Mount of Zion. In the prophet's vision natural calamity in the form of the locust is merged with the ravages of a swarming enemy. These in turn serve as a background to Joel's eschatological message.

JOHANAN BAR NAPPAḤA (or Naphḥa, generally known just as R. Johanan; 3rd cent.): The most outstanding of the Palestinian *amoraim*. A brilliant halakhist and aggadist, he taught in Sephoris and later in Tiberias where his pupils included distinguished rabbis who laid the foundation for the Palestine TALMUD. J. was involved in many halakhic discussions with his brother-in-law SIMEON BEN LAKISH and the two profoundly analyzed the Mishnah. After the death of RAV and SAMUEL, J. was regarded as the outstanding rabbinical authority, and his decisions and views were respected in Babylonia, being frequently quoted in the Babylonian Talmud.

JOHANAN BEN ZAKKAI (known as *Rabban* "our master"; 1st cent. C.E.): *Tanna* who survived the destruction of the Temple and founded the ACADEMY at YAVNEH; a pupil of Hillel, who called him "a father of wisdom and a father of the generation to come". The re-establishment of the Yavneh academy was one of the great turning points in Jewish religious history, ensuring the continuance of tradition despite the cessation of the Temple service, around which religious activity had previously revolved. Yavneh took the place of Jerusalem as the seat of the SANHEDRIN, which became the central body in Jewish life and developed Jewish law and practice in new directions. J. himself based this approach on the biblical verse "For I desire mercy rather than sacrifice" (Hos. 6:6) and taught that the continuation of Judaism depended on loyalty to tradition rather than on the possession of a particular land or Temple. Under his guidance the synagogue and the house of study took the place of the Temple. J. established unity among the scholars and secured the supremacy of Yavneh's authority. He paid particular attention to the compilation and recording of all aspects of the Temple ritual in anticipation of a possible restoration.

JOHN THE BAPTIST: Ascetic preacher who exercised a powerful influence upon JESUS. Possibly connected with the ESSENE sect, he lived as a hermit in the desert until about 15 C.E. when he emerged from his seclusion in order to preach the need for repentance in view of the imminence of the Kingdom of God. BAPTISM, which he regarded as of supreme importance, was to be the sign of that repentance. Among those who answered the call was Jesus, in whom J. saw the Messiah to bring about the Kingdom of God. He was beheaded by Herod Antipas.

JOINT OWNERSHIP, see **PARTNERSHIP**

JONAH: Fifth of the Minor Prophets; fl. late 9th-early 8th cent. B.C.E. The Book of J. is the only one of the prophetic books to present its lesson solely by narrative. Directed by God to deliver a message of doom to Nineveh, J. flees to Tarshish. On the way a storm overtakes his ship and the fugitive is cast into the sea, but he is swallowed by a fish and miraculously disgorged onto the coast. He finally reaches Nineveh to preach God's message, effecting repentance and Divine forgiveness. The prophet's vehement disapproval at the outcome is met by an object lesson in the nature of God's mercy. God's concern, power, and grace, he is told, extend to all humanity as well as beasts and it is not possible to escape His will. Critical attempts to assign the book to the period 600-200 B.C.E. are based upon linguistic and ideological considerations. Kabbalists and others have interpreted the story allegorically and mystically. The Book of J. is read in its entirety in the Afternoon Service on the Day of Atonement.

JONAH, RABBENU, see **GERONDI, JONAH**

JONATHAN BEN UZZIEL (1st cent): *Tanna*, known as an outstanding pupil of HILLEL, though no *halakhot* have been preserved in his name. The Talmud attributes to him a TARGUM of the Prophetical Books, but the Targum commonly known by his name dates in its present form from much later (4th-5th cent.; Babylonian). A Targum on the Pentateuch has also been attributed to J., but it dates from the 3rd-4th cent. and the ascription appears erroneous.

JORDAN (Heb. *yarden,* from the root *yarad,* "descend"): The largest river in the Land of Israel. From the foothills of Mt. Hermon, it winds its way along the Great Rift through the Sea of Galilee to the Dead Sea 1,292 ft. below sea level. For the Israelites under Joshua the crossing of the Jordan in miraculous circumstances heralded the first stage of the predestined conquest of Canaan (Josh. 3:15-17). The river figures in a number of biblical narratives while in the Second Temple Period a number of sects centered their baptismal rites around the J. (see ESSENES: JOHN THE BAPTIST). The river has been prominent in both Jewish and Christian tradition and folklore.

JOSE, see **YOSE**

JOSEPH: Son of JACOB and Rachel; his story is related in Gen. 37-50. A favorite of his father, he was hated by his brothers who plotted his downfall and abandoned him in a ditch. Picked up by a band of Midianites, J. was taken to Egypt as a slave. After a series of vicissitudes, his fame as an interpreter of dreams reached Pharaoh. Deeply impressed by J.'s perspicacity, Pharaoh promptly elevated him to the rank of viceroy. He was married to Asenath, daughter of a leading priest at Heliopolis, who bore him Manasseh and Ephraim. Foreseeing famine, he prudently accumulated vast stocks of grain which he eventually distributed in a manner that changed the feudal system of land tenure into state ownership. It was that famine which brought Jacob and his remaining 11 sons into Egypt where, after a dramatic encounter, the latter were reconciled with J. He died at the age of 110. Critical scholarship is divided as to the extent of historicity in the story, taking into account certain parallel mythological motifs and the absence of external historical confirmation. It has also been suggested that he was the eponymous personification of a group of tribes. Other scholars have stressed the verisimilitude of the realistic element.

JOSEPH BEN ABRAHAM HA-COHEN (Al-Basir; 11th cent.): The first KARAITE philosopher; lived in Persia or Babylonia. Despite his blindness, he traveled extensively. His thought lacks originality and his philosophy is virtually indistinguishable from that of the Arab *kalam*; nevertheless it influenced Karaite thought in following centuries. J. was a rationalist, holding that knowledge must precede revelation. Man has complete free will, though God knows beforehand how he will act. J. tended to be stringent in his halakhic decisions but was responsible for easing the Karaite laws regulating the degrees of forbidden marriage with relatives.

JOSEPHUS FLAVIUS (Hebrew name: Joseph ben Mattityahu ha-Cohen): Politician, soldier, and historian (c. 38-c. 100). During the great revolt against the Romans he was commander in Galilee, but when his fortress Jotapata was conquered he went over to the Romans and adopted the name of Vespasian's family, Flavius. He accompanied Vespasian and Titus during the siege of Jerusalem, and later lived in Rome where he wrote books on Jewish history (*The Jewish War* and *The Antiquities of the Jews*), a defense of the Jewish people *Against Apion* (an anti-Jewish Alexandrian writer), and an *Autobiography.* His writings, which cannot always be implicitly trusted, were for a long time the only source of knowledge of the religious scene at the end of the Second Temple Period. All discussions regarding the PHARISEES, SADDUCEES, ESSENES, and the DEAD SEA SECT have to take J. into account. The medieval historiographical work YOSIPPON is mainly based on J.

JOSHUA (originally Hoshea, cf. Num. 13): According to the biblical account, first the servant and subsequently the successor of MOSES as leader of the children of Israel. Conqueror of Canaan, he ruled for 28 years and during this period the ARK was brought to Shiloh and the Land of Canaan apportioned among the tribes. The biblical Book of Joshua is the first among the FORMER PROPHETS and deals with events from the death of Moses to the death of Joshua: (1) the conquest of Canaan (chaps. 1-12); (2) the division of the land (chaps. 13-21); (3) final acts and exhortations of J. and his death (22-24). Stylistic and other analogies between the Book of J. and the Five Books of Moses have led critics to include them all in a literary unit called the Hexateuch. The Talmud ascribes to J. the authorship of the Book of J. as well as the eight concluding verses of DEUTERONOMY (*Bava Batra* 15a).

JOSHUA BEN HANANIAH (1st-2nd cents.): *Tanna*; pupil of R. Johanan ben Zakkai. Noted for his wisdom, J. held many discussions with Christians and Romans. He accompanied R. Gamaliel to Rome where he answered philosophical problems in behalf of the *Nasi*. According to the Midrash he once restrained the people from rebelling against Rome after the Emperor Hadrian's refusal to honor his pledge to rebuild the Temple (*Gen. Rab.* 64). J. succeeded Gamaliel as head of the *Bet Din* in Yavneh. As a legislator he tended toward leniency, permitting, for example, the conversion of Ammonites. One of his best-known aphorisms was "The evil eye, the evil inclination, and hatred of mankind drive a man out of the world" (*Avot* 2:16).

JOSHUA BEN LEVI (3rd cent.): *Amora*; head of the Lydda academy and leader of the Jewish community in Palestine. J. engaged in halakhic discussions with R. JOHANAN and SIMEON BEN LAKISH, and many of his decisions were accepted as *halakhah*. He also instituted many rules regulating the synagogue service. J. was an outstanding aggadist and was himself the subject of miraculous legends (depicting him as the companion of ELIJAH, as visiting paradise, etc.).

JOSHUA BEN PERAḤYAH (1st cent. B.C.E.): *Tanna; Nasi* of the Sanhedrin. Together with Nittai the Arbelite, he constituted one of the ZUGOT who transmitted the ORAL LAW tradition. Only one *halakhah* is quoted in his name. According to a legend, J. was the teacher of Jesus.

JOSIAH: King of Judah, 640-609 B.C.E. Taking advantage of the crumbling conditions of the Assyrian Empire, he strengthened Judah, and expanded its frontiers to the north. Making common cause with the Chaldean Nabopolassar he marched against the Egyptian pharaoh Necho and was killed in the battle of Megiddo. J. inaugurated an important program of religious reform probably connected with his break with Assyrian suzerainty. Resolving to put the Temple in order, he chanced upon a book of the law (identified by many scholars with the Book of DEUTERONOMY) and upon learning its contents destroyed all the emblems of Canaanite and Assyrian idolatry, and centralized worship in the Temple. Practices such as sacred prostitution and child sacrifice were banned. Baal priests were put to death. At a festive convocation the covenant between God and Israel was solemnly reaffirmed and Jerusalem once again became the exclusive religious center of Judah; for the first time after the conquest of Canaan, the Passover was observed in Jerusalem in accordance with biblical injunction (in 622 B.C.E.). J.'s reforms were of historic significance in the development of the monotheistic Israelite cult.

JOURNEY, PRAYER ON SETTING OUT FOR A (Heb. *tephillat ha-derekh*): Prayer enjoined in the Talmud (*Ber.* 29b), from which its form (with additions from *Derekh Eretz Rabbah* 11, and of appropriate biblical verses) has entered the rites of both *Ashkenazim* and *Sephardim.* Different versions exist for land, sea, and air voyages. The *Sephardi* rite has the prayer in the first person singular, the *Ashkenazi* version in the first person plural, following the view (*Ber.* 29b-30a) that all travelers should be included in the prayer. Recited upon reaching a spot about 100 yards from the outskirts of the place of departure, the prayer is for a minimum journey of some 3 miles, or for a shorter one if dangerous.

JOY: A spirit of j. is regarded by Judaism as an essential prerequisite to the true worship of God. "Serve the Lord with j., come before Him with exulting" (Ps. 100:2). The rabbis said "The Divine Presence does not rest upon a man while he is in a state of gloom... but only through the j. with which he fulfills the commandments" (*Shab.* 30b) and "The Holy Spirit descends only upon a joyful heart" Y. *Suk.* 5a). Special occasions of j. in Jewish life are family festivals (such as circumcision and *bar-mitzvah* ceremonies and especially weddings), the married state as such ("he who dwells without a wife dwells without j." — *Yev.* 62b), the Sabbath and festivals, as well as the general performance of the commandments. The Water Libation ceremony in the Temple was described as a ceremony of such j. that "he who has not seen it has not seen true j." (Mishnah *Suk.* 5:1), and the celebration of the Rejoicing of the Law (see SIMḤAT TORAH) in the synagogue is to this day a public demonstration of the conviction that "the precepts of the Lord are right, rejoicing the heart" (Ps. 19:8). The Ḥasidim have made joyful enthusiasm (*hitlahavut*) a central feature of their worship. The emphasis on the spirit of j. prevented the sterner and more ascetic aspects of religion from turning into morbidity and helped the Jew to overcome the horrors of exile and persecution through the "gladness of the Lord".

JUBILEE (Heb. *yovel*): According to the Bible,

every fiftieth year is to be proclaimed as a Jubilee. All the laws which govern land cultivation and its produce during the SABBATICAL YEAR apply also to the J. The J. is however characterized by further distinctive provisions. The J. began in *Tishri,* and on the Day of Atonement the *shophar* was blown and "liberty proclaimed throughout the land unto all its inhabitants" (Lev. 25:9-10). All slaves were released and all land reverted to the original owner. It is with regard to the sale or gift of land that the provisions of the J. are of paramount importance. Only such possession of land as has been obtained through INHERITANCE is permanent in Jewish law. Land obtained in any other way (including land mortgaged for debt) reverts to its original owner with the advent of the J. This institution prevents the alienation of an inherited share of the land and converts all sales or gifts (*Bek.* 52b) of land into leases for a known, fixed, and limited period (Lev. 25:28). The emancipation of both persons and property enjoined by the institution of the J. was originally meant to act as a safeguard against complete pauperism, prevent the accumulation of property in the hands of the few (an evil vehemently inveighed against by the prophets), and ensure the continued existence of independent freeholders. The custom lapsed with the destruction of the Temple and according to Jewish law only applies when all Jews live in Israel, each tribe in its own territory.

JUBILEES, BOOK OF: Jewish pseudepigraphal work; a kind of commentary or Midrash on the Book of Genesis and the first chapters of Exodus, written in the form of an angelic revelation to Moses. Composed originally in Hebrew — as has been proved by the discovery of Hebrew fragments of this work among the DEAD SEA SCROLLS—the complete version of J. is extant only in Ethiopic. The book derives its name from the fact that the author divides the history of Israel into "jubilee" periods (7×7 year-weeks = 49 years). Composed during the latter half of the 2nd cent. B.C.E., the work apparently stems from an Essene rather than, as was previously held, a Pharisaic milieu. The B. of J. insists, as do also the Dead Sea Scrolls, that the religious holiday be observed according to a solar calendar. The Law is glorified and projected back into the distant past of Israel. The author's purpose was evidently to remind Israel of its unique calling and to recall its duty to the Law.

JUDAH: Fourth son of JACOB and Leah. Through his son Perez he was the ancestor of DAVID. The tribe of J. was the largest and most important of the twelve TRIBES and gave its name to the southern kingdom after the split which followed the death of Solomon. The kingdom of J. continued in existence until the Babylonian conquest of 586 B.C.E. From "Judah" was derived the name "JEW", and according to Jewish belief, the MESSIAH will also come from J. — the tribe of David.

JUDAH BAR EZEKIEL (3rd cent.): Babylonian *amora.* A pupil of RAV and SAMUEL, he meticulously preserved their teachings, and hundreds of their *halakhot* are quoted in the Talmud in his name. J. founded the ACADEMY at PUMBEDITA, developing an approach to talmudic dialectics which became standard.

JUDAH BEN BARZILLAI ALBARGELONI (11th-12th cents.): Rabbi in Barcelona. His halakhic works (none of which has survived in its entirety) aimed at a straight-forward summary of talmudic discussions; his object was to codify decisions, for which he depended largely on the *geonim,* in particular HANANEL. J., who was one of the early kabbalists, also wrote a commentary on the Book of YETZIRAH.

JUDAH BEN BAVA (2nd cent.): *Tanna,* one of the Ten MARTYRS. He disputed many halakhic subjects with R. Akiva. His own most noteworthy *halakhah* was the decision that only one witness was required to testify to a man's death in order to permit his widow to remarry. During the Hadrianic persecutions when the Romans forbade the teaching of the *Torah,* he ordained several of R. Akiva's outstanding pupils (including R. MEIR, and R. SIMEON BAR YOḤAI) thereby ensuring the continuity of tradition. Caught by the Romans in the act of ordination, he bade the disciples escape and himself suffered martyrdom.

JUDAH BEN ILAI (2nd cent.): *Tanna;* teacher of R. JUDAH HA-NASI, who later incorporated in the Mishnah many of the traditions he had received from J. After the Hadrianic persecutions, J., who had been ordained by JUDAH BEN BAVA, established with a few colleagues the ACADEMY at Usha (his birthplace). J. taught in the form of halakhic MIDRASH, and the SIPHRA is based on his teachings. He was greatly revered for his humility and saintliness.

JUDAH BEN ISAAC (Sir Leon of Paris; 1166-1224): Tosaphist; grandson of RASHI. He re-established the Paris *yeshivah* in 1198 and under his direction it became an important center. His main literary work was his TOSAPHOT on the Talmud in which he was greatly influenced by his teacher Isaac ben Samuel of Dampierre.

JUDAH BEN KALONYMOS OF SPIRE (12th cent.): Lexicographer. His works include *Agron* (a dictionary of technical talmudic terms) and a critical dictionary of talmudic and midrashic sages analyzing all known information about their lives and teachings (*Yiḥusei Tannaim va-Amoraim*).

JUDAH BEN SAMUEL HE-ḤASID OF REGENSBURG (d. 1217): Talmudic scholar and mystic and one of the leading personalities in the movement known as the "Ḥasidei Ashkenaz". His reputation for asceticism and saintliness made him the the subject of many legends. The ethical work Sepher Ḥasidim has been ascribed to him; actually it is a composite work, containing writings of J., his father Samuel, and his pupil Eleazar ben Judah of Worms. He is also credited with the authorship of Shir ha-Kavod. J.'s mysticism was ethical and devotional, but also embodied many elements of popular folk religion, and this combination successfully appealed to the piety of the German Jews, who appreciated his stress on the Bible and devout prayer (as compared with the traditional rabbinical emphasis on talmudic scholarship) as expressed, for instance, in the advice that those who knew no Hebrew should pray in a language they understood.

JUDAH BEN TABBAI (1st cent. B.C.E.): *Tanna; Av Bet Din* of the Sanhedrin and — together with Simeon ben Shetaḥ — one of the zugot responsible for transmitting the oral tradition.

JUDAH HA-LEVI (c. 1075-1141): Spanish poet and religious thinker. A physician by profession, J. expressed his true genius in his poetry and his theological prose work *The Kuzari.* Upon completion of this last work he set out for the Holy Land, staying some time in Alexandria and visiting Tyre and Damascus en route; his eventual fate is unknown. According to legend he was killed by an Arab horseman while reciting his famous "Elegy for Zion" before the gates of Jerusalem. J. was the outstanding Hebrew poet of the Middle Ages; like his friend Moses Ibn Ezra, he applied the forms and conventions of Arabic poetry, e.g. rhyme and meter, to classical Hebrew. The body of his poetry falls under three main headings: secular (e.g. songs of love, wine, and friendship), religious, and national. His religious verse, marked by an intense and at times mystical love of God, has found its way into Jewish liturgy as have some of his national poems. The profound yearning for Zion which characterizes his national poetry is based on J.'s essentially religious belief that life in exile is by definition incomplete and that only in Zion can a Jew achieve the maximum degree of communion with God. *The Kuzari* — the only major Jewish classic written in platonic dialogue form — uses as its setting the historical conversion to Judaism of the king of the Khazars and consists primarily of a conversation between that king and a rabbi. Unlike other medieval Jewish philosophers, J. aimed, not to reconcile Judaism with current philosophical thought, but rather to demonstrate the intrinsic inadequacy of philosophy and the superiority of revelation. But as is to be seen from his attack on philosophy, an attack which itself makes use of philosophical arguments, J. was no mere dogmatist but would expound his faith philosophically. Although rational proofs can be misleading, there is, he maintains, nothing in the Bible which contradicts reason; but at the same time the Bible is a source of higher and surer truth than can be attained rationally. The Jewish religion is hence not irrational but suprarational. The existence of God cannot be proved philosophically neither does it require such proof. God is known through His revelation and through His manifestation in Jewish history, and long before Pascal, J. emphasized the difference between the "God of Abraham" (i.e., of living experience and history) and the "God of Aristotle" (i.e., an abstract philosophical principle, such as a first cause, etc.). J.'s philosophy of history and of the contact between God and man culminates in his doctrine of prophecy. Prophecy is both the mission and the ground of the spiritual superiority of Israel which is conceived as "the heart of the nations" — the intermediary between God and the world. The prophet is the highest type of human being and receives his inspiration directly from God, while the prophetic gift is given only to the Jewish people in the Land of Israel. Although J.'s view of the election of Israel as that of a spiritual super-race was not shared by other philosophers, it is true to say that he showed more awareness of the historical and national character of Jewish existence than any other medieval philosopher.

JUDAH HA-NASI (known as *rabbenu ha-kadosh* "our holy rabbi" or more generally merely as *Rabbi* i.e., the teacher *par excellence*; c. 135-c. 217): Patriarch (Nasi) of Palestinian Jewry; son and successor of Simeon ben Gamaliel. He lived most of his life in Galilee, presiding over his academic Sanhedrin in Bet Shearim and later in Sepphoris. A towering personality, he combined wisdom, learning, dignity, statesmanship, and wealth. His crowning achievement was the redaction of the Mishnah, which was both a text book for the study of the Oral Law and the first comprehensive code of rabbinic law (halakhah). Attempts at compilation had been made previously (e.g. by R. Akiva, R. Meir, R. Nathan) but they were uncoordinated and contained great diversities and lacunae. J.'s objective was to determine a unified compilation which would serve as the central legal instrument for Judaism and take the place of the academy which could no longer coordinate all the scattered Jewries. He secured the cooperation of all scholars and determined an agreed, unified text, the finishing touches to which were applied by his son and successor, Gamaliel III. J. decided which traditions were worthy of preservation; his views were accepted, even where they differed from those of his colleagues. According to a tradition J. was born on the day R. Akiva died; this is not merely a chronological speculation but implies that the tremendous task of systematizing the Oral Law to which R. Akiva had devoted his life was continued and completed by J. J. was the last of the TANNAIM; his successors, the AMORAIM, used his compilation as the basis for their studies, out of which eventually emerged the two TALMUDS.

JUDAH ḤASID HA-LEVI (1638-1700): Kabbalist and messianic enthusiast in Poland; a popular preacher, whose homilies stressed the importance of repentance and good deeds. He founded a group, called the "*Ḥasidim*", which devoted itself to prayer and penitence in the hope of realizing ultimate redemption. Believing that redemption to be at hand, J. and 1,500 followers set out for Palestine, arriving in 1700 after an adventurous journey. They bought land in Jerusalem where the synagogue named for J. stood until destroyed by Arabs in 1948. J. died a few days after arrival in Jerusalem and the group — persecuted by local Jews who (rightly) suspected their messianic fervor to be of Sabbataian inspiration — soon broke up, many of its members returning to Europe.

JUDAH LÖW BEN BEZALEL (known as the *Maharal* of Prague; c. 1525-1609): Rabbi and kabbalist. He lived in Prague 1573-1584 and later 1598-1609, and was widely recognized as one of the leading rabbinical authorities of his time. His many writings present profound and at times original interpretations of Judaism which combined philosophical and mystical elements. The creation of the legendary GOLEM was attributed to him.

JUDAH THE MACCABEE (d. 161 B.C.E.): Eldest son of the priest Mattathias of Modiin and military leader in the rebellion against the Seleucids of Syria. After the death of his father (166), J. assumed command of a small force and by utilizing his intimate knowledge of the countryside led his band in a number of harassing guerilla raids. His successes not only drew more men to his cause but called Syrian attention to his activities. In the following years J. repeatedly defeated the numerically superior Syrian armies and by 164 B.C.E. he was able to liberate Jerusalem and reconsecrate the Temple — events commemorated in the celebration of the ḤANUKKAH festival. He then led a campaign to relieve the oppressed Jewish communities in Idumea, Ammon, Galilee, and Gilead. Though the Seleucid rulers were now disposed to grant the Jews complete religious freedom, J. continued the fight to free his people from foreign rule. For a time J. was able to continue his series of triumphs, but he fell at the battle of Elasa (161). The struggle against the Seleucids was continued by his brothers (see HASMONEANS). J.'s piety, qualities of leadership, and military genius have made him one of the great Jewish heroes.

JUDAISM: The Jewish religion; also, in a wider sense, the general characteristics of Jewish values, ethics, attitudes, and *mores*. The term is not found in the Bible; its earliest known usage appears to be in a Midrash of uncertain date (*Est. Rab.* 7:11). "J." (Heb. *yahadut*) is frequently used today to denote the entirety of Jewish thought, starting from its basic idea of MONOTHEISM and its concomitant ethical imperatives (see ETHICS). These two concepts are bound up in turn with the two pivotal events in which the biblical God manifests His relation to the cosmos and to history, i.e., CREATION and the EXODUS. The legal and ritual traditions developed by the PRIESTS, and the ethical message preached by the PROPHETS later became fused in the teaching of the early rabbis (TALMUD, MIDRASH). In its practical application, J. was seen as a series of distinct and detailed MITZVOT (see PRECEPTS, 613); under the influence of PHILOSOPHY, on the other hand, a theory of J. was eventually formulated in intellectual terms, though no formal CREED was ever accepted as universally binding. The character of later-day Judaism was determined by certain medieval developments and achievements, e.g. the formulation of the LITURGY, the evolution of rabbinic scholarship (CODES, RESPONSA, COMMENTARIES, etc.) and the emergence of a strong MYSTIC trend (KABBALAH, ZOHAR). Still later, at the beginning of the Modern Period, the mystic trend found major expression in ḤASIDISM, the rational in HASKALAH. EMANCIPATION also led to other rationalistic and naturalistic attitudes, as expressed in REFORM J., CONSERVATIVE J., and RECONSTRUCTIONISM. Certain movements not formally or explicitly religious (e.g. the national movement, ZIONISM) but imbued with a sense of Jewish loyalties and values are considered also to be an aspect of J.

JUDGE: According to the biblical account, the ELDERS of the tribes served as judges before the settlement in Canaan. Later, acting upon the advice of Jethro, Moses appointed judges at various levels (Exod. 18:25-26). Afterward, the function of supreme j. was occasionally merged with that of the leader, king, priest, or prophet. In the Second Temple Period, cases were brought before the 71 judges who constituted the great SANHEDRIN while lesser Sanhedrins sat in other towns. After the Bar Kokhba revolt, Roman authorities forbade the ORDINATION of judges (*Sanh.* 14a) but in the course of time the function of the j. was combined with that of RABBI and in medieval times Jewish judges in many countries enjoyed a considerable degree of autonomy. A single j. was deemed competent to try a case if he was recognized as an outstanding scholar (*mumḥeh*) or if all parties agreed to accept his decision; otherwise cases were heard by more than one j. — generally, three. A judge must reach his decision only according to *halakhah,* except in exceptional cases in which he is empowered to act as he thinks fit. A proselyte is disqualified from acting as a j., since it is feared that due to his upbringing he may tend to render decisions on grounds other than traditional Jewish law. Since the lapse of ordination, a judge's authority is vested in him by the will of the people who bind themselves to abide by his decisions, while his competence to adjudicate in law is limited in certain spheres. The qualities required include "expert knowledge of Mishnah and Talmud, ability to weigh, sift, and decide, application over a period of years to the study of practical *halakhah,* and experience gained in a number of cases without committing errors of judgment". Great stress is also laid upon the ethical qualities demanded of a j.; beside wisdom he must be possessed of "humility, fear of God, detestation of money, love of truth, love of his fellow-men, and a good name". According to the Talmud, judges should also be familiar with languages and secular subjects. An imposing physical presence is also desirable. Once appointed, the j. is to be held in the highest esteem and respect, and the Bible (Exod. 22:27) expressly forbids his disparagement. Those disqualified from acting as witnesses (e.g. women) are also disqualified from acting as judges.

JUDGES, BOOK OF (Heb. *Sepher Shophetim*): Second book of the second part of the BIBLE (the Prophets); a direct continuation of the Book of JOSHUA, describing Israel's varying fortunes from the death of Joshua to the rise of the prophet SAMUEL. The period was one of general instability and lack of cohesion between the tribes, and is best characterized in the verse (21:25, etc.) "In those days there was no king in Israel; every man did what was right in his own eyes". The "Judges" were inspired leaders, arising in moments of severe crisis and impelled to action by the spirit of God. As temporary leaders in war, their influence rarely exceeded local or tribal boundaries. There were twelve Judges, six major ones (Othniel, Ehud, Barak [with Deborah], Gideon [with his son Abimelech], Jephthah, and Samson) and six minor (Shamgar, Tola, Jair, Ibzan, Elon, and Abdon). The book consists of three parts: 1) an account of the conquest of Canaan (chaps. 1-2:5); 2) the stories of the J. (2:6-16:31); 3) an appendix telling the stories of Micah's sanctuary and the idol therein, and of the war of the tribes against Benjamin, following the outrage at Gibeah (17-21). The purpose of the book is to present Israel's vicissitudes in Canaan in terms of an alternating rhythm of apostasy (as a result of the failure to exterminate the Canaanite population), foreign oppression, return to God, deliverance through a judge, reversion to idolatry, and so on (see 2:6-3:6). Rabbinic tradition ascribes the authorship to Samuel.

JUDGMENT, DAY OF, see **DAY OF JUDGMENT**

JUDITH: Apocryphal book which relates the cunning murder of Holofernes, commander of the forces of Nebuchadnezzar, king of Assyria, by the pious and beautiful Judith who succeeded thereby in raising the siege of her town, Bethulia. Some scholars have held that the story is fictitious and dates from the Hasmonean Period, when it was written to inspire the people in this fight for independence; in support of this contention several internal contradictions and anachronisms have been cited. However, indications have been growing that a historical basis for the incident may be found dating from the late Persian Period in Palestine (4th cent. B.C.E.). The work was apparently written originally in Hebrew but was preserved in its entirety only in Greek translation. Some late Hebrew Midrashim contain the same story but connect it with the Hasmoneans and the festival of *Ḥanukkah.*

JUS (or LEX) TALIONIS: The law of retaliation. The Bible states "An eye for an eye, a tooth for a tooth, a hand for a hand... etc." (Exod. 21:24-5; Lev. 24:20; Deut. 19:21), as the punishment to be inflicted upon one who has caused bodily injury to another. There is no evidence that this was ever applied literally (although according to an early source the Sadducees maintained that it should be so interpreted) and in rabbinical law it was interpreted to mean appropriate money compensation for personal injury and financial restitution in cases of damage to property. The only exception to this rule is the case of murder, where the life of the murderer is forfeit (see HOMICIDE). However, even in this case the practice (found in some ancient codes) of exacting vengeance from the children of the criminal is expressly prohibited — "The fathers shall not be put to death for the children neither shall the children be put to death for the fathers, every man shall be put to death for his own sin" (Deut. 24:16).

JUSTICE: A Divine ATTRIBUTE expressed in God's intolerance of evil and punishment of sin. Rabbinic literature frequently refers to the conflict between God's j. (His attribute expressed through the use of the Divine name *Elohim*) and His MERCY (expressed through the Tetragrammaton). A corollary of the doctrine of Divine j. is belief in REWARD AND PUNISHMENT. Divine j. must be reflected in human j. "What doth the Lord require of thee but to do justly, to love mercy, and to walk humbly with thy God" says the prophet Micah (6:8). The passion for j. can be regarded as the keynote of biblical legislation, and the basis of the demand for social righteousness on the part of the prophets. "Justice, justice shalt thou pursue, that thou mayest live to inherit the land which the Lord thy God giveth thee" (Deut. 16:20), expresses the legal basis, and "the Holy God is sanctified by justice" (Is. 5:16), the ethical. This insistence on j. as the foundation of Judaism is emphasized not only by contrasting it with injustice, but by insisting on its superiority over two other supreme virtues, peace and mercy. Thus, although R. Simeon ben Gamaliel said "By three things is the world preserved — by truth, justice, and peace" (*Avot* 1:18), the rabbis make Moses the prototype and protagonist of strict j. and Aaron that of peace (*Sanh.* 6b); they further interpret Aaron's sin in making the Golden Calf to be that he preferred peace to j. (*Exod. Rab.* 41:6). Similarly the rabbis were at great pains to define the precise legitimate bounds of j. and mercy. The world cannot exist if governed solely by j., and it must therefore be tempered by mercy, but the element of mercy must not be permitted to deflect the straight course of j. and can only modify the verdict. This is strikingly exemplified by the injunction "Thou shalt not favor a poor man in his cause" (Exod. 23:3) which, in its unbending insistence on the strictest impartiality, lays down that even a wrongful verdict to favor the poorer party in a suit on the grounds that the rich man would not thereby be harmed, is an act of injustice. The statement "sympathy and compassion are great virtues but even these feelings must be silenced in the presence of j." aptly sums up the Jewish view. In the administration of j. the verse, "Thou shalt not wrest justice; thou shalt not respect persons; neither shalt thou take a gift" (Deut. 16:9), was developed and practiced to an extraordinary extent by the rabbis. Anything which might in the remotest degree be interpreted as showing favor to one party against the other, or as liable even unconsciously to influence the JUDGE one way or the other, was rigidly forbidden. The application of the principles of j. in society is one of the great Jewish contributions to mankind. In the words of one of its more modern formulations (the "Guiding Principles" of the U.S. Reform Movement): "Judaism seeks the attainment of a just society by the application of its teaching to the economic order, to industry and commerce, and to national and international affairs".

K

KABBALAH: Hebrew word meaning "receiving" or "that which is received", hence also TRADITION. In talmudic Hebrew K. signifies post-Mosaic tradition, i.e., traditional (rabbinic and even biblical) laws and doctrines that are not contained in the Pentateuch (see WRITTEN LAW). In the 13th cent. the term came to be applied to the new mystical doctrines and systems that had been developing in southern France and Spain since the 12th cent. and which reached their literary climax in the ZOHAR. Since this particular mystical movement determined the subsequent development of Jewish mysticism, K. is often used in a broad sense as synonymous with the latter. Kabbalistic sources also distinguish between *K. iyyunit* ("speculative K.", esoteric philosophy) and *K. maasit* ("practical K.", the magical use of kabbalistic teaching for spiritual or temporal purposes). The distinction was never very sharp, since the study of theoretical K., including the meditation on the Divine mysteries and the use of proper *kavvanot* (see DEVOTION), was held to affect powerfully both the heavenly spheres and the soul of man. This form of K. particularly was developed by the school of Isaac LURIA. The more magical side of the "practical" K. flourished in N. Africa, Yemen, and E. Europe (see BAAL SHEM) and was based on the belief in the potency of mystic formulas and Divine names (see AMULETS). For the doctrines of K., see MYSTICISM.

KABBALAT SHABBAT (Heb. "reception of the Sabbath"): Service preceding *Maariv* on Friday evenings. See SABBATH; SABBATH PRAYERS.

KABRONIM (Heb.): Gravediggers. Many Jewish communities had a society (*ḥevrah*) of *k.*

KADDISH (Aram. "sanctification"; cognate with Hebrew KIDDUSH and KEDUSHAH): Doxology recited at the conclusion of each principal section of every service. It was originally not part of the fixed liturgy and — despite the fact that it has become best known as a mourner's recitation — was unrelated to MOURNING. The *k.* was an expression of praise to God recited by the preacher at the close of his discourse or after the study of AGGADAH. Its central feature was the congregational response: "May His great name be praised for all eternity" (cf. Dan. 2:20). There is no clear evidence as to when the *k.* was composed, but it probably achieved approximately its present form by the 8th or 9th cent. The simplicity of its language (Aramaic) and the absence of any reference to the destruction of the Temple seem to indicate an origin prior to 70 C.E. As the *k.* passed from the school to the synagogue and became part of the liturgy, its text was expanded. There are five forms of *k.*:

1) The short, or half, *k.* recited by the reader before or after certain sections of the service.
2) The full *k.* recited at the end of the main part of the service. This contains the additional sentence "May the prayers and entreaties of the whole House of Israel be accepted by its Father in heaven".
3) The mourner's *k.*
4) The rabbinical *k.*, recited after the study of rabbinical literature or after a sermon.
5) The "*k.* of renewal", used at funerals. It is recited at the graveside immediately after the burial. In its opening section, the messianic prayer is elaborated and specific requests for the revival of the dead, the rebuilding of the Temple, etc. are added. According to Maimonides, this *k.* should be recited after the study of *aggadah*, a practice followed by some oriental Jews.

There are minor differences in wording on the festivals in various rites. In American Reform liturgies, a sentence is added referring to the dead who have departed this world. (The sentence also appears in the *Sephardi* liturgy in the HASHKAVAH prayer for the dead but not in the *k.*). In the West London Synagogue of British Jews, the *k.* is recited in Hebrew instead of Aramaic. It is not clear when the *k.* came to be regarded as a mourner's prayer. Its appeal is due to its exhortation to sanctify God's Name and glorify His sovereign kingdom, and its expression of hope for the speedy advent of the Messiah. It also conveys the idea of the necessity to accept God's judgment, though His ways are inscrutable. Originally, the mourner would recite the *k.* during the course of the liturgy. Soon, however, it became customary to place the mourner's *k.* at the end of the service. The practice of having it recited by the bereaved son did not gain general acceptance until the 13th cent., and its recitation on the YAHRZEIT dates from about the 15th cent. According to tradition, the punishment of sinners in Gehenna lasts for a full year, and so as not to make it appear that the deceased was unrighteous, *k.* is recited for eleven months and one day only. When there is no son to recite the *k.*, it may be said by any adult male member of the immediate family or any male Jew who volunteers. The *k.* can only be recited when a *minyan* is present. In Conservative and Reform services, it is the practice for female as well as male kin to recite the *k.*

KADOSH, see **MARTYRDOM**

KAHAL, see **COMMUNITY**

KALISCHER, TZEVI HIRSCH (1795-1874): Orthodox rabbi and forerunner of Zionism. The first rabbi of modern times to bring the doctrine of the return to Zion from the sphere of mystical messianic speculation to the practical level of colonization, he fought tirelessly against both assimilationists and Orthodox opponents in his efforts to propagate his views. The rabbinical conference convened by him in 1860 in Thorn (Prussia), where he was rabbi, and his work *Derishat Zion* ("Seeking Zion") are landmarks in the history of pre-Herzlian practical Zionism.

KALLAH (Heb. "bride"), see **MARRIAGE**

KALLAH MONTH: Month during which study conventions were held in the Babylonian ACADEMIES at the time of the *amoraim* and *geonim.* The *k.*m. was usually held twice a year, during the months of *Adar* and *Elul,* and was attended by students and scholars from all over Babylonia. The choice of these two months, immediately before the spring and autumn season respectively, enabled farmers to attend, as they were then comparatively free from agricultural labor. A popular tone seems in general to have marked the *kallah* conventions. A separate treatise of the Talmud was studied at each *kallah,* but the answers to many practical problems received by the academies were also discussed and publicized during the study month. An attempt to revive the idea of the *kallah* has recently been made by leading *yeshivot* in Israel.

KALLIR, ELEAZAR (c. 7th-8th cent.): Liturgical poet; pupil of YANNAI. One of the earliest Palestinian PAYTANIM, his home town, which he calls Kirjath Sepher (cf. Judg. 1:11), has never been precisely identified. K. was the first of the liturgical poets to embellish the entire liturgy with elaborate hymns. His poetry is full of midrashic allusions and is couched in language which showed daring innovations and departures from accepted Hebrew usage; his meaning is often obscure, and his compositions were severely criticized (e.g. by Abraham Ibn Ezra) for their artificial and intricate diction. On the other hand he was so highly regarded by the N. French scholars that R. TAM actually identifies him with the *tanna* R. Eleazar (*Tos. Ḥag.* 13a). His influence, especially on ASHKENAZI liturgy, has been immense, both by virtue of the number of his compositions and through his influence on later *paytanim.*

KALONYMOS BEN KALONYMOS (1286-after 1328): Author and translator. His *Even Boḥan* ("Touchstone") is a didactic work satirizing the moral life and social position of the Jews in his native Provence. Among other things he complained, for example, that the Jewish festivals were observed in their externals — as regards food, festivities, etc. — but that their real significance was ignored. K. also wrote *Masekhet Purim* ("Purim Tractate"), a parody of a talmudic tractate and its rabbinical argumentation.

KANAH, BOOK OF: Kabbalistic work by the author of the Book of *Peliah* (Spain, 14th cent.). Both works are in the form of dialogues between the wonder child Nahum, who received heavenly revelations at the age of five, and his father Kanah. The books contain in the main material from earlier mystical writings, but are characterized by an unusual anti-halakhic tendency. The doctrine that the real meaning of the Talmud is contained in the kabbalistic writings is taught in a manner which expresses contempt for the ordinary, exoteric forms of rabbinic Judaism. The antinomian ideas of the *K.* seem to have influenced SHABBETAI TZEVI.

KAPLAN, MORDECAI MENAHEM (1881-1983): U.S. rabbi; founder of the Reconstructionist Movement (see RECONSTRUCTIONISM). He called for the formulation of a new "covenant" by means of which Jews throughout the world would give expression to the new status which he believed they would have to adopt for themselves in order to ensure Jewish survival in the modern world. K. aroused considerable debate by his naturalist theology, which has no room for the traditional notions of REVELATION and a transcendent GOD, but assumes religion to be a human creation, like language or art, expressive of a people's culture. K.'s positive attitude to Jewish tradition was thus not based on the acceptance of a Divinely revealed LAW, but on the affirmation of historical Jewish peoplehood with its specific forms of expression. Although K.'s thinking was in many ways more radical than that of REFORM, he considered himself as belonging to the CONSERVATIVE Movement, and for many years taught at the Jewish THEOLOGICAL SEMINARY. His revised version of the prayer book was burned by a group of Orthodox rabbis.

KAPOTA (Yidd.?): Long outer garment at one time generally worn in E. Europe. It has survived as the distinctive garb of certain groups of extreme Orthodox and ḥasidic Jews.

KAPPARAH, see **ATONEMENT**

KAPPAROT (Heb. "expiations"): A custom performed on the morning preceding the Day of Atonement which consists of taking a fowl in the right hand and reciting specified verses from Psalms (107:17-20) and Job (33:23-4). After recitation the fowl is waved around the head while the following is said three times: "This is my change, this is my redemption. This rooster shall be killed, while I shall be admitted to and allowed a long, happy, and peaceful life". A cock is used by a male, a hen by a female. Nowadays many who still practice *k.* use eighteen coins (in Heb., the numerical value of the word "life" is eighteen) instead of a fowl. The fowl or the money is then given to charity. The custom may be ancient but is not mentioned before the Gaonic Period and may have arisen in Babylonia, where an analogous ritual of casting a basket filled with seeds into a river was sometimes performed. Several authorities (e.g. Solomon ben Adret, Naḥmanides, Joseph Karo) opposed the practice because of its pagan and superstitious character, but the weight of opinion and tradition, and kabbalistic influence in particular, have caused it to be continued in observant circles.

KARAITES (originally Ananites): Jewish sect rejecting the ORAL LAW, founded by ANAN BEN DAVID. The K. emerged in the 8th cent. and spread rapidly among Middle Eastern communities, and after the 12th cent., into Crimea and E. Europe. The vigorous counterattack of the rabbis, starting with SAADYAH, checked their spread, particularly from the 12th cent. on. Intermarriage with K. ceased completely and they became a separate "schismatic" sect. Culturally as well they remained stagnant after their great "Golden Age" (11th-12th cents.), which witnessed remarkable literary activity. There was a minor revival among the Russian K. in the 19th cent., but after World War II, only a few thousand K. survived in the USSR and in the Middle East; most of the latter emigrated to the State of Israel. As its name (from *kara,* "a reader of Scripture") indicates, the sect claimed its message to be a rejection of the authority of the Oral Law as developed by the rabbis, and a return to the pure doctrine of the written text of the Bible. In this respect it bears a distinct resemblance to SADDUCEEISM, many of the elements of which are found in Karaism. However even Anan, the founder of the sect, adopted some of the principles of rabbinic interpretation of the Bible, including the use of verbal analogy (*gezerah shavah*). The most striking difference between rabbinic Judaism and Karaism is the absence of "rabbinic" customs (e.g. TEPHILLIN, MEZUZAH) and festivals (e.g. ḤANUKKAH) among the latter and the rigid interpretation given to the biblical laws relating to the Sabbath, ritual cleanness, and the degrees of propinquity that forbid marriage. The K. not only insist upon the letter of the biblical law but even increase its severity. As regards the Sabbath, no light or fire of any kind whatsoever is permitted on that day (cf. Exod. 30:3) and the rabbinic legislation permitting one to move up to 2,000 cubits from one's dwelling or the limits of the town on that day is denied. No work may be done for a Karaite by a non-Jew. Whereas the "primary" laws concerning those degrees of relationship that preclude marriage, as given in Lev. 18 and 20, were expanded by the rabbis to include "secondary" degrees of prohibition, the K. extended the prohibited relationship to an infinite descent of collaterals and to such an inordinate degree that their later authorities were forced to modify the rules. Ritual uncleanness was extended to every issue of the body, and K. require the washing of both hands and feet and the removal of shoes before entering the synagogue or reading from the *Torah.* Such verses as Deut. 6:8, taken by the rabbis as enjoining the wearing of phylacteries, are regarded by the K. as symbolic, but on the other hand the laws enjoining the four fringes are given great importance and the words "And ye shall see them" (Num. 15:39) are taken to mean they must be prominently displayed in synagogue. The Karaite liturgy (which has no afternoon service) consists largely of scriptural readings. Recent research suggests a strong influence on the K. by the sect of the DEAD SEA SCROLLS, and analogies have been found between their methods of Bible exegesis and those of the PESHER of the Qumran sect.

KARKASANI, see **KIRKISANI**

KARLIN: Suburb of Pinsk; seat of ḥasidic dynasty and center of Lithuanian ḤASIDISM. The dynasty was founded by Aaron of K. (d. 1772), who was outstandingly successful in winning adherents to his cause. He inaugurated a custom of devoting one day a week to solitary meditation. He was succeeded by his pupil Solomon of K. (1738-1772) who was noted for his fervor, as expressed notably through his self-surrender in prayer. According to a tradition of his followers he was the suffering Messiah son of Joseph.

KARLITZ, ABRAHAM ISAIAH (known by the title of his work *Ḥazon Ish;* 1878-1953): Halakhic authority; lived in Vilna until 1935 when he settled in Benei Berak in Palestine. The numerous volumes of his published works form a halakhic commentary to the Talmud and later codes. K. dealt at length with halakhic problems connected with the emerging State of Israel, devoting particular attention to the largely neglected agricultural laws of the Bible, such as *shemittah,* tithing, etc. Although he occupied no official position, his halakhic authority was universally acknowledged. He was also consulted on moral, public, and personal problems, and was widely revered for his ascetic and saintly life.

KARO, JOSEPH (1488-1575): Codifier and kabbalist. K. was born in Spain, but after the expulsion (1492) the family settled in Turkey where he served for many years as rabbi in Adrianople and Nicopolis. In 1536 he went to Palestine and settled in SAFED, where he was soon acknowledged as one of the leading personalities in the distinguished community of scholars and saints, many of whom were his disciples and friends (e.g. Moses CORDOVERO and Solomon ALKABETZ). Soon after his arrival he joined in Jacob BERAV's attempt to renew ORDINATION, and was himself ordained by Berav. His most outstanding work is the monumental commentary *Bet Yoseph* ("House of Joseph") on JACOB BEN ASHER'S CODE *Arbaah Turim*, in which he reviewed and discussed practically the whole relevant halakhic literature. On the basis of this work he next produced his own shorter code, SHULḤAN ARUKH ("Prepared Table"), which soon became established as the standard code of rabbinic law and practice, particularly after Moses ISSERLES of Cracow had added glosses embodying the divergent rulings and customs of the *Ashkenazi* tradition. K. also wrote many responsa, a commentary *Keseph Mishneh* on Maimonides' code *Mishneh Torah*, and a diary, parts of which were published subsequently under the title *Maggid Meisharim*, in which he recorded the mystical revelations which he experienced at night time.

KASHER (Heb. "fit" or "proper"; *Ashkenazi* pronunciation *kosher*): Food prepared in accordance with the DIETARY LAWS; in this sense the opposite of TEREPHAH. It can be used to designate the ritual fitness of any object according to Jewish law, such as a SHOPHAR, a LULAV, or a MIKVEH. It is also used as a verb; one is said for example, to "kosher" vessels, and the ritual preparation of meat is also commonly described as "koshering". In many states of the U.S., in some European countries, and in the State of Israel, the term is legally protected, and merchants or food dispensers who advertise their products as *k.* may be prosecuted if they violate the rabbinic requirements.

KASHRUT, see **DIETARY LAWS**

KAVVANAH, see **DEVOTION**

KAZARS, see **KHAZARS**

KEDESHAH (Heb.): Sacred harlot. Prostitution was part of the official rites in temples and high places throughout the ancient Near East, being regarded as a magical means for the preservation of fertility and as an act of devotion to the gods. The practice was strongly condemned and outlawed both in the Pentateuch and by the Prophets as pagan immorality and as an abomination to the Lord (Deut. 23:18) but was probably not completely eradicated until the end of the First Temple Period. Both male and female prostitutes (*kedeshot* and *kedeshim,* from *kadosh,* "sacred" or "consecrated") are mentioned (e.g. I Kings 14:24) as are the attempts of several kings of Judah to stamp out the custom (I Kings 15:12; 22:47; II Kings 23:7).

KEDUSHAH, see **HOLINESS**

KEDUSHAH (Heb. "sanctification"): Name given to prayers describing the sanctification of God by the angels in heaven and its imitation on earth. The *k.* contains the verses Is. 6:3 ("Holy, Holy, Holy", etc.) and Ezek. 3:12 ("Blessed be the glory of the Lord from His place"). One *k.,* said while sitting (*k. de-yeshivah*), is interwoven with the YOTZER benediction. Another is known as the *k. de-sidra,* contained in the prayer *u-va le-tziyyon.* The main *k.* (*k. de-amidah*) forms part of the third benediction of the AMIDAH when recited aloud by the reader (the congregational responses are later than the prayer and probably originated in the Gaonic Period). It opens by expressing Israel's readiness "to sanctify His name in the world, as the angels sanctify it in the heavens above"; Israel, too, joins the angelic choir (according to the enlarged form of the *k.* — the *k. rabbah* — used in MUSAPH) by professing "Hear, O Israel, etc." and is answered by God Himself who proclaims "I am the Lord, your God". The *k.* is of early date and originated among mystics. It belongs to the most solemn and exalted portions of the service. The *k.* as part of the *amidah* is recited only when a *minyan* is present; there are variations in formulation between the *Ashkenazi* and *Sephardi* versions. In gaonic times, the *k.* was not a generally accepted practice in the Palestinian rite, except on Sabbaths and festivals; but in the Babylonian rite and those prevailing today, it became part of the daily liturgy. Many piyyutic compositions elaborated the theme of the *k.*; some are still in use on the New Year and Day of Atonement. The basic part of the *k.* (the "Trisagion" and its preface) also became prominent in Christian liturgy.

KEHILLAH, see **COMMUNITY**

KEIN EIN HA-RA (Yidd. "no EVIL EYE"; in Heb. *beli ein ha-ra*): Popular exclamation expressing hope that a present satisfactory situation is not to be spoiled. Its superstitious origin has been generally forgotten.

KELAL ISRAEL (Heb. "total community of Israel"): Although this phrase is rarely found in rabbinical sources, it is widely used to convey the conception of what has been called "catholic Israel" i.e., the totality of the Jewish people as one indivisible unit. The underlying idea is expressed in a Midrash which compares the FOUR SPECIES to the four types of Jews who make up

KETER:
Torah crown;
East Europe, 18th cent.;
Feinberg Collection, Detroit.

INCENSE:
Incense (Silver *besamim*) box;
Eastern Europe, late 18th cent.
Jewish Museum, New York.

KETUBBAH: Marriage contract; Padua, 1670; Israel Museum, Jerusalem.

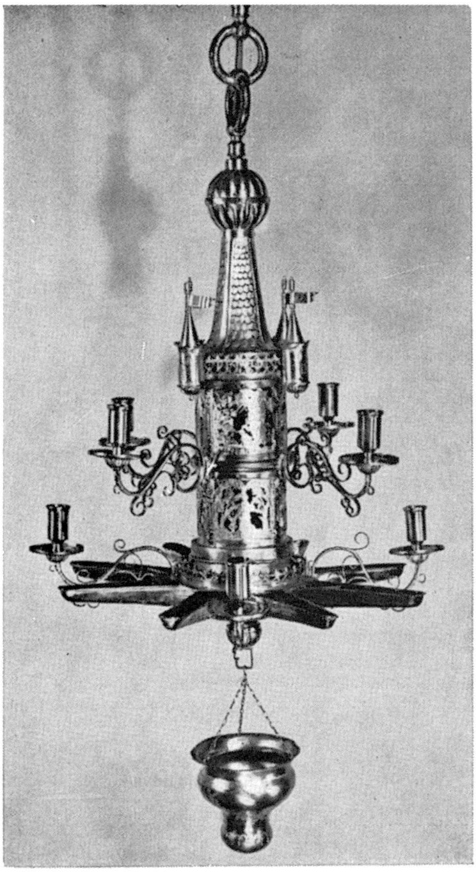

LAMP: Silver synagogue lamp; Metz, early 19th cent.

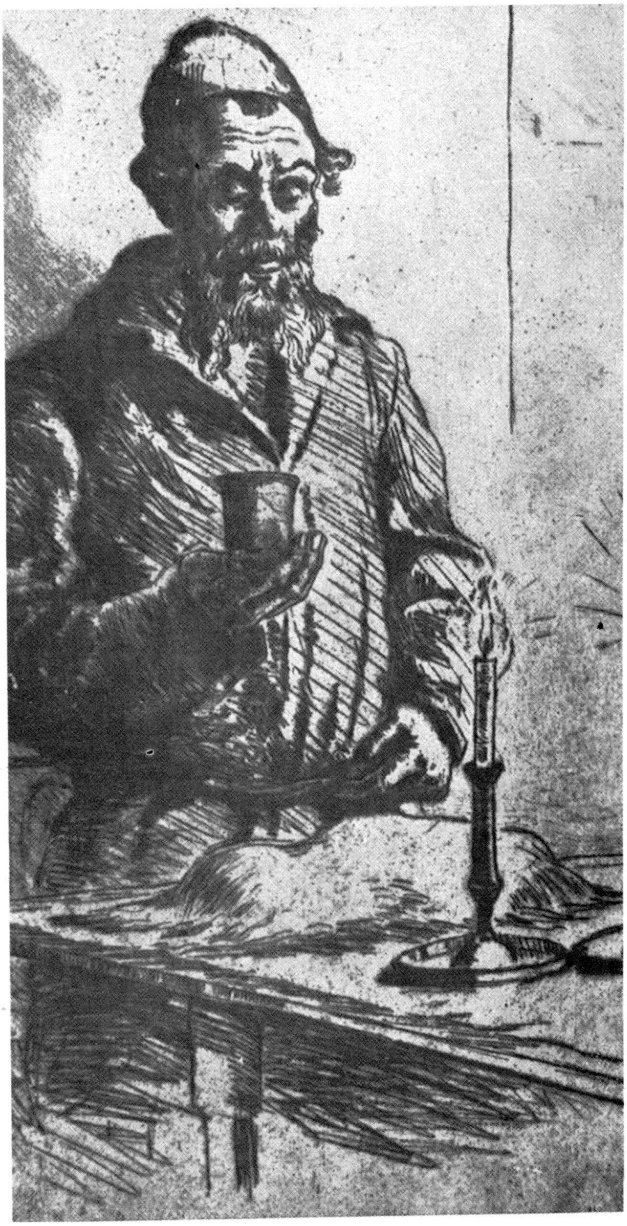

KIDDUSH:
by Hermann Struck
(1876-1944).

KOL NIDREI:
Kol Nidrei prayer
from festival prayer-book;
Germany, c. 14th cent.;
Cologne Municipal Museum.

LEVIRATE MARRIAGE: Ḥalitzah, from Bernard Picart's *Cérémonies et coutumes religieuses.*

MARRIAGE: "Jewish Wedding" by Jozef Israels (1824-1911); Rijksmuseum, Amsterdam.

MARRIAGE: "The Wedding" by Moritz Oppenheim (1800-1882);
Oscar Gruss collection;
(photo archiv. Jewish Theological Seminary of America, N.Y.; Frank J. Darmstaedter).

MARRIAGE: Betrothal ring designed for Samson Wertheimer (1658-1724); Feinberg Collection, Detroit.

MATZAH: *Matzah* baking and eating; from the Nuremberg *Haggadah*, late 14th cent.; Schocken Library, Jerusalem (Photo Bernheim).

MEZUZAH:
Wood;
France, 18th cent.
(Private collection).

MOSES AND THE BURNING BUSH: detail from fresco at Dura-Europos synagogue (3rd cent.).

MEZUZAH:
Porcelain;
Germany, 18th cent.;
Israel Museum, Jerusalem

וְאֵת עֲמָלֵנוּ אֵלוּ הַבָּנִים כְּמוֹ שֶׁנֶּאֱמַר כָּל הַבֵּן הַיִּלּוֹד הַיְאֹרָה תַּשְׁלִיכֻהוּ וְכָל הַבַּת תְּחַיּוּן : וְאֶת לַחֲצֵנוּ זוֹ הַדְּחַק כְּמוֹ שֶׁנֶּאֱמַר וְגַם רָאִיתִי אֶת הַלַּחַץ

ומעלתו שהות חדש ניסן ומלני הסבות התלה דתה השם יתברך לעשות הגדולה הזאת בעצמו כי מי שידד מערכות השמימיות ומי ישנדה הטבעים המוחזקים ומי יבטל כחותם נברים העליונים והשפלותיהב כי תס הש"יתברך תבר יוגרס ותל ג בחיורא הזלה. כיון בחמרו ובעברתו כתלן מעריס. וגומר כ' בתומרו ובעברתי ב כתרן מעריס מורה. מעט היות המערכה העליונה. מחייבת שלא יכתו ישראל ממנריס מעבודתו ההגחתיות תמדד החערבה וויניקס. וכן דרם ה ההעבדה תני ולא מלאך לב' שהמכוון בה הות לשדד כח המערכה. תבר ה"ק שיהיה ב' תס ברוגינו התשוט וביכלתו וכונגד הבחינה

ה:ב:

MOSES FOUND BY PHARAOH'S DAUGHTER:
from *Haggadah* of 1740.
British Museum, London.

the community — those who have both *Torah* and good works, those who possess only one or the other of them, and those who are completely devoid of any virtue. "Yet I cannot destroy them", the Midrash has God say, "let them all be bound together and they will complement and atone for one another". The concept of *K.I.* played a central part in the thought of Solomon SCHECHTER.

KELIM (Heb. "vessels"): First tractate in the Mishnah order of *Toharot,* devoted to amplifying the laws governing the ritual uncleanness contracted by various types of utensils, as stipulated in Lev. 6:20 ff.; 11:32 ff.; Num. 19:14 ff. and 31:20 ff. There is no *gemara* in either Talmud.

KENAS, see **FINES**

KENE HORA: Popular abbreviation of KEIN EIN HA-RA.

KENESET HA-GEDOLAH (Heb. "Great Synagogue" or "Assembly"): Spiritual and legislative institution of the post-prophetic era, variously estimated as consisting of 120 or 85 sages. It is usually cited in the sources as *Anshei K.H.* ("the Men of the Great Assembly") and is listed in the chronological chain of tradition between the prophets and the High Priest Simeon Ha-Tzaddik (c. 200 B.C.E.). Its contribution to Judaism was fundamental and enduring in three fields: 1) Liturgy. The Men of the Great Synagogue instituted the AMIDAH to be recited three times daily; the benedictions before and after meals, and before the performance of commandments; *kiddush* and *havdalah,* at the commencement and termination, respectively, of Sabbaths and festivals. They are also credited with initiating the custom of reading the Law publicly on Sabbaths and festivals and on Mondays and Thursdays. 2) Preservation of Scripture. They are reported to have canonized the Book of Ezekiel, the Twelve Minor Prophets, Daniel, and Esther. 3) ORAL LAW. They laid the foundations of the *halakhah,* the *Midrash,* and the *aggadah.* In sum, they formulated what became known as normative Judaism. But the basic contribution of the Men of the *K.H.* was their success in transferring religious authority from the hereditary priesthood to the scholars (*hakhamim*). Religious authority in Judaism has ever since been in the hands of scholars. The revolutionary effect of the work of the *K.H.* is reflected in the triple maxim which tradition has attributed to the Men of *K.H.*: 1. "Be slow in giving judgment". Previously the meting out of justice on the part of the elders was a simple process. But the new judges had to take into consideration legal principles and precedents, and the judicial processes were slowed down. 2. "Establish many disciples". This represents much more than mere popularization of knowledge which had been begun by Ezra. The raising of many disciples meant the training of numerous experts who were neither levites nor priests. The rise of the scholarly SOPHERIM established forever the supremacy and authority of learning in Judaism. 3. "And make a barrier about the Law". These barriers — known as *gezerot* (decrees) and *takkanot* (ordinances) — not only reduced the violations of biblical laws but created a halo of sanctity about Jewish private and public life.

KENESET ISRAEL (Heb. "Assembly of Israel"): Concept often used homiletically in the Midrash as a synonym for the Jewish people as a collective whole, usually in a spiritual sense. More or less identical with "Israel", it is used to emphasize the characteristics which distinguish the Jewish people as a separate entity and in its special relation to God. Midrashic literature abounds in references portraying *K.I.* as speaking to or pleading before God, and the rabbinic concept of an earthly community which is at the same time spiritual and heavenly, seems to have influenced the Christian theological concept of the "church". The symbol of *K.I.* also played an important role in kabbalistic mysticism.

KERI AND KETIV, see **MASORAH**

KERIAH, see **RENDING**

KERIAT HA-TORAH, see **READING OF THE LAW**

KERIAT SHEMA, see **SHEMA**

KERIAT SHEMA AL HA-MITTAH, see **NIGHT PRAYERS**

KERITOT (Heb. "Excisions"): Seventh tractate in the Mishnah order of *Kodashim.* It deals with the Divine punishment of *karet* ("cutting off", cf. Gen. 17:14; Exod. 12:15, etc.) rabbinically interpreted as natural death in the prime of life (generally without offspring). Thirty-six sins are listed which merit this punishment. The tractate has *gemara* in the Babylonian, but not the Palestinian, Talmud.

KEROVAH (pl. *kerovot*; also under old French influence, *kerovetz*): *Piyyutim* inserted mainly in the repetition of the *amidah*: originally in all 18 benedictions for special weekdays, but surviving in present-day usage chiefly in the 14th (on *Av* 9) and 16th benedictions (on all fasts); inserted also in the first benedictions of the Morning Service *amidah* for Special Sabbaths and for festivals. Additional Service *kerovot* are the prayer for DEW on Passover (1st day) and for RAIN on *Shemini Atzeret.* The *k.* usually has a *reshut* (introduction) in which the *hazzan,* expressing his own unworthiness, prays for Divine guidance, and a *silluk* (conclusion) leading to the KEDUSHAH.

KETER MALKHUT (Heb. "crown of royalty" cf. Est. 2:18 and *Avot* 4:17): Phrase representing the enthronement of God by angels and man, not so much through their acceptance of His sovereignty as by "crowning" Him with praise. The

Talmud (*Ḥag.* 13b) describes Sandalphon, one of the archangels, as standing behind the Divine chariot and "binding crowns on the head of his Maker". Similarly *Yalkut Isaiah* 272 states, "Daily the heavenly angels crown the Holy One, Blessed be He, with the threefold *kedushah* (see Is. 6:3), and a midrash states that the angels take the words of prayer and praise uttered by Israel, and weave them into a crown for the supreme King of kings. The name *K.M.* was given by Ibn Gabirol to his great poem in praise of God and subsequently also by other poets to similar compositions. *K.M.* poems, particularly Ibn Gabirol's, are frequently recited after the Evening Service of the Day of Atonement.

KETER TORAH (Heb. "crown of Law"): Symbol of learning. In *Avot* 4:17, the *K.T.* is mentioned together with the "crown of royalty" (KETER MALKHUT) and the "crown of priesthood", but the "crown of a good name" is regarded as greater than them all. Unlike the others, the *K.T.* can be acquired by anyone, and does not depend on birth or descent. The phrase also applies to one of the most ornate appurtenances of religious worship with which the synagogal Scrolls of the Law are often crowned. The *K.T.*, usually of silver, is in the shape of a large crown, with two sockets into which the tops of the rollers are inserted. Precious Bible manuscripts, carefully written and revised, were also called *keter* by Oriental Jews, the best known being the *k.* of Aleppo.

KETUBBAH (Heb. "writ"): An Aramaic document containing a statement of the obligations which the bridegroom undertakes toward his bride and which in rabbinic law is a prerequisite of MARRIAGE. In all traditional weddings, the *k.* is prepared before the ceremony. Originally, the officiating rabbi wrote it out shortly before the beginning of the ceremony. In modern times, however, the form is usually printed, leaving the names, date, and other relevant details to be filled in. It is then signed by two male witnesses, not related to the bride, the bridegroom, or each other; in some communities it is also signed by the bridegroom. The groom performs an act of KINYAN as well, a symbolic act in acceptance of the obligations listed. The *k.* is read in Aramaic either just before or during the marriage ceremony. In many congregations a short summary in the vernacular is read by the officiant. The *k.* is then given to the bride who keeps it as legal proof of her husband's obligations toward her. In ancient times the text of the *k.* was not fixed, since the economic clauses (referring to dowry, etc). varied with each case. When a formula was finally adopted, additional clauses (*tenaim,* "conditions") were often appended. The tradition of adding *tenaim* to the *k.* has been revived in modern times. In the State of Israel, the Chief Rabbinate has sanctioned several such appendices. The Rabbinical Assembly of America (the rabbinic arm of the Conservative Movement) has introduced an additional clause in which the bride and groom take a pledge to appear before a rabbinic court in the event of any dispute between them. The purpose of this provision is to enable the religious authorities to counsel couples in marital difficulties and to ensure that all rabbinic regulations affecting DIVORCE will be followed if the marriage is ultimately dissolved. American Reform Jews have abolished the *k.* altogether. According to rabbinic tradition, provision for the payment of a large sum of money to a divorcee or widow was instituted to protect an indigent widow and, even more important, to make the contemplation of divorce more serious, as the prospect of undertaking a heavy financial burden toward a divorced wife might prevent a hasty or frivolous decision in this respect. Under the provisions of the *k.* the minimum amount payable to a widow or divorcee who was a virgin at the time of marriage was 200 *zuzim.* Estimates suggest that this was sufficient to support a family for one year. If the bride had been a widow or divorcee, the amount payable was 100 *zuzim.* The *k.* also specified the dowry and the *tosephet* ("addition") which the bridegroom undertook to repay in the event of divorce (or decease), beyond the legal requirements. The custom at present is to add 100 per cent to the amount of the dowry, which is always equated *pro forma* with 100 silver pieces, for a previously unmarried woman, and fifty for divorcees or widows. Both the real and personal property of the husband is under lien to the wife should a *k.* settlement become necessary.

KETUBBOT (Heb. "Marriage Contracts"; cf. Exod. 22:16): Second tractate in the Mishnah order of *Nashim* with *gemara* in both Talmuds. It deals with the KETUBBAH, both as a document and as the sum settled on a wife in the event of widowhood or divorce. Other subjects discussed include the marital and material rights and duties of husband and wife, and grounds for the dissolution of a marriage. The Babylonian *gemara* on *K.* ranges over so many subjects that it has been described as a complete Talmud in miniature.

KETUVIM, see **HAGIOGRAPHA**

KHAZARS: A tribe of Turkish or Finnish origin who lived along the lower Volga in the region of Crimea. During the 8th-10th cents., they reached the zenith of their power, and during this period a Judaizing movement took place among them. King Bulan (786-809) together with some 4,000 nobles adopted the Jewish faith, and although Moslems, Christians, and pagans formed the great majority of the population and were granted internal autonomy, the state religion was Judaism.

Ḥasdai Ibn Shaprut, vizier to Abdulrahman III of Cordova, is said to have established contact with the then reigning king Joseph by sending him a letter written by Menahem Ibn Saruk (c. 960). In his reply the king gave details concerning the conversion of his ancestor and other information about the state. Doubts have been expressed about the authenticity of the letters. They appear as a preface to Judah Ha-Levi's philosophical work *Kuzari* (i.e., *Khazars*), which uses the historical incident of the king's conversion as the framework for an imaginary dialogue between the king and a Jewish sage. The power of the K. was broken by Archduke Jaroslav in 1083 and they disappeared following the Tatar invasion of 1237.

KIBBUTZ GALUYYOT, see **EXILES, INGATHERING OF**

KI LO NAEH (Heb. "For to Him it is fitting"): Alphabetic hymn eulogizing God, recited by *Ashkenazim* in the last section of the Passover *Seder* service. Of unknown authorship, it is of medieval origin and was probably written in France or Germany. Each stanza ends with the refrain "for to Him it is fitting (to sing praise)".

KIDDUSH (Heb. "sanctification"): A ceremony and prayer by which the holiness of the Sabbath or a festival is proclaimed. The term is an abbreviation of the talmudic expression *kiddush ha-yom* ("sanctification of the day"). The *k.* is recited on Sabbath or festival eve over a cup of wine immediately before the meal. It is chanted by one person, usually the head of the house, while all present identify themselves with the recitation by answering *amen.* In some homes, however, it is recited (in unison or separately), by all present or by all males over the age of thirteen. The reciter takes the cup into his right hand, preferably in the palm, enclosing the cup with his fingers, chants the *k.*, drinks, and gives all present a sip of the wine. If no wine is available the *k.* may be recited over bread. Even when wine is used, there should be on the table two whole loaves of HALLAH (covered by a cloth) which traditionally symbolize the double portion of MANNA gathered by the Children of Israel each Friday during their 40 years in the wilderness. The *k.* is essentially a home ritual associated with the Sabbath or festival meal, but from ancient times it has been customary to recite it on these days in the synagogue at the end of the evening prayer, for the benefit of wayfarers and the poor, who lodged and ate in the synagogue. When the latter custom fell into disuse, some rites abolished the chanting of the *k.* in the house of worship, while others retained it as an act of public sanctification of the Sabbath. Scriptural warrant for the *k.* ceremony is found by the rabbis in Exod. 20:8, which the Talmud interprets as meaning "Remember it over wine" (*Pes.* 106a). The *k.* consists of two BENEDICTIONS: one for the wine (or bread) and one for the Sabbath or festival. The rabbis of the Mishnah differed as to which should be recited first, but Hillel's view that the blessing over wine takes precedence prevailed. In the *k.* for Friday evening it is customary to recite the account of the Sabbath of Creation (Gen. 2:1-3) before making the blessing. It was formerly omitted in Reform liturgies but has now been widely reintroduced, though generally (as in Reconstructionist custom) without the reference to the Chosen People. The *k.* chanted after the Morning Service on Sabbaths or festival days is called *Kiddusha Rabbah* ("the great *k.*") — this by inversion, since it is not the main *k.*; it may be recited over all kinds of drink and not necessarily wine. It contains no benediction apart from the one recited over wine (or other drink), and is preceded by appropriate Bible passages (on Sabbath: Exod. 20:8-11; on the pilgrimage festivals: Lev. 23:44; on *Rosh ha-Shanah*: Ps. 81:4-5 or similar verses). On festivals (except for the last days of Passover), the SHE-HEḤEYANU blessing is recited at the conclusion of the *k.*

KIDDUSH HA-SHEM (Heb. "sanctification of the Name" i.e., of God): Concept stemming from a belief that any worthy action on the part of a Jew which enhances the prestige of Judaism in the eyes of gentiles thereby also "sanctifies" the name of God as embodied in His revelation and covenant to Israel; similarly its opposite, ḤILLUL HA-SHEM, an unworthy act, desecrates the Name. Both terms are usually employed in relation to the conduct of Jews in the eyes of their non-Jewish neighbors. In its narrower (and original) meaning the term *K.H.* signified MARTYRDOM, since the sacrifice of one's life for God's Law was regarded as the supreme sanctification of God's name.

KIDDUSH LEVANAH (Heb. "sanctification of the moon"): The regular reappearance of the NEW MOON is regarded as one of those benefits for which praise and thanksgiving should be given to God. A *baraita* (*Sopherim* 20:1-2) contains the text of the relevant blessing together with the regulations. Various differences in custom exist, but the most prevalent tradition is that the *k.l.* is recited by a *minyan* in the synagogue courtyard on the Saturday night prior to the 10th day of the lunar month, providing the crescent is visible. The Talmud (*Rosh ha-Shanah* 25a) relates that during a period of persecution R. Judah Ha-Nasi instructed R. Ḥiyya to determine the date of the New Moon and told him to quote, "David, king of Israel, is alive and exists" as a kind of slogan. This phrase, with its undertones of hope for the coming of the Messiah, has therefore been incorporated into the *k.l.* prayers. The benediction emphasizes the fact of renewal in nature as evidenced by the moon and interprets it as a symbol of Israel's renewal and redemption. Various other elements, some of a superstitious nature, have also crept into the rite.

KIDDUSHIN, see **MARRIAGE**

KIDDUSHIN (Heb. "Marriage"): Seventh tractate in the Mishnah order of *Nashim,* with *gemara* in both Talmuds. It contains regulations governing weddings and marital status.

KIDNAPPING: The biblical law, "And he that stealeth a man, and selleth him, or if he be found in his hand, he shall surely be put to death" (Exod. 21:16, cf. also Deut. 24:7) marks k. as a capital offense. The Talmud, together with some modern scholars, considers the eighth commandment of the Decalogue to refer not to the stealing of property but to k. (*Sanh.* 86a). To be liable to CAPITAL PUNISHMENT the following four conditions had to be present: (1) The thief had actually to take the abducted person into his possession or domain, thus depriving him of his personal liberty; (2) He had to sell him as a slave; (3) The sale had to be to a stranger (if the kidnaped person was sold to one of his kin, the thief was not culpable since he had not deprived the victim of association with his family); (4) The kidnaper must himself have treated the victim as a slave before selling him. Each stage must have been witnessed by at least two witnesses (*Sanh.* 85b).

KILAYIM, see **MIXED KINDS**

KILAYIM (Heb. "Mixed Kinds"): Fourth tractate in the Mishnah order of *Zeraim* with *gemara* in the Palestinian, but not Babylonian, Talmud. It discusses the prohibitions against mingling plants, animals, and clothing of a single genus but different species (Lev. 19:19; Deut. 22:9).

KIMḤI: Family of grammarians and biblical exegetes in Spain and S. France. Joseph K. (c. 1105-1170) compiled a Hebrew grammar, the *Sepher ha-Zikkaron* ("The Book of Remembrance") in which he examined the language of the liturgy and developed a ten-vowel theory of the Hebrew language as opposed to the seven-vowel theory postulated by his predecessors. His elder son Moses K. (d. c. 1190) compiled several grammatical works in which he developed the "eight conjugations" of the Hebrew verb. The most famed of the family was the younger son, David K. (known as *Radak,* c. 1160-1235) who wrote *Mikhlol* ("Compendium"), a grammatical work and Bible dictionary which became standard, and a lucid commentary on the Bible printed in all subsequent major editions of the rabbinic Bible, greatly influencing both Jews and (through its numerous later translations) Christians. A firm upholder of Maimonides' theories, he attempted in his commentaries to rationalize miracles and to discover the literal meaning of the text. He frequently attacked Christian theology and introduced polemical passages into his commentary.

KINAH (pl. *kinot*: Heb. "lament"): Form of elegy recited in biblical and talmudic times in mourning over an individual (e.g. David's *k.* on Saul and Jonathan, II Sam. 1:17 ff.), or over a national catastrophe (Jeremiah's lament on the destruction of the First Temple and the deportation to Babylonia). The Book of Lamentations was called *Kinot* in the Talmud (*Bava Batra* 14b). In gaonic times, special *seliḥot* (i.e., prayers of a penitential character) were composed in Babylon for *Av* 9 then a day devoted largely to penitence; these resembled the *kinot* of KALLIR, probably the first poet to use this distinctive name, which was later applied specifically to the *piyyutim* for *Av* 9. Many *Kinot* on tragic historical events (e.g. the massacres of whole Jewish communities during the Crusades, the persecutions in Spain in 1391, the Chmielnicki massacres of 1648, etc.) were composed by *Ashkenazi* and *Sephardi* poets and some of them found a permanent place in the respective liturgies. All Day of Atonement rites incorporate the *k.* on the *Ten Martyrs* of the Hadrianic persecutions, while most contain the elegies on Zion by Judah Ha-Levi; these last represent a special type of *k.* expressing yearning for Zion and the hope of redemption.

KINDLING OF LIGHTS (Heb. *hadlakat nerot*): Lights are kindled by the housewife at the beginning of Sabbaths and festivals and indicate the approach of a day of light and cheerfulness. The k. of l. is obligatory, and in the absence of women the obligation falls on men. Before the lighting an appropriate blessing is recited. During the Middle Ages, a controversy arose as to whether the benedictions should precede or follow the kindling of the Sabbath lights: if the benediction is recited first, the woman has already recognized the presence of the Sabbath and may no longer light the candle, but on the other hand a blessing cannot be recited after the precept is fulfilled. As a compromise therefore the woman first kindles the lights, but by putting her hands over her eyes, refrains from looking at them until after she has recited the blessing. It is customary to kindle two lights; this has been associated homiletically with the two versions of the Sabbath commandment (Exod. 20:8 and Deut. 5:12) but may originally go back to the necessity of having one light in the living room and one in the kitchen. The kindling of these lights constituted one of the major practical differences between the KARAITES and the Rabbanites; the former would not allow a light to burn, even if kindled prior to the Sabbath, and sat in darkness throughout the Sabbath eve. Other occasions for the k. of l. are Ḥanukkah, the anniversary of the death of a near relative (Yahrzeit), and on the Day of Atonement. See also Lamp, Sabbath.

KING AND KINGSHIP: The Jewish view of kingship is centered on the antithesis between the biblical regulations concerning the appointment of a king in Deut. 17:13-20 on the one hand and Samuel's vigorous denunciation of the people for desiring such a king on the other. Subsequently rabbinic law regarded the former passage as obligatory, making the appointment of a king a Divine commandment, and explained the prophet's objections as stemming from his fear that a king might not regard himself as subject by the Law to any limitations of his absolute power. Exception to the rabbinic view was taken by Isaac Abravanel, who regarded the passage in Deuteronomy only as a permission and held that the appointment of a king was not really in accordance with God's will; the ideal form of government was non-monarchical. This view notwithstanding, the idea of a hereditary monarchy from the House of David is paramount in Judaism, and prayers are still recited for the restoration of the Davidic line, affirming that "a stranger shall not sit on his throne, nor others inherit his glory, for by Thy Holy name didst Thou swear unto him that his light shall not be quenched forever" (blessing after recitation of the *haphtarah*). Because of this sentiment the first Hasmonean rulers, who were not of Davidic descent, refused to adopt the title of king, and when Alexander Yannai took the title, he was criticized for flaunting Jewish tradition and sentiment. Maimonides deals with the question of the legitimacy of the non-Davidic kings in the secessionist Northern Kingdom and declares that they are to be deemed legitimate if appointed by a prophet and if they walk in the way of God (*Hilkhot Melakhim* 1:8). The rabbinic law of kingship and royal power, its duties and prerogatives, was codified by Maimonides, though on the basis of theoretical conjecture rather than any historical reality.

KINGDOM OF HEAVEN: An eschatological concept, referring to a future state of perfection of the world, free from the taint of sin and suffering, and in which all shall live according to the precepts of the Divine Will. The Israelite prophets not only regarded history as the scene of Divine action rather than as a fortuitous series of events, but also envisaged a glorious consummation. The present sinful and imperfect order would come to an end on the terrible Day of the Lord, but following this judgment God would create a "new heaven and a new earth" and all creatures would be at peace with one another, with nature, and with God, just as they were in the Garden of Eden. Originally the concept of the K. of H. was not identical with the messianic idea. However the two eschatological concepts fused to some extent, until practically no distinction was made between the K. of H. and the "Days (or Realm) of the Messiah". The Pseudepigrapha abound with detailed descriptions of this heavenly realm, and the K. of H. — or Kingdom of God as it was also called — occupied a central position in the teachings of Jesus, whose idea of the K. of H. seems to have been closely related to contemporaneous sectarian views. The members of the Dead Sea sect at Qumran believed that by joining the community they likewise became members of the community of the elect, destined to inherit the K. of H. (see Dead Sea Scrolls). The Qumranites, like the early Christians, believed the K. of H. to be at hand and saw themselves as active participants in the eschatological drama that had already begun to unfold itself on earth. In contrast to the acute apocalyptic mood of the sectarian circles, the Pharisees saw themselves as still living in the Olam ha-Zeh. In talmudic literature the concept of the K. of H. is at times vague and ambiguous. In many instances it is equated with the "Days of Messiah", but at other times it means *Olam ha-Ba* as distinct from the messianic era. According to the latter interpretation, the K. of H. would succeed the messianic era; the reign of the Messiah, preceded by the messianic "birth pangs" and the eschatological war, still belonged to this world. After the messianic era had come to an end, there would be a general resurrection of the dead, followed by the great judgment of all mankind and the establishment of a new creation cleansed of all unrighteousness, i.e., the K. of H. The distinction between the two eschatological eras was also maintained by medieval theologians; its significance resides in the fact that the political and social redemption of Israel and mankind are considered as the penultimate and not the ultimate goal of history. The idea of the K. of H. connects ultimate perfection with a profound and radical transformation of the cosmos as a whole. See Apocalypse; Eschatology.

KINGS, BOOK OF (Heb. *Sepher Melakhim*): The last book in the Former Prophets section of the Bible, recounting Israel's history during a 400-year period from the end of the reign of David to Jehoiachin's release from Babylonian imprisonment. Following the Septuagint, K. is divided into two books, I and II Kings (corresponding to III and IV Kings in the Septuagint, where I and II Samuel appear as I and II Kings). The historical viewpoint is religious throughout, and the men who ruled the two kingdoms are ultimately evaluated in accordance with their degree of loyalty to God's covenant. Authorship of K. is ascribed by the Talmud to Jeremiah (*Bava Batra* 15a). Modern critics believe the writing of its sources to have begun as early as the end of Solomon's reign. The prevalence of a strong Deuteronomic influence in the book has been pointed out by many scholars.

KINNIM (Heb. "Birds' Nests"): Last tractate in the Mishnah order of *Kodashim*; it has no *gemara* in either Talmud. *K.* discusses the regulations for bringing a sacrificial offering of fowl after childbirth (Lev. 12:8), or by the poor in atonement for certain offenses (enumerated in Lev. 5) for which they cannot afford the more expensive guilt-offering (Lev. 5:11).

KINYAN, see **PROPERTY**

KIRKISANI (also **KARKASANI**), **ABU YUSUF YAKUB** (10th cent): KARAITE scholar. His major work *Kitab al-Anwar* (in Hebrew *Sepher ha-Orah* "The Book of Light") describes Ḳaraite beliefs and customs and also contains a valuable survey of Jewish sects from the Samaritans and Sadducees to his own time. It preserves many quotations from books now lost. K. is scathing in his criticism of the RABBANITES, but does not spare his own sect. He was the first Karaite to insist upon the value of reason as an aid to faith. K. also wrote commentaries on books of the Bible, and philosophical and theological works.

KISLEV: Third month in the religious calendar, ninth in the civil. It has 29 or 30 days and its zodiac sign is Sagittarius. The festival of *Ḥanukkah* commences on the 25th of the month.

KISSING: The rabbis disapproved of k., with the exceptions of the kiss given to a man when appointing him to a position of honor, the kiss of meeting and of parting, and the k. of relatives. Other k. is either "shameful" or "silly" (*Exod. Rab.* 5:1). Sacred articles are kissed as a sign of respect, e.g., the fringes (cf. Num. 15:37-41), the Scroll of the Law, the *mezuzah*, or a religious book which has fallen to the ground. Among *Sephardim* children kiss their parents' hands after receiving parental BLESSING, and among oriental Jews it is customary to kiss the hand of the HAKHAM in salutation. The peaceful surrender of one's soul to God is called "death by the kiss (of God)" on the basis of the literal translation of Deut. 34:5 "And Moses died... by the mouth of the Lord".

KITTEL: The white garment traditionally worn in some *Ashkenazi* rites by members of the congregation during prayer on the High Holidays (New Year, Day of Atonement), by the officiant at the Additional Service on the first day of Passover (when the prayer for dew is recited) and the eighth day of Tabernacles (during the prayer for rain), by the celebrant at the *Seder* table, and in some communities by the groom during the marriage ceremony (where it is usually presented to him by his bride). Formerly it was worn every Sabbath and at all solemn occasions (cf. Y. *Rosh ha-Shanah* 1:3). The *k.* is also part of the raiment in which the dead are clothed for BURIAL. The color white is associated with symbolic purity (and hence forgiveness of sins), integrity, and piety.

KLAUS (Ger. "enclosure"): A kind of *Bet Midrash*, usually serving also as a synagogue, in which the Talmud was studied by adults. The *k.* thus functioned as a place of study rather than as a school. The Ḥasidim often called their synagogues *k.* (in Yiddish "*kloiz*"). The term appears in Central and E. Europe from the 17th cent. Among *Sephardim* the corresponding institution was known as *hesger* (Heb. "enclosure").

ḲODASHIM (Heb. "Holy Things"): Fifth of the six orders in the Mishnah and Tosephta. It deals with sacrifice, ritual slaughter, and Temple procedure. In the Mishnah, *K.* consists of eleven tractates (ZEVAḤIM, MENAḤOT, ḤULLIN, BEKHOROT, ARAKHIN, TEMURAH, KERITOT, MEILAH, TAMID, MIDDOT, and KINNIM). Nine of these have *gemara* in the Babylonian Talmud but none in the Palestinian.

KOHELET, see **ECCLESIASTES**

KOHELET RABBAH, see **MIDRASH RABBAH**

KOHEN, see **PRIESTS**

KOHLER, KAUFMANN (1843-1926): U.S. Reform leader of German origin. In his *Jewish Theology* he stated: "Judaism is nothing less than a message concerning the One and holy God and one, undivided humanity with a world-uniting messianic goal, a message intrusted by Divine revelation to the Jewish people". The Jewish people has a mission to perform, viz., teaching ethical monotheism to the world. In accordance with classic Reform, K. had no place for Zionism in his system, nor did he find much justification for most of the rituals of traditional Jewish religion. He regarded legalism and nationalism as perversions of true Judaism, the essence of which he found in the doctrine of prophetic universalism. He attributed Jewish survival to the religious genius of the Jewish people, and considered (under Kantian influence) the idea of God as a postulate of man's moral conscience.

KOHUT, ALEXANDER (1842-1894): Rabbi and scholar. A native of Hungary, he emigrated to the U.S. in 1885 to become rabbi of the congregation *Ahavath Chesed* in New York. He helped to inspire a revival of traditional Judaism in America and was one of the founders of the JEWISH THEOLOGICAL SEMINARY. His main scholarly work was a revised and augmented edition of NATHAN BEN JEHIEL's talmudic dictionary *Arukh*.

KOL BO (Heb. "everything within"): Encyclopedia; compendium. The term is particularly applied to two works — the first is a ritual compendium, probably compiled by Shemariah ben Simḥah of Germany at the beginning of the 14th cent. and containing, apart from the usual laws, a number of religious enactments, legends, and other additions. The name is also applied to the large comprehensive folio prayer book designed for the use of the officiant and including the complete and unabridged liturgy, with all *piyyutim* for every weekday, Sabbath, festival, and fast.

KOL NIDREI (Aram. "all vows"): Opening words of the Evening Service commencing the Day of Atonement. Strictly speaking, *K.N.* is not a prayer but a declaration which states that all vows made unwittingly or rashly during the year (and hence unfulfilled) shall be considered null and void. *K.N.* is recited in Aramaic in most rites, in Hebrew in some (e.g. Roman and Byzantine). Its declaration is a comparatively late custom, which dates from the Gaonic Period and persisted despite the opposition of some of the Babylonian *geonim*. The original version referred to vows made during the preceding year; R. Tam altered the formulation to refer to the forthcoming year, and this version is customary among *Ashkenazim*. The Italians still use the original formulation, while *Sephardim* (and *Ashkenazim* in the Land of Israel) combine both forms. It precedes the Day of Atonement service proper, so that from the outset the worshipers might remove from themselves the guilt of any vow which they had unintentionally failed to observe. Because of its position at the opening of the service on the most sacred day of the year, it has been charged with strong religious sentiments and is chanted to a solemn and impressive melody. It is recited three times to emphasize its significance and also to ensure that it will not be missed by latecomers. During its recitation the Ark is open and two Scrolls of the Law taken out, one held on each side of the reader. This prayer has frequently been used as the basis for malevolent charges against Jews by anti-Semites who have claimed that it absolves Jews from all vows they might make; in fact, as the rabbis have stressed, it refers only to vows made between man and God. Vows made by one man to another can only be annulled by mutual agreement. The impact of this prayer has been so great that its name is generally used to refer to the entire eve of the Day of Atonement.

KOLEL, see **ḤALUKKAH**

KOOK, ABRAHAM ISAAC (1865-1935): Chief Rabbi of Palestine (from 1921) and a spiritual leader whose personality, thought, and writings appealed to religious and non-religious alike. He called for *hakhlalah* ("inclusion") by which he meant, on the political and national level, a perspective which would "include" various points of view, political programs, party philosophies, and even anti-religious tendencies as "branches" of the total Jewish Tree of Life. In personal terms, it meant a Judaism which "included" all the variegated expressions of the Jewish religious genius — its law, legends, poetry, mysticism, etc. K. was inclined to see the hidden mystical streams of Jewish thought as the "soul" of Judaism, as part of the "fuller and deeper" *Torah*. His writings include halakhic responsa, theological and mystic meditations (particularly the volumes called *Orot* ["Lights"]), poetry, and a commentary on the prayer book. His letters, of which several volumes have been published, reveal the personality of a man who was more willing, as he said, to commit the "sin" of "causeless love" than of "causeless hate". They also reveal the trials of an Orthodox leader who was troubled not only by the anti-religious tendencies of secular elements in the new Jewish community of Palestine, but was also accused of "heresy" by extremist elements in the Orthodox camp. K. who was born in N. Russia and served as rabbi in Lithuania before going to Palestine where, in 1904, he became Chief Rabbi of Jaffa, is considered a great original thinker in the tradition of Jewish MYSTICISM.

KORAN (Arab. "reading"): The Holy Scripture of ISLAM. The K. consists of the utterances of MOHAMMED; a standard version of the text was edited on the authority of Othman, the third caliph, in the mid-7th cent., about 19 years after the prophet's death. According to Moslem belief the K., as divinely revealed to Mohammed, is an exact replica of its heavenly prototype. Other holy books, revealed by earlier prophets (e.g. Moses and Jesus), carried essentially the same message as the K., but their text and teaching had been corrupted. Nevertheless, people possessing such Scriptures ("peoples of the book") were to be treated differently from pagans. Mohammed is considered the last in a series of prophets sent by God (the "seal of the prophets"), and supersedes them all. The K. is divided into 114 *suras* or chapters arranged according to their length (from 286 to 3 sentences), with the exception of the first *sura*, which stands in a class by itself. Moslem veneration of the K. and the practice of reading it at Friday assemblies and other religious holidays follow the Jewish pattern. In Moslem theology the K. is one of two sources of authority; it represents the written law but is supplemented by tradition (*ḥadith*), i.e., reliable testimonies of what Mohammed said or did on certain occasions. The K. contains much biblical and aggadic material, frequently in garbled form due to misunderstandings and errors on the part of either Mohammed or of his informants. Sarcastic criticism of his errors contributed much to Mohammed's increasing hostility toward Jews. Many biblical heroes figure prominently in the K. e.g., Adam, Noah, Abraham, Ishmael, Lot, Joseph, Saul, David, Solomon, Elijah, Job, Jonah. Moses' name occurs in 34 *suras*. Modern scholars have made detailed studies tracing some of the Koranic references back to their Jewish sources. Some formulations in MAIMONIDES' THIRTEEN PRINCIPLES OF FAITH (e.g. that Moses is the greatest of all prophets, that the TORAH as presently extant is the one given to him, and that it will never be superseded) have been explained as directed against Moslem claims regarding the K.

KORBAN, see **SACRIFICE**

KOSHER, see **DIETARY LAWS; KASHER**

KOTEL MAARAVI, see **WESTERN WALL**

KROCHMAL, NACHMAN (known as *Ranak*: 1785-1840): Philosopher of history; lived in Galicia. He was the first Jewish scholar to view Judaism not as an independent, detached sphere of inquiry but an integral part of the flowing stream of human culture. K. set for himself the task of studying the ever-changing manifestations of the Jewish spirit in different epochs and under varying circumstances. As a historian he assembled facts which he submitted to critical analysis, and as philosopher he sought to synthesize them into a system which bears some analogy to the Hegelian view of the unfolding of the spirit in history. The tension between these two foci of interest gave his work an uneven character. K. saw the world as an arena of conflicting forces in which man was the creator and bearer of the historical process. The hand of God is evident in this process (influence of Vico) and Israel's mission is to spread the knowledge of the Absolute Spirit and instruct mankind (influence of Lessing), a task which did not cease with the advent of Jesus. K., however, also wanted to understand the human elements in Israel's Divine history. Hence, he went beyond Maimonides' identification of Judaism with the abstractions of Reason and beyond the antihistorical views of the Enlightenment with its hero-worship, belief in infinite progress, and its strong assurance of man's intellectual integrity; instead he turned his attention to the role of the masses and the *Volksgeist* (influence of Montesquieu, Fichte, and Hegel). This new mode of thinking saw history as the reflection of the soul of a people and the unique nature of its spirit as it unfolds under the peculiar circumstances of time and place, custom and tradition. His *Moreh Nevukhei Ha-Zeman* ("Guide for the Perplexed of the Time") is considered the most original product of 19th cent. philosophical writing in Hebrew. Its concept of the Jewish mission influenced Jewish Reform thinkers, while its justification of the fundamentals of Judaism by the use of Western philosophy impressed many 19th cent. Jewish writers. By basing his historical approach on the historical reality of the Jewish people, and not solely on a theological or philosophical abstraction called "Judaism", K. laid the foundation for a new approach to Jewish tradition.

KUNTRAS (etymology uncertain): Term used in medieval sources for a register or notebook (cf. *Git.* 28a). Its most common application is by the tosaphists who invariably refer to RASHI's commentary by that name. Consequently Zunz inferred that Rashi's commentary was in the form of "lecture notebooks".

KUPPAH (Heb.): Poor box to which Jews contributed on joyful (Purim or weddings) as well as sad and solemn (eve of the Day of Atonement; *yahrzeit*) occasions and at weekday prayer services. The distribution of the money — generally made on Fridays — was supervised by a group of overseers. The word *k.*, came to refer to general relief (in contrast to *tamḥui* — feeding the poor). The overseers fixed the amount to be raised by the community and each member — man, woman, and child — was expected to contribute according to his means. Even the poor themselves were taxed as they too were obligated to fulfill the commandment of CHARITY.

KUTIM: Inhabitants of Cuthah, brought into the Land of Israel by King Sargon of Assyria to take the place of the ten tribes following the fall of the Israelite kingdom (721 B.C.E.). Settling in Samaria they became known as SAMARITANS (II Kings 17:24, 30), though rabbinic literature calls them K. exclusively. At first they continued to worship the god Nergal but subsequently requested the Assyrian king to send one of the exiled Israelite priests to instruct them in the religion of the land. The result was a syncretic amalgam of old and new customs. After the fall of Jerusalem (586 B.C.E.) the K. reverted to their former cult. However, when the Second Temple was being built they claimed a right to participate. Suspecting insidious motives the Jews rejected the plea. Relations deteriorated to downright hostility, leading ultimately to the creation of a rival Samaritan temple on Mt. GERIZIM. In rabbinic law the K. were given a special status as they were considered neither Jews nor heathens.

KUZARI, BOOK OF, see **JUDAH HA-LEVI**

L

LABOR: Judaism generally takes a positive attitude toward the dignity and social value of l. R. Simeon bar Yoḥai stated that the phrase "Six days shalt thou work" is a commandment as binding as the phrase which follows it "and on the seventh day thou shalt rest" (*Mekhilta* on Exod. 20:9-10). Even Adam was enjoined to work in the Garden of Eden (Gen. 2:15) and such biblical verses as "when thou eatest of the l. of thine hands, happy shalt thou be and it will be well with thee" (Ps. 128:2); "sweet is the sleep of the laborer whether he eat little or much" (Ecc. 5:13); and "go to the ant thou sluggard" (Prov. 6:6), etc., all emphasize the value of l. Rabbinic thought developed this attitude to l. even further, cf. "idleness leads to immorality... and to degeneration" (Mishnah *Ket.* 5:5); "he who does not teach his son a trade teaches him brigandage" (*Kidd.* 30b); "great is l. for it lends dignity to man" (*Ned.* 49b); and "the man who lives from the l. of his hands is greater than one who fears Heaven" (*Ber.* 8a). In one respect only does a sharp difference of opinion develop, over the question whether a man is entitled to abandon work in order to devote himself to sacred study. Against the statement of R. Gamaliel III "Study without l. must be futile and lead to sin" (*Avot* 2:2), the counter-statement is made that insofar as the righteous are concerned "their l. is performed for them by others" (*Ber.* 35b). In answer to the injunction of R. Meir: "a man should always teach his son a light and clean trade", R. Nehorai said "I eschew every trade in the world and will teach my son only *Torah*" (Mishnah *Kidd.* 4:14). The rights of the laborer laid down in the Bible are reinforced in the Talmud. Whereas the Bible legislates simply that the day laborer should be paid at the end of his day's work (Lev. 19:3; Deut. 24:5) the Talmud states that to break this regulation would constitute a breach of four distinct and separate biblical commandments (*Bava Metzia* 111a). In the legal sphere the general rule which states that a man cannot establish his right to a financial claim merely by swearing to it was set aside in the case of a laborer who swears he has not received his wages; such an oath did establish his claim, and the rabbis made this exception explicitly to protect the interests of the laborer (*Shav.* 45a). In modern rabbinic law attempts have been made to cope with recent developments which affect the character of l., wages, the relationship between l. and management, etc.

LADINO: Spanish ("Spanioli") dialect spoken by many *Sephardi* groups. Basically a medieval (primarily Castilian) Spanish dialect, L. also contains Hebrew, Turkish, and other elements. In modern times the Latin alphabet is used instead of the original Hebrew characters. Since the 15th cent. L. literature has been mainly religious (prayers and devotional tracts, translations of moral and ascetic works), but has also included folk poetry, songs (the *romancero*), belles-lettres, and journalism. L. is slowly dying out in the *Sephardi* centers where it used to be spoken (Greece, Turkey, Israel).

LAG BA-OMER: Minor festival. The 33rd (Heb. *lag*) day (falling on *Iyyar* 18) of the seven-week period of the Counting of the Omer, which extends from the second day of Passover to Pentecost (Lev. 23:15). On *Lag ba-Omer* the period of semi-mourning is lifted, and weddings, haircuts, etc. are permitted. The reason for the institution of *Lag ba-Omer* is obscure. A talmudic passage (*Yev.* 62b), telling of the plague which killed the 24,000 disciples of R. Akiva during the *Omer* period also provides the rationale for the mourning observed during this period and is taken as a reference to the disasters of the Bar Kokhba war; this passage, however, makes no mention of *Lag ba-Omer*, though one complicated gloss on the statement, "the plague ceased at the middle of the period to Pentecost", relates it to *Lag ba-Omer*, which subsequently became known as the Scholars' Festival. According to another view the day was selected because only 32 of the 49 days of the *Omer* period are days of mourning when Taḥanun is said; the 33rd day therefore, marks the lifting of the ban. According to other traditions, the great flood commenced on this day and, in the time of Moses, manna began to fall from heaven. A later tradition established the date as the day of death of R. Simeon bar Yoḥai, to whom the Zohar is attributed and hence it is celebrated in particular by kabbalists. R. Simeon's burial place — Meron in Galilee — has remained the scene of a picturesque ceremony on this day when Ḥasidim and others bring their young children for their first haircut, and light bonfires and dance throughout the night. The ceremony incurred the severe displeasure of R. Moses Sopher, but without detriment to its popularity.

LAMDAN (from Heb. *lamad* "learn"): A talmudic scholar; usually a layman who has acquired competence in talmudic studies.

LAMED VAV: According to a statement of Abbaye in the Talmud (*Sanh.* 97b), "the world must contain not less than 36 (in Heb. *lamed vav*) righteous men who are vouchsafed the sight of the Divine Presence". The Talmud also says that these 36 differ from other righteous persons in that they behold the Divine Presence with special clarity. On this basis arose the legend of the *Lamed Vav,* men of usually humble vocation whose special spiritual gifts are not generally recognized or appreciated but by whose merit the world exists. In times of crisis and danger they reveal themselves and bring salvation to the people. According to the *Tikkunei Zohar* (chap. 21) there are two such groups of 36 secret saints, one for the Land of Israel and one for elsewhere. The legend formed a basis for many Jewish folk tales.

LAMENTATION, see **KINAH**

LAMENTATIONS (Heb. *Eikhah,* after its opening word; in the Talmud, called *Kinot* — "dirges"): Sixth book in the Hagiographa section of the Bible and third of the Five SCROLLS. Traditionally ascribed to Jeremiah (on the basis of II Chron. 35:25), the book is placed in the Septuagint version after that of the prophet. It consists of five chapters, four of which elegiacally bemoan Israel's sorrowful plight during the siege and fall of Jerusalem in 587-586 B.C.E. and the subsequent sufferings during the Exile. In the fifth chapter the plaint fuses into a prayer for Israel's redemption. The prevalent motif is that a causal connection exists between Divine punishment and the sins of the people — prophets and priests included — and that genuine repentance is needed before an appeal to God's mercy will be answered. Chapters 1-4, written in elegiac meter, are arranged acrostically according to the alphabet. Critical scholarship denies the book's single authorship, but dates the composition close in time to the catastrophic events it describes. The book is read in the synagogue during the evening and morning services on *Av* 9.

LAMENTATIONS RABBATI, see **MIDRASH RABBAH**

LAMP, see **LAMPS, SABBATH; MENORAH**

LAMPRONTI, ISAAC (1679-1756): Italian rabbi, scholar, and physician. He practiced medicine in Ferrara where (from 1743) he was rabbi and head of the *yeshivah.* He is best known for his *Paḥad Yitzḥak* ("Awe of Isaac") an extensive talmudic encyclopedia arranged in alphabetical order. The articles in this work are generally exhaustive dissertations on their subject, and are valuable for their quotations of rabbinic responsa and other often unpublished sources.

LAMPS, SABBATH: The emphasis laid by the Pharisees on the duty of kindling S. L. was probably by way of a demonstrative refutation of Sadducean and later Karaite interpretation whereby Exod. 35:3 was taken to prohibit the burning of any lights on the Sabbath. A whole chapter of the Mishnah (*Shab.* 2) is devoted to the subject. Although the Talmud does not mention the number of lights, later tradition established it as two (corresponding to *shamor* and *zakhor* — the introductory words to the two versions of the fourth of the TEN COMMANDMENTS). The S. L. became a central feature of Sabbath observance, and special oil lamps (later, candlesticks) were designed for the purpose. See KINDLING OF LIGHTS.

LAND LAWS, see **AGRARIAN LAWS**

LANDAU, EZEKIEL (1713-1793): Talmudist; born in Poland. From 1755 he was rabbi of Prague, where he founded a celebrated *yeshivah.* An uncompromising opponent of both Ḥasidism (he ordered the burning of JACOB JOSEPH OF POLONNOYE's *Toledot Yaakov Yoseph*) and Enlightenment. L. enjoyed great moral prestige and halakhic authority; he also tried to mediate in the conflict between Jacob EMDEN and Jonathan EIBESCHUTZ. For his own congregation L. issued SUMPTUARY LAWS and other regulations. The best known of his halakhic works is *Noda bi-Yehudah* (responsa).

LANDESRABBINER (Ger.): Title given from the 17th cent. on in Germany and Austria to rabbis appointed or recognized by the government. Their jurisdiction extended over the political unit known as a *Land,* of which there were many in Germany. Their function was often civic and representative (in the 19th cent., they were generally expected to Germanize the Jews) rather than strictly religious.

LANDLORD AND TENANT, see **TENANCY**

LA-SHANAH HA-BAAH BI-YERUSHALAYIM (Heb. "next year in Jerusalem"): A wish traditionally expressed at the conclusion of the Passover *Seder* and, in some rites, of the Concluding Service of the Day of Atonement. In the State of Israel the wording is *. . . bi-Yerushalayim ha-benuyah* rebuilt Jerusalem").

LATTER PROPHETS, see **PROPHETS**

LAVADORES (Span. "washers"): *Sephardi* name for members of a burial society (see ḤEVRAH KADDISHA).

LAVER: Basins for the ritual ABLUTIONS required of PRIESTS were provided both in the Tent of Meeting (see Exod. 30:18-20) and in the Temple (see BRAZEN SEA). In many synagogues artistic lavers are used for washing the priests' hands before the PRIESTLY BLESSING.

LAW, see **HALAKHAH; TORAH**

LAW, CIVIL, see **CIVIL LAW**

LAW, CODIFICATION OF, see **CODES OF LAW**

LAW, ORAL (Heb. *Torah she-be-al peh*): The part of the Divine revelation to Moses which is not recorded in the Pentateuch but was transmitted by oral tradition. In the rabbinic view, TORAH in its widest sense, denoting the whole body of Jewish teaching, is comprised of two parts, both imparted to Moses at Mt. Sinai: the WRITTEN LAW (i.e., the Pentateuch) and the unwritten or Oral Law committed to writing in the Mishnah (see TALMUD). Belief in the O.L. does not therefore mean that the Talmud was inspired, but that Moses received at Sinai both (a) the explanation of the precepts contained in the written *Torah,* together with the manner of their fulfillment; and (b) the methods by means of which the written text was to be interpreted, developed, and expanded. The doctrine of an O.L. was held and developed in particular by the PHARISEES, and it enabled them to formulate biblical precepts with greater detail as well as apply the law of the *Torah* to varied and changing circumstances. Oral traditions existed, no doubt, from very early times, and much of rabbinic exegesis was originally evolved for the purpose of providing scriptural basis for practice already traditionally current. The HERMENEUTIC RULES of biblical exegesis used in determining HALAKHAH were crystallized by Hillel into seven rules and expanded by Ishmael ben Elisha into thirteen. *Halakhot* deduced by these methods are considered as possessing biblical authority. The application of these rules and the continuous development of criteria, norms, and precedents to which they gave rise, not only ensured that the Law was related to changing economic, social, and political situations, but also greatly enlarged the body of *Torah.* In spite of its steady growth, the O. L. was for a long time not formally committed to writing, though many private written collections ("scrolls") of *halakhot* existed long before the compilation of the MISHNAH, into the text of which material from several of these collections was incorporated. The prohibition against committing the O. L. to writing was finally overridden when it became apparent that the integrity of tradition could not otherwise be guaranteed and that *halakhot* might be forgotten. The classical texts of the O. L. are the tannaitic *Midrash* and the two versions of the TALMUD. These sources reflect the twofold approach of the O. L. to the written text of Scripture: the *Midrash Halakhah* applies rabbinic exegesis to the biblical text in order to prove an organic relationship between the traditionally received *halakhah* and the written text, whereas collections of the Mishnah type organize their material according to systematic criteria. Which of the two literary forms of the O. L. is earlier is a subject of scholarly debate. The body of O. L. is made up of: (1) Interpretations of the precepts handed down from Sinai and supported, however remotely, by Scripture. (2) Traditional *halakhot* for which no support is found in Scripture; this class is called *halakhah le-Mosheh mi-Sinai* ("law of Moses from Sinai"). These two categories were never subject to controversy. Whenever a scholar stated that he had received a particular matter by tradition, it was accepted unreservedly. (3) Laws derived by means of the hermeneutical rules. (4) Cases decided by reasoning and logical analysis. It is with the latter two categories that most of the controversies recorded in the Talmud are concerned. (5) Rabbinic enactments and decrees. In a wider sense the O. L. also includes the teachings of the *aggadah,* particularly of the aggadic *midrash,* in which Scripture is often used by the rabbis as a peg upon which to hang exegetic homilies. In a statement that was evidently meant as a polemical rejoinder to Christian claims, the rabbis declared Israel's peculiar distinction to lie in its acceptance of the O. L., as contrasted with the Written Law which was accepted by many other nations as well. The O.L. was evolved by the teachers of the Second Temple Period, the Pharisees, and their successors. The Sadducees and Essenes possessed their own traditions for developing biblical legislation but these groups disappeared after 70 C.E. The O. L. was rejected by the KARAITES (8th cent. ff.) who preached a return to a pure scriptural Judaism. Reform Judaism considers both the concept and the contents of the O. L. as historically conditioned phenomena and hence rejects the Orthodox claim that they are permanently and unalterably valid. Conservative Judaism tries to steer its course in full awareness of the history-based development of the O. L. but in a spirit of fidelity to its rôle and significance in Jewish tradition.

LAW, READING OF, see **READING OF THE LAW**

LAW, REJOICING OF, see **SIMḤAT TORAH**

LAW, SCROLL OF, see **SEPHER TORAH**

LAW, TABLES OF, see **TABLETS OF THE LAW**

LAWS OF NOAH, see **NOAH, LAWS OF**

LAYMAN: The Hebrew term *hedyot* was used in Temple times to designate a private person, as opposed to a member of royalty or the priesthood. It is also found as an appellation for an ignorant man, one of low character or ill-manners and the unskilled as opposed to the skilled worker. *Leshon hedyot* thus means popular, everyday, or vulgar parlance; *kohen hedyot* refers to the ordinary PRIEST. With the destruction of the Temple most distinctions between laymen and priests disappeared. Exceptions are (1) the right of priests to bestow the priestly blessing; (2) impurity incurred by priests through contact with corpses; (3) restrictions on priestly marriage; and (4) certain signs of respect to priests, e.g. the right to be called first to the reading of the *Torah*. Nowadays "layman" is used to designate the members of a congregation in contrast to the officiants.

LEAP YEAR, see **CALENDAR**

LEAVEN (Heb. *ḥametz*): As an agent of fermentation, l. is the subject of biblical prohibitions of a ritual nature. The *halakhah* defines l. as dough that has been kneaded from flour and water and allowed to stand until it has soured. In commemoration of the EXODUS, when the Israelites in leaving Egypt could not wait until their dough leavened (Exod. 12:39), only unleavened foods are permitted during the PASSOVER Festival; for, "whosoever shall consume l., that soul shall be cut off from the congregation of Israel" (*ibid.* 19). L. was also barred in the Temple meal-offering. For a dough to be considered l. it must have stood for approximately eighteen minutes. Biblical law considers l. only such dough as is made from the five kinds of grain — wheat, barley, spelt, maize, and oats. All l., including that absorbed by utensils, is to be removed and destroyed before Passover. Utensils that have been used for unleavened food are rendered fit for the festival only after complete scouring. On the eve preceding Passover (*Nisan* 13) a thorough search of one's premises is undertaken in order to ensure that no l. remains there (BEDIKAT ḤAMETZ). Any l. found is burnt the following morning, after which no benefit may be derived from l. until after the festival. L. which may unknowingly have remained is declared ownerless (in Yidd. *ḥametz bateln*). The search is traditionally made by candlelight and small pieces of l. are intentionally left around to be burned on the following morning (*Nisan* 14). Where there is a large amount of l., it is feared that the owner may not wholeheartedly nullify his possession of it or destroy it. The custom therefore arose of selling the l. to a non-Jew for a nominal sum and repurchasing it after Passover. Transgression is thereby avoided as the law only prohibits the retention of one's own l.

LEESER, ISAAC (1806-1868): U.S. rabbi and author. A native of Germany, he went to the U.S. in 1824. *Ḥazzan* in Philadelphia from 1829, he edited both *Sephardi* and *Ashkenazi* prayer books which were in use for a long time, made an independent translation of the Bible into English, and founded the first congregational Hebrew school in the U.S. as well as the Maimonides College for training rabbis. Through *The Occident and Jewish Advocate* which he edited, his influence extended to many Jewish communities throughout the U.S. Although an Orthodox rabbi, and a bitter opponent of the Reform movement, L. advocated certain liberalizations in traditions.

LEGACY, see **INHERITANCE**

LEGALISM: The preference of legal rules and norms above moral and spiritual values. The term has a pejorative quality and has usually been applied by Christian controversialists to Judaism.

LEGEND, see **AGGADAH**

LEIL SHIMMURIM (Heb. "night of watching"): Name given by the Bible (Exod. 12:42) to the night of the EXODUS and hence to the first night (in the Diaspora, first two nights) of Passover. As the night was thought to lie under special Divine protection, doors were often left unlocked and the night prayer omitted. Some scholars suggest that the term *l.s.* is similar to the Bedouin *samarum* (staying up all night and telling stories) and refers to the custom of staying awake all night and recounting the exodus from Egypt.

LEKAḤ TOV (Heb. "Good Doctrine"): Midrash on the Pentateuch and the Five Scrolls composed in Germany at the end of the 11th cent. by TOBIAH BEN ELIEZER. Based on older Midrashim, the work is also known as PESIKTA ZUTARTA.

LEKET (Heb. "gleanings"): Term for GLEANINGS which fall aside during the harvest and which must be left for the poor (see Lev. 19:9-10). A description of *l.* in ancient Israel is given in Ruth 2. The laws of *l.* belong in the same group as SHIKHḤAH and PEAH; see AGRARIAN LAWS.

LEKHAH DODI (Heb. "Come my beloved"): Introductory words of a 16th cent. composition (one of the last to be included in the prayer book) sung at the inauguration of the Sabbath. The author's name, Shelomoh (Solomon) Ha-Levi (ALKABETZ) is given in acrostic in eight of the nine stanzas. Incorporating many biblical phrases, particularly from Isaiah, the poem personifies the Sabbath as a bride (cf. *Shab.* 119a), symbolically welcomed by the congregation's bowing toward the entrance during the last stanza. It is a relic of a more elaborate processional greeting of the Sabbath. Replete with references to the peace and joy of the Sabbath and the larger peace and joy of messianic times and the restoration of Jerusalem and Israel, it was quickly adopted in all rites. The hymn is sung after the introductory Psalm 29.

LEKHU NERANANAH (Heb. "O come, let us exult"): The opening words of Ps. 95, and hence of the group of six psalms (95-99 and 29) recited in the *Ashkenazi* rite for the inauguration of the Sabbath at the beginning of the Friday evening service; the *Sephardi* rite has only Ps. 29. The six psalms, which describe the grandeur of God's work in nature and His righteous judgment of the world, were said to correspond to the six working days of the week. (The Sabbath Psalm [92] is recited after Ps. 29 and the Lekhah Dodi). The custom of reciting this group of psalms was introduced by the kabbalists of Safed in the 16th cent.; previously the beginning of the Sabbath eve service had been the same as on weekdays.

LEON, MOSES DE, see **MOSES DE LEON**

LEON OF MODENA, see **MODENA, LEONE**

LEON (SIR LEON) OF PARIS, see **JUDAH BEN ISAAC**

LEPROSY: The usual (though possibly incorrect) translation of the biblical *tzoraat*, an affection of the skin and other surfaces which renders the person or object unclean. Signs of l., which may appear on persons, the walls of houses, or in fabrics are described at length in Lev. 13. On being pronounced as leprous by a priest, the affected person or object is to be quarantined until the scourge disappears. On being healed, a leper must undergo a service of cleansing and bring special offerings to the Temple (*ibid.* 14) The rabbis consider the attitude to the leper in the Pentateuch to be not medical but moral; they suggest that l. is the result of scandalmongering and evil talk (Leshon ha-ra), as evidenced in the instance of Moses in speaking against Israel (Exod. 4:7), and Miriam in speaking against Moses (Deut. 24:8-9). The laws concerning l. are discussed in the talmudic tractate Negaim.

LE-SHANAH HA-BAAH BI-YERUSHALAYIM, see **LA-SHANAH HA-BAAH BI-YERUSHALAYIM**

LESHON HA-RA (Heb. "the tongue of evil"): Scandalmongering. *L. H.* is considered to be prohibited by the Bible on the basis of Lev. 19:16, "You shall not go up and down as a slanderer among your people", and is frequently condemned in the Book of Proverbs. The rabbis, in inveighing against it, often resorted to hyperbolic language, e.g. in saying that slander, talebearing, and evil talk were worse than the three cardinal sins of murder, immorality, and idolatry. Of one who indulges in *l.h.* they say that he denies the existence of God, and that the Almighty declares "I and he cannot live in the same world" (*Erak.* 15b). Rabbinic law distinguishes between various categories of talebearing (*rekhilut*), slandering, scandalmongering, etc. Every kind of trafficking in evil reports or rumors — whether true or not — by carrying them from one person to another, or by relating unpleasant or harmful facts about another, is forbidden. The rabbis forbade even "the dust of *leshon ha-ra*", i.e., *l.h.* by insinuation, as in saying "do not mention so-and-so for I do not wish to tell in what he was involved", or in praising a person to his enemy since this also invites *l.h.* Both the teller of and the listener to *l.h.* are guilty of transgression, even if the person spoken about is present at the conversation. If a person publicizes unpleasant facts about himself, he who repeats them has not indulged in *l.h.* The most thorough discussion of the halakhic and moral aspects of *l.h.* is in Israel Meir Cohen's *Ḥaphetz Ḥayyim.*

LETTING, see **HIRING**

LEVAYAH, see **BURIAL**

LEVI, see **LEVITES**

LEVI BEN GERSHON (also known as Gersonides or by his initials as *Ralbag*; 1288-1344): Bible commentator, philosopher, talmudist, mathematician, and astronomer. His *Milḥamot Adonai* ("Wars of the Lord") does not present a complete system but discusses the major philosophical and theological problems of his time — creation of the world, Divine Providence, the nature of the soul, miracles, and prophecy, both supplementing Maimonides and criticizing him on many points. Although L. exhibits a formal attachment to traditional Jewish doctrines, his thinking was more radically Aristotelian than that of most of his predecessors, and he was greatly influenced by the Arab philosopher Averroes, on several of whose works L. wrote supercommentaries. Whereas Maimonides, if necessary, gave precedence to revelation over Aristotelian doctrine, L. endeavored to adapt traditional concepts to Averroistic rationalism; e.g. he differs from Maimonides in holding that the world was created of eternal matter and not *ex nihilo.* Divine Providence is concerned with universals but not individuals since God cannot know particulars. Immortality depends on the degree of philosophical knowledge which the soul absorbs as a result of its contact with the Active Intellect; the most advanced stage of this contact is prophecy. Miracles are possible for God, who created the world from formless primal matter by an act of Divine will. L.'s Bible commentaries tend to the philosophical and ethical rather than to plain exposition of the text; his endeavor to give a rational interpretation of every detail in the sacred text led him to make far-reaching use of allegory. L., who was practically the last Jewish Aristotelian, aroused much controversy and his views were attacked by Ḥasdai Crescas.

LEVI BEN JAPHETH (early 11th cent.): Karaite writer. Son of the Karaite scholar Japheth ben Ali, he probably lived in Jerusalem. He is best known for his work on Karaite law, *Sepher Mitzvot* ("Book of Precepts") written in Arabic but soon translated into Hebrew.

LEVI ISAAC OF BERDICHEV (1740-1809): Ḥasidic leader; known as the "merciful one" or the "defender of Israel" because of his reputation for upholding the virtues of the Jewish people against all charges, even against God's judgment. His famous "*Din Torah* with God" in which L.I. summons God to a court of judgment because of His alleged mistreatment of Israel, but which ends with his fervent submission to God's holy will, is the subject of a classic folk song. Popular legend made the personality of L.I. the object of many ḥasidic tales. In addition to being a typical ḥasidic *tzaddik*, L.I. was a recognized rabbinic scholar. He served as rabbi of the community of Berdichev which, as a tribute to his unique greatness, never appointed a successor after his death. L.I.'s work, *Kedushat Levi,* was much studied by Ḥasidim. In popular memory he lives on as the man of whom it was said that he loved God and that he loved the *Torah,* but that both these loves were excelled by his love for Israel.

LEVIATHAN: Primeval sea monster mentioned in Job 40:25-32 and described as powerless against the might of God (cf. Ps. 104:26). Echoes of the ancient myth according to which God defeated the mighty serpent are preserved in Is. 27:1 and in Ps. 74:14, where, however, the meaning is allegorical and signifies the downfall of the empires of Egypt and Assyria. According to the Talmud (*Bava Batra* 74b) the l. was among the "sea monsters" mentioned in Gen. 1:21. Plotting to destroy the world, the monster was slain by the Lord and its flesh was cut up and preserved as sustenance for the righteous in the World to Come. The l. figures prominently in Middle Eastern mythologies where it symbolizes the forces of chaos and evil, defeated by the power of good. The kabbalists found esoteric significance in the story of the l. by identifying the male and female of the species with SAMAEL and LILITH. Maimonides suggested that the l. legends were veiled prophecies referring to future events.

LEVIRATE MARRIAGE (Heb. *yibbum*): The biblical injunction to marry the widow of one's brother who has died childless (Deut. 25:5-10). The obligation of l.m. (*levir* — Lat. "husband's brother", in Heb. *yavam*) applies even though the widow has children of her own from a previous marriage, the sole criterion being the childlessness of her deceased husband. Thus, should there exist a viable child from the husband at the time of his demise, though born out of wedlock or illegitimate in law (but not if born of a non-Jewess), l.m. cannot take place. The obligation of l.m. falls upon brothers born of the same father (but not if born only of the same mother) as that of the deceased; all such brothers are liable but preference is given to the oldest (who is however relieved from the duty if a younger brother volunteers). Biblical law does not require a formal marriage ceremony between the widow and the levir who becomes her husband, but the rabbis forbade l.m. to take place without first following the normal marriage ceremony. The pre-l.m. procedure (called *maamar*) does not yet make the widow fully the wife of the levir, but merely "bespeaks" her to him, to the exclusion of the remaining brothers. On the performance of l.m., the widow is considered to be the wife of the levir in all respects and she can thus be freed from the union only by formal divorce. The inheritance of the deceased passes to the brother who marries the widow. Where impediments in law stand in the way of the l.m., or the brother refuses to fulfill the obligation, or the widow refuses to marry her brother-in-law, or where l.m. may be inadvisable on other grounds, the rite of *ḥalitzah* (Heb. "drawing off") is performed instead. If the deceased husband is survived by a brother, the widow is not allowed to remarry without either l.m. or *ḥalitzah.* Only if the widow is incapable of bearing children is she freed entirely from both of these alternatives. *Ḥalitzah* must take place before a court of five; it consists in a reading by the widow of the relevant biblical verses (Deut. 25:7-10), drawing off the right shoe of the levir, and spitting on the ground in front of him as a sign of contempt and rebuke for one who brings disgrace upon himself by shirking the duty of perpetuating the name of his brother. After *ḥalitzah* has been performed neither the levir who performed it nor any of his brothers may marry the widow and she is free to marry whomever else she chooses. She may not however marry a priest as her status is similar to that of the divorcee. L.m. was practiced in patriarchal times (cf. Gen. 38) but it appears that the widow was to become the wife of the brother only until a child was born (Malbim on Deut. 25:5). Ruth's marriage to Boaz (Ruth 4), which has been quoted in proof of the fact that l.m. was practiced by all relatives of the deceased, was not a case of l.m. at all. The drawing off of the shoe was effected in order to legalize the transference of the rights of the first redeemer to Boaz. The regulations concerning l.m. are discussed in the talmudic treatise YEVAMOT. The levirate custom had gradually declined by talmudic times, and the later rabbis generally encouraged those upon whom the duty fell to avail themselves of the biblical provision for its evasion, i.e., *ḥalitzah* — though differences of opinion were also recorded. The reasons for the more lenient tendency were: a) the fact that the biblical law of l.m. is unusual in that it sanctions a union which is incestuous by normal standards; b) the likelihood that the surviving brother would already be married, and the l.m. thus clash with the medieval prohibition against POLYGAMY among *Ashkenazi* Jews (see also R. GERSHOM). Maimonides and the Spanish school upheld l.m. The Israeli rabbinate has established that in the State of Israel the obligation of *ḥalitzah* takes precedence over that of l.m., and it is forbidden to make a l.m.; a brother who refuses to give *ḥalitzah* to his deceased brother's widow is liable to imprisonment. Reform Judaism has dispensed with the duty of l.m. and the concomitant necessity of *ḥalitzah*.

LEVITA, ELIJAH, see **BAḤUR, ELIJAH**

LEVITES: Descendants of Levi, third of the twelve sons of Jacob. Levi's three sons — Gershon, Kohath, and Merari — formed clans within the tribe of Levi. However, biblical reference to l. as a secular tribe is almost nonexistent. Various theories have been advanced for this; some scholars even deny a secular origin for the l. and suggest they were a heterogeneous sacerdotal guild which acquired tribal status as it became a socially dominant factor. According to the Bible (Exod. 32:25-29) the l. supplanted the first-born of Israel in the task of sacral ministration when the latter defected to worship the Golden CALF and the l. alone remained faithful. The tribe was subdivided into (a) the PRIESTS, descendants of AARON, who performed ritual service in the Tabernacle and later in the Temple; and (b) the l. charged with the ancillary duties of carrying the sanctuary and its vessels throughout Israel's wandering in the wilderness. The l. also functioned as assistants to the priests (Num. 1:50-53; 4:1-33). A count of the l. in the wilderness of Sinai recorded some 22,000 (Num. 3:39). The age at which they were eligible for service varied. Thus in Num. 4:3 they served from the age of 30 until 50, while according to Num. 8:24 they began to serve at 25 years, and in I Chron. 23:24, at 20. This apparent discrepancy has been explained by the assumption that the younger age groups were directed to the less important functions and only at 30 were they eligible for the more important ones, e.g., Temple administration, judicial office, gatekeeping, and the performance of sacred music (I Chron. 23:3-6). No fixed territory was allotted to the l. by Joshua upon the conquest of Canaan, "for the Lord is their inheritance" (Josh. 13:14). With the exception of those connected with the Temple service, and who lived in Jerusalem, the l. dwelt in 48 cities apportioned to them throughout the country (Num. 35). There they apparently assimilated among their fellow Israelites, a process which would explain why their numbers were less than those of the priests. They received a TITHE of agricultural produce for their sustenance (Num. 18:20-21), a second tithe of which they had to pass on to the priests. No mention of the LEVITICAL CITIES is made during the Second Temple Period. The l. were known as instructors in sacred lore (cf. Deut. 35:10) and it is hence that the Scribes (SOPHERIM) originated. The precedence of the priest over the levite and of the levite over the "Israelite" is still maintained by the custom of calling up a priest before a levite at the Reading of the Law in the synagogue. The levite washes the hands of the priest before the latter utters the priestly benediction in the synagogue.

LEVITICAL CITIES: The 48 towns which God commanded Moses to set apart for the tribe of Levi; each was surrounded by a specified area of open land (Num. 35). These towns included the six Cities of Refuge for sheltering the accidental homicide (see ASYLUM). According to some commentators the LEVITES, being thus dispersed throughout Israel, could discharge their task as instructors of the people (Deut. 35:10) more effectively. The actual apportioning of the cities by each tribe to the levites is described in Josh. 21.

LEVITICUS: Third book of the PENTATEUCH; in Hebrew, called *Va-yikra* after its first word (formerly known also as *Torat ha-Kohanim* — "Law of the Priests"). Continuing the Mosaic legislation commenced in the previous book (EXODUS), it concentrates on ritual and legal subjects. Chaps. 1-7 deal with sacrificial ritual; 8-10, installation of priests; 11-15, cleanness and uncleanness; 16, Day of Atonement; 17-26 the "Holiness Code" (a collection of ritual and ethical injunctions including the original formulation of the GOLDEN RULE "Thou shalt love thy neighbor as thyself" — 19:18); 27, vows and tithes. Bible critics assign a separate pre-exilic authorship (H) to the Holiness Code.

LEVITICUS RABBAH, see **MIDRASH RABBAH**

LEX TALIONIS, see **JUS TALIONIS**

LIBATION (Heb. *nesekh*): Offering of wine or oil. Every animal SACRIFICE in the Temple was accompanied by a MEAL-OFFERING and a l. (Num. 15:1-16) of wine which was poured into a bowl in the S.W. corner of the ALTAR whence it flowed through a shallow cavity into the *shittin* — the depths of the altar foundations (*Suk.* 48a). In the case of a lamb the l. consisted of a quarter *hin* of wine, for a ram a third of a *hin*, and for an ox a half *hin*. Sometimes the sacrifice (especially a meal-offering) was offered with OIL (either poured over the sacrifice or the sacrifice being soaked in it). During Tabernacles, when prayers are offered for rain, water l. formed part of the Temple service.

LIBEL, see **SLANDER**

LIBERAL JUDAISM, see **REFORM JUDAISM**

LIBERTY, see **FREEDOM**

LIFE: L. is considered God's supreme blessing, and it is hence often identified with the good as such — cf. Deut. 30:19: "I have set before you l. and death, blessing and curse; therefore choose l., that both you and your seed may live". The *Torah* itself is a "Tree of Life", and the purpose of its commandments is "that man shall live by them" (Lev. 18:5), a phrase to which the rabbis added "and not die by them" (*Yoma* 85b). Hence all laws — with the exception only of the cardinal sins of idolatry, bloodshed, and adultery — are liable to suspension in case of DANGER to l. (*Sanh.* 74a). As long as there is l. there is hope, and "a living dog is better than a dead lion" (Ecc. 9:4). The biblical emphasis on l. in this world as a supreme value (see Ps. 115:17 "The dead praise not the Lord, neither any that go down into silence") was generally maintained in Jewish tradition, in spite of the increasing importance of belief in an afterlife. DEATH is regarded as the principal source of impurity, and priests, Nazirites, or anyone wishing to enter the Temple were forbidden to defile themselves by contact with the dead (Lev. 21:1; Num. 5:2 ff.; 6:6). The infinite value of every human l. is solemnly affirmed in the court's instruction to witnesses in capital trials: "Whoever destroys one l. is as if he destroyed a whole world, and whoever preserves one l. is as if he preserved a whole world" (*Sanh.* 4:5). Hastening death even by one minute is considered tantamount to bloodshed, and rabbinic law prohibits euthanasia. The motif of l. is particularly conspicuous in the additional prayers of the period between New Year and the Day of Atonement. Many of the biblical references to l. have later been interpreted as meaning the IMMORTALITY of the soul or the RESURRECTION OF THE DEAD.

LIFE, BOOK OF, see **BOOK OF LIFE**

LIGHT: In addition to its physical properties l. serves almost universally as a symbol of life, blessing, peace, knowledge, understanding, redemption, the soul, and good, whereas darkness represents chaos, death, ignorance, sin, suffering, and evil. God's first creation was l. (Gen. 1:3-4) and in later theology He Himself was defined as l., the source of l., etc. The *Torah* too is "a l."; and to be blessed is to "walk in the l. of God's face". In the Second Temple Period the "theology of l." was further developed. Sectarian circles (see DEAD SEA SCROLLS) expressed the opposition between God's elect and the reprobate as one between the children of l. and the children of darkness, and this usage subsequently passed into the NEW TESTAMENT. Hellenistic philosophers, PHILO in particular, and Neo-Platonists made much use of l. symbolism when speaking of spiritual and Divine realities. In mystical literature both the symbolism and the experience of higher, heavenly (viz., spiritual) l. played an important rôle. Kabbalistic writers especially use l. as synonymous with Divine substance, spiritual essences and the like, and describe cosmic and mystical processes in terms of EMANATION, retraction (TZIMTZUM), etc. of supernal lights. The symbolic significance of l. is reflected by the frequent ritual use of lights, and in particular of CANDLES, candelabra, etc. From the MENORAH in the Temple to the Sabbath (see LAMP, SABBATH) and *Ḥanukkah* lights, from the NER TAMID in the synagogue to the medieval custom of lighting a candle for the soul of the deceased (in the mourning period and on the YAHRZEIT), Jewish practice attests the perennial symbolic significance of l.

LIGHT, PERPETUAL, see **NER TAMID**

LIGHTS, FEAST OF, see **ḤANUKKAH**

LIPKIN, ISRAEL, see **SALANTER, ISRAEL**

LITURGY: While individual, spontaneous prayer was practiced in Israel from earliest times, fixed obligatory community prayers originated only after the Babylonian Exile. Some of the psalms date from the days of the First Temple and were used there for liturgical purposes, but they were recited by levitical choirs and not as a rule by the worshipers themselves. The creation of regular community prayers to be recited by all Jews at certain times and in the same form, marks a significant change in religious life; for through it a new form of *avodah* (= "Divine service", "worship") was fashioned, the *avodah she-ba-lev* ("service of the heart") which — in contrast to the Temple service — could be performed anywhere by ordinary people and without the assistance of priests. Even though the regular prayers were conceived, in the first place, as community prayers to be recited preferably in the presence of a MINYAN, the individual may nevertheless recite most of them on his own and is indeed obliged to do so, according to the rules laid down eventually by the *halakhah*. However even when spoken by an individual, these prayers retain the character of community prayers; the first person plural is used throughout, so that the worshiper reciting them feels himself part of the community of Israel. The custom of praying at fixed times and according to a fixed form developed gradually in the course of the early Second Temple Period. Some talmudic sources ascribe the establishment of these prayers to the Men of the Great Synagogue (*Meg.* 17b; 25a), but they also state that the final "arrangement" took place only in the days of R. Gamaliel II, following the destruction of the Temple (*ibid.*; *Ber.* 28b). After the loss of the Temple, additional emphasis was undoubtedly laid on the regular prayers, now considered as replacing the sacrifices which could no longer be offered. Regular prayer assemblies were at first probably held mainly on Sabbaths, festivals, and fast days. A regular weekday service was held in the Second Temple Period by the MAAMADOT, i.e., delegations from the twenty-four districts of the country who took turns in representing the people at the Temple service. A brief daily morning service of the priests in the Temple is also on record. Probably, different "orders of prayers" were used on various occasions, and out of these eventually developed the accepted standard "orders" of the AMIDAH, such as the "seven benedictions" for Sabbaths and festivals and the "eighteen benedictions" for weekdays. By the end of the 2nd cent. C.E. the "order of prayers" had been firmly established and, except for minor changes and additions which are not obligatory, has remained unaltered in its basic structure. Differences between the various "rites" (e.g. *Ashkenazi, Sephardi,* Yemenite, ancient Palestinian) are limited to details of formulation, but do not concern the actual order and outline of the statutory prayers themselves; as regards the latter, a high degree of unity was reached and preserved at least from the 2nd cent. on. Great variety prevails, on the other hand, regarding the "additions" and non-obligatory parts of the liturgy, especially the PIYYUTIM, SELIḤOT, etc. Hence the different "rites" present the appearance of great diversity in spite of the identity of the underlying structure common to all. The basic fixed component parts of Jewish l. comprise the AMIDAH (essential in one of its various forms for any of the statutory prayers); the SHEMA and the benedictions attached to it (for SHAḤARIT and MAARIV); later also the KADDISH and, for Shaḥarit, the PESUKEI DE-ZIMRA. On festivals HALLEL must be recited; on certain days, including Sabbaths and festivals, a portion from the Bible is read in synagogue. Obligatory too — though intended for individual or domestic worship — are GRACE, KIDDUSH, etc. and the many BENEDICTIONS to be recited on various occasions, e.g. the benedictions to be recited in the morning (nowadays mostly recited by the reader in synagogue at the beginning of the Morning Service). At first, the prayers — like the ORAL LAW — were not committed to writing. Hence they did not possess a single uniform text; only the general content of each benediction was defined, not the wording. In fact, the Talmud encourages individual additions even to the obligatory prayers and rejects the mechanical repetition day after day of the same formula, thus stressing the necessity of preserving the spontaneous character of PRAYER (*Ber.* 29b; Y. *Ber.* 4:3). In synagogue the *amidah* was recited aloud by the reader, while the congregation would either pray along with him word for word in an undertone or listen silently and respond with *amen.* The *Shema* and its benedictions, too, were recited aloud (though for this part of the service the reader would not leave his seat) either in unison or antiphonically. Eventually, as knowledge of Hebrew decreased, definite texts were memorized and used regularly. Only with the introduction of printed prayer books did it become customary (in European congregations especially) for each individual to recite the various prayers silently, while the reader would chant aloud only the opening and conclusion of each; in the case of the *amidah*, the silent recitation by each individual would be followed by its repetition, chanted aloud by the reader. The use of printed prayer books also resulted in the fixing — according to the custom of each region or locality — of the *piyyutim* and other non-obligatory parts of the l., which were no longer freely interchanged as in olden times (though in many places a considerable number of the *piyyutim* included in the printed editions are in practice omitted). According to the *halakhah,* prayers may be recited in any language; but in spite of this ruling, prayers were recited only in Hebrew throughout Jewish history; the few exceptions to this rule include the Greek-speaking Egyptian Diaspora of 2000 years ago and some modern Reform (and to a lesser extent Conservative) congregations.

LIUBAVICH: Russian village near Mohilev; until the Soviet revolution, seat of the SHNEERSON dynasty, the leaders of ḤABAD Ḥasidism, founded by R. SHNEOUR ZALMAN OF LYADY. (*Ḥabad* ḥasidim are also known as L. ḥasidim). The rabbi of L. has settled in the U.S. and the headquarters of the group are now in New York. L. is one of the most active ḥasidic groups maintaining schools, *yeshivot,* orphanages, etc., and sometimes working clandestinely — as in Russia after the Soviet revolution. Its spiritual life centers on the study of its founder's writings (TANYA) and joyful meetings (*farbrengungen*) of the ḥasidim. The rabbi functions as a spiritual guide and teacher, rather than as a miracle worker.

LOANS: The injunction to lend money to one in need is a positive precept (Exod. 22:24; Lev. 25:36), while the refusal to grant a loan involves the transgression of a prohibition. The Bible warns against refusing to lend money at the approach of the SABBATICAL YEAR for fear that it would be rendered unclaimable due to remission (see PROSBUL). The rabbis enacted several ordinances to facilitate borrowing, and regarded the lending of money as more important than charity (*Shab.* 63a) since it enables the borrower to stand on his own feet without feeling shame or humiliation. As a potential recipient of l., a poor man takes precedence over a rich man, relatives over strangers, local persons over those from other towns. Having loaned money, one may not act as a "usurer" (Exod. 22:24) toward the borrower. Where no date for repayment is stipulated, the normal loan period is thirty days and repayment may not be claimed before the lapse of this period (*Mak.* 3b). Thirty days is also allowed when, on default of the borrower, claim is made from the guarantor. A loan contracted without recourse to a written DEED is secured only by the moveable property of the borrower; one contracted by deed is secured also by his immoveable property. No interest may be demanded or offered between a borrower and lender who are both Jews (see USURY).

LOGOS (Gk. "word", "speech", "reason"): The concept of *l.* in the sense of Divine reason plays a considerable role in Greek, particularly Stoic, philosophy, especially in philosophical accounts of the origin of the cosmos. It is by means of the creative and sustaining principle of the Divine *l.* that the world exists. Although in a sense an aspect of the Divine, the *l.* often appears as a separate entity, viz., a half-personal EMANATION of God. The concept was appropriated by PHILO in order to bridge the gap between the transcendent God of Judaism and the Divine principle experienced by man. This view of the *l.* as a mediating principle between God and material creation could link up with biblical references to the creative Word of the Lord by which the heavens were made (Ps. 33:6) and with the concept of *memra* (Aram. "word") in TARGUM literature (especially as it appears in *Targum Onkelos*). In Proverbs, Job, and in certain apocryphal books the concept of Divine Wisdom (*ḥokhmah*) has some of the qualities of the *l.* Early Christianity took up the notion of *l.* and in the gospel of John, the *l.* as an eternal, Divine principle is said to have been made flesh in the person of Jesus. This emphasizes the redemptive function of the *l.* as an exclusive vehicle of salvation, rather than its creative or revelatory function. As such it has become a major feature of Christian theology, and this fact possibly contributed to the disappearance of *l.* speculations, together with the whole Philonic tradition, from Jewish thought. In kabbalistic literature concepts similar to that of *l.* reappear in the doctrine of SEPHIROT.

LOST PROPERTY: The finder of l.p. is required to seek out its owner and restore his property to him (Deut. 22:1-3). With the exception of certain articles which lack any identification mark and which their owner would presumably despair (Heb. *yiush*) of finding as soon as he knows they are lost (e.g. scattered coins), advertisement of the found property is to be made (in post-Temple times, this was done in the synagogue or study center). The announcement is to be worded in general terms and the applicant must be able to prove his ownership by describing marks of identification. The lost article is to be kept in good order by the finder until claimed, the finder being considered in law as a bailee. If the owner does not claim the property, the finder is regarded as the owner. Regulations vary according to the kind of property lost and found (e.g. animals whose upkeep involves expense for the finder). The subject is discussed in the talmudic tractate *Bava Metzia.*

LOST TEN TRIBES, see **TRIBES, LOST TEN**

LOTS, FEAST OF, see **PURIM**

LOVE: The natural l. of men and women is frequently referred to in the Bible, (cf. e.g., Gen. 29:18, 20; Deut. 21:5; Judg. 16:4), but the same word (*ahav*) is also applied to non-sensual, moral and spiritual relationships, e.g. between parents and children, between man and his fellow man (Lev. 19:18, 34) and between man and God (Deut. 6:5). It was the allegorical interpretation of erotic l. as spiritual l. which was responsible for the inclusion, or the retention, of the SONG OF SONGS in the biblical canon. The prophets frequently use the image of matrimonial l. to describe the relationship between God and Israel — perhaps none more drastically than the prophet Hosea. In rabbinic literature the idea of the l. of God as a supreme religious value is further developed, and in the Middle Ages it also acquired mystical connotations. According to the Talmud the highest form of service of God is service "out of l." as contrasted with "service out fear" (*Ned.* 31a). The Mishnah (*Avot* 5:19) differentiates between l. "dependent on a motive" which disappears when the motive no longer obtains, and disinterested love which is eternal. The example cited of the former is the l. of Amnon for Tamar, and the latter, David and Jonathan. *Ahavat Yisrael* ("l. of Israel"), an all-embracing love comprehending all Jews, is regarded as a great virtue by the rabbis, and the Midrash reproves several of the greatest figures in the Bible such as Moses (cf. Num. 20:10) and Isaiah (cf. 6:5) for not rising on occasions to the highest level of that all-embracing l. (*Ahavat Yisrael* later became an important ḥasidic concept). L. of one's fellow men is enjoined not only toward Jews (Lev. 19:18), but also toward the stranger (cf. Lev. 19:34; Deut. 10:19). Hillel's dictum (*Avot* 1:12), "Be as the disciples of Aaron, loving peace and pursuing peace" continues, "loving thy fellow creatures and drawing them near to the *Torah*". Some medieval writers imply that l. of God necessarily excludes all l. of created beings, but the main stream of rabbinic tradition eschews such radicalism and holds that in the l. of God the natural forms of l. (between spouses, members of the family, fellow men) are hallowed rather than abolished.

LÖW, LEOPOLD (1811-1875): Hungarian rabbi and scholar; from 1850 rabbi at Szeged. The son of Eleazar L., a noted talmudist and opponent of REFORM, L. became one of the most forceful spokesmen of extreme religious reform and was involved in bitter controversies with the Orthodox. An outstanding preacher, he was the first rabbi to give sermons in Hungarian. He edited a scholarly journal, "*Ben Chananja*", and published important studies in which he sought to show that Judaism as a religion had always developed and never remained stationary.

LUBLIN, MEIR BEN GEDALIAH (known as *Maharam Lublin*; 1558-1616): Codifier and Talmud commentator; head of *yeshivot* in Lublin and Cracow. His novellae *Meir Einei Ḥakhamim*, elucidations of halakhic difficulties raised in the commentaries of Rashi and the *tosaphot*, are printed in many Talmud editions. L. was an independent and original commentator who relied more on later than earlier authorities. In his responsa, he inclined to leniency to assist *agunah* cases and in other matters of personal status.

LUDOMIR, MAID OF (c. 1815-c. 1905): Popular name of Hannah Rachel Werbermacher, the only woman to become a ḥasidic leader. After a severe emotional and spiritual crisis, she adopted the customs of a male *ḥasid*, donning *tallit*, *tephillin*, and *tzitzit*, and she built her own synagogue to which thousands flocked to hear her teaching. She also gained a reputation as a miracle worker. Her reputation declined after her marriage to the *tzaddik* Mordecai of Czernobyl. Toward the end of her life she settled in Palestine.

LUḤOT HA-BERIT, see **TABLETS OF THE LAW**

LULAV (Heb. "sprout"): Rabbinic term for the palm branch, taken together with other vegetable species on the Feast of Tabernacles. As the *l.* is the most conspicuous of the FOUR SPECIES (see Lev. 23:40), the term is used in the benediction to refer to the whole. The *l.* is taken in the hand after the *amidah* of the Morning Service and waved in the air at certain points in the *Hallel* service (except on Sabbaths). It is also carried in the HOSHANOT procession (HAKKAPHOT) and, in the *Sephardi* rite, during the Additional Service. The *l.* with the myrtle and the willow is held in the right hand, the ETROG in the left.

LURIA, ISAAC (known as *Ari*, i.e., the "holy lion"; 1534-1572): Kabbalist in Safed, and founder of a new school of MYSTICISM which exerted a profound influence on the whole Jewish world and formed the theoretical basis for much of late ḥasidic thought. L. was born in Jerusalem; he lived for a time in Cairo, returning to settle in Safed about 1569. He died at an early age, soon becoming a legendary figure in Jewish tradition and literature. He was a talmudic scholar and a highly original mystic who lived an ascetic life and imparted his teachings to a very small circle of disciples among whom were Joseph Ibn Tabul and Ḥayyim VITAL. The latter's notes on his master's teachings were widely circulated after his death, and the Lurianic system was also widely disseminated by the school of the Italian kabbalist Israel SARUK. L.'s ideas are exceedingly complex and difficult. On the one hand his mystic experiences include direct visions and communications with spirits and souls from "other worlds", and on the other hand his theological speculations reveal an extraordinary capacity for imaginative symbolic thinking. According to L. creation became possible by a preceding act of TZIMTZUM — a voluntary "contraction" or withdrawal of God from "Himself into Himself", thereby creating the possibility of existence outside the Divine, including that of evil. The incipient creation was thrown into confusion by the catastrophe of the "breaking of the vessels" (*shevirat ha-kelim*) whereby the primordial light of creation spilled over, as it were, and its sparks fell into lower and even demonic spheres of being. The purpose of history is the healing of this breach in the Divine and cosmic order; hence the concept of TIKKUN ("restoration"), whereby all the fallen sparks and souls are returned to their proper place, is of paramount importance in the Lurianic system. The achievement of the cosmic *tikkun* is identified with the messianic consummation of history. The doctrine of *tikkun* is associated with that of *gilgul* (TRANSMIGRATION OF SOULS). There is a great emphasis on the unique spiritual significance of every human act, since by his acts man fulfills a redemptive rôle. In addition to the elaboration of his doctrines, L. composed a number of hymns, some of which have been included in the prayer books influenced by the ḥasidic tradition.

LURIA, SOLOMON (known as *Maharshal*; c. 1510-1573): Russian talmudist; rabbi of Brest-Litovsk, Ostraha, and, after 1555, Lublin. Despite his great reputation as a scholar, he encountered much opposition because of his independence of mind and incisive criticism. He insisted on recourse to the basic source (i.e., the Talmud) rather than later codes in all halakhic decisions, on a rational understanding of the plain meaning of the talmudic text, and on establishing correct readings of that text. Only a part of his commentary on the Talmud, *Yam shel Shelomoh* ("Solomon's Sea"), has been published, but his brief notes *Ḥokhmat Shelomoh* ("Solomon's Wisdom") are printed in almost every Talmud edition.

LUST, see **YETZER HA-RA**

LUSTRATION, see **ABLUTION**

LUZZATTO, MOSES ḤAYYIM (known as *Ramḥal*; 1707-1747): Italian mystic and poet, born in Padua. He is often, though not very appropriately, called the father of modern Hebrew poetry. L. was an inspired and inspiring personality and soon attracted a circle of fervent disciples and admirers who shared his kabbalistic meditations and messianic expectations. In his states of mystic trance L. heard angelic voices, received celestial messages, and composed kabbalistic works. These, together with the messianic character of his circle, provoked the hostility of many rabbis who had not yet forgotten the disastrous outcome of the activity of the kabbalistic messiah SHABBETAI TZEVI. L. was censured, and forced to promise to abstain from kabbalistic writing, and to render up his manuscripts to the authorities. As rabbinic persecution continued, he left Italy via Frankfort for Amsterdam, where he earned his living as a diamond polisher. It was there that he composed *Mesillat Yesharim* ("Path of Upright Ones"), one of the most beautiful and widely read of Jewish ethical classics. In 1743-4 he went to Palestine and settled in Acre. He and his family perished in the plague of 1747.

LUZZATTO, SAMUEL DAVID (known as *Shadal*; 1800-1865): Italian scholar. L. taught at the Padua Rabbinical College and published studies on Jewish history and literature, as well as on religious philosophy. His commentaries on the Bible are conservative, though not Orthodox, and are opposed to Higher BIBLICAL CRITICISM. In his basic outlook L. was a romantic, and contrasted his idea of a "Judaism of feeling" to the rationalism of Maimonides, as well as to the theosophy of the kabbalists. L. is counted among the fathers of the WISSENSCHAFT DES JUDENTUMS.

LXX, see **SEPTUAGINT**

LYING: Any act of l., even if not taking the more serious forms of FALSE WITNESS or PERJURY, is considered a violation of both a prohibition (Lev. 19:11) and a positive precept (Exod. 23:7), and an offense to the God whose "seal is truth" and of whom it is said that He "lieth not" (I Sam. 15:29; Ps. 89:34-5). According to the rabbis "liars cannot behold the glory of God" (*Sot.* 42a). R. Jonah of Gerona lists the following nine types of lies: — (1) Untruths spoken in the course of business dealings; (2) l. without intending and causing harm; (3) l. with an eye on some future benefit; (4) deliberate falsification of facts heard; (5) promise made with the intention of not keeping it; (6) a promise made and left unfulfilled; (7) causing another to assume that one has done him a favor; (8) priding oneself on qualities one does not possess; and (9) the falsehoods of children who, while not lying deliberately, nonetheless do not speak the truth.

M

MAAMADOT (Heb. "stands"): In the Second Temple Period, those Israelites present in the Temple during the daily sacrifice. Priests, levites, and Israelites were divided into twenty-four groups, each group officiating and participating in the Temple service in weekly turns. Since only a token number of Israelites could be present in Jerusalem, the others whose turn it was to be present celebrated by attendance at special services in their own towns and villages. In memory of Temple times the custom arose of reciting special prayers (called *m.*) at the conclusion of the Morning Service; these are said only by individuals and were never intended for public recitation.

MAARAVOT, see **MAARIV; PIYYUT**

MAARIV (Heb. "who brings on the evening twilight"): Evening Service, also called *arevit*, recited daily after nightfall, and named after one of the opening words of its first prayer; its institution is ascribed (*Ber.* 26b) to the patriarch Jacob (on the basis of Gen. 28:11). Opinions in the Talmud differ as to whether it is obligatory or optional to recite the *M.* AMIDAH; the accepted ruling is that it is optional — unlike in SHAHARIT and MINHAH (which correspond to the two daily communal sacrifices in the Temple). The established custom is nevertheless to recite it daily, though in *M.* — in contrast to all other prayers — the *amidah* is not repeated by the reader. Biblical verses adduced to support a third daily prayer include Ps. 55:18 and Dan. 6:11. *M.* consists of two parts — corresponding to the two main parts of *Shaharit*: The SHEMA and its benedictions, and the *amidah*. The recital of the *Shema* each morning and evening is prescribed by the earliest law (though according to the ancient Palestinian custom only the first two passages were recited at night). The benedictions before and after the *Shema* follow the same scheme as in the morning, though their wording is different; after BAREKHU (preceded by Ps. 78:38 and 20:10), instead of YOTZER there is *maariv aravim* ("Blessed... who brings on the evening twilight"), followed by AHAVAH: after the *Shema* and the GEULLAH, there follows a further benediction, HASHKIVEINU — a typical evening petition for peace and protection during the night. On weekdays another benediction, composed of a collection of Bible verses beginning with Ps. 135:21, is recited in most *Ashkenazi* congregations; it is of post-talmudic origin. The short KADDISH precedes the *amidah*, while the full *kaddish* and ALEINU follow it. On Sabbath eve (when the service is preceded by *kabbalat Shabbat*), the reader recites one single benediction following the *amidah*, containing an abbreviated version of the latter (*magen avot*) and concluding "Blessed... who sanctifies the Sabbath". Otherwise *M.* for Sabbaths and festivals is no different from that of weekdays (except for the *amidah*) in most rites; only the conclusion of *hashkiveinu* has a different wording and is followed (in most congregations) by Bible verses appropriate to the day (e.g. Exod. 31:16-17 for Sabbath). In some *Ashkenazi* congregations, however, it is customary to interpolate on festivals piyyutic portions (called *maaravot*) into each of the benedictions of the *Shema*. On Saturday nights, *M.* is preceded by Psalms 144 and 67 while Psalm 91 is interpolated following the *amidah*.

MAASEH BERESHIT (Heb. "work of creation"): Rabbinic term derived from the first word of the Hebrew Bible (*bereshit* "in the beginning") and designating an esoteric discipline of mystical COSMOGONY AND COSMOLOGY. Essentially an exposition of the first chapter of Genesis, *M.B.* was not to be taught in public, but had to be transmitted from master to disciple "under four eyes" (Mishnah *Hag.* 2:1) because of the danger of gnostic and heretical misunderstanding of the difficult and subtle subject-matter. The rabbinic attitude to the study of *M.B.* is summed up in the saying: "Thou art not allowed to investigate that which is above and that which is below, that which is before (in the ultimate future) and that which is behind (at the beginning of things), but only that which is from Creation on" (*Gen. Rab.* 1). Nevertheless fragmentary remains of teaching on the subject are preserved in the Talmud, Midrashim, and HEIKHALOT literature. MAIMONIDES identified *M.B.* with the physical sciences. See also MAASEH MERKAVAH; MYSTICISM.

MAASEH BOOKS: Yiddish collections of folklore with an ethical content, first appearing in the 15th cent. The sources are talmudic and midrashic *aggadah* (with much additional embellishment), as well as medieval legend of both Jewish and non-

Jewish origin, but in all cases given a religious application.

MAASEH MERKAVAH (Heb. "work of the chariot"): Term designating the principal subject-matter of Jewish MYSTICISM in the Tannaitic and Post-Tannaitic Periods. Essentially an exposition of Ezekiel's vision of the Divine throne-chariot (Ezek. 1), the study and teaching of *M.M.* was restricted by the rabbis even more than that of MAASEH BERESHIT (Mishnah *Ḥag.* 1). The two esoteric disciplines were connected in the sense that, according to the ancient mystical COSMOGONY, the heavens and the sphere of the Divine THRONE were situated "above" the earth and the firmament. In fact, the practitioners of ecstatic *Merkavah* mysticism experienced an ascent of the soul, in which they passed through the various heavenly spheres until they finally beheld the vision of the "chariot" i.e., the Throne of Glory. Much of the *M.M.* tradition is embodied in talmudic and midrashic literature. Maimonides interpreted the term *M.M.* rationalistically as theology.

MAASER, see **TITHE**

MAASER SHENI (Heb. "Second Tithe"): Eighth tractate in the Mishnah order ZERAIM with *gemara* in the Palestinian Talmud; its five chapters deal with the regulations concerning the consumption of the TITHE in Jerusalem or alternatively its "redemption" (see Deut. 14:22-7). See also AGRARIAN LAWS.

MAASEROT (Heb. "Tithes"): Seventh tractate in the Mishnah order ZERAIM, with *gemara* in the Palestinian Talmud. Its five chapters deal with the TITHE given to the levites.

MACCABEES, see **HASMONEANS**

MACCABEES, BOOKS OF THE: Four separate books of the APOCRYPHA. *I Maccabees* is primarily a historical account of the Maccabean revolt, covering the period between 175-135 B.C.E. Written in Hebrew during the latter part of the 2nd cent. B.C.E. from the standpoint of strict legal Judaism and by an ardent admirer of the Maccabeans, this work has been preserved only in a secondary Greek translation. *II Maccabees* is, according to its author, a condensed version of Jason of Cyrene's history of the Maccabean revolt. In contrast to I *Maccabees,* this book has a religious rather than historical aim, and stresses God's miraculous deliverance of His people. Though II *Maccabees* contains additional information on the Maccabean Period it is not generally reliable. It was probably written in Greek (perhaps in Egypt) in the 2nd cent. B.C.E. *III Maccabees* is in no way connected with the history of the Maccabees, but is a Greek work relating the wondrous deliverance of the Temple from the profane hands of Ptolemy Philopater. It goes on to describe Ptolemy's subsequent attempts to destroy the Jewish populace of Alexandria and how his plans were thwarted in each instance until he finally recognized the intervention of the Divinity. This work appears to be by the hand of an Alexandrian Jew who wrote it either in the last cent. B.C.E. or the first cent. C.E. *IV Maccabees* is a philosophical work influenced by Pharisaism and Stoicism; it has no bearing on the Maccabees except that its author illustrates his points by examples taken from II *Maccabees;* it was written in Greek by a Jewish author some time between 100 B.C.E.-100 C.E. See HASMONEANS.

MACHPELAH, CAVE OF: Cave near Hebron. When Sarah died at Hebron, Abraham approached the local dignitaries with a view to buying a plot for her burial. Negotiations took place with Ephron the Hittite who sold the cave of M. to Abraham for 400 silver shekels (Gen. 23). In this cave were also buried the three PATRIARCHS and their wives (except Rachel). In Byzantine times a church was built on the site, later a synagogue; and since the 12th cent., a mosque, with entry generally prohibited to non-Moslems until 1967.

MACROCOSM, see **MICROCOSM**

MAGEN AVOT (Heb. "a shield of our forefathers"): Opening words of an abbreviated form of the seven benedictions of the Friday evening AMIDAH (hence known also as *me'en sheva* "an abstract of the seven benedictions"), recited by the cantor after the *amidah.* It was originally instituted to enable late-comers to conclude their prayers and return home with the other congregants (since synagogues were situated outside towns and it was dangerous to be out alone at night; see Rashi on *Shab.* 24b).

MAGEN DAVID (Heb. "shield of David"): Symbol consisting of two superimposed equilateral triangles, forming a hexagram. It has neither biblical nor talmudic authority and its origin as a Jewish symbol is extremely obscure; though it occurs occasionally in early Jewish synagogues, graves, etc. it is found much more extensively in non-Jewish environments (Roman pavements, churches, etc.). The *m.d.* is mentioned by the 12th cent. Karaite writer Judah Hadassi, but developed into a distinctive and representative Jewish symbol only after the 17th cent. It was adopted by the Zionist Organization at the First Zionist Congress (1897) and subsequently incorporated in the flag of the State of Israel. In Israel a red *m.d.* corresponds to the Red Cross in western countries. The term *m.d.* is earlier than its application to the hexagram and occurs as a designation of God (similar to the expression "shield of Abraham" in the first benediction of the AMIDAH) in the third benediction after the reading of the HAPHTARAH.

MAGGID (Heb.): 1) Popular preacher. Wandering preachers are known to have existed as far back as

11th cent. France and Germany, but the name and institution of *m.* became a characteristic feature of the Russian and Polish communities. From the 17th cent. on, the rabbis preached twice a year only (on the Sabbaths preceding Passover and the Day of Atonement); the preaching throughout the year for purposes of edification, instruction, and repentance was left to the *m.* the larger congregations often appointing a permanent *m.* along with a rabbi (e.g. R. JACOB BEN WOLF KRANTZ, the celebrated *m.* of Dubno). It was mainly by means of wandering preachers that ḤASIDISM was spread in the 18th cent. 2) In mystical literature a technical term for a heavenly agent (voice, angel, or spirit) communicating supernatural illumination to the mystic. Many kabbalists had *maggidim* (pl.), the best-known instance being that of R. Joseph KARO.

MAGIC: The Bible forbids the practice of m.; the prescribed penalty for transgression of the prohibition is death. Its exponents are usually referred to in the feminine and the Talmud infers (*Sanh.* 67a) that it was mostly practiced by women. The most complete list of the various forms of m. is to be found in Deut. 18:10-11. The story of Saul and the witch of Endor (I Sam. 28) illustrates the extent to which m. was practiced in early times, despite the biblical prohibition. The Talmud, however, seems to differentiate between what might be called "black m." and "white m.", depending on the source of the occult powers. Thus while it ascribes, for instance, the acts practiced by Balaam to "black m." (*Sanh.* 106b), it also refers to sorcery which is entirely permitted such as the feat ascribed to R. Ḥanina and R. Oshaiah of creating a three-year-old calf every Sabbath eve through study and application of the mystical "Book of Creation". The statement is quoted to prove that m. deriving from a pure source is permitted. As for the efficacy of m., the generally held opinion was that, though its practice was possible, it was prohibited as "an abomination unto the Lord" (Deut. 18:12). Rationalist thinkers, including Maimonides (*Hilkhot Avodah Zarah* 11:15) denied its efficacy, and regarded all those who believed in it as fools and lacking in faith. Nevertheless a folk belief in m. persisted among Jews until a late date and was stimulated by the KABBALAH (e.g. through AMULETS), while EXORCISM of evil spirits has been practiced up to modern times.

MAGOG, see **GOG AND MAGOG**

MAH NISHTANNAH (Heb. "Wherein is different?"): The opening words of the four questions asked at the Passover *Seder,* usually by the youngest child. Originally the HAGGADAH was recited after the meal, and the questions were prompted by what the child had already observed. The Mishnah (*Pes.* 10:4) reflects both the earlier custom of leaving it to the child's spontaneous curiosity to inquire about the meaning of the *Seder* ceremonies, and the later formalized version of the four questions to which the father replies with the recital of the *Haggadah,* telling the story of the exodus from Egypt.

MAH TOVU (Heb. "How goodly"): Opening words of prayer recited in the *Ashkenazi* ritual upon entering the synagogue. It is composed of biblical verses, all taken from Psalms and mentioning prayer or a house of prayer, the one exception being the quotation from BALAAM "How goodly are thy tents, O Jacob, thy dwellings, O Israel" (Num. 24:5), though this too is interpreted (*Sanh.* 105b) as referring to the synagogue and *bet midrash.* In the *Sephardi* ritual, one verse (Ps. 5:8) is generally said on entering and another (*ibid.*, verse 9) on leaving the synagogue.

MAHAMAD: Western *Sephardi* transliteration of Heb. MAAMAD — originally the representatives of the people who assisted at the daily sacrifice in Second Temple times. In *Sephardi* usage *m.* came to mean the board or governing body of the synagogue elected by the *yeḥidim* ("members").

MAḤLOKET (Heb. "division"): The word can signify both "dissension" and "difference of opinion". The former is naturally deplored by the rabbis, who rule, for instance, that a man coming to a new locality must abide by local custom even if he disagrees with it "lest he cause *m.*" (Mishnah *Pes.* 4:1). On the other hand, genuine difference of opinion, based upon principle, and especially in the elucidation of the meaning of Scripture, is also called *m.* and is used (together with its cognate verb) for those differences of interpretation among the *tannaim* and *amoraim* with which the Talmud is replete. The difference between the two kinds of *m.* is stated in *Avot* 5:20, the classical example of the former being that of Korah against Moses (Num. 16) whereas "*M.* for the sake of heaven" is exemplified by the controversies between HILLEL and SHAMMAI.

MAḤZOR (Heb. "cycle"): Originally the LITURGY of the prayer book, arranged chronologically according to the annual cycle (cf. *M. Vitry, M. Romania,* etc.). In *Ashkenazi* usage *m.* came to mean the festival prayer book (see FESTIVAL PRAYERS) as distinct from the prayer book for ordinary weekdays and Sabbaths (SIDDUR).

MAIMON, ABRAHAM BEN MOSES, see **ABRAHAM BEN MOSES BEN MAIMON**

MAIMONIDES, see **MOSES BEN MAIMON**

MAINTENANCE: According to rabbinic law, a man, upon marriage, assumes obligations to feed, clothe, house, "cure", and "ransom" (namely, redeem from any form of detention) his wife, provide for her burial, and make certain provisions for her children. In accordance with his means a husband must maintain his wife on a scale of living suited to his station (but not inferior to her previous one) and allow her pocket-money and extra indulgence. In exchange for m. the wife must not shirk her domestic duties, and her earnings and chance gains are her husband's. If the husband defaults in m., the wife may borrow on his credit and he must pay; chronic defaulting constitutes grounds for divorce. By blameful conduct a wife forfeits her right to m.

MAJORITY: The Bible ordains "Thou shalt not not follow a multitude to do evil" (Exod. 23:2). The rabbis interpret this homiletically to stress that a m. must be followed to do good or justice e.g. in cases of legal and halakhic decisions where a m. vote was binding. An individual is advised to abandon his opinion in the face of that held by the majority (*Eduy.* 5:7). See DEMOCRACY.

MAJORITY, see **ADULT**

MAKHSHIRIN (Heb. "Predisposings"): Eighth tractate in the Mishnah order *Toharot* with six chapters (to which no *gemara* is extant). It deals with the imparting of ritual impurity to a solid or dry food following contact with an unclean object after the food has been moistened by one of seven liquids.

MAKKOT (Heb. "Stripes"): Fifth tractate (originally the end of the tractate SANHEDRIN) of the Mishnah order *Nezikin,* with *gemara* in both Talmuds. Its 3 chapters deal with the rules of flogging, prescribed as a punishment for certain offenses (Deut. 25:1-3); false witnesses (Deut. 19:15-21); and the CITIES OF REFUGE for unintentional murderers (Num. 35:9-28).

MALACHI: Last of the twelve Minor Prophets. Of unspecified date, but probably approximately contemporaneous with Ezra, he marked the transition between the era of the Prophets and the era generally (though incorrectly) named that of the Scribes. Nothing is known of his personal history — not even the name is certain as M. may be merely an appellation meaning "my messenger". His words were directed against the dishonoring of Temple ritual by the priests, the profanation of marriage, and the oppression of the hireling, the widow, the orphan, and the stranger. M. proclaimed the universal rule of God (1:11) and ultimate vindication of His justice.

MALAKH HA-MAVET (Heb. "Angel of Death"): See ANGELOLOGY.

MALBIM, MEIR LEIBUSH (1809-1879): Rabbinical scholar. He served as rabbi in many communities (including Bucharest, Mohilev, and Koenigsberg) but was opposed by the modernists on account of his Orthodoxy, and by the Orthodox on account of his leaning to HASKALAH. He was prompted to write his Bible commentary *Ha-Torah veha-Mitzvah* ("The *Torah* and the Commandment") in answer to the 1849 Reform Assembly at Brunswick which attacked the authority of the TALMUD and the ORAL LAW. M. drew for his argument on *halakhah, aggadah,* kabbalistic mysticism, philosophy, and ethics, and his exposition is characterized by a pilpulistic approach, seeking the significance of every synonym and parallelism in the Bible. M. strictly opposes the view that the biblical quotations cited by the rabbis in support of their halakhic decisions were merely mnemonic techniques to facilitate the remembering of orally transmitted laws. Much of his commentary is therefore devoted to establishing the logical and philological basis of rabbinic exegesis by attempting to reconstruct rabbinic grammar, penetrate the spirit and nuance of the Hebrew language, and analyze the phraseology of the text of the *Torah.* His other writings include sermons and novellae on the *Shulḥan Arukh.*

MALKHUYYOT (Heb. "sovereignties"): Section of the AMIDAH of the Additional Service of the ROSH HA-SHANAH liturgy, devoted to the theme of God's sovereignty. The theme is expressed by appropriate biblical verses — three each from the Pentateuch, the Prophets, and the Hagiographa, with the concluding verse from the Pentateuch (as laid down in Mishnah *R.H.* 4:6) — ALEINU and a prayer. After *m.*, the SHOPHAR is sounded (except on a Sabbath) — in the *Sephardi* rite during both the silent *amidah* and its repetition by the cantor, in the *Ashkenazi* rite during the latter only.

MALSHIN, see **DENUNCIATION**

MAMZER: Bastard, a child born from a union within the biblically forbidden degrees of propinquity (see INCEST) or of a married woman by a man other than her husband, i.e., a child born out of her ADULTERY. The child of an unmarried mother is not a *m.* according to Jewish law. The Bible states that a *m.* "even to the tenth generation" cannot marry into the Jewish fold (Deut. 23:3). The only legal marriage permitted him is to a freed bondswoman, a convert, or another *m.* (*Kidd.* 4:1). A *m.* nevertheless inherits from his father equally with legitimate children. See also ILLEGITIMACY.

MAN: The two common names in the Bible for man are *adam* and *ish.* The first form generally refers to any member of the human species (as is implied by its original use as the name of the first man) and is etymologically connected with the word for earth (*adamah* — Gen. 1:26). Other names are *enosh* (an archaic form of *ish*) and *gever* which suggests masculine qualities. M. is considered the lord of creation (Gen. 1:28) and is insignificant only when compared to GOD. The contrast between his majesty in one sphere and his insignificance in another is expressed by the Bible: "What is man that Thou art mindful of him, and the son of man that Thou visitest him? Yet Thou hast made him little less than the angels, and hast crowned him with glory and honor. Thou madest him to have dominion over the work of Thy hands and hast put all things under his feet" (Ps. 8:4-6). The creation of m., together with that of other living creatures took place on the sixth day; though placed in the same physical category, his claim to pre-eminence lies in the fact that he was created "after the image and likeness of God" (Gen. 1:26-27). The rabbis emphasized that this distinction is a sign of the special love of God for m.: "Beloved is man, for he was created in the image of God; but it was by special love that it was made known to him that he was created in the image of God" (*Avot* 3:18), i.e., is endowed not only with special dignity but also with the consciousness of his dignity. There is no initial distinction between one m. and another. The rabbis declare that the verse "This is the Book of the Generations of Man" (Gen. 5:1) conveys a "fundamental principle" for the Bible since it teaches the common descent of all mankind. Subsequent formulations and elaborations of the doctrine of m. by hellenistic thinkers, talmudic AGGADAH, medieval philosophy, Kabbalah, and modern writers are generally indebted to contemporary philosophical theories and terminologies. See FALL OF MAN; IMMORTALITY; RESURRECTION; SOUL; YETZER HA-RA.

MAN, SON OF: With one exception, the phrase "son of man" is used in the Bible to convey the idea of an "ordinary man", "a mortal": cf. "God is not a man that He should lie, neither the son of man that He should repent" (Num. 23:19). The phrase is found most extensively in Ezekiel, who applies it to himself 90 times in all. This usage should be correlated with Ezekiel's insistence that he possessed no special gift but was rather chosen by God as one of the people and to be a watchman (chap. 33). The term occurs for the first time in an apocalyptic context in the Book of Daniel, in the vision "Behold, one like the son of man came with the clouds of heaven, and came to the Ancient of Days" (7:13), and hence passed into eschatological usage as a messianic title. As such, it played a great rôle in Christian phraseology; the opposite, rabbinic view, was stated by R. Abbahu in a comment on the aforementioned verse from Numbers: "If a man say 'I am the Lord', he lies; if he says 'I am the son of man' he will repent" (Y. *Taan.* 2:65).

MANASSEH, PRAYER OF: A short, poetic work in Greek, purporting to be the confession of sin and prayer of repentance uttered by Manasseh king of Judah during his captivity in Babylon (cf. II Chron. 33:12). Though the composition is undoubtedly of Jewish origin, it has been preserved only in Christian sources where it is included in the books of the APOCRYPHA. The date of its authorship is uncertain.

MANASSEH BEN ISRAEL (1604-1657): Dutch rabbi. Born of Marrano parents, he went to Amsterdam as a child and was appointed rabbi at the age of 18. Though best known to posterity for those activities which ultimately resulted in the return of the Jews to England, M. was in his time a popular and widely read religious thinker. His *El Conciliador* ("The Conciliator"), written in Spanish, wherein he undertook to resolve biblical inconsistencies and contradictions in accordance with Jewish tradition, won him fame also among Christian biblical scholars and was followed by other works in Spanish and Latin which helped to acquaint Christian readers with Jewish teachings. During his visit to England he published his *Vindiciae Judaeorum* ("The Answer of the Jews", 1656), an apologetic work in reply to Prynne's *Short Demurrer* which opposed the return of the Jews to England. In the *Hope of Israel* (1650) he dealt with the traditions concerning the Lost Ten Tribes, reputed to have been discovered in S. America.

MANNA: Food miraculously provided for the Israelites during their wandering in the wilderness (Exod. 16:4-35). It is described as a thin layer of seedlike substance like hoar frost (Exod. 16:14) or like coriander seed and suitable for varied processing (Num. 11:6-8). A double portion was gathered on each Friday, when for the only time m. remained fresh until the next day (the custom of placing two loaves on the Sabbath eve table has been traced to this historical precedent). Only when the Israelites had crossed the Jordan did m. cease to appear, but as a memorial, a jar of m. was placed in the Sanctuary. Its spiritual significance was explained in the passage "...and fed thee with m. that He might make thee know that man doth not live by bread only but by everything that proceedeth out of the mouth of the Lord..." (Deut. 8:3). The rabbis suggested that m. was created on the first Sabbath eve of creation (*Avot* 5:9).

MANNERS, see **DERELH ERETZ**

MANTLE OF THE LAW, see **ME'IL**

MANUAL OF DISCIPLINE, see **DEAD SEA SCROLLS**

MAOT ḤITTIM (Heb. "wheat money"): Money distributed on the eve of Passover to the poor, enabling them to make the requisite preparations for the festival. The Mishnah and Talmud required this provision for the needy as a communal obligation (known as *kimḥe de-Pisḥah* — "flour for Passover"), and in medieval times *M.Ḥ.* was accepted as a communal tax. Although monetary gifts have largely supplanted gifts in kind, it is still known for communal organizations or individuals to supply those in need with unleavened bread and wine for the festival.

MAOZ TZUR (Heb. "O Fortress, Rock of my salvation"): Hymn sung on Ḥanukkah after the kindling of lights, in the *Ashkenazi* but not the *Sephardi* ritual. The song was composed by Mordecai (possibly 13th cent.), whose name appears in acrostic. Originally intended for the home, it has been also transferred to the synagogue. Its stirring tune, adapted from an old German folk song, forms a fitting accompaniment to its theme of the Jewish people's salvation from the oppression of the Egyptians, Babylonians, Haman, and the Syrian Greeks.

MAPHTIR, see **HAPHTARAH**

MAPPAH (Heb. "cloth"): (a) A binder wound around the *Torah* scroll; (b) Cover, often elaborately decorated, for the reading desk or TEBAH; (c) The name of a commentary on Karo's Shulḥan Arukh by Moses Isserles; it expounds *Ashkenazi* customs and practice.

MAR (Aram. "master"): Honorific title ("sir") given in Babylonia to the EXILARCHS and to some amoraic teachers.

MAR SAMUEL, see **SAMUEL**

MARBITZ TORAH, see **RABBI**

MARḤESHVAN (popularly known as *Ḥeshvan*): Second month in the religious calendar, eighth in the civil (occurring in Oct.-Nov.); known in the Bible as *Bul.* It has 29 or 30 days and its zodiac sign is the scorpion. In Israel, a daily prayer for rain is incorporated in the *amidah* from the 7th of the month until Passover.

MAROR (Heb. "bitter herb"): The regulations for the paschal lamb include the injunction, "With unleavened bread and with bitter herbs shall they eat it" (Exod. 12:8). Originally a condiment eaten with meat, *m.* was invested with symbolic significance as a memorial of the fact that the Egyptians "embittered the lives" of the children of Israel (Exod. 1:14). With the destruction of the Temple the paschal sacrifice ceased, but both unleavened bread and bitter herbs (*maror*) became an integral part of the *Seder* on the first night (in the Diaspora, first two nights) of Passover. The HAGGADAH is to be recited only "when MATZAH and bitter herbs are lying before you", and the *m.* is ceremoniously eaten twice, once with HAROSET and once with *matzah.*

MARRANOS: Crypto-Jews of Spain and Portugal who under the pressure of circumstances outwardly adopted Christianity while in various degrees maintaining Jewish rites and customs in secret. The M. of the Balearic Islands are known as Chuetas. The abusive term (Span. "swine") was applied to the forced converts and their descendants after the anti-Jewish outbreaks which occurred in Spain in 1391 and which were followed by more anti-Jewish campaigns throughout the 15th cent. Thousands of Jews were massacred during 1391, and thousands adopted Christianity in order to escape the fury of the mob. Every successive wave of persecution or discriminatory laws against the Jews during the subsequent century added to the numbers of M. who soon became a socially, economically, and politically prominent group, thereby provoking more resentment and hatred. Although the M. are usually regarded as equivalent to the *anusim* ("forced converts") of rabbinical literature, the identification is not exact from the legal point of view. The only true *anusim,* i.e., those who were given no choice, were the Jews of Portugal who in 1497 were forcibly dragged to the baptismal font after the time limit for their departure from the country had expired and they had been prevented from reaching the coast. M. in general were those who did not make the supreme sacrifice of MARTYRDOM. The majority of M. reconciled themselves to their double life of outwardly practicing the new faith, while retaining a knowledge of their Jewish origin and the observance of many of its customs and laws. Eventually many escaped to more tolerant lands and publicly embraced Judaism. The rabbis generally accepted the viewpoint that M. who continued to observe Jewish customs in secret were not to be regarded as voluntary apostates, and specifically forbade any discrimination against a Marrano who returned to Judaism ruling that despite the passing of a generation, he should be recognized as a Jew by birth and therefore not requiring ritual immersion. It was this group persisting in their Jewish customs, which incurred the fury of the Inquisition when it was established in 1480. The Inquisition had jurisdiction only over M. and not against professing Jews who, never having been Christians, could not be accused of heresy. In the subsequent four centuries tens of thousands of M. both in Spain and Portugal as well as in their overseas possessions were charged with heresy by the Inquisition and went to the stake or suffered confiscation of goods and imprisonment. The *Sephardi* communities of the West were founded mainly by M. escaping from Spanish and Portuguese territories. Those who did not escape gradually assimilated to their environment, although a few groups of M., conscious of their Jewish origins, still seem to exist.

MARRIAGE: Jewish m. is achieved in two distinct stages *Kiddushim* (or *Kiddushin*) and *Nissuim* (or *Nissuin*). The rite of *Kiddushim* creates the binding relationship of husband and wife, while *Nissuim* bestows upon the spouses full conjugal rights and imposes the mutual obligations of married life. Of the three original forms of acquiring a wife by *Kiddushim* — by money, by a written deed, or by cohabitation — only that of money, i.e., any article of value but commonly a simple gold ring, is actually practiced. In the presence of two witnesses the bridegroom hands the bride a ring and says: "Behold thou art consecrated unto me by this ring according to the Law of Moses and Israel". The free consent of both parties is essential to *Kiddushim.* The *Nissuim* ceremony marks the inauguration of full married life, and it is customary for the bride and groom to fast until the ceremony. In some communities, the bride walks seven times around the groom before the ceremony. After the blessings, the bride and groom are isolated in privacy sufficient for actual union to take place. The *ḥuppah* (the bridal canopy) symbolically satisfies this requirement, and the whole period of isolation (*yiḥud*) during *Nissuim* is now also generally symbolic. Prior to *Nissuim* the husband is required to accept in writing all the obligations of a "Jewish husband" to his wife. These include duties during married life and provisions for the wife's maintenance in the event of divorce or widowhood (see DIVORCE; MAINTENANCE). The talmudic rabbis endeavored to protect the wife by forbidding a husband to live with his wife without a m. document — called a KETUBBAH — always in her possession. Though an unlimited interval of time could elapse between the two rites of marriage, in modern times the *Kiddushim,* the reading of the *ketubbah,* and the *Nissuim* take place consecutively as component parts of one wedding ceremony. A series of benedictions is recited — two for the *Kiddushim* and seven for the *Nissuim* — that give emphasis to the religious character of the m. tie, express thanks to God for having implanted His image in the human race and granted the joy of married life, and include prayers for the happiness of the bride and groom and for the restoration of Jerusalem. At the end of the *Kiddushim* ceremony a glass is broken to commemorate the destruction of Jerusalem. As "wine gladdens the heart of man" (Ps. 104:15), both the *Kiddushim* and *Nissuim* ceremonies begin with a cup of wine. The wedding ceremony (Heb. *ḥatunnah*; in Yidd., *ḥassene*) is followed by a m. feast and, in the case of first weddings, by a week of celebrations. Marriages are not celebrated on Sabbaths, holy days, or during seasons associated with historic memories of national tragedy such as the three weeks culminating in *Av* 9 and the period of counting the *Omer* (with the exception of the 33rd day of the *Omer* and several other exceptions which are not uniform among all communities). Parties to a m. must be of marriageable age, namely thirteen and a day for males and a day over twelve and a half for females. In practice the ages were often raised by rabbinic enactment. A minor daughter could be given in marriage by her father or, if fatherless, by her mother or brothers. Males are admonished not to delay m. beyond the age of twenty. Where the degree of relationship between a man and woman disqualifies them as marriage partners according to biblical injunction (Lev. 18, 20), any wedding ceremony performed between them is regarded as incestuous and void from the beginning. M. to the sister of a former wife is forbidden during the latter's lifetime. M. with uncles (but not with aunts) and m. of first cousins are allowed. M. with a brother's former wife is forbidden. However, where a man has died without issue, an obligation is placed on one of his surviving brothers to marry the widow (see LEVIRATE MARRIAGE). The eldest son of such a m. perpetuates his deceased uncle's memory. Should the brother refuse to carry out this obligation he must grant the widow her freedom to marry a stranger. This he does by the rite known as *ḥalitzah,* which is usually resorted to nowadays, in place of the alternative obligatory m. Other marriages that are forbidden, though not void, are between a priest and a divorcee or a proselyte; between a man and his divorcee who had in the meantime been married to another man; between an adulterous divorcee and her paramour; with a widow requiring *ḥalitzah*; and of graver severity, with the issue of an incestuous union. Marriages between Jews and non-Jews are not possible under Jewish law. Fundamental Jewish law does not require monogamy. Rabbi Gershom (11th cent.) prohibited the practice of POLYGAMY among *Ashkenazim.* The recent removal of Jewish communities previously living in countries where polygamy is still legal has almost brought to an end polygamous marriages among Jews. With few exceptions all marriages celebrated in the State of Israel are monogamous. A contemporary problem is that of the religious status of civil m. Certain rabbinical authorities see in such m. a reflection of m. by cohabitation which, though in abeyance since ancient days, is of undisputed validity. Hence these authorities require the dissolution of civil m. by a religious divorce before permitting subsequent remarriage. Rabbinical courts in the State of Israel lean to the view that modern civil m. and the ancient mode of m. by cohabitation are two different things.

The rabbis say that among the first questions asked of a man on the day of judgment are "Did you marry?" and "Have you founded a family?". The Jewish view of the conjugal relation was always a deeply moral and spiritual one. A wife was not looked on solely as a necessary agent for fulfilling the commandment of "be fruitful and multiply" or for safeguarding the proper use of natural instincts. Nor was she merely man's companion.

She was intended for his very completion, and according to the rabbis "a wifeless man is a deficient man". Man is dependent on woman "for joy, for happiness, for blessing". "I have never called my wife 'wife' but 'home'". These and similar sayings of the ancient rabbis shaped the ideals and practice of married life for the people at large. A wife should be both tended and cherished. The husband's obligations for the provision of his wife's material needs are clearly defined. He was, moreover, bade to "love her as himself but honor her more than he honors himself". Assigned by God to fulfill the modest role of man's "help-mate", the Jewish wife is honored as a "woman of valor" whose "price is far above rubies" and whose praises (Prov. 31:10-31) are sung in the Jewish home at the beginning of each Sabbath eve. See MATRIMONY.

MARRIAGE BROKER, see SHADKHAN

MARTYRDOM (in Hebrew idiom *kiddush ha-shem,* i.e., death for "the Sanctification of the Name" of God): The supreme act of faith and final proof of man's willingness to "Love the Lord thy God with all thy soul' (Deut. 6:6) — even though He take thy soul" (*Ber.* 61b). The ideal of m. in Judaism stems from the AKEDAH, God's test of Abraham through a command to offer up his only son Isaac; in that case the supreme sacrifice was not exacted, and essentially m. thus represents the willingness to make such a sacrifice. The martyr "sanctifies the name of God in public" and he is called *kadosh* ("holy one"). On the other hand SUICIDE, the deliberate throwing away of life without reason, is regarded as the most heinous of crimes, and the various regulations in talmudic and post-talmudic literature attempting to establish those instances when m. is justified are designed to show, as far as possible, the frontiers between the two acts. The duty of preserving life is paramount in Judaism, and it is laid down as a general rule that in order to save life one may transgress all the commandments of the *Torah* with the exception of the three cardinal sins of idolatry, shedding of innocent blood, and adultery. In the case of these three, one should endure m. rather than transgress. However in times of religious persecution, when the observance of the Law becomes a public demonstration of religious loyalty, the Jew was obliged to submit to m. rather than transgress even the most insignificant commandment (*Sanh.* 74a-b). During the Middle Ages, mostly in connection with the massacres which accompanied the CRUSADES, whole communities underwent self-immolation at the behest of their leaders rather than submit to baptism (the example of the Jewish community of York in 1190 is outstanding). These tragic episodes are usually regarded as the classic examples of m. in Jewish thought and history, and to this day a prayer is recited on Sabbath for "the holy congregations who laid down their lives for the Sanctification of the Divine name", and *Sephardi* communities recite a special memorial prayer (HASHKAVAH) in memory of the victims of the Inquisition. According to Jewish law, the wife of a martyr may not remarry. See also MARTYRS, THE TEN: MEMORBUCH.

MARTYRS, THE TEN: During the Hadrianic persecution following the defeat of Bar Kokhba in 135 C.E., many *tannaim* suffered martyrdom at the hands of the Romans. They were charged with various "offenses" and executed at different times; e.g. the offense of R. Ḥanina ben Teradyon was the public teaching of the Law and that of Judah ben Bava the conferring of the prohibited ORDINATION (*semikhah*) upon five of his disciples. This gave rise to the legend of the T.M. (as found, for example, in the Midrash of the Ten Martyrs, varying versions of which have been preserved) which turned these individual cases into a tale of a single collective martyrdom. This Midrash occurs in two poetic versions: *Eleh Ezkerah,* incorporated in the penitential prayers of the Day of Atonement; and *Arzei Levanon,* in the elegies for *Av* 9. The latter only enumerates seven martyrs by name; the former, in addition to the two mentioned above, lists Akiva, Ishmael ben Elisha, Ḥutzpit the Interpreter, Yeshevav the Scribe of the Sanhedrin, Eleazar ben Shammua, Hananiah ben Ḥakhinai, Simeon ben Gamaliel, and Eleazar ben Dama.

MASHIAḤ, see MESSIAH

MASHGIAḤ (Heb. "supervisor"): Title of one who performs *hashgaḥah* — religious supervision — particularly in the observance of KASHRUT. Beside being halakhically expert in his particular field, the *m.* must be a God-fearing and trustworthy person. The ignorant, and those motivated solely by financial gain, are precluded from serving as *m.* The term is also applied to the rabbi responsible for moral instruction and guidance in a *yeshivah.*

MASHIV HA-RUAḤ U-MORID HA-GASHEM (Heb. "Who causes the wind to blow and the rain to fall"): Phrase (taken from Mishnah *Taan* 1:1) introduced in all rites before the second benediction of the *amidah.* It is said between *Shemini Atzeret* (when first recited in the prayer for RAIN) and the first day of Passover, after which the *Sephardi* (and Israeli *Ashkenazi*) ritual replaces it with *morid ha-tal* ("who causes the DEW to fall").

MASKIL (Heb. "intelligent", "knowing"): Originally — particularly in *Sephardi* usage — a title of honor for a learned man, the term came to designate, in the 19th cent., a follower of the HASKALAH ("enlightenment") movement; hence it had a pejorative implication when used by the Orthodox.

MASORAH (Heb.): The body of textual notes relating to the "authorized" text of the Hebrew BIBLE. The name probably derives from the root *asar*, meaning "to fetter" (cf. *masoret*, Ezek. 20:37); subsequently it was associated with the verb *masar*, "to hand down", in the sense of "traditional transmission". The M. had its origin in the period of the SOPHERIM and some of its earliest features may date back to the time of EZRA. The purpose of the Masoretes was to safeguard the integrity of the biblical text, and, at the same time, to facilitate its study. Since the Scriptures as a whole, and the Pentateuch in particular, were Divinely inspired and considered as the ultimate source of Jewish doctrine and observance, the slightest change could have far-reaching consequences (cf. *Eruv.* 13a). The labors of the Masoretes extended over many centuries. The Talmud (cf. *Sopherim* 6:4) records that three scrolls of the *Torah*, exhibiting only the slightest textual divergences, were kept in the Temple court to provide a standard copy. A standard text of the extant canon was probably in existence before 200 B.C.E.; nevertheless, for a long time manuscripts continued to show considerable diversity (cf. the DEAD SEA SCROLLS). In order to achieve uniformity, scholars proceeded to compile, first orally and subsequently in writing, numerous notes and rules with which to "fence round" the correct text. Originally, it seems, the Bible was written in continuous script. The Masoretes (including the early *Sopherim*) divided the words, books, sections, paragraphs (large and small), verses, and clauses; they fixed the spelling, pronunciation, and cantillation; they were responsible for the change from the old to the square type of ALPHABET; they prescribed the manner of setting out poetic passages; they determined that some letters be written large (Gen. 1:1) and others small (Lev. 1:1), or suspended (Judg. 18:30), or inverted (Num. 10:35 ff.), or dotted (Deut. 29:28), with a view to drawing attention to textual data or to halakhic and aggadic interpretations. The M. also recorded full and defective spelling as well as orthographic and grammatical abnormalities, and enumerated the letters, words, verses, etc. Even textual emendations were indicated, by the use of the words *kerei* ("to be read") and *ketiv* ("written"), while *sevirin* ("of opinion") pointed out unacceptable alterations; but the text itself was left unchanged, since it was forbidden to add to Holy Writ (Deut. 13:1). Other emendations attributed to the Scribes (TIKKUNEI SOPHERIM) appear to represent midrashic exegesis rather than textual criticism. In the 7th and 8th cents. the creative period came to an end with the introduction of elaborate systems of ACCENTS and vocalization (the Tiberian vowels were sublinear and the Babylonian supralinear). This vocalization reflected the Hebrew pronunciation obtaining at the end of the Talmudic Era, but not necessarily the manner in which the language was spoken in biblical times. For practical purposes, Aaron BEN ASHER brought masoretic activity to a close. Although various schools differed on minor points, and manuscripts long continued to be eclectic, Ben Asher's code (930) was accepted, on Maimonides' recommendation, as the standard text. In the 13th and 14th cents. the scholars who specialized in biblical vocalization were called NAKDANIM ("punctuators"). The division into chapters and the numbering of the verses were taken over from the Latin Bible in the 16th cent. The masoretic notes are placed on the side margins (Minor M.) and on the top and bottom ends of the page (Major M.), while the longer annotations are reserved for the end of the Bible (Final M.). Separate works (e.g. *Okhlah ve-Okhlah; Minḥat Shai*) have also been devoted to the subject. The M. prepared by Jacob Ḥayyim ibn Adonijah for the second Bomberg edition of the Bible (Venice, 1525-26) is regarded, despite its faults, as the *textus receptus*; while Elijah Levita's *Masoret ha-Masoret* (1538) was the first notable attempt at a critical study of the material. In modern times, C.D. Ginsburg and P. Kahle, among others, have made important contributions to knowledge of the M.

MASSEKHET (Heb. [Aram. *masekhta*] "woven fabric"): A tractate of the Mishnah(hence of the Tosephta or Talmud) dealing with a specific subject, and subdivided into chapters. Originally the Mishnah had 60 such tractates, but with the division of tractate *Nezikin* into three BAVAS and the separation of *Makkot* from *Sanhedrin* the number rose to 63. The Palestinian *gemara* has 39, the Babylonian 37 tractates.

MATMID (from Heb. *tamid* "perpetual"): One who persists, particularly in his study of the Talmud. The fervent student who devotes days and nights to talmudic learning has been immortalized in Hebrew literature by Bialik's poem *Ha-Matmid.*

MATRIARCHS: The "full" wives of the three PATRIARCHS — SARAH, REBECCA, LEAH, and RACHEL. Unlike the Patriarchs they are not mentioned in the daily prayers, but prayers for sick females begin "He who blessed our Matriarchs Sarah, Rebecca, etc." and blessings for girls invoke their names. Rabbinic legend wove many stories about the four m., extolling their virtues.

MATRIMONY: Jewish tradition is emphatic in regarding the matrimonial state as a social, moral, and religious ideal, and as a necessary condition of spiritual perfection. CELIBACY was frowned upon, and even ascetic and mystical writers never suggested that the perfect life was possible without m. The rabbis are eloquent in extolling the virtues of the married state, e.g. "He who dwells without a wife dwells without joy, without blessing, without good, and without happiness" (*Yev.* 62b), and "He who has no wife is less than a man" (*ibid.* 67a). MARRIAGE is a religious duty, enjoined by the first biblical commandment "Be fruitful and multiply" (Gen. 1:28); since its purpose is procreation, ten years of childless marriage was regarded as a valid and natural cause for DIVORCE. Although monogamy was envisaged as the ideal state (see Gen. 1 and 2), the Jewish legal system presupposes POLYGAMY. It was not until the time of R. GERSHOM BEN JUDAH (c. 965-1028) that monogamy became legally binding upon *Ashkenazi* Jews, but the decree enforcing it seems to have been the legal formulation of existing practice rather than a reform. It is significant that the ideal relationship between God and Israel is depicted by the biblical prophets as well as in later aggadic literature and liturgical poetry not so much in the language of erotic love (as in the allegorical exegesis of the Song of Songs) as in imagery drawn from the matrimonial bond between husband and wife.

MATTAN TORAH, see **GIVING OF THE LAW; REVELATION**

MATTATHIAS, see **HASMONEANS**

MATZAH (Heb.): Unleavened bread. Since it does not require fermentation of the dough, *m.* can be baked hurriedly, and is therefore specified as the bread prepared for unexpected visitors (cf. Gen. 19:4). For the same reason it became the bread of the EXODUS: "And they baked unleavened cakes of the dough... for it was not leavened, because they were thrust out of Egypt and could not tarry" (Exod. 12:39). As a result, the main ritual in the observance of the Festival of PASSOVER, also called the Festival of *Matzot*, is the prohibition against eating any LEAVEN and the religious duty of eating *m.* The two regulations are not identical; the positive duty of eating *m.* applies only on the first night (the first two nights in the Diaspora) while the prohibition against leaven applies to the whole period of the festival. The principal regulation concerning the baking of *m.* is that the ingredients be only specially prepared flour and cooled water. The addition of salt is prohibited for no clear reason, and the dough must be continuously kneaded and baked with such rapidity as to prevent any possibility of fermentation. Eighteen minutes is usually regarded as the maximum amount of time. Normally it is sufficient to exercise care that the flour does not come into contact with moisture from the time of the grinding of the corn. In view of the positive obligation of eating *m.* on the first night, many very Orthodox Jews bake a specially prepared *m.* for that occasion. This is called *shemurah m.* or *m. shemurah* (i.e. *m.* which has been specially guarded) and the flour for this *m.* is supervised from the time the wheat is harvested. Spiritually and allegorically leaven is regarded as the symbol of impurity and *m.* that of purity (*Ber.* 17a). All the meal-offerings in the Temple were of *m.* and were disqualified in the event of fermentation.

MATZEVAH (Heb.): Monument, originally a raised stone. *Matzevot* (pl.) were known in biblical times as religious monuments (Gen. 28:18-21; for pagan *m.* see Exod. 24:24; Deut. 7:5) and as memorial stones (cf. Josh. 4:20-3). The term came principally to signify a TOMBSTONE.

MAZZAL (Heb.): Literally a "constellation", its common connotation as "fortune" is due to ancient widespread belief in ASTROLOGY and the doctrine that the fate of each person is decided by the constellation under the influence of which he was born. Hence also the talmudic dictum *ein mazzal le-yisrael,* i.e., Israel is ruled directly by Divine Providence and is not subject to fate, or rule of the stars. The word now is completely devoid of any such astrological or superstitious significance. Such fortune can be either good or bad and the Talmud differentiates between *mazzal tov* ("good luck") and *mazzal bish* ("bad luck"). The common usage nowadays however is to limit the full phrase *mazzal tov* to formal expressions of CONGRATULATION and to use the word *m.* as the equivalent of "good luck".

MAZZIK (Heb. "harmer"): A harmful spirit or DEMON; synonymous with *ruaḥ* and *shed,* but expressing more clearly its dangerous nature.

MEAL-OFFERING (Heb. *minḥah*): Although flour, oil, and frankincense form the ingredients of all meal-offerings, different kinds of such offering are specified in the Bible (Lev. 2). They include 1) *Solet* — flour (generally of wheat) mixed with oil; 2) *Maaphei Tanur* — offering baked in the oven in the form of *ḥallot* (loaves) or *rekikin* (thin, wafer-like forms); 3) *Maḥavat* — baked in a flat pan; and 4) *Marḥeshet* — prepared in a deep pot. Only a *kometz* — a handful of the mixture grasped by three fingers — plus the frankincense, were placed on the altar, the remainder being eaten by the priest. The m. was salted (*ibid.* v.13) but was not allowed to leaven. In cases of sin-offering, the frankincense and oil were omitted. A m. always accompanied an animal sacrifice (Num. 15:1-16), but could also be offered independently (one was offered in the Temple each morning and evening).

MEAT: The soft part of the animal, as opposed to the bones, sinews, horns, hoofs, and skin, which are not classed as m. The flesh of fowl and birds is considered m. in rabbinic law but not in the Bible. The flesh of fish or permitted insects is not considered m., nor is blood or forbidden fat. Certain parts of the hide and skin are considered m., though after the hide has been processed and becomes leather it is no longer so considered (*Ḥul.* 122a). M. is mentioned in halakhic discussion in a variety of contexts e.g., in connection with the laws regarding the paschal lamb (Exod. 12:8), sacrificial flesh (*ibid.* 29:33), m. torn from a living animal (see Ever Min Ha-Ḥai), permitted and forbidden animals (Lev. 11), defects which render flesh unfit for consumption (see Terephah), the impurities to which flesh is subject (Deut. 14:21, etc.), flesh from which no benefit may be derived (e.g. Exod. 21:28), the prohibition against cooking m. and milk together (based on Exod. 23:19, etc.), the preparation of the m. of clean animals for consumption, or the determination of what, in popular parlance, is considered m. as far as vows are concerned (*Ned.* 54b). Only m. of clean animals (Lev. 11) that have been ritually slaughtered (see Sheḥitah) may be eaten. Since, however, the Bible forbids the consumption of certain fats and blood (Lev. 3:17), the m., after slaughter, requires porging (see Nikkur) in order to rid it of forbidden fat, and "kashering" in order to rid it of any remaining blood. The "kashering" is effected by soaking the m. in water for a half-hour and then covering it lightly with salt. The salt should not be so fine as to melt on contact with the m. but should be of a fairly coarse variety. If the m. is roasted directly on the flame it does not require soaking and salting. Liver may in fact only be "kashered" in this way — if it is done in any other way it becomes forbidden and renders the utensils used in its preparation also forbidden. M. may not be cooked together with MILK or in utensils in which milk foods have been cooked. Such cooking renders the m. and utensils forbidden and no benefit may be derived from either. Although the Bible says "Thou shalt not seethe a kid in its mother's milk" (Exod. 23:19), all clean animals and fowl are included in the m.-milk prohibition. Milk may not be eaten after the partaking of m.; custom varies as to the period of time which should elapse (see Dietary Laws). M. is considered both a substantial food and one that gives "joy", and is therefore to be eaten on festivals as it is conducive to the joy of the occasion, and on Sabbaths as it contributes to the Sabbath delight. For the same reason, it is not eaten by the mourner on the day of the burial nor during periods of national mourning like the week of the fast of *Av* 9.

MEDICINE: While the Bible expressly mentions "physicians" only in connection with the embalming of Jacob (Gen. 50:2) and King Asa's recourse to them (II Chron. 16:12), it frequently refers to acts of healing, especially by God, "thy Healer" (Exod. 15:26). Both legal and moral literature, from the Bible to the latest rabbinic responsa, contain numerous references to m. Of special historical interest are many passages in the Talmud testifying to some advanced medical knowledge and achievements by the ancient rabbis, several of whom were themselves medical practitioners. Such passages include references to anesthesia ("sleeping drug") for surgical operations (*Bava Metzia* 83b), amputations (*Y. Naz.* 9:5), artificial teeth and limbs (*Shab.* 6:5, 8), caesarian sections on living mothers and subsequent childbirths (*Bekh.* 8:2), and the feasibility of "artificial" human conception (*sine concubito*) by impregnation through sperm in tub-water (*Ḥag.* 15a) — the latter two being by far the first such references known in the history of m. Although occasionally the view was expressed that resort to m. indicated a lack of trust in the will of God who alone "woundeth and healeth" (Deut. 32:39), the rabbis found scriptural sanction for the practice of m. in Exod. 21:19, pointing out that the provision "Thou shalt surely cause him to be healed" implied the right of an injured party to consult a physician and sue his attacker for medical expenses. The legal codes devote chapters to "The Laws of the Physician" — listing his responsibilities, liabilities, and claims to payment (*Yoreh Deah*, 336) to the visiting of and prayers for the sick (*ibid.*, 335), and to the conditions under which the Sabbath and other precepts may be violated to protect life and health (*Oraḥ Ḥayyim* 228-230; 618; etc.), apart from dealing with such medical subjects as ABORTION, CHILDBIRTH, CIRCUMCISION, and STERILIZATION. The extraordinary Jewish proclivity to m. — engendered at least partly by Judaism's this-worldly outlook, its religious concern for life and health, and its rational approach to healing — found fullest expression in the Middle Ages when, it has been estimated, over one half of all best-known Jewish intellectuals — rabbis, philosophers, poets, grammarians, etc. — were physicians by occupation. Since then Jews have continued to play a prominent part in all branches of medical research and practice. Certain medical developments have faced rabbinic law with grave problems, e.g. the need of POST MORTEM autopsies and dissections both for establishing the causes of death and for the training of medical students.

MEGILLAH (Heb. "scroll"): Parchment scrolls were the traditional form of BOOKS until the introduction of bound leaves (codices); letters too were in the form of scrolls. The *Torah* scroll, rolled around two staves at its two ends, is not usually designated a *m.;* the term is applied more specifically to the five short books, Song of Songs, Ruth, Lamentations, Ecclesiastes, and Esther (see SCROLLS, FIVE), the Book of Esther being the *m. par excellence.*

MEGILLAH: Tenth tractate in the Mishnah order *Moed,* with *gemara* in both Talmuds. Its four chapters deal with the rules for reading the Scroll of Esther on PURIM, the synagogal reading of the *Torah,* and rules concerning synagogues in general.

MEGILLAT ESTHER, see **ESTHER; SCROLLS, FIVE**

MEGILLAT TAANIT (Heb. "Scroll of Fast"): An ancient tannaitic chronicle compiled at the beginning of the Common Era and recording thirty-five anniversaries of glorious deeds or joyous events in Jewish history. Public mourning was forbidden on most of these days as was fasting on all of them. The scroll, written in Aramaic with Hebrew additions, is divided into twelve chapters coinciding with the months of the year and enumerating events from different periods of Jewish history. The significance of the dates lapsed in the course of time, and since the 3rd cent. the festival days of *M.T.* have not been distinguished from ordinary days, even as regards fasting and mourning.

MEGILLOT, THE FIVE, see **SCROLLS, THE FIVE**

MEḤITZAH (Heb. "partition"): a) A division in the synagogue separating men from women during public prayer. The practice of separating the sexes during prayer is of ancient origin; in the Temple there was a separate court for women, and the Mishnah (*Suk.* 5:2) records the special care taken to maintain the separation of the sexes, especially during Tabernacles, when the Temple festivities attracted large crowds of worshipers. Reform and Conservative synagogues, and even some Orthodox, dispense with the *m.* b) In *halakhah, m.* is also a technical term for a division (e.g. wall or fence) which creates a separate domain; to be legally effective it must be at least ten handbreadths in height.

ME'IL (Heb. "mantle"): One of the priestly garments (Exod. 28:4). The term came to be used for the often richly embroidered covering of the *Torah* scroll.

ME'ILAH (Heb. "Transgression" — with regard to holy objects, i.e., those belonging or consecrated to the Temple): Eighth tractate in the Mishnah order *Kodashim* with *gemara* in the Babylonian Talmud. Its six chapters deal with the consequences of the profane use of objects consecrated to the sanctuary (see Lev. 5:15-16).

MEIR (2nd cent. C.E.): *Tanna*; pupil of R. Akiva. After the Hadrianic persecution he was a prominent member of the Sanhedrin established at Usha. M. had a brilliant intellect and was said to to have been able to adduce 150 reasons for declaring an object unclean and another 150 for declaring it clean. His teaching formed an important basis for R. Judah Ha-Nasi in his compilation of the MISHNAH so that traditionally a mishnaic teaching, the source of which is not specifically named, was ascribed to M. (*Sanh.* 86a). He was famous for his parables and fables. In his personal character he emerged as a man of humility and resignation. His wife BERURYAH is also quoted as a talmudic authority. Toward the end of his life he left the Sanhedrin as a result of his opposition to the patriarch R. Simeon and his further statements are introduced as the remarks of "the others" (*aḥerim*).

MEIR BAAL HA-NES (Heb. "Meir the Miracle Worker"): Name given to a certain Meir whose tomb is venerated in Tiberias by both *Ashkenazi* and *Sephardi* Jews. Although he is generally identified with the *tanna* R. MEIR, of whom miracles are told in aggadic literature (see BAAL NES), it is doubtful whether the identification is correct The name became widespread only during the 19th cent. when collections throughout the world for charitable causes in Palestine were made with collecting boxes labeled "The Charity of R. Meir Baal Ha-Nes". The custom is first attributed to Israel BAAL SHEM TOV.

MEIR BEN BARUCH OF ROTHENBURG (c. 1220-1293): German rabbinic authority; died in prison in Alsace, having refused to allow the Jewish community to ransom him and thereby encourage future extortion on the part of the rulers. M. was the most influential German rabbi of his day and was one of the last and greatest of the tosaphists. His rulings on Jewish law — which directed the religious trend of German Jewry in the direction of *halakhah* rather than mysticism — were incorporated by his pupil ASHER BEN JEHIEL into his famous code. M. also wrote liturgical poems, the best-known of which, composed after the burning of the Talmud in Paris, became part of the liturgy for *Av* 9.

MEIR BEN GEDALIAH OF LUBLIN, see **LUBLIN, MEIR**

MEIR BEN SAMUEL (known as *Ram*; 11th-12th cents.): French tosaphist; son-in-law of Rashi and father of the tosaphists Isaac Samuel ben Meir, and *Rabbenu* Tam. M. established a distinguished acedemy at Ramerupt and was one of the founders of the school of tosaphists (see TOSAPHOT).

MEIRI, MENAHEM (c. 1249-c. 1310): Talmudist in Perpignan, S. France. Both as a theological thinker and as a halakhist he gave proof of independence of mind and a liberal outlook, and he opposed the condemnation of the study of philosophy by many rabbis during the controversy about the works of Maimonides. His rationalistic outlook appears in his denial of the existence of evil spirits and of the efficacy of amulets or astrology. His works are distinguished by their method and logic.

MEKHILTA (Aram. "measure" i.e., form or rule for deducing the *halakhah* from Scripture): Tannaitic Midrash on the latter part of Exodus, emanating from the school of R. ISHMAEL. It consists of a mainly halakhic commentary on Exod. 12-23:19 and concludes with two sections on the Sabbath (related to Exod. 31 and 35). The original work was more extensive than the version that has survived. Fragments of another *M.* on Exodus, deriving from the school of R. SIMEON BAR YOḤAI, have been preserved in the recently discovered *Midrash ha-Gadol.* See MIDRASHIC LITERATURE.

MELAMMED (Heb.): A teacher, usually a teacher of smaller children (*m. dardekei* or *m. tinokot*). The Talmud stresses his importance. In the course of time the term came to have a certain derogatory meaning, being applied to those in the lowest category of the teaching profession.

MELAVVEH MALKAH (Heb. "accompanying the Queen" i.e., the Sabbath): A festive board conducted at the termination of the Sabbath and lasting as long as possible in order to retain the Sabbath atmosphere after its conclusion. Just as the Sabbath is welcomed in song as a bride and as a queen (the *Sephardi* version of LEKHAH DODI, based on the Talmud, ends "Come, O bride, come O Sabbath Queen"), so it is also solemnly bidden farewell. Kabbalistic and ḥasidic practice (based on the belief that at the close of the Sabbath wicked souls return to Gehinnom and Sabbath angels to heaven) enhanced the observance of the custom. Authority for the *m.m.* meal is found in the Talmud (*Shab.* 119b) where R. Ḥanina enjoins laying the table on Sabbath night even if one is not hungry. Special ZEMIROT have been composed for this celebration, of which the most important is in praise of the prophet Elijah who, according to a Midrash, sits on this night under the Tree of Life and records the merits of those who have faithfully observed the Sabbath.

MELIḤAH (Heb. "salting"): See MEAT.

MEMORBUCH (Ger. "memorial book"): Martyrology containing a list of the countries and localities in which massacres took place during the Middle Ages, together with the names of the martyrs (usually confined to scholars and communal leaders) who lost their lives on those occasions. They were solemnly read out in many European synagogues on all occasions upon which the memorial prayer for the dead was recited. The word is a translation of a phrase in Mal. 3:16.

MEMORIAL SERVICE (also called *mazkir* or *yizkor*): A M.S., in which prayers are offered for the repose of the dead is customary in the *Ashkenazi* rite on the last days of the three pilgrimage festivals and the Day of Atonement. It consists of brief prayers beginning *yizkor* ("May God remember...") and EL MALE RAḤAMIM ("God who is full of compassion..."), in which each individual may insert the names of his departed relations. It is recited after the READING OF THE LAW, before the scrolls are returned to the Ark. Though only of late medieval origin and not common to all rites, the M.S. has become in the popular mind one of the most important parts of the liturgy. It is unknown among the *Sephardi* communities, where a short memorial prayer (*Hashkavah*) for deceased relatives can be offered by those called up to the *Torah*.

MEMRA, see **LOGOS**

MENAḤEM AV, see **AV**

MENAHEM MENDEL OF RYMANOV (d. 1815): Ḥasidic rabbi in Galicia. Disciple and successor of R. ELIMELECH OF LIZENSK, he lived a life of poverty and ascetic mortification, and had a reputation as a healer of the sick and a clairvoyant. He believed the Napoleonic wars to be the War of Gog and Magog heralding the advent of the Messiah.

MENAHEM MENDEL OF PRZEMYSLANY (d. 1772): Ḥasidic rabbi, disciple of the BAAL SHEM TOV. In 1764 he settled with a group of followers in Tiberias; his example stimulated other ḥasidic groups to go to the Holy Land. He emphasized contemplative prayer and is noted for the saying "May I be vouchsafed to pray one genuine prayer in my life".

MENAHEM MENDEL OF VITEBSK (1730-1788): Ḥasidic rabbi in Russia. A disciple of R. DOV BER OF MEZHIRICH, he traveled to Vilna together with R. SHNEOUR ZALMAN of Lyady in order to represent the ḥasidic movement to the Gaon ELIJAH BEN SOLOMON and dissuade him from excommunicating its adherents, but Elijah refused to receive them. In 1777, *M.M.* went to Palestine with 300 followers, settled in Safed and subsequently in Tiberias, and encouraged others to follow his example. His doctrine emphasized the omnipresence of God, and hence the possibility of communing with God and redeeming the SHEKHINAH inherent in all things.

MENAHEM NAHUM OF CHERNOBYL (1730-1789): Ḥasidic rabbi in Russia, founder of a noted dynasty of TZADDIKIM. At first a practitioner of severe ascetic mortifications, he later became a disciple of the BAAL SHEM TOV and preached Ḥasidism in Russia and the Ukraine. His teaching emphasizes DEVEKUT (mystical communion with God) and the importance of the TZADDIK as mediator between the ordinary believer and God.

MENAḤOT (Heb. "Meal-Offerings"): Second tractate in the Mishnah order *Kodashim* with *gemara* in the Babylonian Talmud. Its thirteen chapters deal with the rules of the MEAL-OFFERING (Lev. 2:1-14; 5:11-13) and similar offerings (e.g. the SHEWBREAD, Lev. 24:5-9 and the two loaves of *Shavuot*, Lev. 23:17) as well as with other ceremonial laws (e.g. TZITZIT and TEPHILLIN).

MENAKKER, see **NIKKUR**

MENDELSSOHN, MOSES (1729-1786): German philosopher, exegete, and translator of the Bible. Upon their emergence from the ghetto at the end of the 18th cent., the Jews of Europe faced the task of reconciling their traditional faith with the prevailing concepts of the Enlightenment. M. was a pioneer in accomplishing this transition from the ghetto to the new world; his career inaugurated the modern era in Judaism, and also adumbrated its peculiar problems. He both identified himself with the nation in which he lived and insisted on loyalty to traditional Judaism. His interpretation of Judaism, elaborated chiefly in his book *Jerusalem*, exerted a profound influence on the future development of Jewish thought. The Jewish religion, according to M., has no dogmas or articles of faith; its spirit is "freedom in doctrine and conformity in action". Judaism consists of ceremonial laws which are continuous, immutable, and eternally valid. Even if these laws are opaque to speculative reason, they have preserved the Jewish community and ensured the continuation of its corporate life. And though these laws can no longer be enforced by a theocratic state, Jews are morally obligated to live by them without reservation or equivocation. The doctrines and ethical teachings of Judaism are those of "reason", and hence universal. Religion must forego coercive methods and confine itself to instructing the ignorant, persuading the faltering, and comforting the penitent. M.'s views were attacked by Christians, chiefly Hamann and Lavater. The former maintained that if Judaism has no dogmas but only laws, it was no religion but only a political system; the latter challenged M. either to refute the truths of Christianity or embrace it. His Jewish detractors reproached him for seeking inspiration from non-Jewish sources, for contracting Judaism into a mere set of observances, for his lack of historical sense, and his denial of Jewish nationalism. Yet, M.'s fundamental principle, that Judaism is only a "religion", and loyalty to it compatible with an identification with the national state, was accepted by the three schools of religious thought that arose in the 19th cent. — the Neo-Orthodox (S. R. Hirsch), the radical Reformers (A. Geiger), and the "Conservatives" (Z. Frankel). In his own time M. was considered equal or even superior to Kant as a philosopher. His significance for Judaism lies in the fact that he marks a turning point in Jewish history. He roused his coreligionists from their mental apathy, elevated their mental state, quickened their sense of the beautiful, imbued them with a desire of culture and helped to abrogate anti-Jewish laws. With his translation of the Bible into German and his Hebrew commentary (*Biur*) M. also founded a new school of biblical exegetes (*Biurists*).

MENORAH (Heb. "candelabrum"): There are two candelabra of religious significance, the seven-branched *m.* of the Temple, and the later eight-branched one (with an additional socket for the "server") used at ḤANUKKAH (in modern usage called a *ḥanukkiyyah*). The Temple *m.*, described in Exod. 33:17 ff., was made by Bezalel for the Sanctuary in the wilderness and was later transferred to the Temple (I Kings 7:49). The Arch of Titus in Rome depicts what purports to be the *m.* of the Second Temple. Its base consists of rectangular squares, but recent research has proved almost conclusively that this is an imaginative reconstruction since the Temple *m.* stood on three legs. The Temple *m.* had to be carved out of a solid block of gold and its reproduction or use outside the Temple was forbidden. The seven-branched *m.* became one of the most familiar Jewish symbols and is frequently found in synagogue decorations, tombs, etc., from the 1st cent. C.E. on. In Kabbalah, the *m.* symbolized the tree of life and its seven branches were held to represent the planets, the firmaments, and the days of creation. The *Ḥanukkah* candelabrum was modeled after the tradition of the Temple *m.*, and its fashioning gave opportunity for considerable artistic embellishment and variety.

MENSTRUATION, see **NIDDAH**

MERCY, see **COMPASSION**

MERITS, DOCTRINE OF: The doctrine that by performing those works commanded by and pleasing to God ("meritorious works"), a man may obtain Divine favor which benefits not only him but also others (his descendants, his city or people, even the world). Merit (*zekhut*) is not negative (avoidance of sin) but positive; God "wanted to enable Israel to obtain merits, therefore He gave many laws and commandments" (*Lev. Rab.* 31). The conception of solidarity that underlies the d. of m. also implies, albeit to a lesser degree, a doctrine of demerits: the consequence of sin may fall not only on the sinner but on others as well.

MERITS OF THE FATHERS (Heb. *zekhut avot*): The traditional doctrine of MERITS emphasizes that the pious deeds of parent secure blessings for their descendants too. Rabbinic *aggadah* and liturgical texts accord a unique place in this respect to the lasting merit of the PATRIARCHS Abraham, Isaac, and Jacob, though the view was also expressed that even their merits were not limitless (*Shab.* 55a). R. TAM (*Tosaphot in loco*) held that even if the m. of the f. could be exhausted, God's COVENANT with them was unbounded.

MERKAVAH, see **MAASEH MERKAVAH**

MESHULLAḤ (Heb. "emissary"): Emissary sent by rabbinical academies to distant lands to collect funds for the upkeep of these institutions. *Meshullaḥim* (pl.) have been common whenever a Jewish dispersion has existed far removed from the centers of learning, as in the following three distinct periods: (1) The *meshullaḥim* sent by the Babylonian academies of Sura and Pumbedita during the later Gaonic Period when Jewish communities sprang up in all countries of the Mediterranean littoral; (2) Emissaries sent by the *yeshivot* and *kolelim* in the Holy Land from the 16th cent. on, usually referred to as *shadarim* (SHADAR from the initials of *shelihei de-raḥmana* "emissaries of the All-Merciful"); (3) *Meshullaḥim* sent by the *yeshivot* of E. Europe to the lands of the *Ashkenazi* dispersion in the 19th and 20th cents. Some of these emissaries were men of great learning and played a rôle in the dissemination of Jewish culture.

MESHUMMAD, see **MUMAR**

MESIRAH, see **DENUNCIATION**

MESIVTA, see **METIVTA**

MESSIAH: The eschatological king who is to rule over Israel at the end of days. The word "M." is derived from the Hebrew *mashiaḥ* (literally "anointed") which, in biblical usage refers to any person charged with a Divine office (e.g. kings, priests, prophets); once it is even applied to a gentile king, Cyrus of Persia (Is. 45:1). In the specifically eschatological passages of the Bible, the word "M." does not occur at all, and it was only in the course of the later development of Jewish ESCHATOLOGY, that "M." became a technical term for the long-awaited, Divinely chosen king of the Davidic line who would rule over a new golden age. The prophets, in their unsparing criticism of specific monarchs, had occasionally compared them with the ideal figure of a Divinely ordained, righteous king. In post-exilic eschatological thought this image of an ideal monarch took on new meaning. The messianic king would not be simply another "anointed" ruler, but "the anointed" *par excellence* who would destroy the enemies of Israel and establish a paradise-like reign of peace and prosperity. After the return of the Babylonian exiles, messianic hopes were centered on ZERUBBABEL, a descendant of David, but these expectations were not realized. Despite its disappointment the Jewish nation continued to cherish the messianic hope. The Maccabean uprising against the Seleucid policy of enforced Hellenization had messianic overtones (cf. the Book of DANIEL). The growth of an acute-eschatological movement within Palestinian Jewry during the last two centuries B.C.E. gave rise to a number of messianic sects. The popular concept of the M. — the eschatological ruler from the line of David — was that adopted by the Pharisees and subsequently by what has been termed "normative Judaism" in general, but it was by no means the only messianic concept current in that period. The adherents of the Dead Sea Community (cf. DEAD SEA SCROLLS) awaited two messiahs: together with and superior to the Davidic king, a messianic High Priest was expected. In other circles, faith was placed in a transcendental deliverer, the "SON OF MAN", an expression which was given an eschatological connotation in the Book of Daniel and was further developed in the "Parables" of the Book of ENOCH. This particular concept seems to have played an important rôle in the formation of JESUS' messianic ideology. The Pseudepigrapha of this period abound in messianic descriptions and Josephus reports the existence of several messianic groups, some of which are also mentioned in the New Testament. Many of those Jewish patriots who participated in the Great Revolt against Rome (66-70 C.E.) believed themselves to be fighting in the great eschatological battle which was to be followed by the reign of the M. Even after the ensuing fall of Jerusalem and the destruction of the Temple, messianic expectations did not die out; this terrrible disaster was thought to be one of the messianic "birth-pangs". In both the revolt of 115-117 and the Bar Kokhba uprising (132-135) messianic speculations influenced the insurgents. Bar Kokhba was regarded as the M. by R. Akiva himself and after the fall of Betar, Akiva's disciples were convinced that the brutal retaliatory measures of the Romans could be nothing other than the dark and terrible period preceding the advent of the M. Some time after this national desaster there arose the concept of a warrior M. — the M. ben Joseph — who was to die on the eschatological battlefield and only thereafter was the Davidic M. to appear on the scene. By the fourth generation of the *tannaim,* messianic belief no longer played such a dominant rôle; it had become the subject of scholarly rabbinical speculation and of faith in an ultimate redemption rather than an impassioned call to immediate revolt. Nonetheless, in times of persecution or major crisis messianic hopes broke out anew (see MESSIAHS, FALSE). The disintegration of the Persian Empire and the dwindling of Byzantine might before the Arab invaders in the 7th cent. occasioned the appearance of several pseudo-messiahs in the East. The following century witnessed a resurgence of messianic hope among the followers of Serene in Syria and Abu Issa Al-Isfahani in Persia. The excitement evoked by the Crusades in Europe and Asia Minor also gripped the Jewish communities of the Diaspora who were all too often the victims of the crusading spirit. During the 11th and 12th cents. a wave of pseudo-messiahs appeared in Europe, particularly in France and Spain. During the First Crusade (1096-1099) messianic hopes rose to a fever pitch among the Jews in the Byzantine Empire and their excitement was shared throughout Europe. The pseudo-m. David Alroy, a leader of a messianic movement in Persia and Kurdistan in the 12th cent. saw in the Crusades a portent of messianic fulfillment. In the same century Maimonides, writing from Egypt to the Jews of Yemen, warned against uncritical messianic enthusiasm, while reaffirming belief in the M. The expulsion from Spain and the persecutions inflicted on the Jews by the Spanish Inquisition called forth renewed hope in the imminent advent of the M. A number of messianic claimants appeared and at times gained some following, but none made as large an impact as SHABBETAI TZEVI (1626-1676). Though the rabbinate was divided in its opinion of him, he fully captured the imagination of the masses. Even after his conversion to Islam, he retained a considerable following. Though several other pseudo-messiahs subsequently appeared, one as late as the 19th cent., messianic enthusiasm never reattained its Sabbataian zenith. The general disillusionment which followed Shabbetai Tzevi's conversion and the growing force of the *Haskalah* among European Jewry both served to dampen excessive messianic zeal. But in different — and partly secularized — forms the messianic idea remained a central factor in Jewish faith and played a role in the development of Zionism. Reform Judaism has tended to reject the concept of a personal M. substituting for it the optimistic faith in the advent of a messianic era with "the unity of all men as the children of God in the confession of the One and Sole God" (Philadelphia program, 1869) or "the establishment of the kingdom of truth, justice, and peace" (Pittsburgh program, 1885).

MESSIAHS, FALSE: The conviction that the MESSIAH has not yet arrived but that redemption is still to come has rendered the Jew particularly prone to acute messianic expectation, especially in times of overwhelming persecution and hardship. Consequently, claimants to the messianic rôle were frequently able to recruit support until circumstances discredited their claims. Whether BAR KOKHBA, the warrior hero of the war of 132-135 C.E., claimed to be the Messiah is doubtful. According to the Talmud (Y. *Taan.* 68d), R. Akiva said of him "This is the King Messiah"; according to another passage (*Sanh.* 93b) he made the claim himself, although in his recently discovered letters he signs himself only NASI (prince or chief). Among the more notable false messiahs were the 8th cent. Persian, Abu Issa Al-Isfahani, who led his 10,000 followers into a futile battle against Abbasid forces; and in the 12th cent. David Alroy of Kurdistan, who proclaimed himself the Messiah and staged a revolt against the Seljuk sultan, promising his supporters to recapture Jerusalem where he would establish an independent kingdom. In the 16th cent., David Reubeni, claiming to be the brother of the ruler of an independent kingdom of Jews from the Ten Tribes at Chaibar, persuaded both the Pope and King Manuel of Portugal of the genuineness of his mission and caused some messianic agitation, though he did not himself claim to be the Messiah. The most famous and most widely accepted of the f. m. was SHABBETAI TZEVI of Smyrna, who set the Jewish world of the 17th cent. agog. His acceptance of Islam to save his own life disillusioned most of his followers, with the exception of certain groups of enthusiasts (such as the DONMEH) who continued to believe in him and followed his example. In the 18th cent. Jacob FRANK stood at the head of an offshoot of this movement in Poland and preached a grossly antinomian and morally corrupt messianism.

METATRON (etymology uncertain): Name of an angel who, though not mentioned in Scripture, plays a dominant rôle in both early and later ANGELOLOGY and mysticism (MAASEH MERKAVAH, KABBALAH). He is variously identified with the Prince of the World, the Angel of the Presence, and ENOCH after his ascent to heaven, and is described as the celestial scribe, the "lesser YHVH", or one "whose name is like that of his Master (i.e., God)". M. is also reminiscent in some ways of PHILO's LOGOS, and this analogy, as well as the frequently mentioned likeness of M. to his Master, may account for the rabbis' explanation of ELISHA BEN AVUYAH's mystical (gnostic?) apostasy as stemming from a vision in which he beheld M. (*Ḥag.* 15a).

METEMPSYCHOSIS, see **TRANSMIGRATION OF SOULS**

METIVTA: Aramaic form of *yeshivah* (ACADEMY), the two words being identical and interchangeable. Hence also the customary abbreviation *Ram* (i.e., the initials of *rosh* ["head"] *metivta* = Heb. *rosh yeshivah*) as the designation of a head of a rabbinic school.

METURGEMAN (Aram. "interpreter"): (1) In early times, the translator of the Law and Prophets when these were read in public. His translation accompanied the reading, verse by verse, and consisted of the officially approved Aramaic version of the Bible (see TARGUM). The office of *m.* is still extant among Yemenite Jews. (2) Spokesman of the talmudic teachers when they lectured in public. The teacher would speak quietly to the *m.* who then explained the discourse to the audience in a loud voice.

MEZUMMAN (Heb.): Invitation to recite Grace After Meals in the presence of three or more adult male Jews.

MEZUZAH (Heb. "doorpost"): Small parchment on which are inscribed the first two paragraphs of the *Shema* (Deut. 6:4-9; 11:13-21). It is rolled tightly and placed in a small case through an aperture of which can be seen the word *Shaddai* ("Almighty") inscribed on the back of the scroll The *m.* is affixed to doorposts in the Jewish home in accordance with the precept in Deut. 6:9. Writing out a *m.* may be undertaken only by a qualified scribe and is to be executed with the same care taken in the writing of a Scroll of the Law. The *m.* is nailed in a sloping position on the upper righthand doorpost of the entry to the home and each of its living rooms. A special blessing is recited before securing it in position. Its purpose has been described as the sanctification of the home by the continual reminder of Divine omnipresence. Among pious Jews, it became customary to kiss the *m.* on entering or leaving a room.

MI SHE-BERAKH (Heb. "He who blessed"): Opening words of synagogal prayer in which God's blessing is requested for any individual(s). Its recitation (in various forms) is customary in most rites after the Reading of the Law; it is offered by the reader for each person called to the reading, after which that person may request prayers to be added in honor of his relations or anyone else he cares to name. The prayer frequently states that the one requesting it has vowed a sum for charity. Special formulae are introduced for sick people, women who have just given birth, and babies at the time of their circumcision.

MICAH: Sixth of the Minor Prophets. He began to preach shortly before the fall of Samaria, being a later contemporary of Hosea and Isaiah. Unlike the latter he did not hail from a princely estate but from a peasant background and referred to the oppressed poor as "my people". He also witnessed Sennacherib's siege of Jerusalem and ascribed the punishment to the moral turpitude of his generation. To the exponents of an empty ritual he gave the classic retort: "He hath shewed thee, O man, what is good; and what doth the Lord require of thee, but to do justly, and to love mercy, and to walk humbly with thy God" (6:8).

MICHAEL (Heb. literally "Who is like unto God?"): Prince of angels (Dan. 10:13). One of the four archangels, he figures prominently in apocryphal and aggadic literature, where he is variously described as God's viceregent, celestial high priest, protector and advocate of Israel (*Yoma* 77a), and keeper of the heavenly keys. As Satan's main adversary he also has certain eschatological functions (e.g. calling the dead to the resurrection). M. is also prominent in Christian and Moslem legend.

MICROCOSM: The view that man represented an epitome or "miniature version" of the larger universe was widely held in the Middle Ages, and correspondences were asserted between the human organism, the cosmos, and even the Deity in whose image man was said to be fashioned. Hence by knowing himself, man may also arrive at a better knowledge of God. The microcosm-macrocosm analogy was elaborated in midrashic and philosophical works, of which Joseph Ibn Tzaddik's *Olam Katon* (i.e., microcosm) is one of the best-known. The m. idea was developed by the kabbalists in terms of their doctrine of sephirot. See also Adam Kadmon.

MIDDOT (Heb. "measurements", "rules", "[moral] qualities"): In rabbinic Hebrew, the hermeneutical rules (see Hermeneutics).

MIDDOT (Heb. "Measurements"): Tenth tractate in the Mishnah order of *Kodashim* with no *gemara* in the Talmud. It describes the design, measurements, appointments, and organization of the Second Temple.

MIDDOT, THIRTEEN, see **THIRTEEN ATTRIBUTES OF GOD**

MIDNIGHT TIKKUN, see **TIKKUN (ḤATZOT)**

MIDRASH: The discovery of meanings other than literal in the Bible. The word "Midrash", derived from the root *darash* meaning "to inquire" or "investigate", denotes that literature which interprets Scripture in order to extract its full implications and meaning. These interpretations usually formed a response to the need of a particular age or environment. The term "M." is found in the Bible (cf. I Chron. 13:22; 24:27). It is supposed by Jewish tradition that some kind of M., in the form of a commentary on Scripture — particularly its legal portions — must have existed from earliest times. Indeed it would seem to be required by the Written Law, which often omits the details of those observances covered by some general command or prohibition. Thus the method of slaughtering animals or the kinds of work forbidden on the Sabbath are never specified. In such cases Scripture often uses the phrase "as the Lord commanded Moses" to indicate the details of the law. This would suggest the existence of a more detailed legislation, completing and complementing the written word of Scripture. Like other branches of the Oral Law, therefore, M. goes back to very early origins. It appears that with the Return from Babylon, the sopherim headed by Ezra, who were both scribes and scholars, began to study the traditional interpretation of the Written Law and apply it to the everyday needs of the community (cf. Ezra 7:6, 10-11). They seem to have continued in this function up to the time of Simeon Ha-Tzaddik who was both the last of the *sopherim* and the first of the teachers of the Mishnah. Later, M. was committed to writing. The very early Midrashim originated with the same teachers whose sayings are preserved in the Mishnah, and they are for the most part halakhic Midrashim, i.e., they deal with the Mosaic Law. A second type of M., the Midrash Aggadah, expounds the non-legal parts of Scripture, and while traces of this genre are also to be found early, its great period of efflorescence began after the Mishnaic Era and continued as late as the 12th and 13th cents. Aggadic Midrashim range over the whole of Scripture and their subject matter includes theology, ethical teaching, exhortation, popular philosophy, imaginative exposition, legend, allegory, animal fables, etc. MIDRASHIC LITERATURE contains some of the most distinctive features of Rabbinic Judaism. It was a way of delving more deeply than the literal meaning of the word of Scripture, and a method of linking the various parts of the Bible together by the discovery of typological patterns, verbal echoes, and rhythms of repetition. This last function is expressed in the phrase "the happenings of the Fathers are a sign to their posterity". Thus, the exile of Jacob and his flight from his brother Esau became a symbol for all subsequent Jewish exile and wandering both in the Biblical and Post-Biblical Periods. The aggadic Midrashim in particular were an instrument for imparting contemporary relevance to biblical events. In this respect the function of M. is the opposite of PESHAT, which aims rather at reconstructing the literal meaning of Scripture, its local setting, and original system of reference. The balance between M. and *peshat* is basic to the rabbinic mentality in its approach to Scripture. Whereas the *peshat* performed its rigorous office of research into the exact meaning of Scripture as far as the available historical and lexicographical knowledge allowed, M. made possible a vivid application of the scriptural word to a later situation or a later system of ideas. It operated according to certain HERMENEUTIC LAWS of interpretation which were, however, never strictly applied, and frequently the rabbis allowed themselves to indulge in far-fetched interpretations and narratives which were clearly intended to delight the fancy as well as to instruct.

MIDRASH RABBAH: A MIDRASH on the Pentateuch and the Five SCROLLS, containing mostly AGGADAH, with the exception of the Midrash on the Book of Numbers, where about a third consists of HALAKHAH. It originated in Palestine and incorporates interpretive dissertations by aggadic teachers from various periods. *Exodus*, *Numbers*, and *Deuteronomy Rabbah* are of much later date than *Genesis* and *Leviticus Rabbah*, the first two having been compiled (according to some authorities) as late as the 12th cent.; they are never quoted by Nathan Ben Jehiel, Rashi, or Maimonides, who otherwise frequently quoted *Genesis* and *Leviticus Rabbah* (as well as the *M.R.* on the Five Scrolls). Some scholars attribute the authorship of *Genesis Rabbah* to R. Hoshaya Rabbah (hence its name) but the work must be later as several of its sayings are attributed to rabbis who lived many generations after Hoshaya. The language of *Genesis Rabbah* is generally Hebrew, but similes, proverbs, and some stories are in Aramaic. *Leviticus Rabbah* is not a commentary on every verse of the Book of Leviticus but a collection of homilies, as is *Deuteronomy Rabbah*, where each section begins with *halakhah*. *M.R.* on the Five Scrolls — Ecclesiastes, Lamentations, Song of Songs (also called *Midrash Ḥasit*), Ruth, and Esther — are classed among the more ancient Midrashim. The oldest of these is *Ruth Rabbah*, which is written in the style of Palestinian *aggadot* and also includes Babylonian aggadic traditions. *Lamentations Rabbah* begins with a long introduction containing 36 sections (corresponding to the numerical value of *Eikhah*, the first word of the book) which consists of descriptions of and meditations on the destruction of Jerusalem and the national tragedy. One section is attributed to R. Simeon bar Yoḥai. The Midrash proper contains stories about the destruction of Jerusalem and Betar and the greatness of Jerusalem. *Esther Rabbah* is a collection of Babylonian and Palestinian *aggadot*.

MIDRASH SAMUEL, see SAMUEL, MIDRASH

MIDRASHIC LITERATURE: Whereas halakhic Midrashim aim at extracting the practical law from the Scriptures, aggadic Midrashim penetrate into their ethical and moral background (see MIDRASH). Midrashic interpretations were current from earliest times (cf. Neh. 8:8) but they really began to flourish in the Tannaitic Period, when teachers expounded the weekly portions of the Pentateuch and Prophets on Sabbaths and festivals during the service in the synagogue (cf. *Ber.* 28a). At first these expositions were recorded in several booklets called *Siphrei de-Aggadeta* — even before the HALAKHAH and GEMARA were committed to writing (cf. *Git.* 60a). Subsequently, they were unified and edited in complete works. Some of these Midrashim have been lost in the course of time. The principal *halakhic* Midrashim extant today are SIPHREI on Numbers and Deuteronomy, SIPHRA on Leviticus, and MEKHILTA on Exodus, but Maimonides (introd. to *Mishneh Torah*) speaks of *Mekhilta* on the last four books of the Pentateuch by R. Ishmael and another *Mekhilta* by R. Akiva. It is now clear that the latter is identical with the *Mekhilta de Rabbi Simeon bar Yoḥai* and *Siphrei Zuta* which originated in the school of R. Akiva. The ancient halakhic Midrashim and the MISHNAH, TOSEPHTA, and each TALMUD, though mainly halakhic, also contain much aggadic material. TANHUMA on the Pentateuch is the oldest aggadic Midrash. An older text of *Tanhuma* was published by S. Buber (Vilna, 1885), and according to him antedates the Babylonian Talmud. Another recension of *Tanhuma*, also called YELAMMEDENU, has been lost and is known only from quotations in medieval works. The Midrash on Psalms, also called Midrash SHOHER Tov, is classed among the oldest Midrashim. MIDRASH RABBAH is of later date and draws largely upon *Tanhuma*. Among the many other Midrashim, mention should be made of PESIKTA DE-RAV KAHANA and PESIKTA RABBATI consisting of homilies on the Pentateuch and prophetic lessons assigned to special Sabbaths. Classic midrashic literature came to a close in the late 10th or early 11th cent. Important compilations of midrashic literature, both halakhic and aggadic, include YALKUT SHIMONI and MIDRASH HA-GADOL, the authors of which have preserved invaluable and otherwise unknown Midrashim.

MIKVAOT (Heb. "Ritual Baths"): Sixth tractate in the Mishnah order of *Toharot*; it has a Tosephta but no *gemara*. Its ten chapters deal with the size and other requirements of a ritual bath (see MIKVEH) and the rules for ritual immersion.

MIKVEH (Heb.): Literally any gathering of waters (Gen. 1:10), but specifically used in *halakhah* for that which forms a bath for the ritual IMMERSION of persons or utensils that have contracted ritual IMPURITY. Although many of the rules of impurity have become irrelevant since the destruction of the Temple, the *m.* has retained its religious rôle in the case of CONVERTS and for the immersion of women who have suffered some venereal discharge, or after menstruation (see NIDDAH) or CHILDBIRTH (see also ABLUTION; BAPTISM). Immersion in a *m.* — either daily or on certain occasions — is still practiced by pious ascetics, Hasidim, and others. The initial source of the *m.* water must be a natural spring, rain, or water obtained from the melting of natural ice. If the water was drawn by a vessel it is invalid for use. Once however the minimum *m.* requirement of 40 *seahs* (approximately 185 gallons) has been met, other water may be added. The *m.* was considered of paramount importance in Jewish life as normal marital life depended on it, and the building of the *m.* was said to take precedence over the construction of a synagogue (which may even be sold to raise money to build a *m.*). The symbolic and ritual significance of regeneration and purification through immersion in natural water is evidently distinct from the hygienic procedure of washing, and a woman's monthly visit to the *m.* helped contribute to the atmosphere of sanctity in traditional Jewish family life.

MILAH, see CIRCUMCISION

MILK: The only halakhic restrictions on the consumption of m. are (1) that it be drawn from a permitted species of animal; (2) that m. or m. products not be mixed or cooked together with MEAT or meat products (it is strictly forbidden even to derive benefit from such a mixture. See DIETARY LAWS). To prevent any doubts regarding a possible admixture of m. from prohibited ("unclean") species, the animal should be milked either by a Jew or in the presence of a Jew (see MASHGIAH). M. from the breast of a woman may be imbibed only by a suckling but not by a child already weaned or by an adult.

MILLENNIUM: The one-thousand year period of messianic rule, sometimes referred to as the "days of the MESSIAH", which is to precede the Last Judgment and the world to come (*ha-olam ha-ba*). The term has entered the European languages from the New Testament description of the 1000 year reign of Jesus and his resurrected saints (*Revelation* 20). Though the idea of an interregnal messianic period is to be found in pseudepigraphal and tannaitic literature, the duration of this era was variously assessed from 40 to 7000 years. The expectation was very much alive in the early Church but was subsequently suppressed, though it broke out time and time again in millenarian or "chiliast" (from Greek *chilias* "thousand") movements. The concept of 1000 years as the duration of the messianic era may have been derived from the idea of a "world week", each day of which was to be 1000 years long. The notion, which can be found in the Slavonic version of the pseudepigraphal Book of ENOCH (33:1-2), was further developed by the *tannaim* who — basing their interpretation on Ps. 90:4 ("For a thousand years in thy sight are but as yesterday") — explained that as the days of creation were six in number, the world would last for 6000 years. The seventh "world day", the Sabbath, was to be the 1000 years of the Messiah (cf. *Sanh.* 97a; *A.Z.* 9a). In modern English usage the term m. refers to a messianic future in general and not necessarily to its duration. See ESCHATOLOGY; MESSIANISM.

MIN, see MINIM

MINHAG (Heb. "custom"): Religious custom or rite; hence the traditional rite of a particular community. Though religious rituals are laid down by *halakhah*, there is great variety in the details of performance as well as in non-statutory observances. More specifically *m.* refers to a liturgical rite. The basic foundations of the LITURGY, especially of the Morning Service, are laid down in tractate BERAKHOT. In the course of the centuries, however, individual additions and modifications have been made, and considerable and significant differences have developed in the rites of various countries and sects. The main differences are between the *Ashkenazi* ritual, evolving from the original Palestinian usage, and the *Sephardi*, deriving from the Babylonian. Within these broad divisions, however, there are many variations of local CUSTOM, such as the Roman, the Italian, the Avignon, the Polish, and the German *minhagim*. The Ḥasidim have adopted the ritual of Isaac Luria (*Nusakh Ari*) which shows slight variations from the standard *Sephardi* usage, while the present *minhag* of Jerusalem is based upon the meticulous regulations for prayer laid down by R. Elijah the Gaon of Vilna, whose disciples (*Perushim*) established the modern *Ashkenazi* community of Jerusalem. The greatest divergence between the various rites is found in the use of PIYYUTIM, or poetic additions for the High Holy Days (originally — but now seldom — for other festivals as well). Considerable modification of the traditional liturgy has been introduced under Reform, Conservative, and Reconstructionist influence. The validity of traditional *m.* is acknowledged by rabbinic law, occasionally even in the face of apparently contradictory *halakhah*. The Mishnah enumerates differences in *m.* between Judea and Galilee, while still others developed between Palestine and Babylonia, and in the various parts of the Diaspora. Some *minhagim* (pl.) have halakhic, others a popular (folkloristic, superstitious) basis. Two examples of widespread *minhagim* are the eating of apples and honey on *Rosh ha-Shanah* and the KAPPAROT rites before the Day of Atonement.

MINḤAH, see MEAL-OFFERING

MINḤAH (Heb. "offering"): The second of the two statutory daily prayers, the other being SHAḤARIT. It is recited any time during the afternoon until sunset and corresponds to the daily "evening" sacrifice in the Temple (in practice offered several hours before sunset). Its institution is ascribed by the Talmud (*Ber.* 26b) to the patriarch Isaac (on the basis of Gen. 24:63). *M.* consists mainly of the AMIDAH (preceded and followed by KADDISH), said silently first by each worshiper and then repeated aloud by the reader. It is customary to recite ASHREI (Ps. 145) by way of opening and to conclude with ALEINU. On Sabbaths, the Day of Atonement, and other public fasts a short reading from the Bible precedes the *amidah*; on Sabbaths, the first part of the following week's portion is read. On fast days, a prophetical reading is also recited at *M.* in some rites. The *amidah* for *M.* is the same as for *Shaḥarit*, but no priestly blessing is pronounced, except on fast days (in the Land of Israel); in the *Ashkenazi* rite *shalom rav* is substituted in the last benediction for *sim shalom*. In many synagogues *M.* is recited late in the afternoon and followed immediately by MAARIV. In gaonic times an abbreviated form of the *amidah* was widely used at *M.* For *M.*, the reader wears the TALLIT, the congregation donning the *tallit* only on the Day of Atonement and *Av* 9. Traditionally the *M.*-service was instituted by the Patriarch ISAAC.

MINIM (Heb. pl. of *min*): Term used in Talmud and Midrash for sectarians, heretics, or gnostics. Its etymological meaning is unknown, though popular etymologies derive *m.* from Mani (founder of the Manicheans) or by way of abbreviation from *Maamin Yeshu Notzeri* (Believer in Jesus the Nazarene). Although the precise meaning of *m.* varied with the circumstances — it is used in talmudic and midrashic sources for the Sadducees, the Samaritans, the Judeo-Christians, and other heretical sectarians — there is no doubt that it later came to mean Judeo-Christians in particular. The Talmud (Y. *Sanh.* 10:6) states that at the time of the destruction of the Temple there were twenty-four kinds of *m.* "The writings of the *m.*", said R. Tarphon, "deserve to be burned, even though they may contain the name of God, for sectarianism is more dangerous than paganism" (*Shab.* 116a). A prayer against the *m.* which was added to the AMIDAH was composed by Samuel Ha-Katan at the request of the *nasi*, R. Gamaliel, as part of the Jewish struggle against Christianity, which at the time was still considered a Jewish sect. The wording of the prayer underwent repeated changes for fear of censorship and to obviate anti-Jewish criticism; thus *malshinim* (informers) was substituted for *m.* Maimonides (*Hilkhot Teshuvah* 3:7) enumerates five classes of *m.* (in the sense of "heretics") who have no share in the World to Come: (1) those who deny the existence of God and His providence; (2) those who believe in several gods; (3) those who attribute to God form and figure; (4) those who believe in the eternity of matter from which God created the world; (5) those who worship stars, planets, etc., believing that these act as intermediaries between man and God. *M.* were disqualified for all religious and ritual functions, and relatives were forbidden to mourn their death but rather instructed to rejoice (*Sem.* 2:10). See HERESY.

MINISTER, see RABBI

MINOR PROPHETS: Twelve shorter works, contained in the PROPHETS section of the BIBLE. They are traditionally termed *Terei Asar* (Aram. "twelve"). The books are HOSEA, JOEL, AMOS, OBADIAH, JONAH, MICAH, NAHUM, HABAKKUK, ZEPHANIAH, HAGGAI, ZECHARIAH, and MALACHI.

MINORS, see ADULT; CHILDREN

MINYAN (Heb. "number"): Minimum quorum of ten adult males required for liturgical purposes, such as the recital of KADDISH, KEDUSHAH, BAREKHU, the repetition by the reader of the AMIDAH;

also for the READING OF THE LAW and the HAPHTARAH. All the above are considered parts of the corporate service and are not recited by individuals when praying alone. Ten adult males constitute a representative section of the "community of Israel" for all purposes; hence the recital of these prayers does not depend on the place (in or outside the synagogue) but on the number of participants. If no *m.* is present, a service containing the above prayers, may not be held even in the synagogue. For the purpose of *m.*, a boy is considered adult when he is BAR-MITZVAH. A *m.* is required for SHEVA BERAKHOT. See also GRACE AFTER MEALS.

MINYAN MAN: One who for payment attends religious services in the synagogue or in private homes (during periods of mourning) in order to make up a MINYAN.

MIR: Small town in Poland famous for its *yeshivah*, founded in 1817, which flourished until World War II and which combined talmudic scholarship with the MUSAR teaching initiated by R. Israel Lipkin SALANTER. Successor schools of the original *yeshivah* exist in the State of Israel and the U.S.

MIRACLES: Extraordinary events that provoke "wonderment" and are ascribed to Divine or at least supernatural action. The more fully developed concept of m. presupposes a fixed natural order from which the miraculous event is a departure. The religious belief in m. assumes that God can set aside for His purposes the order of nature which He has created, e.g. to reveal His saving presence, His omnipotence, etc. Many m. are recorded in Scripture, mainly in connection with the history of the Jewish people, e.g. the splitting of the sea after the EXODUS from Egypt, the Divine revelation at Sinai, Joshua's stopping of the sun, or the m. related of Elijah and Elisha. M. are also recorded in rabbinic literature, though the rabbis do not offer a systematic theory or doctrine of m. Thus the Mishnah lists a number of miraculous things that were created on the eve of the first Sabbath, i.e., before the work of creation ended, and of miraculous phenomena in the Temple. M. were often worked by God through his messengers or through saintly men (e.g. ḤONI HA-MEAGGEL, ḤANINA BEN DOSA). Many talmudic rabbis are described as "experienced in m.". However, not everything called a miracle by the rabbis is a spectacular or manifestly supernatural event, and the term is sometimes used to denote God's salvation in everyday matters, e.g. the finding of daily bread or recovery after an illness; these are in the language of the AMIDAH prayer "the m. that are daily with us — morning, noon, and night". The rabbis emphasize that man is surrounded at all times by m., many of which he is not even aware of. Both usages of the term, however, refer to the work of God, either directly executed by Him or through the mediation of a human or natural agency. With the development of the philosophical concepts of natural order and causality, it became increasingly difficult to defend m., and the more rationalist medieval thinkers (e.g. MAIMONIDES, LEVI BEN GERSHON) tried to reduce the significance of even the biblical m. to a minimum, explaining most of them as symbolic allegories or dreams. This cautious rationalism of the philosophers stands in marked contrast to the avidity for m. that characterizes popular religion and certain forms of mysticism. Belief in m. often bordered on MAGIC and SUPERSTITION, and once more flourished in the ḥasidic movement, which ascribed the power of working m. to the saintly leader or TZADDIK (see also BAAL SHEM).

MISHKAN, see **TEMPLE**

MISHNAH, see **TALMUD**

MISHNEH TORAH, see **MOSES BEN MAIMON**

MISSION, RELIGIOUS, see **PROSELYTES**

MITNAGGEDIM (Heb. "opponents"): Opponents of the ḥasidic movement which spread in Eastern Europe in the second half of the 18th and in the first half of the 19th cent. ELIJAH BEN SOLOMON OF VILNA was acknowledged to be the foremost leader of the party of *M.* whose criticisms were directed at both the behavior and the theology of the ḤASIDIM. Ḥasidic behavior during prayer in the synagogue ("strange movements", uninhibited shouting, and similar expressions of religious enthusiasm) was resented, as was also the claim of the ḥasidic TZADDIK to act as an intermediary between the simple believer and God. Even more serious, in the eyes of the *M.*, were rumors that the Ḥasidim made light of the details of the Law and taught an heretical form of pantheism. In 1772, Elijah of Vilna issued severe bans of excommunication against all ḥasidic communities and their leaders. After the death of Elijah, the struggle between the Ḥasidim and the *M.* assumed even more bitter proportions, and it was only in the latter part of the 19th cent. that hostility began to subside, partly because the Emancipation and Enlightenment movements provided common foes, although important differences of ritual and religious atmosphere continued to divide the communities. On the whole, the *M.* prided themselves on being more respectful of the traditional rabbinic disciplines of learning (Talmud) than were the Ḥasidim. As time passed, it became obvious to both groups that the differences between them were more a matter of emphasis than of principle, and today little remains of the original bitterness that existed between the two groups in E. Europe.

MITZVAH (Heb. "commandment"): The term

mitzvah is employed in two senses, one technical, the other general. Technically it denotes the individual injunctions of the Bible which in their totality make up the TORAH. The number of *mitzvot* (pl.) in the *Torah* has traditionally been counted as 613 (see PRECEPTS, 613), consisting of 365 negative (*m. lo taaseh* or *lav*) and 248 positive (*m. aseh*) *mitzvot*. In addition to the biblical *mitzvot*, there are innumerable *mitzvot* of rabbinic origin. Some of these rabbinic ordinances are treated as if they had Divine authority, and the blessing recited prior to their performance contains the formula otherwise confined to biblical precepts ("Blessed art Thou our God who hath sanctified us with His commandments and commanded us to..."). These include the *m.* of washing the hands before meals, kindling the Sabbath and festival lights, making the *Eruv*, reciting *Hallel* on festival days, kindling ḤANUKKAH lights, and reading the Scroll of Esther (MEGILLAH) on *Purim*. The rabbis admit that there may be differences of value and importance between the *mitzvot* (of some, such as TZITZIT [*Ned.* 25a], circumcision [*Ned.* 32a], and charity [*Bava Batra* 9a], it is stated that their performance is equivalent to the performance of the *Torah* as a whole), but nevertheless enjoin that one must "be as heedful of a light *m.* as of a grave one, for thou knowest not what is the reward for the performance of a *m.*" (*Avot* 2:1). The opposite of a *m.* is an AVERAH ("transgression"). The rabbis say that "A *m.* which is fulfilled through an *averah* is reckoned as an *averah*" i.e., with regard to *mitzvot* the end does not justify the means. Liability for the performance of *mitzvot* comes with the attainment of one's religious majority, for which reason a boy on attaining this age is termed a BAR MITZVAH and a girl BAT MITZVAH. A woman is exempted from the performance of such *mitzvot* that depend upon a fixed time for their performance (*Kidd.* 29a). Some rabbis taught that there is no reward in this world for the performance of *mitzvot* (*Ḥul.* end). In a general sense, the word *m.* is also used for any good deed or act of piety or kindness even though it is not specifically enjoined in the Bible, e.g. "It is a *m.* to fulfill the wishes of the departed" (*Ket.* 70a). In addition to the division of *mitzvot* into those of biblical and rabbinic authority, many other classifications exist, e.g. *mitzvot* concerning relations with one's fellow men. The importance of the concept of *m.* in Jewish theology reflects the basic view that every human activity is also an act of obedience to the Divine will. See also DUTY.

MIXED KINDS (Heb. *kilayim*): The sowing, grafting, breeding, or mixing of diverse kinds of seeds, trees, animals, or fabrics is prohibited by the Bible (Lev. 19:19; Deut. 22:9-11). The laws governing m.k. fall under four major headings, the first of which applies only in the Land of Israel, the remainder elsewhere as well.

(1) *Zeraim* ("seeds") — It is forbidden to plant together two types of seed which differ in name, appearance, or taste. The prohibition applies only to seed normally planted for food but not to seed planted normally only for medical use. The space to be left unplanted between the various kinds of seed varies with the plant in question. Under this heading is also included the grafting of trees.

(2) *Kerem* ("vine"). The regulations concerning planting of two kinds of seed together with the vine are stricter than those of *Zeraim* and it is forbidden to derive any benefit whatsoever from the product (*Kidd.* 56b).

(3) *Behemah* ("animal") — It is forbidden to crossbreed any two species of animal, nor may they be tied or yoked together for purposes of work, such as plowing or pulling (Deut. 22:10).

(4) *Shaatnez* ("mingling of fabrics") — Garments containing mixed wool and linen are forbidden to be worn. Any intermingling whatsoever of hackled, spun, or woven wool with linen, renders the cloth or garment *shaatnez*. Exceptions to this law are the priestly garments, of which the girdle contained both wool and linen, and fringes (TZITZIT) which in former times were made by adding a woolen thread even to a linen garment. The laws of m.k. are among those called *ḥukkim* in the Bible (Lev. 19:19) and this is rabbinically interpreted as meaning that their subject is a Divine decree, the explanation of which is beyond human comprehension. Attempts have been made to explain the legislation concerning the m.k. by reference to the first chapter of Genesis where the creation of plant, marine, and animal species is described, each "according to its kind", i.e., each species was created distinctly and endowed with a natural propensity for distinctive growth. Hence some commentators hold that the law of m.k. intends to safeguard the distinctiveness of the species, and mingling them would be a violation of the laws of nature established by God.

MIXED MARRIAGE, see INTERMARRIAGE

MIZMOR (Heb. "song": see also ZEMIROT). The word occurs in the superscriptions of more than a third of all PSALMS, and hence is used as synonymous with "psalm".

MIZRAḤ (Heb. "east"): In fulfillment of Solomon's prayer at the dedication of the Temple "And they shall pray unto Thee toward their land which Thou gavest unto their fathers, the city which Thou hast chosen and the house which I have built to Thy Name" (I Kings 8:48), Jews everywhere turn in prayer in the direction of the Temple mount. Thus, in countries west of Israel, they turn toward the east, and the Ark is placed in the eastern wall of the synagogue. This practice meant that the "*m.*" side of the synagogue came to be considered especially distinguished, and the seats there were reserved for the honored members of the community. Wall plaques bearing the word "*mizraḥ*" (and known by that name) surrounded by artistically drawn figures and biblical or kabbalistic inscriptions adorned most synagogues in Europe and even many homes.

MIZRAḤI, see **RELIGIOUS PARTIES**

MIZRAḤI, ELIJAH (c. 1455-1526): Turkish rabbi and mathematician. As Chief Rabbi of Turkey (from 1495) he adopted a tolerant attitude toward the KARAITES. He wrote halakhic works and responsa as well as *Sepher ha-Mizraḥi,* a supercommentary on Rashi's commentary to the Pentateuch.

MNEMONICS: Actual or artificial words used as aids in memorizing. M. were common both in literary composition (e.g. alphabetic and other ACROSTICS in the Psalms and in PIYYUT) and for memorizing halakhic discussions and conclusions (cf. YAKNEHAZ or — as a non-halakhic instance — the three meaningless words quoted at the SEDER service which constitute a mnemonic for the Ten Plagues). Most mnemonic devices are ABBREVIATIONS.

MOAB, see **AMMON**

MOADIM LE-SIMḤAH (Heb. [May you have] "festivals for rejoicing"): The traditional greeting among *Sephardim* on festival days. The formula comes from the festival *amidah* and is now generally used in the State of Israel. The usual reply is *ḥagim u-zemannim le-sason.* ("feasts and festal seasons for joy"). See also ḤAG SAMEAḤ.

MODEH ANI (Heb. "I give thanks [unto Thee]"): Prayer said immediately upon waking in the morning. It does not appear in medieval sources, and seems to have been composed about the 17th cent. in order to avoid saying the traditional (already mentioned in the Talmud) *Elohai Neshamah* ("O my God, the soul which Thou gavest me") while still in bed and before performing the prescribed morning ablutions. (*M.A.* — which does not mention the Divine Name — could be recited under such circumstances). The prayer *Elohai Neshamah* was transferred to the MORNING BENEDICTIONS. *M.A.* expresses thanks to the "living and eternal King" for the refreshment of mind and body after sleep and welcomes the presence of God immediately upon waking.

MODENA, AARON BERAHIAH, see **AARON BERAHIAH BEN MOSES OF MODENA**

MODENA, LEONE (Judah Aryeh, 1571-1648): Italian rabbi. As brilliant and gifted as he was unstable, M. was a prolific author (in Hebrew and Italian) and fascinating preacher. His versatile if shallow mind combined rationalism, skepticism, faith, and superstition. Among other works he wrote a book in defense of religion and two devastating attacks on the kabbalah (he later denied the authorship of the second of these treatises). M. also dabbled in alchemy, directed the theater and music academy in the ghetto of Venice, and was a member of a circle of gamblers. M.'s writings became influential again when the struggle between kabbalists and rationalists was resumed in the 18th cent.

MOED (Heb. "Appointed Time", hence "Set Feasts"): The second order of the Mishnah, dealing with the laws of Sabbath and festivals. It has twelve tractates, each of which also has a Tosephta, as well as *gemara* in both Talmuds (except SHEKALIM which lacks *gemara* in the Babylonian Talmud). The twelve are SHABBAT, ERUVIN, SHEKALIM, YOMA, SUKKAH, BEITZAH, ROSH HA-SHANAH, TAANIT, MEGILLAH, MOED KATAN, and ḤAGIGAH.

MOED KATAN (Heb. "Minor Festival" also known after its opening word as "*Mashkin*" i.e., one may irrigate): Eleventh (in some codices twelfth) tractate of the Mishnah order *Moed.* Its three chapters deal with the nature of work permitted on the intermediate days (ḤOL HA-MOED) of Passover and Tabernacles and with the rules of mourning on Sabbaths and holidays.

MOHAMMED (570-632): Founder of ISLAM. He grew up in Mecca and was familiar with both Jews and Christians, by whose traditions and lore he was considerably influenced. At first M. had no intention of establishing Islam as a new religion. Considering himself the messenger and prophet of *Allah* to the Arabs, he wished to convert his people to MONOTHEISM and to warn them of God's wrath on the Day of Judgment. He believed his revelations to be identical with those given by earlier prophets to Jews and Christians and was therefore disappointed when they rejected his claims. He consequently accused them of intentionally deleting predictions of his advent from the Bible. Rejected at first by his own people, he attempted to win the approval of the large Jewish community, especially that of Medina. In 622, after failing to gain the support of the Meccans, he made his famous flight (*Hijra*) to Medina, and proclaimed Islam as a new faith, leaning heavily on Judaism for its formulation. But embittered by the refusal of the Jews to recognize him he cruelly attacked several Jewish tribes killing the men and enslaving the women and children (625). Nevertheless M. legislated that Jews should not be forced to embrace Islam, but like other "Peoples of the Book", be permitted to practice their religion while suffering certain ignominies. See KORAN.

MOHEL (Heb. "circumciser"): Person authorized to perform CIRCUMCISION. The duty of circumcising a newborn male child rests formally on the father, but the actual execution is entrusted to a person duly trained and declared competent both in theory and practice. The *m.* thus acts as the agent of the parent. Although according to law any competent Jew may perform circumcision, preference is given to one of genuine piety who performs the act "for the sake of Heaven". A woman may act as *m.* only where no competent male Jew is available. The Talmud states that a "sage should be able to perform ritual slaughter and circumcision" (*Ḥul.* 9a).

MOHILEVER, SAMUEL (1824-1898): Russian rabbi and Zionist. He officiated in various Polish communities and in 1882 founded in Warsaw the *Bnai Zion,* the first local group of the pioneer Zionist movement *Ḥibbat Zion.* His decision to co-operate with the secular Zionists within the framework of the *Ḥovevei Zion* proved a major event in the development of the Zionist movement and aroused the opposition of the more extreme Orthodox. M. welcomed and enthusiastically supported Herzl.

MOLCHO, SOLOMON (c. 1500-1532): Kabbalist, messianic enthusiast, and martyr. Born of a Marrano family in Portugal, he returned to Judaism and escaped to Salonica where he studied with — and greatly influenced — the kabbalistic circle of R. Joseph Taytazak, which also included Joseph KARO and Solomon ALKABETZ. From Turkey he went to Italy where he spent thirty days in prayer and fasting among the beggars in front of the Pope's palace. This and other messianic gestures alarmed some of the Jewish leaders, but most Jews and Christians revered M. as a man of God and a prophet. Even Pope Clement VII was greatly impressed by him and protected him from the Inquisition. From Italy he traveled to Regensburg with David Reuveni to seek an audience with the Emperor Charles V, who had both of them arrested and delivered to the Inquisition. M. was burned at the stake in Mantua. His kabbalistic homilies are printed in his *Sepher ha-Mephoar* which includes his forecast that the Messiah would appear in the year 1540.

MOLECH (also **MOLOCH; MILKOM**): Semitic deity worshiped by the Ammonites. A high place was erected for this idol by the aging Solomon (I Kings 11:5-8). In ancient Israel M. was worshiped as an aspect of BAAL by offering children to a sacrificial fire, though both talmudic and modern opinion differ as to whether the burning was real or symbolical. The Bible strongly condemned this practice (Lev. 18:11; 20:2-5; Deut. 18:10; Jer. 12:35). M. worship was practiced at TOPHETH in the valley of Hinnom outside Jerusalem (II Kings 23:10).

MOLKHO, see **MOLCHO**

MÖLLN, see **JACOB BEN MOSES HALEVI MÖLLN**

MOLOCH, see **MOLECH**

MONASTICISM: M. which plays an important rôle in Christianity and other religions is practically unknown among Jews. The only examples in Jewish history date from the late Second Temple Period and include the ESSENES, the sect of the DEAD SEA SCROLLS (identified by many scholars with the Essenes), and the THERAPEUTAE. CELIBACY is frowned upon by Judaism, and extreme ascetic tendencies (see ASCETICISM) were generally counteracted by the social and world-affirming orientation of the Jewish tradition. In general the idea of m. which requires withdrawal from the "world" in order to achieve spiritual perfection, is contrary to the Jewish demand of hallowing life in the world by the discipline of SANCTIFICATION.

MONDAYS AND THURSDAYS: Two weekdays characterized liturgically by the Reading of the Law (the first section of the Pentateuch portion for the following Sabbath) and the recitation of additional penitential and supplicatory prayers at the Morning Service. They are also the preferred days for voluntary fasts. In ancient times villagers went to town on M. and T. to attend the markets and the law courts, and the Talmud credits EZRA with instituting instruction in the law on those days. The three voluntary fasts known as *Behab,* i.e., Monday-Thursday-Monday, and observed shortly after Passover and Tabernacles, are meant to atone for unintentional sins and levity during the festive season, after the example of Job (Job 1:5).

MONEYLENDING, see **LOANS; USURY**

MONOGAMY, see **POLYGAMY**

MONOTHEISM: Belief in, and worship of, one GOD. M. is the decisive characteristic of the Israelite conception of God, though different stages of development and definition are discernible (see HENOTHEISM). Biblical m. differs from polytheistic paganism not only in the number of gods professed, but in its understanding of God as absolutely above nature and in complete mastery of it. The world and its individual parts — stars, sun, earth, and sea — exist solely by God's will; they tremble before Him and perform His bidding. The biblical conception of God is non-mythological: God was not born, He does not beget other divinities, and He is independent of matter or other beings. He cannot be coerced by magic, is omnipotent, and depends upon no sacrificial cult to sustain His being. At the same time He enters into a direct, personal relationship with His creatures, is concerned with their plight and even elects individuals or groups for special purposes. This idea of God is different from philosophical m.; it is an original religious intuition rather than the result of intellectual speculation, though the precise moment in the history of Israel at which it came into full blossom may be difficult to determine. The rabbis of the Talmudic Period ascribed the monotheistic revolution to Abraham. Critical scholarship associated the emergence of m. with the literary prophets, but some modern scholars accept the biblical account according to which the monotheistic intuition was arrived at by Moses (cf. Exod. 20:1-6), possibly in the experience of the Burning Bush, which was not only a prophetic calling but a revelation of the Divine name (Exod. 3:14). Whereas in the Pentateuch God demands obedience to a law which is at once ritual and moral, that is, without sharp distinction between the two, prophetic m. becomes emphatically moral and at times anti-ritualistic. The biblical historians do not recognize a gradual evolution of ethical m., but rather a gradual falling away from Israel's pristine faith. Even in the days of Moses there was occasional backsliding, as when the Golden Calf was manufactured to serve as a material symbol of God. After the conquest of Canaan, the influence of the local population and its religious cults made itself felt. The Book of Judges describes alternate cycles of faith and faithlessness. The sporadic worship of Baal was followed by a resurgence of m. in the time of Saul, David, and Solomon, but SYNCRETISM and IDOLATRY held sway again from then until the Exile. After the Exile, idolatry ceased completely among Jews, and Ezra and his successors no longer found it necessary to inveigh against it. Subsequently the main stages in the history of Jewish m. were the struggle of the rabbis against the DUALISTIC tendencies of GNOSTICISM, and the attempts of the medieval philosophers to formulate a m. free from the taint of ANTHROPOMORPHISM. Medieval apologists frequently contrasted the pure and uncompromising m. of Judaism with what seemed to them the polytheism implicit in the Christian doctrine of the trinity. The kabbalistic doctrine of God (see SEPHIROT) has been criticized by its opponents as a departure from strict Jewish m., but the kabbalists held that their mystical theology, which described the dynamic unity of the Godhead in symbolic language, was perfectly monotheistic. Under the influence of Enlightenment rationalism, which emphasized the moral aspects of religion to the neglect of its ritual and irrational aspects, Judaism has often been described as "ethical m.".

MONTH, see **CALENDAR**

MOON: According to Gen. 1:16 the m. was created together with the SUN on the fourth day of creation. It was regarded throughout the Middle East as a deity, as in Ur and Haran where Abraham spent his early years. Moon worship was however strictly forbidden to the Israelites (Deut. 17:3). The m. formed the basis of the monthly CALENDAR reckoning and the proclamation of the NEW MOON was a prerogative of the SANHEDRIN. The monthly ceremony of blessing the moon (KIDDUSH LEVANAH) generally takes place between the 3rd and 15th of each month when the light of the m. is regarded as being at its strongest.

MOON, NEW, see **NEW MOON**

MOON, BLESSING OF, see **KIDDUSH LEVANAH**

MORAIS, SABATO (1823-1897): U.S. rabbi. Born and educated in Italy, he lived for five years in London and went to the U.S. in 1851, succeeding Isaac LEESER as minister of the *Sephardi* congregation Mikveh Israel in Philadelphia. A leading traditionalist, M. was profoundly concerned at the spread among U.S. Jews of both the Reform movement and religious indifference, and exerted a decisive influence on the incipient CONSERVATIVE Movement. He was one of the founders (in 1886) of the JEWISH THEOLOGICAL SEMINARY in New York, serving as its first president until his death.

MORALISTS, see **ETHICS; MUSAR**

MORDECAI: A descendant of a Benjamite family of Babylonian exiles who saved Persian Jewry from the evil designs of HAMAN when he bid Queen ESTHER, his daughter by adoption, to intercede with King Ahasuerus. According to the Book of Esther — the sole source for this story — M. became viceroy of Persia and conferred considerable benefits upon his brethren. Talmudic *aggadah* identifies M. with the prophet Malachi (*Meg.* 10b).

MORDECAI BEN HILLEL (d. 1298): German talmudist. He was martyred at Nuremberg together with his wife and five children. His talmudic compendium *Mordekhai* quotes many medieval authorities and was highly esteemed as a source book; it was printed in major editions of the Talmud. M. also wrote liturgical poetry.

MORE JUDAICO, see **JEWISH OATH**

MOREH NEVUKHIM (Heb. "Guide for the Perplexed"): See **MOSES BEN MAIMON**

MOREH TZEDEK (Heb. "Teacher of righteousness"): See **DEAD SEA SCROLLS.**

MORENU (Heb. "our teacher"): Title originally given to distinguished rabbis (Germany, 14th cent.) and subsequently to all rabbis. Later it became an honorific used either indiscriminately (as in E. Europe), or bestowed by the rabbi on exceptionally learned and pious laymen (in Germany).

MORNING: Despite the fact that in the Bible the m. actually begins at sunrise (cf. Judg. 9:33, "And it shall be in the m. when the sun rises"), halakhically m. is considered to begin with the appearance of the m. star, even though the sun has not yet risen. This dawn is referred to as "the m. of the night" (*Yoma* 20b), i.e., the sign of m. which marks the end of the night. There is a difference of opinion in the Talmud as to when m. ends. According to the majority opinion it continues until midday, but R. Johanan ben Zakkai holds that it extends only to the end of the fourth hour — the hour in this case being a twelfth part of the period of daylight (*Ber.* 26b-27a), and hence variable with the seasons.

MORNING BENEDICTIONS: Series of blessings recited originally in talmudic times, upon wakening, each individual benediction suiting the particular occasion or action. Thus, immediately upon stirring from sleep, *Elohai Neshamah,* ("O my God, the soul which Thou gavest me") was said, while upon hearing the cock crow, opening the eyes, rising, dressing, washing the hands, etc., the appropriate blessings were pronounced, concluding with a prayer for guidance through the *Torah* and salvation from sin (*Ber.* 60b). The *geonim* later transferred the M.B. to the commencement of the synagogue service, where they are followed by passages from the Written and Oral Laws. There were added a prayer for deliverance from arrogant men and mishaps (*Ber.* 16b), an exhortation to fear God privately and publicly, the remembrance of man's insignificance before God, and the assertion of God's covenant with the Patriarchs. The three M.B. in the negative ("who has not made me a heathen, a slave, a woman", cf. *Men.* 43b), whose content is partly modeled on similar Greek prayers, have been reformulated in some modern rites (e.g. the Conservative) in positive fashion ("who hast made me a Jew", etc.). See MODEH ANI.

MORNING SERVICE, see **SHAḤARIT**

MOSER, see **DENUNCIATION**

MOSES: Leader and lawgiver. The Bible portrays M. as the greatest of all prophets, who, alone among men, knew God "face to face" and whom God chose to be the mediator of His REVELATION and the leader who would transform a horde of slaves into a potential "kingdom of priests" and "a treasured people". From birth to death M.'s life is depicted as an integral part of the Divine design of redemption. According to the biblical account, the future liberator of Israel, son of Amram and Jochebed of the tribe of Levi, was born (probably in the 13th cent. B.C.E.) at the height of the Egyptian persecution, when Hebrew male infants were drowned at birth. After a period of concealment, M.'s mother placed him in a casket among the Nile reeds, entrusting his life to Providence. M. was rescued by Pharaoh's own daughter and brought up in the royal palace. But heredity triumphed over environment; he was drawn to his brethren. Seeing an Egyptian taskmaster maltreat a Hebrew, he slew the Egyptian. The next day he beheld Israelite smiting Israelite; when he intervened his brother Hebrew betrayed him and he had to flee to Midian. In the desert, shepherding the flock of his father-in-law Jethro, M.'s spirit matured. At the age of eighty he was vouchsafed a theophany in the form of a BURNING BUSH that was not consumed, and in which the God of his fathers, laid upon him the mission to lead His people out of Egypt. In vain M. attempted to resist the call, and finally accepting the Divine charge, he appeared, together with his brother AARON, before Pharaoh, and demanded in the Lord's name "Let My people go!" TEN PLAGUES reinforced his demand; the last plague, the slaying of the Egyptian first-born, brought the Hebrews freedom. The urgency with which the Israelites left Egypt was matched by the haste with which Pharaoh sought to recapture his erstwhile bondmen, whom he overtook at the shores of the Sea of Reeds or "Red Sea" (probably in the region of the Bitter Lakes). There an event occurred which left an indelible mark in Jewish tradition: the Israelites crossed dryshod, while the pursuing Egyptians were drowned. The EXODUS was only the beginning of the way that was to lead the Israelites to the Promised Land. The next major event was the GIVING OF THE LAW at SINAI. There the DECALOGUE, and other legislation, was promulgated and M. bound the people in a solemn Covenant to the Lord. He also built the first national sanctuary, the TABERNACLE or "Tent of Meeting", which was to serve as the visible symbol of the Invisible God's presence in their midst. The unique theophany at Mt. Sinai was followed by the anticlimax of the sin of the Golden CALF, described by the Bible as Israel's first lapse into idolatry. M. shattered the Tablets of the Covenant; but although his life's work was seemingly undone, faith triumphed over despair. M. interceded with God, obtained God's pardon for the people, and carved the tablets anew. The camp, however, continued to simmer with potential or actual rebellion. The tragic climax came when ten of the twelve spies sent to reconnoiter the Promised Land brought back a discouraging report. Clearly the former slaves were not ready to enter upon their national inheritance. M. led Israel for forty years through the wilderness until the old generation died and a new generation had grown up. After annexing the lands of Sihon and Og in Transjordan M.'s work drew to its close. The Lord forbade him to cross the Jordan in punishment for an act of disobedience (Num. 20:1-13). In three valedictory addresses, delivered in the Plains of Moab, M. reviewed the story of the Exodus and recapitulated the terms and the law of the Covenant. Then, having exhorted and blessed his people he died "but no man knoweth of his sepulcher unto this day" (Deut. 34:6) and no cult could ever become attached to his person. The *aggadah,* in all its forms, embellished the biography of M. more than that of any other biblical personage. But through all the variegated and often contradictory legends runs the assumption that in spite of his unique career as the faithful "servant of God", M. always remained a mortal, fallible human being. In modern times the historicity of M., as of the Exodus tradition as a whole, has been challenged; but many scholars agree that some of the tribes were in fact enslaved in Egypt and freed; that the Israelite religion was probably founded by some kind of solemn covenant; and that a heroic figure like M. played a central rôle in these events. However no critical hypothesis can in any way affect the towering image of M. as it has developed in biblical, rabbinic, and kabbalistic tradition. Both a historical personality and a spiritual symbol, M. represents the passionate and self-sacrificing leader, liberator, intercessor, lawgiver, teacher (*Mosheh Rabbenu,* i.e., M. our master), "faithful shepherd", founder of Judaism, and prophet of MONOTHEISM. Tradition attributes to him the authorship of the entire PENTATEUCH and regards him as the fountainhead of the ORAL LAW. Eschatological speculation also ascribed to him a rôle in the future, messianic redemption.

MOSES, ASSUMPTION OF: Apocryphal work of Jewish origin written in Hebrew or Aramaic during the first part of the 1st cent. C.E. Now extant only in a Greek version, it contains a revelation purportedly made to Joshua by Moses who relates the coming history of Israel down to the reign of Herod and the ensuing messianic era. The acute-eschatological expectations voiced in this work, together with its harsh condemnation of the Temple priesthood, suggest that it originated in circles related to the ESSENES.

MOSES, SEAT OF: In *Matthew* 23:2 Jesus refers to the Scribes and Pharisees as "sitting in the seat of Moses"; a further reference to the S. of M. is found in *Pesikta de-Rav Kahana* 12 in the name of the 4th cent. R. Aḥa. Opinions differ as to the signification of the term — some scholars have maintained that the reference is to a place of honor, others that it was the stand on which the Scroll of the Law was placed during the service. If the former, examples of such seats, designated for the most distinguished elder and placed close to the Ark, have been discovered in ancient synagogues at Dura-Europos, Ḥammat (near Tiberias), and Ḥorazin.

MOSES, SONG OF: (1) Hymn of praise, known in Heb. as *Shirat ha-yam* ("Song of the Sea") or merely as the *Shirah* ("Song"), sung by the Israelites after their miraculous crossing of the Sea of Reeds, also known as the "Red Sea" (Exod. 15:1-18), and belonging to the same literary *genre* as the Song of Deborah (Judg. 5) and David's song of victory (II Sam. 22). It is recited every day in the MORNING SERVICE and figures as the Pentateuchal reading on the seventh day of Passover. On that occasion, as well as on *Shabbat Shirah* (i.e., when read as part of the pentateuchal portion in the yearly cycle) it is sung to a special solemn tune. (2) Words of Moses — an exhortation and prophecy in poetic language — spoken before his death (Deut. 32).

MOSES, SONS OF: Legendary Jewish tribe, having their own independent kingdom in some faraway country. According to the 9th cent. traveler Eldad the Danite, they lived beyond the river SAMBATYON. The legend of the S. of M. is similar to that of the ten lost TRIBES.

MOSES BEN ENOCH (10th cent.): One of the four rabbis who according to legend were captured by pirates in the Mediterranean and sold to foreign lands, where they spread talmudic knowledge. M. was responsible for bringing profound talmudic learning to Spain, where he founded a school and was later succeeded by his son Enoch ben Moses.

MOSES BEN JACOB OF COUCY (13th cent.): French talmudist and preacher who took part in the DISPUTATION of Paris (1240). Inspired by a dream, he went preaching through S. France and Spain and raised the level of religious life in these communities considerably. Critical of philosophy, he preached (like the German Ḥasidim) a piety that implied the highest moral standards. He is best known for his popular codification *Sepher Mitzvot Gadol* (abbreviated, *SeMaG*).

MOSES BEN MAIMON (MAIMONIDES or *Rambam*; 1135-1204) Philosopher and codifier; born in Spain, lived most of his life in Egypt where he was physician to the court. M. concluded at the age of 30 his commentary (in Arabic) on the Mishnah. Unlike RASHI who explains each sentence separately, M.'s method was to give a short review of a talmudic treatise on the Mishnah, explain individual words, and determine the law, so that the student obtained a clear picture of the whole subject. His Mishnah commentary was widely appreciated, and several Hebrew translations were produced. As an introduction to his major work *Mishneh Torah* ("Second *Torah*", also known as *Yad Ḥazakah,* "Strong Hand", after its 14 sections — *Yad* having the numerical value of 14), M. wrote *Sepher ha-Mitzvot* ("The Book of Commandments") consisting of a methodological preface to, and an enumeration and definition of, the 613 Precepts. This work, too, was written in Arabic, while the *Mish-*

neh Torah was in mishnaic Hebrew. His objective in all his halakhic work was to define the actual law in the most concise manner possible. The *Mishneh Torah* is a monument of analytical power. Drawing upon the whole range of rabbinic literature, where subjects occur in the most unexpected contexts, M. sifted his material from the "sea of the Talmud", grouped it under appropriate headings, and extracted the final *halakhah* from the labyrinth of numerous and complicated discussions. M. rejected customs based on belief in demons and similar superstitions, coining the motto: "Man should never cast his sound reason behind him, for the eyes are in front and not in back". This work, the first of its kind, provoked much criticism, mainly because it codified the whole Oral Law without indicating sources. R. Abraham ben David of Posquières was its most outspoken opponent, and M. in a letter to one of his critics, expressed regret at not having listed out-of-the-way sources in a separate work. He indicated that he intended to compile such a reference book, but though he never did write this work, numerous attempts were made by later scholars to trace M.'s sources and reconstruct the arguments that led to his decisions. Nevertheless, many passages in the *Mishneh Torah* still remain unaccounted for and very often its decisions run counter to the Talmud itself. It appears that M. occasionally deviates from the opinion of early teachers, following instead the plain meaning of the biblical text (see *Hilkhot Ned.* 12:1); he also added laws not mentioned in any source but which accorded with his medical knowledge and could be deduced from the Mishnah (e.g. *Hilkhot Sheḥitah* 8:23). M. included in his legal code a number of theological and philosophical ideas, as well as moral and practical rules, which, he held, formed part of the aggadic teaching of the Oral Law. The *Mishneh Torah* became a standard work of Jewish law and a major source for subsequent codes. Even more significant, in many respects, was M.'s philosophical *Moreh Nevukhim* ("Guide for the Perplexed"), thus entitled because it was intended neither for ordinary people nor for those who occupy themselves exclusively with the study of the *Torah*, but for those who follow both *Torah* and philosophy and who are "perplexed" by the contradictions between the teachings of the two. In interpreting the *Torah* in the light of philosophy, M. rejects the literal understanding of certain texts, particularly of all ANTHROPOMORPHISMS. Phrases ascribing human qualities to God merely represent human phraseology used by the *Torah* as metaphors for His actions. Faith is, ideally, a matter of conviction based on philosophical understanding. M.'s reconciliation of philosophy with Jewish tradition was based on his assumption that Aristotle's philosophy was the truth. However, he rejected the Aristotelian theory of the eternity of the universe, which he held to be unproved, and accepted the biblical doctrine of *creatio ex nihilo*. Prophecy, according to M., is that state of intellectual and moral perfection in which the human mind becomes illuminated by "Active Intellect" proceeding from God. All prophets received the Divine message by mediation, i.e., in a vision; only the prophecy of Moses came immediately from God. To know God and His relationship to creation, one must understand the nature of the universe and its parts. Man's free will is not affected by God's omniscience and foreknowledge, hence man's responsibility for his actions. The Divine commandments are not capricious decrees but designed to develop man's moral and intellectual potentialities, though some precepts are beyond human understanding. M.'s theological views are concisely summed up in his THIRTEEN ARTICLES OF FAITH which have been included in the liturgy in poetical form (YIGDAL). The *Guide for the Perplexed*, which has been translated into several languages, dominated the subsequent development of Jewish thought and also influenced non-Jewish philosophers, although immediately on its publication it provoked a storm of Orthodox protest. M. and his followers were accused of excessive rationalism, bordering on — or at least encouraging — heresy, and of undermining the belief in revelation and in traditional dogmas and law. For over a century the conflict between Maimonists and anti-Maimonists rent Judaism into almost two camps, but finally the name of M. became established as the symbol of the pure and orthodox faith. The popular evaluation was expressed by the later inscription on M.'s tombstone "From Moses to Moses there was none like unto Moses".

MOSES BEN NAḤMAN (NAḤMANIDES or *Ramban*; 1194-1270): Spanish talmudist, kabbalist, and Bible commentator. The spiritual leader of Spanish Jewry, he had to leave the country as a result of his impressive stand in the 1263 DISPUTATION at Barcelona, and spent his last years in Palestine, being the first outstanding rabbi to pronounce the resettlement of the land of Israel a biblical precept. M. raised talmudic study in Spain to new levels, and his *novellae*, in which selected passages from the Talmud were expertly analyzed, virtually inaugurated this branch of rabbinic literature. Despite his originality, M. was essentially a defender of traditional authority. His original and profound commentary on the Pentateuch opened broad theological and philosophical vistas, and combined philological precision, fidelity to the rabbinic sources, and kabbalistic mysticism. Respecting the authority of reason within its limits, but refusing to acknowledge it as the final arbiter, he opposed Maimonides' rationalization of miracles and of certain commandments (e.g. SACRIFICES). While never neglecting the literal, aggadic, and halakhic interpretation of the biblical text, he insisted that its ultimate meaning was essentially mystical. In addition to his importance as talmudist and commentator, M. was also one of the most influential personalities in the history of early Spanish Kabbalah.

MOSES DE LEON (1250-1305): Spanish kabbalist in Guadalajara and (from 1290) in Avila. He had a wide acquaintance with previous mystical literature, and was a prolific writer. His name is chiefly connected with the controversy regarding the publication and authorship of the ZOHAR, alleged to have been composed in the circle of the 2nd cent. *tanna* Simeon bar Yoḥai. Modern scholarship attributes the authorship of this classic of KABBALAH to M. de L. himself. See MYSTICISM.

MOSES HA-DARSHAN (i.e., "the Preacher", 10th-11th cents.): Scholar and biblical commentator. He lived in Narbonne in S. France. M.'s commentary (Midrash) on Genesis (BERESHIT RABBATI) quoted by both Rashi and the 13th cent. Christian polemicist Raimund Martini, has only recently been published.

MOSES LEIB OF SASSOV (c. 1745-1807): Ḥasidic rabbi; founder of the Sassov dynasty and pupil of R. Samuel Shmelke of Nikolsburg. He was partly responsible for the development of music and dance as an expression of ḥasidic piety.

MOSES ḤAYYIM EPHRAIM OF SADILKOV (c. 1737-c. 1800): Ḥasidic rabbi; son of the BAAL SHEM Tov's daughter Odel, and disciple of his grandfather and of R. Dov Ber of Mezhirich. His *Degel Maḥaneh Ephraim* ("Flag of the Camp of Ephraim") is a classic of ḥasidic literature. Whether or not, the work precisely and reliably reflects the Baal Shem Tov's doctrines, it constitutes a valuable presentation of ḥasidic teaching on humility, DEVEKUT, and the function of the TZADDIK in the community.

MOSHAV ZEKENIM, see **OLD AGE**

MOTHER: Although legally "the FATHER takes precedence over the m. in all matters" (*Ker.* 28a), both the Bible and Talmud insist with unvarying emphasis on the equal rights of both PARENTS in the moral and ethical sphere. The Fifth Commandment, enjoining the duty of honoring parents, mentions the father before the m.; in Lev. 19:2, enjoining fear (or reverence) for parents, the m. is mentioned before the father. This difference in phraseology forms the basis for the rabbinic statement that since God knows that the natural tendency of a child is to honor the m. more than the father, and fear the father more than the m., the order in each case is reversed, in order to teach the duty of equal reverence and honor to both parents (*Kidd.* 30b-31a). Similarly the dire punishment for smiting or cursing parents specifically mentions both father and m. (Exod. 21:15-17). The Four Mothers, or MATRIARCHS (Sarah, Rebekah, Rachel, and Leah), rank equally in Jewish sentiment with the Three Patriarchs (Abraham, Isaac, and Jacob). In valid marriages the child is accorded the status of his father (e.g. the son of a priest and an Israelite mother is a priest; of an Israelite father and the daughter of a priest, an Israelite), but with regard to mixed marriages the child receives the status of the mother (the son of a non-Jewish father and a Jewish m. is considered Jewish, etc.) Only the woman bearing the child is regarded as the m., since ADOPTION has no validity in Jewish law. The Talmud contains many stories of the extreme respect paid by the rabbis to their mothers; of one rabbi it is related that "when he heard his m.'s footsteps, he used to remark "I stand up before the Divine presence" (*Kidd.* 31b), and several medieval rabbis declared that their best teachers had been their mothers. Throughout Jewish history, the m. has symbolized home and FAMILY life, which centered around her and which to a great extent was regarded as her responsibility. (See also WOMAN).

MOUNT ZION: Hill in Jerusalem. Originally a Jebusite fortress, it was captured by David and renamed the "City of David" (II Sam. 5:6-7). Already in the Second Temple Period various views were held as to the exact location of the biblical M.Z. The hill sloping down to the Valley of Hinnom (S.W. of the present Old City Wall) has been identified with Mt. Zion for over 1,000 years, though scholars agree that the original Zion is actually elsewhere. The identification of the present Mt. Zion is of ancient Christian tradition (the site of the Last Supper; later also that of the "Dormition" of Mary); since the Crusader Period the "TOMB OF DAVID" has also been located on the hill and the tradition has been adopted by Jews. Until 1967, with the Western Wall (Wailing Wall) of the Herodian Temple in Arab hands, attempts were made to make "Mt. Zion" and the Tomb of David a center of Jewish pilgrimage and a national shrine.

MOURNERS FOR ZION, see **AVELEI ZION**

MOURNING (Heb. *avelut*); M. rites are undertaken in times of both individual loss and national calamity (cf. Josh. 7:6, etc.). The first mention of m. in the Bible is that of Abraham weeping for his wife Sarah (Gen. 23:2). The injunction to Ezekiel after losing his wife bidding him refrain from making excessive lamentation, "weep not, neither shall thy tears run down, sigh in silence... bind thy headtire upon thee and put thy shoes upon thy feet, and cover not thine upper lip and eat not the bread of men" (Ezek. 24:16-17), is the basis from which the normal rites of m. have been inferred. The Bible in addition mentions many other such rites, some approvingly, such as RENDING one's garments (still symbolically observed), wearing sackcloth and placing earth or ashes upon the head, and others negatively, such as cutting the flesh or making oneself bald by tearing out the hair. It was also customary in talmudic times to hire professional mourners to lament and wail (cf. Jer. 9:16ff.). But on the whole the Bible admonishes mourners against excessive grief, particularly that involving bodily affliction. Various periods for observing m. are mentioned in the Bible, from thirty days (for Moses, Deut. 34:8) to seven (for Saul, I Sam. 31:13). The Egyptians devoted seventy days of m. to Jacob, who was also mourned for seven more days at the threshing floor of Atad (Gen. 50:3, 10). M. rites are undertaken for immediate relatives, viz., father, mother, son, daughter, brother, sister, and spouse, these being the relatives in whose behalf a priest is obliged to defile himself in m. (Lev. 21:2-3). Definite biblical obligation to mourn is derived from the remarks of Aaron (Maimonides on Lev. 10:3), but the biblical obligation extends only to the *onen*, i.e., to the mourner on the day of death and burial of his relative. The *onen* is forbidden to consume meat and wine and is freed from all religious obligations such as prayer, *tephillin*, etc. On returning from the burial the first food is provided for the mourner by others (*seudat havraah*). The rabbis figured the period of m. in conformity with the different periods mentioned in the Bible, each suggesting a period involving a lesser degree of mourning. Thus they say "Three days for weeping, seven days for eulogy, thirty days for pressing garments and haircutting" (*M.K.* 27b). During the first seven days (SHIVAH) the mourner is forbidden to leave his home, to study *Torah* (except Job, Lamentations, and the laws of m.), to greet another person (from the third day he may respond if greeted first), to wear leather footgear or any new garment, to bathe, use make-up, shave or cut his hair, engage in any work or business activity, or have marital relations. The mourner sits on the floor or a low stool. The day of burial and one hour of the seventh day count as full days for *shivah*. It is customary to keep a lamp burning in memory of the deceased during the entire seven days, and prayers are recited with a *minyan* at the home of the deceased. On the Sabbath of the *shivah*, the mourner attends synagogue but does not occupy his usual seat. During *shivah* it is customary to visit the mourner and comfort him with the phrase, "May the Almighty comfort you together with those who mourn for Zion and Jerusalem" (among British Jews it is customary to wish the mourner "long life"). From the seventh to the thirtieth day (SHELOSHIM) the mourner may not shave or wear new clothes; he must refrain from participating in festive activity for a full twelve months. During the *shivah*, when prayers are said at home, certain of the usual prayers are omitted and it is usual to study a section of the Mishnah at the conclusion of the service. The mourner recites KADDISH at each service for eleven months for parents and for thirty days in the case of other relatives. The day of the anniversary of death (according to the Hebrew date) is observed yearly in semi-m. (YAHRZEIT), *kaddish* is recited, and amusement avoided. At a comparatively late period, it became customary to kindle a light on occasions of *yahrzeit*. It is also usual to distribute charity on such occasions, and visit the grave of the departed. M. rites are not observed during festivals, and the advent of a festival terminates the *shivah*. Similarly, a festival occurring after the seventh day terminates the *sheloshim* period. The mourner may not marry during *sheloshim*. The general rabbinic attitude toward m. is reflected in the statement (*M.K.* 27b) "it is forbidden to overstress m. for the departed", and the Talmud lays it down as a general rule that "the law in matters pertaining to m. is decided in accord with the more lenient opinion" (*ibid.* 26b). See also TAHARAH; TOMBSTONE; YIZKOR.

MUHAMMAD, see **MOHAMMED**

MÜHLHAUSEN, YOMTOV LIPMANN (fl. c. 1400): Scholar and anti-Christian polemicist; rabbi in Prague, Cracow, and Erfurt. Arrested in 1399 with other Jewish notables, he was forced to engage in a DISPUTATION with the apostate Peter (Pesaḥ). M. was released but 80 other Jews were martyred. M., who was familiar with Latin and Christian literature, composed a famous work of polemics, the *Sepher ha-Nitzaḥon* ("The Book of Triumph") in which he summarized the Prague disputation and others. The book made a great impression on Christian theologians, who attempted to answer it in polemical tracts known as "anti-Lipmanniana".

MUKTZEH (Heb. "set aside", "excluded"): Objects which it is forbidden to handle on Sabbaths and festivals. The Talmud enumerates 12 categories of *m.* including (1) objects whose nature renders them unfit for use on the Sabbath (e.g. because of their connection with secular work, such as tools or money); (2) objects not normally used at all (e.g. broken crockery, pebbles); (3) objects which were not in existence or were inaccessible at the commencement of the Sabbath (e.g. a new-laid egg, fruit fallen from a tree during the Sabbath): this category is called *nolad*; (4) any object which at the commencement of the Sabbath served as a base for an object forbidden on the Sabbath (e.g. a tray upon which the Friday night candles were placed). Though forbidden to be moved directly, a *m.* object may be moved indirectly, e.g. broken crockery may be cleared away by the use of a broom.

MUMAR (from Heb. *hemir* "to change" — i.e., one's religion): APOSTATE; one who has forsaken Judaism for a different faith (also called *meshummad*). In this sense the word has often been substituted, at the behest of Christian censors, for the original *meshummad* to be found in the rabbinic texts. The *m.*, although a sinner, is still regarded essentially as a Jew, though in some respects he is treated as a non-Jew; he loses certain rights and privileges of an Israelite and is disqualified from giving testimony or performing ritual slaughter. The Talmud classifies apostates in various categories, e.g. a "*m.* as regards one commandment only", i.e., one who regularly violates a particular precept, and a "*m.* as regards the whole *Torah*". The former disqualifies himself in particular aspects but is not considered an apostate from Judaism. Another distinction is made between the *m. le-hakhis* who violates a precept in a spirit of rebellion and denial of its Divine authority and the *m. le-te'avon,* who violates the precept because he is not strong enough to withstand temptation. Many of the talmudic laws regarding the treatment of the various categories of *m.* have fallen into disuse.

MURDER, see **HOMICIDE**

MUSAPH (Heb. "additional sacrifice", later "Additional Service"): Service recited only on Sabbaths and festivals (New Moon, pilgrim festivals, New Year, Day of Atonement) for which the "additional sacrifices" were prescribed (Num. 28-29). It is usually read immediately after SHAḤARIT and the READING OF THE LAW but may also be said later. It consists of the AMIDAH (preceded and followed by KADDISH) spoken first silently by each worshiper and then repeated aloud by the reader. It is customary to conclude it with EIN K-ELOHEINU and ALEINU, often followed by the singing of various hymns. Except on ROSH HA-SHANAH, when it consists of 9 benedictions, the *M. amidah* invariably has 7 benedictions, the first and last three as in every *amidah,* while the intermediate one (*kedushat ha-yom*) speaks of the special significance of the day. It differs from the same benediction in the other prayers of Sabbaths and festivals in that special mention is made here of the sacrifices prescribed for the day, and a prayer is offered for speedy redemption and the rebuilding of the Temple. On *Rosh ha-Shanah* and the Day of Atonement the *M. amidah* is greatly extended by the addition of piyyutic compositions, etc. (see FESTIVAL PRAYERS). On *Rosh ha-Shanah* the SHOPHAR is sounded at the conclusion of each of the three intermediate benedictions. On the Day of Atonement, the *avodah* — a detailed poetic description of the Temple service — is recited during the repetition of the *M. amidah.* On the first day of Passover a prayer for dew and on *Shemini Atzeret* a prayer for rain, also in piyyutic form, are added. In the *Ashkenazi* rite the priests recite the priestly blessing toward the end of the *M. amidah* on festival days (in the Land of Israel, on all occasions when *M.* is recited).

MUSAR AND MUSAR LITERATURE: In biblical Hebrew *m.* signifies "punishment", "chastisement" and hence "instruction" as to right behavior. In later usage the word came to mean morals, ethics, moral instruction, etc., and more particularly religious ethics (including ascetic and devotional instruction). Unlike formal ETHICS, *m.* literature is practical in character, often preferring the homiletic approach to systematic exposition, and developing its teaching by way of aggadic interpretation of Scripture (see AGGADAH), e.g. by attributing to biblical and talmudic figures the virtues it wished to stress. Thus, although the Talmud and Midrash abound in moral teaching of the kind which later periods would have called *m.*, there is only one small tractate (*Avot*) wholly devoted to it, and that by way of presenting the moral maxims of various rabbis. It was only in the latter half of the Middle Ages that *m.* literature developed as a distinct branch of writing, often in the form of spiritual manuals, penitential tracts, and ETHICAL WILLS. The first book of Maimonides' *Code* and the *Eight Chapters* which form an introduction to his commentary on *Avot* are presentations of Aristotelian ethics rather than characteristic examples of the vast *m.* literature, which ranges from the philosophical and highly spiritual (e.g. Baḥya's *Ḥovot ha-Levavot;* also the *Hegyon ha-Nephesh* of Abraham bar Ḥiyya) to the popular and unsophisticated. A late classic of *m.* was the *Mesillat Yesharim* of Moses Ḥayyim Luzzatto (which served as a favorite textbook in the MUSAR MOVEMENT), while another popular work was the *Ḥeshbon ha-Nephesh* ("Examination of the Conscience") of Mendel Levin (known as Mendel Satanover 1741-1819), a pioneer *maskil* and member of the circle of Moses Mendelssohn. In modern, post-Emancipation Jewry, *m.* has been superseded by a more sermonizing kind of literature of edification.

MUSAR MOVEMENT: Pietistic movement, taking its name from its moral earnestness and its stress on the practice of the virtues; founded in the 19th cent. by R. Israel SALANTER. Unlike the ḥasidic movement, with which it has points in common, it did not minimize the value of the academic study of the Talmud but emphasized the emotional and spiritual character of study as distinct from mere intellectual exercise. According to Salanter, the knowledge by heart of all four sections of the *Shulḥan Arukh* does not necessarily impart immunity from vice; hence talmudic study should be supplemented by meditation on *musar* works. The M.M. introduced the study of religio-ethical classics into the curriculum of the Lithuanian *yeshivot* which became its strongholds. It demanded from its adherents rabbinic learning and punctilious observance of the Law combined with purity of mind and intention, regard for one's fellow man, and continual self-examination. In pursuit of his aims Salanter founded a MUSAR Society in Vilna (1842), where a number of the classics of *musar* literature were soon republished. In 1848 he moved to Kovno where he established a larger society but was opposed by the local rabbis who did not reject *m.* in particular but resented innovations as such; a schism however was avoided. After Salanter's death, the movement was led by R. Isaac Blaser, known as R. Itzele Peterburger who arrived in Kovno in 1879 and made the *yeshivah* of SLOBODKA the center of his activities, himself leading the life of a recluse. The M.M. posited as its main principles an inner peace of mind, forebearance, orderly thought, humility, personal cleanliness, and a lively religious awareness. Every student was encouraged to keep a notebook in which he recorded his moral and ethical failings. *Musar* classics were read aloud to a special tune. Next to Slobodka, the main centers of the M.M. were the *yeshivot* of Telz, Mir, and Navahardok, and their offshoots in Israel, the U.S., and Western Europe. To a varying extent the principles of the movement have been accepted in most *yeshivot* which now include in their curriculum at least a weekly *musar shmooz*, i.e., a a causerie on *musar* by the *mashgiaḥ* (supervisor).

MUSIC: Many of the instruments mentioned in the Bible, including those which later served for liturgical purposes in the Temple (harp, lyre, shepherd flute, trumpet), originated among Oriental peoples, particularly the Egyptians. Only the SHOPHAR (ram's horn), the sound of which is more cultist than musical, is a typical Jewish instrument, from its initial use in announcing the Jubilee year down to its surviving use in the synagogue. DAVID was traditionally the first to organize Jewish musical life, for which he designated trained groups of levites. He also seems to have been responsible for establishing a repertoire of melodies and hymns ("PSALMS") for cultic use. M. thus became an integral feature of the Temple service. In the Mishnaic Period and in talmudic times when instrumental m. was no longer practiced, partly out of mourning for the destruction of the Temple, partly because of the association of m. with pagan religious rituals, prayers and the Scriptures were recited or sung to a traditional melody. More particularly the ACCENTS of the scriptural reading came to be regarded as characteristic of Jewish m. The final graphic form of these accents was determined in the 10th cent. by the Masorete scholars of Tiberias. Some authorities regard these accents as the primary source for the system of musical notation which developed in Europe at the end of the Middle Ages. However, it is impossible to reconstruct the exact original musical significance of the accents or the tones. There are great differences between the *Ashkenazi* (N. European) and *Sephardi* (especially Near Eastern and Balkan) communities with respect to the melodic and dynamic aspects of the reading of the weekly portions from the Pentateuch and the Prophets in the synagogue. The *Ashkenazi* communities were apparently influenced by the music of the late Middle Ages in Europe, and the Oriental *Sephardim*, who brought a musical tradition with them from Spain, were later influenced by Arabic music. The Italian and Yemenite communities preserved the formulas of more ancient times. However, the syntactical system for joining the various accents into melodies is the same for all communities. The musical form of declaiming a sacred text current among the Byzantine Greeks (*ekphonesis*), was apparently taken over from Jewish religious tradition. The singing of the various FESTIVAL PRAYERS was influenced not only by the traditional melodies of the accents, but also by the popular tunes of various musical environments. However, the parallelistic structure of the Psalms and of most biblical verses in the liturgy — which possibly originated in the antiphonal singing of two choruses or of a chief singer and the congregation in the Temple — influenced the "two-part" structure of much liturgical poetry (PIYYUT). Rhyme, which appeared early in Hebrew liturgical poetry, also points to popular religious singing forms. With the development of folk singing in Europe at the end of the Middle Ages, non-Jewish tunes were adopted into the synagogue repertoire, often over the opposition of rabbis and religious authorities. There is also evidence of the use of musical instruments to accompany formal liturgical occasions, and not only celebrations such as weddings. Few Jews in Germany and Spain participated in the musical culture of the *ars nova* period, but in other countries (e.g. Italy, Netherlands), Jews took an active part in musical life and often developed a flourishing musical life of their own, producing accomplished compositions in the styles of the period. However, it was only in the 19th cent., as a result of the REFORM Movement, that Jewish written music became a major cultural phenomenon chiefly in Germany, Austria, and France. Leading cantors — e.g. Sulzer, Lewandowsky, and Baer — tried to adapt compositions to synagogal use "in the spirit of the times" and their compositions were partly inspired by traditional *Ashkenazi* tunes. At the same time, secular composers, including many Jews (e.g. Ernest Bloch), came to seek inspiration in traditional Jewish themes. An effort was also made to restore instrumental polyphonic music to the synagogue. A unique musical art developed in E. Europe at the end of the 18th cent. in the ḥasidic courts, influenced to a certain degree by the style of Oriental and popular gypsy players. The art of instrumental virtuosity and of vocal cantorial music developed under the impact of Ḥasidism. E. European cantorial music, rich in coloratura, left its stamp also on the beginnings of Israeli music two generations ago. Today, a renewed trend to orientalization is noticeable in Israeli m. The abundant musical traditions of new immigrants from the Orient (chiefly from Yemen, the Balkans, Arabic-speaking lands, and Iran) expressed in tunes of "petitions", liturgical poetry, and secular traditional songs (Spanish romances, Yemenite women's songs, etc.) has increasingly permeated modern compositions; a synthesis of this heritage is however much more difficult in the synagogue, since each community tends to cling to its own melodic tradition. See also CANTORIAL MUSIC; ORGAN.

MUSIC, CANTORIAL, see CANTORIAL MUSIC

MYRTLE, see FOUR SPECIES

MYSTICISM: A religious term originally associated with the Greek mysteries which were revealed only to initiates. Scholars have pointed out that although m. is an almost universal religious phenomenon, there is no such thing as m. in abstract, but only the mystical forms of particular religious systems—Christian, Islamic, Jewish, etc. Judaism, like other religions, has many varieties of m. They all have in common the conviction of an "inner" or "higher" reality, beyond all "external" reality or permeating it. M. is the attempt to "know", on an experimental as well as cognitive level, this inner reality which Jewish mystics associate with the Divine. To the extent that m. means an immediate contact with the Divine it can be said that all religion has an element of m. The prophets, the psalmists, and the ordinary religious practitioner all attempt to "know" God. In Judaism, the pursuit of mystical studies originally confined to small circles whose intellectual and religious background fortified them against the dangers of straying into the paths of heresy. Hence m. was often cultivated in esoteric circles who passed on their "secrets" from "mouth to ear". Later generations gave to this mystical stream within Judaism the term KABBALAH — "received" tradition. Lurianic kabbalism (see LURIA, Isaac) seized wider circles, and in the last few centuries, Jewish m. found popular expression in the folk movement called ḤASIDISM. A historical survey of Jewish m., taking the term in its broadest sense of a particular intense and personal experience of the Divine, would have to start with the Bible. The request of Moses to "know" the ways of God, and his "seeing" of God which was confined to the "back" rather than the "face" of the Divine Glory suggests mystical qualities. The visions of the prophets could also be included under the category of mystic experiences, as could numerous expressions of the psalmists. Apocalyptic literature, such as the Book of Enoch and IV Ezra, abounds in mystical visions and in revelations of hidden things. Reserved for initiates and the elect few, the esoteric teachings of a mystical "way" were normally cultivated in sectarian circles or in small conventicle groups. Among the great teachers of the Tannaitic Period, some (e.g. R. Johanan ben Zakkai) are known to have been exponents of mystical teaching and practice. The ancient rabbis divided the field of mystical lore into two broad categories; 1) MAASEH BERESHIT — the "work of creation", i.e., mystical COSMOLOGY AND COSMOGONY; and 2) MAASEH MERKAVAH — the "work of the chariot". The latter is the greater mystery, being concerned with the vision of the Divine Majesty (KAVOD) on its throne of glory. Its imagery was largely drawn from the description in the Book of Ezekiel, of the heavenly hosts and the Divine throne, to which certain gnostic elements were added. The vision was attained by an ascent of the soul — in mystical ecstasy — to the heavenly spheres. The practitioners of this kind of m. were sometimes called *Yordei Merkavah* — the "descenders of the chariot" and the mystical experience was described as "entering *Pardes*" ("PARADISE" i.e., a celestial region). Attempts to enter *Pardes* were associated with grave mental and even physical danger, and the rabbis warned that "Only one who is over forty, whose belly is full (with talmudic knowledge), and who is married should be admitted to mystical exercises and speculations". A well-known talmudic story reports that "Four entered *Pardes*, namely BEN AZZAI, BEN ZOMA, AḤER, and AKIVA. Ben Azzai looked and died. Ben Zoma looked and went mad. Aḥer became an apostate. Only R. Akiva entered in peace and came out in peace" (*Ḥag.* 14b). The Talmud does not specify the nature of the mystic visions experienced by the "descenders of the chariot", but some small post-talmudic writings known as the HEIKHALOT tracts, probably composed in Babylonia during the 6th-8th cents., contain more detailed information. "The

Greater and Lesser *Heikhalot*;" the "SHIUR KOMAH"; the "Alphabet of Rabbi AKIVA", Midrash *Konen* — are some of the works which have survived from this period. The characteristic mood of these works is a sense of awe and trembling before the Divine Majesty. Often they describe the experiences of those who have attempted to pass through the various chambers of the celestial palaces, guarded by heavenly hosts, until they approach the Throne of Glory. The books include ecstatic hymns, references to a complex system of ANGELOLOGY, speculation about the mystical import of numbers and letters, references to the fasting and purification rites which precede the ecstatic visions, etc. This literature has left its imprint on Jewish liturgy (e.g. the KEDUSHAH prayer and many hymns used in the liturgy of the "Days of Awe"). Two mystic texts of the Post-Talmudic Period which played an important part in later kabbalistic speculations were the *Sepher* YETZIRAH ("Book of Creation") and the Book of BAHIR (of "Brightness"). The former expounds the creative powers of the Hebrew ALPHABET and speaks of ten SEPHIROT which, in combination with the alphabet, are the elements of creation. The latter, the first kabbalistic work in the narrow technical sense, appeared in southern France in the 12th cent., but contained material and traditions from the East. During the 12th and 13th cents., mystic traditions from the East (Palestine and Babylonia) entered Europe through Italy. One strong mystical stream cf theological speculation and devotional life developed among the 12th cent. ḤASIDEI ASHKENAZ (the "pious of Germany and Western Europe"). R. JUDAH BEN SAMUEL HE-ḤASID (d. 1217) and R. ELEAZAR OF WORMS (d. 1238) were among the leaders of this movement, which propagated an other-worldly asceticism, "equanimity" in the face of all wordly joys or trials, humility, and piety. It also stressed the value of the proper *kavvanot* (DEVOTIONS) accompanying prayer. Its mystic speculations centered about the mystery of the Cherubim and the Glory of God, looking upon these as manifestations of the utterly hidden and transcendent Godhead. Another mystic tradition — the one later associated with the term Kabbalah — originated in the part of S. France known as Provence. Abraham ben David and his son R. Isaac the Blind, were the leading teachers of mystic circles in this part of Europe. Their disciples used the term Kabbalah to refer to esoteric teachings which had been "received" either by private revelation or by ancient tradition. The Book of *Bahir*, which appeared at this time in Provence, already contains allusions to the specifically kabbalistic doctrine of the *sephirot*, which assumes a series of Divine forces or EMANATIONS mediating between the utterly transcendent and infinite God, and this finite, created universe. Echoes of certain oriental doctrines about the TRANSMIGRATION of souls also found their way into the *Bahir* and the kabbalistic speculations of Provence, and from there into the Spanish mystical schools. Among those who helped transplant the m. of southern France to Spain was Rabbi Azriel, who was a disciple of Asher ben David, a nephew of Isaac the Blind. R. Azriel settled in Gerona, which soon became the center of an important kabbalistic school. Other kabbalistic centers in Spain were Burgos, Toledo, and Barcelona. It was in Spain that classical Kabbalah developed its characteristic theosophical systems in which ancient gnostic elements combined with medieval neo-Platonism. Somewhat outside the main stream of Spanish Kabbalah was Abraham ABULAFIA (flourished c. 1270), whose "prophetic" Kabbalah aspired to the experience of mystical illumination which, he thought, could be achieved by meditation on combinations of Hebrew letters. This meditation was combined with other physical-psychic techniques designed to make the mystic a proper vessel for receiving the Divine light.

The most important literary product of Spanish Kabbalah is the ZOHAR. Traditional kabbalists attributed its authorship to the 2nd cent. Palestinian *tanna* R. Simeon bar Yoḥai. Modern scholars agree with earlier critics who held it to be the work of the 13th cent. Spanish kabbalist MOSES DE LEON. The book appeared in Spain in the second half of the 13th cent. and soon became the most influential single source of kabbalistic speculation. The basic premise of the Zohar, as, indeed, of all Kabbalah, is that the material world is merely the visible aspect of an unseen reality. As such, it is both symbol and part of that larger reality which is not to be perceived by the physical senses but can be partly revealed to the "Masters of the Mystery, or the Hidden Wisdom". The essential unity of all the "worlds", both the hidden and the manifest, is a basic affirmation of the Kabbalah. Everything "below" draws sustenance from "above"; everything in the lower world is connected with its spiritual counterpart in the higher worlds. The mystic's task is to be aware of this mystery, to attune the dynamics of life so that they are harmoniously united with the invisible sustaining structure, and to effect by action and prayer a greater harmony and unity between the upper and lower worlds. This correspondence between upper and lower spheres exists in all parts of the Divine creation. "The Lord made this world corresponding to the world above, and everything which is above has its counterpart below... and yet they all constitute one mystery". The central and most complete symbol of this correspondence between the "upper" and "lower" is man. "When the Holy One created man, He set in him all the images of the supernal mysteries of the world above, and all the lower mysteries of the world below, and all are designed in man who stands in the image of God". A basic idea of the Kabbalah is that the "lower" cannot only be influenced by the "higher" but may also influence it. Every move on this earth calls forth a corresponding movement in the spheres above. Man is therefore an active co-worker, even co-creator, with God. To guide him in his work, man has been given the *Torah,* which contains much more than appears on a surface reading. The kabbalist reads the *Torah* not only as a document of history or a code of law, but as a mystical account, in "cipher language" as it were, of the dynamics of the hidden Divine life underlying creation. The kabbalist knows how to "decode" the esoteric meaning of Scripture. To be sure, no man can penetrate into the innermost mystery of the utterly transcendent Godhead, sometimes referred to as *Ein Soph* — the Infinite which is the "Most Hidden of the Hidden". But this *Ein Soph* clothes itself in "garments", i.e., manifests itself as the living God of religion in Being, creation, and revelation. These "garments" are, in a sense, "emanations" of God; manifestations of the hidden Godhead as well as the "channels" through which the Divine influence flows and operates in all the "worlds". Generally known as *sephirot*, they are described in the various kabbalistic systems by a variety of terms. The *Bahir* compares them to an inverted tree, whose roots are above and the foliage below. Another frequent image is that of the human body, considered as a paradigm of the Divine Life manifesting itself in the symbolic figure of ADAM KADMON, the primordial man (see also MICROCOSM). The Divine world of the *sephirot* is conceived by the kabbalists as a mystical organism in which the dynamics of the Divine life manifests and fulfills itself. The usual schematic description of the *sephirot* includes ten entities: 1. *Keter Elyon*, the "supreme crown" of God; 2. *Ḥokhmah*, the "wisdom" or primordial idea of God; 3. *Binah*, the "intelligence" of God; 4. *Ḥesed,* the "love" or mercy of God; 5. *Gevurah* or *Din*, the "power" of God, chiefly manifested as the power of stern judgment and punishment; 6. *Raḥamim* or *Tipheret*, the "compassion" or "beauty" of God, to which falls the task of mediating between the two preceding *Sephirot;* 7. *Netzaḥ*, the "lasting endurance" of God; 8. *Hod,* the "majesty" of God; 9. *Yesod*, the "basis" or "foundation" of all active forces in God; 10. *Malkhut*, the "kingdom" of God, usually described in the Zohar as the *Keneset Yisrael*, the mystical archetype of Israel's community, or as the SHEKHINAH. The relationships between these *sephirot*, their separations and conjunctions represent for the kabbalist the mystery of the inner life and unity of God, as well as the key to that cosmic harmony and unity between "lower" and "higher" which assures the continuous flow of grace (*shepha*) into this world. Spanish Kabbalah continued to develop in the 14th and 15th centuries, and reached a fresh climax in the century following the expulsion from Spain. The new *Sephardi* communities in the Turkish empire became centers of kabbalistic activity. The most important of these centers was SAFED in Upper Galilee which, in the 16th cent., became the spiritual capital of a mystical Judaism. While Moses CORDOVERO brought traditional Kabbalah to new heights of systematic synthesis and intellectual penetration, Isaac Luria initiated a new school which profoundly transformed mystical theology and practice by adding new gnostic, mythical, and messianic motifs. One of the basic images of Lurianic doctrine is the "Breaking of the Vessels", a cosmic catrastrophe associated with the early stages of creation, as a result of which sparks of the Divine Light-Essence fell into chaos and into what was subsequently to become the sphere of the demonic. To restore the broken or disarrayed order of creation by lifting the sparks to their proper place by a process called TIKKUN ("repair") is man's mission on earth. This theme of a cosmic fall and eventual redempton of the sparks of Divinity from the "shells" which enclosed them, is related to the Lurianic doctrine of TZIMTZUM ("retraction"). The latter concept refers to the process whereby the Infinite God "withdrew", as it were, "from Himself into Himself", thereby creating a vacuum empty of His Presence— in which creation could take place, but in which also the root ground of evil could come into being. The eschatological character of Lurianism contributed greatly to the messianic ferment of the 17th cent. which led to the great messianic outburst connected with the name of SHABBETAI TZEVI. The Sabbataian movement gave rise to a heretical Kabbalah which flourished in secret conventicles and whose furtive but dangerous existence explains much of the rabbinic hostility and suspicion directed against the founders of ḤASIDISM, the last great mystical movement in Judaism. Severely condemned by 19th cent. critics as irrational, superstitious, and downright foolish, Jewish m. has found more systematic treatment in modern scholarship and literature. In recent years, Abraham Isaac KOOK formulated a mystical theology based on traditional kabbalistic doctrines as well as contemporary Jewish experience.

N

NAHAVENDI, BENJAMIN, see **BENJAMIN BEN MOSES NAHAVENDI**

NAḤEM (Heb. "comfort"): Prayer instituted by Palestinian *amoraim* and recited in the Afternoon Service *amidah* on *Av* 9. It prays for the comforting of those who mourn Zion and for the rebuilding of the city. Joseph Karo suggested that it is recited at the Afternoon Service to correspond to the time of the actual destruction of the Temple.

NAḤMAN OF BRATZLAV (1772-1810): One of the most original of the hasidic leaders. A great-grandson of Israel BAAL SHEM Tov, he regarded himself as the only true interpreter of the teachings of his ancestor, and incurred the hostility of other ḥasidic rabbis by his criticism of them. He visited Palestine in 1798 and on his return settled in Bratzlav. N. stressed simple faith and prayer as against intellectualism and developed the theory of the TZADDIK as the intermediary between man and God. His outstanding contribution to ḥasidic literature is his collection of folk tales (*Sippurei Maasiyyot* — homely parables which his followers believe to enshrine the most recondite and esoteric mysteries. He did not establish a dynasty; as he emphasized to his followers that he would still be with them even after his death, they never appointed a successor.

NAḤMANI BAR KAYLIL, see **ABBAYE**

NAḤMANIDES, see **MOSES BEN NAḤMAN**

NAHUM: Seventh MINOR PROPHET; prophesied in Judah toward the end of the 7th cent. B.C.E. He foretold the destruction of Nineveh in 612 B.C.E., and interpreted it as heralding the downfall of Assyria. According to N., God's justice — which extends over the whole world — might at times appear to tarry but is nevertheless assured. His book consists of three chapters, marked by a rich, pungent, and alliterative style.

NAHUM OF GIMZO (1st-2nd cents. C.E.): *Tanna* noted for his learning, poverty, and pious resignation in the face of misfortune(which he accepted with the phrase *gam zu le-tovah* "this too is for the best"). His teachings became influential through his pupil R. Akiva, who was responsible for the general acceptance of N.'s methods for the halakhic interpretation of Scripture (see HERMENEUTICS).

NAJARA, ISRAEL BEN MOSES (c. 1555-1628): Palestinian rabbi, kabbalist, and poet. The outstanding Jewish poet of his period, he composed sacred and secular poems in Hebrew and Aramaic, restoring PIYYUT to its former importance. His main themes are praise of God, laments for the sufferings of Israel, and longing for redemption. His poetic description of the mystical union between God and Israel often resorted to an erotic imagery that was condemned by other rabbis. Several hundred of his religious poems are extant, including *piyyutim* for each Sabbath and festival. Many passed into the liturgy, particularly in Italy, Palestine, and the Orient. Best known is YAH RIBBON OLAM, which was incorporated into the Sabbath ZEMIROT in all rites. The outstanding collection of his poems is *Zemirot Yisrael* ("Songs of Israel").

NAKDANIM (Heb. "punctuators"): Scholars who provided biblical manuscripts with masoretic apparatus, accentuations, and punctuation. They were the successors of the MASORETES, whose work they conserved. The *n.* flourished from the 9th cent. until the invention of printing.

NAME, CHANGE OF, see **CHANGE OF NAMES**

NAMES: Proper n. in ancient times had a significance to which no parallel exists at the present day. The name was taken as representing the essence of its bearer; hence people were often given new n. upon entering a new mode of being. The earlier books of the Bible often explain why individuals were called by certain n. or why the n. of Abram, Sarai, Jacob, and Hoshea were changed to Abraham, Sarah, Israel, and Joshua. N. of gods often formed a part of personal names, and it was not uncommon at first for Israelite n. to contain the element BAAL, though this was discontinued under the influence of monotheism, when the elements *El, Eli, Jeho* were substituted. According to the Talmud (*Ber.* 3b) the name given to a person affects his future, and rabbinic literature abounds in etymologies for the n. of persons, as well as of places and even animals mentioned in the Bible. Rabbinic law requires the most extreme and meticulous care in the correct orthography of all names in documents, particularly a bill of divorce, which can be invalidated by a misspelling or omission. A Jew is known by his own Hebrew name and that of his father (X.

son of Y.) and in this form he is "called up" to the Reading of the Law in the synagogue. The Talmud states that "the majority of Jews in the Diaspora adopt the non-Jewish names of their environment" (*Git.* 11a), but the rabbis saw a special virtue in the fact that "the children of Israel did not change their names in Egypt; as Reuben and Simeon they descended and as Reuben and Simeon they went out". The notion of a connection between name and essence also underlies the rabbinic statement (*R.H.* 16b) that a "CHANGE OF NAME" was one of the four things which could avert the evil decree. This gave rise to the ritual of "changing" the name of a dangerously ill person, usually by adding an auspicious name such as "Ḥayyim" (Life) or "Joshua" (Salvation). See also GOD, NAMES OF.

NAMES OF GOD, see **GOD, NAMES OF**

NARBONI, MOSES, see **MOSES HA-DARSHAN**

NASHIM (Heb. "Women"): Third order of the MISHNAH comprising the tractates YEVAMOT, KETUBBOT, NEDARIM, NAZIR, SOTAH, GITTIN, and KIDDUSHIN. All have *gemara* in both Talmuds and are also in the Tosephta. Their subject matter covers betrothal, marriage, divorce, marital relationships, and vows.

NASI (Heb. "prince"): According to the Talmud the presiding officer of the Great SANHEDRIN in the Temple bore the title *nasi*, though some scholars regard this as an anachronism and believe that in the days of the Temple the High Priest was president of the Sanhedrin and that the title *n.* belonged to the head of the Pharisaic party. The title *n.* is said to have been borne at first by one member each of the ZUGOT (the other being *Av Bet Din*), beginning with Yose ben Joezer (c. 160 B.C.E.). Hillel established a dynasty and his descendants continued to hold this office till the first quarter of the 5th cent. Various *nesiim* (pl.) are credited with having introduced far-reaching innovations in Jewish law. Thus Simeon ben Shetaḥ (c. 70 B.C.E.) introduced the KETUBBAH by which the husband pledged himself to pay his wife two hundred *zuzim* in the case of his death or of divorce. Simeon also established elementary schools. R. Gamaliel I ruled that the testimony of one witness to the death of a man was sufficient to permit his widow to remarry. Hillel II's (c. 350 C.E.) formulation of the principles of the CALENDAR was the last great *takkanah* (ordinance) of the *nesiim*. Soon after the destruction of the Jewish state, the *nesiim* obtained official recognition as the political heads of the Jewish communities throughout the Roman Empire. Their new title of "patriarch" was the equivalent of the Greek *ethnarch* borne by the early Hasmonean princes. In their new rôle, the *nesiim* were in constant communication with the Roman government. Thus it is related of R. Gamaliel II of Yavneh that he maintained a school for the study of Greek in order to train qualified officials. The *n.* carried on varied activities. He headed the board which fixed and proclaimed the New Moon and the leap years; he proclaimed national fast days in emergencies; he visited distant communities in order to strengthen the religious loyalty of the people, particularly in places where they had come under hellenistic influence. In order to maintain his educational and political activities, the *n.* dispatched emissaries to collect funds in the Jewish communities. The ordination of scholars and the appointment of judges were in the hands of the *n.* while through their apostles, the *nesiim* actually governed the Jewish communities throughout the Roman Empire. Outside Palestine, the title was often applied to the lay leader of the Jewish community.

NATHAN: Prophet ministering during the reigns of David and Solomon. His apposite parable of the ewe-lamb brought home to King David the wickedness of his crime against Uriah the Hittite (II Sam. 12:1-14). It was N. who also informed David that the Temple would be built by his son and not by himself. The prophet's intervention against Adonijah's usurpation of the throne ensured the anointing of Solomon as king of Israel (I Kings 1:5-39).

NATHAN BEN JEHIEL OF ROME (1035-1106): Talmudic lexicographer. His *Arukh* was the only medieval dictionary of the Talmud and Midrash. A comprehensive work, it not only quotes but also explains difficult talmudic passages. The material is arranged alphabetically and includes many sources otherwise unknown (down to the Gaonic Period) as well as important variant readings of the text. This book was the basis of subsequent talmudic lexicography and constituted an outstanding philological achievement for its period.

NATHAN OF GAZA (Ghazzati; c. 1644-1690): Kabbalist and messianic enthusiast. He met SHABBETAI TZEVI in 1665 and became his "prophet", and the theologian of the messianic movement. In his tracts and epistles he proclamed Shabbetai's messiahship and the imminence of redemption. It was N. who developed Shabbetai's personality and sense of mission. N. traveled extensively in behalf of the movement and remained faithful to Shabbetai even after the latter's apostasy, spending his last years in misery and poverty among fellow Sabbataians in Macedonia. His doctrines were based on a new interpretation of the KABBALAH of Isaac LURIA. He taught that the soul of the Messiah must first descend to the realm of darkness in order to redeem the Divine sparks imprisoned there through the process of restoration (TIKKUN); only after this was accomplished would the soul of the Messiah be revealed in its earthly incarnation. This theory allowed for an acceptable explanation of Shabbetai's apostasy and for the movement's antinomianism.

NATOREI KARTA (Aram. "The Guardians of the City"): Name adopted by a group of Orthodox extremists in Jerusalem who refuse to recognize the existence or the authority of the State of Israel, in view of the secular nature of its creation and orientation. The phrase originates from an incident in which R. Judah Ha-Nasi sent R. Ḥiyya and R. Ashi on a pastoral tour of inspection. In one town they asked to see the "guardians of the city" and the city guard was paraded before them. "These are not the guardians of the city but its destroyers" they declared. "Who then are the guardians?" they were asked, and they answered "The scribes and the scholars", referring them to Ps. 127:1 (Y. *Ḥag.* 76c).

NATRONAI II BEN ḤILAI (9th cent.): *Gaon* of Sura, 853-858. He was the author of many responsa, those dealing with liturgical custom being particularly significant. His arrangement of the "hundred daily blessings" (prepared at the request of the community of Lucena in Spain) laid the foundation for the prayer book compiled by N.'s successor AMRAM GAON. A bitter opponent of the Karaites, N. sought to establish uniform custom so as to strengthen Rabbanite Judaism.

NATURAL LAW: 1. The law by which NATURE, i.e., the cosmic order, operates; and 2. the moral law inherent in the natural order and discoverable by man's contemplation of nature (his own and that of all things around him) even without a special REVELATION from God. Whereas the rabbinic doctrine of seven NOACHIAN LAWS does not refer to n.l. but rather to an original revelation for all mankind, many other rabbinic dicta suggest the more or less vaguely assumed existence of a n.l. Medieval philosophers stressed that revelation was necessary for such ritual regulations or details as would not occur to human beings, or for such insights and precepts as the human intellect might well, but not necessarily, arrive at unaided. In order not to leave the formulation of the basic rules of religion and morals to the vicissitudes of human intellectual development, God also revealed laws that actually form part of n.l. (e.g. the prohibition against murder, or the duty of honoring one's father and mother). Non-philosophical theologians held that the purpose of the TORAH was to lift Israel above n.l. to a supernatural order reflected by the revealed law.

NATURE: The concept of n. as a system operating according to fixed laws of its own, derives from Greek philosophy rather than from the Bible. The biblical writers, while evincing an appreciation of the regular workings of the universe (cf. Ps. 104 and 148), are nevertheless primarily concerned with the acts of the Creator and His permanent and direct responsibility for the cosmic order (see also Ps. 19). The rabbis held a similar view: the regularity of natural phenomena was an expression of God's will, just as were miracles. In fact "he who commanded the oil to burn, can command the vinegar to burn". Some medieval thinkers (e.g. BAḤYA IBN PAKUDA) held that admitting the existence of n. and an autonomous NATURAL LAW was tantamount to denying the sole and exclusive rôle of God's will and PROVIDENCE. However most philosophers argued that there was no contradiction between belief in God as the First Cause of all things, and an established secondary order ("Creation" which He had made to function according to a causality of its own. It was generally admitted that the Creator could suspend or "break through" the natural order by MIRACLES. Modern philosophers of n. often require a theological reformulation of the relationship of n. to God. Whereas most traditional systems agreed that God was "outside" — viz., "above" — n., some modern "naturalistic" (viz., anti-supernaturalistic) doctrines take a different view. Spinoza's pantheism identifies God and n. The ancient rabbis and medieval thinkers insisted that the contemplation of n. led to a recognition of God, and Abraham is said by the Midrash to have become convinced of the existence of God by speculating on the nature and origin of the universe. He therefore possessed a Natural Religion, arrived at by Natural Theology, even before God manifested Himself to him and introduced him to the order of revealed religion.

NAZARENES, see **EBIONITES; JEWISH CHRISTIANS**

NAZIR (Heb. "NAZIRITE"): Fourth tractate of the Mishnah order of *Nashim*, with *gemara* in both Talmuds. It discusses laws connected with the nazirite (Num. 6:1-21).

NAZIRITE (Heb. *nazir* from *nazar* "to dedicate"): Ascetic person who takes the nazirite vow. This vow prohibits the n. from (1) partaking of wine, the products of the vine, or strong drink; (2) cutting his hair; and (3) contracting impurity from a dead body, even that of his closest relatives. If no period of time is specified in undertaking the vow, it is held to be binding for thirty days. If the n. becomes ritually unclean, the continuity of his period of consecration is broken and he must shave, bring certain sacrifices, and then recommence his naziriteship (Num. 6:1-21). One may become a n. for life (*nazir olam*) in which case the heavy growth of hair may be thinned each year but this must be accompanied by bringing the sacrifices specified for a n. who has completed his vow; or a n. like SAMSON who, consecrated at birth, may never cut his hair and if ritually unclean is not obligated to offer sacrifices normally brought for n. defilement (*Nazir* 1:2). Women and slaves (but not heathens) could take the vow with the permission of their husbands or masters. While recognizing the sanctity attaching to the true n., the n. vow was not recommended by the rabbis except in cases where a clear break with the past seemed necessary and beneficial for the individual; moderation rather than abstention was advocated by the rabbis, who also stated that the institution of the n. could exist only in the Land of Israel which alone is blessed with the appropriate holiness (although instances of n.'s outside Israel are recorded). The subject is discussed in the talmudic tractate NAZIR.

NECROMANCY: DIVINATION through communication with the dead. N. is forbidden in the Bible (Deut. 18:11) and is termed "an abomination unto the Lord". The detailed vocabulary used in the Bible (*ov, yiddeoni,* "inquiring of the dead") suggests the existence of different kinds of n., but the only actual account of its practice in the Bible is Saul's request to the witch of Endor to raise the soul of Samuel (I Sam. 28:7-20). Most earlier Jewish authorities regarded the practice as efficacious but forbidden, though the more rationalistically inclined thinkers (Phineas ben Ḥophni Gaon, Maimonides, etc.) denounced it as a gross superstition and explained the story of Saul at Endor as a dream. (See MAGIC).

NEDARIM (Heb. "Vows"): Third tractate of the Mishnah order of *Nashim*, dealing with vows and their annulment (Num. 30:2-17). It has *gemara* in both Talmuds.

NEDAVAH, see **FREE-WILL-OFFERING**

NEDER, see **VOWS**

NEGAIM (Heb. "Plagues" i.e., leprosy): Third tractate of the Mishnah order of *Toharot*. It deals with the laws concerning LEPROSY in a person, in clothing, and in habitations, as well as with the purification of the leper (cf. Lev. 13-14).

NEGINOT (Heb. "melodies"): The signs serving as musical indications for the reading of the Bible. See ACCENTS.

NEGLIGENCE: Charges of n. arise when work given to an artisan or laborer is performed badly, or with disregard for the instructions of the owner, or if the materials entrusted to the artisan are ruined by him. In these instances full compensation must be made by the artisan. Beside total n., *halakhah* recognizes "n. which borders upon intention" and also "n. bordering upon accident" in which cases the ordinary penalty for n. does not apply — in the former instance because it would be too light a penalty, in the latter because it would be too severe. For ritual n. see ERROR. In the case of movable property given in trust without payment, the bailee ("unpaid guardian") is responsible for criminal n. (*peshiah*) only.

NEHARDEA: City in Babylonia situated near the junction of the Euphrates river and the Nahr Malka. As seat of the EXILARCH its Jewish origins were traditionally traced back to King Jehoiachin who was said to have erected a synagogue there for which earth and stones were brought from Jerusalem. The ancient ACADEMY at N. reached its zenith under the *amora* SAMUEL; shortly after his death the city was destroyed by the Palmyrenes (259). The Nehardean tradition of Jewish scholarship passed to the academy of PUMBEDITA which was founded by Samuel's pupil JUDAH BAR EZEKIEL. Although many scholars continued to reside in N. after it was rebuilt, the town never regained its former prominence as a center of Jewish learning.

NEHEMIAH: Cupbearer to the Persian king Artaxerxes by whom he was appointed governor of Judea. According to the traditional account, he collaborated with EZRA in reforming the Jewish community at Jerusalem and countering its spiritual and physical stagnation. In the teeth of SAMARITAN opposition he rebuilt the walls of Jerusalem (Neh. 6:15) and supported Ezra's reforms with the weight of his authority. The Temple services were reorganized, strong action was taken against mixed marriages and the desecration of the Sabbath, and the people's fidelity to the Law reaffirmed in a solemn covenant (chaps. 8-10). His vigor and drive and the success of his campaign testify to a character of singular power, zealously devoted to the cause of God and His people. N.'s own memoirs form the basis of the biblical account. Traditionally regarded as a unit, the books of Ezra-Nehemiah (now divided into two separate works) are 10th in the Hagiographa. Modern scholars believe the book was compiled by the author of Chronicles, but are not certain of the exact chronological relationship between Ezra and N.

NEHUNYAH BEN HA-KANAH (1st cent. C.E.): *Tanna* quoted frequently in the Talmud especially as a halakhist. He was the teacher of R. ISHMAEL and consequently was highly regarded by the kabbalists who ascribed to him the Book of BAHIR, the prayer *Anna be-Koaḥ*, and other mystical compositions.

NEHUSHTAN (from Heb. *naḥash* — snake, and *neḥoshet* — copper): Term used by HEZEKIAH (II Kings 18:4) in derogation of the figure of a copper snake worshiped by the Israelites. According to Num. 21:6-9, the brazen serpent was originally fashioned by Moses in the wilderness and put upon a pole; the Israelites who had been bitten by "fiery serpents" sent by God as a punishment were to look at this serpent of brass and be healed.

The association of the N. with heathen snake worship induced Hezekiah to destroy it in the course of his campaign for religious reform.

NEILAH (Heb. "closing", i.e., of the gates): Originally a prayer offered on all public fast days at sunset when the Temple gates were closed; now recited only on the Day of Atonement. It is the last of the five prayers of the Day of Atonement and its recital is concluded at nightfall, when the fast ends. It is recited with particular solemnity and to impressive melodies. The medieval poets interpreted the word *N.* as referring to the closing of the heavenly gates at the sealing of Divine judgment on the Day of Atonement. After *Ashrei* (Ps. 145), the AMIDAH (preceded and followed by KADDISH) is first said silently by each worshiper and then repeated aloud by the reader. It differs from the other *amidot* of the Day of Atonement in that it contains only the shorter confession of sins (*vidduy*) and not the long version, which is replaced by a prayer *attah noten* extolling God's mercy in forgiving the repentant sinner. After the *amidah,* the first verse of the SHEMA is proclaimed (once) by the reader and repeated by the congregation, followed by "*barukh shem,* etc." ("Blessed be the name of the glory of His kingdom for ever and ever") said three times, and "the Lord is God" (I Kings 18:39) said seven times. After this, the SHOPHAR is sounded once (if night has fallen) to indicate the termination of the solemn fast day. The TALLIT is worn by the congregation at *N.* as at all Day of Atonement services.

NEO-ORTHODOXY, see **ORTHODOXY**

NEO-PLATONISM, see **PLATONISM**

NER TAMID (Heb.): "Eternal Lamp" prescribed in Exod. 27:20-21 and Lev. 24:2 as an essential appointment of the Sanctuary in the wilderness and later of the Temple. It had to be placed "without the veil of testimony in the tabernacle of the Congregation" and was part of the seven-branched candelabrum. The priests had to see that it was kept continually burning. Only pure olive oil could be used for it. The ever-burning lamp was taken to symbolize, among other things, the eternal watchfulness and providence of God over His people. The account of the origin of ḤANUKKAH given in the Talmud (*Shab.* 21b) centers round the miracle by which a single day's supply of pure oil found in the Temple by the victorious Maccabees burnt for eight days until new oil could be prepared. The Eternal Lamp was situated in the west of the Temple and faced westward; it was therefore called "the Western Lamp" (Mishnah *Tam.* 6:1; *Shab.* 22b). Since the synagogue is called a "minor sanctuary" (*Meg.* 29a) it became customary, but not obligatory, for it too to incorporate a *N.T.* There was, however, considerable initial objection to the now universal practice of suspending it in front of the Ark, on the grounds that this was a gentile custom, and it was felt that as in the Temple the *N.T.* should be suspended on the western wall.

NESEKH: WINE used or intended for use in heathen worship. Anything used in connection with pagan worship was forbidden as food, drink, or for any other purpose, nor was benefit to be derived from it. The wine of the heathen was, in former times, always suspect of having been used for a LIBATION or similar ceremonial, and was thus strictly prohibited. Even though such libations have largely ceased nowadays, the ban on drinking gentile wine — one of several prohibitions ascribed to the GREAT SYNAGOGUE and intended to limit social contact and conviviality with non-Jews (*Shab.* 17b) — is still considered binding in rabbinic law. Such wine, because not actually libation wine, is technically described as *setam yeinam* ("their wine") but is popularly called *n.*; it must not be drunk, though benefit from it (e.g. selling) is permitted. The prohibition also extends to unbottled wine that has been merely touched by a gentile, but does not include liquids not made from grapes. "Kosher" wine signifies wine guaranteed not to have been touched by a gentile before the bottle has been sealed.

NESHAMAH YETERAH (Heb. "extra soul"): According to legend, God gave Adam a higher soul which dwelt within him and elevated him throughout the Sabbath. This soul is granted to every man for the duration of the Sabbath (*Betz.* 16a) and, according to one interpretation, the custom of smelling SPICES during the HAVDALAH service at the termination of the Sabbath is meant to comfort man for the loss of this extra soul.

NETHINIM: Servants in the Temple; according to tradition they were originally the conquered Canaanites ("hewers of wood and drawers of water") given by David to the levites to perform menial tasks in the sanctuary along with Gibeonites. N. went into the Babylonian Exile and returned with Zerubbabel and Ezra. Though subscribing to the commandments as incorporated in Ezra's covenant, they were still regarded as inferior and intermarriage with them remained forbidden. They lived in a special section of Jerusalem and in other cities of Judah; the N. were still known at the time of R. Judah Ha-Nasi, while in amoraic times mention is made of a village of N.

NETILAT YADAYIM, see **ABLUTION**

NEVELAH, see **CARCASS**

NEW CHRISTIANS, see **MARRANOS**

NEW MONTH, ANNOUNCEMENT OF (Heb. *birkat ha-ḥodesh,* literally the "blessing of the New Moon"): Public announcement of the day(s) of the forthcoming *Rosh Ḥodesh* (NEW MOON) made in the synagogue on the preceding Sabbath after the

READING OF THE LAW; this is a survival of the ancient custom of *kiddush ha-hodesh* by which the official date of the beginning of the new month was determined by the Sanhedrin (*Soph.* 19:9). It is accompanied by various prayers; the opening passage *yehi ratzon* (found only in the *Ashkenazi* rite) is an adaptation of a private prayer of the 3rd cent. *amora* Rav (*Ber.* 16b). Though not part of the obligatory prayers, the "blessing" is invested with great solemnity and chanted to a moving tune.

NEW MOON (Heb. *Rosh Ḥodesh*): The beginning of the Hebrew month. During the period of the First Temple the N.M. was regarded as a semi-festival (possibly the continuation of an ancient moon-festival tradition) when the people abstained from business (Amos 8:5), thronged the Temple (Is. 1:13-14; 66:23), held family feasts (I Sam. 20:5), and visited the prophet (II Kings 4:23). The festive character of the day was equally signified by its special sacrifice (Num. 28:11-15) and by the blowing of the trumpet (Num. 10:10). The festiveness of the N.M. disappeared during the Second Temple Period except for another waning custom by which women were granted freedom from work on that day as a reward for their reluctance to give their ornaments for the fashioning of the Golden Calf (*Turei Zahav* to *Oraḥ Ḥayyim* 417). Nevertheless considerable attention was paid to the determination of the N.M. by the SANHEDRIN through the testimony of witnesses (see CALENDAR), and the liturgy of the day reflects its ancient importance. When in the 3rd cent. Rav on a visit to Babylon from Palestine heard a community reciting the Half-HALLEL on that day, for which there was no apparent authority, he decided to retain the custom as it was obviously based on an old tradition; this practice has since become universal. Its festive nature is further stressed by the scriptural reading, the recitation of YAALEH VE-YAVO, and the MUSAPH service, before the recital of which the *tephillin* are removed. Fasting and mourning are forbidden on the N.M. (which is observed for two days when the preceding month has 30 days). The blessing recited on the Sabbath preceding the N.M. (*Shabbat Mevarekhim*) is a relic of a custom in the synagogue — antedating the fixing of the CALENDAR — to establish the N.M. on the evidence of eye-witnesses. See NEW MONTH, ANNOUNCEMENT OF; YOM KIPPUR KATAN.

NEW MOON, BLESSING OF, see **KIDDUSH LEVANAH**

NEW TESTAMENT: Name given to the specifically Christian holy scriptures, as distinct from the Jewish Bible which is called by Christians the OLD TESTAMENT. The expression itself is biblical, occurring in Jer. 31:31 "Behold the days come, saith the Lord, that I will make a new covenant with the House of Israel and the House of Judah". Christians applied this verse to accord with their belief in the abrogation of the Law through the fulfillment of the messianic prophecies in the person of JESUS.

NEW YEAR: The first Mishnah of tractate ROSH HA-SHANAH enumerates four days of the year which are regarded as New Years for different and specific purposes; *Nisan* 1 for dating the reigns of kings, and the order of festivals and months; *Elul* 1 for tithing cattle; *Tishri* 1 for calendrical purposes and for the seventh year of release (SHEMITTAH) and JUBILEE; and *Shevat* 15 (or 1) as the NEW YEAR FOR TREES. Of these four only *Tishri* 1 is celebrated as a religious N.Y. festival (ROSH HA-SHANAH) since on that day "all who have entered into the world pass before Him (in judgment) like a flock of sheep" (Mishnah *R.H.* 1:2).

NEW YEAR FOR TREES (Heb. *Rosh ha-Shanah la-Ilanot*; also *Tu bi-Shevat*, i.e., *Shevat* 15): Originally the New Year for Trees had no religious significance, except that according to the School of Hillel the age of a tree for purposes of fruit tithes and similar laws (e.g. ORLAH) is reckoned from that date — *Shevat* 15 — when with the approaching end of winter, the sap begins to shoot up in the trees. According to the School of Shammai the date is *Shevat* 1. The Talmud gives no indication of any celebration or liturgical observance connected with *Shevat* 15, though certain penitential prayers are omitted and fasting is forbidden. Since the 17th cent., partly under the influence of the kabbalists, who saw profound esoteric meaning in the verse "For man is like the tree of the field" (Deut. 20:19), a special ceremonial developed for the day. Among *Ashkenazim* it consisted merely of eating fruit from the Holy Land, but Oriental Jews observed an elaborate ritual in which 15 different fruits were eaten to the accompaniment of appropriate readings from the Bible, Talmud, and Zohar. In the State of Israel it has become an arbor day marked by ceremonial planting of trees by school-children.

NEXT YEAR IN JERUSALEM, see **LA-SHANAH HA-BAAH BI-YERUSHALAYIM**

NEZIKIN (Heb. "Damages"): Fourth order in the Mishnah, Tosephta, and Talmud, dealing primarily with monetary subjects and damages which are legally adjudicated. It contains ten tractates — BAVA KAMMA, BAVA METZIA, BAVA BATRA (these three originally constituted a single tractate called *N.*), SANHEDRIN, MAKKOT, SHEVUOT, EDUYYOT, AVODAH ZARAH, AVOT, and HORAYOT. Eight of these have *gemara* in both Talmuds (the exceptions are *Avot* and *Eduyyot* which have no *gemara* in either Talmud).

NIDDAH: A menstruating women, who is separrated from and forbidden intimate contact with her husband (Lev. 15:19-24; 18:19; 20:18). The separation is to commence twelve hours before the expected onset of the menses. With the beginning of the menstrual flow a minimum five day period is to be observed (longer if warranted), which is then followed by a seven day "clean" period (*libbun*). At the end of these twelve days (which the slightest show of blood invalidates, making a recount of seven further clean days necessary) marital relations may be resumed, but only after immersion in a MIKVEH. The slightest drop of blood renders a seven day separation necessary, even if unconnected with the menstrual flow.

NIDDAH (Heb. "Menstruation"): Second treatise in the Mishnah order of *Toharot* with *gemara* in both Talmuds. It deals with the ritual uncleanness contracted by woman as a result of menstruation (Lev. 15:19-24) or childbirth (Lev. 12:1-5), and the regulations governing her purification.

NIDDUY, see **EXCOMMUNICATION**

NIGGUN (Heb. "melody"): The traditional tune to which a prayer is chanted. Among Ḥasidim, the *n.* (often a wordless melody hummed repeatedly) was prominent in religious services and on other ceremonial occasions (e.g. gatherings at the home of the *tzaddik*). Many rites, as well as ḥasidic sects, have their own characteristic *n.*

NIGHT: The Jewish DAY lasts from sunset to sunset, and that portion from sunset until the "rising of the morning star" constitutes the n. There is however some doubt as to the exact incidence of the two outer limits. In discussing the advent of n. the rabbis differ as to whether its hour is to be reckoned from sunset or from the appearance of the stars; for this reason the Sabbath and festivals are regarded as beginning with sunset, or "when the sun is at the top of the trees" but conclude with the appearance of three stars of medium magnitude on the following night. Similarly the end of n. is reckoned either when one can distinguish between blue and white, or between blue and green (Mishnah *Ber.* 1:2). The n. is divided into three (*Ber.* 3a) or four (*ibid* 3b) watches. In Jewish law various activities cannot be undertaken at n., such as the beginning of court sessions, the signing of documents, and the passing of a capital verdict.

NIGHT OF WATCHING, see **LEIL SHIMMURIM**

NIGHT PRAYERS (Heb. *keriat Shema al ha-mittah*, i.e., "the reading of the *Shema* in bed"): Special night prayer which includes a prayer for undisturbed repose, the first paragraph of the SHEMA, Psalms 92 and 3, the HASHKIVENU prayer, appropriate scriptural verses, and ADON OLAM. The recitation of the *Shema* before sleeping is based on a saying of R. Joshua ben Levi (*Ber.* 4b).

NIKKUR (Heb. "porging"): The fat of those species of animal fit to be brought as sacrifice in the Temple is forbidden for consumption (Lev. 7:25). The removal of such forbidden fat (termed ḤELEV) is called *nikkur*. Generally the forbidden fats are those which were burnt on the altar (Lev. 3:3-4) and are recognizable by the fact that they form a separate solid layer of fat surrounded by a skin or membrane, which is easily peeled off. There are however some threads of forbidden fat which must be porged out with great skill and care. (The rabbis legislate the porging of 51 out of 121 sinews). *N.* may be undertaken only by a person (*menakker*) who is fully conversant with its intricate regulations and has received practical training from a recognized expert in the subject.

NINE DAYS: Period of mourning (*Av* 1-9), observed in the *Ashkenazi* rite during the latter part of the THREE WEEKS of mourning culminating in the fast of *Tisha be'Av* (see AV, NINTH OF). For the entire three weeks (commencing on the fast of SHIVA ASAR BE-TAMMUZ) no festivities are celebrated or marriages solemnized. During the Nine Day period, Orthodox Jews abstain from meat and wine. On the Sabbath before *Av* 9 (*Shabbat Ḥazon*) an appropriately somber prophetical portion is read from Is. 1:1-27 in which the people are rebuked for their sins and destruction is foretold). *Sephardim* generally observe the last period of mourning only during the week of *Av* 9.

NINTH OF AV, see **AV, NINTH OF**

NISAN: First month of the religious year, seventh of the civil. It has 30 days and its zodiac sign is the lamb. In the earlier biblical books its name is given as AVIV, "*N.*" being derived from the Assyrian. According to tradition *N.* is the month of the creation of the world, the birth of the patriarchs, the exodus from Egypt, the erection of the tabernacle, and it will also be the month of redemption. *Nisan* 1 was the "New Year of Kings", and reigns were reckoned from that date. *N.* 14 is the Fast of the First-born, *N.* 15 is PASSOVER, and the OMER period is counted from the 16th. *N.* is a festive month when public mourning is avoided and TAḤANUN omitted from the daily prayers.

NISHMAT KOL ḤAI (Heb. "The breath of every living thing"): Concluding doxology in the Sabbath and festival PESUKEI DE-ZIMRAH in all rites (though with differences in wording). Its language is early and the prayer is mentioned in the Talmud; the earlier section is quoted as the concluding blessing of the *Seder* service (*Pes.* 118a) and the middle section as a thanksgiving for rainfall (*Ber.* 59b). The last part was added in gaonic times. A medieval legend, according to which the author of the prayer was none other than the apostle Peter, was vehemently rejected by Rashi.

N. concludes with the YISHTABBAH prayer, the *Ashkenazi* and *Sephardi* versions of which differ.

NISSIM, RABBENU, see **GERONDI, NISSIM**

NISSUIM, see **MARRIAGE**

NOACHIAN LAWS: Injunctions traditionally given to NOAH and therefore binding upon Jew and gentile alike. According to the Talmud there were seven such laws derived from the early chapters of Genesis and they consisted of prohibitions against (1) Blasphemy, (2) Idolatry, (3) Sexual immorality, (4) Murder, (5) Robbery, (6) Eating a portion of a living animal; and an injunction concerning (7) The administration of justice (*Sanh.* 56a). The last of these is interpreted by Naḥmanides to include the entire range of social legislation. Another talmudic source (*Ḥul.* 92a) counts 30 such laws, but they are seen as mere derivations from the basic seven. A gentile who observed the N. l., acknowledging their Divine source, was considered a pious man who merited the Kingdom of Heaven (*Sanh.* 105a).

NOAH: Hero of the biblical story of the FLOOD; son of Lamech (Gen. 5:28-29). N. was a just and righteous man who "walked with God" (Gen. 6:9). He was saved from the destruction of mankind in an ARK which he built at God's command for himself, his family, and specimens of all living species. N.'s first act upon leaving the ark after the flood was to make a sacrifice to God. His sacrifice was accepted and the blessing of fertility and dominion previously vouchsafed to Adam was now bestowed in a covenant upon him (*ibid.* 9:1-17). Unlike heroes of other ancient accounts of Floods, e.g. the Sumerian Ziusudra and the Babylonian Utnapishtim, where the escape from the deluge resulted in the apotheosis of the hero, N. retained the rôle of a mortal champion of humanity. Talmudic controversy over the proper evaluation of N.'s virtue derived from the passage "N. was a righteous and wholehearted man in his generation" (Gen. 6:9). The rabbis commented that "in his generation" could have either a derogatory or a laudatory implication (*Sanh.* 108a). He is described as a husbandman, but the story of his planting a vineyard and his subsequent intoxication contributed to the division of opinion among the rabbis as to the strength of his character and virtue. Humanity as a whole, descended from N.'s three sons, Shem, Ham, and Japheth.

NOMISM: Rule or predominance of LAW. The Jewish religion has often been defined as n. because of its characteristic manner of expressing religious values and attitudes in terms of laws and commandments. See also HALAKHAH; TORAH.

NOTARIKON (Gk.): Representation of a word or phrase by a single letter, usually the initial; hence also a method of interpreting of a word by taking its letters as initials for other words, as opposed to GEMATRIA which represents the numerical equivalent of a word (each Hebrew letter having a numerical value). Interpretation by *n.* consists of moral and homiletical lessons derived from the reading of a word as composed of initial letters of other words. Thus a rabbinical *n.* explains the word *mizbeaḥ* ("altar") as constituting an ABBREVIATION *of meḥilah, zekhut, berakhah, ḥayyim* ("forgiveness, merit, blessing, life"). It was recognized by the rabbis as one of the 32 methods of homiletical interpretation, and on certain occasions was adduced to support a halakhic ruling.

NOVELLAE (Heb. *ḥiddushim*): Customary designation of a certain type of talmudic commentary, one of the main branches of rabbinic literature. The two main types of such literature stem from the two classical commentaries to the Talmud — that of RASHI, consisting of a running commentary, the purpose of which is to explain the text, and that of the TOSAPHOT, consisting of a penetrating analysis of individual points for the purpose of elucidation or resolving contradictions. The n. correspond to the *tosaphot* (which incorporate n. from French and German rabbinical authorities); they investigate specific problems or passages of the Talmud — generally halakhic — in order to reveal "new" solutions. Until the 16th cent. the n. consisted of sober, rigorous, and often profound analysis and interpretation, but with the development of the Polish method of PILPUL they tended to become exercises in ingenuity and hairsplitting dialectics. Whereas the purpose of the older n. was elucidation, that of the later n. was by way of response to the challenge to say something strikingly "novel", a *ḥiddush.* The considerable body of n. literature includes both n. on the various tractates of the Talmud and super-n. on the older n.

NUMBERS: Although n. play a great rôle in religious symbolism, there are practically no n. with special significance in the Bible, except the number 7 (cf. at the conquest of Jericho, 7 priests with 7 horns circumambulating the city 7 times, Jos. 6:1 ff.). Post-biblical literature attaches more significance to certain numbers, particularly 7 and 10, and the attribution of numerical values to the letters of the Hebrew ALPHABET gave a further impetus to the use of n. as a key for mystical exegesis and speculation. The fact that every Hebrew word has its numerical equivalent gave rise to interpretation by GEMATRIA — a method extensively employed in the Midrash for homiletical purposes. It is one of the 32 HERMENEUTICAL RULES of R. Yose Ha-Galili, as used for instance in numerical symbolism. These methods are developed to extremes in Jewish mystical literature (see YETZIRAH) and particularly in the KABBALAH.

NUMBERS (Heb. *Be-Midbar* = "In the Wilderness"): Fourth book of the PENTATEUCH, containing mostly historical material. The first portion (chaps. 1-19) deals with the generation of the Exodus, the second (20-36) with those about to enter the Promised Land. The story of the spies (13-14) explains Israel's prolonged sojourn in the desert as a punishment for their lack of faith. For a similar reason Moses and Aaron were not permitted to enter the promised land (20:1-13) and Moses was bidden to bestow the leadership of the people upon Joshua (27:12-23). Most legislative portions of the book are an expansion of or supplement to the laws already contained in the books of EXODUS and LEVITICUS.

NUMBERS RABBAH, see **MIDRASH RABBAH**

NUSAKH (Heb.): Originally meaning "removal" and hence "copying", it is now used in three different ways, each conveying the idea of "accepted formula". *N.* is used: (1) to refer to textual variants, called "differing *nuskhaot*". Rashi and the tosaphists, however, introduced the word *girsa* to signify different readings; (2) to distinguish the differing liturgical RITES of the various communities and groups. Thus *Nusakh Ashkenaz, Nusakh Sephard*, *Nusakh Romi*, and *Nusakh Ari* refer respectively to the prayer books and liturgical customs of the German, Spanish, Roman communities and those established by R. Isaac LURIA; (3) to denote the *Nusakh ha-Tephillah*, the traditional manner in which the prayers are chanted as they have been handed down through the centuries.

O

OATH MORE JUDAICO, see **JEWISH OATH**
OATH, see **JEWISH OATH; VOWS**
OBADIAH: Fourth in the books of the Minor Prophets, O. consists of a single chapter announcing the downfall of Edom. There are no biographical data but the contents indicate that O. witnessed Edomite complicity in the Babylonian destruction of Jerusalem in 586 B.C.E. (v. 11-14). Punishment was to overtake the arrogant Edomites on the approaching Day of the Lord. The Talmud describes the prophet as an Idumean proselyte identical with the O. in I Kings 18:3 ff., who sheltered a hundred prophets from the wrath of Jezebel (*Sanh.* 39b).
OBADIAH OF BERTINORO, see **BERTINORO, OBADIAH OF**
OBLATION, see **MEAL-OFFERING**
ODEL (or Adel; 18th cent.): Only daughter of the BAAL SHEM Tov and mother of the *tzaddikim* BARUCH OF MEDZIBOZH and MOSES ḤAYYIM EPHRAIM OF SADILKOV. In ḥasidic tradition, she is depicted as the ideal of righteous womanhood.
OFFERINGS, see **SACRIFICES**
OHALOT (Heb. "Tents"): Second tractate in the Mishnah order of *Toharot*; it has no *gemara* in either Talmud. It discusses the ritual impurity spread by a corpse, which defiles not only that which touches it but whatever is under the same roof (or OHEL, i.e., tent) with it for a period of seven days (Num. 19:13-20).
OHEL (Heb. "tent", technically "overshadowing"): From Num. 19:14, it is inferred that all utensils or humans under the same "tent" or roof with a corpse or part of a corpse, or in the shadows of something which also overshadows a corpse, contract ritual uncleanness for a period of seven days. As priests are not permitted to contract ritual uncleanness, they must not enter a house where a corpse lies, nor a cemetery where they might cast shadow over a grave. The term *o.* is also used for a structure over a tomb and was especially applied to those over the graves of outstanding ḥasidic rabbis, which were visited regularly on the anniversary of death — by their ḥasidim.
OIL: In the Sanctuary and Temple only "pure olive oil beaten for the light, to cause the lamp to burn always" (Exod. 27:20) was permitted for use; among Oriental Jews this is still the only o. permitted for the Eternal Lamp in the synagogue. R. Tarphon similarly declared that only olive o. could be used for the Sabbath Lamps, but the accepted ruling is that, with few exceptions, any o. may be used (Mishnah *Shab.* 2). O. was used for the ANOINTING of High Priests and kings. CANDLES have largely replaced o., though many still prefer the use of o. for the ḤANUKKAH-lamp. O. also formed part of some sacrificial offerings.
OKHLAH VE-OKHLAH: Work on the MASORAH, probably composed in Babylonia in the 10th cent. and listing peculiarities and distinctive features in the spelling of the biblical text (in alphabetic order of the words). The opening words of the book are *O. va-O.* — two words sounding alike but of different grammatical structure. In its present form the work contains additions by later *Sephardi* and *Ashkenazi* scholars.
OLAH, see **BURNT-OFFERING**
OLAM HA-ZEH and OLAM HA-BA (Heb. "this world" and "the world to come"): Eschatological concepts developed during the Second Temple Period and in subsequent rabbinic literature. Originally the meaning of the word *olam* was temporal ("age") rather than spatial ("world"), and the terms under discussion signified respectively the present age, with all its shortcomings and miseries, and the future or messianic age (often identified with the KINGDOM OF GOD). It was believed that same major catastrophic event (e.g. the DAY OF JUDGMENT, RESURRECTION) would terminate the *O.h-Z.* and usher in the *O.h-B.* The concept of *O.h-B.* is thus different from that of HEAVEN or PARADISE (see also EDEN, GARDEN OF), which is the abode of departed souls pending the advent of the "coming age". However, the distinction was not always maintained in later literature and many rabbinic sayings concerning the future state of the world were understood as referring to the "other world", i.e., the celestial realm of blessed souls; cf. the statement in *Ber.* 17a: "The World to Come is unlike This World. In the World to Come there is no eating or drinking or propagation or business or jealousy or hatred or rivalry, but the righteous sit with crowns upon their heads, enjoying the radiance of the Divine Presence". The Divine punishment declared for certain heretics

is a denial of their "share in the World to Come", a state to which every Jew, as well as the righteous gentile, is entitled (Mishnah *Sanh.* 10:1). The relationship between *O.h.-Z.* and *O.h.-B.* is expressed in two mishnaic statements (*Avot* 4:21-22): "*O.h.-Z.* is like an antechamber to *O.h.-B.* Prepare thyself in the antechamber that thou mayest enter the palace". Thus *O.h.-Z* is regarded as the place for performing good deeds and acquiring merits, which are then stored up in *O.h.-B.*, the place of reward and bliss. The other statement reads "Better is one hour of repentance and good deeds in *O.h.-Z.* than the whole life of *O.h.-B.*; and one hour of bliss in *O.h.-B.* is better than the whole life of *O.h.-Z.*" See also ESCHATOLOGY.

OLD AGE: The Bible says "Thou shalt rise up before the hoary head and honor the face of the old man" (Lev. 19:32), and the Talmud (*Kidd.* 32b) explains that "old man" should be taken to refer to the scholar. Respect and consideration for o.a. has always been an outstanding characteristic of Jewish social ethics. The prayer of David "Cast me not off in the time of old age; forsake me not when my strength faileth" (Ps. 7:9) occupies (in plural form) a prominent place in the liturgy of the High Festivals and Penitential Days, and finds practical expression in the Homes for the Aged that constitute an important form of Jewish philanthropic activity in modern times.

OLD TESTAMENT: Name given by Christians to the Jewish Bible, based upon their belief that the messianic prophecies had been fulfilled by the advent of Jesus, as recounted in their supplementary scriptures, the "NEW TESTAMENT". The Hebrew name for the O.T. is TANAKH.

OMEN: see **DIVINATION**

OMER: Sheaf cut in the barley harvest. The children of Israel were commanded to bring an *o.* "on the morrow of the Sabbath" and only after offering the *o.* and the appropriate accompanying sacrifice were they permitted to eat the grain of the new harvest (Lev. 23:10-14). The PHARISEES, in opposition to the SADDUCEES, maintained that the "Sabbath" mentioned in this verse refers to the Festival of Passover, which is the subject of the previous paragraph; in other words the *o.* was to be offered on the second day of Passover and was to consist of an *omer* (the tenth of an *ephah*) of barley. From this day seven full weeks were counted and the fiftieth day was observed as the Festival of Weeks (SHAVUOT). This counting which is observed to the present day, is called the "Counting of the *O.*". The announcement of each day is generally incorporated into the Evening Service (as the *o.* was reaped by night) after the recitation of an appropriate benediction, and is followed by a prayer for the restoration of the Temple service. The period between the first harvest and the first fruit harvest, which the counting of the *o.* commemorates must originally have been one of joy, but tradition has established it as a period of sadness and semi-mourning during which — with the exception of LAG BA-OMER — merriment, the celebration of marriages, haircutting, and the wearing of new clothes are all forbidden. The only basis for this abstinence is a vague statement in the Talmud (*Yev.* 62b) that "12,000 pairs of the disciples of R. Akiva died in one period" and that that period was "between Passover and Weeks". The passage is taken by most scholars to refer to the War of Bar Kokhba. The ceremonious cutting of the first sheaf of corn on the morrow of the first day of Passover has been revived in many agricultural settlements of the State of Israel. The Israel Chief Rabbinate has permitted the holding of INDEPENDENCE DAY celebrations and the recital of sections of the HALLEL prayer on *Iyyar* 5 during the Counting of the *O.*

OMER, 33rd DAY OF, see **LAG BA-OMER**

ONEN, see **ANINUT**

OMNAM KEN (Heb. "Indeed it is so"): Penitential poem (*seliḥah*) recited in the Polish rite during the Evening Service of the Day of Atonement. Each verse concludes *salaḥti* ("I have forgiven"). Its author has been identified as R. Yomtov of Joigny, who met a martyr's death in the York massacre of 1190.

ONAAH (Heb.): Fraudulent representation; overreaching; unfair profit. The rabbis interpreted the biblical prohibition "ye shall not wrong one another" (Lev. 25:14) as applying to transactions in which the profit obtained was so great that the overcharging was tantamount to fraud. They ruled that overcharging by the seller or underpayment by the purchaser by 1/6th of the market value constitute grounds for canceling a transaction. The reference was to movable goods; the rule was not generally applied to real estate but in that case the overcharging had to exceed 50% to be annulled. The rabbis also ruled that the deal was only regarded as fraudulent where the seller concealed his profit margin; where this was openly stated and accepted by the purchaser, the deal could not be canceled. The term *o.* was also applied to wounded feelings which, the Talmud says, is a worse offense than monetary imposition (*Bava Metzia* 58b).

ONEG SHABBAT (Heb. "Sabbath delight"): Phrase based on Is. 58:13 — "And thou shalt call the Sabbath a delight" — and expressive of the traditional attitude toward the Sabbath. The rabbis approved of everything that would enhance the "Sabbath delight", recommending that additional dishes be served at the Sabbath meal and insisting on a minimum of three meals in honor of the day. Since the SEUDAH SHELISHIT was the specific additional meal of the Sabbath, it became the principal occasion for *O.S.* and is marked by the singing of ZEMIROT and the delivery of discourses on the biblical lesson of the day. The modern *O.S.*, a cultural rather than a strictly religious occasion, is a partly secularized form of the ḥasidic tradition, and attempts to capture the spirit of the Sabbath without necessarily adhering to its ritual forms; it was introduced in Tel-Aviv by the poet Bialik.

ONIAS, TEMPLE OF: Temple erected in the mid-2nd cent. B.C.E. at Leontopolis in Egypt by Onias III, deposed High Priest (who had fled to Egypt during persecutions by Antiochus in Jerusalem) or possibly by his son Onias IV. It was built at the site of the shrine of an Egyptian goddess and seems to have served the local Jewish military colony which may have included members of the priestly family who had fled with Onias. Various suggestions have been made to explain why Onias built a temple and not a synagogue (e.g. personal ambition; Egyptian political aspirations). The Temple was closed by the Romans in 71 C.E.

ONKELOS, TARGUM, see **TARGUM**

OPHANNIM: Class of ANGELS. The term is derived from Ezekiel's vision of the Divine throne-chariot (Ezek. 1:15ff.) and originally refers to the "wheels" that bear the throne. In later literature the O. became a class of the angelic hierarchy, similar to CHERUBIM, SERAPHIM, and *ḥayyot*.

ORACLE: Medium whereby the Divine purpose, the future, or some unknown fact is revealed. In ancient times, it was customary among all people to consult an o. in times of crisis. The Bible forbids the traditional pagan methods of DIVINATION but does refer to accepted Israelite methods, as in the passage "And when Saul enquired of the Lord, the Lord answered him not, neither by dreams, nor by Urim, nor by prophets" (I Sam. 28:6), where the three sources mentioned indicate methods of Divine communication which may be regarded as oracular. There are many instances of specific enquiries being answered by means of a DREAM or a PROPHET (cf. e.g. Gen. 31:24), or other oracular media. Among the last the most important were the Urim and Thummim and the EPHOD, though their precise nature and mode of operation are not known. When Joshua was appointed to succeed Moses he was told that Eleazar the High Priest would "ask counsel of him after the Urim" (Num. 28:21). It has been assumed that when mention is made of asking Divine counsel (e.g. Josh. 9:14; Judg. 1:1-2) this was sought through the Urim and Thummim. There is, however, nothing to indicate of what they consisted, apart from the statement that in putting the breastplate on Aaron, Moses "also put in the breastplate the Urim and the Thummim" (Lev. 8:8). They probably served as a form of divination by lots that were kept in the breastplate of the High Priest — and to this should be correlated the references to oracular divination by means of the ephod (I Sam. 23:9) and lots (Num. 26:55). The Urim and Thummim were used in the Pre-Exilic Period but are not mentioned after the time of Solomon, although the omission may be due more to the stress on the growing rôle of the prophet than to the actual cessation of consulting the Urim and Thummim. The oracular use of an ephod is referred to in I Sam. 23:9 ff.

ORAL LAW, see **LAW, ORAL**

ORAḤ ḤAYYIM, see **SHULḤAN ARUKH**

ORDEAL: Method for determining the truth of an accusation or a claim by supernatural aid rather than by human evidence; usually referring to the test to which the suspected person is subjected. The test was generally painful, and the emergence of the victim unscathed was regarded as proof of his innocence. The only clear instance of trial by o. in Jewish literature is to be found in the test of bitter waters imposed upon a SOTAH, a married woman suspected of adultery that cannot be proved (Num. 5:11-31). This was practiced during the Second Temple Period up to tannaitic times (cf. Mishnah *Sot.* 1:5; *Eduy* 5:6) but was abolished by R. Johanan ben Zakkai (*Sot.* 9:9).

ORDINANCE, see **TAKKANAH**

ORDINATION: In rabbinic law the formal transmission of judicial authority. The traditional theory holds that original authority was given by God to Moses. Before his death Moses asked God to appoint a successor, and Joshua was selected with the words "Take thee Joshua the son of Nun... and lay thine hand upon him" (Num. 27:18). This "laying on of hands" constitutes *semikhah*, or o., whereby a master formally transfers authority to his disciple. Nowhere else in the Bible is there mention of this manner of o. or transfer of authority, but Jewish tradition accepted that the o. thus conferred upon Joshua was in turn transferred by him to his successor, and so on, in an unbroken chain throughout the centuries up to the period of the Second Temple. The mishnaic statement concerning the transmission of tradition ("Moses received the *Torah* from Sinai and handed it down to Joshua, and Joshua to the elders, the elders to the prophets, and the prophets handed it to the Men of the Great Assembly", *Avot* 1:1) was interpreted as referring also to the succession of authority. Only a duly ordained person was empowered in turn to ordain others, and the continuation of o. depended therefore on an unbroken chain of tradition. During the Hadrianic persecution which followed the defeat of Bar Kokhba in 135 C.E., the Romans, wishing to destroy religious authority, decreed capital punishment upon those conferring or receiving o. One of the Ten MARTYRS, Judah ben Bava, was stabbed to death by Roman soldiers who surprised him in the act of ordaining five of his disciples (*Sanh.* 14a). Rabbinic law stated that o. could be conferred only in the Land of Israel in order to ensure that the land remain the spiritual center of Jewry. Only ordained rabbis could determine the CALENDAR, judge certain cases, or impose fines. After the time of Hillel, the title "RABBI" was given to those ordained, and the Babylonian *amoraim* were then limited to the title of "*rav*", but not "rabbi". O. came to an end about the 4th cent. as a result of the political, spiritual, and economic decline of Palestinian Jewry. Theoretically, once the chain had been broken, it could not be re-established. In the 12th cent., however, MAIMONIDES suggested the possibility of renewing o. by the unanimous decision of all the rabbis assembled in the Land of Israel, who could invest one of their number with this authority, and he, in turn, would then be able to ordain others. It was on the basis of this suggestion that in 1538 Jacob BERAV made an attempt in Safed to reintroduce o., and had it conferred upon himself. A violent controversy ensued and the attempt failed because of the determined opposition of R. Levi IBN ḤAVIV the rabbi of Jerusalem who had not been consulted and who rallied other scholars to his view that the undertaking was illegitimate. Modern discussions on the possibility of re-establishing the SANHEDRIN, which depends upon o., center around this incident in which all possible arguments, for and against, had been brought forward and discussed. The *semikhah* conferred on a rabbi today, though it is called by its old name, is not the same as the ancient o. There is neither the laying on of hands nor the conferring of that judicial authority which resides in talmudic *semikhah* alone. It is rather the *hattarat horaah* (Heb. "permission to teach"), which replaced the ancient *semikhah* and which certifies competence to serve as a rabbi.

OREN (from Latin *orare* "pray"): Among German Jews, a term for prayer.

ORGAN: Though instrumental MUSIC figured prominently in the liturgy of the Temple, it was virtually absent from the traditional synagogue service as it developed in the Middle Ages. The admission of an o. into this service, especially on the Sabbath, constituted one of the main subjects of contention between Orthodox and Reform factions in the 19th cent. In Germany it was first introduced by Israel Jacobson at Seesen (1810) and Berlin (1815). Among its outstanding Orthodox opponents were Moses SOPHER and Akiva EGER, who regarded the practice as assimilationist. A Christian organist was engaged by the Hamburg Reformists in 1818. In the U.S. the o. was first introduced in the Reform temple at Charleston S.C. in 1841 and has since become a regular feature in Reform and some Conservative services. It is also common in France and Italy and is used in certain Orthodox synagogues on weekdays (e.g. at weddings). Orthodox objections emphasized not only the technical infringements of rabbinic law (e.g. when a Jewish organist plays the instrument on Sabbaths and festivals), but also the very specific association of the o. with church music.

ORIGINAL SIN, see **FALL OF MAN**

ORLAH (Heb. "uncircumcision"): The fruit of young trees during their first three years of producing; such fruit is forbidden for use (Lev. 19:23-25). In the fourth year the fruit is termed "holy" (*ibid.*) and was to be taken to Jerusalem to be consumed amid praise and thanksgiving. This fruit, called *neta revai* ("planting in its fourth year") could, however, be redeemed and so rendered free for use outside Jerusalem, while the money value plus a fifth was to be taken to Jerusalem and spent there. Today *neta revai* is regarded as the same as *o.* and the fruit is wholly permitted from the fifth year. *O.* is one of the few AGRARIAN LAWS which apply even outside the Land of Israel.

ORLAH (Heb. "Uncircumcision"; cf. Lev. 19:23-25): Tenth tractate in the Mishnah order of *Zeraim.* It deals with the laws of ORLAH, according to which the fruit of a tree or vine is regarded as "uncircumcised" — and therefore forbidden for consumption — during its first three years. *O.* has *gemara* in the Palestinian Talmud only.

ORPHANS: Together with widows and strangers, o. were, in the social and economic system of ancient Israel, among the most helpless members of society and hence special objects of solicitude in biblical legislation, which emphasized the claims of o. to justice (Deut. 24:17; Is. 1:17; Ps. 82:3), protection from oppression (Exod. 22:22), charity (Deut. 14:28; 24:19; 26:12), and hospitality (Deut. 16:11, 14). In their denunciation of evil, the prophets frequently singled out the exploitation and inconsiderate treatment of o. (Is. 1:23; 10:2; Ezek. 22:7; Mal. 3:5). God Himself, "the Father of o." (Ps. 68:6), is the guardian of their rights (Deut. 10:18); He hears their cries and His judgment may turn those who oppress them into o. themselves (Exod. 22:22-23). In talmudic law the general biblical injunctions are elaborated and expanded to grant o. many legal privileges and concessions. O. are exempt from taxation (*Bava Batra* 8a); they are not required to pay compensation for damage caused by their animals under certain conditions (*Bava Kamma* 39a); they need no PROSBUL to claim the repayment of loans after the Sabbatical year (*Git.* 37a); and their property is regarded as equivalent to sacred property (*Bava Metzia* 56b). Altogether, o. are to be treated with special gentleness and dignity, to be addressed in soft words, and to have their possessions guarded more zealously than one's own. All these regulations apply to rich as well as poor o. It is particularly meritorious to provide a home for o., and whoever brings up an o. is regarded as his father (*Sanh.* 19b). O. are required to observe a full year's mourning after the death of a parent and to say KADDISH for eleven months.

ORTHODOXY: Modern designation for the strictly traditional section of Jewry. The term itself is borrowed from Christian usage and was first applied by REFORM Jews to describe, somewhat disparagingly, those who remained rigidly faithful to traditional Judaism. Though O. is widely diversified among its many religious groupings and nuances of belief and practice (e.g. Ḥasidim and *Mitnaggedim*; Jews following *Ashkenazi* and *Sephardi* rites, etc.), all Orthodox Jews are united in their belief in the historical event of revelation at Sinai, as described in the TORAH; in their acceptance of the Divine Law, in its Written and Oral forms, as immutable and binding for all times; in their acknowledgment of the authority of duly qualified rabbis — who themselves recognize the validity of the TALMUD, the SHULḤAN ARUKH, and all other traditional sources of the HALAKHAH — to interpret and administer Jewish law; and in their adherence to traditional Jewish beliefs as enshrined in the THIRTEEN ARTICLES OF FAITH enumerated by Maimonides. Unlike Reform and Liberal groups, O. rejects the doctrine of "progressive revelation", denies the assumptions and conclusions of higher BIBLE CRITICISM, especially with regard to the Pentateuch, and generally opposes radical departures from traditional attitudes and practices. Thus O. opposes proselytizing propaganda and objects to ORGAN music and to mixed seating of men and women in synagogue worship. Its halakhic observance does not admit distinction between ethical *versus* merely ceremonial precepts. Historically speaking the relative position of rabbinic O. *vis-à-vis* its opponents has undergone a reversal in modern times. In the past, opposition to normative rabbinic Judaism often came from extremist religious movements (e.g. the KARAITES in medieval times) which made O. appear flexible and liberal by comparison. In the face of modern movements (reform, liberal, "progressive"), however, O. is rigorous and unbending. O. has exhibited a reluctance to co-operate with non-Orthodox groups in religious areas. The relations between O. and non-O. are especially troubled by Orthodox refusal to recognize the marriages, divorces, and conversions carried out by rabbis who do not submit to the authority of traditional Jewish law. To distinguish the "modern" type of O. as developed in Germany during the second half of the 19th cent. under the guidance of S. R. HIRSCH and E. HILDESHEIMER (modern dress, use of the vernacular, study of secular sciences, and participation in the general culture) from the earlier ghetto-type of O., the term "Neo-Orthodoxy" is occasionally used.

OSSUARY: Container for the bones of the dead. The Mishnah mentions the custom of gathering up the bones of the dead after decomposition of the flesh (Mishnah *Sanh.* 6:6) and giving them a secondary burial in an o. (*Pes.* 8:8; *M.K.* 1:5). Contrary to the accepted opinion that relatives observe that day as one of mourning, R. Meir suggests that since the act of giving the dead final burial is a cause of satisfaction, it may even be performed on the intermediate days of festivals (*M.K.* 8a). The bones were collected in a sheet and then deposited in stone ossuaries, many examples of which have been found dating from the 2nd and 3rd cents. with inscriptions in Hebrew, Aramaic, or Greek.

OWNERSHIP, see **PROPERTY**

P

PAGANISM, see **IDOLATRY**
PAIRS, see **ZUGOT**
PALESTINE, see **HOLY LAND; ISRAEL, LAND OF**
PALESTINIAN TALMUD, see **TALMUD**
PALM, see **LULAV**

PANTHEISM: Term used since the 18th cent. to designate the theory that "all" (viz., the universe, or nature) is God. Among the various types of p. may be mentioned such individual views as God is everything (theopanism); everything that exists is Divine; God is immanent in everything. Neo-Platonism (see PLATONISM) which holds that all being flows out of God (see EMANATION) is much closer to p. than is ARISTOTELIANISM. And MYSTICISM, by obliterating the difference between God and the human soul in the ecstasy of mystical union, also tends toward p. All forms of p. are opposed to classical THEISM which assumes the non-identity of Creator and creation and thus the non-identity of God and the human soul. For theism the relationship between God and the soul is not one of ultimate unity, but an I – Thou confrontation. Jewish Orthodoxy has always adhered to the basic pattern of biblical theism and p. was considered heretical. Kabbalistic doctrines often exhibited pantheistic tendencies and were consequently regarded with suspicion. The classical kabbalistic statement of a limited p. was formulated by Moses CORDOVERO: "God is all reality, but not all reality is God". The traditional formula "*Elohim* (God) equals *teva* (nature)" (the numerical value of the two words are identical) does not imply genuine p. In a famous anti-deistic sermon preached in 1703, David Nieto, Haham of the London *Sephardi* congregation, used expressions which led to accusations of Spinozistic p. See also ḤASIDISM; KABBALAH; SPINOZA.

PARADISE (from Gk.*paradeisos,* "garden"): Common designation for the abode of the blessed after death, based on the SEPTUAGINT translation of the biblical "GARDEN OF EDEN". The idea that the souls of the righteous enjoy celestial bliss in a (heavenly) Garden of Eden was current in rabbinic literature. The Hebrew equivalent of p., *pardes,* occurs three times in the sense of "garden"; in the Talmud (*Ḥag.* 14b) the word is used for the realm of mystical experiences, of the ascent of the soul to the vision of the celestial. The Apocrypha and midrashic literature contain many descriptions of both the earthly p. and the heavenly p. of souls. The latter is usually described as a place of spiritual delights. See also OLAM HA-BA; PARDES.

PARAH (Heb. "Cow"): Fourth tractate of the Mishnah order of *Toharot,* dealing with the laws concerning the RED HEIFER (cf. Num. 19). It has no *gemara* in either Talmud.

PARASHAH, see **READING OF THE LAW**
PARASHIYYOT, THE FOUR, see **SABBATHS, SPECIAL**

PARDES: In late biblical (cf. Song of Songs 4:3; Ecc. 2:15; Neh. 2:8) and talmudic Hebrew "garden", "orchard". The word is derived from the Greek *paradeisos* (see PARADISE). In the Middle Ages the word *p.* was also used as an abbreviation for the four types of biblical exegesis from a combination of the initial letters of *peshat* (literal meaning), *remez* (veiled allusion), *derash* (homiletic interpretation), and *sod* (esoteric significance).

PARENTS: Biblical Hebrew has no generic word to denote p. but refers to them always as "FATHER and MOTHER" (e.g. Exod. 20:12; Lev. 19:3; Prov. 1:9). Later Hebrew adopted the word *horim,* which occurs only once in the Bible (Gen. 49:26) and probably means "forebears". Respect for p. is enjoined by the DECALOGUE and was inculcated to an extreme degree by the rabbis. Rabbinic law admits of only two exceptions to the duty of unquestioning obedience: p. must be disobeyed when they order their children to transgress the *Torah* (Mishnah *Bava Metzia* 2:10), and a son may ignore his parents' wishes in choosing a wife (*Rama* to *Yoreh Deah* 250, 25). Otherwise the duty of honoring and revering p. knows no bounds. The Talmud specifies "The son should not stand nor sit in his father's place nor contradict him. He must provide for his father's material wants and lead him in and out" (*Kidd.* 31b). The father has the legal duty to support his children up to the age of six; after that his support is regarded as an act of charity (*Ket.* 49b, 65b). He is permitted to chastise his children, but only while they are minors (*M.K.* 17a). Father and mother are equal as far as the duties owed them by the child are concerned and their special status is attributed to the fact that in every man's life "there are three partners: his father, his mother, and God" (*Kidd.* 30b).

PARNAS (Heb. "provider"): The term *p.* occurs both in the general sense of a leader or guide of a whole generation, and in the more specific sense of a religious and administrative functionary. Thus the Talmud describes Moses, Aaron, and Miriam as "three good *parnasim* of Israel" (*Taan.* 9a), and Joshua ben Hananiah referred to R. Gamaliel as "the *p.* of his generation" (*Ber.* 28a). When religious leadership passed to the rabbis, the term *p.* came to mean the lay leader of a community or congregation. Though they were supposed to be learned men (cf. "Who is a scholar worthy of being appointed *p.*? He who is asked about a law from any source, and is able to answer" — *Shab.* 114a), *parnasim* (pl.) were nevertheless not necessarily chosen from the aristocracy of learning or exemplary conduct, and there are many references in the Talmud and later sources to their autocratic behavior. In modern times, the word is applied to the elders, viz., members of the governing board of a congregation, and more particularly to its president.

PAROKHET (Heb.): The curtain of the Sanctuary, made of "blue and purple and scarlet and fine twined linen" (Exod. 26:31). It was placed in the Sanctuary to make the division "between the holy place and the most holy" (*ibid.* 33). In the Temple the task of making the *p.* was entrusted to women (*Ket.* 106b). The *p.* in the Sanctuary and Temple served as the origin for the modern *p.* (the term is used only by *Ashkenazim*) which is an integral part of the furnishings of the synagogue, and is placed in front of the Ark. On the High Holidays and *Hoshana Rabbah* a white *p.* is used; otherwise it may be of any color, and there are many magnificent examples of embroidered *parokhot* (pl.). The *Sephardi* rite has no *p.*, except on TISHA BE-AV when the Ark is draped with a black curtain (among *Ashkenazim*, the *p.* is removed altogether).

PARTITION, see **MEḤITZAH**

PARTNERSHIP (Heb. *shutaphut*): A p. in Jewish law is established by joint acquisition or inheritance and involves joint investment, even if only one of the partners is active. The p. is effected by means of a KINYAN and the conditions are usually set down in writing. Unless agreed otherwise, capital gains or losses are shared equally. Each partner can obligate the firm through his contracts. A p. may be dissolved by mutual agreement or predetermined conditions, involving actual partition or by allowing one partner the option of buying or selling a half share for an agreed sum. The death of a partner immediately voids the p.

PARVEH (Yidd.): Term applied to foods which can be classified neither as MILK dishes nor as MEAT, and which may consequently be eaten with either, without infringing the DIETARY LAWS forbidding the simultaneous consumption of "meat and milk". Care is taken to keep *p.* utensils separate and not to cleanse them together with either milk or meat utensils.

PASCHAL LAMB, see **PASSOVER**

PASKAN (or **POSEK**; Heb. "decisor"): One qualified and recognized as a decisor in Jewish law; see CODES. To render a decision on a point of religious law is called *pasken* in Yiddish, a usage common among *Ashkenazi* Jews.

PASSOVER: First of the three PILGRIM FESTIVALS, observed for 8 days in the Diaspora (see SECOND DAY OF FESTIVALS) and 7 days in Israel and by Reform Jews. P. is the universally accepted, if inexact, name for this festival, which commemorates the EXODUS of the children of Israel from Egypt ("the festival of freedom"). Actually the Hebrew word *pesaḥ* and its English equivalent "Passover" — indicating the "passing over" or "sparing" of the houses of the Children of Israel during the plague of the first-born (Exod. 12:13)— is used in the Bible solely with respect to the sacrifice of the paschal lamb which took place on the eve of the Exodus (*Nisan* 14). The seven-day festival which follows (*Nisan* 15-22) is in the Bible called "the festival of unleavened bread" (MATZAH — cf. Lev. 23:5-6: "On the fourteenth day of the first month at even is the Lord's Passover. And on the fifteenth day of the same month is the feast of unleavened bread to the Lord"). The agricultural aspect of the festival is connected with the spring season and the beginning of the barley harvest, and was expressed in ancient times by the offering of the OMER in the Temple on the second day of the festival. Both the first and last day (two days in each case in the Diaspora) are considered holy days and all work is prohibited, though the special dietary laws apply to the entire duration of the festival. These laws are (a) the strict prohibition against eating any LEAVEN; and (b) the commandment to eat *matzah* on the first night(s). The rabbis added extra stringency to the first of these regulations by ordaining that — unlike in other accidental admixtures of prohibited food which may be disregarded if the quantity is less than a sixtieth of the total — the tiniest amount of leaven in food renders it unfit for use on P. Hence the most rigid care must be exercised in the preparation of food for P., in order to ensure that no trace of leaven be found in it. The rabbis also laid down that leaven which has been in the possession of a Jew during P. remains forbidden even after the festival. This has given rise to the ceremony of "selling leaven", whereby such leaven as remains in the possession of a Jew is transferred by formal sale to a non-Jew, and reacquired after the festival. The *Seder* ceremony (see HAGGADAH), celebrated on the first night(s) of the festival, is the most important home ceremony in the liturgical year. The laws of the festival are discussed in the talmudic tractate PESAḤIM. The synagogue service is identical, basically, with that of the other two Pilgrim Festivals except that after the first day(s) only the shorter form ("half") of the HALLEL is said. A prayer for DEW, recited on the first day of the festival, marks the end of the winter season and the beginning of summer. On the intermediate Sabbath of P., the Song of Songs is recited in *Ashkenazi* synagogues. Allegorically this book represents the bond established at the Exodus between God and the Children of Israel, but the spirit of spring with which it is infused (cf. Song of Songs 2:11-13) serves as a reminder of the agricultural aspect of the festival. In Temple times, those unable to observe the festival had another opportunity to offer the paschal sacrifice a month later (see PASSOVER, SECOND). The coincidence of P. with Easter led in the Middle Ages to the linking of the RITUAL MURDER LIBEL with the P. festival, which thus often became a time of fear and actual terror for Jews. SAMARITAN Jews still sacrifice a paschal lamb at their annual P. ceremony in Shechem (Nablus). See also FESTIVAL PRAYERS.

PASSOVER, SECOND (Heb. *pesaḥ sheni*): The celebration of the Second PASSOVER (Num. 9:9-25) was strictly limited to those who, through ritual uncleanness or unavoidable absence from Jerusalem, were precluded from sacrificing the paschal lamb on its proper date, *Nisan* 14. A concession was made to enable such persons to offer the sacrifice a month later. The only recorded instance of the celebration of the S.P. was by King Hezekiah, after consultation with "the princes of the congregation in Israel" (II Chron. 30:2). S.P. (on *Iyar* 14) is marked today by the omission of supplicatory prayers (TAḤANUN) in the synagogue service and in some communities by eating a piece of unleavened bread.

PASSOVER SEDER, see **HAGGADAH**

PATER SYNAGOGAE (Lat. "Father of the Synagogue"): Title conferred in the Classical Period on an outstanding member of a congregation. The office was probably honorary and involved no active duties. It has been found in the Diaspora (in both Greek and Latin inscriptions) but not in Palestine. A parallel title of honor — *mater synagogae* — was applied on occasion to a venerated female member of the congregation.

PATERNITY: Unlike maternity, for which — in principle — evidence (e.g. the testimony of eyewitnesses) can be produced, p. is incapable of strict proof. Yet p. is of the utmost consequence both in civil and ritual law (e.g. inheritance, incest and forbidden marriages, claims to the priesthood, etc.). Rabbinic law lays down that reasonable assumption is sufficient, and if a man says "this is my son" he is believed. See FATHER.

PATRIARCHATE, see **GAON; NASI**

PATRIARCHS (Heb. *avot*): The founding fathers of the Jewish people, ABRAHAM, ISAAC, and JACOB. The p. were Divinely elected and were the human parties to God's COVENANT. Their seed, the Children of Israel, inherited the blessings, promises, and duties given to them (i.e., the land of Canaan, the *Torah*, and the obligation to walk in the ways of God). Abraham, the first patriarch, stands in a special category, as is reflected in the first paragraph of the *amidah* (called *Avot*, i.e., p.) which mentions all three p. by name, but concludes "Blessed art thou, O God of Abraham". The Morning Prayer is traditionally regarded as having been instituted by Abraham, the Afternoon Prayer by Isaac, and the Evening Prayer by Jacob. The significance of the p. and their enduring merits are constant themes of synagogal poetry. See also MATRIARCHS; MERITS OF THE FATHERS.

PAUL: The "Apostle to the gentiles". Originally a Jew named Saul from Tarsus in Asia Minor, he studied for some time under the Patriarch GAMALIEL I (*Acts* 22:3), but his spiritual background was Hellenism rather than Palestinian Judaism. P. wrote in Greek, and his Bible quotations are drawn from the SEPTUAGINT. At first a zealous adherent of the Pharisaic party and a violent opponent of CHRISTIANITY (at that time a Jewish sect), he became an enthusiastic convert as a result of a visionary experience on the road to Damascus, while on a mission from the SANHEDRIN to put down the nascent Christian movement in that city. Changing his name from Saul to P., he embarked on missionary journeys to Asia Minor, Greece, and Rome. P.'s activity was largely instrumental in bringing about the development of Christianity from a Jewish sect to a world religion. He not only founded the Church of the "gentiles", but also evolved the theology of the new dispensation, according to which the Law of Moses and the promises of the prophets had been fulfilled in JESUS. Thus in his view Israel and its Law were now superseded by the Church and faith in Christ. Many of the terms in which P. elaborated his thought go back to sectarian, non-Pharisaic Jewish sources; e.g. the notions of children of light *versus* children of darkness, flesh *versus* spirit, election of grace, predestination, etc. which are prominent in the DEAD SEA SCROLLS. P.'s *Epistles* became part of the New Testament, and hence his ideas regarding the *Torah* (he held that the Law could not lead to true "salvation" but only to consciousness of man's innate sinfulness) have decisively influenced Christian attitudes toward Judaism.

PAYTAN (Heb.): Author of PIYYUT.

PEACE: The word *shalom* (from the root *sh-l-m* "wholeness, completion, perfection") in biblical Hebrew signifies well-being in the widest sense, and the full, undisturbed unfolding of the blessed life. In a narrower sense it means p. as the absence of war and violence. The passion for p. as the *summum bonum* runs throughout all Jewish literature and thought. It applies both to the messianic vision of universal p. when "nation shall not lift up sword against nation, neither shall they learn war any more" (Is. 2:4; Mic. 4:3) and to the more homely sphere of domestic p. "between man and his fellow man and between husband and wife" (see SHALOM BAYIT). AARON the High Priest is regarded as the prototype of those who "love p. and pursue p. and love all creatures", and the Jew is enjoined to follow his example (*Avot* 1:12). R. Simeon ben Ḥalaphta said, "God could find no better vessel of blessing for Israel than p." (*Uktzin* 3:12). Every single prayer of importance (e.g. the Priestly Blessing, the *kaddish*, the *amidah*, the Grace after Meals) ends with a prayer for p. and the hope that the same p. which exists among the heavenly spheres shall also reign on earth. The original, full signification of the term is still preserved in the traditional Jewish greeting "p. unto you" (*shalom aleikhem*); the shorter version of *shalom* is the usual formula of greeting in modern Hebrew.

PEACE-OFFERINGS (Heb. *shelamim*): A class of SACRIFICE. There were three kinds of p.-o.: (1) the THANKSGIVING-OFFERING (*todah*); (2) the votive-offering (*neder*); and (3) the FREE-WILL-OFFERING (*nedavah*). The p.-o., of oxen, sheep, or goats, was slaughtered after the owner had placed his hands (*semikhah*) on the head of the animal, confessed, and offered prayer. Its fat was offered and burned on the altar, the priest receiving the right shoulder and breast, and the worshiper the remainder.

PEAH (Heb. "corner"): One of the obligatory gifts to the poor (Lev. 19:9-10; 23:22). The Bible ordained that GLEANINGS for the poor should be left at the corners of a field that was being harvested. The rabbis applied the law only to the Land of Israel but the custom was also observed by Jews in Babylonia. Although halakhically the obligation is met by leaving a single stalk for the poor, the rabbis taught that at least one-sixtieth of the harvest should be left and that this proportion should be increased in the event of a good crop or a large number of poor gleaners.

PEAH (Heb. "Corner"): Second tractate of the Mishnah order of ZERAIM, with *gemara* in the Palestinian Talmud only. It deals with the laws of PEAH and other gifts to the poor made from agricultural produce (e.g. LEKET, the poor TITHE).

PENITENCE, see REPENTANCE

PENITENCE, TEN DAYS OF (Heb. *aseret yemei teshuvah*): Penitential period commencing with ROSH HA-SHANAH and concluding with the DAY OF ATONEMENT. According to the Mishnah (*R.H.* 1:2), *Tishri* 1 (New Year) is the Day of Judgment. The Talmud, however, explains (*ibid.* 16b) that on this day final judgment is passed only on the "perfectly righteous" and the "utterly wicked", whereas judgment of the intermediate categories is suspended until the Day of Atonement on the tenth of the month. As a result the entire ten-day period became one of penitence, in anticipation of that final judgment. Only slight changes are made in the liturgy for the days between the two festivals. The reading of SELIḤOT continues during these days. Prayers for life are inserted in the *amidah*, the wording of the 3rd and 8th benedictions is changed to emphasize the concept of the sovereignty of God, and the *amidah* is followed by the recitation of AVINU MALKENU. These days constitute a period of solemnity though not of mourning; fasting, where it is practiced, has a purely penitential character. It became customary prior to the Day of Atonement to visit cemeteries, to make contributions to charity, and among Oriental Jews to undergo flagellation as a mark of penitence.

PENITENTIAL PRAYERS, see SELIḤOT

PENTATEUCH: The five books of Moses (GENESIS; EXODUS; LEVITICUS; NUMBERS; DEUTERONOMY). See BIBLE; TORAH.

PENTECOST, see WEEKS, FEAST OF

PEOT (Heb. "corners"): According to the Bible (Lev. 19:27) it is forbidden to remove the hair at the corners of the head. The rabbis interpret this regulation as meaning that the temples must not be rendered as smooth as the forehead (*Mak.* 20b). No obligatory measure is laid down for the length of hair to remain, but it has been taken as the length of a line drawn from the top of the forehead to the base of the earlobe. The custom arose among Orthodox Jews (at first in Hungary and Galicia, as well as in Yemen) of allowing the *p.* to grow completely uncut. The biblical injunction not to "mar the corners of the beard" (*loc. cit.*) has been traditionally interpreted as a prohibition against SHAVING.

PEREK SHIRAH (Heb. "Chapter of Song"): A collection of hymns of praise to the Creator as sung by the heavenly bodies, the earth, animals and birds, and vegetation. The idea that all creation praises God is frequently expressed in the Bible (e.g. Ps. 148) and seems to have given rise to the selection of appropriate scriptural verses to represent the "hymnal of creation". *P.S.* is only indirectly mentioned in the Talmud, but it appears to be an ancient *baraita* known to have existed in the Gaonic Period, although the version extant today is certainly late. Its authorship was variously ascribed to R. Eliezer Ha-Gadol, to R. Judah Ha-Nasi, and even to David. It is printed in several editions of the prayer book, and is recited by some as a private devotion after the Morning Service.

PERJURY: The violation of an OATH, though not prosecuted, is regarded as a great sin (see Zech. 5:4), the punishment for which is reserved to God. For p. in civil transactions, if admitted, atonement is made by means of a special offering (Lev. 5). There is no obligation on WITNESSES to take an oath guaranteeing the truth of their EVIDENCE.

PERPETUAL LIGHT, see **NER TAMID**

PERPETUAL OFFERING, see **TAMID**

PESAḤ, see **PASSOVER**

PESAḤ SHENI, see **PASSOVER, SECOND**

PESAḤIM (Heb. "Paschal Lambs"): Third tractate in the Mishnah order of *Moed* with *gemara* in both Talmuds. It deals with the laws of PASSOVER, based on Exod. 12; 23:15; 34:15 ff.; Lev. 23:5 ff.; Num. 28:16 ff.; and Deut. 16:1. Subjects discussed include the prohibition against leaven, the duty of partaking of unleavened bread and bitter herbs, the *seder* service, the paschal offering, and SECOND PASSOVER.

PESHAT: The literal meaning of the biblical text, as distinct from DERASH (homiletical lessons read into the text for purposes of moral edification). The explicit distinction between *p.* and *derash* seems to date from the Middle Ages, and Rashi in particular sharply differentiates in his biblical commentary between the two approaches. In the Talmud *p.* means "the accepted interpretation as taught in the schools" (cf. *Ḥul.* 6a; *Ket.* 111b). See also PARDES.

PESHER (Heb. "interpretation" or "explanation"; pl. *pesharim*): Name given to a number of biblical commentaries discovered among the DEAD SEA SCROLLS. The term is derived from the authors' method of introducing their commentaries, which were interspersed between biblical passages, with the phrase "its interpretation refers to" (*pishro al*). According to these interpretations the key to the meaning of the books of the Bible was given to the "Teacher of Righteousness", one of the leaders of the Dead Sea community. The authors of the *pesharim* believed the scriptural prophecies to have been written for their own time and predicament, and they interpreted the biblical texts in the light of their acute-eschatological expectations. *Pesharim* have been discovered on Habakkuk, Isaiah, Nahum, Micah, Hosea, and Psalms.

PESHITTA: The Syriac version of the BIBLE (including the New Testament). It is called *Peshitta*, or *Peshitto* ("Simple"), because the Old Testament was rendered directly from the Hebrew, in contrast to the Syrio-Hexapla which is a literal translation of the SEPTUAGINT in Origen's *Hexapla.* The greater part of the rendering, which was produced by many translators working at different periods, is of Jewish origin, and still retains traces of Judeo-Aramaisms and rabbinical interpretations. It also contains some divergences from the masoretic text. Although the translation may have been initiated in the 2nd or even the 1st cent., and was originally intended for use by Jews in certain synagogues, by the 3rd cent. it had become the Bible of the Syriac speaking Christians. The P. was revised in the light of the Septuagint whose influence is particularly noticeable in Genesis, Isaiah, the Minor Prophets, and Psalms. Ezekiel and Proverbs, however, accord closely with the TARGUM, while I Chronicles (a late addition) reflects midrashic exegesis. Originally the Syriac Bible lacked Esther, Ezra, Nehemiah, Chronicles, and the Apocrypha. The present text is a revision made early in the 5th cent.

PESIKTA (Aram. "section"): Cycle of Midrashim, so called because instead of following the biblical books in sequence, it deals only with selected passages. Two versions are extant. The first is usually called *P. of Rabbi Kahana,* because the opening section commences with his name. Though much of it is of ancient origin, the work as a whole is late, and was completed about the 7th cent. The other version — *P. Rabbati* — is still later (845). Earlier scholars confused the two texts both with each other and with the 11th cent. Midrash LEKAḤ TOV, which was also known as *P. Zutarta.* The *P.* consists of distinct sections, each complete in itself, and each relating either to the weekly section of the Law read in the synagogue or the portions read on special Sabbaths, festivals, etc. In addition to *aggadah,* the *P.* contains much important halakhic material.

PESUKEI DE-ZIMRAH (Heb. "verses of song or praise": called by *Sephardim "zemirot"* i.e., "songs"): A collection of biblical hymns recited daily at the beginning of the Morning Service. They are preceded and followed by a benediction (*barukh she-amar* and *yishtabbaḥ* respectively). The *P.d.-Z.* are not mentioned in the Talmud, though they or a similar selection of hymns were probably already recited then by pious worshipers. The main components are Ps. 145-150 and Exod. 15. On Sabbaths and festivals several more psalms are added, and the hymn of praise, NISHMAT, precedes the opening blessing. The *P. d.-Z.* are followed by the short KADDISH and BAREKHU. In the *Ashkenazi* service, it is usual for worshipers to read the *P. d.-Z.* silently, while the reader chants only opening or concluding verses; in other rites they are often recited aloud either in unison or antiphonally. No MINYAN is required for the recitation of the *P. d.-Z.* and their insertion in the early part of the Morning Service is in accord with the rabbinic teaching that man should first praise God and then present his own petitions (*Ber.* 32a).

PFEFFERKORN, JOHANN JOSEPH (1469-after 1521): Apostate. A butcher by trade, he converted to Christianity in 1505 and, encouraged by the Dominicans, denounced Jewish literature as containing anti-Christian blasphemies. Emperor Maximilian empowered him to examine all Jewish books in Germany except the Bible and to destroy any that were anti-Christian. The order was eventually rescinded after a bitter dispute in which several Christians took part; P.'s sponsors (the "obscurantists") were opposed by the humanists led by Johannes Reuchlin.

PHARAOH (Heb. form of Egyptian word meaning "great House" i.e., the palace of the king): During the early dynasties, honorary title for the king of Egypt. Among the Pharaohs mentioned in the Bible are those contemporary with Abraham (Gen. 12:14-20); with Joseph (Gen. 41:37-57); the P. of the oppression (Exod. 1:8) and of the Exodus (Exod. 5 ff.); the father-in-law and ally of Solomon (I Kings 3:1; 7:8); P. Shishak who sacked Jerusalem (I Kings 14:25); and Necho who defeated Josiah (II Kings 23:29-34).

PHARISEES (Heb. *perushim* "separatists" — probably separatists from ritual impurity and defilement): One of the three main sects in Judaism reported in some ancient sources to have existed centuries prior to the destruction of the Jewish state in 70 C.E.; probably a successor group to the HASIDEANS. According to JOSEPHUS the P. were distinguished from the other sects by their adherence to the Oral Law, and he adds that they were noted for their skillful interpretation of the *Torah*. Both Josephus and the New Testament describe the P. as the most rigidly observant group, though the followers of the other sects, the SADDUCEES and ESSENES, were no less conscientious in their adherence to their respective interpretations of the *Torah*. Modern scholars have advanced sociological explanations for the sectarian divisions, with the Sadducees representing the priestly aristocracy and the P. the scholars with popular backing. Rabbinic literature describes the special discipline which members of the Pharisaic party observed: 1) they (re-) tithed any doubtful fruit, i.e., any produce obtained from a non-member; and 2) they kept themselves in ritual purity at all times. In their theology, the P. differed from their Sadducee opponents in maintaining a belief in the immortality of the soul and the resurrection of the body; in the existence of angels; in Divine Providence; and in freedom of will. The masses looked to the P. for religious leadership. In the synagogues, the conduct of the prayers and the reading and exposition of Scriptures were conducted by the scribes of the P. That popular sympathies lay with the P. is illustrated by an incident related of Alexander Yannai. When this king in his capacity as High Priest performed a ceremony at the Feast of Tabernacles in the Temple not in accord with the Pharisaic rite, he was pelted with citrons. The king thereupon let loose his foreign mercenaries upon the people, killing six thousand. The spiritual superiority of the P. derived from their doctrine of the Oral Law (see LAW, ORAL), which gave their approach to religion a more dynamic quality than that exhibited by their opponents. One of the main points at issue between the P. and the other sects was the question of the religious authority of the High Priest. The Sadducees and the Dead Sea sect — probably identical with the Essenes — insisted on the scriptural prerogative of the High Priests — who up to the Maccabean revolt were of the family of Ẓadok — to decide on all matters pertaining to the *Torah*. The P., following the leadership of Ezra and the Men of the Great Synagogue, demanded the submission of the High Priests to the authority of the scholars. Thus they compelled the High Priest to take an oath on the night of the Day of Atonement that he would conduct the ceremonies on the following day in accordance with the instructions of the Pharisaic authorities. Pharisaic ethics and piety were characterized by a profoundly humane attitude which extended even to slaves and criminals. Thus Pharisaic *halakhah* held a slave responsible for his actions, in contrast to the Sadducees who held the master responsible for the actions of his slave. Pharisaic interpretation of the Written Law was often in the direction of leniency; e.g. they interpreted the biblical rule of "an eye for an eye" as referring to monetary compensation for personal damage. In European languages the word "Pharisee" has acquired a pejorative connotation, due to the tendentious description of the P. by the authors of the New Testament. The resentment of the early Christians toward the Pharisees resulted from their being forced by Pharisaic Judaism to change from a Jewish sect into a gentile religion. The Pharisaic line was continued by talmudic and later rabbis, who together form the tradition of rabbinic Judaism, so that the entire subsequent development of Judaism bears the indelible stamp of Pharisaism.

PHILANTHROPY, see **CHARITY**

PHILISTINES: People originating in the Aegean basin, with a culture of the Mycenean type. The

P. settled on the southern coast of Palestine (the name is derived from Philistia) in the 12th cent. B.C.E. and were one of the Israelites' chief rivals in the conquest of the country. Their possession of iron ore (which they turned into a monopoly, cf. I Sam. 13:19 ff.) gave them a considerable military advantage. At one of their successful battles against the Israelites they captured the Ark (I Sam. 4-6), and the resultant demoralization precipitated the Israelite demand for a monarchy (I Sam. 8). Fighting with the Philistines continued throughout the reign of Saul, who though initially victorious, finally suffered defeat and death at Philistine hands in the battle of Gilboa (I Sam. 31:1-13). Only under Saul's successor David, who set himself the goal of removing the Philistine danger, were they conclusively routed in a series of battles which culminated in the capture of Gath (II Sam. 3:18; 5:17-25; 8:1; 19:9; 21:15-22; 23:9-17). Although not pure Semites (they were for instance, not circumcised), the P. adopted the Semitic god Dagan, and their religion was repeatedly denounced by the prophets (e.g. Amos 1:6-8; Jer. 47).

PHILO (c. 25 B.C.E.-40 C.E.): Alexandrian philosopher. By combining contemporary hellenistic (Platonic, Stoic, etc.) philosophy and piety with Jewish belief in REVELATION and Holy Scripture, he became the first representative of theological philosophy. P. read his philosophy into the Bible through allegorical interpretation. By explaining scriptural statements and narratives as ALLEGORY, he could divest them of their apparently concrete, material, and at times trivial character, and demonstrate their higher, spiritual meaning. The purpose of P.'s many writings was to impress gentiles as well as cultured Jews with the greatness of Scripture and Mosaic law by presenting the latter as conforming to the law of nature and philosophical reason. P.'s thought is characterized by a basic DUALISM between spirit and matter. A purely spiritual God is so completely separate from the material world that He acts upon the latter only by means of mediating agencies (see LOGOS). The spiritual soul is imprisoned in the body during this earthly life, and its task is to liberate itself from the world of the senses and reascend to its Divine home. In rare moments of mystical ecstasy, the soul may rise above its bondage to matter even during this life and hence achieve the spiritual contemplation of God. P.'s work is the noblest expression of the fusion of Judaism and Hellenism, but it consisted more of a projection of hellenistic ideas and values into Jewish tradition than a genuine interpretation and development of that tradition. Christian thinkers found some of P.'s ideas (e.g. his other-world orientation, his doctrine of the mediating *logos*) particularly congenial, and his influence on the beginnings of Christian theology is very strongly marked. This fact may have further contributed to the almost total neglect of P. and his work in the subsequent development of Judaism.

PHILOSOPHY: As the systematic study of reality and of its general principles, p. frequently borders on, and overlaps with, religion. The relationship between the two is conceived differently by different thinkers. An extreme orthodox-fundamentalist school condemns p. as a vain exercise of human reason which should be guided by REVELATION alone. At the opposite extreme the rationalist approach exalts p. to the rank of sole arbiter of the rightness or wrongness of religious doctrines. Traditional theology and p. of religion occupy various positions between these extremes. Since the subject matter of p. often coincides with that of religion (e.g. the existence and nature of GOD, the origin and nature of the universe, the nature and destiny of man and his soul, the source and sanctions of morality, etc.), p. has often been called upon to prove, confirm, or buttress religious doctrines, or to interpret the dogmas of religion and elucidate their implications and presuppositions in the light of philosophical understanding. Thus, though the Bible is essentially non-philosophical in character, yet underlying its symbolism and concrete imagery there are ideas and concepts that lend themselves to philosophic elaboration: God, revelation, transcendence, monotheism, Divine justice (THEODICY), the meaning of history, etc. The biblical manner of speaking in non-philosophical, concrete images of things which others might have expressed in more abstract and conceptual terms, was also followed by the ancient rabbis (AGGADAH; see also ANTHROPOMORPHISM); only occasionally would they raise a genuine philosophical problem in epigrammatic form, but without going into systematic, philosophical discussion. Therefore, the history of Jewish p. suggests that it appeared as the result of contact with the philosophical thought of other civilizations (HELLENISM, Islamic Aristotelianism and Neo-Platonism, post-Kantian idealism, modern existentialism, etc). It may thus be defined as the effort of Jewish thinkers to use the categories of contemporary philosophies as a means of arriving at a philosophical understanding of Judaism. Jewish p. in this sense is distinct from the contributions of Jewish thinkers to general p. No doubt Jewish philosophers occupy a prominent place in the history of modern p., but even SPINOZA's contribution is to general rather than to Jewish p., if one reserves the latter term for philosophical attempts to elucidate the nature, contents, meaning, presuppositions, and implications of Judaism as a religion or as a historical phenomenon. Jewish p. flourished for the first time in the orbit of hellentistic civilization, where its foremost representative was PHILO of Alexandria. Philo interpreted Judaism in terms of Neo-Platonic and Stoic ideas, but he left little or no mark on Jewish posterity. Of far greater significance was the medieval revival of Greek p. among the Arabs and the use to which it was put by the theological schools of ISLAM (*Mu'tazila*, *Kalam*). The fact that two competing universal religions both rejecting Judaism, claimed exclusive validity, as well as the rationalist criticism of religion in general, gave an enormous impulse to the theological effort of proving the validity of religion by rational means. The first major medieval Jewish philosopher, SAADYAH GAON, still depended on the *Kalam* school as did David AL-MUKAMMAS and many others, both orthodox Rabbanites and Karaites. But, whereas the latter's p. remainded in the *Mu'tazilite* tradition, rabbinic thought developed under the decisive influence of the two main streams of Greco-Arab p., NEO-PLATONISM and ARISTOTELIANISM. Neo-Platonism was the major influence in the thought of Isaac ISRAELI and reached its height in the *Fountain of Life* (*Fons Vitae*) of Solomon IBN GABIROL; its moral and ascetic theology is also manifest in *The Duties of the Heart* by BAHYA IBN PAKUDA, in Joseph IBN TZADDIK's *Microcosm*, and in the *Kuzari* by JUDAH HA-LEVI. Aristotelianism, however, proved by far the more powerful trend. Established by some of the greatest thinkers of Islam, Aristotelianism had appeared in the thinking of Abraham IBN DAUD and reached its height in *Guide for the Perplexed*, the major work of the outstanding medieval Jewish philosopher, MOSES BEN MAIMON (Maimonides), which posits the most comprehensive justification and reconciliation of Judaism and philosophy along Aristotelian lines. The caliber of his work made it inevitable that most subsequent writings be dependent on it, either commenting on and developing its ideas or criticizing and combating them. The controversy caused by Maimonides' works rent Jewry into two hostile camps, but could not, in the long run, prevent the victory of Maimonides' p. Jewish p., exemplified in the works of ISAAC ALBALAG, LEVI BEN GERSHON, Ḥasdai CRESCAS, and many lesser figures like Joseph ALBO, continued generally to build on the Aristotelian foundations laid by Maimonides and was further accentuated by developments in Arabic thought, especially by the work of the Arab Aristotelian, Averroes. The prolific and versatile Isaac ABRAVANEL marks the end of the Spanish-Jewish philosophic tradition which was cultivated, though not really continued, in Italy where Jews had philosophized in a Christian environment since at least the time of HILLEL BEN SAMUEL of Verona. Modern Jewish p. begins with Moses MENDELSSOHN. His p., in many ways typical of the European HASKALAH, was soon superseded by the triumph of German idealism, applied to Judaism by Solomon Formstecher and Samuel Hirsch. Naḥman KROCHMAL, a pioneer of the new WISSENSCHAFT DES JUDENTUMS, in his *Guide to the Perplexed of Our Times* used historical research in the service of an ambitious p. of history in which Hegelian overtones are distinct. Ludwig Steinheim propounded a decidedly antirationalist p. of revelation. The turn of the 20th century witnessed a revival of Kantianism, exemplified by Moritz LAZARUS' *The Ethics of Judaism* and particularly by the work of Hermann COHEN. The modern, anti-idealist (or existentialist) trend came to the fore in Jewish thought with Franz ROSENZWEIG's *The Star of Redemption*. The last decades of German Jewry were marked by the activity of other great religious thinkers, in particular Leo BAECK and Martin BUBER. Since the destruction of German Jewry, the centers of Jewish religious p. have shifted to the U.S. and the State of Israel. Another trend initiated by the HASKALAH movement was the growth of a secular attitude in philosophizing about Judaism. Though the trend expressed itself more in literature and journalism, it determined the climate in which the developing Jewish nationalism (ZIONISM) formulated its ideology and its evaluations of the past and present. The most outstanding of these philosophical essayists was AḤAD HA-AM, whose doctrine of Zion as a "spiritual center" was opposed both by the historian Simon Dubnow, whose theory of successive social and cultural centers affirmed the Diaspora as a legitimate form of Jewish existence, and by Jacob Klatzkin who preached a radical "negation of the Diaspora". Others, such as the Socialist-Zionist Ber Borochov, tried to bring Zionism in line with radical Marxist or Socialist views. With the establishment of the State of Israel, the philosophical problems of statehood and political existence have come to take a more prominent place in the wider context of Jewish philosophy (such as p. of history, religion, individual and collective destiny).

PHINEHAS: Son of Eleazar and grandson of AARON. When Israel "began to commit harlotry with the daughters of Moab", P. ran a spear through Zimri, a chief of the tribe of Simeon, who had defiantly entered the encampment at Shittim with a Midianite woman. P.'s zeal persuaded God to end the plague which was ravaging Israel in punishment for their infidelity, and P. and his offspring were rewarded with eternal PRIESTHOOD (Num. 25:1-15). The ZADOKITES traced their descent to him. Rabbinic *aggadah* identifies P. with the prophet Elijah, both of whom served as prototypes for zealous action in the name of the Lord.

PHYLACTERIES, see **TEPHILLIN**

PIDYON HA-BEN, see **FIRST-BORN, REDEMPTION OF**

PIDYON SHEVUYIM (Heb.): Ransom of CAPTIVES.

PIG: A cloven-hoofed quadruped which is forbidden as food as it does not chew its cud (Lev. 11:7). Since it also wallows in dirt, the p. became for Jews a symbol of filth (Y. *Ber.* 2) and of all that is unseemly and abominable. The use of the p. in pagan sacrifices, such as some pagan rulers attempted to force upon the Jews, may also have contributed to the particular abhorrence in which the p. is held above all other "unclean" animals. In due course it became so abhorred that it was often referred to not by name but by the euphemism "the other thing". One who raises swine is considered accursed (*Men.* 64b), and it was forbidden to trade in or have benefit from them. Some authorities (e.g. Maimonides) interpreted the ban as being based on physical considerations but others (including the kabbalists) stressed the spiritual aspect. (See DIETARY LAWS).

PIGGUL (Heb. "abomination"): Term for the invalidation of sacrifice because the sacrificer, at the time of slaughter, intends to partake of it outside its proper place or beyond its allotted time.

PIKUAḤ NEPHESH, see **DANGER**

PILGRIM FESTIVALS (Heb. *shalosh regalim*): Every male Israelite was enjoined to make the PILGRIMAGE to Jerusalem three times a year, on the festivals of PASSOVER, WEEKS, and TABERNACLES (Exod. 23:17; Deut. 16:16), which were therefore termed the three p. f. (cf. Exod. 23:14). The pilgrim had to offer a sacrifice, the minimum value of which was laid down in the Mishnah as three pieces of silver (*Ḥag.* 1:1-2). The pilgrims also brought with them the second TITHE of their produce, which had to be consumed in Jerusalem. In the synagogue, FESTIVAL PRAYERS, including the HALLEL, are recited on the p.f. These vary from one festival to another only by the mention of the specific festival and its sacrifice, and in the relevant scriptural readings. In addition to statutory festival prayers, each festival has its specific liturgical features, ceremonies, and customs, e.g. the recitation of AKDAMUT on Weeks (among *Ashkenazim*), and the waving and procession of the FOUR SPECIES on Tabernacles. The Song of Songs is read on Passover; Ruth on Weeks; and Ecclesiastes on Tabernacles. Doubt is expressed in the Talmud as to whether SHEMINI ATZERET is to be regarded as the final day of Tabernacles or as an independent festival.

PILGRIMAGE: The Bible enjoins pilgrimages to Jerusalem and the Temple on the occasion of the three PILGRIM FESTIVALS (Exod. 23:17; Deut. 16:16). The institution of this custom evoked a ready response from the people, and when Jeroboam I established the secessionist Northern Kingdom he deliberately set up rival shrines at Dan and Bethel in order to wean the people away from these pilgrimages (I Kings 12:26-33). The custom of making the p. to Jerusalem reached its fullest development during the Second Temple Period, when it was followed even by Diaspora Jewry. The popularity of the Tabernacles p. is attested to by the fact that the daily prayers for rain were postponed until fifteen days after the festival "in order to grant time for the last of the Israelites to return to the Euphrates" (Mishnah *Taan.* 1:3). The vast throngs who made the p. on Passover are mentioned by Josephus (*Wars* 6:9) who reports that the census taken by the Roman procurator Gestus Florius on the eve of the outbreak of the Roman War in 66 gave the number of paschal lambs slaughtered on this holiday as 256,500; this number would indicate a total of almost 3,000,000 pilgrims. (The figure of 1,200,000 lambs given by the Tosephta *Pes.* 4 seems an exaggeration). The fact that accommodation was found for all the pilgrims is listed among the minor miracles (*Avot* 5:4). The custom continued even after the destruction of the Temple, especially on *Av* 9, but pilgrimages were now occasions for mourning, and pilgrims would rend their garments and cry out in bitter lamentation (*M.K.* 26a). During the Middle Ages individual Jewish pilgrimages to the Western Wall were of regular occurrence, and it is to the heart-rending scenes there that the (non-Jewish) name "Wailing Wall" refers. Organized pilgrimages to HOLY PLACES other than the site of the Temple appear to have been instituted after Jews began to immigrate to the Holy Land following the expulsion from Spain in 1492. At first the main goal of the popular pilgrimages was the traditional tomb of the prophet Samuel at Ramah. Gradually, however, this was superseded by pilgrimages to the grave of R. Simeon bar Yoḥai at Meron. Though initially no fixed day existed for this particular p., in the course of time it came to be fixed on LAG BA-OMER, and the custom of making this p. continues to the present day. In the 16th cent. Isaac Luria claimed to have established the identification of many graves of talmudic rabbis in Galilee, and pious Jews would make pilgrimages to the Holy Land to prostrate themselves on these tombs, and utter the special prayers composed for the occasion. When access to the Western Wall was denied after the establishment of the State of Israel in 1948, its place as the center of p. was taken to some extent by Mt. Zion, the spot in Israel nearest to the site of the Temple. Oriental Jews from almost every country make regular pilgrimages to the real or reputed graves of biblical figures and distinguished rabbis; similar customs existed among the Ḥasidim.

PILPUL (Heb.): The process of dialectical reasoning applied in the study of the Oral Law. P. could mean the application of the HERMENEUTIC RULES to the halakhic parts of the Bible, but more particularly it signifies the logical analysis and argumentation characteristic of legal casuistry. The process was occasionally carried to extremes of casuistic hairsplitting in order to sharpen the acumen of the student (*Eruv.* 13a), but because of the misuse to which unrestrained dialectic could be put (*Sot.* 47b) pilpulistic method was controlled by the rabbis, who did not hesitate to exclaim "The sharper one is, the more prone to error" (*Bava Metzia* 96b). P. used to demonstrate intellectual brilliance, or to erect detailed halakhic edifices without solid scholarly foundation, aroused the ire and disapproval of scholars of all ages, who characterized such pursuit as a waste of time and vain mental gymnastics. The pilpulistic approach was highly developed by the tosaphists and by ghetto *yeshivot*; it thus played an important part in E. European rabbinic scholarship, despite the protests of some leading talmudists.

PIRKEI AVOT, see **AVOT**

PIRKEI DE-RABBI ELIEZER (or **BARAITA DE-RABBI ELIEZER**); Pseudepigraphic Midrash on the early part of the Bible ascribed to the *tanna* R. Eliezer ben Hyrcanus whose life story is told in the first chapter; in fact, however, the composition of much of the work has been dated to the 8th cent. *P. de-R. E.* is aggadic Midrash, the avowed purpose of which is to "declare the glory of God". Many sections are devoted to the creation chapters of Genesis and the early history of the patriarchs; its sudden conclusion with the punishment of Miriam for slandering Moses indicates that the work was unfinished or that its continuation has been lost. Three chapters (6-9) are devoted to the calendar, others to particular topics such as the Sabbath (18), repentance (43), and circumcision (29). The author often relates certain precepts to events in the lives of the patriarchs.

PITTUM HA-KETORET (Heb. "The compound forming the incense"): *Baraita* (*Ker.* 6a; also Y. *Yoma* 4:5) describing the preparation of INCENSE in the Temple (Exod. 30:34-38). It is recited at the end of the Morning Service, or — among *Sephardim* — prior to the Afternoon Service. The mystics attached great significance to its meticulous recitation, and for fear that the worshiper might be negligent in his recital on weekday mornings, they restricted the passage to the liturgy of Sabbaths and festivals, a practice which has remained the *Ashkenazi* custom in the Diaspora.

PIYYUT (Heb.): Synagogal POETRY. As a genre referring specifically to those liturgical poems added to the statutory prayers, *p.* originated in Palestine, probably in the 5th cent.; *piyyutim* (pl.) were subsequently composed also in Babylonia and especially in Germany, France, Spain, and Italy. This creative flowering of poetic spirit continued until the 18th cent., although from the 14th cent. on *paytanim* (i.e., composers of *p.*) were less prolific, and their *piyyutim* were rarely incorporated into the official LITURGY. Numerous *piyyutim* dealt with some local event and, as they had but limited significance, fell eventually into oblivion. Many others have been brought to light as a result of the discovery of the Cairo GENIZAH. Israel Davidson (*Thesaurus of Medieval Hebrew Poetry*) enumerated some 35,000 poems of the *p.* type and listed nearly 3,000 *paytanim* and poets. *P.* was first composed anonymously; the oldest known *paytanim* are Yose ben Yose (c. 5th cent.) and Yannai and his pupil Eleazar Kallir. With these the *p.* reached its first peak, and their compositions occur in the FESTIVAL PRAYERS. The early Palestinian *paytanim* introduced rhyme into Hebrew poetry, and there is evidence suggesting that they influenced Christian liturgical poets. They were followed by Saadyah Gaon (Babylonia), R. Meshullam ben Kalonymos the Great and Amittai ben Shephatiah (Italy) — 10th cent.; Rashi (France), Solomon Ibn Gabirol and Judah Ha-Levi (Spain), Solomon ben Judah Ha-Bavli (Italy), Moses ben Kalonymos and Jekuthiel ben Moses (Germany) — 11th cent.; R. Tam (France) and R. Yom Tov of York (England) — 12th cent.; and Meir ben Baruch of Rothenburg (Germany) 13th cent. While *paytanim* generally set out to supplement the existing prayers, Yannai and Kallir may have been prompted by more pressing motives. Justinian (527-565) had, with missionary intent, prohibited instruction in the Oral Law while permitting the reading of the weekly scriptural portion. This prohibition has been suggested as an explanation for the unusual halakhic character of the *p.* of Yannai whose elaboration of the themes of the SIDRAH and stress on *halakhah* may have been designed as a substitute for more formal teaching. Similar considerations have been advanced in connection with the compositions of Eleazar Kallir. *P.* is often distinguished by a normal or reverse alphabetic acrostic, both serving as aids to memory, especially when the *piyyutim* were being transmitted orally. Early Palestinian *p.* reflected the needs and conditions of its country of origin, and some compositions, especially those of Yannai and Kallir, showed dependence in halakhic matters on the Palestinian Talmud. But when from the 8th cent. on, Babylonia began to contest the spiritual supremacy of Palestine in the Jewish world and in W. Europe, the Babylonian

Talmud came to be increasingly accepted as authoritative over the Palestinian, voices were soon raised in opposition to the introduction of *p.* into the liturgy at all. Maimonides objected to the extravagant and theologically objectionable imagery with which some *paytanim* referred to God or described His attributes. Ibn Ezra (on Ecc. 5:1) attacked the *paytanim* for the artificiality and obscurity of their language and for their abuse of the grammar and pure forms of Hebrew. Despite such opposition, however, *piyyutim* have continued to be an integral part of the prayers, and have enriched and developed the Hebrew language. They are classified according to their general character (e.g. penitential prayers; KINOT — elegies, especially for *Av* 9) or their position in the liturgy, e.g. *maaravot*, which are inserted in the MAARIV prayer, and YOTZEROT, which are named after the word *yotzer* (creator) found in the first blessing before the *Shema*. The *yotzerot* are divided into the *ophan* (dealing with the mystical heavenly creatures), the *zulat* (from "there is no God beside Thee" — *zulatekha*), and the *geullah* (from *gaal* — "who hast redeemed Israel"). *Kerovot*, sometimes known as *shivata* (from *shiva*, "seven", after the seven benedictions of the Sabbath and festival *amidah*) are inserted into the repetition of the *amidah*. Poetical forms used are the *sheniyyah*, *shelishiyyah*, and *shalmonit* — two, three, and four line stanzas respectively — and the *mostejab*, in which each stanza begins with a biblical verse.

PLAGUES, THE TEN: Punishments inflicted by God upon the Egyptians in order to force Pharaoh to release Israel from bondage. Various traditions seem to have existed regarding the exact number and details of the p. (cf. Ps. 78:43-51). The fullest and most detailed account (Exod. 7:14-12:30) mentions ten p., following one another in three groups of three plus a final one. In each group the first two plagues were unleashed after a warning by Moses, while the third followed unannounced. The miraculous character of the p. is emphasized both by the biblical account and later *aggadah*, and the recital of the names of the plagues is a central feature of the *Seder* service.

PLATONISM AND NEO-PLATONISM: The philosophical systems of Plato (427-347 B.C.E.) and of the later philosophers — ancient and medieval — whose thinking followed Platonic lines. P. proved a congenial philosophy to many religious minds (e.g. PHILO of Alexandria), but it was not until the Middle Ages that the Neo-Platonic tradition, initiated by Plotinus (3rd cent. C.E.) and his successors and mediated by Islamic and Christian sources, made a profound and lasting mark on Jewish thought. The Platonic "forms" were identified with the creative thoughts of God, and God was defined as the Good, the First Principle, and "The One", i.e., as absolutely single and self-sufficient. From this ultimate One descended or emanated (see EMANATION) the intelligible world of ideas and the lower forms of being down to the material world. The human SOUL was a particle from a higher realm of being (the "World Soul" according to Plotinus, the THRONE of Glory, according to the Jewish Neo-Platonists) to which it longed to return. N.-P. provided a philosophical basis not only for the rational, but also for the spiritual and even mystical life. Its aim was to reach the ultimate One lying behind all concrete experience; its method was that of intellectual abstraction (viz., of contemplative ascent) by which it divested experience of all that was specifically human until nothing was left but God. Medieval N.-P. received a powerful impetus through the *Liber de Causis* (attributed to Aristotle but actually written in the 9th cent. by a Moslem philosopher, and containing extracts from the 5th cent. Neo-Platonist Proclus) and profoundly affected Jewish philosophical and religious thought. Beginning with Isaac ISRAELI (c. 850-c. 950), Jewish N.-P. reached its height with Solomon IBN GABIROL in the purely philosophical sphere, and with BAHYA Ibn Pakuda and JUDAH HA-LEVI's *Kuzari* in the ascetic and theological sphere. Other representatives of N.-P. were Abraham IBN EZRA and Joseph IBN TZADDIK. While N.-P. was soon eclipsed by ARISTOTELIANISM in philosophy, it continued to exert a powerful influence on mystical speculation and, in particular, on the emergent KABBALAH in the 13th cent. In contrast to the ancient and medieval predilection for N.-P. as the most adequate philosophy from the religious point of view, many modern critics maintain that N.-P. with its monistic tendency, its exaltation of the abstract above the concrete, and its hostility to the material order of Creation, is essentially incompatible with biblical teaching and spirituality.

PLEDGES: Personal property offered as security against the repayment of a debt. The pledge may be any object belonging to the borrower. The creditor may not enter the home of the debtor to take or choose the pledge, but must accept whatever pledge the debtor chooses to give him. The debtor's tools of trade (Deut. 24:6) or necessary clothes or covering (Exod. 22:26) cannot be taken during the time of the day or night when they are normally used, nor may the clothing of a widow, or vessels required to prepare food, be taken as a pledge (Deut. 24:10-17). The indiscriminate taking of p., and the resultant hardship and evil were severely denounced by the prophets.

POETRY: The early books of the Bible contain fragments of ancient p., (e.g. Gen. 4:23-4; Gen. 49; Exod. 15; Num. 2:17-18; Deut. 32-33) but biblical

OMER: Tablet for
Counting of the *Omer;*
Italian, 18 cent.
Feinberg Collection, Detroit.

PASSOVER:
Seder dish;
Italian, 1673.
Roth Collection,
Jerusalem.

PASSOVER: *Seder* dish; German, 1802. Feinberg Collection, Detroit.

PASSOVER:
"Passover Meal"
by Moritz Oppenheim (1800-1882);

PLAGUES:
The ten plagues,
from a Venetian *Haggadah,* 1609.

סאנגרי ·

ל אקוה סי קונבירטי אין
סאנגרי · טוטו מצרים
סוספירה אי לאנגרי :

דם

צפרדע

ראנוקייו ·

פיר לה גראן קואנטיטה די
ראני · נון סי דורמי ני
איספאסטה ני קוצי איל פאני :

פידוקייו

ג׳יאנדרי איירה לה קואנטיטה
די פידוקייו · גרוסי קומי
גראני די פינוקייו :

כנים

ערוב

מיסקולייו ·

לופי אורסי טיגרי אי
ליאוני · איראנו אין מצרים
אין טוטי אי קאנטוני :

פיסטי ·

פיסטיאמי די אוני סורטי ·
פוקי סקאמפאנו די לה
מורטי :

דבר

שחין

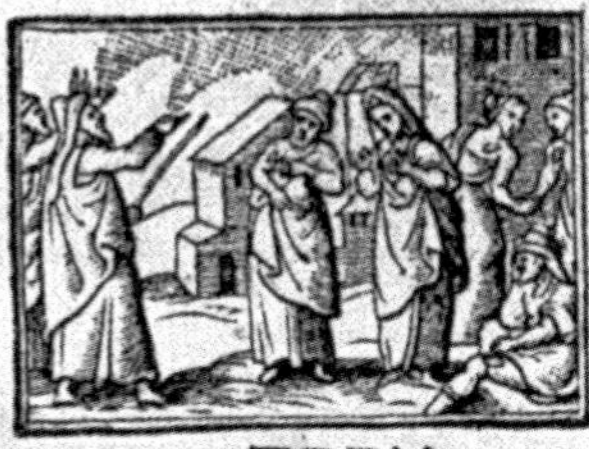

פיסטולה ·

משה ספארסי קאליגיני
דינאנצי פאראוני · קאסקו
סופרה מצריים אי פיצי
בוניוני :

טימפיסטה ·

טימפיסטה אקומפאניאטה
קון פוקו · קונסומאורה
מצרים אין אוני לוקו :

ברד

ארבה

גרילו ·

אונה גראן קואנטיטה די
קאואליטי · קי דיוראוה
לה ויידורה · די לי ארבורי
אי לי אירביטי :

סקוריטו ·

טרי גיורני די טיניברה
אי סקורורי · אויאנו לי
מצריי׳ אי ישרא׳ ספלינדורי

חושך

מכת בכורות ;

פירקוסה די פרימי
נאיטי ;

פיאנטי ספירי אי גיימיטי
סי סינטיוה פיר לה מורטי
די פרימי גייניטי :

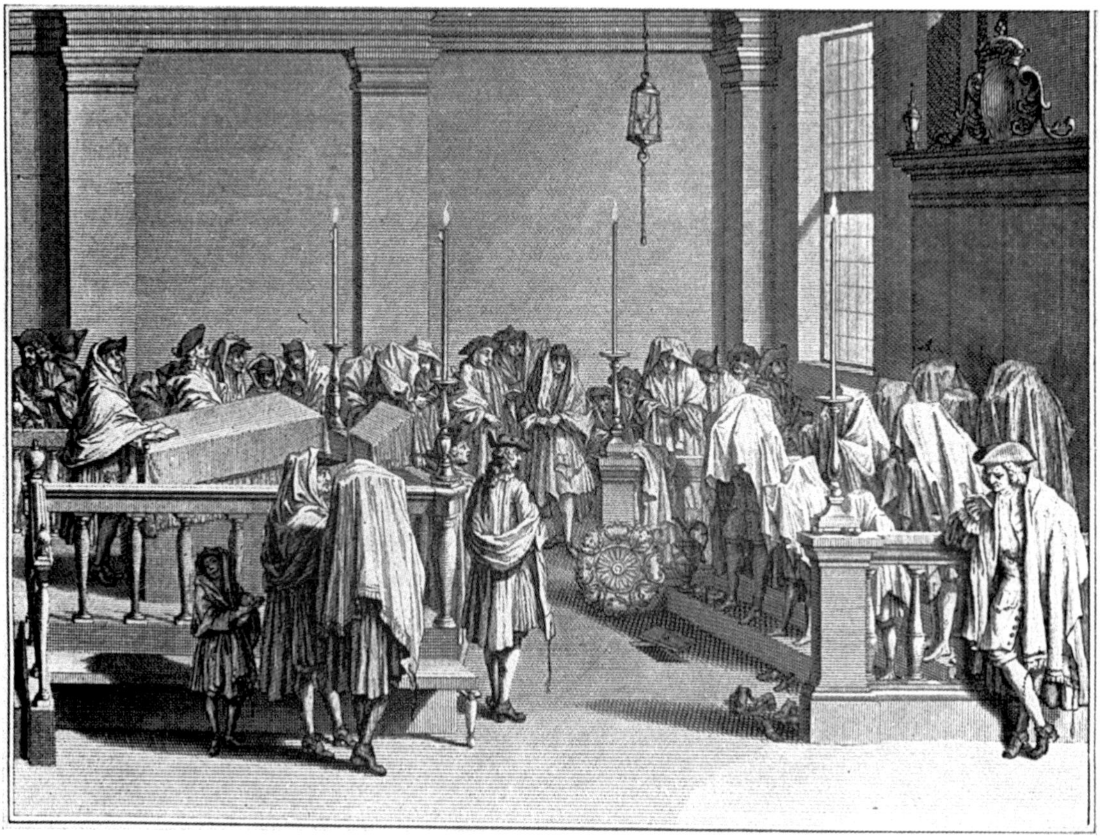

PRIESTLY BLESSING: from Bernard Picart's *Cérémonies et coutumes religieuses* (Amsterdam, 1723).

PURIM: A Purim rattle (*gregger*);
Central Europe.
Feinberg Collection, Detroit.

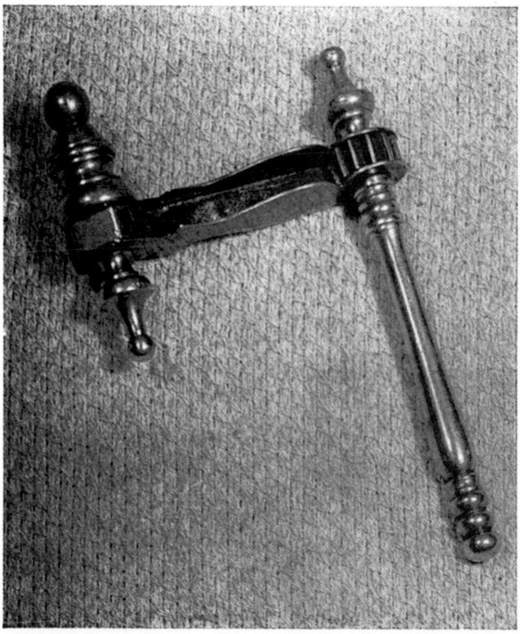

PURIM: *Purim* Plate;
Strasbourg, 18th cent.
Cluny Museum, Paris.

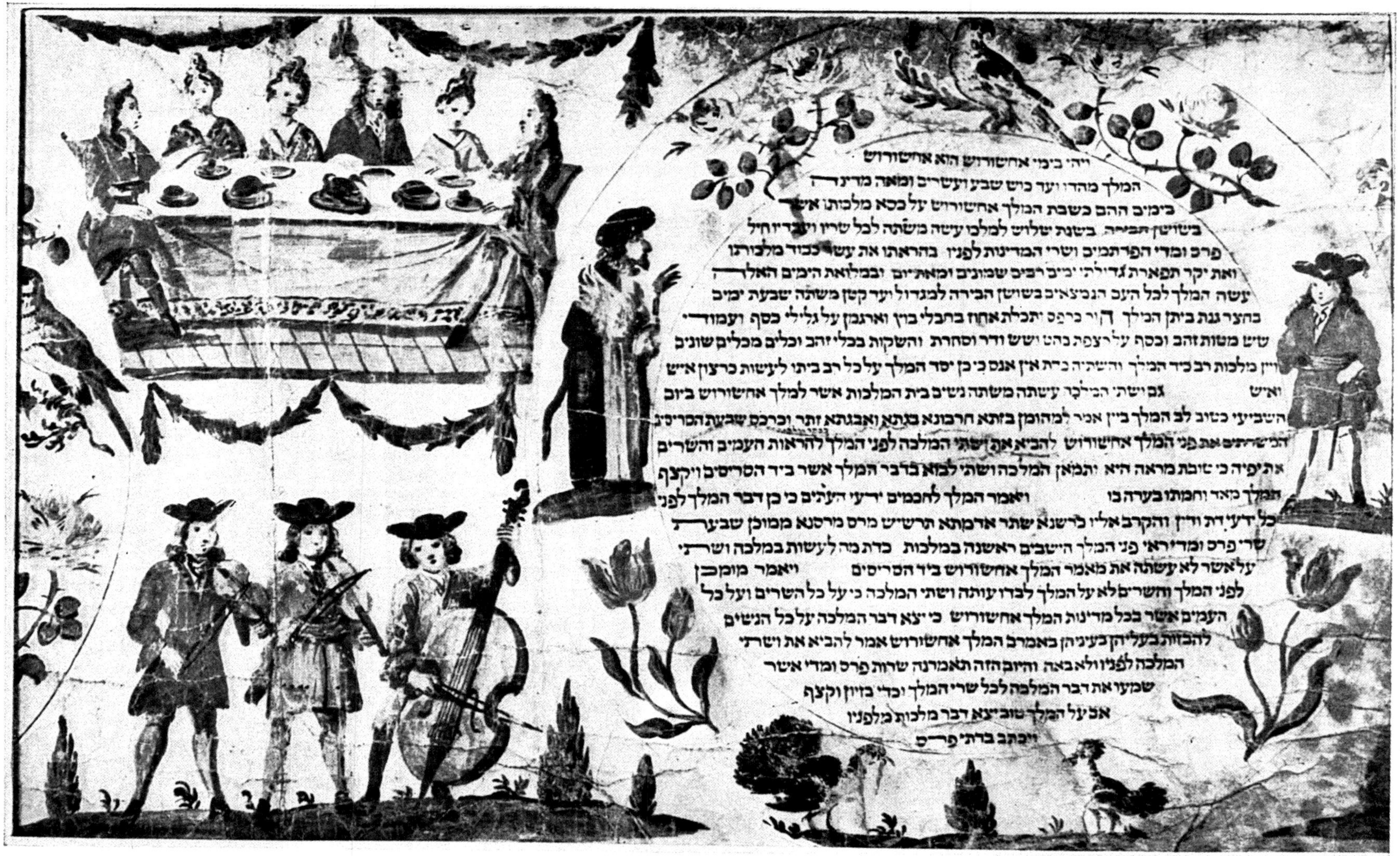

PURIM: "*Ahasuerus' Feast*", from Scroll of Esther, 1730. Israel Museum, Jerusalem.

PURIM:
"Purim at Home"
by Moritz Oppenheim
(1800-1882).

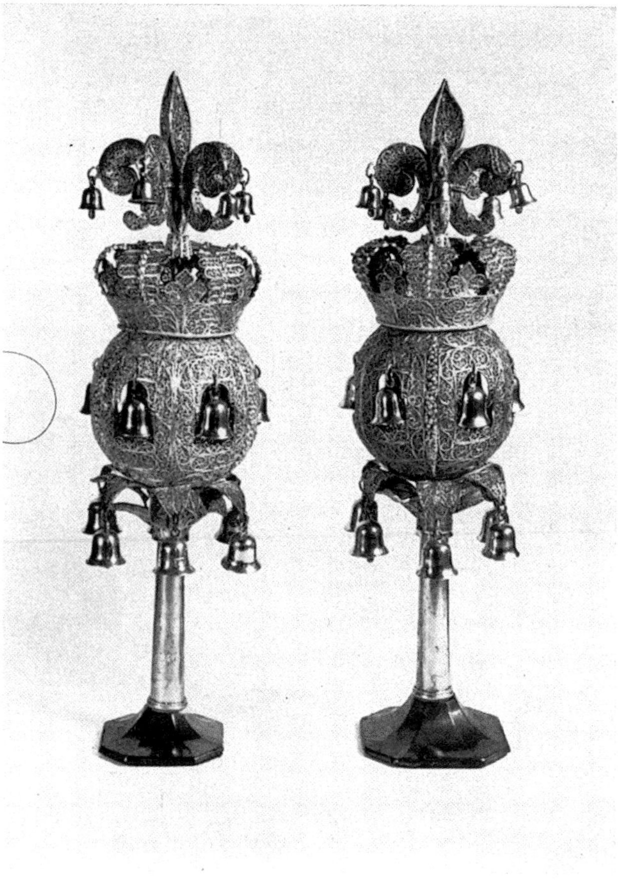

RIMMONIM: Silver filigree bells from the *Sephardi* congregation; Amsterdam, 17th. cent. Victoria and Albert Museum, London.

RIMMONIM: One of a pair of *Rimmonim* in tree-form (symbolizing the Tree of Life); Breslau, c. 1770; Jewish Museum, New York.

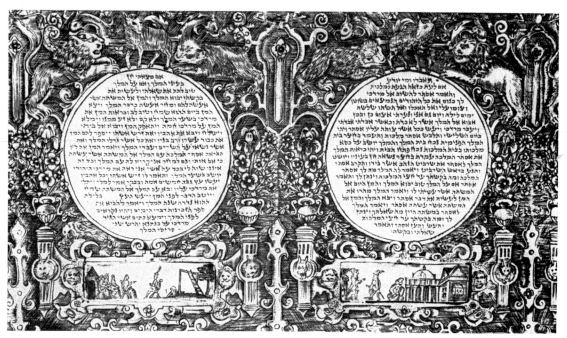

PURIM: Scroll of Esther. Italian, 17th cent. Cologne Municipal Museum.

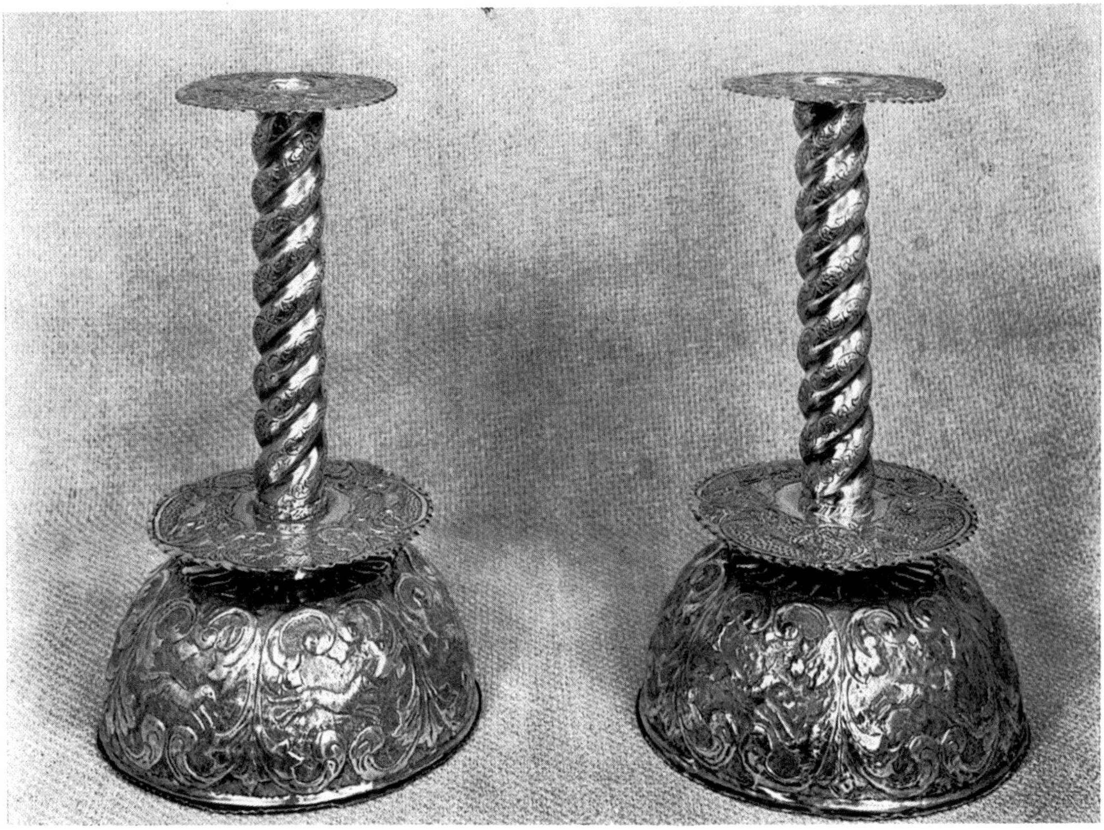

SABBATH: Sabbath lamps; German, 17th cent. Feinberg Collection, Detroit.

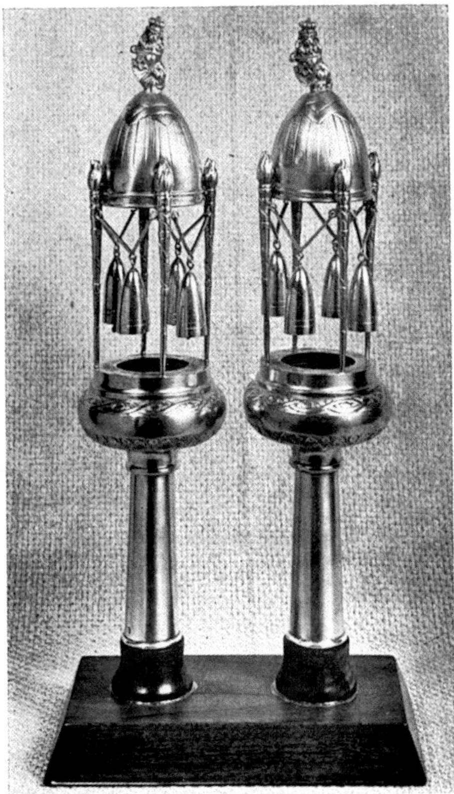

RIMMONIM: French, c. 1800. Feinberg Collection, Detroit.

SAMARITANS: Samaritan High Priest with *Torah* by E. M. Lilien (1874-1925).

p. reaches its full development in later works such as the Books of Psalms, Song of Songs, Job, Ecclesiastes, and the prophetical writings. In form, biblical p. resembles the p. prevalent in the Middle East of the time; its particular characteristic is parallelism according to which the second half of a verse echoes, repeats in other words, or provides an antithesis to the first half. During the First Temple Period, PRAYER was generally the utterance of the individual (cf. I Sam. 2:1-11; I Kings, 8:22-64) but the LITURGY developed during Second Temple times and especially after the destruction of the Temple. The prayers took a fixed format; hymns — many of them emanating from Babylonia — were written and were incorporated in the service. Alphabetical and nominal acrostics proved a favorite device and served a mnemonic purpose since books were not generally available and the congregation had to pray by heart. Further additions were made during the Gaonic Period when, largely under Arabic influence, rhyme became a prominent feature of Hebrew p. The concept of meter was introduced later into Hebrew p. by Dunash ben Labrat (10th cent.). Hebrew sacred p. flourished from the 5th-14th centuries, starting with the period of *paytanim* (see PIYYUT) when many of the best-known *piyyutim*, SELIḤOT, and KINNOT were composed. Outstanding poets in medieval Spain included Solomon IBN GABIROL (whose *Keter Malkhut* is a classic of religious p.); Moses IBN EZRA (whose *seliḥot* received wide currency); JUDAH HA-LEVI (whose sacred poems were imbued with national sentiments and the love of Zion); and Abraham IBN EZRA. Distinguished religious poets in Italy, France, and Germany carried on the ancient Palestinian tradition. The Crusader massacres inspired many moving dirges, some of which found permanent places in the prayer services. From the 13th cent., much sacred p. continued to be written but was marked by quantity rather than originality. Among the exceptions were the kabbalist poets of Safed (NAJARA, ALKABETZ) and the Yemenite poet SHABBAZI. Few poetic additions to the liturgy have won a permanent place in recent centuries, although the Reconstructionist prayer book includes poems by modern Hebrew poets.

POLEMICS: Controversies conducted in writing (for verbal p., see DISPUTATIONS). Religious p. are frequent in Jewish literature. There is much implicit and explicit polemicizing in the Bible, though the exact references are not always clear. The first famous polemic in post-biblical literature was the controversy between JOSEPHUS and Apion, an Alexandrian author who repeated the anti-Semitic libels of earlier Greek writers, including accusations that the Israelites were expelled from Egypt because they were afflicted with leprosy and that they worshiped the head of an ass in the Temple. Josephus' reply, *Against Apion* — a classic of its type — is to a large extent the model for all Jewish defensive p. With the rise of Christianity, anti-Jewish polemical literature emerged in which Christian writers tried to prove that the biblical prophecies had been fulfilled by the advent of Jesus. Justin Martyr's *Dialogue with the Jew Tryphon* (2nd cent.) — in which the disputants part with mutual expressions of goodwill — was followed by a host of anti-Jewish writings by the CHURCH FATHERS, of which the best known are the *Adversus Judaeos* of Tertullian and the *Dialogue of the Jew and the Christian concerning the Holy Trinity* of Jerome. The KARAITE schism gave rise to a number of polemical works between Rabbanites and Karaites; among the most prominent Rabbanite polemicists was SAADYAH Gaon. During the Middle Ages a considerable number of anti-Christian polemical works were written, e.g. Joseph Kimḥi's *Sepher ha-Berit* (Provence, 12th cent.) and the *Sepher ha-Nitzaḥon* of Lipmann MÜHLHAUSEN (Austria, 15th cent.). One of the most successful and impressive polemical works, and one which especially aroused Christian antagonism, was the *Ḥizzuk Emunah* of the 16th cent. Karaite, Isaac of Troki. Johann Eisenmenger's crudely anti-Semitic *Entdecktes Judenthum* (17th cent.) served as a model for later anti-Jewish writers.

POLYGAMY: P. is taken for granted in the Bible, even though the account of creation (Gen. 1:27; 2:18-24) indicates that monogamy was the original state envisaged by the Creator. In spite of frequent instances of p. (the first being Lamech, Gen. 4:19, and the most outstanding being Solomon, I Kings 11:3), monogamy appears to have been the rule, polygamy the exception; indeed the biblical hymn in praise of the ideal wife (Prov. 31) presupposes a monogamous society. The same holds true for the Talmud. Rabbinic law as set forth in the tractate NASHIM is based upon the assumption of p., yet the ethical approach clearly favors monogamy. Hardly any of the rabbis of the Talmud is known to have had more than one wife, and the first Mishnah of *Yoma* requires the High Priest to be married to one wife. The edict formally outlawing p. among *Ashkenazi* Jewry (c. 1000; see R. GERSHOM) merely gave legal effect to a state of affairs which had already long prevailed. Probably under Moslem influence, p. was still found among *Sephardi* and oriental Jews until recent times, but is dying out as the result of immigration to the State of Israel where monogamy is the law of the state. In exceptional cases rabbinic practice provides for the suspension of the "ban of R. Gershom". For example, in the case of a wife's insanity, since it is halakhically impossible to divorce an insane partner, the husband may be permitted to remarry in what is technically a bigamous marriage, provided a hundred rabbis sign the dispensation.

PORGING, see **NIKKUR**

POSEKIM, see **CODES**

POST-MORTEM: In compliance with the DIETARY LAWS, Jewish law required extensive p.-m. examinations on all animals after slaughter, to ensure the absence of physical defects, particularly perforations or abnormalities in the vital organs which would compromise their validity as food. A thorough knowledge of precise rules laid down in the Talmud and codes for examining animals after death is a prominent characteristic of the qualifications of all traditional rabbis, and it has provided them with considerable competence and experience in the morbid anatomy and pathology of animals. Jewish law objects to p.-m. operations on human beings, and bases its argument on the inviolability of the body and the duty to inter every part of it after death without delay (cf. Deut. 21:23). The sole consideration which may override these objections in exceptional cases is the immediate prospect of saving other human life. Hence rabbinic permission to perform an autopsy is granted only in instances of obscure or hereditary diseases where the findings may reasonably be expected to yield information of value in the treatment of patients suffering from similar diseases, and on condition that the operation is reduced to a minimum and that all parts removed are treated and eventually buried with due reverence. See also DISSECTION.

POTTERY (Heb. *kelei ḥeres*): P. is distinguished halakhically from other utensils because its material is held to be more porous than any other — consequently no method is recognized of purging it from either (1) ritual uncleanness, or (2) the absorbed taste of forbidden foods. Thus, p. which has been used for foods containing LEAVEN cannot be rendered (as can metal utensils) fit for PASSOVER use, nor can an earthenware vessel that has contracted ritual uncleanness be rendered ritually clean by immersion in a *mikveh*.

POVERTY: Biblical and rabbinic writers tended generally to regard p. as an unmitigated misfortune. God's blessing upon His people is meant to include material prosperity along with the other felicities of life, but as the Bible recognizes that "the poor shall not cease out of the land", it commands those more fortunate to "open thine hand wide unto thy brother, to thy poor, and to the needy in thy land" (Deut. 15:11). Care and consideration for the poor were insisted upon not only as a moral virtue but also as a legal requirement. But although p. was considered one of the worst of afflictions, too much wealth was also regarded as a danger and temptation (cf. Deut. 8:11-18; also Deut. 32:15 "But Jeshurun waxed fat and kicked... then he forsook the God which made him", and throughout the prophetic books) and it was thought most desirable to achieve a mean between these two extremes. Nevertheless other views of p. are in evidence too; occasionally the rabbis even praise p. as a positive virtue. On the verse (Is. 48:10) "I have tried thee in the furnace of affliction", the Talmud comments "This teaches that the Holy One, Blessed be He, went through all the virtues in order to bestow them upon Israel and found none more becoming than p." (*Ḥag.* 9b). This view of p. as a positive religious value was expressed by ascetic moralists (e.g. BAḤYA Ibn Pakuda) and mystics (cf. the *Sepher Ḥasidim* and the Zohar) but never became dominant. (See CHARITY).

PRAYER: The Bible contains many individual prayers (e.g. of Moses, Num. 12:13; Hannah, I Sam. 2:1-10; Solomon, I Kings 8:15-23; Hezekiah, II Kings 19:15-19); in addition many psalms are, in fact, prayers. The institution of three daily prayers is ascribed by the rabbis to the three PATRIARCHS, while the introduction of set formulas for p. is generally attributed to the Men of the Great Synagogue (KENESET GEDOLAH). Though the Bible makes no statements about the actual nature of p., the rabbis found its theological essence expressed in the biblical phrase "serving God with the heart". Whereas *avodah* (Divine "service") had originally signified the sacrificial worship in the Temple, the Babylonian Exile had stimulated the development of corporate p. as the principal form of worship. Communal prayer continued to develop, and in the Second Temple Period the SYNAGOGUE was, in many respects, even more significant than the Temple with its priestly ritual. After the destruction of Jerusalem by the Romans, the synagogue — whose functions often merged with that of the "House of Study" (BET MIDRASH) — became the center of communal and religious life. Although occasionally referred to as merely a substitute for the sacrifices of the Temple, p. has always been considered an essential and major expression of religion. Traditionally p. consists of two essential elements: supplication and petition on the one hand, and praise and thanksgiving on the other. In due course a fixed pattern emerged, particularly for the p. *par excellence*, the AMIDAH. The full liturgical p. service included opening BENEDICTIONS, the recitation of the SHEMA with its benedictions, the *amidah*, and the Reading of the Law. (See also SHAḤARIT; MINḤAH; MAARIV; MUSAPH; FESTIVAL PRAYERS). Prayers of various kinds (see KINNOT; PIYYUT; SELIHOT) continued to be composed throughout the ages and were added to the PRAYER BOOK. P. should be a genuine outpouring of the heart, and even after the introduction of fixed prayers, the rabbis emphasized the need to retain an element of spontaneity. Man should pray only in a devout and reverential frame of mind (Mishnah *Ber.* 5:1) and "he who makes his prayer a fixed, routine exercise, does not make his prayer a supplication" (*ibid.* 4:4). The Mishnah condemns p. undertaken as a burden to be discharged, or p. that contains no original thought (*ibid.* 29b). It should be recited "not in a spirit of sorrow, or of idleness, or of laughter or chatter or frivolity or idle talk, but with the joyousness of the performance of a religious act" (*ibid.* 31a). The manner of p. is equally important: "he who raises his voice in prayer is of little faith" (*ibid.* 24a), but one should rather form the words of the prayer with the lips (*ibid.* 31a). At the same time, however, p. obligations can be discharged by listening with devotion to the person conducting the prayer and answering AMEN to his blessings (cf. *Ber.* 52b. and *Shav.* 29a). Although, as a general rule, it is laid down that the person who leads the congregation in prayer (SHELIAH TZIBBUR) should be of irreproachable moral character and that the p. of the righteous son of a righteous father is more acceptable than that of the righteous son of a sinner (*Yev.* 64a), the rabbis loved to expatiate on incidents illustrating that the p. of a reprobate who has a single redeeming feature can be more efficacious than that of the most blameless person (cf. Y. *Taan.* 1:64b). God is said to "listen to p." and the rabbis had no doubts as to the efficacy of p. R. Ḥanina ben Dosa, after praying for the sick, could tell whether or not his p. would be answered (Mishnah *Ber.* 5:5). P. has the effect of averting the evil fate decreed for an individual in the New Year (*R.H.* 18a), but prayers about past events are considered vain and useless (Mishnah *Ber.* 9:3). The rabbis never systematically discussed the theological and philosophical problems inherent in p., and in petitionary p. in particular (e.g. will an all-knowing and all-good God change His designs — which are, by definition, for the good of His creatures — because man expresses his own desires? Should p. consist only of praise and thanksgiving, and of expressions of thanksgiving to the Divine will?). For the medieval mystics p. was an occasion for specific DEVOTIONS (*kavvanot*); for others it was a spiritual exercise to increase the communion with God. For rabbinic tradition in general p. was primarily the fulfillment of a commandment, i.e., part of the wider discipline of serving God (*avodah*): God wants man to bring his personal fears and wishes to Him, as a child would to his father. In this view the philosophical objections are not so much answered as irrelevant. P. can be private or corporate statutory or non-statutory. The most common of the non-statutory prayers are those for rain in time of drought. Many of the prayers included in the LITURGY for public and statutory worship were originally composed as private prayers. The statutory liturgy should be recited in community (see MINYAN); if said privately, certain prayers are omitted.

PRAYER BOOK: The Hebrew p.b. (in Heb. *siddur* or *seder tephillah*) contains the entire LITURGY used in the synagogue and at home, including many prayers which are not obligatory such as ZEMIROT (table-songs for Sabbath), SELIḤOT for various occasions, in some editions the whole Book of Psalms (for devotional use), the text of the READING OF THE LAW for weekdays, chapters from the Mishnah which it is customary to recite before or after prayers, and, in effect, anything the worshiper may require during synagogue services or at domestic liturgical occasions (e.g. meals). Often detailed rules concerning the *halakhot* of prayer are also given. P.B.'s differ greatly in size according to the amount of additional material included and depending also on whether the same prayers (e.g. the AMIDAH) are printed for every occasion they are to be recited. All p.b.'s contain at least weekday and Sabbath prayers, GRACE, and other BENEDICTIONS. For festivals, the *Ashkenazi* p.b. usually contains only the text of the *amidah*, KIDDUSH, and HALLEL, since the full festival liturgy, including the poetic additions, is too extensive to be included in one volume. Hence special books of prayers for the various festivals, called MAḤZORIM are used for these occasions. In ancient times prayers were not written down; the first known written p.b. dates from the 9th cent. In the Middle Ages it was usual for at least the reader to use a p.b. With the invention of printing, the p.b. became widespread and its use by every worshiper, a matter of course. Because of the variety of RITES and, more particularly, of the non-obligatory material (minor variations in the wording of some prayers, differences in the order of prayers and — in particular — in the choice of non-statutory material such as *piyyutim*, *seliḥot*, etc.; see also NUSAKH), different editions of the p.b. exist. Many include vernacular translations of the prayers; the U.S. Reform p.b., for example, is primarily an English liturgy with certain prayers incorporated in Hebrew.

PRAYER OF MANASSEH, see **MANASSEH, PRAYER OF**

PREACHING, see **HOMILETICS**

PRECEPT, see **MITZVAH**

PRECEPTS, 613 (Heb. *taryag mitzvot*): According to ancient rabbinic tradition (e.g. *Mak.* 23b), the number of the commandments of the Law of Moses is 613. They are subdivided into 248 positive and 365 negative commandments, said to correspond to the 248 bones and 365 muscles of the human body (also to the 365 days of the solar year). As no count of the pentateuchal laws yields precisely this number, various rules have been formulated defining the principles according to which the biblical injunctions and prohibitions should be counted (cf. Maimonides' Introduction to his *Book of Precepts*). Several scholars have produced slightly divergent lists of the 613 p. both in prose and in poetry; the latter are known as AZHAROT and are recited in the *Sephardi* rite at the Afternoon Service of the FEAST OF WEEKS. See MITZVAH.

PRECENTOR, see **ḤAZZAN**

PREDESTINATION: The doctrine that man's life, and its ultimate destiny (salvation or damnation) in particular, are determined solely by the inscrutable will of God and not by anything that man himself can do. The doctrine is well known from Islam and Christianity (in the latter religion it is associated more particularly with the names of Paul, Augustine, and Calvin) but has generally been held to be alien to the Jewish tradition. The DEAD SEA SCROLLS have shown, however, that predestinarian views were held by Jewish sectarians and it may be from them that Paul inherited his doctrine. See also DETERMINISM; FREE WILL.

PRE-EXISTENCE: The existence in time of something before the creation of this universe. The notion of p. presupposes belief in a higher, spiritual, and possibly eternal sphere in which things can pre-exist. Thus, according to Platonic and Neo-Platonic doctrine individual souls are not created together with the physical body, but are pre-existent and merely enter the physical body destined for them. This belief was adopted by the ancient rabbis and underlies the kabbalistic doctrine of *gilgul* (TRANSMIGRATION). According to one rabbinic statement (*Pes.* 54a) seven things were created before the creation of the world: the TORAH, repentance, the Garden of Eden, Gehinnom, the throne of God's glory, the heavenly temple (of which the TEMPLE in Jerusalem was regarded as an earthly reproduction), and the names of the Messiah.

PRIESTLY BLESSING: Blessing prescribed in Num. 6:23-27, to be said in the Temple by the priestly descendants of Aaron; the Tetragrammaton, which occurs three times in the p.b., was pronounced until the death of Simeon Ha-Tzaddik (*Yoma* 39b). The p.b. was subsequently transferred to the synagogue and introduced into the repetition of the *amidah* in the Morning and Additional Services; it is recited by priests in the Diaspora only during the Additional Service on festivals (except on a Sabbath) and the Day of Atonement, the reader alone reciting it on all other occasions. In the State of Israel the priests recite it on weekdays, on Sabbaths, New Moons, and festivals both at Morning and Additional Services, on the Day of Atonement also at the Concluding Service, and on *Av* 9 at the Afternoon Service. After removing their shoes and having their hands washed by the LEVITES, the priests ascend the *dukhan* (the platform before the ark; hence the *Ashkenazi* expression *dukhen*, "to recite the p.b."), and with fingers outstretched to form five gaps, arms raised to shoulder height, and head covered with a *tallit*, they recite the benediction in unison ("...who hast sanctified us with the sanctity of Aaron, and hast commanded us to bless thy people Israel in love") and then repeat the blessing word for word after the reader. The p.b. is explained by the rabbis as: "The Lord bless thee" — with wealth; "and keep thee" — accepting your prayers; "make His face to shine upon thee" — with knowledge and understanding; "the Lord lift up His countenance upon thee" — accepting your prayers, "and give thee peace" — at all times and with all men (*Num. Rab.* 11, 13 ff.).

PRIESTLY CODE: One of the literary sources (denoted as "P") composing the PENTATEUCH, according to the documentary hypothesis of BIBLICAL CRITICISM. P. itself may be composed of several older sources. It is characterized by a preoccupation with ritual legislation (e.g. sacrifices and purity), genealogies, and certain stylistic stereotypes. The largest units of P. are found in LEVITICUS, but critics ascribe many parts in other biblical books to the priestly source.

PRIESTLY PRIVILEGES (in Heb. *mattenot kehunnah*): In return for their service in the Temple, the priests enjoyed 24 p.p., consisting of various sacrifices and offerings or parts thereof, the first of the fruits and of the shorn wool, the firstling of a pure animal, five shekels from the redemption of a first-born son, a lamb from the redemption of the firstling of an ass, the priest's share of the crops, of the dough, of slaughtered animals, etc. Ten p.p. were distributed and had to be consumed in the Temple courtyard, four within Jerusalem and the remaining ten anywhere in the Land of Israel (*Ḥul.* 133b), the owner giving them to any observant priest he wished. Of the p.p., only the Redemption of the first-born son has remained in effect (see FIRST-BORN, REDEMPTION OF).

PRIESTLY VESTMENTS: Ordinary priests wore four white linen vestments when ministering in the Temple: a tunic, girdle, breeches, and cap (Exod. 28:40 ff.). These, with a miter replacing the cap, were also worn by the HIGH PRIEST when entering the Holy of Holies on the Day of Atonement (Lev. 16:4) and for certain services (*Yoma* 3:6; 7:1). Otherwise, the High Priest wore four additional vestments (Exod. 28:4), or eight in all: the extra four were a blue, sleeveless robe with bells at its hem; an EPHOD, worn over the robe and made of gold, blue, purple, scarlet, and fine linen, with two onyx stones bearing the names of the children of Israel on its shoulder straps; a breastplate of the same materials as the ephod and containing the URIM AND THUMMIM and twelve precious stones, in four rows, engraved with the names of the twelve tribes; and a golden plate, engraved with the phrase "Holy to the Lord" and worn on the forehead with the miter.

PRIESTS AND PRIESTHOOD: According to the biblical account, the male descendants of AARON, from the tribe of LEVI, were endowed with the hereditary functions, responsibilities, and privileges of the priestly office. The p. were not allowed to possess any land, but were consecrated to the service of God: "I [the Lord] am thy [Aaron] portion and thine inheritance among the children of Israel" (Num. 18:20). The duties of their office included not only cultic mediation and officiation at sacrifices and oracles, but also, to some extent, teaching and administering the Law, "for the priest's lips should keep knowledge and they should seek the Law at his mouth" (Mal. 2:7). P. received the twenty-four PRIESTLY PRIVILEGES (which included the meat of various SACRIFICES, flour and oil from the MEAL-OFFERINGS, the SHEWBREAD, the first ripe fruits, the HEAVE-OFFERING, ḤALLAH, the first wool from the sheep shearing), and being thus freed from the worry of earning a livelihood were able to devote themselves to primary tasks of teaching and officiating at the Temple service (*avodah*). P. also gave the PRIESTLY BLESSING, determined the purity of the leper, and officiated at the redemption of the FIRST-BORN of man and beast. In ancient times the HIGH PRIEST also gave oracular guidance by means of the URIM AND THUMMIM (see also EPHOD) in times of national emergency or distress. The priestly tribe was divided into twenty-four sections, each of which took a turn at officiating in the Temple for a week at a time. Priestly ministration in the Temple, as well as the consumption of sacrificial meat and other sacred gifts such as the heave-offering, required the strict observance of the rules of ritual PURITY. P. were forbidden to defile themselves by contact with a corpse except in the case of seven immediate relatives (father, mother, brother, sister, son, daughter, and spouse); the High Priest was forbidden to defile himself even in these cases. A priest must not marry a divorcee, a harlot, a woman born of an illicit priestly marriage (*ḥelallah*), a proselyte, or, in the case of the High Priest, a widow. The laws concerning the forbidden marriages of p. are still considered valid by Orthodox Jews, as is the law against defilement by contact with a corpse, and the duty of bestowing the priestly blessing and officiating at the redemption of the first-born. P. are also granted precedence in such matters as being called to the Reading of the Law or the recital of Grace After Meals.

The hierarchy of the priesthood contained several grades: (1) The High Priest (*kohen gadol*) was inducted into office by anointment with sacred oil (Exod. 30:22-33), donning the eight vestments (breastplate, ephod, blue robe, tunic, miter, girdle, plate, and drawers — Exod. 28) which he wore when officiating. From the time of King Josiah, when the sacred oil ceased to be manufactured, the High Priest assumed office without anointment. He conducted the entire service of the Day of ATONEMENT and was the only person allowed to enter the Holy of Holies in the Temple (and then only on that day). (2) The *segen* ("deputy") was appointed to accompany and aid the High Priest, acting on occasions as his deputy in directing the priests. (3) The *meshuaḥ milhamah* ("priest anointed for war"), who accompanied any kind of military expedition (Deut. 20:2 ff.), enjoyed a status similar in some respects to that of the High Priest (e.g. he could not marry a widow. (4) *Amarkalim* and *gizbarim* ("overseers and treasurers") in charge of the income and expenditure of the Temple treasury. (5) *Rosh hamishmar* ("head of the watch"), who was responsible for the priests on duty in the Temple precincts, and (6) *rosh bet av* ("head of the priests having charge of the daily service") who determined the particular work of each priest during his turn of office at the Temple. (7) The ordinary rank-and-file priest, known as *kohen*. Certain bodily BLEMISHES and disabilities disqualified a priest (*baal mum*) from officiating in the Temple.

PRIMOGENITURE, see BIRTH-RIGHT; FIRST-BORN; INHERITANCE

PROFANATION: Desecration of holy things. The Temple and all its appurtenances, including the priestly garments and the animals donated to it or used for sacrifices, were regarded as sacred, and their use for non-ritual purposes was forbidden. Anyone committing such an act of p. was required to bring a sacrifice and pay for the value of the article profaned with an increment of one-fifth (Lev. 5:14). However, if an animal was donated as a sacrifice and was then disqualified for that purpose because of some physical BLEMISH, the donor could redeem it by paying the value of the animal plus the same increment; the same law applied to houses "consecrated", i.e., donated to the sanctuary (Lev. 27:13-15). The priestly order was similarly regarded as consecrated, and a priest was forbidden to marry a divorcee or harlot. Should he enter into such a union the offspring was declared "profaned" from the priesthood (Lev. 21 and commentaries). On the principle that "one can aid sanctity but not diminish it" (*Shab.* 21b), a consecrated object could be used for a higher degree of sanctity but not for a lower. The term p. is also used in a wider, non-cultic sense, e.g. in the expressions "p. of God's Name" (see ḤILLUL HA-SHEM) and "p. of the Sabbath" (see ḤILLUL SHABBAT). See also SACRILEGE.

PROFANE: That which is permitted for secular use, as distinct from that which is set aside for sacred purposes (see HOLINESS). The mishnaic tractate dealing with the laws of ritual slaughter of animals for human consumption is called ḤULLIN ("Profane Things") to distinguish it from KODASHIM ("Holy Things"), dealing with sacrificial animals and articles consecrated to the Temple. Similarly when animals or things which have been consecrated are "redeemed" i.e., to be employed for non-sacred use, they are said to "pass into the state of *ḥullin*". The fruit of trees during the first three years of growth are forbidden for normal use; in the fourth year they become p. and can be eaten (see ORLAH).

PROFIAT DURAN, see **DURAN**

PROOF, see **EVIDENCE**

PROPERTY: Jewish law recognises two kinds of p.: personal, movable p. (*mittaltelim*) which can be disposed of at will; and fixed p. (real estate — *karkaot*) which, while also disposable at will, can never be absolutely alienated in the Land of Israel (Lev. 25:23). Beside the ability and right of the individual to dispose of his p., the court has the full power, by declaration, to divest an individual of p. (*Git.* 36b). The act of possession or agreement, without which no commercial transaction is ultimately binding, is called *kinyan;* the development of the *kinyan,* which in its various forms symbolizes the actual transfer of ownership of goods or land, and binds the parties, led to free and easy economic intercourse. The forms of *kinyan* prescribed for the transfer of real estate are: 1) payment of the purchase price (or part thereof if the seller is agreeable); 2) composing a document containing the words "my field is sold to you"; 3) seizing (*ḥazakah*), i.e., performance of an action regarded as a declaration of ownership or unchallenged occupation for a specific period of time. Movable p. is exchanged by means of the following *kinyanim*: 1) actual grasping of the object (*hagbahah*); 2) exchange (*suddar* or *ḥaliphin*), or symbolic transfer of the actual goods (cf. Ruth 4:7); 3) *ḥatzer* (court), i.e., the bringing of the object into the territory of the acquirer; 4) *agav,* i.e., transference of the movable goods together with the REAL ESTATE upon which they are situated. The laws of transference of p. take cognizance of custom and business usage; consequently, forms of acquisition such as payment, shaking hands, handing over keys, and various other commercial customs are all recognized in Jewish law. Promises of p. gifts to the Temple or to charitable institutions require no formal *kinyan* but are legally binding upon utterance.

PROPHETS AND PROPHECY: The Greek word *prophetes* signifies one who "tells forth" a Divinely inspired message; occasionally this may also include the "foretelling" of the future. The word "prophet" is used in the Septuagint to translate the biblical term *navi* and from there it passed into other Bible translations and into most European languages. Beside *navi,* the Hebrew Bible also used the earlier terms *roeh* and *ḥozeh* ("seer"; cf. I Sam. 9:9 and Is. 29:10). The phenomenon of prophecy was known in other religions as well; and the ancient rabbis speak of seven prophets, including BALAAM, who had been sent to the gentiles (*Bava Batra* 15b). Although only one of the three main divisions of the Bible is known as PROPHETS (BOOKS OF), the Pentateuch too, is in a sense a prophetic book, since it contains God's word as delivered by Moses. Essentially the prophet is the spokesman or "mouthpiece" (cf. Exod. 4:16; 7:1) of a Divine power. However, the Bible (cf. Num. 12:6-8; Deut. 33:10) and later Jewish tradition placed both Moses and the Pentateuch (TORAH) in a category apart. The gift of prophecy, as a channel of Divine guidance supplementing the normal methods of instruction by PRIESTS and teachers, was always considered part of the promise to Israel (cf. Deut. 18:15; Amos 2:11), though it also raised the problem of distinguishing between true and false prophets (cf. Deut. 13:1-6; 18:15-22). The outstanding characteristic of ancient Israelite prophecy is the emergence of a series of prophets — and particularly literary prophets — who did not belong to the associations and schools of prophets often connected with the sanctuary (cf. I Kings 22; Amos 7:12-14) and whose teaching shows a remarkable emphasis on moral values as the main content of God's covenant with Israel. At times this emphasis actually appeared to denigrate the more formal, ritual aspects of religion (see CEREMONIAL LAW; SACRIFICE). From their belief in a moral God, the prophets derive their relentless demand for a just society ("Let justice well up as waters, and righteousness as a mighty stream" — Amos 5.24), and their conviction of the final establishment of peace on earth ("And they shall beat their swords to plowshares, and their spears into pruning-hooks; nation shall not lift up sword against nation, neither shall they learn war any more" — Is. 2:4). The rabbis held that many true prophets including seven prophetesses appeared in Israel, but that only those prophecies of permanent significance were preserved in Holy Scripture. Drawn from all strata of society (Isaiah seems to have been connected with the royal house of Judah; Jeremiah and Ezekiel were of priestly descent; Amos was a herdsman and dresser of sycamore trees) and independent of any office or institution, the prophets showed favor to no man, however exalted his rank (cf. Nathan's rebuke of King David: "Wherefore hast thou despised the word of the Lord, to do that which is evil in My sight?" — II Sam. 12:9; or Elijah's denunciation of King Ahab for Naboth's murder — I Kings 21:17 ff.) and paid no consideration to the established forms of society, however strongly supported by king, leaders, or the masses (Elijah against the prophets of Baal — I Kings 18:16 ff.). As they derived their authority only from God, the prophets felt an irresistible inner compulsion to proclaim their Divine message ("And I heard the voice of the Lord, saying: 'Whom shall I send, and who will go for us?' Then I said: 'Here I am; send me'" — Is. 6:8; cf. Jer. 20:9 ff.). Thus driven by the hand of God, the prophets fulfilled their mission in the teeth of the most formidable obstacles as well as inner conflict and resistance (cf. e.g. JEREMIAH and JONAH): "To whomsoever I shall send thee thou shalt go, and whatsoever I shall command thee thou shalt speak. Be not afraid of them" (Jer. 1:7-8). Underneath their bitter and scathing denunciations, there looms an abiding love for their people ("He that scattered Israel doth gather him, and keep him, as a shepherd doth his flock" — Jer. 31:9) and a comforting message of spiritual rebirth, social reconstruction, and national revival that suffuses the insistent call to repentance and the promise of better days, even though fulfillment and redemption may come to only a remnant of the people. The Bible describes different types of prophets. ABRAHAM, the first to be called a prophet (Gen. 20:7), qualified for the title by virtue of his close relationship to God, and his characteristically prophetic intercession for those under God's judgment, as in the case of Sodom (Gen. 18:16 ff.). His legacy to his descendants was the prophetic demand to keep "the way of the Lord, to do righteousness and justice" (Gen. 18:19). Greatest of all the prophets was MOSES, of whom it is said that "there hath not arisen a prophet since in Israel like unto Moses, whom the Lord knew face to face" (Deut. 34:10). SAMUEL resembles Moses in his quality of judge and leader. The type of militant prophet was represented by ELIJAH and ELISHA who, faced with the increasing influence of Baal worship in the Northern Kingdom, led the opposition of the faithful minority. NATHAN and GAD were the royal mentors of David. Literary prophecy, commencing with AMOS and HOSEA, ranges through the majestic poetry of ISAIAH, the strange symbolism of EZEKIEL, until its final expression in HAGGAI, ZECHARIAH, and MALACHI during the rebuilding and completion of the Second Temple; with their deaths the "spirit of prophecy departed from Israel" (*Sot.* 48b). Its return was expected as an eschatological event (cf. Joel 3:1-2). Unique as was each individual prophet, a common theme runs throughout all prophetic utterance and is expressed most succinctly by Zechariah (4:6): "Not by might, nor by power, but by My spirit, saith the Lord of hosts". The medieval philosophers and theologians in seeking to explain prophecy, offered — in general — two contrasting interpretations. Rationalistic philosophers (Abraham Ibn Daud, Maimonides, Gersonides) held that a prophet was naturally endowed with perfection of reason, of imagination, and of moral character, coupled with an acquired perfection of wisdom and knowledge. By the grace of God, and moved by the Active Intellect, the faculties of imagination (e.g. in dreams) and reason are activated, and prophetic experience and illumination take place. Prophecy is thus the perfection of the human mind. Other thinkers (e.g. Judah Ha-Levi, Crescas) maintained that prophecy was totally a supernatural gift bestowed by God; the prophet is thus a higher species of mortal, chosen by God and endowed by Him with higher powers, who receives his inspiration and his visions by a special act, either directly from God or through some intermediary (e.g. an angel).

PROPHETS, BOOKS OF (Heb. *Neviim*): The second section of the Bible, preceded by the Pentateuch and followed by the Hagiographa. It is subdivided into 1) Former Prophets (*Neviim Rishonim*): JOSHUA, JUDGES, SAMUEL, KINGS; and 2) Latter Prophets (*Neviim Aḥaronim*): ISAIAH, JEREMIAH, EZEKIEL, and the twelve MINOR PROPHETS. This division was unknown to the Talmud in which the terms "former" and "latter" referred to prophets flourishing during the First or Second Temple respectively. The division of Samuel and Kings into two books each in the Hebrew Bible is also post-talmudic and derives from the Greek Septuagint by way of the Latin Vulgate. The Former Prophets have also been called "oral" and the Latter Prophets "literary", i.e., having committed their prophecies to writing.

PROPHETS, FALSE: Wherever prophecy is recognized as a channel of Divine revelation, the problem almost inevitably poses itself of how to distinguish between true and false prophets. In many instances the acuity of this problem added tragic poignancy to the ministry of a true prophet. The Pentateuch defines several criteria for recognizing the false prophet, i.e., one who falsely claims to speak in God's name. Such a prophet on the strength of a true prediction, propagates idolatry (Deut. 13:2-6), falsely claims Divine inspiration, or prophesies in the name of false gods (*ibid.* 18: 20). If a prophet predicts an event in the name of God and it does not materialize, then the people shall know him to have lied (*ibid.* 21:22). The Bible records numerous struggles between true and false prophets. Elijah successfully challenged the prophets of Baal (I Kings 18:19 ff.), Micaiah was thrown into prison for contradicting the prophets of success with a prophecy of woe (I Kings 22), and Jeremiah's entire life consisted of an unrelenting struggle against the comforting demagogy of false prophets who soothed the conscience of the people and announced peace instead of alarming them. The rabbinic criteria for distinguishing between true and false prophecy have been codified by Maimonides (*Yesodei ha-Torah* chaps. 8-10).

PROSBUL (Gk.: "for the court"): Legal instrument annulling the Sabbatical release of debts (see SABBATICAL YEAR). All private loans are automatically remitted at the end of the Sabbatical Year (Deut. 15:2) and hence it became difficult to obtain loans immediately before the onset of that year. In order to avoid hardship and encourage lending, HILLEL instituted the *p.*, which is a declaration made before a court of law by the creditor, and signed by witnesses, stating that all debts due to him are given over to the court for collection. Since the remission of loans during the seventh year applies only to individuals but not to public loans, the effect of the *p.* is to render the individual's loan public, and it is therefore not remitted (see DISPENSATION). Amoraic rabbis criticized the *p.* as circumventing a biblical law, but the authority of Hillel ensured its retention.

PROSELYTES (from the Septuagint translation [*proselytos*] of the Hebrew *ger* originally meaning a stranger; later, one converted to Judaism): The Bible refers to p. in Exod. 12:48 etc. (cf. also Is. 56:3, 6), and to actual conversion in Ruth 2:12 and Est. 8:17. The rabbis distinguished between two types of p.: (1). The half-p., called *ger toshav* (i.e., settler p.: Lev. 25:47), or *ger ha-shaar* (the p. of the gate: cf. Exod. 20:10). The half-p. undertook in the presence of three *ḥaverim* (scholars) to observe some of the basic principles (but not the ceremonies) of Judaism, such as the renunciation of idolatry or the keeping of the seven Noachian laws (A.Z. 64b); Maimonides calls these "the righteous gentiles". (2). The full p., *ger tzedek* ("righteous p.") who, having converted out of love of Judaism, accepts all its laws and ceremonies. Specially blessed in the 13th benediction of the *amidah*, he is to be shown every consideration, and even his forebears may not be disparaged. Sincerity of motive is an indispensable prerequisite for conversion, though Maimonides (*Issurei Biah* 13, 14) accepts as Jews those who convert for personal reasons. Conversion of a full-p., but not of a half-p., entails circumcision (for men), immersion in a ritual bath (for men and women), and (during the existence of the Temple) a sacrifice.

Active propaganda, though not by professional missionaries, was early directed toward gaining p., and according to R. Eleazar ben Pedat, this was actually the Divine purpose for the dispersion of the Jewish people (*Pes.* 87b). Thus the rabbis interpret "the souls that they had gotten in Haran" (Gen. 12:5) as referring to the p. made by Abraham (*Siphrei* to Deut. 6:5). Hillel's lenient attitude toward intending p., in contrast to the somewhat sterner approach of Shammai (*Shab.* 31a), most probably reflected the dominant view. Immediately before and after the destruction of the Second Temple, many converts were made both among the masses and the upper classes. Josephus states that there was no city anywhere into which Jewish observances had not penetrated (*Against Apion* 2, 40), that almost all the women in Damascus were "addicted to the Jewish religion" (*Wars* 2, 20, 2), and that Queen Helena and her son King Izates of Adiabene were converted to Judaism (*Ant.* 20, 2, 1-4). Rabbinic literature tells, for example, of many converts in Maḥoza in Babylonia (*Kidd.* 73a), while among scholars of note, R. Meir, Shemaiah, Avtalyon, R. Akiva, and Onkelos, the author of the Targum on the Pentateuch, were regarded as p. or descendants of p. When, however, Christianity began to gain successes among p. and half-p., the Jewish attitude to proselytism changed. Josephus (*Against Apion* 2, 11) reported that of the many Greek p. only some had remained faithful, while others had forsaken Judaism. This may have prompted R. Eliezer ben Hyrcanus to speak of the unreliability of p. (*Bava Metzia* 59b). It was said that spies, under the guise of p., were planted among the Jews by the Romans, which was doubtless a major reason that conversion was difficult "in these days" (*Yev.* 47a referring probably to the period of the Hadrianic persecutions). Bitter historical experiences led to the statement of R. Ḥelbo (*Kidd.* 70b) that p. are as grievous to Israel as a scab on the skin. To this inner resistance against p. were added the outer restrictions imposed by Christianity, which in the 4th and 5th cents. prohibited conversion to Judaism as a criminal offense, punishable at first by the confiscation of property and later by the death of the proselytizing Jew. During the following centuries, comparatively few p. were made, although Dhu Nuwas, the Jewish king of Yemen (6th cent.) and the Khazars in S. Russia (8th cent.) constitute important exceptions. In the Middle

Ages occasional conversions to Judaism, even by clerics, occurred in Europe. Traditional rabbis still make every effort to dissuade the intending p. from conversion in order to test the sincerity of his motives; whereas the policy of Reform regarding the acceptance of p. is more liberal. Once he is formally converted (following a period of instruction in the teachings and practices of Judaism), the p. ranks as a full member of the Jewish people; the only halakhic disability is the prohibition against a priest marrying a female p.

PROSTRATION: Casting oneself flat on the ground. Like bowing and kneeling, p. is a gesture or attitude of reverence to God and was practiced in the ancient Temple. Four forms of p. are mentioned in the Talmud: — *berikhah*: apparently, bending the knee (Y. *Ber.* I, 8); *kidah*: bowing with face to the ground; *keriah*: kneeling; *hishtaḥavvayah*: prostration with outstretched hands and feet (*Ber.* 34b). Practiced also in biblical times, *hishtaḥavvayah* was performed by the priests and people in the Temple at thirteen different locations (corresponding to the thirteen Temple court gates: *Shek.* 6:3; *Mid.* 2:3) when the High Priest pronounced the Tetragrammaton during the Day of Atonement service (*Yoma* 6:2). A form of p. is still practiced in the *Ashkenazi* rite during the recital of the Day of Atonement Avodah, and during the Aleinu prayer on the New Year and Day of Atonement. A still more modified form is performed (seated, with the head resting on the arm) when Taḥanun is said in the presence of a Scroll of the Law.

PROVERBS, BOOK OF (Heb. *Sepher Mishlei*): Second book in the Hagiographa section of the Bible. The work belongs to Hebrew Wisdom Literature and exhibits many of the characteristics which that genre shares with oriental literature in general. Its 31 chapters contain collections of didactic aphorisms, generally optimistic in tone, wherein man is exhorted to be mindful of the dictates of wisdom for his own good. In spite of the somewhat utilitarian character of its teaching, the book emphasizes that true wisdom is associated with fear of God (1:7). Though poetically personified (chap. 8), the idea of wisdom in P. is not to be confused with the hypostatized concept of *sophia* in later gnostic writings. The opening verse of the book ascribes its authorship to Solomon. This however does not apply to the entire work, which according to the Talmud received its definitive form through Hezekiah and his scribes (*Bava Batra* 15a). It teaches that the wise will be duly rewarded and the wicked — in particular the ignorant — punished. The book consists of (1) Praise of Wisdom (1-9); (2) "Proverbs of Solomon" (10:1-22:16); (3) "Words of the Wise" (22:17-24:22); (4) "Sayings of the Wise" (24:23-4); (5) "Proverbs of Solomon which the men of Hezekiah king of Judah copied out" (25:1-29:27); (6) "Words of Agur son of Jakeh" (30:1-33); (7) Words of King Lemuel (31:1-9); (8) Praise of virtuous wife (31:10-31). Critical scholarship admits the possibility that some of the proverbial Wisdom Literature goes as far back as King Solomon's court (cf. I Kings 5:12), but holds that the constituent parts of the Book of P. date from various periods, some even from post-exilic times. The final redaction of the compilation in written form is attributed to the period of the Great Synagogue.

PROVIDENCE (Heb. *hashgaḥah*): The power which rules both the world and human destiny, sustaining all and guiding everything in accordance with its purposes. Originating in Stoic philosophy, the term p. has been adopted by theistic theologies to designate the fundamental belief that God is "great in counsel and mighty in work" and that His eyes "are open upon all the ways of the sons of men, to give every one according to his ways, and according to the fruits of his doings" (Jer. 32:19). Biblical history is a record of God's immediate participation in the affairs of man; in fact "by Him actions are weighed... The Lord killeth and maketh alive... maketh poor and maketh rich; He bringeth low and lifteth up" (I Sam. 2:3-9). God's p. extends also to the non-human part of creation (cf. Ps. 104:21-33; 145:15-16). The ancient rabbis further emphasized these beliefs: "Know what is above thee — a seeing eye, and a hearing ear, and all thy deeds written in a book" (*Avot* 2:1) and, "no one lifts even a finger here below, unless it is ordained above" (*Ḥul.* 7). Belief in a Divine p. was confronted by contrary views (scientific, philosophical, or religious), which emphasized the ineluctable rule of necessity in the cosmos. In the Hellenistic Period this inflexible cosmic law was identified with the stars, and the rabbis taught that Israel, being under God's immediate p. as His chosen people, was not subject to the sway of the stars (the *mazzal*). In medieval times, the emergence of the concepts of nature and natural causality also challenged belief in p. The tightly-knit and autonomous causal nexus seemed to leave room for a Divine First Cause but not for the exercise of immediate and direct p. (such as miracles, answer to prayer). All medieval philosophers (e.g. Saadyah, Baḥya, Judah Ha-Levi, Maimonides) wrestled with this problem, which was further complicated by considerations of man's free will in relation to God's — possibly determining — foreknowledge. Some thinkers (e.g. Abraham Ibn Ezra) held that Divine p. extended only to general categories and processes (general p.) but not to the fate of individuals. Traditional Orthodoxy, however, assumed an "individual p." (Heb. *hashgaḥah peratit*). The fact that modern definitions of nature, causality, or God differ from their medieval counterparts does not seem essentially to affect the problem of p. as it was stated by the great thinkers of the Middle Ages. See also ASTROLOGY; DETERMINISM; PREDESTINATION.

PSALM, DAILY: Psalm recited at the conclusion of the Morning Service — a different one on each day of the week (Sunday — Ps. 24; Monday — 48; Tuesday — 82; Wednesday — 94; Thursday — 81; Friday — 93; Saturday — 92). The same psalms were recited by levites in the Temple service (Mishnah *Tamid* 7:4) and the custom was continued after the destruction of the Temple (*Sopherim* 18:4). The Talmud finds a connection between the contents of the seven psalms and the seven days of creation (*R.H.* 31a).

PSALMS (or **PSALTER**): First work in the Hagiographa section of the Bible and the foremost collection of Hebrew religious poetry. It contains 150 sacred poems, divided — in analogy to the Pentateuch — into five books (I:1-41; II:42-72; III:73-89; IV:90-106; V:107-150) each ending with a doxology, while Ps. 150 in its entirety constitutes an apt doxological conclusion to the collection as a whole. The English title derives from the Septuagint *psalmos* or *psalterion* — Greek for a stringed instrument which is the translation of Heb. MIZMOR (from the root "to pluck"), a term used to describe 57 p. The Hebrew title is *Tehillim* ("Hymns of Praise"). The collection is traditionally associated with King David, who is indicated as author in 72 p. Eleven p. are ascribed to the sons of Korah, 12 to Asaph. Other authors mentioned are: Moses (90), Solomon (72, 129), Heman the Ezrahite (88) and Ethan the Ezrahite (89), and Jeduthun (39). Fifteen "Songs of Ascents" (*shirei ha-maalot*) and 15 Hallelujah p. are anonymous. A general classification of the p. can be made under three headings:

1. Supplication — relating to national disaster (e.g. 44, 60, 80, 102, 137) or individual entreaty (e.g. 6, 30, 38, 39, 41, 88) — about 60 in all.
2. Glorification — national thanksgiving and praise (e.g. 46, 66, 118, 129), individual thanksgiving (e.g. 107, 115, 138), praise of the *Torah* (19:8-11, 119) and of Jerusalem (48, 87, 122), and the "Royal Psalms" (2, 18, 21, 45, 72, 101, 110, 132, 144).
3. Didactic p. — on right belief and action (1, 15, 37, 50, 112); historic lessons (78, 105, 106); theodicy (49, 73, 139).

The religious and literary influence of p. upon the Jews can hardly be overestimated. By Second Temple times the book was used in the synagogue, where it has continued to form an important part of the LITURGY. Its heartfelt poetry has enabled the worshiper to give vent to his innermost longing for communion with God. Moreover, in its variegated range of themes, the Jew has found fitting expression for all the events of his life, whether joyous or sorrowful. The essential spirit is one of optimism and unshakable belief in God's redemptive grace and justice, no matter how painful the suffering of the moment. Similarly profound has been the influence of P. through Christianity upon Western culture. A large number of psalms was used liturgically in the sacred service of both the First and Second Temples. Evidence of this is found in their captions, which contain technical instructions regarding choral and instrumental rendering. The interpretation of the titles of individual psalms is uncertain and has been the subject of much controversy; their precise meaning had already been lost by the time of the Septuagint (3rd cent. B.C.E.). The most frequent title is *Mizmor*, denoting a sacred song with stringed accompaniment. How this differed from *Shir Mizmor* (Pss. 48, 66, 83, 88, 108) or *Mizmor Shir* (65, 67, 68, 75, 87, 92) is unknown. *Shir ha-Maalot* (120-134) — "Song of Ascents" — may refer to the pilgrims ascending to Jerusalem or more likely to a levitical musical rendering performed on the 15 steps separating the Women's Court from the Men's Court at the Temple, during the Feast of the Water Libation (Mishnah *Suk.* 5:4). *La-Menatzeaḥ* (a word prefacing 55 psalms) appears to refer to the chief musician; *Al ha-Gittit* — to a vintage song; *Al Shoshannim* (45, 69) *Al Tashḥet* (57, 58, 59, 75), *Al Maḥalat* (53, 88) may mean that the psalm was to be sung to the tune of a popular song opening with these words. *Maskil* (13 times) may refer to the intellectual character of the psalm. David's intimate association with P. is based upon ancient tradition and on biblical indications (cf. II Sam. 6; I Chron. 15-16 which indicate an organized religious service in which elements of the Book of P. were no doubt in use). Whereas earlier criticism had ascribed most of the psalms to a post-exilic date, more recent scholarship has increasingly emphasized the affinities with ancient Canaanite poetry. The general tendency is to view the core of the collections which compose P. as pre-exilic, Ps. 137 being one of the latest (and exilic). A comparison of P. with the hymns of ancient Egypt and Babylonia has raised problems of literary influence, but there is no doubt that the Hebrew religious genius has stamped the P. with its own unique world view and style. See POETRY.

PSALMS, MIDRASH, see **SHOḤER TOV**

PSALMS OF SOLOMON: Pseudepigraphical collection of 18 psalms attributed to King Solomon. They were in fact written 70-40 B.C.E. as they describe Pompey's conquest of Jerusalem (63), the ensuing desecration of the Temple, and Pompey's death (48). Though these P. of S. are extant only in a Greek version, they were originally composed in Hebrew or Aramaic. Long attributed to Pharisaic circles, they are now held to form part of the literature of the general eschatological movement of that period.

PSEUDEPIGRAPHA, see **APOCRYPHA**

PSEUDO-JONATHAN, TARGUM: The Talmud (*Meg.* 3a) attributes the TARGUM of the Prophets to JONATHAN BEN UZZIEL, "from the mouths of Haggai, Zechariah, and Malachi", and says that he also intended to translate the Hagiographa, but was prevented from doing so by a heavenly voice. Modern scholars — on stylistic and other grounds — doubt that Jonathan composed the extant Targum to the Prophets traditionally ascribed to him. This Targum is not strictly a translation, as it frequently paraphrases the text and adds homiletical interpretations.

PSEUDO-MESSIAHS, see **MESSIAHS, FALSE**

PUBERTY, see **ADULT**

PULPIT: In Neh. 8:4, it is stated that "Ezra the scribe stood upon a p. of wood in order to read the Law to the assembled people". The Hebrew word *migdal*, here translated "pulpit", is rendered by the Septuagint as *bema* "rostrum". This latter word is used in the Talmud to describe: (a) the platform for the Reading of the Law set up for the king in the Temple once in seven years in accordance with Deut. 31:10-11, (Mishnah *Sot.* 7:8); and (b) the platform in the center of the famous synagogue of Alexandria (*Suk.* 51a). In both cases Rashi translates the word as "our ALMEMAR". *Ashkenazi* Jewry has retained this originally Arabic word (*al-minbar*) while *Sephardi* Jewry uses the talmudic word TEBAH, and Russian Jews use *bimah* (from Gk. *bema*). The *almemar, tebah*, or *bimah* is usually placed in the center of the synagogue as a raised platform from which the Scroll of the Law is read (and, in some rites, from which the whole service is conducted). Later usage introduced a special p. for sermons near the ark. The moving of the *almemar* to the front of the synagogue because of exigencies of space was for long a point of controversy between Orthodox and Reform Jews, but it is no longer generally regarded as a breach of Orthodox practice to have it moved forward. Sermons were originally delivered from the *almemar* or from before the Ark, and the special p. for the preacher is a late innovation. Many American synagogues combine p., reading desk, and Ark into one architectural unit. The importance attached by modern congregations to the weekly sermon is indicative of a profound change in the conception of the rabbinate and of the influence of the Christian environment on Jewish liturgical patterns. The Protestant influence has found even verbal expression in the phrase "to occupy a p." which has become synonymous with holding rabbinic office.

PUMBEDITA: City in N. Babylonia on the Euphrates river; for eight centuries home of an important ACADEMY, rivaled only by that of SURA. The P. academy was founded by JUDAH BAR EZEKIEL, pupil of SAMUEL (contemporary of RAV, the founder of Sura), c. 260. The academy continued the traditions of NEHARDEA, and for seven hundred years the famous "Nehardean row" of students at P. was a living memorial to the parent institution. R. Judah was succeeded by RABBAH, R. JOSEPH BAR ḤIYYA, ABBAYE, and RAVA, names which appear throughout the Babylonian TALMUD and bear witness to the enormous part played by P. in the formulation of this code. With the passing of Rava (353 C.E.) decline set in, and many rabbis from P., such as R. Pappa, founded academies in other cities of Babylonia. From the time of R. ASHI, P. took second place to Sura. It again became of great importance in the 10th-11th cents. (when it had been transferred to Baghdad) under SHERIRA and HAI, and closed finally with the latter's death in 1038.

PUNCTUATION, see **MASORAH; VOCALIZATION**

PUNISHMENT: The following types of p. are provided for in Jewish jurisprudence: (1) Death by stoning, burning, decapitation, or strangulation; (2) excision (Heb. *karet*); there is a difference of opinion as to whether *karet* refers to premature death or childlessness (cf. Lev. 20:20); (3) death at the hands of Heaven; (4) BANISHMENT; (5) corporal punishment ("stripes"), including *makkat mardut* i.e., FLOGGING for infraction of certain rabbinical injunctions; (6) monetary FINES; (7) servitude; (8) IMPRISONMENT; (9) EXCOMMUNICATION (*ḥerem*); and (10) "death at the hand of the zealot (e.g. the death of Zimri at the hands of Phineas, see Num. 25:6-8 and *Sanh.* 9:6). CAPITAL PUNISHMENT is described in the Bible as a deterrent (e.g. "All Israel shall hear and fear and shall do no more any such wickedness in the midst of thee" Deut. 13:12), as a means of rooting out evil elements from the nation (Deut. 17:7, etc.), and as expiatory (Num. 35:31-33). Thus MURDER is considered a crime against the sanctity of the land, and "no expiation can be made... for the blood shed therein but by the blood of him that sheds it." In practice capital p. ceased to be inflicted by Jewish courts some time before the destruction of the Second Temple. Corporal punishment (derived from Deut. 25:1-3) is applicable in the transgression of biblical prohibitions. However, of the 365 prohibitions, only 207 are punishable by flogging. Offenses against property are punishable in Jewish law only by the imposition of a fine. Personal injury likewise requires of the offender financial restitution only, the sole exception being when a man is unable to repay the value of a theft, in which case he is sold to the one from whom he stole and must work off the value (Exod. 22:2). A woman must not be sold into servitude for her theft. A minor is not liable for any p. Many of the detailed talmudic provisions date from a period when certain forms of p. were no longer administered, and the discussions do not, therefore, necessarily reflect earlier or actual practice. On the other hand Jewish courts (see BET DIN) enjoyed a measure of autonomy throughout the Middle Ages, including the power to inflict fines and corporal p. In the absence of ORDINATION, the courts derived their authority to inflict p. from legal principles permitting extraordinary action. Already the Talmud had conceded to the courts the power to "administer corporal or other p. not in accord with biblical law" (*Yev.* 90), that is, when circumstances so warranted (see also TAKKANAH). In modern times the practice of p. by rabbinic courts has ceased altogether and even excommunication is rarely if ever resorted to.

PUPILS, see **EDUCATION**

PURIFICATION, see **ABLUTION; PURITY, RITUAL**

PURIM (Heb. "lots"): A festival commemorating the deliverance of the Jews of the Persian Empire from extermination, probably during the reign of Xerxes I (485-465 B.C.E.). The story of P. is told in the biblical Book of ESTHER. HAMAN, chief minister of AHASUERUS (Xerxes), plotted to destroy the Jews of the Empire. With the king's consent, he fixed the date of their doom by lot as *Adar* 13. Esther (Hadassah), the king's Jewish wife, courageously interceded with Ahasuerus; as a result, the king authorized the Jews to defend themselves, and on the appointed day they routed their enemies. On the morrow they celebrated their victory and called the day *Purim*, in allusion to the lots Haman had drawn. To commemorate this event, *Adar* 14 is marked with festivities and rejoicing. In Shushan (Susa), capital of the Persian Empire, fighting occured on *Adar* 14 as well, and the victory there was celebrated only on the 15th. The tradition subsequently arose that ancient cities which had already been walled in at the time of Joshua (e.g. Jerusalem), observe *P.* on the Shushan anniversary (Shushan *P.*). Many laws and customs as well as a rich folklore are associated with *P.* The most important ceremony is the reading of the Book of Esther from a specially prepared and handwritten parchment scroll. The regulations for the reading, as for the celebration of *P.* in general, are discussed in the tractate MEGILLAH. Both men and women are obliged to hear the reading of the *P.* MEGILLAH ("scroll"); children too should hear the story. The *megillah* is read both on the preceding night and on *P.* day itself. Before the reading, three special blessings are pronounced. There is also a custom of making a din by sounding rattles, called "*gregers*", at every mention of the name of Haman. The AL HA-NISSIM prayer is recited in the *amidah* and in the Grace after Meals. The pentateuchal reading at the Morning Service recounts the attack of AMALEK (the traditional ancestor of Haman) on the Jews. Other customs, made obligatory by Jewish law, are the sending of gifts (*mishloaḥ manot*) — to friends, usually two kinds of sweetmeats, and to the poor (*mattanot la-evyonim*), food or money. An important feature of the celebration is the *P.* banquet (*seudah*) when inebriation is encouraged. In general a certain amount of levity and popular amusement was permitted on *P.* and masquerades and *P.* plays became a widespread feature of the celebration in medieval times (possibly under the influence of the Christian carnival). In some European talmudic academies it was customary to elect one of the students as rabbi for a day (*P.* rabbi). In the State of Israel, *P.* is a carnival period, especially for children, and the occasion for the ADLOYADA procession. In leap year, *P.* is observed in the second month of *Adar*. See also PURIM KATAN; PURIMS, LOCAL.

PURIM KATAN (Heb. "minor *Purim*"): The festival of PURIM falls on *Adar* 14 (or 15). In a leap year, however, there are two months of *Adar*, in which case the festival is celebrated during the second of them. In such a year the corresponding days of the first *Adar* are called *P.K. P.K.* is not marked by any celebration apart from the fact that supplicatory prayers (TAḤANUN) are omitted from the Morning and Afternoon Services, and fasting and funeral eulogies are forbidden.

PURIM, SHUSHAN, see **PURIM**

PURIMS, LOCAL: Local festivals commemorating a signal deliverance from danger. The custom to celebrate the anniversary of such deliverance — on the analogy of the festival of PURIM — developed both among individual families and whole communities. The forms of the celebration were often patterned on the original *Purim*: the particular event would be recorded in a MEGILLAH, special prayers of thanksgiving recited, a banquet held, and the day observed as a holiday. Among such local *P.*'s are the *P.* of Narbonne (*Adar* 29, instituted 1236), of Cairo (*Adar* 28, instituted 1524), of Frankfurt-on-Main (*Adar* 20, instituted 1616), and of Leghorn (*Shevat* 22, instituted 1743). An example of a family *Purim* is that observed by the family of Yom-Tov Lipmann HELLER to commemorate his release from prison on *Adar* 1.

PURITY, RITUAL: Concept in ritual law denoting a state of fitness of "holy" objects (see HOLINESS) for ritual use, or of persons for contact with such objects. The opposite of *tahor* (Heb. "ritually pure") is *tame* (Heb. "ritually impure", viz., polluted or defiled). The law recognizes different degrees of ritual defilement. The chief source of impurity is a dead body (cf. Num. 19:11 ff.), but there are many other sources (cf. e.g. Lev. 12-13). Persons or objects coming into specified forms of contact with a source of impurity become themselves impure and may in certain cases transmit their pollution — albeit to a lesser degree — to other persons and objects. Holy objects (e.g. sacrificial meat, heave-offerings, etc.) that are thus defiled become unfit for consumption and must be burned. Persons in a state of impurity must not touch holy objects or enter the Temple precincts. PRIESTS are forbidden to contract ritual impurity from a dead body (Lev. 21:1-3, 10-12). Human beings in certain degrees of defilement, as well as certain classes of objects, can regain r.p. after ritual IMMERSION (see also ABLUTION) and a period of waiting. In some kinds of defilement the ceremony of purification requires the ashes of a RED HEIFER (Num. 19). Even in biblical literature the terms *tahor* and *tame* occasionally have a wider meaning and the usage is also extended to symbolize moral and spiritual states. The latter usage is frequent in ethical and ascetic literature.

Q

QUERIDO, JACOB: Turkish heresiarch (d. c. 1690). Follower and successor of the pseudo-messiah SHABBETAI TZEVI. He led a group of 300 families in Salonica who, in 1683, followed the example of their messiah and outwardly apostatized to Islam. This was the origin of the crypto-Sabbataian sect known as the DONMEH.

QUMRAN, see **DEAD SEA SCROLLS**

QUORUM, see **MINYAN**

R

RAAYA MEHEIMANA (Aram. "Faithful Shepherd"): The appellation of Moses in kabbalistic literature and especially in the ZOHAR, based on a midrashic legend according to which Moses' devotion to his flock of sheep (cf. Exod. 3:1) merited him the Divine choice to become the shepherd of Israel. *R.M.* is also the title of a mystical work by an anonymous Spanish kabbalist, written toward the end of the 13th cent. and subsequently incorporated into the Zohar. The work is in the form of a conversation between Moses (hence its name), the prophet Elijah, and Simeon bar Yoḥai.

RABBAH BAR NAḤMANI (3rd-4th cents.): Babylonian *amora;* head of the PUMBEDITA ACADEMY. Although his legal interpretations tended to be severe, he was nonetheless a popular teacher and attracted many pupils (including ABBAYE and RAVA). His halakhic views are often quoted in the Talmud, as are his legal disputes with his colleague R. Joseph.

RABBAN (Heb. "our master"): Title of honor. There were no titles of this nature in ancient times, but in the Mishnaic Period, . — which is a variant form of the more usual "RABBI" — was applied honorifically to leading scholars and, more particularly to presidents of the SANHEDRIN.

RABBANITES: Followers of the rabbinical tradition. The term was first applied to adherents of the Oral Law and Rabbinic Judaism by the KARAITES, who employed the term in a contemptuous sense to designate the partisans of rabbinic, as opposed to purely biblical, Judaism.

RABBENU TAM, see **JACOB BEN MOSES TAM**

RABBI (Heb. "my master"): Honorific term originally used in Palestine in addressing sages, but developing gradually into a title for any person qualified to give decisions on Jewish law. The conferring of ORDINATION in the Land of Israel was curtailed in the 4th cent., but a limited authorization (*hattarat horaah*) was subsequently introduced (*Sanh.* 5a; *Ket.* 79a). At a later period it was decreed that a candidate for the office of r. must sit for an examination in Talmud and codes. The formal conferment of a MORENU diploma was first introduced in Germany in the 14th cent.; it entitled the recipient to act as a rabbinical DAYYAN, or judge. Only men steeped in knowledge of the Talmud and rabbinic literature after many years of intensive study were admitted to full rabbinic honors. The examination of candidates for the rabbinate was administered by institutions (e.g. *yeshivot*) or by individual rabbis of repute, and could bear on any subject in the Talmud and codes. In the 19th cent., RABBINICAL SEMINARIES and special theological institutions for training rabbis were founded in western countries and America. Many of these added a body of secular studies to the traditional rabbinical requirements. Until medieval times the r. received no salary from his congregation, in accordance with the mishnaic law which prohibits deriving any income or benefits from the *Torah*. Thus a r. had always a private occupation — as an artisan, doctor, merchant, farmer, or even a laborer. If a r. gave up his vocation for his office or was otherwise unable to find an alternative living, he could claim compensation only for bare necessities. This situation changed during the Middle Ages especially after the persecutions in Spain (14th-15th cents.): the refugee rabbis who fled to countries of asylum found little opportunity for making an outside livelihood, and at the same time new communities of exiles had need for full-time professional rabbis to minister to them. Some rabbis achieved an international reputation and authority beyond the limits of their own congregations. The RESPONSA which they sent to correspondents often formed a link between the scattered communities of Jews in many parts of the world, and unity was also strengthened by rabbinic codifications of Jewish law and custom. Rabbinical SYNODS established unified norms on many important problems, such as monogamy, inheritance, marriage and divorce, and the promulgation of laws against informers. In matters such as the administration of the communities and their relations with civil authorities, the rabbinate acted in concert with (and was to some extent subject to) the lay leadership. Often the election of a r. was subject to confirmation by the civil authorities. In Poland during the reign of Sigismund I, the r. was confirmed by the king and was thus in a sense an agent for the crown who collected the poll-tax and enjoyed large powers of civil and criminal jurisdiction. Outside interference, however, was strongly resented (e.g. Simeon Duran was elected

r. in Algiers on the express condition that he forego the custom of seeking ratification of his appointment from the government). In spite of external influence, the internal management of the Jewish communities was largely left to Jews themselves. Very often Jewish courts, which were always constituted of rabbinical judges, were permitted to try even criminal cases in which Jews were involved. The main duties of a r. lay in deciding legal questions in all branches of Jewish law, acting as judge in civil and criminal cases, forming a BET DIN, supervising religious institutions such as *sheḥitah* and *mikveh*, etc. Some rabbis also acted as the head of local talmudic colleges. Until the 19th cent., preaching was of secondary importance (see MAGGID): r. usually preached only on *Shabbat ha-Gadol* and *Shabbat Shuvah* and during the months of *Elul* and *Adar*. In certain Middle Eastern countries, the r. was known as *Marbitz Torah*. In modern times, the emphasis in rabbinical function has largely changed. The r. is a communal official whose duties include not only religious activities (in which preaching and public speaking play an important part) but also embrace educational, pastoral, social, and interfaith activities; not all modern rabbis are qualified as *dayyanim*, i.e., entitled to render decisions in matters of rabbinic law. In the British Commonwealth the term "minister" is used for a person who is allowed to carry out the traditional functions but who lacks full rabbinic qualification. The training and manner of ordination of rabbis vary according to the character (rabbinical seminary, YESHIVAH) and affiliation (Orthodox, Conservative, Reform) of the institution of study.

RABBI, see **JUDAH HA-NASI**

RABBINATE, see **RABBI**

RABBINICAL ASSEMBLY OF AMERICA: The rabbinical arm of the CONSERVATIVE MOVEMENT. Organized in 1901, it has about 700 members, most of whom are graduates of the JEWISH THEOLOGICAL SEMINARY of America. The R.A. functions through various committees which deal with such matters as social action, education, prayer and worship, family ethics, etc. Its law committee serves in an advisory capacity to members of the R.A. The R.A. is responsible for placing rabbis in suitable congregations and has its own draft system for supplying chaplains to the armed forces.

RABBINICAL CONFERENCES: With the establishment of REFORM JUDAISM during the first half of the 19th cent. in Germany, its advocates felt the need to lay down the principles of the new movement and to establish a uniform policy with regard to departures from the accepted norms. This need was supplied by the convening of conferences of Reform Rabbis (which differed from medieval synods in that they were confined solely to rabbis). The first of the r.c. was the Brunswick Conference held in 1844; it concerned itself mainly with such matters as might impair Jewish-Christian relations, e.g. the ***Kol Nidrei*** **prayer**, the Jewish oath, and the prohibition against intermarriage. It was followed by the conference at Frankfort-on-Main the following year (at which such radical innovation as the use of the organ, the introduction of the vernacular in the service, and the triennial cycle of scriptural reading were adopted) and the Breslau Conference in 1846. The first conferences of American Reform Rabbis were held at Philadelphia in 1869 and Pittsburg 1885. It was at the Philadelphia Conference that the traditional belief in a restoration of a Jewish state was formally renounced, and the principle affirmed that the Diaspora, far from being a punishment for sin, was in accordance with the Divine will and essential to the "Jewish mission". Since the beginning of this century the three religious groups in the U.S. — Orthodox, Conservative, and Reform — have convened annual r.c. In recent years, on the initiative of the Chief Rabbi of Gt. Britain, several conferences of Orthodox European Chief Rabbis have been convened. See also COUNCILS AND SYNODS.

RABBINICAL COUNCIL OF AMERICA: U.S. organization of Orthodox rabbis. Early in the 20th cent. tensions began to develop between the UNION OF ORTHODOX RABBIS, which represented the old school of Yiddish-speaking E. European rabbis, and the body of younger, more modern, English-speaking rabbis, who were growing in both members and influence. As a result, in 1936 these younger rabbis formed the R.C. of A., a separate organization to which most of the modern Orthodox rabbinate is now affiliated. In addition to its professional activities, it maintains a *bet din*, and as the ecclesiastical arm of the Union of Orthodox Congregations, is the main body supervising the *kashrut* of manufactured goods. It has some 800 members.

RABBINICAL COURTS, see **BET DIN**

RABBINICAL SEMINARIES: Until the 19th cent. the only institutions of higher Jewish learning (after the ACADEMIES) were the YESHIVOT, where study was confined to the Talmud and codes. The *yeshivot* were not specifically designed for the training of RABBIS, since Jewish tradition in its insistence on TALMUD TORAH, does not distinguish between professional rabbis and laymen. As long as the function of the rabbi was largely confined to making decisions on questions of ritual law, the *yeshivah* continued to provide the necessary knowledge for those of its students who wished to enter the rabbinate. With the dawn of the modern age, however, it was increasingly felt that rabbis needed to acquire not only a knowledge of such Jewish subjects as homiletics, history, Bible, theology, philosophy, ethics, liturgy, and Hebrew literature, but also — since the rabbi was expected to represent the community on all public occasions — a knowledge of general secular culture. Out of this need arose the r.s., specifically created for the professional training of rabbis in Western countries. The first such seminary was the Instituto Rabbinico Lombardo-Veneto, established in Padua in 1827 and later transferred to Rome. Two years later the Séminaire Israélite de France was founded in Metz (later moving to Paris). The second half of the century saw the establishment of a number of important seminaries. Orthodox Jews founded the Breslau Seminary under the leadership of Zacharias Frankel in 1854, Jews' College in London in 1856, the *Bet ha-Midrash* in Vienna in 1872, the *Rabbiner Seminar für das Orthodoxe Judenthum* under Hildesheimer in Berlin in 1873, and the *Israelitische Theologische Lehranstalt* in Vienna in 1893. In 1886, a rabbinical seminary was established in New York by Sabato Morais, and in 1901, under the direction of Solomon Schechter it became the Jewish Theological Seminary. This school developed into the rabbinical seminary of the Conservative Movement; its place as a seminary for Orthodox rabbis was taken by the Isaac Elhanan Theological Seminary (founded 1896; later Yeshiva University). The Reform Movement established in 1873 the *Lehranstalt für die Wissenschaft des Judenthums und Rabbiner Seminar* in Berlin and the Hebrew Union College in Cincinnati (1871), integrated since 1950 with the Jewish Institute of Religion in New York (founded 1922).

RABBINITES, see **RABBANITES**

RACHEL, TOMB OF, see **TOMB OF RACHEL**

RADAK, see **KIMḤI**

RAIN: In the land of Israel rain is seasonal; the early rains (*yoreh*) fall in *Ḥeshvan* (c. October), the latter rains (*malkosh*) come to an end during *Nisan* (c. April). R. which falls out of season or with undue force is considered harmful (Ezek. 13:13), while that which falls in good quantity and at the expected time is called a blessing (*ibid.* 34:26). The abundance or lack of r. is considered by the *Torah* as one of the Divine means of rewarding or punishing the people of Israel, because the "keys of r." have been retained by the Almighty to chasten man and cause him to repent. Both unseasonal r. (I Sam. 12:18ff.) and drought (I Kings 17) are invoked by the prophets as signs of God's displeasure. Supplication for the blessing of rain, and recognition of God's instrumentality in the bestowal of this blessing, is to be found in the daily service during the winter months (see MASHIV HA-RUAḤ). The Festival of Tabernacles and its practices are particularly associated with r. and water (e.g. the WATER-DRAWING FEAST), and the additional service for *Shemini Atzeret*, called *Geshem* (i.e., "rain"), opens with a petition for r. which is timed in accordance with the seasons of the Holy Land. In many synagogues, it is customary for the precentor to clothe himself in white — as on the Day of Atonement — during the recitation of this prayer. A series of special services and fasts, varying in intensity with the progression of the drought, are inaugurated if the rains fail to arrive in due season. The talmudic tractate *Taanit* is devoted to the description of these services and the regulations governing the fasts.

RAINBOW: After the FLOOD, God placed a r. in the sky as a visible sign of His covenant with NOAH (Gen. 9:12-17). Consequently a Jew upon seeing a r., makes the blessing "Blessed art Thou... Who remembers the covenant, art faithful to Thy covenant, and keeps His promise". According to a rabbinic dictum the r. was created at twilight on the last day of creation.

RAMBAM, see **MOSES BEN MAIMON**

RAMBAN, see **MOSES BEN NAḤMAN**

RAMḤAL, see **LUZZATTO, MOSES ḤAYYIM**

RAM'S HORN, see **SHOPHAR**

RAN, see **GERONDI, NISSIM**

RANSOM (Heb. *kopher*): The Bible explicitly prohibits the taking of r. (blood-money) in the case of murder (Num. 35:31-2) and the only trace of the ancient legal institution of r. in Jewish law is the indemnification paid by the owner of an ox that has killed a man by goring (Exod. 21:30). At the taking of the CENSUS each individual was to give "a ransom for his soul unto the Lord... a half shekel" (Exod. 30:12). The ransoming (Heb. *pidyon*) of CAPTIVES played an important part in Jewish history both in talmudic times and during the Middle Ages and was considered a supreme duty of charity. The Heb. term *pidyon* is also used for the redeeming of the FIRST-BORN.

RAPHAEL: Archangel. Unlike MICHAEL and GABRIEL, R. is not mentioned in the Bible, but he figures prominently in both the Apocrypha (e.g. *Tobit* 12:18; *Enoch* 20:1-7) and in kabbalistic literature. With Michael, Gabriel, and URIEL, he constitutes one of the four archangels who together fulfill various quadrilateral functions, such as taking command of the four points of the camp of Israel and the four points of the compass, or standing right and left above and below the Heavenly Choir which sings the praises of God. More particularly R. is also the Angel of Healing (his name being a compound of the Heb. *rapha*, "healed", and *el*, "God").

RAPOPORT, SOLOMON JUDAH (1790-1867): One of the founders of modern Jewish studies (WISSENSCHAFT *des Judentums*); rabbi in Tarnopol and Prague. R. was a pioneer in applying the methods of modern scholarship to Jewish cultural history; his works include monographs on Jewish personalities (e.g. Saadyah, Hai, Kallir) and the first (and only) volume of a projected Jewish encyclopedia, *Erekh Millin*. R. insisted on freedom of inquiry (thus arousing the bitter enmity of the ultra-Orthodox and the Ḥasidim) but opposed Reform Judaism and severely attacked the views of GEIGER.

RASHBA, see **ADRET, SOLOMON BEN**

RASHBAM, see **SAMUEL BEN MEIR**

RASHBASH, see **DURAN, SOLOMON BEN SIMEON**

RASHBATZ, see DURAN, SIMEON BEN TZEMAḤ

RASHI (abbrev. of Rabbi Shelomoh [Solomon] Yitzḥaki; 1040-1105): French Bible and Talmud scholar. At an early age he went to Germany to study in the academies at Mainz and Worms; at 25 he returned to his native town of Troyes and founded his own academy which attracted many students. The pressing need for an adequate and complete commentary on the Bible and Talmud prompted R. to set about writing his famous, definitive interpretation of these two works. His commentaries excel all others by the lucidity and precision with which they explain even the most intricate subject. Though his primary objective was to establish the plain and exact meaning of the biblical text, R. also included interpretations from the Midrash whenever he felt they contributed to a better understanding of Scripture. Rather than suggest forced interpretations, however, he would on occasion admit that "I cannot explain this". R.'s commentary on the Bible was the first dated Hebrew book printed (1475) and had a great influence upon Jew and non-Jew alike; it was translated into Latin, studied by Nicolas of Lyra (13th cent.), and used in the preparation of the first German translation of the Bible. Several supercommentaries have been written on it. R.'s commentary on the Babylonian Talmud was based on a preliminary study of the textual tradition with a view to establishing correct readings. In this work too his style is characterized by lucidity, logic, and terseness. His commentary on the Talmud was left incomplete, ending at tractate *Makkot*, page 19b; it was continued by his grandson, SAMUEL BEN MEIR. R. often translated difficult words into French; his commentaries contain about 10,000 French words and incidentally constitute a valuable source for the study of old French. It was said of R. that but for his commentary, the Talmud would have been forgotten. Unlike the TOSAPHISTS, he did not enter into dialectical discussions, but would obviate questions and difficulties by a judicious word or phrase. R.'s interpretations of talmudic passages have often determined halakhic decisions; in his responsa he emerges as one of the great authorities of Jewish law. It was due to the influence of R. and his school that France soon became the classical land of Bible — and Talmud — study, while Spain remained the center of Jewish poetry and philosophy. For many centuries, study of the Pentateuch and the Talmud meant, in essence, study of R.'s commentaries; his work formed an essential part of Jewish basic education, and has to this day continued to retain its freshness and value.

RASHI SCRIPT: The cursive script of Spanish Jews, a modification of the usual square Assyrian script designed to expedite writing. The *ḥet*, *gimmel*, and *shin*, for instance, are reduced by this script from 2 or 3 strokes to one each. When the first Hebrew book was printed — a Bible with Rashi's commentary (Reggio de Calabria, 1475) — this script was selected as the model for the type used for the commentary, hence the name R.S. (i.e., the script in which Rashi was first printed, not, as is commonly supposed, the script in which he wrote). R.S. was frequently used in printing rabbinical works.

RAV: While the term RABBI ("my master") was used in Palestine as a title for those who were ordained there and authorized to judge penal cases, *Rav* (Heb. "great") was the title used in Babylonia for those qualified for the rabbinical office but unable to receive ORDINATION, as this honor could be conferred only in Palestine. The title is still used in communities where Hebrew or Yiddish is spoken.

RAV (3rd cent.): Babylonian *amora* who studied for many years with R. JUDAH HA-NASI in Palestine. His period of scholarly activity spanned the last generation of the *tannaim* and the first generation of *amoraim*, and his status is sometimes considered to be equal to that of a *tanna*. Some time after his return to Babylonia he left NEHARDEA, seat of his colleague SAMUEL, to found the ACADEMY of SURA; it was the authority of the two men that ensured the independent status and prestige of the Babylonian academies. The TALMUD reports many of the discussions of R. and Samuel and ruled that in matters of ritual law R.'s opinion was to be followed. Rav also gave to the *bet din* power to excommunicate any person refusing to answer its summons. R. was a noted aggadist, many of whose homilies dealt with ethical questions. Several prayers composed by him (e.g. ALEINU) were included in the liturgy. R. has been called the father of Jewish learning in Babylonia.

RAV KAHANA, PESIKTA OF, see **PESIKTA**

RAVA (4th cent.): Babylonian *amora*. Almost every page of the Talmud reports discussions between R. and his colleague ABBAYE, based on their profound knowledge of the Oral Law and great analytical powers. With six exceptions, the decision in each case is in accordance with the views of R. R. stressed the importance of study and also emphasized ethical conduct. He headed the ACADEMY at MAḤOZA; after the death of Abbaye, the PUMBEDITA school merged with the academy at Maḥoza and R. thus became the undisputed talmudic authority in Babylonia.

RAZIEL: ANGEL entrusted with guarding or transmitting Divine secrets. The name occurs in the Slavonic Book of Enoch, the Targum on Ecc. 10:20, and later pseudepigrapha, but is far less prominent than that of the archangels.

RAZIEL, BOOK OF: A mystical work ascribed to the angel RAZIEL. According to its author, its secrets were imparted by Raziel to Adam when he was driven from the Garden of Eden, and to Noah before he entered the Ark, and ultimately came into the possession of Solomon. The work contains much ancient magical material as well as mystical hymns going back to the *Merkavah* mystics (see MYSTICISM). The Book of R. had an unusually large circulation in E. Europe for a work of its kind, owing to the belief that a house in which it was found would be protected from conflagration.

READING OF THE LAW (Heb. *keriat ha-torah*): Public reading from the Pentateuch constitutes part of the synagogue service on Sabbaths, all festivals, the New Moon, *Ḥanukkah, Purim,* and fast days; also on ordinary Mondays and Thursdays. The R. of the L. takes place at the end of SHAḤARIT; on Sabbaths and fast days also during MINḤAH. Special handwritten parchment scrolls must be used; the persons called up to "read" (*aliyah la-torah*) recite a BENEDICTION both before and after the reading. The written text has no vowels, punctuation, or ACCENTS and requires considerable skill to read. In most congregations (excepting the Yemenite) the one "called up" no longer reads his portion; instead, the entire text is chanted by an appointed reader. The number of persons to be "called" is fixed in accordance with the status of the day; on Sabbath at least seven people are called, on the Day of Atonement six, on festivals five (all the above apart from the *maphtir*; see HAPHTARAH); on New Moon and *Ḥol ha-Moed* four; on all other occasions three. The Law was read as part of the service even as far back as Temple times (rabbinic tradition ascribes the institution of the Sabbath, festival, and New Moon reading to Moses, and the reading on Mondays, Thursdays, and during Sabbath *Minḥah* to Ezra), but — unlike the later and present custom — the portions to be read were not definitively marked out. On festivals, portions appropriate to the day were read (cf. Mishnah *Meg.* 3-4); if too short, they were repeated several times. On Sabbaths, it was usual to continue where the reading had been terminated the previous Sabbath and a minimum of 21 verses had to be read — 3 for each person "called"; but there is no indication that even by the Mishnaic Period definite portions had been allocated to each Sabbath. Every verse was translated orally into Aramaic after it had been read in Hebrew (see TARGUM). In some countries of the Diaspora, the reading took place in the vernacular, e.g. Greek. Two "cycles" of the R. of the L. emerged: a triennial one in Palestine, which divided the Pentateuch into over 150 *sedarim;* and an annual one in Babylonia, based on a division into 54 *parashiyyot* (some of which are combined in years with less than 54 Sabbaths none of which is also a festival). Eventually the Babylonian cycle prevailed and was adopted by all congregations in the Diaspora and even in Palestine. The annual reading concludes on SIMḤAT TORAH, whereupon the new cycle is begun. Each Sabbath is known by the name of its portion. For festivals too, suitable portions were determined, and those are followed by an appropriate passage from Num. 28-29 for the *maphtir.* On Sabbath afternoons, Mondays and Thursdays, the beginning of the *parashah* (portion) of the following Sabbath is read. The Reading, with the accompanying benedictions, can only be held when a MINYAN is present and a scroll available. The scroll is taken out from the ARK to be read from and then returned with great ceremony, while the congregation stands and recites psalms and hymns. When a *kohen* is present, he must be called first, followed by a levite; often the rabbi is called third. In some congregations *maphtir* is considered a special honor. A *bar mitzvah* is usually called for *maphtir,* and generally reads this portion himself. Reform congregations generally read selected portions only; some have dispensed altogether with the R. of the L., and the scroll is merely held up before the worshipers in a symbolic gesture. Some Conservative congregations have reintroduced the ancient Palestinian triennial cycle. See also MI SHE-BERAKH.

REAL ESTATE: Real estate is acquired by (1) purchase, (2) presumptive right, or (3) deed (see KINYAN). If intention is present, all movable property within the area of the r.e. is automatically transferred at the same time without a separate *kinyan;* this is called *agav*. R.e. serves as security for a loan contracted by deed, but not for one contracted verbally. No oath is taken on claims involving r.e., nor do the laws of the bailee apply to it. Unless the purchase price exceeds the value of the land by more than half, no claim of overcharging can be brought against the seller. R.e. cannot be stolen; thus however many times it may have been resold without permission of the

TABLE OF SCRIPTURAL READINGS IN THE SYNAGOGUE

	Pentateuch		Prophets
Genesis	*Bereshit*	1:1 — 6:8	Isaiah 42:5—43:11 (42:5—21)*
	Noaḥ	6:9 —11:32	Isaiah 54:1—55:5 (54:1—10)
	Lekh Lekha	12:1 —17:27	Isaiah 40:27—41:16
	Vayera	18:1 —22:24	II Kings 4:1—37 (4:1—23)
	Ḥayei Sarah	23:1 —25:18	I Kings 1:1—31
	Toledot	25:19—28:9	Malachi 1:1—2:7
	Vayetze	28:10—32:3	Hosea 12:13—14:10 (11:7—12:12)
	Vayishlaḥ	32:4 —36:43	Hosea 11:7—12:12 (Obadiah 1:1—21)
	Vayeshev	37:1 —40:23	Amos 2:6—3:8
	Miketz	41:1 —44:17	I Kings 3:15—4:1
	Vayigash	44:18—47:27	Ezekiel 37:15—28
	Vayeḥi	47:28—50:26	I Kings 2:1—12
Exodus	*Shemot*	1:1 —6:1	Isaiah 27:6—28:13; 29:22, 23 (Jeremiah 1:1—2:3)
	Vaere	6:2 — 9:35	Ezekiel 28:25—29:21
	Bo	10:1 —13:16	Jeremiah 46:13—28
	Beshalaḥ	13:17—17:16	Judges 4:4—5:31 (5:1—31)
	Yitro	18:1 —20:23	Isaiah 6:1—7:6; 9:5, 6 (6:1—13)
	Mishpatim	21:1 —24:18	Jeremiah 34:8—22; 33:25, 26
	Terumah	25:1 —27:19	I Kings 5:26—6:13
	Tetzavveh	27:20—30:10	Ezekiel 43:10—27
	Ki Tisa	30:11—34:35	I Kings 18:1—39 (18:20—39)
	Vayakhel	35:1 —38:20	I Kings 7:40—50 (7:13—26)
	Pekudei	38:21—40:38	I Kings 7:51—8:21 (7:40—50)
Leviticus	*Vayikra*	1:1 — 5:26	Isaiah 43:21—44:23
	Tzav	6:1 — 8:36	Jeremiah 7:21—8:3; 9:22, 23
	Shemini	9:1 —11:47	II Samuel 6:1—7:17 (6:1—19)
	Tazria	12:1 —13:59	II Kings 4:42—5:19
	Metzora	14:1 —15:33	II Kings 7:3—20
	Aḥarei Mot	16:1 —18:30	Ezekiel 22:1—19 (22:1—16)
	Kedoshim	19:1 —20:27	Amos 9:7—15 (Ezekiel 20:2—20)
	Emor	21:1 —24:23	Ezekiel 44:15—31
	Behar	25:1 —26:2	Jeremiah 32:6—27
	Beḥukotai	26:3 —27:34	Jeremiah 16:19—17:14
Numbers	*Bemidbar*	1:1 — 4:20	Hosea 2:1—22
	Naso	4:21— 7:89	Judges 13:2—25
	Behaalotekha	8:1 —12:16	Zechariah 2:14—4:7
	Shelaḥ	13:1 —15:41	Joshua 2:1—24
	Koraḥ	16:1 —18:32	I Samuel 11:14—12:22
	Ḥukkat	19:1 —22:1	Judges 11:1—33
	Balak	22:2 —25:9	Micah 5:6—6:8
	Pinḥas	25:10—30:1	I Kings 18:46—19:21
	Mattot	30:2 —32:42	Jeremiah 1:1—2:3
	Masei	33:1 —36:13	Jeremiah 2:4—28; 3:4 (2:4—28; 4:1, 2)

* Parentheses indicate the *Sephardi* rite where this differs from the *Ashkenazi*.

	Pentateuch	Prophets
Deuteronomy *Devarim*	1:1 — 3:22	Isaiah 1:1—27
Vaethanan	3:23— 7:11	Isaiah 40:1—26
Ekev	7:12—11:25	Isaiah 49:14—51:3
Reeh	11:26—16:17	Isaiah 54:11—55:5
Shophetim	16:18—21:9	Isaiah 51:12—52:12
Ki Tetze	21:10—25:19	Isaiah 54:1—10
Ki Tavo	26:1 —29:8	Isaiah 60:1—22
Nitzavim	29:9 —30:20	Isaiah 61:10—63:9
Vayelekh	31:1 —30	Isaiah 55:6—56:8
Haazinu	32:1 —52	II Samuel 22:1—51
Vezot Haberakhah	33:1 —34:12	Joshua 1:1—18 (1:1—9)
New Year, 1st Day	Genesis 21:1—34; Numbers 29:1—6	I Samuel 1:1—2:10
2nd Day	Genesis 22:1—24; Numbers 29:1—6	Jeremiah 31:2—20
Sabbath *Shuvah*	Weekly portion	Hosea 14:2—10; Micah 7:18–20, or Hosea 14:2—10; Joe 2:15—17 (Hosea 14:2—10 Micah 7:18—20)
Day of Atonement, Morning	Leviticus 16:1—34; Numbers 29:7—11	Isaiah 57:14—58:14
Afternoon	Leviticus 18:1—30	Jonah 1:1—4:11; Micah 7:18—20
Tabernacles, 1st Day	Leviticus 22:26—23:44; Numbers 29:12—16	Zechariah 14:1—21
2nd Day	Leviticus 22:26—23:44; Numbers 29:12—16	I Kings 8:2—21
Sabbath During *Ḥol ha-Moed*	Exodus 33:12—34:26; Daily portion from Numbers 29	Ezekiel 38:18—39:16
8th Day	Deuteronomy 14:22—16:17 Numbers 29:35—30:1	I Kings 8:54—66
Rejoicing of the Law	Deuteronomy 33:1—34:12; Genesis 1:1—2:3; Numbers 29:35—30:1	Joshua 1:1—18 (1:1—9)
First Sabbath *Ḥanukkah*	Weekly and *Ḥanukkah* Portions	Zechariah 2:14—4:7
Second Sabbath *Ḥanukkah*	Weekly and *Ḥanukkah* Portions	I Kings 7:40—50
Shekalim	Weekly portion; Exodus 30:11—16	II Kings 12:1—17 (11:17—12:17)
Zakhor	Weekly portion; Deuteronomy 25:17—19	I Samuel 15:2—34 (15:1—34)
Parah	Weekly portion; Numbers 19:1—22	Ezekiel 36:16—38 (36:16—36)
Ha-Ḥodesh	Weekly portion; Exodus 12:1—20	Ezekiel 45:16—46:18 (45:18—46:15)

	Pentateuch	Prophets
Sabbath *ha-Gadol*	Weekly portion	Malachi 3:4—24
Passover, 1st Day	Exodus 12:21—51; Numbers 28:16—25	Joshua 3:5—7; 5:2—6:1; 6:27 (5:2—6:1)
2nd Day	Leviticus 22:26—23:44; Numbers 28:16—25	II Kings 23:1—9; 21—25
Sabbath During *Ḥol ha-Moed*	Exodus 33:12—34:26; Numbers 28:19—25	Ezekiel 36:37—37:14 (37:1—14)
7th Day	Exodus 13:17—15:26; Numbers 28:19—25	II Samuel 22:1—51
8th Day	Deuteronomy 15:19—16:17;* Numbers 28:19—25	Isaiah 10:32—12:6
Pentecost, 1st Day	Exodus 19:1—20:23; Numbers 28:26—31	Ezekiel 1:1—28; 3:12
2nd Day	Deuteronomy 15:19—16:17;* Numbers 28:26—31	Habakkuk 3:1—19 (2:20—3:19)
Ninth of *Av*, Morning	Deuteronomy 4:25—40	Jeremiah 8:13—9:23
Afternoon	Exodus 32:11—14; 34:1—10	Isaiah 55:6—56:8; (Hosea 14:2—10; Micah 7:18—20)
Other Fasts	Exodus 32:11—14; 34:1—10	Isaiah 55:6—56:8 (none)
Sabbath and New Moon	Weekly portion; Numbers 28:9—15	Isaiah 66:1—24
Sabbath immediately preceding New Moon	Weekly portion	I Samuel 20:18—42

* On Sabbath, 14:22—16:17

owner, or whatever improvements have been made on it by pseudo-owners, it always reverts to the original owner. The "thief" is not reimbursed for improvements and he must indemnify the owner for any usufruct enjoyed. Land or anything joined to it cannot contract ritual uncleanness.

REBBE: Term used for ḥasidic leaders and spiritual guides. The *r.* or TZADDIK is not necessarily a halakhic scholar or teacher, but guides his followers by virtue of the spiritual power and holiness thought to be inherent in him. See ḤASIDISM.

REBELLIOUS SON: According to Deut. 21:18-21, an utterly incorrigible and r.s. should, on the complaint of his parents to the "elders of the city", be sentenced to death, even though he has not committed any capital crime. The Talmud considers the law virtually incomprehensible, and the explanation that the execution is preventive (on the assumption that the *Torah* foresaw the future of such a lad who, if allowed to grow up, would undoubtedly commit a capital offense and that "it is better that he die innocent than die guilty") is homiletical rather than legal in character. The rabbis defined the law of the r.s. in such a manner that it was practically inapplicable, and concluded (*Sanh.* 71a) that "the case of the r.s. has never occurred and never will occur. The law was written merely that 'you may study and receive reward for that study'".

REBUKE AND REPROOF: The offering of rebuke to the violator of religious practice is a positive precept (Lev. 19:17) but may not be undertaken indiscriminately. Thus it is forbidden so to rebuke another that he is publicly shamed (*Erak.* 16b); the rabbis declared, "just as it is a *mitzvah* to rebuke one who will listen and profit thereby, so it is a *mitzvah* to refrain from rebuke when it will obviously be of no avail" (*Yev.* 65b).

RECHABITES: A clan headed by Jonadab (Jehonadab), son of Rechab, tracing its ancestry to Caleb and the Kenites. The R. dwelt among the Israelites, living a nomadic life and abstaining from intoxicating drink and even the cultivation of the vine. Their ideal was the pristine austerity of the desert life as against the corruption and sophistication of Canaanite civilization to which Israel gradually succumbed. Zealous anti-Baalists, they co-operated with Jehu in extirpating the household of Ahab (II Kings 10:15-27). They still existed in the time of Jeremiah, who held them up as an example of fidelity and self-discipline to the recalcitrant Israelites (Jer. 35). According to the Midrash, the descendants of the R. were drawn into the Sanhedrin and became prominent expounders of the Law.

RECONSTRUCTIONISM: Religious movement originated in the U.S. by Mordecai M. KAPLAN, and noted for its distinctive attempt to elaborate and apply the consequences of modern naturalism for Judaism. The movement has developed a number of activities (including a magazine, press, and several synagogues and — in New York — the Society for the Advancement of Judaism), and its adherents come from a cross-section of the Reform, Conservative, and secularist wings of American Judaism. While ardently Zionist, R. holds that it is neither feasible nor desirable for all Jews to concentrate in the State of Israel; it believes rather that the Jewish people should be dedicated to a kind of spiritual nationalism, in accordance with which world Jewry would possess both a center in Israel and a Diaspora in which it would have the benefit of cultural contact with many peoples. To foster this kind of peoplehood, R. urges the formation of a new covenant among all Jews. In the manner of modern rationalism and naturalism, it assumes that Jewish religion, like all religions, is a natural outgrowth of the Jewish people's efforts to ensure its survival and find answers to the questions of human existence. Being a human enterprise, religion must be organically related to the advance of human knowledge, to which, in turn, it makes its own contributions. R. proposes complete freedom for Jews to work out their religious ideas on the basis of a respect for facts and tolerance for differing views. It urges Jews to accept freedom and variety in religious practices as a normal and desirable phenomenon and calls for freedom of, for, and from religion *per se*. Beyond the internal needs of the Jewish community, it urges an ethic founded on the unity of all mankind, respect for individual differences, and the need for all groups to be open to each other's insights into human welfare. Judaism is viewed as a religious civilization evolving in response to the changes in the world about it. God is the power in the universe that impels or helps the Jew to achieve salvation or make the most of his life. The Reconstructionist liturgy is similar to the Conservative but incorporates appropriate supplementary medieval and modern texts.

RED HEIFER (Heb. *parah adummah*): Sacrifice enjoined by the Bible (Num. 19) in connection with the purification ritual for persons who had become polluted through contact with the dead. The R.H. had to be free from blemish and never yoked. It was sacrificed outside the Israelite camp (or later in Jerusalem, on the Mount of Olives), and its blood sprinkled by the priest seven times toward the Tabernacle. The entire carcass was then burned in a fire to which cedar wood, hyssop, and a scarlet thread had been added. The ashes were transferred by a layman to a clean place. All participants in the rite were rendered unclean until the evening. The ashes were mixed with fresh water in an earthen vessel and it was by sprinkling with this "water of purification" that ritual purity could be regained. While considering the symbolism of the R.H. as incomprehensible to human reason, rabbinic *aggadah* associates the purifying function of the red cow with the sin of the Golden CALF Modern scholars point to the analogy of the scapegoat, the sin-offering of the High Priest (Lev. 16:26-27), and the heifer sacrificed by a community in the vicinity of which murder had been committed (Deut. 21:3). In commemoration of this commandment, and because all who were contaminated by corpses had to be cleansed for the Passover, the chapter of R.H. is read in the synagogue on the Sabbath called *Shabbat Parah*, a few weeks before Passover.

REDAK, see **KIMḤI, DAVID**

REDEMPTION (Heb. *geullah*): The religious and theological meanings of r. are derived from ancient Israelite law and social custom. To "redeem" meant to fulfill the duty of next of kin ("redeemer") by ransoming a kinsman who had sold himself into slavery, or by exercising the option to buy back family property that had been alienated. The next of kin who acts as BLOOD AVENGER is also called *goel*. To describe God as *goel* (cf. Job 19:25 "I know that my redeemer liveth") is to imply that He is, as it were, the closest and nearest relative. In saving His people (cf. Is. 11:11; Jer. 31:10) He acts the part of the kinsman in ancient law. Liturgical reference to God as Israel's redeemer is made daily in the benediction following the SHEMA and in the seventh benediction of the weekday AMIDAH. The idea of redemption operates on a variety of levels: as social and political liberation (the prototype being the EXODUS from Egypt, and the expected consummation in the messianic r.), as freedom from sin, and as a general cosmic transformation. Accordingly concepts of r. range from the historical to the transcendental and mystical (see ESCHATOLOGY). The KABBALAH in particular developed the notion of a r. (TIKKUN) in which God Himself shares, since He too (in the aspect of the Godhead called the SHEKHINAH) was involved in the suffering of a disarranged and "fallen" world. It has been suggested that modern Zionism is merely the national and secularized reinterpretation of the ancient Jewish striving for r.

REDEMPTION OF FIRST-BORN, see **FIRST-BORN, REDEMPTION OF**

REFORM JUDAISM: Religious trend advocating modification of ORTHODOX tradition in conformity with the exigencies of contemporary life and thought. The essential difference between Reform and Orthodox Judaism revolves around the authority of the *halakhah*: whereas Orthodoxy maintains the Divine authority of the *halakhah* in both its biblical and rabbinic expressions, R.J. subjects religious law and customs to the judgment of man. While granting the elements of Divine inspiration in the Bible and Jewish tradition, it attempts to differentiate between those elements of the law which are "eternal" and those legal forms and customs which it believes are the product of a particular age. It thus maintains its right to adapt and change Jewish tradition in such a fashion as it thinks will make this tradition more relevant and attractive to each generation. The historic origins of the organized Reform movement were motivated less by theological or ideological attitudes than by a desire for a more pleasant form of religious service. A prominent German Jew, Israel Jacobson, organized a Jewish school and then a synagogue in Seesen. He later moved to Berlin where religious services along the lines he had initiated were conducted in his home and in the home of Jacob Herz Beer. In 1818, a group of Jews in Hamburg built a synagogue which they called a Temple. The organizers of these early Reform services conducted some of the prayers in the vernacular, shortened the service, eliminated some ideas that they felt were "out of date", used musical accompaniment, and delivered the sermon in German. Jacobson also introduced the ceremony of confirmation into the religious calendar of the new community. The new "sectarians", as they were called by the Orthodox rabbis, evoked strong criticism from the traditional segments of the Jewish community who tried and at times succeeded in persuading government authorities to ban the new religious movement. But the ideas of the French Revolution and liberal tendencies in Germany evoked in the hearts of many Jews the feeling that a new age, of which the EMANCIPATION of the Jews was a symptom, was dawning in the religious and ethical consciousness of mankind. This outlook influenced the ideological development of the Reform leaders who relinquished the belief in a personal Messiah who would lead the Jews back to Palestine. They insisted that Jews look upon the lands of their residence as their permanent homes and not a place of temporary exile. Practices like covering the head during services, dietary restrictions, the donning of phylacteries, and other traditional customs and laws, were also regarded by some of the early reformers as outmoded. The prophetic and ethical rather than the ritual elements of biblical Judaism were looked to for inspiration. The negation of ritual aroused resentment not only on the part of the Orthodox authorities but also among a large segment of the newly emerging "Reform" Movement. At a series of conferences in Germany at Brunswick (1844), Frankfort (1845), and Breslau (1846), the new movement split into "radicals", like Samuel HOLDHEIM, and "CONSERVATIVES", like Zacharias FRANKEL. Others, like Abraham GEIGER, tried to occupy a middle position and worked for a platform of religious principles and order of prayers acceptable to all groups. As an organized religious movement, R.J. in Germany achieved only modest growth. It organized a seminary as well as a number of congregations. Many great scholars and contributors to Jewish WISSENSCHAFT were associated with it in one form or another. In France and England too, the Reform Movement made slow organizational headway. In 1903, the *Union Israélite Libérale* was formed in France and built its own Temple in Paris. In England a Jewish Religious Union was founded in 1902 and later established a Reform congregation. In the U.S., however, the Reform Movement enjoyed remarkable growth. As early as 1824, some members of the Beth Elohim congregation in Charleston, S. Carolina, tried to introduce changes in the ritual of prayer. After some years of controversy, their synagogue became the first Reform congregation in the U.S. About the middle of the 19th cent. other "liberal" congregations were formed and led by rabbis who had recently emigrated from Germany. Among these early German-American Reform leaders were David EINHORN, Leo Merzbacher, Benjamin Szold, and Isaac Mayer WISE. Wise, at the beginning of his career in America, ranked himself among the more traditional of the liberal rabbis who strove to avoid a religious breach in the American religious community. But a number of RABBINICAL CONFERENCES and personal experiences in congregations convinced him that there was a deep and genuine division of religious opinion. In 1873, he succeeded in forming the UNION OF AMERICAN HEBREW CONGREGATIONS and in 1875, this Union established the HEBREW UNION COLLEGE in Cincinnati. In 1889, Wise organized the CENTRAL CONFERENCE OF AMERICAN RABBIS. In the U.S. the Reform Movement was able to achieve what it could not attain in Germany — a consensus of opinion about the principles of R.J. As early as 1869, a dozen Reform rabbis met in Philadelphia to affirm that they no longer looked forward to returning to Palestine; that they did not believe in bodily resurrection after death; that the scattering of Jews throughout the Diaspora aided Judaism in fulfilling its religious mission; and that while Hebrew was to be preserved as a language of prayer, religious services should also be made understandable to modern Jews. In many ways, the early American Reform Movement was more radical than its German progenitor. In 1885, a group of nineteen rabbis answered a call by Kaufmann KOHLER, a prominent rabbi and theologian, to convene a meeting which later became known as the Pittsburgh Conference. The Pittsburgh "Platform" followed the general lines of the Philadelphia principles with respect to Palestine and belief in bodily resurrection after death. It emphasized the prophetic ideals of the Bible as against the precepts and regulations of the Talmud and openly declared that some Mosaic legislation, such as the dietary laws, need no longer be obeyed. It also emphasized the need for expressing religion through concrete efforts for social justice — a principle that received increasing emphasis in later Reform conferences. Between 1885 and 1937, the American Reform Jewish community grew tremendously in organizational strength and underwent a considerable inner religious revolution. The Columbus Platform of 1937 differed from the Pittsburgh Platform in a number of essentials. It urged, rather than discouraged, a greater emphasis on Hebrew, traditional customs, and ceremonies. It emphasized that Jews were bound to each other not only in a religious faith but as a people with a common history and fate. Its most controversial and startling change was a reversal of the earlier Reform attitude toward Palestine. It urged all Jews to participate in the rebuilding of Palestine and thus, by implication, followed the leadership of Zionist Reform leaders like Stephen S. Wise and Abba Hillel Silver. The trend toward more tradition and greater emphasis on Hebrew continues within the Reform Movement of today. There are now more than 600 Reform congregations joined together in the WORLD UNION FOR PROGRESSIVE JUDAISM and Reform congregations can be found in many lands.

REFUGE, see **ASYLUM**

REFUGE, CITIES OF, see **CITIES OF REFUGE**

REJOICING OF THE LAW, see **SIMḤAT TORAH**

RELEASE, see **VOW**

RELEASE, YEAR OF, see **SABBATICAL YEAR**

RELIGIOUS PARTIES: The political Zionist movement and the Zionist Organization founded by Theodore Herzl were in essence secular and nationalist, though some of their earliest impulses came from a religious motivation (as expressed, e.g., by Judah ALKALAI and Tzevi Hirsch KALISCHER). Apart from a vague statement by Herzl to the effect that the Return to Zion must be preceded by a Return to Judaism, the movement ignored the specifically religious aspect of Judaism and confined itself to the conception of the Jewish people as a national entity. However, after the Fifth Zionist Congress in 1901, when the Swiss and other student organizations formed a radical fraction and adopted a positive anti-religious attitude, R. Isaac Jacob Reines of Lida (district of Vilna) who had joined the movement, founded a specifically religious wing of the Zionist Organization which he called *Mizraḥi* (abb. of "spiritual center"). The motto of the movement was "The Land of Israel to the People of Israel according to the *Torah* of Israel". The *Mizraḥi* movement was therefore from its inception an integral part of the Zionist Organization. This co-operation between Orthodox Jews and anti-religious elements aroused the determined opposition of the leading rabbis of the time, both *Mitnaggedim* and Ḥasidim. When the Tenth Zionist Congress (1911) decided, in the face of *Mizraḥi* opposition, to make itself responsible for educational and cultural activities, religious elements, at a Congress held at Kattowitz in May, 1912, founded the *Agudat Israel*, a world religious movement opposing political Zionism of any kind. The *Agudat Israel* therefore stood outside, and in opposition to, the Zionist Organization and the Jewish Agency. With the establishment of the State of Israel, however, a representative of *Agudat Israel* joined the Provisional Government; after the advent of the Likud government in 1977, the party entered the government coalition, but refused any cabinet appointments. *Agudat Israel* has also participated in municipal elections. Whereas *Mizrahi* participated in both the Zionist Organization and the State, *Agudat Israel* only participated in the latter. A small extremist group located mostly in Jerusalem, the NATOREI KARTA, acknowledges neither. From both the *Mizrahi* and *Agudat Israel* there subsequently arose Socialist groups, the *Poel Mizrahi* and *Poalei Agudat Israel* respectively; a complete merger was achieved by the two *Mizrahi* groups, which is now known as the National Religious Party, but the two *Agudah* groups remain separate and sometimes even in opposition to one another. In 1949 the four religious parties established a united front for the national elections, but subsequently they have run independently. In recent years, splinter parties have broken off from both *Mizrahi* and *Agudah*, leaving both with small parliamentary delegations. With the absence of a clear majority for any one party in the *Knesset*, the religious parties, primarily *Mizrahi*, have been able to have legislation implemented in the religious field, such as the transfer to the rabbinic courts of all questions of personal status (marriage, divorce, legitimacy, etc.) and regulations governing the Sabbath and dietary laws.

REMA, see **ISSERLES, MOSES**

REMAK, see **CORDOVERO, MOSES**
REMEZ, see **PARDES**
REMNANT OF ISRAEL (Heb. *She'erit Yisrael*): The idea of the remnant is expressed by nearly all the literary prophets. Despite the catastrophes and dire punishments visited upon the sinful people of Israel, either directly by God or at the hands of other nations before the Day of Judgment, the people will not be utterly destroyed: a repentant and righteous remnant will survive and ultimately constitute the kingdom of God. This doctrine, hinted at in Lev. 26:44-45, is clearly enunciated by Isaiah, who thought of the remnant as a small minority ("a tenth part") of the people (Is. 6:3) and who gave one of his children the symbolic name *Shear Yashuv* ("the remnant will return") in token of this belief (7:3). Jeremiah elaborated upon the theme: "And I will gather the remnant of my flock out of all the countries whither I have driven them and bring them again to their folds" (23:3). Ezekiel also accepted the doctrine to the extent that he designated the Babylonian exiles as "the remnant of Israel" (cf. 9:8; 11:13).
RENDING OF CLOTHES (Heb. *keriah*): The practice of rending one's garments is found in the Bible as a sign of mourning (Gen. 37:34) and of national (Josh. 7:6) and personal (Gen. 37:29) distress. A Jewish mourner (male or female) rends his garments upon the demise of any one of the following seven close relatives: father, mother, brother, sister, son, daughter, wife, or husband. While doing so he recites the blessing ***barukh dayyan ha-emet*** ("Blessed is the righteous Judge"). The rent is made on the left side over the heart in the case of parents; on the right side for other relatives. For parents all garments are rent and the tear is left permanently; in the case of other relatives, only the upper garment is rent and crudely sewed together again after the week of mourning. Other occasions upon which Orthodox Jews rend their garments are: (1) when beholding the Temple site for the first time; (2) for a Scroll of the Law which has been burnt; and (3) upon receiving news of a communal or national Jewish calamity.
REPENTANCE: The Hebrew word for r. is *teshuvah* (lit. "return"), which clearly indicates that the Jewish concept of r. means a return to God and to the right path (cf. Hos. 14:2; II Kings 17:13; Jer. 13:14; 18:11; Joel 2:12-13, etc.). According to rabbinic teaching, man was created with an evil inclination — a tendency to sin — to which r. is the antidote. It is within each man's power to redeem himself from sin by sincerely changing his ways and returning to God. The rabbis frequently extol the merits and significance of r., e.g. "Great is r., for it brings healing to the world. Great is r., for it reaches to the throne of God. Great is r., it brings redemption near. Great is r., for it lengthens a man's life" (*Yoma* 86a); "Where the penitent stand, there is no place for the perfectly righteous" (*Ber.* 34b). A fundamental biblical text is the statement by Ezekiel that God delights not in the death of the wicked but that he turn from his evil way and live (Ezek. 33:11). The importance of r. as a moral act became emphasized all the more after the destruction of the Temple and the cessation of atonement offerings. Particular stress was laid on the penitential season — the TEN DAYS OF PENITENCE (as well as the preparatory month of ELUL). A distinction is made between r. for sins committed against God and those committed against one's fellow man. Whereas the former demands only regret, confession, and abnegation of the offense, the latter involves complete restitution for the wrong committed or, in the case of a non-material offense, reconciliation and forgiveness. R. is regarded as so fundamental that it is enumerated in the Talmud as one of the seven things created by God before He created the world (*Pes.* 54a; see PRE-EXISTENCE). A penitent must not be reminded of his past sins. Providing it is sincere, r. has the power of completely erasing all man's previous transgressions — "R. and good works are man's advocates". R. is a major theme in the ethical, devotional, spiritual, and ascetic writings of the medieval philosophers (e.g. Maimonides, Baḥya), kabbalists (e.g. Isaac Luria), moralists, and later of the MUSAR MOVEMENT. See also ATONEMENT: CONFESSION.
REPENTANCE, TEN DAYS OF, see **PENITENCE, TEN DAYS OF**
RESH GALUTA, see **EXILARCH**
RESH KALLAH (Aram. "head of the *kallah*"): The term *kallah* (orig. probably "round") came to mean, in Babylonian usage, a rabbinic lecture or discourse, apparently because the audience was seated in a circle or half-circle. The *r.k.* was the sage who presided over the bi-annual assembly; he is mentioned, together with the EXILARCH and the heads of the academies, in the YEKUM PURKAN prayer. Outside the KALLAH MONTHS, the *r.k.* also delivered homiletic or halakhic discourses on Sabbaths (*Bava Batra* 22a).
RESH LAKISH, see **SIMEON BEN LAKISH**
RESPONSA (Heb. *she'elot u-teshuvot* "questions and answers"): Answers to questions on Jewish law and observance given by halakhic scholars in reply to inquiries addressed to them. R. literature originated as a distinct branch of Jewish law during the Gaonic Period, and became especially important after the Mohammedan conquest. The unquestioned central spiritual authority of the *geonim* — the heads of the two Babylonian aca-
EXISTENCE). A penitent must not be reminded of

communication which resulted from the extensive caravan routes established throughout the Islamic world, allowed far-flung communities to send their questions on disputed or unknown points of Jewish procedure or law to the authorities for solution. At first the r. were couched in the briefest of terms, and consisted of a single sentence, or even a word ("forbidden" or "permitted"); gradually, however, they developed into monographs which dealt exhaustively with the subject at hand. The proliferation of gaonic r. can be seen in the fact that over 10,000 are still extant, those of Hai Gaon (d. 1038) alone numbering about 1,000. Each country and each period produced its rabbinic authorities and its r. literature. The respondents are divided into the RISHONIM, those earlier authorities whose decisions were usually based directly on the Talmud, and the AḤARONIM, later authorities who take into consideration both the Talmud and earlier r. *Rishonim* include the r. of R. Meir of Rothenburg in Germany, R. Asher ben Jehiel of Germany and Spain, R. Solomon ben Adret of Barcelona, R. Isaac ben Sheshet and R. Simeon ben Tzemaḥ Duran of Algiers. Important *aḥaronim* are found in many countries e.g., Joseph Colon of Italy, Israel Bruna of Germany. The best-known r. collections of recent centuries include the *Noda bi-Yehudah* of Ezekiel ben Judah Landau of Prague, the *Ḥatam Sopher* of Moses Sopher of Pressburg, and the r. of Isaac Elhanan Spektor of Kovno. As the questions addressed to these rabbis were not confined to ritual or ceremonial matters but covered every aspect of Jewish life, rabbinic r. serve as a mine of information about the social, economic, religious, and communal history of the Jews in each country. The first prayer book was a responsum sent to the Jewish community of Lucena that had inquired about the correct liturgy; again, the only connected history of the Gaonic Period, the Letter of R. SHERIRA Gaon, was a responsum sent by him to the community of Kairouan; and most of our information about the mysterious Eldad Ha-Dani who appeared in the 9th cent. in Kairouan, is contained in the query about him sent by that community to the *gaon* Cohen Tzedek. Each new problem that arose, as a result of new conditions of life, soon became the subject of r., and the r. literature faithfully reflects the continuous process of adjustment and modification which Jewish law underwent throughout the centuries. The rôle of r. is similar to that of case law in the English system; they are taken increasingly into account by the civil judiciary of the State of Israel and also serve to guide not only Orthodox, but also Conservative and Reform practice.

RESURRECTION (Heb. *teḥiyyat ha-metim*): The doctrine of r. teaches that the bodies of the dead will arise from their graves at some future period. Belief in r. began to develop toward the end of the Biblical Period, possibly under Persian influence, and is referred to in the Book of DANIEL (12:2). By the end of the Second Temple Period it had developed into a fundamental dogma of the Pharisees, who sought biblical warrant for it by means of midrashic methods of exegesis (see HERMENEUTICS) and declared it heresy to deny, as did the Sadducees (Josephus, *Ant.* 18, 1, 4; *Sanh.* 90b), that the doctrine possessed Mosaic authority (Mishnah *Sanh.* 10:1). R. is one of the few dogmas expressly stated in the liturgy, where it is the subject of the second paragraph of the AMIDAH. Since rabbinic times it has been accepted as a fundamental doctrine of Judaism, and is commonly associated with the Messianic Era (see ESCHATOLOGY). Maimonides enumerates it as the last of the THIRTEEN PRINCIPLES OF FAITH. However, the dogma proved a stumbling block to those thinkers who conceived of eschatological perfection in a more purely spiritual way, and to whom the heavenly bliss of the soul seemed a more worthy consummation than the possibility of continued life in a material body. Maimonides himself seems to have identified r. with the immortality of the soul and was later obliged to compose a special treatise in which he argued that a spiritual view of immortality was not in conflict with the doctrine of the return of the soul to the body. Most Orthodox thinkers took the doctrine of r. in its literal sense, though views differed as to whether r. would embrace all mankind, or the Jewish people as a whole, or only the righteous. Maimonides and Crescas regarded it as confined to the righteous only; Abravanel conceded it to all Israel; and Manasseh ben Israel to all mankind. Under the impact of natural philosophy the belief in the r. of the body has been greatly shaken. Reform Judaism has denied the literal concept of bodily r. (and revised the liturgy accordingly), and has asserted that the belief is non-indigenous, a foreign import into Jewish history which should be rejected. The moderate Reform and the Conservatives tend to identify it with the doctrine of the immortality of the soul.

RETALIATION, see **JUS TALIONIS**

RETRIBUTION, DIVINE: Divine r., i.e., the reward of the righteous and the punishment of the wicked, either in this world or in the hereafter, is a fundamental biblical and rabbinic belief. It is a corollary of the belief in Divine JUSTICE and hence is also connected with the doctrine of FREE WILL. Maimonides enumerates r. as the eleventh of his THIRTEEN ARTICLES OF FAITH, and Albo, whose *Ikkarim* is a critique of these principles, nevertheless accepts the doctrine of r. as one of the three basic principles of Judaism (alongside belief in

God and revelation). Whereas the biblical doctrine of r. envisages earthly reward and punishment (cf., e.g., Deut. 11:13-15. "If ye will harken to My commandments... I will give you the rain of your land in its due season... and I will give grass in thy fields for thy cattle and thou shalt eat and be satisfied"), the rabbis increasingly placed r. in an eschatological perspective. Thus it was taught that "there is no reward for good deeds in this world" and that the happiness and "length of days" promised by the Bible as the reward for honoring one's parents refers to the future world "which is everlasting and wholly good" (*Ḥul.* end). But, although r. is taken for granted by the rabbis, they insisted that it should not serve as the primary motive for virtue. Fear of punishment is an inferior sort of FEAR OF GOD, and a good deed (MITZVAH) should be considered its own reward. One of the earliest mishnaic teachers, Antigonus of Sokho, said, "Be not as servants that serve their master with a thought of obtaining reward" (*Avot* 1:3). Medieval Jewish philosophers subscribed fully to the rabbinic view of the otherworldly quality of r. In modern times, many liberal thinkers have denied the possibility of Divine r. or endeavored to rationalize it in terms of historical processes.

REVELATION: The act by which God manifests Himself (His saving presence, His will, His commandments) to man. Biblical and rabbinic Hebrew have no specific term corresponding to r. God is said to "appear" to the patriarchs and prophets, and the appearances are described in varying degrees of ANTHROPOMORPHISM and concrete imagery (cf. Gen. 3:8; 18:1, 38; Exod. 19:20). Sometimes the Divine manifestation takes place "in a vision" or "in a dream" (Gen. 31:13 ff.; Num. 12:6) or by means of an ANGEL. At the same time the Bible emphasizes that no direct, sensory perception of God is possible, and hence various circumscriptions were used when describing Divine manifestations, e.g. *kavod* ("glory"; see Exod.33: 18-23; Lev. 9:6; Exod. 24:9-11) and, in later rabbinic usage, *shekhinah* (e.g. *gilluy shekhinah*, "Divine manifestation"). Sometimes the agent of r. is described as the "word" (*davar;* see also LOGOS) or as the "spirit" (see HOLY SPIRIT). Although any event in which the Divine majesty or presence becomes immediately manifest (e.g. THEOPHANY; see also MIRACLE) is called r., the term has come to be applied more particularly to the communications of the Divine will as revealed to God's messengers. According to the traditional view, Mosaic Law (see also TORAH, WRITTEN LAW, ORAL LAW) represents the highest type of r. The PROPHETS experienced lesser degrees of r., whereas for other parts of Scripture the term INSPIRATION rather than r. would be appropriate. Rabbinic theology correlates the different DIVINE NAMES with different manifestations of the Divine (see also ATTRIBUTES). In the Talmudic Period a "celestial voice" (BAT KOL) is reported to have sometimes communicated Divine approval or disapproval. For medieval thinkers r. was identical with prophecy and they considered such problems as the degrees of prophetic r., the relationship between supra-rational r. and reason, and the rôle of human faculties in r. While JUDAH HA-LEVI held r. to be essentially different from, and superior to, rational knowledge, others (e.g. SAADYAH, MAIMONIDES) held prophecy to be the perfection of the intellect itself, and supernaturally revealed laws to be, in the main, anticipations of subsequent rational insight. The view that r. was essentially the manifestation of a Divine Law, since reason itself was sufficient for insight into the principles of religious truth and ethics, was still held by Moses MENDELSSOHN. In the 19th cent. Ludwig Steinheim was exceptional in formulating a radical philosophy of r., maintaining that reason had to abdicate in the face of r. The anti-supernaturalist and rationalist character of modernism in general, and BIBLICAL CRITICISM in particular, challenged the traditional conceptions of r., revealed laws, and revealed scriptures. Liberal and Reform theologians spoke of r. as a subjective mode of experience or as a growing (and increasingly refined) perception of the Divine creative power and of moral values in human history. Hence the notion of a "progressive r." rather than that of r. as a distinct, objective, and supranatural event. The concept, however, has not been sufficiently elaborated, and r. is used more as a figure of speech than as a precise term. In the philosophy of Franz ROSENZWEIG, r. is the term for the specific mode of relationship between God and man (i.e., individual man and not humanity as a collective). Charismatic revelatory experiences, often defined as lower forms of r. (e.g. illuminations, visions, infusions of Holy Spirit, etc.), played a considerable rôle in the history of Jewish MYSTICISM.

REVENGE, see **BLOOD AVENGER; VENGEANCE**

REWARD AND PUNISHMENT, see **RETRIBUTION**

RIBASH, see **ISAAC BEN SHESHET**

RIF, see **ALFASI, ISAAC**

RIGHTEOUSNESS: Usual English translation of the Hebrew words *tzedek, tzedakah,* meaning uprightness, honesty, and freedom from wickedness, sin, and deceit. A TZADDIK ("righteous man") is one who lives righteously by adhering to the Divine law, i.e., one in whom no fault or transgression is to be found. R. is the keynote of biblical legislation and prophetic preaching. Abraham was admitted to God's COVENANT in order that he and his seed might "keep the way of the Lord, to do r. and justice" (Gen. 18:19) and in Deut. 16:20 Israel is exhorted, "that which is wholly righteous shalt thou follow, that thou mayest live and inherit the land". It is assumed throughout rabbinic literature that no perfectly righteous man exists, but that a man's status depends on the balance of his deeds. Legend, however, knows of 36 perfectly righteous men (LAMED VAV) through whose r. the world exists. As against the minimum ideal of r., which consists of conformity to the requirements of the law, the higher ideal of boundless devotion to God is exemplified by the ḤASID (as distinct from the *tzaddik*). In rabbinic and medieval Hebrew the word *tzedakah* became narrowed down to denote only one aspect of r., that of almsgiving and CHARITY.

RIMMONIM (Heb. "pomegranates"): The pomegranate was one of the favorite and characteristic fruits of the Land of Israel (cf. Deut. 8:8). Pomegranate-shaped adornments (called *r.*) embellished both the skirt of the garment of the High Priest (Exod. 28:33-34) and the Temple of Solomon ("400 *r.* for the two networks" — I Kings 7:42). The rabbis regarded the fruits as a symbol of the 613 precepts of the *Torah*, and said that "even the worthless members of the Jewish people are as full of good deeds as is the pomegranate of seeds" (*Eruv* 82a). Originally the silver or gold adornments placed on top of the rollers of the Scrolls of the Law (see BELLS) were often made in the shape of pomegranates, and among *Sephardim* they were called *r.*

RISHON LE-ZION (Heb. "First in Zion" from Is. 41:27): Title given to the *Sephardi* CHIEF RABBI of Israel at least since the 16th cent. and probably much earlier. According to one tradition, when Moses GALANTE was appointed spiritual head of the Jerusalem community in 1597, he modestly refused to assume the title of *Ravad* (Rabbi, head of the *bet din*) hitherto held by the Chief Rabbi, but agreed to the title of *Rishon le-Zion* on the principle of first among equals. After his death the *Sephardi* community decided that in the future all their Chief Rabbis would be known by this appellation.

RISHONIM (Heb. "first ones"): The distinction between *r.* and AHARONIM ("later ones") is found with reference to the prophets, the *tannaim*, and the *amoraim;* now, however, the term *rishonim* is technically used when referring to codifiers of talmudic law active during the period between the completion of the Talmud and Joseph Karo's compilation of the *Shulḥan Arukh* (16th cent.). Later talmudic authorities are called *aḥaronim*.

RITES, see MINHAG; NUSAKH

RITUAL BATH, see MIKVEH

RITUAL MURDER ACCUSATION, see BLOOD LIBEL

RITUAL PURITY, see PURITY, RITUAL

RITUAL SLAUGHTER, see SHEḤITAH

RIZHIN, see RUZHIN

ROBBERY: The open and forcible appropriation of another's goods (as opposed to THEFT). The prohibition against r. (Lev. 19:13) carries no corporal punishment since the felony can be rectified by restoration of the stolen property. Rabbinic leniency in cases of r. was based on hope of the robber's repentance. Withholding another's property, even though it has come legitimately into one's possession, is considered "oppression" (Lev. 19:13) and is included in the prohibition against r., as is the misappropriation of funds entrusted to one's care. The forcible taking of a pledge and borrowing without permission also fall under this prohibition. If the stolen goods have meanwhile undergone a change as in the case of a beam which has been built into a building, the equivalent may be restored in money (*Git.* 55a). The penalty for falsely denying a r. while under oath is an additional quarter of the restitution. The prohibition against r. is one of the seven NOACHIAN LAWS.

ROGACHOVER, see ROZIN, JOSEPH

ROKEAḤ, see BELZ

ROKEAḤ, ELEAZAR, see ELEAZAR BEN JUDAH

ROSENZWEIG, FRANZ (1886-1929): German philosopher and theologian. Born of an assimilated family, his religious interests and struggles brought him to the brink of conversion to Christianity, but he decided to learn Judaism first, and an experience of an Orthodox Day of Atonement service made him fully accept his ancestral religion and devote his life and philosophical gifts to its interpretation. In his main work, *The Star of Redemption,* which he wrote as a soldier during World War I, R. anticipated some of the characteristic positions of later existentialist philosophy. According to R., God, man, and the world are three distinct kinds of being, none of which can be dissolved in the other though they are related one to another. The relation between God and the world is called creation, that between God and man revelation, and that between man and the world, redemption. R. stressed the religious, transhistoric quality of Jewish existence and consequently opposed Zionism. He was also unique among Jewish philosophers in his evaluation of the relationship between Judaism and Christianity which he considered as mutually exclusive yet complementary. His poetic gift and power of interpretative penetration found full scope in his translation into German with commentary of some of JUDAH HA-LEVI's poems, and in the translation of the Bible which he undertook together with Martin BUBER. In 1920 he founded the *Freies Jüdisches Lehrhaus* in Frankfort-on-Main as part of his work for Jewish adult education.

ROSH, see **ASHER BEN JEHIEL**

ROSH HA-SHANAH (Heb. "beginning of the year"): Four different dates in the CALENDAR are mentioned in the Mishnah (tractate ROSH HA-SHANAH) as being the NEW YEAR for different specific purposes. One of these dates had acquired the religious significance of an annual day of judgment and the Mishnah states: "On *R.H.* all that comes into the world pass before Him like flocks of sheep". The Talmud connects this reference to *Tishri* 1, the beginning of the ancient agricultural year (and not with *Nisan* 1 which, since the Babylonian Exile, begins the civil calendar). *Tishri* 1 is the only one of the four New Years to be specified in the Bible as a festival (cf. Lev. 23:23-4: "A Sabbath, a memorial of the sounding of the *shophar*" — and Num. 29:1-6: "A day of sounding the *shophar*"), although no mention is made of it there as the New Year. The sounding of the *shophar* is one of the distinctive features of the religious celebration of the festival, and has largely determined the character of the liturgy of the day, particularly the Additional Service (see FESTIVAL PRAYERS). Three groups of prayers, each consisting of ten scriptural verses selected from all three portions of the Bible, are inserted into the Additional Service, each with a beautiful introduction and closing paragraph compiled by Rav in the 3rd cent. The first section consists of verses describing the sovereignty of God (hence called MALKHUYYOT); the second speaks of God's remembrance of His creatures (ZIKHRONOT); and the third is related to the sounding of the *shophar* (SHOPHAROT). After each section, the *shophar* is sounded according to a fixed pattern (with minor differences between the *Sephardi* and *Ashkenazi* rites). *R.H.* takes on additional significance since it stands at the beginning of the TEN DAYS OF PENITENCE, which culminate on the Day of ATONEMENT. *R.H.* does not commemorate any historical event in Jewish history, but rather the creation of the world. It is a period of self-examination and Divine judgment, a judgment in this case universal, since it is "the day on which the world was conceived, the day on which all creatures pass before Thee". The liturgy for the day stresses man's yearning for the establishment of God's sovereignty over the entire world and the ushering in of the millennium. *R.H.* is the only festival observed for two days in the Land of Israel (see SECOND DAY OF FESTIVALS). Various customs are connected with its celebration. On the first night dishes are prepared that are meant to augur well for the New Year: for example, apples dipped in honey are eaten while a prayer is recited for a "good and sweet year". On the second night one partakes of new fruit for the first time in order to be able to say the SHE-HEHEYANU blessing. It is also customary to go to a river or pond to recite TASHLIKH.

ROSH HA-SHANAH (Heb. "New Year"): Eighth tractate in the Mishnah order of *Moed* with *gemara* in both Talmuds. After mentioning the four NEW YEARS, it deals at length with the rules for the sanctification of the NEW MOON, and the laws for ROSH HA-SHANAH (sounding of the SHOPHAR, liturgy, etc.).

ROSH HA-SHANAH LE-ILANOT, see **NEW YEAR FOR TREES**

ROSH ḤODESH, see **NEW MOON**

ROSH YESHIVAH (Heb. "head of the YESHIVAH"): The head of an institution for the study of the Talmud. In the YEKUM PURKAN prayer, the phrase occurs in the Aramaic plural as *reishei metivata*; they rank after the *geonim* (see GAON) and exilarchs but take precedence over "judges in the gates". The title is also used today not only for the principals of various *yeshivot* but also for the permanent members of the teaching staff.

ROZIN, JOSEPH ("the Rogachover *gaon*"; 1858-1936): Talmudist; rabbi in Dvinsk and Petrograd. He was the author of tens of thousands of responsa noted for their independence, originality, and subtlety as well as their cryptic style. Many of his responsa were published under the title *Tzaphenat Paneaḥ*.

RUTH, BOOK OF: Second of the five SCROLLS, the Book of R. tells the story of a widowed Moabite proselyte who refuses to forsake her impoverished mother-in-law, Naomi, upon the latter's return to Bethlehem after a ten-year absence. While gleaning in the fields Ruth meets the owner of the land, Boaz — a kinsman of Naomi — who treats her with great kindness. At the end of the harvest Ruth, acting on Naomi's advice, seeks out Boaz by night on the threshing floor and entreats him to assume the responsibilities of next of kin and redeem the fortunes of her family. Boaz accedes to her wishes and takes Ruth for a wife; their son is the grandfather of DAVID. Rabbinic tradition ascribes the book to Samuel (*Bava Batra* 14b), but critics have regarded the composition as post-exilic. The Book of Ruth is read in the synagogue on the Feast of Weeks.

RUTH RABBAH, see **MIDRASH RABBAH**

RUZHIN, ISRAEL (FRIEDMANN) OF (1797-1851): Ḥasidic rabbi. A grandson of R. ABRAHAM MALAKH, Israel of R. succeeded his father at the age of 16. He was distinguished for his natural charm, brilliance, and wisdom, and held a splendid court, granting audiences seated on a throne, driving in a magnificent carriage drawn by four horses with outriders and generally affecting royal manners which suggested messianic qualities to his followers. He was denounced to the Russian authorities for setting himself up as a monarch and spent 22 months in prison. After being released he fled to Kishinev and then to Austria, but was finally cleared of all charges and re-established himself at Sadagora in Bukovina where he conducted himself in even grander style. The Sadagora rabbis of the Friedmann family are his descendants.

S

SAADYAH BEN JOSEPH (882-942: Scholar. S. was born in Egypt but wandered through Palestine and other lands until he finally settled in Babylonia. *Gaon* of the ACADEMY at Sura (928-930, 936-942), he was also a prolific writer in many areas: *halakhah*, liturgy, philosophy, biblical exegesis, and Hebrew grammar. His *Siddur* with Arabic rubrics is one of the earliest systematic compilations of the PRAYER BOOK. His religious poetry, which is often exceedingly involved and difficult, influenced a whole school of writers of PIYYUT. Of great importance, both for its scientific value and for its profound influence on Arabic speaking Jewry, was his translation of the Bible into Arabic. This, as well as his Arabic commentaries to many of the biblical books, were pioneer works and were frequently quoted by the later commentators. Much of his literary work resulted from the controversies in which he was involved, e.g. the *Sepher Zikkaron* (establishing the authority of Babylonian rabbis to fix the calendar, against the counter-claims of the Palestinian rabbinate) and his many polemical writings against the KARAITES and other heretics. His *Book of Beliefs and Opinions,* written in Arabic and known in Hebrew under the title *Emunot ve-Deot*, is the first great Jewish philosophical classic. This work is indebted to Aristotelianism and Moslem *kalam* philosophy, and clearly states the view held by most medieval philosophers that there was a distinction but no contradiction between reason and revealed religion. According to S. the Divine commandments fall into two categories: ethical commandments, which conform to reason and would be observed even without revelation and ceremonial commandments which have the authority of revelation only. S.'s definitions of God and His ATTRIBUTES influenced philosophers and mystics (e.g. the ḤASIDEI ASHKENAZ).

SABBATAI TZEVI, see **SHABBETAI TZEVI**

SABBATAIANISM, see **SHABBETAI TZEVI**

SABBATH: The weekly day of rest, observed from sunset on Friday until nightfall Saturday. It has been suggested that the biblical S. displays certain similarities to the Babylonian *shappatu*, but the connection is a dubious one, and the origin of this institution remains obscure. According to Gen. 2:1-3 the S. was established as a day of sanctity and blessing on the seventh day of creation; the commandment in the DECALOGUE. "Remember the S. day, to keep it holy" (Exod. 20:8) refers to this first S. of creation. Although the institution of the S. is also of paramount social significance, its primary purpose is strictly religious; it is "a S. unto the Lord, thy God", and serves as an eternal reminder that God is the creator and ruler of the universe, and that man who has been granted dominion over creation must not regard it as his own domain but administer it in accordance with the will of God as manifested in His Law. The S. is referred to (Exod. 31:16-17) as a symbol of the COVENANT between God and Israel (for that reason the TEPHILLIN, being also a symbol of the Divine covenant, are dispensed with on the S.), and as a sign commemorating both the creation and the exodus. The public desecration of the S. is punishable by death according to biblical law (cf. Num. 15:32-6) and was held by the rabbis to be a sin equal to idolatry. The holiness of the day is expressed primarily by the prohibition against doing any work. In positive terms, S. observance means a 24-hour period of rest and leisure to be devoted to prayer, study, and relaxation; in negative terms it means the abstention from all work, i.e., the renunciation by man of that dominion over the rest of creation which he enjoys during the "six days of work". The activities forbidden on the S. conform to certain criteria specified by rabbinic law, which enumerates 39 principal types of "work" (each of which is further subdivided). Since the lighting of fires and cooking are among these forbidden actions, the preparations of the festive S. meals must be made in advance (cf. the biblical precedent in Exod. 13:22-24). The observance of this prohibition subsequently gave rise to a variety of special pre-cooked S. dishes. The suspension of all trade and business activities on the S. was enforced by Nehemiah (Neh. 13:14-22) after a period of some laxity with regard to these rules. At the time of the Maccabean revolt, observance of the S. was so strict that Jewish warriors preferred to be killed rather than offer resistance on that day; a rule, however, was later promulgated that preservation of life overrides the observance of the S. (see DANGER). The scriptural reference for this *halakhah* was taken to be Exod. 31:14, "for it (viz. the S.) is holy unto you", implying that "the S. is given unto you; you are not to be delivered unto the S." (*Yoma* 85b). Essentially the S. is a day of physical and spiritual joy, to be honored by festive food and dress and the kindling of lights. The rabbis referred to the commandment "Remember the S. day, to keep it holy" to establish the rule that the sanctity of the S. must be pronounced over a cup of wine both at the inception (KIDDUSH) and termination (HAVDALAH) of the day in order to emphasize its distinctiveness from weekdays (*Pes.* 106a). The obligation to light a special LAMP or special CANDLES on S. eve (*Shab.* 25b) devolves upon the housewife, who pronounces a special blessing on the occasion. For the distinctive liturgy of the day, see SABBATH PRAYERS. In homiletic and mystical literature the S. is interpreted as a symbol for the messianic age or the World to Come. S. observance has been one of the most distinctive features of Jewish life, and its rôle in Jewish history has aptly been summed up in the saying, "More than that Israel has kept the S., it is the S. that has kept Israel". See also ERUV; MELAVVEH MALKAH; ONEG SABBATH; SABBATH PRAYERS; SABBATHS, SPECIAL; ZEMIROT.

SABBATH PRAYERS: As far as their basic structure is concerned, the prayers recited on SABBATH do not differ from those of other days, except that the AMIDAH consists of only seven benedictions and that in addition to the three regular daily prayers a fourth — MUSAPH — is added as on festivals. On the other hand, there are many additional psalms and poetic compositions in the S.P. and in the morning the SHAHARIT prayer is followed by the READING OF THE LAW. On Friday evenings, MAARIV is preceded by *kabbalat shabbat* ("the reception of the Sabbath"), a ceremony which consists in most rites of a number of psalms (among them Ps. 92, the "Sabbath psalm") and the hymn LEKHA DODI. The BENEDICTIONS before and after the SHEMA are in most rites today the same as on weekdays, except for a different conclusion to *hashkiveinu* and the addition of Exod. 31:16-17. The Sabbath *amidah,* too, does not contain the series of petitions prescribed for weekdays; one of the reasons suggested for this omission is that the requests for material blessings (health, sustenance, etc.) are liable to remind the worshiper of his wants and troubles and thus impair the enjoyment of the Sabbath. The intermediate benedictions of the *amidah,* which is devoted to the "sanctification of the day" (*kedushat ha-yom*), open differently in each Sabbath service, though the conclusion is always the same ("Blessed... who sanctifies the Sabbath"). During *Maariv,* the opening *atta kiddashta* ("Thou hast sanctified"), followed by Gen. 2:1-3, emphasizes the Sabbath of Creation. In *Shaharit,* the opening *yismah Mosheh* ("Moses rejoiced"), followed by Exod. 31:16-17, refers to the revelation on Sinai; in MINHAH, the opening *atta ehad* ("Thou art One") evokes the "perfect rest and peace" of messianic times. Taken together, these three benedictions express three different aspects of the Sabbath — as a commemoration of creation and revelation and as a symbol of future redemption. In the *Musaph* prayer the intermediate benediction of the *Ashkenazi* rite opens with *tikkanta Shabbat* ("Thou hast instituted the Sabbath") — a paragraph whose words are arranged in reverse alphabetical order. In *Maariv,* the *amidah* is followed by the recital of Gen. 2:1-3. The reader then repeats aloud a summary of the *amidah* (MAGEN AVOT) in a single benediction. It is customary to read the second chapter of Mishnah *Shabbat* (BA-MEH MADLIKIN), and in many congregations KIDDUSH is also recited by the reader. At home, *kiddush* precedes the meal, and the latter is accompanied by the singing of ZEMIROT (Sabbath songs). During *Shaharit* the PESUKEI DE-ZIMRA are said in extended form and are followed by NISHMAT. YOTZER is enlarged by *piyyutim,* which combine the Sabbath motif with the prayer text. The *amidah* is followed by the Reading of the Law and HAPHTARAH; the *Torah* scroll is taken out and returned to the ARK with great ceremony, including various prayers not used on weekdays. Then follows *Musaph.* Before the morning meal *kiddush* must again be recited. For *Minhah* there is again a short Reading of the Law; it is customary after *Minhah* to read (in summer) one of the chapters of Mishnah *Avot* ("Sayings of the Fathers") or (in winter) a collection of psalms (Ps. 104 and the "songs of ascent", Ps. 120-134). Upon the termination of the Sabbath, *Maariv* is recited as on weekdays and is followed by HAVDALAH.

SABBATH, THE GREAT, see **SHABBAT HA-GADOL**

SABBATH LIGHTS, see **LAMP, SABBATH; KINDLING OF THE LIGHTS**

SABBATH SOUL, see **NESHAMAH YETERAH**

SABBATHS, SPECIAL: Four Sabbaths between the end of the month of *Shevat* and *Nisan* 1 are each named after the additional reading from the Pentateuch which replaces the ordinary weekly MAPHTIR. (1) *Shekalim*: On or before *Adar* 1, Exod. 30:11-16 is read; this passage contains the commandment to give an offering of half a shekel (in Second Temple times this 'tax" was collected at the beginning of *Adar*). (2) *Zakhor*: Deut. 25:17-19 is read on the Sabbath before *Purim* as it contains the admonition to "remember (*zakhor*) what Amalek did unto you" (HAMAN — the *Purim* villain — is held by rabbinic tradition to have been a descendant of Amalek). (3) *Parah*: On the Sabbath before *Ha-Hodesh* (see 4) the chapter dealing with the RED HEIFER (Num. 19:1-22) is read as a reminder that the approaching Passover sacrifice requires each person to be in a state of ritual purity. (4) *Ha-Ḥodesh*: Read on or before *Nisan* 1 as a reminder of the approach of Passover (Exod. 12:1-20). These four Sabbaths are known as *arba parashot* ("four Bible portions"). The Sabbath directly before Passover is called *Shabbat ha-Gadol* ("the Great Sabbath" — the origin of this name is in doubt). Three Sabbaths are named after the first word of the prophetic reading for the respective days; Sabbath *Ḥazon* (Is. 1:1; read before *Av* 9); *Sabbath Naḥamu* (Is. 40:1; the Sabbath following *Av* 9); and Sabbath *Shuvah* (Hos. 14:2; preceding the Day of Atonement). It was customary for the rabbi to deliver a sermon on *Shabbat ha-Gadol* and on *Shabbat Shuvah* (see HOMILETICS). Other specially-named Sabbaths are Sabbath *Bereshit* (when the annual reading of the Pentateuch cycle is commenced), Sabbath *Shirah* (when the Song of Moses in Exod. 15 is recited); and Sabbath *Ḥol ha-Moed* (a Sabbath that falls on an intermediate day of a festival).

SABBATIANISM, SABBATIANS, see **DONMEH; SHABBETAI TZEVI**

SABBATICAL YEAR (Heb. *shemittah*, or *sheviit*): Every seventh year is called a year of *shemittah*, when "the land must keep Sabbath unto the Lord" (Lev. 25:2). During this year land must lie fallow; whatever grows on it is designated ownerless property (*hephker*) to which all enjoy equal rights with the owner. It is forbidden to trade with produce of the *shemittah* year which, in its ownerless state, is also free from tithes. At the end of the year all debts are remitted (Lev. 25; Exod. 23:10-11; Deut. 15:1-3). The precept of the s.y. is meant to emphasize the conditional nature of the possession of the Holy Land by the Jewish people ("for the land is Mine... you are strangers and sojourners with Me", Lev. 25:23); the land is the gift of God, granted to the people on condition that they abide by His Law. Failure to observe *shemittah* was traditionally regarded as one of the causes of exile (Lev. 26:34; *Shab.* 33a). The laws of the s.y. are discussed in the talmudic treatise SHEVIIT and in later rabbinical literature. *Shemittah* constitutes a problem for Orthodox Jews in the State of Israel. The Israeli rabbinate permits the land to be temporarily sold to a non-Jew and worked during the *shemittah* year. The actual yearly reckoning of the s.y. is no longer certain, but Orthodox tradition has agreed on a certain count; a s.y. will be observed in Israel, for instance, in 5747 (1986-7). See also DISPENSATION; JUBILEE YEAR; PROSBUL; TITHES.

SABORAIM, see **SAVORAIM**

SACRIFICE OF ISAAC, see **AKEDAH**

SACRIFICES: The Hebrew term for sacrifice, ***korban*** (from *karav* "draw near"), originally denoted that which is brought near, i.e., offered, to God; a later, homiletical interpretation also suggested "that which is meant to bring man near to God". S. as an expression of worship are first mentioned in the Bible in the story of Cain and Abel, and again in the accounts of Noah and the patriarchs. The story of the exodus mentions the sacrifice of the paschal lamb, and with the erection of the portable Sanctuary in the wilderness, the Pentateuch (particularly Exod. 29 ff. and Lev.) prescribes regular s. of various types for all occasions. Animals could be brought from the following clean species: the bullock and the ox, the cow and the calf; the sheep (male or female) and the lamb; the goat (male or female) and the kid; turtle-doves and pigeons. Other sacrificial offerings were made of wine, and various kinds of spices for incense. There were different types and classes of s., such as sin- and guilt-offerings to atone for certain transgressions, peace-offerings (thanks and votive), private s. brought by individual worshipers and public s. (e.g. the daily morning and evening s.) offered by the priests in the Temple in behalf of the whole nation, holocaust-offerings (when the whole animal was burned on the altar), and s. whose meat was shared both by the offerer and the priests. An essential part of the sacrificial ritual was the sprinkling or pouring out of the blood of the animal on or near the altar. S. were accompanied by meal-offerings, libations, and, where appropriate, by confessional prayers (see Num. 5:7; Lev. 16:21). Characteristic of the history of the Israelite cult was the struggle for the centralization of all sacrificial worship at the Temple in Jerusalem, especially as s. at local HIGH PLACES were easily contaminated by Canaanite paganism. This struggle was only intermittently successful (e.g. in the reign of King JOSIAH). The rabbinic theory was that prior to the building of the Tabernacle in the wilderness, the Israelites had been allowed to make their offerings on a *bamah* (High Place), but that this had been forbidden during the 39 years when the Tabernacle existed in the wilderness. When the Israelites entered the Holy Land and reached Gilgal, where they had a temporary sanctuary for a period of 14 years, *bamot* were again permitted. With the erection of the Sanctuary at Shiloh which remained in existence 369 years, *bamot* were once more prohibited. After the destruction of the Sanctuary at Shiloh in the time of Eli, when sacrificial worship was transferred first to Nob and after Saul's destruction of Nob to Gibeon for a period of 57 years, *bamot* were again permitted. They were finally forbidden when the Temple was built in Jerusalem (*Zev.* 18b, 112b). Originally every animal slaughter had a sacrificial character. With the prohibition of all s. outside Jerusalem, the concept of the PROFANE slaughter and consumption of meat, hitherto unknown, had to be introduced (cf. Deut. 12:20-27). Some of the prophets were less concerned with the abolition of the High Places than with the sacrificial cult as such, which they denounced in harsh words. There are scholars who take this condemnation of s. in a literal sense; traditional interpretation on the other hand takes it to refer to the external, mechanical performance of ritual unaccompanied by penitence, genuine piety, and a contrite heart. All s. ceased after the destruction of the Second Temple, and PRAYER — which had existed long before and even formed part of the Temple ritual — became a "substitute for s." Opinions differ as to the religious and moral value of s. S., together with prayer, have been among the basic expressions of worship since the very dawn of human history, but precisely for that reason it has also been argued that s. belong to a more primitive stage of religious evolution. MAIMONIDES thought that the biblical s. were instituted by way of a compromise, since the people could not have grasped the idea of a religion without s., and that they were intended to wean the people away from the corresponding idolatrous practices. NAHMANIDES and others insist on the moral and spiritual symbolism of the details of the ritual, as well as on the significance of the sacrificial idea as such. Whereas the Orthodox prayer books retain the prayers for the restoration of the sacrificial cult in the rebuilt Temple, Reform usage has omitted or rephrased these passages in keeping with the conception of s. as a once adequate but now outmoded form of worship. See also BURNT-OFFERING; FIRST FRUITS; FREEWILL-OFFERING; GUILT-OFFERING; LIBATIONS; MEAL-OFFERING; PEACE-OFFERING; SIN-OFFERING; TAMID; TRESPASS-OFFERING; WHOLE-OFFERING.

SACRILEGE: The profane use of an object dedicated to a holy purpose. One who inadvertently makes use of or derives benefit from property dedicated to the Sanctuary is required to make restitution, pay a fine, and sacrifice a TRESPASS-OFFERING. If benefit from such property has been derived deliberately, then beside restitution the offender also incurs corporal punishment; neither the fine nor the offering, however, are exacted from him. Stealing a vessel used for the Temple service constitutes one of the three instances in which zealots are allowed to take the law into their own hands and put the offender to death if caught during the commission of the crime (Mishnah *Sanh.* 9:6). The concept of s. (in Heb. *ḥillul ha-kodesh*) is further extended to include any desecration of holiness either in the Temple (e.g. in the case of a High Priest contracting a forbidden marriage) or, more generally, in breaking the Sabbath laws. The punishment for s. is, in most cases, excommunication or death "at the hands of Heaven".

SADDUCEES (Heb. *tzedukim*): A Judean sect which flourished during the last two centuries of the Second Temple. While JOSEPHUS and later rabbinic literature describe the S. as essentially a religious sect, defined by specific theological tenets and ceremonial practices, some historians suggest that the differences between the S. and their opponents the PHARISEES derived from social and political considerations. The origin of the name too is uncertain, but is possibly derived from the priestly house of ZADOK, the ancestors of the HASMONEANS. This would account for the close connection of the S. both with the Hasmonean dynasty and with the Temple hierarchy, as well as with the priestly and aristocratic classes in general; the Pharisees for their part were more concerned with developing the Law and influencing the masses. Feeling ran high between the two parties and more than once led to massacres and civil war, particularly in the reign of Alexander Yannai (103-76 B.C.E.). According to Josephus the distinctive Sadducean doctrine was a rejection of the ORAL LAW, but both he and the Talmud record several other specific differences between S. and Pharisees on ritual, legal, and theological issues. Thus the S. held that the Feast of Weeks always had to fall on a Sunday. They also insisted that the High Priest enter the Holy of Holies in the Temple on the Day of Atonement with the incense burning on a censer. When Pharisaic influence increased under the reign of Queen Salome Alexandra (76-67), they exacted an oath from the High Priest binding him to perform the ritual according to Pharisaic rules, i.e., place the glowing coals in the censer only after having entered the Holy of Holies. The S. also allowed individuals to finance the daily public sacrifices, in contrast to the Pharisees who insisted that the sacrifice be offered out of the *shekalim* collected from a tax imposed on all Jewry. In contrast to Pharisaic penal law, the S. held the master responsible for damages committed by his slaves, and they tended toward severity in meting out punishment to criminals. The S. objected to many rituals and ceremonies established or countenanced by the Pharisees, such as washing the hands before meals or the water-festivals on the Feast of Tabernacles, nor did the S. recognize the validity of the *eruv*, a legal provision by which objects could be carried from one's home into a common court on the Sabbath. Conversely, the S. had their own legal and ceremonial traditions and institutions which the Pharisees rejected. Theologically the S. rejected the doctrines of resurrection and the immortality of the soul as well as belief in angels. According to Josephus the S. also denied

Divine providence in the affairs of man. Whatever their origins, the S. emerge into view as a clearly defined party only during the Hasmonean Period. This was a time when the contrast became more sharply polarized between the non-priestly, popular, "rabbinic" type of Judaism which had been developed since Ezra and which was close to the life of the mass of peasants and artisans, and the more conservative tendencies of a powerful and wealthy priesthood, whose interests were allied with those of the aristocracy and the landowners. With the destruction of the Temple the S. lost their social and ideological center and no more is heard of them.

SAFED: Small town in Galilee which became the center of remarkable literary and spiritual activity in the 16th cent. It was probably chosen as a place of residence on account of its proximity to Meron, the traditional burial place of the *tanna* R. SIMEON BAR YOHAI to whom the authorship of the ZOHAR was ascribed. Many kabbalists and talmudists (e.g. Cordovero, Joseph Karo, etc.) were concentrated in S., and it was from here that the new Kabbalah associated with the name of Isaac LURIA spread. S. was also the scene of an attempt by Jacob BERAV to renew rabbinic ORDINATION.

SALANTER, ISRAEL (1810-1883): Founder of the MUSAR MOVEMENT. Though his real name was Israel Lipkin, he became known as Israel Salanter from the town Salant where he married and studied. Appointed head of a *yeshivah* in Vilna in 1840, he was involved in a fierce controversy with R. Mordecai Melzer of that town who opposed his systems of study; S. was forced to leave. He then established a *yeshivah* in Kovno, but left in 1857 to lead a wandering life, traveling to Germany and Paris. His main innovation was the establishment of "MUSAR houses" where both professional scholars and earnestly devout people would retire for one or more hours each day for "examination of conscience" and the study of *musar* writings. Under the influence of S. and his disciples the study of *musar* was accepted as part of the curriculum of the Lithuanian *yeshivot*. S.'s *musar* writings were collected by his disciple R. Isaac Blaser (R. Isaac of Petersburg) and published under the title *Or Yisrael*.

SALE: To become legally binding, any s. or purchase requires a *kinyan* (see PROPERTY). An oral agreement to buy or sell an article is not binding, and either party may retract. If the vendee pays money to the vendor after an agreement for the s. of movable property has been reached, the vendor still has the legal right to void the s. if the formal *kinyan* has not yet taken place. However it is considered morally dishonest to retract under such circumstances. A s. is effected in cases of immovable property by payment of the full price or by writing and signing the deed of s.; for movable property, an action of ownership (e.g pulling or raising the object) is required.

SALT: S. as a preservative was a symbol of the eternal covenant between God and His people (Num. 18:19; II Chron. 13:5). All sacrifices and meal-offerings had to be salted prior to being placed on the altar (Lev. 2:13); the s. used for this purpose was stored in a special place known as the Salt Chamber on the north side of the Temple court (*Mid.* 5:3). After the Temple Period, a table at which meals were taken came to be regarded as symbolizing the altar, and it therefore became customary to place s. on the table at each mealtime, and to dip the bread into s. after making the HA-MOTZI blessing. According to Jewish DIETARY LAWS, all MEAT must be thoroughly salted for one hour after having been soaked in water in order to be drained of blood and become permissible for consumption.

SALVATION: Acts whereby God delivers His people from distress, and the resultant state of such deliverance. The term (Heb. *yeshuah,* also *teshuah*) occurs very frequently in biblical and liturgical texts (cf. Gen. 49:18; Exod. 14:13, 30) and particularly in Isaiah (cf. 45:17, "Israel is saved by the Lord with an everlasting s.") and the Psalms, but almost always refers to deliverance from concrete and specific sufferings, oppression, exile, etc. It is not used in connection with the remission of sin, ATONEMENT, and the like. A favorite image is that of the "sprouting" or "flourishing" of s. (cf. the second and the fifteenth benedictions of the AMIDAH, "who causest the horn of s. to flourish"), connected with the idea of the messianic sprouting of the "shoot of David". See also REDEMPTION.

SAMAEL: The prince of demons in Jewish folklore, hence identical with SATAN. His name occurs in the Slavonic Book of ENOCH, and together with his wife LILITH, he plays an important rôle in popular legend and in kabbalistic literature. As the evil one, S. acts as seducer, accuser, and destroyer as well as the guardian angel of the gentiles. His antagonist is the archangel MICHAEL, the guardian angel of Israel. PIRKEI DE-R. ELIEZER describes S.'s initiative in planning Adam's fall, his descent from heaven, and his use of the serpent to seduce Eve. He acted as the accuser against the Children of Israel to persuade God not to redeem them from the bondage of Egypt (*Exod. Rab.* 21:7), and it was he who was sent by God to take the soul of Moses (*Deut. Rab.* end). He continues throughout history to act as the accuser of Israel, except on the Day of Atonement, when his power is invalid.

SAMARIA (Heb. *Shomron*): Capital of the northern Kingdom of Israel. It was founded by King Omri who had bought the site from Shemer (I Kings 16:24). A sanctuary for Baal was erected there by Ahab (*ibid.* 16:32), and the luxury and corruption of S. were the subject of rebuke by many of the prophets. The capital was conquered by the Assyrians during the reign of Hosea after a siege of 3 years (II Kings 17:1-7) in 721 B.C.E.; the Israelite population was deported and replaced by foreign colonists (see SAMARITANS). A Greek colony after the time of Alexander the Great, S. was destroyed by John Hyrcanus but rebuilt by the Romans, presented to Herod, and named Sebaste; the remains of the rebuilt city are still extant (now in the Kingdom of Jordan).

SAMARITANS: The population of SAMARIA after the destruction of the Northern Kingdom in 721 B.C.E. Known in Hebrew as *Shomeronim* (cf. II Kings 17:29), or, in the Talmud, as *Kutim* ("Cutheans"), they call themselves *Benei Yisrael* ("Children of Israel") or *Shamerim* ("Observant Ones"). According to their own tradition, the S. are the descendants of that part of the Israelite population that remained in the country after the deportation of the ten tribes by Sargon II of Assyria. The biblical account describes them as descendants of the heathen colonists from various parts of Mesopotamia, especially Cuthan, whom Sargon II settled in the depopulated Samaria. The heterogeneous ethnic character of the new population (II Kings 17:24) also produced a heterogeneous syncretistic religion which provided fertile soil for friction, both political and religious, with the Judean exiles returning from Babylonia. According to the biblical account (Neh. 6), the S. wished to participate in the rebuilding of the Temple but were rebuffed by the Jewish leadership. The resultant breach between the two groups developed into a permanent schism after Sanballat's son-in-law, a priest at Jerusalem, was expelled (432 B.C.E.) for marrying the daughter of a Samaritan (Neh. 13:28; Josephus, *Ant.* 11:8). In the 4th cent., by permission of Alexander the Great, the S. built a temple on Mt. GERIZIM; this was destroyed by John Hyrcanus c. 128 B.C.E. A second Samaritan temple was destroyed by the emperor Zeno in 486 C.E. The Samaritan religion has its origin in the Israelite traditions of the Northern Kingdom and resembles Sadducean Judaism (see SADDUCEES) in many respects; hence also its resemblance to KARAISM, which likewise exhibits certain Sadducean features. The S. believe in (1) God, who is unique; (2) Moses, the only prophet; (3) the *Torah*; (4) the sanctity of Mt. Gerizim; (5) future reward and punishment, a concept linked with the advent of the messianic restorer (*taheb*), who will end the period of *fanuta* (God's displeasure) and introduce that of *rahuta* (Divine favor). The Samaritans observe seven biblical festivals — *Pesaḥ, Matzot, Shavuot, Yom Teruah, Yom Kippur, Sukkot,* and *Moed Shemini* — and two minor feasts — *Tzimmut* ("conjunction of") *Pesaḥ* (*Shevat* 15) and *Tzimmut Sukkot* (*Av* 15). In some respects the rabbis regarded the S. as Jews (e.g. *Ber.* 7:1), and held that "when the S. adopt a commandment they observe it more scrupulously than do the Jews" (*Ḥul.* 4a). But in respect of marriage and other laws they are treated like non-Jews. Talmudic law with regard to the S. is summarized in tractate *Kutim.* The S. recognize as Holy Scripture only the Pentateuch, which they have preserved in a pre-Masoretic Hebrew recension, written in archaic script (developed from Phoenician writing). The addition, at the end of the Decalogue (Exod. 20:17; Deut. 5:21), of a commandment to build an altar and to sacrifice on Mt. Gerizim (cf. Deut. 27:6 ff.) and the substitution of Gerizim for Ebal in Deut. 27:4 are obvious interpolations. There is also a TARGUM (4th cent.) to the Pentateuch composed in the original Samaritan tongue, a dialect of Western Aramaic. Some of the early liturgical compositions (*dephter*) and midrashic writings (e.g. the *Memer Marka*) are likewise in Aramaic. After the Moslem conquest of Palestine (632), the S. gradually adopted Arabic as their vernacular (except for prayers, for which they continued to use Hebrew), translating the Bible into Arabic (11th-12th cents.), and producing a considerable body of literature, mainly religious, in that language. The history of the S. under Moslem rule is one of persecution and decline. The group, which in 1955 had dwindled to about 250 in Nablus (Shechem) and 70 in Holon, near Tel Aviv, and which seemed to be dying out, has shown some signs of recovery.

SAMARITAN PENTATEUCH: A recension (not a version) of the Hebrew text of the Pentateuch, written in an archaic script evolved from the old Hebrew (Phoenician) writing. Its antiquity is attested to, *inter alia,* by the shape of the letters as well as the fact that a dot is placed after each word. Possibly the S.P. dates back, in its primary form, to the time of Josiah, but it has been much altered in the course of the generations, and the surviving mss. belong mostly to the 12th cent. It nevertheless constitutes the earliest external witness to the Hebrew text. Although independent of Jewish tradition from the time of Nehemiah (c. 432 B.C.E.; cf. Neh. 13:23-31), it substantially corroborates the masoretic recension, while containing some 6,000 variant readings. Most of the divergences are due to scribal errors, ignorance, or a desire to facilitate the comprehension of difficult texts and to harmonize related passages. Doctrinal reasons account for other emendations (e.g. the substitution of Gerizim for Ebal in Deut. 27:4). But a residual number of variants are of critical value, especially where these agree with the Septuagint. There exist Aramaic and Arabic translations of the S.P.; but a Greek version is known chiefly from patristic references.

SAMBATYON: Name of the legendary "Sabbath River". The Pseudo-Jonathan Targum to Exod. 34:10 identifies it with the River Gozan across which the Ten TRIBES were led into exile (II Kings 17:6). According to legend it is a mighty torrential river, not of water but of stones and rubble which tumble down during six days of the week and prevent the exiles from returning to their land; only on the Sabbath, when Jewish law prevents them from crossing, does the river rest. So widespread was the belief in the existence of this miraculous river that it is mentioned by Josephus (*Wars* 7, 5, 1) as having been seen by Titus, and it is referred to by R. Akiva in his discussions with the Roman general Turnus Rufius as irrefutable proof of the Divine sanctity of the Sabbath (*Sanh.* 65b). The 9th cent. adventurer Eldad Ha-Dani claimed that only the "sons of Moses" dwelt beyond it. During the Middle Ages attempts to discover the Lost Tribes generally began with a search for the S.

SAMSON BEN ABRAHAM OF SENS (c. 1150-1230): French TOSAPHIST, compiler of the standard *tosaphot* to the tractates *Shabbat* and *Menaḥot.* S. also wrote commentaries on the Mishnah orders, *Zeraim* and *Toharot,* which lacked *gemara* in the Babylonian Talmud; the commentary on *Zeraim* frequently quotes the Palestinian Talmud to elucidate its points. In 1211, S. went to Palestine with a group of 300 rabbis from France and England, settling first in Jerusalem and later in Acre.

SAMUEL (11th cent. B.C.E.): Prophet and last of the Israelite JUDGES. Born to Hanna after many years of childlessness and in answer to fervent prayer, he was dedicated by her to serve in the sanctuary as a NAZIRITE. S. was therefore brought up at Shiloh by the High Priest, Eli. As a child, he received his first prophetic revelation which foretold the destruction of the House of Eli. After the Philistine victory at Aphek (where the ARK OF THE COVENANT was captured) and the death of Eli and his sons, S. became a leading national figure, acknowledged "from Dan to Beersheba" as a prophet and judge. Residing in Ramah, he stood at the head of several groups of prophets, tried to restore traditional religious worship, and judged cases in Israel on his regular circuit of the sacred towns of Bethel, Gilgal, and Mizpah. The need for greater national unity, emphasized by growing Philistine pressure, resulted, in S.'s old age, in the popular demand for a KING. S. considered the institution of monarchy as a breach of the original covenant according to which Israel was to have no king but God; in obedience to God's word, however, he anointed Saul as the first king of Israel. Relations with Saul deteriorated over the years and ended in complete break, whereupon S. anointed DAVID as Saul's successor. The Book of S. (originally third in the section of the BIBLE known as the Former Prophets) is now divided into two books which form a unit and contain an account of Israel's history from the end of the period of the Judges until David's old age. At the center of this formative period are the personalities of Samuel (whose death is related in I Sam. 28:3), Saul, and David. The chief purpose of the book is to describe the factors that led to the rise of the monarchy, to show the Divine roots of this institution, and to emphasize that the king, no less than his people, is bound by the terms of the Divine covenant and is subject to God's will. According to one talmudic view, the book (as well as the Books of Judges and Ruth) was written by Samuel himself. Modern scholars distinguish two or more historical sources, worked over by Deuteronomistic redactors.

SAMUEL, MIDRASH: A late Midrash to the Book of Samuel, first quoted by Rashi in the 11th cent. in his commentary to I Sam. 2:30. It consists of aggadic commentaries taken from earlier midrashic compilations and arranged in sequence by the collator. It is of Palestinian origin. Another book of the same name by Samuel Uzeda, a disciple of Isaac Luria, is a commentary on *Avot.*

SAMUEL (3rd cent. C.E.): Babylonian *amora*; younger contemporary of RAV. He was already established as a *dayyan* in NEHARDEA when Rav returned from Palestine. The Talmud rules that in matters of civil law S.'s opinion is to be followed; his dictum "The law of the land is binding on Jews who live there" (*Git.* 10b) became of far-reaching importance for Jewish civil law in the Diaspora. S. was a distinguished astronomer who composed a fixed CALENDAR, though out of respect for the Palestinian gaonate he refrained from circulating it. His discussions with Rav laid the foundation for the Babylonian Talmud.

SAMUEL BEN HOPHNI: *Gaon* of Sura, 997-1013. S. translated the Pentateuch into Arabic and wrote a Bible commentary marked by a literal (*peshat*) and rationalist approach. He was the author of responsa in Hebrew, Aramaic, and Arabic, halakhic works (in Arabic), and polemics directed against the Karaites, in which he upheld the immutable nature of the *Torah.*

SAMUEL BEN MEIR (*Rashbam*; c. 1080-after 1158): French commentator on the Bible and Talmud; grandson and pupil of Rashi and brother of Rabbenu Tam. His commentary on the Pentateuch is based on a literal exposition (*peshat*) of the meaning and is marked by erudition and clarity of thought and expression. In it S. made use of his extensive knowledge of Targum, Mishnah, and Talmud as well as of Hebrew linguistics. His completion of his grandfather's Talmud commentary (e.g. in *Bava Batra, Pesahim*) is printed in all editions. S. was also a noted TOSAPHIST.

SAMUEL HA-KATAN (late 1st cent. C.E.): *Tanna.* None of S.'s *halakhot* is recorded, but he was well-known for his gentleness, humility, and pacifism. At the request of the patriarch Gamaliel II he composed (probably c. 80-90 C.E.) the *birkat ha-minim* (*u-le-malshinim*) which was inserted as a 19th benediction in the AMIDAH (*Ber.* 28a). It has been suggested that the original version of this prayer, which is directed against Jewish heretics (MINIM), was specifically worded so that Judeo-Christians, who at that time still worshiped in synagogues, would henceforth be unable to participate in Jewish prayers. This move, in reaction to the teachings of Paul, would have led to the final separation between Judaism and Christianity.

SANCTIFICATION: S. can mean: 1) the religious discipline and the process of spiritual growth by which a person increases in HOLINESS (cf. the talmudic saying "If a man sanctify himself a little, he becomes sanctified much; if he sanctify himself below, he becomes sanctified from on high"); 2) CONSECRATION usually by a vow, of objects, persons, or specific times, which are thereby "set apart" (*kadosh*) and made subject to special ritual rules; 3) the formal acknowledgment of the character of sanctity attaching to persons or times. Thus the immanent "holiness" of the Sabbath, festivals, the priestly order, and the Jewish people, are liturgically acknowledged by benedictions which give thanks to God "who has sanctified" them (see also KIDDUSH: NAZIR). The liturgical acknowledgment of God's holiness is known as KEDUSHAH, while "S. of the Name" is the acknowledgment of God's holiness through martyrdom. Examples of s. by consecration are *kiddush ha-hodesh* (see NEW MONTH, ANNOUNCEMENT OF), the DEDICATION of an animal or inanimate object to the Temple, or the consecration of something for religious use whereby it ceases to be "profane" and becomes reserved for a sacred purpose. In some cases a consecrated object can revert to its previous state by redemption. The legal and practical corollaries of the action of s. are well illustrated by the laws of priesthood. The priest is invested with an inherent sanctity as a result of his priestly descent ("They shall be holy unto the Lord their God", Lev. 21:6), and has the duty to preserve this sanctity ("and they shall not profane the name of their God", *loc. cit.*). For this reason they are forbidden to contaminate themselves with the dead. It is solely on account of this duty to preserve unsullied their state of sanctity and transmit it to their descendants that a priest is forbidden to marry a divorcee or a convert, since the offspring of such a union would be profane i.e., disqualified from the priesthood. In moral and ascetic literature the term signifies the human effort as well as the Divine assistance that lead to the higher stages of spiritual perfection.

SANCTIFICATION OF THE MONTH, see **NEW MONTH, ANNOUNCEMENT OF; NEW MOON**

SANCTIFICATION OF THE NAME, see **MARTYRDOM**

SANCTUARY, see **ASYLUM; TEMPLE**

SANDAK, SANDEK: Person given the honor of holding the child on his knees during the CIRCUMCISION ceremony. The word is of Greek origin, derived either from *syndicus*, meaning "patron" or — more probably — *synteknos*, "companion to the father". The word is found in the Talmud, though in the prayer book the *s.* is called *baal berit ha-milah.*

SANDALFON: Angel. The name is Greek (and means "co-brother") but it does not occur in non-Jewish sources. S. figures prominently in the ancient mysticism of the Divine chariot (*merkavah*), where he is identified with the *ophan*, the "wheel" of Ezek. 1:15, and is said to stand "on earth but his head reaches to the heavens, being higher than his fellow angels by a distance of 500 years' journey". S. stands behind the Divine chariot weaving crowns of prayer for his Maker (*Hag.* 13b). The name may be due to his identification as a brother of METATRON. He figures prominently in kabbalistic AMULETS. See ANGELOLOGY.

SANDEK, see **SANDAK**

SANHEDRIN: Term derived from the Greek and meaning council court. The exact nature and functions of this body, which flourished during the latter part of the Second Temple Period, are not quite clear, particularly as the information contained in the rabbinic sources (which are in part later than the S.) and in the Greek texts (JOSEPHUS, NEW TESTAMENT) is conflicting. According to the Talmud, the S. par excellence, i.e., the "Great S." in Jerusalem, consisting of seventy-one members, met in the Hall of Hewn Stones in the Temple. The inferior courts of twenty-three members were known as Small Sanhedrins. Small Sanhedrins functioned in every city or region, while the Great S. was largely a legislative body as well as court of appeal to which the inferior courts submitted queries. The Small S. of Jerusalem consisted of at least twenty-three members out of the seventy-one which comprised the Great S. The judicial function of the Great S. was confined to the trying of national figures, such as the king and the High Priest, and to cases involving definition of the Law, as in the case of a false prophet. The S. was also an educative body, attended by students who even participated in its deliberations. Some of the trials described in the gospels are reported to have taken place in the home of the High Priest and thus not in the Temple; this may imply that the reference here is not to the Great S. but to a special political council court, set up by the High Priest in his capacity of head of the state. This body, acting as a grand jury, assembled the facts concerning the charges against Jesus and presented them to the Roman governor, Pontius Pilate. In the early days of the Hasmonean dynasty the Great S., consisting of Pharisees, probably shared the government with the king. The Great S. was headed by two senior officials — the NASI and the AV BET DIN. John Hyrcanus later broke with the Pharisees, expelled them from the S., and annulled their religious rulings. They were reinstated only after the death of Alexander Yannai, when his widow, Salome Alexandra, held the reins of government. Under Herod and his successors (all of them Roman appointees) the authority of the Great S. was confined to purely religious affairs. After the destruction of Jerusalem in 70 C.E., the name of S. designated the assemblies of leading Jewish scholars which functioned as a religious legislature first in Yavneh (in Judea) and subsequently in Usha, Shepharam, Bet Shearim, Sepphoris, and Tiberias (in Galilee) up to the 5th cent. Outside Palestine, the authority of the S. depended entirely upon its voluntary acceptance by the people. This was achieved through the intensive educational activity of Jewish scholars, who frequently undertook journeys to distant countries in order to disseminate Jewish knowledge and inspiration. The S. continued not only to interpret the Law but also to issue *gezerot* (decrees) and *takkanot* (ordinances) to meet the needs of the times.The question of a possible renewal of the institution of the S. has been debated at various times; see ORDINATION. The name S. was also given to the rabbinical assembly convened by Napoleon in Paris (1807) in order to approve Jewish adherence to his civil code.

SANHEDRIN: Fourth tractate of the Mishnah order of NEZIKIN with *gemara* in both Talmuds. It deals with the authority of all types of law courts; legal procedure, particularly in criminal cases (investigation of witnesses, judgments, decisions, etc.); and CAPITAL PUNISHMENT (when and how applicable). Other subjects include the privileges of the High Priest and king; the law of the rebellious son (Deut. 21:18 ff.) and the banned city (Deut. 13:13 ff.); and false prophets. The tenth chapter, which opens with the words "All Israel has a portion in the World to Come" (although it proceeds to list exceptions) deals with life after death and has been one of the main sources of rabbinic theology. The tractate MAKKOT may originally have formed part of the tractate S.

SARUG (or SARUK), ISRAEL (16th cent.): Italian kabbalist; one of the earliest propagandists of Lurianic Kabbalah. He claimed to be a disciple of Isaac LURIA and disseminated the latter's doctrines while giving them a distinctly quasi-Platonic turn of his own. His influence dominated the kabbalistic schools of Italy.

SASPORTAS, JACOB (17th cent.): Rabbi and kabbalist. He held rabbinical posts successively in his native North Africa, London (where he was the first HAHAM), Hamburg, and Amsterdam. When the Jewish world was swept with messianic expectation at the time of SHABBETAI TZEVI, S. was one of the few outstanding scholars who refused to be carried away by the general fervor and expectancy. He wrote a series of bitter letters against Sabbatianism and was one of the movement's leading opponents.

SATAN: The word S., probably meaning "adversary", occurs in the greater part of the Bible as a common noun and refers often to human antagonists (e.g. I Sam. 29:4; I Kings 5:18). There are, however, intimations even in pre-exilic biblical literature of a malign influence, variously described, that seeks to mislead human beings (e.g. I Kings 22:22). But in only three passages, all of them late, is S. depicted as an individualized superhuman being. In Zech. 3:1-2, he appears as accuser; in Job 1:2, he is the heavenly prosecutor (included among "the sons of God") who tests Job's piety on the rack of affliction; in I Chron. 21:1 he functions as seducer, taking over a negative rôle originally ascribed to the Lord (II Sam. 24:1). In all these passages S., though hostile to man, remains obedient to God (cf. Is. 45:6-7). In the apocryphal and apocalyptic literature, however, and to an even greater degree in the New Testament, the concept of S., under Zoroastrian influence, evolves as the incarnation of evil and the supreme enemy of the Deity. He is the ruler of countless demons and his kingdom extends throughout the world. He is cast out from heaven (a misinterpretation of Is. 14:12), but continues with other fallen angels (cf. Gen. 6:1-4) to work evil upon earth. In tannaitic literature S. is rarely mentioned. It is the later, chiefly Babylonian, *aggadah* that enlarges the scope of his influence and activities. He is identified — among others — with ASMODEUS, SAMAEL (chief of the DEMONS), the evil inclination, and the angel of death. He first tempts, then accuses and slays. But monotheism has circumscribed his powers: on *Rosh ha-Shanah* he is confused by the *shophar*; on the Day of Atonement his authority is annulled. Ultimately he will be vanquished by the Messiah. Kabbalah gives even greater prominence to the concept of evil and uses a variety of synonyms for S. (e.g. *kelippah*, "evil shell"). There are also occasional allusions to S. in the liturgy, but these have the general connotation of "corrupting desires", and possess no doctrinal significance.

SAVORAIM (Heb. "expositors"): Title given to scholars and heads of the Babylonian ACADEMIES in the period following that of the AMORAIM and preceding that of the *geonim* (see GAON) (6th-7th cents.). While the *amoraim* were the authors of the *gemara*, interpreting the Mishnah and giving decisions on practical law, the *s.* merely expounded certain obscure passages in the Talmud and added their explanatory notes to the text of the Babylonian Talmud. They were also responsible for the final editing of the amoraic redaction of the Babylonian Talmud.

SAYINGS OF THE FATHERS, see **AVOT**

SCANDAL-MONGERING, see **LESHON HA-RA**

SCAPEGOAT, see **AZAZEL**

SCHECHTER, SOLOMON (1848-1915): Scholar and theologian; born in Rumania, he was in 1890-1902 lecturer in rabbinics at Cambridge (to where he brought the bulk of the Cairo GENIZAH), and thereafter in New York where he headed the JEWISH THEOLOGICAL SEMINARY and laid the groundwork for the CONSERVATIVE Movement. S. avoided broad programmatic statements and formal systems, but the philosophy of Judaism implicit in his scholarly as well as popular writings still provides a major part of the ideological foundation of Conservatism. Characteristic of his theology is a shift of emphasis from God, as a philosophical concept, to Israel, as a historical entity. According to S. revelation is manifest in tradition: the Scriptures reveal history, and it is in the history of the Jewish people that the raw material for any Jewish theology has to be found. S.'s most influential contribution to American Jewish life was his popularization of the concept of a "catholic (i.e., all-embracing) Israel", which was meant to provide a theoretical basis for the continuation of the Historical School's search for Jewish unity, without, however, providing definite criteria for determining which phenomena or groups actually formed part of this "catholic Israel" and which lay outside it. He maintained contact with Reform leaders, though continuing to criticize them. His writings include editions of rabbinic texts (*Avot de-Rabbi Natan*, Damascus Documents) and many essays on Jewish history and rabbinic theology.

SCHISMS, see **CONTROVERSIES, RELIGIOUS; MINIM**

SCHOOL, see **EDUCATION**

SCHREIBER, MOSES, see **SOPHER, MOSES**

SCIENCE: Systematic knowledge arrived at by observation, experiment, induction, logical deduction, etc. Different branches of s. recognize varying premises and require the use of different methods — hence also the usage that restricts the term s. to the natural and "exact" sciences. S. and religion have clashed in modern times, but the conflict is merely a modern variation of the medieval conflict between the spirit of rational enquiry and that of mute acceptance of traditional dogma. The conflict arises whenever contradictions are discovered between the findings or claims of s., and the real or alleged teachings of religion. Sometimes not only specific religious doctrines (e.g. the account of creation, the manner of the composition of Bible, etc.) are contested in the name of natural or historical s., but religion itself is turned into an object of rational enquiry (e.g. by psychology or sociology). Attempts to resolve the ensuing conflicts usually take the form of: 1) limiting the sphere of competence of science e.g., by pointing out the *a priori* character of its axiomatic assumptions or by showing that some of its claims are not "scientific" at all but philosophical; 2) limiting and defining the proper sphere of religious teaching, e.g. by distinguishing between what is held to be genuinely and essentially religious doctrine, and what is outmoded s. falsely claiming religious authority; 3) reinterpreting, by various methods of exegesis, the meaning of traditional statements and of biblical and other authoritative texts, so as to make them appear consonant with scientific views (e.g. when the six days of creation are said to correspond to geological ages). Whereas Reform and Liberal Judaism generally accept the authority of the sciences in their respective spheres, ORTHODOXY tends to be more fundamentalist and to insist on the literal acceptance of biblical and even rabbinic statements. Thus biblical criticism, theories of evolution, and other scientific or critical views are still considered heretical in certain Orthodox circles.

SCIENCE OF JUDAISM, see **WISSENSCHAFT DES JUDENTUMS**

SCRIBE, see **SOPHERIM**

SCRIPT: Ancient Hebrew s., as it is found on coins, seals, and other inscriptions from the First Temple Period, was similar to the neighboring Semitic (Phoenician, Canaanite) scripts, but was replaced, after the Babylonian Exile, by the square s. currently in use. The Talmud refers to the former as *ketav ivri* ("Hebrew s."), and to the latter as *ketav ashuri* ("Assyrian script", although in *Sanh.* 21b the Talmud explains the latter term as meaning "upright, square script"). Most talmudic rabbis hold that Scripture was originally written in the ancient s. but was rewritten by EZRA in accordance with the injunction of "a prophet who came up from Babylon". A different view, found in the Talmud and accepted by Azariah dei Rossi in the 16th cent. claims priority for the square s. and maintains that the Bible was originally written (i.e., by Moses) in "the Assyrian script", and then changed to the "Hebrew script", after which the "Assyrian script" was reintroduced. Detailed regulations are laid down as to the ink and parchment or hide which may be used for sacred scrolls, as well as the manner of writing to be employed. From the standard square s. various types of cursive s. have developed; see also Rashi Script. The ancient Hebrew s. is still used by the Samaritans.

SCRIPTURE, see **BIBLE**

SCROLL OF ESTHER, see **SCROLLS, FIVE**

SCROLL OF THE LAW, see **SEPHER TORAH**

SCROLLS, THE FIVE: The Five Scrolls (Heb. *megillot*) — i.e., the biblical books Song of Songs, Ruth, Ecclesiastes, Esther, and Lamentations — are five books of the Hagiographa read from a scroll in the synagogue on special occasions. The reading of the Book of Esther on *Purim* morning is regulated in detail in the Mishnah; later it came to be read also on *Purim* eve. The custom of reading the other four books from a scroll is post-talmudic. Reading from Lamentations on *Av* 9 is known at least from early gaonic times. The Song of Songs is read on the Sabbath of Passover week (by *Sephardim* on *Seder* night and Friday afternoons), Ecclesiastes on the Sabbath of the week of Tabernacles (although not by *Sephardim*), and Ruth on the Feast of Weeks. In most congregations today only the Book of Esther is read from an actual scroll, and only Esther and Lamentations are read aloud and according to a special cantillation of their own; however certain congregations (e.g. some of the *Ashkenazi* synagogues in Jerusalem) read all five books aloud from a scroll and precede the reading (even on *Av* 9) with the blessing "Blessed... who has sanctified us and commanded us regarding the reading of the scroll." Only in the case of Esther is a further benediction recited at the conclusion of the reading.

SEA, BRAZEN, see **BRAZEN SEA**

SEARCH FOR LEAVEN, see **BEDIKAT ḤAMETZ; LEAVEN**

SEAT OF MOSES, see **MOSES, SEAT OF**

SECOND DAY OF FESTIVALS: The fixing of the calendar originally depended on the verbal testimony of witnesses who came to the Sanhedrin in Jerusalem to assert that they had seen the New Moon. Messengers were then sent out to announce the fact, but as they could not reach the Diaspora communities speedily, these communities were in doubt as to which of two days was the first of the month, and consequently as to which day marked the actual beginning of the festival in question; as a precaution two days were observed. Since *Rosh ha-Shanah* falls on the first day of the month, this information could not be passed on in time even in the Land of Israel and this festival alone was, and still is, celebrated for two days even there. Strictly speaking the Day of Atonement should also be observed for two days, but this custom was dispensed with; nevertheless some pietists in the Middle Ages observed a two-day fast, despite rabbinical disapproval of the custom as being injurious to health. Doubt regarding the Second Day was ignored with respect to the Counting of the Omer. By the 4th cent. the question was raised as to why the observance of a Second Day of festivals should be continued since the calendar had already been fixed by astronomical calculation; the answer came that established custom and tradition should not be lightly discarded (*Beitz.* 4b) and this ruling was sent to Babylonia by the authorities of the Land of Israel. Reform Judaism has abolished Second Day observances in the Diaspora.

SECOND PASSOVER, see **PASSOVER, SECOND**

SECOND TEMPLE, see **TEMPLE**

SECTS AND SECTARIANS, see **CONTROVERSIES, RELIGIOUS; MINIM**

SEDER (PASSOVER), see **HAGGADAH**

SEDER ELIYYAHU (Heb. "Order of Elijah"; also known as *Tanna de-vei Eliyyahu*): Ethical religious work in Hebrew probably written in the 10th cent. although it has been assigned to the Talmudic Period. Opinions as to the place of authorship vary between Palestine and Italy. The book consists of two parts: *Eliyyahu Rabba* ("The Large Order of Elijah") and *Eliyyahu Zuta* ("The Small Order of Elijah"). It comprises a series of moral homilies stressing the love and study of *Torah,* love of Israel, and social justice.

SEDER OLAM (Heb. "Order of the World"): Name given to two early historical works. The more ancient, the *Seder Olam Rabbah* ("The Great *S.O.*") summarizes the history of the world and particularly of the Jews up to the 2nd cent. It was edited by the *tanna* R. Yose ben Ḥalaphta and his school. The *Seder Olam Zuta* ("The Lesser *S.O.*"), dating from the 8th cent., contains similar contents with particular stress on the genealogy of the Babylonian exilarchs which is traced back to the House of David.

SEER (Heb. *roeh* or *ḥozeh*): Alternative and early designation for prophet; indicative of the visionary aspect of prophecy (cf. Num. 12:6 ff.). *Roeh* was the popular title for a man of God prior to the time of Samuel (I Sam. 9:8) and probably referred to his function as a clairvoyant diviner who would be consulted for practical ends (cf. the case of Saul and his servant turning to Samuel in order to find the lost she-asses; I Sam. 9:6 ff.). The Ḥasidim gave the title s. (*ḥozeh*) to R. Jacob Isaac of Lublin, who was reputed to possess the gift of second sight.

SEFARDI(M), see **SEPHARDI(M)**

SELAH: Word of uncertain etymology and meaning, found 71 times in the Psalms, three times in Habakkuk (chap. 3) and in the 3rd and 18th benedictions of the AMIDAH. It has been interpreted as (1) A word meaning "forever" (Targum), "eternally, without interruption" (*Eruv.* 54a), or "it is so" (Ibn Ezra on Ps. 3:3); (2) A musical instruction: a change in rhythm or tune, *fortissimo* ("lift up" your voices), an interlude to be played by the musical instruments while the singers are hushed, or a pause whose significance was concealed from those not engaged in the Temple service; (3) A liturgical note: a eulogistic response that is to be made by bystanders ("lift up" your benediction); (4) A word composed of initial letters and meaning "return to the beginning" (*da capo*).

SELF-DEFENSE: The law concerning the BURGLAR who is slain in the act of breaking in (Exod. 22:1-2) is taken by the Talmud (*Sanh.* 72 a-b) as the basis for its theory of justifiable homicide, i.e., homicide committed in s.-d. Taking the life of a criminal is considered justifiable not only in case of a direct threat to life but also where there exists reasonable certainty that life is being threatened. However such action in s.-d. is to be taken only as a last resort; if no previous attempt is made to restrain the attacker, e.g. by wounding or maiming rather than killing him, his death is considered murder, though punishable only by Divine intervention and not by a human court.

SELIḤOT (Heb. "penitential prayers", lit. "forgiveness"): A type of PIYYUT requesting forgiveness for sins. Originally composed for the Day of Atonement and fast days, *s.* were later extended to other services. The kernel of all *s.* consists of the enumeration of the thirteen Divine attributes (Exod. 34:6-7) — traditionally given to Israel as a formula with which to beg Divine forgiveness — the *viddui* (CONFESSION), and appropriate biblical verses. The *s.* were incorporated within the framework of the AMIDAH, though early Palestinian *paytanim* connected them with the KEROVAH (as is still to be found in certain fast day rites). In the Middle Ages, the amplified version of *s.* came to be used on *Rosh ha-Shanah* and the Ten Days of Penitence, and then during the whole period preceding *Rosh ha-Shanah* (from *Elul* 1 among *Sephardim;* among *Ashkenazim* from the Sunday before *Rosh ha-Shanah* — or from two previous Sundays when *Rosh ha-Shanah* falls on a Monday or Tuesday). According to subject-matter, *s.* are divided into: (1) *tokhaḥah*, "admonition", in which the worshiper is called upon to consider his ultimate destiny; (2) *bakkashah*, "petition" (not always poetical), dealing with the suffering of Israel and a request for God's mercy (beginning with *anna*, etc.); (3) *gezerah*, "evil decree", describing persecutions and sufferings, particularly those of the Crusades in the 11th and 12th centuries; (4) *akedah*, "the binding of Isaac", telling of martyrdom; (5) *teḥinnah*, "supplication", on the theme of the relationship between God and Israel; (6) *viddui*, "confession" (in prose). The poetical forms of *s.* — *sheniyyah*, *shelishiyyah*, *motsejab* — are identical with those of the *piyyutim*. In addition, there are the *pizmon*, a *seliḥah* consisting of strophes of more than four lines with a refrain, and the *ḥatanu*, dealing with Jewish martyrdom, especially that of the Ten MARTYRS (e.g. *Eleh Ezkerah*, recited during the Additional Service on the Day of Atonement). The earliest known writer of *s.* is YOSE BEN YOSE (c. 5th cent.), one of whose compositions, *Omnan ashameinu*, ("Truly our transgressions"), is included in the Evening Service of the Day of Atonement. In the Italian rite, the *s.* service is called *taḥanunim* ("supplications").

SEMAKHOT (Heb. "Joys"): Euphemistic title of the small tractate EVEL RABBATI which deals with the laws of mourning.

SEMIKHAH (Heb. "laying-on" of hands): The laying of hands on the SACRIFICE (see Lev. 1:4). The obligation of *s.* applied to all sacrifices brought by individuals, but not to those offered in behalf of the community. The sacrificer placed his hands between the horns of the animal and, where required, made his confession. The term is also used for ORDINATION, and in this sense is derived from the biblical account of the transfer of authority from Moses to Joshua accomplished by Moses placing his hands on Joshua's head (Num. 27:23).

SEMINAIRE ISRAÉLITE (originally **ÉCOLE RABBINIQUE) DE FRANCE:** French rabbinical college developing from a *yeshivah* founded in 1704 in Metz. In 1859 it was transferred to Paris and was supervised by the Central *Consistoire.* It graduates rabbis after a five-year course.

SEMITES: Group of kindred nations speaking kindred languages, originating from the Arabian peninsula and eventually occupying the areas from the Mediterranean coast to the mountains of Iran and Armenia. They included the Arabs, Hebrews, Phoenicians, Arameans, Babylonians, and Assyrians. The primitive Semitic religion had common characteristics which can often be discerned behind the three great religions of JUDAISM, CHRISTIANITY, and ISLAM which emerged from it. The Bible ascribes the common origin of all these nations to Noah's son Shem. See ARAMAIC; HEBREW LANGUAGE.

SEPHARDI(M): Early commentators identified the word *Sepharad*, which appears in Obad. 9:20, with the country of Spain (and Zarephath, in the same verse, with France). As a result, the Jews of the Iberian peninsula and their descendants came to be known as *Sephardim*, in distinction to the Jews of the Franco-German tradition who are known as ASHKENAZIM (*Ashkenaz* in Gen. 10:3 having been identified with Germany). In ritual and liturgical matters, *Sephardi* Jewry represents a continuation of the Babylonian tradition, since all the countries of the Mediterranean littoral came under the influence of the Babylonian *geonim* during the period of Mohammedan rule, while *Ashkenazi* Jewry largely followed the tradition of the Palestinian scholars. After the expulsion of the Jews from Spain in 1492 the word *Sephardi* was given wider connotation as the Jews from Spain imposed their culture and traditions upon the Jewish communities of N. Africa and the Middle East. The word *Sephardi* today is thus frequently used for a Jew belonging to one of the Oriental communities which adopted the *Sephardi* rite, whether or not the community is originally of Spanish provenance. When JACOB BEN ASHER compiled his *Arbaah Turim*, he took as his main authorities ALFASI, MAIMONIDES, and his own father, ASHER BEN JEHIEL; the resulting work was a code of standard *Sephardi* practice. See LADINO.

SEPHER ḤASIDIM (Heb. "Book of the Pious"): The main literary product of medieval German Ḥasidim (ḤASIDEI ASHKENAZ). It incorporated the teachings of the movement's three outstanding figures, JUDAH BEN SAMUEL HE-ḤASID OF REGENSBURG, his father, and ELEAZAR BEN JUDAH OF WORMS. The work — originally consisting of three sections devoted to piety, humility, and fear of God — mirrors the religious life of medieval German Jewry. Its object is to serve as a guide to everyday religious conduct and it emphasizes the practice of asceticism, humility, and adherence to strict ethical standards.

SEPHER HA-YASHAR (Heb.): Book of Jashar. See BIBLE, LOST BOOKS OF.

SEPHER MILḤAMOT ADONAI (Heb.): Book of the Wars of the Lord. See BIBLE, LOST BOOKS OF.

SEPHER MITZVOT GADOL, see **MOSES BEN JACOB OF COUCY**

SEPHER MITZVOT KATAN, see **ISAAC BEN JOSEPH OF CORBEIL**

SEPHER TORAH (Heb. "Scroll of the Law"): Manuscript of the Pentateuch used for synagogue readings (on Mondays, Thursdays, Sabbaths, and Holy Days). It is written by a scribe on strips of specially treated (so as to be durable) vellum or parchment made from the leather of a clean animal (although not necessarily slaughtered ritually). Originally a reed pen was obligatory but later a quill was permitted. The strips of parchment are sewn together with threads made from the tendons of ritually clean beasts to form a long roll, both ends of which are wound around wooden staves (*etz ḥayyim*). It is then tied round with a sash and in *Ashkenazi* synagogues, covered with an embroidered mantle (*me'il*) with each stave surmounted by silver finials (*rimmonim*) and a silver crown (*keter torah*); a breast plate (*ḥoshen*) and pointer (*yad*) used during the reading are suspended from the finials. In oriental synagogues the *s.t.* is put inside a wooden or metal cylindrical chest (*tik*). When the scroll is being written, the scribe must maintain a devout frame of mind and utter each word aloud before writing it. Each letter must be separated from the next by a space. In the event of a mistake, the scribe may erase a letter unless this occurs during the writing of a Divine name in which case he must recommence the entire strip. If three or more mistakes are discovered in a *s.t.*, the scroll can no longer be used. The text is written without vocalization or accentuation. Decorative titles (*tagin*) are appended to the top of 13 letters. There is no punctuation or verse-division but sections are indicated either by leaving a space in a line (*setumah* — a "closed" section) or by leaving the rest of the line blank (*petuḥah* — an "open" section). The conclusion (SIYYUM) of the writing of a *s.t.* is an occasion for celebration with male members of the congregation each writing in one of the last letters and the women participating in sewing together the last parchments. The *s.t.* is the central object of veneration in the synagogue. When it is carried, the congregation stands and those nearest to it kiss the mantle as it is carried past. Should a scroll be dropped, the entire congregation is under obligation to fast. In early times, the rabbis would not allow any worshiper to leave the synagogue until after the *s.t.* had been replaced in the ARK following the READING OF THE LAW. The *s.t.* is kept in the ark (*aron* or *heikhal*) at the side of the synagogue facing Jerusalem. One *s.t.* may be placed on top of another but a scroll of the law may not lie under a scroll of the prophets. The open scroll is displayed to the congregation before (in *Sephardi* practice) or after (*Ashkenazi*) the reading of the portion of the law. Usually readings are taken from a single scroll but on occasions two or even three scrolls are used. On SIMḤAT TORAH all available scrolls are taken from the ark and carried in procession seven times around the synagogue. If a synagogue is in danger, the scrolls must be rescued first. A *s.t.* which is worn out or disqualified for other reasons is not destroyed but either placed in a special storeroom (GENIZAH) or ceremoniously buried. In Second Temple times, a *s.t.* was deposited in the Sanctuary and taken out on solemn occasions when the High Priest or king would read portions to the public. In medieval times, it was customary in some communities for each

Jew to carry a small *s.t.* with him at all times for magical or superstitious reasons.

SEPHER YETZIRAH, see **YETZIRAH, BOOK OF**

SEPHIROT (Heb. "numbers"): A term probably originating in the Book of YETZIRAH where it refers to the primordial numbers. In later kabbalistic writings, under Neo-Platonic and gnostic influence, *s.* refers to the EMANATIONS and manifestations of the Godhead. The usual arrangement of the *s.* in the kabbalistic tree was in the following order: *Keter Elyon* — the "supreme" crown of God; *Ḥokhmah* — the "wisdom" or primordial idea of God; *Binah* — the "understanding" of God; these form the first triad. *Ḥesed* — "love" or mercy of God; *Gevurah* or *Din* — His "power", in particular the power of stern judgment; and *Tipheret* or *Raḥamim* — the "beauty" or "compassion" of God, form a second triad. *Netzaḥ* — the "lasting endurance" of God; *Hod* — the "majesty" of God; and *Yesod* — the "foundation" of all active forces in God form the last triad, while *Malkhut* — the "kingdom" of God, identified with the SHEKHINAH and with *Keneset Yisrael* — the mystical archetype of Israel — is the last of the *s.* and functions as the recipient of the Divine life which flows into it from all the others. (The names of the seven lower *s.* are based upon I Chron. 29:11). A large part of kabbalistic speculation is concerned with describing the nature of the *s.*, their relationship with each other as well as with their fountainhead, which is the unfathomable Godhead or EIN SOPH, and with the lower worlds. See KABBALAH.

SEPTUAGINT: Oldest Greek version of the Bible. The name (*septuaginta* in Latin means 70) derives from a legend (*Letter of Aristeas; Meg.* 9a; *Sopherim* 1:8) according to which Eleazar the High Priest, at the command of Ptolemy Philadelphus (288-247 B.C.E.) sent 72 scholars from Jerusalem to Alexandria to render the *Torah* into Greek for the Royal Library. Each translator worked in his own cell, yet, guided by Divine inspiration they finished simultaneously and the translations were all identical. According to the Church Fathers the 70 sages translated not only the Pentateuch but the whole Bible. On the other hand, in *Sopherim* 1:7 five translators are mentioned, one apparently for each book of the Pentateuch. Actually the S. owes its existence to the fact that the growing Jewish population of Egypt had become sufficiently hellenized to need a Greek translation of the Scriptures, especially for liturgical purposes in synagogue. At first the Greek renderings were probably oral and accompanied the reading of the Hebrew text; later a written translation emerged, and in time the Greek version often took the place of the original. Nevertheless the legend appears to contain a core of fact. The Pentateuch was translated in the 3rd cent., possibly with the encouragement of Ptolemy II. The first translators may have been born in Palestine, or else received guidance from Palestinian scholars; but the translation was made in Egypt. The Prophets and part of the Hagiographa were rendered in the 2nd cent. B.C.E., and the entire translation was completed before the Christian era. In the S. the canonical books are arranged in a different order (law, history, poetry, prophecy) from that of the Hebrew Bible, and a number of apocryphal works have been added. The Greek translation is a composite and uneven work and occasionally of poor quality; at times it is literal to the point of unintelligibility. The translators' knowledge of Hebrew often seems to have been inadequate, and the texts they used were not faultless. Nevertheless the S. is a pioneer work of the greatest significance. Based on a Hebrew text that differed in many respects from the Masoretic recension, it is of utmost importance for biblical criticism, though it must be used with caution as the version contains obvious errors, glosses, emendations, and interpolations. The original text has not yet been established; the three main codices (Vaticanus, Sinaiticus, and Alexandrinus) vary one from another.

At first the S. was viewed with favor by the Palestinian rabbis (*Meg.* 9b; *Sopherim* 1:8; cf. *Meg.* 1:8). Hellenistic Jewry revered it, and even instituted an annual celebration in its honor (Philo, *Life of Moses*, 2:7). But the growing divergences between the accepted Hebrew text and the Greek, the doctrinal use made of the latter by sectarians, and, in particular, its subsequent recognition as the official Christian Bible created a hostile reaction, increasingly marked from 70 C.E. onward. The day on which the S. was completed was likened to that on which the Golden Calf was made (*Sopherim* 1:7), and the study of the Greek language, once highly esteemed, was frowned upon (*Sot.* 9:14; *ibid.* 49b). Thus the S., which initially marked the fusion of Hebraism and HELLENISM and helped to spread the concept of monotheism in the gentile world, ultimately became a barrier between the two cultures and an instrument for the propagation of a rival religion. A new Greek translation became necessary for Hellenistic Jewry, and in the 3rd cent. the versions of AQUILA, of THEODOTION, and of SYMMACHUS were composed. See BIBLE TRANSLATIONS.

SERAPH: A heavenly being mentioned only once in the Bible — in Is. 6:2 where the seraphim are described as six-winged creatures who sing the Trishagion. In the Apocryphal Book of ENOCH the seraphim are identified with the "burning serpents" (*neḥashim seraphim*) of Num. 21:6. They are also mentioned in the liturgical elaboration of the *kedushah* in the daily Morning Service. See ANGELS.

SERKES, JOEL BEN SAMUEL (known from the initials of his book as *Baḥ*; 1561-1640): Rabbi in Poland and Lithuania; author of *Bayit Ḥadash* ("New House"), a commentary on JACOB BEN ASHER's *Arbaah Turim*, discussing the talmudic and early rabbinical sources of Ben Asher's work. His glosses on the Talmud are included in most modern editions of the Talmud. S. strongly opposed philosophy and expressed his opinion that a scholar who devoted himself to philosophy and neglected Kabbalah should be excommunicated.

SERMONS, see **HOMILETICS**

SERPENT: Reptile denoted by a number of different terms in the Bible. The s. was regarded as a symbol of evil, and as such figures as the tempter in the story of the Garden of Eden (Gen. 3). Its negative association with the Tree of Life stands in contrast to Babylonian myth in which the s. appears on a tree as a bestower of life. As proof of Moses' Divine mission to Pharaoh, his staff turned into a s. (Exod. 4:2-4). A brazen s. (NEHUSHTAN) served to cure the stricken Israelites in the wilderness (Num. 21), but the representation was kept in the Temple and must have constituted an object of superstitious worship until destroyed by Hezekiah (II Kings 18:4). The rabbis counted among the wonders of the Temple in Jerusalem the fact that serpents never caused any harm within its precincts (*Avot* 5:8).

SERPENT, BRAZEN, see **NEHUSHTAN**

SERVANT OF THE LORD: Both Moses and Israel are termed Servants of the Lord in the Bible. The concept of a servant through whose suffering light and salvation will come to the world is found in the second part of the book of ISAIAH (42:1-4; 49:1-6; 50:4-11; 52:13-53:12). The s. is said to proclaim justice and truth to the people through the Divine spirit. His path is strewn with obstacles: his own people do not recognize him, he is smitten by his adversaries and submits silently to suffering for the sins of others. God, however, is destined to raise him up, and his message will ultimately triumph throughout the world. The interpretation of these somewhat obscure prophecies has been complicated by the fact that the problem has been moved from the sphere of biblical exegesis to that of religious polemics by early Christian identification of Jesus with the suffering servant. Commentators disagree on whether to refer the symbol of the servant to an individual (contemporary with the prophet or a future messianic figure) or to a group (Israel as a whole, the ideal Israel — cf. Is. 49:3 — or the righteous and loyal minority of the people). Jewish exegetes have, as a rule, favored the collective interpretation.

SEUDAH SHELISHIT (Heb. "third meal"): In talmudic times it was customary to eat only two meals per day (cf. e.g. *Suk.* 27a) and since the commandment to honor the Sabbath and call it a delight was interpreted as including food and drink, the rabbis insisted that three meals be taken on the Sabbath (i.e., one on Friday evening and the two others during the day). To eat three meals on the Sabbath became synonymous with giving the day full honors; hence such talmudic statements as, "May my portion be with those who eat three meals on the Sabbath" (*Shab.* 118b) and "he who observes the three meals on the Sabbath is delivered from three evils" (*Shab.* 118a). Although the *s.s.* has no KIDDUSH, in the course of time a special sanctity became attached to it, particularly under kabbalistic influence. With the Polish *Ḥasidim* the *s.s.* became a major feature of religious and social life. Gathering at the table of the *tzaddik* they would spend hours at the sacred meal till late after the end of the Sabbath, listening to their master's mystical discourse and singing hymns or wordless tunes that produced both ecstatic enthusiasm and quiet meditation. The traditional *s.s.* gave rise to the custom of foregathering on Sabbath afternoons for ONEG SHABBAT ("delight of the Sabbath", see Is. 58:13) meetings.

SEUDAT HAVRAAH (Heb.): Meal provided for mourners by sympathetic neighbors on return from funeral. Tradition requires that the mourners be given round foods (such as eggs and rolls) to symbolize the recurring cycle of life and death. An appropriate addition is made to the GRACE AFTER MEALS on this occasion.

SEUDAH MAPHSEKET (Heb. "The meal which separates"): Name given to the last meal taken before commencing the fast of the Day of Atonement and of *Av* 9. Whereas the *s.m.* in the former case has a festive character, the last meal on *Av* 8 expresses the mournful nature of the occasion: one course only (no meat or wine) should be served, and it frequently consists of only a piece of bread and an egg dipped in ashes.

SEUDAT MITZVAH (Heb. "meal of the commandment" i.e., a meal which is a religious occasion): A meal connected with a religious ceremony or celebration. The term has a specific technical connotation, beyond the general rabbinic idea that every meal should be spiritualized by some religious content, such as the exposition of words of *Torah* which turns the physical act of eating into a service of God (*Avot* 3:4); it applies specifically to banquets or meals held in connection with certain religious rites or with festive occasions qualifying as such, e.g. a circumcision, *bar mitzvah*, betrothal, or wedding; originally a *s.m.* was held in conjunction with the declaration of the NEW MOON. The rabbis held (*Shab.* 118b) the completion of the study of a tractate of the Talmud to be an occasion for a festive gathering, and the banquet held in connection with it is therefore classified as a *s.m.* A first-born son is free from the obligation of fasting on the day before Passover if he is present at a *s.m.* — hence the custom of arranging a SIYYUM (the completion of the study of a tractate) to take place on that day.

SEVEN BENEDICTIONS, see **SHEVA BERAKHOT**

SEVORAIM, see **SAVORAIM**

SEX: The treatment of s. in both biblical and rabbinic literature is natural and frank, equally removed from licence (which is considered pagan) as it is from sheer negation. In both its legislative and moral teachings Judaism is concerned to control and hallow man's s. drives through an effective regimen of self-discipline in thought and action. In fact, the highest ideal of "holiness" is often defined as abstinence from sexual licentiousness (Lev. 19:2 and commentaries). The Jewish s. code condemns unchaste conduct as among the most heinous offenses against God and society, branding as capital crimes such perversions as sodomy and pederasty (Lev. 20:13, 15-16) as well as adultery (*ibid.* 10) and incestuous relationship (*ibid.* 11ff.). Also biblically forbidden are s. relations with a menstruant woman (*ibid.* 18), with a man "that is crushed or maimed in his privy parts" (Deut. 23:2, see STERILIZATION), between Jews and non-Jews (Deut. 7:3), and with male or female prostitutes (Deut. 23:18), or indeed with any person outside lawful wedlock (see Maimonides, *Hilkhot Ishut,* 1:1-4). The prohibition against wearing the clothes of the opposite sex (Deut. 22:5) is designed to prevent levity and promiscuity. Many additional rabbinic regulations seek to curb lewd thought and illicit intimacy between the sexes (see CHASTITY). Moral and homiletical writers interpret the rite of CIRCUMCISION as symbolizing the primacy of controlling the s. instinct and hallowing the sexual act by token of the "covenant" between God and Israel, given as the first law to the first Jew (Gen. 17). The rabbis recognize that "there is nothing harder in the entire *Torah* than to abstain from s. and forbidden relationships" (*ibid.* 18). Since "there is no guardian against unchastity" (*Ket.* 13b), laws concerning incest and forbidden relations should not be expounded in public (*Ḥag.* 11b); nevertheless, the most intimate and frank discussions on s. feature frequently in the Talmud and have always been a natural part of religious education. Judaism strongly opposes the notion of regarding the s. instinct as intrinsically sinful or shameful. It should be sublimated rather than suppressed, for "were it not for the evil inclination (i.e., the s. urge), no man would build a home and marry" (*Gen. Rab.* 9:8). Hence to the rabbis, who discouraged CELIBACY, it was this instinct which completed the creation of the world and caused God to pronounce His work as "very good" (*ibid.* on Gen. 1:31).

SEXTON, see **SHAMMASH**

SFORNO, OBADIAH (1475-1550): Italian philosopher and Bible exegete. His biblical commentaries relied on the literal interpretation of the text (*peshat*); they were influenced by S.'s philosophical propensities but rejected the then prevalent mysticism. S. also wrote *Or Ammim* ("Light of Nations"), a polemic (which he himself translated into Latin) attacking Aristotelian theories on the eternity of matter, Divine omniscience, and the nature of the soul. S. was also the author of a philosophical commentary on *Avot.*

SHAATNEZ, see **MIXED KINDS**

SHABBAT, see **SABBATH**

SHABBAT (Heb. "Sabbath"): First tractate in the Mishnah order of *Moed* with *gemara* in both Talmuds. It comprehensively surveys legislation connected with SABBATH observance including regulations concerning carrying from one place to another, the Sabbath lamp, the 39 classes of forbidden labor, and the care of animals on the Sabbath.

SHABBAT HA-GADOL (Heb.): Name given to the Sabbath before Passover. Unlike the four Special Sabbaths which precede this Sabbath (see SABBATHS, SPECIAL), *Shabbat ha-Gadol* has no special pentateuchal reading, but there is a special prophetic reading (Mal. 3). Various fanciful reasons have been adduced for the name (lit. "the great Sabbath"), the most popular being that the day the Children of Israel in Egypt were commanded to prepare the paschal lambs happened to be the Sabbath before Passover. In all probability, however, it owes its name to the distinctive word *ha-gadol* in the prophetical lesson (Mal. 3:23; cf. similar Sabbaths such as *Ḥazon, Naḥamu, Shuvah*). Certain *Ashkenazi* communities recite special *piyyutim* in the Morning and Additional Services and read a section of the *Haggadah* in the afternoon. This is also one of the two Sabbaths in the year (the other being *Shabbat Shuvah*) when the rabbi traditionally delivers a public discourse.

SHABBAZI, SHALOM BEN JOSEPH (17th cent.): Greatest of the Yemenite *paytanim.* Influenced by the medieval Spanish poets and by the 16th cent. kabbalist poet Israel Najara, he wrote hundreds of religious and secular poems in Hebrew and Arabic (sometimes using both languages in the same poem). Many of his *piyyutim* have been incorporated into the Yemenite liturgy. His songs, suffused with the love of Zion and the love of the soul for God, are often strongly marked by kabbalistic influences. Legends are told among Yemenite Jews about S., and his tomb became a center of pilgrimage.

SHABBES GOY (Yidd.): Non-Jew who performs particular tasks in behalf of a Jew during the Sabbath. It is forbidden for a Jew to ask a non-Jew to do work for him which he himself is forbidden to do on the Sabbath, and he is not allowed, moreover, to benefit from work done by the non-Jew even when unbidden. The activity of the *s.g.* is therefore confined to: (1) cases of non-serious illness (for serious illness, even the Jew is permitted to break the Sabbath laws); (2) lighting a fire in cold weather; (3) relieving an animal from pain; and (4) such acts as are done for both non-Jews and Jews when the former are in the majority. In practice, however, the restrictions on the use of the services of the *s.g.* are often circumvented.

SHABBETAI BEN MEIR COHEN, see **COHEN, SHABBETAI BEN MEIR**

SHABBETAI TZEVI (1626-1676): Pseudo-messiah. Born in Smyrna, he devoted himself to talmudic as well as kabbalistic studies and gave himself over to ascetic practices. He was surrounded by a circle of companions and disciples to whom, at the early age of 22, he made mystical revelations, possibly containing hints of his messianic calling. The fact that he was born on *Av* 9, the traditional date of the birth of the Messiah, supported his claim. His behavior, however, caused a scandal and he was forced to wander, but wherever he went (Salonica, Constantinople, Jerusalem) his mystical enthusiasm caused an uproar and frequently led to his expulsion from the community. In Cairo he married a certain Sarah, a waif of the Chmielnicki massacres; the marriage was given mystic import by S. and his followers. Of decisive importance was his meeting (in the summer of 1665) with NATHAN OF GAZA, who recognized S. as the Messiah and became his "prophet". In December 1665 he publicly proclaimed himself the Messiah in the synagogue at Smyrna. Practically the entire Jewish world was seized with a delirium of excitement. Prayers were offered up for S.T. and many Jews sold their houses in the sure hope of their imminent and miraculous transportation to the Land of Israel. In 1666 he proceeded to Constantinople in order to claim his kingdom from the sultan. Immediately on his arrival, however, he was arrested, and after two months of imprisonment in the capital was incarcerated at Abydos. Since he was allowed considerable freedom, his imprisonment did nothing to diminish belief in his messianic claims. His followers referred to Abydos as *Migdal Oz*, ("Tower of Strength") and on Passover a paschal lamb was sacrificed there by S.T. himself. Then, denounced by a certain Nehemiah Cohen, he was summoned before the sultan, and following the advice of the sultan's physician, an apostate Jew, he adopted Islam to save his life. His apostasy led to confusion and shame except among his most fervent followers (the Sabbatians) who still clung to their belief that his conversion was part of a Divine plan (a belief retained by the DONMEH). Ultimately banished to a small village in Albania, S. died in obscurity. The movement connected with S.T. — the last major messianic outbreak in Jewish history — left a long and bitter aftermath of confusion, kabbalistic heresy and heresy-hunting, and clandestine Sabbatian groups which demoralized Jewish life and led to a reaction against KABBALAH and active messianism. See also EIBESCHÜTZ, JONATHAN; FRANK, JACOB.

SHADAR, see **MESHULLAH; SHALIAH**

SHADDAI, see **GOD, NAMES OF**

SHADKHAN (Heb.): Marriage broker. The verb from which the word is derived is found in the Talmud (*Shab.* 150a) where it signifies "to arrange a marriage" (a transaction which is permitted even on the Sabbath). The *s.* as a professional intermediary fulfilled an important social function in the traditional Jewish community which considered it unseemly for young people to do their own courting, and he was indispensable in the Medieval Period when Jews lived in small and scattered groups. Jews regarded it as a highly praiseworthy and honorable occupation, and famous rabbis were proud to engage in it. Brokerage commission (usually a percentage of the dowry) was regulated by custom, and litigation on the subject (particularly when the marriage did not take place) is occasionally mentioned in rabbinic responsa. In Jewish folklore and humor, the *s.* and his profession have become the subject of many jokes.

SHAHARIT (Heb. "dawn prayer"): Morning prayer, recited daily before the first quarter of the day has passed. The Talmud (*Ber.* 26b) ascribes the institution of this prayer to the patriarch Abraham (on the basis of Gen. 19:27); it corresponds to the daily dawn sacrifice (TAMID) in the Temple. In its present form S. is the most extensive of all daily prayers. First, various BENEDICTIONS of thanks and praise (the *birkot ha-shahar*) are recited (though these were originally intended to be spoken by each individual upon arising) followed by various private prayers and Bible passages (not obligatory). Then come PESUKEI DE-ZIMRA, with their benedictions (for which no MINYAN is required). The synagogue service proper begins with BAREKHU, followed by the SHEMA and its benedictions (YOTZER, AHAVAH). After the last of these — GEULLAH — the AMIDAH follows without interruption, thus welding **the**

SCRIBE: *"Sopher Setam"* by Boris Schatz (1866-1932).

SARCOPHAGUS:
Sarcophagus from the Herodian Period.

SHOPHAR:
Shopharot from the 18th cent.; German.
Israel Museum, Jerusalem.

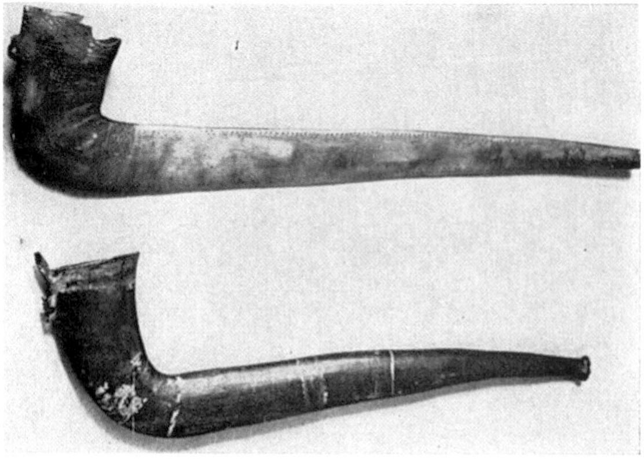

SEPHER TORAH:
Torah miniature scroll; probably English, 1765.
Jewish Museum, London.

SYNAGOGUE: Interior of Ezra synagogue, Cairo.

SYNAGOGUE: New Synagogue, Brussels, 1880.

SYNAGOGUE: From the Transito synagogue at Toledo, 14th cent.

SYNAGOGUE: Wooden synagogue in Wolpa.

SYNAGOGUE: The *Altneuschul* in Prague.

SYNAGOGUE: The Israel Goldstein Campus Synagogue at the Hebrew University, Jerusalem.

SYNAGOGUE:
Now Santa Maria La Blanca.
Toledo, 13th cent.

Waare afbeeldinge van Sabetha Sebi den genaemden
herfteller des Joodtschen Rycks.
Vray pourtrait de Sabbathai Sevi qui se dict Restaura:
teur du Royaume de Juda & Israel.

SHABBETAI TSEVI:
A contemporary picture
Amsterdam, 1669.

SYNAGOGUE:
Municipal Museum of Amsterdam.
by Eduard Frankfort.

מאימתי

מאימתי

מאימתי

קרין את שמע בערבים משע' שהכהני' נכנסים
לאכול בתרומתן עד סוף האשמור' הראשונה
דברי ר' אליעזר וחכמים אומר עד חצות רבן
גמליאל אומר עד שיעלה עמוד השחר מעשה
ובאו בניו מבית המשתה אמרו לו לא קרינו
את שמע אמר להם אם לא עלה עמוד השחר
חייבין אתם לקרות ולא זו בלבד אמרו אלא
כל מה שאמרו חכמים עד חצות מצותו עד
שיעלה עמוד השח' הקטר חלבי' ואברי' מצותן
עד שיעלה עמו' השחר וכל הנאכלים ליו' אחד
מצותן עד שיעלה עמוד השחר אם כן למה
אמרו חכמים עד חצות כדי להרחיק אדם מן
העבירה גמ' תנא היכא קאי דקתני
מאימתי ותו מאי שנא דתני בערבית ברישא
לתני דשחרית ברישא תנא אקרא קאי דכתיב
בשכבך ובקומך והכי קתני זמן ק"ש דשכיב'
אימת משע' שהכהני' נכנסין לאכול בתרומתן
ואי בעי' אימא יליף מברייתו של עולם דכתיב
ויהי ערב ויהי בקר יו' אחד אי הכי סיפ' דקתני
בשחר מברך שתי' לפני' ואחת לאחרי' בערב
מברך שתים לפניה ושתים לאחרי' לתני ערבי'
ברישא תנא פתח בערבי' והדר תני בשחרית
עד דקאי בשחרי' פריש מילי דשחרי' והדר פרי'
מילי דערבית אמר מר משעת שהכהני' נכנסי' לאכול בתרומה מכדי כהנים אימת
קא אכלי תרומה משע' צאת הככבים לתני משעת צאת הככבי' מלתא אגב אורחי'
קמ"ל כהני' אימת קא אכלי בתרומה משעת צאת הככבים והא קמ"ל דכפר'

ברכות א ב

TALMUD: A page from the Bomberg edition of the Talmud, 1522.

Shema and the *amidah* into one single, continuous entity. In Jerusalem, the PRIESTLY BLESSING is recited daily in the course of the S. *amidah*. After the *amidah* on ordinary weekdays there follow *taḥanun* (originally individual, spontaneous prayers of supplication, today with fixed wording); and half-KADDISH; then Ps. 145 and *u-va le-tziyyon* (see KEDUSHAH), full *kaddish, aleinu*. On Mondays and Thursdays, a section from the week's Pentateuch portion is read from the Scroll of the Law (see READING OF THE LAW) after *taḥanun*. Further additions are customary in some congregations. On the NEW MOON and most festivals HALLEL is read immediately after the *amidah*, followed by the full *kaddish*, then the Reading of the Law; on Sabbath, too, the latter two follow the conclusion of the *amidah*. On Sabbaths and festivals, it is usual to recite MUSAPH immediately after the reading. For S., male worshipers clothe themselves in the TALLIT and on weekdays also put on TEPHILLIN. On festivals, especially the New Year and Day of Atonement, S. is extended considerably by the addition of *piyyutim*.

SHALIAḤ (Heb. "messenger"): 1) An AGENT appointed by and empowered to act in behalf of his principal. 2) Emissary appointed to fulfill religious functions. The general name for this kind of *s.* is *sheliaḥ mitzvah*, of whom the Talmud says that he is Divinely protected from harm while fulfilling his duties (*Pes.* 8a). The *sheliaḥ mitzvah* can belong to one of two categories — the SHELIAḤ TZIBBUR and the *s.* in behalf of an institution (also known as *shadar*; see MESHULLAḤ). When the latter's mission is for an institution in the Land of Israel he is sometimes referred to as a *sheliaḥ Zion* (cf. *Beitz.* 25b).

SHALOM ALEIKHEM (Heb. "Peace be upon you"): Opening words of hymn welcoming the Sabbath angels to the home. It is sung on the eve of the Sabbath by the master of the house on his return from synagogue, before the KIDDUSH. The hymn, which is known in the *Ashkenazi* rite only, is of late composition; its basic idea derives from the talmudic statement (*Shab.* 119b) that on Sabbath eve two ministering angels accompany the Jew from the synagogue to his home.

SHALOM BAYIT (Heb.): Domestic peace and harmony between husband and wife. Many rabbinic regulations are stated to have been made in order to promote *s.b.* and to protect the home from disturbance. "Where there is peace between husband and wife the Divine Presence dwells among them" (e.g. *Sot.* 17a). The kindling of the Sabbath lights is regarded as the outstanding symbol of *s.b.* (*Shab.* 23b). Where the *Ashkenazi* prayer book quotes as one of the supreme virtues "making peace between man and his fellow" (based on Mishnah *Peah* 1:1), the *Sephardi* prayer book adds "and between man and wife". See MATRIMONY.

SHALOSH SEUDOT, see **SEUDAH SHELISHIT**

SHAMMAI: *Tanna.* Colleague of HILLEL (forming with him the last of the ZUGOT) and vice-president of the Sanhedrin, succeeding Menahem the Essene (Mishnah *Ḥag.* 2:2) in the first decades C.E. The severe character of S. is often presented in contrast to the gentle personality of Hillel, who tended toward a liberal and progressive interpretation of the *halakhah*. S. is represented as irascible and as favoring a strict and conservative interpretation of the law. Nevertheless his favorite maxim concludes "Receive every man with a cheerful countenance" (*Avot.* 1:16). Both Hillel and S. established schools, known as BET HILLEL AND BET SHAMMAI, whose members continued the traditions of their founders.

SHAMMASH (Heb. "servant"): The equivalent in the synagogue to a church sexton or the usher of the *bet din;* the corresponding talmudic term is ḤAZZAN. During the Middle Ages the *s.* fulfilled a number of extra-synagogal functions such as acting as the public crier, calling worshipers to prayer, making communal announcements, etc., but subsequently his duties became confined to matters pertaining to the synagogue. The word is also used for the additional candle which kindles the ḤANUKKAH lights. The Talmud also applied the verb *shammesh* ("serve") to a student attending the practicing rabbi who is his master; this practical apprenticeship was regarded as more important than academic study (*Ber.* 7b, 47b).

SHAS: Word made up of the initial letters of *Shisha Sidrei* (Mishnah), the "Six Orders" into which R. Judah Ha-Nasi divided the Mishnah. The word came to be applied universally to the Talmud as a whole, and was widely used after Catholic censorship forbade the use of the word "Talmud" in the 16th cent.

SHATZ, see **SHELIAḤ TZIBBUR**

SHAVING: The Bible forbids rounding the corners of the head (removing the hair from the temples) or destroying corners of the BEARD (Lev. 19:27). The corners of the beard were held to be five in number — two on each cheek and one on the chin (*Mak.* 20a). Rabbinic law interprets the prohibition as excluding the use of a razor but not of scissors, clippers, or depilatory powder; modern authorities have also permitted the use of an electric razor. A razor may be used on the neck or on top of the head. The two prohibitions subsequently led to the custom of allowing the sidecurls ("corners", see PEOT) to grow untrimmed, and to the recognition of the beard as a sign of respect among Jews. S. is prohibited on Sabbaths and festivals and during a period of mourning. Strict Orthodox custom also forbids s.

for 33 days during the *Omer* weeks and the three weeks preceding *Av* 9. Oriental and ḥasidic custom celebrates a boy's first haircut on his third or fourth birthday with great pomp and ceremony. In the State of Israel the ceremony usually takes place at Meron on *Lag Ba-Omer*. The cleansing ritual of the leper demands the s. of his entire body (Lev. 14:9). The Nazirite is forbidden to shave at all during the period of his vow (Num. 6:5).

SHAVUOT, see **WEEKS, FEAST OF**

SHEDIM, see **DEMONOLOGY**

SHE'ELOT U-TESHUVOT, see **RESPONSA**

SHE-HEḤEYANU (Heb. "who has kept us in life"): Name given to a benediction of which *s.* is the first distinctive word. It is recited as a blessing of thanksgiving for certain things when they are enjoyed for the first time. The occasions may be (a) general, e.g. the acquisition of new property, clothes, etc. ("He who acquires a new house or purchases new vessels" — *Ber.* 9:1), or (b) seasonal, e.g. on eating the fruit of a new season or on the advent of festivals. The wording of the benediction is "Blessed art Thou, ...who hast kept us in life, and preserved us, and enabled us to reach this season."

SHEḤITAH (Heb. "ritual slaughter"): The act of ritual slaughter which alone renders an animal or bird fit for consumption according to Jewish law. It consists in cutting through both the windpipe and the gullet by means of a sharp implement. Fish and those species of locust permitted as food (Lev. 11) do not require *s.* The SHOHET must examine both windpipe and gullet after *s.* in order to ascertain that at least the major portion of both (or of one in the case of fowl) has been cut through. A knife or any sharp instrument may be used for *s.*, but the implement (*ḥallaph*) must be so sharp that the slit is effected by the sharpness of the knife without requiring downward pressure by the *shoḥet*. The cutting edge must be free from even the slightest imperfection (*pegimah*), or notch, and the sides of the cutting edge must be perfectly smooth. The implement is to be examined both before and after the *s.* This examination is made by drawing the cutting edge and sides forward and backward slowly and carefully over the tip of the finger and nail in order to feel any imperfection, or by holding the edge against the light so that an imperfection would cast a shadow, or by drawing it across the surface of still water, in which case an imperfection in the cutting edge would leave a ripple. Five factors render the *s.* invalid. (1) *Shehiyyah* — if after commencing to slaughter, the *shoḥet* interrupted or stayed the progress of the knife; (2) *Derasah* — if the knife was pressed downward instead of being drawn across the throat; (3) *Haḥladdah* — if the gullet and windpipe or one of them were cut from the inside; (4) *Hagramah* — if the cut was made too close to the head or body of the animal, thus going beyond the bounds of what is legally considered the neck; (5) *Ikkur* — if the implement used was notched or otherwise unfit. S. is preceded by a special blessing but is not invalidated in the event of its non-recital. S. has been both attacked and defended on humanitarian grounds. Loss of consciousness after the severance of the jugular vein is almost instantaneous. Efforts have been made by anti-Semites and by those acting in behalf of humane societies to ban *s.* in various parts of the world on the grounds of cruelty to animals, though scientific evidence has also been adduced to uphold the humane character of *s.*

SHEITEL, see **WIG**

SHEKALIM (Heb. "Shekels"): Fourth tractate of the Mishnah order of *Moed*, with *gemara* in the Palestinian Talmud only. It deals with the half-SHEKEL tax which defrayed the expenses of maintaining worship in the Second Temple; the tax was discontinued with the Temple's destruction.

SHEKEL: Ancient Hebrew monetary unit containing 20 *gerah* (Num. 3:47). Abraham bought the Cave of Machpelah for 400 shekels of silver (Gen. 23:15). Originally a standard weight of silver (about 14 grams) the s. became a current coin in Maccabean times. A half-s., called *beka*, was paid into the treasury by all participants in the national census (Exod. 30:13-15). A per capita tax of 1/3 s. was extracted for work connected with the restoration of the Second Temple (Neh. 10:33-34). During the Second Temple Period, Jews everywhere paid an annual levy of a half-s. for the maintenance of the Sanctuary. The Mishnah tractate SHEKALIM describes regulations concerning this levy, which is still commemorated in the symbolic "ceremony of the half-s." which takes place in many synagogues on the eve of *Purim*, before the reading of the *megillah*. The Zionist Movement revived the idea of the s. by giving the name to the small annual contribution which entitles members to participate in elections..

SHEKHINAH (Heb. lit. "indwelling"): Divine Presence. The term, derived from biblical verses (e.g. Exod. 25:8; Lev. 16:16) speaking of God's "dwelling" — i.e., presence — in the midst of Israel, might be regarded at first sight as one of the many circumlocutions employed by the Talmud to avoid mentioning the name of God directly. Closer analysis, however, shows that the rabbis used the term in the more specific sense of the manifestation of the Divine Presence in the life of man, or the principle of Divine immanence in creation. According to aggadic teaching the S. dwells only among Israel (*Ber.* 7a), and probably for this reason conversion to Judaism is called "being brought under the wings of the S." The S. dwells among the Children of Israel "even in their impurity" i.e., sin (*Yoma* 56b, based on Lev. 16:16). The S. may also rest upon individuals. "The S. rests upon man not through gloom, indolence, frivolity, or idle chatter, but only through the joy experienced in fulfilling Divine commandments" (*Shab.* 30a). The S. is present in every home where there is domestic peace, and blesses that home (*Sot.* 17a). Study (*Avot* 3:7) and congregational prayer (*Ber.* 6a) bring about the presence of the S., whereas sin (*Sot.* 3b) and injustice (*Sanh.* 7a) drive it away. When Israel goes into exile, the S. accompanies them, as it will accompany them on their return (*Meg.* 29a). The bliss of the beatific vision in the future world is expressed in the words "there the righteous sit and enjoy the splendor of the S." (*Ber.* 17a). In KABBALAH, S. is the tenth *sephirah* and represents the "feminine" aspect of the Divinity.

SHELOH, see **HURWITZ, ISAIAH**

SHELIAḤ TZIBBUR (Heb. "messenger of the congregation"): Designation for the leader of prayer in the synagogue. The term is first mentioned in the Mishnah (*R.H.* end). The office of *S. T.* ("*Shatz*") was introduced in the synagogue to fulfill the obligations of those who could not recite the prayers themselves. In the course of time the term *S. T.* was replaced by ḤAZZAN.

SHELOSHIM, see **MOURNING**

SHEM HA-MEPHORASH (TETRAGRAMMATON), see **GOD, NAMES OF**

SHEM TOV, see **IBN SHEM TOV**

SHEMA (Heb. "Hear"; the first word of Deut. 6:4: "Hear, O Israel, the Lord is our God, the Lord is One"): The name given to three Bible passages (Deut. 6:4-9; 11:13-21; Num. 15:37-41) which must be read (hence: *keriat Shema*= "the reading of the S.") every morning and evening. The custom of *keriat Shema* was part of the Temple service (Mishnah *Tamid* 5:1) and was taken over by the synagogue. It is considered an obligation prescribed by the Bible itself on the basis of the verse: "and thou shalt speak of them... when thou liest down and when thou risest up" (Deut. 6:7). In the morning, the S. should be recited before the first quarter of the day has passed; in the evening, before midnight (although if this is impossible it may be read any time during the night). The S., though not strictly speaking a prayer, has become an integral part of the Morning and Evening Services; BENEDICTIONS must be recited before and after it (three in the morning; YOTZER, AHAVAH, and GEULLAH; four in the evening) after which the AMIDAH should follow immediately, without interruption. No MINYAN is required for the recitation of the S. or its benedictions (except for the recital of BAREKHU, which precedes the benedictions). In olden times, the S. was recited antiphonally, with the reader saying one verse, the congregation the next, and so on. Today in *Ashkenazi* communities the S. is recited silently by the entire congregation; among oriental Jews it is customary to read it aloud in unison. Its recitation is immediately preceded by the phrase EL MELEKH NE'EMAN and after the first verse a doxology is added silently: *barukh shem kevod malkhuto*, etc. (="Blessed be the name of the glory of His Kingdom for ever and ever"); on the Day of Atonement this doxology is recited aloud. Apart from the twice-daily reading of the S. with its benedictions, the first passage is read by the individual before retiring at night, and the first verse is also recited when the Scrolls of the Law are taken out of the ARK, as part of the KEDUSHAH of MUSAPH (possibly having been inserted during a Byzantine persecution when recitation of the S. proper was forbidden), and at the conclusion of NEILAH on the Day of Atonement. Because of its emphasis on the unity of God, the S. is considered the Jewish "confession of faith" and a vital part of the liturgy; it is spoken by a Jew on his deathbed, and throughout the centuries Jews undergoing martyrdom have died with the S. on their lips.

SHEMA KOLI (Heb. "Hear my voice"): Rhymed hymn recited in the *Sephardi* ritual on the eve of the DAY OF ATONEMENT preceding the KOL NIDREI prayer. It has been ascribed to R. HAI GAON.

SHEMAIAH (1st cent. B.C.E.): President (*nasi*) of the Sanhedrin; together with AVTALYON, the fourth of the ZUGOT. Traditionally (see *Git.* 57b) both S. and Avtalyon were converts (or sons of converts). They were widely admired and respected as authorities, although no *halakhot* are directly quoted in their names.

SHEMINI ATZERET (Heb. "the eighth day of Solemn Assembly", cf. Num. 30:35): Last day (outside the Land of Israel, last two days) of the Festival of TABERNACLES. The Talmud (*Suk.* 47a) discusses whether S.A. should be considered an independent festival immediately following Tabernacles or whether it is actually the concluding day of that festival, comparable to the last day of Passover (cf. Num. 28:16, 25). The compromise solution which the rabbis reach regards S.A. as an independent festival in certain respects (one of which is its name) but otherwise as a continuation of *Sukkot*. However meals are not eaten in the tabernacle, nor do the *lulav* and *etrog* figure in the service for that day. The striking difference between the number of sacrifices offered during the previous seven days, which total seventy in all (Num. 29:12-32) and the solitary "one ram, one bullock" of this festival (*ibid.* 36), is the basis of a Midrash to the effect that the 70 sacrifices correspond to the "seventy nations" (i.e., mankind), while S.A. symbolizes the special relationship between God and Israel. In the Diaspora, where the biblical festivals are extended to two days, the conclusion of the *Torah* is read on the Second Day, which is called SIMHAT TORAH (in the liturgy, however, the name S.A. is retained); in the Land of Israel the day of S.A. is also *Simhat Torah*. The prayer for RAIN is recited in the Additional Service on S.A.

SHEMITTAH, see **SABBATICAL YEAR**

SHEMONEH ESREH, see **AMIDAH**

SHEMOT, see **EXODUS**

SHEMOT RABBAH, see **MIDRASH RABBAH**

SHEOL, see **GEHINNOM**

SHERIRA (10th cent.): *Gaon* of Pumbedita, whose declining prestige he restored. His responsa are largely concerned with religious practice but also contain important expositions of the Talmud and Midrash. Best known is the letter he wrote as a responsum to the Kairouan (N. Africa) community, which was concerned about Karaite questioning of the authenticity of Mishnah and Talmud tradition. S. in reply provided a history of Jewish tradition with details of the sequence of generations of *amoraim, savoraim,* and *geonim,* as well as rich general historical and methodological data. He stressed that the Talmud represents an unbroken ancient tradition and not a gradual accretion while its authorities are interpreters, not authors.

SHETAR, see **DEED**

SHEVA BERAKHOT (Heb.): The "seven benedictions" recited at the wedding ceremony after the bridegroom has "consecrated" his bride by placing the ring on her finger. The *s.b.* are of ancient origin and are already quoted in the Talmud (*Ket.* 8a). The first benediction is over the wine, and the following three praise God who has created all things for His glory, formed man, and created him male and female in His image. The fifth benediction mentions the joy of the restoration of Zion, and the sixth evokes the joy of the first couple in Paradise. The seventh blessing gives thanks to God for having created "joy and gladness, bride and bridegroom", etc. and concludes "Blessed... who makes the bridegroom rejoice with the bride". During the seven days following the marriage, the *s.b.* are recited during GRACE after every meal at which a MINYAN is available (the *minyan* must include some new guests on each occasion).

SHEVARIM, see **SHOPHAR**

SHEVAT: Eleventh month of the religious calendar, fifth of the civil. S. has thirty days and its zodiac sign is the water carrier. It is the month of the NEW YEAR FOR TREES which falls, following the tradition of BET HILLEL, on the 15th of the month (the *Bet Shammai* date — *Shevat* 1 — did not gain acceptance).

SHEVAT, FIFTEENTH DAY OF, see **NEW YEAR FOR TREES**

SHEVIIT (Heb. "Seventh Year"): Fifth tractate of the Mishnah order of *Zeraim* with *gemara* in the Palestinian Talmud only. It deals with the law of SHEMITTAH (the seventh year when the land lies fallow and debts are released) including the institution of the PROSBUL.

SHEVUOT (Heb. "Oaths"): Sixth tractate of the Mishnah order of *Nezikin* dealing with various types of OATHS (cf. Lev. 5:2ff.) and incidentally with laws concerning ritual uncleanness and BAILMENT (describing the four types of bailee). It has *gemara* in both Talmuds.

SHEW BREAD or SHOWBREAD (Heb. *lehem panim*): In accordance with biblical precept (Exod. 25:30; Lev. 24:1-9), twelve loaves of fine flour (representing the twelve tribes), arranged in two rows, were placed each Sabbath on the golden table in the Sanctuary (and later in the Temple). They remained there until the following Sabbath, when they were replaced by twelve fresh loaves. The old loaves were then divided among the outgoing and incoming watches of priests for their consumption. The two rows of s. were placed on golden chalices filled with frankincense which was burnt on the altar after the bread was removed from the table each Sabbath. S. may have been so called because it was baked in a mold with two open sides.

SHIELD OF DAVID, see **MAGEN DAVID**

SHIKHHAH (Heb. "forgotten"): Forgotten sheaf, i.e., sheaves which the landowner had overlooked in the reaping and which must be left for the poor to take.

SHIR HA-KAVOD (Heb. "The Hymn of Glory"; also known after its opening words as *anim zemirot* "I shall sing songs"): Alphabetic acrostic recited responsively by *Ashkenazim* at the end of the Morning Service (in some rites restricted to the conclusion of the Sabbath Additional Service, in others omitted entirely). It is often recited by a small boy with the congregation reading the responses. In certain rites it is also sung on the eve of the Day of Atonement. The composition of the hymn, a Divine doxology that is often anthropomorphic, has been attributed to R. JUDAH HE-HASID.

SHIR HA-MAALOT (Heb. "The Song of Degrees"): Superscription of a group of PSALMS (120-134). The title may refer to the custom of reciting the psalms while traveling from Babylonia to Palestine, up to Jerusalem, or ascending the Temple steps. One of these psalms (126) is sung before GRACE AFTER MEALS on Sabbaths and festivals as a reminder of Zion. This custom, based on passages from the Zohar, is late and first appears in print in the 17th cent.

SHIR HA-SHIRIM, see **SONGS OF SONGS**

SHIR HA-SHIRIM RABBAH, see **MIDRASH RABBAH**

SHIR HA-YIHUD (Heb. "The Song of Unity"): Hymn divided into seven sections, one of which is read (by *Ashkenazim*) on each day of the week, although in practice only the Sabbath section is recited in many congregations. The hymn, glorifying the characteristics of God, seems to have been partly inspired by Ibn Gabirol's *Keter Malkhut*. It is a product of the 13th cent. German school of Hasideans and has been attributed to R. SAMUEL BEN KALONYMOS HE-HASID.

SHIRAH, PEREK, see **PEREK SHIRAH**

SHIRAT HA-YAM, see **MOSES, SONG OF**

SHIRAYIM (or **SHEYARIM**; Heb. "remainders"): Term used by Hasidim to refer to the "remainders" of the food eaten by the holy *tzaddik*, or leader of the hasidic community. The rabbi's *hasidim* frequently struggle with one another for these scraps since, in their eyes, they have been sanctified and endowed with holy power by the *rebbe*. A signal mark of honor bestowed by the *rebbe* is to invite a certain follower to share these "remainders".

SHIUR KOMAH (Heb. "Dimensions of Stature" i.e., of God): Mystical work dating from the Gaonic Period, but possibly much earlier. It attempts to convey the greatness and majesty of God by attributing to him colossal dimensions of stupendous magnitude, e.g. "The soles of His feet cover the whole universe; the height of His soles is 30,000 thousand parasangs; from the sole to the heel 1,000 times 1,000 plus 500 parasangs; his square beard is 11,500 parasangs. Each parasang is 3 miles and each mile 10,000 cubits". Many authorities denounced the work as grossly anthropomorphic and spurious, and Maimonides declared that it ought to be burned. Defenders of the *S.K.* claimed that it was not to be taken literally but had an esoteric meaning.

SHIVAH, see **MOURNING**

SHIVAH ASAR BE-TAMMUZ (Heb. "the 17th day of the month of *Tammuz*"): FAST day: the "fast of the fourth month" mentioned in Zech. 8:19 commemorating the breach of the walls of Jerusalem three weeks before the complete fall of the city and the destruction of the Temple. According to Jer. 39:2 the breach of the walls by Nebuchadnezzar in 586 B.C.E. took place on *Tammuz* 9, but since the break made by Titus in 70 C.E. fell on *Tammuz* 17, the latter date was chosen for the fast (*Taan.* 26a). The Mishnah (*Taan.* 4:6) adds four other mournful anniversaries on this date: the breaking of the Two Tablets, the cessation of the daily sacrifice, the burning of the Scrolls of the Law by an otherwise unknown Apostomus, and the erection of an idol in the Sanctuary. *Tammuz* 17 begins the THREE WEEKS of mourning which last until *Av* 9.

SHNEERSON: Hasidic family, descended from SHNEOUR ZALMAN OF LYADY. The leaders (*rebbes*) of the LIUBAVICH or HABAD Hasidim, all belong to the S. dynasty.

SHNEOUR ZALMAN OF LYADY (1747-1813): The founder of HABAD Hasidism, i.e., the school of hasidic thought and of the grouping that later came to be known as the LIUBAVICHER Movement. As a young boy, he achieved a reputation as a brilliant talmudic student. Instead of continuing his studies in Vilna, the center of talmudic studies, he went to Mezhirich where he spent three years with Dov BER of Mezhirich who recognized the unusual talents of his young disciple from Lithuania and urged him to compose a revised version of the *Shulhan Arukh*. S.Z. completed this prodigious task at the age of twenty-five. Dov Ber then assigned to him and to R. Menahem Mendel of Vitebsk the mission of "capturing" Lithuania, the stronghold of the MITNAGGEDIM (as the opponents of HASIDISM were called). After Menahem Mendel left for Palestine, S.Z. became one of the foremost leaders of Hasidism in the northern part of Russia. His prominence, due to his erudition and personality, caused him to be dragged unwillingly into the center of the bitter controversy between the *Mitnaggedim* and the Hasidim. He went to Vilna in an attempt to meet the Vilna Gaon, the leader of the anti-hasidic opposition, in order to bring about a reconciliation, but the latter refused to see him. As a result of false accusations by the *Mitnaggedim*, S.Z. was twice imprisoned by the Russian authorities in St. Petersburg. His release confirmed his disciples in the justice of their cause, and his followers to this day observe the date of his release, *Kislev* 19, as a festival. S.Z. developed his own system of mystical theology in several important works, of which the best-known, called *Likkutei Torah* (or the TANYA), was regarded by his followers as the fundamental text of hasidic spirituality. S.Z.'s teachings have a strong psychological element and stress the importance of intellectual effort in achieving the proper levels of devotion and piety. Though considered by his followers a TZADDIK, he denied the alleged miracle-working powers of the *tzaddik* and stressed instead the need for the Hasid and his REBBE to work together as friends and mutual helpers. When Napoleon's army approached Russia, S.Z. fled toward the interior and died on the way.

SHNODDER: The amount of the contribution to the synagogue or to charity which is made by a person called to the Reading of the Law is formally announced and introduced by the formula "*ba-*

avur she-nodar" (in the *Ashkenazi* pronunciation), i.e., "on account of which he offers". The second word was taken over into Yiddish and regarded as a verb (*shnoddern*) meaning "to make a contribution".

SHOḤER TOV: (Heb. "he that diligently seeketh good", cf. Prov. 11:27): Midrash on the Psalms, named after its opening words. It contains homilies and interpretations on 143 psalms and has been collated from many aggadic sources. The work is not uniform and falls into two sections — 1) homilies on Psalms 1-118, and 2) on 119-150 (much of the latter being taken from *Yalkut*). The date of the work is uncertain but it was known extensively by the 11th cent. It has been suggested that the place of composition was S. Italy.

SHOḤET (Heb.): One trained and ordained to perform ritual slaughter (SHEḤITAH). In order to receive his diploma, (called *kabbalah*), a *s.* must not only know the laws and theory of *sheḥitah* but must also have had practical experience under the guidance of experts. In awarding the diploma, the personal habits and character of the candidate are fully considered; a person who is not punctiliously observant, or who is not thought to be Godfearing or who rejects rabbinic tradition (e.g. a Karaite) is not to receive the *kabbalah*. The ordained is, by custom, to be not less than eighteen years of age, is not to be prone to drunkenness, and his fingers are not to have lost their delicacy of touch. Women, although permitted to perform *sheḥitah*, are not in fact so ordained. A non-Jew may not act as a *s.*

SHOMER YISRAEL (Heb. "Guardian of Israel"): A late *piyyut* of unknown date and authorship, first found among the *seliḥot* for *Tevet* 10 in a 13th cent. manuscript. It was originally recited on fast days, but later (apparently only in the 19th cent.) was incorporated into TAḤANUN in the *Ashkenazi* and ḥasidic rituals, while in other rites it is still reserved for fast days and also, with an additional stanza, for penitential days. The version given in the prayer book is obviously greatly shortened, and further stanzas are found in some manuscripts.

SHOPHAR (Heb.): A ram's horn sounded on ceremonial occasions, such as in proclaiming the JUBILEE year (Lev. 25:9) or the anointing of a new king (e.g. I Kings 1:34); it is now almost entirely confined to use in the synagogue, during the High Festival period. Although later *Ashkenazi* custom introduced the sounding of the *s.* daily during the month of *Elul* (except on the day before *Rosh ha-Shanah*), and the Western *Sephardi* custom on *Hoshana Rabbah*, and all rites at the close of the service on the Day of ATONEMENT, it is enjoined in the Bible only for *Rosh ha-Shanah*, in the phrase "it shall be a day of sounding to you" (Num. 29:1). The alternate reading (Lev. 23:24), "A memorial of sounding", serves as the justification for not sounding the *s.* on the Sabbath (which is regarded as being a sufficient memorial in itself), though in the Temple it was sounded on Sabbaths as well. Whereas the Bible gives neither the order of the blasts nor their meaning, the rabbis evolved an elaborate order of sounding, the essence of which is that the *s.* should sound broken notes resembling sobbing (the *shevarim* sound) and wailing (the *teruah* sound), which are both preceded and followed by a long unbroken sound (*tekiah*); this order is repeated three times after the recital of each of the three sections of the *amidah* of the Additional Service. Saadyah Gaon adduces ten reasons for the sounding of the *s.* (e.g., to proclaim God's sovereignty, as a symbol of the Ingathering of the Exiles, etc.). Maimonides gives as its message (*Laws of Repentance* 3:4) "Awake ye sleepers from your sleep, and ye that are in slumber, rouse yourselves. Consider your ways, remember God, turn unto Him". The use of the *s.* has been reintroduced in the State of Israel for official occasions such as the swearing-in of the president of the State. It is also sounded in Orthodox residential neighborhoods to herald the advent of the Sabbath.

SHOPHAROT: Name given to ten biblical verses which mention the sounding of the SHOPHAR and which are recited during the Additional Service on *Rosh ha-Shanah* (together with the ten MALKHUYYOT and the ten ZIKHRONOT) and after which the *shophar* is sounded. The selection is made up of 3 verses from each of the three portions of the Bible, the tenth verse being taken once again from the Pentateuch. The introductory and concluding prayers have been ascribed to RAV.

SHOPHETIM, see JUDGES, BOOK OF

SHOSHANAT YAAKOV (Heb. "The lily of Jacob"): The concluding section of the PIYYUT of *Asher Heni* ("Who brought the counsel of the heathen to nought"), which is recited on *Purim* after the reading of the Scroll of Esther both in the evening and in the morning. While *Asher Heni* dates from the Gaonic Period, S.Y. is a later addition, consisting of two parts, the first of which is not contained in the *Sephardi* ritual.

SHOWBREAD, see **SHEW BREAD**

SHROUDS, see **BURIAL**

SHULḤAN ARUKH (Heb. "Prepared Table"): The standard CODE of Jewish law and practice compiled by Joseph KARO and first published in 1565; *Ashkenazi* custom was added by Moses ISSERLES in his *Mappah*. The S.A. succeeded in standardizing and creating a normative framework and guide for Jewish practice. Karo wrote the S.A. as a key to and synopsis of his larger work *Bet Yoseph*, which was based in turn on the

Turim of Jacob Ben Asher. Following the pattern of the *Turim*, the S.A. is divided into four parts: (1) *Oraḥ Ḥayyim,* dealing with the ritual obligations of daily life from waking to sundown and covering blessings, prayers, Sabbaths, festivals, etc. (2) *Yoreh Deah,* dealing mainly with dietary and ritual laws including mourning, vows, respect to parents, charity, etc. (3) *Even ha-Ezer,* on personal status, marriage, divorce, etc. (4) *Ḥoshen Mishpat,* which embraces the entire body of Jewish civil law as far as it is applicable in Diaspora conditions.

SHULKLAPPER (Yidd. "synagogue knocker"): Name given to the synagogue official whose duty was to make the rounds of the houses in villages of E. Europe and call the men to prayer, usually for the Morning Service and for Seliḥot which were recited in the small hours of the morning. He would knock at the bedroom window with a stick — sometimes with an artistically carved hammer — and announce in plaintive chant "Arise for the service of the Creator".

SHUSHAN PURIM, see **PURIM**

SIBYLLINE ORACLES: A series of quasi-prophetic books written under the pseudonym of a Sibyl (pagan prophetess) and dating from the 2nd cent. B.C.E. to the 4th cent. C.E. Ancient sources report the existence of some 15 S.O., but only 12 are now extant. The S.O., composed in Greek hexameters, are of Jewish, Christian, and pagan origin. Of special Jewish interest are the Sibylline books, IV, V, and XI, which show a marked Jewish influence, though Christian interpolations have evidently been added. The Sibyl, "Babylonian" by name, rebukes the gentiles for their sins, threatens with destruction those who persecute the Jews, and foretells the birthpangs and the advent of the Messiah, the eschatological war against Gog and Magog, and an era of everlasting spiritual peace and material prosperity.

SICK, PRAYER FOR: In addition to the eighth benediction of the weekday amidah, which is a petition for the healing of the sick in general, any individual may offer prayers for sick friends or relatives. These can be added to the above benediction or else to the 16th benediction of the *amidah* (which is used freely as a framework into which personal requests may be inserted). Such prayers can, of course, also be offered anywhere and at any time in free style and in the words of the individual worshiper. Prayers for the sick may also be offered in the synagogue after the Reading of the Law; in the latter case, it is usual for the person requesting such a prayer to vow an offering to charity (see Mi She-Berakh). It is also customary to read psalms for the sake of the sick. A form of prayer to be recited by a sick person, incorporating psalms, prayers, and a brief confession of sin, also became customary, and special prayers, including the solemn change of Name, were composed for those very gravely ill.

SICK, VISITING THE (Heb. *bikkur ḥolim*): The duty of visiting the sick ranks among the major acts of charity and is regarded as one of the great social virtues of Judaism. The passage from the Mishnah (*Peah* I) which describes it as one of the six things from which man derives benefit in this world while the stock remains for him in the World to Come is recited every day at the beginning of the Morning Service. When the rabbis wished to emphasize the special sanctity of an ethical act they ascribed its performance to God Himself; thus they explained that God appeared to Abraham (Gen. 18:1) in order to fulfill the duty of visiting the sick after Abraham had undergone the ceremony of circumcision. The rabbis said "whosoever visits the sick reduces his ailment by one sixtieth" (*Ned.* 39b) and "visiting the sick can hasten recovery, just as refraining from doing so can hasten the death of the patient" (*Ned.* 40a). Societies for Visiting the Sick have been a prominent feature of Jewish social services throughout the ages. The visitor recites a special prayer for the patient's recovery. It is also customary for worshipers to visit invalids after service on Sabbath morning, before they return to their own homes.

SIDDUR, see **PRAYER BOOK**

SIDELOCKS, see **PEOT; SHAVING**

SIDRAH (Heb. "arrangement"; pl. *sidrot* or *sedarim*): The weekly portion of the Pentateuch read publicly in the synagogues on Sabbath. The term is found in talmudic times (*Shab.* 116b; *Yoma* 87a), *Sephardim* use the term *parashah* (pl. *parashiyyot*). The 54 *sidrot* are so arranged (two being sometimes joined together) that the public reading of the Pentateuch commences on the first Sabbath after *Simḥat Torah* (*Shabbat Bereshit*) and concludes annually on *Simḥat Torah.* This follows ancient custom and is in contrast to the Palestinian custom whereby the Pentateuch, variously divided into 154 (the Masoretic total of *sedarim*), 167 (Yemenite scrolls), or 175 (*Soph.* 16:10) *sidrot,* was read once in three years (the Triennial Cycle). Each *s.* is named after one of its initial words. See Reading of the Law.

SILENT PRAYER (Heb. *tephillah be-laḥash*): S.P. seems to have been unknown in ancient times, when worshipers called on God with a loud voice. When Hannah, praying to God in the bitterness of her soul, "spake in her heart, only her lips moved but her voice was not heard" the High Priest Eli thought that she was drunk (I Sam. 1:13). In rabbinic usage s.p. means the silent, individual recital of the amidah by the congregation, prior to its repetition by the reader. Originally a communal prayer, the *amidah* was recited publicly by the reader in behalf of the congregation whose participation was restricted to the responses "amen" after each benediction and in the Temple with "Blessed be His name, whose glorious kingdom is for ever and ever". Later the practice arose that each member of the congregation say the *amidah* silently; the subsequent public recital was for the sake of those unable to say the prayer for themselves (*R.H.* 34b), but has been retained in order to preserve the original character of the *amidah* as a congregational rather than as an individual prayer. Private petitions may be added in the 16th benediction of the silent *amidah*. According to the rabbis the s.p. should be heard by the worshiper himself, though not by others, i.e., s.p. too should be clearly articulated and must not be confused with meditation.

SIMEON BAR YOḤAI (2nd cent. C.E.): *Tanna*; pupil of R. Akiva. He conducted his school at Tekoa in Upper Galilee where his pupils included R. Judah Ha-Nasi. The halakhic Midrashim SIPHREI and MEKHILTA evolved from the teachings of his academy, which was noted for systematic classification of *halakhot* and attempts to adduce a rational basis for the law. S. is frequently quoted in the Mishnah and other tannaitic sources as "R. Simeon" and had a reputation as a miracle worker. For speaking against the Romans he was condemned to death, and he and his son Eleazar consequently had to go into hiding—traditionally they spent 12-13 years in a cave until the death decree was annulled. Many legends were woven around this period, and kabbalists subsequently claimed that the ZOHAR itself was the result of the mystical doctrines evolved by S. during that time. Folk tradition observes the date of his death — LAG BA-OMER — as a feast, especially at his reputed grave in Meron where bonfires are lit and special poems, composed in his honor, are sung.

SIMEON BEN GAMALIEL: (1) *Tanna* (1st cent. C.E.). *Nasi* of the Sanhedrin in the years immediately preceding the destruction of the Second Temple (when Johanan ben Zakkai was *av bet din*). He became an adherent of the School of Shammai and belittled intellectual argument and pedagogic activity (he himself had no disciples), saying "Not the study but the practice of the law is essential". He served as a leader in the early stages of the rebellion against Rome, though later his views became more moderate. According to tradition he was one of the ten martyrs executed by the Romans, but it is possible that he was put to death by the Zealots during the last year of the war. (2) *Tanna* (2nd cent. C.E.). *Nasi* of the Sanhedrin at Usha in the generation after the Bar Kokhba revolt. Under his statesmanship, the Sanhedrin recovered much of its significance. S. was noted for his humility and leniency, and many *halakhot* are quoted in his name.

SIMEON BEN LAKISH (also known as Resh Lakish; 3rd cent.): Palestinian *amora*. Originally a gladiator, he was influenced by R. Johanan bar Nappaḥa to turn to sacred studies. S. became an outstanding and independent scholar and noted aggadist; he was deputy (and brother-in-law) to R. Johanan, and their legal discussions constitute one of the main elements of the Palestinian Talmud.

SIMEON BEN SHETAḤ (1st cent. B.C.E.): Scholar and NASI of the SANHEDRIN. A Pharisaic leader during the reign of Alexander Yannai and his widow Salome Alexandra (sister of S.), S. was renowned for his courageous integrity. S. and Salome Alexandra transformed the Sanhedrin from a Sadducee to a Pharisaic body (possibly by introducing SCRIBES into its ranks, which hitherto had been composed of priests and lay aristocracy). He recalled JUDAH BEN TABBAI from exile in Alexandria and together they constituted one of the ZUGOT. S. initiated several important religious enactments, e.g. concerning the marriage contract, and laid the foundation for elementary education for Jewish children.

SIMEON HA-TZADDIK (i.e., "the pious"): High Priest. Views are divided, as to whether he flourished in the 4th-3rd cent. B.C.E. (following *Yoma* 69b which describes his meeting with Alexander the Great) or in the 3rd-2nd cent. B.C.E. (following *Ecclesiasticus* 50). He was a dominant personality who played an important part in the KENESET HA-GEDOLAH, which formulated the liturgy, closed the canon, and established the SANHEDRIN. Scholars have suggested that he belonged to the HASIDEANS; that he was a strong supporter of the Seleucids who recognized him as the *de facto* ruler of Judea; that he was responsible for establishing the central rôle of study in Jewish tradition; that in his time the Oral Law was accepted as the authoritative interpretation of the Sinaitic legislation; and that at a crucial moment, he stemmed the current of Hellenization.

SIMḤAH BEN SAMUEL OF VITRY (d. 1105): French scholar; pupil of RASHI. He compiled the *Maḥzor Vitry* which in its complete version is an encyclopedic work incorporating midrashic excerpts, responsa, a commentary on *Avot*, a treatise on the calendar, etc. and the complete annual cycle of prayers together with a codification of laws related to the liturgy and the synagogue service. The MAHZOR represents the ancient French rite, which is closely connected with the more widespread German (*Ashkenazi*) ritual. It has been a valuable source book for all students of the liturgy and *piyyut*.

SIMḤAH BUNAM OF PRZYSUCHA (1765-

1827): Polish ḥasidic rabbi; spiritual heir of Jacob of Przysucha whose teachings he interpreted. S. opposed the popular ḥasidic *rebbes* and wonder workers, stressing instead the rôle of the tzaddik as the spiritual guide to his *ḥasidim*. A man must above all be true to himself and seek for truth in thought and action. He preferred Jewish medieval philosophy and the teachings of Judah Loew ben Bezalel of Prague (*Maharil*) to the study of the Kabbalah which was accepted by other ḥasidic leaders. His highly individual approach aroused the opposition of contemporary *tzaddikim*.

SIMḤAT TORAH (Heb. "Rejoicing of the Law"): Name given in the Diaspora to the second day of Shemini Atzeret; in the Land of Israel, it is an additional name of the latter festival. *S.T.* is an outstanding example of a comparatively late custom becoming entrenched so firmly in the affections of the people that it came to rank as a major celebration. The Talmud knows nothing of it; during the Gaonic Period there are only the vaguest intimations of this day having any special character. Its inception followed the abolition of the Palestinian custom of completing the synagogal cycle of Pentateuch reading every three years (*Meg.* 29b) and the universal adoption of the Babylonian custom of finishing the reading of the *Torah* each year. In the 14th cent. Jacob ben Asher codified the custom of immediately recommencing the reading of the *Torah* after its completion on *S.T.* "in order that Satan shall have no opportunity of accusing the Jews of having finished with the *Torah*". In the 16th cent. Moses Isserles mentioned the *Ashkenazi* customs of taking all the scrolls out of the Ark and making seven circuits of the synagogue with them on the analogy of the seven circuits (hakkaphot) with the Four Species on Hoshana Rabbah; of calling up an indefinite number of worshipers to the Reading of the Law; of calling up children *en masse* to the reading; and of celebrating the occasion with feasting. Later came the custom of appointing a Ḥatan Torah and Ḥatan Bereshit for the coveted honor of reading the concluding and the commencing portions of the Pentateuch respectively. All these customs have now become "statutory law" and the celebrations are accompanied by merrymaking in the synagogue, and much dancing and song.

SIMON, see SIMEON

SIN: Any departure from the right path enjoined upon man by God; in more formally legal terms, any transgression of the Divine commandments. In addition to the eloquent imagery of the expressions "transgression" and "departing from the way", biblical, talmudic, and liturgical literature employ a great number of terms to signify s. The most important of these are *ḥet*, *avon*, and *pesha* (cf. the High Priest's confession of s. in behalf of the people, Lev. 16:21) — usually interpreted as unwillful s., knowledgeable s., and rebellious s. The rabbis distinguish between additional categories of s.: lighter and more serious sins (according to the punishment decreed by biblical law), sins against a fellow-man as opposed to sins against God (the former requiring restitution and placation as a condition of atonement), sins involving the community, etc. However, a man should "not consider the gravity or lightness of the s., but the greatness of Him who has given the commandment". Generally speaking rabbinic (as distinct from kabbalistic) theology has no formal doctrine of original sin, but it is assumed that no man is completely free of s. No s. is unpardonable, however, since "man's power to sin cannot be greater than God's power to forgive" (Joseph Albo), but atonement requires repentance, confession to God, restitution (where applicable), and sacrifice (in Temple times). For certain sins only the Day of Atonement and death bring complete forgiveness. Medieval ascetic manuals gave detailed penitential prescriptions for specific sins.

SIN, ORIGINAL, see FALL OF MAN

SIN-OFFERING (Heb. *ḥattat*): Sacrifice brought (1) by an individual who has inadvertently transgressed a law involving the punishment of extirpation (*karet*), e.g. eating leaven during Passover; (2) by the High Priest or (3) the Sanhedrin in the event of a mistaken decision concerning such a law; and (4) by the priest in behalf of the people on the Day of Atonement. In the last three instances a special procedure was followed and the s. was called a *ḥattat penimit* ("inner s.") since its blood was sprinkled on the inner, golden altar, between the staves of the Ark and in front of the curtain. Sin-offerings were also made in behalf of the public on New Moon and festival days, and by individuals as part of the purification ceremony after (a) childbirth, (b) leprosy, (c) flux, and (d) the termination of the nazirite vow.

SINAI, MOUNT: Mountain located in the Sinai peninsula; also called Horeb (cf. Exod. 3:1). At its foot the Israelites encamped in the third month after the Exodus from Egypt (Exod. 19:1). Moses ascended to the top of the mountain to receive the Ten Commandments in the course of a unique and majestic theophany (Exod. 20:1-24:8). The mountain did not subsequently become connected with a specific cult, however, and the only record in the Bible of a later visit is that made by the fleeing Elijah (I Kings 19:8). Several conjectures have been made as to the exact location of the site, but it remains uncertain. The rabbis related many legends concerning M.S., which is regarded as the epitome of holiness and one of the two sacred mountains (the other being Moriah) on which — spiritually speaking — the world rests.

SINAITIC COMMANDMENTS, see **ORAL LAW; WRITTEN LAW**

SIPHRA, see **MIDRASH**

SIPHREI, see **MIDRASH**

SIRACH, WISDOM OF, see **BEN SIRA**

SIVAN: Ninth month of the civil, third of the religious year; zodiac sign, twins. The name is mentioned in the Bible (Est. 8:9). S. has thirty days, outstanding among them being the 6th-7th (in the Land of Israel the 6th only), the Feast of WEEKS (*Shavuot*), traditional anniversary of the giving of the Law (and also of the death of King David). According to MEGILLAT TAANIT, miracles were performed for the Jews in the Hasmonean Period on the 15th, 16th, and 25th of S., and fasting is therefore forbidden on these days. In Eastern Europe a fast was observed on the 20th of S. in commemoration of the Chmielnicki massacres of 1648-49 (*gezerot taḥ.*).

SIYYUM (Heb. "end"): Celebration held at the conclusion of the study of a tractate of the Talmud. The occasion is considered a SEUDAT MITZVAH and is usually accompanied by a *hadran*, i.e., a halakhic discourse relating to the tractate just studied. Individuals or study groups about to finish a tractate usually leave the last few lines for completion at the *s.* These are followed by the recital of a special KADDISH and a brief reading of the first lines of the tractate to be studied next. It is customary to arrange for a *s.* to be held on *Nisan* 14 (Fast of the First-born) so as to exempt the participating first-born from the obligation of fasting. Another type of S. is held upon completing the writing of a Scroll of the Law. Each man present writes one of the final letters (generally a letter contained in his own name), and the ceremony is followed by a festivity.

SKEPTICISM, see **AGNOSTICISM**

SLANDER: The verse "Thou shalt not take up a false report" (Exod. 23:1) forbids originating a calumny or encouraging its propagation. Injury to another person's reputation by falsehood, s., talebearing, or careless gossip is often mentioned in the Bible and severely denounced by the rabbis. The Talmud says "Calumny kills three — the slanderer himself, the one who listens, and the person spoken of", while "thou shalt not curse the deaf" (Lev. 19:14) is interpreted by the rabbis to apply to all kinds of s. about those absent or dead. In certain cases rabbinic law provides for monetary fines or even excommunication until the s. is retracted. The spreading of false reports is to be distinguished from talebearing and the spreading of injurious but true reports. See LESHON HA-RA.

SLAUGHTER, RITUAL, see **SHEḤITAH**

SLAVES AND SLAVERY: The institution of slavery, whereby a person forfeits his individual liberty and becomes the bondsman of his owner, is accepted by the Bible and Talmud as a normal aspect of the economic and social system. Both works endeavored, however, to institute human regulations to ensure considerate treatment of the slave. There was a considerable difference between the status of the Hebrew and the non-Hebrew (called "Canaanite") slave. The Hebrew could become a slave only through being sold by the *bet din* in payment of debt (Exod. 21) or by voluntarily selling himself on account of poverty (Lev. 25:39). He had to be released after six years of service or before that if he paid off the outstanding balance of his debt. Special regulations applied to the Hebrew female slave (Exod. 21:7-11). So liberal was the interpretation of the injunction not to treat the slave harshly that the Talmud declares in a somewhat hyperbolic statement "Whoso acquires a slave to himself acquires a master to himself" (*Kidd.* 20a). The position with regard to the Canaanite bondsman was very different. He was regarded as the property of his master and could be bequeathed to one's heirs together with the other possessions of the legator (Lev. 25:46). On the other hand any ill-treatment resulting in the loss of an eye or a tooth brought about his automatic release (Exod. 21:26-7) as did also the advent of the JUBILEE year. The slave was circumcised and regarded as a member of the community, bound to perform certain religious duties. In addition every encouragement was given for his manumission, if he became a full Jew. Slavery disappeared among Jews in the Middle Ages.

SLOBODKA: Suburb of Kovno in Lithuania and seat of a famous *yeshivah*. In 1892 the VOLOZHIN *yeshivah* was compulsorily closed by the Russian authorities for refusing to introduce secular studies; its place was taken by the S. *yeshivah* which five years later numbered some 200 students. Its curriculum was influenced by the MUSAR MOVEMENT. In 1925 a section of the *yeshivah* was established at Hebron in Palestine but after the 1929 riots moved to Jerusalem where it is called the Hebron *yeshivah*, carrying on the traditions of S. A S. *yeshivah* has been established at Benei Brak.

SOCIAL JUSTICE: While the plea for s.j. is one of the main themes of the PROPHETS — and their most specific and important contribution to religious thought and action — the idea of s.j. also infuses the whole of biblical legislation. Biblical instances of righteousness often include the concept of s.j. Commandments enjoining charity and consideration to the poor (Deut. 15 and elsewhere) emphasized the duty of the individual and society to the underprivileged and dispossessed. Whereas the Pentateuch does not distinguish between s.j. and ritual and ceremonial obligations (cf. e.g. Lev. 19 where ordinances concerning peace-offerings, leaving part of one's agricultural produce to the poor, talebearing, malice and vengeance, mixed seeds, etc. appear as one piece of legislation) the prophets laid an almost exclusive stress on the need for s.j., condemning in the strongest words those who combine an outward formal piety and ritual observance with a disregard for s.j. (cf. Is. 58; Amos 8:4-5). According to the prophets, the continued survival of nations, whether Jewish or gentile (cf. Amos 1-2; Jonah), is dependent upon national righteousness and s.j. With the loss of national independence the emphasis in the appeal for s.j. shifted even more to the community as a whole. Rabbinic and medieval Jewish communal legislation continued the constant preoccupation with s.j. The prominent part played by Jews in many countries in philanthropic initiatives as well as in socialist movements has often been attributed to the traditional Jewish emphasis on s.j. which tends to manifest itself even in secularist contexts that have become divorced from the religious roots of Judaism.

SOD (Heb. "secret"): Esoteric allegorical method of Bible interpretation (see Pardes) based on the belief that Scripture may have more than one level of meaning. It was especially used for interpreting the creation story (Gen. 1, Maaseh Bereshit) and Ezekiel's vision of the Divine Chariot (Ezek. 1, *Maaseh Merkavah*), and was only to be expounded to mature, reliable students.

SOLOMON (10th cent. B.C.E.): Israelite king; son of David. His great lifework was the construction of the Temple which he dedicated with a lofty prayer (I Kings 8:12-53) in the eleventh year of his reign. S. achieved a wide reputation for wisdom and was the subject of many legends in Jewish and Moslem tradition. Several biblical books (Proverbs, Ecclesiastes, Song of Songs, Ps. 72) were attributed to his authorship.

SOLOMON, PROVERBS OF, see **PROVERBS, BOOK OF**

SOLOMON, PSALMS OF, see **PSALMS OF SOLOMON**

SOLOMON, SONG OF, see **SONG OF SONGS**

SOLOMON, TEMPLE OF, see **TEMPLE**

SOLOMON, WISDOM OF, see **WISDOM OF SOLOMON**

SON OF GOD: Term occasionally found in Jewish literature, biblical and post-biblical, but nowhere implying physical descent from the Godhead. In general terms, the Jewish people are referred to as "the children of the Lord your God" (Deut. 14:1; cf. Exod. 4:22 and Hos. 11:1), in relation to the concept of the Fatherhood of God. Gen. 6:2 mentions the "sons of God" who intermarried with the daughters of man; the phrase is generally taken to refer to angels (also in Ps. 82:6), and is used in this sense in the *Berikh Shemei* prayer (in its Aramaic form) from the Zohar which is recited in some rites at the opening of the Ark. The application of the term to Jesus by the early Church was probably a combination of the metaphorical use of the term in Jewish apocryphal literature (e.g. *Wisdom of Solomon* 2:18) with the literal conception of the term in pagan tradition. When used by the rabbis, the reference was to Israel or to man in general.

SON OF MAN, see **MAN, SON OF**

SONG OF MOSES, see **MOSES, SONG OF**

SONG OF SONGS (Heb. *Shir ha-Shirim,* also known as Canticles and as the Song of Solomon); Fourth book in the Hagiographa section of the Bible and first of the five Scrolls. Its eight chapters consist of the poetic dialogues and monologues of two lovers who express yearning, suffering through separation, the bliss of re-encounter, and the virtue of loyalty. The comeliness of each partner is expressed in a delicate though at times frankly erotic manner. The descriptions of scenery are of a beautiful simplicity and point to a love of nature and the land. The apparent artlessness, purity, and intensity of the S. of S. have made it a classic prototype of love lyrics throughout the ages. As a result of its manifest secular character its canonization was opposed, and final acceptance was only effected as late as the end of the first cent. C.E. at the Synod of Yavneh, on the basis of an allegorical interpretation according to which God was considered as the bridegroom and Israel the bride. This tradition of allegorical interpretation was inherited by Christian exegetes, for whom Jesus became the royal bridegroom and the church the bride. In late medieval exegesis, Jewish and Christian, the collective allegory gave way to an individual-mystical one; and the bride and bridegroom symbolized the human soul and its Divine beloved. Traditionally the work is of Solomonic authorship; according to the Talmud (*Bava Batra* 15a) it was written by Hezekiah "and his contemporaries". Modern scholars assign it a post-exilic date on stylistic grounds, though the setting of the poetry echoes the Solomonic era, but have reached no unanimity as to the original meaning and character of the poem (lyrical drama, collection of wedding songs, etc.) The book, redolent of a spring-like atmosphere, is read in synagogues of the *Ashkenazi* rite on Passover; according to the *Sephardi* rite it is recited on Friday afternoon in preparation for the Sabbath (the beloved bride) as well as on *Seder* night.

SONG OF SONGS RABBAH, see **MIDRASH RABBAH**

SONG OF DEGREES, see **SHIR HA-MAALOT**
SONS OF LIGHT AND DARKNESS, see **DEAD SEA SCROLLS**
SOPHER (SCHREIBER), MOSES (1762-1839): Hungarian rabbinical authority; son-in-law of Akiva EGER. From 1803, he was rabbi in Pressburg (Bratislava) where he founded and headed a distinguished *yeshivah*. S. was generally known as *Ḥatam Sopher* (abbreviation for "Novellae and Responsa of Moses Sopher"), after his six-volume *chef d'œuvre*. One of the outstanding halakhists of his time, he issued responsa to queries from Jewish scholars in many parts of the world. From 1819, he took a leading part in the struggle against the REFORM Movement, strongly opposing any change or innovation. He objected to any substitutions for Hebrew in the liturgy, holding that the introduction of the vernacular would harm Jewish unity. S.'s views — which affected the development of Hungarian Orthodoxy — were summarized in his last testament which warned against Reform and especially against reading the works of Moses MENDELSSOHN. He was succeeded as rabbi in Pressburg and head of the *yeshivah* by his elder son ABRAHAM SAMUEL BENJAMIN S. (1815-1871), known as *Ketav Sopher* after the name he gave all his works, which included commentaries on the Bible, on the *Shulḥan Arukh*, and on certain talmudic tractates. He continued his father's struggle against Reform and was active in the foundation of a separate Orthodox community (1868-69). His brother SIMEON S. (1821-1882) served as rabbi in various communities and from 1860 in Cracow where he was the chief spokesman for Orthodox Jewry in Galicia.
SOPHERIM (Heb. "scribes"): Whereas in biblical usage the term "scribe" signifies a high administrative official, in the early Second Temple Period it came to mean the literate man, engaged in the interpretation of the *Torah* and the transmission of the ORAL LAW. Hence the *s.* are generally considered as the precursors of PHARISAISM and the initiators of the "Jewish" as distinct from "Israelite" period of history. From their ranks came the Men of the Great Assembly (KENESET GEDOLAH). These *s.* were active in the two centuries after EZRA (cf. also the *mevinim* — "expounders" — mentioned in Ezra 8:18 and Neh. 8:7). Information as to their activities is meager, but there are many talmudic references to *divrei sopherim* ("words of the Scribes", i.e., ancient post-biblical regulations), *dikdukei s.* ('legal minutiae"), and *takkanot s.* ("enactments" not derived from the *Torah*). Many of their ordinances had the character of forming a *seyag* ("FENCE") for the protection of the *Torah*. The Talmud ascribes to them regulations relating to prayer, *tephillin*, *tzitzit*, ritual slaughter, the blowing of the *shophar*, the institution of the feasts of *Ḥanukkah* and *Purim*, and the introduction of eighteen emendations into the biblical text (see TIKKUN SOPHERIM). Subsequently the term underwent another change of meaning and denoted one who taught the Bible to children (cf. the later talmudic usage "local scribe" for elementary teacher). The sages and rabbis of the Tannaitic Period were never called "scribes". In the New Testament "Scribes and Pharisees" appear as pejorative terms connoting hypocrisy. Eventually the meaning of the term was limited to penmen occupied in the writing of *Torah* scrolls, *mezuzot*, and *tephillin* (known as *sopher setam*) as well as documents which are valid only if written by hand e.g. bills of divorce. The tractate *Sopherim*, appended to the Babylonian Talmud, contains the meticulous laws which such scribes have to observe.
SOTAH (Heb.): A married woman suspected of adultery (Num. 5:11-31). The procedure prescribed by the Bible to prove her innocence or guilt is the only clear example of trial by ordeal to be found in Judaism. The *s.* is the subject of a complete tractate of the Talmud but the last Mishnah in the tractate declares that the trial was abolished by R. Johanan ben Zakkai (1st cent. C.E.). The reason for its abolition, "because of the spread of immorality" (*Sot.* 47a), has been explained as meaning that the trial can be effective only if the husband himself has been entirely blameless in his sexual life.
SOTAH (Heb. "Woman suspected of adultery"): Sixth tractate in the Mishnah order of NASHIM with *gemara* in both Talmuds. It contains the laws of SOTAH (Num. 5:11-31), a discussion of the laws contained in Deut. 20:2-9, and legislation regarding the breaking of the neck of a heifer in accordance with Deut. 21:1-9.
SOUL: The belief that "something" in man survives his physical death was current in biblical times, although the notion of a s. as an independent, spiritual, or heavenly principle had not yet emerged. Life was not so much the presence of a s. as the animation of a body, and the original meanings of the biblical terms for s. are "breath", "wind", etc. (cf. Gen. 2:17). The seat of life is BLOOD. After death the individual leads a "lifeless", shadowy existence in a Hades-like underworld (*sheol*); cf. Saul's raising of Samuel's spirit from below rather than calling down his s. from above (I Sam. 28). During the latter half of the Second Temple Period the notion of a distinct s.-substance, joined to the body at birth and leaving it again at death, began to gain some ground. In accord with the Platonic tradition, the s. was held by the rabbis to be pre-existent (see PRE-EXISTENCE) and of heavenly origin. Accor-

ding to the medieval thinkers it was "hewn from the THRONE of Glory"; by being sent down into a body it is contaminated, or at least exposed to the danger of contamination through sin. Rabbinic thought generally steered clear of the radical hellenistic DUALISM, exemplified by PHILO, which equated spirit, soul, and good on the one hand, and matter, the body, and evil on the other. The traditional view on the subject is summarized in the daily morning prayer: "O my God, the soul which thou gavest me is pure; thou didst create it, thou didst form it, thou didst breathe it into me... and thou wilt take it from me, but wilt restore it to me in the future" (see RESURRECTION). The Platonic and Neo-Platonic assumption of a spiritual and pre-existent s.-substance also underlies the doctrine of the TRANSMIGRATION of souls which was taken up by the medieval kabbalists. The Aristotelian thinkers (e.g. Maimonides), who defined the s. as the "form" of a living organism, had greater difficulty than the Platonists in giving a philosophical account and justification of the doctrine of IMMORTALITY which, they held, extended only to that part of the mind which man acquired by intellectual effort and insight (the "acquired intellect"). The usual view was that after death the s. was judged for its life on earth, twelve months (see GEHINNOM) was admitted to celestial bliss (see PARADISE). In the late Middle Ages various rites arose, which were meant to improve the lot of departed souls in the hereafter; some of these have become permanent features of the synagogue service (YIZKOR, HASHKAVAH, KADDISH).

SOUL, TRANSMIGRATION OF, see **TRANSMIGRATION**

SPEKTOR, ISAAC ELHANAN (1817-1896): Lithuanian rabbi; lived in Kovno from 1864. The outstanding rabbinical authority of his time both in E. Europe and beyond, S. issued responsa to queries received from many communities. Noteworthy was his tendency to leniency in rulings concerning AGUNOT — a problem that became particularly prevalent as a result of the vast migration from E. Europe. The Isaac Elhanan Yeshiva (later Yeshiva University) in New York was named in his honor.

SPICES (Heb. *besamim*): The use of s. both as condiments and for perfume was widespread in ancient times. The maiden in the Song of Songs was perfumed with "myrrh and frankincense and with all the powders of the merchant" (3:6), and the maidens brought before Ahasuerus were prepared "six months with oil of myrrh and six months with sweet odors" (Est. 2:12). According to the Midrash only women perfumed themselves (*Gen. Rab.* 17:13) and it was regarded as unseemly for a scholar to do so (*Ber.* 43b). It was customary to burn s. after a meal (*Ber.* 42b) and a blessing is to be said before smelling them; this is probably the origin of the one instance where s. are used in Jewish ritual today in the *havdalah* service marking the conclusion of the Sabbath, which includes the smelling of s. together with the appropriate blessing. Spice boxes for use on this occasion became a favorite object of Jewish ritual art. For the use of s. in the Sanctuary and Temple, see INCENSE.

SPINOZA, BARUCH (BENEDICT) (1632-1677): Dutch philosopher of a Portuguese MARRANO family that had escaped to Amsterdam. S. had a traditional Jewish education and a good knowledge of the medieval Jewish philosophers, but his own philosophic development, greatly influenced by Descartes, led him away from traditional Orthodoxy. His profound and rigorously elaborated pantheistic metaphysics, his radical demand for unfettered freedom of inquiry, and his moral stature have made of him one of the great figures in modern European philosophy. His place, however, is in the history of general Western thought rather than specifically Jewish philosophy. His unorthodox views, which came close to "atheism" as understood by the Calvinist authorities at Amsterdam, led to his excommunication by the *Sephardi* community in 1656. Jewish judgment of S. varies according to the emphasis placed on his integrity and nobility of character, his devotion to the search for truth and his profound piety on the one hand, or on his denial of a personal, transcendent God, his rejection of the authority of revelation and the law, and his critical analysis of the Bible (he was one of the pioneers of biblical criticism) on the other.

STAR OF DAVID, see **MAGEN DAVID**

STARGAZING, see **ASTROLOGY**

STAR WORSHIP, see **IDOLATRY**

STERILIZATION: The two principal laws in the Bible bearing on the subject of s. are the prohibitions against CASTRATION and against marriage to a man "'crushed or maimed in his privy parts" (Deut. 23:2). From these biblical prohibitions rabbinic law concludes that it is forbidden to impair the reproductive organs in men, beasts, or birds (*Even ha-Ezer* 5:11). In males the prohibition includes any mutilation of the penic, testicles, or seminal ducts, even after any previous impairment. Forbidden too, though not as culpable an offense, is s. by means of "a cup of sterility" (*ibid.* 12), an oral contraceptive or sterilizing agent evidently known to the ancients and frequently mentioned in the Talmud. The same applies to the s. of females (*ibid.* 11). These laws, like any other, are set aside if necessary to obviate danger to life (such as in cancer or certain prostate operations), but Jewish law never condones s. for social, punitive, or even eugenic reasons. The marriage ban applies to men whose organs have been mutilated or injured "by the hand of man" only, not to those so injured by an act of God, and suffering from defects which are congenital or caused by illness. This sterility as such, in either party, is not to be an impediment to marriage or conjugal relations.

STIEBEL (Yidd. "a little house", "conventicle"): A room used for prayer gatherings as distinct from a regularly consecrated SYNAGOGUE. In the 18th cent., adherents of the emergent ḥasidic sect, which was violently opposed by the rabbis, particularly in Lithuania, used such temporary prayer rooms for their services, with the result that the *s.* has become the characteristic prayer house of the ḥasidim. Partly due to ḥasidic influence, partly to the desire on the part of various groups to maintain their specific liturgical customs, and partly for economic reasons, the *s.* is more characteristic in the State of Israel than is the formal synagogue.

STOICISM: Philosophical school (founded c. 300 B.C.E. in Athens) which flourished in the Greco-Roman era. Its main emphasis was on ethics, and it stressed the ideal of the wise man whose virtue consists in liberating himself from the sway of the passions and living in conformity with nature and the cosmic law. This cosmic law was conceived by the Stoics as an immanent Divine principle (cosmic Reason, see also LOGOS); life in accordance with it was of the highest felicity. In spite of its pantheistic character (see PANTHEISM) and pagan origin, S., and particularly its stern morality, its belief in a universal governing principle, and its conception of the Divine principle active in the cosmos as Reason, profoundly influenced Jewish thought (PHILO, the mishnaic and talmudic teachers) as well as Christian religious ethics and philosophy. To the extent that Stoic elements became part of Greek philosophical tradition, the influence of S. is evident throughout medieval Jewish philosophy.

STONES AND STONE-WORSHIP: The use of s. in religious worship was widespread in ancient times (cf. Gen. 28:18), and rocks and megaliths frequently served as cultic objects among the Semites. Transmitted to the Hebrews through the Canaanites, stone-worship was prohibited as idolatrous. The Israelites were enjoined not to erect a pillar (*matzevah*) or bow down to figured stone (*even maskit*; Lev. 26:1). Stones were, however, used as memorials of historic events (cf. Josh. 4:9; 8:32; I Sam. 7:12) and as "witnesses" (Gen. 31:48-52).

STONING, see **CAPITAL PUNISHMENT**

STRANGER: In ancient times strangers (i.e., those who were not members of the ethnic or tribal group) were normally without legal or other protection. Hence the grave insistence of the Bible on the duty of showing every consideration to the "s. within thy gates" and treating him like the homeborn Israelite. God "loveth the s. in giving him food and raiment" (Deut. 10:18) and has commanded man to love the s. (*ibid.* 19), for "the s. that dwelleth with you shall be unto you as one born among you" (Lev. 19:33-34). In the rabbinic view the "stranger", in order to qualify for the protection provided by Jewish law, was expected to adhere to the seven NOACHIAN LAWS. A certain confusion has been caused by the fact that the word *ger*, which in the Bible almost without exception means the s. (*ger toshav* cf. e.g.; Gen. 23:4; Deut. 10:19) is used in the Talmud for the PROSELYTE (*ger tzedek*).

STRANGULATION, see **CAPITAL PUNISHMENT**

STRASHON, SAMUEL (1794-1872): Lithuanian talmudist. His novellae on the Babylonian Talmud (*Ḥiddushei ha-Rashash*) were incorporated in many subsequent Talmud editions and helped to establish accurate readings through their extensive references and explanations of complicated subjects.

STRIPES, see **FLOGGING**

STUDY: The s. of the *Torah* (*Talmud Torah*) is considered a positive religious duty of the highest importance. A blessing is included in the daily morning prayer for fulfilling the commandment "to engage in the s. of the *Torah*". This duty is included among those precepts the fruits of which "are enjoyed in this world while the stock remains for the World to Come", and it is, indeed, "the greatest of them all" (Mishnah *Peah* 1:1). The blessing preceding the reading of the *Shema* in both the Morning and Evening Service asks for the grace to be enabled to study the *Torah.* When groups, or even an individual, engage in the s. of the *Torah*, the Divine Presence dwells among them. S. should be regular habit (*Avot* 1:15). Indeed man should devote all his free time to the s. of the *Torah*, giving one third to the Pentateuch, one third to the Mishnah, and one third to Talmud (*Kidd.* 30a). The relative value of s. *versus* observance is expressed in the paradoxical summing up of a famous debate on the subject: "s. is the more important since it leads to observance" (*Kidd.* 40b). EDUCATION has at all times been central to Jewish life and the student its ideal — to the extent that it became accepted (e.g. in E. Europe) for the wife to earn the family's livelihood so as to enable the husband to devote himself to s. Until modern times, s. meant, as a rule, rabbinic learning. The emphasis on intellectual achievement, which was the inevitable result of the high regard in which *Talmud Torah* was held, occasionally led to reactions stressing the more inward (devotional and moral) values of Judaism; cf. Ḥasidei Ashkenaz; Ḥasidism; Musar.

SUBBOTNIKI (Russ. "Sabbatarians"): Name given to a Judaizing sect in Russia which first emerged at the end of the 18th cent. Their main characteristic was their observance of the Jewish Sabbath, but they also adopted various other biblical and Jewish customs such as circumcision, abstention from unclean animals, rejection of the New Testament, and a strict monotheism. Subjected to cruel persecution by the Russian authorities at the beginning of the 19th cent., they were exiled to Siberia in 1826. They obtained religious freedom only at the beginning of the 20th cent. A number of their descendants adopted Judaism and settled in Palestine.

SUFFERING: S. becomes a theological problem if one maintains religious belief in a just God who rewards virtue and goodness, in which case s. must be conceived as Divine punishment for sin. This simple theological scheme, however, is not always confirmed by reality, and the problem of s. occupies a prominent place in both the Bible and Talmud. It is the subject of the Book of Job, whose theme is that the righteous man can be made to undergo s. in order to prove that he is capable of selfless piety. Other books of the Bible seem to assume a direct relation between s. and sin. There is a distinct ambivalence in the approach of the rabbis to the problem. On the one hand they lay down that s. is the result of sin (*Shab.* 55a), and that it acts as an expiation for sin (*Yoma* 86a). On the other, they concede that s. can come upon an innocent person and that, in fact, it is the fate of the righteous in this world. According to a rabbinic legend Moses protested against the agony of R. Akiva's martyrdom and torture which he beheld in a vision, but God's reply was "Be silent! Such is my decree" (*Men.* 29b). Both views are combined in the passage: "If a person is visited by s. let him examine his actions. Should he find them blameless let him attribute it to neglect of the study of *Torah*. If he still finds no cause, let him accept that they are the chastenings of love, as it is said (Ps. 94:12) 'For whom the Lord loveth He chasteneth'" (*Ber.* 5a). The usual explanation of s. resorts to eschatology and to the doctrine of retribution in the World to Come. The standard rabbinic view is that the righteous person expiates his few sins on this earth in order to enjoy the full reward for his righteousness in the World to Come (cf. *Kidd.* 40b). See also Theodicy.

SUFISM: The traditional designation of Mohammedan mysticism (from *suf*, the coarse woolen cloth which the early Moslem ascetics used to wear). The ultimate aim of the sufis was mystical union with God by passing through the stages of abstinence, renunciation, poverty, trust, purity of will and mind, and love of God. The teachings of s. were greatly influenced by the philosophy of Neo-Platonism and in some branches at least, exhibited gnostic traits. Long suspected of heresy and opposed by the orthodox theologians, Sufi mysticism was finally reconciled with orthodox thought in the 12th cent. S. also exerted considerable influence on medieval Jewish piety and ascetic theology, notably on Baḥya Ibn Pakuda whose *Ḥovot ha-Levavot* contains Sufi terminology, ideas, and quotations. Another Jewish thinker deeply influenced by S. was Abraham, the son of Moses Maimonides.

SUICIDE: Judaism does not consider the individual as the owner or unlimited master of his own life; consequently s., which amounts in rabbinic thought to murder, is strictly forbidden. "And surely the blood of your lives shall I require" (Gen. 9:5) is considered a prohibition referring to the s. Man is not permitted to sacrifice his life even to avoid violating biblical commands unless it be to avoid committing one of the three cardinal sins (murder, adultery, idol-worship); indeed, concerning the three for which he must lay down his life, many authorities hold that he is to allow himself to be killed rather than violate them, but must not actively destroy himself. Many instances are recorded in Jewish history of individual and collective s. committed by fighters (e.g. at Masada in 72 C.E.) and martyrs (e.g. at York in 1190) to escape the hand of the enemy and the threat of slavery or apostasy. That suicides have no share in the World to Come is recorded as a Jewish doctrine by Josephus but does not appear in the Talmud. The s. is to be buried in a separate part of the cemetery. However a recent rabbinic ruling considers the s. as being of unsound mind, and as such he is allowed to be interred with others.

SUKKAH (Heb.): The booth or tabernacle in which the Children of Israel were enjoined to dwell for seven days "in order that your generations may know that I caused the Children of Israel to dwell in tabernacles when I brought them out of the Land of Egypt" (Lev. 23:42-43), and which gives the name to the Festival of Tabernacles. Booths probably played a part in the ancient harvest festivals, hence their association with *Sukkot*, which is also called the "harvest festival" in the Bible. I Maccabees also associates the *s.* with the first celebration of Ḥanukkah. The *s.* must be a temporary structure, its roof covered with cut vegetation and open to the sun, though it must give "more shade than light". Orthodox Jews take their meals in the *s.* and many also sleep there during the first seven days of the festival. In Western communities a *s.* is built adjacent to the synagogue and visited by the congregation for light refreshments after the services on the festival. Although the FOUR SPECIES are considered a separate rite independent of the *s.* (Lev. 23:40), it appears that NEHEMIAH (8:15) regarded them as the materials from which the *s.* was to be constructed; a similar opinion voiced in the Talmud by R. Judah (*Suk.* 37a) was overruled. A *s.* must have a minimum of three walls and be not more than 20 cubits high. It must be at least large enough for the major part of the body to enter standing up. Inclement weather absolves one from the duty of dwelling in the *s.* Women are exempt from the obligation to dwell in a *s.* (as they are from all commandments which depend upon a fixed time for their performance) but they may do so if they wish. The kabbalistic custom of USHPIZIN ("guests") associates Abraham, Isaac, Jacob, Joseph, Moses, Aaron, and David each with one day of the festival; one of the unseen guests is welcomed each day to the *s.* and an appropriate invocation recited.

SUKKAH (Heb. "Booth"): Sixth tractate in the Mishnah tractate of *Moed*, with *gemara* in both Talmuds. It sets forth the laws of the Festival of Tabernacles (cf. Lev. 23:34ff.; Num. 29:12ff.; Deut. 16:13ff.) including the regulations concerning the *lulav*, the Water-Drawing Festival, and the erection of the booth.

SUKKOT, FESTIVAL OF, see **TABERNACLES**

SUN: In the Bible the s. is a symbol of joy and light (cf. Ps. 19:6-7); and an eclipse of the s. presages impending judgment and doom (cf. Is. 13:10; 40:2; Amos 8:9; Mic. 3:6). Calendrical needs, both for the purpose of establishing the solar year and its solstices and for accurately determining the beginning and the conclusion of Sabbath and festivals and the times for prayer and sacrifices, stimulated close study of the s. by the rabbis. The length of the year, the exact determination of sunset and sunrise, and the onset of TWILIGHT were all exhaustively debated and finally established. One of the rarest ceremonies in Judaism is the Blessing of the Sun, recited when the s. enters a new cycle (and according to tradition stands at the same position as at its creation), which according to the Talmud (*Ber.* 68a) occurs every 28 years. The ceremony is held on the first Wednesday in the month of *Nisan* in that year. The order of service comprises appropriate scriptural verses, Ps. 148 followed by the prescribed blessing of God "who fashions the works of creation", and talmudic passages. The last occasion on which the blessing was recited was in 1981 and the next is due in 2009.

SUPERSTITION: Superstitious practices such as DIVINATION and MAGIC are prohibited in the Bible. Part of the opposition to them was due to the fact that they led to idolatrous and immoral practices and were therefore "an abomination to the Lord" (Deut. 18:9). With the complete triumph of monotheism among the Jews during the period of the Second Temple, s. lost its idolatrous character; the Talmud forbids only "the ways of the Amorites" (cf. Tos. *Shab.* 6:7), i.e., superstitious customs tinged with positively heathen and idolatrous features. However superstitious practices and beliefs are rife in the Talmud, ranging over the whole area of belief in DEMONS, AMULETS, sorcery, DREAMS, and chance occurrences. ABBAYE, in particular, reports a host of superstitious beliefs conveyed to him by his foster-mother. Many medieval authorities declared all forms of s. to be outright nonsense. Nevertheless, superstitious beliefs and practices, often abetted by mystical and kabbalistic influences, have persisted in Jewish circles to this day, mainly in the form of folk customs.

SUPPLICATION, see **BAKASHAH**

SURA: City in S. Babylonia, also called Matta Mahaseia, where RAV founded (c. 219) a famous ACADEMY which flourished for eight centuries. It was in S. that the Babylonian TALMUD was largely compiled by R. ASHI and RAVINA during the 4th-5th cents. From the time of R. Mar bar R. Huna (591), the heads of the S. academy bore the title GAON. The most renowned *gaon* of S. was SAADYAH. The academy at S. enjoyed continuous interchange with its sister academy at PUMBEDITA, with which it ultimately merged.

SUSANNA AND THE ELDERS: Book in the Apocrypha. It tells how Susanna, the beautiful and pious wife of Joachim, excites the lust of two elders. When she rejects their advances they concoct a charge of adultery against her. She is found guilty and sentenced to death, but as she is led forth to her execution the young Daniel is able to expose the falsity of the accusation by a clever stratagem, and the elders are put to death instead. The book dates from the second or first century B.C.E. It has been suggested that it originated as a polemic concerning the difference of opinion between Sadducees and Pharisees over the laws governing conspiring witnesses and reforms in the administration of justice.

SWINE, see **PIG**

SYMMACHUS (c. 2nd-3rd cent.): Translator of the Bible into Greek. Fragments of his translation have been preserved in Origen's *Hexapla*. In contrast to the SEPTUAGINT, which in some places deviates from the masoretic text, and to AQUILA, whose version is a literal interpretation of the text written in a poor Greek style, S. produced a polished Greek translation which often paraphrases the text but maintains the meaning. There are various conjectures as to his identity (e.g. he may have been a Christian of the Ebionite sect; a

Samaritan convert to Judaism; or the *tanna* Symmachus ben Joseph).

SYNAGOGUE (from Gk. *synagoge*: "a place of meeting" or "assembling"): Greek term translating the Heb. *bet ha-keneset*. The exact origin of the s. is unknown. Though PRAYER was an integral part of sacrificial service at an early time (see SACRIFICES), there is no record of the existence of special prayer houses. The s. may have originated during the period of Babylonian captivity, although some scholars trace its beginnings to the period of the Kingdom. The first Babylonian exiles (597 B.C.E.) seem to have met for the purpose of exposition of the Scriptures and public worship on Sabbaths and festivals; when the bulk of the people were exiled to Babylonia (586 B.C.E.) they already found the institution of meeting for prayer and instruction in existence. Such gatherings are recorded in the Book of Ezekiel, and the reference in Ezek. 11:16 possibly reflects the emergence of the s. in the Babylonian Exile. To the allegation of the inhabitants of Jerusalem that the exiles, being far removed from the Temple, had forfeited the presence and protection of God, the prophet replied with the Divine message that God Himself would be a *mikdash me'at* ("a little sanctuary") to Israel in exile (Ezek. 11:15-16). This was interpreted by the rabbis to refer to the "houses of worship and houses of learning". No definite reference to the existence of the s. is known until long after the return from the Babylonian Exile. It is possible that by the time Ezra instituted the reading of the *Torah* on Sabbath afternoon and on the second and fifth day of the week (*Bava Kamma* 82a), and statutory daily prayers (*Meg.* 17b; *Ber.* 33a), assemblies for worship were already in existence throughout the land. By the end of the Second Temple Period the s. was a well-established institution both in Palestine and in the Diaspora; cf. the matter-of-course references in the New Testament to Jesus' preaching in the synagogues in Galilee. A s. existed even within the precincts of the TEMPLE (Mishnah *Yoma* 7:1; Tosephta *Suk.* 4:3), but the date of its establishment is unknown. The s. had so much become the focus of religious life that the destruction of the Second Temple left much less of a vacuum than had the destruction of the First Temple. The rabbis taught that a s. should be erected wherever there existed a Jewish community. Where possible they were built on hills so that they should not be overlooked by other buildings. After the destruction of the Temple in 70 C.E., the s. became the spiritual fortress of the Jewish people. Religious life, and to some extent communal life in general, centered around the s. and its dual rôle of prayer house and place of religious instruction. Architecturally the central feature in a s. is the ARK on the east wall (i.e., oriented "toward Jerusalem") containing the Scrolls of the Law. In front of the Ark burns the "perpetual light", reminiscent of the LIGHTS kindled by the priest in the seven-branched candelabrum in the Temple (Num. 8:14). Originally the stand for the reader (or whoever led the service) was slightly below floor level — a feature with which the rabbis associated the verse "From out of the depths I call upon Thee" (Ps. 130:1), but it subsequently became customary for the officiant to read from a raised platform (BIMAH). As in the precincts of the Temple, a special compartment or gallery is reserved in the traditional s. for women; Conservative and Reform synagogues, however, have men and women seated together. No priest or ordained minister is required to conduct the service or preach in the s., though men so trained (see CANTOR, ḤAZZAN, RABBI), are now usually employed for these functions. However, anyone who is religiously and morally fit and able to lead the congregation in prayer and to communicate knowledge of the *Torah* is qualified to officiate in the s. The entrance to the s. must be opposite the side toward which the worshipers turn in prayer (facing Jerusalem). In many, the seats along the eastern wall of the s. are regarded as especially privileged and are much coveted. The s., in contrast to the Temple, constituted a gathering place for congregational worship — a major innovation in religious history profoundly influencing both Christian (church) and Moslem (mosque) forms of worship. In modern times, especially in the U.S. the s. (or "temple") has developed into a community center, the function of which is to provide not only for religious but also for educational and social activities.

SYNAGOGUE COUNCIL OF AMERICA: Organization established in 1926 to present a united front of varying Jewish religious trends in activities involving non-Jewish (mainly, Christian) organizations. Its constituents are Orthodox (Rabbinical Council of America and the Union of Orthodox Jewish Congregations of America), Conservative (Rabbinical Assembly of America and the United Synagogue of America), and Reform (Central Conference of American Rabbis and the Union of American Hebrew Congregations). It participates in interfaith activities and in fighting religious prejudice.

SYNAGOGUE, GREAT, see **KENESET GEDOLAH**

SYNCRETISM: The act or system of blending or reconciling heterogeneous elements. In the history of religion s. signifies the mixing of beliefs and practices of different — and at times conflicting — character and origin. S. occurs wherever different cultures meet. The biblical record contains indications of much popular s. between Israelite and Canaanite religion, an amalgamation which the prophets had continually to combat. An example of conscious theological s. can be found in Gen. 14:22, where Abraham identifies his God with Melchizedek's *el elyon*. In a narrower sense s. generally refers to the blending of Greek and Oriental religions in the Hellenistic Period; from the point of view of Jewish monotheism this s. was merely another form of paganism (see MACCABEES).

SYNOD, see **COUNCILS**

T

TAAMEI MIKRA, see **ACCENTS**
TAANIT (Heb.): Fast.
TAANIT (Heb. "Fast"): Ninth tractate in the Mishnah order of *Moed* with *gemara* in both Talmuds. It deals with fasting in time of drought, prayers for rain, and regulations concerning minor Fasts.
TAANIT ESTER, see **ESTHER, FAST OF**
TAANIT SCROLL, see **MEGILLAT TAANIT**
TAANIT TZIBBUR: Public fast.
TABERNACLE, see **SUKKAH**
TABERNACLES: The third of the Pilgrim Festivals, in Hebrew *Sukkot* from the main aspect of the festival which involves the celebrant's dwelling in a Sukkah. Originally a Harvest Festival (Exod. 23:16; Deut. 16:13), it was given added historical significance as a commemoration of the forty years' wandering in the wilderness (Lev. 23:43). The festival became so popular that in mishnaic times it was known simply as *ḥag* i.e., "festival" *par excellence.* Liturgically it is described as *zeman simḥatenu,* "the time of our rejoicing". The biblical regulations concerning the holiday mention the injunctions to dwell in the *sukkah* and to take the Four Species. A circuit of the synagogue with the Four Species in hand is made daily to the accompaniment of chanted *hosannas,* and the Four Species are waved in prescribed fashion during the recitation of the Hallel. The seventh day of the festival has been given the name Hoshana Rabbah, when — among other ceremonies — a sevenfold circuit of the synagogue is made with the Four Species. Most of these ceremonies originate in ancient Temple custom. During the intermediate days of the festival, the Water-Drawing Festival, of which a vivid description is given in the Talmud (*Suk.* 53a), was celebrated as the most joyous occasion of the year. The festival begins on *Tishri* 15 and lasts seven days; the eighth day (according to some, a separate festival) is Shemini Atzeret. In the Diaspora a ninth day is added for Simḥat Torah (in the Land of Israel, this is combined with *Shemini Atzeret*). Work is prohibited only on the first and last days (in the Diaspora, the first two and last two), and the intermediate days are hol ha-moed. *Hallel* and the Additional Service are recited each day (see Festival Prayers). The unusual order of the sacrifices offered during the festival in Temple times (Num. 29:12-32: 13 bullocks were offered on the first day, and the number was progressively reduced by one daily until on the seventh day only seven were offered, making a total of 70) has given rise to the tradition that these sacrifices represent the offerings made by Israel in behalf of the 70 nations which traditionally inhabit the earth. There is evidence that in Second Temple times the pilgrimage to Jerusalem was of greater proportions on this festival than on the other pilgrim festivals, since at this time the harvest had been fully gathered and farmers were free to leave their fields.
TABLETS (or **TABLES**) **OF THE LAW** (Heb. *luḥot ha-edut; luḥot ha-berit*): Two tablets of stone were received by Moses from God at Sinai as a sign of His covenant with Israel. The Decalogue was engraved upon them "by the finger of God" (Exod. 31:18). After Israel's apostasy (see Calf, Golden), Moses broke the tablets and was bidden to hew a new set on which the identical text was engraved (Exod. 34:1). The tablets were deposited in the Ark, which was therefore known as the Ark of the Covenant (Deut. 10:2), and was subsequently kept in Solomon's Temple (I Kings 8:9) until its destruction. According to the rabbis the size of the tablets was $6 \times 3 \times 6$ cubits (*Bava Batra* 14a). Aggadic and kabbalistic comment deals copiously with the substance of the tablets, the nature of the script, and the circumstances of their transmission. According to one tradition they were hidden by Jonah; to another, they were taken into the Babylonian Exile. In modern times an emblem of the tablets traditionally adorns the ark in the synagogue. Until the end of the Middle Ages the tablets did not figure as a Jewish symbol.
TADSHE: Midrash, also called *Baraita de-Rabbi Pinḥas ben Yair* after the 2nd cent. *tanna* to whom the work is traditionally ascribed. The book opens with a commentary on "Let the earth bring forth", (Heb. *tadshe ha-aretz*: Gen. 1:11), hence its title. *T.* contains speculations on the mystical significance of numbers along lines developed in the Book of Yetzirah, as well as astrological matter. It has been suggested that its author was the 11th cent. S. French scholar Moses Ha-Darshan.
TAGIN (Aram. "crowns"): Decorative crownlike

flourishes on certain letters in masoretic Bible scrolls. Their origin is traditionally ascribed to Sinaitic revelation, and talmudic and midrashic sources assign them a mystical significance. A Book of *T.* (*Sepher Tagin*) sets out the rules for their correct application. *T.* also appear on the MEZUZAH and TEPHILLIN, but not in printed texts of the Bible.

TAḤANUN (Heb. "supplication"): Petition for grace and forgiveness (the name is derived from the original introduction: "...and receive my supplications" — *taḥanunai*) said daily, except on Sabbaths, festivals, and days of joy (e.g. in the presence of a bridegroom) after the morning and afternoon *amidah.* The liturgical *t.* replaces the earlier silent, personal petitions for mercy. *T.* is also called *nephilat appayim* ("falling on the face") from the attitude in which it was originally recited (this was a complete prostration still practiced in France as late as the beginning of the 13th cent.); since gaonic times, however, the posture has been modified into an inclination of the head on the left arm (or on the right when the *tephillin* is on the left). SAADYAH described the worshiper as "half sitting and half kneeling" during *t.*, but the western tradition is to sit. "Falling on the face is practiced only in the presence of a Scroll of the Law, the attitude being considered a sign of reverence. The prayer is introduced (since the 18th cent.) with the verse "And David said... 'I am in a great strait; let us fall now into the hand of the Lord'" (II Sam. 24:14). This is followed by Ps. 6, the *piyyut* "Guardian of Israel" (SHOMER YISRAEL), and the conclusion "As for us, we know not what to do", composed of biblical verses. The *Sephardi* ritual omits "Guardian of Israel" and substitutes Ps. 25 for Ps. 6. In the Israeli *Sephardi* and ḥasidic rites *t.* commences with the confession of sins (*viddui*) and the thirteen Divine attributes; in the Israeli *Ashkenazi* and the Diaspora *Sephardi* rituals these are said on MONDAYS AND THURSDAYS only (see VE-HU RAḤUM).

TAHARAH, see **PURITY, RITUAL**

TAHARAT MISHPAḤAH, see **FAMILY**

TAKHRIKHIN (Heb.): Shrouds. See BURIAL.

TAKKANAH (Heb.): Regulation or ordinance promulgated for the public welfare or for the strengthening of religious and moral life, and supplementing the law of the *Torah.* Rabbinical authorities have introduced ordinances, throughout the ages, but those enacted after the closing of the Talmud are regarded as binding only on the country or community directly under the jurisdiction of the promulgating authority. The Talmud attributes to Moses himself the *t.* of reading excerpts from the Pentateuch on Sabbaths, festivals, the New Moon, and on the intermediate days of festivals (Y. *Meg.* 4:1). The AMIDAH prayer is traditionally considered a *t.* issued by the men of the Great Synagogue. Among tannaitic *takkanot* are included provisions that a wife's marriage settlement (KETUBBAH) is to be a general mortgage on the whole of the husband's property (issued by SIMEON BEN SHETAH); communities must appoint elementary school teachers (by Joshua ben Gamla); a father must support his minor children (by the SANHEDRIN at Usha); compulsory education is to be provided for children from the age of six (*Bava Batra* 21a). Among the first *takkanot* introduced by rabbinical authorities in Christian Europe are those of R. GERSHOM BEN JUDAH (11th cent.). His twenty-five ordinances (including the prohibitions against POLYGAMY and against opening letters addressed to others) were accepted as binding in *Ashkenazi* custom. An ordinance enacted by a *bet din* for a particular reason is not invalidated even if that reason no longer exists, and only another *bet din* of greater authority can annul it. Nevertheless many *takkanot*, particularly those of a local or communal nature, did in fact lapse in the course of time.

TAL, see **DEW**

TALLIT (Heb.): Four-cornered cloth with fringes (cf. Num. 15:38) used by males as a prayer shawl during the Morning (and Additional) Service; called *tallit gadol* ("big *t.*") in order to distinguish it from the *tallit katan* ("small *t.*"), or TZITZIT, worn beneath the outer garments. The *t.* is donned before putting on the TEPHILLIN. After the recital of a special blessing (*le-hitatteph ba-tzitzit*) it is wrapped around the head and shoulders and let down so that two of its fringe-bearing corners fall behind and two in front of the wearer. The minimal size of a *t. gadol* is that of a garment large enough to envelop the head and upper body of a youngster. In some areas, particularly in Eastern Europe, only married men wore the *t.*, and even where an unmarried man wore one, he would not cover his head with the *t.* during prayer. The *t.* should be made of wool and have woolen fringes attached. It may, however be made of other fabrics, in which case the fringes must be made from the same fabric as the *t.* It is now frequently made from silk. Unless it is impossible to obtain an alternative, a linen *t.* is not to be used. At the Afternoon and Evening Service the *t.* is worn by the officiant only; on the Day of Atonement it is worn by male worshipers at all five services. On *Av* 9, the *t.* is donned at the Afternoon instead of at the Morning Service.

TALMID ḤAKHAM (Heb. "disciple of the wise"): The favorite term in rabbinical literature for a scholar. It implies that the true scholar is always a student and that the study of the *Torah* is never ending. The *t.ḥ.* embodies a Jewish ideal of perfection; the Talmud states that "a bastard who is a *t.ḥ.* takes precedence over a High Priest who is an ignoramus" (*Hor.* 13a). But while excessive in their praise of the *t.ḥ.* (he "increases peace in the world", *Ber.* end), the rabbis also demand from him the most exacting standards of personal conduct; certain actions that are normal and legitimate for others would be a "profanation of God's name" (*ḥillul ha-Shem*) in a scholar. Nevertheless rabbinic law provides certain privileges (e.g. exemption from taxes) for the *t.ḥ.*

TALMUD (Heb. "teaching"): The word T. is most commonly used as a comprehensive term for the Mishnah (see below) and GEMARA regarded as a single unit; it is applied specifically to two compilations, the Palestinian (incorrectly, Jerusalem) T. (*Talmud Yerushalmi*) and the Babylonian T. (*Talmud Bavli*). The T. is a unique literary work, the result and record of study and discussions over a period of some eight centuries by the scholars of the entire nation working continually in the ACADEMIES of Palestine and Babylonia. Its spiritual roots are the Bible and the traditions of HALAKHAH and MIDRASH that crystallized during the Second Temple Period. Though considering itself grounded in the Bible, the T. itself clearly distinguishes between the "WRITTEN LAW", i.e., Scripture, and the ORAL LAW, which was transmitted by word of mouth from the time of Moses (*Avot* 1:1). It is claimed, however, that both derive from Sinai and are complementary expressions of the same Divine law: the precepts of the *Torah* required elucidation and elaboration at innumerable points, and a living, unwritten interpretation must have existed from earliest times. The activities and institutions that gave rise to the origin of talmudic Judaism can be traced back to the period of the Babylonian Exile which provided an impetus for the formation in embryonic form of the *bet ha-keneset* ("SYNAGOGUE"), with its non-sacrificial form of worship (cf. Ezek. 11:16), and the BET HA-MIDRASH ("schoolhouse") where Divine service assumed the form of *Torah* study. Ezra "the SCRIBE" (Ezra 7:6) inaugurated a new era of *Torah* teaching (Neh. 8:7) which provided the religious dynamic of Jewish life from the 5th cent. B.C.E. down to modern times. The institution of the Great Assembly, also attributed to him, is still the subject of scholarly dispute (see KENESET GEDOLAH), but the existence of an organization of this nature appears to be postulated by the spiritual creativity of the epoch. This early formative period is considered to have come to an end with the age of the *sopherim*, which concluded with SIMEON HA-TZADDIK (*Avot* 1:2), who was followed by a succession of ZUGOT ("pairs"), the first of each duumvirate being the NASI ("prince", "president"), and the other the AV BET DIN ("head of the court") of the SANHEDRIN. HILLEL and SHAMMAI were the last of the "pairs"; thereafter the scholars of the Mishnaic Period are called TANNAIM ("teachers"). The oral tradition was linked to Scripture by a method of exegesis which gradually evolved HERMENEUTICAL RULES. Hillel recognized seven of these (later expanded by R. Ishmael into 13; subsequently 32 were enumerated). He also sought to bring some system into the bewildering accumulation of traditions by dividing the laws into six sections. The work of systematization was continued by later generations of scholars, notably by R. AKIVA and R. MEIR, and a final authorized compilation was made by R. JUDAH HA-NASI, c. 220 C.E., under the title "Mishnah" ("teaching"). The Mishnah was not so much a code as a textbook, giving the essence of the Oral Law as it was known to the sages of the time. It recorded conflicting opinions and very often named the disputants. It included, however, only a part of the available material; of the rest a portion was incorporated in a parallel collection called TOSEPHTA ("supplement") while numerous tannaitic statements excluded from the Mishnah (though sometimes found in the *Tosephta*) are cited in the discussions of the post-mishnaic scholars and are called *baraita* ("extraneous" teaching). Other collections of tannaitic dicta are to be found in the halakhic and aggadic MIDRASHIM.

The Mishnah consists of six orders (*Shishah Sedarim;* hence the abbreviation *ShaS* for Talmud); each order is divided into tractates (*Massekhtot*), each tractate into chapters, and each chapter into paragraphs. The following are the names and themes of the orders:

1. ZERAIM ("Seeds"), mainly agricultural laws; 11 tractates.
2. MOED ("Appointed times"), laws of festivals and feasts; 12 tractates.
3. NASHIM ("Women"), chiefly on marriage, divorce, and vows; 7 tractates.
4. NEZIKIN ("Damages"), civil and criminal law; 10 tractates.
5. KODASHIM ("Holy things"), pertaining primarily to Temple service; 11 tractates.
6. TOHAROT ("Purity"), laws of ritual purity and impurity; 12 tractates.

The language of the Mishnah is new (i.e., rabbinic) Hebrew, as distinct from classical (biblical) Hebrew. Mishnaic Hebrew, which developed during the period of the Second Temple, contains many Greek and some Latin loanwords and shows marked Aramaic influence. It is an idiom well-adapted to deal with practical matters, but lacks the vigor and poetic grandeur of the biblical tongue.

No sooner was the Mishnah completed than it became the subject of intensive study in the

Jewish academies of both Palestine and Babylonia. The discussion focused on the Mishnah is called *gemara* ("completion" or "teaching"), and the sages of the period bear the name AMORAIM ("discoursers"). The *gemara* proceeds by way of question and answer, and generally follows the method of analogy and association, as a result of which a discussion may cover a wide range of subjects and often end up with a completely different subject-matter. Thus a discussion on a point of law between two rabbis may lead to an enumeration and elucidation of all other questions about which these two teachers were at variance. The second chapter of the tractate *Shabbat* starts with the explanation of the list of oils suitable for the Sabbath lamp and leads, by way of association, to a discussion regarding the lighting of the *Ḥanukkah* lamp, and this, in turn, leads to a brief account of the *Ḥanukkah* miracle, which is thus mentioned in the T. only incidentally. Talmudic exposition combines records of actual discussions in the academies, traditions of the schools, tannaitic texts, and the redactor's glosses. Discussions that took place in different schools and at different times were often juxtaposed by the redactors when they chose what they considered relevant to the argument from the vast accumulated material at their disposal. R. JOHANAN was one of the chief architects, though hardly the compiler, of the Palestinian T., the redaction of which was hastily finished at Tiberias, c. 400 C.E., under the pressure of growing persecution; the order *Nezikin* was probably completed earlier at Caesarea, c. 350. The foundations of the Babylonian *gemara* were laid by RAV and SAMUEL, while the final redaction was the work of R. ASHI and RAVINA, c. 500. Minor additions were made by the SAVORAIM ("reasoners") in the 6th and 7th cents. The rabbis ruled that the Oral Law might not be written down (*Git.* 60b; *Tem.* 14b). Notwithstanding this interdict, private manuscripts of at least parts of the talmudic literature were used, it appears, by many scholars in order to assist their memory; subsequently, the whole of talmudic literature was committed to writing. Both Talmuds have, with slight variations, the same Mishnah; but they differ in respect of the size and content of their *gemara* and its arrangement in relation to the Mishnah. The language of the *gemara* is composed of new Hebrew and Aramaic; in the Palestinian T. Western Aramaic is used, in the Babylonian T. Eastern Aramaic. The Palestinian recension contains 39 tractates, belonging mainly to the first four orders; the text, which is obviously incomplete, may originally have extended to the whole order of *Kodashim*. The Babylonian T. has only 36 tractates (belonging chiefly to orders 2-5), but is nearly four times as large (2,500,000 words) as its Palestinian counterpart (750,000 words). The style of the two Talmuds, and more especially the Palestinian, is terse to the point of obscurity. The only complete manuscript of the Palestinian T. is that of Leyden; while the Munich Codex (1334) is the sole surviving manuscript of the whole Babylonian T. Daniel Bomberg printed the first complete edition of the Palestinian T. in Venice in 1522-3, and that of the Babylonian version in the same city in 1520-23. All subsequent editions of the Babylonian T. have retained the pagination of the first edition. Of the two Talmuds, the Babylonian recension has received more continuous and intensive study and is regarded as the more authoritative.

The rabbis themselves distinguish in their teaching between *halakhah* ("the way to walk", "the legal section") and AGGADAH ("narration"). The former comprises all aspects of Jewish law — ritual, civil, and criminal; the latter, which forms more than a seventh of the Palestinian, and nearly a third of the Babylonian T., is a generic term for all non-legal subject-matter, and includes homiletics and ethics, history and legend, scientific facts and philosophical reflection. Both *halakhah* and *aggadah* are anchored in the Bible by means of midrashic methods of interpretation, but each uses a different method and practical purpose. The *halakhah* endeavored to translate the ideal of doing God's will and obeying His law into the practical details of a way of life. It used the methods of logical argument, analysis, and consideration of traditional customs and norms that had long been established in the schools or in general practice. It is a rabbinic axiom that there is nothing superfluous in Scripture. Every nuance, every word, every letter is made to yield a meaning in support of ancient usage, or new enactment (TAKKANAH), or to build a "FENCE" (*seyag*) around the sacred heritage of the *Torah* in order to safeguard it from careless or ignorant trespass. Consequently halakhic conclusions are considered as rigorously binding in rabbinic Judaism. It is different with the aggadic dicta, most of which are designed to direct man's faith and devotion toward God. "Would you know your Maker?" ask the rabbis; "Then go study the *aggadah* — for there you will learn to know Him and to imitate His ways" (*Siphrei, Ekev*). It has therefore been the tradition to exercise greater freedom in the interpretation of the *aggadah*, though literalist and fundamentalist movements have been not infrequent. But in spite of the different character of the two types of teaching, they are not presented separately in the T. A halakhic discussion may be followed by a few pages of *aggadah* or even interpreted by an aggadic dictum or reflection.

In the evolution of Judaism the T. is the sequel

to the Bible. Like so many sequels it does not match the simple grandeur of its predecessor. Nevertheless rabbinic Judaism considers it the necessary complement and fulfillment of Scripture. Since the redaction of the T., the study of its contents has been the basis of Jewish religious life. The leading talmudic academies, after Babylonia, were in N. Africa from where they spread to Spain and Italy and to Germany and France. The commentary by RASHI on the Babylonian T. and its further elucidation by the TOSAPHISTS were major factors in the exclusive popularity of the Babylonian version. The codifiers systematized the vast and often unorderly mass of material and organized the juridical sections under relevant heads (see CODES). In more recent centuries the center of talmudic study was in the *yeshivot* of E. Europe which concentrated on the exclusive, and often hypercasuistic, study of the text and commentators. During the past century, and as a result of the application of modern historical and philological methods by the WISSENSCHAFT DES JUDENTUMS, the scientific study of the text and background of the T. has greatly advanced the understanding of the nature and composition of the T. Throughout the centuries countless rabbis and scholars have written NOVELLAE, commentaries, glosses, and RESPONSA, examining the problems raised by the text and seeking to explain difficulties as well as to relate the conclusions to circumstances of later ages. However, most of these related to the Babylonian T. and it is only in recent centuries that the Palestinian T. has formed the basis for major commentaries and comparative study. Opposition to the T. has also emerged on occasion. The KARAITES rejected the rabbinic tradition and sought their sole inspiration in Scriptures. The REFORM Movement considered the T. as the expression of one phase in the history of Judaism and hence rejected its authority, although adopting some of its ethical teaching. The T. was throughout the Medieval Period the object of continuing attacks from Christian and anti-Jewish sources and copies were collected and destroyed or subjected to severe censorship. In recent decades, however, Christian scholars (e.g. Strack, G.F. Moore, Travers Herford) have written important scholarly works on the T. and the Talmudic Period.

TALMUD, BURNING OF: In the year 1240 the apostate Nicholas Donin laid a charge before the authorities in N. France that the TALMUD contained blasphemies against Jesus. The Jews were compelled to surrender their copies of the Talmud pending clarification of the charge; this took the form of a DISPUTATION between Donin and rabbis Jehiel of Paris, Moses of Coucy, Judah ben David of Melun, and Samuel ben Solomon of Chateau Thierry. The disputation lasted for three days, at the end of which time the charge was decided as proved. Louis IX ordered that all copies of the Talmud be confiscated and burned; 24 carloads were consigned to the flames in 1242. The occasion was commemorated in the dirge *shaali seruphah be-esh* which was subsequently included in the dirge of the *Ashkenazi* rite recited on *Av* 9. The precedent of 1242 was followed in later centuries; instances of Talmud burnings are recorded in Italy, Poland, and elsewhere.

TALMUD TORAH (Heb. "Study of the TORAH"): The literal meaning of the term gave rise to its secondary meaning as the place where EDUCATION, in particular of an elementary nature, was provided. During the Middle Ages, and right up to the threshold of the modern period in E. Europe, elementary Jewish education was provided by private tuition, or in the ḤEDER, or through a *T.T.* (a school supported by the community). Although the famous *T.T.* established in Amsterdam in the 16th cent. was for both rich and poor alike, in E. Europe the *T.T.* was for poor and orphaned children only. The expense was met by the community and was levied in different ways in different communities. Classes were in session throughout the whole day and the curriculum consisted entirely of religious subjects, the *T.T.* being regarded as a preparatory school for the YESHIVAH. Under the influence of the HASKALAH a system of "modernized" *Talmud Torahs* was set up, particularly in Russia, with more up-to-date methods of instruction. The old-type *T.T.* still obtains in Jerusalem and elsewhere. In the Diaspora many religious day schools call themselves *T.T.*

TAM, JACOB BEN MEIR (or *Rabbenu Tam* "our perfect rabbi", 1100-1171): N. French rabbinical authority; grandson of RASHI and younger brother of SAMUEL BEN MEIR. The outstanding figure among the TOSAPHISTS, T. used his undisputed authority to convene rabbinical synods at which rules binding on the Jewry of all N. France were enacted. His most famous work is the *Sepher ha-Yashar* ("The Book of the Righteous") which collates responsa and analytic novellae on 30 talmudic tractates. His disagreement with Rashi over the correct order of the verses inscribed in TEPHILLIN led to the custom whereby very Orthodox Jews wear two pairs of phylacteries, one according to each version.

TAMID (in full, *olat tamid*: Heb. "perpetual burnt-offering"): Burnt-offering of a lamb offered twice daily in the Temple, once in the morning and once at nightfall (Exod. 29:38; Num. 28:1-8). See SACRIFICES.

TAMID (Heb. "Perpetual-Offering"): Ninth tractate in the Mishnah order of *Kodashim* with *gemara* in the Babylonian Talmud only. Dealing primarily with the daily morning and evening offering

(TAMID), it also touches on many general details of Temple organization and the sacrificial rite (e.g. the occasions upon which the High Priest officiated in person, the priestly benediction, and the night watch of the priests).

TAMMUZ: 4th month of the religious, tenth of the civil year. The name is of Babylonian origin, T. being the name of a god figuring prominently in the Sumerian and Babylonian pantheon (cf. Ezek. 8:14). It has 29 days and its zodiac sign is the crab. *T.* 17th (SHIVAH ASAR BE-TAMMUZ) commemorates the breaching of the walls of Jerusalem by Nebuchadnezzar in 586 B.C.E. and by Titus in 70 C.E.; this date marks the commencement of the annual THREE WEEKS of mourning culminating in the fast of *Av* 9.

TANAKH (initial letters of *Torah, Neviim, Ketuvim,* i.e., Pentateuch, Prophets, Hagiographa): Usual Hebrew name for the Jewish BIBLE.

TANḤUM BEN JOSEPH OF JERUSALEM (13th cent.): Palestinian scholar. His Bible commentary (in Arabic) contained a comprehensive introduction dealing with grammatical principles. A follower of Maimonides, his commentary displays critical acumen and a philosophical approach. His other works include a lexicon to Maimonides' *Mishneh Torah.*

TANḤUMA: Name given to various midrashic compilations. They were not written or compiled by R. Tanḥuma bar Abba, a Palestinian *amora* after whom they are named, but his collection may have been used as a basis. The first (*Tanḥuma* A) is probably the oldest midrashic collection in existence; it is quoted in the Babylonian Talmud, and was probably edited in the 5th cent. Another midrashic collection, no longer extant (apart from quotations), and properly known as the YELAMMEDENU from the opening words of its sections *yelammedenu rabbenu* ("Let our master teach us"), is sometimes referred to as *Tanḥuma* B. As a result the second *Tanḥuma* MIDRASH, (the "popular" *Tanḥuma*) is referred to as *Tanḥuma* C. It is a digest of *Tanḥuma* A and B. The *Tanḥuma,* like the *Midrash Rabbah,* follows the weekly biblical portions; there is, however, no *Tanḥuma* to the Five Scrolls.

TANNA (Aram. "one who studies and teaches" especially the ORAL LAW): A teacher mentioned in the MISHNAH or BARAITA. The period of the *tannaim* began after HILLEL and SHAMMAI (the last of the ZUGOT) and ended with the generation after R. JUDAH HA-NASI in the 2nd cent. C.E.; the last generations of *tannaim* thus lived after the destruction of the Second Temple. They were succeeded by the AMORAIM, the interpreters of the Mishnah. In the Talmudic Period the term *t.* was also applied to the "reciter" of the Mishnah and other tannaitic texts who was to be found in every academy (at that time the Oral Law — i.e., *Mishnah* — had not yet been committed to writing and had to be recited or quoted from memory). Maimonides (at the end of his introduction to *Zeraim*) enumerates 128 *tannaim* mentioned in the Mishnah.

TANNA DE-VEI ELIYYAHU, see **SEDER ELIYYAHU**

TANYA (also known as *Likkutei Amarim,* "Collections of Sayings"): Ḥasidic classic written by SHNEOUR ZALMAN OF LYADY, the founder of ḤABAD. The word *Ḥabad* is an abbreviation formed by the initial letters of *ḥokhmah, binah,* and *daat* which represent, according to Shneour Zalman, an ascending scale in the awareness of God. *Ḥokhmah* means simple faith, which in itself is insufficient to achieve a true knowledge (*daat*) of God. Only through contemplation and study (*binah*) can this be attained. The book is divided into two parts: "The Book of the *Beinonim*" (the "average men"), who through study and contemplation can achieve love and reverence for God; and "The Book of Unity and Faith" a commentary on the *Shema.* The book is greatly venerated by *Ḥabad* ḥasidim who study it daily.

TAREPH, TARPHUT, see **TEREPHAH**

TARGUM (Aram. "translation"): The ARAMAIC translation of the BIBLE. After the Babylonian Exile Aramaic became the language commonly spoken by Jews in Palestine as well as in Babylonia, and it became necessary to translate the biblical portions read in the synagogue into the vernacular (cf. Neh. 8:8; *Meg.* 3a). Each Hebrew verse of the pentateuchal reading was consecutively translated aloud, and to some extent interpreted, by the METURGEMAN ("translator"). The need for accurate translations became particularly pressing with the spread of Christianity, when proponents of the new religion began to interpret certain passages to accord with their own doctrines. According to the Talmud two translations of the Pentateuch were then made: one, by Akylas (AQUILA) the proselyte (2nd cent.), into Greek, and one by ONKELOS the proselyte, into Aramaic, both at the dictation of R. Eliezer and R. Joshua (Y. *Meg.* 1:11). Modern scholars doubt the reliability of this tradition which, they think, arose from a confusion of the name of Onkelos (who was no translator at all) with Aquila. The T. of Onkelos, it is argued by some, reflects Babylonian and not Palestinian Aramaic. Some scholars think that the anonymous 2nd cent. Aramaic translator used Aquila's Greek version, and his T. was hence called "T. Onkelos" by the Babylonian Jews. The T. Onkelos came to be accepted as the official and authorized translation of the Pentateuch, and it was obligatory to read it in conjunction with the Hebrew text of the weekly portion (the Hebrew was read twice and T. once, as was the custom in public worship; *Ber.* 8a). Another T. of the Pentateuch is known as T. *Yerushalmi,* while the T. Jonathan (attributed to Jonathan ben Uzziel; *Meg.* 3a) extends also to the Prophets and part of the Hagiographa. There are also Targumim (pl.) to the Five Scrolls and a Second T. of Esther. These Targumim are mainly aggadic paraphrases, and their authorship is unknown. T. Onkelos gives the plain meaning of the Hebrew text except in a few instances where it translates according to halakhic interpretation; T. Jonathan and *Yerushalmi,* on the other hand, paraphrase the text more freely and add homiletical interpretations. Onkelos paraphrases all anthropomorphisms more strictly than any other T. Various opinions have been expressed as to the authorship and date of T. Jonathan and T. *Yerushalmi,* but all scholars agree that these two Targumim were written in Palestine for the Jews living there. Whether composed in Palestine or Babylonia, T. Onkelos was adopted by the Babylonian Jews and was hence called the "Babylonian T." by the tosaphists.

TARPHON (1st-2nd cent.): *Tanna*; teacher of R. Akiva with whom he differed on a number of halakhic issues. Of extraordinary modesty and humility and an advocate of the abolition of the death penalty (Mishnah *Mak.* 1:10), T. also became one of the most vehement opponents of the JEWISH CHRISTIANS, declaring that he would unhesitatingly burn their gospels, even though they contained the name of God (*Shab.* 116b). In a year of famine, T., who was a priest, underwent a formal ceremony of betrothal with 300 women so that they might share in his priestly emoluments.

TARYAG MITZVOT, see **PRECEPTS, 613**

TASHLIKH (Heb.): On the first day of ROSH HA-SHANAH (or on the second day, if the first falls on a Sabbath), it is customary for Orthodox Jews after reciting the Afternoon Service to visit a river, the seashore, or some other place where water is found, and to recite verses from Scripture concerning repentance and the forgiveness of sins. These verses include: "He will again have compassion upon us; He will subdue our iniquities; and Thou wilt cast (Hebrew: *tashlikh*) all their sins into the depths of the sea" (Micah 7:19). The custom, which apparently originated in the late Middle Ages (being first mentioned by R. Jacob ben Moses Mölln), possibly on the basis of non-Jewish custom or superstition, symbolizes "the casting of the sins into the sea"; some Jews even turn out the pockets of their garments and let crumbs etc. fall into the water. Later rabbinic authorities (e.g. Elijah of Vilna) interpreted *t.* — on the basis of a *midrash* — as a reminder to God of the merits of Abraham and Isaac.

TASHMISHEI KEDUSHAH (Heb. "appurtenances of holiness"): Religious articles and synagogue appurtenances such as TALLIT, SHOPHAR, *Torah* ornaments, and the like. *T.K.* are to be treated with reverence, and must not be put to secular use, though sacrilege (see MEILAH), in the strict sense of the term, does not apply to them. See also VESSELS, SACRED.

TAZ, see **DAVID BEN SAMUEL HA-LEVI**

TEACHER OF RIGHTEOUSNESS, see **DEAD SEA SCROLLS**

TEBAH, see **ALMEMAR**

TEHILLIM, see **PSALMS**

TEḤINNAH (Heb. "supplication"): Private devotions. Certain private supplications are introduced according to individual need into the appropriate benediction of the AMIDAH (in the 8th, 9th, and 16th, respectively, for recovery from sickness, for the granting of livelihood, and for any personal petition). In talmudic times *teḥinnot* (pl.) were said after the *amidah*; these were later replaced by TAḤANUN. *Teḥinnot* from the Talmudic Period include prayers for forgiveness of sin, for the study of the *Torah*, and for Divine blessing and protection in general; many were incorporated into the statutory prayer book, e.g. the *t.*, "Deliver me this day, and every day, from arrogant men" (Morning Benedictions), and "Grant us long life, a life of peace, of good, of blessing" (the Sabbath preceding the New Moon). Particularly prevalent during the 16th-18th cents. was the *t.* that formed part of *Tikkun Ḥatzot* ("midnight devotion"), which was recited at midnight or in the early morning for the advent of redemption and the rebuilding of the Temple. From the Gaonic Period on, many *teḥinnot* were composed in the vernacular (Aramaic, Yiddish, Spanish, Arabic, Dutch, English, etc.) for the benefit of those unfamiliar with Hebrew. Many collections of such private devotions exist; they include prayers upon visiting the sick or at a cemetery, supplications to be recited by women for the blessing of scholarly and pious children or when baking Sabbath cakes or lighting Sabbath candles, as well as prayers for different occasions like a *bar mitzvah*, for a teacher beginning to instruct his pupils, and even for a preacher that he might deliver a stirring and acceptable sermon. Devotional books in Yiddish, meant for women, were also known as *teḥinnot*.

TEITELBAUM, MOSES (1759-1841): Ḥasidic leader. A profound talmudic scholar, he became a ḥasid on his appointment as rabbi of Ujhely in Hungary in 1808 and established a dynasty of Hungarian ḥasidim. He was held in the utmost veneration by his followers who referred to him as the *Saba Kaddisha* ("The Holy Old Man"). The ḥasidic dynasty which he founded comprises today the Satmer and the Sigut ḥasidim who are distinguished by their fanatical separatism and their violent opposition to the State of Israel.

TEKIAH, see **SHOPHAR**

TELS: Town in Lithuania; seat of a famous *yeshivah* established in 1875 and rising to renown under R. Eliezer Gordon (1851-1910) who was appointed rabbi of T. in 1882 and brought his disciples with him from Kelm. R. Simeon Shkop headed the *yeshivah* from 1885, and the tradition of T. was carried on later by the son-in-law of Eliezer Gordon, R. Joseph Leib Bloch. At the outbreak of World War II some of the students and their teachers escaped to Japan, whence they made ther way ultimately to the U.S. and re-established their *yeshivah* in Cleveland.

TEMPLE: The first T. in Jerusalem, built by Solomon on Mount Moriah, is called in Scripture by various names: "the house of the Lord", "the house of God", "the holy T." (*heikhal* or *mikdash*), "the T. of the Lord", and "Sanctuary". Its usual name in rabbinic literature is *bet ha-mikdash* ("the house of the Sanctuary"), a name which occurs only once in Scripture (II Chron. 36:17). The T. consisted of three parts: 1. The Holy of Holies (*devir*) — on the west — containing the Ark of the Covenant. 2. The Holy Place (*heikhal*), containing the altar of incense, the table of shewbread, the seven-branched candlestick, etc. 3. The court (*azarah*) — on the east — containing the sacrificial altar. Surrounding the T. on 3 sides (the east excepted) were buildings with cells for storage, etc. The general architectural lay-out of the T. in Jerusalem was similar to that of other Semitic sanctuaries in Palestine, but it contained no image of God and was considered His dwelling place (*mishkan*) in a spiritual sense only; cf. Solomon's dedication prayer, "Behold, heaven and the heaven of heavens cannot contain Thee; how much less this house that I have builded" (I Kings 8:27). The T. served a two-fold purpose: 1) To shelter the Ark of the Lord, which symbolized the covenant between God and the people (*ibid.* 21); 2) To serve as a meeting-place for the people for sacrifice, prayer, and thanksgiving. The sacrifices were accompanied by songs (Ps. 26:6; 56:13; 100:2,4; 116:19) and processionals (cf. Jer. 33:11). Many of the Psalms that call for giving thanks (e.g. Ps. 107, 118, 136) and rendering praises (113-116, 135, etc.) were associated with the bringing of these thanksgiving offerings. Processionals of great multitudes used to form on Tabernacles (Ezek. 46:3; Is. 1:13; 66:23) and other festivals when the people came as pilgrims from all parts of Judah and beyond (cf. Jer. 17:26; 41:5). The prophets' high regard for the T. may be seen from the fact that though they frequently condemned sacrifices and prayers as mechanical performances, they never spoke disparagingly of the T. itself. The T. is "the Lord's house" and the "house of the God of Jacob" (Is. 2:2-3), filled with "the glory of the Lord" (Ezek. 9:3; 43:4 ff.; Hab. 2:20, etc.), and in the end of days will be a place of worship for all nations (Is. 2:2-3; 56:7; 66:20). The T. was repaired from time to time, as in the days of King Joash, under the supervision of Jehoiada (II Kings 12), and of King Josiah (*ibid.* 22). A religious nadir was reached when Manasseh introduced pagan forms of worship into the T., apparently as a mark of submission to the king of Assyria. Josiah re-established the T. as the only national sanctuary and abolished sacrifices in the High Places. The destruction of the T. by Nebuchadnezzar (587 B.C.E.) marked the end of an era in the history of the Jews and their religion. As a corroboration of the prophecies of Micah, Jeremiah, and Uriah that the T. would be destroyed as a punishment for moral and ethical sins, the calamity gave fresh impetus to faith in the prophets' teachings and hope that their assurances with regard to rebuilding of the T. would be fulfilled. Fourteen years after the fall of Jerusalem, Ezekiel in Babylonia foretold the rebuilding of the T. and described in detail its structure, the form and order of its service, etc. At about the same time the four annual fast days commemorating events that led to the destruction of the T. were fixed and the Book of Lamentations was composed in memory of the destruction of the T. In 538 B.C.E. Cyrus issued an edict permitting the rebuilding of the T. in Jerusalem and encouraging the exiled Jews of his empire to return to their homeland. The captured vessels of the T. were turned over to "Sheshbazzar the prince of Judah". The returning exiles set up an altar and laid the foundations of the Second T. Subsequently, the institution of maamadot ("stations") was established. The priests and the levites had previously been divided into 24 *mishmarot* ("courses"), each *mishmeret* (sing.) performing the T. services during its allotted week, twice each year. The Israelites throughout the country were now also divided into 24 *maamadot*, each representing a section of the country. Every week at least 5 men from a *maamad* went to Jerusalem, to "stand by" at the offering of the tamid (the public sacrifice). In addition, during the time of the *tamid* offering, the rest of the people of the *maamad* whose week it was, gathered in their own cities for prayer and *Torah* reading. Thus the offering of the daily *tamid* sacrifices became a national affair in which every individual Jew had a share. Antiochus III, upon conquering Judea in 198 B.C.E., showered great gifts upon the T., and his son and successor, Seleucus IV, followed his example. Antiochus IV ("Epiphanes"), however, in his contempt for non-hellenistic cultures, first looted the T. vessels (169) and then set up a statue of Zeus on the altar (167). The T. services were interrupted for three years, to be renewed only with the reconquest of Jerusalem by JUDAH THE MACCABEE, who purified and rededicated the T. (165), an event commemorated annually by the Festival of ḤANNUKKAH. When Pompey conquered Jerusalem in 63 B.C.E. he desecrated the T. by entering the Holy of Holies. Herod completely rebuilt the T. at great expense, doubling its size. The masons of Herod's T. were 1,000 priests specially trained for the purpose. Beginning with Herod, the High Priesthood ceased to be an hereditary office. He introduced the custom whereby High Priests were appointed by Roman procurators, chiefly on the basis of political loyalty but later also for financial considerations. This situation led to a considerable lowering of the prestige of the High Priesthood, but at the same time strengthened the authority of the Pharisaic scholars, even in T. affairs. The Roman emperor Caligula (40 C.E.) ordered that his imperial image be set up in the T., but was compelled by Jewish protests to rescind his edict. In the struggle against Rome the Jewish rebels were confident that God would not permit His T. to be conquered, much less destroyed. But in the year 70, Titus ordered the destruction of the T. The day of the destruction, *Av* 9, has ever since been a day of fasting and prayer in Judaism. The T. area is now the site of the Mosque of Omar, erected c. 700 C.E.

According to the accounts in the talmudic sources the preparations for the daily services began each morning before cockcrow, when the priest in charge of the distribution of the various functions awakened the elders of the priests whose turn it was to perform the services. Walking in procession and bearing torchlights, they inspected the T. vessels, making certain that they were in their proper place. The ashes and unburned pieces were removed from the altar, and the wood on the altar arranged. Then followed the sacrifice of the morning *tamid* and the lighting of the candelabrum, the various tasks being divided among the 13 priests. Thereupon the priests gathered in the *lishkat gazit* ("chamber of hewn stones" — the seat of the Sanhedrin) and recited prayers, the DECALOGUE, and the three chapters of the SHEMA. They pronounced three benedictions with the people: EMET VE-YATZIV, "May the service of Thy people be ever acceptable unto Thee" (*retzeh*), and the PRIESTLY BLESSING. The levites sang the psalm of the day, and the people prostrated themselves. The evening *tamid*, offered usually in the early afternoon, followed the same order as that of the morning sacrifice, but without the lighting of the candelabra and the incense-offering. On Sabbaths and festivals, there was an additional (*musaph*) sacrifice. On the Day of Atonement, the High Priest brought the atoning sacrifices for the whole people, in the course of which he also entered the Holy of Holies to offer incense. In the Second T. Period the censer was placed on the rock (*even shetiyyah*) which earlier had supported the Holy ARK. The Mishnah relates that the king and the High Priest used to utter a special benediction at the conclusion of their reading from the *Torah* that the T. may stand and the Divine Presence dwell there. Prayers for the T. are to be found frequently in the traditional liturgy. The third benediction in the Grace after Meals includes a prayer for "the great and holy house over which Thy name has been called". In T. days the prayer was for the continuation of the existence of the T., but after the destruction the prayer was for its rebuilding. After each recital of the *amidah*, a petition is added: "May it be Thy will that the T. be rebuilt soon in our days". The same petition is offered after the COUNTING OF THE OMER. The Additional Service on Sabbaths and festivals contains a prayer that "Thou mayest have mercy on Thy T. and rebuild it soon, etc." Reform Jews have omitted prayers for the rebuilding of the T. and the reinstitution of the sacrificial system. Wherever a Jew prays, he faces in the direction of the T. in Jerusalem. There is hardly a traditional occasion or a prayer in which reference is not made to the destruction of the T.; the ancient custom of having the groom break a glass at the wedding has likewise been interpreted as a commemoration of the destruction of the T. Some pious Jews, sitting on a low stool in the manner of mourners, recite prayers known as *Ḥatzot* ("Midnight") each midnight for the rebuilding of the T. Most talmudic authorities held that the site of the T. remained sacred even after the destruction.

TEMPLE: Name adopted in the REFORM movement for the SYNAGOGUE. It was first applied to the Hamburg t. (1818) and probably derived from the Reform viewpoint that the synagogue had replaced the ancient t., unlike the Orthodox belief that the Jerusalem t. would be ultimately restored. The term t. is frequently used in the U.S.

TEMPLE OF ONIAS, see **ONIAS, TEMPLE OF**

TEMURAH (Heb. "Exchange"): Sixth tractate in the Mishnah order of *Kodashim* with *gemara* in the Babylonian Talmud only. It deals with the circumstances under which a sacrificial animal may be exchanged (according to Lev. 27:10, 33).

TEN COMMANDMENTS, see **DECALOGUE**

TEN DAYS OF REPENTANCE, see **PENITENCE, TEN DAYS OF**

TEN MARTYRS, see **MARTYRS, TEN**
TEN PLAGUES, see **PLAGUES, TEN**
TEN LOST TRIBES, see **TRIBES, LOST TEN**
TENAIM, see **BETROTHAL**

TENANCY: The Mosaic code lacks any legislation for determining the duties and obligations of the tenant except for the provision for the SABBATICAL YEAR. In rabbinic law the conditions of t. are subject to both contract and local custom and can be changed only by common agreement between the parties. The presumptive rights of the person in possession are of great force in *halakhah* and render summary eviction extremely difficult. Rabbinic legislation differentiates between a tenant (*aris*) who pays rent proportionate to his produce and one (*ḥokher* or *sokher*) who pays fixed rental. During the Middle Ages special *takkanot* dealing with "tenant rights" were enacted and applied by Jewish communities in order to ensure equitable regulation of the crowded ghetto tenements where Jews were forced to live.

TEPHILLAH: Hebrew for PRAYER. Specifically used to refer to the AMIDAH.

TEPHILLIN (Heb.): Phylacteries worn by Jewish males of thirteen years of age and over at the weekday Morning Service (originally they were worn throughout the day). The injunction to wear them is based on four paragraphs in the Bible (Exod. 13:1; Exod 13:11; Deut. 6:4-9; Deut. 11:13-21; see *Sanh.* 88b). These four paragraphs are written twice on parchment, once all together on one piece and once on four separate pieces with each piece containing one paragraph. The two sets are placed in specially made leather cases, one of which containing four parchments (*shel rosh* i.e., "of the head") is placed on the head so that the front edge of the case lies just above the spot where the hair begins to grow and directly above the space between the eyes. It is held in position by a strap (*retzuah*) which circles the head and is fastened by a knot at the nape of the neck. The knot is made to resemble the Hebrew letter *dalet*. The case containing the single parchment (*shel yad* i.e., "of the hand") is placed on the muscle of the inner side of the left forearm, so that the section through which the strap passes is toward the shoulder. A strap knotted in the form of the Hebrew letter *yod* secures it and is then wound seven times around the arm and three times around the middle finger. The remainder of the strap is passed under the palm and wound around it, thus forming the Hebrew letter *shin*. The three letters form the Divine name *Shaddai*. A separate benediction is recited after putting on the head *t.*, since it is regarded as a distinct commandment. When the *t.* are removed at the close of the service, the order is reversed and the head *t.* is taken off before the hand *t.* The object of the *t.* commandment is to direct the thoughts of the wearer to God and to the teaching contained in the four paragraphs. A tannaitic text has God say to Israel "Observe the commandment of *t.* and I shall account it to you as though you were engaged in the study of the *Torah* day and night". Maimonides (*Hilkhot Teph.* 4) expresses this as follows — "The holiness of *t.* is great, for as long as the *t.* are on the head and the arm of a man, he is humble and Godfearing, he eschews levity and idle talk, and does not conceive evil thoughts, but turns his heart exclusively to words of truth and justice". RASHI and Rabbenu TAM, renewing an ancient dispute (illustrated by variant *t.* found in the Dead Sea caves from the late Second Temple Period), differed as to the order of the texts on the four parchments; some pious Jews, particularly among Ḥasidim and oriental communities, put on two pairs of *t.*, according to the two versions. *T.* are not worn on Sabbath and festivals (since these days are regarded as sufficient reminders in themselves of the events and concepts which the *t.* are also worn to recall). Custom differs as to the wearing of the *t.* on the intermediate days of festivals (in the Land of Israel, they are not worn). *T.* are not worn by a mourner on the first day of mourning, while on *Av* 9, they are put on at the Afternoon instead of the Morning Service. It is customary to have the *t.* examined once in seven years. The Reform Movement dropped the tradition of wearing *t.* and Abraham GEIGER maintained that they were originally pagan amulets; their retention was advocated by ZUNZ.

TERAPHIM (Heb.): Human images used as household gods and consulted for purposes of DIVINATION. Rachel stole Laban's t. (Gen. 31:19), probably because according to local law her husband would thereby become her father's heir. Samuel denounced the *t.* as witchcraft (I Sam. 15:23), and their banishment from Israel was part of Josiah's drive for religious reform; they retained their popularity until the Babylonian Exile. The prevalence of household *t.* is attested by the story of David's wife Michal (I Sam. 19:11-16).

TEREPHAH (or, among *Sephardim*, *tareph*): Originally, the tearing or mauling of an animal by a wild beast (e.g. Gen. 31:39) but used as a generic term for (1) any defect which renders an animal unfit for food; and (2) any food prepared contrary to the DIETARY LAWS. Early tradition lists the major classes of defect which render an animal *t.* These were expanded by the Mishnah to eighteen (*Ḥul.* 3:11) and by Maimonides to seventy (*Hilkhot Sheḥ.* 1039). The eighteen *terephot* (pl.) are: —

(1) if the gullet is pierced; (2) if the windpipe is torn; (3) if the membrane of the brain is pierced; (4) if the heart is pierced; (5) if the

spine is broken; (6) if the spinal chord is severed; (7) if the liver is missing; (8) if the lung, (9) maw, (10) gall bladder, (11) intestines, or (12) inner stomach is pierced; (13) if the greater part of the outer coating is torn; (14) if the second or (15) third stomach is pierced on the outside; (16) if the beast has fallen from a height, or (17) has most of its ribs broken, or (18) has been mauled. As a guiding principle in cases of doubt the rabbis laid down that an animal suffering from a particular sickness or injury which made its survival for the next twelve months unlikely, was to be considered *t.* (*Ḥul.* 42a). If it definitely suffered from one of the eighteen defects, it was *t.* even though it might survive for more than twelve months. *T.* may not be eaten, but other benefit (e.g. sale to a non-Jew) may be derived from it (Exod. 22:30).

TERUAH, see **SHOPHAR**

TERUMAH, see **HEAVE-OFFERING**

TERUMOT (Heb. "Heave-Offerings"): Sixth tractate in the Mishnah order of *Zeraim* with *gemara* in the Palestinian Talmud only. It deals with the laws regulating the HEAVE-OFFERINGS brought to the priests from the Israelites (Num. 18:8 ff.) and the levites (*ibid.* 25 ff.).

TESHUVAH, see **REPENTANCE**

TESTAMENT, see **WILL**

TESTAMENT, NEW, see **NEW TESTAMENT**

TESTAMENT, OLD, see **OLD TESTAMENT**

TESTAMENTS OF THE TWELVE PATRIARCHS: A Jewish pseudepigraphical work, purporting to be the testaments of the twelve sons of Jacob and comprising 12 separate testaments, written originally in Hebrew or Aramaic during the 2nd cent. B.C.E. The Testaments are patterned after the blessing of Jacob to his sons (Gen. 49). Each of the tribal patriarchs recounts the virtues and sins of his own life and then exhorts his children to live a life of righteousness. Most of the testaments end on an apocalyptic note. The T. contain several Christian interpolations but the number of these is much smaller than was at one time assumed. Because of the emphasis on Levi (the priest) and Judah (the king), the testaments were thought to be either a Christian work reflecting the belief in the royal and priestly nature of Jesus, or a composite Jewish work — the priestly element reflecting the period of the Hasmonean priest-kings and the Testament of Judah echoing the traditional messianic hopes placed in the house of David. The discovery of the DEAD SEA SCROLLS, with their doctrine of a royal and a priestly messiah, has thrown new light on the testaments and revealed them as belonging to the literature of the eschatological movement, probably related to ESSENE-like circles.

TETRAGRAMMATON, see **GOD, NAMES OF**

TEVEL (Heb.): Agricultural produce which has not yet been tithed and is therefore forbidden for profane use. The rabbis ruled, on the basis of Deut. 26:13, that liability for TITHES commenced only "when it (i.e. the crop) has seen the front of the house", i.e., when the crop is gathered in, thus permitting *t.* to be eaten by the agricultural worker in the field (*Ber.* 35b; *Bava Metzia* 87a). The Talmud reports that this rule was often abused, in order to circumvent the liability for tithes and that people would bring in their produce through the roof, so that it would not have "seen the front of the house".

TEVET: Fourth month of the civil year, tenth of the religious year; zodiac sign, a kid. The 10th of *T.* is a fast day in commemoration of the commencement of the siege of Jerusalem by Nebuchadnezzer (II Kings 25:1). According to tradition the 9th is the anniversary of the death of Ezra and the 20th, of Maimonides.

TEVILAH, see **ABLUTION; BAPTISM; IMMERSION**

TEVUL YOM (Heb. "One who bathes in the day"): Tenth tractate in the Mishnah order of *Tohorot* with no *gemara* in either Talmud. It deals with the minor instances of ritual impurity which still apply after ritual immersion until sundown (Lev. 15:7 ff.; 22:6).

TEXTUAL CRITICISM, see **BIBLE CRITICISM**

THANKSGIVING: Biblical expressions of t. frequently commence with *barukh* ("blessed be"; e.g. Gen. 24:27; Exod. 18:10; II Sam. 18:28; Is. 28:6), and hence the statutory opening formula ("Blessed art Thou O Lord, our God, King of the Universe...") of the BENEDICTIONS uttered in t. to God before enjoying anything in this world (*Ber.* 35a). Other benedictions of t. are recited on special occasions, e.g. on hearing good news ("...who art good and dispenseth good", *Ber.* 9:2), on recurring joyful events ("...who hast kept us in life", *Ber.* 9:3), and on deliverance from peril (e.g. after safely journeying through desert regions or returning from the sea, or being released from captivity or prison, and on recovering from sickness). The latter blessing is known as GOMEL ("...who doest good... and hast also rendered all good unto me", *Ber.* 54b). T. is the theme of many PSALMS which have, for this reason, been included in the LITURGY (e.g. the HALLEL). Sectarian psalms of t. have been discovered among the DEAD SEA SCROLLS. The introductory part of the daily Morning Service is known by the name of "passages of song" (*Ashkenazi* PESUKEI DE-ZIMRA, *Sephardi* ZEMIROT) and includes the t. of David (I. Chron. 16:8-36; *hodu*: "Give thanks unto the Lord"). The 18th benediction of the AMIDAH is referred to in the *Mishnah* under the title *hodaah,* i.e., t., the shorter form of which, recited by the congregation during the reader's repetition, is known as the *modim de-rabbanan* i.e., "the *modim* ("t.") of the rabbis" because the passage is compounded of several rabbinic prayers. The special t. additions for *Purim* and *Ḥanukkah*, are appropriately inserted at this point to commemorate the deliverance granted on these days (AL HA-NISSIM). In the second and third paragraphs of the GRACE AFTER MEALS (*nodeh*: "we thank Thee" and *ve-al ha-kol*: "for all this... we thank... Thee"), t. is offered, *inter alia*, for the "desirable, good, and ample land" God has given His people, for His covenant, and His *Torah* (*Ber.* 48b-49a). In messianic times, says a rabbinic statement (*Lev. Rab.* 9:7), all sacrifices and prayers will be abolished, except the t. offering and the prayer of t. to God — for man will always desire to express his t. to Him who is the source of all blessing.

THANKSGIVING-OFFERING (Heb. *todah*): Sacrifice offered in the Temple by individuals as a mark of THANKSGIVING to God. The regulations of the offering are given in Lev. 7:12-15 and it is enumerated among the holy things of lesser sanctity (Mishnah *Zev.* 5:6). The breast and the shoulders were given to the priest, while the hide and flesh were retained by the person who brought the offering. It could be eaten until midnight on the day of sacrifice. The Midrash (*Lev. Rab.* 27:12) declares that in the Messianic age when sin, and hence also the need of SACRIFICES of expiation, will have ceased the T.O. alone will continue.

THANKSGIVING PSALMS, see **DEAD SEA SCROLLS**

THEFT (AND STOLEN GOODS): A thief is one who purloins without the knowledge of the owner, as opposed to the robber who openly and forcibly appropriates another's goods (see ROBBERY). The prohibition "Thou shalt not steal" (Lev. 19:11) carries no CORPORAL PUNISHMENT with it since the felony of t. may be rectified by restoration of the stolen goods. The thief who admits his t. of his own free will must restore the goods or their value and is free from further obligation or punishment. If however he is convicted by a court, or the goods are traced to him by the authorities, he is fined and must restore double their value to the owner (Exod. 22:3); for the t. of an animal followed by its sale or slaughter, four-or fivefold restitution must be made (Exod. 21:37). T. of sacred property (*hekdesh*), or from another who had stolen such, carries no double fine. If the thief is unable to repay the amount he stole (but not if he is only unable to pay the additional fine) he may be sold into the service of the owner of the property (Exod. 22:2). A woman is not sold into service even if she is unable to repay the value of the stolen goods. It is forbidden to receive or deal in stolen goods and one who receives such goods from a known thief is obliged to restore them to the original owner without receiving compensation from him. See also BURGLARY; KIDNAPING.

THEISM: Philosophical term designating a specific form of belief in GOD. T. maintains the existence (against ATHEISM) of one and only one God (against polytheism and DUALISM), distinct from the world which is His creation (against PANTHEISM), and conceived in personal terms i.e., as active and willing (against DEISM). The philosophical concept of t. provided a rationale of the Jewish biblical conception of God. For some of the specific theological problems connected with t. see ANTHROPOMORPHISM; ATTRIBUTES; MONOTHEISM.

THEOCRACY: Term used by JOSEPHUS to describe the constitution of the post-exilic Jewish commonwealth. Since then the term has come to mean any system of government where power is vested in the spiritual leadership wielding its authority in the name of God. The concept of a t. has often been identified with the biblical idea of a "kingdom of priests and a holy nation" and the prophetic vision of the kingdom of God on earth. References to God's kingship abound in the liturgy, e.g. the standard opening of every benediction "Blessed art Thou O Lord, our God, King of the Universe". The prayer for the establishment of the sovereignty of God occupies the most prominent place in the liturgy of the High Festivals, especially the New Year with its enthronement of God as King and the concluding blessing of the MALKHUYYOT "Reign Thou in Thy glory over the whole Universe, that... whatever hath breath in its nostrils may say, 'The Lord God of Israel is King and His dominion ruleth over all'... Blessed art Thou O Lord, King over all the earth". The opening passage of that section praying for the ideal time when "the Lord will be King over all the earth" has been taken over into the daily prayers and is recited at the conclusion of each service. The opposition of the prophet Samuel to the people's demand for a king was made explicitly on the grounds that they wished to substitute a human monarchy for the kingship of God (I Sam. 8:7). A sacerdotal t. developed in Israel during early Second Temple times, under Persian domination. According to Josephus the motives of the Zealot rebellion were less political than religious, in their insistence that God alone should rule over them (*Wars* 2, 8, 1; *Ant.* 18, 1, 1-6). During the Middle Ages and until the period of Emancipation Jewish life was, in a sense, theocratically governed, since it was dominated by the rabbinate which exercised legislative functions based on the *halakhah*, especially in the frequent instances where Jewish communities enjoyed internal autonomy.

In the State of Israel the term t. is occasionally used in discussions regarding the demand of religious groups that the state be subject to religious *halakhah*.

THEODICY: The vindication of God's JUSTICE in the face of the existence of moral evil and what appears to be innocent SUFFERING. The problem of t. arises whenever a personal God is believed to be both good and all-powerful. Since biblical times Jewish theology has always affirmed God's justice (see also TZIDDUK HA-DIN). The resultant problem of the suffering of the righteous (cf. Hab. 1:13; JOB), and in particular that of Israel at the hands of the gentiles, exercised biblical writers, apocalyptists, ancient rabbis, and medieval philosophers and kabbalists. The traditional explanation attributed suffering to sin and human inadequacy, hence the usual reaction to catastrophe and disaster was penitence and prayer for the forgiveness of the sins for which these misfortunes were the just retribution. "Wilt thou put Me in the wrong, in order to put yourself in the right?" (Job 40:8) is the retort of God to Job when he questions the justice of God. Often the view is advanced that evil exists only on a partial and short-range view of God's designs and "whatever the Holy One, blessed be He, does, He does for good" (*Ber.* 60a). More fundamental than the problem of suffering is the metaphysical problem of evil as such which constitutes one of the major themes of philosophy as well as kabbalah. See also ESCHATOLOGY; GOOD AND EVIL.

THEODOTION (c. 2nd cent. C.E.): Translator of the Bible into Greek; reputedly a convert to Judaism. His version is an improvement on that of AQUILA both in style and interpretation. T.'s Greek version, like that of SYMMACHUS, has been preserved in fragments only in Origen's *Hexapla*. The most important fragment is T.'s Greek version of the Book of Daniel with the apocryphal additions, which gained great popularity in early Christian circles and entirely displaced the SEPTUAGINT version. T. probably based his version on the Septuagint, correcting faulty passages in accordance with the Hebrew text.

THEOLOGY, see **JUDAISM**

THEOPHANY, see **REVELATION**

THERAPEUTAE: An ancient sect of Jewish ascetics who lived near Lake Mareotis, not far from Alexandria in Egypt. The existence of this sect is attested to solely in the writing of PHILO (*De Vita Contemplativa*). The T., both men and women, lived in individual chambers apart from society. They devoted themselves throughout the entire course of the day to solitude, prayer, and the study of the Scriptures. So strict was their devotion that the needs of nature were attended to only in the hours of darkness so as not to lose a single moment of study during the daylight hours. On the Sabbath, the T. assembled for communal study followed by a communal meal which consisted of bread with salt, herbs, and spring water. Most of the T. ate only twice a week while others fasted from one Sabbath to the next. In many aspects, the T. bear a marked resemblance to the ESSENES, but the scanty sources of information do not permit an objective comparison.

THIEF, see **THEFT**

THIRTEEN ATTRIBUTES (Heb. *middot*): Based on Exod. 34:6-7, rabbinic tradition frequently refers to God's t.a. of MERCY. There is no unanimity among the commentators as to the precise nature of these ATTRIBUTES and the distinctions between them, as well as to their correlation to the words of the biblical text. The divisions of the scriptural verses are artificial, e.g. (1) the Lord; (2) the Lord; (3) God; (4) merciful; (5) gracious; (6) long-suffering; (7) abundant in lovingkindness; (8) truth; (9) keeping mercy unto the thousandth generation; (10) forgiving iniquity; (11) forgiving transgression; (12) forgiving sin; (13) clearing (the guilty). There are alternative enumerations, some of which include only one mention of the Divine Name, some none, but always the words are divided so as to make a total of thirteen. The tradition associating this particular verse with God's attribute of mercy, as well as the number 13, seem to be ancient, though other numerical traditions also appear to have existed. Some of these are preserved by the KARAITES who list 9-11 attributes. The Talmud quotes R. Johanan as stating that the Almighty said to Moses "Whenever Israel sins, let them recite these *middot* before Me and I will forgive them"; while R. Judah states, "A covenant has been made with the 13 *middot* — when the children of Israel recite them they will not be turned away empty-handed". As a result they form the central motif of supplicatory prayers on all special occasions. The chapter in which the passage occurs is read as the pentateuchal lesson on all public fasts, and the verses of the t.a. are recited by the whole congregation before being repeated by the reader. In some rites they are solemnly recited on festivals (but not if these occur on the Sabbath) when the Ark is opened, and they form the most important element of the SELIḤOT prayers. During the Concluding Service (*Neilah*) on the Day of Atonement they form the refrain of a composite *seliḥah*.

THIRTEEN PRINCIPLES (or ARTICLES) OF FAITH: Customary designation for MAIMONIDES' formulation of the DOGMAS of Judaism. The first Mishnah of the tenth chapter of tractate *Sanhedrin* reads "All Israel has a share in the World to Come... and these are they that have no share in the world to come". Maimonides takes the last clause as meaning that those guilty of the departures from Judaism therein enumerated are heretics who forfeit their rights and privileges as Jews. In his otherwise succinct commentary to the Mishnah, he expands his explanation of this particular Mishnah into a long and detailed examination of the principles of Judaism, evolving thirteen principles of faith: (1) The existence of GOD the Creator; (2) the unity of God; (3) the incorporeality of God; (4) His eternity; (5) prayer is for God alone; (6) the prophets are true; (7) the supremacy of Moses above all other prophets; (8) the Pentateuch was given to Moses; (9) the immutability of the *Torah*; (10) God's omniscience; (11) Divine RETRIBUTION; (12) the belief in the advent of the MESSIAH; and (13) the RESURRECTION of the dead. The formulation of such a dogma aroused considerable opposition, and a long controversy ensued both around the attempt to draft a CREED and around the actual details. The Thirteen Principles are found in the prayer book in two versions: a prose version in which each principle is introduced with the words "I believe (ANI MAAMIN) with perfect faith" and a rhymed version — YIGDAL (composed by Daniel ben Judah of Rome, c. 1300). The Thirteen Principles were never formally adopted as fundamentals, and many philosophers disputed the number, the formulation, or the very concept of formal dogmas. See CREED; DOGMA.

THIRTY-TWO PATHS OF WISDOM: Mystical concept occurring in the Book of YETZIRAH, where the term "32 Paths of Hidden Wisdom" refers to the 22 letters of the Hebrew alphabet which with the 10 elementary and primordial numbers constitute the elements of creation (an interpretation also given by SAADYAH and JUDAH HA-LEVI). In kabbalistic literature the notion of the 32 paths was reinterpreted in terms of the doctrine of SEPHIROT. The highest *sephirah* (disregarding the almost utterly transcendent first *sephirah* — "Crown") is Wisdom — the first recognizable "flash" of the Divine reality manifesting itself. This "flash" then assumes form and structure, and emanates or "descends" into the lower *sephirot* by "32 paths" or channels. These paths reflect the manner in which the various *sephirot* unite with each other in order to draw the Divine flow into the world.

THIRTY-SIX SAINTS, see **LAMED-VAV**

THREE WEEKS: The period from *Tammuz* 17 (SHIVAH ASAR BE-TAMMUZ), when the walls of Jerusalem were breached by Nebuchadnezzar, to *Av* 9, the anniversary of the destruction of the Temple. This period is called *bein ha-meitzarim* ("between the straits", cf. Lam. 1:3) and is a period of mourning which falls into two parts: one of lesser intensity from *Tammuz* 17 to *Av* 1 and a period of greater intensity from *Av* 1-9 (NINE DAYS). The celebration of marriages and all festive occasions, as well as haircutting, are forbidden during the whole period, while during the latter portion the eating of meat and drinking of wine is proscribed except on the Sabbath. On the three Sabbaths of the T.W. the prophetical readings in the synagogue consist of prophecies of doom (Jer. 1, 2, and Is. 1), chanted, in some rites, to a special tune.

THRONE OF GOD: Ancient image associated with the idea of Divine majesty. In I Kings 22:19 Micaiah the prophet says to Jehoshaphat, "I saw the Lord sitting on His throne and all the hosts of heaven standing by Him on His right hand and left", while the call of God came to Isaiah when he beheld Him "sitting upon a throne high and exalted" (Is. 6:1). A vivid vision of the Divine throne was experienced by Ezekiel (Ezek. 1:10) and by the author of the Ethiopic Book of Enoch. This "throne of glory" is frequently mentioned in the Talmud, e.g. "Great is repentance for it reaches to the throne of glory" (*Yoma* 86b) and mention is made of God moving "from the throne of judgment to the throne of mercy" (A.Z. 3b). Throne-mysticism (MAASEH MERKAVAH) is one of the earliest forms of Jewish MYSTICISM. Partly under the inspiration of Ezekiel's vision, a school of esoteric mystics developed, which practiced meditation leading to a vision of the celestial throne (see also HEIKHALOT). The idea of the T. of G. was also connected with that of the *Kavod*, the Divine glory, as the visible manifestation of the incorporeal God, and in the mystical theology of the ḤASIDEI ASHKENAZ the *Kavod* is personified as sitting on the throne, i.e., as the mystical appearance of the Divine glory and majesty manifest. Throne mysticism fell into desuetude, but its literary and theological traditions profoundly influenced the liturgy, PIYYUT, and medieval KABBALAH. The motif of the T. of G. is particularly dominant in the hymns of the liturgy for the High Holidays. See also KEDUSHAH; SHIR HA-KAVOD.

TIBBON, see **IBN TIBBON**

TIK (from Gk. *theke*): A casing or sheath. The term is used to designate (1) a TEPHILLIN (*Shab.* 16:1); (2) a case in which a Scroll of the Law is contained (*Meg.* 26b). Oriental communities apply the word to the casing of wood or silver in which the Scroll of the Law is rolled up and which is placed upright in the ALMEMAR, the *Torah* being read in this vertical position.

TIKKUN (Heb. "repair"): A term which has its origin in the kabbalistic idea of a spiritual "catastrophe" which once occurred on a cosmic — even Divine — level, and which also occurs in man conceived as a microcosm. This "disarrangement"

TABERNACLES: Tabernacle from S. Germany, 19th cent. Israel Museum, Jerusalem. (Photo: Alfred Bernheim).

TASHLIKH IN POLAND: painting by W. Stryowski.

TEMPLE: The Holy Temple vessels carried in Titus' triumphal procession; Arch of Titus, Rome.

TIK: Silver *Torah* case;
Persia, 1764.
Jewish Museum, New York.

TEPHILLIN: with silver cases;
Central Europe, 18th cent.;
Feinberg Collection, Detroit.

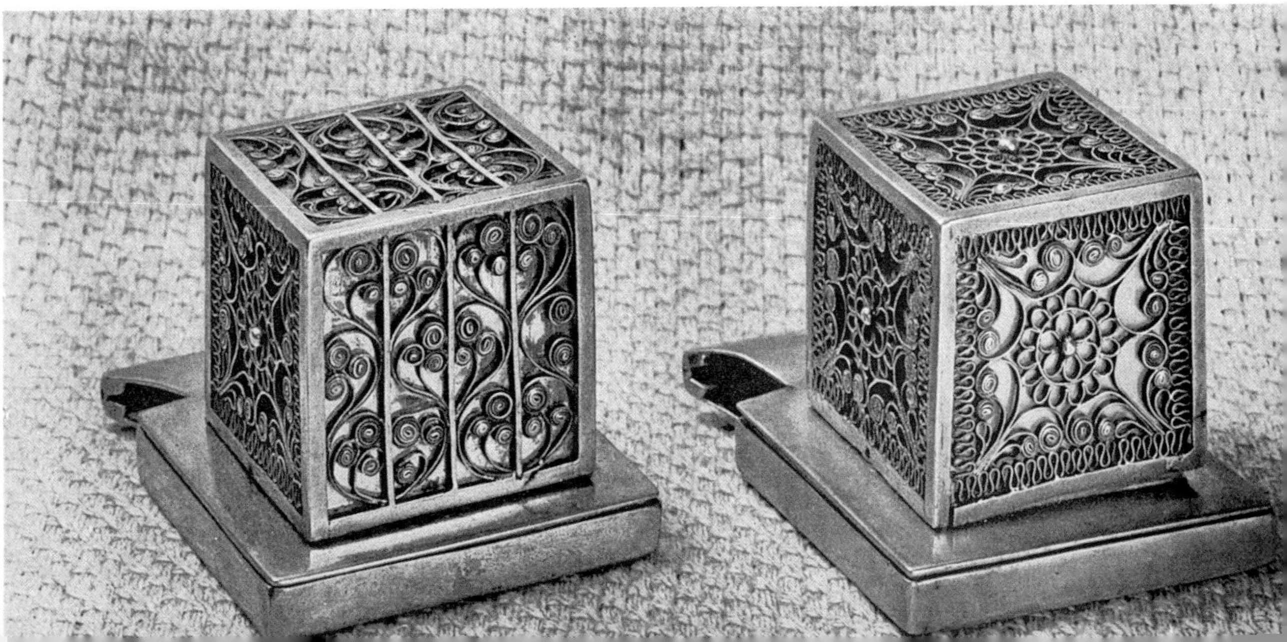

TIK:
Ornamental *Torah* case
from Aleppo.

TORAH ORNAMENTS:
Silver *Torah* case;
Paris, c. 1860.
Benguiat Collection.

TORAH ORNAMENTS:
Silver breastplate;
Nuremberg, c. 1700.
Jewish Museum, New York

TORAH ORNAMENTS:
Breastplate;
Feinberg Collection, Detroit.

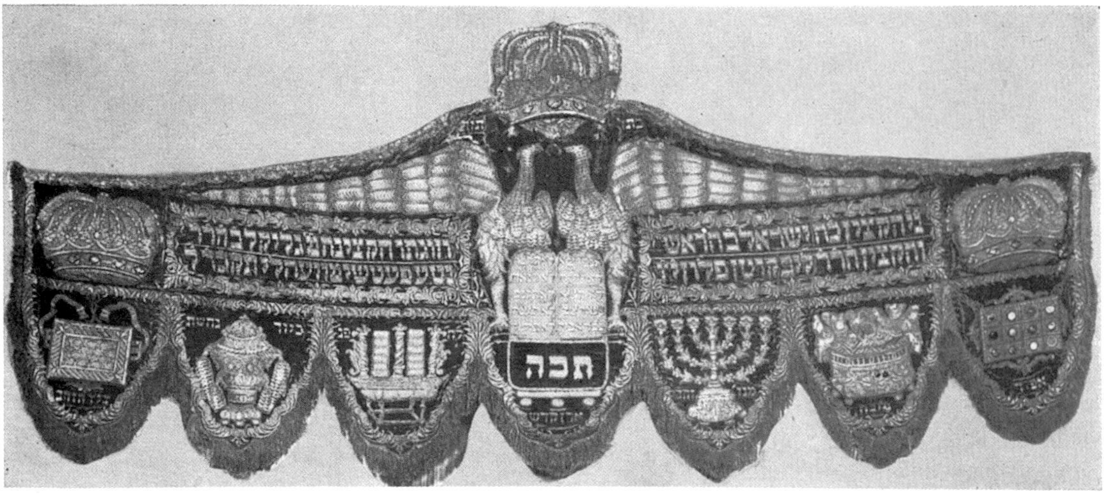

TORAH ORNAMENTS: *Kaporet*, Prague, 1764.

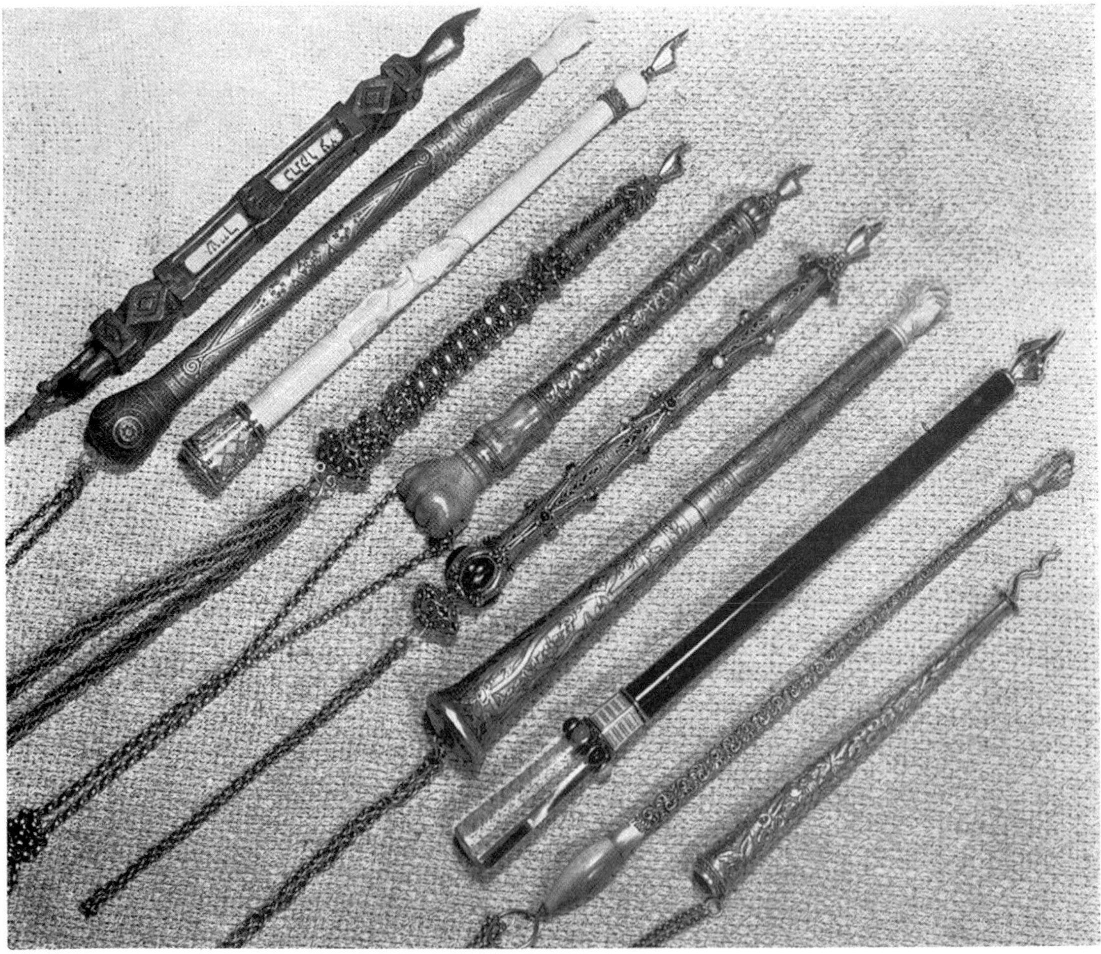

YAD: Selection of *Yadayim* made in the 18th-19th cents. Feinberg Collection, Detroit.

WAILING WALL, 1947: Zionist Archives, Jerusalem.

WEEKS: *Shavuot* bowl; Jewish Museum, Frankfort.

ZODIAC:
From the Bet Alpha Synagogue. (Dept. of Archeology, Hebrew University, Jerusalem).

in the cosmic or individual spiritual harmony results in a *pegam* — an inner defect in the channels that effect the flow of grace from the "higher" to the "lower" forms of being. Man can help bring about a "repair" — *tikkun* — of this condition by his behavior (observance of the commandments, piety, virtue) and mystical meditations (KAVVANOT). The notion of *t.* played a central rôle in Lurianic KABBALAH (see also Isaac LURIA; MYSTICISM). In ḥasidic communities, the *rebbe* would often be asked by penitents to provide them with spiritual help and advice for achieving the proper *t.* of their souls.

TIKKUN: Order of service for certain occasions; mostly recited at night. (1) *T. Ḥatzot* ("midnight *t.*"): Prayers, generally (but not uniformly) consisting of Ps. 79, 102, and 137, the *vidduy* (confessional), the Thirteen Divine Attributes, and dirges (*kinot*) recited at midnight by individuals or small groups, sitting on the ground, in mourning over the destruction of the Temple and the Jewish state. Instituted in the 16th cent. by kabbalistic circles in Safed, the custom of *T. Ḥatzot* spread quickly and was very popular throughout the 17th and 18th cents. (2) *T. Shomerim La-Boker* ("*t.* of watchmen for the morning": cf. Ps. 130: 6): Similar to (1), but said shortly before sunrise. (3) *T. Leil Hoshana Rabbah* ("*t.* for the eve of HOSHANA RABBAH"): Includes the reading of Deuteronomy, Psalms, and passages from the Talmud, Midrash, and Zohar. This *t.* continues through the night, a custom originating in the 14th cent. when the Pentateuch was read during this night. (4) *T. Leil Shavuot* ("*t.* for the eve of SHAVUOT"): Contains extracts from the Bible, Mishnah, Talmud, Midrash, and Zohar, as well as prayers and *azharot* on the 613 precepts; recited throughout the night. (5) *T. Shabbat* ("Sabbath *t.*"): A collection of *piyyutim*, excerpts from Mishnah *Shabbat*, etc. Its composition is attributed to the kabbalist Isaac LURIA and it is recited on Friday evenings and Sabbaths. Some rites observed *tikkunim* on various other occasions, e.g. on the traditional anniversary of the death of Moses (*Adar* 7) and of the death of Isaac Luria (*Av* 5).

TIKKUN SOPHERIM (Heb. "correction of the scribes"): (1) Emendations of the biblical text (mostly changes in pronominal suffixes) traditionally ascribed to the men of the KENESET GEDOLAH (see SOPHERIM). There are — according to various opinions — 11, 12, or 18 such changes, intended to avoid anthropomorphism (e.g. Gen. 18:22 — "but Abraham stood yet before the Lord" instead of the original "but the Lord stood yet before Abraham") or to eliminate offensive terms by a resort to euphemism, (e.g. Job 2:9, where Job is counseled to "bless God and die", meaning, "to curse, etc."). (2) Colloquial term for an unpointed printed text of the Pentateuch used in preparation for READING OF THE LAW.

TISHA BE-AV, see **AV, 9th OF**

TISHBI, ELIJAH, see **LEVITA, ELIJAH**

TITHES: The tenth part of one's income, set aside for a specific purpose. The earliest biblical reference concerns Abraham's tithe to Melchizedek (Gen. 14:18-20). All produce, fruit and vegetable, is liable to be tithed. Untithed it is called TEVEL and may not be eaten except incidentally while it is still in the field. The following t. must be separated, in addition to the HEAVE-OFFERING: (1) first tithe (*maaser rishon*), (2) second tithe (*maaser sheni*), and (3) poor tithe (*maaser ani*). Produce of HEKDESH, or of ownerless property (HEPHKER) or of the SABBATICAL YEAR or of the GLEANINGS and corners left for the poor are not liable to be tithed. For the purposes of tithing the years are divided into cycles of seven, the seventh year being free from t. The first tithe is to be separated in all six years; the second tithe in the first, second, fourth, and fifth years; the poor tithe in the third and sixth years. The first tithe (Num. 18:24) is given to the LEVITE who himself could own no land and who in turn must give one-tenth of what he receives (i.e., one hundredth of the total produce, called *terumat maaser* ["the heave-offering of the tithe"], to the priest (Num. 18:26). The levite may then use the remainder as he wishes. The second tithe (Lev. 27:30-31; Deut. 14:22-26) must be taken to Jerusalem and consumed there. It may however be exchanged for its money value, and this amount, together with an additional fifth, must be taken to Jerusalem and spent there. The poor tithe (Deut. 14:28-29; 26:12) is distributed to the needy anywhere. Its cash equivalent may however be used instead. Produce untithed at its source is liable to tithing by whoever has it in his possession. One may not tithe from one product for another, nor from bad for good produce, nor from produce in one location for produce situated elsewhere. Twice during the seven year cycle, before Passover of the fourth and seventh years, all tithing obligations are to be brought up to date and the tithes removed (*biur*; cf. Deut 26:12 ff.; *Maaser Sheni* 5) and a relevant confession recited. Rabbinical discussion of the subject can be found in the talmudic tractates TERUMOT, MAASEROT, MAASER SHENI.

TOBIAH BEN ELIEZER (11th cent.): Biblical exegete living in Castoria (Bulgaria). His main work LEKAḤ TOV ("Good Counsel") is a largely midrashic commentary upon the Pentateuch and Five Scrolls, drawing mainly on talmudic and other rabbinic and elucidated sources and arranging the material according to the biblical sequence. T. shows a keen sense for the plain meaning of the Bible, and authorities such as R. Tam and Samuel ben Meir quoted him with respect, though Ibn Ezra was critical of him on grammatical grounds.

TOBIAH BEN MOSES (11th cent.): Karaite scholar, biblical exegete, and liturgical poet in Constantinople. He originated from a Rabbanite family but was converted to KARAISM and studied in Jerusalem under a leading Karaite authority — Yeshuah ben Judah. Having mastered Arabic, T. proceeded to translate the Arabic works of his sect into Hebrew. Among his original works are *Yehi Meorot* ("Let there be Luminaries") on the biblical commandments; *Otzar Neḥmad* ("Pleasant Thesaurus") on Leviticus; and *Zot ha-Torah* ("This is the Pentateuch") a commentary on the Pentateuch.

TOBIT, BOOK OF: An apocryphal work of uncertain authorship and date which has been variously assigned, from the 2nd cent. B.C.E. to the 2nd cent. C.E. It has also not been established whether the original was written in Greek, Aramaic, or Hebrew. T. was a righteous man exiled with the ten tribes. His lost eyesight is regained by magical means disclosed to his son Tobias by the angel Raphael who delivers him from the evil Asmodeus. The motif is one of righteous suffering which ends in the restoration of happiness.

TOHORAH, see **PURITY, RITUAL**

TOHOROT (or **TOHAROT**; Heb. "purities", euphemism for ritual impurities): (1) Sixth and last order of the MISHNAH dealing with various classifications of ritual impurity and the rites of purification. It comprises the tractates KELIM, OHALOT, NEGAIM, PARAH, TOHOROT, MIKVAOT, NIDDAH, MAKHSHIRIN, ZAVIM, TEVUL YOM, YADAYIM, and UKTZIM, to which only *Niddah* has a *gemara.* (2) Fifth tractate of the order of *T.* with no *gemara* in either Talmud. It deals with minor ritual impurities which defile only until sunset.

TOKHAḤAH (Heb. "rebuke"): Two sections of the Pentateuch (Lev. 26 and Deut. 28) which prophesy a series of drastic punishments to be visited upon the Israelites should they forsake the *Torah.* When these sections are recited as part of the Reading of the Law, it is customary for the reader to call himself up and to read in an undertone.

TOLEDOT YESHU (Heb. "History of Jesus"): Scurrilous account of the life and activity of JESUS which circulated in different versions among the Jews during the Middle Ages; its Hebrew version probably dates from the 13th cent. but it may be based on an earlier work in Aramaic. It gives the most ignoble interpretations to such details as the birth, the supernatural powers, and the tragic death of Jesus. Thus Jesus is made the illegitimate son of Mary by a Roman soldier Panthera (as first stated by Celsus in the 2nd cent.), his powers are said to derive from black magic, and his death is a shameful one. The dates do not correspond with those of the historical Jesus of Nazareth, and the work is an expression of the vulgar polemic which was, at times, the Jewish reaction to the even more vulgar attacks to which Judaism was subjected in popular Christian preaching and writing.

TOMB OF RACHEL: Unlike the three patriarchs and their wives Sarah, Rebecca, and Leah, Rachel was not interred in the family sepulcher of Machpelah near Hebron but "was buried on the way to Ephrath which is Bethlehem" (Gen. 35:19). The biblical narrative also records that "Jacob set up a monument upon her grave, that is the monument of the grave of Rachel to this day" (*ibid* 20). The traditional identification of the tomb dates at least from the Byzantine Period. A Midrash (*Gen. Rab.* 82:11) to the effect that Jacob buried his beloved wife in that place so that she might intercede for her descendants when they passed by on their way to exile in Babylonia (based on Jer. 31:15) caused the Tomb of Rachel to become a favorite place of pilgrimage for Jews. Since 1967 the tomb has been under Israeli control.

TOMBS AND TOMBSTONES: In the Bible the word *kavar* ("to bury") is used both for BURIAL in the earth and for interment in tombs, burial being the only permitted method for the reverential disposal of the dead. In talmudic times, however, the word *kever* was confined to a grave in the soil, while the word *kokh* was used for the rock-hewn tombs which were a prominent feature of the hill country of Judah and Galilee. The traditional tombs of the members of the Sanhedrin in Sanhedria in Jerusalem and the discovery in recent years of the extensive burial place at BEIT SHEARIM in Galilee are outstanding examples of these tombs. In the latter place there are examples of sarcophagi as well as rock-hewn tombs. The Bible makes occasional mention of a *matzevah*, i.e., some kind of monument or pillar placed over a tomb (e.g. that placed by Jacob over the TOMB OF RACHEL and that which Absalom prepared for himself, II Sam. 18:18), but the custom of erecting tombstones over graves is of comparatively recent origin among Jews and as late as the 16th cent. Joseph KARO (*Yoreh Deah* 364) declared it not obligatory. Among *Sephardim* the tombstones are laid flat whereas the *Ashkenazi* custom is to place them in an upright position. The usual custom is to erect them during the twelfth month after burial (in the State of Israel, within thirty days). Few inscriptions on Jewish tombs have been found from before the 1st cent. B.C.E. but from that period on they are a regular feature of Jewish tombs. The inscriptions though mostly in Hebrew, appear in the Classical Period in other languages as well, especially Greek, and are frequently decorated with typical Jewish symbols (*menorah*, *etrog*, *lulav*, etc.). In the Middle Ages, inscriptions were entirely in Hebrew, but in recent centuries the vernacular has again appeared in tombstones — with or without Hebrew. On the tombstones of priests, it is customary to portray two hands in the traditional gesture of the PRIESTLY BLESSING.

TOPHETH: High Places dedicated to the rites of MOLOCH in the valley of Hinnom, west of the walls of Jerusalem (Jer. 7:31-32; II Kings 23:10). Its exact location as well as etymology is uncertain. The Moloch rites included the sacrifice and burning of children, and hence the name T. came to mean a place of horror and abomination. In his drive against idolatry Josiah defiled the T., but it was revived and continued until the Babylonian Exile. In later Hebrew literature the word T. (and also GEHINNOM, the "valley of Hinnom") became synonymous with "hell".

TORAH: Hebrew word meaning "teaching", "instruction", or "guidance" (probably derived from *yarah* "throw", throw lots for Divine guidance by oracle). In biblical usage the word has no particular prominence, and appears together with similar terms (e.g. commandments, laws, ordinances, etc.). Only in the Second Temple Period did *T.* come to mean LAW in a more specific sense, translated by the hellenistic Jews as *nomos*. In rabbinic literature *T.* is used in a variety of senses, all based on the general understanding of *T.* as the guidance and teaching imparted to Israel by Divine REVELATION. Thus *T.* designates the PENTATEUCH as distinct from the other two main sections of the Hebrew Bible — the Prophets and the Hagiographa (see TANAKH), but in a wider sense is also applied to Scripture as a whole and to biblical legislation in contradistinction to rabbinical enactments. Scripture, however, is only the *Torah she-bi-khetav*, the WRITTEN LAW, which is supplemented by the equally Divine *Torah she-be-al-peh*, the ORAL LAW. Both these *Torahs* together constitute "the *Torah*" in its most comprehensive sense. In the Bible the term is often applied to specific laws and regulations, e.g. "the *T.* of the meal-offering" (Lev. 6-7), "the *T.* of the leper" (*ibid.* 14:2), where rabbinic writing would have used *din* or HALAKHAH. The concept of *T.* is wider than that of *halakhah*, which is only part of *T.* The study of *T.* was considered by the rabbis a major religious duty (see EDUCATION, STUDY, TALMUD TORAH), and its fulfillment the highest goal of piety and virtue. Unlike WISDOM, which is shared by all nations, *T.* is the exclusive possession of the Jewish people: "If one shall say to you that there is wisdom in Edom, believe it; if he says there is *Torah* in Edom, believe it not" (*Lam. Rab.* 2). The Divine injunction to Joshua (Josh. 1:8) "This book of the *Torah* shall not depart from thy mouth, but thou shalt meditate on it day and night" was interpreted as an exhortation to devote the whole of one's time to the study of the *T.* The daily prayers include a blessing to God for the commandment to occupy oneself with the study of the *T.*, while the blessing immediately preceding the reading of the *Shema*, both in the morning and the evening, is one of praise to God for giving the *T.* and of prayer for Divine grace in its acquisition. The rabbinic passage enumerating those things the fruit of which man enjoys in this world while the main reward is reserved for the World to Come (Mishnah *Peah.* 1:1) concludes "but the study of the *T.* is equivalent to them all". The idea that the *T.* is the source of life of the Jewish people, is expressed in many rabbinic parables and homilies, but particularly in the liturgical BLESSINGS recited by the person called to the synagogal reading of the Pentateuch, and in the daily morning prayer: "Blessed is our God, who hath created us for His glory and hath separated us from them that go astray, and hath given us the *T.* and thus planted everlasting life in our midst. May He open our heart unto His *T.*"

TORAH ORNAMENTS: The Scroll of the *Torah* (see SEPHER TORAH) is adorned with ornaments (varying in different rites and traditions) to express the reverence and love in which it is held. The *Ashkenazi* and Western *Sephardi* custom is to drape the Scroll in a mantle (MEIL) of costly material (velvet or silk, often richly embroidered) which is removed during reading when the parchment scroll is laid down flat on the reading desk. Other ornaments include the band (MAPPAH; *Sephardi, faire*) with which the two halves of the roll are bound together after use (among German Jews this is a VIMPEL inscribed with an appropriate biblical verse); a crown (KETER) and/or other ornaments (RIMMONIM) placed on top of the rollers; a breastplate, sometimes a reproduction of the breastplate of the High Priest (cf. Exod. 28:13-30); a pointer (YAD) of precious metal for use by the reader. Among the oriental *Sephardim* the *Torah* scroll is encased in a hinged box of wood (TIK) either plain or overlaid with precious metal, and read in an upright position. Such a usage provides for only two of the above ornaments — the pointer and the *rimmonim* — which are placed on holders protruding from the case. In the Italian rite both a crown and *rimmonim* are placed on the top of the Scroll.

TORAH, READING OF, see **READING OF THE LAW**

TORAT KOHANIM, see **LEVITICUS**

TORTS (Heb. *nezikin*): An act whereby damage which requires compensation is caused to the person, property, or reputation of another. Default on contract is also a tort, responsibility and compensation being determined by the terms of the contract. Where no contract exists, compensation is decided by law. A tort may be caused by the property of the individual as well as by the individual himself. As a general rule the Mishnah states that "a man is always considered forewarned (and therefore liable for any tort caused by him), whether the damage is done in error or wantonly, awake or asleep" (*Bava Kamma* 2:6). In cases of error, however, he is only liable for the actual damage done but not for the incidental payments, such as pain, shame, etc., normally incurred in the injury of another. The responsibility for t. caused by property is based on the grounds that a person is responsible for guarding his property and taking reasonable precautions to see that no damage occurs through negligence in this regard. Cases where the owner could not reasonably have been obliged to guard against the contingency from which the damage arose incur payment of only half the damage. The major types of tort by property are classified under the headings:

(1) Ox (*shor*) — damage done directly by an animal;
(2) Pit (*bor*) — stationary obstacles placed in a public thoroughfare;
(3) Grazing (*maveh*) — damage in which advantage accrues to the animal;
(4) Fire (*haver*) — inanimate property which travels to do damage.

Slander, insult, and betrayal are t. in law. The subject is fully treated in the talmudic order Nezikin.

TOSAPHOT (Heb. "additions") **and TOSAPHISTS:** The *tosaphot* are the novellae on the Talmud printed in the outer column of all Talmud editions. There is a difference of opinion as to the origin of the name. The general view is that they constitute additions to the commentary of Rashi, and this is supported by the fact that the most frequent words of introduction are "the *kuntras* (i.e., Rashi's commentary) explains". The term may mean additions to the Talmud itself. Unlike the commentary of Rashi, the *t.* are not a consecutive commentary, but consist of learned discussions and excursuses on specific points and problems. The tosaphists (i.e., the authors of the *tosaphot*) originated in North France, the home of Rashi, and their activity lasted from the 12th to the 14th cent. The first tosaphists were the two sons-in-law of Rashi, Meir ben Samuel and Judah ben Nathan, but the greatest was his grandson Jacob ben Meir, known as *Rabbenu* Tam. Of the 300 tosaphists, outstanding are Samuel ben Meir, Samson ben Abraham of Sens, Judah ben Isaac of Paris, and Samuel (Sir Morel) of Falaise. The tosaphist school also spread to Germany, the most distinguished of the German tosaphists being Isaac ben Asher (*Riba*). The printed *tosaphot*, which cover 38 tractates of the Talmud, are a composite collection based upon the separate editions of *tosaphot* made by various scholars. These collections are known by the place names of their authors, such as *tosaphot* of Sens (by Samson of Sens), Evreux (Moses of Evereux), Touques (Eliezer of Touques), as well as the *tosaphot* of Perez ben Elijah of Corbeil. The *tosaphot* of tractate *Yoma* were written in Germany by Meir of Rothenburg, a pupil of Jehiel of Paris.

TOSEPHTA (Aram. "Addition"): Tannaitic work, partly parallel to the Mishnah and supplementing it; its text often provides variant readings of the Mishnah (see also Baraita). The extant T., like the Mishnah, is divided into six "orders" which are subdivided into treatises bearing the same names as those of the Mishnah (missing are *Kinnim, Middot*, and *Tamid* from the order *Kodashim*, and also *Avot*, although Avot De-Rabbi Natan may be part of an aggadic section of the T. enlarging on *Avot*). Various theories have been advanced as to the relationship between the two works, among them the view that after the concise formulation of the Mishnah, the T. was meant to serve as a fuller record of the tannaitic traditions. The foundations of this work were laid by R. Akiva (cf. *Eduy.* 2:1; 8:1; *Kil.* 1:3). The Talmud (*Sanh.* 86a) states "whenever an anonymous opinion is given in the Mishnah, it is R. Meir's; in the T., it is R. Nehemiah's; all however originate from R. Akiva" (both R. Meir and R. Nehemiah were pupils of R. Akiva). Some authorities, including Maimonides, attributed the authorship of the T. to R. Ḥiyya but this theory has been disproved. Probably the final redactor of the T. was one of the last of the *amoraim* who combined several collections of *tosaphot* (pl.). The hitherto only critical text of the T. (by Zuckermandel, 1886) is now being superseded by S. Lieberman's edition with commentary *Tosephta ki-pheshuta.* See Talmud.

TOWER OF BABEL, see **BABEL, TOWER OF**

TRADITION: Doctrines or rules handed down from generation to generation by word of mouth. The technical terms for t. in Hebrew are *kabbalah* ("that which is received") and Masorah ("that which is passed on"). The terms can refer to historical t. such as the one claiming that Amoz, the father of Isaiah, and Amaziah, king of Judah, were brothers (*Sot.* 10b) or to traditions handed down by a teacher, as in the phrase "I have received a t. from the mouth of Shemaiah and Avtalyon" (*Pes.* 66a). The most common use of the word, however, refers to those ordinances of the ORAL LAW for which no proof can be adduced from the Bible but which are regarded as of equal authority with biblical laws. These are called *"halakhot* of Moses from Mt. Sinai". Thus R. Eliezer ben Hyrcanus told R. Yose to ignore a vote taken on a certain occasion since "I have a *kabbalah* from R. Johanan ben Zakkai who heard it from his teacher, and his teacher from his teacher that it is a *halakhah* of Moses from Mt. Sinai that in Ammon and Moab the poor man's tithe is given in the seventh year" (Mishnah *Yad.* 4:3; *Ḥag.* 3b). Again, finding no biblical authority for the traditional Jewish method of animal slaughter for food, the Talmud declares it to be a t. (*Ḥul.* 28a). The phrase *"halakhah* of Moses from Mt. Sinai" is not always to be taken literally but is used for any t. of immemorial antiquity. According to Maimonides all laws and enactments which have no biblical authority but are accepted in the Talmud without dissent belong to this class of traditional teaching. Traditional CUSTOM is known as *minhag.*

TRANSGRESSION, see **SIN**

TRANSLATIONS OF BIBLE, see **BIBLE TRANSLATIONS**

TRANSMIGRATION OF SOULS: The belief that after death the SOUL enters into a new body, though known in Eastern religions, is never encountered in biblical and talmudic Judaism. It is mentioned for the first time in the 10th cent. by SAADYAH who reports that some "foolish" Jews held the belief. The theory reappears as an esoteric Jewish doctrine in the 12th cent. kabbalistic Book of BAHIR, which may have derived it from earlier Jewish sources or from the Catharist heresy which flourished in Provence at that time. Various expressions were used in early kabbalistic literature for the concept of t., but ultimately the term GILGUL ("revolving") became generally accepted. For the early kabbalists and for the author of the ZOHAR, t. or reincarnation of the soul was a punishment and a grace inflicted on individuals who had committed certain sins or failed to fulfill certain commandments of God, particularly the commandment of procreation. By assuming a new bodily existence, they would have another opportunity to make good where they had failed and to fulfill their destiny. As time went on, the concept of t. was extended, and three transmigrations were held to be the minimum for every individual soul. In the KABBALAH of the 16th cent., and later, the doctrine of t. assumed a prominent position. Isaac LURIA and his disciples in Safed associated the doctrine of t. with the fate of Adam's soul after its "fall". Adam's soul contains within itself the souls of all men, and its fall expresses its state of alienation from God. The individual soul has it's place within the soul of Adam, and as such it shares the fate of the general fall and also endures its individual "exile" brought about by its own sins. Its misdeeds on earth may even bring about the reincarnation of a soul in a lower form of life, and it must continue on its transmigration until it achieves its "TIKKUN", i.e., the restoration to its proper place in the soul of Adam. The determining of one's previous existences and the search for the proper *tikkun* became an important element of folk religion in Eastern Europe, especially within the Ḥasidic Movement. A soul that is not reborn with a new body but enters and "possesses" another human being is known as a DYBBUK.

TRAVEL, PRAYER FOR, see **JOURNEY, PRAYER FOR**

TREASON: The Bible does not mention an instance of the betrayal of one's country, but it contains many instances of rebellion and regicide (e.g. II Sam. 18:14; II Kings 11:1). The penalty of death for disobedience to the king is based (*Sanh.* 49a) upon the declaration made by the people to Joshua: "whosoever rebels against your word shall be put to death" (Josh. 1:18). Any disobedience toward the royal command is considered rebellion: the king may punish the offender in any manner considered fit, but he may not confiscate his property. Rabbinic law has transferred to the state the rights previously enjoyed by the king. In the State of Israel, wartime t. is one of the two instances in which the death penalty is applicable.

TREE OF LIFE (Heb. *etz ḥayyim*): The T. of L. i.e., a tree whose fruit gives life to those partaking of it, is a frequent mythological symbol found in Semitic and other cultures (e.g. Babylonia, Greece, Persia, and India). The motif is used in the biblical account of the GARDEN OF EDEN, where the T. of L. is mentioned alongside the Tree of Knowledge (Gen. 2:9). Adam's expulsion from the Garden of Eden (Gen. 3:23-24) after eating from the Tree of Knowledge is motivated (*ibid.* 22) by the concern that he might also partake of the T. of L. and thus gain immortality. In the Book of Proverbs the tree figures as a metaphor signifying WISDOM (3:18) or the path of the righteous (4:30). There is much difference of opinion among commentators as to the precise meaning and relationship of the two trees in the paradise story. Apocalyptic literature promises the righteous that they will partake of the T. of L. after the final judgment (e.g. Enoch 24:4; 25:4-6; II Esdras 8:52). In kabbalistic literature the symbolism of the two trees, and of the T. of L. in particular, is developed in mystical fashion.

TREES, NEW YEAR FOR, see **NEW YEAR FOR TREES**

TRESPASS: The English term t. applies to a

variety of acts, expressed in Hebrew by different words. The most important of these are (1) offenses against another person's rights or property (*nezek, nezikin*), see TORTS; (2) transgressions against the Divine Law in general, see AVERAH; (3) certain specific offenses, atonement for which requires a special kind of sacrifice, see TRESPASS-OFFERING.

TRESPASS-OFFERING (Heb. *asham*): An offering brought by one guilty of the "trespasses" of perjury in denying a committed robbery, profane use of sacred objects, or violating a betrothed handmaid; by a Nazirite after being cleansed from ritual defilement; and by a leper after his purification. In addition there is a "suspended trespass-offering" for cases of doubtful trespass (Mishnah *Zev.* 5:5). The offering, which was eaten by the priests, consisted of a two-year-old ram.

TRIAL, see **CRIMINAL PROCEDURE**

TRIBES, TEN LOST: The schism that followed the death of Solomon ended in the secession of ten tribes (Reuben, Simeon, Dan, Naphtali, Gad, Asher, Issachar, Zebulun, Ephraim, and Manasseh) who under JEROBOAM formed the Northern Kingdom of Israel. Lasting less than 200 years, the kingdom fell to the Assyrians in 721 B.C.E., when the majority of the Israelites were deported to Assyria (II Kings 17:6). Unlike the Judeans of the Southern Kingdom (who survived a similar fate 135 years later), they soon assimilated and lost their separate identity. Those remaining in the homeland commingled with foreign colonists and subsequently became known as SAMARITANS. The loss of the ten tribes was never accepted as final by the Jews. From the time of Jeremiah who prophesied their return (31:4 ff.) and Ezekiel who connected their eventual return with the era of redemption (37:16) — a concept developed in apocalyptic literature — hope of their eventual restoration was never relinquished. The Midrash mentions different places as their dwelling-place (e.g. across the river SAMBATYON, under a blanket of clouds, or within the walls of Antioch) and fantastic reports regarding the lost t. were a frequent feature of Jewish legend and folklore, particularly in periods of messianic ferment. A vivid description purporting to be of the lost tribes was given by the 9th cent. Jewish traveler, Eldad Ha-Dani.

TRIBES, TWELVE: In the time of the JUDGES, and before the consolidation of a unifying national consciousness, Israelite society was a loose association of tribes, held together by a common religion and common ancestry (cf. Judg. 5). According to the biblical account the tribal grouping of Israel originated with the twelve sons of Jacob, grouped as: 1) the children of Leah — Reuben, Simeon, Levi, Judah, Issachar, and Zebulun; 2) those of Bilhah — Dan and Naphtali; 3) those of Zilpah — Gad and Asher; and 4) those of Rachel — Joseph and Benjamin. Joseph's two sons — Manasseh and Ephraim — formed separate tribes but this did not increase the overall number since the tribe of LEVI, having been selected for sacred duty, was not included in the general census and there was no tribe of Joseph as such. Each tribe, moreover, was divided into several clans or families each consisting of a number of households. Leading the tribes were the princes or chieftains. Joshua divided the land of Canaan among the t.t. and although the tribal boundaries were effaced during the period of the monarchy, consciousness of tribal origins remained; in Ezekiel's closing eschatological vision of Jerusalem the city's gates bear the names of the t.t. (Ezek. 48:31-34).

TRIBUNALS, see **BET DIN**

TRIENNIAL CYCLE, see **READING OF THE LAW**

TROKI, ISAAC OF (1533-1594): KARAITE scholar born in the Lithuanian Karaite center of Troki. Frequently called upon to participate in religious controversies with Christians, he made a special study of Christian theology and as a result wrote a classic work of anti-Christian polemic *Ḥizzuk Emunah* ("Strengthening of Faith"). T.'s criticism of Christian dogma was so successful that the work was translated into Latin and other languages and became the subject of passionate debate. It was also extensively used by freethinkers in their attacks on Christianity. So popular was the work among Jews that it was emended by Rabbanite writers to remove its Karaite character, and talmudic statements were inserted into the original text.

TROP: The Judeo-German form of the medieval *tropes*, signifying the cadences of church plainsong. It refers to the traditional notes to which the *Torah* is chanted (cantillation, ACCENTS). These are of ancient origin, and are mentioned by early commentators such as Rashi and Ibn Ezra and regarded as being invested with the same authority as the MASORAH. T. is invaluable both for establishing the correct accentuation of words and as an aid to the proper division of sentences to establish their correct meaning. Elijah Gaon of Vilna used the various names of the notes of the *t.* (which are in Aramaic) as a basis for homiletical interpretation.

TRUTH AND TRUTHFULNESS: The word truth (*emet*) in biblical and rabbinic language does not so much signify scientific or theological truth as honesty, truthfulness, sincerity, loyalty, integrity, etc. When referring to actions and judgments it can also mean "right" and "just" (cf. Zech. 8:16); in connection with facts it signifies "authenticated", "substantiated". It is thus a practical rather than a logical concept. God is true, i.e., ever faithful (cf. Jer. 10:10; Ps. 31:6) and His word, law, and precepts are true (Ps. 19:10; 119:43; 142). Being one of God's chief ATTRIBUTES (Exod. 34:6; Ps. 117:2), truth is stressed both in the Bible and Talmud as one of the greatest virtues. Only he "who speaks truth in his heart" shall "abide in Thy tabernacle and dwell in Thy holy mountain" (Ps. 15:2) and the daily morning prayer exhorts the worshiper: "at all times let a man fear God secretly as well as publicly, acknowledge the truth and speak the truth in his heart". The talmudic description of a hypocrite and a liar is that of a person who has "one thing in his heart and another on his lips" (*Pes.* 113b). R. Simeon ben Gamaliel enumerates truth as the first of the three pillars upon which the continued existence of the world depends (*Avot* 1:1), while "truth is the seal of the Holy One, blessed be He" (*Yoma* 69b). Truth will ultimately triumph while falsehood will not endure (*Shab.* 104a), and liars are one of the four groups with whom the Divine Presence does not abide (*Sotah* 42a). Parents are bidden never to make a promise to a child and not keep it, lest thereby they encourage untruthfulness in the child (*Suk.* 46b). The reinforcement of a statement by an OATH, though at times required by law, was discouraged by the rabbis, since it tended to create a double standard of truth. In spite of the command to speak truth (Zech. 8:16) and the prohibition against LYING (Exod. 23:7), truthfulness must take account of specific situations and in certain circumstances there may be other overriding demands (*Yev.* 65b). Thus the Midrash adduces the difference in wording between Gen. 18:12 ("my husband is old") and v. 13 ("I am old" which is how God repeats Sarah's statement to Abraham) as proof of the propriety of modifying a statement for the sake of domestic harmony. The rabbis in extolling AARON as a lover of peace explain that he was not averse to telling a "white lie" if peace could thereby be established or restored. The use of *emet* in a logical sense (e.g. "necessary truth", "eternal truth", "revealed t.", etc.) only appears in the course of medieval philosophical literature.

TU BI-SHEVAT, see **NEW YEAR FOR TREES**

TURIM, see **JACOB BEN ASHER**

TWILIGHT: Period of evening when it is still doubtful whether it is DAY or NIGHT. R. Yose alone (*Shab.* 34b) holds tha "t. is as the twinkling of the eye", i.e., there is no t. The accepted view, however, is that it is the period between sunset and darkness, opinions differing as to whether this is to be determined by the appearance of the sky or by a measurement of time (*loc. cit.*). For halakhic purposes it is accepted that as long as only two stars of medium magnitude are visible it is still t., the appearance of the third star marking the onset of night. The time period differs according to the latitude and the period of the year.

TZADDIK (Heb. "righteous"): God is described in the Bible as a *t.* (e.g. Deut. 32:14), but generally the word denotes the "righteous man". As such it embodies one of the ideals of moral and religious perfection in Judaism. The righteous man lives by his faith (Hab. 2:4) and scrupulously obeys God's Law; he is beloved by God, who answers his prayers. A rabbinic hyperbole expresses this idea by stating that "God decrees and the righteous man annuls" (*M.K.* 16b), i.e., the prayers of the *t.* can avert disasters decreed by God. In talmudic usage the *t.* is different from the ḤASID (another ideal type) in that the latter goes to more extreme lengths of piety and devotion. Since the 18th cent. the term *t.* has been especially applied to the ḥasidic rabbi who was held to act as intermediary between man and God and was accordingly regarded by his followers with the utmost reverence. The ḥasidic *t.* does not require ordination and the position was generally hereditary — but not necessarily so. His followers would visit him to receive his advice and *segullot* (formulas for success, health, etc.) and in return would donate money which would be devoted either to charity or to the *t.*'s own household. Some of the *tzaddikim* (pl.) lived in luxurious opulence and their excesses contributed to the discrediting of the concept of the *t.* in many circles — although many other *tzaddikim* continued to live in poverty or modesty and acquired a reputation for their learning and saintliness. Nevertheless the fanatic devotion of the *ḥasid* (i.e., his follower) toward his *t.* increased the suspicion with which he was regarded by the MITNAGGED. The ideal embodied by the ḥasidic *t.* is not in accordance with the traditional Jewish reverence for the rabbi as a scholar (*talmid ḥakham*); in this case personality replaced doctrine and religious value was imparted not by the *t.*'s knowledge but by the saintly quality of his personality. See also LAMED VAV.

TZEDAKAH, see **CHARITY; RIGHTEOUSNESS**

TZE'ENAH U-RE'ENAH (Heb. "Go forth and behold"; words derived from the Song of Songs "Go forth, O ye daughters of Zion, and behold"): A Yiddish homiletical commentary and exposition of the Pentateuch (arranged according to the weekly portions) by Jacob ben Isaac Ashkenazi of Janov written especially for the use of women. The biblical narrative is embellished by expositions of relevant *Midrashim*. Immediately upon publication (early 17th cent.) the work attained immense popularity and became the favorite reading matter for pious women, especially on

Sabbath afternoons. The same author's *Sepher ha-Maggid* ("Book of the Preacher") deals similarly with the Prophetical Books and Hagiographa.

TZIDDUK HA-DIN (Heb. "justification of the judgment"): The acceptance of the justice of the Divine decree, especially in the sense of resigned submission to God's justice in the face of a person's death. The term therefore signifies specifically the prayer which is recited at a funeral. The basis of this moving prayer is found in A.Z. 18a; R. Ḥanina ben Teradyon and his wife were sentenced to death by the Romans, and their daughter committed to a brothel. On hearing the sentence R. Ḥanina quoted, in acceptance of the Divine will, the first half of Deut. 32:4, his wife completed the verse, and the daughter quoted Jer. 32:19. These verses are included in the *tzidduk ha-din* prayer.

TZIMTZUM (Heb. "contraction"): In Lurianic KABBALAH, the process whereby God, who is "All", "withdraws" or contracts Himself so as to leave a kind of primordial space or non-divine vacuum within which creation can take place. The doctrine was meant to account for the possibility of creation, when all is filled with God, since the infinite being of God does not permit the existence of anything else. Yet even the space of *t.* is not conceived as completely empty of the Divine Light. An impression of the Divine remains "as the fragrance which lingers in the vial after it has been emptied of its perfume". In the system of Isaac LURIA the notion of *t.* also served as an explanation for the origin of evil, as well as a theistic qualification of the pantheism inherent in the thought that all creation is included within God. Connected with the doctrine of *t.* is that of the BREAKING OF THE VESSELS, which developed the traditional idea that the Divine, no less than Israel, suffers EXILE.

TZITZIT (Heb. "fringes"): Fringes appended to each of the four corners of a garment (Deut. 22:12). Since modern dress rarely includes four-cornered garments a special one (*arba kanphot* "four corners", or *tallit katan*, "small *tallit*", so-called to differentiate from the large TALLIT worn at prayer) is worn during the day by observant male Jews (including children) beneath the outer clothing in order to fulfill the biblical precept "and they shall put upon the fringe of the corner a thread of blue (*tekhelet*)" (Num. 15:38). Since the exact shade of blue referred to is unknown, white strands are often used nowadays. The reason for the commandment is that "it shall be unto you for a fringe, that you shall look upon it, and remember all the commandments of the Lord and do them, so that you turn not after your heart and eyes after which you go astray; that you may remember and do all my commandments and be holy unto your God" (Num. 15:39-40). A blessing is recited when putting on the *t.* The *t.* consists of four long strands drawn through a small hole about an inch and a half from the corner. The two parts of the strands are tied together by a double knot. The longest strand (*shammash*) is then wound seven, eight, eleven, and thirteen times around the other seven halves of the four threads. After each set of windings a double knot is made. The total length of the *t.* should be not less than eleven and a half inches.

TZOM, see **FAST**

TZOM GEDALIAH, see **GEDALIAH, FAST OF**

TZUR MI-SHELLO (Heb. "Rock from whose store we have eaten"): Song sung at the Sabbath table though containing no specific reference to the Sabbath. *T.M.* is of unknown authorship, its four stanzas corresponding to the first four paragraphs of the Grace after Meals and hence usually sung immediately before it. The refrain is based partly on II Kings 4:44.

U

UGARIT: Ancient N. Syrian town on the site of the present Ras Shamra, discovered in 1929. The discovery there of a large quantity of clay tablets, including a group written in a cuneiform alphabet, has revolutionized the study of Canaanite mythology and its bearing upon biblical scholarship. The inscriptions date from the 14th cent. B.C.E., are written in a language closely resembling Aramaic and Hebrew, and have thrown light on the literary and cultural background of the Bible in general, as well as on many phrases and mythological allusions. Though the state of the tablets' preservation often makes their rendering controversial, there is general agreement about the main outlines of most of the myths and legends, some of which are paralleled in the biblical narratives. There are three main cycles: —

1. The deeds and conflicts and final ascendancy of the god Baal over his enemies. Other mythological figures with biblical associations are the sun-god El (sometimes represented by a bull) and his consort Ashtoreth, or Asherah, their son Hadad, Anath, Yam-Nahar, Moth, and others. Baal's palace is at Mt. Zafon.
2. The story of King Keret of Hubut.
3. The tale of Haquhat, son of the righteous king Daniel (cf. Ezek. 14:14, 20, 28).

UKTZIN (Heb. "Stalks"): Twelfth tractate in the Mishnah order of *Toharot* with no *gemara* in either Talmud. It discusses ritual defilement conveyed to a plant when its stalks, husks, or kernels come in contact with ritual impurity.

UNCLEANNESS, see **PURITY, RITUAL**

U-NETANNEH TOKEPH, see **AMNON OF MAINZ**

UNION OF AMERICAN HEBREW CONGREGATIONS: Organization representing the Reform congregations and their members in the U.S. It was founded by Isaac Mayer Wise in Cincinnati in 1873. Its purpose, as stated in its constitution, is "to encourage and aid the organization and development of Jewish congregations; to promote Jewish education and enrich and intensify Jewish life; to maintain the Hebrew Union College - Jewish Institute of Religion; to foster other activities for the perpetuation and advancement of Judaism". It was the earliest Jewish congregational federation in the United States. Affiliated with the Union are various Reform Jewish religious organizations representing the men, women, youth, and administrative officials of Reform temples. Its headquarters are located in New York City, and its membership totals several hundreds of thousands of families.

UNION OF ORTHODOX HEBREW CONGREGATIONS: The official representative organization of Orthodox congregations in the U.S. It has an affiliation of over 700 congregations and serves as the national central body of Orthodox synagogues, representing them in civic bodies and the Jewish community. The Rabbinical Council of America is its ecclesiastical arm, and it supports Orthodox rabbinical seminaries. The Union is responsible for a *kashrut* certification service whose symbol is a "U" within a circle.

UNITED SYNAGOGUE: Orthodox synagogue organization in England, constituted by an Act of Parliament in 1870. The U.S. embraces synagogues in Greater London and certain provincial towns; these are divided into Constituent, District, and Associated Synagogues. It is administered by a council, and according to its constitution the British Chief Rabbi is its sole recognized religious authority.

UNITED SYNAGOGUE OF AMERICA: Association of over 750 Conservative congregations in the U.S. and Canada. Founded in 1913 by Solomon Schechter, it has grown steadily and was responsible for the establishment in 1957 of the World Council of Synagogues with affiliates in Israel and several S. American and European countries. Essentially a lay body, the U.S. of A. endeavors to secure a greater participation by the laity in the conduct of Jewish education and ritual practice.

UNITY OF GOD, see **MONOTHEISM**

UNIVERSALISM: The wish or claim of a religion, or of certain of its ideals and values, to apply to the whole world. Its opposite is particularism. Judaism displays a distinct ambivalence — or rather an unrelieved dialectical tension — in its attitude toward particularism and u. The vision of a united humanity and the prayers and yearnings for its fulfillment are as prominent in Jewish thought as the ideal of the survival of the Jewish people as a distinct and chosen entity. Jewish u. was based on the one hand on the recognition of the universal sovereignty of God (cf. Abraham's reference to God as "the Judge of all the earth" in Gen. 18:25), and on the other hand on its messianic vision (cf. the messianic vision of Micah 4:1-4 or of Is. 2:2-4). There are many other expressions of the universalist ideal in the Bible as well as in rabbinic literature. The liturgy of the High Holidays is largely devoted to the theme of God's sovereignty over mankind, almost to the exclusion of Israel's specifically particularistic and national concerns. The second part of the ALEINU prayer, praying for the perfection of mankind in the Kingdom of God, is a noble and sublime expression of the universalist approach. However, the particularistic attitude is very strong and all but dominant in Israel's national and social consciousness as well as in theological tradition (see CHOSEN PEOPLE). Some thinkers have endeavored to reconcile the two outlooks by interpreting Israel's mission as that of a herald and witness of the Divine promise for all mankind. Reform Judaism has been particularly emphatic in its reaction against the particularistic elements in Jewish tradition and in its emphasis on the view that the Jews were entrusted with a moral mission to mankind.

UNLEAVENED BREAD, see MATZAH

UNTERFIRER (Yidd.): The person who leads the bride or bridegroom "under the wedding canopy". The *unterfirers* are usually the parents of the bride and groom or, in their absence, married couples, if possible closely related to them.

URIEL: The fourth and least important of the four archangels (the others being MICHAEL, GABRIEL, and RAPHAEL), who preside over the four quarters of the globe. U. is placed in the north. Unlike the other three, he is not mentioned in rabbinical literature but is frequently referred to in the Apocrypha and Pseudepigrapha whence he entered into medieval mystical literature, where he also figures as the angel of fire (*ur* = "fire").

URIM AND THUMMIM, see ORACLE

USHPIZIN (Aram. "guests"): A legend first mentioned by the Zohar (*Emor* 103b-104a) to the effect that on each of the seven days of the Festival of Tabernacles one of seven patriarchs or heroes of biblical history (Abraham, Isaac, Jacob, Joseph, Moses, Aaron, and David) is welcomed as a spiritual guest to the Tabernacle (see SUKKAH). The formula of greeting was composed by Isaac Luria in 16th cent. Safed. Originally practiced only by the kabbalists, the custom of reciting *u.* became widespread and its formula (in Aramaic) is found in many festival prayer books. It also became a custom to invite poor students to the tabernacle as a symbol of the spiritual visitors.

USUCAPION, see ḤAZAKKAH

USURY: Modern usage limits the word usury to mean the exaction of interest at a rate higher than law or custom, but since any charging of interest is strictly forbidden in the Bible (Exod. 22:24; Lev. 25:36-37; Deut. 23:20-21) the Hebrew word refers to interest of any kind. There are however two words used for interest, both to be found in Lev. 25:36 — *neshekh* (literally "biting"), and *tarbit* (literally "increase"). The Mishnah (*Bava Metzia* 5:1) differentiates between the two, saying that the former refers to a direct addition to the money or produce lent, the latter to increase in the value of the produce. The prohibition against interest seems to have been frequently disregarded in biblical times, for Ps. 15 enumerates among the qualities of the virtuous men that "he putteth not out his money to u." The law against both receiving and giving interest applies only to the Jew, the non-Jew being explicitly excluded from the prohibition (Deut. 23:21). Advantage was taken of this to circumvent the law by introducing a non-Jew as an intermediate strawman (cf. Mishnah *Bava Metzia* 5:6). The biblical prohibition against u. reflects the simple economy of an agricultural society where LOANS were needed to provide immediate relief in moments of distress (e.g. failure of crops). With the development of a money economy, industry, and trade, the ancient prohibitions became economically obsolete and (in part) morally irrelevant. Unable to disregard a plain biblical prohibition, Jewish practice evolved — against long resistance — the legal fiction known as *hetter iska* by which a loan is contracted in the form of a partnership. Although this procedure is considered legitimate for business transactions and investments, loans to a fellow man in need should be free of interest (GEMILUT ḤESED). The Catholic Church in the Middle Ages enforced a similar prohibition between Christians, and hence the Jews, being outside Christian society and its laws, when debarred from other occupations, were often forced into the rôle of moneylenders and usurers. The financial operations of all banks in Israel are covered by a general *hetter iska*.

U-VA LE-ZION (Heb. "And a redeemer shall come unto Zion"): Opening phrase of one of the concluding prayers in the Morning Service. It consists of (1) Is. 59:20-21. (2) *Kedusha de-Sidra* (Aram. "the *kedushah* of the biblical lesson") — the recitation of Is. 6:3 in Hebrew and Aramaic. This was originally instituted either to enable latecomers to recite the KEDUSHAH or else, at an early period when ten verses from the prophetical books were read each morning, to parallel the blessings after the HAPHTARAH. (3) Prayer based on verses from I Chron., Psalms, and Micah thanking God for His continuing mercies. (4) Prayer for enlightenment in the Law, made up of citations from Psalms, Jeremiah, and Isaiah. On Sabbaths and festivals when the Morning Service is lengthened, ***u-va le-zion*** is recited in the Afternoon Prayer; on the Day of Atonement, in the Concluding Service. With the exception of the first section, the prayer is also incorporated in the Saturday Evening Service.

V

VA-ANI TEPHILLATI (Heb. "And as for me, may my prayer"): Biblical verse (Ps. 69:14) recited at the opening of the Sabbath Afternoon Service. According to Abudraham, it was inserted to ask Divine acceptance of the prayer even though the worshiper may have drunk liberally at the Sabbath morning meal (and the *halakhah* states that a person who has imbibed a quantity of wine should not pray). The verse is also incorporated in the MAH TOVU prayer at the commencement of the Morning Service.

VACHNACHT: Yiddish designation of the festal gathering and watch over a male child originally held on the night before circumcision but later transferred, in most rites, to the eve of the Sabbath preceding the circumcision. The custom is first mentioned in the Talmud (*Sanh.* 32b). Although medical considerations have been adduced for the custom (i.e., to enable prior examination of the child's fitness for the operation), its origin seems to be an ancient folkrite to protect the child from demonic dangers and in particular the babe-snatching LILITH. In some rites the feast is known as *zakhar* or *shelom zakhar*.

VA-YEKHULLU (Heb.): Opening word, serving also as the name, of the concluding paragraph of the creation account in Genesis (Gen. 2:1-3, "And the heaven and the earth were finished", etc.). The verses are recited three times on Friday evenings: (1) during the *amidah*, (2) after the *amidah* — in order not to differentiate between a festival Sabbath (when *V*., not included in the *amidah*, is said immediately after it) and a normal Sabbath, (3) in the KIDDUSH at home — for the sake of the members of the household (*Tosaphot Pes.* 106a).

VA-YIKRA, see **LEVITICUS**

VA-YIKRA RABBAH, see **MIDRASH RABBAH**

VEGETARIANISM: Although abstention from animal food was occasionally suggested for ascetic reasons, v. as a religious principle was never encouraged in the history of Judaism. Indeed, most of the DIETARY LAWS deal with the specification of permitted meats and their preparation, and the consumption of meat is considered as one of the essential delights of the Sabbath and the festivals. Nevertheless, the rabbis point out that the permission to partake of animal food was not part of the original dispensation at the time of creation. Though man was given dominion over the animal kingdom, only "every herb bearing seed... and every tree in which there is fruit" (Gen. 1:30) was granted to him for food. Only after the Deluge, the covenant with Noah permitted "every moving thing that liveth... even as the green herb" (Gen. 9:3) while strictly prohibiting the consumption of blood (*ibid.* 4). The ancient rabbis clearly regarded the killing of ANIMALS for human consumption as a privilege granted to man only because of his superior moral and intellectual faculties. This is expressed by the teaching of R. Judah Ha-Nasi that "an *am ha-aretz* (a boorish ignoramus) should not eat meat" (*Pes.* 49a), and by the rabbis' legal definition of a "glutton" as one who eats an inordinate measure of meat (*Sanh.* 70a). "Since there is no joy without meat" (*Pes.* 109a), its consumption is to be avoided in times of distress or mourning. Thus meat should not be eaten following the death of a close relative until after the funeral and customarily should also be avoided during the period of national mourning culminating in the fast of *Av* 9, but the prohibition does not extend to fish. Isaiah's prophecy that in messianic times "the lion shall eat straw like the ox" (Is. 11:7; 65:25) has been interpreted by some commentators as meaning that even the carnivorous animals would becаme vegetarians; others simply take it for a metaphorical image of universal peace.

VE-HU RAḤUM (Heb. "And He, being merciful" — opening words of Ps. 78:38): The verse occurs in the prayerbook as (1) the introduction to the weekday Evening Service where it is meant as a plea for forgiveness for sins committed during the day. (2) The opening of a SELIHAH, known as the "long" *V.R.*, recited before TAHANUN on MONDAYS AND THURSDAYS. The *seliḥah*, which is composed mainly of biblical verses, seems to have originated in a period of persecution — Zunz suggests the Gothic and Frankish persecutions in the 7th cent.

VENGEANCE: Different attitudes to v. are expressed in various biblical, rabbinic, moral, and legal texts; any particular attitude depends partly on historical circumstances, and partly on whether v. appears as a Divine or a human attribute. Such verses as "Vengeance is mine and I will repay" (Deut. 32:35) and "He will avenge the blood of His servants and will render vengeance unto His adversaries" (*ibid.* 44) show that v. is regarded as a Divine prerogative and is part of the system of Divine RETRIBUTION whereby human injustice is corrected by Divine justice. As a human act, v. is explicitly restricted: "Thou shalt not avenge, nor bear any grudge against the children of thy people" (Lev. 19:18), the only exception to this rule being the law of the BLOOD AVENGER, though even this type of v. was restricted by the institution of the CITIES OF REFUGE (see also ASYLUM). The difference between taking v. and bearing a grudge is explained by the Talmud: if a man asks his neighbor to lend him an article and is refused, and on the morrow that neighbor asks something of him, he should not say "As you refused me yesterday so I refuse you today" since that would constitute v. If he says "though you refused me a favor, I shall not do likewise", this is bearing a grudge (*Yoma* 23a). The virtue of the *maavir al middotav* i.e., he who forebears and suppresses his natural emotions of wrath and vindictiveness, is highly praised. The Bible contains many examples of forebearance and abstention from v. as well as of savage revenge, the best-known instance being the massacre of the inhabitants of Shechem by Simeon and Levi, an act which was denounced by Jacob both at the time (Gen. 34:30) and on his deathbed (*ibid.* 49:5-7).

VE-SHAMERU (Heb.): First word of the verses (Exod. 31:16-17) recited before the *amidah* in the Friday Evening Service and on Sabbaths during the Morning Service *amidah*, as well as in the Sabbath morning *kiddush*.

VESSELS, SACRED (Heb. *kelei kodesh*): Vessels used by the Israelites in the desert Sanctuary and in the two Temples e.g., the ark (*aron*), candlestick (*menorah*), veil (*parokhet*), table, (*shulḥan*), laver (*kiyyor*), altar (*mizbeaḥ*), coal shovels (*maḥtah*), large shovel (*magrephah*). The Vessel Chamber contained numerous vessels of silver and gold. Nebuzaradan took the s.v. to Babylon (II Kings 25:13-17) where Belshazzar used them at a royal feast, paying for the sacrilege with his life (Dan. 5). The vessels returned to Jerusalem with the homecoming exiles after Cyrus' edict (Ezra 1:7-11). They were looted from the Second Temple by Titus and taken to Rome where a representation of the act can still be seen upon the Arch of Titus. Sometimes the term is used of synagogue appurtenances such as the ark, *tallit*, *shophar*, *siddur*, etc. which, however, are more correctly classified under TASHMISHEI KEDUSHAH. The Hebrew expression *kelei kodesh* is also popularly used to refer to synagogue personnel and religious officials (rabbis, cantors, beadles, etc.).

VIDDUI, see **CONFESSION**

VILNA GAON, see **ELIJAH BEN SOLOMON**

VIMPEL (or **WIMPEL**; Yidd.): An embroidered band of linen, usually including a scriptural verse as part of the design, and used as a binder (see MAPPAH) for the *Torah* Scroll. Among German Jews it was customary to cut the *v.* from the swathing sheet used on the occasion of a circumcision, and thereafter dedicate it for use as a wrapper at the first presentation of the boy at the synagogue (usually on his first birthday). See also TORAH ORNAMENTS.

VINE, see **WINE**

VIRTUE: There is no Hebrew term corresponding exactly to v., moral excellence or particular moral qualities ("virtues") being generally referred to as *middot tovot* (see MIDDOT). V. in the traditional Jewish sense consists of the practices, actions, and state of mind which conform to the will of God, i.e., in the wholehearted service of God. V. in a general sense is therefore identified with adherence to the *Torah*. Certain types of v. and of virtuous life are specifically described and extolled — sometimes incidentally — in the Bible; cf. Ps. 15 and 24:3-4 for the virtuous man and Prov. 31 for the ideal virtuous woman. In rabbinic and medieval literature (moral, philosophic, and ascetic) the moral virtues and vices are discussed and analyzed according to various principles of classification, and treated either as points of halakhic law (cf. the biblical commandment to help one's neighbor, or the prohibition against slander and rumor-mongering) or as mental and temperamental qualities conducive (or harmful) to the good life (e.g. under such headings as pride, humility, contentment, patience, etc.). See also ETHICS; MUSAR.

VISION: The experience of beholding something with the "eyes of the spirit". A v. may be sought or induced by mystical practices, or be spontaneous and unexpected. Its contents may be terrestrial events removed in space ("second sight") or time ("foresight", prophecy) or spiritual realities and symbols. On the highest religious level visions are experienced as God's REVELATION to the PROPHET. Different categories of v. are implied in Num. 12:6-8, where a distinction is made between the manner in which God revealed Himself to Moses, speaking to him "mouth to mouth, manifestly and not in dark speeches, and the similitude of God doth he behold" and His appearance to other prophets to whom He was to make Himself known "in an appearance and speaking with him in a dream". This may mean that the message of God came to other prophets in a dream or trance-like state, whereas Moses was in full possession of normal cognitive faculties. The Bible often records visions, many of them THEOPHANIES; with some prophets (e.g. Ezekiel, Zechariah) they are more frequent than with others. The identification of v. with prophetic experiences seems to be implied by I Sam. 3:1. Often the prophet received his calling in a v. (e.g. Is. 6). Visionary accounts abound in APOCALYPTIC literature. According to the Talmud most prophets beheld their visions "as in a cloudy mirror", thus accounting for a certain lack of clarity which often requires verbal interpretation. Talmudic literature, though discussing prophetic v., does not itself record visions, though visionary experiences were cultivated in mystical circles among the ancient rabbis as well as the medieval kabbalists. See KABBALAH; MAASEH MERKAVAH; MYSTICISM; THRONE OF GOD.

VISITING THE SICK, see **SICK, VISITING THE**

VITAL, ḤAYYIM (1543-1620): Mystic; foremost disciple of Isaac LURIA, and heir and guardian of his teaching. He was born in Safed, where he also studied under Moses Alshech and Moses Cordovero. From about 1595 until his death he lived in Damascus. V., who seems to have considered himself the potential "Messiah son of Joseph", wrote the standard exposition of Lurianic KABBALAH, known under the title *Etz Ḥayyim* ("Tree of Life") and sub-divided into several books, e.g. *Peri Etz Ḥayyim* ("Fruit of the Tree of Life"), the *Book of Kavvanot*, and the *Book of Metempsychoses.* He also left an interesting and revealing autobiographical *Book of Dreams.*

VITAL, SAMUEL (17th cent.): Rabbi and kabbalist in Damascus; son of Ḥayyim VITAL. He edited his father's works on Lurianic kabbalah, which he also propagated in his sermons and addresses. In later life he moved to Cairo.

VOCALIZATION: The Hebrew ALPHABET is entirely consonantal and for the traditional pronunciation of a biblical word it is necessary to rely on the MASORAH. The earliest method used to give some kind of vocalic indication was the insertion of vocalic letters in the consonantal text. This method was superseded by a full system of v. through punctuation. Although later orthodox theory attributed Mosaic antiquity to this system, there is little doubt that it was first introduced after the conclusion of the Talmudic Period; Saadyah Gaon (892-942) is the first to mention it. The system of sublinear v. evolved by the Masoretes of Tiberias became universal although a Babylonian and a Palestinian supralinear system was also prevalent for a time in the Middle Ages.

VOLOZHIN: Town in Lithuania, seat of a famous *yeshivah* established in 1803 by Ḥayyim Volozhin, disciple of Elijah Gaon of Vilna. He was succeeded by his son Isaac who in turn was succeeded by his son-in-law Naphtali Tzevi Judah BERLIN under whose leadership the *yeshivah* rose to its greatest fame, with 400 students. Closed by the Czarist government in 1879, it was reopened in 1881 but was closed again in 1892 for its refusal to introduce secular studies. It was refounded in 1899 but did not reattain its previous position of eminence.

VOWS AND OATHS: Solemn affirmation (oaths) and promises to perform, or abstain from, specific actions (vows). Jewish law knows many more or less synonymous terms (cf. the opening of KOL NIDREI: "All vows, bonds, oaths, anathemas, excommunications," etc.) and the line of division between o. and v. is not always clearly drawn particularly since swearing to do a certain thing is tantamount to a vow. Reserving the term o. for the most solemn kind of affirmation made in a court of law, v. (*nedarim*, singular *neder*) can be divided into positive and negative. The first is a solemn undertaking or pledge to (1) consecrate something to God, or (2) do something in His honor; the second, called *issar*, is the voluntary abstention from an otherwise legitimate activity or enjoyment. Akin to *neder* is *nedavah* which, by contrast, is the pledging or consecration of a designated gift to God; hence in the case of *nedavah* the destruction or theft of the article or the death of the consecrated animal nullifies the vow. The vow, which must be voluntarily undertaken in full consciousness of its implications, becomes effective in both instances upon utterance, and the violation of such a spoken vow constitutes a transgression of the prohibition "he shall not profane his word" (Num. 30:33). As far as v. are concerned the everyday, local meaning of the words used determines the limits and conditions of the vow. A *neder* or *nedavah* is to be fulfilled before three Pilgrim Festivals have passed lest the prohibition against laxity in the fulfillment of v. is infringed (Deut. 23:22). V. were usually undertaken either in times of distress, as in the case of Jacob (Gen. 28:20-22), or as an expression of thanksgiving for favor and kindness received (cf. Ps. 116:16-18). They were also undertaken as a sign of penitence or to free oneself from severe temptation (*Avot* 3:13). In matters affecting the physical well-being of the wife or the mutual relations of married life, a husband may void the v. of his wife on the day he hears them (*hapharah*). He may also void the v. of his unmarried daughter (Num. 30 ff.). After careful examination of the circumstances surrounding the taking of the vow, a competent *bet din* may nullify it and absolve the vower (*hattarah*). There must exist, however, reasonable grounds for such nullification. It is customary to nullify v. (except those contracted between man and man) before the advent of the High Festivals (see KOL NIDREI). In general the talmudic attitude toward taking v. is negative. It finds expression in such statements as "He who makes a vow, though he fulfills it, is called wicked", or "for sins arising from unfulfilled vows, children die". Even in attempting to rid oneself of bad habits, vowing should be resorted to only when all else has failed. There are two kinds of forbidden oaths. (1) A vain oath, forbidden in the Decalogue — "Thou shalt not take the Name of the Lord thy God in vain" (Exod. 20:7). (2) A false oath — "Thou shalt not swear by My Name falsely" (Lev. 19:12). A vain oath is one which (a) attempts to deny a self-evident fact, or (b) affirms a self-evident fact, or (c) involves one in undertaking the impossible, or (d) is directed against the fulfillment of a religious precept. In each of these instances the oath, which has no validity or effect, is punishable on utterance. The penalty for a false oath is restitution of the intended loss plus an additional fifth of the monetary value (or estimated damage), and the obligation to bring a guilt-offering "for the Lord will not hold him guiltless who taketh His Name in vain" (Exod. *loc. cit.*). The misuse of God's Name is the greatest sacrilege possible, since the basic notion of an oath is the total submission of one's words, thoughts, deeds, and in fact entire personality to the judgment of God. Undertaken lightly, the wrath of Heaven is evoked. An oath may in certain circumstances be undertaken for the purpose of strengthening one's moral character and observance, but the taking of oaths, like that of v., is discouraged in Judaism. An oath is only administered in a law court when other evidence has proved inadequate. To be valid an oath need not mention any of the names of God, and may be uttered in any language.

VULGATE, see **BIBLE TRANSLATION**

W

WAGES: The fee paid for labor or service. The employer is strictly enjoined to pay such fees without delay upon completion of the labor or service — "The w. of a hired man shall not abide with thee all night until morning" (Lev. 19:13). The Talmud explains that one hired for the day is to be paid not later than the next morning, one hired for the night by the following evening (see Deut. 24:15). One who withholds such w. transgresses several biblical prohibitions. Crediting the laborer at a shop or bank is considered due payment but, in order to protect the laborer against possible exploitation in the form of inferior merchandise at inflated prices and values, payment in kind is strictly forbidden. The terms of hire do not require witnesses or a KINYAN in order to bind the parties. When doubt arises concerning the terms, the custom of the place and trade is to be followed. Payment of substandard w. is forbidden as part of the prohibition against oppressing the hired man (Deut. 24:14). Government drafted workers in time of emergency or war are to be paid fair w. and even prisoners of war are to receive due compensation if made to work. The SABBATICAL YEAR (which cancels all debts) does not cancel w. due.

WAILING WALL, see **WESTERN WALL**

WANDERING JEW: Figure of medieval Christian legend, later connected with the prophecy in *Matthew* 16:28 — "There be some standing here which shall not taste of death till they see the son of man coming in his kingdom". According to the legend, a cobbler of Jerusalem, by name of Ahasuer, taunted Jesus on his way to the crucifixion and was cursed to live and wander for ever until the return of Jesus. The W.J. came to serve as a symbol of the Jewish people as a whole who according to a medieval Christian belief, were doomed to wander in exile until they adopt Christianity; the legend thus provided a concrete expression of the pejorative explanation given by Christians for the immortality of the Jewish people. Various claims to have seen the W.J. have been made from time to time, and the legend has formed a favorite subject for fiction.

WAR: Wars and customs connected with warfare are described in many of the biblical books, particularly the historical ones. A fairly systematic exposition of the laws and usages of w. is given in Deut. 20:1-21, and the rules of w. developed in the Talmud, though owing much to the experience of later periods, are almost entirely based upon rabbinic exegesis of this passage. Different categories of w. are distinguished: *milḥemet ḥovah* (obligatory w.) regarded by some authorities as identical with the *milḥemet mitzvah* (a war which is commanded by God), and *milḥemet reshut* (the "permitted w."). To the former category belong the w. of extermination of the seven Canaanitish nations and wars to defend the territorial integrity of the land of Israel. The *milḥemet mitzvah* could be declared by the king alone and the various exemptions detailed in Deut. 20:5-8 are suspended. To wage such a w. one could take "even the bridegroom from his chamber and the bride from her bridal canopy" (Mishnah *Sot.* 8:7; the phrase is from Joel 2:16 and may be meant as a hyperbole. There is no reference in Jewish literature to women soldiers). The permissive w. could be declared only by the decision of the Sanhedrin with the application of the exemptions to conscription detailed in the Pentateuch. Various concessions and absolutions, such as the permission to make free use of fuel, to disregard the dietary laws, and to eat doubtfully tithed produce, were made to soldiers. A vivid account of an apocalyptic w. probably based on contemporary military experience is contained in the DEAD SEA SCROLL of "The War of the Sons of Light and the Sons of Darkness".

WAR SCROLL, see **DEAD SEA SCROLLS**

WAR OF GOG & MAGOG, see **GOG & MAGOG**

WARD, see **GUARDIAN**

WARS OF THE LORD, BOOK OF, see **BIBLE, LOST BOOKS OF**

WARNING, see **HATRAAH**

WASHING, see **ABLUTION**

WATER: The cleansing and refreshing properties of w. assure it a prominent place both in the symbolism and in the rituals of religion. Transferring the idea of PURIFICATION by w. from the physical to the ceremonial level, biblical and rabbinic law prescribe ABLUTIONS and IMMERSIONS for various occasions (see also MIKVEH), e.g. washing one's hands before (and after) meals, and the ritual bath taken by married women (see NIDDAH). On the other hand, the *halakhah* (based on Lev. 11:38) rules that plants are not susceptible to ritual contamination until they come into contact with w. The most spectacular ceremonial use of water was at the annual rite of w. LIBATION, preceded by the solemn drawing of the w., which was held on the Feast of TABERNACLES, against the opposition of the Sadducees who maintained that there was no scriptural authority for the ritual (see also WATER-DRAWING, FEAST OF). In the *aggadah*, w. is regarded as a symbol of the *Torah* (e.g. *Taan.* 7a, based on Is. 55:1).

WATER-DRAWING, FEAST OF (Heb. *Simḥat Beit ha-Shoevah*): The ceremony of the water LIBATION which took place in the Temple, amid great popular rejoicing, on the last six days of the Festival of Tabernacles. The cryptic reference in Is. 12:3 has been taken as indicating the ancient origin of the celebration. The Pharisees considered it a Mosaic tradition but this view was opposed by the Sadducees. The popularity of this feast can be gathered from the statement that whosoever had not seen it did not know what joy meant (*Suk.* 53a). When the Sadducee king Alexander Yannai contemptuously threw the water on his feet he was pelted with *etrogim* by the outraged crowd at the Temple. Huge bonfires were lit in the outer court of the Temple as in every household (*Suk.* 51a) so that the whole of Jerusalem was ablaze with light. The men danced and sang to the accompaniment of levitical musicians, and even the leading sages took part in the public rejoicing. The rite ceased with the destruction of the Temple.

WAVE-OFFERING (or **HEAVE-OFFERING;** Heb. *tenuphah*): The raising or separation, by a waving motion, of a sacrifice dedicated to the Lord. Among sacrifices which had to be "waved" were first fruits of oil, fruit, and grain; flesh or redeemed fatlings (Num. 18:15-18); and cakes from new meal dough and certain tithes (Num. 15:20ff.). The waving was performed by the priest and the regulations for the ceremony are described in the Talmud (*Men.* 61-2).

WAYS OF THE GENTILE, see **ḤUKKAT HA-GOY**

WEDDING, see **MARRIAGE**

WEEKS, FEAST OF (or **PENTECOST;** Heb. *Shavuot*): The second of the PILGRIM FESTIVALS. It is so called because it occurs on the completion of seven full weeks after the "morrow of the Sabbath" when the "sheaf of the wave-offering" of barley was offered up (Lev. 23:15). These seven weeks are marked by the Counting of the OMER (hence the name *atzeret* — "termination" — given to the festival in the Mishnah). The interpretation of the words "on the morrow of the Sabbath" was a subject of controversy between the Pharisees and the Sadducees, the former maintaining that the word Sabbath in this context refers to the first day of PASSOVER (with the result that the F. of W. always fell on the same day of the week as the second day of Passover) while the Sadducees (as the Samaritans, and later the Karaites) maintained that the reference is to the first Sunday after the first day of Passover (according to which the F. of W. would always fall on a Sunday). The FALASHAS took "morrow" as the morrow of the Festival of Passover, and hence observe the F. of W. on *Sivan* 12. The Pharisaic interpretation was accepted as normative. Although like the other two Pilgrim Festivals (Passover and TABERNACLES), W. has its agricultural significance — it is the festival celebrating the conclusion of the grain harvest (*ḥag ha-katzir* "the HARVEST FESTIVAL") — its celebration became almost exclusively concentrated on the aspect of the festival commemorating the revelation on Mt. Sinai and in the liturgy it is called "The Season of the Giving of our *Torah*". Nowhere in the Bible is this date explicitly given, and it is deduced by calculation based upon the narrative in Exod. 19:1-16; the Talmud records a difference of opinion as to whether the revelation took place on the 6th or the 7th of *Sivan* (*Shab.* 86b). The decision was given in favor of the former date; the celebration of the festival for both these days in the Diaspora is however not because of the controversy but because of the custom of observing a SECOND DAY of festivals outside the Land of Israel. The liturgy follows the same pattern as that of the other two Pilgrim Festivals. The Scriptural reading — which is preceded by the recitation of AKDAMUT — includes the Decalogue, and the Book of RUTH is read in the synagogue because it mentions the barley and wheat harvests and also because its heroine is a proselyte who accepted the *Torah;* another explanation is that Ruth's grandchild, DAVID, was born and died on *Shavuot.* The agricultural aspect of the feast is stressed by the customs of decorating the synagogue with plants and greenery and consuming dairy food instead of meat. Under the influence of the Kabbalah, a custom obtains of sitting up all night on the festival and reading excerpts from the Bible and rabbinic texts (TIKKUN).

WEIGHTS & MEASURES, see **MEASURES**

WEISS, ISAAC HIRSCH (1815-1905): Talmudical scholar and historian. Born in Moravia, he settled in 1861 in Vienna. W. published critical annotations of SIPHRA and MEKHILTA, and his outstanding *Dor Dor ve-Dorshav* ("Each generation and its homilists"), a five volume history of oral tradition from earliest times to the Spanish expulsion, incorporates biographies of the main rabbis of the Talmudic Period. This was a pioneer work in the critical analysis of rabbinic sources.

WESTERN WALL (Heb. *Kotel Maaravi*): The last remnant of the Jerusalem Temple court and the main object of traditional Jewish pilgrimages; also known as the Wailing Wall. The earliest layers, consisting of large blocks date from Herod's reconstruction of the Second Temple. They are followed by a layer built during the reign of Hadrian and lastly by Arab masonry. Whenever circumstances permitted, Jews gathered at the Wall for prayer; the Midrash says, "The Divine Presence never departs from the W.W.". In modern times, this Jewish custom met with Arab opposition, and at times interference on the grounds that the Wall adjoined the *Haram es-Sherif* – a Moslem holy site. After the War of Independence, Jews were denied access to the Wall, which was under Jordanian control, in spite of the armistice agreement stipulating free access to holy sites. Since 1967 though, the Israeli government has expanded the plaza tremendously, and the W.W. has become the foremost HOLY PLACE for Jewish visitors from the entire world.

WHOLE-OFFERING (or **HOLOCAUST**: Heb. *olah*, from the root "to ascend", or *kalil*): SACRIFICE in which the offering was wholly consumed by fire upon the altar. The entire animal was placed on the altar with the exception of the hide and those parts that could not be washed clean. Whole-offerings included the communal *olat ha-tamid* ("perpetual offering") brought by the community every morning and evening and freewill-offerings from individuals (cf. Lev. 1:3-17; 6:1-7). Later the w.-o. became associated with the sin-offering and was offered even by foreign heathens (*Shek.* 7:6). According to some interpreters the w.-o. symbolized the ascent of the soul in worship to God and its total submission to Him.

WIDOW: In the ancient world, a w. was largely deprived of legal redress, hence the biblical emphasis on special consideration to be shown toward the w. (generally classified together with the ORPHAN; cf. Exod. 22:21-23) and the assurance that God Himself protects her (Deut. 10:18; Ps. 68:6). A w. can remarry anyone except a High Priest; in the event of her husband having died without issue, she may only remarry after receiving *ḥalitzah* (see LEVIRATE MARRIAGE). She may not remarry before three full months of widowhood have elapsed. In the event of her remarriage with a widower the seven festive blessings (SHEVA BERAKHOT) are not recited for the seven days of the wedding festivities. The provisions of the marriage contract (KETUBBAH) provide the w. with support from the deceased husband's estate as long as she remains unmarried; upon remarriage complete settlement of all her claims and rights is effected.

WIFE, see **MATRIMONY**

WIG (in Yidd. *sheitel*): In talmudic times, wigs were worn by women for adornment or to hide the lack of hair. The Talmud forbids the loose exposure of the hair in the street by married women (citing this even as grounds for divorce) but the rigid development of this regulation — whereby a woman shaves off her hair at marriage and thereafter never appears in public without a w. — dates only from the 15th cent. In some Orthodox circles, married women cover their hair with wigs although among oriental and ḥasidic Jews, a kerchief is used as the covering.

WILL, FREE, see **FREE WILL**

WILLOW (Heb. *aravim* — Is. 15:7; Ps. 137:2; or *arvei naḥal* — Lev. 23:40; Job. 40:32): *Salix*, which grows abundantly in the Land of Israel. "Willow of the brook" were required on the Feast of TABERNACLES for the FOUR SPECIES. Willows growing in the vicinity of Jerusalem (at Motza) were picked for the adornment of the altar on the Feast and branches were carried at the HAKKAPHOT circuits. They were called HOSHANA after the responsive refrain of the ceremony. The shaking of w. twigs and shower of leaves on HOSHANA RABBAH give a symbolic expression to the quest for RAIN.

WILLS, see **INHERITANCE**

WILLS, ETHICAL, see **ETHICAL WILLS**

WIMPEL, see **VIMPEL**

WINE: Despite the fact that the first references to w. in the Bible are connected with the drunkenness of Noah (Gen. 9:20-27) and the account of the incest committed by the two daughters of Lot with their father (*ibid.* 19:31-38), w. is generally praised in Jewish tradition for its wholesome qualities and its capacity to "gladden the heart of man" (cf. Ps. 104:15). W. was regularly used as a LIBATION in the sacrificial services (Num. 28-29). Rabbinic law further amplified and expanded the ritual use of w. As the symbol of JOY its use was an essential element on all festive occasions, e.g. the KIDDUSH, HAVDALAH, the FOUR CUPS at the *Seder* service, at weddings, and at circumcisions. It was granted a special blessing distinct from that of all other agricultural produce ("Blessed art Thou... who createst the fruit of the vine"), and it is the only item of a meal which is not covered by the GRACE BEFORE MEALS but requires a separate benediction. Where the Written *Torah* is compared to water, the Oral Law is compared to wine (Midrash on Song of Songs 1:2) and this comparison extends to everything which is praiseworthy — Jerusalem, Israel, the Messiah, and the righteous. According to one rabbinic statement the NAZIRITE is regarded as a "sinner" for depriving himself of the legitimate pleasure of w. (*Nazir* 19a). Excessive drinking was encouraged on PURIM and in greater moderation on SIMHAT TORAH. Only over-indulgence is condemned. The tradition of moderation was so firmly entrenched that alcoholism has never been a social problem among Jews and no reactions to drink in the form of abstinence and prohibition movements were ever necessary. As a result of the ancient link between w. and idolatrous ritual, a strict prohibition has been enforced against partaking of w. prepared by GENTILES (*yein nesekh*); when the original reason became obsolete the prohibition was maintained (*setam yeinam*) in order to prevent conviviality — leading to intermarriage — between Jews and gentiles.

WISDOM (Heb. *ḥokhmah*): In biblical usage w. is conceived as a human characteristic, partly the result of experience and learning, but mainly a gift of God. The praise of w. sung in some texts (see WISDOM LITERATURE) and its description as God's first creation, prior to the creation of the world (cf. Prov. 8:22-32), led to its subsequent identification with the concept of TORAH. Since the *Torah* was conceived as a primordial manifestation of Divine w., the rabbis could use the words spoken by w. (Prov. 8:22), "The Lord possessed me in the beginning of His way, before the works of old", as a proof text for the doctrine of the PRE-EXISTENCE of the *Torah* (*Pes.* 54a). Elsewhere the rabbis identify w. with practical intelligence and secular knowledge, e.g. in the midrashic statement (*Lam. Rab.* 2:17) "If a person says to you that there is w. among the nations, believe him; if he says there is *Torah* among the nations, do not believe him". The blessing prescribed to be recited on seeing a gentile sage is "Blessed be He who hath imparted His w. to flesh and blood" (*Ber.* 58b). Rashi seems to have been the first to differentiate between *ḥokhmah* and *binah* ("understanding"), the former referring to the acquisition of facts, and the latter to the knowledge which is deduced from these facts by the use of the intelligence (in his commentary on Exod. 31:3 and elsewhere). In medieval thought w. was considered one of the Divine ATTRIBUTES and in KABBALAH the term *ḥokhmah* denoted one of the ten manifestations, or SEPHIROT, of the Godhead. The term also figures in the triad — w., understanding, and knowledge — of ḤABAD Ḥasidism. The ideal of Jewish EDUCATION was generally defined as the wise man or sage (*ḥakham*), a title which is still used in some communities as synonymous with RABBI.

WISDOM LITERATURE: Type of literature based on the praise of WISDOM as the quintessence of human perfection and virtue. One trend in W.L. personified wisdom as a near-Divine entity, a development which linked the concept of w. with that of LOGOS. W.L., which flourished in the Ancient Orient (e.g. Egypt, Mesopotamia), is represented in the Bible by the books of Proverbs, Job, and Ecclesiastes, as well as the didactic Psalms. They contain counsel based upon the rational insight and practical experience of sages, as distinct from the absolute demands based on prophetic experience. Often the words of instruction are addressed to the young and couched in pragmatic terms, the main stress being on practical conduct and personal sagacity. However, in spite of its utilitarian morality, biblical W.L. leaves no doubt that piety and the fear of the Lord are the beginning of all wisdom (see Ps. 111:10). Another outstanding feature of W.L. is its universalism. There is no mention of specific Jewish rituals or national interest in any of the three books referred to. The lessons, moreover, are addressed to the individual and not to society. The same pragmatic and humanistic tendencies combined with biblical piety are characteristic of post-biblical W.L., e.g. the apocryphal Book of ECCLESIASTICUS and the pseudepigraphic WISDOM OF SOLOMON. Certain elements and literary forms of W.L. were developed by the exponents of the Oral Law in such works as *Avot* and *Avot de-Rabbi Natan*.

WISDOM OF SOLOMON (or **BOOK OF WISDOM**): Pseudepigraphic work ascribed to Solomon but in fact written in Greek by an Alexandrian Jew of a philosophic bent, probably during the 1st cent. B.C.E. It contrasts the bliss of piety with the short-lived happiness of the godless. God draws near to Israel when the latter adheres to the dictates of wisdom. The main object of the book is to counter the dangers of Hellenization by advocating the wisdom of the Bible. The author displays considerable knowledge of the popular Greek philosophy of the period, by which he was profoundly influenced. See WISDOM LITERATURE.

WISE, ISAAC MAYER (1819-1900): U.S. Reform leader. Immigrating to the U.S. from Bohemia in 1846, he officiated for two years in Albany and thereafter in Cincinnati. W. was responsible for organizing the main instruments of the U.S. REFORM Movement, namely the UNION OF AMERICAN HEBREW CONGREGATIONS (1873), the HEBREW UNION COLLEGE (1875) of which he was the first president, and the CENTRAL CONFERENCE OF AMERICAN RABBIS (1889). He compiled the Reform prayer book *Minhag America* (1857; replaced in 1896 by the *Union Prayer Book*) and was an advocate of shorter services, the use of English and the organ in the synagogue, and the Friday evening lecture-service. Convinced of the profound harmony between American and Jewish ideals, he stressed the Ten Commandments as the basis of Judaism under the slogan "Back to Mosaism". He envisioned the creation of a universal faith to be pioneered by Judaism; this was to be based on 1) monotheism; 2) the concept that man is created in the image of God and is accountable to Him; 3) the idea that Israel has been Divinely chosen to convey these truths to the world.

WISSENSCHAFT DES JUDENTUMS (Ger. "Science of Judaism"): The scientific study, in accordance with the recognized scholarly methods of historical and philological research, of Jewish religion, literature, and history. *W.d.J.*, as distinct from the traditional forms of learning to which, indeed, it appeared as heretical, developed in the 19th cent. as part of the movement for EMANCIPATION and religious REFORM. Its inspiration was to a large extent apologetic: Judaism had a proud past (hence Jews should not be impressed by gentile arguments about Jewish cultural inferiority), it had evolved in various forms throughout its long history (hence reform and change were legitimate), and it had often existed in close cultural contact with the surrounding civilizations (hence there was no justification for denying Jews civil rights). 19th cent. *W.d.J.* originated in Germany (ZUNZ; GEIGER; see also FRANKEL; GRAETZ), but it soon spread to Italy (S.D. LUZZATTO), France (S. Munk), and, later, also to England and the U.S. (see S. SCHECHTER). A parallel school, writing in Hebrew, emerged in Eastern Europe (S.J. RAPOPORT; N. KROCHMAL). Originally concerned mainly with history of literature (biblical and post-biblical, rabbinic, medieval) and of ideas, *W.d.J.* eventually developed into the modern type of "Jewish studies" with their greater range and their stronger emphasis on social and economic history. There is also a greater awareness of the cultural and ideological conditioning of historical research.

WITCHES AND WITCHCRAFT: "Thou shalt not suffer a witch to live" (Exod. 22:17), clearly expresses the biblical viewpoint on witchcraft. The verse is preceded by the enumeration of the penalties for sexual offenses (*ibid.* 15) and followed by the denunciation of unnatural vice and idolatry (*ibid.* 18-19), thus furnishing the general pagan milieu in which witchcraft was seen by the Bible. Different kinds of witchcraft were practiced among the ancient Israelites and their neighbors, and the variety is reflected by the biblical vocabulary, which mentions diviners, soothsayers, enchanters, charmers, consulters of ghosts, attendant spirits, and necromancers (Deut. 18:10-11). All contact with witchcraft and its practitioners was forbidden by the Bible, which demands man's wholehearted allegiance to God (*ibid.* 13). The Israelite, moreover, having been granted the privilege of prophetic guidance, should have no need of magic DIVINATION. Saul took stern measures against witches, though he consulted one in his hour of despair (I Sam. 28:7). The prevalence of witchcraft among women is attested to in numerous talmudic passages, and according to one tradition SIMEON BEN SHETAH hanged eighty witches in one day in Ascalon (*Sanh.* 6:4). A concession was granted for the use of certain MAGIC formulae for healing the sick. Medieval authorities were divided in their views of witchcraft: some held that it did not really exist and was practiced as deceit and illusion; others believed in its reality and in its connection with the demonic powers. See also AMULETS; DEMONOLOGY; MAGIC; SUPERSTITION.

WITNESS: Each individual enjoys a presumption of trustworthiness, and his EVIDENCE is therefore acceptable without substantiation by OATH. Every man is obliged to appear before the court and deliver any relevant testimony in his knowledge. A witness who has given false testimony becomes a *rasha* ("wicked one") and forfeits his trustworthiness as a witness in future cases until such time as his veracity is re-established. The law that a *rasha* is ineligible as a witness (*Sanh.* 27a) is derived from the verse "put not thy hand with the wicked to be an unrighteous witness" (Exod. 23:1). The *rasha* is further defined as (1) one who intentionally violates a prohibition punishable by stripes; (2) one who unlawfully takes money or property belonging to another. The former may be reinstated after repentance, the latter after the restoration of the unlawfully acquired property to its owner. A general reservation on grounds akin to the second instance disqualifies those engaged in certain disreputable occupations, such as the professional gambler. Relatives are disqualified as witnesses in cases involving their kinsfolk (*Sanh.* 3:4), but neither intimate friendship nor extreme enmity are disqualifying factors. Except in a limited number of cases, women are not eligible to act as witnesses. No one may testify against himself. See also EVIDENCE; FALSE WITNESS.

WOMEN: Like other ancient Semitic and non-Semitic cultures, biblical and post-biblical Judaism was markedly patriarchal in character, though in many ways greater provision was made for the rights of w. The Creation account represents w. not as equal, but as an equally valuable counterpart (Heb. *ezer ke-negdo*: Gen: 2:18) to men. They are both equally created in the image of God (*ibid.* 1:27); together they are called "man" (*ibid.* 5:2) and form one unit. Hence the rabbis could say that "he who is not married is not a man" (*Yev.* 63a). In many spheres rabbinic law recognized equality of men and w.; they are subject to the same laws, religious prohibitions, and penalties (*Kidd.* 35a), and w., like men, may offer sacrifices in the Temple (Maimonides, *Maaseh ha-Korbanot*, 2:3). Father and MOTHER are deserving of the same honor (Exod. 20:12) and respect (Lev. 19:3). WIDOWS, like ORPHANS, being among the weakest and most underprivileged members of society, are to be treated with special consideration. The four MATRIARCHS feature alongside the three Patriarchs as the founders of the Jewish people. The biblical record mentions many other female heroines, outstanding in their rôles of prophetess (Miriam, Huldah), judge (Deborah), exemplary mother (Hannah), or proselyte (Ruth). Nevertheless in many areas it is taken for granted that men and women are meant to be different in status, rights, and obligations and to complement rather than equal each other. In general, corresponding to their endowments and relationship in nature, men are assigned functions which are active, protecting, and outgoing — "it is the way of men to go out to war... to go round searching for a spouse, and not the way of w." (*Kidd.* 2b) — while the virtues of w. are supposed to shine within the home: "All the glory of the king's daughter is within the palace" (Ps. 45:14). Accordingly, in the acts of MARRIAGE and DIVORCE, for instance, the man is the active party (i.e., giving the ring or deed, reciting the legal formula divorcing his wife) and the woman the passive, receiving party. For similar reasons, INHERITANCE and certain property rights are vested mainly in men (but see ZELOPHEHAD, DAUGHTERS OF) though even married w. have some such independent rights. According to rabbinic law, w. are not eligible for ecclesiastical office and positions of authority in general, in spite of biblical and post-biblical precedents of reigning queens (Athaliah, Salome Alexandra). W. are not admitted as WITNESSES in court (except in cases of AGUNAH) and are debarred from the active as well as passive vote as this would be tantamount to conceding them authority in public affairs. Many Orthodox synagogues do not permit feminine voters, at least in religious matters, and the introduction of universal franchise in the State of Israel met with a certain amount of Orthodox opposition. Traditionally women were supposed to make their influence felt indirectly by their strength of character and personality (as in the case of R. Meir's wife BERURYAH). Theoretically — though rarely in practice — w. are admitted as ritual slaughterers (*Zev.* 3:1) and circumcisers (*A.Z.* 27a; cf. Exod. 4:25). They are also legally entitled to recite, and be called up to, the Reading of the Law, but a rabbinical enactment forbade this in order to preserve decorum at public services (*Meg.* 23a). Since the primary duty of w. is in the home they are exempted from the performance of such positive precepts as are bound to a particular time (*Kidd.* 1:7) i.e., from a considerable part of ceremonial and liturgical life. The rabbis placed great emphasis on the affectionate regard and tender treatment due to women. They urged a man "to love his wife like himself, and to honor her more than himself" (*Yev.* 62b); to spend on his own food less, and on honoring his wife more, than he can afford (*Ḥul.* 84b); and never to hurt her or to bring her to tears (*Bava Metzia* 59a). For a wife "is the crown of her husband" (Prov. 12:4); she "is his home" (*Yoma* 1:1). W. have priority over men in law court appearances (*Yev.* 100a) and in claims to redemption as captives (*Hor.* 3:6). Among the special virtues of w. the Talmud lists their superior compassion (*Meg.* 14b), charity (*Taan* 23b), chastity (*Eruv* 21b), piety (*Sot.* 11b), and their primary share in educating their children and in keeping their husbands from sin (*Yev.* 63a). On the other hand, they are said to be disposed to curiosity (*Tah.* 7:9), gossip (*Ber.* 48b), superstition (*Pes.* 100b), and lightmindedness (*Shab.* 33b). Compared to the great stress laid on the EDUCATION of men, that of w. was sadly neglected — in spite of notable exceptions — until modern times. Rabbinic law exhibits a marked tendency toward progressively improving the legal rights and status of w. (e.g. in regulations concerning the KETUBBAH and divorce; R. GERSHOM's *ḥerem* on polygamy), but modern developments such as the emancipation of w. have outstripped rabbinic law which has not yet completely adjusted to recent changes.

WORLD TO COME, see **OLAM HA-BA**

WORLD UNION FOR PROGRESSIVE JUDAISM: Founded in London, England, in 1926, the W.U. links Jews in Reform, Liberal and Progressive communities in over 20 countries. It has been headquartered in Jerusalem since 1973, and is dedicated to preserving Jewish identity and perpetuating the Jewish heritage worlwide. The Israel Movement of the W. U. coordinates the activities of its schools, settlements, youth movements and congregations throughout Israel. The W.U. is committed to the development in Israel of an open, democratic and pluralistic society, and to providing Diaspora Jewry with affirmative learning experiences in Israel.

WORSHIP, see **PRAYER**; **SACRIFICE**

WRITTEN LAW: Rabbinic term, referring to the Law given by God to Moses in written form, as distinct from the ORAL LAW. The Talmud (*Git.* 60b) interprets the verse: "Write thou these words, for according to the mouth of these words I have made a covenant with thee and with Israel" (Exod. 34:27) as referring to two complementary "TORAHS" — that contained in the word "write" (*ketav*, hence *Torah she-bi-khetav*, the W. L.) and that contained in the words "according to the mouth" (*al pi,* hence *Torah she-be-al-peh,* the Oral Law). In the strict sense, only the Pentateuch qualifies as W. L., since legal material contained in the Prophets and Hagiographa is described by the rabbis as "tradition" (*divrei kabbalah*) and hence part of the Oral Law. Nevertheless the term W. L. is at times used in a wider sense, covering the Bible (i.e., Holy Writ) as a whole. In the rabbinic view the W. L. and the Oral Law are complementary and of equal validity, both having been given to Moses on Mt. Sinai.

Y

YAALEH (Heb. "Let [our prayer] ascend"): *Piyyut* recited in the *Ashkenazi* rite after the *amidah* on the Evening Service of the Day of Atonement. Of unknown authorship *y.* consists of 8 three-line stanzas, each having three words to a line, the middle word forming a reverse alphabetical acrostic, with *aleph* repeated three times; each line in each three-line stanza commences with *yaaleh* ("may it ascend"), *ve-yavo* ("and may it come"), *va-yeraeh* ("and may it appear"), respectively.

YAALEH VE-YAVO (Heb. "May [our remembrance] rise and come... [before Thee]"): Prayer recited in each *amidah* on New Moons and festivals and in the Grace after Meals on those occasions. *Y.V.* is mentioned in the Talmud (*Sopherim* 19:7; *Ber.* 29b) and its style is regarded as reflecting the early period of *paytanim.*

YAD (Heb. "Hand"): A pointer, usually of silver but also of wood or ivory, used by the reader as a guide in reading the Scroll of the Law. Although its use is not obligatory, it is nevertheless recommended in order to prevent touching the revered parchment with the finger.

YAD ḤAZAKAH, see **MOSES BEN MAIMON**

YADAYIM (Heb. "Hands"): Eleventh tractate in the Mishnah order of *Toharot* with no *gemara* in either Talmud. It deals with ritual impurity of the hands and their purification through ablution. Other topics discussed include the canonical status of certain biblical books and the differences between Pharisees and Sadducees.

YAH: One of the names of God, considered by some as an abbreviated form of the Tetragrammaton *YHVH*; it occurs in the poetical parts of the Bible. The composite HALLELUJAH ("Praise ye Yah") of the Psalms has gained universal currency as an expression of glorification of God. Also frequent are theophorous names containing the element "*Yah*" e.g. Isaiah (Heb. *Yeshayah* = "*Yah* saves"), or Hezekiah ("*Yah* is my strength"). See GOD, NAMES OF; YAHVEH.

YAH RIBBON OLAM (Aram. "God, Master of the Universe"): Hymn in Aramaic, composed by the kabbalist poet Israel ben Moses NAJARA whose name "Israel" forms the acrostic. It is generally sung as a table hymn accompanying the Sabbath meals. The melodies now associated with *Y.R.* are much later than its date of composition.

YAHRZEIT (Yidd.): The anniversary of the death of a relative for whom MOURNING is enjoined. During the Talmudic Period this anniversary was commemorated by a voluntary fast (*Ned.* 12a). In addition it was the custom to visit the grave on that day (Rashi on *Yev.* 122a). In the course of time, and especially during the late Middle Ages, the customs appertaining to the *y.* were regulated. Fasting on the *y.* has fallen largely into abeyance. The day is observed by the lighting of a candle to burn for the full 24 hours (in support of which the verse is adduced "the soul of man is the lamp of the Lord" — Prov. 20:27) and by the mourner reciting KADDISH at the three statutory services. On all years subsequent to the first anniversary, the (Hebrew) date of death is regarded as the *y.* On the first anniversary, the date of burial is generally (though not universally) commemorated since mourning begins with the funeral and a full year of mourning should be observed. Among the ḤASIDIM the custom developed of regarding the *y.* of their great rabbis as an occasion for celebration and not of sorrow, since it marked the anniversary of the translation of the soul to higher spheres to receive its reward: it is celebrated by the omission of supplicatory prayers, as on all semi-festivals, and even by dancing. This custom is frowned upon by the MITNAGGEDIM. However the traditional anniversary of the death of R. Simeon bar Yoḥai on LAG BA-OMER has been celebrated since the 16th cent. as a popular festival, particularly at his tomb in Meron. It is also customary to permit a person observing *y.* to lead the congregational prayer and to be called to the Reading of the Law. *Sephardim* in particular attach great value to reading the HAPHTARAH on the Sabbath preceding the *y.* for one's parents.

YAHVEH: According to scholarly opinion, the original pronunciation of the TETRAGRAMMATON (*YHVH*), the particular name of the God of Israel (also called the *Shem ha-Mephorash* — "the explicit Name"). By Second Temple times, it was regarded as too sacred to be pronounced (except by the High Priest on the Day of Atonement) and was read as ADONAI ("Lord"). Of the varied attempts at elucidating the meaning of YHVH the most plausible are: "He is that He is", or "He causes to be". See also GOD, NAMES OF; JEHOVAH.

YAKNEHAZ: Acrostic abbreviation of the words: *yayin* = wine, *kiddush* = sanctification, *ner* = light, HAVDALAH = prayer of "separation", and *zeman* = "time" i.e., hallowing of the festive day. The abbreviation served as a mnemotechnic aid for the correct sequence of benedictions in the *kiddush* prayer on the eve of a festival which coincides with the conclusion of the Sabbath. The word *y.* sounds similar to German *jagt den Has* ("hunt the hare"), hence the hare-hunting scenes in many illustrated Passover *haggadot.*

YALKUT (Heb. "compilation"): Title given to several midrashic compilations. Best-known are the YALKUT SHIMONI (13th cent.); *Yalkut ha-Meiri* (date and identity of author not established); and YALKUT REUVENI (17th cent.).

YALKUT REUVENI: An anthology of homiletic and mystical commentary to the Pentateuch arranged in order of the weekly portions. Its author was the 17th cent. kabbalist, Reuben Kahana of Prague. The work is particularly valuable for its quotations from kabbalistic compositions over the preceding 500 years, many of which are no longer extant.

YALKUT SHIMONI: Midrashic thesaurus to the Bible arranging halakhic and aggadic passages of the Talmud and midrashic works according to biblical order. There are two parts, the first relating to the Pentateuch, the other to the remaining biblical books. Beside serving as a useful handbook for homiletic purposes, the Y.S. has considerably aided comparative and critical evaluation of midrashic material. Of the 50 sources quoted some are no longer extant. The work is attributed to R. Simeon Ha-Darshan (c. 13th cent.) about whose identity there are conflicting views.

YAMIM NORAIM (Heb. "Days of Awe"): The TEN DAYS OF PENITENCE. The Bible does not connect the festival of the first day of the seventh month (ROSH HA-SHANAH) with the solemn fast of the Day of Atonement which is observed on the tenth. The Talmud however regards them as the beginning and the end of a period of self-examination and judgment, and a later term (first found in the *Sepher Maharil* of the 14th cent. JACOB BEN MOSES MÖLLN) coined for this period is *Y.N.* For details of their observance, see ROSH HA-SHANAH and ATONEMENT, DAY OF.

YANNAI (6th or 7th cent.): One of the earliest *paytanim* (Hebrew liturgical poets.). Little is known of his life and even his Palestinian origin is only a matter of inference. Most of his considerable poetic output is lost. He is the first known *paytan* to have composed rhymed verse and to sign his name acrostically. The KEROVAH form has been associated with Y. His compositions include *Az Rov Nissim* (in the *Ashkenazi* version of the *Seder* service) and other *piyyutim* which have been discovered in the Cairo GENIZAH.

YARMULKA: A word of Polish origin adopted in Yiddish for the skull cap (as distinct from the hat) worn as a COVERING OF THE HEAD in accordance with Orthodox Jewish custom. The Hebrew equivalent is *kippah.*

YASHAR, BOOK OF, see **BIBLE, LOST BOOKS OF**

YAVNEH (Gk. Jamnia): Palestinian town near Ashdod; significant Jewish settlement dated only from the reign of Alexander Yannai. In 68 C.E., R. JOHANAN BEN ZAKKAI interceded with Titus to spare Y. and its sages. When this was granted, R. Johanan proceeded to organize an academy which was able to receive the scholars who fled from Jerusalem in 70. At a meeting held in a vineyard, he declared the Y. academy the successor of the Jerusalem SANHEDRIN. In the course of the next sixty years, the sages at Y. reorganized Judaism to meet the new situation resulting from the destruction of the Temple and put the stamp on the form of Judaism that came to be accepted as normative. Under Hadrianic rule, the Roman governor — fearing the authority established by the academy at Y. — moved the school to Lydda.

YEAR, see **CALENDAR**

YEAR OF RELEASE, see **SABBATICAL YEAR**

YEB (or Elephantine): Island in the Nile, opposite Aswan in Upper Egypt. Aramaic papyri discovered there have revealed the existence in the 5th cent. B.C.E. of a Jewish garrison which maintained its own Temple — with its altar, sacrificial system, and priesthood — while remaining in communication with the religious authorities in Jerusalem. In 407 an Egyptian rabble destroyed this temple but the garrison received the approval of the Persian satrap of Judea to rebuild it.

YEHUDAI GAON (8th cent.): Head of the talmudic academy at SURA. His *Halakhot Pesukot* ("Halakhic Decisions"), of which only fragments are extant, constitutes one of the first attempts at systematic codification of talmudic material for practical purposes and was the first such work to quote decisions without identifying the source (a method later followed by Maimonides in his *Mishneh Torah*). His talmudic glosses were so popular that some were mistakenly embodied in certain copies of the Talmud. Y.'s contact with the N. African communities established the relationships and avenues of communication by which Babylonian tradition ultimately became the standard for Spanish Jewry.

YEKUM PORKAN (or **PURKAN**; Aram. "May salvation... be granted"): Two Aramaic prayers recited in the *Ashkenazi* ritual on Sabbaths before the Additional Service. One prayer is in behalf of rabbis and teachers in Israel and Babylonia and in all the lands of the Diaspora (this last being a late addition), and the other in behalf of the congregation. The first *Y.P.*, containing reference to the exilarchs and heads of the academies, was composed in Babylonia.

YELAMMEDENU (Heb.): Palestinian midrashic collection of unestablished date, covering the entire Pentateuch and associated with the TANḤUMA. In its present form it is incomplete. The name is derived from the halakhic address: "*yelammedenu rabbenu*" ("let our teacher pronounce") with which each section opens. The pertinent *halakhah* or sometimes *aggadah* enables the introduction of ethical and theological material connected with the biblical readings.

YESHIVAH: The oldest institution for higher learning in Judaism; see ACADEMY. After flourishing in Babylonia from the 2nd cent., it was introduced in Narbonne in S. France about the 10th cent. and from there spread to the Rhineland communities and to France and Germany. Jacob Pollak (15th-16th cents.) was responsible for its introduction in E. Europe, where it flourished in Poland, Lithuania, Hungary, and Galicia until the 20th cent. *Yeshivot* exist today in various countries; the State of Israel has (as of 1985) over 70,000 *y.* students in 650 *yeshivot.* See EDUCATION.

YETZER HA-RA AND YETZER HA-TOV (Heb. "The evil inclination and the good inclination"): The Bible refers to the "inclination of man which is evil from his youth" (Gen. 6:5; 8:21) but the Talmud complements this by positing the existence of an opposing instinct within man which draws him toward the good. The rabbis also taught that the evil inclination could be disciplined and pressed into the service of God and interpreted the commandment to love God "with all thy heart" (Deut. 6:5) as meaning with both the good and evil inclination — (*Siphrei,* Deut. 32). According to another rabbinic statement God created both the evil inclination (i.e., human nature with its desires and passions) as well as the *Torah* containing the antidote with which to master it (*Kidd.* 30b). The identification of the good inclination with *Torah* resulted in the view that the evil inclination was with man from his birth, whereas the good inclination came to him at BAR MITZVAH, i.e., at his full acceptance of *Torah.* The rabbinic doctrine of the two inclinations was clearly intended to substitute a psychological DUALISM for the cosmic dualism of other systems which connected man's inner struggle between GOOD AND EVIL with a cosmic division between forces of light and darkness. The more radically dualistic view (e.g. the talmudic identification of the *yetzer ha-ra* with SATAN) of the nature of the two inclinations came to the fore again in the KABBALAH.

YETZIRAH, BOOK OF (*yetzirah* — "creation"): A brief text of ancient origin and of great influence in the development of the Jewish mystic tradition. Traditional kabbalists ascribed its origins to Abraham, but most modern scholars suggest that it was written between the 3rd and 6th cents., though containing later interpolations. A Book of Y. is mentioned in the Talmud (*Suk.* 65b, 67b) but is not identical with the extant work of that name. The book identifies the elements of creation in the ten primordial numbers, called SEPHIROT, and the twenty-two letters of the Hebrew ALPHABET. These together, through their convergence and combination, form the "THIRTY-TWO SECRET PATHS OF WISDOM". The book also contains elements of MERKAVAH mysticism with allusions to the *ḥayyot* ("animals") mentioned in the Book of Ezekiel, and the theurgic power of mystic names. Some scholars see a connection between Y. and the number mysticism of the Pythagorean school. The letter-MYSTICISM of the book, however, would seem to indicate more indigenous Jewish origins.

YEVAMAH, see **LEVIRATE MARRIAGE**

YEVAMOT (Heb. "Levirates"; also formerly known as *nashim* "women"): First tractate in the Mishnah order of *Nashim* with *gemara* in both Talmuds. It deals with the laws of LEVIRATE MARRIAGE (Deut. 25:5 ff.) and the ceremony of *ḥalitzah,* and also discusses prohibited marriages (Lev. 18 ff.).

YIBBUM, see **LEVIRATE MARRIAGE**

YIDDISH: Judeo-German dialect which became the sole vernacular of the Jews of E. Europe. It contains a large admixture of Hebrew words (particularly the religious vocabulary) as well as of some Slavic, but the basic stratum of the language derives from medieval German. As the language of the E. European ghetto and its intensive Jewish culture, Y. became invested in the minds of the people with a sanctity of its own. It was regarded as the only language in which the intricacies of the Talmud and codes could be properly expounded. Many popular devotional and edifying writings, such as the TZE'ENAH U-RE'ENAH and TEḤINNOT were composed in Y. in addition to the popular homiletic version of the Bible known as *Ivri-Teutsch.* Y. remains the language of instruction in the older *yeshivot* in the State of Israel, the U.S., and elsewhere, while certain ultra-religious Jews (including the NATOREI KARTA), regarding Hebrew as the Holy Tongue which must not be profaned by secular use, continue to speak Y. as their vernacular. Secular Y. literature reached a zenith in the 19th and early 20th cent., but with the annihilation of E. European Jewry, Y. is slowly declining, being supplanted in Israel by Hebrew, and in Europe and America by the native languages.

YIDDISHKEIT (Yidd. "Jewishness"): The Jewish way of life as expressed in the practices of the traditional Jewish religion and its customs. The term has a warm ring for the *Ashkenazi* Jew, denoting the positive aspects of Jewish habits, often of folk origin.

YIGDAL (Heb. "Magnified and praised be the living God"): Hymn sung at the conclusion of Sabbath and festival Evening Services; among *Ashkenazim*, it is also recited before the daily Morning Service. It is based on Maimonides' THIRTEEN ARTICLES OF FAITH (each line treating of one of the Articles). The *Sephardi* version has a fourteenth, concluding line (a later addition), which reads: "These are the Thirteen Principles..." The authorship of *y.* has been assigned to Daniel ben Judah of Rome (14th cent.).

YIḤUS (Heb.): Distinguished connections or genealogy. In Bible times the highest distinction was to belong to the Davidic family while the priestly and levitical families were also regarded with great respect. Later Jewish tradition particularly valued a relationship with an outstanding scholar. In medieval Europe, pride was also taken in the martyrdom of ancestors.

YIMAḤ SHEMO (Heb. "May his name be blotted out"): An execratory appellation added to the mention of the name of an inveterate enemy of the Jewish people. Its origin is attributed to the commandment (Deut. 25:10) to "blot out the memory of Amalek" and the phrase is sometimes therefore extended to *yimaḥ shemo ve-zikhro* "May his name and memory be blotted out". From Deut. 25:6 however it would appear that the phrase means that he should leave no posterity to continue his name (cf. Ps. 109:14).

YISHAR KOAḤ or **KOḤAKHA** (Heb. "May [thy] strength remain firm"): An exclamation of approval, appreciation, or thanks. It derives from a passage in the Talmud (*Shab.* 87a) where Resh Lakish, by a play on the word *asher* in Exod. 34:1, has God say approvingly to Moses *yishar koḥakha* for smashing the Tablets of the Law. In *Ashkenazi* synagogues the phrase is used as an expression of thanks to the preacher (after a sermon), priest (after giving the PRIESTLY BLESSING), or the performer of a *mitzvah*; it corresponds to the *ḥazak (u-) varukh* of the *Sephardim*.

YISHTABBAḤ (Heb. "May His Name be praised"): The opening word of the concluding blessing of the PESUKEI DE-ZIMRA, used as the name for the whole prayer. The benediction contains fifteen terms of praise and adoration; in some rites it is recited standing.

YIZKOR, see **MEMORIAL SERVICE**

YOM HA-DIN, see **DAY OF JUDGMENT**

YOM HA-KIPPURIM or **YOM KIPPUR**, see **ATONEMENT, DAY OF**

YOM KIPPUR KATAN (Heb. "Minor Day of Atonement"): Observance of the day preceding the New Moon as a period of atonement and fasting. A special order of service (including *seliḥot* and Psalms) was drawn up to be recited at midnight and at the Afternoon Service. The custom, which originated with the 16th cent. kabbalists in Safed, is not widely observed nowadays.

YOM TOV, see **FESTIVAL**

YOMA (Aram. "The Day" i.e., of atonement, cf. its original Heb. name of *kippurim*): Fifth tractate in the Mishnah order of *Moed* with *gemara* in both Talmuds. It deals with the laws of the Day of ATONEMENT including a detailed account of the ritual to be observed by the High Priest on that occasion.

YOMTOV BEN ABRAHAM ISHBILI (known as *Ritba;* 13th-14th cents.): Spanish talmudic scholar. His compositions included novellae on most talmudic tractates, commentaries on the Passover *Haggadah* and the halakhic compendium of Alfasi, and a philosophic treatise *Sepher ha-Zikkaron* ("The Book of Remembrance") in which he attacked Naḥmanides' strictures on Maimonides' theology.

YOMTOV LIPMANN, see **MÜHLHAUSEN**

YOREH DEAH, see **SHULḤAN ARUKH**

YOSE BEN ḤALAPHTA (2nd cent. C.E.): Palestinian *tanna*; pupil of R. AKIVA. He was forced to flee during the Hadrianic persecutions but eventually settled at Sepphoris where he headed the ACADEMY. His halakhic pre-eminence and the respect in which he was held by R. JUDAH HA-NASI and R. SIMEON BEN GAMALIEL led to his views being accepted in legal disputations (*Eruv.* 46b). He is the reputed author of the historical work SEDER OLAM.

YOSE BEN JOEZER (2nd cent. B.C.E.): Scholar; president of the Sanhedrin. Together with Yose ben Johanan he constituted the first of the five "pairs" (ZUGOT). He belonged to the party of the HASIDEANS and strongly opposed the Hellenists.

YOSE BEN JOHANAN, see **YOSE BEN JOEZER**

YOSE BEN YOSE (5th, 6th, or 7th cent.): The earliest known Palestinian liturgical poet (*paytan*). Some of his PIYYUTIM have been incorporated into the *Sephardi* liturgy on the Day of Atonement (e.g., *Azkir Gevurot Eloah* — a picturesque portrayal of the Temple ritual of that day) and *Rosh ha-Shanah* (*Ahalelah Elohai Ashirah Uzo* — on the majesty of the Creator). His compositions are alphabetic with rhythmic pattern and occasional alliteration, but lack rhyme or meter.

YOTZER: The first of the two BENEDICTIONS preceding the SHEMA in the Morning Service, so called because it opens "Blessed... who forms (Heb. *yotzer*) light and creates darkness, etc." (cf. Is. 45:7). Its theme is praise to God who restores light to the earth every morning. However, the Talmud rules that God's power to bring darkness must be mentioned together with the praise for bringing light (and *vice versa* in the Evening Service) in order to protest the ancient dualistic belief in two separate deities of light and darkness respectively (*Ber.* 11b). In the form now used, Y. contains the alphabetic hymn *El Barukh*, a poetic description of the angels praising God in heaven and proclaiming "Holy, holy, holy is the Lord" etc. (see KEDUSHAH), originating in early mystic circles. Brief *piyyutim* are inserted into the Y., especially on the Sabbath (e.g. *el adon*) and festivals; these are generally known as Y. hymns (*yotzerot*). Before the conclusion (*yotzer ha-meorot*) some rites (but not the *Sephardi*) insert a messianic petition: "Cause a new light to shine upon Zion"; this was opposed, however, by some authorities in gaonic times on the grounds that the subject of the benediction is the physical light of creation and not the spiritual light of redemption. The term Y. is loosely applied to all the extra hymns which were introduced into the Morning Service (the general tendency in recent times is to omit these accretions).

YUDGHAN (8th cent.): Sectarian leader in Hamadan, Persia. Like his teacher ABU ISSA, Y. prohibited the partaking of meat and wine, and stressed the virtue of prayer and fasting. He considered the Sabbath and holidays to have lost their binding character with the destruction of the Temple. His theology, which taught a spiritual and mystic approach to the Bible, opposed anthropomorphism and upheld free will. His followers (Yudghanites) dwindled away or were absorbed by the KARAITE Movement.

Z

ZACUTO, MOSES (c. 1625-1697): Italian kabbalist and liturgical poet. Born in Amsterdam, he set out on a pilgrimage to the Holy Land, but was persuaded to remain in Italy where he served as rabbi, first in Venice and then in Mantua. In addition to his kabbalistic and devotional compositions, Z. wrote halakhic responsa, a drama on the patriarch Abraham (*Yesod Olam*), and a poetic vision of the soul's fate in the hereafter.

ZADOK: Priest; descendant of Eleazar, son of Aaron (I Chron. 5:34). He sided with David against Absalom (II Sam. 19:12) and anointed Solomon as king against his rival Adonijah, who was banished (*ibid.* 2:35). The house of Z. ruled as HIGH PRIESTS until the time of the Hasmoneans. The "sons of Z." are also mentioned in the DEAD SEA SCROLLS ("Zadokite Fragments"), where the reference is possibly to the ancient priestly family. The party of the SADDUCEES also is thought to have been connected with the house of Z.

ZADOKITE FRAGMENTS, see **DEAD SEA SCROLLS**

ZAKHUR LA-TOV (Heb. "May he be remembered for good"): Honorific phrase added to the name of a deceased person held in fond remembrance; now generally replaced by ZIKHRONO LIVERAKHAH. The former phrase occurs several times in the Talmud and once in the liturgy for PURIM ("and may Hasbonah also be remembered for good").

ZAVIM (Heb. "Persons with unclean flux"): Ninth tractate in the Mishnah order of *Toharot* with no *gemara* in either *Talmud.* It gives the regulations concerning ritual uncleanness contracted as a result of a flux (Lev. 15) or as a result of contact with a person so afflicted.

ZEALOTS: Extreme and uncompromising partisans of a cause; nowadays often used as synonymous with "fanatics". In a more specific sense the term is applied to a sect that existed during the last decades of the Second Temple and uncompromisingly rejected the Roman dominion. Their political intransigence was based on theological and messianic beliefs, and they opposed both the Romans and those of their fellow Jews who accepted Roman rule. They took a leading part in the revolt against Rome (66-70 C.E.) but were also engaged in intensive strife with the other Jewish parties, terrorizing and massacring their opponents on more than one occasion. Attempts have been made to identify the Z. with the Qumran sect (see DEAD SEA SCROLLS). In Rabbinic theology a zealot is a person who, moved by "zeal for his God", acts spontaneously when the duly constituted authorities are unable to act; the prototype is PHINEHAS (see Num. 25:6-13).

ZECHARIAH: Eleventh of the twelve Minor Prophets; contemporary of HAGGAI (Ezra 5:1). His prophecies were uttered in 520-518 B.C.E. when national morale in Judah was low. Disappointed at the barrenness of the land, harassed by covetous neighbors and resenting the Persian yoke, the returning exiles were further depressed by a series of natural misfortunes (Hag. 10:6, 9-10; 2:17). Z. pitted words of comfort (1:13) and encouragement (8:13) against the despair and weariness which had seized the community and had delayed the restoration of the Temple. In line with his predecessors, he stressed the religious significance of repentance (1:3-4), truth and justice (7:9-10; 8:16-17) as against mere practices of fasting (7:5-6). He also regulated the constitutional relationship between the High Priest Joshua and the governor ZERUBBABEL, whom he considered the Messiah. Structural divergences between chapters 1-8 and 9-14 have led critics to suggest a composite authorship.

ZEKHOR BERIT (Heb. "Remember the Covenant"): The opening words of a penitential hymn composed by R. GERSHOM BEN JUDAH and recited in the *Ashkenazi* SELIḤOT ritual on the day before *Rosh ha-Shanah.* It is recited with the Ark open, and is so highly regarded that the *seliḥot* service of that day is commonly referred to as *Z.B.* It is also recited during the Concluding Service on the Day of Atonement.

ZEKHUT AVOT, see **MERITS OF THE FATHERS**

ZELOPHEHAD, DAUGHTERS OF: The five daughters and only children of a Manassite called Z. (Num. 26:33ff.). Upon their father's death they approached Moses for a ruling upon their title to their father's property and received an affirmative reply, which served as a precedent for all subsequent generations (*ibid.* 27:6-8). Upon Joshua's conquest of Canaan the claim of the daughters was put into effect (Josh. 17:3-6). In order to keep the inheritance within the tribe, the daughters of Z. married their cousins (Num. 36:6).

ZEMIROT (Heb. "songs"): (1) Name applied by *Sephardim* and Yemenites to the Psalms and other scriptural passages of praise, which serve as an introduction to the Morning Service proper (the *Ashkenazi* PESUKEI DE-ZIMRA). (2) Hymns sung at the table on Sabbaths (but not on festivals). Hymn singing, although originating earlier, received a powerful impetus wih the spread of the Kabbalah in 16th cent. Safed, where a large number of *z.* was composed. Among MITNAGGEDIM the *z.* were generally limited to YAH RIBBON OLAM and TZUR MI-SHELLO. The ḤASIDIM, on the other hand, used a much larger repertoire, especially on Sabbath afternoon (during the SEUDAH SHELISHIT) in order to extend the sanctity of the Sabbath into the "profane" week (cf. *Shab.* 115a). Today, however, there is little difference in custom, the popularity of *z.* having grown among all observant Jews. Among Oriental Jews *z.* are also sung in the vernacular language (Arabic, Persian). One characteristic feature of the *z.* are the traditional melodies handed down from generation to generation.

ZEPHANIAH: Ninth of the twelve Minor Prophets. A descendant of King Hezekiah, he is the only prophet known to possess a direct royal pedigree. Z. was a contemporary of Jeremiah, and his prophecies, directed mainly to the aristocratic elements, were uttered during the early period of the reign of Josiah (c. 630 B.C.E.) before that king's reformatory campaign. Z.'s admonitions of Judah, his forecast of the doom of the Philistines (2:4-7), Ammon and Moab (2:3-11), Egypt, (2:12), and Assyria (2:13-14) must be seen against the background of incursions by the Scythians and the imminent fall of Nineveh, and the profound effect, which these events had upon the historical scene of the day. In clear and concise language, dispensing with poetic embellishment, Z. sets forth his message of the coming Day of the Lord when evil will meet its due fate in Israel as well as among the gentiles and when all peoples will return to the Lord, and accept His dominion.

ZERAIM (Heb. "Seeds"): First order of the Mishnah. Its first tractate BERAKHOT deals with benedictions and prayers, the other tractates (PEAH, DEMAI, KILAYIM, SHEVIIT, TERUMOT, MAASEROT, MAASER SHENI, ḤALLAH, ORLAH, and BIKKURIM) describing various aspects of agricultural legislation. The Palestinian Talmud contains *gemara* on the entire order, but the Babylonian only to *Berakhot.*

ZERUBBABEL: Leader of the Jewish exiles returning from Babylonia. Z. was a grandson of King Jehoiachin and hence of Davidic descent. With the consent of Cyrus, he returned to Judah at the head of the home-coming exiles in order to rebuild the land and the Temple (EZRA 3:2). He set up an altar for burnt-offerings, and ensured the observance of the festivals. Z. was appointed governor of Judah under Darius I in 521 B.C.E. The reconstruction of the Temple was suspended in the face of opposition, and the prophets HAGGAI and ZECHARIAH had to urge Z. to complete the building. The work was recommenced in 520 B.C.E. after a 17-year suspension and the Temple was dedicated in 516 B.C.E., though there is no mention of Z. in connection with the dedication. Some scholars have suggested that Z. is identical with Sheshbazzar (Ezra 1:8) while the Talmud identifies him with NEHEMIAH (*Sanh.* 38a). In any case the messianic expectations connected with Z. were not realized. According to one tradition Z. returned to Babylonia and died there.

ZEVAḤIM (Heb. "Animal Sacrifices"; also known formerly as *Sheḥitat Kodashim,* "the slaughter of consecrated animals" and *Korbanot,* "sacrifices"): First tractate in the Mishnah order of *Kodashim* with *gemara* in the Babylonian Talmud only. Its subject matter is animal (including bird) offerings, and it discusses the selection of the animal, the procedure of sacrifice, the allocation of the sacrificial meat among the priests, etc.

ZIKHRONO LI-VERAKHAH (more properly, *Zikhro li-Verakhah;* Heb. "May his memory be for a blessing"): Honorific phrase added to the mention of the name of a person held in fond and pious remembrance (cf. ZAKHUR LA-TOV). It derives from the verse "The memory of the righteous is a blessing, but the name of the wicked shall rot" (Prov. 10:7). It is the custom, in writing the name of the deceased in Hebrew, to add the initial letters of the two words ("*zal*").

ZIKHRONOT (Heb. "remembrances"): The second of three sections of the Additional Service *amidah* on *Rosh ha-Shanah,* the other two being MALKHUYYOT and SHOPHAROT. Each consists of ten appropriate biblical verses, with an introductory paragraph and a concluding blessing. The ten verses in the *z.* refer to God as "remembering" (his mercies, his covenant, etc.). After their recital the SHOPHAR is sounded.

ZIMRA, DAVID BEN SOLOMON IBN AVI (known as *Radbaz;* fl. 16th cent.): Talmudic scholar and kabbalist. Born in Spain, he was Chief Rabbi of Egypt for 40 years and eventually settled in Safed. Among the many subjects incidentally dealt with in his 2,400 published responsa are Palestinian topography, numismatics, and the Falashas. Enjoying great prestige and authority among his colleagues, he opposed harshness in the interpretation of the *halakhah,* chiding those who "heap restrictions upon restrictions".

ZIMMUN, see **GRACE AFTER MEALS**

ZION: Originally a Jebusite hill fortress in southern JERUSALEM conquered by David (II Sam. 5:6-9) and named the City of David. As the city expanded to the north, Z. also denoted the site of the TEMPLE. The exact location of Z. is a matter of dispute. Josephus identified it with the western hill or upper city of Jerusalem. Modern scholarship favors the so-called "Ophel" — the hill of the temple Mount (*Har ha-Bayit*) as the true position. The presently designated MOUNT Z., S.W. of the Old City wall, was until 1967 a Jewish pilgrim site especially during the festivals. In poetic usage Z. embraced the whole of Jerusalem (Amos 6:1) and even the entire Jewish kingdom (Is. 1:27). In the image of a forsaken spouse, Z. symbolized the fate of the Jewish people in distress (Is. 49:14), while in prophecies of redemption, it is depicted as the mother of a reborn Israel (Is. 66:8). By a further extension of meaning, Z. was visualized as the spiritual capital of the world — the messianic City of God (Is. 60:40). As an ideal hope and aspiration, the concept of Z. became charged with an intense religious and eschatological current, fed by the prophetic vision of Z. as the Divine seat from which the Word of God was to issue forth for the salvation of all mankind (Is. 2:3) and as the source of justice and righteousness (Is. 33:5). Z. has been a symbol of Jewish restoration throughout the ages (cf. ZIONISM) and is frequently mentioned in the liturgy, and personified — both in poetry and midrashic legend — as a virgin, mother, or widow in mourning (cf. Lam. 1:11). Judah Ha-Levi's famous elegies addressed to Z. are known as Zionides.

ZIONISM: Movement to secure the return of the Jews to the Land of Israel. Modern political Z., as founded by Theodor Herzl at the First Zionist Congress (1897), although a consciously secular movement aimed at solving the "Jewish problem", could draw emotionally as well as ideologically on a long religious tradition of messianic hope in an ultimate restoration of ZION. This hope, vividly expressed in the prophets, aggadic literature, and the liturgy, had often found explosive vent in messianic movements and caused some rabbis (e.g. MOHILEVER) to support first *Ḥibbat Zion* and, subsequently, Herzl's Political Z., which soon included a strong religious faction. Nevertheless Z. was at first violently opposed on religious grounds by a large section of Orthodoxy (who claimed that Divine Providence should not be anticipated by human, let alone by ungodly and secular, action), as well as by Reform (which held national aspirations to be a betrayal of the purely religious mission of Israel). The essence and nature of Z. became a renewed subject of probing discussion after the achievement of its primary objective: the establishment of the State of Israel. The relation of "religious" and "secular" factors in the history as well as in the present situation of Z. is still a hotly disputed ideological issue. (See RELIGIOUS PARTIES).

ZODIAC: An imaginary broad celestial belt within which ancient astronomers visualized the sun, moon, and planets as passing. It was divided into 12 equal parts, each of which was given a sign representing a zodiacal constellation (see below). The signs are listed in the Hebrew calendar as corresponding to the 12 months of the year beginning with *Nisan*. The first Jewish source to mention the 12 signs in their present form is the Book of YETZIRAH where they also correspond to 12 organs of the human body. The relationship of the 12 Tribes to the Zodiacal signs has also been noted (*Yalkut Shimoni* Num. 418). The origin of the signs is unknown; rabbis interpreted them symbolically, thus *Moznayim* ("Scales") is the sign of *Tishri*, the month of judgment. The theme of the Z. formed a favorite theme of Jewish art and was prominent in ancient synagogal decoration. The signs of the Z. are:

Hebrew	*Latin*	*English*
Taleh	*Aries*	Ram
Shor	*Taurus*	Bull
Teomim	*Gemini*	Twins
Sartan	*Cancer*	Crab
Aryeh	*Leo*	Lion
Betulah	*Virgo*	Virgin
Moznayim	*Libra*	Scales
Akrav	*Scorpio*	Scorpion
Keshet	*Sagittarius*	Archer
Gedi	*Capricornus*	Goat
Deli	*Aquarius*	Water carrier
Dagim	*Pisces*	Fishes

ZOGERIN (Yidd. *zogen* "to say"): Woman reciter who — in E. Europe — read the synagogue prayers in Yiddish to other women unable to follow the text on their own.

ZOHAR, THE BOOK OF (*Zohar* = Heb. "splendor"): A kabbalistic work composed of several literary units not all by the same author. Kabbalists since the 14th cent. have recognized the Z. as the most important work of mystical teaching, and the book achieved in some circles a sanctity only slightly less than that of the Bible. The largest section, the Z. proper, consists of a mystical commentary on parts of the Bible, delivered in the form of discussions of a group of 2nd cent. rabbis and scholars in Palestine led by Simeon bar Yoḥai. Most of their reflections and exchanges deal with the "inner", i.e., esoteric meaning of Scripture. Other sections of the Z. like the *Idra Rabba* — ("the Greater Assembly") and the *Idra Zuta* — ("the Lesser Assembly") also depict scenes in the life of Simeon bar Yoḥai and his disciples.

All these parts are in Aramaic. Another section, the *Midrash Ha-Ne'eman* ("The Mystical Midrash") is written partly in Hebrew and attempts a more straightforward mystical interpretation of biblical passages. The *Raaya Meheimana* ("The Faithful Shepherd") is a kabbalistic interpretation of the commandments and prohibitions in the *Torah.* The *Raza de-Razin* ("Secret of Secrets") contains material on physiognomy and chiromancy. These and other parts of the Z. are characterized by an enthusiastic style, theosophical speculation, and mythological imagery. Traditional kabbalists ascribe all or most of these books to the authorship of Simeon bar Yoḥai and his contemporaries. Modern scholarship has shown that the main part of the Z. was written toward the end of the 13th cent. by Moses de LEON, a Castilian kabbalist who died in 1305. Some parts of the Z. were written shortly afterward and added to the main work.

The Z. has been described as a mixture of theosophic theology, mystical psychology, anthropology, myth, and poetry. Old gnostic doctrines, mystical traditions, theurgic speculations, popular superstitions, and mythological motifs dwell side by side with echoes of Neo-Platonic and Aristotelian philosophic theories about the nature of the cosmos and about the relationship between a transcendent God and a finite world. The problem of the manner in which the inscrutable mystery of the Godhead, the EIN SOPH (the "Infinite"), manifests itself in the Divine creative process, is one of the Z.'s major themes. The doctrine of the SEPHIROT is the kabbalistic answer to this problem. The *sephirot* are the ten stages of the inner-Divine world through which God descends, from the innermost recesses of His hiddenness down to His manifestation in the SHEKHINAH. The *Shekhinah* — the last of the *sephirot* — is also the heavenly archetype of the community of Israel. When the inner contrasting forces of the Life Divine (e.g. grace and stern judgment) are harmoniously balanced, then reality is in order, the *Shekhinah* (conceived in "female" imagery) is united with the upper ("male") *sephirot* and the abundance of Divine life flows harmoniously into the world. When there is a defect in the proper conjunction of the upper *sephirot,* disorder, chaos, and evil result. The problem of evil occupies a large place in the discussions of the Z. At times, evil is described as a negative but powerful reality, resulting from the ascendancy of certain Divine qualities (e.g. destructive judgment) over others (e.g. pure grace). The central doctrine of the Z. is that the harmonious union of the Divine Life is brought about as well as disturbed by human action (i.e., by a religious life, good works and mystical meditations, and by sins and improper thought respectively). The *Torah,* for the Z., is an essential key to the mysteries of the Divine processes. For the kabbalist it is an actual manifestation of the Divine and a kind of *corpus symbolicum.* Hence the author of the Z. is less interested in the literal meaning of the historical events described in the Bible, than in the theosophical mysteries that are their "inner" and therefore more "real" meaning. The basic premise of the Z. is that there exists a complete correspondence between the "lower" and "upper" worlds. Therefore a "quickening" from below can arouse a "quickening" above. Hence man's deeds and prayers have cosmic significance. See KABBALAH; MYSTICISM.

ZOROASTRIANISM, see **DUALISM**

ZUGOT (Heb. "pairs"): Name given to each of five pairs of scholars representing five generations of leading exponents of Oral Law spanning the period between the Maccabean revolt and the time of Herod. The pairs held the office of president (*nasi*) and vice-president (*av bet din,* literally "father of the court") respectively. They were: 1) Yose ben Joezer and Yose ben Johanan; 2) Joshua ben Peraḥiah and Nittai of Arbel; 3) Judah ben Tabbai and Simeon ben Shetaḥ; 4) Shemaiah and Avtalyon; 5) Hillel and Shammai. Louis Finkelstein has suggested that each member of the *z.* represented either the plebeian or patrician party on a bipartisan basis.

ZUNZ, LEOPOLD (1794-1886): German scholar; founder of the modern scientific (historical and philological) study of Judaism (WISSENSCHAFT DES JUDENTUMS). Z. was the first to employ consistently modern methods of historical and literary research in his study of Jewish works. His purpose was to indicate the inner relations and mutual influences of Jewish thought (Talmud, Kabbalah, Hebrew grammar, *piyyutim*) with a wealth of historical and philosophical details in order to demonstrate their continuity. On religious matters, he was guided by his basic conviction that true reform must preserve the essential identity of historic Judaism which is not a static law but a growing original force. In his *Gottesdienstliche Vortrage der Juden,* he traced the historical evolution of the Jewish sermon and endeavored to show that preaching in the vernacular was no modern innovation but an ancient custom.